ACTS

Baker Exegetical Commentary on the New Testament

ROBERT W. YARBROUGH
AND ROBERT H. STEIN, EDITORS

Volumes now available

Luke *Darrell L. Bock*
John *Andreas J. Köstenberger*
Acts *Darrell L. Bock*
Romans *Thomas R. Schreiner*
1 Corinthians *David E. Garland*
Philippians *Moisés Silva*
1 Peter *Karen H. Jobes*
Revelation *Grant R. Osborne*

Darrell L. Bock (PhD, University of Aberdeen) is research professor of New Testament studies at Dallas Theological Seminary. He is the author or editor of more than twenty books, including *Jesus according to Scripture, Studying the Historical Jesus*, and *Luke* in the Baker Exegetical Commentary on the New Testament series.

ACTS

DARRELL L. BOCK

Baker Exegetical Commentary on the New Testament

Baker Academic
Grand Rapids, Michigan

Published by Baker Academic
a division of Baker Publishing Group
P.O. Box 6287, Grand Rapids, MI 49516-6287
www.bakeracademic.com

Printed in the United States of America

Library of Congress Cataloging-in-Publication Data

Bock, Darrell L.
    Acts / Darrell L. Bock.
        p.   cm.   — (Baker exegetical commentary on the New Testament)
    Includes bibliographical references and indexes.
    ISBN 10: 0-8010-2668-7 (cloth)
    ISBN 978-0-8010-2668-3 (cloth)
    1. Bible. N.T. Acts—Commentaries. I. Title.
    BS2625.53.B63 2007
    226.4'077—dc22   2007010840

10   11   12   13   14   15   16   10   9   8   7   6   5   4

To my colleagues at Dallas Theological Seminary,
Talbot Theological Seminary, Tyndale House, Bengelhaus,
and the universities of Aberdeen and Tübingen for their friendship,
fellowship, encouragement, and instruction

And, most especially, to Sally Bock, whose life defines faithfulness

Contents

Series Preface

The chief concern of the Baker Exegetical Commentary on the New Testament (BECNT) is to provide, within the framework of informed evangelical thought, commentaries that blend scholarly depth with readability, exegetical detail with sensitivity to the whole, and attention to critical problems with theological awareness. We hope thereby to attract the interest of a fairly wide audience, from the scholar who is looking for a thoughtful and independent examination of the text to the motivated lay Christian who craves a solid but accessible exposition.

Nevertheless, a major purpose is to address the needs of pastors and others involved in the preaching and exposition of the Scriptures as the uniquely inspired word of God. This consideration affects directly the parameters of the series. For example, serious biblical expositors cannot afford to depend on a superficial treatment that avoids the difficult questions, but neither are they interested in encyclopedic commentaries that seek to cover every conceivable issue that may arise. Our aim therefore is to focus on problems that have a direct bearing on the meaning of the text (although selected technical details are treated in the additional notes).

Similarly, a special effort is made to avoid treating exegetical questions for their own sake, that is, in relative isolation from the thrust of the argument as a whole. This effort may involve (at the discretion of the individual contributors) abandoning the verse-by-verse approach in favor of an exposition that focuses on the paragraph as the main unit of thought. In all cases, however, the commentaries stress the development of the argument and explicitly relate each passage to what precedes and follows it so as to identify its function in context as clearly as possible.

We believe, moreover, that a responsible exegetical commentary must take fully into account the latest scholarly research, regardless of its source. The attempt to do this in the context of a conservative theological tradition presents certain challenges, and in the past the results have not always been commendable. In some cases, evangelicals appear to make use of critical scholarship not for the purpose of genuine interaction but only to dismiss it. In other cases, the interaction glides over into assimilation, theological distinctives are ignored or suppressed, and the end product cannot be differentiated from works that arise from a fundamentally different starting point.

The contributors to this series attempt to avoid these pitfalls. On one hand, they do not consider traditional opinions to be sacrosanct, and they are certainly committed to doing justice to the biblical text whether or not it supports such opinions. On the other hand, they will not quickly abandon a long-standing view, if there is persuasive evidence to support it, for the sake of fashionable theories. What is more important, the contributors share a belief in the trustworthiness and essential unity of Scripture. They also consider that the historic formulations of Christian doctrine, such as the ecumenical creeds and many of the documents originating in the sixteenth-century Reformation, arose from a legitimate reading of Scripture, thus providing a proper framework for its further interpretation. No doubt, the use of such a starting point sometimes results in the imposition of a foreign construct on the text, but we deny that it must necessarily do so or that the writers who claim to approach the text without prejudices are invulnerable to the same danger.

Accordingly, we do not consider theological assumptions—from which, in any case, no commentator is free—to be obstacles to biblical interpretation. On the contrary, an exegete who hopes to understand the apostle Paul in a theological vacuum might just as easily try to interpret Aristotle without regard for the philosophical framework of his whole work or without having recourse to the subsequent philosophical categories that make possible a meaningful contextualization of his thought. It must be emphasized, however, that the contributors to the present series come from a variety of theological traditions and that they do not all have identical views with regard to the proper implementation of these general principles. In the end, all that really matters is whether the series succeeds in representing the original text accurately, clearly, and meaningfully to the contemporary reader.

Shading has been used to assist the reader in locating the introductory comments for each section. Textual variants in the Greek text are signaled in the author's translation by means of half-brackets around the relevant word or phrase (e.g., ⌜Gerasenes⌝), thereby alerting the reader to turn to the additional notes at the end of each exegetical unit for a discussion of the textual problem. The documentation uses the author-date method, in which the basic reference consists of author's surname + year + page number(s): Fitzmyer 1992: 58. The only exceptions to this system are well-known reference works (e.g., BDAG, LSJ, *TDNT*). Full publication data and a complete set of indexes can be found at the end of the volume.

Robert Yarbrough
Robert H. Stein

Author's Preface

This work represents the completion of a commitment made in the early 1980s to produce a commentary on both Luke and Acts. There were times when I wondered if I was crazy to agree to this. On the one hand, there are many excellent commentaries on both books, although there were fewer when I originally agreed to do both books. Second, the life of Jesus and the issues raised by Acts are two very distinct areas of NT studies, each representing its own specialty and having a unique literature. One could say, like the old chewing-gum commercial, "Double your pleasure, double your fun," but I often sensed that I had doubled the bibliography and the issues to tackle. Nonetheless, what I have learned in this study and tried to convey has been richly rewarding. The examples of these first saints have much to teach us today.

I took on this assignment at the time because no one recently had written a major commentary on both works and because Luke-Acts is the product of one author telling one story in two volumes. That Luke-Acts was a single work had been little appreciated in the way commentaries handled both works. Luke's innovation needed a careful treatment, especially from an evangelical perspective. So much skepticism had mounted around both Jesus and the earliest church in twentieth-century NT study that a fresh look at these two works was needed. Since the time of that commitment, two authors, Joseph Fitzmyer and Luke Timothy Johnson, have produced an excellent set of critical commentaries on Luke-Acts. Fitzmyer brings a superb understanding of the first-century context to his work, and Johnson knows the Greco-Roman context and the literary themes that enlighten the work. Still, my sense is that issues of importance about the nature of our text, what it can teach the church today, and certain historical issues still needed work. So I offer this commentary, well aware that there is much more that could be said. There comes a time, however, when a commentator must decide that his labor is sufficient to serve the reader well. That is my prayer, especially for those who preach Luke-Acts, rich as it is with history, theology, and pastoral concern for the identity of Christianity and the Christian message.

I owe special thanks to many who encouraged the development of this commentary. Professor Doctor Martin Hengel of the University of Tübingen hosted me on a 2004–5 Humboldt Stiftung scholarship, which allowed me to complete this work. It was my third opportunity to spend a year in a place that has become a second *Heimat*. Our numerous conversations about the early church and its history, held in his home, provided a wealth of insight and wisdom for which I am grateful. The administration and the Department of New Testament at Dallas Theological Seminary afforded me a sabbatical leave and allowed me to function as a research professor so that I was free for this work. Brittany Burnette performed an admirable task as research assistant and conversation partner, as did Stratton Ladewig and John Edwards. My editors at Baker Academic deserve praise for the thoroughness of their work: Jim Kinney, Wells Turner, and series editor Robert Yarbrough. Finally, my wife, Sally, with whom I will celebrate thirty years of marriage this year, has had to live with this project for most of our married life. Our last child went to college two years ago, but in many ways our nest has not been empty because of this work. Yet she also faithfully looked at all the material so that I could be sure I had written in such a way that someone without excessive training could benefit. For such faithfulness I dedicate this work to her, for she has borne the greatest sacrifice with the highest level of grace.

I complete this work on the sixtieth anniversary of the freeing of the prisoners of Auschwitz, effectively ending the Holocaust. As one of Jewish descent, this has special meaning for me. No act against humanity shows the searing reality of sin within us as much as this event from our own recent past. Acts is a story about God's work of love in Jesus to liberate us from what is so destructive for all of us. If this commentary helps give but a glimpse of the great light that Jesus brought to the world, which was experienced by his followers, then my intentions will be met. I have written for both the scholar and the pastor, as well as for the student of Acts, but more than that, I have written in the hope that the gospel, which is so powerfully described and presented in this biblical book, will become more real for those who study Acts.

January 27, 2005
Tübingen, Germany

Abbreviations

Bibliographic and General

Alex. Codex Alexandrinus

BAGD *A Greek-English Lexicon of the New Testament and Other Early Christian Literature.* By W. Bauer, W. F. Arndt, F. W. Gingrich, and F. W. Danker. 2nd edition. Chicago: University of Chicago Press, 1979.

BDAG *A Greek-English Lexicon of the New Testament and Other Early Christian Literature.* By W. Bauer, F. W. Danker, W. F. Arndt, and F. W. Gingrich. 3rd edition. Chicago: University of Chicago Press, 2000.

BDF *A Greek Grammar of the New Testament and Other Early Christian Literature.* By F. Blass, A. Debrunner, and R. W. Funk. Chicago: University of Chicago Press, 1961.

BDR *Grammatik des neutestamentlichen Griechisch.* By F. Blass, A. Debrunner, and F. Rehkopf, Göttingen: Vandenhoeck & Ruprecht, 1984.

BMI British Museum collection of ancient Greek inscriptions

Byz Majority text family

CIG *Corpus inscriptionum graecarum.* Edited by A. Boeckh. 4 vols. Berlin: Ex Officina Academica, 1828–77.

CII *Corpus inscriptionum iudaicarum.* Edited by J. B. Frey. 2 vols. Rome: Pontificio Istituto di Archeologia Cristiana, 1936–52.

CIL *Corpus inscriptionum latinarum.* Berlin: Reimer, 1862–.

CMRDM *Corpus monumentorum religionis dei Menis.* Edited by Eugene Lane. 4 vols. Leiden: Brill, 1971–78.

CPJ *Corpus papyrorum judaicarum.* Edited by V. Tcherikover. 3 vols. Cambridge: Harvard University Press, 1957–64.

EDNT *Exegetical Dictionary of the New Testament.* Edited by H. Balz and G. Schneider. 3 vols. Grand Rapids: Eerdmans, 1990–93.

Eng. English Bible versification

esp. especially

ESV English Standard Version

HCSB Holman Christian Standard Bible

IG *Inscriptiones graecae.* Berlin: Reimer, 1873–.

IGRR *Inscriptiones graecae ad res romanas pertinentes.* Edited by R. Cagnat et al. 3 of 4 vols. published. Rome: L'Erma, 1964.

ILS *Inscriptiones latinae selectae.* Edited by H. Dessau. 3 vols. in 5. Berlin: Weidmann, 1896–1916.

Inschr. Eph. *Die Inschriften von Ephesos.* Edited by H. Wankel. 8 vols. in 10. Bonn: Habelt, 1979–84.

KJV King James Version

L&N *Greek-English Lexicon of the New Testament: Based on Semantic Domains.* Edited by J. P. Louw and E. A. Nida. 2 vols. 2nd edition. New York: United Bible Societies, 1989.

LSJ	*A Greek-English Lexicon.* By H. G. Liddell, R. Scott, and H. S. Jones. 9th edition. Oxford: Clarendon, 1968.
LXX	Septuagint
MAMA	*Monumenta Asiae Minoris antiqua.* Manchester, UK: Manchester University Press, 1928–.
MM	*The Vocabulary of the Greek Testament.* By J. H. Moulton and G. Milligan. London: Hodder & Stoughton, 1930. Reprint, Peabody, MA: Hendrickson, 1997.
MS(S)	manuscript(s)
MT	Masoretic Text
NA[27]	*Novum Testamentum Graece.* Edited by (E. and E. Nestle), B. Aland, et al. 27th revised edition. Stuttgart: Deutsche Bibelgesellschaft, 1993.
NASB	New American Standard Bible
NET	New English Translation
NewDocs	*New Documents Illustrating Early Christianity.* Edited by G. H. R. Horsley and S. Llewelyn. North Ryde, NSW: Ancient History Documentary Research Center, 1976–.
NIDNTT	*The New International Dictionary of New Testament Theology.* Edited by L. Coenen, E. Beyreuther, and H. Bietenhard; English translation edited by C. Brown. 4 vols. Grand Rapids: Zondervan, 1975–86.
NIV	New International Version
NKJV	New King James Version
NLT	New Living Translation
NRSV	New Revised Standard Version
NT	New Testament
OGIS	*Orientis graeci inscriptiones selectae.* Edited by W. Dittenberger. 2 vols. Leipzig: Hirzel, 1903–5.
OT	Old Testament
pl.	plural
P.Lond.	Papyrus London
P.Magd.	Papyrus Magdalen
P.Mich.	Papyrus Michigan (University of Michigan, Ann Arbor)
P.Oxy.	Papyrus Oxyrhynchus
PGM	*Papyri graecae magicae.* Edited by K. Preisendanz. 2 vols. Berlin: Teubner, 1928–31.
RSV	Revised Standard Version
sg.	singular
SIG	*Sylloge inscriptionum graecarum.* Edited by W. Dittenberger. 3rd edition. 4 vols. Leipzig: Hirzel, 1898–1901, 1915–24.
Str-B	*Kommentar zum Neuen Testament aus Talmud und Midrasch.* By H. L. Strack and P. Billerbeck. 6 vols. Munich: Beck, 1922–61.
TDNT	*Theological Dictionary of the New Testament.* Edited by G. Kittel and G. Friedrich. Translated by G. W. Bromiley. 10 vols. Grand Rapids: Eerdmans, 1964–76.

Hebrew Bible

Gen.	Genesis	2 Chron.	2 Chronicles	Dan.	Daniel
Exod.	Exodus	Ezra	Ezra	Hos.	Hosea
Lev.	Leviticus	Neh.	Nehemiah	Joel	Joel
Num.	Numbers	Esth.	Esther	Amos	Amos
Deut.	Deuteronomy	Job	Job	Obad.	Obadiah
Josh.	Joshua	Ps(s).	Psalms	Jon.	Jonah
Judg.	Judges	Prov.	Proverbs	Mic.	Micah
Ruth	Ruth	Eccles.	Ecclesiastes	Nah.	Nahum
1 Sam.	1 Samuel	Song	Song of Songs	Hab.	Habakkuk
2 Sam.	2 Samuel	Isa.	Isaiah	Zeph.	Zephaniah
1 Kings	1 Kings	Jer.	Jeremiah	Hag.	Haggai
2 Kings	2 Kings	Lam.	Lamentations	Zech.	Zechariah
1 Chron.	1 Chronicles	Ezek.	Ezekiel	Mal.	Malachi

Greek Testament

Matt.	Matthew	Eph.	Ephesians	Heb.	Hebrews
Mark	Mark	Phil.	Philippians	James	James
Luke	Luke	Col.	Colossians	1 Pet.	1 Peter
John	John	1 Thess.	1 Thessalonians	2 Pet.	2 Peter
Acts	Acts	2 Thess.	2 Thessalonians	1 John	1 John
Rom.	Romans	1 Tim.	1 Timothy	2 John	2 John
1 Cor.	1 Corinthians	2 Tim.	2 Timothy	3 John	3 John
2 Cor.	2 Corinthians	Titus	Titus	Jude	Jude
Gal.	Galatians	Philem.	Philemon	Rev.	Revelation

Josephus

Ag. Ap.	Against Apion
Ant.	Jewish Antiquities
J.W.	Jewish War
Life	Life of Josephus

Philo

Abraham	On the Life of Abraham
Cherubim	On the Cherubim
Creation	On the Creation of the World
Decalogue	On the Decalogue
Embassy	On the Embassy to Gaius
Flaccus	Against Flaccus
Good Person	That Every Good Person Is Free
Hypothetica	Hypothetica
Joseph	On the Life of Joseph
Migration	On the Migration of Abraham
Moses	On the Life of Moses
QG	Questions and Answers on Genesis
Rewards	On Rewards and Punishments
Spec. Laws	On the Special Laws
Unchangeable	That God Is Unchangeable

Other Jewish and Christian Writings

Add. Esth.	Additions to Esther
Ag. Her.	Irenaeus, *Against Heresies*
1 Apol.	Justin Martyr, *First Apology*
As. Mos.	Assumption of Moses
Bar.	Baruch
2 Bar.	2 (Syriac Apocalypse of) Baruch
3 Bar.	3 (Greek Apocalypse of) Baruch
4 Bar.	4 Baruch
Barn.	Barnabas
1 Clem.	1 Clement
2 Clem.	2 Clement
Dial.	Justin Martyr, *Dialogue with Trypho*
Did.	Didache
Eccl. Hist.	*Ecclesiastical History*
1 En.	1 Enoch
2 En.	2 Enoch
1 Esd.	1 Esdras
2 Esd.	2 Esdras (4 Ezra)
Herm. *Mand.*	Shepherd of Hermas, *Mandate*
Hom. Acts	John Chrysostom, *Homilies on Acts of the Apostles*
Ign. *Eph.*	Ignatius, *To the Ephesians*
Ign. *Magn.*	Ignatius, *To the Magnesians*
Ign. *Phld.*	Ignatius, *To the Philadelphians*
Ign. *Rom.*	Ignatius, *To the Romans*
Ign. *Smyrn.*	Ignatius, *To the Smyrnaeans*
Ign. *Trall.*	Ignatius, *To the Trallians*
Jdt.	Judith
Jos. Asen.	Joseph and Aseneth
Jub.	Jubilees
L.A.B.	Pseudo-Philo, *Liber antiquitatum biblicarum*
Let. Aris.	Letter of Aristeas
1 Macc.	1 Maccabees
2 Macc.	2 Maccabees
3 Macc.	3 Maccabees
4 Macc.	4 Maccabees
Mart. Ascen. Isa.	Martyrdom and Ascension of Isaiah
Mart. Pol.	Martyrdom of Polycarp
Odes Sol.	Odes of Solomon
Pol. *Phil.*	Polycarp, *Letter to the Philippians*
Ps. Sol.	Psalms of Solomon
Sib. Or.	Sibylline Oracles
Sir.	Sirach (Ecclesiasticus)
T. Ash.	Testament of Asher
T. Benj.	Testament of Benjamin
T. Dan	Testament of Dan
T. Gad	Testament of Gad
T. Iss.	Testament of Issachar
T. Jac.	Testament of Jacob
T. Job	Testament of Job

T. Jos.	Testament of Joseph
T. Jud.	Testament of Judah
T. Levi	Testament of Levi
T. Mos.	Testament of Moses
T. Naph.	Testament of Naphtali
T. Reu.	Testament of Reuben
T. Sim.	Testament of Simeon
Tob.	Tobit
Wis.	Wisdom of Solomon

Rabbinic Tractates

The abbreviations below are used for the names of the tractates in the Babylonian Talmud (indicated by a prefixed *b.*); Palestinian, or Jerusalem, Talmud (*y.*); Mishnah (*m.*); and Tosefta (*t.*).

'Abod. Zar.	'Abodah Zarah	Naz.	Nazir
'Abot	'Abot	Ned.	Nedarim
B. Bat.	Baba Batra	Neg.	Nega'im
B. Meṣi'a	Baba Meṣi'a	Nid.	Niddah
Ber.	Berakot	'Ohol.	'Oholot
Beṣah	Beṣah	Pe'ah	Pe'ah
Bik.	Bikkurim	Pesaḥ.	Pesaḥim
Demai	Demai	Qidd.	Qiddušin
'Erub.	'Erubin	Roš Haš.	Roš Haššanah
Giṭ.	Giṭṭin	Šabb.	Šabbat
Ḥag.	Ḥagigah	Sanh.	Sanhedrin
Ḥul.	Ḥullin	Šeb.	Šebi'it
Kelim	Kelim	Šebu.	Šebu'ot
Ker.	Kerithot	Šeqal.	Šeqalim
Ketub.	Ketubbot	Soṭah	Soṭah
Kil.	Kil'ayim	Sukkah	Sukkah
Ma'aś. Š.	Ma'aśer Šeni	Ta'an.	Ta'anit
Mak.	Makkot	Tamid	Tamid
Meg.	Megillah	Ṭohar.	Ṭoharot
Mid.	Middot	Yebam.	Yebamot
Miqw.	Miqwa'ot	Yoma	Yoma (= Kippurim)
Mo'ed Qaṭ.	Mo'ed Qaṭan		

Qumran / Dead Sea Scrolls

1Q29	Liturgy of the Three Tongues of Fire
1Q35	Festival Prayers
1QapGen	Genesis Apocryphon
1QH	Thanksgiving Hymns/Psalms (*Hodayot*)
1QIsa[a]	Isaiah Scroll[a]
1QM	War Scroll (*Milḥamah*)
1QpHab	*Pesher* on Habakkuk
1QS	Manual of Discipline (*Serek Hayaḥad*, Rule of the Community)
1QSa	Appendix *a* to 1QS (Manual of Discipline)
4Q158	Reworked Pentateuch
4Q174	Florilegium (4QFlor)

4Q175	Testimonia (4QTest)
4Q181	Ages of Creation
4Q428	Hymn
4Q501	Apocryphal Lamentations
4Q503	Daily Prayers
4Q511	Songs of the Sage
4Q521	Messianic Apocalypse
4QEn[b]	Book of Enoch[b]
4QExod[a]	Exodus[a]
4QExod[b]	Exodus[b]
4QGen-Exod[a]	Genesis-Exodus[a]
4QpNah	*Pesher* on Nahum
4QpPs	*Pesher* on Psalms
6Q18	Hymn
11QPs[a]	Psalms Scroll[a]
11QT	Temple Scroll
11QtgJob	Targum to Job
CD	Damascus Document

Classical Writers

Ann.	Tacitus, *Annals*
Apology	Plato, *Apology of Socrates*
Chaer.	Chariton of Aphrodisias, *Chaereas and Callirhoe*
Descr.	Pausanius, *Description of Greece*
Ep.	*Epistles*
Eph. Tale	Xenophon of Ephesus, *Ephesian Tale of Anthia and Habrocomes*
Geogr.	*Geography*
Hist.	*Histories*
Hist. Alex.	Aristobulus , *History of Alexander*
Hist. Rom.	Livy, *History of Rome*
Il.	Homer, *Iliad*
Leuc. Cleit.	Achilles Tatius, *The Adventures of Leucippe and Cleitophon*
Life Apoll.	Philostratus, *Life of Apollonius of Tyana*
Lives	Diogenes Laertius, *Lives of the Philosophers*
Metam.	Ovid, *Metamorphoses*
Nat.	Pliny the Elder, *Natural History*
Od.	Homer, *Odyssey*
Pel. War	Thucydides, *Peloponnesian War*
Rom. Hist.	Dio Cassius, *Roman History*

Transliteration

Greek

α	a	ζ	z	λ	l	π	p	φ	ph
β	b	η	ē	μ	m	ρ	r	χ	ch
γ	g/n	θ	th	ν	n	σ/ς	s	ψ	ps
δ	d	ι	i	ξ	x	τ	t	ω	ō
ε	e	κ	k	ο	o	υ	y/u	ʽ	h

Notes on the Transliteration of Greek

1. Accents, lenis (smooth breathing), and *iota* subscript are not shown in transliteration.
2. The transliteration of asper (rough breathing) precedes a vowel or diphthong (e.g., ἁ = *ha*; αἱ = *hai*) and follows ρ (i.e., ῥ = *rh*).
3. *Gamma* is transliterated *n* only when it precedes γ, κ, ξ, or χ.
4. *Upsilon* is transliterated *u* only when it is part of a diphthong (i.e., αυ, ευ, ου, υι).

Hebrew

א	ʼ	בָ	ā	*qāmeṣ*
ב	b	בַ	a	*pataḥ*
ג	g	חָ	a	furtive *pataḥ*
ד	d	בֶ	e	*sĕgôl*
ה	h	בֵ	ē	*ṣērê*
ו	w	בִ	i	short *ḥîreq*
ז	z	בִ	ī	long *ḥîreq* written defectively
ח	ḥ	בָ	o	*qāmeṣ ḥāṭûp*
ט	ṭ	בוֹ	ô	*ḥôlem* written fully
י	y	בֹ	ō	*ḥôlem* written defectively
כ/ך	k	בוּ	û	*šûreq*
ל	l	בֻ	u	short *qibbûṣ*
מ/ם	m	בֻ	ū	long *qibbûṣ* written defectively
נ/ן	n	בָה	â	final *qāmeṣ hēʼ* (בָה = *āh*)
ס	s	בֵי	ê	*sĕgôl yôd* (בֶי = *êy*)
ע	ʻ	בֵי	ê	*ṣērê yôd* (בֵי = *êy*)
פ/ף	p	בִי	î	*ḥîreq yôd* (בִי = *îy*)
צ/ץ	ṣ	בַ	ă	*ḥāṭēp pataḥ*
ק	q	בֶ	ĕ	*ḥāṭēp sĕgôl*
ר	r	בָ	ŏ	*ḥāṭēp qāmeṣ*
שׂ	ś	בְ	ĕ	vocal *šĕwāʼ*
שׁ	š			
ת	t			

Notes on the Transliteration of Hebrew

1. Accents are not shown in transliteration.
2. Silent *šĕwā'* is not indicated in transliteration.
3. The spirant forms בּ גּ דּ כּ פּ תּ are usually not specially indicated in transliteration.
4. *Dāgeš forte* is indicated by doubling the consonant. Euphonic *dāgeš* and *dāgeš lene* are not indicated in transliteration.
5. *Maqqēp* is represented by a hyphen.

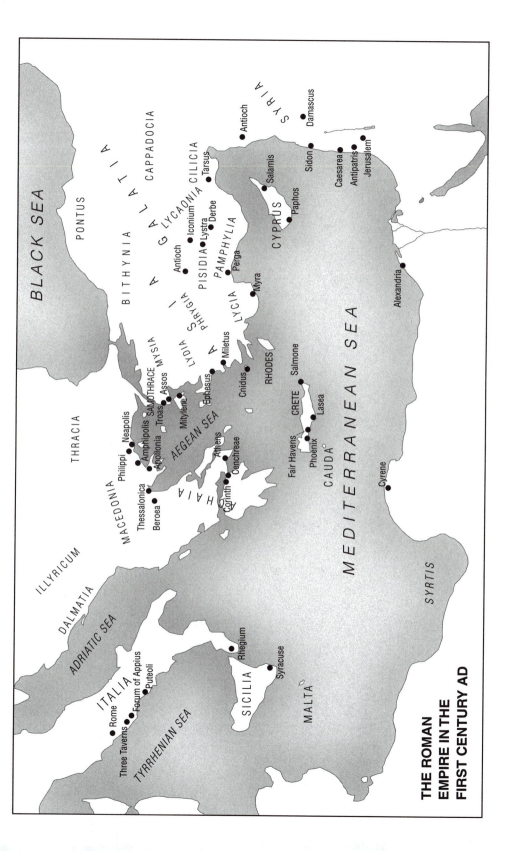

THE ROMAN
EMPIRE IN THE
FIRST CENTURY AD

Introduction to Acts

This introduction makes no claim to be comprehensive. It introduces the discussion of issues associated with Acts that the commentary will treat in more detail. It thus helps these general issues not to get lost in the details that will often emerge later. At the same time, it points the way to more comprehensive examination of the issues.

Genre and Overview

The Title of the Book, Relationship to Luke's Gospel, and Genre

The title "Acts of the Apostles" (ΠΡΑΞΕΙΣ ΑΠΟΣΤΟΛΩΝ, *Praxeis Apostolōn*) appears in $\mathfrak{P}^{74}$ (the title here is at the end of the book, not the beginning), ℵ, B, D (with the singular "Act," likely due to itacism),[1] and Ψ. These are MSS from the fourth to ninth centuries. Manuscript 1175 has only "Acts" as the title. Other MSS, such as 33, 189, 1891, and 2344, mention Luke the evangelist in a longer version of the title ("Luke the evangelist's Acts of the Holy Apostles"). Latin versions possess similar titles. Most likely none of these titles was originally part of the book; they probably emerged in the late first or early second century.[2] The fathers and lists of the second and third centuries confirm the use of such titles.[3] In addition, Tertullian also called the book a "commentary of Luke" (*On Fasting* 10), and Irenaeus (*Ag. Her.* 3.13.3) speaks of the "testimony of Luke regarding the apostles." The variations show that by the end of the second century there were many ways to identify this book of Luke.

In Hellenistic writing, the genre of "acts" normally recounts the deeds of a single great individual, such as Alexander the Great (Diodorus Siculus, *Library of History* 17.15; 18.1.6) or Augustus (*Res gestae divi Augusti*), but sometimes it covers a group, such as "Acts of the Early

---

1. Itacism is the tendency for οι, η, ει, and υ to be pronounced as ι. Failure to distinguish these sounds led to spelling variants when manuscripts were copied by dictation.

2. This suggestion is based on analogy with titles in the Gospels; Hengel 1985: 64–84. Harrison 1975: 11 argues for a second-century date for these titles.

3. Irenaeus, *Ag. Her.* 3.13.3 ("Acts of the Apostles"); Clement of Alexandria, *Stromata* 5.12.82.4 ("Luke in the Acts of the Apostles"); Tertullian, *On Baptism* 10.4 ("Acts of the Apostles"); Muratorian Canon, lines 34–39 ("The Acts of All the Apostles were written in one volume. Luke addresses it to the most excellent Theophilus"); Bruce 1988b: 160; Eusebius, *Eccl. Hist.* 3.4.1 ("in the Acts"); Pesch 1986a: 22–23; for a late-second-century date for the Muratorian Canon, see Ferguson 1982: 677–83. Luke's Acts also does not match in genre the "hero" accounts of second-century accounts of "Acts" (Jervell 1998: 58; Roloff 1988: 1).

Kings" (Diodorus Siculus, *Library of History* 3.1.1; Wikenhauser 1921: 94–104; Talbert 1997: 7; Fitzmyer 1998: 47–48). Such "acts" often were designed to present the hero as a kind of divine man or at least a man sent from God. This genre normally details the hero's acts, including miracles and anecdotes. It is likely that the title "Acts of the Apostles" was intended to highlight that the characters God uses in Acts are to be seen as sent from God. Acts, however, is less focused on individuals than it is on the selective presentation of the growth of the community and its message. The book moves from locale to locale as God directs, starting in Jerusalem and culminating in the travels of Paul to Rome. In fact, the key character in Acts is God, his activity, and his plan.

The work does follow many of the basic rules of Hellenistic histories. Van Unnik (1979: 37–60) identifies two key characteristics of such histories: political understanding and power of expression, and he lists ten rules of such writing, most of which Luke follows.[4]

The title highlights the role of witnesses in the book, but the apostolic band is not the central character of Acts. Rather, God's activity stands at the core of the account. Acts narrates God's work in establishing the church through Jesus's activity. Both Jews and Gentiles make up the church, the new people and community of Jesus. The work of Jesus and the establishment of this community of the Spirit represent the initial fulfillment of God's promises (Schneider 1980: 73; Roloff 1988: 2).[5] Furthermore, only some of the Twelve are highlighted: Peter and John are prominent in this group, but other key players in Acts are not part of the Twelve. These include Stephen, Philip, Paul, and James. Paul is called apostle in only one scene in Acts (14:4, 14) and this is when he appears with Barnabas. Others wish to highlight the Holy Spirit as key, but the Spirit's work is under God's sovereign direction and that of Jesus, the one mediating the Spirit's distribution (Acts 2:32–36; discussed in Gaebelein 1912: 8; Ehrhardt 1958: 67, "gospel of the Holy Spirit"; Bruce 1990: 21–22).

In sum, Acts is a sociological, historical, and theological work explaining the roots of this new community, as a sequel to Luke's story of

4. The rules are (1) a noble subject, (2) the usefulness of the subject for readers, (3) independence of mind and absence of partiality, (4) good narrative construction, (5) adequate collection of preparatory material, (6) the selection and variety of treatment of that material, (7) correct disposition and ordering of the account, (8) lively narration, (9) moderation in topographical detail, and (10) the composition of speeches adapted to the orator and rhetorical situation. Marguerat 2002: 14 holds that Luke follows eight of the ten rules. Only the choice of subject and the lack of impartiality deviate from the list. But as Marguerat is aware (2002: 22), it is precisely because Luke is presenting divine acts and their significance that the subject matter is noble and a perspective that is not partial is undertaken, a perspective that is more in line with Jewish historiography.

5. Without specifying the book's genre, Marguerat 1998 compares Acts to a colony foundation narrative, which seeks to trace the origins of a community, something Acts does in terms of God's promise and provision. He reaffirms this in a later work, calling it apologetic historiography, that is, a "narrative of beginnings" (2002: 34).

Jesus portrayed in his Gospel.[6] It is not part of the genre of "acts" in the Greco-Roman sense; it is, rather, a "historical monograph" in the ancient sense of the term (Hengel 1979: 13–14, 36; Sterling 1992; Witherington 1998: 2–39). This classification also rejects the idea that the appropriate genre for this material is ancient epic (*pace* Bonz 2000). Acts lacks the poetic nature of such works, is concerned with the church's relationship to Israel more than to Rome, and gives evidence, where we can check Luke's work, of being in touch with historical detail rather than being as creative with such detail as the epic classification suggests (Hemer 1989; see the introduction to 16:11–40 and comments on 16:16–40 where Paul's trials are discussed).

Our careful attention to such background will reveal that Luke is a historian in the ancient mold, whose historiography is rooted more in Jewish models than in Greco-Roman ones. Acts is, however, not a full treatment of origins but quite a selective one, highlighting themes and parallels Luke wants the reader to appreciate. That it does not fill in the gaps distinguishes it from later apocryphal "Acts" and speaks to its authenticity (Hengel and Schwemer 1997: 106, 385n554). Luke reveals the selective nature of his treatment as he tells his story. For example, he does not give us the origin of every community he treats, even important ones such as Antioch and Rome. As I noted in the commentary on Luke's Gospel (Bock 1994a: 52), precedents for such a story of God's work among his people are the various works about the Maccabean period (1–2 Maccabees). Acts, however, is a unique account of the origins of God's new community and is best understood as a part of the two volumes Luke composed. Luke was innovative in creating this account of how God worked to bring about a new era and community (Roloff 1988: 1). Nothing indicates the sequel nature of the work more clearly than the reference to "the first account" in Acts 1:1, looking back to Luke's Gospel. The linkage between the works is further reinforced by the overlapping accounts of Jesus's ascension at the end of Luke and the beginning of Acts.

An Aside on Philosophy of History and Recent Study of Acts

It has become popular in our postmodern age to define history itself as a construct and a type of fictive act. Marguerat (2002: 5–7) says

---

6. Shauf 2005: 60–61 notes ten subcategories of historical genre that scholars have attributed to Acts: general history, Greco-Roman political history, apologetic history, institutional history, continuation of biblical history, pathetic history, tragic-pathetic history, rhetorical history, succession narrative, and historical monograph. The problem is that Acts can be connected to many of these subgenres at once, and so such detailed classification probably is too specific. Acts shares traits with a variety of ancient historical genres. For example, Sterling 1992: 17 speaks of apologetic historiography, but then also describes Acts as establishing group identity. Shauf 2005: 65–66 notes that whatever the classification, when it comes to function, most scholars agree that the identity of the community is the point (so also Marguerat 2002: xi).

that "historiography should not be regarded as descriptive, but rather (re)constructive."[7] By this he means that histories are facts interpreted. Marguerat (2002: 8–13) utilizes Ricoeur's distinctions between documentary history, which looks at facts; explicative history, which looks at events from a social, economic, and political viewpoint; and poetic history, which is rooted in founding myths and interprets the past to give a community its sense of identity. For Marguerat, the fact that God is so active in the account makes Acts "poetic history" in many of its sections, rather than reflecting the other two categories. He observes that although Acts includes all the types of history, God's activity makes key sections "poetic" in thrust. There is a major worldview and definitional problem here. How does one treat Jesus's appearance to Paul—as metaphorical and poetic or as a real documentary event? If it is a documentary event, then why are other similar events in Acts moved into this poetic category? What is one to do with the myriad scenes in Acts where God is the reason events take place? Does the description "poetic" really suffice? Such a move risks becoming a worldview, a metaphorical catchall category to rule out God's activity as historically out of bounds in terms of explicative social history. Acts becomes secularized before a page is read or an event is narrated. A key call is being made before the game even begins.

The plurality of interpretations one can give to events affects the way history is viewed. One should be careful, however, not to go too far in making this point. The recent work of Shauf (2005: 66–84) goes in an exaggerated direction. Shauf sidesteps the historicity question by defining historiography as "imaginative narration" simply because the historian assembles a narrative from already limited resources, which themselves are socially constructed as well as tied to what the author himself may see (2005: 66–75). This type of philosophical reading of history is becoming popular in our postmodern world. It gives history and historiography a "linguistic" spin (Clark 2005).

Clark's work, which is an excellent historical-philosophical overview of historiographic discussion, endorses this tendency and is quite skeptical about the historical accuracy of ancient works. She says of the historical critic, "The critic's task, then, is to show how 'seemingly politically innocent objects, forms of subjectivity, actions, and events' are the effects of power and authority, that is, the task to denaturalize and rehistoricize what ideology has produced. By an Althusserian symptomatic reading, the critic looks at gaps and absences in the text, reads what in effect is 'illegible,' and notes how the answers given by a writer do not answer the questions posed" (Clark 2005: 176). This type of ideological deconstruction also itself needs deconstructing, since it often fails to show that the author does not, in fact, answer the question raised. Often an ancient

---

7. Similar in treatment is Schröter 2005.

author gives an answer that deftly moves from the initial question to a more comprehensive but appropriate response. The reading of the deconstructionist turns out to be culturally superficial and illiterate. We shall have occasion to see this move missed regularly in the skepticism with which Haenchen and others read Acts. They argue that Luke fails to address either the questions or the charges the text raises. We shall see just as often that this skeptical reading of Luke often badly misreads the text, undercutting the method's claim to credibility. Even more, Luke does not write from a position of power and authority, since the church of the first century did not have a powerful social position in the ancient world. Luke's appeal to God makes a claim of power but only because Luke was convinced God had really acted in history. It seems clear that Luke's view of Paul's experience and the autobiographical claims of Paul overlap here. Some concrete act transformed Saul into Paul, just as another concrete act provided justification for proclaiming a dead Galilean teacher, crucified for claiming to be a king, as Savior and Lord.

Such a philosophical and skeptical reading of history ignores the fact that certain events are intrinsically significant or may acquire multiple significances as they are tied to or properly associated with later events, so that this significance can be drawn in a variety of ways. That certain events are significant and transforming can be seen by the effects they generated, the expectations they created, or even the impression they initially conveyed. It is possible for ideology and historical data to be combined in a way that reflects an appropriate historical perspective. For example, was D-day merely a social construct, or was it not an inherently significant World War II event that generated initial impressions, expectations, and results? It is true that it could be viewed as a victory or as a defeat, depending on what side one was on, but no one can deny that it was a key event seen as potentially significant from its inception. One need only examine General Rommel's initial reaction to the event to realize that events can and do have an inherent quality to them, especially when they are key events, and that aspects of those events can be read symbolically as reflecting an ultimate significance of such an event. In other words, it is a case not of poetry or history exclusively but of poetry plus history. Nor is the mere collection of events into a sequence that notes the events' relationship and significance to other (often later) events a distortion of history if such connections exist or can be reasonably established. To see the founding of the United Nations as a product, among others, of events in World War II does not distort history.

Thus, although one should not deny that a historian can and does create relationships and can be creative (insightful?) in connecting events, this does not mean that such constructs misrepresent history. This historian's perceptions are very much a part of what history is and how it works itself out. Historical insights can be particularly useful in showing us where history has gone or what might have driven it. One must distinguish between the idea that there is one interpretation of a given set of events (for there are surely more) and the idea that particular interpretations are very useful in pointing to what was hoped for or what resulted from a set of events. History may entail more than digging up brute facts, as recent historiography loves to point out, since these facts are interpreted, but some interpretations and points of view often do mirror what the events produced, enlightening and/or revealing the events' later historical significance and role.

Nor should one read Acts and rule the role of its key player (God) out of bounds before Luke starts to string together the events and their circumstances in ways that point to God's or Jesus's presence and action. It is interesting to note that (1) classical historians respect Luke as a historian as they use him (Nobbs 2006) and that (2) a careful look at the details of Acts shows that, where we can check him, Luke is a credible historian (see the discussion of this theme in the introduction to Acts 16:11–40 as it relates to Paul's trials). Here the work of Sherwin-White 1963; Hemer 1989; and the six-volume series launched by Winter and Clarke (1993) suggest that we should not be so skeptical about Luke. This also shows the crucial importance of doing careful work in backgrounds, especially Jewish and Greco-Roman sources. More NT scholars need to be better equipped in Second Temple Jewish study and classical literature. One must read Acts open to such a balanced view of its historical approach—in terms of its poetry, history, and cultural setting—as well as to the option of divine activity.

Overview of Acts

Acts is one of the longest books of the NT and contains 1,003 verses as compared to 1,151 in Luke and 1,071 in Matthew. It covers eighty-eight pages of the Nestle-Aland text, in comparison to Luke's ninety-six pages and Matthew's eighty-seven pages. Witherington (1998: 6) notes that Acts has 18,374 words as compared with Luke's 19,404 words. Of the 5,436 hapax terms in the NT, 2,038 occur in Acts (Culy and Parsons 2003: xiii).

We have already noted that this work is the sequel to Luke's Gospel. The Acts of the Apostles highlights God's plan of salvation and how God established the new era that resulted from Jesus's ministry, death, and resurrection. It explains how a seemingly new movement is actually rooted in ancient promises associated with Judaism and yet includes Gentiles.

As I noted in the Luke commentary (Bock 1994a: 1–4), four issues dominate these two volumes. (1) The issue of how salvation could claim to be related to the God of Israel and include Gentiles is a major burden of this second volume. How did this happen? What did God do to bring it about? This question is largely answered in Acts 2–11. (2) How could this movement claim to be the promise of God when the Jewish people remained so unresponsive? The Gospel is more concerned with this question than Acts is. In the sequel, this theme emerges as most Jews continue to reject the message, even as many Jews do come to faith. Another major subtheme here is how what started out as the natural extension and realization of Judaism came to develop its own structure, the church. (3) Key to all of this is Jesus's role and function. Whereas Luke's Gospel outlines his ministry, the book of Acts shows how the risen Lord continued to be active and how the new community preached Jesus as central to God's plan. Whether we are looking at what Jesus realized in his ministry and resurrection (Acts 2:16–36) or what he will do when he returns (Acts 3:19–23), he is the Lord, who is seated at God's right hand and appointed to be the judge of the living and the dead (Acts 10:40–42). (4) Finally, there is the story of various faithful witnesses who respond to Jesus in the face of opposition. Whether this theme concerns Peter and John, Stephen, Philip, Paul, or Barnabas, the book is filled with those sharing in the calling to take the message of fulfillment to the end of the earth. They serve as examples for those who carry out the mission of God.

The real center of the book, however, is God. At key junctures God enables, directs, protects, and orchestrates. Nothing shows this as much as the story of Paul, who comes to faith by Jesus's direct intervention and is protected as he travels to Rome, despite shipwreck. It is no accident that in discussing God, we also cover the activity of Jesus and the Spirit he sends. Jesus mediates the Spirit, who in turn enables. The Spirit is sent as "power from on high" to lead the new community (Luke 24:49) and to empower its members as powerful witnesses to the events that eyewitnesses around Jesus saw and experienced (Acts 1:8; Bauckham 2006, esp. p. 390 with discussion of αὐτόπται [autoptai, eyewitnesses] in Luke 1:1). This sending of the Spirit is another link between the end of Luke and the beginning of Acts. The Spirit in particular is the spirit of enablement and testimony in Acts.

Most of the book is told from the perspective of certain locales and key figures. As Acts 1:8 suggests, it proceeds from Jerusalem into Judea and Samaria and to the end of the earth. Peter dominates early as the new community gathers and grows in Jerusalem (Acts 1–5). The theological burden of the book is carried in this section by key speeches that dominate this unit. But others of Hellenistic Jewish background are also active, moving out from Jerusalem as the result of persecution. Stephen gives his life by testifying in Jerusalem, and Philip takes the gospel to Samaria in a prelude to the spread of the gospel to all people (Acts 7–8). Meanwhile, God is preparing another vessel to take God's word out, as Saul is called to faith (Acts 9). A return of the focus to Peter allows him to bring the gospel to Gentiles at Caesarea (Acts 10:1–11:18). During that time, Acts also introduces more detail about an important community in Antioch (Acts 11:19–30). The pressure in Jerusalem is shown to be great when James, not the Lord's brother, is slain and Peter is imprisoned (Acts 12). Still, God protects Peter there.

The scene then shifts to Antioch, a major community that launches the missionary travels of Paul and Barnabas (Acts 13–14). The issue of exactly how Gentiles should be included brings all the key players to Jerusalem for a council to decide the matter (Acts 15). More missionary travel for Paul follows, beginning from Antioch, with several of the famous churches being established or strengthened during this time. So we hear of communities in Philippi, Thessalonica, and Corinth as well as work in Athens (Acts 16:1–18:23). Paul's third journey focuses on Ephesus, but then he returns to Jerusalem and is making a vow in the temple when he is arrested (Acts 18:24–21:36). Paul's ministry in each case has a great impact, even though it also meets with stern opposition. The rest of the book is taken up with Paul's journey to Rome (Acts 22–28). The major elements of this unit are Paul's defense speeches, in which the position of the church relative to God's promise again shows forth. The theme of divine protection closes the book: Paul experiences a shipwreck on the way to Rome, but he arrives safely and awaits his trial, eagerly sharing Jesus as Lord with all who will visit him.

Acts as Ancient Rhetorical History

We consider the literary genre of Acts before we turn to the question of authorship. As already suggested, Acts is a sociological, historical, and theological monograph with parallels in works such as the Maccabees. Jervell (1998: 76–79) calls it a history of God's people. Comparisons to other ancient works must be made with qualifications, as we shall see. First, the nature of the work and its tradition base indicate that this is not an ancient novel or romance. Pervo's claim (1987) that Acts is more like a novel represents a skeptical handling of the book at one end of the spectrum in the discussion of the work as history. In varying degrees, writers such as Dibelius, Conzelmann, Haenchen, and others treat Acts as having little historical value. The roots of this view go back to the old Tübingen school and F. C. Baur in the nineteenth century, with its portrait of Christianity in conflict and Luke as the mediator of the tension in Acts, trying to smooth over real differences between Peter and Paul.[8] According to this view, Luke tries to present a more idealized picture of the church than what really existed. Even though the later

---

8. As Gasque 1989: 24–26 and Marguerat 2002: 2–4 note, the issue of the Lukan portrayal of Paul is also the oldest complaint raised against Luke's presentation of history, going back to W. M. L. DeWette (1780–1849) in the early nineteenth century. The question was pursued by F. C. Baur (1792–1860) and his *Tendenzkritik*, where Peter and Paul represent competing Christianities that Luke seeks to reconcile. Marguerat calls Baur "the real detonator in the criticism of Luke's historiography." Overbeck 1919: 78 calls Luke's work a "gaffe on the scale of world history."

date for Acts that this view implies has been abandoned, some of what this perspective argues for in terms of church tension is still retained by those who doubt the credibility of Acts. Through Dibelius (1956) this approach came to appeal also to form criticism (on the problems with form criticism, see Bauckham 2006: 241–52). In this view, Luke was more about theology than history, and the two were almost competing concerns (Marshall 1980: 34–36). Nothing exemplifies this approach more than the commentary by Haenchen (1987), who at almost every turn sees historical problems and regards Luke as more concerned to edify than to inform.

Another group of scholars, however, dating back to Ramsey and extending to Bruce, Gasque, Hemer, Hengel, Marshall, Sherwin-White, and Witherington, have high regard for Luke as an ancient historian.[9] Ramsey, in particular, in a careful study of Acts found that many of its details are more trustworthy than he thought before he began his study. To argue this is not to deny that Luke writes a theology and has a perspective that he brings to the account. There is not the disjunction, however, between history and theology that the other approach to Acts often brings. Since, in many ways, a consideration of historicity in detail requires going through the data of the book unit by unit, only some general remarks are made here, noting that the conservative and more moderate approaches to Acts often speak with respect for Luke's approach as a historian.

For some scholars, the most troubling aspect of the book is the range of miracles and the direct invoking of divine involvement. For those who question such categories, Acts is automatically suspect because of the way God functions as the central, and even most active, character. Luke's perspective and testimony are that God has acted in such a manner, representing proof that God was at work. This is a worldview issue when it comes to Acts. If one doubts God's activity in things such as miracles, then Acts instantly becomes suspect historically, and interpretation quickly moves in a more "poetic" direction.

When we move to events that have documentary or historical corroboration, then Luke fares well. Fitzmyer (1998: 126–27) notes nine elements of the account that have external attestation, either through the Pauline Epistles or through outside historical sources. These are Paul's escape from Damascus, Paul's trip to Rome, the earning of Paul's livelihood, Herod Agrippa's sudden death, Gallio as proconsul of Achaia, Felix and Festus as procurators in Judea, Drusilla as wife of Felix, Bernice as wife of Herod Agrippa II, and Ananias as high priest. He also notes minor

9. Fitzmyer 1998: 124 places himself in the middle, between skeptical and conservative handlings of the book. Barrett 1994; 1998 also likely belongs here. We shall interact with this more moderate approach in more detail as we proceed from passage to passage, since discussions of historicity ultimately boil down to working through the details.

details that are correct, such as proper descriptions of cities (Philippi as a "colony") and officials (politarchs in Thessalonica). Much of what we can test shows that Acts is a credible historical source. The work of Hemer (1989) has shown how careful Luke is in Acts in numerous details. Hengel (1979: 60) affirms that Luke is no less trustworthy than other historians of antiquity, an assessment that might seem like faint praise, but in the environment of extreme skepticism, this is saying a great deal. Hengel says that comparisons to largely fictitious, romance-like writings are a disservice.

The treatment of the individual units will also show that trustworthiness is a prominent feature in Acts. We shall sort out the places where some scholars are most suspicious of Luke as a historian, namely, the Jerusalem Council and other points related to Paul, especially his effort to gather a collection for Jerusalem. For example, Barrett (1998: xxxvi–xlii) focuses on the council passage as a historical problem and argues that Baur was right about the tension between Peter and Paul, so that such an event could scarcely have occurred. Indeed, Paul's relationship to Jerusalem and the Jews of that city is where the issue of Luke's history versus his theology is most often questioned. We shall pay careful attention to such questions in the commentary as they arise.

In general, what kind of history is Acts? Often a writer's *Tendenz* or that he or she argues an apologetic case is used to suggest that we should expect something less than general accuracy. Penner (2004) devotes an entire monograph to arguing that ancient historiography was about persuasion, plot, and characterization—even the rewriting of history to make a convincing case—and he challenges approaches to ancient history such as those of Hengel or Witherington. In Penner's view, the line between ancient history and romance is thin. He also argues that ancient history is not about the veracity of the event but verisimilitude rooted in later personal experience (2004: 110). An appeal to experience, however, that was direct and early also fits into such ancient historical writing, a point Penner minimizes. Penner also emphasizes how all recognize Luke as the creator of the text's wording, which makes it hard to reach the actual history (2004: 108, 111). But *Tendenz* merely reflects a point of view on events that themselves are open to interpretation. Good history is about more than merely what happened and when; it also treats causes and effects, also revealing motivations and rationale. One must avoid appealing to false oppositions here. Luke's creativity is seen not in his creating an event but in his summarizing of it, an option Penner seems to exclude. Luke's summary can have connections to the real event and need not disregard it. In addition, sometimes verisimilitude may appear to exist because there is connection to a real event and background the author or his source portrayed. There is also the real possibility that tensions between early and later times overlapped, making texts relevant for both the time of the event and the time when Luke is writing. Thus we should be careful in suggesting that the relevance of a scene to a later setting means that it could not have been relevant earlier.

What Acts seeks to do is to teach and persuade, even by the use of powerful examples, but to do so by showing, through the selective choice of events and summary, what originally took place on a grander scale. There is no doubt that Acts has a case to argue, as both the preface to the Gospel and Acts itself suggest. It seeks to give assurance, but this assurance is rooted, in part, in the essential character of the events Luke portrays. It may not be the only possible point of view on these events, but it is the one for which Luke contends.

The book of Acts is like other ancient histories in its approach. The ancients understood history as the relating of deeds for edification, as Lucian's discussion in *How to Write History* 49–55, 63 shows and as do the remarks of Polybius (*Hist.* 2.56.11) and Quintilian (*Institutio oratoria* 2.4.2).[10] Lucian says that a historian should get his facts right. The study of Fornara (1983) distinguishes between Roman histories and Greek history such as that of Thucydides and Polybius. Penner (2004: 110) dismisses the appeal to such experts on the classics, seeing them as too conservative about their task, but perhaps classical scholars such as Fornara recognize that efforts to move the historical task away from the events that sources attempt to portray risk abandoning history altogether. Greek historians valued personal observation and participation in events where they could find such sources. The "we sections" of Acts reflect this Greek tradition, as does the concern for a variety of races and cities. Such ancient writers used speeches as summaries of events and as a means of tying their history together, but they also disliked the idea of inventing speeches. Polybius (*Hist.* 12.25A–B) condemns inventing speeches or replacing with fictitious exposition the words spoken. Polybius also notes that such orations have the goal of ascertaining the words spoken and "may be regarded as summaries of events" (Witherington 1998: 33). Bruce (1990: 28) notes parallels between Luke's writing and Thucydides, such as Luke's preface and his synchronic use of dating. Luke seems to write with an awareness of such historical conventions. One Lukan contrast to this Greco-Roman tradition is that the key events are not political or military as in most Greek history; instead, they are social and communal, showing where the emphasis is in seeing God at work. To find God at work, look especially among God's people.

The work also fits into the genre of Jewish historiography. Here the primary concern is to tell "the story of a subgroup of people in an ex-

---

10. Witherington 1998: 10–11, 24–39 has a more complete discussion, where he shows that Lucian argued for care about detail and accuracy as well as for concern for the accuracy of sources; see also Mosley 1965–66; Bruce 1990: 27–34; and esp. van Unnik 1979: 46–47.

tended prose narrative" (Sterling 1992: 17) while highlighting God's activity. As Marguerat (2002: 25) says, "Judeao-Christian *historia* has no other ambition than to point to God behind the event." However, a difference between Luke and these ethnic narratives is a key feature of his book: he is trying to explain how God directed that the new faith *expand* from its Jewish subgroup roots to include people of all sorts of backgrounds. Finally, a key theme in Jewish historiography is to show that what people are experiencing is part of the way God has acted for ages. This explains why such histories constantly appeal to the Scriptures by quotation and allusion. The model for accounts such as the Maccabees is the historical narrative sections of the OT itself, which tells Israel's story as God directed it in the past through Moses, Joshua, the judges, and then a succession of kings (Rosner 1993: 65–82). Schneider (1980: 122–25) even stresses that this connection to how God has always acted is the key to understanding Luke's work. In this sense, the account is a piece of salvation history, telling how God has acted to save. We shall have occasion to return to these issues when we consider the preface of Acts. Those listening to the story of Acts (most of Luke's ancient audience would have experienced the book by hearing it read) would have recognized it as a treatment of history with antecedents in Greek and Jewish history.

In sum, Acts is a piece of Hellenist and Jewish historiography that treats the theme of how the new community is rooted in God's old promises, the Lord Jesus's current activity, and the Spirit's effective presence. Acts focuses on key human players as well, such as Peter, Stephen, Philip, Paul, and James. The book places these characters and events in the context of the world's larger history. Its details are correct regarding provinces and governors, as well as in elements of local color and judicial practice (for the latter, see Sherwin-White 1963). Barrett (1998: cxiv–cxviii) gives Luke a "mostly favorable" verdict as a historian, noting that even where his sources are not corroborated, Luke must be taken seriously. But Barrett also regards Luke as getting more off the track once Paul and the Jerusalem Council are treated. We shall have occasion to assess this view of Acts 15 and Luke's handling of Paul. Our take is not as skeptical as Barrett's, but this is a discussion that cannot be undertaken without considering the details. So this topic awaits the commentary.

Acts seeks to inform and instruct about the outcome and aftermath of Jesus's coming to earth as God's unique representative. By examining the impact of Jesus, Luke was an innovator in seeing that the story of the earliest community was worth telling in connection with what Jesus had done. Luke hoped that others would come to appreciate what God had done and was doing through what became the church. In this way, those in the community could be encouraged and come to a deeper appreciation of their heritage, while others could be exhorted to be a part of what God was doing.

Language, Style, and Form

Luke's language reflects Koine Greek written by someone in contact with Jewish tradition (de Zwann 1922; Cadbury 1958: 213–38). Fitzmyer (1998: 114–15) notes an array of Jewish Greek vocabulary as well as several Septuagintisms and Latin terms. More debated is whether there is evidence of Aramaisms, which is hard to separate from Septuagintal influence since the style of the LXX itself is full of Hebraisms or Aramaisms.[11] Luke has the largest vocabulary of any NT writer, but this may reflect the wide variety of settings presented in his work. Almost 90 percent of the vocabulary is also found in the LXX (Clarke 1922: 69; Polhill 1992: 43), and 85 percent overlaps with Plutarch (Haenchen 1987: 72). Much of the vocabulary mirrors other accounts, such as Judges, Samuel, Kings, and 2 Maccabees (Schille 1984: 29). This usage shows a "well educated" writer (Haenchen 1987: 72). It also indicates a desire to give a "biblical" feel to his account. Only Paul and the author of Hebrews are comparable in their range and use of Greek.

The style shifts as Acts proceeds. In the early chapters of Acts, Luke presents a series of mostly short scenes and speeches in a variety of settings (Pesch 1986a: 34–36; Roloff 1988: 11). As the account moves to consider Paul, he becomes more of a focus, and the scenes in general have more detailed development. It is fair to say that the style of speeches early on has a more Semitic feel than later speeches, showing some sensitivity to setting.[12] Important scenes are retold, such as Paul's conversion and the arrival of the Spirit to the Gentiles when Peter speaks to Cornelius's household.

Extensions of style are the forms that Luke uses: narrative, miracle accounts, summaries, "we section" travel notes, and especially the speeches where the bulk of the conceptual theology is expressed (Fitzmyer 1998: 96–108). The narratives are more like stories about the key characters than any other form subtype. Yet the flow of the narrative is also designed to suggest how Luke sees God active in the world. Certain events told in a favorable light point to key examples of faithfulness to be emulated. Summaries are both major (2:42–47; 4:32–35; 5:12–16) and minor (1:14; 6:7; 9:31; 12:24; 16:5; 19:20; 28:30–31). Some summaries indicate growth (2:41; 4:4; 5:14; 6:1; 9:31; 11:21, 24; 12:24; 14:1; 19:20).

No form is more discussed by scholars than the "we sections." The haphazard way these sections appear, sometimes with events of less significance, speaks against the idea that Luke has created the sections to give the impression he was present in these locales (*pace* Rothschild 2004: 264–67, who sees them as part of the mainly rhetorical element

---

11. Barrett 1998: xlv–xlviii lists a series of constructions, common in Acts, showing a Greek influenced by Hebrew style; see also Haenchen 1987: 74–75.

12. See Witherington 1998: 44. One can note the lack of citations in the speeches in Acts 10 and 17, where Gentiles do not need or necessarily appreciate references to Scripture.

in Acts, inserted by the author "to indulge the audience in a fantasy meant to transport them beyond argument to belief").[13] Why create the impression of eyewitness presence at some of the less significant events in the book if one is inserting such claims? The lack of significance for the locales of such sections speaks to their authenticity. Fitzmyer (1998: 100–102) notes the lack of any literary precedent for a travel narrative that is a literary creation. He also challenges the idea that such conventions exist for sea voyages. Rather, as Fitzmyer argues, these notes indicate when the writer of Acts was present at some of the events being portrayed, part of the valued "eyewitness motif" in Greek historiography. Hengel (1979: 66–68) agrees that this work needs to be taken "seriously as a source." More debated is whether the "we" represents Luke himself or an eyewitness other than Luke. For a good case that the author is someone other than Luke, see Porter 1999: 10–66, who notes how Paul is presented in more muted tones in the "we sections" than elsewhere in Acts. This seems to be a reason he thinks the source does not go back to Luke. The muted tones, however, may be due to the nature of the original genre itself, which was more of a summarizing travel narrative than a full account with a wide variety of detail. Despite efforts to place the source with someone other than Luke, a view that is plausible, it is hard to overcome the impression given by the text that the author includes himself as present at these various occasions. The question remains: Why would Luke treat this "we" source in a manner different from all the other sources he used, which also came from other people or communities? It may well be that Luke left his summaries alone as he inserted them into his account. Still, the likelihood is that the "we" is an indication of when Luke was present. The role of the speeches is so important to Acts that we shall discuss them separately later when we consider sources.

13. This is but one example of Rothschild's appeal to various rhetorical devices as means of persuasion instead of reflections of genuine, historiographical concerns (Rothschild 2004: 291). She examines the following five devices: patterns of recurrence, prediction, predictive exploitation of the Greek auxiliary verb δεῖ, amplification of eyewitnesses, and epitomizing. She claims that these techniques are representative of Hellenistic historiography and lead to a conclusion that history and theology should not be placed in competing categories, as is often the case for Luke-Acts. The reason for the opposition, however, is the view that the use of rhetoric at the expense of genuine history is what is taking place. A second take on the "we passages" comes from Phillips 2005. He analyzes them from a narrative perspective and argues two points: (1) the narrator shares a place in postapostolic times with Paul, and (2) this approach allows the narrator to historicize the earlier events tied to the apostles, especially the community of goods. Both of these observations need qualification. Actually, with regard to point 1, Luke sees Paul as overlapping with the apostolic times, although his role becomes significant later as shifts are taking place in Jerusalem, where the apostles become less central. This apostolic overlap undercuts the idea that Paul is the only example of how to handle goods in contrast to the earlier actions of the apostles in idea 2. Acts never portrays the sharing of goods in a negative light. In fact, it shows an ethic that takes seriously the needs of a neighbor.

Luke is a skilled ancient historian who writes with vividness and variety. His goal is to instruct, inform, and persuade his audience that God has been at work in Jesus and those who followed him. Rothschild's attempt, noted above, to argue that Luke lacks genuine historical concern appeals to specific ancient forms in a useful study of such forms' presence in a wide array of ancient literature. She presents forms, however, that appear in all kinds of ancient historiographic texts, both trustworthy and not. So their presence is not able to define the exact type of historiographic text we possess. Fornara (1983) and Hemer (1989) indicate that matters are not so simple.

For a contrasting approach to Acts, appealing to a sophisticated use of the ancient biographical genre, the essay by Porter (2005) is of significance. He compares ancient historical romance to historical monograph: "Many of these elements ascribed to fiction can be contained within the historiographical hypothesis" (Porter 2005: 8–9). What Porter says of fiction can also be applied to rhetorical claims. He appeals to the category of ancient biography for Acts. The problem here with classification is that the key character of Acts is God, not any of his servants. So if it is a biography, it is of a special kind, a "theography," if you will. This blurring of the genre lines points to the uniqueness of Acts and makes it hard to know if it should be classified as an ancient history (story of great deeds) or a special form of biography (story of God's directive, salvific work).

Author, Roots, and Purpose

Authorship, Internal Evidence, External Evidence, and the Critical Debate

Much of the discussion of authorship parallels the issues raised about the authorship of the Gospel of Luke, since the two works are linked (Bock 1994a: 4–7; Cadbury 1922 reviews in detail the tradition tied to Luke). It is clear that the two volumes are the work of the same author, since the two prefaces are linked by the mention of Theophilus (Luke 1:1–4; Acts 1:1–5).

Regarding internal evidence, the key element is the "we sections" and the debate that swirls around this material (Acts 16:10–17; 20:5–15; 21:1–18; 27:1–28:16). If these units are what they seem to be, then the author was a witness to some events recounted in Acts and was a sometime companion of Paul (Bruce 1990: 3–5). We have already noted that the haphazard use of these sections and the lack of precedent for literarily created "we sections" speak for its authenticity as reflective of the author.[14] The author is not a witness to Jesus's ministry; he is a second-generation convert, a sometime companion of Paul.

14. But see Barrett 1998: xxvii–xxix, who attributes the "we sections" to an itinerary list. Porter 1999: 10–66 argues that this section is a source distinct from the author's

The external evidence is most revealing. Candidates who knew Paul are numerous (Mark, Aristarchus, Demas, Luke, Timothy, Titus, Silas, Epaphras, and Barnabas). Colossians 4:14 names Luke as one known to Paul, but that tradition also names many of the others we have listed. Luke is also mentioned in Philem. 24 and 2 Tim. 4:11. Despite the number of possibilities, the external tradition is united around one figure, Luke. This is significant, especially since Luke is not a prominent figure in the period, according to the NT (Bruce 1990: 6). This stands in contrast to Haenchen (1987: 14), who argues that the tradition should be read critically and has little value on its own. He claims that Luke emerges by a process of elimination from information in the second century. Haenchen's view, however, ignores the unanimity in the tradition when many candidates could fulfill the general evidence emerging from within Acts. Would such unanimity emerge if someone were just trying to guess who the author might be? There would be no reason to pick Luke out of the blue as the author. This tradition was firmly in place by AD 200. Justin Martyr in *Dial.* 103 speaks of Luke, citing the third Gospel, as a companion of the apostles. The Muratorian Canon, lines 34–39, refers to Luke as the author who compiled the Acts for Theophilus, as do the Anti-Marcionite Prologues. Irenaeus (*Ag. Her.* 3.1, 14) refers to Luke as Paul's companion and the recorder of his gospel. He also says that Luke was inseparable from Paul.[15] Clement of Alexandria (*Stromata* 5.12), when alluding to Acts 17, calls Luke the author of Acts. Tertullian in *Against Marcion* 4.2 also connects Luke and Paul, as does Origen, according to Eusebius, *Eccl. Hist.* 6.25.

The debate about these references concerns the seemingly different portrait of Paul in his epistles from that in Acts; this is said to bring doubt on the tradition of Luke's association with Paul (Windisch 1922: 316–48 has one of the fullest and earliest defenses of this view). Marshall (1980: 42) notes that this is a key reason many doubt the historical value of Acts. Vielhauer (1966) states this view most compactly and powerfully, citing four alleged inconsistencies between Paul and the portrait of Paul in Acts relating to natural law, Jewish law, Christology, and eschatology. He claims that Luke has a place for natural theology, as seen in Acts 17, whereas Paul, according to Rom. 1, has none; that Luke has no place for the cross, but it is central for Paul; and that Luke has virtually abandoned the end-time eschatology that Paul affirms. He also notes how little of Paul's own writing shows up in Acts.

---

general emphases in Acts but that it cannot be ruled out or shown that it goes back to the author.

15. Irenaeus's idea that Luke was constantly with Paul is clearly an exaggeration, given the brief references to Luke's presence in the "we sections." By contrast, Eusebius (*Eccl. Hist.* 3.4) says Luke was with Paul "a good deal" (also noted in 3.24, where Luke is said also to have had contact with "the rest of the apostles").

Credible responses to Vielhauer exist (Ellis 1974: 45–47; Bruce 1976; Fitzmyer 1998: 145–47 calls Vielhauer's view "clearly exaggerated"). The difference between Acts 17 and Rom. 1 is the difference between the writing of someone reaching out to share the gospel while making an effort to find common ground (Acts 17) and the more forthright critique of what pagan culture was in the eyes of a monotheist (Rom. 1). The difference is merely one of contextualizing. Paul's speech in Acts 17 is not as philosophically grounded as Vielhauer suggests. Gärtner (1955) shows this by arguing that the speech is rooted in Jewish natural theology, a point we shall underscore in the commentary. Luke does have a view of the cross like Paul's. It shows up in the speech to the elders at Miletus (Acts 20:28) as well as at the Last Supper (Luke 22:18–20). As Moule (1966: 159–86) shows, Luke's Christology is not adoptionist, as some claim.[16] Luke too affirms an end-time eschatology, whether it be in the explanation of Peter in Acts 3:18–22, in brief notes about Jesus being the one appointed to be the judge of the living and the dead (Acts 10:40–42; 17:30–31), or in the affirmation of Jesus's return in Acts 1:11. The issue of the law is more complex and will be treated in the relevant commentary sections, but the key is the recognition that Paul again contextualizes, being a Jew to the Jews and a Greek to the Greeks (1 Cor. 9:19–23). This is something hard-line Jewish believers might have objected to but that he saw as entirely consistent. That Paul could be sensitive to Jewish concerns about circumcision (in line with 1 Cor. 9) is shown by Acts 16:3 (and in 1 Cor. 7:19 Paul says that circumcision is of no account). As Ellis (1974: 47) says about Vielhauer's essay, "When he [Vielhauer] has difficulty in recognizing Luke's Paul, this writer often finds a similar difficulty in recognizing Vielhauer's Luke."

Haenchen (1987: 112–16) argues that the unknown author of the work was not a collaborator with Paul but a writer from a later generation. First, he presents the view that both Paul and this writer deal with the mission to the Gentiles without the law but that Luke did not know of Paul's solution, namely, that Christ is the end of the law. One can see, however, the law-mission issue in Acts 13:38–39, 48–50; 15:2; 21:20–21, 28. In contrast to Haenchen's solution, which argues that Paul reasoned his way to a gentile mission, Luke views the matter from the outside, namely, that God willed the mission. There are hints in Acts 13 that things are not as Haenchen suggests here.

16. Adoptionism is the view that Jesus became the Christ or was appointed to that position sometime during his earthly ministry (e.g., at his baptism or after his resurrection). For the case that Luke (along with Matthew and Mark) presents Jesus as possessing a heavenly identity before Easter, see Gathercole 2006. How much some of these texts Gathercole appeals to implied in their original historical setting is debatable, but that Luke uses them with full force is quite likely given his post-Easter perspective. Ambiguity became clarity in light of divine events.

Second, Haenchen argues that there is a discrepancy between the "Lukan" Paul and the Paul of the letters. He begins by asserting that Paul considers himself to be an apostle, something that Luke does not affirm. Haenchen also states that Luke presents Paul as a miracle worker and a great orator, two things that Paul does not emphasize. But Haenchen is not correct here. In several texts, Paul indicates that he performed miracles (Rom. 15:18–19; 1 Cor. 5:4–5; 2 Cor. 4:7; 12:9; 12:12; 1 Thess. 1:5), and his letters themselves are proof of his oratorical skills. Moreover, Haenchen's claim that Acts portrays Paul as "a great orator" is exaggerated, considering that Paul does not move most of the Athenians, leaves Festus with the impression that he is mad, and puts Eutychus to sleep. When Paul hesitates about his gifts, we may have evidence of a humility that does not want to take excessive personal credit for gifts that God is responsible for giving.

Third, Haenchen alleges that Luke's portrayal of Jewish-Christian relations contradicts Paul. In Acts, Paul is persecuted for preaching that, according to the age-old Jewish promise, Jesus rose from the dead. In the Pauline writings, and as Acts also hints, Paul is persecuted for having Jews abandon the law and practices such as circumcision. In this critique, Haenchen is guilty of reductionism, as if Jewish reaction to Paul were limited to one issue or concern. Paul seems quite clear that a crucified, risen Messiah is a stumbling block to the Jews (1 Cor. 1:23). Resolution of this dispute will require looking at the details of the passages, but the initial case against a Lukan-Pauline connection is not as strong as it might at first appear (Porter 1999: 187–206).

Three observations are helpful in analyzing the issue. The first is that how one presents oneself and how another sees and summarizes one's arguments are not always the same. Sometimes what impacts a listener and resonates with him or her is different from what even the speaker expected. The second is that the emphasis and concerns of a student may not always mirror those of the teacher. Luke is often said to ignore Paul's teaching about the cross and justification by faith alone, but it may well be that Luke has merely highlighted the "who" of salvation more than the "how." He is aware of the cross and of justification, but Luke does not dwell on these themes. He may simply take the cross as a given, as the discussion at the Last Supper and at Miletus suggest (Luke 22:18–22; Acts 20:17–35). The exalted Jesus and the mission to the Gentiles are two major themes that both Paul and Luke share, but Paul, a theologian with a rabbinic background, goes beyond these to show how salvation is accomplished. Paul expounds this process of salvation in great detail (more detail, in fact, than almost any other NT writer). Luke, on the other hand, is more of a lay theologian and is not interested in probing these details. For Luke, salvation is about identifying with and turning to faith in Jesus. Thus Luke's "difference" may simply reflect his own concerns and emphases. The third is that Luke's concerns at points are distinct from

Paul's. For the most part, Paul writes to those inside the church about specific, local issues, whereas Luke writes about more global issues. These elements mean that one needs to be careful in making an assessment that one figure does not know the other (Marshall 1980: 43n4).

Regarding Luke's lack of references to Paul's letters, it is not necessary for Luke to cite or note correspondence about specific, local issues that he does not treat in Acts. Bruce (1990: 54) suggests that the book was written too close to the time when Paul wrote his letters, so that there was no collection of them available. Issues that need more detailed consideration are the debate over circumcision and Paul's relationship to Jerusalem and its Jewish Christian community. Witherington (1998: 88–97) discusses in some detail the issue of Paul, Galatians, and the debate over circumcision and sees the accounts as reconcilable with Lukan authorship. My treatment of Acts 15 comes to a similar conclusion: I argue that this conclave of leaders took place after the writing of Gal. 2 (see introduction to Acts 15:1–35 in the commentary).

Bruce (1990: 52–59) has an important treatment of these questions and also does not see the differences as precluding Lukan authorship. In particular, he notes that Paul's willingness to be a Jew to the Jews and a Greek to the Greeks (1 Cor. 9:19–23) is a key to understanding how Paul handles the issues of the vow request in Jerusalem and of Timothy's circumcision.

In sum, the external evidence strongly favors Luke as the writer of Acts. That no other Pauline companion was ever put forward as the author of this work when many such candidates existed is key evidence. It is true that the internal considerations and theological emphases raise questions about whether Luke is the author, but not to a degree that cancels out the likelihood that he was the author and that the tradition has the identification correct.[17]

Sources

We have already noted the "we sections" and how they help us understand the origins of Acts by showing when the author himself was a source. Harder to determine is the extent to which Luke used other source material and whether we are able to identify such sources. Bruce (1990: 40) notes that some scholars have rightly called such efforts "largely guess-work." There is no good way to determine the existence of such sources.[18]

In Acts 1–12, it appears there are sources from the Jerusalem community and perhaps from Hellenistic Jewish communities as well, since Acts 6:8–8:40 seems to be told from the latter perspective, whereas most

17. Bock 1994a: 5–6 suggests that Luke was a doctor and likely a Gentile who may have been a God-fearer before becoming a Christian.
18. For a discussion of sources, see Schneider 1980: 82–89, who rejects as unlikely a Semitic source for Acts 1–15.

everything else up to this point has a Jerusalem perspective. Acts 12 seems to be Jerusalem-based, and the source for Acts 9 could well be Paul. More difficult to determine is the origin for Acts 10–11. Either locale for the source (the Jewish Jerusalem or the Hellenist Jerusalem community) could be present here. What makes the discussion so difficult is that Luke has taken over his sources and put the entire story into his own style.

In Acts 13–28 Paul likely had some impact, but beyond this it is hard to know if Luke worked with local traditions of either an oral or a written nature or with a combination of both types. Barrett (1994: 51–56) proposes Philip, Caesarea, Antioch, and Paul as potential sources, with Antioch having a key role even in the Pauline conversion account, the early journey, and the Jerusalem Council (Barrett 1998: xxiv). This Antioch thesis has its roots in the work of Harnack (1908: 131–58, 169–73), who argues for two distinct sources, one from Jerusalem and another from Antioch (Fitzmyer 1998: 82–83). Hengel (1983: 4) has a variation of this, with a source about Peter and an Antiochene source for Acts 1–15. For the second and third journey, we have the "we source" and thus possible contact with Paul or those of his circle.[19] This source was quite familiar with Corinth and Ephesus, as there is much local color in these sections. Josephus and Paul's letters seem unlikely sources (Bruce 1990: 43–44).

In sum, Marshall (1980: 37) is correct when he speaks of the difficulty of discovering the sources for Acts.[20] He then raises the question of how one can think about reliability when the sources are not known, and he makes two points. First, there is good evidence for the church having a well-circulated, reliable tradition, as Jervell (1972: 19–39) argues. Second, in the places where we can check Luke against his sources, such as his likely use of Mark, he is shown to be careful with them.

The Speeches in Acts

The scholarly positions about the speeches in Acts mainly parallel the debate over the historicity of Acts. This is, in part, because fully one-third of the book consists of speech material.[21]

19. Barrett 1998: xxx argues for a Pauline or a Pauline-circle connection for the parts of this material that are not, in his view, fictitious.

20. For a detailed presentation of potential sources, see Fitzmyer 1998: 85–88, who has Palestinian, Antiochene, Pauline, and "we section" sources. He explicitly rejects an Aramaic source for Acts 1–15.

21. Polhill 1992: 42–47 notes that about three hundred of its about one thousand verses are speech material. Fitzmyer 1998: 104–5 lists twenty-eight speeches in the book, of which eight are tied to Peter and ten to Paul. Forms include missionary speeches to Jews, evangelistic speeches to Gentiles, a prophetic indictment from Stephen, two speeches that teach, two defense speeches, and one defense-debate speech. Fitzmyer 1998: 106 is agnostic on the ability to decide the historicity of the speeches, other than to say that Luke had the input of sources.

On one side of opinion belong those who doubt the speeches' general accuracy. The claim is that the style and parallel themes of the speeches along with the "convention" of ancient historiographic handling of such material mean that Luke is responsible for their content with only a minimal concern to reflect what originally took place. This position was set forth by Dibelius (1956: 138–85) and has been defended by many scholars (Schweizer 1966). Dibelius presented his view as early as 1926, but his classic statement is a 1944 essay published in English in 1956. Wilckens reaffirms this position in a monograph on the speeches.[22] An updated version of this argument comes from Marion Soards (1994: 1–17). He argues that the speeches are a literary device, a convention of historiography, and a theological-ideological device and that they help Acts form a unity in its argument.

On the other side stand those who agree that the wording of the speeches comes from Luke but argue that Luke is summarizing tradition with a concern to report what was said (Dodd 1936; Bruce 1942; Ridderbos 1962; Marshall 1980: 39–42; Bruce 1990: 34–40; Witherington 1998: 46–49). In favor of this position is the fact that Luke circulated through the church communities and would have had access to such tradition and heard apostolic speeches on a regular basis. More important, the content of these speeches and their Christology differ enough in the titles used to indicate that some input from tradition is likely. One need only compare the heavy use of the OT in Acts 2 or 3 with the lack of such use in Acts 10, or the shift in those same chapters from Messiah, Holy One, or servant to a singular appeal to Lord or judge of the living and the dead to see the difference (Bruce 1990: 37–39). Polhill (1992: 46) notes the uniqueness of Stephen's speech in the collection as well as Paul's addresses at Mars Hill and Miletus. Dodd's work on the themes of apostolic preaching still has merit in making the case that the church's public teaching did consistently address certain themes in the midst of this kind of variation. The length of the speeches in Acts, most of which are very short and can be read in a few minutes at most, speaks for their character as summaries. Witherington argues that the Lukan speeches are tightly fitted into their settings, suggesting their authenticity.

When it comes to the conventions of ancient historiography, the debate turns on the remarks of Thucydides in *Pel. War* 1.22.1. Here the author admits that he cannot recollect the exact words, but states that his goal is to place in the speakers' mouths sentiments proper to the occasion

---

22. The original monograph, published in 1961, is now in a third edition, published in 1974. Similar is Haenchen 1987: 129–32, who argues that Wilckens showed that the early speeches also have Hellenistic elements in them, proving that they are not authentic. Conzelmann 1987: xliii–xlv maintains that the speeches are inserted into the narrative and are literary creations.

and to give the general purport of what was actually said (Bruce 1990: 34). Thus he claims the freedom to use wording summarizing what in fact was said. Dionysius of Halicarnassus (*Letter to Pompey* 3) criticizes Thucydides for being so committed to history over entertaining (Witherington 1998: 48). Polybius (*Hist.* 2.56.10–12) also embraces this approach to history, noting that the historian is "to instruct and convince for all time serious students by the truth of the facts and the speeches he narrates." He goes on to stress that the truth has precedent for the historian over the goal of entertaining. Fornara (1983) in a monograph on ancient historical writing affirms this technique in *some but not all* classical authors. So the question becomes, "What type of ancient historical writer is Luke?"

To answer this question, we must remember that Luke has shown that he can carefully follow sources where we can test him—namely, in his use of sources in the Gospels (e.g., also outside the Gospels, Acts 17:1–9).[23] In addition, Luke lived in closer proximity to his sources than Thucydides did, giving Luke a good opportunity to know what the apostles preached. Bruce (1990: 39) refers to Luke as a writer who is Thucydidean but with "considerable restraint." Quoting Foakes-Jackson and Lake (1931: xvi), Bruce (1990: 39) argues that the speeches give us "an extraordinarily accurate picture of the undeveloped theology of the earliest Christians, and so enable us to determine the character of the most primitive presentation of the gospel." Hengel (1979: 61) says it this way:

> On the other hand, one can hardly accuse him [Luke] of simply having invented events, created scenes out of nothing and depicted them on a broad canvas, deliberately falsifying the traditions in an unrestrained way for the sake of cheap effect. He is quite simply not concerned with pious edification at the expense of truth. He is not just an "edifying writer," but a historian and theologian who needs to be taken seriously. His account always remains within the limits of what was considered reliable by ancient standards of antiquity. . . . True, the speeches interspersed through Acts always also serve to develop Luke's own theological ideas, but as a rule he does this by use of older traditions, and often attempts to give an appropriate characterization of individual speakers.

In sum, Luke is a careful, ancient historian. He writes with style and flair, often summarizing more complex events. But he is also interested in more than entertaining. He wishes to inform and persuade at the same time. What happened is as important for him as engaging the reader in

23. There is no doubt that Luke often is responsible for the final composition of his units. The question is whether he had access to sources and community oral traditions in constructing his work. Word usage statistics are cited throughout the commentary so that the reader can keep an eye on how often key vocabulary appears in both Luke-Acts and the NT. Such statistics can be a clue that a source is in use.

his topic. Luke is selective in presenting his history and functions very much as an author, but he also is careful in doing so.

Purpose(s) of Acts

Many suggestions have been made on the purpose of Acts.[24] Some themes form subplots in the book but are not comprehensive enough to encompass the whole. Is it a political apologetic on behalf of the church or Paul? This was once a popular view, but it seems unlikely, especially when one recalls that Acts is tied to Luke's Gospel and that Paul is the topic only in the last quarter of the two volumes (Pesch 1986a: 29). Although elements of such concerns appear in the latter part of Acts, there is too much about the communities, their development, and message for this to be the main point.

The idea that Luke wrote in response to the delay of the parousia is also overdrawn (but so Conzelmann 1960). The theme of end-time eschatology is not comprehensive enough throughout the book to be the major theme.

Nor is the work written to counter the Gnostics, who were not an organized movement this early (but so Talbert 1966; see Fitzmyer 1998: 60).

A place to begin is the prologue of Luke's Gospel (Luke 1:1–4), which says the goal is to reassure Theophilus about what he was instructed. Acts 1:1–5 goes in the same direction, picking up from what Jesus began to do and teach. Bruce (1990: 21–22) suggests that the book would be better entitled "The Acts of the Risen Jesus" or "The Acts of the Holy Spirit." This points to the fact that the book's key topics concern major activity from heaven. The time spent explaining how God directed Jews and Gentiles to be connected to each other through Jesus tells us that God is the primary mover in the action (Acts 10–11, 15). What God has done through reconciliation and what Jesus and the Spirit do comprise key themes of the book, but always with an eye to what has taken place in the community God is forming through Jesus and the Spirit. Thus the book parallels Paul's words in Romans: "to the Jew first and then to the Greek" (1:15–17). God's activity through Jesus and the Spirit has brought people of all types into his family.

Another key feature that points to the purpose of Acts is the constant appeal, especially in the early speeches, to the Scripture of Israel. "All the prophets declared these days," as Acts 3:24 puts it (Schneider 1977: 51). Here the point is that what appears to be a new movement is really rooted in old, divinely made promises. This shows Luke's sensitivity to the question of how Christianity is perceived. In the ancient world,

---

24. Van Unnik 1960–61 traces the earlier history of this discussion. Schneider 1977 covers German interpretation in the nineteenth and twentieth centuries. Maddox 1982 surveys and assesses the variety of views.

something new was not necessarily better. What was tested by time was respected. This is part of Luke's point. The new movement is the realization of promises God had made long ago (Squires 1993). This underscores the fact that Luke is seeking to legitimize the claims of the new movement. God's salvation program is as much the topic, then, as God's activity. In a sense, the theme of Acts is that salvation is for all because Jesus is Lord of all, a view that has roots in a program God set forth through the sacred promises. The Spirit's arrival is the indication that promises have moved from being made to being realized, as the speech in Acts 2 shows. This hope extends not only to Gentiles but to all sorts of people: the diseased (Acts 5:12–16), the possessed (8:4–8), the poor (6:1; 9:36–42), and women (9:36–42; 16:12–15; 21:8–9; Witherington 1998: 71). How the church carried out Jesus's commission rooted in this promise is also a key element of the story (Fitzmyer 1998: 55).

Luke Timothy Johnson (1992: 6–9) calls the work a theodicy in explaining how Gentiles could be so present and Jews so hesitant in a movement that is supposed to realize Israel's hope. Is God faithful to his promises? Acts explains that God is faithful and that rejection was also predicted. This idea is a key part of the work's purpose, as both Gentile inclusion and the nature of Jewish rejection are traced. This theme also develops another point of the book: Christianity, or "the Way," as Luke calls it, did not seek to be a distinct faith but was forced to become such because of the rejection the movement met within official Judaism. The important point here is that the message and preaching are an extension of God's promises to Israel and that the new community is now the place where these promises are realized. In a sense, Luke's point is that one who is a good Jew will join in this fulfillment and be joined to others in the process. Therefore Theophilus can be assured that this is God's way.

In sum, Luke, a sometime companion of Paul, put the content of tradition into his own words. He did this in order to indicate how a new movement emerging out of Judaism came to incorporate Gentiles into the community of God. At the core of the activity and preaching stands the work of God through the now exalted Jesus, who in turn distributes the Spirit as a sign that the new era and salvation have come to both Jews and Gentiles. Acts is a testimony about the early church's witness and God's role in bringing it to pass. There is an element of triumph in Luke's account. As Kistemaker (1990: 34) says, it is "to convince Theophilus that no one is able to hinder the victorious march of Christ's gospel." Luke may be reassuring a God-fearer who has come to faith that being a Gentile in an originally Jewish movement was by God's design. This testimony is rooted in early church tradition, even though Luke frames it into a unified story and style.

Date, Destination, Readers, and Canonicity

Date

The date of Acts is tied to discussion of the date of Luke's Gospel (Bock 1994a: 16–18). As the sequel, Acts would have come after the completion of the Gospel, and so the discussion is tied to the two books as well as to the Gospel of Luke's relationship to the other Gospels (Fitzmyer 1998: 51–55 has a solid survey of the issues here). Acts could have been written no earlier than AD 62, since there is discussion of Paul's imprisonment in Rome. Some scholars argue for allusions to Acts in the Pastoral Epistles, such as in 2 Tim. 3:11 or the mention of Luke in 2 Tim. 4:11, but such connections are not certain (Conzelmann 1987: xxvii).

Conzelmann (1987: xxvii–xxxiii) covers potential allusions to Acts in the later writings of the church, as does Bruce (1990: 10–12). Potential allusions include 1 Clem. 2.2 (Acts 2:17); 1 Clem. 5.4, 7 (Acts 1:25); Pol. *Phil.* 2.3 (Acts 20:35); Pol. *Phil.* 6.3 (Acts 7:52); Pol. *Phil.* 12.2 (Acts 2:5; 4:12; 8:21; 20:32); Justin Martyr, *1 Apol.* 50.12 (Acts 1:8). Such allusions would mean that the work was completed by the turn of the first century.

Two options dominate the discussion of the date of writing. One possibility is sometime in the 60s. The other is the period AD 70–100. Hemer (1989: 367–70) has a good list of adherents for all such options over about the last century, including those who opt for a date as late as AD 135, a decidedly minority third view. The latter date assumes that a noncompanion of Paul wrote this work and that the unified tradition surrounding Luke is completely wrong, as he would not have lived to such a late date.

The major arguments for a date in the 60s are the absence of references to Paul's death and/or the lack of resolution of his Roman imprisonment (Kistemaker 1990: 22–24, opts for a date before Nero's persecutions in AD 64). Reasons are as follows: (1) Those who point to the lack of resolution on the imprisonment favor an early 60s date. Those who emphasize no mention of Paul's death favor a date in the mid- to late 60s. The rationale here is that if a writer had written after AD 70, then how could the outcome of this imprisonment or the eventual death of Paul in about AD 67 not have been noted? The argument is more against a later date than for the earlier date, since it is an argument from silence. (2) The absence of any mention of Nero's persecution also suggests an earlier date in a time before Rome attacked the new movement. Bruce (1990: 14) responds, however, that the Romans themselves regarded Nero's behavior as an aberration of Roman standards, so nothing need change in how someone writing after AD 62–64 saw the Romans as a whole. (3) There also is no hint of the war with the Jews in the late 60s. Here too the argument is more against a late date and is grounded on what is not covered. (4) It is also suggested that the positive tone in engaging

Judaism comes before there was a major split. (5) Finally, the lack of discussion of Paul's letters is said to favor an earlier date. The argument for a late date must suppose that the author of Acts ignored these letters, which would have been well known by the later period.[25]

A date in the early 60s relies a great deal on the lack of resolution of Paul's fate. Hemer (1989: 383) asks rhetorically about the argument for the nonresolution of Paul's fate, "If Paul's fate were immaterial, why tantalize the reader with a cryptic and unnecessary focus on it?" If there are reasons to suggest a resolution is not necessary to the author's account, however, then the rationale for an early 60s date is weakened. And there is such an explanation: whether Paul (or any messenger of the gospel) dies or not in bringing the message is not as relevant as the message being proclaimed, which is exactly where Acts ends. The message reaches Rome as God had promised Paul. In Acts, we have martyrs for the faith such as Stephen and those who are merely persecuted. In each case, the gospel message is shared (Bruce 1990: 13). This is Luke's key point. It must be admitted that this argument for an early date has some force. The question is whether it is compelling enough in light of other factors that also are at work in determining the date of Acts.

Critics of a date in the 60s, or at least the early 60s, note that abrupt endings occur elsewhere in the canon and do not impact dating. For example, Mark's Gospel likely does not develop the resurrection appearances—a surprise—and such an omission is the clear choice of its author. So how much can one make of such an argument (Fitzmyer 1998: 52)? It may well be that the death of Paul is alluded to delicately in Acts 20:24–25. But the real reason for objecting to this date is that it requires an early date for Mark's Gospel, which most place, at the earliest, in the 60s as well (Fitzmyer 1998: 53). A late-60s date or a post-70 date for Acts escapes this objection.

Those favoring a late date tend to base it on the fact that Acts follows Luke's Gospel and then argue that Luke's Gospel was written in a post-70 setting. This view depends more on how Luke's Gospel is dated than on evidence from Acts. The key to this discussion is whether Luke's treatment of the Olivet Discourse and its focus on the city of Jerusalem more than the temple reflect a post-70 perspective, something that is also debated. In addition, those holding this view appeal to allusions to Israel's house being desolate or the unique description of Rome's forces surrounding Jerusalem in Luke 19:41–44. The argument is that these texts with their unique details about how Jerusalem was put under siege require that Jerusalem had already

---

25. Hemer 1989: 376–82 gives fifteen reasons for an early date, but five are the most important for him. He opts for AD 62, which is early for some who see Luke's Gospel as written later, whether in the mid- to late 60s or after AD 70. Larkin 1995: 18 also prefers such a date.

experienced judgment, which means a date after AD 70.[26] Since all these passages that are invoked for the date of Luke's Gospel appear in prophetic contexts, the possibility of prediction cannot be excluded; this renders their use for dating problematic, especially when it is possible that Jesus saw Israel headed for covenantal judgment because of its rejection of his message, something taught in Jewish sacred texts (Bock 1994a: 17).

Those who favor an AD 80–100 date also refute the idea that the book could be later in origin, such as AD 115–30, because its theology does not reflect the period of the early second century.[27]

A decision here is difficult. In favor of an early date are the use of Paul in Acts and the lack of explicit development of the fall of Jerusalem. For a date after AD 65 but before AD 90 stands the connection of Acts to issues tied to the date of the Gospels and details in Luke. For reasons argued in Bock 1994a: 17, I do not find the post-70 dating of Luke on the basis of eschatological texts convincing, but the relationship of Acts to the dating of the Gospels is an important factor for this topic. The latter would tend to favor a date in the late 60s. Marshall (1980: 46–48) speaks of a "towards AD 70" date. This date is suggested by the lack of explicit reference to AD 70 and by the lack of any effort to draw upon the "legacy" of Paul in contrast to Acts' focus on Paul's own ministry activity. Luke might even be writing when he can sense the approach of Jerusalem's defeat by Rome. Either Acts is written so much after AD 70 that these issues are no longer worth noting, because they are a given, or it is written before it. On balance, the latter is more likely.

Place of Writing and Destination

We really do not know where Acts was written (Schneider 1980: 121). Irenaeus places its origin in Rome (*Ag. Her.* 3.1.1, 14). Eusebius agrees (*Eccl. Hist.* 2.22.6). Achaia (Anti-Marcionite Prologues; Jerome, *Commentary on Matthew*, preface) and Caesarea are also noted as possibilities, and Corinth and Ephesus have been modern suggestions (Pesch 1986a: 28). Palestine and Syria seem unlikely locales (Fitzmyer 1998: 54–55), although the use of sources from such locations is likely. We also do not know the work's destination. Was it for someone in Rome or simply someone in the upper level of society? Theophilus likely had

26. Holding this view are Schneider 1980: 118–21, who opts for AD 80–90; Pesch 1986a: 28, who opts for a date near AD 90; Barrett 1998: cxii, cxviii, who opts for the 80s; Roloff 1988: 6, around AD 90; Fitzmyer 1998: 54, AD 80–85; Hengel 1979: 66, AD 80–90; Witherington 1998: 62, late 70s or early 80s; so also Bruce 1990: 12–18, a change from his earlier view; Polhill 1992: 30, slightly earlier, in AD 70–80.

27. So Conzelmann 1987: xxxiii against O'Neill 1961: 1–58, one of several who hold to this late option and appeal to Luke's use of Josephus, written in the 90s, as a key point for this view, something that likewise has not won wide consent.

a background in Judaism and the synagogue, and so he may well have been a God-fearer (Witherington 1998: 64; Nolland 1977). The saturation of this work with the sacred Scriptures of Judaism suggests that this background had relevance for the reader.

Canonicity

Acts had a life beyond Theophilus. It eventually circulated in the church (Bruce 1990: 19–21). We have already noted allusions to use of the book, but use is not the same as recognition of its inherent authority. Like the four Gospels, Acts appears to have been well established as an authoritative source by the end of the second century. It is listed in the Muratorian Canon, in the Anti-Marcionite Prologues, and in Irenaeus (*Ag. Her.* 3.15.1, where he defends Acts' portrait of Saul's conversion in the face of some who challenge Paul's apostolic authority). The presence of apocryphal versions of Acts seems to assume the original version. Acts appears as the link between the Gospels and the letters of Paul. This is important because by this time both Paul's letters and the four Gospels were likewise well established as authorities. When Tertullian wrote against heretical views, he twice affirmed the authority of Acts (*Prescription against Heretics* 22.11; 23.3).

Key Manuscripts of Acts

The discussion of MSS in Acts includes not only observing what texts exist but also noting the special situation of the Western text in Acts (Barrett 1194: 2–29; Fitzmyer 1998: 66–72; Epp 1966; Head 1993). Here we survey mostly the key Greek MSS.

Major uncial and versional witnesses for the Alexandrian family include ℵ, or Sinaiticus (fourth century); A, or Alexandrinus (fifth century); and B, or Vaticanus (fourth century). The Byzantine text (Byz) is best represented by H (ninth century), L (ninth century), P (ninth century), Ψ (eighth or ninth century), and 049 (ninth century). The Western text has witnesses in D, also known as Codex Bezae (fifth century), and the Harclean Syriac (seventh century). Codex D lacks Acts 8:29–10:14; 21:2–10, 16–18; 22:10–20; and 22:29–28:31. Codex E (sixth or seventh century) is a Greek-and-Latin text with a mix of mostly Western and some Byzantine readings. Key minuscules include 614 (thirteenth century, Western and Byzantine mix) and 1739 (tenth century, eclectic).

Most of the fifteen papyri of Acts contain fragmentary portions of the book (Fitzmyer 1998: 66–67 has the complete list and identifies verses tied to each). Among the more important are $\mathfrak{P}^8$ (fourth century, Acts 4:31–37; 5:2–9; 6:1–6, 8–15), $\mathfrak{P}^{29}$ (third century, Acts 26:7–8, 20, Western), $\mathfrak{P}^{38}$ (ca. AD 300; Acts 18:27–19:6, 12–16, Western), $\mathfrak{P}^{45}$ (a major witness containing large portions of 4:27–17:17, it is a third-century mix of Western and mostly Alexandrian readings; sometimes called Caesarean), $\mathfrak{P}^{48}$

(late third century, Acts 23:11–17, 23–29, Western), $\mathfrak{P}^{53}$ (third century, Acts 9:33–10:1), $\mathfrak{P}^{74}$ (seventh century, large portions of Acts from 1:2 to 28:31, Alexandrian), and $\mathfrak{P}^{91}$ (third century, Acts 2:30–37; 2:46–3:2). Other papyri are $\mathfrak{P}^{33+58}$, $\mathfrak{P}^{41}$, $\mathfrak{P}^{50}$ (Alexandrian), $\mathfrak{P}^{53}$, $\mathfrak{P}^{56}$, and $\mathfrak{P}^{57}$. Alexandrian minuscules include 33 (Acts 11:26–28:31), 81, 104, 326, and 1175. Western minuscules are 383 and 614. The Byzantine text dominates the minuscules, including MS 33 for Acts 1:1–11:25.

On the versions and the fathers, Clement of Alexandria and Origen are witnesses to the Alexandrian text whereas Tertullian, Cyprian, Old Latin, and probably the Syriac and some Coptic texts witness the Western family (Barrett 1994: 27). The text-type of Irenaeus's work is disputed.

My introduction to the Gospel of Luke discusses the Byzantine family and its later origin (Bock 1994a: 19–20; also Witherington 1998: 65–66). There is a wider range of variants in Acts, especially because of D, than in Matthew, Luke, or the Pauline Epistles. Some scholars argue that this suggests that its recognition as a sacred text took longer, so that it was not copied with quite the same care (Barrett 1998: xxii). What we may have, however, is the impact of the Western variations on Acts as well as the movement in Greek vocabulary in the Byzantine period. None of this means that Acts was slower to gain recognition than these other books, as our section on canonicity argues.

The MS evidence for Acts is strong. Three families of text appear in Acts: Alexandrian, Western, and Majority (I use the siglum "Byz" for this latter family; Barrett 1994: 21–22; Fitzmyer 1998: 69). In general, the Western text is longer and more periphrastic than the Alexandrian.

The Western text is the subject of debate (Head 1993: 415–44). Barrett (1998: xix–xxii) discusses the theory of Boismard and Lamouille (1984), which argues for the originality of the Western text. A variation of this view is that two versions of Acts existed early on, an option also treated by Barrett (1994: 22–23). Head (1993) discusses the theory of two versions of Acts, with one version being found in the Western tradition, and he finds it unpersuasive. Such a theory means that Acts did not circulate until the middle of the second century, which seems very unlikely. Most scholars see the Western text as an attempt by a later copyist to improve the literary style of Acts. The period it was undertaken is early enough that its readings may on occasion be original. The dates of this period are also debated, as the mid–second century and the third to fourth centuries have been suggested. Although the evidence suggests that the Alexandrian text is likely the closest to the original, readings and variants must be assessed one at a time.

Chronological Keys to Acts

A few events give us some indication of when the story of Acts took place. The date of many events, however, is a matter for discussion. For example, the date of Jesus's crucifixion is disputed, with AD 30 and 33 the most plausible candidates.[28] The later date can explain Pilate's hesitation about Jesus and his care in dealing with the Jews during Jesus's trial, since his protector Sejanus is no longer present. The earlier date allows more room for the later events concerning Paul. Either date is possible.

Events within Acts can be dated mostly with the help of extrabiblical information about the figures the book discusses (Fitzmyer 1998: 138–39). A key in figuring out much of this is the Delphic Inscription, noted above, which names Gallio and gives us a firm date for him.

Key Dates for Acts

Date	Event	Source
AD 14–37	Reign of Tiberius	
AD 36	Pilate's rule as procurator in Judea ends	Josephus, *Ant.* 18.4.2 §89
AD 41–54	Reign of Claudius	
AD 44	Death of Herod Agrippa I	Josephus, *Ant.* 19.8.2 §§350–51; Acts 12:20–23
AD 49	Edict of Claudius expelling Jews from Rome	Acts 18:2c; Suetonius, *Claudius* 25
AD 52–53 (twelfth year of Claudius's reign)	L. Junius Gallio Annaeus is proconsul in Achaia and Corinth	Delphic Inscription
AD 52–60	M. Antonio Felix is procurator of Judea	Josephus, *Ant.* 20.7.1 §137; *J.W.* 2.12.8 §247; 2.13.2 §252
AD 54–68	Reign of Nero	
ca. AD 60–62	Portius Festus is procurator of Judea	Acts 25:9–12; Josephus, *Ant.* 20.8.9–10 §§182–88; 20.9.1 §§197, 200; *J.W.* 2.14.1 §§271–72

Several factors enter into debates about the dates tied to Paul. First, how does one correlate Acts and Gal. 1–2, especially the timing and nature of the Jerusalem Council? Second, whether one takes Gal. 1:18 and 2:1 as sequential or as overlapping determines whether a fourteen-year or a seventeen-year gap ensues between the two visits to Jerusalem that Paul notes. Most scholars see Paul covering seventeen years in this sequence, but the case is not certain. When one adds a possible three-year difference in the dating of Jesus's crucifixion, complicating factors multiply. Finally, there is the issue of whether one counts the fourteen or seventeen years inclusively or not, which impacts the dates

28. Bock 1996: 1821 prefers AD 33 for the crucifixion, as does Hoehner 1977: 95–114. Riesner 1998: 52–58 fully discusses the issues and takes the more common AD 30 position; an oft-cited study of Pauline chronology is Jewett 1979; see also Finegan 1998.

by a year or so.[29] Such considerations could also apply to Paul's reference to the phrase "after three years," found in Gal. 1:18. This final possibility impacts the result by as much as a year. Witherington counts inclusively and argues that Paul was converted in AD 34, assuming an AD 30 crucifixion for Jesus, with Paul making a second visit to Jerusalem in AD 48. Alternatively, one could have an AD 33 crucifixion and argue that events in Acts 1–9 are highly compressed, having taken place largely within a couple of years.[30] Counting inclusively from AD 33 and yet seeing a relatively quick conversion by Paul, one could arrive at a similar timing for Paul's second visit to Jerusalem before Acts 15. All such options are possible.

As a result of these issues and other more minor details, various models for the dating of events in Acts exist.[31] One can compare Fitzmyer (1998: 139–41) with Witherington (1998: 81–86). They share an AD 30 date for the crucifixion. But Witherington connects Acts 11:27–30 with Gal. 2:1–10, placing that visit in AD 48. He also has Paul's first missionary journey occurring in AD 48. The Jerusalem Council is then dated at AD 49. Fitzmyer has the council in AD 49 but ties Gal. 2 to Acts 15. Fitzmyer (1998: 136–37, 139) dates the first journey of Paul to AD 46–49, the historicity of which he also defends against the complaints of some that Paul never treats this period. The lack of detailed information allows for differing judgments here, but the result is determined mainly by how one puts Galatians and Acts together.

There is more agreement regarding dates right after the Jerusalem Council. The second journey is AD 50–52, but the third journey is variously dated again as we move away from the firm date of Gallio. Fitzmyer has the third journey in AD 54–57, whereas Witherington has it in AD 53–57 or 58. They also do not agree on the date of Paul's house arrest in Rome; Fitzmyer has this in AD 61–63, whereas Witherington has it in AD 60–62.

I agree with Witherington (1998: 92–94) that Acts 11 and Gal. 2 belong together, for reasons that will be defended in the introduction to Acts 15:1–35. This is the minority view among scholars, but it has good justification.[32] Witherington gives seven reasons for his view, but three are

29. As Witherington 1998: 88–90 notes. For example, does one count fourteen or seventeen full years, or does a part of a year count as a year?

30. For example, Riesner 1998: 322 has an AD 30 date for the crucifixion, yet he argues that Paul was converted in the second year after Jesus's death, in AD 31–32, and so he counts years in Galatians in a noninclusive manner.

31. For a comparison of seven models, see Schneider 1980: 129–33. For a comparison of more than thirty proposals, see Riesner 1998: 3–28. Riesner 1998: 39–40 correctly insists that these issues cannot be decided without taking Acts seriously in terms of historicity.

32. Riesner 1998: 320–22, 396 holds to the South Galatia theory for the letter, making it the earliest of Paul's epistles, written in either AD 48 or AD 50. He appears to lean in the direction of Acts 15 ≠ Gal. 2, but the point is not entirely clear.

the most important: (1) Paul's claim that he went to Jerusalem a second time in Gal. 2 by means of revelation is something that can be tied to Agabus's prophecy in Acts 11:27–29. (2) An Acts 11–Gal. 2 connection also ties nicely to the instruction in Gal. 2:10 that Paul remember the poor, since he is bringing famine relief in Acts 11. (3) Galatians 2 is discussing table fellowship, which also is the topic of Acts 10–11, whereas Acts 15 covers circumcision. Thus I prefer Witherington's chronology to Fitzmyer's, but with the caveat of only a slight preference for an AD 33 date for Jesus's crucifixion. Those who support Acts 15 as equaling Gal. 2 usually argue that all the same figures appear in both passages and that the years of Paul's visits as noted in Galatians match this setting.

Witherington and Fitzmyer also proceed on differing premises for assessing historically the data from Paul and Acts. Fitzmyer (1998: 133) argues another commonly held view, that Paul's information in his letters has historical precedence over Luke's information, probably because we have a difference between what was experienced by Paul and Luke using sources (Jewett 1979 also defends this view). Witherington (1998: 86–88) suggests the Lukan data need to be taken more seriously, particularly in light of the fact that Luke is consciously writing a history and provides to us many people and events to work with in making judgments. Witherington notes that Paul's dating in his letters is made in passing as the apostle discusses various issues. So Luke's evidence is direct evidence to such events and their timing. When one adds to this the fact that the "we sections" also point to Luke's experience, then Acts should be weighed almost equally with Paul. Witherington pays careful attention to Paul when the two works overlap at points where Luke was not present. I share this view as well.

This survey and introductory treatment of various models shows how complex it is to obtain clear dates for events in Acts. This is why dates among commentators differ, although usually those differences are within the range of a year or so. This commentary will not take a firm stand on specific dates, given all the judgments about correlation that this requires. My view is that Jesus was crucified in AD 33, that Paul was converted by AD 35, that Gal. 2 and Acts 11 belong together, and that the Jerusalem Council took place in AD 49. Paul's imprisonment in Rome is probably to be dated to AD 60–62. Where relevant, I will note other dates but always with a caveat that often a variation of a year or so is possible.

The Theology of Acts

In my commentary on Luke's Gospel (Bock 1994a: 27–43), I surveyed the theology of Luke-Acts, something I have also done in a longer form elsewhere (Bock 1994b: 87–166). There is no need to repeat it here. This survey will focus on the main theological themes of Acts alone, something done in more detail by O'Toole (1984) and Jervell (1996). As noted, the key subject of Acts is God in his actions through Jesus and the Spirit. We start with the mighty God who has a plan and saves.

The Plan and Work of the Mighty God

Three speeches and one set of terms sum up this theme. Peter's speech in Acts 2, his address to Cornelius in Acts 10, and the discussion of God's activity in Acts 15 summarize the work of God through Jesus. In each case, the Spirit also plays an essential role in what takes place, as the Spirit is the promise of the arrival of the new era (Acts 1:1–8; Luke 3:15–17; 24:49). The threefold telling of the conversion of Saul also highlights the theme of an active God. In addition, the use of ideas such as the plan (βουλή, boulē) that is foreknown, foretold, predestined, promised, ordained, or worked out through God's choice also shows this emphasis (Acts 2:23; 4:27–28). Squires (1998: 19–39) surveys this theme in more detail as it runs through the entire book, while his monograph (1993) traces the theme in fullest detail. God acts constantly in Acts: in the distribution of the Spirit in Acts 2, in miraculous activity through the apostles in Acts 3, in judgment in Acts 5, in the vindication of Stephen in Acts 7, in leading Philip in Acts 8, in Saul's conversion in Acts 9, in taking Peter to Cornelius in Acts 10, in calling for mission by Paul and Barnabas in Acts 13 and empowering them throughout the mission (Acts 13:2; 14:27), in guiding the church at the council in Acts 15, in leading Paul in mission in Acts 16–19, in empowering Paul in his work in Acts 16–21 (Acts 21:14–16), and in protecting Paul as he heads to Rome in Acts 27–28. God is Savior in Acts (Green 1998).

Secondary agents also reveal Acts' emphasis on the plan; guidance by the Spirit, such as when Philip is led to the eunuch (Acts 8:26–40); the repeated fulfillment of divine prophecy (Acts 2:16–36; 13:47; 15:15–17; 28:25–27; Bock 1987; Peterson 1993; Bock 1998b); the direction by divine agents (Moses in Acts 7:30–38 as a precursor to Jesus; Acts 22:7–11; 26:13–18 in the conversion of Saul) whether angelic (Acts 5:19–20; 8:26; 27:23) or with revelatory gifts (Acts 11:28; 21:10–11); and the use of miracles. Also important here is the use of the idea that things are "necessary" (Cosgrove 1984; Acts 3:21–22; 4:12; 5:29, 40–41; 9:6; 14:22; 26:23).

God's actions in accord with his promise show that God is acting in continuity with long-standing commitments (Marshall 1980: 23–24). The explicit use of Scripture concerns five key themes: Christ's exalted position and work in giving the Spirit, covenant and promise, community mission and guidance, commission to the Gentiles, and challenge and warning to Israel of the consequences of rejection (Evans and Sanders 1993; Bock 1998b). Echoes of Scripture concern, in addition, issues of identity, affirming the new community as the people of God (Litwak 2005). Acts appeals to the major covenants as pointing in this direction

(Bruce 1990: 64; Abraham: Acts 3:25; Moses: Acts 3:22–24; David: use of Isa. 55:3 and Ps. 16:10 in Acts 13:34–35). All the prophets bore witness to Jesus (Acts 10:43).

Mission, Opposition, and the Inclusion of the Gentiles

Most of this divine activity is designed to spread the message of the word of the gospel to humanity (Green 1998). God is a Savior and has reconciled humanity to himself through the person of Jesus. Again the speeches in Acts 2 and 10 raise the theme. Acts 3 shows that this is part of God's promise made to Abraham. Salvation leads to becoming a part of God's new community, composed of both Jew and Gentile, as Acts 15 makes clear. Even the persecution that surfaces often results in the spreading of the word. The persecution in Acts 8, which leads to the message going out into Judea and Samaria, is an example of how mission, suffering, and opposition combine in an important way in Acts. There is not only the idea of mission; there is also the recognition that the opposition this mission faces is often a blessing, even though it is hard to endure (Acts 14:22; Cunningham 1997; Rapske 1998).

The note of mission is struck right at the start in Acts 1:8, with its roots going back to the commission in Luke 24:47–49. The key central portion of Acts shows how God took a predominantly Jewish movement and called its members to reach out and include Gentiles, since Jesus's work and the Spirit were for all people. The message they preached centered on what God had done through Jesus but even more on who Jesus was, one who now was vindicated and seated at God's side, appointed to bless and to judge (Acts 2:30–36; 3:18–26; 10:40–42). Less is made of how Jesus saves, which was what Paul emphasized. More is made of Jesus as the Lord, Christ, or judge of the living and the dead who offers forgiveness to those who turn to him in faith and repentance. In fact, the two key gifts of salvation for Luke are forgiveness and the Spirit (2:36–40), leading one day to believers' receiving the promised vindication (3:20–26). Luke indicates the message's progress by means of the book's geographical focus, found in Paul's three journeys and the book's many summaries. These factors point to the progress of God's word. Acts possesses a selective look at such expansion, with Paul's ministry serving as a kind of example of mission to the Gentiles. In a sense, Acts is a "mission history" (Hengel 1971–72; Schnabel 2004).

The inclusion of the Gentiles is also a promise of Scripture (Acts 13:47; 15:16–18). This mission works out God's call (15:11). All types of people benefit: the powerful and the weak, the rich and the poor, male and female, old and young (2:17–18), poor widows (9:36–41), provincials (14:15–18), merchants (16:14), jailers (16:30–32), sailors (27:25), centurions in the military (10:34–48), proconsuls (13:7), governors (24:10), kings (26:2), and philosophers (17:18; Johnson 1992: 17). Movement in the direction of the Gentiles starts with Philip and the eunuch in Acts 8, but it is solidified with the elaborate means God uses to direct Peter to Cornelius in Acts 10. The many missions of Paul show how such efforts were directed from and rooted in the church in Antioch.

A full study by Stenschke (1999) examines the rationale for a mission to Gentiles. He considers the Lukan portrait of Gentiles before they come to faith, noting seven ways Gentiles are described that point to their need for salvation: (1) ignorant, with an ignorance that leads to idolatry (Acts 17:22–31); (2) rejecting God's purpose and revelation in history, especially in their hostility to God's people the Jews and in Pilate's rejection of Jesus (7:36; 4:25–28); (3) idolaters (most evident in Ephesus in Acts 19); (4) materialistic (16:16–19; 19:24–27); (5) engaged in unethical behavior (20:17–35); (6) under Satan's power (26:18); and (7) subject to judgment (10:38–42). An exceptional category of Gentiles is the God-fearers. Their association with Judaism means they are not subject to all of these criticisms and are viewed with some respect for their religious quest. Nonetheless, they still need to respond to the need for salvation, just as Jews who had access to God's revelation and promise do. The account concerning Cornelius in Acts 10 points to such a portrait of the God-fearer. The gospel makes a great impact among this group. Stenschke successfully challenges the thesis of Taeger (1982), who sees Gentiles as needing only correction not salvation in the call to repentance.[33]

Jesus, the Lord of All for a Gospel Sent to All

The key to Luke's Christology in Acts is Jesus's vindicated and exalted position, which has him ministering from God's side as Savior, Christ, and Lord (Bock 1987; Strauss 1995; Buckwalter 1996; Buckwalter 1998: 107–23). Acts begins with Jesus raised and vindicated in his claims as he prepares his followers for their calling in appearances that take place over a period of forty days. The Christology is mainly presented, however, in the speeches. In Acts 2, Jesus is the promised Lord and Christ who mediates the long-promised Spirit from the right hand of God. In Acts 3 he fulfills the promise to Abraham and is the Holy One killed but now raised as he waits in heaven to return as judge, just as the prophets promised. In Acts 10, he is appointed the judge of the living and the dead in fulfillment of the prophets. As Bruce notes (1990: 60), Jesus is the sent Messiah (Acts 2:36; 3:20; 5:42; 8:5; 17:3b; 18:5), son of David (2:30; 13:23), Lord (2:36; 10:36), Son of God (9:20; 13:33), prophet like Moses (3:22–23; 7:37), servant of the Lord (3:13, 26; 4:30; 8:32–33), and

---

33. Note especially the discussion in Stenschke 1999: 386–88. He observes that the speech at the Areopagus is the key text for many espousing this view (Acts 17), and he challenges the dichotomy that Vielhauer 1966 sees between Pauline and Lukan anthropology based on this assumption. Stenschke also questions the claims of Parsons and Pervo 1993 that Luke's theology is not unified in its various portrayals in Luke-Acts.

Son of Man (7:56). He is also the righteous one (3:14; 7:52; 22:14), the author of life (3:15), leader and Savior (5:31), and one destined to suffer (3:18; 17:3a; 26:23) and be rejected (2:23–24; 3:13–15; 8:32–33; 13:28). Jesus shares the name of the Lord and a variety of acts are performed in his name, from exorcism to baptism (2:21 read with 2:36, 38; 3:6; 4:12, 30; 5:28, 40–41; 8:16; 9:14–16, 21, 27–28; 10:48; 15:14, 17; 16:18; 19:5, 13, 17; 21:13; 22:16; 26:9). He is an agent for miracles (3:6; 4:10; 9:34). Jesus is an active, exalted figure in Acts. He is not passive as he sits at God's right hand, but is at work for his people.

Although it is often suggested that Acts 2:36 indicates adoptionist Christology, that is, a belief that Jesus came to his exalted position as a result of the resurrection, this is not Luke's view. For Luke, the resurrection made evident what Jesus always was. Barrett (1998: lxxxv–lxxxvi) argues that Acts 2 stops short of identifying Jesus as being on the same level as the God of the OT, but this is less than likely. The very idea that Jesus could exist and labor at God's side is an affirmation of his equal status. Barrett's position also ignores the midrashic link between Acts 2:21 and 2:36, where Joel's reference to calling on the "Lord" to save includes calling on Jesus. Luke has a "high" Christology, expressed in how Jesus functions as a mediator for God and is responsive to the Father, but his status is nonetheless the same. Any "subordinationism" in the book is strictly functional, of Father to Son, and not ontological. Luke's Christology ultimately unites around this idea of an exalted Jesus who serves the Father faithfully from God's side in heaven. Because Jesus is Lord of all (Acts 10:36), the gospel can go to all, as Peter affirms in the key, groundbreaking speech to Cornelius.

This Jesus also serves from his high position (Buckwalter 1998). His death was the ultimate act of service, but he also guides and instructs (Acts 16:7; 18:9–10), gives the benefits of salvation (2:38; 5:31; 10:43; 13:38–39), and exorcises and heals (3:6, 16; 4:10; 9:34; 16:18).

The Holy Spirit

John Chrysostom (*Hom. Acts* 1.5) says that Acts is the "gospel of the Holy Spirit" because the Spirit's presence is so evident in the book. The Spirit was promised by the Father (Acts 1:4) and has now come (Acts 2:16–21). The Spirit's presence at Pentecost was a visible indication that the new era of the Messiah had arrived (Luke 3:15–17; 24:49; Acts 1:4, 8). The Spirit is, in a real sense, the "gift" that makes salvation what it should be for one's relationship to God (Acts 2:39–40). The bestowal of the Spirit on both Jews and Gentiles gives evidence that God treats everyone the same and calls on all to respond to Jesus (Acts 10:34–43). In a sense, the Spirit is an empowering presence (Luke 24:49; Acts 1:8) but also a Spirit of witness and testimony (Acts 2:4–12; 4:8). Some have spoken of the Spirit's role in Acts as exclusively that of the "Spirit of prophecy" (assessed in Turner 1998), but this narrows the focus of the

Spirit's work too much, even though this theme is a major emphasis. Prophetic ability includes the experience of visions and dreams, guidance, charismatic wisdom, praise, witness, and teaching (Turner 1998: 334–35), although not everyone has all of these experiences. The manifestation of tongues from the Spirit shows this revelatory, declarative role for the Spirit (Acts 2:4, 11; 10:46; 19:6). The Spirit's guidance stands behind the apostolic decree (15:28) and is responsible for the call of Saul and Barnabas (13:1–2). Luke emphasizes what the Spirit does for the community more than what the Spirit does in each believer. Dishonoring the Spirit can also be a cause for judgment (5:1–11). The Spirit can be called the "Spirit of Christ" (16:7). For Luke, this refers to the mediation of the Spirit from Jesus: the Spirit comes from Jesus, and so Jesus can direct the believer (2:30–36). The Spirit is a witness to the Christ event and is initially mediated through Christ—elements of emphasis that develop Jewish hope in new directions. In sum, the Spirit is the key to the renewal and mission of God's people. The Spirit ensures an intimate connection between the disciple and Jesus. This entire activity is part of the reason that the Spirit is seen as a central eschatological gift. The many references to being filled with the Spirit help to make this final point (4:8, 31; 6:3, 5; 7:55; 9:17; 11:24; 13:9, 52).

The New Community's Emerging Separate Identity

The themes of inclusion of the Gentiles and growth in the face of opposition have already been treated. Acts also has glimpses of community life. Some scholars feel that Luke idealizes the church and minimizes the tension that existed early on, especially between Paul and others on matters of Gentile inclusion. In fact, Acts does give us indications of such major tensions, as Acts 6–7, 9, and 15 clearly show. But they are not told with the intensity of one in the midst of the dispute as much as by one who now lives after its basic resolution.

At the core of this discussion was whether Gentiles should be treated as proselytes were in Judaism, with expectation that they be circumcised and observe other legal practices (Marshall 1980: 29–30). The rejection of the gospel message by many Jews and the tension this produced was one factor in the new community's response. This need to resolve the issue became more intense as Gentiles began to come in and the community's character became clearer. The new community was no longer going to be a purely Jewish institution, but it also did not sense a calling to abandon its connection to Judaism. Once the church decided that Gentiles could enter without being circumcised, the issue became how law-sensitive Jewish believers and Gentiles could coexist. For Acts, the solution was not an all-or-nothing decision in favor of one side or the other; instead we see a kind of ethnic sensitivity that called on Jews not to force Gentiles to become Jews and asked Gentiles to be sensitive to Jewish practices. The solution at the Jerusalem Council shows this kind of compromise.

Gentiles should not alienate Jews with the freedoms they have in Jesus and apart from the law, and so they should avoid meat offered to idols or slaughtered in a manner that reflected uncleanness and should strive to be morally pure. The rules about meals and meat may have applied only to "mixed" meals, where Jews and Gentiles were present. If so, the solution differs little from that discussed by Paul in 1 Cor. 10. It is also unclear if these limitations continued or eventually ceased.

Although the influx of Gentiles certainly helped the new community to develop a distinct identity and character, the Jewish rejection of the gospel and the persecution that followed had the same impact. The new locale of the people of God became the messianic community that now also included Gentiles (Seccombe 1998). Meeting regularly in the synagogue was no longer possible for the new community. They were forced to meet elsewhere, and they did so in house churches (Gehring 2004, esp. chaps. 3–4). The new community began to meet in homes and became the church not so much because the new community sought to be separate. Rather, the realities of the reaction to the church forced it to become separate. Acts recounts this change as well.

The community itself is a place of baptism, worship, table fellowship, and instruction (Peterson 1998; Acts 2:38–47). It is a place of prayer for the work of God (4:23–31). It also is a place where those in the church can obtain support and relief if they are materially at risk (4:32–37; 6:1–6). The Spirit guides the church in active mission to take the message to those who are not a part of the community (13:1–2). This mission often meant that people worked out of places where they had established themselves, such as Antioch. They sent out teams to key locales, as Paul's ministry with Barnabas and others indicates (Towner 1998). By the end of Acts, it is clear that at each locale leadership existed in the form of elders who are to instruct, guide, and protect the flock (11:29–30; 14:23; 15:1–16:4; 20:17–35; 21:18). Whether this new community saw itself as "restored Israel" (so Polhill 1992: 65–67) is a matter of debate. They did, however, view themselves as a community that had been formed by God in conjunction with promises made long ago. The remnant of Jews who believed in the Messiah was the link to Israel of the past. The new community's existence meant that God was also doing something fresh from a structural point of view, distinct from the Israel of old. The way in which the law was handled also pointed to a fresh work of God.

The Law

In many ways, the issue of how Gentiles entered the new community suggests how the law is handled in Acts. God's revelation showed that circumcision is not to be a concern for Gentiles (S. Wilson 1983; Blomberg 1984; 1998; Acts 10–11; Barrett 1998: xcviii–ci). Wilson argues that Luke favored law observance, and this is the common view, but as Blomberg shows, the picture is more complex. There is no doubt that early in Acts, the new community still participates at the temple and preaches there. This shows that the earliest believers saw their faith as the natural extension of Jewish faith and hope. But the view of the temple in Acts is not one dimensional; Stephen's speech includes an element of caution about overemphasizing the temple as sacred space (also 17:24).

The key passages for the discussion of law observance are the vision in Acts 10 and the Jerusalem Council in Acts 15. Acts 10 appears to argue that dietary laws should not get in the way of Jew-Gentile fellowship; in Peter's vision, all foods are clean and so, he infers, are all people. Acts 15 is where the final decision about circumcision takes place, an important decision where this physical sign of the covenant is declared unnecessary. Circumcision represents a "yoke" that Gentiles need not bear, as neither the disciples nor the fathers were able to bear it in the past. This final remark suggests that the issue is not merely circumcision but all that circumcision implied about keeping the law. Barrett (1998: c) argues that this perspective is different from Paul's, but this claim is overdrawn. Although Barrett claims that there is no mention of Christ in Acts, unlike in Paul, Jesus's role is in fact presumed in the response to the gospel in Acts 10–11. So what is explicit in Paul is implicit in Acts. And the declaration that the law cannot provide forgiveness (13:39) shows that Luke does include a critique of the law or a call for its renovation in Acts.

Two other events are important to this discussion: Paul's vow in 18:18 and the purification request made to Paul by believers in Jerusalem in 21:23–24a. The first is an expression of Jewish piety and reflects the fact that Paul continued to observe some practices of Judaism in conformity with Jewish custom (Josephus, *Ant.* 19.6.1 §§292–96; *J.W.* 2.15.1 §§309–14). Paul's agreement about purification to show his respect for the law in the heavily Jewish context of Jerusalem is nothing more than Paul being a Jew to the Jews (1 Cor. 9:19–23). When Luke speaks of the new community fulfilling the old hope, it is not the law that is central but promise, hope, and resurrection (note the speeches of Acts 2 and 3; 23:6; 26:6; 28:20).

In sum, Luke's handling of the law is nuanced. Many Jews show sensitivity to the issue, especially if they are ministering to other Jews, but law observance is not something that the new community emphasized, and when it came to Gentiles, the new era meant new ways.

The Debate over "Early Catholicism"

Among scholars, one of the more discussed points is whether Acts reflects an increasing structuring of the new community and what has been called "early Catholicism," with its apostles and elders, baptism and Eucharist (Barrett 1998: xciii–xcvii). Ernst Käsemann defined and argued for the view (1964a: 89–94; 1969: 236–51; noted by Bruce 1990: 47). Part of the point here is that the movement shifted from being purely Spirit-directed to being overseen by a growing group of appointed leaders. Elements of this new Catholicism include apostolic succession and authority in a hierarchy, a clergy-laity distinction, sacramentalism, concern to consolidate, and development of a doctrinal core. Some of this evolution was merely natural as the new community grew and tried to cope with its expansion, but the claims of the early-Catholic view seem to outweigh the evidence, since most of the above-mentioned elements do not appear as structured in Acts as this view alleges. It is implied that this structure reflects the later time to which Acts belongs. The early community is also said to shift from hope in the soon return of the Lord to the realization that he might not return for some time (Polhill 1992: 52–54 also summarizes this early-Catholic view). As Barrett (1998: xciv) notes about this position, eschatology is replaced by salvation history.

Barrett correctly challenges the presence of early Catholicism in Acts. He notes that the apostles drop from the account after Acts 15 and execute no clear administrative authority other than occasionally to affirm the message's expansion, such as in Samaria. There is no transmission of their authority to others. A variety of people, including preachers of the gospel and elders, carry out the church's ministry with no clear hierarchy between them. Sacraments are noted but hardly highlighted. All of this suggests that the description "early Catholic" does not fit the events in Acts.

Triumph of the Gospel

Above all, Acts is about the expansion and triumph of the gospel as it penetrates the world from Jerusalem to Rome by means of God's guidance and despite intense opposition (Polhill 1992: 71–72). The new community formed around it is divinely wrought. Part of the power of the new community is its faithfulness and its members' determination to lead lives that honor God. This is sometimes expressed as the ethics of Acts. A second dimension of this response to the revealed word of God about Jesus is the conscious mission of the new community (Bolt 1998; Capper 1998; Barrett 1998: civ–cvi). Acts tells the story of a community centered on God's work in Christ and preaching that message (Marshall 1980: 25–27), alongside lives lived in a manner that honors and serves others. Acts emphasizes these two elements, evangelism and a God-honoring life, as making up the central character of this new people of God.

The geographic expansion of the preaching moves from Jerusalem (Acts 1–7) to Samaria and beyond (Acts 8–11), and then out beyond Jerusalem and Israel as far as Rome (Acts 12–28). This shows the movement of God's word into the entire world. The expression "end of the earth" summarizes the call. This call is rooted in Isa. 49:6 and looks toward bringing the message to everyone. Rome is the symbol for this call to preach to all, since Rome is the first-century hub of the world. Peter takes the word to the Gentiles (Acts 10–11), and Paul takes it into much of the world outside Israel (Acts 13–28). The God-honoring life shares that word, even in the face of opposition, and relies on God in the midst of that opposition. Those who preach know how to present what they believe. They know how to defend their faith, as the speeches of defense by both Stephen and Paul show. In short, they witness and engage in mission (Bolt 1998). They present the hope of life in the Spirit as well as the assurance of resurrection alongside the forgiveness of sins. These are gifts of grace from God, given through faith in Jesus, that is, through turning to him.

The preachers of the gospel speak in places where people who seek God gather, such as the synagogues. But they also show up in places where people discuss all kinds of ideas, such as Mars Hill. They engage in the public square. In a sense, they convey the special witness of those such as the Twelve, Stephen, and Paul, giving testimony to what these original believers saw and taught but also to what they themselves are now experiencing. The community also cares for itself, sharing its resources to ensure that basic needs are met (Acts 6:1–6). One community gathers its resources to help another in need, such as when Paul takes a collection back to Jerusalem (11:27–30). The community of believers faithfully responds to God despite charges from the Jewish leadership and others that their views are either a distortion of God's will or a reflection of strange ideas. Key to the idea of the triumph and expansion of the word's scope are the summaries (6:7; 9:31; 12:24; 16:5; 19:20). In one way or another, they all declare that the word of God increased or that the church increased. The theme is the progress of the word (Rosner 1998).

The church serves, preaches, teaches, heals, and prays. This community values peace, promotes unity, settles disputes, shares goods, and exemplifies grace. In this way it shows its health as it grows (Rosner 1998: 221). The major actor of Acts, God, is responsible for this growth through the work of the Spirit, mediated through Jesus (Acts 13:47; 14:27; 15:12; 28:28). The book has an open ending, as the work is not yet done but continues into the future. The book thus brings us into the present, telling us that the acts of God and the advance of God's word have a future into which we join. Those who are a part of this community are asked to press ahead in the continuing task (Rosner 1998: 232).

Eschatology

Luke's view of the end is simple. It will come. With it will come an accounting that Jesus will perform on behalf of God. This is the flip side of God's role as Creator. God is also Judge. All are responsible to God and will give an account to God. When the Lord will come is not a matter of concern for believers. Their task is the mission. As the study of eschatology by John Carroll (1988) shows, the issue is not "when" but "that" it will come.

Uncertainty as to the time is indicated in Acts 1:6–7. That Jesus will come and act as judge is shown in 1:9–11; 3:18–22; 10:38–42; 17:30–31.[34]

History of Interpretation

Obtaining a sense of how the book of Acts has influenced the church over the centuries has been a difficult task until recently. But the emergence of a commentary series dedicated to the theological reading of passages through the centuries provides a starting point for such study. Pelikan's (2005) treatment of Acts is not so much a commentary as a discussion of the subsequent impact on the church of issues raised in Acts, its *Wirkungsgeschichte* (the history of its interpretive impact). My commentary will not comment a great deal on this activity except here and there where it directly touches on the historical exegesis or is an implication of such exegesis. Pelikan's volume does an excellent job of introducing the key discussions that Acts helped to generate.

The Fundamental Social Context of Acts

The social context of Acts centers on the Jewish presence in Judea, the impact of Diaspora Judaism in some of the regions outside Judea, and the presence and power of the Roman Empire. This world was a complex mix of Hellenistic influence and Jewish practice. Hengel (1974) presents a detailed study of how complex this interrelationship was. We see monotheism and polytheism side by side in a kind of ancient diversity that led to various mixtures of perspectives.

The history of Judaism in Judea reflects this cultural mix. The Jews had suffered through intense efforts to hellenize them, leading to the controversial Maccabean War, a heroic effort to preserve Jewish identity in the face of edicts by the Seleucid king Antiochus Epiphanes IV in 167–164 BC prohibiting Jewish practice (1 Macc. 1–2). Bock (2002b: 79–136) discusses in detail this cultural history, the troubled relations between Jews and Gentiles, and the social strata of first-century society.

The various sects in Judaism at the time of Acts had their origins in diverse reactions to the presence of hellenization. With the coming of the Roman Empire, however, Judaism was tolerated as an acceptable religion, in accordance with the Roman view of allowing all to worship as they pleased as long as they did not challenge the state or the emperor. The Sadducees cooperated with the Romans as much as possible. The Pharisees held an uneasy relationship with Rome but did not withdraw as the Essenes had done during what they regarded as the unacceptable rule of the Hasmoneans, who had combined the priestly and regal office into one person. The Zealots and others opposed Rome and sought the

---

34. Carroll's study does not develop the judgment side of the eschatology of Acts. Here what is said to Gentiles in Acts 10 and 17 is particularly significant.

removal of Rome's control. Thus there was a wide spectrum of religious, political, and social views during the time of Acts.

Jews of the Diaspora tried to uphold their Jewish identity by gathering in community around houses of prayer and the study of the law at synagogues in various locations. These houses of worship will be important centers of activity in Acts.

The Roman Empire had an estimated population of fifty to eighty million, with about seven million free Roman citizens (Schnabel 2004: 558–59). About two and a half million people inhabited Judea, and there were about five million Jews altogether in the empire, 10 percent of the whole population. Schnabel (2004: 557–652) presents a solid overview of the many elements of the social and cultural world of this period. Since Judaism was a minority religion, the earliest Christianity was barely a dot on the demographic map.

Acts is the amazing account of how this tiny religious movement made its way into the much larger Roman world. For Luke, nothing else could explain its growth but the work of God in association with God's promise and direction. It is important to keep in mind, however, the ethnic history of the region and the turbulent relationship between Jews and Gentiles in order to truly appreciate the reconciliation that the gospel message sought to bring, not only between individuals and God but also between ethnic groups that had experienced so much hostility.

The Foci of This Commentary and Notes on Characterization in Acts and on Acts as Narrative

The first goal of this commentary is to lead the reader through the fundamental argument of the book by paying special attention to the Greek and its historical context. The terms used by Luke and the historical background that informs the text are richly noted so that it is clear what Luke intended and how the text makes such an intention clear. This special attention to Luke's terms often includes word counts, not for merely statistical reasons but to show how common a term is in both of his volumes. The plethora of extrabiblical references, both Jewish and Greco-Roman, are designed to show where Luke's expression fits in his time.

This commentary also informs the reader of the key exegetical discussions about meaning, noting options about what the text might mean and indicating where one might find other discussions of the question or a particular view, especially the "commentary tradition" of such discussions. It cites studies that are particularly beneficial for understanding what Luke means.

The question of historicity is discussed in some detail. I have interacted with other commentators' judgments with special attention to the more historically skeptical treatment of Haenchen (1987). Most of these discussions come in the introductory sections to each unit, although treatment of important details appears at points in the exegetical section. These opening units also contain discussions of the form of the passage unit and observations of a narrative or literary nature.

Discussions of the application of the texts are restricted to summary sections that appear at the end of the unit, following the exegesis. These units are introduced with the opening phrase "In sum" to make clear the transition to a summary of the passage and its application. These summaries are important because they state the central teaching and ethical points emerging from the narrative.

This commentary does not develop the narrative-critical and literary levels. It would have required an entire additional level of commentary that in some cases would have been redundant in terms of the meaning, especially if the characterization of key figures in the book were developed. The most important observations of this type are included, but a thorough discussion of such observations at a micro level has not been pursued. Observations about how a character is portrayed are made as they appear in the argument of the book, but an entire portrait is not attempted. Instead a full list of references to a figure is provided so that the reader can easily pursue this subject.

Perhaps the basic point about Acts is that its most important characters are God, Jesus, and the Spirit, for the human characters are assessed and described in terms of how they relate and respond to these key characters (Gaventa 2003: 27).

Brawley (1990) in a full study develops this idea from a narrative perspective for both Luke and Acts. He treats the discussion of the characterization of God in a key chapter of his work (1990: 107–38), observing that characters are developed through information, action, personal traits, and evaluation. These elements can be presented explicitly in the account by the narrator or implied. How, how often, and with what kind of variations is a figure described? For God and Jesus, numerous titles point to important characteristics, along with the actions each undertakes. God and Jesus are the major players in the book, whether through specific interventions by God, the portrayal of God as Creator, the appearances by Jesus, or the fact that much happens in Jesus's name. The redundancy is seen in prolepsis (anticipated action), analepsis (recalled action, which is common in the treatment of Pentecost, the conversion of Paul, the Cornelius event, and the Jerusalem Council), evaluation (sanctioning or disapproving characters), and relation (clarifying relationships among characters).

God as Creator is bigger than the temple (Acts 7:48–50). God can enable (2; 4:24–29). God's promises direct history (2:29–36; 3:25–26). He is the God of promise and of the fathers (3:13; 22:14; 24:14). He is Father, as Jesus is Son (1:4). God's actions are evaluated as directing and as positive, especially in the case of Cornelius (10:45; 11:18; 15:7–9, 14) and of Paul's work with Gentiles (21:19–20). Also, in numerous places God directs action by sending an angel or by giving enablement through the distribution of the Spirit as the outworking of his promise, themes that run through the entire book. Clearly, God is a key character in the book, as is Jesus, who often mediates God's will and distributes his blessings (Acts 2, 9).

The key role of the human characters in the church is that of witnesses engaged in the pursuit of mission outreach and fostering growth to maturity in the church. Peter, Stephen, Philip, Barnabas, and Paul are the most "rounded" of the characters in Acts. Such characters are legitimated or given approval not just as believers and active witnesses but in other ways as well. Brawley (1987: 55) names six types of legitimating techniques: divine approval, access to divine power, high motivation, benefiting others, a high level of culture, and adherence to ancient tradition. Most of the key human characters in Acts are described with multiple levels of legitimization.

There also are important foil characters who, although they are not Christian, treat Christians with a greater sense of fairness than do most who do not believe. These include individuals such as Gamaliel, Sergius Paulus, Claudius Lysias, Festus, and Agrippa. They also include groups, with the Sadducees and chief priests consistently appearing far worse than the Pharisees in Acts (Brawley 1987: 84–132). For Luke, the Pharisees believe in God's hope of resurrection and at times are not as harsh toward the testimony of believers as are the other groups. Gamaliel's caution to the Sanhedrin in Acts 5 is an example of such a foil character. The failure of the Pharisees is spiritual obtuseness (Darr 1998: 132). The Roman leaders play another role. They are the "neutral" evaluators of the new message of the Way. Their consistent evaluation is that the message of the Way represents no crime of sedition before Rome and no threat to Rome. What has caused the turmoil is a religious dispute among Jews, a point made by Gallio, Claudius Lysias, and Festus (Acts 18:14–15; 23:29; 25:24–27). The repetition of this theme from various witnesses indicates how important a point it is for Luke's narrative.

A third important class of characters includes the God-fearers, who, with more revelation, turn to embrace Jesus. Important examples are the Ethiopian eunuch, Cornelius, and Lydia. The Philippian jailer is not a God-fearer, but he falls into this category because of his response. His conversion comes because, after seeing God work, he falls under instant fear. Luke shows that people come to God in different ways. The example of an instant conversion is Saul/Paul himself. These three classes of human characters drive the narrative as types of response to God.

The fourth class of characters includes those who oppose Jesus. They come from the Jewish leadership as well as from Gentile contexts. Usually there is something at stake in power or self-perception that leads to the opposition and what Luke portrays as hardness of heart—failure to see what God is saying and doing through his servants. Thompson (1998) details how the Jewish leadership is contrasted to believers in Acts 1–7: (1) believers share the presence of God, but the leaders do not; (2) believers are united by this divine presence, but the leaders are jealous and oppose it; (3) believers care for the needs of others, but the leaders are self-serving or jealous; and (4) believers unite the Jews under God's promise, but the religious leaders are divisive in rejecting this opportunity. This portrait persists when Jewish leaders oppose Paul. These leaders help to cause riots in Jerusalem (Acts 21) and other cities that are a part of Paul's missionary efforts. Pagan Gentiles wedded to idolatry, however, respond similarly in Ephesus, also causing a near riot (Acts 19). Luke thus shows how opposing God leads to a division in the midst of a lost opportunity to experience God.

Those who wish a full narrative focus in a more concentrated way through a commentary can consult the fine treatments by Gaventa (2003) and Spencer (2004).

Outline of Acts

This commentary's working outline of Acts uses the summaries and Paul's missionary journeys as keys to its division.

I. Introduction: Jesus Ascends to the Father and Gives a Mission (1:1–11)

Acts begins with a short prologue that connects the book to Luke's Gospel and introduces the key themes of Acts: (1) Jesus is alive and functioning at God's right hand; (2) the promised Spirit will come and enable the new mission in fulfillment of divine promise; (3) the message of the kingdom is to go out into all the world, starting from Jerusalem. The Father is active through the Son by means of the Spirit to enable Jesus's followers to proclaim God's forgiveness. The new faith, rooted as it is in God's promise, reaches into commitments Israel's God made long ago. All of this sets the stage for the expectation of the Spirit and the launch of the mission from within the new community in Jerusalem. The language is that of a historical monograph in the Greco-Roman sense. Plümacher (1979: 457–66) notes terminological and conceptual overlap with a series of epistles by Cicero, Sallust (*Jugurthine War* 5.1; *Conspiracy of Cataline* 4.4), and Diodorus Siculus (*Library of History* prologue to book 16) in referring to events and their linkage to each other. So also Palmer (1993), who cites Cicero's letters to Atticus (1.19.10; 1.20.6; 2.1.1–2) and to family (5.12.10) as examples of works focused on one theme or person. Palmer argues that this approach is paralleled by Sallust, 1 Esdras, and 1 and 2 Maccabees.

This unit has two parts. First is the review of Jesus's activity in the forty-day period between his death, resurrection, and ascension. Here Jesus issues a charge to await the promised Spirit in Jerusalem and reminds his followers that the work of John the Baptist contrasts with the greater work of God to come in the arrival of the Spirit (1:1–5). Second is the quelling of eschatological curiosity with a call to mission. Jesus is taken up to the Father's side after the commission. From here on, the Spirit will empower the new mission, and at some unspecified later point in time Jesus will return to complete the work God started through him (1:6–11). As Jesus departs, so he will return. All remaining questions and promises will then be realized.

The length of this introduction is disputed. Barrett (1994: 57) takes it to verse 14, arguing that everything in these verses recapitulates things known from Luke's Gospel. Schneider (1980: 188, 195) argues that Acts 1:1–3 is the introduction and that verses 4–14 are about the ascension. Barrett's option looks more likely than Schneider's, as there is too tight a conceptual linkage between issues in verses 3–5 to separate them. On the other hand, 1:12 shows the response to the command to wait in

Jerusalem and sets up the "waiting" commanded by Jesus (note τότε, *tote*, then, in v. 12), moving directly into the replacement of Judas (with a mere καί, *kai*, and, in v. 15). So I have chosen to view this waiting as the first act of the church gathered in Jerusalem rather than a part of the introduction (with Gaventa 2003: 62). In verses 12–14 the initial participants are specified. As in Luke's Gospel, Jerusalem is a hub of activity at the beginning of Acts. By the end of the book, however, the center of activity will change. Rome becomes the hub, a move that vividly illustrates how the gospel has gone out into the world as Jesus commanded. God's activity will move far outside Israel but in keeping with promises made to it.

Traditionally, the title of the book has been "Acts of the Apostles," but this ignores the role of God as the main player. "Acts of the Holy Spirit" is a second suggestion, but this title overemphasizes the Spirit when Jesus is also at work over his new entity, not to mention the direction of the Father over all of these events. Stott (1990: 33–34) has suggested the title "The Continuing Words and Deeds of Jesus by His Spirit through the Apostles." This title is good but also tends to underplay God's sovereign work in the book. More appropriate would be "The Acts of the Sovereign God through the Lord Messiah Jesus by His Spirit on Behalf of the Way." The apostles are not noted in this title because many others besides the apostles are the human agents in the book. "The Way" is mentioned because this is Luke's most prominent title for the new movement. The title underscores the divine support for the new community God has formed and is expanding. The name also explains that the community's identity is rooted in divine provision and promise, as well as possessing a direction God points to on behalf of humanity.

A. Review of Book 1 to the Ascension (1:1–5)

Acts begins by linking this second volume to Luke's first, his Gospel. Luke 24 is especially important to this linkage. There Jesus is raised and appears to the disciples after a ministry that involved both word and deed (Luke 24:50–53). In this section of Acts, Jesus proves himself to be alive to the apostles for a period of forty days. The disciples and readers such as Theophilus can be assured that Jesus is alive. His divine mission is alive and well on earth. More than that, he gives instruction to prepare them for mission, while also promising that enablement for this mission will come to accomplish what is needed for God's kingdom. So Jesus instructs them to remain in Jerusalem and not to begin the mission until the long-promised enabling Spirit comes from the Father. What they have to do is so important and will require so much from them that God must equip them for the task. God will not let them down. He will give them the one they need to accomplish taking the message to the end of the world. Thus this review introduces, reassures, and prepares the reader for what God has called the new community to do. The church's primary task is to represent God faithfully, including witnessing to God's work in Jesus through the Holy Spirit.

Exegesis and Exposition

[1]In the first account, O Theophilus, I treated all that Jesus began to do and also to teach, [2]until the day God took him up, after he had given a command through the Holy Spirit to the apostles he had elected. [3]To them also he had presented himself living after his suffering by many proofs, appearing to them through forty days and speaking things concerning God's kingdom. [4]And while [sharing table] with them, he commanded them not to leave Jerusalem, but await the Father's promise, which, he said, "You heard from me, [5]for John, on the one hand, baptized with water, but before many days, on the other, you shall be baptized with the Holy Spirit."

Luke begins Acts with a renewed dedication and refers back to his Gospel. Five elements connect Acts and the Gospel. First, Luke calls the first book a "former account" (πρῶτον λόγον, *prōton logon*; "first" has the force of "former" here, so "former account"; Pesch 1986a: 60n4; BDF §62). Second, the address to Theophilus recalls the figure introduced

1:1

to us in Luke 1:3. The overlapping address shows that Luke composed Acts as a single story line extending from his Gospel. Everything about this introduction to Acts confirms this linkage. The prologue parallels the style of other ancient introductions (Philo, *Good Person* 1 §§1–7).[1] Third, this link to Luke's Gospel is further affirmed in Acts 1:4–5, which makes the connection to John the Baptist, the figure with whom Luke's Gospel begins. A fourth connection in the introduction is the overlapping accounts of the ascension in Luke 24 and Acts 1. A fifth connection, noted in Acts 1:2, is the direct allusion back to the instruction given in Luke 24:47, 49 to await the Spirit and be witnesses. Witherington (1998: 107–8) plausibly suggests that Luke 24 is telescoped (condensed) and that Acts 1 recapitulates what took place over the forty days (also Bock 1996: 1944 and n. 23). Unlike Luke 1:1–4, which is a sentence in periodic style, this passage is simply a collection of clauses (BDF §464).

In treating Luke 1:3, Bock (1994a: 63–64) suggests that Theophilus's identity is unknown but that he appears to be a person of high social standing and could well be a Christian Gentile wavering in his faith because of the pressure placed on the church (see also Polhill 1992: 79). The name means "friend or beloved by God." He could be a patron or simply the most important intended reader. Barrett (1994: 65) notes that the name is common and that Luke 1:3 with "most excellent" in its address speaks to a person, not an "ideal" figure. In other words, Theophilus is not a symbolic reference to those beloved of God (Bruce 1990: 98 agrees).

Luke's first book treats all that Jesus began to do and teach. The linkage to Luke's Gospel suggests this interpretation over the alternative, that Luke is claiming rhetorically and hyperbolically to cover everything Jesus did and taught (but so Witherington 1998: 9–10, 106). The combination of deed and word is a theme in Luke's Gospel (as the pattern of preaching, Luke 4:16–30, and activity, 4:31–44, shows).[2] The particle τε (*te*) tightly links the preaching and the action, almost suggesting that they are a package ("a holy knot," Calvin). The particle is often left untranslated but indicates a close connection (which I render "and also"). The idea that Jesus "began" (ἤρξατο, *ērxato*) such activity may well suggest that he is still at work as Luke writes his story of the church in volume 2. Acts 9 describes Jesus's direct involvement, but the claim is wider than his direct, visible involvement (Bruce 1990: 98). This

---

1. Alexander 1996: 73–103 discusses how Luke's work fits the middle level of scientific writing from a Greek perspective, although one could question this connection to scientific works, since Acts is not about science but history. See Witherington 1998: 105n2; Eckey 2000: 43.

2. Wikenhauser 1961: 24 speaks of the miracles and the passion as the key activities, and Pesch 1986a: 61 notes the kingdom (Acts 1:3) as the key teaching topic. Jervell 1998: 109 speaks of the demonstration of the power of God's word as the purpose of Jesus's actions.

link is important. What the early church said and did was rooted in and connected to activity in which the risen Jesus was involved. Indeed, the point is that without Jesus and his work, one cannot make sense of the church's existence and activity.

The account in Luke proceeds to the ascension, an event that Luke alone details in the NT. The ascension stands as a key divine act vindicating Jesus and placing him in authority at the right hand of God (Ps. 110:1; Acts 2:32–35). The "taking up" of Jesus is where Luke 24 ended (see Luke 24:51). The language that is used parallels passages where God has taken up righteous men directly to heaven.[3] Acts 1 will review this departure, and Acts 2 will explain it.

     1:2

The commandment alluded to here (ἐντειλάμενος, enteilamenos) refers to the call to a mission that these chosen apostles should lead. This mission represents the next phase of God's work and takes place in fulfillment of Scripture about the Christ, as Luke 24:47 declares. For Luke, Scripture is the voice of God (Jervell 1998: 110). So the plan to take the message of the kingdom out to the world by preaching repentance and the forgiveness of sins takes place as part of the divine program. Except at Acts 14:4 and 14, where Barnabas and Paul are called apostles, the term ἀπόστολος (apostolos) refers to the Twelve (or the Eleven, minus Judas; Bruce 1990: 99). In normal usage an apostle is merely a "commissioned, sent agent," and this is what these Twelve are for Jesus (Le Cornu and Shulam 2003: 8). In Judaism, such a representative speaks for the one who sends him. "A man's agent is like to himself" (m. Ber. 5.5). BDAG (122) notes that the term can simply mean "delegate, envoy, messenger," but it especially refers to this special group in Acts (1:2; 2:42–43; 4:33, 35, 37; 5:2, 12, 18, 40; 6:6; 8:1, 14, 18; 9:27; 11:1; 14:4; from here on linked with elders: 15:2, 4, 6, 22–23; 16:4). They are to preach repentance for the forgiveness of sins to all the nations, beginning from Jerusalem, as witnesses empowered by the Spirit ("power from on high") sent from the Father (Luke 24:47–49). The linkage between the Spirit's work and the apostles is frequent in Acts (1:5, 8; 2:4; 4:8; 5:32; 8:17–18, 29; 13:4; 15:28; Jervell 1998: 110).

    At this point a question emerges about how to take the preposition διά (dia) with the genitive reference to the Spirit. One view is that Jesus gives this command through or by means of the Spirit (Luke 24:49; Acts 1:8). In other words, his followers are given a mission through the Spirit and will be enabled for it by the Spirit (Acts 1:5). So the translation "he had given a command through the Holy Spirit." A second view wishes to connect grammatically the activity of the Spirit to the choosing of the Twelve here (so "the apostles whom he chose through the Holy

---

3. On the use of the verb ἀναλαμβάνω (analambanō, to be taken up) in Acts for the ascension, see Acts 1:11, 22; also 2 Kings 2:9–11 LXX; 1 Macc. 2:58; Sir. 48:9 (of Elijah); 49:14 (of Enoch); Conzelmann 1987: 4.

Spirit").[4] Key here is Luke 6:13, which lacks any mention of the Spirit with the choosing of the Twelve, whereas all through Acts the Spirit is connected to preaching and mission activity (Acts 1:8, 16; 2:4, 17–18; 4:8). Barrett (1994: 68–69) argues that the relative clause works better with this sense.[5] Kilgallen (2000: 414–17) opts for a third view, taking διά with the genitive as meaning "because of" the Spirit. The idea is that the apostles are those who are chosen because of the promise of the coming of the Spirit. This promise of the Spirit's coming, however, requires an understanding that involves a rare usage of the preposition and this meaning seems too subtle to be likely, for the coming of the Spirit in Acts 2 is upon all, not just the apostles, and so does not explain why just the Eleven are chosen. The theme of how the Spirit is associated with mission favors the first reading (NET, HCSB, RSV).

The mention of the Spirit reinforces the role of this key figure in Acts for the church's mission. Jesus and the Spirit operate in concert on behalf of God. Does this connection possibly allude to John 20:22 (Bruce 1988a: 31)? The Spirit in Acts is almost always an aid in proclamation and an enabler (esp. Acts 2:17–18), a point that argues against tying the Spirit to mission and the choosing of the Twelve as Johnson argues. There is continuity between Jesus's ministry and the apostles' mission as they seek to call Israel to reenter the program of God (A. Robinson and Wall 2006: 30).

1:3   After his suffering (παθεῖν, *pathein*; Acts 17:3; 26:23), Jesus's activity from his resurrection to his ascension entails presenting himself to his followers alive (ζῶντα, *zōnta*) by many proofs. These appearances last forty days; ἡμερῶν τεσσεράκοντα (*hēmerōn tesserakonta*) is a genitive of time (BDF §186.2). The term for "proof," τεκμήριον (*tekmērion*), refers to "that which causes something to be known in a convincing and decisive manner, proof" (BDAG 994; Josephus, *Ant.* 17.5.6 §128; 3 Macc. 3:24). Witherington (1998: 108) notes that the term is reserved for Greek historical texts (Quintilian, *Institutio oratoria* 5.9.3 says the term indicates that the proof points to a conclusion; also Mealand 1989 in a search of the Thesaurus Linguae Graecae [a database of ancient Greek writings]). Barrett (1994: 69) argues that παρέστησεν (*parestēsen*, presented) can bear the meaning "proof" as well (see Lysias, *Against*

---

4. Larkin 1995: 38–39 argues that the command through the Spirit adds nothing to the meaning. Also Haenchen 1987: 139 and n3 argues that Luke moved the stressed words of the recipients forward. In this view, the resultant sense is, "He commanded the apostles whom he chose through the Spirit." See also Pesch 1986a: 61n11; and Schneider 1980: 192–93—citing Luke 6:12–16 as background. Moule 1959: 169 speaks of the clause being displaced and calls the passage "notoriously problematic." He makes no decision about the reading. Moulton and Turner 1963: 350 note the clause's unnatural order, which suggests a connection to mission.

5. Johnson 1992: 24 connects it with both, arguing that the Spirit works in all of Jesus's activities.

Eratosthenes 12.51, which, like Acts 1:3, also has both terms for "proof." Jesus's appearances were convincing to those who had not expected a resurrection. These appearances showed that Jesus was still alive. They are part of the confirmation and encouragement Theophilus needs (Luke 1:4). To have seen the resurrection was a qualification for being a "witness" to Jesus (Luke 24:44–48). These appearances gave Jesus the opportunity to continue to instruct about the kingdom of God. He was teaching the witnesses that the rule of God he was bringing now would move on with the next stage of the apostles' mission (on the kingdom of God, see Bock 2002a: 565–93; Acts 3:14–26 discusses the two-stage messianic-kingdom program of Jesus).

There is no OT symbolic/figurative sense for forty days (Balz, *TDNT* 8:139); forty *years* in the wilderness or as the length of a king's reign is perhaps the closest type.[6] This divergence from the common use of the number makes it quite likely that this is a specific period of time, and so the number is literal in force even if it might convey something more. The idea is not that Jesus was continuously with them for forty days but that he appeared at intervals within that period as the appearances in the Gospels indicate. The expression οὐ μετὰ πολλὰς ταύτας ἡμέρας (*ou meta pollas tautas hēmeras*) in 1:5 is a way to say "after a short period" or "before long" (cf. Moulton and Turner 1963: 193). This indicates that the forty days and the coming of the Spirit fit into a tightly linked time sequence of days.

Jesus taught his followers about the kingdom, which also was the central theme of his earthly ministry (Bock 2002a: 565–93).[7] "God's Kingdom" (τῆς βασιλείας τοῦ θεοῦ, *tēs basileias tou theou*) refers to God's promised rule that comes with Jesus's messianic program and activity. This expression is not as prevalent in Acts as it is in Luke. It appears thirty-two times in Luke and six times in Acts (1:3; 8:12; 14:22; 19:8; 28:23, 31). For Luke, the idea summarizes a key component of the gospel

6. Discussing the origin of the length of forty days, some try to turn it into some type of symbolically developed or "sacred" number (see Haenchen 1987: 141n1; Bauernfeind 1980: 20; Pesch 1986a: 62; A. Robinson and Wall 2006: 31–32). Jervell 1998: 111 speaks of forty as the fulfillment number in the history of Israel (Exod. 16:35; Ps. 95:10; Amos 5:25; 2 Sam. 2:10; 5:4; 1 Kings 2:11; 11:42; 2 Kings 12:1; 2 Chron. 9:30). It does function this way in a generic sense, but it is most common to have forty years point to such a significance. The best explanation is that this was the period of Christ's appearances, as no symbolism is transparently evident ("not a typical expression," Conzelmann 1987: 5). The timing fits because fifty days is the gap between Passover and Pentecost (Williams 1990: 20; Tertullian, *Apology* 21.29 mentions these details and appears to follow the account of Acts 1).

7. Pelikan 2005: 38–41 notes that many teachers in the early centuries of the church saw these forty days as an important period of teaching for the apostles and invoked this postresurrection "gospel of the forty days" as the putative source of subsequent church traditions. In particular, Pelikan mentions the third-century teaching of Cyprian of Carthage in his *Three Books of Testimonies against the Jews*.

(Luke 9:2, 6) that already had shown signs of arriving during Jesus's ministry (Luke 11:20; 17:21). Jesus's resurrection allows the kingdom to be preached (Acts 28:23, 31). From a literary point of view, the probable content or themes of what is meant here show up in the early speeches of Acts 2–4. So this remark in Acts 1 serves as a thematic introduction (Bruce 1988a: 32–33 looks back to Luke 24:44–47 as well as forward to Acts 10:42; 17:31).

Kistemaker (1990: 48) lists ten appearances of Jesus: to the women at the tomb, Mary Magdalene, the Emmaus disciples, Peter in Jerusalem, ten disciples, eleven disciples, seven disciples fishing in Galilee, eleven disciples in Galilee, the five hundred, and James the Lord's brother.

1:4   As Jesus stays with the apostles and engages them in table fellowship (see additional note on Acts 1:4), he commands them not to depart from Jerusalem but to begin the mission from there, waiting for the "promise of the Father" (τὴν ἐπαγγελίαν τοῦ πατρός, tēn epangelian tou patros) to come. This promise they had heard about from Jesus. This theme of the Father's promise is an allusion to the Holy Spirit (Luke 24:49, clothed with power from on high) and is a theme Luke traces from early on in his two volumes (Luke 3:13–17) and develops especially in Acts 2 and 10–11, when the Spirit comes on the believing community at Pentecost and on Cornelius and the Gentiles respectively (Acts 2:16–39; 10:34–45; 11:15–17). Acts 1:5 will allude to teaching that parallels Luke 3:15–17 and the words of John the Baptist, which Jesus apparently reinforced, since Acts 1:4–5 makes the point that Jesus taught them this. The promise's OT sources are Joel 2:28–32, Isa. 44:3, and especially 32:15: "A spirit is emptied out on us from on high." These sources show that although this faith appears to be new, it is rooted in divine promises of old, an important idea to the ancients, who desired their religions to be time-tested (Witherington 1998: 109). The link between the Spirit and promise is frequent in the NT (John 14:16–17, 26; 15:26–27; 16:7–15; Eph. 1:13; Bruce 1990: 101). Indeed, the Spirit is a major gift provided by the gospel, as Rom. 5–8 teaches (Rom. 5:5; 8:2–17).

The timing of this command is not specified. It could have come anytime during the forty-day period, especially if the ending of Luke's Gospel is telescoped (so Harrison 1975: 37 and Larkin 1995: 39 imply; discussion in Bock 1996: 1929). Its key point in conjunction with Acts 1:8 is that the mission will be launched from Jerusalem after the promise (the Spirit) has come (Acts 3:25–26). Jesus speaks prominently of the Spirit in John 14–16. With enablement (Rackham 1901: 5), the mission of preaching the kingdom and Jesus can proceed. Effective ministry requires God's direction and enablement. The mission command provides the direction for the church, and the Spirit gives the enablement. The end of the verse shifts to direct address as Jesus recalls what they heard from him earlier.

Jesus recalls and explains (ὅτι, *hoti*, is explanatory: for) why they must   **1:5**
remain in Jerusalem in salvation-historical terms (Schneider 1980: 200).
This includes a contrast using μὲν . . . δέ (*men . . . de: on the one hand*,
there was John the Baptist . . . *on the other hand*, there is the Spirit's
coming). The baptism of John the Baptist was an eschatological, preparatory washing. Participation in it meant that one was ready for God
to come. The gift of the Spirit, however, was the sign that the Messiah
had come and the new era had begun (Luke 3:1–17, esp. vv. 3–6, 16;
Mark 1:8; Matt. 3:11; Acts 1:8; 2:4, 16–39); ἐν πνεύματι (*en pneumati*,
with the Spirit) is instrumental in the current verse (Barrett 1994: 74).[8]
Only Luke's Gospel puts this promise from John in the context of being
asked if he is the Messiah. Thus his answer in Luke indicates how one
can know the Messiah has come. It is when the baptism of the Spirit
comes. Jervell (1998: 113) rightly calls this baptism an "eschatological
salvation and judgment baptism." It saves and protects from judgment,
portraying not only the cleansing from sin but also the indwelling of
God as a result of the cleansing. The bridge from the old era to the new
is crossed when Jesus brings the Spirit. Jesus's ministry itself is the
connection point.

Apparently Jesus also made this point about the Spirit to them, as
he reminds them here (Luke 12:12 has the concept, as does 24:49).
This will be the point of Peter's speech in Acts 2, but Peter will add the
explicit connection that Jesus as the risen Messiah has bestowed the
Spirit, having received the Spirit from the Father (Acts 2:32–33). In Acts
1 the Father does this work, reflecting Jesus's tendency to highlight the
Father as the key to Jesus's activity. The new-era baptism promised by
the Father (see v. 4) is what they are to await in Jerusalem. The Spirit
will cleanse and enable them to be indwelt in order to empower them
for mission (Ezek. 36:25–26; 1QS 4.21 pictures washing as a cleansing;
Conzelmann 1987: 6). By associating baptism with repentance, Acts
2:38 alludes to this cleansing imagery.

Marshall (1980: 58) notes that power, not cleansing alone, is the point
(so Acts 1:8). This is why indwelling or clothing is often the point of
comparison when the Spirit is pictured as remaining with the believer
(see the important verse Luke 24:49 for the clothing metaphor). Luke
repeats the John-Jesus contrast in Acts 11:16 and 13:24. Acts here also
reflects the John-Jesus contrast of Luke's infancy narrative (Luke 1–2).
Luke repeats things that are extremely important to him, and this teaching of the coming of the Spirit as the sign of Messiah's presence and
the arrival of new-era blessing is one of his most important themes. In

8. On Luke 3, John's baptism, and the coming Spirit, see Bock 1994a: 287–89, 324.
Schneider 1980: 200 notes that the Greek wording about baptizing with the Spirit is closer
to Mark 1:8 in its grammar than to Luke 3. Bauernfeind 1980: 21 sees evidence for the
use of tradition in this terminological connection to Mark's version.

the NT view, this coming of the Spirit is something new and previously unavailable, or else the Twelve and those with them would not have had to wait for the event (see also John 7:39; Rackham 1901: 5). Stott (1990: 40) mentions four requisites for this mission: a mandate to witness, the ascended Lord who directs the mission, the central role of the apostles for the task, and the coming of the Spirit to empower them (also R. Longenecker 1981: 353–55).

The disciples perceive this event as an indication of the full arrival of the end, which leads to their question in verse 6 about the restoration of the kingdom to Israel. It is here that Jesus will nuance how the end works and what their responsibility is as it unfolds. The speech in Acts 3 shows how the apostles put together what they learn here. Jesus indicates the wait will not be long, following "after these few days."[9] Indeed, according to the chronology of Acts, the wait was about ten days, since Pentecost was fifty days after Passover and Jesus appeared for forty days.

In sum, Acts 1:1–5 reviews the resurrection of Jesus and his setting up of their enablement for mission. The apostles benefit from Jesus's choice, his revelation, his commission, and God's promise of the Spirit (Stott 1990: 35–37). They cannot proceed without the enablement of the new era, the Spirit of God. This provision from the Father was promised long ago. The faith has ancient roots. As the apostles return to Jerusalem, they can be assured that the suffering of Jesus did not end the story of the kingdom but was part of God's program. Jesus is raised, alive, and ready to bestow the blessing they need to carry out the mission he will give them. How he is able to do this is what the ascension will show, as he prepares to tell them their mission. These are the goals of the next section of the introduction along with one other point, namely, what is left for Jesus to do.

There will be a day when Jesus returns from heaven to complete what God has started through him. The introduction to Acts not only highlights key themes of the book; it also proclaims with assurance that God's program is on track. This is the major application of the unit: Jesus's resurrection and the coming of the Spirit assure us that God is at work and the plan of salvation is intact. The Spirit's coming and indwelling guarantee this conclusion. It is a central goal of the Spirit operating in the church that God's community be committed to mission. Since the time of the apostles, other believers are also beneficiaries of Jesus's choice, his revelation of himself, his commission, and his provision of the Spirit, but the roots of our experience go back to Jesus's

---

9. Barrett 1994: 75 argues that οὐ (*ou*, not) with πολλάς (*pollas*, many) converts to the idea of "few" and that the demonstrative pronoun that immediately follows is in effect redundant. On the grammar and word order involving the preposition μετά (*meta*, after), see BDF §433.3.

resurrection appearance to these disciples, who are different from us in that they saw him face to face.

Additional Notes

1:1. That μέν is not followed by a corresponding δέ is not unusual in Acts (3:13, 21; 21:39; 27:21; 28:22; Barrett 1994: 65). It is left untranslated, as normally it would mean "on the one hand" but here it works as an introductory particle without carrying any easily translated meaning.

1:2. There is a text-critical difference between the Western tradition and B here. At the end of the verse, D refers specifically to a command to preach the gospel and has moved up the verb that refers to the ascension. Barrett (1994: 67–68) argues for the shorter reading in B, which is what our translation reflects.

1:4. The meaning of the verb συναλίζω (*synalizō*) is disputed (LSJ 1694; BDAG 964; Eckey 2000: 45n125). It literally translates as "eating salt with" and thus appears to refer to table fellowship (Barrett 1994: 71). Some argue that this fits the context poorly and that this sense is not attested elsewhere, and so they prefer the sense of "to stay with" someone (so RSV), seeing it as a variation of συναυλιζόμενος (*synaulizomenos*), which has this other meaning. The lexicon appeals to Acts 10:41 as supporting the option of sharing the table (see BDAG 964 §1). So I have translated it accordingly (see notes in HCSB and NET). The remark may well look back to Luke 24:41–43 or John 21:9–14, as the Gospels narrate various scenes of this type to which the tradition may be alluding. The remark either refers back to such a previous meal, or else it is a final instruction toward the end of the period (so Haenchen 1987: 141). Schneider (1980: 199) holds that the verse connects with Acts 1:2 as a final appearing, with verse 3 functioning as a parenthesis in the account. Schneider also maintains that one should not connect this scene to Luke 24:41–43, since the tone is different here in that there is mention of the Spirit. If Haenchen is right, then this remark sets up Acts 1:6, but the καί beginning verse 4 seems to look back to Acts 1:3 and not present a new event. The taking of food indicates the physical and material nature of Jesus's resurrection. His appearances were not merely visions or a phantom (Bruce 1988a: 34). Viewing this instruction as occurring toward the end of the forty-day period frees us from having to identify it with previous appearances taking place in Galilee and Jerusalem. Wikenhauser (1961: 26) correctly notes, however, that the time and place of this meal is difficult to establish.

I. Introduction: Jesus Ascends to the Father and Gives a Mission (1:1–11)
  A. Review of Book 1 to the Ascension (1:1–5)
➤ B. The Ascension and Final Testament: A Promise for the Disciples Now and a Promise to Return
  (1:6–11)

B. The Ascension and Final Testament: A Promise for the Disciples Now and a Promise to Return (1:6–11)

This scene reconstructs the eschatological priorities and calendar anticipated by the Jews and the disciples. It also sets forth a mission that supplies the outline for Acts and reflects the church's fundamental call. In explaining the mission, Jesus clarifies the calendar for the disciples, who still need instruction about God's plan. In verse 7 Jesus does not answer the question in verse 6 about whether the restoration of the kingdom for Israel is around the corner. Instead he tells them it is not their business to know what time the Father has set for this event. The reply does not deny that this will happen; it just affirms that the timing will not be revealed and that they have another calling to pursue in the meantime. This splitting of the coming of the Messiah from the future restoration creates room for what the church came to call the second coming of Christ. What Judaism had believed would come all at once is split into two parts, with a mission in between.

This mission is defined in verse 8. They are to receive power in the Spirit of God. As a result, they can be witnesses to Jesus from Jerusalem to Judea and Samaria and finally to the end of the earth. Instead of worrying about when God will consummate the program, they are to take to the world the news of salvation's coming.

The scene ends with Jesus ascending into heaven, taken up in a cloud to God's side to share in administering God's program, and a pair of angels appear to explain that as Jesus has departed, so will he return (vv. 9–11). This note of assurance, tinged with rebuke, says that they should not be surprised that Jesus has gone to reside in God's presence in heaven and that they should be certain that he will return as he has departed. That the hope of return is associated with the clouds of heaven is something Paul reassures the Thessalonians about in 1 Thess. 4:13–18 as he gives a word of comfort. Luke's purpose here is similar. Jesus may not be visibly present, but the plan moves on and the new community has a task to perform until he returns. The point of the unit is really a command: do not look up and merely be idle, waiting for the return, but move out and share what God's program in Jesus is all about.

Exegesis and Exposition

[6]So, on the one hand, when they had come together, they asked him, "Lord, will you at this time restore the kingdom to Israel?" [7]But he, on the other hand, said to them, "It is not for you to know the times or seasons that the Father has set through his own authority, [8]but you shall receive power when the Holy Spirit comes upon you, and you shall be my witnesses in Jerusalem, in all of Judea and Samaria and as far as the end of the earth." [9]And after he said these things, as they were looking, he was lifted up and a cloud received him from their sight. [10]And while they were gazing into heaven as he departed, behold, two men stood by them in white robes, [11]and they said to them, "Men of Galilee, why do you stand looking into heaven? This Jesus, the one taken from you into heaven, this one will come in a manner similar to the way you saw him depart into heaven."

Acts often uses a μὲν . . . δέ (men . . . de) construction simply to resume the narrative, as here (BDF §251). The construction implies a contrast between the disciples' question and Jesus's reply, as the translation shows.

1:6

Jesus's announcement of the Spirit's coming makes the apostles think that the time of restoration for Israel has come (Jervell 1998: 114). But the coming of the Spirit does not mean the completion of the kingdom promise. Acts 2–3 will make the sequence clearer.

Nothing indicates that the primary subject of Jesus's earlier discussion, the apostles, has changed from verse 2. Nonetheless, the promise of Acts 1:8 and the nature of the provision of the Spirit make clear that they represent the community as a whole. Acts 1:12 tells us that their coming together for this announcement took place at the Mount of Olives, located just outside Jerusalem. Bethany, noted as the locale of an ascension into heaven in Luke 24:50, is on the eastern side of the Mount of Olives (see Bock 1996: 1944).

So the apostles ask a question to see if the time of Israel's restoration has come. The direct question is introduced with εἰ (ei; Robertson 1934: 916 notes that it mirrors Semitic and LXX style; also Moulton and Turner 1963: 333), which is untranslated. The term χρόνῳ (chronō, time) suggests a specific interval of time (Barrett 1994: 76). Many Jewish texts, as well as OT hope in general, expected that in the end Israel would be restored to a place of great blessing (Jer. 16:15; 23:8; 31:27–34 [where the new covenant is mentioned]; Ezek. 34–37; Isa. 2:2–4; 49:6; Amos 9:11–15; Sir. 48:10; Ps. Sol. 17–18; 1 En. 24–25; Tob. 13–14; Eighteen Benedictions 14).[1] The question is a natural one for Jews who have embraced the messianic hope. Luke 1–2 expressed this hope vividly (1:69–74; 2:25,

---

1. On ἀποκαθίστημι (apokathistēmi, restore), see Mal. 3:23 LXX (4:6 Eng.), where it is an eschatological technical term, and Dan. 4:36 LXX. Acts 3:21 will return to this idea. Isaiah 49:6 has the concept, not the term.

38). What was debated in Judaism is whether the centrality of Israel would be positive or negative for Gentiles. Would it come with salvation or judgment for the nations? The disciples are not even thinking in mission terms here. Their question reflects a nationalistic concern for Israel's vindication and the completion of the promise.

1:7   Jesus's reply in verses 7–8 does not reject the premise of the question, that the kingdom will one day be restored to Israel (Barrett 1994: 77), but it does change its focus, and it is debated whether the definition of Israel changes as the book proceeds (Barrett argues that it does). This reading is in contrast to Stott (1990: 41), who sees the question as full of errors. In Stott's view, they should not have asked about restoration, since that implied a political kingdom; nor should they have asked about Israel, since that anticipated a national kingdom; nor should they have asked about "at this time," since that implied the kingdom's immediate establishment. There is no indication in Jesus's reply, however, that anything they asked was wrong except that they are excessively concerned about when all of this would take place (Le Cornu and Shulam 2003:15). The other major argument Stott makes is that there is no mention of the land in the NT. It is not surprising, however, that the land is not mentioned, since (1) Israel is in its land when the NT is written, and (2) the rule of Jesus is anticipated to extend over the entire earth, so why focus just on the land?

In fact, it is not that the definition of Israel or that expectation for Israel changes but rather that being blessed of God is now centered in the figure of the eschaton, Jesus, rather than in an ethnic or legal emphasis. Throughout Acts Jesus is preached as the mediator of blessing. We shall see that throughout Acts the role of Israel remains and the hope is preached as the natural extension of Jewish expectation, the divinely promised hope of restoration. How this works itself out in detail is part of the story of Acts, especially Acts 10–15, where the manner in which Gentiles are included is worked out. Romans 9–11 suggests that this new emphasis emerging from the new era did not remove hope for Israel or replace the nation in God's plan, as Paul has a concern for ethnic Israel in these chapters in line with OT promise, which looks to include Israel in the end (Polhill 1992: 84n27 shows the options; see additional note on 1:7 and the idea of a future for Israel). What does change, in terms of normal Jewish anticipation, is an emphasis on the scope of the blessing. Acts will show that concern for Israel alone is not the point of the gospel. The message will go to all and is for all because Jesus is Lord of all, a role that includes his being judge of the living and the dead.

Jesus does not answer the question about Israel's restoration and its timing. Nor is his response a renunciation of an imminent end (*pace* Haenchen 1987: 143). It makes no commitment at all as to when the end comes; it just points out that there are things to do in the meantime.

The times or seasons (χρόνους ἢ καιρούς, *chronous ē kairous*) the Father has set by his own authority are not for them to know. The question about the specific time in verse 6 is answered with respect to all times and seasons in verse 7 (Jervell 1998: 115). The expression οὐχ ὑμῶν ἐστιν γνῶναι (*ouch hymōn estin gnōnai*) means that this matter is of no concern to them (BDF §162.7). Barrett (1994: 78) cites Mekilta Exodus 16.32 (59b): "No one knows . . . when the kingdom of the house of David will be put back in its place, and when the evil kingdom will be wiped out." This nicely summarizes an important Jewish view of the unknown timing of restoration and hope. Jesus here says more than this Jewish text. Not only do people not know the time; it is also not to be a matter of excessive concern to them. One is to be ready for Jesus's return whenever God decides to bring it.

It is most likely that the Greek terms for "times" and "seasons" are synonymous, and they appear to reflect a traditional phrase (Dan. 2:21; Wis. 8:8; 1 Thess. 5:1; Schneider 1980: 220, although the LXX texts reverse the order). It is possible, however, that the first refers to a specific time period and the second to a broader time frame, given the use of "times" (καιροί, *kairoi*) of the Gentiles in Luke 21:24 and the specific question about the "time" (χρόνος, *chronos*) of the end in verse 6. The point is clear: the timing of the promise's completion, however it is conceived, is set by God and will not be revealed (Mark 13:32 and parallels make a similar point). The Father has "set" (ἔθετο, *etheto*) the timing in his own sovereign authority. This verb in the middle voice means "fix" or "establish" something (BDAG 1004 §4b; 1 Cor. 12:18 has a similar force).

The disciples' calling, concern, and mission are not to focus on the timing of the end. Rather they are to receive the enablement that God will give in the Spirit. They will be Jesus's witnesses from Jerusalem to the end of the earth.[2] The Spirit is tied to power (δύναμιν, *dynamin*), which refers here to being empowered to speak boldly by testifying to the message of God's work through Jesus. Paul says something similar of the gospel in Rom. 1:16–17; for him, responding to the gospel gives power to live in a way that is honoring to God and allows one to experience fullness of life. The term "power" appears ten times in Acts, sometimes referring to miracles or other effects of power (2:22; 3:12; 4:7; 8:13; 10:38; 19:11) and other times to enablement (4:33; 6:8). The enablement is in word and act (Jervell 1998: 115: "miraculous power in miracle and word").

So they are to be "witnesses" (μάρτυρες, *martyres*) for Jesus. The idea has OT roots in the concept of witness (Num. 35:30; Deut. 17:6–7; Isa.

1:8

2. On Jerusalem as the "navel," or center, of the world, see Ezek. 5:5 (Jerusalem at the center of a circle of the nations); 38:12; 1 En. 26.1 (Jerusalem at the center of the world's geography); and esp. Jub. 8–9 (J. M. Scott 1995: 99–103; Le Cornu and Shulam 2003: 19). Conceptually, see Isa. 2:2–4; Mic. 4:5; Deut. 32:8.

43:10–12; 44:8–9). Jesus also spoke of witnesses in a legal sense (Matt. 18:16), as do passages discussing activity or potential activity in the church (2 Cor. 13:1; 1 Tim. 5:19). A witness in this sense is someone who helps establish facts objectively through verifiable observation. As such, a witness is more than someone with merely subjective and personal impressions. This objectivity and fact-based quality of the witness are why the direct experience of Jesus's ministry and resurrection are required of Judas's replacement in Acts 1:21–22, a passage that shows what stands behind Luke's use of this term. Thus "witness" is a key term in Acts for those who experienced Jesus and saw him in a resurrection appearance (1:22). This experience means that they can testify directly to what God did through Jesus (Luke 24:48).

The disciples' direct and real experience of Jesus and his resurrection qualifies them as witnesses, but the Spirit will give them the capability to articulate their experience with boldness. Acts 2 will show the initial enablement in Peter, who is transformed from the person who denied Jesus three times. Thirteen of the thirty-five NT uses of "witness" are in Acts. Other NT uses outside Acts refer simply to the broader sense of someone who saw or experienced something. Most its uses in Acts, however, are narrower than the term's general use and have this special force (BAGD 494 §2c; BDAG 620; Acts 1:22; 2:32; 3:15; 5:32; 10:39, 41; 13:31; 22:15; 22:20 have this more narrow sense). The roots of this use go back to Luke 24:47 (Strathmann, *TDNT* 4:492–93). This testimony will start in Jerusalem, but it will spread to Judea and Samaria and to the end of the earth. Jerusalem will be important in Acts 1–7. Judea and Samaria will become a concern in Acts 8–10. After a brief return to Jerusalem in Acts 11–12, the gospel will spread, primarily focused on the mission from Antioch, eventually reaching Rome through Paul. In this sense, 1:8 introduces the book by showing a concern for the geographical expansion that Luke loves to note.

Instead of worrying about the end of the plan, they are to be equipped to carry the message to the end of the earth. There is dispute about what "end of the earth" (ἐσχάτου τῆς γῆς, *eschatou tēs gēs*) means.[3] The phrase has OT roots (Isa. 48:20; 49:6; Jer. 10:13). Does it refer here to Spain (as in 1 Clem. 5.7) and thus cover the earth (so Witherington 1998: 110–11),[4] or to Rome (of Pompey's roots in Ps. Sol. 8.15, see Conzelmann 1987: 7), or is it ethnic in force, looking to the Gentiles? Against this last option is that Paul engages Jews in Rome as well as Gentiles. Moore (1997: 389–99) has a full discussion of the issue and

---

3. The Greek phrase is in the singular, "end of the earth." A literal translation has been adopted in this commentary, though it differs from the more idiomatic English plural.

4. For Marshall 1980: 61 and Jervell 1998: 116, Rome ends the "first phase" (Marshall) or the goal of "Jewish mission" (Jervell), but the goal of the entire mission is wider and goes out from Rome.

notes that Palestine and Ethiopia have also been suggested as options (though, I think, less likely). Pao (2000: 93) also presents a full list of options, either geographic or ethnic: Is the "end of the earth" Ethiopia, Israel, Diaspora Jews, Rome, Spain, the whole world, Gentiles, or the farthest end of the earth?[5]

Acts does show an interest in Rome (19:21; 23:11; chap. 28). From a literary standpoint within Acts, the reference to Rome after a long providential sea journey in Acts 27 would mean that the message has now reached the hub of the Gentile world, from which it can proceed everywhere (Barrett 1994: 80). Thus the difference between interpreting "end of the earth" as specifying Rome or as looking at the broader edges of the world is not great. If Isa. 49:6 is in the background, as is possible (see Acts 13:47), then the point is that the message is going out to the world (but its reaching Rome is an important part of that task).

Moore (1997) notes that Luke uses Isaiah extensively, so that an allusion to it is likely. He cites eighteen texts with allusions to Isaiah in Luke-Acts. Pao (2000: 84–86, 92–95) supports this view and regards the allusion to Isa. 49:6 as solid, while observing that in Acts 13:47 and Isaiah the emphasis is on Gentiles, which rules out references to Ethiopia, Israel, or Diaspora Jews. Pao also argues that the expression is not a stock phrase in Greco-Roman expression, as it appears only five times in the LXX, twice in Luke, and nowhere else in ancient Greek literature not influenced by Isaiah or Acts (although why this biblical limitation should be imposed on the use of the expression in Greek sources is not clear). Moore (1997: 393) notes six LXX texts—Isa. 45:22; 49:6; 48:20; 62:10–11; Jer. 16:19; 38:8 [31:8 Eng.]—but regards 49:6 as key. In these LXX passages the emphasis is on the extension into all the earth (van Unnik 1966). In Ps. Sol. 1.4, the phrase is parallel to πᾶσαν τὴν γῆν (*pasan tēn gēn*, all the earth), indicating that the two expressions are synonymous or nearly so. Pao excludes Spain as not adequately attested in Greek sources. Schnabel (2004: 375) adds that Spain has no role to play in Acts, so he prefers to see a reference to the edges of the empire. Thus the expression is likely intended to refer primarily to the Gentiles, allowing an allusion within it to Rome as its center or to the world. Moore (1997: 397–98) says it nicely: Rome "points to the end of the earth" and an "expansion of the gospel into the Gentile world without implying a final withdrawal of the gospel from the Jews." An intended reference in the phrase to the Gentiles in the world is quite likely.

The phrase "end of the earth," then, is geographic and ethnic in scope, inclusive of all people and locales. As Schnabel (2002: 369 =

5. Schnabel 2004: 372–76, studying the case for and against each option, opts for the farthest regions of the earth, bounded by Gaul-Britannia-Spain (west), the Arctic-Scythia (north), Ethiopia (south), and lands beyond India-China (east). He cites Strabo, Philostratus, and Philo for this meaning, but these are all Hellenist or Hellenistic Jewish writers.

2004: 375) says, "Die Mission der Jünger ist Weltmission" (The mission of the disciples is world mission). The kingdom message will move out gradually and encompass all. The church's call is to be missionary in direction and eschatological in focus. The world is the end goal, pointing to complete deliverance that drives the present mission and gives it focus (Stott 1990: 44).

This does not exhaust the discussion, since at a literary level the involvement of Gentiles is not clear at this point in Acts. A reader of Acts must be open to the possibility of, and be sensitive to, the fact that what Jesus or Luke meant and how an expression originally might have been understood are not necessarily the same thing. The disciples probably originally thought of Jews everywhere. To Luke, it probably anticipates the offer of the gospel to all people. Such a double meaning is possible in literature and also in historical understanding that is developing. In fact, it will take the apostles and others time to realize that Jesus does not intend for the message to go just to Jews dispersed throughout the world but also to Gentiles (as correctly noted by Williams 1990: 24). An indication of this double significance is how God must lead the church into Gentile mission in Acts 10–11. God's intention was the world, but perhaps originally the disciples thought it would be Israel's restoration that would bring the nations to Jerusalem, as Israel's Scripture suggested.

S. Wilson (1973: 91–92) rejects the idea that the passage could be understood ambiguously as referring to Diaspora Jews. His reading fails to distinguish adequately between what Jesus or Luke meant by the commission as an introduction to the apostles' task and how the disciples may have originally heard it. The commission did have a universal thrust but was originally heard in a limited, Jewish scope by the disciples (correctly, Rengstorf 1962: 186–87). God will clarify this realization, as Acts 8–11 shows, and it may well be that at a later point the significance of Isa. 49:6 became more evident. Larkin (1995: 41) rightly calls the verse a "command-promise" (so also Haenchen 1987: 144). Thus part of the concern of Acts is to show how the church came to be so inclusive of Gentiles. There was a commission from Jesus, but it took some time for its extent to be appreciated. Nonetheless, this commission describes the church's key assignment of what to do until the Lord returns. The priority for the church until Jesus returns, a mission of which the community must never lose sight, is to witness to Jesus to the end of the earth. The church exists, in major part, to extend the apostolic witness to Jesus everywhere. In fact, the church does not *have* a mission; it is to be missional and *is* a mission (A. Robinson and Wall 2006: 43–45).

These early verses raise a series of major themes that carry over into application (Fernando 1998: 64–70). They include an expression of the importance and centrality of the equipping Spirit for ministry, a warning not to be unbalanced or be excessively inquisitive about the exact timing of the end, and a call not to be parochial or ethnically exclusive about the gospel but to be committed to carrying out Jesus's commission and witnessing in word and deed. S. Wilson (1973: 94–95) sees the point of the commission as rooting the Gentile mission in Jesus's command, showing Jerusalem as the central base, revealing mission as the essence of the church, and establishing that this mission is part of a gradually developing plan. Acts shows, however, that the plan did not emerge as one gradually developed by the church but as one gradually revealed and extended by God.

After Jesus completes this commission (καὶ ταῦτα εἰπών, *kai tauta eipōn*, **1:9** after saying these things; εἰπών is an aorist participle) and as they are still looking (βλεπόντων αὐτῶν, *blepontōn autōn*; note the shift to the present participle), Jesus is "lifted up" and a cloud takes him out of their sight. This verse uses the verb ἐπαίρω (*epairō*, lift up) in the passive voice (ἐπήρθη, *epērthē*; "taken up" in NIV, NLT) to indicate Jesus's ascension to heaven.[6] This is the term's only use with this force in the NT. Jesus is "taken up" by God as he is taken up (ὑπέλαβεν, *hypelaben*) into the clouds "from their eyes" (i.e., from their sight, ἀπὸ τῶν ὀφθαλμῶν, *apo tōn ophthalmōn*).

The compound verb ἐπαίρω, with its idea of "taking up in support" placed alongside the mention of the cloud, suggests that the cloud enveloped him from underneath and took him away (Dan. 7:13). The description has biblical and Jewish precedent. Other biblically rooted raptures described in Judaism include Enoch (Gen. 5:24) and Elijah (2 Kings 2:11) in Philo, *QG* 1 §86. Josephus, *Ant.* 4.8.48 §326, speaks of Moses, who ascended according to Jewish tradition (Barrett 1994: 82). The rapture of Enoch appears in 1 En. 39.3; 71.1 and 2 En. 3.1–3 (Johnson 1992: 27; Haenchen 1987: 149n6). A rapture of Ezra appears in 2 Esd. (4 Ezra) 14:49. Baruch is raptured in 2 Bar. 76.2 (Pesch 1986a: 76). The cloud is not merely a vehicle for their ascension but probably is also a sign of God's heavenly glory (Marshall 1980: 61; Fernando 1998: 72; Exod. 16:10; Ps. 104:3; Luke 9:34–35; Rev. 11:12) or the divine presence (Jervell 1998: 117; 1 Thess. 4:17; 1 En. 39.3). The last thing Jesus does on earth before ascending to the Father's side is to give this commission, which shows its importance. Witherington (1998: 112) observes that, like the passing of the mantle from Elijah to Elisha, Acts 1 points to the passing on of Jesus's power and authority to his witnesses. It is not so much that Jesus passes his power on to them, however, but that he will share it with them, as they are obedient to the call of mission. This enablement will be provided by the Spirit, as verse 8 suggests with its reference to "power" (Luke 24:47–49).

6. On this term, see BAGD 282 §2a; BDAG 357 §1; and 1 Clem. 45.8, which speaks of the names of the persecuted righteous being lifted up.

This verse describes Jesus's exaltation-ascension, which brings him to God's side ("the right hand of God," Acts 2:33). Luke is the only writer to record this event, but he also is the only writer to cover this period.[7] Witherington (1998: 112–13), in discussing the entire scene, defends its historicity and notes its discussion in Justin Martyr, *1 Apol.* 50, who reviews the story line of the end of Luke and Acts. Justin's treatment shows that this event was a part of the church's tradition by the mid–second century and among its summary of events tied to Jesus.[8] Most NT books speak of Jesus's resurrection or simply speak of him being exalted to the side of God (Eph. 1:19–22; 1 Tim. 3:16; Heb. 1:3; 4:14; 6:19–20; 9:24; 1 Pet. 3:21–22; Wikenhauser 1961: 29). An ascension may be implied, however, in John 20:17 (Polhill 1992: 86). Wikenhauser (1961: 29–32) argues that these texts presuppose an ascension event as do John 20:17 and Matt. 28:18–19, even though they do not mention it.

Wikenhauser also defends the antiquity of belief in bodily resurrection. This is not the mere ascent of a soul. A bodily ascension fits the Jewish background, especially after a physical resurrection. The event is portrayed as one that was seen by the apostles, with three different verbs for seeing appearing in verses 9–11 to emphasize the point (Hauck and Schulz, *TDNT* 6:576). The eyewitness motif in key events is present here. Acts will stress that the point of the resurrection was not merely to vindicate Jesus's claims and show him to be alive but also to bring him to the side of God to indicate his current and future authority. Such executive power involves the distribution of salvation's benefits now (Acts 2:32–36) and the exercise of judgment in the future (3:18–22; 10:40–42). Bruce (1990: 103) is correct to point out that Jesus does not come to the Father's side out of the blue at the end of the forty days but rather that resurrection-exaltation-ascension are seen as part of "one continuous movement" and together point to exaltation. In other words, what takes place here illustrates what had already taken place as a result of the resurrection.

1:10 The disciples are transfixed at what is taking place, "gazing" heavenward. The term ἀτενίζοντες (*atenizontes*, gazing) is another present participle showing contemporaneous action.[9] Luke likes this verb. Twelve of the fourteen NT occurrences are in Luke-Acts, with ten of them in this book alone (Acts 3:4, 12; 6:15; 7:55; 10:4; 11:6; 13:9; 14:9; 23:1). It refers to a fixed gaze and means giving something significant attention. As they are looking, something else takes place.

7. Barrett 1994: 81 speaks of Luke here writing up traditional material that is neither old nor widespread, but Schille 1984: 75–76 argues it is an older tradition.

8. On the form of a "transport" to heaven, which is what is present here, versus a mere heavenly journey account, see Schneider 1980: 208–11. He discusses parallel forms in Greco-Roman and Jewish contexts.

9. This construction is a periphrastic imperfect, which Luke loves to use. It appears in Luke-Acts fifty-two out of the eighty-six NT uses; Bruce 1990: 104.

More amazing actions unfold, for two men appear, standing among them "in white robes" (ἐν ἐσθήσεσι λευκαῖς, *en esthēsesi leukais*). The pluperfect verb for "stand" (παρειστήκεισαν, *pareistēkeisan*) works like a simple imperfect or past tense (Wallace 1996: 586). The use of "behold" (ἰδού, *idou*) tells us the appearance was sudden. This scene recalls the description of angelic figures in Luke 24:4, where the apparel was "dazzling" (ἀστραπτούσῃ, *astraptousē*).[10] The white robes are probably indicative not so much of color as of the transcendent glory of the agents (Kittel, *TDNT* 1:84n67; Polhill 1992: 87n37; 2 Macc. 3:26; T. Levi 8.2; Mark 9:3; 16:5; John 20:12; Acts 10:30). The two men who appear probably evoke the two-witness motif (Deut. 19:15; Larkin 1995: 43) that their testimony is true. By what they say in verse 11, they will give the heavenly commentary and explanation of what is taking place. The apostles are multiple witnesses to this event.

With a mild rebuke, the angels explain the importance of what is taking place. The opening address using the noun ἀνήρ (*anēr*, man, here in the plural ἄνδρες, *andres*) is common in Acts and in Greek. The address is often qualified by the Galilean home of the inhabitants, as here (see also Acts 2:14, 22; 3:12; 5:35; 17:22; 19:35; 21:28). In some of the cases in Acts where this generic term is used, it may be that not just men are addressed but the crowd as a whole. But here the apostles are the focus, and so they are addressed as men of Galilee (literally, "Men, Galileans"). A variation of this address is to follow ἄνδρες with the plural "brothers" (ἀδελφοί, *adelphoi*) or some other qualifier (Acts 1:16; 2:14, 22, 29, 37; 7:2; 13:38; 15:13; 22:1; 23:1; 28:17). The Gospels make clear that these eleven are Galilean.

1:11

The mild rebuke is expressed in the question "Why do you stand looking into heaven?" The interrogative τί (*ti*) has the force of an adverb, asking "Why?" (Wallace 2000: 154). The idea is that they should not be surprised that the risen Jesus is lifted up into God's presence. His departure means that they now have work to do. Jesus's command means that they are not to gaze into the heavens idly, awaiting his return, but engage in the task Jesus has given them to do in the meantime.

But there is more. In a statement that contains a promise, the two tell the group emphatically with an element of repetition that Jesus shall return "thus, in this manner" (οὕτως ἐλεύσεται ὃν τρόπον, *houtōs eleusetai hon tropon*, he will come thus, in the manner that . . .). In the

10. For discussion of Luke 24:4, see Bock 1996: 1890. This passage uses a different verb for standing as well. Acts 1 uses παρίστημι (*paristēmi*), which Luke utilizes in nineteen of its forty-one NT occurrences, with thirteen of them in Acts. Luke 24:4 has ἐφίστημι (*ephistēmi*), which Luke uses eighteen times out of twenty-one NT occurrences, with eleven in Acts. The idea that these figures are Moses and Elijah is unlikely (since no names are given), and the description of them as "dazzling" suggests angelic messengers (*pace* A. Robinson and Wall 2006: 36–37).

way he was taken up from them, he shall also return. The promise that Jesus will come is a classic example of a "predictive" future (Wallace 2000: 244). The verb used for "taken up" (ἀναλαμβάνω, *analambanō*) is the same as was used in Acts 1:2;[11] only here it is in the form of a substantival participle standing in apposition to Jesus (this Jesus, "the one who was taken up"). Taken up in a cloud, he will return in a cloud to render judgment (Dan. 7:9–14; Mark 13:26; 14:62; Luke 21:27; Rev. 1:7). Thus the angels' remark does not answer the disciples' question of when restoration occurs, but it assures them that a return will complete the messianic task. Peter himself affirms this in Acts 3:18–22, putting together in that speech what the angel says here into a conclusion about the certainty of Jesus's return to deliver and judge. This scene, then, is one that reassures that God will complete the plan—this same Jesus, taken up to the side of God, will return to work God's will (so correctly Gaventa 2003: 67; *pace* any idea that Luke writes because of a delay of the parousia). Bruce (1954: 41) speaks of a "pledge of the coming consummation of glory" and notes that Jesus's departure does not lead to inactivity in the interim but an effectual presence (Matt. 28:20; Eph. 4:10). There is no need to deny that there will be a return (S. Wilson 1973: 106). The unit deemphasizes an excessive eschatological hope that engages in date setting, but it assures that the end will come.

In sum, there is one central application for the unit: the church is called to engage in mission to the world, knowing that Jesus's return is assured. In major part, it is for mission that the Spirit is sent.

Additional Notes

1:6. Interrogative εἰ (*ei*) introduces a direct question (BDR §440): "Will you restore at this time?"

1:7. Views on how ethnic Israel is handled in Acts are quite diverse. J. Sanders (1987) argues the nation is tossed aside. Jervell (1972) sees Luke still very concerned for Israel. Tiede (1980; 1986) also discusses the possibility of a restored Israel. Nowhere in Acts does preaching to Jews stop, a point that argues against Sanders. Acts 3:20–21 suggests that the church preached that what the OT had said would come to pass; a major part of this message concerns the full restoration of Israel in the end. Luke's view that the word of God comes to pass, as was highlighted in Luke 1–2, speaks also for the idea that Israel still has a future in God's plan. The idea that there is a "time of the Gentiles" in Luke 21:24 also suggests that a time for Israel may well come in the future, after a period when Gentiles are the center of attention.

1:9. Codex D has the cloud envelop Jesus and then take him up, an order that is the reverse of most MSS. Luke's description in the original text is less concerned than D with such detailed sequence, first summarizing that Jesus was taken up and then telling how.

11. See discussion there; also 2 Kings 2:11 LXX; 1QH 11.20 (sometimes numbered 3.20).

1:9–11. Stott (1990: 45–49) discusses in some detail the issue of the timing of this ascension as well as its historicity. He argues that what Luke collapsed at the end of Luke 24, he gives in more detail here, both accounts presenting a single event of ascension (*pace* Haenchen 1987: 145, who argues that the accounts contradict each other by having the events forty days apart). If Stott is correct, and this is quite possible, then this event would still have taken place at the end of Jesus's appearances. Stott also covers the historicity of this event, stressing its report by eyewitnesses, the simplicity with which it is told, and its function in giving an adequate explanation for why appearances stopped. He argues that the public visibility of this departure versus other appearances was designed to indicate that something different had taken place. It points to the fact that a new phase is approaching when the Spirit comes in a fresh way.

1:11. The use of ἐμβλέποντες (*emblepontes*) is slightly more likely than the nonprefixed form of the verb (βλέποντες). The textual evidence is nicely split. Reading the nonprefixed verb "to see" are 𝔓⁷⁴, ℵ*, B, E, 33, and 81. Reading the prefixed form are 𝔓⁵⁶, ℵ², A, C, D, Ψ, and Byz. Since the nonprefixed form appears in verse 9, the prefixed verb is the more difficult reading.

II. The Early Church in Jerusalem (1:12–6:7)

The first major section of Acts covers activity in Jerusalem. The first scene is about replacing Judas. The leadership is reconfigured as the Twelve. These leaders represent the base of the faithful remnant nation (1:12–26). They also serve as key witnesses, since the criterion is direct experience with Jesus's ministry and resurrection. Then comes a major event of the book, the promised distribution of the Spirit at Pentecost. With the Spirit's coming, Peter gives a key speech explaining that the new era is a part of Jesus's continued work that shows him to be the promised Christ and Lord (2:1–41). A short scene follows with the group members engaged in worship, instruction, and fellowship as they work to be a community (2:42–47).

Next Luke juxtaposes word and deed, as he often did in his Gospel, with Peter's healing of a lame man the occasion for yet another speech that overviews Jesus's current and future ministry. This activity fits the promise of Torah but meets with official resistance as Peter and John are arrested. The prayer of the community to be steadfast in testimony is juxtaposed with the release of, and a warning to, those arrested (3:1–4:31). The cycle of activity and community life continues with the observation that all things are held in common and with the example of Barnabas. But all is not well. Ananias and Sapphira claim to lay at the apostles' feet all the proceeds from the sale of a property but engage in deception by keeping some of the proceeds for themselves. Peter confronts them one at a time for lying to the Spirit, and they are judged (4:32–5:11). Another summary about the signs and wonders the apostles perform follows. The attention they are gaining shows that the ministry they are engaged in is making an impact (5:12–16).

One more cycle of persecution follows as the apostles continue to minister contrary to the admonition of the Jewish leadership. An arrest leads to a miraculous release to allow them to continue to preach, something the guards report to the leadership, who arrest them yet again. In the examination before the leadership, Peter claims to obey God, not them, something the narrative itself indicates as well. God has exalted Jesus, and they are witnesses of these things, as is the Spirit whom they obey. In a meeting of the leadership, Gamaliel counsels that the movement will die if it is not of God, but if it is of God, they cannot oppose it successfully. The remarks set up a key theme of the book, as the growth and expansion of the new community gives the narrative's answer to these options (5:17–42).

Once again Luke switches back to community life and shows how the group resolves an issue of racial favoritism regarding the care of Hebrew and Hellenist widows. The Hellenists who make the complaint are told to appoint some of their own people to help solve the problem (6:1–6). The unit ends with a summary noting the growth of the community (6:7). In this unit Luke juxtaposes mission with community activity and formation. The Jesus community is a place for growth and witness.

A. Community Life: Replacing Judas by Depending on God and Reconstituting the Twelve (1:12–26)

In this scene we see the church responding to Jesus's command to wait for the Spirit in Jerusalem. The disciples are not idle as they wait. They pray and are unified. They act to replace Judas among the Twelve. Judas is judged, having chosen to separate himself from the group. Acts 1:12–14 names some of the key figures present. Acts 1:15–17 reveals that the group is one hundred twenty in size and has Peter address the fact that Scripture predicted Judas's defection. The explanation is interrupted in verses 18–19, where Luke explains to his readers what happened to Judas. Acts 1:20–22 completes Peter's speech calling for the replacement of Judas. Acts 1:23–26 presents the selection of Matthias instead of Barsabbas as the Lord indicates his choice through the casting of lots. The community is preparing itself for the coming of the Spirit with prayer. Through scriptural reflection, they also consider what they should do. The unit begins a pattern for this section of Acts: we gain a glimpse of community life and then observe the community engaging the larger culture in witness. The juxtaposition is intentional. The community is not only to be inwardly focused on its worship, obedience, growth, and nurture; it is also to move out into the world in testimony.

Zwiep (2004: 178–79) notes four key biblical-theological elements underscoring the divine control of salvation history in the passage: (1) the advance of the gospel was not halted by Judas's disobedience; (2) Jesus was not mistaken when he picked him; (3) the leaders who remained continued faithfully to represent the new movement; and (4) a circle of the Twelve existed at Pentecost to serve as Jesus's chosen leaders of eschatological Israel in continuity with God's promise. It can be added that the rest of Acts makes clear that this community became a new, fresh institution of God, distinct from Israel, but it did so because of the opposition of Jewish leaders throughout the Diaspora. The new community represented the realization of divine promises appearing with God's chosen one and the coming of the Spirit, whom the chosen one would distribute. This point is made abundantly clear in Acts 2. None of this happened as a surprise to the plan or as a revision of it. God's program for now was being realized in what became the church.

This new community's existence, however, cannot cancel out promises and commitments a faithful God has made to Israel, a point made clear in Acts 3, where Peter affirms the realization of Israel's promises in line with the prophets' teaching to Israel. Zwiep (2004: 179–82) also notes that this text is the first in Acts to elevate Peter as the key figure of the earliest Jerusalem community. The choice of Matthias provides a figure for the twelfth throne discussed by Jesus in Luke 22:30b. With that slot now refilled, the program moves ahead, as Jesus's eschatological promise in this regard still stands.

Exegesis and Exposition

[12]Then they returned to Jerusalem from the Mount of Olives, which is near Jerusalem, a Sabbath day's trip away; [13]and when they entered, they went up to the upper room, where they were staying, Peter and John and James and Andrew, Philip and Thomas, Bartholomew and Matthew, James the son of Alphaeus and Simon the Zealot and Judas the son of James. [14]These all with one purpose devoted themselves to prayer, together with the women, Mary the mother of Jesus, and his brothers.

[15]And in those days Peter rose up in the midst of the brothers (and the crowd of persons was in all about one hundred and twenty) and said, [16]"Brethren, ⌐it was necessary⌐ that the Scripture be fulfilled, which the Holy Spirit spoke beforehand through David's mouth, concerning Judas, the one who became a guide to those who arrested Jesus. [17]For he was numbered among us, and was allotted a share in this ministry. [18](Now this one bought a field with the reward of his unrighteousness; and he fell headlong, burst open in the middle, and all his bowels poured out. [19]And this became known to all those who lived in Jerusalem, so that they called the field in their language ⌐Akeldama⌐, that is, Field of Blood.) [20]For it stands written in the book of Psalms, 'Let his habitation become desolate, and let no one dwell in it'; and 'His office let another take.' [21]Therefore, it is necessary that one of the men who came with us all the time in which the Lord Jesus came in and went out among us, [22]beginning from the baptism of John until the day he was taken from us—one of these men should become with us a witness to his resurrection." [23]And they sent forward two, Joseph, the one called Barsabbas, who was surnamed Justus, and Matthias. [24]And praying they said, "You, Lord, the one who knows the hearts of all, point out whom you have selected from these two [25]to take the ⌐place⌐ in this ministry and apostleship from which Judas turned aside, to go to his own place." [26]And they cast ⌐lots⌐ for them, and the lot fell to Matthias; and he was counted with the eleven apostles.

The disciples are obedient to Jesus's instruction, returning to Jerusalem from the Mount of Olives to await the promised arrival of the Holy Spirit. The term for the locale, Ἐλαιῶνος (Elaiōnos), can mean "olive orchard" (Robertson 1934: 154n2) or "olive grove" (HCSB). Rabbinic texts call

1:12

the mount Har ha-Zêtîm or Har ha-Mišḥâ (Le Cornu and Shulam 2003: 29). The text calls Jerusalem a Sabbath's day journey away, probably a distance of anywhere from about 900 to 1,120 meters or a little over 1,000–1,200 yards, about three-quarters of a mile. Jervell (1998: 117) suggests about 880 meters. Barrett (1994: 85) gives a larger figure (1,120 meters) by measuring from Jerusalem to the summit, figuring on the idea that a Sabbath's journey is a traditional 2,000 cubits and a cubit is 56 centimeters, as in Mekilta Exodus 16.29 (59a) and *b. 'Erub.* 51a. The exact distance is disputed. Haenchen (1987: 150n11) speaks of 200 ells equaling 960 yards, a slightly shorter distance, whereas Bruce (1988a: 39n43) notes the 2,000 cubits mentioned in *m. Soṭah* 5.3 and appears to agree with Haenchen, saying the distance is slightly less than 1 kilometer, which is 0.62 miles. Marshall (1980: 62) opts for a longer distance, about 1.2 kilometers. This 2,000-cubit limit was derived by combining Exod. 16:29 ("stay where he is") with Num. 35:5, which measured a city's length as 2,000 cubits (Polhill 1992: 88n43).

In other words, Sabbath travel was limited to a distance equal to the diameter of one's village. This 2,000-cubit limit would mean that Qumran's stricter Sabbath's journey limit of 1,000 cubits outside a city (CD 10.21) is not how Luke reckoned this, although pasturing a beast there did allow for the 2,000-cubit limit outside the city (CD 11.5–60). Josephus puts the distance between the mount and Jerusalem alternately as five (*Ant.* 20.8.6 §169) or six stadia (*J.W.* 5.2.3 §70), where a stadion equals 192 meters or about 219 yards. So the various descriptions reflect the same basic distance, but it is not entirely clear which precise distance is intended. Haenchen (1987: 150) notes that Zech. 14:4 has the Messiah descend to the Mount of Olives. Thus the locale carries eschatological overtones and is an appropriate place to have discussed Jesus's return.

All of this reckoning suggests Jewish roots for this scene, but it does not mean the ascension took place on the Sabbath; by Luke's reckoning, it likely did not. This is because forty days of appearances from resurrection to ascension, with the resurrection taking place one day after the Sabbath, means a Sabbath is not in view. Reckoning the distance as a Sabbath's walk is merely a way to give a measurement, not the timing of the event.

1:13　The Eleven gather in an upper room where they are staying in Jerusalem. Acts 1:14 notes others who are with them as they wait and pray. The mood of piety is a positive note in the narrative, as is the discussion of their unity. The upper room (τὸ ὑπερῷον, *to hyperōon*) was built on "the flat roof of an oriental house" (BAGD 842; BDAG 1034; "upstairs room" in NET; Robertson 1934: 629; Dan. 6:10–11).[1] The term appears only in Acts (9:37, 39; 20:8). Often such rooms were rented out (*m. Ned.* 7.4; *m. Šabb.*

---

1. On the role of such rooms in Judaism as places of assembly, study, and prayer, see Str-B 2:594.

1.4; Le Cornu and Shulam 2003: 30–31). Pilgrims were not charged to use these rooms during feasts, if later sources are correct (*t. Maʿaś. Š.* 1.12; *t. Neg.* 6.2). It is not clear if the upper room is the same locale as the Last Supper, given that Luke 22:11–12 uses a different term for the latter's locale, as does Mark 14:15 (ἀνάγαιον, *anagaion*, in Luke 22:12 and Mark; κατάλυμα, *katalyma*, in Luke 22:11). Nor is it at all clear that this was the house of John Mark's mother, Mary (Acts 12:12, as Polhill 1992: 89 correctly notes). The size of the room required suggests a locale in a wealthy area (Le Cornu and Shulam 2003: 31–32).

The Twelve are reduced to eleven because of Judas's defection and suicide, which is described in verses 17–19. Jesus chose and assembled them as an identifiable group in Luke 6:14–16 (also Matt. 10:2–4; Mark 3:16–19). Their formation was a symbolic way of saying Jesus was leading a reorganization of Israel. This was an indication that the new era had come and that the old Israel was not responding to God in a proper manner and needed restructuring under the direction and ministry of Jesus, whom God had sent (Luke 22:29–30; Matt. 19:28; McKnight 2001: 203–31).

Luke's list of the Eleven matches the order of his list in Luke 6:14–16 except at four points: (1) John and James are moved ahead of Andrew in the first grouping of four. (2) Thomas is moved to the second slot in the second group of four rather than standing last in this group. (3) Matthew is last in that group, not third. (4) Simon the Zealot is referred to as a Zealot in a slightly different way in the last group of three.[2] Acts groups the list in two sets of four, and then the final three. John may be moved forward because he is prominent in Acts (3:1, 3, 4, 11; 4:13, 19; 8:14; Barrett 1994: 87). Might these differences indicate that this material possesses a traditional base distinct from the source for Mark and Luke? The difference in the list plus the fact that the term for the upper room differs from Luke 22:11–12 may well suggest this. Simon Peter leads the list as always, and John and James of Zebedee are placed side by side in the first group. The last name associates Judas with a James. Is James the father or the brother? The grammar leaves this less than clear, but normally the father is meant (BDF §162.4). Jude 1 shows that a brother could be intended, but this is less than likely given the history of the list. This Judas may be the Thaddeus of Matt. 10:3 and Mark 3:18 and the "Judas, not Iscariot" of John 14:22. Of these figures, Acts names only Peter, James, and John again (Le Cornu and Shulam 2003: 32).

The group has both piety and unity. The verse reads as a summary, a 1:14 form common in Acts (6:7; 9:31; 16:5; 19:20). The group gathered in the room also consists of more than the Eleven (see v. 15); present are the

---

2. For a comparative chart of all lists of the Twelve and a discussion of each of them, see Bock 1994a: 543; on the Zealots, see Josephus *Ant.* 18.1.6 §§23–25 (they have a "passion for liberty") and *J.W.* 2.22.1 §651.

"women," who likely include witnesses of the crucifixion and resurrection, since they are otherwise undescribed (Luke 23:49; 24:1, 9, 22). Luke loves to mention the presence of women: Mary, John Mark's mother, as well as Rhoda (Acts 2:12–13), Lydia (16:14–15), and Tabitha (9:36–43). Barrett (1994: 89) suggests that the women of Acts 1 are wives, but less clear for him is that they also are witnesses who have followed Jesus for a long period (Luke 8:1–3).[3] Luke often notes the participation of women among the disciples in his Gospel (for the unique passages in Luke's Gospel, see Bock 1994a: 710). It is not clear why one would have to choose between the options. The gathering could well include some of the women who had faithfully followed Jesus and among whom were the witnesses as well as wives. In Acts women will share in the Spirit (Acts 2:17; some will be prophetesses, 21:9). This larger group has been together before, and extensive overlap between the groups is likely (Luke 24:9, 33; Pesch 1986a: 81). Jesus's mother, Mary, and his brothers are also present. James will be noted as the leader in Jerusalem after the apostles move out in mission (Acts 12:17; 15:13; 21:18). This is the last mention of Mary in the NT.[4]

The gathered community is of "one mind" (ὁμοθυμαδόν, homothymadon) as it prays. Ten of the eleven NT occurrences of this term appear in Acts. The word refers to a group acting as one ("with one accord" in KJV, ESV, RSV; "with one mind" in NASB, NET; "met together continually" in NLT; "continually united" in HCSB; "all together" in Robertson 1934: 602). Often it describes Jews or others acting in protest against something (Acts 7:57; 12:20; 18:12; 19:29). In other cases it describes the disciples who are in accord about something (2:46; 4:24; 5:12; 15:25). As the examples concerning disciples show, it is a term that points to the fundamental unity within the church. Here the group is operating in obedience, waiting for the Spirit and praying in preparation as they wait. The nascent church is showing some of its most fundamental characteristics: gathered, seeking the Lord's will with one mind in prayer, and assembled to carry out God's mission (Pesch 1986a: 82).

The point is driven home by saying that they are devoted to or persevering (ἦσαν προσκαρτεροῦντες, ēsan proskarterountes) in prayer together. The construction is another example of periphrasis using the imperfect, so the prayer is pictured as ongoing (BDAG 881 §2b). This term does not appear in Luke but appears six times in Acts out of ten

---

3. See Haenchen 1987: 154n3, who says Codex D's later reading referring clearly to wives (the addition of καὶ τέκνοις forces one to read γυναιξίν in this way) reflects D's hesitancy to see the women's independent activity; note also the discussion in Witherington 1998: 113.

4. For the various church views of the relationship of Jesus to these brothers, see Bruce 1990: 106–7, who notes that views include cousins, brothers through Joseph, and brothers through Mary. The most natural reading is that they were brothers through their shared connection to Mary. On Mary as *theotokos* (mother of God) later in church tradition, see Pelikan 2005: 44–46.

NT occurrences (Acts 1:14; 2:42, 46; 6:4; 8:13; 10:7; Mark 3:9 is the only use in the Gospels). It is often tied to prayer in the NT (Acts 1:14; 2:42, 46; Rom. 12:12; Col. 4:2). The Acts communities often pray, especially about their mission (Acts 2:46–47; 4:24–30; 13:3). Fernando (1998: 74) notes that prayer is mentioned thirty-one times in Acts and in twenty of its twenty-eight chapters. As they patiently wait on God's timing, the disciples are praying and readying themselves for their task as a group. Williams (1990: 30) notes that praying together often builds or maintains unity. Acts 1:15 tells us that about 120 are present, and so the room must be of some size. The whole of 1:13–14 makes a transition to the replacement of Judas so that the Eleven can again become the Twelve. This small group, which began as 120, will grow throughout the book as Luke narrates the expansion of the group in mission. The first such note of an addition of three thousand appears in Acts 2:41.

At some point during those interim days (ἐν ταῖς ἡμέραις ταύταις, *en tais hēmerais tautais*, in those days) Peter, taking the lead role, addresses the group about a problem. The structure of the group is not right. The Twelve are now eleven and need to be constituted correctly. It is debated whether Peter acts without the Spirit in dealing with this problem. Nothing about the narrative, however, portrays this event negatively. The group has been obedient in coming to Jerusalem. They are of one mind and engaged in prayer. Scripture will be invoked, and God's leading will be sought as well, allowing God to make the choice by lot, which is not an unprecedented method of selection (see additional note on 1:26). The lots probably were stones with a name on them, shaken in a bag or vessel until one fell out (1 Sam. 14:41–42; Prov. 16:33; Livy, *Hist. Rom.* 23.3.7; 1QS 5.3; Beardslee 1960: 245–52). The lot may have prevented rivalry or done away with any need to campaign for the post. So everything about the scene is told in a positive light. Paul, although not counted as one of the Twelve by Luke, is seen as a special, directly appointed witness when the Lord directly brings him into the church.

Barrett (1994: 94) is skeptical about this scene, any traditions concerning Peter, and its details about Judas, although he does accept that there was a tradition about Matthias's selection. In favor of the scene's authenticity is the obscurity of the figure chosen (S. Wilson 1973: 108, although he questions some details). But why doubt that this was done at the behest of the Eleven and that some record of its taking place was known? Marshall (1980: 63) calls the choice of Matthias an event about which there should be "no doubt." The authenticity debates over the details about Judas hinge on the differences between this account and Matt. 27:3–10, and Peter's speech is part of a larger debate over such speeches in Acts.

There are numerous elements to this discussion. First is the NT treatment of these two events and their relationship to each other. For example, A. Gordon (1971: 97–100) defends the credibility of Matthew and Acts, saying as a lawyer that the accounts are not inconsistent. Second is the issue of Peter's speech. Wilcox (1972–73: 438–52) presents evidence of both Lukan wording and more traditional expression in the speech. He argues that the use of Scripture here looks to Judas's death and his replacement as a part of a tradition about the Twelve. Third are the speeches in Acts, of which Peter's speech is a part. Witherington (1998: 39–51, 116–20) notes that one-third of Acts is speech material and defends its roots as part of the tradition. Finally, there is the study of Judas in the NT and especially in Acts 1. Zwiep (2004: 5–31) surveys the state of this study and then devotes an entire monograph to this passage. He questions some efforts of revisionism about Judas that try to make him an innocent figure (Zwiep 2004: 176: "The historical Judas was not a devil, but neither was he a saint"). All of this discussion gains renewed significance in light of the recent discovery of the Gospel of Judas, which attempts to rehabilitate Judas's image, although it lacks any historical value in telling us about the historical Judas (Bock 2006: 215–17). Zwiep suggests that the failure to say much about Judas in the NT and the early church is because of the sense of embarrassment his actions caused. Zwiep's primary goal is to examine Judas in the literary light of Acts. He notes that Judas is the first of many figures to experience judgment in Acts, an antagonist God deals with, turning what Judas meant for evil regarding Jesus into good while Judas suffers his own justice. The account seems a credible account of Matthias's election (so Zwiep 2004: 178, who is less confident about knowing the details of Judas's death, but see A. Gordon 1971, noted just above). Gaventa (2003: 72) reminds us that in Luke 22:3 Judas is said to be filled with Satan, making this the initial note of Satan's effort to sidetrack the disciples from within.

We are told that the group's size is around 120. The verse uses ὄνομα (*onoma*) to refer to persons, not to someone's name, which is its more common usage.[5] Scholars debate whether this is the size that permitted a local sanhedrin (a leaders' council, where there is one leader for every ten members, as at Qumran, 1QS 6.3–4; CD 13.1–2). Barrett (1994: 96) rejects the idea. Polhill (1992: 91n52) accepts it, pointing to *m. Sanh.* 1.6 but noting that the inclusion of women in the count makes the analogy less exact. Williams (1990: 31) appears to accept it as well, but with an explanation that the 120 people allow a local sanhedrin of 23 to be formed, which is the topic of the larger section of the Mishnah just noted (so also Schille 1984: 82). The Mishnah reads, "And how many residents must there be in a town so that it may be suitable for a sanhedrin? One hundred and twenty." A dissenting opinion in the Mishnah says that

5. See BDAG 714 §2; Acts 18:15; Rev. 3:4; 11:13; on τέ (*te*) as introducing an explanatory remark, see Robertson 1934: 434; ἐπὶ τὸ αὐτό (*epi to auto*) means "all together," Robertson 1934: 602.

230 are needed. The same text also notes that the great Sanhedrin has 71 members and the small (or local) one has 23. Regardless of the debate over the local sanhedrin background, this is seen as an authentic community of decent size. The number 120 in this verse is approximate (ὡσεί, *hōsei*, about), however, which makes such a possible allusion or a developed symbolism as a made-up number less than clear or likely. Jervell (1998: 123) makes this argument against such symbolism and also notes that the "council" of the group is already present in the Eleven. If Luke were making the number up to attain 12 x 10, or a Sanhedrin, then why does he give an approximation?

Peter addresses the entire group with the frequent expression ἄνδρες ἀδελφοί (*andres adelphoi*; see Acts 1:11 for discussion; the second term in apposition, "brothers," bears the emphasis, Robertson 1934: 399). In this context, where men and women have been named, it is possible that all are addressed, and so the translation "brothers and sisters" would be possible, much as some in the northern United States use "you guys" for men and women in a group. Although it is claimed that there is no linguistic justification for such a broad rendering, Acts 17:34 is an example where ἄνδρες includes a reference to a woman, namely, Damaris. Polhill (1992: 61) renders it "believers," making the same point. Others see only men addressed (Jervell 1998: 123). The translation above has opted for the ambiguous term "brethren." It is clear women are present and Peter is speaking to the group, but since Peter is directing the action, it is unclear who would have been involved or would have been responsible for giving approval to Peter's suggestion. Was it only the men? Was it only the Eleven? Or did it seem like a good idea to all present? The text does not tell us.

1:16

Peter sees in Judas's defection the fulfillment of Scripture.[6] Luke uses the verb πληρόω (*plēroō*) twenty-five times in his two volumes (Luke nine times, Acts sixteen times), often with a note that a divine utterance (Luke 1:20) or a passage (Luke 4:21) is fulfilled (Luke 1:20; 2:40; 3:5; 4:21; 7:1; 9:31; 21:24; 22:16; 24:44; Acts 1:16; 2:2, 28; 3:18; 5:3, 28; 7:23, 30; 9:23; 12:25; 13:25, 27, 52; 14:26; 19:21; 24:27). Only here and in Luke 4:21 is "Scripture" combined with the verb. It can be events in the divine plan that are fulfilled (Luke 9:31 [Jesus's suffering and exodus in Jerusalem]; 21:24 [the times of the Gentiles]; 22:16 [the final coming of the kingdom]; 24:44–47 [what Moses, the Prophets, and the Psalms said about the Christ]). When the verb is tied neither to an event nor to Scripture, it often refers to a person being full, to an attribute, to an emotion, or to a place being full (Luke 2:40; Acts 2:2, 28; 5:3), such as Jerusalem being full of the apostles' teaching (Acts 5:28). Time can also

---

6. Note that ἔδει, *edei*, is in the imperfect tense: "it was necessary"; on this verb in Luke-Acts, see Cosgrove 1984: 168–90; Luke 9:22; 17:25; 24:7, 26, 44; Acts 3:21; 9:16; 14:22. God's plan is being played out.

be filled up (7:30 [forty years]; 9:23). The invoking of Scripture for this horrible event of Judas's defection and for Jesus's death, which came from it, shows that Jesus's death and the betrayal of one of the original Twelve were not outside God's plan or awareness (Jervell 1998: 124).

Peter sees the Scripture he is about to cite as having come from the Holy Spirit through the mouth of David (διὰ στόματος Δαυίδ, *dia stomatos Dauid*, where the preposition has the idea of means; Moule 1959: 56–57). Scripture is ultimately a revelation from God (Acts 2:16; 3:18, 21, 25; 4:25; 15:7; 28:25; Williams 1990: 31). God speaks in it. Scripture can guide the disciples because it is the Spirit of God at work. The psalms Peter will cite in verse 20 are no exception.

The topics are Judas, the one who guided the arrest of Jesus, as Luke 22:39–54 detailed, and the need to replace him to restore the apostles to twelve. The psalms Peter cites (69:25; 109:8) are about the unrighteous or the enemies of God, who ultimately are judged. Judas belongs in this category, so Peter applies the text to him in what is called hermeneutically a typological-prophetic manner (on the hermeneutics of early-church *testimonia* such as this, see Bruce 1988a: 44–45). The texts are cited in Acts 1:20. The first text is Ps. 69:25: since the defection has occurred, there is a reference to the enemy's house being left desolate. The second text, Ps. 109:8, refers to what needs to be done to replace Judas. Someone must take his place of responsibility (Polhill 1992: 91).[7] Conzelmann (1987: 11) takes this initial reference to Scripture as generic to the Judas story as a whole and not tied to any particular text (more on this in the discussion of Acts 1:20). He rejects a connection to the second passage because it is not yet fulfilled. However, given what is to take place, Peter is using the text as justification for acting, and so a prophetic use is at work.

Scripture leads Peter to ensure that the core apostolic circle consists of twelve members. The move to replace Judas is part of the judgment Judas experiences. Williams (1990: 109) makes the point that it is Judas's apostasy, not his death, that requires his replacement because, after the death of James son of Zebedee in Acts 12:2, no replacement is made or noted. Once a faithful member becomes the replacement, the effort to have twelve is not to be continued perpetually. Wikenhauser (1961: 33) recalls Jesus's promise to the Twelve that they would inherit twelve thrones on his return. This promise might well have motivated Peter here (Matt. 19:28; Luke 22:28–30). So the slot must be filled, and when Matthias is elected, he will fill the twelfth slot of this special class of apostles once and for all.

---

7. Barrett 1994: 96–97 thinks Ps. 41:9 [41:10 MT; 40:10 LXX] is in view, where the psalmist laments that a trusted friend has betrayed him. If so, the move is hermeneutically the same as the psalms cited, but Acts lacks a reference to this text. At best, it is a conceptual allusion.

Peter gives two reasons (ὅτι, *hoti*, for) the Judas matter is important to settle: (1) he was numbered among the Twelve (Luke 22:3), and (2) he had a share in the ministry (διακονία, *diakonia*; Luke-Acts has nine of thirty-four NT uses, eight of which are in Acts; Luke 10:40; Acts 1:17, 25; 6:1, 4; 11:29; 12:25; 20:24; 21:19). The term is a general one for ministry pictured as service. Only the uses in Acts 1 refer to the specific apostolic ministry of the Twelve. Judas's portion of the work of the Twelve must be redistributed. The term κλῆρον (*klēron*, share) is also used to describe the lots cast in verse 26, as the lot indicates who obtains the twelfth spot and shares a role among the Twelve (BDAG 548 §§1–2, 581).[8] The idea is to share in something. In 2 Pet. 1:1, one obtains a lot from God or Christ (Hanse, *TDNT* 4:1–2). Wilcox (1972–73: 447) notes parallel wording in Targum D on Gen. 44:18 and calls the source for this verse a traditional one. Marshall (1980: 64) also notes the possibility of tradition being present here.

1:17

In an aside consisting of two verses, Luke explains what happened to Judas, to underscore the horrific judgment he experienced. Dormeyer and Galindo (2003: 39) call this description an "antibiography" and the first negative example of a follower in Acts. The detail differs from Matt. 27:3–10, leading to much discussion about what is said here and its relationship to what Matthew says. Matthew has Judas repent and try to return the money. When the return is refused, Judas tosses the money in the temple, and the priests use the proceeds to purchase the Field of Blood (see Acts 1:19). He then hangs himself (Matt. 27:5). Matthew sees in this a fulfillment of Zech. 11:13. There is no mention of Judas's hanging or of his repentance in Acts.

1:18

Barrett (1994: 93) claims that no harmonization of these accounts is possible. But things are not so clear. It is evident that Matthew tells his account not only to discuss Judas but also to focus on the Jewish leadership and critique them for their involvement in what the evangelist sees as an unrighteous act. This fits Matthew's polemic against the leadership. Acts is interested only in Judas's eventual fate, not in any intervening activity, including any regret Judas may have felt. Judas's money led to the purchase of the field. Thus it may well be that, in a "causative" sense, he purchased the field. Another example of this sense would be a judge who sentences a criminal to death but does not personally execute him.[9] The fact that Judas died a horrific death there soon after his defection indicates that God was aware of and judged

8. Luke's Gospel uses the verb λαγχάνω (*lanchanō*, obtain a share) in 1:9 and has two of its four NT uses; the others are in 2 Pet. 1:1 and John 19:24. The "lot" of the Levites reflects a similar usage (Num. 18:21–26; cf. Johnson 1992: 35).

9. On the term for "field," χωρίον, *chōrion*, see BDAG 1095 §1, possibly a term for a small estate; Wallace 1996: 424–25; Barrett 1994: 98. Bruce 1990: 109 notes a view that it may have been bought in Judas's name.

his unrighteousness (like the divine judgment that befalls Ananias and Sapphira in Acts 5). Such judgments of bodily destruction are common, especially associated with dropsy, conditions of severe bodily swelling, or severe bodily damage (2 Sam. 20:10; Prov. 20:30; Acts 12:20–23; Bruce 1990: 109). Different purposes and concerns lead to the differing details, which are reconcilable.

The verse notes that Judas bought the field with the money he obtained, money that is described as μισθοῦ τῆς ἀδικίας (*misthou tēs adikias*, the reward of his wickedness). The term for "wickedness" (τῆς ἀδικίας) is in the genitive case, which is often translated "of," so that the relationship to the word it qualifies is left ambiguous. There are a variety of translations for the phrase that all make the same basic point: "the price of his wickedness" (NASB), "the reward he got for his wickedness" (NIV), "the money he received for his treachery" (NLT), and "his unrighteous wages" (HCSB).[10] In this case the genitive qualifies the description of the reward as having its roots in Judas's wicked act of betrayal. Luke notes the lack of morality in the act of betrayal, underscoring again that Jesus died as an innocent, with his death rooted in betrayal by a "colleague" in ministry. Second Peter 2:13 and 15 have similar expressions (Williams 1990: 32). Matthew 27:19 places the amount given to Judas at thirty shekels. Witherington (1198: 121) points to indications of Judas's greed in the tradition (John 12:4–6).

The death is described very briefly. He "fell headlong" or "became prone" (πρηνὴς γενόμενος, *prēnēs genomenos*), meaning that he fell forward in such a way that he burst open (ἐλάκησεν, *elakēsen*) and his insides poured out.[11] This is the only use of λακάω (*lakaō*) in the NT. This kind of gruesome detail matches the description of the death of Herod Agrippa I in Acts 12:23, making a similar point about God's judgment. The description is also like the judgment of Amasa in 2 Sam. 20:10 and conceptually like the judgment of Antiochus in 2 Macc. 9:1–18 (cf. also Catullus in Josephus, *J.W.* 7.11.4 §453; Wis. 4:18–19). It is sometimes said that Judas hanged himself on this site, but nothing in Acts directly indicates this (correctly Barrett 1994: 99, but his hesitation on other options is not to be embraced). That detail comes from Matthew. Conzelmann (1987: 11) says the account suggests a fall from a roof or cliff, but again whether there was an earlier hanging is not precluded by what Acts does say.[12] Luke is interested in the event simply as a judgment. The

10. On "unrighteous," see Luke 16:8–9; 18:6; Wallace 1996: 125n143. Jervell 1998: 125n106 calls this a Semitism.

11. BDAG 863 notes that the other suggested option, that he swelled up (for πρηνής), is not attested for this term; also Barrett 1994: 98; for λακάω, see BDAG 581.

12. For a possible combination, see Marshall 1980: 65. Apollinaris of Laodicea appears to be aware of a less dependable, independent version of Judas's death through Papias; see Papias, *Fragments* 18.1, where Judas is described as bloated and is said to have been cut down after hanging himself and then to have burst open. Papias's version does seem

verb for the "pouring out" of Judas's insides is the same as will be used to describe the "pouring out" of the Spirit in Acts 2:17 (ἐκχέω, *ekcheō*; BDAG 312). The image is vivid and graphic, intended not only to describe but also to leave an emotive impression on readers to prevent their following Judas's negative example of unfaithfulness and betrayal.

The event became well known to all in Jerusalem, so well known that the field was named, in "their own dialect" (τῇ ἰδίᾳ διαλέκτῳ αὐτῶν, *tē idia dialektō autōn*) of Aramaic, Akeldama (Ἀκελδαμάχ, *Hakeldamach*), or Field of Blood. There is no doubt that the reference to a dialect refers to Aramaic (Le Cornu and Shulam 2003: 42; Fitzmyer 1998: 224–25). Matthew 27:9 shares this detail. One wonders why Luke would make such a remark if he created the event. He would have been exposing himself to criticism for presenting a well-known event, complete with detail, that had not occurred. This side note about the name of the field, which is shared with Matthew, suggests that the core of the story is authentic, rooted in tradition. This verse indicates that we have a parenthesis, for Peter and his audience would have known Aramaic, and so there would be no need to translate the meaning of the name (Haenchen 1987: 160–61). **1:19**

The text now returns to Peter's address and the citation of Psalms. It begins with the typical early-church introductory formula γέγραπται (*gegraptai*, it stands written; Luke 2:23; 3:4; 4:4, 8, 10; 7:27; 10:26; 19:46; 24:46; Acts 1:20; 7:42; 13:33; 15:15; 23:5).[13] The book of Psalms is named directly four times in the NT, all in Luke-Acts (Luke 20:42; 24:44; Acts 1:20; 13:33). **1:20**

The first-cited passage is Ps. 69:25 (69:26 MT; 68:26 LXX). The psalm discusses the enemies of God. The psalmist cries to God to be delivered from them and calls for God's judgment so that their camp is left desolate and no one is able to live in their tents. Peter applies the psalm typically-prophetically to indicate that Judas has experienced such a judgment. The type of death Judas experienced left the field desolate for him and others. Matthew 27:7 notes that the field became a cemetery. The wording differs from the LXX:

Acts 1:20a	Ps. 68:26 LXX
Γενηθήτω ἡ ἔπαυλις αὐτοῦ ἔρημος καὶ μὴ ἔστω ὁ κατοικῶν ἐν αὐτῇ	Γενηθήτω ἡ ἔπαυλις αὐτῶν ἠρημωμένη καὶ ἐν τοῖς σκηνώμασιν αὐτῶν μὴ ἔστω ὁ κατοικῶν
Genēthētō hē epaulis autou erēmos kai mē estō ho katoikōn en autē	*Genēthētō hē epaulis autōn erēmōmenē kai en tois skēnōmasin autōn mē estō ho katoikōn*

to be exaggerated, since Papias says that Judas was so bloated that he was unable to pass where a wagon could, and his eyelids were so swollen that no light could enter.

13. Luke has fourteen of the sixty-seven NT occurrences; Matthew has nine; Mark has seven; Romans has sixteen; and 1 Corinthians has nine.

Acts 1:20a	Ps. 68:26 LXX
Let his habitation become desolate, and let no one dwell in it	Let their habitation become desolate, and in their tents let no one dwell

There are two important differences between the texts. The first is that Acts has a simplified rendering of the passage ("their tents" has become simply "in it," referring to the habitation or homestead). The second is that the rendering has been turned into a singular (αὐτοῦ, *autou*) from a plural (αὐτῶν, *autōn*) to focus the application on Judas. The differences from the LXX may point to a traditional source for Luke's version, since the LXX is a good rendering of the MT. The point of Peter's citation is that judgment has fallen on this enemy of the righteous Jesus.

The term ἡ ἔπαυλις (*hē epaulis*) refers to a dwelling place, suggesting that the field may well have been intended as a home or had a dwelling on it already (Johnson 1992: 36, who notes the frequent use of Ps. 69 in the NT: Mark 15:23, 36; John 2:17; 15:25; Rom. 11:9–10; 15:3). It refers to "property that serves as a dwelling place, whether personally owned or by contract" (BAGD 283; BDAG 360).[14] This is the only use of the term in the NT.

The second passage is from Ps. 109:8 (108:8 LXX). The link between the two passages Peter cites is the use of the third-person pronoun αὐτοῦ. Such linking of passages through a shared word is common in Judaism. This first-century technique is called *gezerah shewa*, which translates as "an equivalent regulation." Once again the psalm in the MT is a lament of the psalmist asking for God's judgment. The request is that the enemy's days may be few and "another may seize his position [or goods]." Peter also uses this text typologically-prophetically to declare Judas judged. Judas's position is free to go to another. Scripture justifies the new election. Again the wording differs slightly from the LXX:

Acts 1:20b	Ps. 108:8 LXX
τὴν ἐπισκοπὴν αὐτοῦ λαβέτω ἕτερος	τὴν ἐπισκοπὴν αὐτοῦ λάβοι ἕτερος
tēn episkopēn autou labetō heteros	*tēn episkopēn autou laboi heteros*
His office let another take	His office may another take

The shift here is from an optative in the LXX ("may another take") to an imperative in Acts ("let another take"). The point is similar but slightly more emphatic in Acts.

14. Bruce 1990: 111 notes papyri use meaning "homestead" (so NASB); other renderings include "place" (NIV), "home" (NLT), "habitation" (KJV, RSV), "dwelling place" (NKJV), "house" (NET), "camp" (ESV).

The main point here is that the office (τὴν ἐπισκοπήν, *tēn episkopēn*) is open to be filled. This term refers to a "position of responsibility," in this case the responsibility of Judas to be a key, event-grounded witness to Jesus, a role his betrayal forfeited (BDAG 379 §2). Luke-Acts has two of the four NT occurrences of the term: Luke 1:20; 19:44, where it refers to a visit; 1 Tim. 3:1; and 1 Pet. 2:12). Scripture and a mood of prayer have prompted this decision, which Luke sees as a legitimate act by the group as they await the Spirit's coming.

Barrett's claim (1994: 100) here that "it cannot be said that any attention is given to the context, still less to the original meaning and reference, of the passage cited" is overstated. Agreed, Peter is not exegeting in a modern sense, by merely making a reference to the original event and context. But the passage is in the Psalter so that God's people will reflect upon the way God acts and cares for the righteous who cry out to God. Peter takes the principle expressed in the psalm as a summary of how God acts and applies it to an event where God has judged. In this sense, Peter is certainly within the psalm's meaning and spirit. So the use of the text is not as far-fetched as Barrett's remark might suggest. Speaking of the use of Ps. 69, Marshall (1980: 65 and also n3) says, "It would be natural to find in this Psalm a prophecy or type of the betrayer of Jesus." He also notes that both passages could be used this way from their wording in the MT (so also Pesch 1986a: 89; *pace* Haenchen 1987: 161, who says the text is rooted in a Hellenistic Christian reading). Bruce (1990: 110) speaks of Jesus as a type of David, as a hermeneutical backdrop for how Peter reads the psalm.

So Peter speaks of the current necessity (δεῖ, *dei*, it is necessary [present tense]) of replacing Judas. This appeal to necessity stands in contrast to the betrayal noted in verse 16, which uses ἔδει (*edei*, it was necessary). The replacement will restore the foundational group to twelve, as verse 26 indicates. This candidate must be a man qualified as a "witness to the resurrection," one who accompanied them during the entire time the Lord Jesus was with them, from the baptism of John until the day he was "taken up" (ἀνελήμφθη, *anelēmphthē*; see Acts 1:2 for this term and 1:8 for μάρτυς, *martys*, witness). A figure of speech called a zeugma is present. It refers to a list that covers the A to Z of something to express the entirety of it. The replacement will have a complete experience of Jesus's ministry and teaching, from the A (baptism of John) to the Z (ascension). The baptism is probably the one John performed to prepare the nation, not his baptism of Jesus, as John's baptism set the stage for Jesus. A time frame starting with John's work is the scope of the message that the apostles will preach (Acts 10:36–41; 13:24–31; Bruce 1990: 111). Such a starting point parallels the role of Luke 3:1–14.

The resurrection is the key event to give testimony to, but this witness must be from someone who also has knowledge of what Jesus did on

1:21–22

earth as well as the results of resurrection and subsequently the ascension. The continuity of exposure to Jesus is central to the special role of the witness and underscores the credibility of the eyewitness tradition the apostles produced (Larkin 1995: 46; Bauckham 2006; *pace* Jervell 1998: 127, who says the witness is about the resurrection alone). The speeches in Acts 2 and 10 show how resurrection and Jesus's ministry are linked in the preaching. Acts 2:22–24 and 10:36–39 refer to Jesus's ministry as a backdrop for the proclamation of resurrection.

The unique qualifications of this office show its singular and foundational role for the church. No one of succeeding generations would have these qualifications (Fernando 1998: 76). Luke 22:28–30 appears to be at the root of this belief. Conzelmann (1987: 11–12) sees traditional roots in both the use of Scripture and the story of the need to replace Judas. Eusebius alludes to Judas's death but refers directly to Acts in *Eccl. Hist.* 3.39.10 and even more briefly treats it in 5.16.13. Conzelmann also notes the Papias tradition discussed in Acts 1:18 above. Weiser (1981: 65) sees Luke working with two traditions: the death of Judas and the selection of Matthias. He also believes Ps. 69 was already tied to the Judas tradition whereas Luke added the connection to Ps. 109. But although this is the only place Ps. 109 is quoted in the NT (allusions occur elsewhere), it is also the only place where the replacement of Judas is taken up, so the unique use may well relate directly to the unique event being treated.

1:23 Two men are put forward: Joseph Barsabbas, who has the surname Justus, and Matthias. Barsabbas was associated with a tradition in the later church that had him survive swallowing snake poison (Papias, *Fragments* 3.9–10; Eusebius, *Eccl. Hist.* 3.39.9). Barsabbas means "son of the Sabbath" or "son of Saba" (Barrett 1994: 102). According to Eusebius, Matthias, whose name means "gift of God," was among the seventy before replacing Judas (*Eccl. Hist.* 1.12.3; 2.1.1). Nicephorus Callistus (*Eccl. Hist.* 2.40) says he suffered martyrdom in Ethiopia. Neither man is mentioned again in the NT.

1:24 The choice is left to prayer and God. The prayer is simply for the choice to be made by the Lord, the one who knows the "hearts of all men" (καρδιογνῶστα πάντων, *kardiognōsta pantōn*). God as "the knower of hearts" appears only here and in Acts 15:8 and not at all in the LXX, but it is conceptually in 1 Sam. 16:7.[15] God is to reveal his choice (ἐξελέξω, *exelexō*). This verb for "select" appears twenty-two times in the NT with eleven occurrences in Luke-Acts: Luke 6:13; 9:35; 10:42; 14:7; Acts 1:2,

15. This description of God became popular in the early church: Herm. *Mand.* 4.3.4; Apostolic Constitutions 2.3.24.6; 3.1.7.8; 4.2.6.8; Pseudo-Clement, *Homilies* 10.13; Clement of Alexandria, *Stromata* 5.14, 16; Jervell 1998: 128. Conceptually in the OT: Pss. 44:21; 94:9; Jer. 11:20; 17:10; 20:12.

24; 6:5; 13:17; 15:7, 22, 25. Here is a good case where the aorist participle and the aorist verb are contemporaneous, as the praying and speaking occur together (BDF §339.1). The casting of lots will make the Lord's choice clear.

Who is the Lord referred to here? Is the Father meant or the Lord Jesus? Barrett (1994: 103) and Marshall (1980: 66) believe the latter, pointing to verse 2, where Jesus is the selector of the apostles, as well as to Luke 6:13; John 6:70; 13:18; 15:16, 19. Jesus is also addressed as Lord in Acts 1:21. The answer is less than clear. Usually, however, the Father performs the action, and Jesus mediates in Acts. In addition, the Father knows hearts in Acts 15, so the Father is probably the actor here (Conzelmann 1987: 12; parabolically, Luke 16:15; Rom. 8:27; 1 Thess. 2:4; Weiser 1981: 71).

Peter states the purpose of the election: to select someone to take (λαβεῖν, **1:25** labein) Judas's place in this ministry (on διακονία, diakonia, see Acts 1:17) and apostleship (defined in vv. 21–22), a role from which Judas deviated (παρέβη, parebē) to go to his own place. The infinitive λαβεῖν indicates purpose (Moulton and Turner 1963: 135; BDF §390.3). The combination of ministry and apostleship is really a hendiadys that can mean "apostolic ministry," that is, service consisting of apostleship.[16]

Judas's transgression and fate are treated next. The term παραβαίνω (parabainō) appears two other times in the NT (Matt. 15:2–3 [2x]; BDAG 758 §1). It means to go aside from a way or turn aside. It can mean to transgress. The ministry of apostleship was a commission to testify to Jesus and his resurrection (Köster, TDNT 8:205) for those who had had a direct experience of the Lord through his teaching and vindication. Luke defines apostleship in terms of mission and an exercise of judgment at the end (Witherington 1998: 126). Judas's act led to the forfeit of this office. He appeared to be a follower of Jesus but was not a genuine follower. The idea that Judas went "to his own place" (εἰς τὸν τόπον τὸν ἴδιον, eis ton topon ton idion) suggests a choice to be separate from the Eleven and implies his judgment to hell. This is an early-church euphemism for where one ends up after death.[17] To describe Judas as having gone "to his own place" means that he ended up in a place different from the Eleven, a euphemism for eternal judgment among the lost.

So they cast lots "for them" (αὐτοῖς, autois, a dative of advantage) to **1:26** see the Lord's decision. This is one of two notes about casting lots in the NT ("gave forth their lots" in KJV). The other is about soldiers cast-

16. See BDF §442.16; HCSB; Barrett 1994: 103. It means a form of ministry equaling, in this case, apostleship; so Wallace 2000: 128.

17. There are numerous references to "the place" in the early centuries of the church: Ign. Magn. 5.1 (of either fate); Pol. Phil. 9.2 (positively of glory); 1 Clem. 5.4 (positively of glory); Bruce 1988a: 47n82; Str-B 4:1097–98; BDAG 1011 §1g (τόπος); with a genitive, Luke 16:28; Köster, TDNT 8:205.

ing lots for Jesus's grave clothes, a detail recounted in all four Gospels (Matt. 27:35; Mark 15:24; Luke 23:34b; John 19:24, in allusion to Ps. 22:18). Nevertheless, the term here is positive, surrounded as it is by piety, prayer, unity, and Scripture. In the OT one can examine texts such as Lev. 16:8 and Josh. 18:6 and 19:51, where the allotment to the nation's tribes was done by casting lots. One can also see the use of lots in Josh. 23:4; 1 Sam. 14:42; 1 Chron. 6:65; 24–26; Neh. 10:34; 11:1; Isa. 34:17; and Jon. 1:7. Several texts use the image negatively as a sign of judgment in which spoils are divided (Joel 3:3; Obad. 11; Nah. 3:10).[18] These texts in Joshua and 1 Chronicles show that such an act is tied to elements of the foundation of Israel.

How lots were viewed is seen in Prov. 16:33, where the decision belongs to God, and in 18:18, where lots serve as an arbiter in disputes. Fernando (1998: 79) observes that lots cease to be used after the Spirit comes, as the next two selections in Acts 6 and 13 take place with only prayer. The supposition in their use was that God has allotted the place that the lot indicates. Names may have been put on one stone each and placed in a cloth bag or vessel, and then the first stone drawn out named the one selected (Conzelmann 1987: 12). If stones were not used, other possibilities include wood, animal bones, or arrows (Le Cornu and Shulam 2003: 49; *m. Yoma* 4.1). With the selection, Matthias is "enrolled" (συγκατεψηφίσθη, *synkatepsēphisthē*) with the Eleven. The term for "enroll" is an NT hapax that refers to being added, usually by a vote (συγκαταψηφίζομαι, *synkatapsēphizomai*; BDAG 951). So now the Eleven are restored to Twelve.

In sum, Acts 1:12–26 covers the obedience of the church as its members wait in Jerusalem for the Spirit. There Peter moves to replace Judas and bring the number of apostles to twelve. The community is unified, praying and seeing what to do through Scripture. Here is a picture of active community life, one of several such snapshots in 1:12–6:7. Peter is leading the congregation, and the choice is left to prayer and the Lord. Everything about the community's actions suggests that this is a community walking with God. The community understands Judas's death to be a judgment from God and part of the divine plan. Peter leads by pointing the community to Scripture, and the community shares in the deliberations, appealing to God to select one who has the heart for the ministry. With the Twelve restored, the table is set for the coming of the Spirit. Readers of Acts are to understand the unit not only as an explanation of how Judas was replaced but also as a precedent for how to seek God as a community in decisions, looking to God to show the way.

18. For the use of lots in Judaism, see Tob. 3:6; *m. Tamid* 1.2; 3.1; *m. Yoma* 2.2; 3.9; 4.1; 1QS 5.3 (legal decisions by lot); 6.16 (lot determines the truthfulness of an outside speaker to the council); 1QSa 1.19–20 (a "simpleton" shall not be allowed to enter the "lot" for an office); Eckey 2000: 66. See also the additional note on 1:26.

Additional Notes

1:16. Codex D has the present tense δεῖ (*dei*, it is necessary) instead of the imperfect ἔδει (*edei*) to suggest that Peter is looking to scriptural support for the present action of replacing Judas, not the defection. The reading of D, however, is not well attested externally.

1:19. The spelling Ἀχελδαμάχ is the most difficult reading among the five options (with 𝔓⁷⁴, ℵ, A, and 81; Barrett 1994: 99). It may be original. But κ is a better rendering of the second letter of the Aramaic, and so the text adopts that reading. The term is transliterated from Aramaic.

1:25. The text reads τόπον (*topon*, place or position), which appears in 𝔓⁷⁴, A, B, C*, D, and Ψ. The alternate reading (κλῆρον, *klēron*, lot) is probably influenced by the wording of Acts 1:17. It is read by ℵ, C³, E, 33, and Byz. The more difficult reading is chosen for the text.

1:26. That Jewish groups in the first century would use lots for making difficult choices is indicated by the Zealots' use of them at Masada in determining the executioners for the murder-suicide pact they formed to avoid capture by the Romans (see Josephus, *J.W.* 7.9.1 §§395–98). In Israel today, a marker at Masada notes the discovery of such lots and includes a picture of them. There were names on the stones that made up the lots. Whether the event happened just as Josephus portrays it is debated by scholars, but his mention of the use of lots would suggest that it was a customary practice.

B. Pentecost (2:1–41)

This event is a fulcrum account in Luke-Acts. Much of Luke's Gospel has been leading up to the Messiah's pouring out of the Spirit (Luke 3:15–17; 24:47–49; Acts 1:4–5). Peter's explanation is the first missionary speech in Acts and one of the most significant because of its detailed explanatory use of the OT and its possession of the core elements of gospel preaching. The unit is important, as the juxtaposition of the ascension and Pentecost in terms of proximate literary space shows (Spencer 2004: 33). Spencer also notes a few parallels between the events: (1) unusual manifestations (to and from heaven); (2) prophecy and fulfillment; (3) Galilean disciples experiencing important events in Judea; and (4) twelve apostles as major figures. Two key events of the earliest church are placed one after the other.

The unit has three parts: (1) the pouring out of the Spirit (vv. 1–13); (2) Peter's speech proclaiming that Jesus is Lord and Christ (vv. 14–36); and (3) the reaction to the speech by three thousand people (vv. 37–41). A large series of link words tie the argument together (see comments at vv. 34–35). Although there is Lukan summary terminology throughout, the speech reflects the church's basic early Christology, as all that is necessary to come to Peter's conclusion is the belief in Jesus's resurrection-ascension, an event that is attested to from the community's earliest days. As we proceed through the speech, we shall see that scholars are wrong to claim that the Christology is late because it requires the LXX to make the scriptural point. In many cases, Peter's point was possible without the LXX, and for some of these texts, such readings already existed in Judaism (Bock 1987: 155–259, 271–72). The issue of where Jesus was as a result of his resurrection and what this meant for who he was must have come up instantly once the disciples found out that he was raised. So Peter's explanation is not only important to Acts, it is also a crucial witness to the early church's basic christological thinking. Peter's speech is the first fulfillment of Acts 1:8, a witness that has echoed around the world ever since Luke recorded it.

1. The Event: The Coming of the Spirit (2:1–13)

This event is one of the key moments in Acts. God pours out the Spirit promised in Luke 24:49 and Acts 1:4–5. This coming of the Spirit enables God's people to carry out the mission assigned to them in Luke 24:47 and Acts 1:8.

Acts 2:1 gives the setting. Acts 2:2–4 describes the event. Acts 2:5–13 gives the perplexed crowd's reaction and a list of all the nations represented who are now hearing about God's mighty work in their own native languages, not in Greek or Aramaic. These tongues are a visible manifestation of the Spirit's arrival and include the disciples speaking in foreign languages. Following the event is an explanation, continuing the pattern of event and word or act and explanation that appeared with Jesus's ministry in Luke's Gospel.

The issue of sources is complex. Wedderburn (1994: 27–54) argues that there were multiple sources and that Luke did not use or recognize all of the symbolism in them, even misunderstanding those sources at points. This final conclusion is unlikely, as it is too speculative in terms of knowing exactly what the sources may have contained and how Luke altered them; his evidence for Luke using such sources is more likely.

A good example of this nonuse of source symbolism is the Sinai-law background to Pentecost, which, as Wedderburn correctly notes, Luke does not employ in Acts 2. Van der Horst (1985) lists numerous conceptual parallels for Acts 2 from the Greco-Roman world. Examples include wind and fire as a figure for divine presence, the existence of divinely inspired speech, lists of nations, signs and wonders, the idea of an eclipse as doom, enemies as a footstool, and collective property. We shall trace the Jewish background for many of these themes as we proceed through the texts. The list and our tracing of such themes shows us, however, that many ideas are neither particularly Jewish nor particularly Greek but stock metaphors of the culture, metaphors whose particular force depends on the context.

Exegesis and Exposition

¹When the day of Pentecost arrived, they were all together in one place. ²And suddenly a sound came out of heaven like the rush of a mighty wind and filled the entire house where they were sitting. ³And there appeared to them tongues like fire being distributed to them and resting on each one of them. ⁴And all

were filled with the Holy Spirit and began to speak in other tongues, even as the Spirit gave utterance to them.

⁵Now there were living ⌜in⌝ ⌜Jerusalem⌝ in those days ⌜Jews⌝, pious men from every nation under heaven. ⁶And when this sound came, the multitude gathered together and were perplexed because each one ⌜heard⌝ them speaking in his own language. ⁷And they ⌜ ⌝ were astonished and wondered, saying ⌜ ⌝, "Are ⌜not⌝ all these who are speaking Galileans? ⁸And how is it we each are hearing our own native language? ⁹Parthians and Medes and Elamites and those who live in Mesopotamia, Judea and Cappadocia, Pontus and Asia, ¹⁰Phrygia and Pamphylia, Egypt and the parts of Libya belonging to Cyrene, and visitors from Rome, ¹¹both Jews and proselytes, Cretans and Arabians, we are hearing them speaking in our own tongues the mighty deeds of God." ¹²And all were astonished and perplexed, saying to one another, "What might this be?" ¹³But others mocking were saying, "They are filled with sweet wine."

2:1   The scene shifts to the day of Pentecost (πεντηκοστή, *pentēkostē*) as the 120 disciples are gathered together in one place (ἐν τῷ, *en tō*, plus the infinitive is temporal; Wallace 1996: 595). It may be that the initial temporal remark is parallel to Luke 9:51 and points to fulfillment, reading, "When the promised day of Pentecost had come" (cf. Lohse, *TDNT* 6:50–52, who also argues that Luke used a tradition here). Reference to Pentecost is common in Hellenistic Judaism but less so in rabbinic expression (Noack 1962: 77–78). That all the disciples are intended by the reference to "they" is indicated by the Spirit's distribution on all, as Peter's later citation of Joel makes clear (vv. 17–18).[1] There is no indication this is the same place as the event in Acts 1, although it could be. It is not at all likely to be the temple, as the term οἶκος (*oikos*, house) appears in verse 2. Luke always refers to the temple (twenty-two times) as τὸ ἱερόν (*to hieron*; Haenchen 1987: 168n1). It is a public place, however, as a crowd quickly is drawn to the event. That houses could hold a group of 120 or so (Acts 1:15) has been shown by an unearthed mansion in the Jewish Quarter of Jerusalem, with its meeting hall of 11 by 6.5 meters (Menzies 1991: 208–9n5; Avigad 1984: 95–103).

God acts to fulfill the promise given in Luke 24:49 and Acts 1:4 when Pentecost arrives (for the use of the verb συμπληρόω, *symplēroō*, meaning "arrive," see Luke 9:51; BDAG 959 §2; Jer. 25:12; Gen. 25:24; Lev. 8:33, using forms of the verb πληρόω, *plēroō*, in the LXX). A wordplay alluding to the idea of being fulfilled cannot, however, be excluded (Polhill 1992: 96; Jervell 1998: 132).[2] Conzelmann (1987: 13) incorrectly rejects the

---

1. Brawley (2005: 25–26) clearly argues for this conclusion, noting that the result is 120 Christian preachers, including women, if one takes Joel as an explanation of the event.

2. The term can point to the completion or arrival of a set time: Luke 9:51 and Acts 9:23. Fulfillment of promise concerning an event or OT Scripture is frequent in Luke-Acts: Luke 1:20; 4:21; 7:1; 9:31, 51; 21:22, 24; 22:16; 24:44; Acts 1:16; 3:18; 13:27.

event's timing, since a day as important as this would be remembered ("The essential historicity of the incident is firmly assured" [Dunn 1975: 135–56]; Marshall 1980: 67; Witherington 1998: 129–30n5). This Jewish festival day falls fifty days after the first Sabbath after Passover (Exod. 23:15–17; 34:22; Lev. 23:15–21; Num. 28:26; Deut. 16:9–12).[3] It was also known as the "Feast of Weeks" or "Day of Firstfruits."

Schreiber (2002: 58–77) emphasizes this firstfruits dimension of the holiday but, because of a lack of mention of this day elsewhere, sees Luke creating the symbolism. In the NT, the Spirit's connection with the resurrection in a text such as Eph. 4:7 does not, however, exclude the day of Pentecost with its idea of firstfruits being tied to the effect of the resurrection and placed in proximity to it. Marshall (1977: 363) notes that the ascension was celebrated on the fiftieth day after Easter in the East Syrian and Palestinian churches until the fourth century, showing the close association between the ascension and Pentecost. Pentecost was one of the three Jewish pilgrimage feasts to Jerusalem during the year, which explains why people from so many nationalities are present in verses 9–11. (The significance of this and its relationship to the Babel incident of Gen. 11:1–9 will be treated later.) This is one of three uses of the term "Pentecost" in the NT (see also Acts 20:16; 1 Cor. 16:8).

It appears that in Judaism it was believed that on this day significant things had taken place in the past (Noack 1962: 81–84).[4] It is possible the Jewish book of Jubilees sees Pentecost and the giving of the law as having fallen on the same day (Weiser, *EDNT* 3:70; BDAG 796; O. Betz, *TDNT* 9:296; Tob. 2:1; 2 Macc. 12:32). Noack (1962: 85–87) distinguishes between the establishment of the covenant of peace tied to Noah, the giving of the law, which is connected but subordinate to it, and the renewal of the law, which is what the fifteenth day of the third month commemorated. He also defends the likelihood that the day is accurately remembered. Marshall (1977: 347–69) suggests that the association may be hinted at in 2 Chron. 15:10–12, and defends the essential historicity of the scene (esp. 1997: 360–65). He also notes that detailed development of this association in Judaism, however, seems to be later (also Lincoln 1984–85:

3. On the differing calendars used by the Sadducees and Pharisees for figuring the date of this feast, see Bruce 1988a: 49n3. Lohse, *TDNT* 6:44–53, suggests that the Pharisaical calendar is in view here, and so it is fifty days after the first day of Passover. Jewish texts discussing this holiday include Josephus, *Ant.* 3.6–7 §§252–57; 13.9.4 §252; Philo, *Decalogue* 9–10 §§32–36; 11 §§44–49; *Spec. Laws* 2.31 §§188–89; Jub. 6.1, 17; 14.1, 20; 22.1–30; Targum Pseudo-Jonathan on Exod. 20:2; Jervell 1998: 132n141. For the Jewish tie between law and Spirit, see T. Jud. 24; Sib. Or. 3.573–74.

4. See Jub. 6.17–18, where the covenant that brings peace was said to have been kept as far back as the time of Noah. Jubilees 1.1 and 15.1 date the event to the middle of the third month, the time of this feast. Qumran may have a similar reckoning (1QS 1.7–2.19, although it is debated if this refers to an annual event; Noack 1962: 89–90). For details of how this holiday worked in Judaism, see Le Cornu and Shulam 2003: 54–58; Exod. 34:22; Lev. 23:15–16; Deut. 16:10, 16; 2 Chron. 8:13; *m. Bik.* 3.2–8.

204–9; in later Judaism, *b. Šabb.* 88b). Barrett (1994: 111) rejects the connection of the giving of the law and Pentecost as being made too late to help with understanding the first-century situation.

Key to the debate on Jewish views is how the book of Jubilees is assessed. Jubilees argues that current feasts are connected to the patriarchs, and this favors an early date for the view, given the second-century BC date for Jubilees. Such connections would suggest that these general associations are older than the time of Jesus. What is harder to ascertain is whether the connection is a broad one to an older covenant tied to Noah, or to the specific event of giving the law, although Jub. 1.1 appears to favor the latter. This belief in the timing, if it is tied to the law, was rooted in Exod. 19:1 and the third new moon, which connects to the festival of the third month. If so, the day Jesus distributed the Holy Spirit was also the day some Jews believed the law came to Israel, although Luke makes nothing explicit of this detail about the giving of the law (Marshall 1977: 365–66; *pace* Le Cornu and Shulam 2003: 59–60).[5] Luke's lack of appeal to this idea means that the debate over the background for Acts is not of such great significance for interpreting Acts, even though it may well have been at work in the cultural backdrop to the event. What Luke sees here is the realization of the divine program tied to the Messiah's promised work, as Peter's speech makes clear. For Luke, the event does not stand as a contrast to Jewish feasts.[6]

2:2 Now God acts to complete the promise of the coming of the Spirit. Luke pictures the event in a way that has an element of "visibility" to it, as verses 2–4 make clear. Its supernatural origin is also obvious, for what he describes came out of heaven. The roots of this promise are in the OT (Num. 11:29; Isa. 32:15; 44:3; Ezek. 36:27; O'Brien 1999: 210).

The first indication that something is taking place is the sound (ἦχος, *ēchos*) like a rushing wind (πνοῆς βιαίας, *pnoēs biaias*) suddenly (ἄφνω, *aphnō*; only here and Acts 16:26; 28:6) filling the room where the disciples are seated. The term for "sound" (ἦχος) appears only here in Acts but also occurs in Luke 4:37; 21:25; and Heb. 12:19. The Acts passage only makes a comparison, and so the sound that is like the wind is the focus (ὥσπερ, *hōsper*, is comparative; Moulton and Turner 1963: 158). This is the only place in the NT where this phrase about wind appears; it does not appear in the LXX. Proverbs 1:23, however, uses πνοῆς for the idea of God's thoughts and teaching, an idea close to this scene. The term also appears to represent the acts of God in a theophany in 2 Sam.

---

5. The texts Le Cornu and Shulam (2003: 59–60) cite for the association of flames with this day are late, including Mekilta de Rabbi Ishmael, *Baḥodesh* 9; Exod. Rabbah 5.9; and Tanḥuma, *Shĕmôt* 25. These late texts make an allusion to Exod. 20:18 less than clear. Other terms, like "multitude" in Acts 2:6, are too general to point clearly to an allusion.

6. For the additional issue of potential exodus-Sinai parallels tied to miracles or a second-Moses theme in Acts 2, see 2:3 and 2:33 below.

22:16; Job 37:10; Ezek. 13:13; and 2 Esd. (4 Ezra) 13:10 (Marshall 1980: 68; Barrett 1994: 113; also perhaps the "storm" of God's presence that greeted Elijah: 1 Kings 19:11–12; Weiser 1981: 83). Philo, *Decalogue* 11 §46, has both a sound of God's voice and fire at Sinai and so is conceptually parallel (Exod. 19:18–19). The term in Acts seems to indicate God's presence with the Spirit's arrival (possibly also an association with life because Gen. 2:7 LXX uses this term for "breath"; Schneider 1980: 249n51). The association of the Spirit with wind, using the Greek term πνεῦμα (*pneuma*; John 3:6–8), may also be present.

The Spirit's presence brings the manifestation of tongues (γλῶσσαι, *glōssai*; BDAG 201 §2). The passive use of ὤφθησαν (*ōphthēsan*, appeared, from the verb ὁράω, *horaō*, to see) points in this context to a divinely directed appearance (Luke 1:11; 24:34; Acts 7:2, 30; 13:31; 16:9; BDAG 719 §1d). These tongues allow the disciples to speak about God's activity in the foreign languages of their audience (vv. 4–11). Thus these tongues function as an evangelistic enablement, so that each person can hear about God's work in his or her own language. 2:3

This immediate use of other languages is how Acts discusses tongues and is different from what 1 Cor. 14 describes. Paul describes a two-step ecstatic process associated with tongues speaking: step one is the utterance in the tongue, and step two is the separate gift of interpretation to be used for the edification of the church and the conviction of unbelievers. Without interpretation, tongues are not to be used in the assembly. Although much is made of this difference, it seems that the phenomenon of tongues in the church had a broad scope in what it covered—a one-step form involving a foreign language and immediate comprehension and a two-step form needing interpretation (Marshall 1980: 69–70; Harrison 1975: 51–52; Larkin 1995: 49; *pace* Johnson 1992: 42, who relates tongues only to a Greco-Roman ecstatic context).

Haenchen (1987: 168) rightly rejects the idea that in Acts there is depicted ecstatic speech that each person heard in his or her own language. There is no miracle of hearing here (Acts 2:6b, 8, 11b).[7] The Spirit is at work only on the believers.

The distribution of these tongues among the believers is compared to a spreading fire, which divided up into bits of flame for each person. The theme of fire (πῦρ, *pyr*) is sometimes associated with divine activity as well (BDAG 898 §2; Isa. 5:24 [in a context of judgment]; the term is frequently used of a simple fire). Luke-Acts has eleven of seventy-one NT uses (Kremer 1973: 112–14). The most common theological image is

---

7. Stott 1990: 66–67 correctly argues there is no miracle of hearing here, although it is less certain that one can merely equate what we have in Acts with what takes place in Corinthians, as he argues; *pace* Pesch 1986a: 100. What Corinthians and Acts share is the view that only when the gift of tongues is intelligible is it to be used in a public setting, meaning it should be coherent.

in association with judgment.[8] We noted the association of fire in Philo with the events of the giving of the law at Sinai when discussing verse 2 drawing on Exod. 19:18 (see also Exod. 24:17). God's presence comes with fire in the burning bush of Exod. 3:2 (Acts 7:30), the pillar of the fire in Exod. 13:21 (Deut. 4:33; 5:24–26; 18:16), before Elijah (1 Kings 18:38), and in association with Ezekiel's call (Ezek. 1:13–14, 27).[9] God is described as a consuming fire in Deut. 4:24 and 9:3 as an image of judgment. Here the emphasis is in the comparison, as with the arrival of the sound in verse 2. The way the Spirit spread was like fire and settled (literally "sat") on each one. The imagery suggests the power of God's presence, but not necessarily Sinai, unless one appeals to the general cultural backdrop of Pentecost and the law, which Luke does not develop. Judgment is not the point, nor is this a complete fulfillment of Luke 3:16–17, as that image is one of purging and judgment (Bock 1994a: 322–24; also Matt. 3:11–12). The distribution of the Spirit does make a distinction here and so a purging is present, but the judgment is yet to come. Thus the image of fire points to the association of heavenly glory in the presence of the Spirit as well as a theophany. Heaven and divine presence come powerfully to the earth to indwell God's people (Lang, *TDNT* 6:947).

2:4   All those present are filled with the Spirit and speak in tongues as the Spirit gives them utterance. The genitive πνεύματος (*pneumatos*) is a genitive of content ("filled with the Holy Spirit"; Wallace 2000: 52). Williams (1990: 44–45) explains that tongues are connected with praise, as these verses note. The connection between the Spirit and prophesying, which will appear in Acts 2:17–18, is present in Num. 11:25 and in Luke 1:67. The description of being filled with the Spirit began in Luke-Acts with the account of John the Baptist (Luke 1:15) and Elizabeth and Zechariah being able to sing a hymn of praise to God (1:41, 67). Those are the only uses of the combination in Luke's Gospel. In Acts 4:8 Peter's being filled allows him to address the crowd and explain what has just taken place, and the community is filled with the Spirit after prayer in 4:31. In 6:3 those chosen to help the widows are full of the Spirit. Paul is promised filling in 9:17 as he is commissioned and is said to have it

---

8. See Gen. 19:24; Lev. 10:2; Joel 2:30, which looks to the salvation that comes from Mount Zion and Jerusalem in a text Luke will cite in Acts 2:17–21; Isa. 66:15; Mark 9:48; Matt. 3:12; 5:22; 18:9; 2 Thess. 1:8; Rev. 19:20; 20:10.

9. Such imagery appears in Judaism, where tongues of fire describe the heavens associated with God's presence. This imagery is in 1 En. 14.8–25, where within heaven there is described a house made of flames of fire where God is present, and the flames represent the power and glory of God's presence; so also more briefly, 71.5; 1Q29 1.3; 2.3; 11QtgJob 41.11; of judgment, 2 Esd. (4 Ezra) 13:10. Later Judaism (Midrash Tanhuma 26c; *b. Šabb.* 88b) speaks of the law given in seventy tongues, using "voices" for "thunderings" in Exod. 20:18 as all the nations hear about the law; *y. Ḥag.* 2.77b.32; Conzelmann 1987: 13; Str-B 2:603.

in 13:9. In 13:52 the community is full of joy and the Spirit as Paul's message goes out to the Gentiles and meets rejection from the Jews. So the phrase in Acts is related to proclamation of the gospel and equipping for mission (Menzies 1991 underscores this point).

In Acts, the Spirit fills for service (9:17) or to speak God's word (4:8, 31; 13:9–10). There can be fresh filling for such ministry (6:3–5; 7:55). Filling with the Spirit in this verse is similar to baptizing with the Spirit in 1:5 and 11:16, the pouring out of the Spirit in 2:17–18 and 10:45, and receiving the Spirit in 10:47. The work of the Spirit, however, involves more than mission; it includes salvation (2:38–39) and transformed lives (2:42–47; Marshall 1980: 69; O'Brien 1999: 210).[10] The fact that this scene fulfills the promise originally noted by John the Baptist with his call for ethical preparation for the coming of the Lord suggests that an ethical dimension to the Spirit's work exists (Luke 3:7–17). Bruce (1988a: 51) proposes that after the phenomenon arrives, the disciples move out into the streets.

These disciples begin to speak in ἑτέραις γλώσσαις (*heterais glōssais*), which refers to other languages, as verse 8 makes clear. In the OT, the expression appears in Isa. 28:11 LXX in the singular. This one-step understanding differs from the description in 1 Corinthians, where two steps (utterance and interpretation) are required for understanding. In Acts this speaking of tongues in foreign languages is done as the Spirit gives them utterance (so also Jervell 1998: 133–34). The term for "utterance" (ἀποφθέγγεσθαι, *apophthengesthai*) is relatively rare, appearing only three times in the NT, all in Acts (2:4, 14; 26:25), and six times in the LXX (BDAG 125; 1 Chron. 25:1 [positively, of prophecy]; Ps. 58:8 [59:7 Eng.]; Mic. 5:11 [5:12 Eng.]; Zech. 10:2; Ezek. 13:9, 19; five of these six uses are negative, of lies or false prophets). Peter will explain in verses 17–18 that all have received the pouring out of the Spirit as an indication of the arrival of God's promised new era (see also Luke 3:15–17, where the Spirit's coming points to the presence of the Messiah, another point Peter makes in Acts 2:36).

The Jewish focus of this description becomes clear with the remarks   **2:5** in this verse that devout men from every nation are among the Jews living in Jerusalem. "Under heaven" (ὑπὸ/ὑποκάτω τὸν οὐρανόν, *hypo/ hypokatō ton ouranon*) is a biblical phrase (Deut. 2:25; 9:14; 29:20). Some

---

10. Turner 1996: esp. 356 correctly argues for the Spirit's working as the Spirit of prophecy who also helps to continue the new exodus liberation and the purging restoration of Israel, although later I question his appeal to "prophet like Moses" and Sinai typology in Acts 2 in the discussion of 2:33. Old Testament background for this understanding of the Spirit's arrival in Judaism includes Exod. 20:18; Isa. 44:3; Jer. 23:29; 31:31–32; Ezek. 36:26–27; 39:29; and the to-be-cited Joel 2:28–29 (Le Cornu and Shulam 2003: 67). On how the Spirit came to be expressed as divine in the development of church doctrine, see Pelikan 2005: 49–50; for the language about the "economy" of the Spirit, see Pelikan 2005: 51.

scholars are surprised that the reference to Jews shows up in a verse speaking of the nations, but the Diaspora is in view, and so the use is not merely ethnic but also geographical (Kremer 1973: 129). The reference to "pious" (εὐλαβεῖς, *eulabeis*) men uses a term that appears four times in the NT, all in Luke-Acts and only of Jews (Luke 2:25 [Simeon]; Acts 2:5; 8:2 [men who buried Stephen]; 22:12 [Ananias]). "Pious" here need not equal "saved," since these people will later be told that they must repent to be delivered. Luke has a degree of respect for those who have an interest in religion, even though they may not be saved. These devout could include proselytes (Acts 8:2; 10:2; 22:12), but the distinction made in 2:10 between Jews and proselytes makes it more likely that proselytes are not yet introduced (Kremer 1973: 129). These more likely are simply faithful Jews who are in Jerusalem. The verse probably pictures a mixed audience. Some may well be "remnant" Jews, who upon hearing the gospel are pious enough to be responsive to it and immediately come into the full faith of the new era.

These Jerusalem pilgrims are present for Pentecost and have come from every direction of the globe, as verses 9–11 will specify (Bruce 1988a: 53). Marshall (1980: 70) notes, however, that many Diaspora Jews returned to Jerusalem to live; and this is more likely meant here (Hengel 1983: 17–18, 57, 175n53; so also Schneider 1980: 251 and n65; Johnson 1992: 43; Acts 6:9).[11] The remark explains that this event had an impact that reached people whose roots spanned the nations, moving in the direction of Luke's more universal concerns, though still within ethnic limits that will not be crossed until Acts 8–11.

2:6   The sound, probably a reference to the tongues in light of the next few verses (not the wind of v. 2), draws a crowd to an unspecified location (Bruce 1988a: 54). They hear the message "in their own language" (τῇ ἰδίᾳ διαλέκτῳ, *tē idia dialektō*) as the disciples speak to them in tongues. This direct communication bewilders or perplexes them. This is the first of three clear references to tongues involving the audience's foreign languages (also vv. 8, 11). Their bewildered response is explained by verses 6–7. The ὅτι (*hoti*, because) of v. 6 gives the reason for bewilderment as they are in the process of hearing (ἤκουον, *ēkouon* is imperfect) their own language, and verse 7 elaborates that it is supposedly uneducated Galileans who are exhibiting this surprising array of linguistic expertise.

11. Josephus, *Ant.* 15.9.3 §320; 17.4.2 §78, refers to the high-priestly family, which also comes from places as far away as Alexandria; *J.W.* 1.22.7 §437; 1.33.9 §672 shows the ethnic variety present in the city, as do graves and inscriptions. On Diaspora Jews and their ties to Jerusalem, see Le Cornu and Shulam 2003: 64–66. Third Macc. 2:31 suggests that some preferred ties to Alexandria over those in Jerusalem, but the pilgrims of Acts made the opposite choice.

The passive form συνεχύθη (*synechythē*) from the verb συγχέω (*syncheō*) refers to being amazed or surprised (BAGD 775; BDAG 953; "bewildered" in RSV, ESV, NASB, NLT; "in confusion" in NET; "confounded" in KJV). The verb shows up in Gen. 11:7, 9 in the LXX. Barrett (1994: 119) correctly notes one should not press the Babel analogy too much to argue for the reversal of that judgment, as the terms are common and the confusion is not ended by the act alone. The tongues still need explanation. There may be only one message, but there are still many languages. In Judaism the idea did exist that at the end there would be one language (T. Jud. 25.3; Conzelmann 1987: 14n6). Acts 2:12 speaks of the people being perplexed, so the sense here is of amazement pointing to bewilderment. They are not able to explain how or why this unusual circumstance has taken place. All five NT occurrences of συγχέω are in Acts (2:6; 9:22; 19:32; 21:27, 31). The reader knows that the Spirit has supplied this supernatural enablement. God is at work.

The range of the emotional response includes amazement and wonder.   **2:7** Amazement will be noted again in 2:12. The term ἐξίστημι (*existēmi*, be amazed) appears seventeen times in the NT, eleven of them in Luke-Acts, and is often connected to miracles in the Gospels.[12] "Be astonished" is a good synonym. "Wonder" (θαυμάζω, *thaumazō*) appears in Luke-Acts in eighteen of forty-three NT uses (in Acts: 2:7; 4:13; 7:31; 13:14; in Luke, often of their wonder at Jesus: 8:25; 9:43; 11:14). Reinforcing the reference to perplexity in verse 6, the combination stresses how surprised they are at what is taking place and that they are unable to explain it. Both verbs, like hearing in verse 6, are imperfects, so the event is portrayed vividly: these people are hearing, are amazed, and are wondering.

Their questions in verses 7–8 express and reinforce the dilemma. The first question expects a positive reply (οὐχ, *ouch*). The audience inquires about the Galilean origin of those who are speaking, "Are they not all Galileans?" Perhaps the meaning is pejorative—how is it that "uneducated" Galileans are using all of these languages?[13] Acts 4:13 shows that the apostles are seen in this light. References to Galileans appear eleven times in the NT, eight in Luke-Acts (Matt. 26:69, where their accent gives them away, and see v. 73; Mark 14:70; Luke 13:1–2 [3x]; 22:59; 23:6; John 4:45; Acts 1:11; 2:7; 5:37). It may be that they are known simply as Jesus's disciples who came from Galilee (Kremer 1973: 139–41), but

---

12. See Mark 2:12; 3:21* (Jesus's alleged insanity); 5:42; 6:51; Matt. 12:23; Luke 2:47* (Jesus in the temple); 8:56; 24:22; Acts 2:7, 12, 8:9*, 11* (both of Simon Magus's magic, which produces a response like miracles); 8:13; 9:21; 10:45; 12:16; 2 Cor. 5:13* (Paul's alleged insanity); Kremer 1973: 138. (Nonmiraculous contexts are indicated with *.)

13. On first-century views of Galileans, see Vermes 1973: 42–57. In later Judaism, *b. ʿErub.* 53b has the phrase "you stupid Galilean" in the midst of a rabbinic anecdote about the fact that Galileans do not speak in a clear language. The region was also known as a place of revolutionaries.

the point either way is the surprise at their diverse linguistic ability. The question is, Where did they get such ability? Haenchen (1987: 169n3) says Luke puts these words in the mouths of the participants, and finds superfluous the question of how they knew these were Galileans. But there are two possibilities: either the accent of their speech gives them away (Bruce 1988a: 54), or the audience knows them as Jesus's disciples and, as a result, likely Galileans. Marshall (1980: 70) suggests that the remarks, possibly coming from just a few, act as a summary of reactions to the event for Luke.

There is a tension between the experience of the event recorded here and the reader, who is privy to the answer to the crowd's question at the text's literary level. God has miraculously supplied this ability through the Spirit. The question has the listeners affirm the miracle (Jervell 1998: 135). At the level of the event's depiction, Peter's speech will supply the explanation with even more theological detail, of which the reader may or may not be aware.

2:8   The second question points to what is taking place. How is it that we are each hearing our own language? Aramaic and Greek would be expected but not each specific language of the diverse homelands represented by the audience (vv. 9–11; on the array of possible languages, such as Coptic, Arabic, and others, see Le Cornu and Shulam 2003: 67–68). The phrase ἰδίᾳ διαλέκτῳ (*idia dialektō*) appears only three times in the NT, all in Acts (1:19; 2:6, 8). This may be a dative of accompaniment (Moule 1959: 45, also appearing in v. 11). The message comes, surprisingly, in their own dialects, with each nation-group hearing its particular language or idiom. Added in this verse is the phrase ἐν ᾗ ἐγεννήθημεν (*en hē egennēthēmen*, in which we were born) to underscore that the native language is meant. God is using for each group the most familiar linguistic means possible to make sure the message reaches to the audience in a form they can appreciate. Thus the miracle underscores the divine initiative in making possible the mission God has commissioned. In a real sense, God is bringing the message of the gospel home to those who hear it.

2:9–11   The list in these verses is not a "table of nations" (but so argues J. M. Scott 2000), nor is it given to distinguish linguistic groupings within the audience, nor is it an astrological list (Kremer 1973: 153–54; Witherington 1998: 136; Bruce 1988a: 116–17; esp. Metzger 1970: 149–69). Gilbert (2002: 503–5) refutes Scott by noting the lack of specific overlap in the lists and prefers a Roman backdrop, where the list counters Rome's claim of universal rule. Such Roman ideas appear in Virgil's *Aeneid* 1.278–79 and its promise of "Rome's empire without end"; Pliny the Elder's list of Pompey's extensive conquests in *Nat.* 7.98; and the list in *Res gestae divi Augusti*. Tertullian (*Against the Jews* 7) also takes the view that Christ overshadows Roman rule by the extent of nations responding.

This list appears to highlight the key communities where Jews of the Diaspora congregated and suggests the gospel's universal scope (Hengel 2000: 161–80). It also suggests that Rome may not have the claim on humanity that this dominant nation thinks it possesses (Gilbert 2002: 527–29). The list mixes peoples (Parthians, Medes, Elamites, Romans, Cretans, and Arabians) with lands (Mesopotamia, Judea, Cappadocia, Pontus, Asia, Phrygia, Pamphylia, Egypt, and Libya; Pesch 1986a: 105; Spencer 2004: 44 presents a schema according to relative location).[14] The structure of the verses is best laid out visually in six parts, in a 4, 2, 2, 2, 2, 4 pattern:

> Parthians and Medes and Elamites and those who dwell in Mesopotamia,
>
> Judea and Cappadocia,
>
> Pontus and Asia,
>
> Phrygia and Pamphylia,
>
> Egypt and parts of Libya belonging to Cyrene,
>
> and visitors from Rome, both Jews and proselytes, Cretans and Arabians.

The table moves from east to west, except that the Parthians and Romans start the first and last pairs respectively as the key powers of east and west (Josephus, *J.W.* 2.16.4 §379). It also moves from northwest to southwest. The list lacks reference to important areas where Paul will travel, such as Greece and Macedonia (Jervell 1998: 135). This lack of connection points to tradition over a "created" story. In all likelihood Judea refers to "larger Judea" (including Syria), as Hengel (2000: 161–80) argues in defending the term's presence in the text (*pace* Haenchen 1987: 170). Jerome (on Isa. 11:6–11) and Eusebius may be correct in suggesting that Judea be rendered as Συρία (*Syria*). There are five basic groupings: those of the Caspian Sea, Asia Minor (modern Turkey) area, North Africa, Rome and the Mediterranean, and then the rest (Stott 1990: 63–65). This list looks like traditional material, but its exact roots are unclear except for its Jewish concern. That languages are not the focus is clear from the inclusion of Jews and proselytes in the list. Rather, the locales likely indicate the scope of Jewish Diaspora settlement. People from these nations have returned to dwell in Jerusalem as an international gathering place for Jews. Syria plays a key role in Acts because of the church in Antioch. Using Judea to refer to

---

14. The Jewish Diaspora dates back to the time of the Babylonian exile. For details on their regions, see Le Cornu and Shulam 2003: 74–87. Jews were seen to be everywhere by Strabo as cited by Josephus (*Ant.* 14.7.2 §§114–15; also Philo, *Moses* 2.4 §20). Le Cornu and Shulam (2003: 84–85) see a table of nations tradition at work here, pointing to the reach of the gospel (Gen. 10:5, 20, 31).

the entire region may suggest messianic Israel, like its boundaries of old under David and Solomon.

The first line lists the communities located to the east in Mesopotamia and beyond. Parthia is the farthest east (for Jews there, see 1 Macc. 15:15–24, which lists kings and the countries where Jews lived, including Arsaces [v. 22], king of Parthia; the location today is in modern Iran), then Media, an area west of the Caspian and south of the Zagros Mountains. Elam is the ancient plain of Khuzistan and is bordered by the Karkheh River, which joins the Tigris north of the Persian Gulf. Mesopotamia covers the Tigris and Euphrates Valley and is where the Parthian and Roman empires met.

The second part of the list covers larger Judea and Cappadocia to the north. The third line looks even farther north, to Pontus on the edge of modern Asia Minor (Turkey) and beyond to Asia, which here is probably western Asia Minor. The middle portion of Acts (chaps. 13–20) will involve this area. The fourth line moves west from Cappadocia to the central and southern edge of Asia Minor, to Phrygia and Pamphylia. The third and fourth lines cover what is today modern Turkey. The fifth line goes farther west and south across the Great Sea (Mediterranean) to Egypt (Philo, *Flaccus* 8 §55 notes that Alexandria was full of Jews in two of its five wards; also 7 §§45–46). Next comes Libya as far west as Cyrene (for Jews there, 1 Macc. 15:23; 2 Macc. 2:23; Barrett 1994: 123).

The last line comes back north to Rome, mentioning that both Jews and Gentile proselytes have come to Jerusalem from there and referring to Crete and the Arabians, probably meaning Nabatea, making almost a full circle as the list is completed. That Rome is in the last grouping is important, for it is where Acts will end (on the Jewish dispersion, see Williams 1990: 45; Str-B 2:606–14; Josephus, *J.W.* 2.16.4 §§345–401; *Ant.* 12.3.1–4 §§119–53; 14.6.2–7.2 §§100–118; Philo, *Embassy* 36 §282). Bruce (1988a: 118) estimates the Jewish population of Rome to be forty to sixty thousand. That is out of about a million citizens in the city, huge by ancient and relatively modern standards (for comparison, London did not reach a million until the early nineteenth century). A proselyte is a Gentile who has received circumcision (if male) and a purifying baptism and has offered a sacrifice (in other words, a Gentile who has become a Jew). More women were proselytes than men (Bruce 1990: 58).

The crowd notes what it is hearing (ἀκούομεν, *akouomen*, presented vividly as a present tense; see v. 8). These Galileans speak of "the mighty deeds of God" (τὰ μεγαλεῖα τοῦ θεοῦ, *ta megaleia tou theou*). The term μεγαλεῖος (*megaleios*, mighty) appears only here in the NT but is frequent in the LXX (Deut. 11:2 [of exodus and wilderness events]; Ps. 70:19 LXX [71:19 Eng.]; Sir. 18:4; 36:7; 42:21; conceptually Jer. 33:3). Thus the tongues lead to a declaration of what God has done through Jesus. The passage is conceptually like Luke 19:37–38, where the miracles of God through Jesus are praised.

Once again the emotional response to the event is highlighted. Some in 2:12
the crowd are astonished and perplexed. Although the term "all" is used
here to suggest that all are inquiring about this, the crowd is in fact split
into two responses, as verse 13 shows, with some not sure what is happening and others offering an explanation. Luke often uses "all" to mean
"many" or even "most." The first verb (ἐξίστημι, existēmi) is repeated
from verse 7 (see discussion there). They are astonished. The second
verb (διαπορέω, diaporeō) is a synonym for the description in verse 6
that they are bewildered. This verb appears four times in the NT, all in
Luke-Acts (Luke 9:7; Acts 2:12; 5:24; 10:17; BDAG 235). The idea is to
be at a loss over something. It appeared in Luke 9:7 to describe Herod's
inability to determine what Jesus's ministry was all about.

One group in the crowd does not understand what is taking place
and admits it. They raise the question "What does this mean?" or, in
effect, "What might this be?" (using an indicative for a direct question;
BDF §386.1). This is a rare idiom that refers to trying to understand the
meaning of an event (BDAG 448 §5; Acts 17:20). So this verse reinforces
verses 7–8 and shows the audience's inability to discern what is taking
place, setting up Peter's speech.

Others in the crowd make an effort to explain, mocking the claims, even 2:13
though this explanation will turn out to be completely wrong. Luke
often has opposing views and reactions to such proclamation (e.g., Luke
9:7–9; Acts 17:32–34; 25:13–22). The Acts 2 narrative notes that these
remarks are given in a mocking tone (διαχλευάζοντες, diachleuazon-
tes, a participle of manner, Robertson 1934: 1127; Wallace 1996: 628;
"sneered" in HCSB; "jeered" in NET). This is the only use of this term in
the NT, nor is it present in the LXX. The nonprefixed form of the verb
appears only in the NT in Acts 17:32, for mocking at Paul's preaching
of resurrection in Athens. This group is clear that it does not believe the
divine claims. So these scoffers render their judgment that the disciples
are filled with sweet, only partially fermented wine (γλεῦκος, gleukos;
BDAG 201, the only use in the NT; Job 32:18–19 is the only LXX use;
Josephus, Ant. 2.5.2 §64). In their skeptical view, only the disciples'
less-than-sober condition can explain the unusual behavior (see other
examples of this drunkenness theme in 1 Sam. 1:13–15; Gen. 19:32–38;
Josephus, Ag. Ap. 2.24 §195).

Bruce (1988a: 59 and n57) observes that the keeping of wine all year
round is described by Cato, On Agriculture 120 (Str-B 2:614). In addition, this is not the season for new or partially fermented wine, as that
normally takes place in the month of August, still two months away. So
the theoretical possibility of having access to wine is available, but it
would not be new wine, merely sweet, cheap wine. The remark cannot
explain the languages but may reflect that some people think that what
they are hearing in unrecognized languages is drunken gibberish (cf.

1 Cor. 14:23, where tongues are seen as being the indicator of someone being "mad"). The verb is yet a third unique term in the verse (μεστόω, mestoō; BDAG 636; 3 Macc. 5:1, 10). Polhill (1992: 104) notes that such events are not self-authenticating and the reaction to them differs. The incorrect surmise leads to Peter's speech, which is presented as a divinely inspired commentary on the event.

In sum, the descent of the Spirit on the day of Pentecost comes with indications that God has acted. In a variety of languages that match the nationalities of Diaspora Jews living in Jerusalem, it includes the praise of God's mighty acts. As it takes place, no one can figure out how Galileans can speak such a variety of languages. God is taking the initiative to enable his people to explain what has taken place through Jesus. Polhill (1992: 106) argues that the passage shows that the mission has begun and the church is enabled to carry it out. From here in Jerusalem, the message will continue to go out into the world (Acts 1:8). The new era also has begun with the promised Spirit's arrival. The national list of Jews is a hint of where the story is going, out into the entire world. Associations with wind and fire point to a theophany. God is powerfully present, directing his mission. As the scene ends, some in the crowd move to mock the events, totally misreading what is happening and handling it with levity by claiming that these Galileans are drunk. Peter's rebuttal follows. Acts is showing God at work. As is often the case when God works, many who see it have no clue what is taking place, making light of it. No one should be surprised at such a variety of reactions when God works. Some do not see what God is doing even after it is explained.

Additional Notes

2:5. The name for Jerusalem ('Ιερουσαλήμ, *Ierousalēm*) appears in its Hebrew spelling here. The alternative spelling is 'Ιεροσόλυμα (*Hierosolyma*). The first form is in the LXX, and the second appears only in the Apocrypha (e.g., 1 Macc. 10:43; 11:34; 2 Macc. 1:1, 10; 3:6, 37; 3 Macc. 1:9; 3:16; 4 Macc. 4:3; 18:5; Lohse, *TDNT* 7:319, 327–28), although the Apocrypha also uses the former spelling. Luke-Acts alternates between the spellings with four uses of the latter in Luke's Gospel (2:22; 13:22; 19:28; 23:7). Only the former term appears in Acts 1–7, except at Acts 1:4. The two spellings alternate in the rest of the book and in Luke's Gospel.[15] The first spelling in Acts accounts for sixty-four of seventy-seven NT occurrences; the second spelling accounts for twenty-six of sixty-two NT occurrences. It is not clear why the spelling differs in Luke's writings.

2:5. There are numerous small text-critical issues in this verse, such as whether εἰς (*eis*) or the more classical ἐν (*en*) precedes the mention of Jerusalem and whether 'Ιουδαῖοι (*Ioudaioi*) belongs in the verse. Metzger (1971: 290–91) has a full discussion of both issues and defends the use of εἰς and the inclusion of 'Ιουδαῖοι.

15. Occurrences of the former spelling: Luke 2:25, 38, 41, 43, 45; 4:9; 5:17; 6:17; 9:31, 51, 53; 10:30; 13:4, 33–34; 17:11; 18:31; 19:11; 21:20, 24; 23:28; 24:13, 18, 33, 47, 52; Acts 1:8, 12, 19; 2:5, 14; 4:5, 16; 5:16, 28; 6:7; 8:26–27; 9:2, 13, 21, 26, 28; 10:39; 11:2, 22; 12:25; 13:27, 31; 15:2, 4; 20:22; 21:11–13, 31; 22:5, 17–18; 23:11; 24:11; 25:3.

2:6. The use of the plural imperfect ἤκουον (*ēkouon*; A, D, E, Ψ) is a more difficult reading than a singular imperfect (C, 81, Vulgate, Syriac) or a singular aorist verb (א, B, 36), or a plural aorist (460) that conforms with other aorists in the verse (Metzger 1971: 291). A copyist changing a plural to a singular is natural in light of the reference to each one (εἷς ἕκαστος, *heis hekastos*) hearing one's own language.

2:7. There are a number of textual issues in this verse. Many MSS read πάντες (*pantes*, all; א*, A, C, E, Ψ) before the reference to being amazed. This could be the reading of the verse, although its absence is a slightly harder reading (B, D). Another variant later in the verse has the crowd speaking "to one another" (πρὸς ἀλλήλους, *pros allēlous*), but this is poorly attested (C³, D, E). The form of the interrogative οὐχί/οὐκ/οὐχ (*ouchi, ouk, ouch*) is also disputed. The first is read by B, while the second, common form is in 𝔓⁷⁴, A, C, Ψ, and 33. The text, which is the more unusual rendering and the slightly more difficult reading with its aspiration before ἰδού (*idou*), is read in א, D, E, 81 (Bruce 1990: 116). Both οὐχί and οὐχ are frequent in Luke-Acts (twenty and fifteen times respectively). Either of the latter two readings is possible.

2. The Explanation: The Spirit's Coming Shows Jesus Is Lord-Messiah (2:14–36)

This initial speech by Peter is entirely about promise, fulfillment, and the resurrection-ascension. What does this pouring out of the Spirit show? Peter strings together three OT citations (Joel 2:28–32 in vv. 17–21; Ps. 16:8–11 in vv. 25–28; Ps. 110:1 in vv. 34–35) with one linking allusion from Ps. 132:11. In verse 30, the allusion refers to God's promise to set a descendant on David's throne to rule, a promise Peter sees as messianic. In fact, all the passages cited in the speech combine to explain God's plan. God had promised an outpouring of the Spirit before the day of the Lord (Joel 2:28–32), a resurrection (Ps. 16:8–11), and an ascension to the side of God (Ps. 110:1). These events initially fulfill OT promises of a Messiah bestowed with divine authority. In between the citations come explanations: the men present are not drunk (vv. 14–15), and Jesus, the one the nation crucified, did mighty works by the power of God and was raised by God (vv. 22–24). David did not write about himself but was a prophet speaking of the Messiah in resurrection and exaltation (vv. 29, 31–33). The combination of Jesus event and OT citation shows God's vindication of Jesus as Lord and Christ, making evident his position by this resurrection. Here is a fundamental christological claim of the church: God raised Jesus to the right hand, where he now is the mediator of God's promised blessing of salvation and the Spirit. A key significance of the resurrection-ascension concerns God's validation of Jesus and the furthering of God's saving work as evidenced by Jesus's mediating of God's Spirit. All of this is rooted in a work that entailed Jesus's death but that death could not contain him. The ascension reveals who Jesus truly is.

This speech is one of the most important theological declarations in the NT. It highlights who Jesus is and explains how one can know what God was doing through him. It nicely complements the presentation of the gospel from Paul and the church tradition, with its emphasis on how Jesus provides salvation as a sacrifice for sin (1 Cor. 15:1–3). Together the speech and the tradition reveal the gospel to be the good news that God's promise has come in Jesus, who died for sin and sits at God's side, distributing the benefits of salvation rooted in forgiveness and the provision of the Spirit. Peter in Acts 2 makes clear that God gave Jesus this authority as a part of the divine plan. The ascension also makes clear that Jesus's authority is rooted in his person and position, as the one who is both Lord and Christ. This is "high" Christology, showing that Jesus shares in God's presence and provision.

Here is a key event in Israel's restoration. Fuller (2006) says that Acts 1–2 is the climax of Israel's restoration, although why he does not discuss Acts 15 and the rebuilt hut of David is not clear. The event is both a continuation of Israel's hope and the beginning of the realization of promise that later in Acts leads to a new entity known as the church. Israel's restoration is not done yet, because as a nation it still needs to say "Blessed is the one who comes in the name of the Lord" (Luke 13:35; Acts 3:18–22). The function of Jesus and the position he has as a result of his ascension discloses the significance of his person as well, because no one shares God's glory but divinity.

Exegesis and Exposition

[14]But Peter, standing with the Eleven, lifted up his voice and addressed them, "Men of Judea and all who dwell in Jerusalem, let this be known to you, and let your ears hear my words, [15]for these men are not drunk, as you suppose, since it is only the third hour of the day; [16]but this is what was spoken through the prophet ⌜Joel⌝: [17]'And it shall be ⌜in the last days⌝, says God, that I will pour out my Spirit upon all flesh, and your sons and your daughters shall prophesy, and your young men shall see visions and your old men shall dream dreams; [18]and, indeed, on my servants and maidservants in those days I will pour out my Spirit and they shall prophesy. [19]And I will give wonders in the heaven above and signs on the earth below, blood and fire and vapor of smoke; [20]the sun shall be turned into darkness and the moon into blood, before the day of the Lord comes, the great and glorious day. [21]And it shall be that all who call upon the name of the Lord shall be saved.'

[22]"Men of Israel, give heed to these words: Jesus the Nazorean, a man attested by God to you with miracles and wonders and signs which God performed through him in your midst—even as you yourselves know—[23]this one, delivered up according to the marked-out will and foreknowledge of God, you killed, having him crucified through the hands of lawless men. [24]But God raised up this one, having loosed the pangs of death because it was not possible for him to be held by it.

[25]"For David says concerning him, 'I saw the Lord before me always, for he is at my right hand that I may not be shaken; [26]therefore my heart was glad, and my tongue rejoiced, even more my flesh shall dwell in hope. [27]For you shall not abandon my soul to hades or permit your Holy One to behold corruption. [28]You have made known to me the ways of life; you will fill me with your gladness in your presence.' [29]Brethren, I say to you with confidence concerning the patriarch David that he both died and was buried, and his tomb is with us to this day. [30]Being therefore a prophet and knowing that with an oath God swore to him

he would set one ⌜ ⌝ from the fruit of his ⌜loins⌝ upon his throne, ³¹foreseeing he spoke about the resurrection of the Christ, that ⌜he⌝ was not abandoned to ⌜hades⌝ nor did his flesh see corruption. ³²This Jesus God raised from the dead, of which we are all witnesses.

³³"Therefore, being lifted up to the right hand of God and also receiving the promise of the Holy Spirit from the Father, he poured out this which you see and hear. ³⁴For it was not David who ascended into the heavens, but he himself says, '⌜The⌝ Lord said to my Lord, "Sit at my right hand, ³⁵until I set your enemies as a footstool for your feet."' ³⁶Therefore let all the house of Israel know with assurance that God established him as both Lord and Christ, this Jesus whom you crucified."

2:14   Peter now rises to represent the Twelve (eleven plus himself) and explain the significance of what is taking place. The combination of ἐπαίρω (*epairō*) and φωνή (*phōnē*) appears only four times in the NT, all in Luke-Acts (Luke 11:27; Acts 2:14; 14:11; 22:22). Peter "lifts up his voice," speaking to the entire crowd about God's work. The verb for "address" (ἀποφθέγγομαι, *apophthengomai*) was used in Acts 2:4 and discussed there. It is another term that only Luke uses in the NT, and it refers to Spirit-inspired utterance. This is no longer tongues speaking but a direct address to the crowd (Bruce 1988a: 60).

Since the topic is God's work and the promise's distribution and availability to all, both men and women are probably highlighted generically in the address (ἄνδρες Ἰουδαῖοι, *andres Ioudaioi*, men of Judea; the only place this combination appears). The opening appeal to those of Judea likely refers to both men and women in the crowd, "people of Judea" or, better, "fellow Jews," although literally the phrase reads "men of Judea" (Bruce 1990: 120; on ἀνήρ, *anēr*, as a term of opening address, see Acts 1:11 and 16; as a term that can include women, 17:34). There is a special focus on those who dwell in the city of Jerusalem (οἱ κατοικοῦντες Ἰερουσαλήμ, *hoi katoikountes Ierousalēm*), the home of the promise's initial distribution and Israel's spiritual center (on the spelling of Jerusalem, see additional note on 2:5). Jerusalem is also highlighted because recent key events about Jesus took place there. Those of Jerusalem know that history. This second address also looks back to 2:5, connecting the units. This speech is clearly for all Jews from start to finish (see v. 22: "men of Israel"; v. 36: "whole house of Israel").

Peter's call to understand opens with a declaration containing two imperatives: "let this be known to you" and "give ear to my words" (= pay attention to my words). Of its fifteen NT occurrences, the adjective γνωστός (*gnōstos*, known) is used twelve times in Luke-Acts. The verb ἐνωτίζομαι (*enōtizomai*) is used only here in the NT and means "pay close attention to something" or "listen carefully" (BDAG 343; thirty-five times in the LXX; e.g., Gen. 4:23; Job 33:1; Ps. 5:2; BDF §123.2, but not in classical Greek; Jervell 1998: 142). Peter wishes to correct a misunderstanding first (v. 15; so also at the start of speeches in Acts 3:12; 14:15). Then he explains what is taking place (vv. 16–36). Such a rhetorical call to hear a speech is not unusual.

This is the first of a number of "missionary speeches" (or kerygmata) in Acts. These speeches share a basic outline that explores Jesus's significance before making a call to faith. Dodd (1936) notes the following themes that appear throughout the speeches, though not in every speech: (1) the age of fulfillment has come; (2) it has come through the life, death, and resurrection of Jesus; (3) the resurrection exalted Jesus; (4) the Holy Spirit is the sign of the church's power; (5) the messianic age's consummation comes in Jesus's return; and (6) God calls for repentance and offers forgiveness, the Holy Spirit, and his promise (also noted by Barrett 1994: 130–31). Dodd (1936: 73) also argues that this material is rooted in tradition. These speeches are probably summaries that have been stylized to a degree since they are so compact and there is so much Lukan vocabulary within them. But they accurately reflect the scope of what was said on these kinds of occasions (Marshall 1980: 72 and esp. Marshall 1970: 99–101; Williams 1990: 48–49).[1] This speech would likely have been in Aramaic (cf. Paul to a similar audience in Acts 22:2) but might have been in Greek, given the mixed audience.

Peter explains (γάρ, *gar*) that the idea that the disciples are drunk is not realistic. The juxtaposition of wine and the Spirit is not unusual, as it appears in Luke 1:15 and Eph. 5:18 (Harrison 1975: 57). The point of the similarity is the "control" that wine or the Spirit can exercise. It is only "the third hour," which means nine in the morning, since the day starts with sunrise. So Peter argues that there must be another explanation for what is taking place. This would be the hour of morning prayer, with the first meal of the day to follow (Polhill 1992: 108).[2]   **2:15**

This verse begins a scriptural defense that runs through verse 21. It is laid out in a this-is-that (τοῦτό ἐστιν, *touto estin*) form that is similar to what one sees in pesher style interpretation found at Qumran (Horgan 1979; CD 10.16). The phrase appears seven times in the NT, twice in Luke-Acts (Luke 22:19 is at the Last Supper and has parallels in all the Synoptics; Matt. 26:26; Mark 14:22, 26—all the Supper; John 6:29; 1 John 4:3). So its use for connecting Scripture in the NT is rare. This idiomatic expression serves to identify and connect two things (BAGD 596 §1a; BDAG 740 §1a). Its role in this speech is to connect what is said in Scripture with the explanation of the Pentecost event (see καὶ ἔσται, *kai estai*, in v. 17, which is a midrashic link using εἰμί). Peter is connecting his cita-   **2:16**

---

1. On its rhetorical elements, see Witherington 1998: 137–39, who notes that unique to the Acts 2 speech are the call for baptism and the reference to the Spirit.

2. Josephus, *Life* 54 §279, speaks of a Sabbath meal at midday. Str-B 2:615 speaks of ten as the usual morning mealtime in later sources; targum on Eccles. 10:16–17; *b. B. Meṣi'a* 83b.

tion of Joel 2:28–32 (3:1–5 MT and LXX) with the events of Pentecost and calling them "last day" events (Isa. 2:2 uses last-day language, the only place in the LXX the phrase ἐσχάταις ἡμέραις [*eschatais hēmerais*] appears). Peter explicitly names the prophet cited, using the preposition διά (*dia*) to make the point that God speaks "through" the intermediate agent, the prophet (see Acts 1:16 for discussion; Luke 1:70; 18:31; Acts 3:18, 21; 28:25; Schneider 1980: 268n33; Wallace 1996: 434).

2:17   Peter now cites Joel. He begins by noting, through an explanatory change made to the Joel text, that these are the last days (see additional note on 2:16–21). Thus the eschatological and fulfillment frame of Pentecost is affirmed at the start. Schweizer argues (*TDNT* 6:410–11) that Luke sees a new age here but not *the* new age. This interpretation is not so clear. The events here are preached as part of God's long-awaited promise in fulfillment of new-covenant hope. It is better to say that Luke sees the start of the decisive eras of fulfillment as happening in these recent events. As with the other three OT texts that will be raised in his speech, this event is seen as fulfilled, at least initially, by what God has done and declared. The apostles read such texts as last-day, kingdom texts and saw themselves in the last days (1 Pet. 1:20; 1 Cor. 10:11; 1 Tim. 4:1; 2 Tim. 3:1; Heb. 1:1–2; 9:26; 1 John 2:18). Since the day of the Lord is also alluded to in this citation, what Peter is really saying here is that the coming of the Spirit is the beginning of "those days." An era of righteousness will conclude them, and that era comes with the day of the Lord. At the end of his speech, Peter will use the coming of judgment as an appeal for the people to repent and thereby experience the blessings of the new era. People must remember that they are accountable to the living God, and so an appeal to judgment is an appeal to reality as Peter sees it.

It is the pouring out of the Spirit that they are seeing and that Joel declares will take place in the last days. Later Jewish interpretation connected the Joel citation to other OT texts that explained the Spirit's coming in the eschaton, a link that was conceptual in nature (Isa. 32:15; Jer. 31:31–33; Ezek. 34–37, esp. 36:22–32; Midrash Psalms 14 §6 [57b]; Midrash Tanḥuma Buber בהל יתך §28 [31a]; Deuteronomy Rabbah 203a on Deut. 6:14; when Ezek. 36:26; Joel 2:28; and Isa. 54:13 are used side by side as God's presence is said to rest on God's people; Str-B 2:615–16). Qumran also expresses the idea of how the Spirit enables discernment in this eschatological community (1QH 15.6–7 [= 7.6–7]; 1Q35 1.1.14; 4Q428 7.6–7; 1QS 4.2–4; Larkin 1995: 52, note on 2:17). This access to the Spirit fulfills the wish, expressed in Num. 11:29, that God would put the Spirit in all God's people. Numbers Rabbah 15.25 declares that in the "world to come all Israel will be made prophets," while citing Joel 2. So the declaration may not be all that surprising, if this late text reflects earlier Jewish tradition (Le Cornu and Shulam 2003: 94–95).

The verb "pour out" (ἐκχέω, *ekcheō*) in reference to the Spirit is important in this speech, reappearing as a midrashic link in verses 18 and 33. The image is of a torrential downpour that is poured out on a parched earth (Larkin 1995: 53). The use of this verb with the Spirit (τοῦ πνεύματός μου, *tou pneumatos mou*, my Spirit) summarizes Joel's key promise—that the Spirit would be poured out "on all flesh" (ἐπὶ πᾶσαν σάρκα, *epi pasan sarka*). The use of ἀπό plus the genitive is partitive here, pointing to the distribution of the Spirit (Schneider 1980: 268n37). The universality of the distribution is one of the main elements of the promise. Before this new period, the Spirit had been distributed to a few people on special occasions for special enablement (see Luke 3:4–6 [Isa. 40:3–5], 16–17). This is a key sign that the new era has come. Right now Peter understands this outpouring as referring to Jews, but he will come to see, as the Lord leads, that this universality includes Gentiles (Witherington 1998: 140–42; Johnson 1992: 49).

The rest of the citation makes clear that people of every gender, age, and class are meant. Except for their occurrence in Acts 1:18 (Judas's demise) and 22:20 (Stephen's martyrdom), the verbs meaning "to pour out" (ἐκχέω and ἐκχύννομαι, *ekchynnomai*) are used only to refer to this event or to its parallel for Gentiles in 10:45 (2:17–18, 33, are the only three occurrences of ἐκχέω in Luke-Acts out of sixteen NT occurrences; ἐκχύννομαι appears six times in Luke-Acts out of eleven times in the NT). The reappearance of ἐκχέω in 2:33 is important because there Jesus is responsible for the outpouring, an act that makes him responsible for mediating the promise's arrival in the last days. This act is evidence of God's vindication of Jesus in the resurrection-ascension as the risen, exalted one who works from God's "right hand" (Rom. 5:5—Spirit poured out; Rom. 8:34—Jesus at the right hand). This Joel citation reappears in a phrase in Acts 2:39; Rom. 10:13; and Rev. 6:12 (Marshall 1980: 73).

The distribution is open with respect to gender. Joel promised that in this new era "your sons and your daughters shall prophesy" (προφητεύσουσιν οἱ υἱοὶ ὑμῶν καὶ αἱ θυγατέρες ὑμῶν, *prophēteusousin hoi huioi hymōn kai hai thygateres hymōn*). This is one of three parallelisms in Acts 2:17–18: sons/daughters, young/old men, male/female servants (the third parallel reads "servants, men and women alike" in NLT; "servants, both men and women" in NIV; "bondslaves, both men and women" in NASB). This third parallel shows that no class is excluded from those who will be gifted in "those" days (i.e., the last days of 2:17). Here the prophesy alludes to the tongues, which are immediately intelligible to the audience. The message declares the acts of God, as was noted in the comments on 2:9–11. The idea is repeated for emphasis in an addition to the Joel citation at the end of verse 18 ("and they shall prophesy"). There was precedent for including women, as in the Hebrew Scripture Sarah, Miriam, Deborah, Hannah, Abigail, Huldah, and Esther were regarded as prophetesses (*b. Meg.* 14a; Exod. 15:20; Num. 12:2; Judg. 4:4; 1 Sam. 2:1–10; 25:23–35; 2 Kings 22:14; 2 Chron. 34:22). Anna was noted by Luke 2:36.

The message the audience is hearing comes directly from God, revealing what God has done and is doing through recent events. The near association of visions and dreams underscores that what is being revealed through the Spirit is not something one would normally know. It comes through the Spirit's disclosing work. The verb "to prophesy" is rare in Acts, appearing only here in 2:18, in 19:6 (also associated with tongues), and in 21:9, tied to the work of Philip's four unmarried daughters. In 1 Cor. 14, tongues are distinguished from prophecy until they are interpreted, and then they are treated like prophecy; there is a close association between the two when tongues are understood.

The distribution is also open with respect to age, as young men will have visions and old men will dream dreams. In both cases the point is that God will be accessible to and direct his people. Later in Acts, Paul will be led by a vision (16:9–10), and Cornelius and Peter each have a vision that sets up their meeting (9:10; 10:3, 10, 17; 18:9; Harrison 1975: 58). Acts 2:17 is the only occurrence of the term ὅρασις (*horasis*, vision) in Acts, one of only four uses in the NT (the others are in Rev. 4:3 [2x]; 9:17). The term is quite common in the LXX, however, appearing more than ninety times, with fifty-two of these in Ezekiel and Daniel (Num. 24:4, 16; Ezek. 1:1; 8:3; Dan. 4:20; 8:1; Johnson 1992: 49). The word for "dream" (ἐνύπνιον, *enypnion*) is an NT hapax but is also common in the LXX, with twenty-four occurrences in Genesis and eighteen in Daniel out of sixty-seven uses (Gen. 37:5; 41:8; Dan. 1:17; 2:1). The verb for "dream" (ἐνυπνιάζομαι, *enypniazomai*) is found only here and in Jude 8 in the NT and appears seventeen times in the LXX, with six uses in Genesis (Gen. 28:12; 37:5, 6, 9, 10; 41:5; Joel 3:1 LXX; most commonly tied to Joseph in Genesis). The use of the dative ἐνυπνίοις (*enypniois*) with a cognate reflects a Hebrew infinitive absolute (Moulton and Turner 1963: 241; BDF §198.6; Wallace 1996: 168–69 notes that the construction has the force of manner). This citation is rooted in tradition and so are its ideas (Dodd 1953: 48; Dunn 1975: 160). The Spirit brings access to understanding God's direction and plan and comes on those who call on the Lord (v. 21).

2:18   The third parallelism in verses 17–18 deals with gender and class. This final parallelism is tightly tied to the previous lists by καί γε (*kai ge*).[3] The Spirit will be poured out "even" or "indeed" on servants, both male and female. Even the lowest of classes will be blessed across both genders. Two often-ignored groups of people, servants and women, will be included. The reference to pouring out the Spirit repeats the language of 2:17. At the end of the verse, the reference to prophesying is added

3. The expression καί γε (the γε is added to the citation), gives an emphatic force of either "yea" or "indeed" to "and," as BDF §439.2 notes. So NET reads "even on my servants."

to the Joel quotation for emphasis and matches the reference in 2:17 as well. Thus the three groups are bookended at a literary level by references to prophesying. The reference to male slaves is one of only three in Acts (the others are 4:29; 16:17) out of 126 NT occurrences. The reference to female slaves is one of only three references in the NT, all in Luke-Acts (the others are Luke 1:38, 48). One final point is that these servants, in contrast to the previous two groups, are described as "my" (μου, *mou*) servants. This is yet another addition to the Joel citation. Thus God highlights the special relationship he has to those who tend to be forgotten in the social scale.

The citation now shifts to God's activity. Wonders and signs shall appear in the heavens and on the earth. An apocalyptic and consummative eschatological edge enters into the speech. Added to the citation are the words "above" and "below," which do not contribute anything conceptually but give the line a rhyme (ἄνω, κάτω, *anō*, *katō*). The term for "wonder" (τέρας, *teras*) appears sixteen times in the NT, nine of which are in Acts with none in Luke (the others are Acts 2:19, 22, 43; 4:30; 5:12; 6:8; 7:36; 14:3; 15:12). The term for "sign" (σημεῖον, *sēmeion*) appears seventy-seven times in the NT, twenty-four of which are in Luke-Acts with thirteen in Acts (the others are Luke 2:12, 34; 11:16, 29–30 [4x]; 21:7, 11, 25; 23:8; Acts 2:19, 22, 43; 4:16, 22, 30; 5:12; 6:8; 7:36; 8:6, 13; 14:3; 15:12). It is another addition to the Joel citation to complete the parallelism, explaining the function of the miracles as signs (Rengstorf, *TDNT* 8:124). The combination appears sixteen times in the NT, including nine times in Acts with none in Luke (the others are Acts 2:19, 22, 43; 4:30; 5:12; 6:8; 7:36; 14:3; 15:12; Matt. 24:24; Mark 13:22; John 4:48; Rom. 15:19; 2 Cor. 12:12; 2 Thess. 2:9; Heb. 2:4). The reference to wonders occurs only in pairing with the reference to signs in Acts. The parallel terms refer to God's miraculous work in the creation. It has OT roots in the exodus story of Moses (Exod. 4:8–9, 17, 28, 30; 7:3, 9; 10:1; 34:10–12). Johnson (1992: 50) connects it to a second-Moses motif. The term's many appearances in Acts, however, point to a highlighting of the events, not a particular person. Some refer to the work of Jesus (2:22), but most look to the work of those in the early church, since the reference is to the significance of Pentecost. This is the time of new deliverance to which God bears witness.

The reference to blood begins to raise the specter of the day of the Lord and judgment. The term αἷμα (*haima*) appears nineteen times in Luke-Acts (the others are Luke 8:43–44 [2x]; 11:50–51 [3x]; 13:1; 22:20, 44; Acts 1:19; 2:19–20 [2x]; 5:28; 15:20, 29; 18:6; 20:26, 28; 21:25; 22:20) out of ninety-seven NT occurrences. None of these uses in Acts alludes to the Luke 23 description of the cross—an important point, as some wish to connect the reference to Jesus's death (*pace* Bruce 1988a: 61–62, who argues for such a connection, as does Larkin 1995: 53, who also

         2:19

notes correctly that the elements tied to Jesus's death are a harbinger or foretaste of the end-time judgment). Marshall (1980: 74) seems to see the allusion as entirely future, as does Conzelmann (1987: 20), who connects the imagery to Luke 21; Schneider (1980: 269) notes a connection to verse 20b. Luke 22:20 does tie blood to Jesus's death in an allusion at the Last Supper. In Acts, Jesus's blood is noted in a similar manner in 5:28 and 20:28 to allude to his death, but none of these texts evokes the theme of judgment against someone. Rather, Acts 20 summarizes Jesus's sacrifice or provision for the church, and Acts 5 notes responsibility for his death in the case of the Jewish leaders. It is better to see these allusions as primarily directed to the future, although there may be some typology in Jesus's death, as Luke 22:20 combined with the descriptions of Jesus's death might suggest. If the reference is future, then the beginning of the new era means that the judgment that consummates it is also drawing nearer.

It is the reference to fire that especially evokes the theme of judgment (Gen. 19:24; Isa. 43:2). The term πῦρ (*pyr*) appears seventy-one times in the NT and eleven times in Luke-Acts (the others are Luke 3:9, 16–17 [2x]; 9:54; 12:49; 17:29; 22:55; Acts 2:3, 19; 7:30; 28:5). Except for Luke 22:55, all the uses in Luke imply an element of judgment. In Acts, by contrast, 2:19 is the only reference to fire as judgment. In combination with the mention of smoke (καπνός, *kapnos*), the connection to judgment is assured. Of its thirteen NT occurrences, all but this appearance of καπνός are in the book of Revelation, and most are associated with judgment (Rev. 9:2–3 [3x], 17–18 [2x]; 14:11; 18:9, 18; 19:3; two uses [8:4; 15:8] allude to God's presence). Thus this part of the Joel citation describes the judgment to come during the day of the Lord (see Acts 2:40 and the call to avoid the judgment). As Haenchen (1987: 179) says, "The cosmic events describe the terrible end which threatens, when only he who calls upon the name of the Lord (= Jesus) shall be saved."[4] The imagery of the sun and the moon changing in the next verse confirms the theme of coming judgment, as these are also signs of the day of the Lord. What is more complicated is how this imagery is related to the cross.

The relationship to events of the cross is tied to the description of cosmic signs in the last part of this verse and in the next. These signs probably have not taken place yet, although the analogy to them was the darkness and reaction of creation to Jesus's crucifixion (Luke 23:44–45; only the sun's darkness is noted there). The juxtaposition of blood, fire, and vapor of smoke, a dark sun, and a bloody moon looks at creation in upheaval and judgment. This is imagery associated with the day of the Lord (see v. 20b) and is tied to the Joel citation. The need for salvation

---

4. Against Haenchen 1987: 179n5, however, such a christological conclusion is not a sign of Hellenistic Christianity; see the discussion below on 2:32–36 and esp. 2:21.

surfaces because of the reality of coming judgment and the accountability that judgment requires.

The description of cosmic signs continues with a reference to the darkened sun and bloody moon. The association of the sun, darkness, and the day of the Lord appears only in Joel 3:4 (2:31 Eng.) in the LXX (Joel 2:10; 4:15 [3:15 Eng.]; Isa. 13:10; and Ezek. 32:7 are conceptually close; stars: Isa. 34:4). The reference to the moon (σελήνη, selēnē) appears only twice in Luke-Acts, here and in Luke 21:25, with the sun as a sign that shows the association Luke makes with the end and the Son of Man's return. The reference to the sun going dark in Luke 23:45, however, complicates the discussion, adding an apocalyptic and eschatological dimension to the cross's description. The usage there may well suggest that the cross portrays judgment and is a type of the day of the Lord (Bock 1996: 1858–60). It is hard to know how literally to take the Joel imagery in Luke-Acts, considering that the initial reference in Joel 2 is describing the effect that an incoming locust plague had for those present during the plague in Joel's time. The example of the cross looks more like nature responding in an unusual way. Either way, the point is that things will happen to make the environment change and be a visible sign of God at work. If the cross is a type for the end and Luke 21:25 refers to it, then some unusual event will cause this condition that is the sign.

2:20

These cosmic signs precede (πρίν, prin, before) the arrival of the day of the Lord, which in this context means the decisive time of judgment that the OT often discusses (Amos 8:9; Joel 2:10; 2:30–31 [3:3–4 MT and LXX]; Zeph. 1:15). The preposition πρίν here looks to subsequent time (Wallace 1996: 596). Peter is saying that the eschatological clock is ticking. With the end the cosmic signs and judgment come (so also Rev. 6:12, alluding to this verse in Joel; Bruce 1990: 121; in the NT: 1 Cor. 1:8; 2 Cor. 1:14; Phil. 1:6, 10; 2:16; 1 Thess. 5:2; 2 Thess. 2:2; 2 Pet. 3:10 [also the day of Christ]). Barrett (1994: 138) discusses Luke's outline of the basic movement of the plan, from Jesus's coming to the coming of the Spirit to mission to portents of the end and then the judgment in Jesus's return. Second Peter shows how comprehensive the judgment is that is associated with this day. It also presents a picture of fire dissolving the creation at the final judgment. That is why Peter describes the day as "great and manifest," a slight change from Joel's "great and terrible" day in the MT but in line with the LXX. The NT rendering makes the point that the day will be obvious, even glorious, when it comes; God will be demonstrably at work. All Jews already knew that the judgment was to be a terrible time for many.

In the midst of judgment's danger and the day's approach comes the exhortation to call on the name of the Lord. This text became traditional to use in the church, as calling on the name was a common expression

2:21

for responding to the gospel message (Acts 9:14; 15:17; Rom. 10:12–13; 1 Cor. 1:2; 2 Tim. 2:22).

The reference to the Lord (κύριος, *kyrios*) needs careful attention. In Joel this means calling out to Yahweh (יְהוָה), Israel's God, for salvation. At a literary level, nothing in Peter's speech up to this point would have anyone think otherwise about the meaning of this reference, because verse 20 speaks of the day of the Lord, which would be the day of God's judgment. But one of the functions of the entire speech is to show that Jesus is Lord, a key title also applied to Yahweh. Peter will give Jesus a place alongside Yahweh as carrying out the plan and will make clear that the name one is to call on belongs to Jesus (Acts 2:38; 4:10–12).[5] If Peter had cited Joel in a Semitic context in the first century, he likely would not have pronounced the divine name and would have used a substitute for the divine name, such as a form of the term "Lord." Haenchen (1987: 179n5) and Conzelmann (1987: 20) are wrong to say that the text presupposes only a Hellenistic setting or the use of the LXX for such a context. The oral practice of Jews in Judea opens up the text to this fresh understanding or fresh ambiguity, in that people would know that "Lord" stood for God. But then if Jesus shares God's position and lordship, what does that connection suggest about the personhood of Jesus?

This speech explains how the church presented its high Christology, something the event of Jesus's exaltation helped it to fully appreciate. These ideas are not made possible only by appeal to the vocabulary of the LXX, as the speech itself indicates. This is not a late realization of the church, for the only supposition this Christology requires is the belief in the resurrection-vindication of Jesus, which placed him at God's right hand. To limit such an understanding to the later Hellenistic church is to fail to appreciate the crucial, deep, and immediate impact of the resurrection on christological understanding. Once the resurrection was experienced and preached, theological reflection would have soon followed.

Peter's ultimate point will be that the only way to be delivered from the day is to call upon the name of the Lord and thereby seek God's salvation. An adequate response can come only through responding to Jesus as the exalted Messiah-Lord. Calling upon this name leads to salvation (σῴζω, *sōzō*; of Jesus saving: Acts 4:12; 11:14; 15:1, 11; 16:30–31; 28:28 [noun form]; in the natural sense of deliverance: 27:31). All (πᾶς, *pas*) who make such a call will be saved. In the speech, Peter is thinking of Jews, but in the literary progression from Acts 10 onward, it will be clear that this is meant to include Gentiles as well. The subjunctive

---

5. For other NT texts applying the term "Lord" for Yahweh to Jesus, see Isa. 45:23 in Phil. 2:10–11 and Rom. 14:11; Ps. 34:8 (33:9 LXX) in 1 Pet. 2:3; and Isa. 8:13 in 1 Pet. 3:15 (Bruce 1990: 122).

mood appears here because the identity of the one who calls upon the name of the Lord is unspecified, given the contingency of the response (Wallace 1996: 478–79).

Peter transitions from the first OT quotation, which explains how the Spirit's outpouring signifies the arrival of the last days, to the point of connection: Jesus the Nazorean, or the one from Nazareth (for other examples of the phrase Ἰησοῦν τὸν Ναζωραῖον, *Iēsoun ton Nazōraion*, Jesus the Nazorean, or similar expressions, see Acts 3:6; 4:10; 6:14; 22:8; 24:5; 26:9). Peter tells the key part of Jesus's story in verses 22–24. The Messiah from Nazareth would be controversial, but Peter does not think this matters, given how God has shown who Jesus is (Witherington 1998: 144).

Addressing Israel again, Peter calls on it to hear his words much as he did at the speech's start in verse 14.[6] Fernando (1998: 107–10) notes that "Christianity is Christ," which means that without him it does not exist. This faith is not an ethic but a work of God. Peter details what God did through Jesus. God accredited him, showed him to be victorious, gave him authority, and calls those who hear the gospel to respond to him. In sum, "Christian preaching begins with the name of Jesus" (Barrett 1994: 140). It also reaches its goal in him. Peter's speech both starts and finishes with Jesus.

Here was a man to whom God gave attestation with powers, wonders, and signs. "Attested" (ἀποδεδειγμένος, *apodedeigmenos*) refers to something that can attest or "show forth the quality of an entity" (BAGD 89 §2; BDAG 108 §2: "approved of God among you" in KJV; "attested to you by God" in NASB, RSV; "accredited by God to you" in NIV; "demonstrated to you to be from God" in NET). The term is rare in the NT, appearing only three other times: Acts 25:7; 1 Cor. 4:9; 2 Thess. 2:4. The perfect form of the participle adds an air of permanence to the attestation. The preposition ἀπό (*apo*, from) looks to God as the ultimate agent who makes the choice (Wallace 1996: 433). Jesus is one who stands attested by God.

Peter describes Jesus's miraculous ministry as evidencing God's demonstration of who Jesus is. The threefold description of his miraculous activity emphasizes the divine means of attestation for him. Two of these terms (τέρασι, σημείοις, *terasi, sēmeiois*) appeared in verse 19 and were discussed there. The third term, δυνάμεσι (*dynamesi*, mighty works), ap-

2:22

---

6. Literally, this is "men of Israel." On the use of ἀνήρ (*anēr*), see Acts 1:16, where a general audience possibly permits a rendering of "people" of Israel. On "men of Israel," see Acts 3:12; 5:35; 13:16; 21:28. An ambiguous rendering, however, makes clear that Peter is addressing everyone with the gospel. In other words, the address is to "men," but probably generically so, as the introduction to the speech addresses "men of Judea and all who dwell in Jerusalem" (v. 14). In verse 29, the same phrase appears as in Acts 1:16; 2:14 has ἄνδρες Ἰουδαῖοι (*andres Ioudaioi*, men of Israel) but also possibly with generic force.

pears ten times in Acts (1:8; 2:22; 3:12; 4:7, 33; 6:8; 8:10, 13; 10:38; 19:11; also Luke 4:14, 36; 5:17; 6:19; 8:46; 9:1; 10:13, 19), mostly referring to the early church's miraculous activity. Here the word looks back to Jesus's miracles, which are also a display of God's "mighty work" (BDAG 263 §3). These works are what God did through Jesus (δι' αὐτοῦ, *di' autou*) in the midst of the very Jewish audience Peter now addresses. Johnson speaks about Jesus being attested as a prophet here (1992: 50), but the speech's burden is that Jesus and the plan relate to the Messiah (v. 36), so that it is the messianic end times that God attests through this work (so Polhill 1992: 111; Pesch 1986a: 120 speaks of the eschatological prophet and Messiah).

The audience well knows that such a display took place. The reputation of Jesus performing miraculous works is something Josephus mentions later in the century in his famous remarks about Jesus in *Ant.* 18.3.3 §§63–64, where he says that Jesus "was a doer of remarkable/strange [παραδόξων, *paradoxōn*] works." Whether Josephus intends παραδόξων ambiguously or positively, he gives evidence of Jesus's reputation as a worker of unusual deeds. The Jewish tradition's belief that Jesus was a "magician" of sorts also attests to this understanding, while viewing the source of Jesus's power differently.[7] Peter sees these "signs" as divine indicators of the fact that God worked in and through Jesus (Acts 10:37–38).

2:23 Peter highlights a contrast between God's work and the nation regarding Jesus. On the one hand, Jesus was delivered up according to God's plan and foreknowledge. Jesus's death was no surprise to God, nor was his suffering. All the texts that Luke-Acts has cited about Jesus's suffering point to the idea that God planned or knew that Jesus would suffer (Luke 9:21–22, 44–45; 13:33; 17:25; 18:31–33; 22:37; 24:46–47). The term for "predetermined" (ὁρίζω, *horizō*) appears eight times in the NT with six uses in Luke-Acts (the others are Luke 22:22; Acts 10:42; 11:29; 17:26, 31; Rom. 1:4; Heb. 4:7). Luke's frequent usage underscores his belief that God is very much in control of events that are tied to Jesus and included a plan for suffering as a part of Jesus's calling. The term for "plan" (βουλή, *boulē*) is similar in force and is favored by Luke. Nine of twelve NT uses are in Luke-Acts (Luke 7:30; 23:51; Acts 2:23; 4:28; 5:38; 13:36; 20:27; 27:12, 42; 1 Cor. 4:5; Eph. 1:11; Heb. 6:17). Reference to foreknowledge (πρόγνωσις, *prognōsis*) is rare, appearing two times in the NT (1 Pet. 1:2 is the other text; two uses in the LXX: Jdt. 9:6; 11:19). Thus from the divine perspective, nothing that happened was outside God's plan. God's attested one was always going to suffer.

On the other hand, Peter is very direct about where human responsibility for the death lies—"You crucified and killed this Jesus by the hands

---

7. See *b. Sanh.* 43a, 107b. Jewish views are also reflected in Justin Martyr, *Dial.* 69.7; Stanton 1994: 164–80. For a careful analysis defending the gist of the Josephus remarks as authentic, see Meier 1991: 56–88.

of lawless men." Most interpreters think the "lawless men" refers only to the Romans who gave out the penalty of crucifixion and executed Jesus. Seen in this light, "lawless men" refers to those who did not have the guidance of the Mosaic law, a phrase expressing a Jewish perspective. But Israel, through its lawless leaders, those who were supposed to support the law, also contributed to the slaying of Jesus, as the end of the verse makes clear.

First he was "delivered over." The term ἔκδοτον (*ekdoton*, given over), an NT hapax with no usage in the LXX in the singular, ties grammatically to the reference to Jesus at the start of the verse. It also follows the reference to the plan of God. As a singular, it appears to refer only to one person, so this would be a reference to Jesus delivered over by God's plan (Luke 24:26–27; Acts 3:18; 13:27; 26:23; Jervell 1998: 145).

This delivery, however, came through (διά, *dia*) the hands of the lawless. The plural reference to lawless men probably means more than Pilate and Herod, and so the Jewish leadership must be in view, given the way Luke tells the story in Luke 22–23 and what Peter goes on to say about who are responsible for the crucifixion at the end of this verse. In addition, there is Acts 4:26–28, where a combination of the Jewish leadership, Pilate, and Herod are held responsible for this death. In Luke 22–23, the driving force behind Jesus's demise is the Jewish leadership (also Acts 13:27–29; Luke 13:34), with the help of the citizens of Jerusalem. Thus Peter says that they, meaning the leadership and Jews of Jerusalem, had him crucified.[8] Peter charges the Jews directly: "By means of having him crucified, you all killed [ἀνείλατε, *aneilate*, second person plural] him." The double charge is emphatic and suggests that the handing over permitted by God included the Jewish leadership and made the nation as a whole culpable. The verb ἀναιρέω (*anaireō*, kill) appears in twenty-one of its twenty-four NT occurrences in Luke-Acts, with nineteen of those in Acts (Luke 22:2; 23:32; Acts 2:23; 5:33, 36; 7:21, 28 [2x]; 9:23–24 [2x], 29; 10:39; 12:2; 13:28; 16:27; 22:20; 23:15, 21, 27; 25:3; 26:10). The verse shows a mix of Lukan and non-Lukan vocabulary, even from the LXX. Jesus, a man attested by God, was put to death in God's plan by the act of lawless people among the Jews and by Roman leaders in Jerusalem. On the Jewish responsibility for Jesus's death, see Acts 2:36; 3:13; 4:10; 5:30; and 7:52 (Bruce 1988a: 123). The remark about the lawless, when it is applied to Jews, is ironic, as it was used by the Jews concerning the Gentiles, as also in some NT texts (Jervell: 1998: 145; Rom. 2:12; 1 Cor. 9:21; Luke 22:37).

8. The term προσπήξαντες (*prospēxantes*, by means of crucifixion) is a participle of means subordinate to the idea of killing; Robertson 1934: 1113. The verb from which it comes, προσπήγνυμι (*prospēgnymi*), is an NT hapax with no LXX usage and means to fasten or affix, so "to nail to a cross," BDAG 884.

This placing of blame on the leadership and the Jews of Jerusalem fits with the overall portrait of Luke-Acts (Weatherly 1994: 50, 64, 70, 82–90). The key texts mentioning the role of the rulers specifically are Luke 22–23; 24:20; Acts 3:17; 4:5, 8, 27; 13:27; and 14:5. Both Josephus (*Ant.* 18.3.3 §§63–64) and the Talmud (*b. Sanh.* 43a) acknowledge a role for the leadership, or at least awareness, in Jesus's death (Le Cornu and Shulam 2003: 107–8). Acts 4:24–27 is especially significant, for there the full blame is placed on a variety of figures, including the leadership, the people of Jerusalem, Herod, Pilate, and the Roman soldiers under his authority. They are all responsible for Jesus's death. Weatherly (1994: 225–42) goes on to argue that this perspective has come to Luke through his traditional sources.

2:24 The attestation continued through what God did with the crucified Jesus. God raised him up. Luke here uses the verb ἀνίστημι (*anistēmi*, raise; Acts 2:32; 3:26; 10:41; 13:32–33; 17:31). In other passages, another verb for "raise" appears (ἐγείρω, *egeirō*, 3:15; 4:10; 5:30; 10:40; 13:30, 37; Barrett 1994: 143).

A mixed metaphor describing Jesus's release follows. God raised Jesus alive, "having loosed the pangs of death" (λύσας τὰς ὠδῖνας τοῦ θανάτου, *lysas tas ōdinas tou thanatou*). "The Abyss can no more hold the Redeemer than a pregnant woman can hold the child in her body" (Bertram, *TDNT* 9:673). The combination has OT roots in 2 Sam. 22:6; Pss. 18:5 (17:6 LXX); and 116:3 (114:3 LXX), where reference is made to the "ropes or snares of Sheol" and the following line mentions pain ("loose pangs"; Job 39:3; Bock 1987: 171; Bratcher 1959: 18–20). There may be a wordplay from Hebrew between חֵבֶל (*ḥēbel*, pangs) and חֶבֶל (*ḥebel*, cord) that fuels the Greek rendering (cf. Ps. 18:5 = 2 Sam. 22:6). Polhill (1992: 113) notes that the idea of birth for new life is appropriate. Barrett (1994: 144) points out that 1QH 3.28 (= 1QH 11.28 in other versification) also has the metaphor: "pangs of death will compass [people] about" (on "pangs" see Bertram, *TDNT* 9:673; Bruce 1990: 64). In 1 QH 11.7–10, a similar extended metaphor is used to describe the sufferings of the Teacher of Righteousness (Le Cornu and Shulam 2003: 112–13). "Pangs" describes death as a painful experience like birth pangs (BAGD 895 §2a; BDAG 1102 §bα; "agony of death" in NASB, NIV; "horrors of death" in NLT; "pangs of death" in RSV, ESV; "pains of death" in NET). The mix in the metaphor is the idea of birth pangs, possibly eschatological pangs, that are loosed like ropes being let loose. Death was not able to encircle Jesus and hold him in its painful grip.

The explanation (καθότι, *kathoti*, because) that follows is that death was unable to hold him. God, the one with power over life and death, was able to overcome death's grip and bring Jesus to life. Luke alone uses καθότι in the NT (Luke 1:7; 19:9; Acts 2:45; 4:35; 17:31). Peter affirms the resurrection, a doctrine some Jews also held (Dan. 12:1–2; Wright

2003: 85–206). Josephus notes that the Pharisees held this view (*Ant.* 18.1.3 §14). Jesus's resurrection was different, however, from Jewish resurrection. Jewish resurrection was a resurrection of all at the end of history. Jesus's resurrection was a singular event within history and involving only one figure. The difference is significant. It suggests that some event has happened to create the new view.

Peter moves to his second scriptural proof text, citing Ps. 16:8–11 (15:8–11   **2:25** LXX, matching its wording). The text is a psalm of confidence that Peter uses to support resurrection. Peter presents the psalm as authored by David. The psalm opens with a word of confidence. The psalmist (note the first person singular) sees the Lord before him always, and God's presence at the psalmist's right hand means that he will not be shaken. The verb σαλεύω (*saleuō*, shake) appears thirty-four times in the Psalter out of seventy-six LXX occurrences (e.g., Pss. 9:27; 14:5; 20:8; 29:7; 45:6; 61:3; 111:6 [10:6; 15:5; 21:7; 30:7; 46:5; 62:2; 112:6 Eng.]). Peter uses the psalm because the kind of defense God gave to the psalmist is like that which Jesus received, a typological-prophetic use. God's protection and the certainty of it are key to the citation's tone and use. Such confidence is reflected in the crucifixion scene as Luke presents it (Luke 23:46 uses Ps. 31:5 [30:6 LXX]; cf. Larkin 1995: 56, who notes that Luke does not use Ps. 22:1 in the crucifixion scene as Mark 15:34 does).

This verse expresses the confidence God's presence gives. It causes   **2:26** the heart to be glad (εὐφραίνω, *euphrainō*; eight uses in Luke-Acts out of fourteen NT uses) and to rejoice (ἀγαλλιάω, *agalliaō*; four uses in Luke-Acts out of eleven NT uses). It causes one's flesh to live in hope. Here flesh (σάρξ, *sarx*) is a figure for the person, used here in parallelism to the heart and tongue, giving a "tour" of the human person. The physical dimension of hope is not lost when one is discussing resurrection, which is why flesh is a major point in the figure. It is especially through the inclusion of the person's entire well-being that one is secure and lives in hope. The LXX reference to "in hope" replaces an MT reference to dwelling "in security," but this simply makes the image more vivid, as does the change from the MT's "my glory" (or perhaps "my liver") to the LXX's "my tongue" in the verse (on the possibilities for the MT, see Bruce 1990: 124). The psalmist can rest in God's care.

This verse is the key to the citation, as it appears a second time in verse   **2:27** 31, where Peter explains his understanding of the psalm. The fundamental assertion is that the one referred to in the psalm has confidence that God will not abandon (ἐγκαταλείψεις, *enkataleipseis*) "my soul" (τὴν ψυχήν μου, *tēn psychēn mou*) in hades. The verb appears 179 times in the LXX, including 21 times in the Psalter, but the combination with hades appears only in this psalm. The use of εἰς (*eis*) in a local sense happens occasionally in the NT ("in hades," BDF §205; Moule 1959: 68, also v. 31).

Hades is the Greek equivalent of Gehenna or Sheol, the place where the dead are gathered for judgment (BAGD 16 §1; BDAG 19; "to the grave" in NIV; "among the dead" in NLT; "to/in hades" in RSV, ESV, NET, NASB; Gen. 37:35; Num. 16:30; Ps. 6:5). Witherington (1998: 145) notes that Jews believed the spirit of a person stayed in the body for three days and then the soul departed (John 11:17, 39). Being in hades stands in contrast here to being in God's presence and expresses the threat that death represents.

As with everything in the psalm up to this point, the language is expressed in the first person. It is "my soul" that will not be abandoned. This gives the impression that the psalmist speaks for himself. In the parallel line that follows, God will not allow "your Holy One" (τὸν ὅσιόν σου, *ton hosion sou*) to see (i.e., experience) "corruption" (διαφθοράν, *diaphthoran*). Both expressions ("Holy One" and "corruption") need careful attention.

The reference to "Holy One" is a non-first-person reference that describes someone who has been "sanctified" before God and has experienced God's mercy, the "saint" (Bruce 1988a: 125; Johnson 1992: 51; Ps. 50:5 [49:5 LXX]). In Acts 13:35 "Holy One" reappears in another use of this OT verse, indicating that this psalm may well have been a part of church tradition explaining Jesus's resurrection. The passage also appears in the later Acts of Philip 78 [15] (Barrett 1994: 146). "Holy One" (ὅσιος, *hosios*) is used seventy-seven times in the LXX. It can refer to a priest (Deut. 33:8), to the pious, or to the faithful. A reference to the faithful is the term's most common usage, especially in the Psalter (2 Sam. 22:26; Pss. 4:3 [4:4 LXX]; 12:1 [11:2 LXX]; 18:25 [17:26 LXX]). In Ps. 16, however, it is a reference to a specific person, as the singulars in the psalm show. It is easy to see why readers might think this is a reference to the psalmist David, given his regal status and the first-person references up to this point in the psalm. What cannot be ruled out, however, is that the psalm could well be read as about God's ultimate protection of the kingship of Israel that David's presence and connection to the psalm suggests. This connection will be alluded to in the promise made to David in Acts 2:30 from Ps. 132:11, which itself reaches back to 2 Sam. 7 and the Davidic covenant. Its placement in the Psalter may well suggest that this hope of protection for the king went beyond the original setting. Peter will make this point explicit later in the speech.

The nonabandonment to hades, the declaration that this one will not see corruption, and the idea of the person being secure, including in his flesh, lead Peter to argue that resurrection, even an immediate bodily resurrection, is affirmed here (Acts 2:30–31). The six appearances of "corruption" in the NT are all in Acts 2 and 13 (2:27, 31; 13:34, 35, 36,

37). The term appears twenty times in the LXX, referring to death and often associated with the Hebrew root שחת (šḥt).[9]

Many scholars argue that the original psalm had in mind only a premature death, which is quite possible given how the term "corruption" is used and how death was seen at the time the psalm was written, but this still reads the psalm too narrowly. As a psalm, it is about an individual but in a way that extends beyond that individual. What this individual experiences is like what others in his class might hope for from God. That is why succeeding generations reflect on this psalm in worship. The hope expressed operates like a promise of God's protection. This protection extends to any threat the "Holy One" faces, and no threat is greater than death. It is in this light that Peter reads the text, as his explanation shows. These hermeneutical observations are important in the face of claims that only the LXX can justify the reading Peter makes and thus the text has its roots in Hellenistic Christianity (so Haenchen 1987: 181–82). That is a far too narrow reading of the Jewish understanding in the first-century context. Luke 23:43 has Jesus express the confidence that his death will take him to paradise "today" and so apparently not to hades.

The concept of an immediate resurrection within history was a fresh idea in Judaism. The Jews believed in a general bodily resurrection at the end of time for all the righteous and wicked together before the judgment (Isa. 66; Dan. 12:1–2; 2 Macc. 7) but did not have an expectation of an earlier, immediate, special resurrection for anyone.[10] This new idea of a resurrection before the end was revealed by Jesus's resurrection. In this speech Peter is arguing that Scripture predicted it, as all can now see.

This final verse contains a note of triumph. The one who experiences God's protection has had the ways of life (LXX is plural, MT is singular, "way of life": speaking of the pleasing life) revealed to him. Some see a connection conceptually to Jesus as the "author of life" in Acts 3:15 (Pesch 1986a: 122). This leaves him glad to be in God's presence. The term for "gladness" (εὐφροσύνη, euphrosynē) appears only twice in the NT, both times in Acts (14:17 is the other use). It also appears 170 times in the LXX (34 times in Isaiah and 11 times in the Psalms). This verse in the psalm expresses trust and confidence in God's deliverance

2:28

9. See 2 Macc. 8:35; Ps. 107:20 (106:20 LXX). The likely force of the word in the MT, with the meaning "the pit," is less vivid, describing the pit one is in as a result of death or catastrophe. These situations are compared to someone caught in a net, as the parallel lines of Pss. 9 and 35 show (Pss. 9:16; 30:9 [29:10 LXX]; 35:7 [34:7 LXX]; 55:23 [54:24 LXX]; Prov. 28:10; Ezek. 19:4). Job 33:28 is close to this use in Ps. 16:10. Conceptually, the fear of death induced by such circumstances is described in Pss. 49:10 (48:10 LXX); 89:48 (88:49 LXX).

10. 2 Macc. 7 is especially clear on how physical this Jewish hope of resurrection was. Here the seven sons of one mother are put to death, and some face their death confident that they will be completely physically restored.

and abiding presence. Again, all of this language, Peter argues, fits resurrection.

2:29 Peter now begins to expound Ps. 16 and justify his interpretation of it. He introduces this fresh point with a direct address to the audience (ἄνδρες ἀδελφοί, *andres adelphoi*). This phrase is intended broadly when the audience is both men and women, especially in Acts 2, where the gift of the Spirit can come to both genders (see Acts 1:16 and 2:14; the "familial" connection [ἀδελφοί] is a part of their Jewish background; Barrett 1994: 146). The explanation of how to read the psalm runs through verse 31, and then verses 32–33 show how the psalm relates to recent events. The justification indicates that God's plan included the resurrection and serves to explain its significance for pointing to Jesus as the Christ. The passage also represents a second proof of fulfillment for the resurrection beyond the eyewitnesses. Both the eyewitnesses and Scripture testify to this expectation (*pace* Polhill 1992: 114). One need not make a choice between the text pointing to Jesus as Messiah and its role as a support for the resurrection, as Polhill does, opting for the messianic point.

Peter's reading presses all the language here in a very literal direction. The text is not about premature death but about not being left in hades. The status of the flesh is part of the text's promise as well. It is Jesus's σάρξ (*sarx*) that does not see corruption; this stresses the bodily nature of his resurrection (Schweizer, *TDNT* 9:646–47).

Peter makes the point that the text is not only about the patriarch David, which is probably the prevalent view, given the fact he addresses the point so directly. This is the only NT text that calls David a patriarch, used in the sense of the head of a family (see 2 Chron. 19:8). The expression is usually reserved for one of the twelve sons of Jacob (Acts 7:8–9; cf. 7:32) or for Abraham (Heb. 7:4). It is used four times in the NT. Sirach 47 includes David in a discussion of the "fathers" that begins in chapter 44 and runs for several chapters (Pesch 1986a: 123).

Peter argues that "it is possible" (ἐξόν, *exon*; BDAG 349 §2; BDF §353.5) to say with confidence (παρρησίας, *parrēsias*) that the psalm is ultimately not about David.[11] David is both dead and buried. His tomb is still ἐν ἡμῖν (*en hēmin*, among us; Moule 1959: 75). Barrett (1994: 146) mentions the later Jewish tradition of *y. Ḥag.* 2.78a.41 and *y. Beṣah* 2.61c.9 that has David die on a Sabbath at Pentecost, along with one other tradition, Derek Eretz Zuta 1, that has corruption not touch David and six other patriarchs (Str-B 2:26, 619). In contrast, *t. B. Bat.* 1.11 has David's tomb in Jerusalem, with uncleanness removed by an underground brook, so that it was eventually moved, according to tradition, to Bethlehem (Le

---

11. Acts 4:13, 29, 31 and 28:31 are the only other Lukan uses of thirty-one occurrences of the term in the NT. On how the later rabbis viewed the hope of the Davidic line, see *b. Sukkah* 52a; Le Cornu and Shulam 2003: 114–15.

Cornu and Shulam 2003: 113). Josephus makes frequent mention of David's grave at that time (Bruce 1988a: 66; Schneider 1980: 274n100; Neh. 3:16). In *Ant.* 7.15.3 §§392–94 he describes John Hyrcanus the high priest and later Herod as raiding or attempting to raid the sepulchre for money in the times of Antiochus VII (ca. 135–134 BC) and Herod, respectively. In both cases, however, the body was not disturbed, and Herod's attempt was rebuffed by fire (also *Ant.* 13.8.4 §249; *J.W.* 1.2.5 §61—both repeating the Hyrcanus story). And in *Ant.* 16.7.1 §§179–83 he details the Herod story, noting that the flames killed two guards and stopped the effort. This also led Herod to build a marble memorial to the tomb, and so it was an impressive site in Peter's day. The location was "probably on the south side of the southeast hill of Jerusalem near the pool of Siloam" (so Polhill 1992: 114; with less certainty, Marshall 1980: 76).

The tomb shows that David cannot fulfill in the fullest sense the psalm's point about the confidence of divine protection, for one can observe David's undisturbed grave, which testifies to David's being in hades.[12] David is mentioned in Luke-Acts twenty-four times, of fifty-nine in the NT (Luke 1:27, 32, 69; 2:4 [2x], 11; 3:31; 6:3; 18:38–39 [2x]; 20:41–42 [2x], 44; Acts 1:16; 2:25, 29, 34; 4:25; 7:45; 13:22 [2x], 34, 36; 15:16). Many of these occurrences suggest Davidic descent, as does this text (Luke 1:27, 32; 3:31; 18:38–39; 20:41–42, 44; Acts 13:22, 34, 36; 15:16). To realize fully the expression of confidence the psalm expresses about God's continual presence, the one referred to must be raised, and this cannot be about a still-buried David, whose grave is undisturbed.

David spoke as a prophet. This explicit reference to David as a prophet   **2:30** is uniquely expressed, even though there was a rich tradition of him as a composer of psalms (Josephus, *Ant.* 6.8.2 §166; 11QPs[a] 27.11; 4Q174 1–3; Fitzmyer 1972: 332–39). Luke-Acts portrays a psalmist and other writers of Scripture as prophets speaking through the Spirit (Luke 20:41–42; 24:44; Acts 1:16; 4:25; 13:33–36; Johnson 1992: 51). Also emphasized is that David knew "God swore to him with an oath" (ὅρκῳ ὤμοσεν αὐτῷ ὁ θεός, *horkō ōmosen autō ho theos*) as a promise. The combination of oath and swearing emphasizes the certainty of God's commitment. The dative ὅρκῳ here is one of association (BDF §198.6). God swore in association with an oath.

The following language comes from Ps. 132:11 (131:11 LXX), which itself describes 2 Sam. 7:12–13 and the Davidic covenant (2 Samuel was considered a messianic text at Qumran; see 4Q174 1.7–13; Marshall 1980: 77). Acts 7:46–47 alludes to the promise as well (see also Ps. Sol. 17.23–51; Bruce 1988a: 66n86). The specific promise is that God "would set one from the fruit of his [David's] loins on his throne" (ἐκ καρποῦ

---

12. The implied idea of an undisturbed grave may well also suggest how physical Peter conceives resurrection to be.

τῆς ὀσφύος αὐτοῦ καθίσαι ἐπὶ τὸν θρόνον αὐτοῦ, *ek karpou tēs osphyos autou kathisai epi ton thronon autou*). This is the promise that a Davidic descendant would sit on the throne of David so that his dynasty would be the fulfillment of God's promise for God's people. The reference in the verse to David's throne looks to the carrying out of this rule with this authority. Peter will say that Jesus begins to fulfill this Davidic promise and messianic authority by pouring out the Spirit, as verses 32–36 declare. The reference to the throne is not concerned with the location of a chair in heaven or on earth, nor with who is ruled over, but with the function that having such a position reflects. The figure portrays the presence of a promised regal personage, the Christ, as verse 36 shows. The expression looks back to Luke 1:32, where the child Jesus is said to be given the throne of David and a kingdom that will never end.

This kingdom is what Jesus taught about throughout his ministry, and although the promise concerns Israel, the concept focuses on the rule he brought in as a result of his first coming. Luke 11:20; 17:21b; and Acts 1:6–8 make this emphasis clear.[13] The allusion is to the Davidic promise. Peter's point is not that Jesus will have this throne one day sometime far in the future. In other words, the point is not that Jesus is merely appointed for the Davidic role now and qualifies for it through his resurrection and then will exercise this authority in the future, in the same way the anointing of David long preceded his actual functioning as king. Rather, Peter's point is that the exercise of messianic authority is on display now in the Spirit's present distribution, as verses 32–36 declare. Psalm 45:6 (44:7 LXX) is a passage about the kingship of Israel at the time of Solomon and expresses the idea of the throne as a place where divine rule functions (see also Pss. 89:14, 29, 36 [88:15, 30, 37 LXX]; 122:5 [121:5 LXX], which stress the function of the rule). Every other OT text cited in this chapter is already initially fulfilled by what Jesus has done. The allusion to this psalm operates in the same way.

This promise stretches back to its initial realization in 1 Kings 8:20, 25; 9:5, and the close connection between the throne of David (or of Israel) and God's kingdom is expressed in 1 Chron. 17:14. In 1 Chron. 29:23 this same throne is called the Lord's throne, showing the close connection between God and God's king and the rule the king exercises on God's behalf. This point of connection also appears in Ps. 2, where sonship and rule are associated. Pesch (1986a: 123) makes the same point by a connection with Ps. 110, where the throne of God and David-Israel overlap. This is why Jesus can ask a messianic question while discussing Ps. 110:1 (Luke 20:41–44). The Son of David can be the Son of God and, ultimately, the Son of Man (2 Sam. 7:7–16).

13. See Acts 1:6–8 above and discussions on the Lukan passages in Bock 1996: 1079–82, 1414–18, and in Bock 2002a: 565–93 on Jesus's view of the kingdom.

The throne discussed in these OT texts is located in Zion, and the promise is that one day such a rule will take place on the earth (Isa. 2:1–4), yet Peter's point throughout his speech is not about the future but about what is evident in the present. Even now Jesus exercises messianic executive authority and prerogatives, as the Spirit's coming shows and the Scripture promised. This is the arrival of that day John the Baptist also predicted in Luke 3:16. Jesus made similar promises in Luke 24:49 and in Acts 1:4–5 (see discussion on Acts 1:4–5). Peter argues that the resurrection makes possible this promise's realization while the Pentecost event shows that the Spirit has come as a function of messianic activity, authority, and promise. Thus Jesus functions now as both Messiah and Lord (v. 36). This divine-human combination is also stressed in Rom. 1:1–4 and through the gospel Paul preached, as set forth in Rom. 1–8 and 15:12. The importance of Jesus's exaltation is a basic theme of NT Christology because it reveals Jesus's uniqueness and points to his qualification to be directly in God's presence, something that has implications for appreciating who Jesus is (also Col. 1:13–14; Eph. 1:19–23; 1 Tim. 3:16; Titus 3:5–7; Heb. 1:1–4; 1 Pet. 3:21b–22; Rev. 1:5–6, using the language of Ps. 89).

2:31   Peter explains that through the language of this psalm David expresses what he foresaw in the promise, namely, the resurrection of the Christ. Peter stresses the point by repeating language from verse 27—he would not be abandoned to hades and his flesh would not see corruption. The differences between verse 27 and the repetition here include the fact that here the "Holy One" is not referred to and that here it is explicitly the flesh (σάρξ, *sarx*) that dwelt in hope, mentioned above in verse 26. The flesh does not see corruption. These emphases show how Peter reads the lines of the psalm and its parallelism. The Jewish "link word" form of *gezerah shewa* appears again in the speech, linking text and exposition together in multiple terms from verses 26–27 (flesh, abandoned, hades, and corruption are all repeated here). If the psalm was ever to be connected to David, it must surely be connected even more to the Christ, whom God has shown Jesus to be by his resurrection. In addition, the verb tenses for "see" and "abandon" are now aorist instead of future, underscoring the verse's current fulfillment.

2:32   From the discussion of Scripture, resurrection, and the Christ, Peter turns to Jesus and his resurrection. Peter puts the two together and declares God's work of fulfilling his promise.

This Jesus, discussed in verses 22–24, is the one whom God raised from the dead. Here the verb used is ἀνίστημι (*anistēmi*, to raise), which appears 108 times in the NT, with 72 occurrences in Luke-Acts (27 times in Luke and 45 in Acts). A few of these occurrences in Acts refer to Jesus's resurrection (2:24; 3:26; 10:41; 13:32–33; 17:31; see discussion of 2:24). The phrase τοῦτον τὸν Ἰησοῦν (*touton ton Iēsoun*, this Jesus), placed at the start of the sentence, is emphatic (Bruce 1990: 126). Peter preaches the very Jesus who has been crucified, the Jesus many think is dead and perhaps to be forgotten.

The theme of witnesses (μάρτυρες, *martyres*) to the resurrection reaches back to Luke 24:48 and Acts 1:8 (see the discussion in 1:8). Peter's point is that the resurrection is neither an idea the apostolic witnesses (note the plural "we") created nor a myth nor a fabrication. Later rabbinic material argues that heaven watches what witnesses say (*t. Šebu.* 3.2; Le Cornu and Shulam 2003: 117). Rather, the resurrection is something the apostolic witnesses experienced and know to be true, and so they can speak to its reality. All the Gospel accounts of resurrection show that it was not anticipated or immediately believed by the apostles. The earliest available source testimony to the resurrection is in 1 Cor. 15:3–5. In that passage, reflecting the early church tradition, the resurrection is treated in parallelism, as an event equal in stature and form to Jesus's dying and being buried, with the proof being the appearances of various sorts. In other words, in this piece of early tradition, the resurrection is a historical fact like the death and burial, not an interpretation of an event. The resurrection is not a symbol or a metaphor for anything; it was a real event that changed the direction of the witnesses' lives. That is precisely the point Peter makes here. Witnesses exist to underscore the resurrection's reality. Its reality points to God's work and vindication, the significance of which follows in verses 33–36. It is a little unclear to what the apostles are witnesses, because the term οὗ (*hou*) can mean "of whom" (referring to a person) or "of what" (referring to a thing). The grammatical ambiguity is in fact quite clear conceptually. The witness is one who has seen Jesus in his resurrected state as shown in Acts 1:22. At this point in the speech, it is the resurrection of Jesus that is highlighted, so a neuter ("thing") referent is slightly more likely. But in a way, the grammatical choice does not make a difference, since it is the resurrection of Jesus that is the point of the witness. There is a kind of syllogism here: (1) The Messiah will rise from the dead as Scripture shows. (2) But God raised Jesus. (3) Therefore Jesus is the Messiah.

2:33   What happened as a result of the resurrection? The verse begins with "therefore" (οὖν, *oun*) to make the application. Peter makes three points, the first two of which set up the third. (1) Jesus was exalted to/by the right hand of God—language that alludes to Ps. 110:1 and sets up the citation of the psalm in verses 34–35. (2) He received from the Father the promise of the Spirit. In light of what Luke already has taught in Luke-Acts, this affirmation points to the realization of the messianic promise (Luke 3:16–17; 24:49; Acts 1:4–5). Jesus serves as an active figure in salvation and a mediator of God's blessing that leads to salvation and righteousness. The distribution of the Spirit is a messianic executive act (Turner 1996: 303–6) that is also in part an act to restore Israel to the fullness promised in the end (1996: 297–302). (3) As a result, Jesus has poured out what the audience sees and hears, that is, the gift of the Spirit. The aorist verb form of ἐκχέω (*ekcheō*) recalls the verb in Acts 2:17 (in the Joel 3 citation) and links the two passages in another example of Jewish *gezerah shewa* (on the verb and the idea it expresses, see the Acts 2:17 discussion and the treatment of Acts 2:20, where the technique is defined). Jesus has now done what Joel promises. Thus the Spirit's outpouring fulfills the promise pointing to the last days and to the Messiah's mediation of salvation from God's side. Indeed, we may well have here a genitive of association: the promise is the Spirit (Robertson 1934: 498).

Two issues concern the mention of the Spirit: (1) In what sense does the Spirit function for Luke: as a figure that initiates into the community (Dunn 1970: 38–54), as the Spirit of prophecy (Menzies 1991; Turner 1996), as a replacement for the giving of the law at Sinai (Kremer 1973: 14–24; already discussed above in 2:1), or as some combination of these (Wenk 2000: 253 includes a "renewed status with God")? (2) Is the background to this text Davidic-royal, is it filled with Sinai and second-Moses motifs, or is it a combination of these?

Regarding the first question, that a combination of initiation into community and Spirit empowerment tied to proclamation in mission is in view can be seen in the combination of Lukan texts introducing the idea of the Spirit's coming, which Acts 2 describes. Luke 3:7–17 has John the Baptist introduce the idea of the Spirit's coming in a context where the ethical preparation of the people is stressed. The Baptist expresses the hope given that the Messiah will do even more to bring about an era where God's people honor God. This points to an initiation or at least the end of a period of transition that enables those who respond to God to carry out God's call. Luke 24:49 and Acts 1:8, on the other hand, look to a distribution of power that fuels mission. The Spirit's filling work also tends to highlight proclamation, as Acts 2:9–11, 17–18 shows. The "Spirit of prophecy" here looks to involve declaring the acts of God through Jesus, something the church does today because of the testimony that the Spirit left with that first generation.

As to whether Davidic-royal or Sinai-Moses themes dominate, it is clear that the psalms chosen to present Jesus in Acts 2 are royal and messianic. They are also traces of Sinai hope, in that the Spirit's coming on all evokes Num. 11:29 and the possible allusion to the ascension may come from Ps. 68:18 in Acts 2:33, which also has Sinai roots. Claims of other Sinai motifs, however, such as the use of flame, smoke, and fire (so Turner 1996: 285–89; Wenk 2000: 249–50), are overdrawn, as Menzies (1991: 229–41) shows that these images come from passages outside the Sinai tradition as well. This more general imagery simply points to a theophany, something that Sinai also has, but is not unique to it. Menzies also highlights the lack of distinctive Sinai elements in Acts 2. Wedderburn (1994: 31–39) correctly notes the contacts with Sinai but also makes the point that Luke does nothing with this theme. Wedderburn distinguishes between what the tradition taught and Luke used and what Luke himself teaches. More important to us is that what Moses expresses in Num. 11:29 is a hope that is not a part of his period and that he did not supply. Thus, Acts 2, if it invokes Sinai, does so more by contrast than by comparison.

In other words, Jesus would in this case be a prophet *unlike* Moses, which is not a point of the normal Sinai-Moses view. When this observation is combined with the explicit multiple invocation of David and promise, the dominant image is Davidic and messianic, as the conclusion in 2:36 also shows. At most, the Sinai parallels point to a theme of God's active presence to deliver, speak, and do powerful works.

So Luke's treatment contains a new-exodus dimension and a deliverance point, but it does not reach the level of making an explicit christological association with Moses. Wenk (2000: 250) argues that "signs and wonders" in Acts 2:19 do evoke a period like the exodus, but only 7:36 moves beyond the use of this generic formula (2:43; 4:30; 5:12; 14:3; 15:12). Still, the generic phrase in the LXX often evokes the exodus acts of deliverance by God (many of the fifty-two occurrences deal with this event). On the other hand, Luke is quite capable of being explicit about Mosaic parallels when he wishes to be, as Acts 3:14–26 and 7:37 show. There is nothing like this in Acts 2. So any Sinai imagery is present not because of some deeply structured Lukan christological point but because of some parallel and contrast with the exodus period in general and with its description of divine activity. Even such exodus imagery, however, is subordinate to Davidic themes in this chapter. Thus exodus-deliverance imagery may well be present in Acts 2, but explicit exodus-Mosaic emphases will appear in Acts 3. It may also well be that whatever Sinai connections exist are a reflection of Lukan sources, not material Luke is highlighting.

The presentation of Christology in Acts 2 hits a crucial point in verses 32–34 and the mention of the ascension to God's right hand. It is disputed whether τῇ δεξιᾷ (*tē dexia*) means "to the right hand" or "by the right hand." Barrett (1994: 149) and Bruce (1988a: 66; 1990: 126) prefer "by" the right hand (so Ps. 118:16 [117:16 LXX][14] and Odes Sol. 25.9), but this seems to ignore the contextual backdrop of Ps. 110:1 in verse 34, which is connected to the occurrence of this term here and points to locale, not means. The expression also is an allusion to verse 30 and seating one on a throne (so correctly BDF §199; Haenchen 1987: 183n1; Conzelmann 1987: 30; Pesch 1986a: 124; Schneider 1980: 275; see Acts

---

14. The LXX reads, "The right hand of the Lord raised me up," in contrast to the MT's "the right hand of Yahweh is exalted."

5:31; conceptually, Heb. 1:3; 12:2). As important as the resurrection is to show that Jesus is alive and vindicated, it is even more significant as an indication of where Jesus went (to God's right hand, to God's presence) and what he does from there (giving the gift of the Spirit). Psalm 68:18 (67:19 LXX) may be in view here conceptually (see Eph. 4:8–10, with its allusion to the gifts of the Spirit). The right hand is the place of favor (1 Kings 2:19; 1 Chron. 6:39; Neh. 8:4; 1 Esd. 4:29; 9:43; Johnson 1992: 52). God's right hand is especially prominent in the OT (Exod. 15:6; LXX of Pss. 17:36 [18:35 Eng.]; 25:10 [26:10 Eng.]; 43:4 [44:3 Eng.]; 97:1 [98:1 Eng.]) and the NT (Luke 22:69; Acts 7:55–56; Rom. 8:34; Eph. 1:20; Col. 3:1; Heb. 1:3, 13; 8:1; 10:12; 12:2; 1 Pet. 3:22 [all as a locale]).

In John's Gospel, Jesus promised to mediate the Spirit (14:16, 26; 16:7). The promise "of the Spirit" (τοῦ πνεύματος, *tou pneumatos*) is an epexegetical genitive (Schneider 1980: 275n113); the promise is the Spirit. The outpouring is now what the crowd is witnessing. The promise realized is what they see and hear (Luke 7:22; 10:23–24; Acts 8:6; 28:26–27). Luke often alludes to promises made to the fathers of old that the events associated with Jesus fulfill (Luke 1:55, 73; Acts 2:39; 3:13, 25; 7:17; 13:23, 32; 26:6). Jesus's resurrection-ascension has led to all of this activity involving the Spirit. Jesus functions as the "middle" figure in God's blessing, as the Father directs to and through him. This is not so much subordinationism (*pace* Jervell 1998: 149) as associative work in the capacity of a mediator who shares God's presence and glorious position.

Peter now turns to his third full OT citation, Ps. 110:1, an important   **2:34–35** proof text throughout the NT that also appeared in Luke 20:42–43.[15] Dodd (1953: 35) calls Ps. 110:1 a "fundamental" text of the early church's preaching.[16] The wording here matches the LXX (109:1) except for the possible exclusion of ὁ (*ho*) before the first use of κύριος (*kyrios*, Lord) in the citation (see additional note). The point made from the psalm differs slightly from the earlier citation of Ps. 110:1 in Luke 20:42–43. There the concern was to raise a question about how the Messiah could be called David's son if David called him Lord. The point was that the lordship of the messianic figure was as important as being David's son. That conclusion, however, was left more as an implication than as an explicit affirmation in Luke's Gospel. In these verses in Acts, Peter makes the explicit point that the resurrection indicates Jesus's position at the Father's right hand, as the one who is seated at God's side. From this place of honor and unique glory, Jesus mediates the blessing of the Spirit

15. For discussion of Ps. 110 and Luke's use in that context, see Bock 1996: 1635–40; see also Matt. 22:44; 26:64; Mark 14:62; Luke 22:69; Rom. 8:34; 1 Cor. 15:25; Eph. 1:20; Col. 3:1; Heb. 1:3, 13; 5:6; 8:1; 10:12. On Ps. 110 and the NT, see Hay 1973.

16. On the hermeneutics applied here, which parallels how Ps. 16 is used, i.e., as a regal text that is ultimately not about David but about Jesus, see Bock 1987: 129–32, 185–86.

and salvation in accord with the promise of God's plan. This reveals who Jesus is. It is Christology of the highest level, tightly associating Jesus with God's unique glory.

That locale is a major topic is clear from the way the passage is introduced (*pace* Jervell 1998: 149, who says locale is not stressed). Luke records the affirmation by an explanatory use of γάρ (*gar*)—"for" it was not David who ascended into heaven (οὐ, *ou*, more likely goes by word position with David, not the verb). Like the point made about David's being buried, this detail says that David cannot be the ultimate referent for the psalm's language. In addition there is a word link involving the terms rendered "right hand" (δεξιᾷ, *dexia*/δεξιῶν, *dexiōn*) between verses 33 and 34. The idea of sitting (κάθου, *kathou*) looks back to the promise of the descendant who is appointed (καθίσαι, *kathisai*) to sit on the throne of David in verse 30. This is accomplished by the word link, or *gezerah shewa*, technique, which is repeatedly used throughout the speech (see vv. 17, 33 [poured out]; vv. 27, 31 [hades]; vv. 21, 36 [Lord]; vv. 26, 31 [flesh]; vv. 27, 31 [abandoned]; vv. 27, 31 [corruption]; vv. 33, 34 [right hand]; vv. 21, 40 [save(d)]). Thus the Messiah is the Christ and Lord (v. 36) who shares exercise of authority with God, an activity that will continue until the job of subjugating God's enemies is done, the point of verse 35. The idea of ultimate subjugation is not developed here but appears in 1 Cor. 15:20–28. As with the citations of Joel 3 and Ps. 16, Peter is pointing to a text that has already begun to be realized. Scripture explains and even proclaims the way of the Messiah that Jesus walked.

The implication of this text is great, because for most in Judaism no person is able to sit permanently in God's presence. God's glory and person are too unique to allow this. Only two texts even entertain this possibility, the slightly later Son of Man texts of 1 Enoch and a ca. 250 BC text in Ezekiel the Tragedian, *Exagoge* (lines 68–89), where Moses has a dream picturing his authority as "god to Pharaoh" (Exod. 7:1) during the exodus. At the end, the Son of Man in 1 Enoch possesses authority to judge from God's side. It is worth remembering that Jesus preferred to call himself Son of Man. In *Exagoge*, Moses is clearly seen in a figurative and noneschatological manner, so his example is not directly relevant.[17] The observation that Jesus has gone to God's side, although it is expressed figuratively since God does not have a limited location or a right hand, led to a high Christology, since it raises the question of who can sit in God's presence. Who is holy enough to do so? This description of Jesus's position suggests an intimate connection between Jesus and the Father and an equality between them. The vindication of Jesus is about more than that he lives and others will be raised. It explains who

17. Bock 1998a has details on all of these Jewish texts and all the other texts that raise the themes of exaltation and blasphemy in Judaism, from the OT to the Talmud.

Jesus is and how God showed him to be the Lord Christ. Here the title "Lord" has its full, heavenly authority because of Jesus's position.

It is sometimes suggested that such a Christology emerged late in the early church or that the argument could have been made only from the Greek LXX (with many others, Jervell 1998: 149n257). But all the LXX did was render the MT while respecting the unique name of God. The MT clearly distinguishes between Yahweh and David's 'ādôn (Lord). Yet, in Second Temple Judaism, Jews did not pronounce God's personal name but replaced it with a form of "Lord," whether in Aramaic, Hebrew, or Greek, as the LXX did in its written form. Qumran shows that they may have inserted dots or an abbreviation to have the same effect of not pronouncing the sacred name (Isaiah Scroll at Qumran; Byington 1957: 57–58). Thus, orally rendering the MT would produce a reading like that in the LXX. What is important here is not just the use of "Lord" as a shared term but the event context in which the text was viewed. So this argument about "late" development is not adequate (*pace* Conzelmann 1987: 21; Schneider 1980: 276).

Everything necessary to make the conclusion that Jesus is the Lord was in place as a result of the resurrection. Thus there is no need to insist that this is a later development. Between the resurrection and the ascension, all the factors to make this conclusion were in place, generating reflection about where Jesus might be as a result of resurrection and what that unique position would mean about Jesus. Sharing God's unique glory points to Jesus's unique, divine position as Messiah, Lord, and Son. Nor is adoptionism present. Jesus did not become Lord but was shown to be Lord through the resurrection-ascension (see Rom. 1:2–4). As verses 21, 36–38 suggest, the "Lord" to be called upon is Jesus—and only God saves (Larkin 1995: 57). He is Lord of all (Acts 10:36; Witherington 1998: 147–53: "It was not that Jesus became *someone* different from who he was before, but that he entered a new stage in his career, or assumed new roles after the ascension" [149]).

Peter draws the combined scriptural argument to a conclusion (οὖν, *oun*). He now believes that the case is made, and so he can bring assurance to them.[18] The audience is explicitly "the entire house of Israel" (πᾶς οἶκος Ἰσραήλ, *pas oikos Israēl*; Moulton and Turner 1963: 200, on anarthrous πᾶς). The expression "house of Israel" is common in the NT (Matt. 10:6; 15:24; Acts 7:42; Heb. 8:8; 10) and the LXX (Lev. 10:6; Num. 20:29; 1 Sam. 7:2–3; 2 Sam. 3:12; 1 Kings 12:23; Jer. 9:25; Ezek. 37:11; and the Jewish prayer the Qaddish; Bruce 1988a: 67n89). The

2:36

---

18. For the term ἀσφαλῶς (*asphalōs*, assuredly), Mark 14:44, Acts 16:23, and this text constitute the three NT occurrences, but the term is very close to Luke 1:4 conceptually. Schneider 1980: 276n123 notes that the root for "assurance" is used fifteen times in the NT and eight times in Luke-Acts; also Schneider, *EDNT* 1:175; Wis. 18:6.

Jews present, mostly those of Jerusalem, are addressed, but they represent the entire nation and what it should now know as a result of these recent events.

The conclusion is that the one "you have crucified" (v. 23) is the one whom God has made Lord and Christ. In this context, the verb ποιέω (*poieō*, make) means that God has shown or established or brought about something by his action (BDAG 840 §2hβ). The idea here is of a designation or role that God has made evident, much as Rom. 1:3–4 argues.

The order of the christological titles is important (κύριον αὐτὸν καὶ χριστόν, *kyrion auton kai christon*) because "Lord" is in the forward and emphatic position. It is the key title, as verses 21 and 34 connect it to the reference to "Lord" in Ps. 110:1 and Joel 3:5 (2:32 Eng.). The Lord to be called upon is Jesus Christ, as it is in his name that they are to be baptized (v. 38). The title "Lord" was used by Palestinian Jews as a title for Yahweh, as is now attested in numerous sources.[19] The point about Jewish sources is important, for it shows that the language is not exclusively Greek and the concept is not exclusively Hellenistic, as some claim. The term "Lord" in this context shows in particular Jesus's lordship over salvation and the distribution of salvation's benefits. Jesus as "Lord" often appears in Acts (4:33; 8:16; 11:17, 20; 15:11, 26; 16:31; 19:5, 13, 17; 20:21, 24, 35; 21:13; 28:31). The sharing of the title with God led the church to apply to Jesus OT passages that were about Yahweh, as Acts 2:21 shows. Similarly the uses of Isa. 45:23 in Phil. 2:10 and of Isa. 8:13 in 1 Pet. 3:15 reflect the same hermeneutical move, indicating that it was common in the church (Bruce 1988a: 68n92; also as a title, 1 Cor. 8:4–6; Rom. 10:9; 1 Cor. 12:3). The resurrection shows that Jesus's authority is one that God attests to be equal to God's own (on the debate over whether this is adoptionism, see the previous verse).

"Christ" is a key title for Luke (Luke 2:11, 26; 3:15; 4:41; 9:20; 20:41; 22:67; 23:2, 35, 39; 24:26, 46; Acts 2:31, 36, 38; 3:6, 18, 20; 4:10, 26; 5:42; 8:5, 12; 9:22, 34; 10:36, 48; 11:17; 15:26; 16:18; 17:3; 18:5, 28; 24:24; 26:23; 28:31; Jones 1970: 69–76). The Christ is the figure of deliverance. God raised Jesus to come directly into God's presence in heaven. The very one the Jewish leaders crucified is the unique, anointed one whom God placed at his side. This point is made to establish their guilt and need to repent (vv. 37–38). "The crucifixion of one who shares the throne of God is a sin against God" (Barrett 1994: 152). On this point, Peter ends his address and leaves the audience to react.

19. See Fitzmyer 1998: 260; 1979: 115–42; Fitzmyer, *EDNT* 2:328–31; 11QtgJob 24.6–7; 1QapGen 20.12–13; 4QEn[b] 1.4.5; 11QPs[a] 28.7–8; Josephus, *Ant.* 20.4.2 §90; T. Levi 18.2; 1 En. 10.9. The Aramaic form also shows early usage in the church: 1 Cor. 16:22 ("Come, Lord"); Did. 10.6.

In sum, Peter's speech proclaims that the distribution of the Spirit is the sign of the last days, the movement to the day of the Lord, the fulfillment of God's promise, and, most important, the indication that Jesus is vindicated, so that this crucified one now sits at God's side, mediating God's salvific blessing as both Lord and Christ. Scripture shows this, as Joel 3 (2 Eng.) is linked to Ps. 16, then to Ps. 132, and finally to Ps. 110. To understand who Jesus is, one must look to both what God did and what Scripture says. The speech highlights that it is God who acted through Jesus. God pours out the Spirit (v. 17), worked miracles through Jesus (v. 22), and then raised and exalted him (vv. 24, 32–33), thereby showing Jesus to be Lord and Christ (v. 36; Weiser 1981: 94). One cannot think of God's activity without thinking of Jesus, and Jesus cannot be who he is without the work of God. The unity of their work is affirmed in the speech.

The speech thus shows how God's activity through Jesus stands at the core of the Christian message. Jesus's resurrection means far more than merely that there is life after death. It is a vindication of Jesus's life and mission, a demonstration that Jesus lives and still rules, and a reflection that Jesus is a unique person, sharing the precious presence and glory of God in a unique way. Christ's death led to Christ's victory and rule (Fernando 1998: 108–9). The reality of the resurrection transformed the apostles from those who were timid to those who were bold to share Jesus with others. Peter also makes clear that the sin of rejecting God's unique messenger stands at the base of why Jesus had to die and that forgiveness and the Spirit are what the gospel offers, as the next unit will show. The Spirit's central place in the promise of God also is highlighted here. The Spirit is the evidence that Jesus is raised and reigns with God. The believer's changed life is a testimony to Jesus's current activity in the world and enables the mission. So God works through the Son and gives the Spirit. Undergirding the salvation message is the united work of Father, Son, and Spirit.

Additional Notes

2:16. In this verse, D and Irenaeus lack a reference to Joel, but the naming of the prophet is too well attested to exclude.

2:16–21. There are twelve small textual issues in these verses (for detailed discussion of each, see Bock 1987: 158–61). Most of the differences are reflected in Codex D. By far the most important of the differences occur in verse 17, where B and 076 with the LXX and the MT read μετὰ ταῦτα (*meta tauta*, after these things) instead of ἐν ταῖς ἐσχάταις ἡμέραις (*en tais eschatais hēmerais*, in the last days), which is read by the rest of the MSS, including ℵ, A, and D. The latter reading is the more difficult, deviating as it does from the Hebrew and Greek. Nor is there anything in the eschatology expressed here that does not match Lukan eschatology (*pace* Haenchen 1954: 162; Haenchen 1987: 179). The "day of the Lord" allusion fits with Luke (Mussner 1966: 263–65). So the text uses "in the last days" to explain the timing of Pentecost and where it fits in God's plan.

On how the text in Acts compares with the MT and the LXX, see Bock 1987: 161–64, who notes seven changes from the LXX, two of which are very significant—the addition of the phrase "says God" within the citation at verse 17 and the repetition of "they shall prophesy" at the end of verse 18, pointing to the work of the Spirit as one of revelatory proclamation. There are two small differences from the MT as well. All the changes are noted above in the exposition. The argument from this citation does not depend on the LXX and therefore is not reflective of a tradition that postdates the setting Luke gives it (*pace* Conzelmann 1987: 19; see Bock 1987: 161–66).

2:25–28. The citation of Ps. 16 reflects the LXX (Ps. 15), leading some to regard the text as late and reflective of a Hellenistic church context (so Conzelmann 1987: 20). The conceptual case could have been made, however, from the Semitic text (Bock 1987: 172–78). There are six differences between the LXX and the MT. (1) "Set before" in verse 8 of the MT version of the psalm is read as "see before" in the LXX. (2) "My glory" in verse 9 is rendered as "my tongue" for reasons that are not clear, except for perhaps the theme of rejoicing. (3) "Sheol" in verse 10 is rendered by the equivalent Greek concept of "hades." None of these differences is significant to the meaning. Three other changes are more important. (4) "In security" in verse 9 is changed to "in hope," a slightly more vivid but conceptually similar image. (5) "The pit" in verse 10 is changed to "corruption." The move is from a description of the place to what happens there, again an image that clarifies. (6) "The life well pleasing to God" in verse 11 becomes "way of life," an idiom for "eternal life" in Greek. This is not so much a change as it is a move to an expression that idiomatically had additional resonances in Greek. The key here is change 5 in this list. Does "to see the pit" mean to avoid an early death whereas "to see corruption" points to resurrection? Or is the expression somewhat open, leading simply to a statement of confidence in God's deliverance, with the nature of that deliverance not specified? Part of the answer may come in the genre of the text as a part of the Psalter. The psalm is not merely highlighting the psalmist's particular experience; it is also affirming the example of that experience, namely, that the righteous one may trust in God, be confident in God's protection, and know his deliverance is sure. The psalmist's point about his experience is that God protects from death. As a representative text in a representative genre, it is less about the particular manner in which that protection comes. Placed in the Psalter, the experience is generic for what it teaches about God, but the particular experience is exemplary, a prime example of how God protects. Most likely, the psalm is being used in this latter typological way, with Jesus's immediate resurrection being a unique realization of this text.

One need not have the LXX text to make the point. Although some make this claim and therefore argue that the tradition represented here is later than the earliest church, this conclusion is not demanded by the text's conceptualization. Bock (1987: 172–81) treats this question in detail and argues that the conceptualization of the psalm in the manner in which Peter understands it could emerge from a Semitic Jewish Christian setting. Williams (1990: 52) says that the rabbis read Ps. 16:9 this way for David but does not specify the text. His appeal may be to the later Midrash Psalms 16 §10 [62a].[20] The parallel to David may well have opened up the text to application to the Messiah. Peter will later argue that the psalm cannot ultimately be about David and so must be about another (stressed by Bruce 1988a: 124). All this may mean that the psalm is true of Jesus in a way it is not true of David. The psalm has a unique application to Jesus, given that Jesus is the ultimate example of the pattern, escaping death through a permanent and unique exaltation to God's right hand.

20. Str-B 2:618 shows that the psalm was read as God saying that his glory exalted over King Messiah and that David, according to one rabbi, did not see the worm (experience decay).

2:30. Various textual variants in 2:30 show the influence of christological concerns about the language of this text. The mention of the Christ according to the flesh is designed to make clear that the deity of Jesus is not compromised by what Peter says. These variants do not reflect the original wording of Acts. They occur with a variety of wordings and reflect later theological concerns of MSS such as D, Ψ, and Byz. A reference to "womb" and not "loins" in this verse in a few Western MSS (some Syriac and the Latin of Irenaeus, but not D) is motivated to bring verbal agreement with Ps. 131:11 LXX (132:11 Eng.) but also is weakly attested.

2:31. The MSS Byz, E, and Ψ add a reference to "his soul" not being abandoned to hades, to create a parallelism to his flesh in the second half of the verse and to reflect what was said in verse 27, but the addition is not well enough attested to be original. These MSS plus D also have a variant, a more classical spelling of "hades" (ᾅδου, *hadou*), but this, too, is not original, as it lacks wide, early attestation.

2:34. It is hard to know if the definite article ὁ (*ho*) is to be read before the first use of κύριος (*kyrios*) in the citation. For the inclusion are 𝔓[74], ℵ[2], A, B[2], C, E, Ψ, and Byz. Against it are ℵ*, B*, and D. The omission does not match the LXX and so is a more difficult reading. It is unclear if the article is original, which explains the brackets in the NA[27] text. Its inclusion or omission has no impact on the text's meaning.

3. The Reaction: Repent and Receive the Promised Gift (2:37–41)

This is the third part of the Pentecost account. The event (vv. 1–13) and Peter's explanation that the Spirit's coming shows Jesus's exaltation as Lord Christ (vv. 14–36) produces a reaction. The convinced crowd asks how they can respond. Peter calls them to repent and be baptized; their identifying with their need for Jesus will yield forgiveness of sins and the gift of the Spirit (v. 38). In a sense, salvation and the gospel can be summarized as new life lived in the context of God's forgiveness and the provision of God's Spirit. This is the gospel, the good news, of the church. In other NT contexts, this turning to Jesus is called faith. Peter then explains that this promise of forgiveness and the Spirit is for everyone, near and far, whom God has called. In a final exhortation, Peter urges them to save themselves from the crooked generation, an allusion to the judgment of the day of the Lord he mentioned in the speech (vv. 39–40 alluding back to vv. 19–20). The call to repent is a success, as three thousand respond, receiving the word, and are baptized, turning to devote themselves to the apostles' teaching, fellowship, the breaking of bread, and prayer (vv. 41–42). Jesus's call to mission, a central theme in Acts, is beginning to be realized. God is forming the new, Spirit-restored community of the now emerging last-days era.

Exegesis and Exposition

[37]Having heard this, they were cut to the heart and so they said to Peter and the rest of the apostles, "What shall we do, brothers?" [38]And Peter said to them, "Repent, and be baptized each one of you in the name of Jesus Christ for forgiveness of your sins and you shall receive the gift, the Holy Spirit. [39]For to you and to your children and to those far off is the promise, to whomever the Lord our God calls to him." [40]And with many other words he testified to and kept exhorting them, saying, "Be saved from this twisted generation." [41]So those who received his word were baptized, and there was added that day about three thousand souls.

2:37   The crowd is deeply impressed by Peter's words. Indeed, they are cut to the heart (κατενύγησαν τὴν καρδίαν, *katenygēsan tēn kardian*). This expression appears only here in the NT, and the same is true of the verb (κατανύσσομαι, *katanyssomai*). The verb refers to a sharp pain or a stab, often associated with emotion (BAGD 415; BDAG 523; Balz, *EDNT* 2:265;

"cut to the heart" in RSV, ESV; "acutely distressed" in NET; "pierced to the heart" in NASB, HCSB; "convicted them deeply" in NLT; "pricked in their heart" in KJV. The phrase may well allude to Ps. 109:16 (108:16 LXX), but only in paralleling its language (Marshall 1980: 80). This psalm has already appeared in Acts 1:20b. The verb covers a range of emotions in the OT: anger (Gen. 34:7), silence (Lev. 10:3), being struck by something (Sir. 12:12), being humbled (Ps. 108:16 LXX [109:16 Eng.]), and having sorrow (Gen. 27:38; Johnson 1992: 57). Polhill (1992: 116) notes that the verb is used in Homer of horses stomping the earth with their hooves. Luke's remark about the heart shows the sincerity and depth of the audience's response (Barrett 1994: 153). "Heart" is a distributive singular; each heart is in view (Moulton and Turner 1963: 23).

The crowd is convinced and wishes to know what to do, a question that recalls an earlier crowd's reaction to John the Baptist in a scene unique to Luke's Gospel (Luke 3:10, 12, 14; also, in various ways, Acts 3:19; 5:31; 8:22; 11:18; 13:24; 17:30; 19:4; 20:21; 26:20, where reactions to remarks appear or are called for from the audience). Moved by an emotional and ethical concern, the crowd senses the need to respond to this message. Peter's answer will be distinct from the earlier response of the Baptist, for now Jesus's ministry has taken place, and responding to him becomes the main point, especially since the issue is the role they had in crucifying the Messiah, as Peter charges (vv. 23, 36). The apostles are respectfully called brothers in a phrase Acts has already used several times (ἄνδρες ἀδελφοί, *andres adelphoi*; see 1:16). Here, in a gender-specific manner, it refers to the Twelve.

This verse presents Peter's response to the question of how the crowd   **2:38**
must react. Whereas verse 36 is the theological conclusion of the speech, here is the application. It has three basic parts: (1) repent, (2) be baptized each one of you in the name of Jesus Christ for the forgiveness of sins, and (3) you shall receive the gift of the Spirit (another epexegetical genitive; the gift is the Spirit; see v. 33). Thus, within his response, Peter presents forgiveness and the Spirit as the principal gifts of God that Jesus provides; he is the entryway into a life with God. Each point calls for specific attention here.

Peter states that the proper response to his message is to repent. The exhortation is expressed as an aorist imperative (μετανοήσατε, *metanoēsate*; BDAG 640 §2). Repentance indicates a turning in direction (in the LXX, see Amos 7:3, 6; Joel 2:13–14; Jer. 4:28; Johnson 1992: 57; also Wis. 11:23; 12:19; Fitzmyer 1998: 265). In this context, it means to make a conscious turn toward God and God's actions through Jesus. This verb appears five times in Acts (2:38; 3:19; 8:22; 17:30; 26:20). It is one of Luke's favorite terms to describe how one should respond to the offer of forgiveness, and he often connects it to forgiveness (Acts 2:38; 3:19; 5:31; 8:22; 26:18, 20; Luke 3:3; 24:47). The Greek word can mean "change one's mind." The idea in Hebrew, however, is "turn," indicating a change of direction. In Luke 24:47 Jesus makes clear that he is referring to the OT sense and that this is what the disciples are to preach.[1] Peter's declaration here is obedient to Jesus's commission and call in Luke 24. Peter is telling his audience to change direction from the attitudes that led them to crucify Jesus, and look to God through Jesus for forgiveness. In some texts in the NT, this act is said to be also part of the gift of God (Acts 5:31; 11:18; 2 Tim. 2:25). Marshall (1980: 80) points out that repentance and faith are two sides of the same coin. I would add that repentance stresses the starting point of the need for forgiveness whereas faith is the resulting trust and understanding that this forgiveness comes from God, the one turned to for the gift (Acts 20:21).

The call is for each one to be baptized in the name of Jesus Christ for the forgiveness of sins. This verse makes several points. First, although all are called upon to repent, each one is to participate individually in a rite of baptism. Despite later controversy about whether one must believe and be baptized in order to be saved, what Peter says here and in his own later epistle shows that the key is the response to God, not the rite per se. This response and its cleansing effect are what the rite signifies. The act of baptism portrays a washing and signifies what repentance produces, cleansing. Peter explains this himself in the very revealing words of 1 Pet. 3:21: "Baptism, which corresponds to this, now saves you, *not as the removal of dirt from the body* but *as an appeal to God for a clear conscience*, through the resurrection of Jesus Christ" (italics added). In other words, it is not the act but the attitude behind it that has the efficacy of yielding forgiveness. Bruce (1990: 129) notes that the Greek term for "repent" often renders a term in Hebrew (*nāḥam*) that means "comfort oneself," indicating the result of what coming to God does. In Jewish thinking, where the context of clean and unclean is common, the washing imagery points to a cleansing that makes one clean so that God can be present, since uncleanness means that one cannot draw near to God. In the present context, the baptismal washing that comes with repentance signifies an inner cleansing that allows the person to be indwelt by the Spirit. How this material connects to the other baptismal texts in Acts is part of an important study by Friedrich Avemarie (2002).[2]

1. As a result, NLT has "each of you must turn from your sins and turn to God," a rendering that may be too particular—"turn from sin and turn to God" might be better, lest one think that every sin must be dealt with consciously ahead of time in order for one to be saved.

2. This work is a very detailed tradition history of all the baptism narratives in Acts. The study covers Acts 2:1–47; 8:4–25; 8:26–40; 9:18; 10:1–11:18; 16:14–15, 30–34; 18:8; 19:1–7; 22:16. He sees much of this material as historically rooted and having "high worth"

The person who turns toward God calls on the name of the Lord by being baptized "in the name of Jesus Christ." This phrase reflects the language of the speech in Acts 2:21, "calling on the name of the Lord to be saved." So Peter's remarks draw upon what he has already proclaimed in Acts 2. The rite is not magical but represents and pictures what repentance is asking God to do, to give forgiveness (Acts 5:31; 10:43; 13:38; 26:18). To agree to baptism is to affirm in a public act what the heart has already done to come into relationship with God. "Baptism is a natural part of the much more important conversion" and a "self-evident expression of conversion" (Schweizer, *TDNT* 6:413–14). Thus, baptism is the representation of the cleansing that belongs to salvation. This washing signifies the forgiveness of sins that Jesus brings and the emergence into a new, clean life with fresh enablement that his work provides (Rom. 6:1–11). Peter calls for each one to be baptized in order to express a personal, visible turning to God.

That baptism takes place in the name of Jesus Christ shows the authority Jesus has at God's side in heaven. Now one appeals to God through this formerly crucified one. One calls upon him to be saved, as stated in verse 21. This interchange between God the Father and the Christ as the one called upon shows the unity of the work between God and the Exalted One. The theme of the name of Jesus is frequent in Acts (3:6, 16; 4:10, 12, 17–18, 30; 5:28, 40–41; 8:12; 9:16, 21, 27, 28; 15:26; 16:18; 19:13, 17; 21:13; 22:16; 26:9). The meaning may be that baptism signifies that one is associated with Jesus as well, that is, is baptized "into" his name, but this is less certain. Fitzmyer (1998: 266) notes that the phrase in Greek has commercial overtones of ascribing something to someone. So salvation is acknowledged as rooted in the work of Jesus Christ. The name of Jesus may well have been confessed publicly at baptism (Acts 22:18; Rom. 10:9–13; 1 Cor. 8:5–6; 12:3; Bruce 1988a: 70). At the least, it was pronounced over the one being baptized (Jervell 1998: 150).

What this turning response leads to is, first of all, "for the forgiveness of your sins" (εἰς ἄφεσιν τῶν ἁμαρτιῶν ὑμῶν, *eis aphesin tōn hamartiōn hymōn*) or, better perhaps, the response comes "with a view to" or "on the basis of" forgiveness of sins (Moulton and Turner 1963: 266; Wallace 1996: 369–71). The term for "forgiveness" (ἄφεσις, *aphesis*) is not common in the NT, appearing only seventeen times, but ten of these are in Luke-Acts (Luke 1:77; 3:3; 4:18 [2x]; 24:47; Acts 2:38; 5:31; 10:43; 13:38; 26:18). It is a commercial term normally referring to the forgiveness of debt (BDAG 155 §2; MM 96). Virtually every passage where "forgiveness" appears is a summary of what Jesus's mission is about (Luke 3:3 is about how John the Baptist prepared for Jesus). God cleanses an unclean object by granting forgiveness so that indwelling and presence can become

---

(Avemarie 2002: 453), although he expresses himself most cautiously on Acts 2, seeing much of the account as reflecting Lukan terminology.

possible (i.e., the Spirit can enter in). As 3:19 shows, repentance, not the rite of baptism, leads to the blotting out of sin (Bruce 1988a: 70). Thus Peter moves directly from forgiveness to the gift of the Spirit.

The second key element in the gospel is the gift (δωρεάν, *dōrean*) that is the Spirit (an epexegetical genitive), already bestowed on those who have followed Jesus but now available as the sign of the new era to anyone who turns to embrace the call of God made through Jesus. In Acts 2:17 this is called the outpouring of the Spirit without discrimination. The Spirit falls on those who call on the name of the Lord for deliverance (see discussion there and at 1:5). At the core of the gospel is the offer of the gift of the Spirit and what the Spirit provides to the one who believes. Paul taught this as well in Rom. 1:16–17 and Rom. 6–8. It reflects core Christian orthodox teaching about the content of the gospel. All four references to a gift in Acts are to the giving of the Holy Spirit to those who respond to the preaching of the church (2:38; 8:20; 10:45; 11:17). In the Spirit is the enablement for new life and for sharing the new message, as Acts 2 itself has shown. The varying way in which the Spirit is distributed, especially on occasions without baptism (Acts 10:44; also Luke 24:47; Acts 3:19; 26:18 [forgiveness mentioned without baptism]), indicates how Spirit baptism signifies primarily the Spirit's washing and consequent presence, rather than representing an emphasis on tongues speaking as a required evidence of salvation or a "second" gift of salvation. In other words, one is baptized in the Spirit so that new life can come and flow forth from cleansing.

Polhill (1992: 117) discusses how εἰς (*eis*) can mean "for the purpose of" or "on the basis of," suggesting baptism is on the basis of the forgiveness of sins, but this is less than certain grammatically, given that this is not a common force for εἰς. Rather, baptism is simply to be associated with the forgiveness it pictures. He also correctly notes, however, that Luke's associating forgiveness simply with responding to Jesus is the more important point (also Acts 10:43; 13:38–39).[3] Repentance is the key response. It leads to public participation in the representative rite of baptism, as well as to the forgiveness that the rite signifies. Repentance also leads to receiving the Spirit.

2:39   The promise's scope is what Peter notes next. The promise certainly alludes back to the Spirit (vv. 33, 38) and possibly to forgiveness as well (v. 38). Barrett (1994: 155) speaks of a background to covenant promise. Bruce (1990: 130) discusses the covenant of grace as well as promises to Noah, Abraham, and David. The Spirit's presence, however, surely invokes the new covenant (so Fitzmyer 1998: 266, looking back to a discussion on 259; Joel 3:1–2 [2:28–29 Eng.]; Isa. 32:15; 44:3; Ezek. 11:19; 36:26–27;

---

3. See also Witherington 1998: 154, who says the issue of sequence is not important to Luke and notes the varying sequences for the Spirit's coming in Acts; *pace* Haenchen 1987: 184, who treats absence of the mention of baptism as the exception.

37:14). This promise is especially important for this Jewish audience and is what they need in light of their plight. The term ὑμῖν (*hymin*, for you) is placed forward in the verse for emphasis and is a good example of a dative of advantage.[4] The promise is also for their children (Ps. Sol. 8.33) and for those far off (Acts 13:33). The language "far off" (τοῖς εἰς μακράν, *tois eis makran*) echoes Isa. 57:19 and, in Peter's mind, possibly alludes to responding Diaspora Jews and God-fearers, since, until the vision in Acts 10, he does not think of Gentiles who are unconnected to Israel's God (Witherington 1998: 155–56; the sense of "far off" as describing distance can be seen through Acts 22:21 and Sir. 24:32). In the development of Luke, however, the expression looks to anyone who responds, which eventually would include Gentiles. The language reappears in Eph. 2:13, 17, where Gentiles are the subject. The "whoever" language of Peter's remark in the verse allows room for the expansion of the promise's scope as God's intention emerges. Thus the expression became a part of tradition to highlight that God's grace has no ethnic preference.

The passage ends with a note about God's direction in the process. The promise is for whomever God might call (προσκαλέσηται, *proskalesētai*). Acts 13:2 and 16:10 use this term with reference to a call for a specific ministry rather than generally of salvation, as here (conceptually, 13:48; 16:14). The entire speech has a dialectic—hearers call on the Lord for salvation (v. 21), and the Lord calls them to himself. The idea of the Lord calling echoes, to a degree, what was not cited from Joel 2:32b (3:5b LXX), and so the Joel passage is still present in the backdrop.

Luke has shared the key portions of the speech and now reports, as is **2:40** common in rhetorical contexts, that Peter said far more than is recorded, as he both testified (aorist) to them and was exhorting/encouraging (imperfect) them (Witherington 1998: 156; Polybius, *Hist.* 3.111.11; Xenophon, *Hellenica* 2.4.42). The verb διαμαρτύρομαι (*diamartyromai*) has the root *martyromai*, which means "witness." With a prefix, however, the term means "testify to [something]." Luke-Acts has ten of its fifteen NT occurrences (Luke 16:28; Acts 2:40; 8:25; 10:42; 18:5; 20:21; 23–24 [2x]; 23:11; 28:23). The verb for "exhort" (παρακαλέω, *parakaleō*) is common, appearing 109 times in the NT with 33 in Luke-Acts, 22 of which are in Acts. The difference in tense means that the speech as a whole is a testimony that includes exhortation throughout. The testimony concerns the facts included in the preaching as well as the exhortation to the audience to respond.[5]

4. BDF §189 prefers dative of possession, but since contingency is in view, a categorization that points to intention is better. In other words, only if they respond does the benefit come.

5. Barrett 1994: 156 argues that Luke has prepared the reader for the speech by statements made earlier about Jesus as Son of David (Luke 1:32), that the *kyrios* of Ps. 110:1

The call to be saved (by God through Jesus) is yet another word link in the speech (see v. 21, "shall be saved"; for a list of word links in Acts 2, see comments on vv. 34–35). The verb σώθητε (*sōthēte*) here is either middle or passive grammatically, but contextually a passive is better, since throughout the speech God is the main acting agent (also 2:47; Johnson 1992: 58). The deliverance is from this crooked or twisted generation. The warning about the fate of this generation alludes back to the mention of the day of the Lord and the judgment that comes at the end (vv. 19–21). The forgiveness that Peter's hearers would obtain by turning to Jesus will also deliver them from this judgment; this shows the spiritual dimensions of the Messiah's work. The reference to a "twisted generation" (τῆς γενεᾶς τῆς σκολιᾶς, *tēs geneas tēs skolias*) appears only here in the NT and alludes to a generation that is ethically crooked, spiritually off the path to God, and thus subject to judgment. With an ethical force, it refers to "social and ethical misconduct which is rooted in ungodliness and unbelief" (Bertram, *TDNT* 7:406–7). The full phrase does not appear in the LXX, but the shorter one without the articles is found in Deut. 32:5 and Ps. 78:8 (77:8 LXX). Both are allusions to the generation that wandered in the wilderness (Larkin 1995: 60; also in the NT, Phil. 2:15; conceptually, Luke 9:41; 11:29; Heb. 3:10; Marshall 1980: 82). Peter urges his audience to experience salvation and deliverance from the coming judgment.

2:41 The response to Peter is significant. About three thousand are baptized, and their "souls" (ψυχαί, *psychai*, i.e., people, reflecting the Hebrew *nepeš*; Bruce 1990: 131; Acts 3:23; 7:14; 27:37) are added to the saved. Jervell (1998: 151) has them added to the "flock of disciples" (*Jüngerschar*), as the church does not yet formally exist, and these are Jews who already belong to Israel. The term "souls" is a way to refer to a person, as a metonymy. The soul is part of the person and makes one a responding being, so it comes to stand for the person as a whole (BDAG 1099 §3), but as BDAG notes, in Greek the soul is not unique to humans but simply describes the nonflesh or nonmaterial aspect of a being.

Luke thus notes growth in the group from about 120 waiting for the Spirit to about 3,000. Bruce (1988a: 73) calls this an example of the "greater works" Jesus said the disciples would perform (John 14:12). The number is significant in a city that swelled to somewhere between 55,000 and 200,000 during feast time.[6] Witherington (1998: 156) notes the pools available in this area for baptism as a way to defend the unit's historicity. Here Luke calls the response "receiving his word" (ἀποδεξάμενοι τὸν λόγον αὐτοῦ, *apodexamenoi ton logon autou*). This

---

is the Messiah (Luke 20:41–44), and that the Son pours out the Spirit through the Father (Luke 2:49 with 24:49). See also Kilgallen 2002: 71–87.

6. Polhill 1992: 118 suggests that the population during feasts was 180,000–200,000. Marshall 1980: 82n1, citing Jeremias 1969a: 83n24, puts the feast's crowd at 55,000–95,000.

combination with the prefixed verb appears only here in the NT. In other texts, the verb "receive" appears without the prefix (Acts 8:13–14; 11:1; 17:11). This is yet another way to summarize the response to the gospel in this chapter. "Receive" goes along with "call on the name of the Lord" (v. 21) and "repent" (v. 38). Each expression points to a different dimension of the embrace of the gospel that saves (indeed, Codex D has "believed" here). Luke will add other descriptions as Acts proceeds. He also favors counts of respondents (2:47; 4:4; 5:14; 6:1, 7; 9:42; 11:24; 13:43; 14:1; 17:10–12; 21:20).

In sum, this concluding unit on Pentecost speaks to Peter's concise reply concerning how to respond to the gospel: repent and show this response by participating in a rite that symbolizes forgiveness and cleansing into life through Christ Jesus. This was the promise of God to all who are called, to all who respond. In addition, salvation means no judgment. Peter's effectiveness in his speech leads to the growth of the believing circle. Peter's focus is not only on what God provides in salvation but also on the identity of Jesus. The resurrection means that an exalted Jesus distributes the Spirit to those who turn to God. This focus on Jesus and what the resurrection means for him is part of what makes Peter's evangelistic effort so effective. People not only know what God is giving (the Spirit in new life on the basis of provided forgiveness) but also have the privilege of knowing and appreciating the work and greatness of the one through whom the gifts of life, forgiveness, and the Spirit come. So, for Luke, this access and offer are the announcement of the gospel. Salvation comes to the one who believes, repents, calls on the Lord's name, and receives the gospel. All four of these responses mean fundamentally the same thing: one has embraced God's grace through Jesus and the Spirit. In Acts the speech not only describes a gospel presentation that is full of important Christology, pneumatology, and soteriology; it also portrays the fact that an appropriate response to this gospel can be described in various parallel ways. This message of hope from God is what the church witnesses to as it calls all people to believe.

All of this assumes one thing: all humanity has a need before God that God himself must take care of in order to make things right. As Fernando (1998: 116–17) states, "Christianity is optimistic about grace, but pessimistic about human nature." Another way to say this is that Christianity is realistic about human nature. A glance at our own history shows the trail of destructiveness that calls for having respect toward God and the life God creates. Such human self-destruction demonstrates the need for transformation where God gives the necessary enablement and direction. One cannot have the gospel and its good news without letting people know about the bad news that is our fault and responsibility. The need for God, however, is not a bad thing. Rather, to need God and respond to God is an opportunity to share in the richness that turning one's life to God can bring. Peter preaches such hope. Out of the ashes from which resurrection emerges is a new life that rests in unending fellowship with God. Stott (1990: 80–81) speaks of the gospel as possessing four components: gospel events, gospel witnesses, gospel promises, and gospel conditions. Jesus's death and resurrection receive attestation from the prophets and apostles and from God's own actions on behalf of Jesus. But this promise is not conferred automatically. One must respond to it with a faith or turning that asks to receive what is promised. Having asked, one can trust God to provide it. After all, it is a promise that God gave much to fulfill.

C. Summary: Community Life (2:42–47)

This passage summarizes the life of the community both internally (v. 42) and with those outside (vv. 43–47). The early believers hold their possessions in common and also go to the temple, reflecting their embrace of the Messiah. This messianic faith has not caused them to separate from Jewish practice and worship. Their interaction and engagement with those outside has sparked even more growth. In Acts we never see a community turned so inward that taking the message to those outside and engaging with those outside is forgotten or ignored.

Exegesis and Exposition

⁴²And they were devoting themselves to the apostles' teaching ⌐ ⌐ and the fellowship, the breaking of bread and the prayers. ⁴³And fear came upon every soul; and many wonders and signs came through the apostles ⌐ ⌐. ⁴⁴And all those who ⌐believed⌐ were together and having all things in common. ⁴⁵And they were selling their possessions and goods and were distributing them to all, as any were having need. ⁴⁶And each day, attending the temple together and breaking bread in their homes, they were partaking of food with glad and grateful hearts, ⁴⁷praising God and finding favor with all the people. And the Lord added to those who were being saved each day.

Community life is summarized as involving four key areas: apostolic teaching, fellowship, the breaking of bread together, and prayer. The newly formed community functions by the believers' devoting themselves (ἦσαν δὲ προσκαρτεροῦντες, ēsan de proskarterountes) to these activities. The expression "devoting themselves" has the idea of persistence or persevering in something (BDAG 881 §2; EDNT 3:172; Barrett 1994: 162). The imperfect periphrastic construction speaks of the ongoing devotion that they have. Of its ten NT occurrences the verb appears six times in Acts (1:14; 2:42; 2:46; 6:4; 8:13; 10:7). It echoes the unity of mind Luke describes in Acts 1:14. In these four ongoing activities, much of the basic work of community appears. Luke favors such summary texts (also Acts 4:32–37; 5:12; 16; Marshall 1980: 83–84; esp. Witherington 1998: 157–59). In Acts 1:6–6:7 Luke uses such summary texts about the community to underscore that this group has bonded together effectively. Schneider (1980: 286) notes that the four items noted appear in two basic groupings: teaching and fellowship, which includes breaking of bread and prayer. If so, the teaching includes the practical art of sharing

2:42

life with each other at all levels, as the discussion of the term "fellowship" below will show. Although the picture here is summarized in ideal terms, Luke is not beyond showing problems and how they were dealt with later (Acts 5–6). The acts are each highlighted with articles—"the" teaching, "the" fellowship, "the" breaking of bread, and "the" prayers (Wallace 1996: 225).

The first activity is the apostolic teaching (διδαχῇ τῶν ἀποστόλων, *didachē tōn apostolōn*). Reference to teaching using the term διδαχή appears thirty times in the NT, five of which are in Luke-Acts (Luke 4:32; Acts 2:42; 5:28; 13:12 [of Paul and Barnabas's teaching]; 17:19 [of Paul's teaching at Athens]). Instruction is an important part of the new community. The centrality of Jesus and the preparation of members to share in the new life and witness are key community concerns. Later the apostolic teaching, called "your" teaching by opponents, will fill Jerusalem, the only other reference to the apostolic teaching (Acts 5:28). Matthew 28:19–20 expresses the task as "teaching them to observe all I commanded you." It likely would have included all kinds of instruction like what we see in the Gospels and Epistles: ethical and practical teaching and a grounding in the central promise God had given in Jesus.

Next comes the mention of fellowship, or, more precisely, sharing in common (κοινωνία, *koinonia*; Witherington 1998: 160). This is the only use of this term in Acts. It occurs nineteen times in the NT, fourteen of which are in Paul. The term speaks of communion or fellowship (its Semitic equivalent, 1QS 6.7; 5.1). It was often used of the type of mutuality that takes place in marriage (BAGD 438–39 §1; BDAG 552; 3 Macc. 4:6). In this verse, the description appears in a context surrounded by terms of shared activity. The term can have overtones of mutual material support that looks to alms and generosity (Rom. 15:26; 2 Cor. 8:4; 9:13), but this is only a part of the sense, not the whole, as verse 44 will indicate explicitly by using other terms (*pace* Johnson 1992: 58). Still, the wordplay with κοινά (*koina*, in common) in verse 44 shows a material element also is involved in the term. Luke points to fellowship to underscore the personal interactive character of relationships in the early church at all levels (so Fitzmyer 1998: 270). There is a real sense of connection to, between, and for each other.

Third is the breaking of bread (κλάσει τοῦ ἄρτου, *klasei tou artou*). The reference to breaking of bread appears only twice in the NT, here and in Luke 24:35, where it refers merely to table fellowship. It is unclear here whether the phrase refers to the Lord's Supper (so NLT) or is a reference to taking some meals together, of which the Lord's Supper was a part. The verb κλάω (*klaō*, break) appears in Acts 2:46; 20:7, 11; and 27:35. In 2:46, the reference seems to be used broadly of meals, suggesting a broad use here as well, although 20:7 appears to refer to the table on the first day of the week. What makes the choice hard to decide is that the Lord's table was part of a larger meal in the earliest church (a full discussion appears in Barrett 1994: 163–65; see also Michiels 1985). Most of the references in this context seem broad, which would suggest a broad reference here. Jervell (1998: 155) argues that a sacramental understanding of this term is not in view, given the generic Jewish understanding of the term. He also notes how verse 46 looks to a broader context for breaking bread. Either way, the phrase suggests the intimate interaction and mutual acceptance that was a part of community life.

Finally, there is reference to prayers (προσευχαῖς, *proseuchais*). This noun appears thirty-six times in the NT, twelve of which are in Luke-Acts and nine of which are in Acts (1:4; 2:42; 3:1; 6:4; 10:4, 31; 12:5; 16:13, 16). Of eighty-five NT occurrences, the verb "pray" (προσεύχομαι, *proseuchomai*) appears thirty-four times in Luke-Acts, sixteen of which are in Acts (Luke 1:10; 3:21; 5:16; 6:12, 28; 9:18, 28–29 [2x]; 11:1–2 [3x]; 18:1, 10–11; 20:47; 22:40–41 [2x], 44, 46; Acts 1:24; 6:6; 8:15; 9:11, 40; 10:9, 30; 11:5; 12:12; 13:3; 14:23; 16:25; 20:36; 21:5; 22:17; 28:8). A community at prayer is something Luke emphasizes about community life. It seeks God's direction and is dependent upon God because God's family of people do not work by feelings or intuition but by actively submitting themselves to the Lord's direction. The plural with the article ("the prayers") could suggest that some set prayers were used. Another option is that the expression refers to an entire range of praying, both set and more spontaneous. The use of set prayer on occasion is likely in light of the facts that (1) set prayers existed in Judaism, (2) a tie to the temple where set prayers were made is expressed in 2:46 and 3:1, and (3) the Lord taught the disciples such a fixed prayer (Luke 11:2–4). The setting here of the community functioning by itself apart from a temple rite suggests, however, that the reference to prayer is broad, although it may well have included such set features (Bruce 1990: 132).

The community generates ongoing fear (φόβος, *phobos*) among "every **2:43** soul" of those outside the community (note the imperfect verb [ἐγίνετο, *egineto*, came] used twice in this verse). The term "soul" (ψυχῇ, *psychē*) matches verse 41 as a reference to people. The fear described here is likely to be similar to that seen in Acts 2:37, where divine activity is associated with the group (Luke 1:12, 65; 2:9; 5:26; 7:16; 8:37). Such activity causes all to take careful, respectful, even nervous notice of what is happening inside the community (Acts 5:5, 11 [reaction to Ananias and Sapphira]; 9:31 [church walks in the fear of the Lord]; 19:17 [after the sons of Sceva's failed attempt to imitate Paul]; 1QH 4.26). Luke-Acts has twelve out of forty-seven NT occurrences of φόβος.

The apostolic activity includes wonders and signs (see discussion at Acts 2:19), one of which will be detailed in 3:1–10, followed by a speech of explanation (see also 5:1–11; 9:32–11:18). This replicates the pattern of deed and word that Luke's Gospel also used to describe Jesus's activity.

God had been at work through Jesus, as Peter's speech in Acts 2:14–40 showed. That work has extended beyond Jesus's crucifixion. Now the work continues through the apostles, indicating that God supports the new community as well.

2:44–45 The quality of mutual caring is highlighted in verses 44–45, as the believers are together and treat everything as belonging to everyone, holding all things as common between them. Like the phrase "those who received" in 2:41, "those who believed" describes those who have responded to the message of this new messianic community ("all the believers" in NIV, NLT; 4:32; 5:14; 10:43; 13:39; 22:19 [all present tense]; only 4:32; 11:21; and 19:2 have the aorist). The members of this new community are called believers because of their response of faith in the preached message.

The expression of their being "together" (ἐπὶ τὸ αὐτό, *epi to auto*) recalls the unity depicted in 1:15 and 2:1. This expression is repeated in verse 47 (4:26 completes the occurrences in Acts, five of ten in the NT). It is disputed how to translate this phrase, but "together" or "at the same place" is likely (BDAG 363 §1cβ).

The believers are also holding items in common (κοινά, *koina*). Out of fourteen occurrences in the NT, this adjective appears only four times with this sense (Acts 4:32; Titus 1:4; Jude 3; Untergassmair, *EDNT* 2:302; in the other cases, it means "impure" or "unclean," e.g., Mark 7:2). Acts will note this "commonness" again (4:32). In both cases, the remark is seen as a favorable indication of the depth of fellowship and mutual care at work in the community. That a community is really functioning with appropriate love and compassion is evident when material needs are also a concern and are being generously provided.[1]

This sharing of material things in common is not a required communalism but a voluntary, caring response to need, as the end of verse 45 shows. The verbs for "sell" (ἐπίπρασκον, *epipraskon*) and "distribute" (διεμέριζον, *diemerizon*) are iterative imperfects (Moulton and Turner 1963: 67): this sharing was done again and again. Everything Luke says about this indicates that he sees such provision as a very positive act, an act of genuine care. The size of the group may well have made this possible, but the later effort by Paul to raise money from Gentiles for this community shows that it functioned across communities as well (2 Cor. 8–9). Acts 5:4 makes clear that such a donation was not required, in contrast to the requirement at Qumran among the Essenes (1QS 1.11–12; 5.1–3; 6.2–3; CD 9.1–15; 1QS 9.3–11, but there the motivation was to ensure purity). That the later church did not keep the practice speaks to the authenticity of this scene. Notes about possessing all things in common are not

---

1. The other reference to this term in Acts refers to "common" (unclean) food (10:14; 11:8). In Acts 10 and 11, the term relates to Jewish ideas of purity. People are no longer seen as unclean by Peter, as a result of his experience in 10:28.

unusual as a sign of ethical virtue in the culture (Philo, *Good Person* 12 §86; *Hypothetica* 11.10–13; *Abraham* 40 §235; Josephus, *Ant.* 18.1.5 §20 [of the Essenes]). The Greek view was that friends share things in common (Plato, *Republic* 4.424A; 5.449C; *Critias* 110C–D; Aristotle, *Nicomachean Ethics* 1168B.31; Iamblichus, *Life of Pythagoras* 30.168).[2] Later rabbinic Judaism argued against it (*m. 'Abot* 5.10; Johnson 1992: 9).

Community members are moved to sell what they own, both possessions and goods, and give the proceeds to those in need (Codex D supplies a clarifying addition: as many as had possessions or goods sold them). Some scholars suggest that this reflects their expectation that Christ would return soon (Barrett 1994: 168), yet the reason given is not eschatological but social. They are motivated by concern for the needs of the community (χρείαν, *chreian*, need; perhaps as Jesus taught in Luke 6:30–36 or from the OT and Deut. 15:4–5; Polhill 1992: 121). Jesus's teaching about not hoarding material provisions from God also may well provide background (Luke 12:13–21). The same motivation appears in Acts 4:35, and failure to meet such needs in 6:3 among Hellenist widows leads to a complaint and resolution in the church (20:34 and 28:10 complete the uses of the term "need" in Acts). The verb in the imperfect shows that this is an ongoing distribution. As people are having (εἶχεν, *eichen*) need, they receive help (Witherington 1998: 162; Haenchen 1987: 192; BDF §325, §367; the verb is used with iterative ἄν, *an*). This means that people did not sell everything all at once. The picture is of a community that cares for all of its members, even those in material need.

The nature of early church worship surfaces in this verse. Each day **2:46** they are at the temple precincts together (3:1–10; 4:1; Solomon's portico: 5:12, 20, 25, 42; προσκαρτεροῦντες ὁμοθυμαδόν, *proskarterountes homothymadon*, persisting together; a phrase that is only here and in 1:14). This is an indication of the Jewish character of their faith in this early period. The phrase καθ' ἡμέρα (*kath' hēmera*) has a distributive sense, meaning "day to day," and of its seventeen NT occurrences, appears five times in Luke and six times in Acts, including twice in this scene (see v. 47). Regular attendance at the temple reflects Jewish practice for those in Jerusalem. Nothing about this is seen as unusual for Jewish believers in Jesus.

This fellowship, like Jewish practice, extends beyond the sacred space (Jervell 1998: 157). They also break bread (20:7, 11) in their homes. The phrase κατ' οἶκον (*kat' oikon*) could mean in various homes, as it is parallel to the distributive reference to each day earlier in the verse (Barrett 1994: 170). So these believers worship and fellowship together in their

2. For discussions of such sharing as an ethical virtue, see Mealand 1977; Klauck 1982; van der Horst 1985; Witherington 1998: 162; Conzelmann 1987: 23n6; and Bruce 1988a: 74n114.

everyday environments. They share the table with joy. This is the only verse where the combination ἀγαλλιάσει καὶ ἀφελότητι (*agalliasei kai aphelotēti*, glad and generous) appears in the NT; the second term is a hapax in the NT and is absent from the LXX. The use of the preposition ἐν (*en*) with these two terms points to association and has the force of an adverb (Moule 1959: 78). Joy and sincerity are present. There is no special sense to the meal here. It is only a reference to regular meals. Luke often notes the joy that comes with faith, a theme that reaches back to the hymns of Luke 1–2.

2:47   The note of joy coming from the fellowship of the community also extends over into praise to God (αἰνοῦντες τὸν θεόν, *ainountes ton theon*) and having favor (ἔχοντες χάριν, *echontes charin*) with those outside the community, or "all the people" (ὅλον τὸν λαόν, *holon ton laon*). This way to express praising God appears in six of its eight NT occurrences in Luke-Acts (Luke 2:13, 20; 19:37; Acts 2:47; 3:8–9 [2x]; Rom. 15:11; Rev. 19:5). The finding of favor is noted only here in Acts. This combination of terms (ἔχω χάριν, *echō charin*) appears in a few NT texts (Luke 17:9 [the phrase means "to thank" here]; 2 Cor. 1:15; 1 Tim. 1:12 [to be thankful]; 2 Tim. 1:3 [to thank]; Heb. 12:28 [to be grateful]; also in the OT: Exod. 33:12; in Judaism: 1 Esd. 6:5; Fitzmyer 1998: 272). The idea is that others are appreciative of this new community ("good will of all the people" in NLT, NET). A vibrant community extends itself in two directions: toward God and toward neighbor. A veiled reference to obedience to the great commandment appears here.

In sum, Luke affirms the internal fellowship, intimacy, and engagement of the community. This positive activity is accompanied by joy and glad hearts, and their worship and praise of God are ongoing. But this is not an isolated, private club or a hermetically sealed community. Their reputation with outsiders also is good.

This good reputation apparently impacts their witness: Luke concludes the summary with a note that as each day passes, the Lord adds to the number who are being saved. The phrase καθ' ἡμέραν (*kath' hēmeran*) is yet another distributive use of κατά.[3] This is an effective community as it is growing at a regular pace. The imperfect προσετίθει (*prosetithei*) is iterative: God is continuously adding to the numbers (Wallace 1996: 547). As it is the Lord God who calls (v. 39), so it is the Lord God who adds to his community. The phrase ἐπὶ τὸ αὐτό (*epi to auto*) probably means simply "to itself," although in the LXX it could refer to the community, which is what the "it" is here (Johnson 1992: 60; Pss. 2:2; 4:9 [4:8 Eng.]; so D adds after it "in the church," an explanatory gloss). The participial use σῳζομένους (*sōzomenous*, those who are saved) appears only here and in Luke 13:23 in Luke-Acts and looks back to Acts 2:21.

---

3. On *kata*, see v. 46, where it is also used for "day by day" and for "various" houses.

It is yet another way to describe believers, with verse 44 (those who believe) and verse 41 (those who receive the word).

This entire unit stresses the solid community start the earliest church enjoyed. It still lived and reflected its Jewish context, going to temple, but, beyond that, gathered in homes for instruction, prayer, fellowship, and the breaking of bread together. Conversion led to immediate follow-up and care for instruction, spiritual nurture, personal fellowship, and the meeting of basic needs (Fernando 1998: 129). The early believers cared so much for each other that they sold or gave personal items to meet those needs. Glad, joyful hearts and praise to God characterized them. Witherington (1998: 163) observes that the community's "presence and witness were infectious." The note of growth at the end of this unit is related to the community work and fellowship God was bringing about within the new community. Their life as a community was a visible part of their testimony. In sharing Christ, they also gave of themselves. One can share Christ not only by what one says about him but also by showing the transformation that following him brings about. As Polhill (1992: 122) suggests, "Luke's summaries present an ideal for the Christian community which it must always strive for, constantly return to, and discover anew, if it is to have the unity of the spirit and purpose essential for an effective witness." Stott (1990: 82–87) speaks of a learning church, a loving church, a worshiping church, and an evangelistic church. In other words, the church is to be a place of spiritual growth and spiritual praise, a place that is relational enough to meet needs, engage the culture, and share Christ.

With Acts 2:42–47 ending as it does, Luke wants to leave no doubt that there is an important connection between community life and the "favor" the community experienced with outsiders. This kind of engagement has a positive effect on mission. Everything about the Gospels and Acts tells us that God's people are to take the initiative to show community and serve those around them. Much in Western culture drives us to an individualism that undercuts this development of community. We are taught to have things our way and that being able to have our individual needs catered to is how to measure the success of an organization. In our culture, our individual needs and rights come before any needs of the group. The biblical picture is not of what someone receives from the church, although one does receive a great deal, but of what one gives and how one contributes to it. The portrait of the early church in Acts shows that community and the welfare of the group were a priority. This attitude reflected spiritual maturity that allowed the church to grow. In the case of this earliest community, the believers' preaching was matched by their community, making a powerful testimony for their mission. When the early church said that God cared, the care they gave their own demonstrated this.

Additional Notes

2:42–44. A few MSS add "in Jerusalem" after "the apostles' teaching" in verse 42 (D and some Vulgate MSS) and at the end of verse 43 after "through the apostles" (E, 33, 104, a few Syriac MSS). Other MSS have the addition of the phrase with a second mention of fear after the discussion of apostolic wonders, a seemingly more natural placement but also repetitive ($\mathfrak{P}^{74}$, ℵ, A, C, and Ψ). The additions are not original because their various locations across the MSS simply indicate that they are trying to make clear that the story is still in Jerusalem. The second reference to fear seems redundant and is placed more logically after the reference to wonders, making it an easier reading. The more difficult reading, placing fear at the front of verse 43, appears in B, D, Byz, and Itala.

2:44. It is hard to know whether the present-tense participle (πιστεύοντες, *pisteuontes*, read by $\mathfrak{P}^{74}$, A, C, D, Ψ, and Byz) or the aorist participle (πιστεύσαντες, *pisteusantes*, read by ℵ, B, 36) is original here. It makes no real difference to the sense. The present tense is common in Acts (see vv. 44–45 above).

D. The Healing of the Lame Man and the Arrest of Peter and John (3:1–4:31)

The first apostolic miracle appears here (3:1–10) and sets off a series of events that leads Peter to preach Jesus from Torah and promise (3:11–26). These events also produce the first official Jewish reaction noted by Luke to the apostolic preaching about Jesus (4:1–22). This is the first of fourteen miracles in Acts (Peter: 3:1–10; 5:1–11; 5:17–26; 9:32–35, 36–42; an angel of God: 12:1–19, 20–23; Paul: 13:4–12; 14:8–11; 16:16–19 with Silas; 16:20–34 with Silas; 20:7–12; 28:3–6, 7–8 [survives a snake bite and performs a healing]; Pesch 1986a: 144–45). There are four healings (three paralytics, one with fever), two raisings from the dead, four liberation miracles (two person-freeings and two exorcisms), three judgment miracles, and one preservation miracle (Paul at Malta). Four of these categories (paralytic healing, raising from the dead, liberation and judgment miracles) have parallels between Peter and Paul, the hero of the last half of Acts. There are also ten summary notices of miracles in the book (Schneider 1980: 305; 2:43; 5:12, 15, 16; 6:8; 8:6–7, 13; 14:3; 19:11–12; 28:9). The paralytic healing is paralleled between Jesus (Luke 5:17–26), Peter (Acts 3:1–10), and Paul (Acts 14:8–11). God's power through Jesus is the point of these accounts, which also portray the release that Jesus's work gives to those who receive it.

Spencer (2004: 51–53) notes that Acts 3–5 concerns the temple, alternating between the temple (3:1–4:22; 5:12–41) and private home settings (4:23–5:11). He points out that both temple scenes begin with apostolic miracles in the name of Jesus. Opposition is from the temple elites. Persecution includes interrogation and incarceration. The apostles consistently declare their loyalty to God. Both speeches issue a call for repentance.

The Acts 3 miracle is an example of 2:43. On the one hand, the healing shows God's power now working through the apostolic group. Such activity represents another way in which the community of believers is obtaining a reputation among those outside the community. On the other hand, the preaching and the reaction it garners show why the Jewish leadership is beginning to become concerned. Luke advances the story of Acts by introducing the opposition that now emerges against the community and its preaching.

1. The Event: The Healing of the Lame Man (3:1–10)

This event shows the community's compassion and how it meets needs beyond merely material concerns. When a lame man asks for alms, Peter and John have no money to give, but instead through the name of Jesus heal the man. This gives the man the capability of an entirely new life; it is an act that portrays what salvation does. Compassion expresses itself in service to others and in meeting their needs. Another emphasis in the account is that God is still active in the authority Jesus possesses, working through the apostles. The account is a miracle event in form (vv. 1–2: setting; vv. 3–5: approach of miracle-workers; v. 6: miracle; vv. 7–10: response and reaction). As in the Gospel of Luke, the miracle is a visual act that points to a deeper reality (Bock 1994a: 463; Bock 2002a: 106–7). Jesus can transform and give new life, and so can the deeds of those he works through. The account closely parallels Luke 5:17–26 and Acts 14:8–11 (Eckey 2000: 101). The key difference from Luke's Gospel is that Peter mediates a healing and then explains what it shows, whereas Jesus declares forgiveness of sins as he heals. The contrast shows that Jesus's act and authority are more direct than Peter's. As is also Luke's pattern, an event leads to an explanatory speech and then the reaction. The apostolic ministry extends Jesus's vindication and presence. This focus on Jesus reflects the mission of the new community Jesus has brought into being. The speech will make clear that thereby God's promise and even expectations originating in the Torah are met. The "new" faith is actually very old, rooted in promises that go back to the beginning of God's work in the world.

Exegesis and Exposition

[1]Peter and John went up to the temple at prayer time, the ninth hour [or three in the afternoon]. [2]And a man lame from his mother's womb was being carried in, whom they set down day by day at the door of the temple precincts called Beautiful, so he could ask for alms from those who entered the temple. [3]When this man saw Peter and John about to go into the temple, he asked for alms. [4]And Peter, gazing at him with John, said, "Look at us." [5]And the man fixed his gaze upon them, expecting to receive something. [6]But Peter said, "Silver and gold I do not have, but what I have, this I give to you; in the name of Jesus

Christ the Nazorean, ⌜ ⌝ walk." [7]And taking him by the right hand, Peter raised him up. Immediately the man's feet and ankles were strengthened. [8]And leaping up, he stood and began walking and entered the temple with them, walking and leaping and praising God. [9]And all the people saw him walking and praising God, [10]and they began to recognize him as ⌜the one⌝ who sat for alms at the Beautiful Gate of the temple; and they were filled with wonder and amazement at what had happened to him.

This verse reaffirms the involvement of the early community at the temple (2:46). The community still reaches out to its Jewish neighbors. Here it is the afternoon time of prayer, the ninth hour on a sunrise schedule, or three in the afternoon. It is also the time of the afternoon Tamid offering (the continual burnt offering; Exod. 29:39; Num. 28:3–4; *m. Tamid*; Fitzmyer 1998: 277).[1] This was one of two key prayer times in the day, the other being at nine in the morning (Dan. 9:21; Jdt. 9:1; Josephus, *Ant.* 14.4.3 §65). The afternoon hour was also the time of the vision of Cornelius in Acts 10:3, 30. Peter and John are the key characters, and this is the first explicit mention of John (they are paired in 4:13, 19; 8:14).[2] In the passage, however, Peter does the speaking. It is natural to speak of going up to the temple, given its elevated location in the city (Luke 18:10; the imperfect in Acts 3:1 is vivid). Haenchen (1987: 198n11) complains that the detail of the time shows the story's inauthenticity because the man would have come in the morning, but this assumes that he would sit out there all day. This complaint is excessively skeptical for three reasons: (1) To come in the morning or afternoon was possible for a Jew. (2) It also would be natural to seek alms whenever a crowd might gather, as at either of these prayer times. (3) The man's appearances were subject to when others could bring him, which could be morning or afternoon. The reference to the temple here is broad, referring to the general area of the temple, as the reference to the Beautiful Gate in verse 2 and the healed man's later entry into the temple proper in verse 8 indicate.

3:1

The setting turns to a man who has been lame from birth (ἐκ κοιλίας μητρός, *ek koilias mētros*, literally, from the mother's womb). The lame are prominent in Jesus's ministry (Matt. 11:5; 15:30–31; 18:8; 21:14; Mark 9:45; Luke 7:22; 14:13, 21; John 5:3). The healing of the lame also appears elsewhere in Acts (8:7; 14:8). The fact that the condition is

3:2

---

1. Hamm 2003 details how often Luke refers to this twice-a-day offering in Luke-Acts, although he overdraws a priestly emphasis out of this usage.

2. Marshall 1980: 87 suggests that the pattern of pairs arises from the ministry of the disciples; see Luke 9:1–6; 10:1. Jervell 1998: 159 speaks of the two-witness motif and sees John inserted into the story by Luke, but the theme does not require that his presence be seen as an insertion. It is unlikely that Peter would go to the temple alone, especially if he seeks to minister in a manner similar to the disciples' earlier efforts.

from birth intensifies its severity. Van der Horst (1989: 37) argues that χωλός (*chōlos*, lame) refers not to complete paralysis but to damage to feet, ankles, knees, or hips. So the man is crippled but not completely paralyzed. This man has never known anything else, nor can he do anything. So "each day" (καθ᾽ ἡμέραν, *kath' hēmeran*) he is set (ἐτίθουν, *etithoun*, they placed) in the temple precincts in the hopes of obtaining financial aid for his condition. The imperfect verb is an example of a habitual imperfect (Wallace 1996: 548).

The locale is given as the Beautiful (ὡραίαν, *hōraian*) Gate (Jeremias, *TDNT* 3:173n5; Schrenk, *TDNT* 3:236; *EDNT* 3:508; BDAG 1103 §2). This is the only reference to this locale in the NT and is otherwise unattested for the temple. It is often associated with the Nicanor Gate (Barrett 1994: 179). Another option for the locale is the Shushan Gate on the eastern side of the temple. It is an old traditional view (so Williams 1990: 66; *m. Mid.* 1.3). Barrett calls the Nicanor Gate the best guess (another Nicanor Gate, described by later rabbis, is sometimes suggested but is less likely). The Shushan Gate was harder to reach and so looks less likely as a possibility for a lame man (Marshall 1980: 88). The Nicanor (or Corinthian) Gate was bronze, larger than the other gates, and heavily adorned. Josephus (*J.W.* 5.5.3 §201) describes the elaborate nature of these gates; eight were overlaid with gold and silver and one with bronze. When opened for special occasions, this gate was a popular way to reach the temple, an important consideration for those seeking alms (*m. Mid.* 2.3; Josephus *J.W.* 5.5.3 §§204–5; Taylor 1999 has a full discussion of the issues). The gate's precise location is not clear, but it allowed access to the Court of Women and Gentiles. Josephus describes the Corinthian gate as even grander than the gates of gold and silver, being larger in size and more adorned. Van der Horst (1989: 38) cites two passages where alms are asked for at synagogues (Cleomedes, *De motu circulari* 2.1, 91; Artemidorus, *Onirocritica* 3.53), noting that we lack texts about such begging at the temple.

The lame man is there to ask alms of the worshipers; giving alms was a responsibility that Judaism took seriously as an expression of compassion that God honored (Luke 11:41; 12:33; Acts 3:3, 10; 9:36; 10:2, 4, 31; 24:17; also Matt. 6:2–4; Bock 1996: 1114, 1166; Sir. 3:30; 7:10; 29:12; Tob. 2:14; 4:7–11; 12:8–9; 14:8–11; 2 En. 63.1–2; *m. Pe'ah* 1.1). Tobit 4:10–11 reads, "For almsgiving delivers from death and keeps you from going into the Darkness. Indeed, almsgiving, for all who practice it, is an excellent offering in the presence of the Most High" (NRSV). So the care of such people was expected in Judaism. Fitzmyer (1198: 278) suggests that the name "Beautiful" is noted because of what is about to take place, but it is unclear whether the name is merely symbolic.

3:3–5   The exchange leading to the miracle follows in these verses. The man is asking (ἡρώτα, *ērōta*) for alms. The imperfect tense points to repeated appeals or some kind of ongoing appeal to the two apostles. The lame man would have made this request of all who were passing by to go to the temple. Peter, with John, gives him attention. The text focuses on Peter, who is the main human character and apostolic spokesperson in these early chapters. His gaze is fixed (ἀτενίσας, *atenisas*) on the man (see BDAG 148: "to look intently at"). Twelve of the fourteen NT uses of this verb are in Luke-Acts (Luke 4:20; 22:56; Acts 1:10; 3:4, 12; 6:15; 7:55; 10:4; 11:6; 13:9; 14:9; 23:1). Peter demands the man's attention by calling on him to look at them. The expression βλέψον εἰς (*blepson eis*) appears in Matt. 22:16 = Mark 12:14; Luke 9:62; John 13:22; and Acts 1:11. Seeking the man's attention tells him that a response is coming, but it will not be what he expects.

The lame man turns his attention (ἐπεῖχεν, *epeichen*) to them in the hope of receiving something. This term means "be especially observant" (Luke 14:7; Acts 19:22; Phil. 2:16; and 1 Tim. 4:16 are the other NT occurrences; BAGD 285 §2a; BDAG 362 §2; "gave them his attention" in NIV; "looked at them eagerly" in NLT; "gave heed unto them" in KJV; "fixed his attention" in RSV, ESV; "paid attention" in NET; "turned to them" in HCSB). Again the verb is presented vividly in the imperfect. He is giving them his attention, hopeful, no doubt, that financial help is on the way.

Peter's reply is emphatic and contains a surprise. There are no alms provided but rather a call to be healed, the core of the miracle event. Silver and gold Peter lacks, and so alms are not possible. In the Greek sentence the phrase about gold and silver is moved forward for emphasis. It is a common expression, especially for a great deal of money (1 Pet. 1:18; Pesch 1986a: 138; Plato, *Republic* 5.464C; Josephus, *Ant.* 15.1.2 §5). Materially, the apostles lived modestly as part of a community that shared its goods (Acts 2:44–45). But Peter does have something he can and will give, the power to walk, through (διά, *dia*; see v. 16) Jesus Christ the Nazorean, the one from Nazareth (BDAG 664–65). It is difficult to determine if the preposition here means "through" or "with," but that Jesus mediates the healing is clear (Moule 1959: 58). No more will people have to bring the lame man up to beg for alms. The present imperative "walk" (περιπάτει, *peripatei*) looks to his being able continuously to walk. In effect, Peter has given him a new life, which is precisely what the miracles represent, as Peter's subsequent speech will show. The NT has thirteen occurrences of the description of Jesus as a Nazorean, seven of which are in Acts (Matt. 2:23; 26:71; Luke 18:37; John 18:5, 7; 19:19; Acts 2:22; 3:6; 4:10; 6:14; 22:8; 24:5; 26:9). Jesus grew up in Nazareth, and this description of Jesus keeps intact his hometown roots. It is in the name of Jesus Christ, that is, in the authority of his still active messianic person, that this man can

3:6

have his legs healed and walk.[3] Peter is now replicating the kind of work Jesus performed in his ministry, but only as one who mediates what Jesus has the authority to do. As Fitzmyer (1998: 278) notes, although the man does not receive the alms he seeks, "he is in the long run not disappointed." Peter gives far more than what money can give (Jervell 1998: 160). Marshall (1980: 88) says the text does not prohibit meeting material needs nor does it advocate giving spiritual help only, not physical help. Peter through Jesus gives what he can give in this case. In giving this gift, Peter enables the man to begin to live and take care of himself. This is how the community is to engage the larger community in which it lives, showing compassion in visible ways that help and even develop people's capabilities.

3:7–8 These verses give the proof of the healing. Peter lifts the man up by taking his right hand. The accusative (αὐτόν, *auton*) with "taking hold" here is a less common construction, since normally this verb takes a genitive (Moule 1959: 36n2). Perhaps the right hand had been extended, expecting alms (Fitzmyer 1998: 279).

The man's feet and ankles are made strong (on taking the hand in healing: Mark 1:31; 9:27; Acts 9:41; Pesch 1986a: 139). The passive "were strengthened" makes clear that divine power is what strengthened the legs. The verb στερεόω (*stereoō*, make strong) appears only three times in the NT, all in Acts (3:7; 3:16 [of this healing]; 16:5 [about the church]). In ancient medical language it was often associated with the feet or the bones (Bruce 1990: 137 refers to Hippocrates and Galen as using the verb; BDAG 943.1). The NT hapax term for "feet" (αἱ βάσεις, *hai baseis*) here can mean "step" and is used in the LXX (Wis. 13:18; Josephus, *Ant.* 7.12.2 §303). The term for "ankles" (τὰ σφυδρά, *ta sphydra*) is also an NT hapax. These can be medical terms but are not exclusively so (BDAG 171, 981).

The healing allows the man to walk into the temple proper for the first time (Lev. 21:17–20; 2 Sam. 5:8 prohibited his entry as a lame man; Polhill 1992: 128). He stood (ἔστη, *estē*, aorist) and was walking (περιεπάτει, *periepatei*, imperfect). He does so with Peter and John. What would normally take months because of muscular atrophy occurs instantly (παραχρῆμα, *parachrēma*). The idea of an immediate healing is common in Luke's miracle accounts (Luke 1:64; 4:39; 5:25 [the paralytic]; 8:44, 55; 13:13; 18:43). He walks, leaps, and praises God, enjoying the gift of his newfound ability. The overload and repetitiveness of movement verbs stresses the healing's complete success. Jesus's work has changed this man's life forever. The miracle portrays what Jesus can do and the

3. On the use of "name," see Acts 2:38; it is especially prominent in Acts 3–4: see 3:16; 4:10, 12, 17–18, 30. Witherington 1998: 175 and Barrett 1994: 182 stress that this is not a magical formula, as Schille 1984: 125 claims, but an "anti-magical" passage together with Acts 19:13–20, where the name points to authority and power. See esp. Zeisler 1979.

joy such work brings. The verb for "leap" (ἄλλομαι, *hallomai*) appears three times in the NT—twice in Acts, as a parallel healing in 14:10 also uses this verb. John 4:14 has water leaping up to eternal life. Isaiah 35:6 LXX uses this verb regarding what will happen in the time of salvation, "Then the lame shall leap like a deer" (Isa. 35:1–10; Johnson 1992: 67; Luke 7:22). The imperfect here may well be ingressive (Wallace 1996: 545): he stood up and began walking. The verb for "praise" (αἰνέω, *aineō*) is also a favorite of Luke's, appearing six times in Luke-Acts out of eight NT occurrences (Luke 2:13, 20; 19:37; Acts 2:47; 3:8–9; Rom. 15:11; Rev. 19:5). The newly healed man knows that God has been at work and that God has been at work through Jesus (v. 6). The man has received a new kind of alms.

These verses give the reaction to the healing. All the people who are at the temple see the formerly lame man now walking and praising God. The observation that the man is able to walk is repeated from verse 8 (for the phrase "all the people," see Acts 2:47, though here it is expressed with πᾶς, *pas*). What is more, these people at the temple all begin to recognize (ἐπεγίνωσκον, *epeginōskon*) him as the man who has been asking for alms at the Beautiful Gate (v. 2).[4]   **3:9–10**

There is no doubt who he is or what his previous condition has been. So wonder and amazement (θάμβους καὶ ἐκστάσεως, *thambous kai ekstaseōs*) fill them. This is the only appearance of this combination in the NT. The term θάμβος (*thambos*) appears three times in the NT, all in reaction to miraculous actions in Luke-Acts (Luke 4:36; 5:9 and here). The term ἔκστασις (*ekstasis*) for amazement appears seven times in the NT, five of them in Luke-Acts (Mark 5:42 [the miracle of Jairus's daughter]; 16:8 [the resurrection announcement]; Luke 5:26 [a paralytic]; Acts 3:9; 10:10 ["vision"]; 11:5 ["vision"]; 22:17 ["vision"]; the verb ἐξίστημι [*existēmi*, to amaze] is in Luke 2:47; 8:56; 24:22; Acts 8:9, 11, 13; 9:21; 10:45; 12:16). This term describes someone emotionally impacted by an experience (BAGD 245 §1; BDAG 309 §1). As these texts show, the reaction is common for miracles. Bruce (1988a: 78–79) compares this healing to Jesus's healing of the paralytic and says that it points to Jesus's authority to forgive sin and thus signals the arrival of the new age (Luke 7:22–23; forgiveness is raised in the speech of Acts 3:12–26). The crowd recognizes what has happened physically to the man. The verb συμβαίνω (*symbainō*, happen) occurs eight times in the NT, four times in Luke-Acts, and two times in the Petrines (Mark 10:32; Luke 24:14; Acts 3:10; 20:19; 21:35; 1 Cor. 10:11; 1 Pet. 4:12; 2 Pet. 2:22). The healing attracts much attention and requires explanation, which verses 11–26 give. It does not yet engender faith (see Acts 4:4) and thus needs Peter's

---

4. On the theme of this type of recognition, see John 9:8–12, 20; on the imperfect as probably ingressive, "began to recognize [him]," see Robertson 1934: 885.

elaboration (Larkin 1995: 66). The healing has the potential, however, to awaken faith and to create controversy (4:16). At the least, admiration for the work of the apostles exists (see 2:43; Pesch 1986a: 140).

In sum, this first miracle by the apostles shows how Jesus can give new life and brings the new era to people. Jesus is now at work through his apostolic representatives. The lame man receives far more than silver and gold could give him. Now he can live a new, full life. Compassion led Peter to meet the man's needs at a spiritual and physical level and to make clear that it was the power of Jesus that enabled the man's new mobile life. Mission led Peter to go where people in need were and to respond. Earlier Jesus had called Peter to be a "fisher of men" (Luke 5:1–11; 24:47). God took the initiative to bring needy people to Peter. Peter took the initiative to bring Jesus to someone who needed him. By doing so, God was working and speaking about his work through his servant Jesus, who in turn is working through his own servants (Acts 3:13–16). None of this took place in a corner. God was impressively at work. In addition, God's promise was being realized, and people were changed as a result.

Additional Notes

3:6. A few key MSS (ℵ, B, D) lack the phrase ἔγειρε καί (*egeire kai*, rise up and) added at the start of Peter's command to the man to walk. It is added in A, C, E, Ψ, and 33. The omission is likely original, given the MS evidence and the fact that the longer phrase fills out the request and replicates Luke 5:23 (but Johnson 1992: 66 is for the longer reading).

3:10. There is fairly evenly divided MS evidence between αὐτός (*autos*, he; 𝔓⁷⁴, ℵ, A, C, 36) and οὗτος (*houtos*, this one; B, D, E, Ψ, Byz). Either reading is possible, but the use of αὐτός is slightly more emphatic.

2. The Explanation: Peter Preaches Jesus from Torah and Promise (3:11–26)

Once again, as in Acts 2, an event leads to an explanation. Peter preaches Jesus as the exalted servant who fulfills God's promise and so possesses the power to heal this lame man. The scriptural argumentation of this speech relies heavily on the Torah, since God is invoked as the God of Abraham, Isaac, and Jacob. Again the offer of forgiveness is made and the opportunity is presented to enter into the era that prophets promised would come one day.

The speech has two movements (Witherington 1998: 176). (1) The first part is the "defense" or "judicial" portion (vv. 12–18). Within this first part is the historical core about what took place before the healing that made it possible. God exalted the one who was crucified, the one by whose power this miracle took place (vv. 12–15). Next comes the explicit declaration that Jesus's name, that is, the authority of his person, is the source of the healing (v. 16). Finally, there is the observation that their acting in ignorance was still a part of God's plan that the Christ would suffer (vv. 17–18). (2) The "deliberative" portion of the speech makes the application. It asks for response from the crowd as they deliberate over the facts (vv. 19–26). Here the appeal is to respond with repentance and a turning to the offer of forgiveness. This response can permit "the times of refreshing" to come, along with the rest of God's promise in Jesus's return (vv. 20–21). The call to turn and the explanation that heaven holds Jesus until the time for completion arrives (vv. 19–21) also contain a warning: failure to respond leaves them culpable before God, for they risk failing to heed the prophet like Moses (vv. 22–23). These events are what the prophets proclaimed in the promise to Abraham's seed. That promise means that blessing can come to those who turn (vv. 24–26).

This speech is one of the most christologically rich addresses in Acts, as Jesus is the servant, the Holy and Righteous One, the Author of life, the prophet like Moses, the Christ, and the seed of Abraham. Hengel (1983: 30–47) makes a strong case that the early church's Christology developed very quickly in the first five years of the church. The proper response to his coming entails turning and repenting (v. 19), as blessing comes from turning to God through Jesus (v. 26).

The speech also introduces eschatological themes, outlining the two comings of Jesus for the first time. Peter declares that what is left to be fulfilled was already laid out in the Hebrew Scriptures in the

II. The Early Church in Jerusalem
D. The Healing of the Lame Man and the Arrest of Peter and John

words of the Law and the Prophets. Again the theological link between Christology and eschatology is the ascension. To call this eschatological part of the speech a digression misses the point of the linkage (but so Fitzmyer 1998: 282, who does, however, note the speech's numerous ancient and traditional touches). If one understands where Jesus is and what his exalted position means, then one can understand the healing. Most scholars appreciate that this speech has many ancient elements in it. Fitzmyer (1998: 282–83) regards "his Messiah should suffer" as a Lukan gloss, but even this could well reflect an ancient view of Jesus's death after the resurrection. Barrett (1994: 188–90) sees Lukan influence in the wording of the complex verse 16 and in the phrase Fitzmyer notes, but sees the bulk of this speech as rooted in tradition with numerous non-Lukan expressions. He notes eleven peculiarities in the speech (also seeing the influence of tradition here is Schneider 1980: 315–16). The speech is unlike Acts 2. The Acts 2 speech developed the historical, kerygmatic facts in detail (2:14–36) and then followed that outline with a short appeal in response to a separate question (2:37–40). In Acts 3 the appeal portion of the speech is more developed (3:19–26) after a relatively short kerygmatic introduction (3:12–18). The reversal provides a type of literary balance and also shows that the gospel was preached with some variety of emphasis between facts and appeal. It may well also assume that the events about Jesus are now better known, so that the issue of response can become the focus.

Exegesis and Exposition

[11]While he held on to Peter and John, all the people ran together to them in the portico that was called Solomon's, completely amazed. [12]And when Peter saw it, he responded to the people, "Men of Israel, why are you amazed at this one, or why do you gaze at us, as though by our own power or piety we had made him walk? [13]The God of Abraham and the God of Isaac and the God of Jacob, the God of our fathers, glorified his servant Jesus, whom you handed over and denied in the presence of Pilate, when he had given a judgment to release him. [14]But you denied the Holy and Righteous One and asked for a murderer to be given to you, [15]and you killed the Author of life, whom God raised from the dead. Of this one we are witnesses. [16]And on the basis of faith in his name, his name strengthened this one whom you see and know; and the faith, the one that comes through Jesus, gave the man this perfect health in your presence. [17]And now, brethren, I know that you ⌜acted⌝ without understanding, just as also your rulers. [18]But what things he foretold through the mouth of all the prophets, that his Christ should suffer, God thus fulfilled.

[19]"Repent, therefore, and turn that your sins may be washed away, [20]so that the times of refreshing from the presence of the Lord might come and he might

send the Christ previously appointed for you, Jesus, [21]whom it is necessary that heaven receive until the seasons of restoration of all, of which God spoke through the mouth of his holy prophets from of old. [22]Moses said ⌐ ⌐, 'The Lord your God shall raise up for you a prophet like me from among your brothers. You shall listen to him according to whatever he tells you. [23]And it shall be that every soul that does not listen to that prophet shall be destroyed from the people.' [24]And all the prophets from Samuel and those who followed afterward spoke and proclaimed these days. [25]You are the sons of the prophets and the covenant that God gave to your fathers, saying to Abraham, 'And in your seed shall all the families of the earth ⌐be blessed⌐.' [26]God, having raised up his servant, sent him to you first, so he might bless you by turning every one of you from your wickedness."

The scene begins with a crowd gathering around the three at Solomon's **3:11** portico.[1] The setting is on the east side of the court of Gentiles (Josephus, *Ant.* 15.11.3–5 §§391–420 [Herod's rebuilding of the temple]; 20.9.7 §221 [Solomon's portico]; *J.W.* 5.5.1 §§184–85). It was a famous location for commerce and discussion (see Acts 5:12b). The location is outside the Nicanor Gate, so they may be leaving the temple.[2] The account does not provide a time reference sufficient to say that the apostles are still going into the temple when the speech is made.[3] It certainly would take a little time for word to spread and a crowd to gather.

As the recently healed man clings to the apostles, the people are astounded (ἔκθαμβοι, *ekthamboi*). Haenchen (1987: 204) suggests that his clinging is the man's way of showing the crowd who healed him. Here is yet another term for "amazement" in the chapter. The intensive form (note the *ek* prefix here) of the word used in Acts 3:10 for "wonder" (*thambous*) gives us a second term in two verses for the crowd's reaction. The verb (*thaumazō*) of this noun (*thambos*) shows up in 3:12 (θαυμάζετε, *thaumazete*) with Peter's remark about why the crowd is in a state of wonder. The term in 3:11 means "utterly astounded." This is its only use in the NT.

Peter seizes the opportunity to explain what is taking place and to pro- **3:12** claim Jesus. He corrects a misunderstanding, just as he did in Acts 2:15. The event and its misunderstanding require a speech. He addresses the

---

1. Jesus taught here, as John 10:23 indicates. Also Luke 2:46 and 19:47 speak of teaching in the temple.

2. This observation is made *pace* Haenchen 1987: 204, who says this shows that Luke does not have good knowledge of the temple, since they would have to be going out, not in, as Haenchen thinks the sequence requires. The charge of Haenchen ignores the possibility of literary compression in the account.

3. So correctly Bruce 1990: 138, who notes the rendering of D as correct (but not original) in its expansion that they were leaving. If the Shushan Gate was the earlier locale, then this is adjacent to it; Marshall 1980: 90.

Israelites (see 2:22) at the temple and asks them why they are so utterly amazed. If they had been paying attention to the events of recent days, they would not be surprised, nor would they stand there gazing at them (for the term ἀτενίζετε, *atenizete*, see on 3:3–5). The reference to "this" (τούτῳ, *toutō*) is probably masculine and refers to "this one," pointing to the healed man (although a neuter—to wonder "at this event"—is possible).

The crowd's attention has turned from the lame man to his two healers. The crowd should be careful to place the credit for the healing in the right place. The question makes clear that it is not by "our own power and piety" (ἰδίᾳ δυνάμει ἢ εὐσεβείᾳ, *idia dynamei ē eusebeia*) that this miracle has occurred. Outside this verse, the term for "piety" appears only in the Pastorals (ten times) and 2 Peter (four times) and refers to someone of good character. Mere piety cannot explain this healing, nor is it their character that has persuaded God to act. They are neither Hellenistic wonder-workers nor "divine men" (correctly Conzelmann 1987: 28; Witherington 1998: 179; also Acts 14:15), nor are they "Jewish charismatics" (correctly Barrett 1994: 193). Their capability comes from another, as Peter will explain.

Peter seeks to give appropriate credit and attention. It is God and his glorification of Jesus that has led to this healing. As Stott (1990: 91) indicates, "The power was Christ's; the hand was Peter's." The idea is not to give undue attention to those through whom Jesus worked. Peter makes sure the credit belongs to God. The infinitive περιπατεῖν (*peripatein*, to walk) gives the purpose and result of the healing (Moule 1959: 128). It is not their power that has resulted in the lame man now walking. Before making the explicit declaration in verse 16, Peter lays some historical, kerygmatic groundwork in verses 13–15. Understanding who Jesus is will help them appreciate what Jesus does.

3:13   When Peter mentions the God of Abraham, Isaac, and Jacob, he invokes the God of promise and the God of the nation.[4] When he says God is the God of *our* fathers, he identifies himself as a member of the nation and an object of that promise along with his audience. God is at work in a fresh way for his people.

This work includes the glorification of God's servant Jesus. The term παῖς (*pais*) is important in the NT when it is used as a title and not as a reference to a son or servant (Matt. 12:18 [alludes to Isa. 42:1]; Luke 1:54 [of Israel]; 1:69 [of David]; Acts 3:13; 3:26 [of Jesus raised]; 4:25 [of David]; 4:27, 30 [of Jesus]; seven of twenty-four NT occurrences). In Luke-Acts the title is used in a somewhat generic sense of one who

4. Exod. 3:6, 15–16; 4:5; 1 Kings 18:36; 1 Chron. 29:18; Acts 7:32; Eighteen Benedictions 1: "Blessed are you, O Lord our God and God of our fathers, God of Abraham, God of Isaac, and God of Jacob." On the God of covenant promise, see Acts 3:25; 5:30; 7:32; 13:17, 32; 22:14; 26:6.

is commissioned by God and serves God. The use of Isa. 53 in Luke 22:37 and Acts 8:32–33 points to an allusion here to the servant figure of Isa. 53. In addition, the expression "God . . . glorified his servant" is similar to Isa. 52:13 (also Acts 3:26; 4:27, 30; Eckey 2000: 107). The juxtaposition of the servant to the servant David in Luke-Acts suggests a regal-messianic dimension to this use and also may open up an allusion to the Isa. 53 image.

The idea of a generic servant of God tied to suffering fits Jewish usage. The term "servant" is used of the rejected righteous man in Wis. 2:13, where it is not messianic in force. A later Jewish text, however, 2 Bar. 70.9, uses it of the Messiah. Bruce (1990: 139–40) argues that Jesus saw his suffering as Son of Man through the lens of the servant image. Witherington (1998: 179–80) notes that the point is that God is at work fulfilling messianic prophecy, as 3:19 also suggests. Williams (1990: 75) surveys the NT use of the Servant Songs (also Menard 1957; Jeremias, *TDNT* 5:709–17). Barrett (1994: 194) sees a clear allusion here but, for reasons that are not clear, says it is a late development in the church. There is no good reason to make the roots of this association late rather than in Jesus's own usage. The tradition is too widely distributed across various early Christian sources to be late (Mark 10:45; 14:24; Luke 22:37; John 12:38; 1 Pet. 2:22–24). The later Jewish Targum Jonathan adds the term "Messiah" to the term "servant" in rendering Isa. 42:1 and 52:13. Thus a messianic overtone is most likely present in the use of this title.

In fact, God glorified (ἐδόξασεν, *edoxasen*) his servant. This reverses the normal pattern associated with glory. God is the one usually glorified (Luke 18:43; 23:47; Acts 4:21; 11:18; 13:48 [God's word]; 21:20), so this expression is unique in Acts (Luke 4:15 is its only use with reference to Jesus in the Gospel). The remark alludes to a product of the resurrection-ascension, namely, this healing, and points to God's acceptance of Jesus after his suffering, a pattern that is like Isa. 52:13–53:12 with suffering followed by glory. Haenchen (1987: 205) denies any allusion to the resurrection-ascension here, but it is the presupposition for Jesus being able to heal. So both the healing and what permits it are in view (so Weiser 1981: 116 with Barrett 1994: 195; see Luke 24:26; 9:26, 32; 21:27). Fitzmyer (1998: 285) sees the force of glorification as bestowing "the status of glory," but he argues that "servant" is not a messianic title. However, by the time of the church and in Jesus's use, suffering and glory were fused together in sequence, as were Messiah and servant. Jesus is alive and still at work, as God promised of the Messiah.

God's activity contrasts with that of the crowd toward Jesus (vv. 13b–15). The crowd delivered up and denied Jesus in the presence of Pilate, a theme in Acts (4:10; 5:30; 7:52; 13:28).[5] The use of "you" (ὑμεῖς, *hymeis*,

---

5. On Pilate, Josephus, see *Ant.* 18.3.1–4.2 §§55–89. Philo, *Embassy* 38 §301 calls him inflexible and relentless.

plural) is emphatic and charges the Jewish crowd with responsibility through actions initiated by Israel's leaders but later approved by Jewish crowds in Jerusalem. The remark describes and summarizes Luke 23:1–25, almost making a commentary on those verses. "Deliver Jesus over" appears in some texts in Luke (9:44; 18:32; 22:4, 6, 21–22, 48; 23:25 [of Pilate giving Jesus over to the Jewish will]; 24:7, 20; also Acts 21:11 [of Paul]; 1 Cor. 11:23) but is an unusual expression in Acts. The idea of Jesus being given over or giving himself is in language that is like Isa. 53. Such allusions run through Christian tradition (Marshall 1980: 91; in NT: Mark 10:45; 14:24; Luke 22:37; John 12:38; 1 Pet. 2:22–24; in the early church: Did. 9.2–3; 1 Clem. 59.2–4; Barn. 6.1; 9.2; Mart. Pol. 14.1; 20.2; on Luke's view of the cross, Moessner 1996). To deny Jesus, as Peter charges here, is to leave a person subject to judgment in Luke (Luke 12:9; Schneider 1980: 319). The charge is repeated in Acts 3:14, but these are the only two references to Jesus in Acts with the verb "deny," making it another unusual expression. These expressions show the traditional touches in the speech. It was the Jerusalem Jews' corporate act that prevented Pilate from releasing Jesus (see Acts 4:27). Thus here we have an elaboration on the charge against the Jewish audience in 2:22–23. The Jewish leaders may have started the process, but the crowd approved it. What "you all" approved (vv. 13–15) can be reversed (vv. 25–26), so there is no hint of anti-Semitism in these remarks (as is correctly noted by Witherington 1998: 181).

3:14 The result of this opposition was that they denied and slew God's Righteous and Holy One, while preferring that a murderer (Barabbas) be released (literally, be granted [χαρισθῆναι, charisthēnai] to them) in his place. This "substitution" is an element of the theological significance of Jesus's work. It also underscores the culpability of choosing a murderer over one who reflects holiness and righteousness. How blind and how culpable could they be for this choice?

Jesus as the Holy One (τὸν ἅγιον, ton hagion) also evokes a theme Luke has highlighted since early in his Gospel. This title shows up in a few places in the NT for Jesus (Mark 1:24; Luke 4:34; John 6:69; 1 John 2:20; Rev. 3:7; in the OT, of Elijah, 2 Kings 4:9; and of Aaron, Ps. 106:16). Twice it appears in the confession of demons (Mark 1:24; Luke 4:34) and once regarding the disciples (John 6:69). Luke 1:35 is close in calling "holy" the child who is Spirit-conceived. Jesus is set apart. Some see here an allusion to a title for God (Lev. 11:44–45; Ps. 77:41 LXX [78:41 Eng.]; Witherington 1998: 181). Jesus's exaltation allows this kind of implication to be possible for this term here. Jesus is worthy through his glorification to be in God's very presence, as verse 21 points out.

Jesus as the Righteous One (δίκαιον, dikaion) is also significant. This term points to a title that has roots in Isa. 53:11 (see also Jer. 23:5–6; Zech. 6:12; Le Cornu and Shulam 2003: 200–201). The "Righteous One" was a messianic description in Judaism (1 En. 38.2; 46.3; 53.6; Ps. Sol. 17.32; see OT: 2 Sam. 23:3; Isa. 32:1; 53:11; Zech. 9:9; Bruce 1990: 141). This description of Jesus looks back at the cross in Luke 23:47, when the centurion declared Jesus to be innocent/righteous. The title reappears in Acts 7:52 and 22:14. An innocent was put to death, one who was righteous before God. Peter holds the audience responsible for this before God.

The charge continues in an even more tightly constructed contrast. "You   **3:15** [all] killed the Author/Prince of life, whom God raised from the dead." There is debate about the meaning of the ambiguous term ἀρχηγόν (*archēgon*). Should it be rendered "Author" or "Prince," since the term can carry both meanings (BAGD 112 §1; BDAG 138–39; Müller, *EDNT* 1:163–64: "leads the way into life")? The term appears four times in the NT (Acts 3:13–15; 5:30–31; Heb. 2:10; 12:1–2). In Acts 3 Jesus is seen as one who leads to life versus one who removes it. Is he the first among many, the one who shows and rules the way (so "Leader" or, as KJV and NASB render this term, "Prince")?[6] Or is he the one who makes life possible (so "Author" in NLT, NIV, RSV, ESV; "Originator" in NET; Heb. 2:10)?[7] The latter sense (despite the claim of Müller in *EDNT*) is slightly more likely, given that Jesus has healed the lame man, as verse 16 indicates. The expression also stands in contrast to a murderer who takes life (Johnson 1992: 68). Jesus not only leads to life; he is its source as a result of faith in him. Schille (1984: 127–28) calls "leader" too weak a translation. There may be a double entendre here (Polhill 1992: 132). The connection of salvation and life in Acts is common (5:20; 11:18; 13:46).

Regardless of the force given to ἀρχηγόν, Jesus's healing shows his authority in relationship to life and makes his healing a rule miracle, that is, a miracle indicating that such authority comes from God and exercises rule over life. It is also clear that God has worked on Jesus's behalf previously, showing his support for Jesus by raising him from the dead (Acts 4:10; 5:30; 10:40; 13:30, 37). The implication is that it is not good to make a judgment that differs from God by killing the one he commissioned. To have agreed to such an act leaves one in a very bad position before God. Of this unique one and the resurrection associated with him, the apostles are witnesses, a theme discussed in Acts 1:8 (Luke 24:49). Peter claims to have direct knowledge of what he testifies.

In sum, there are four charges in verses 13–15: the Jews of Jerusalem handed Jesus over to be killed; they disowned him before Pilate; they

---

6. Supporting this interpretation is Larkin 1995: 67. See Num. 13:2 (leader of the tribe); of David: Ezek. 34:24 (prince); 37:25 (prince). On "leader to life," reading "life" as a genitive of direction, see Haenchen 1987: 206n4.

7. See Josephus, *Ag. Ap.* 1.19 §130; conceptually, Acts 2:32; 26:23; Fitzmyer 1998: 286. Bruce 1988a: 82 appeals to an equivalent term in Aramaic that can mean salvation and life. On use with the idea of "cause," see Josephus, *Ant.* 7.9.4 §207.

asked for a murderer instead of the Author of life; and then they caused the death of the Author of life in the sense that their actions led the way to his death (Stott 1990: 92).

3:16   This verse gives the answer to the question of the source of the healing (see v. 12). It is written in a very contorted syntax (Williams 1990: 75–76), but this is a result of highlighting the role of the name and the person of Jesus, whose "name" is mentioned twice in the verse, as is the twofold mention of faith connected to him. Add to this the single mention of "Jesus," and he is identified three times in the remark.

The verse begins emphatically with the phrase "on the basis of faith in his name" (ἐπὶ τῇ πίστει τοῦ ὀνόματος αὐτοῦ, *epi tē pistei tou onomatos autou*). The use of "faith" as a term for a response is also frequent in Acts, which sometimes speaks of an initial faith and other times of faith as a characteristic of one's life (3:16; 6:5–7; 11:23–24; 13:8; 14:9–10, 21–22, 27; 15:8–9; 16:5; 17:30–31; 20:18–21; 24:24; 26:16–18). In 14:9 it is healing that is believed in, whereas in 20:21 it is the message. In 13:8 the movement itself is simply called the faith, whereas in 6:5–7 men of faith are chosen for a task. This shows the range of the term in Acts. Whose faith is meant here, that of Peter and John (Barrett 1994: 200; Witherington 1998: 182; vv. 12–13), or that of the man (Haenchen 1987: 207; Jervell 1998: 165), or that of all three? Barrett says that it is the faith of the apostles, since the man was looking only for money. But he did respond to the apostles (so correctly Bruce 1988a: 82). Given that faith can refer to the start of faith or its ongoing character, it is not impossible in this case that all three are meant, but certainly the lame man is the key one who responds and whose response is represented in what is said about repentance in verse 19 (14:9 also points to a response in a healing context). The lame man's response to his healing shows that he did respond to what God had done and was thankful for it. So the appeal is to the value of a response, and so the man must be included. In this way, the text shows God's initiative through his servants and then the response such an initiative should bring. The man can now bring strong testimony to God's work through Jesus, even by just standing there with the apostles.

The importance of the idea of Jesus's name is discussed at 2:21, 38 and 3:6. It is a way of pointing to the person. It is his name, the person of Jesus, that has brought strength to legs that previously were weak. The one healed is one they know and see. They know his history as the man at the gate who regularly begged for alms. Now he is whole, restored to "perfect health" (ὁλοκληρίαν, *holoklērian*). This hapax term means to bring something to wholeness or to sound well-being and thus full health ("complete health" in NET; "complete healing" in NIV; "perfect health" in NASB, RSV, ESV). In the LXX it refers to an unblemished animal that is qualified for sacrifice because it is sound (Zech. 11:16;

so it is not merely a technical medical term; Bruce 1990: 142; Witherington 1998: 182). The idea of faith through Jesus is repeated here to drive the point home that the healing took place in their presence. So God working through Jesus is a fact. What should be the response to this present and visible divine work through Jesus?

These verses contain another contrast. Peter speaks of his hearers as   3:17–18
brethren, beginning his transition to the application of his speech (καὶ νῦν, *kai nun*, and now). "Brethren" here reflects their shared Jewish identity, not as "if they were already Christians" (*pace* Haenchen 1987: 207; with Fitzmyer 1998: 287). Since these verses are a bridge, many commentators make this a new section of the speech, but conceptually Peter is still summarizing what took place and how things reached this point. So I opt to leave it as part of the speech's first section, which lays the historical-theological groundwork.

The Jews and their leaders who prodded them acted in ignorance, but what took place fulfilled God's plan as revealed in the prophets. That plan taught that the Christ would suffer. Human responsibility and divine design are side by side. Ignorance does not alleviate the need to repent, because the penalty and responsibility for the ignorance are still present, as verses 19–23 show. Luke 13:33–35 has Jesus declaring Israel's house desolate or in spiritual exile until the nation responds. The term ἄγνοια (*agnoia*, ignorance) appears four times in the NT (Acts 3:17–18; 17:30–31; Eph. 4:17–19; 1 Pet. 1:14–16). Acts 17:30 speaks of God overlooking the past time of ignorance *for the nations* (i.e., not Jews as here), but this is no longer the case. This ignorance does not leave one without responsibility or excuse, which is why the crowd must act. Ignorance cannot provide an ultimate excuse, especially now that Peter has revealed God's program to them. Their sin of not recognizing Jesus as Messiah and of killing him can still be forgiven if they respond (Pesch 1986a: 154; Schneider 1980: 322; Luke 23:34; 1 Tim. 1:13; also perhaps 1 Cor. 2:8, but 1 Corinthians may refer to spiritual powers).

Marshall (1980: 92) suggests that Peter turns their ignorance into a willing sin, for which there is no atonement if they now fail to respond (Num. 15:22–31 notes the distinction in types of sin; Lev. 22:14). That is likely not the case. Both the crowd and the rulers did not act out of knowledge at the time, but it was not because they were not given an opportunity to respond. In other words, the idea is that they were confronted earlier with what they were doing, as Jesus warned them throughout the last week of his ministry. They acted in ignorance, however, in the sense that they did not understand what it was they truly were doing (Acts 13:27). It was not an ignorance of a lack of opportunity to understand, but an ignorance in failing to perceive with understanding. Peter is making this clear, just as God's acting through Jesus in this healing shows what the understanding of Jesus should be. This healing and what it means give them another opportunity to understand what they have done. Later Jewish texts point out the need for Israel to respond anew to God. If the people of Israel do not repent, they will not be redeemed (b. Sanh. 97b), and if they repent for a day, the Son of David will come (y. Ta'an. 1.1 [64a]; Witherington 1998: 183).

Rulers (οἱ ἄρχοντες, hoi archontes) are often mentioned in Acts and are seen as a driving force behind Jesus's death in Luke 23 (Acts 3:17–18; 4:5–10, 26; 7:27, 35; 13:27–28; 14:5–7; 16:19–21; 23:5). Polhill (1992: 133) notes four themes that intertwine in Acts: (1) those who killed Jesus acted in ignorance, not appreciating what they did; (2) the condemnation of Jews is not a blanket one but involves Jerusalemites; (3) Gentiles shared in being culpable; and (4) it was all part of a divine plan.

God foretold these events. The term προκαταγγέλλω (prokatangellō, foretell) is not common in the NT (Acts 3:17–18; 7:52–53). But Luke often notes that the Christ was to suffer (παθεῖν τὸν χριστόν, pathein ton christon) either according to Scripture or by God's plan (Luke 24:25–26, 45–47; Acts 3:17–18; conceptually, Luke 9:22; 17:25; Acts 17:3; 26:22–23; also 1 Pet. 2:21, 23; 3:17–18).[8] Peter is making clear that a Messiah who suffers, which was not an expectation in Judaism, is something God planned and Scripture declared, even though Peter does not note a specific text here. Luke's earlier use of the righteous-sufferer texts (Pss. 22, 69) and his allusion to Isa. 53 in verse 13 show the roots of the concept Peter argues for here at a literary level. With the historical-theological ground now set, Peter can make his call for their response, and his rationale for it, in verses 19–26. Bruce (1990: 143) notes that this work by the Christ allows for sin to be blotted out, implying an atoning significance to Jesus's work (Rom. 3:19–31).[9]

3:19 The application of the speech emerges with the use of οὖν (oun, therefore). Acts 3:19–21 is so important for the presentation of eschatology in Acts that each phrase needs careful attention (Witherington 1998: 184–86). The text shows that Luke, for all his emphasis on what is happening now eschatologically, has not abandoned the idea of a future eschatology. Luke's eschatology is now and not yet. In Acts 2 the now is emphasized. In Acts 3 what is to come is highlighted. No one can know the timing of the end (1:6–7), but one can know what this return means and what it will bring (3:20–21).

The call is made with a double imperative to repent (μετανοήσατε, metanoēsate) and turn (ἐπιστρέψατε, epistrepsate). Both verbs are aorist and thus represent summary calls to repent and turn. It is the crowd's view of Jesus that needs altering (v. 17).

---

8. In Judaism, b. Ber. 34b has all of Scripture speak of the days of the Messiah; so Barrett 1994: 202.

9. For how the church doctrinally came to see Jesus's death as for our sake and in our stead, see Pelikan 2005: 63–66.

Repentance as the summary response to the apostolic message also appears in 2:38 (see discussion there; 3:19–21; 8:22–23; 17:30–31; 26:19–20; also Luke 3:8–14; 5:32). It stresses the need for a change in direction, to change one's mind about where one is. Such a call reappears in Acts 17:30 and 26:20, showing that repentance is for all, both Jews and Gentiles.

The idea of turning also makes this point and highlights the process of ending up in line with God. Ἐπιστρέφω (epistrephō, turn) appears eleven times in Acts, seven of which refer to turning to God or the Lord (see asterisks; 1 Thess. 1:9; *Acts 3:19–21; *9:35, 40; *11:21; *14:15–17; *15:19–20, 36; 16:18; *26:16–20 [2x]; *28:24–27; in the OT: Isa. 6:10; 9:13; 55:7; Hos. 5:4; 6:1; Amos 4:6; Joel 2:12–14; Johnson 1992: 68). Important to note is that whereas "faith" is the term highlighted in verse 16, now repentance and turning are called for. Peter uses a variety of terms to describe properly responding to his message. The variety indicates that the early church had a collection of terms, not just one, to indicate how to respond to the gospel. Williams (1990: 71) speaks of repentance and faith being "almost" synonymous. Each term, however, focuses on an aspect of what is essentially one positive response to the message. Repentance is the starting point of that response, and faith is where the process ends up.

The result of the turning (εἰς, eis) is to blot out (ἐξαλειφθῆναι, exaleiphthēnai; BDF §402.5) sin. This is another way to describe obtaining forgiveness (see also Col. 2:14–15; Rev. 3:5; 7:16–17; 21:3–4). In the LXX the verb is used to describe being blotted out of God's book if one is not forgiven (Exod. 32:32), blotting out sin (2 Macc. 12:42), a request to blot out sin (Ps. 51:9 [50:11 LXX]), and a request not to let the sin of an unrighteous one be blotted out (Ps. 109:14 [108:14 LXX]; Jer. 18:23). Isaiah 43:25 is very close in sense to the use here in Acts, as is Isa. 32:15 Symmachus, highlighting the work of the Spirit (Larkin 1995: 68, note on 3:19). The term means "wipe away," "erase," or "obliterate" (BAGD 272 §2; BDAG 344). It was used of washing papyri to remove letters written in ink. In ancient times ink did not soak into the paper but remained on the surface, so removing writing was straightforward. This then became the metaphor (Stott 1990: 93). Thus it means an obliteration that leaves no trace. Peter offers the opportunity to have the penalty of sin removed completely.

There are further consequences of Jesus's work. The term ὅπως (hopōs)   **3:20–21** usually indicates purpose (Acts 3:19–21; 8:14–16, 24; 9:1–2, 11–12, 17, 24–25; 15:15–18; 20:16; 23:15; 25:26–27; other occurrences of this term in Acts do not indicate purpose; BDF §369.5; Moule 1959: 138). This purpose links to what forgiveness and what the times of refreshing lead to, namely, the ultimate return of Jesus. The idea of divine design expresses the hope and ultimate goal of reaching such an outcome. Divine design is indicated by the use of δεῖ (dei, it is necessary) in verse

21, where heaven *must* hold Jesus until the time of return. Jesus is also referred to as the appointed Christ in this verse. In Jewish understanding, repentance, when it takes place en masse, can set the cycle in place that leads to the completion of God's plan, the arrival of times of refreshing, and the sending of the Christ (see discussion of 3:17–18; other Jewish texts are T. Dan 6.4; T. Sim. 6.2–7; T. Mos. 10.1–10; 2 Esd. [4 Ezra] 4:39; Talbert 1997: 55; Barrett 1994: 203). The Jewish belief was that a corporate response of righteousness could lead to the promise's completion as a righteously prepared people experience blessing's complete fulfillment. The idea of divine design in the rest of this text suggests that this Jewish idea may not be so prominent, since it suggests too much cause and effect from the human response, but the assumption is that in the final era many will be responsive and ready for God's rule to come in fullness. The point of the verse, then, is that these events are associated with one another in a kind of package deal rather than in a strict cause-and-effect relationship. Acts 1:6–7 also underscores that God has a specific timing in place, and so this repentance is not the cause of the return. Peter's appeal is made to each one, but its impact is especially effective if many respond.

The "times of refreshing" (καιροὶ ἀναψύξεως, *kairoi anapsycheōs*) is another NT hapax expression. It looks to a period of time that includes rest and refreshment (Kremer, *EDNT* 1:95). Ἀνάψυξις refers to a "cooling" to relieve trouble or to dry out a wound ("refreshment" in NLT; "refreshing" in NIV, RSV, NET; BAGD 63; BDAG 75; Schweizer, *TDNT* 9:664; Fitzmyer 1998: 288, "to cool by blowing" is the idea of the related verb). In the LXX the only use of ἀνάψυξις is in Exod. 8:11 LXX (= 8:15 Eng.), where it refers to relief from the plague of frogs. The verb ἀναψύχω (*anapsychō*, to refresh) is used of the Sabbath rest of slaves and animals and the soothing of Saul by David's music (Johnson 1992: 69; Exod. 23:12; 1 Sam. 16:23). The arrival, then, is of a period of messianic refreshment, the "definitive age of salvation" (Schweizer, *TDNT* 9:664). The idea has parallels in Judaism (2 Esd. [4 Ezra] 7:75, 91, 95; 11:46; 13:26–29; 2 Bar. 73–74; 1 En. 45.5; 51.4; 96.3; Bruce 1990: 144) and is traditional in its origin (*pace* Kremer, *EDNT* 1:95, who argues that this is a Lukan expression). It refers to entry into a new and unending eschatological life before the Lord. The closest parallel in the NT is the concept of "rest" in Heb. 3–4 (Pesch 1986a: 155). One wonders if ἀνάψυξις alludes to the Spirit's washing work in the messianic age that points to spiritual refreshment.

The reference to times and seasons contains terms that appear in Luke 21:24 (times [καιροί] of the Gentiles—the current era) and Acts 1:6–7.[10] The question in Acts 1 receives a reply that it is not for Peter's hearers

---

10. See discussion there, where the question is whether this is the time (χρόνῳ) to restore the kingdom to Israel (looking to a future time).

to know the times or seasons—a reply that uses both terms for "time." In other words, their repentance brings both times of refreshment and times establishing all things God promised (Barrett 1994: 205). All of this takes place before the Lord, before his presence.

Along with this entry into refreshment is the completion of God's plan with Christ's return. Peter is urging repentance so that one can participate in God's entire planned program from start to finish. A key aspect of that program is Jesus's return, when the Christ will exercise judgment on behalf of righteousness and complete God's promise already outlined in the prophetic teaching of the Hebrew Scripture. Nothing Peter says here indicates that anything promised there has been changed. The timing of the consummation comes down the road, but what will happen has been and remains described in those texts. Peter speaks of God sending the Christ appointed (προκεχειρισμένον, *prokecheirismenon*) for all of them. Note that the second-person pronoun (ὑμῖν, *hymin*) is plural. Both other occurrences of "appointed" in Acts are about Paul as a chosen servant of God (22:14–15; 26:16–18).

This Christ is received in heaven for now. Here is another way to portray the experience of ascension. Heaven holds Jesus at God's side until the day he is revealed in return (Luke 21:25–28). He is not passive until the return, however, as Acts 2 shows that Jesus is quite active now in salvation in distributing the Spirit, and Acts 3 shows him as the source of this healing. As Bruce notes (1988a: 85), "Jesus must reign at God's right hand until all hostile powers are overthrown" (1 Cor. 15:24–28).

Nevertheless, with his return comes "the seasons of the restoration of all things" (χρόνων ἀποκαταστάσεως πάντων, *chronōn apokatastaseōs pantōn*), yet another NT hapax expression. The term ἀποκατάστασις (*apokatastasis*, establishment) does not appear in the LXX (Müller, *EDNT* 1:130). The anticipated end was seen as establishing again the original creation's pristine character. This restoration is what Jesus brings with his return, an idea given later development in Rev. 19–22 but whose roots Peter declares here are already evident in that "of which God spoke through the holy prophets of old." The relative pronoun ὧν (*hōn*, of which) could refer back to "the seasons" of which God spoke (Bauernfeind 1980: 69) or to "all things" of which God spoke (so Conzelmann 1987: 29; Barrett 1994: 206, nearest referent). Acts 3:24 appears to highlight the period of time being addressed by the promise ("these days"), but it is the content that is being highlighted here—that all things will be restored (taking πάντων as the antecedent of ὧν; so Oepke, *TDNT* 1:391: the new world and the messianic creation in a final and complete restoration). In the NT this idea is discussed in Matt. 19:28; Rom. 8:18–23; and Heb. 2:5–8. The point is that God has already indicated what the end will be like. So, to learn about the future, Peter urges them to read what God has already said through the prophets about the new era the eschaton would bring. The expression about the prophets is like Luke 1:70. Texts such as Isa. 65–66 are in view, where Israel is restored to fullness (also Isa. 34:4; 51:6; Jer. 15:18–19; 16:15; 23:8; 24:6; Ezek. 17:23; Amos 9:11–12; Jervell 1998: 167n358). The two expressions for time—καιροί and χρόνοι—probably look at one period, as opposed to distinct periods of time. However, it is seen as one great, extended period (thus the plurals) whose high point is Christ's return, and so the stress is on what participation in the period of messianic blessing ultimately will yield (Marshall 1980: 93–94).

In sum, three blessings are offered in verses 19–21: the forgiveness of sins, the promise of times of refreshing, and the opportunity to participate in the return of the Messiah. Jesus brings all of this over time. Stott (1990: 94) calls these total forgiveness, spiritual refreshment, and universal restoration. The process starts with forgiveness and runs through Jesus's return.

3:22 The promise of a great deliverance figure and what is at stake in responding to him are the topics of verses 22–23. Peter cites Deut. 18:15 with only three minor changes from the MT and LXX. The second-person pronouns are plural rather than singular to make a more direct connection with the audience. At the end of the second sentence of the citation, the call to obey is made to all the listeners (πρὸς ὑμᾶς, *pros hymas*, the second-person pronoun addressing the crowd, is plural also). This addition replicates the call at the beginning of the citation (ὑμῖν, *hymin*), alludes to Deut. 18:15, and also includes the phrase "according to whatever he tells you" as a summary of the point from Deut. 18:19. Finally, the addition at the beginning of the next verse, "it shall be," sets up the linkage to a second OT citation from Lev. 23:29. The pronoun is moved forward (ὑμῖν, *hymin*, for you) to make the point that God's action of raising up a prophet like Moses is for the benefit of the people, a clear example of a dative of advantage.

Peter makes clear that the promise of a great saving leader-prophet like Moses is something the OT declared. Such a prophet God would "raise up" (ἀναστήσει, *anastēsei*). This verb, reused in verse 26, may well have a wordplay built around it (also Acts 13:33). It means to bring someone onto the scene of history but could in this context allude to resurrection, to raise someone up, especially in its second occurrence later in the speech (Larkin 1995: 69; Acts 3:26).

In the original context, this promise of a prophet would have alluded to Joshua or others. Their presence as those who could speak for God would preclude the need to appeal to magic or divination. This passage came to be seen by first-century Judaism, however, as a typological promise of a prophet of the Mosaic leader-deliverer pattern who was a part of the eschaton (Bock 1987: 191–94). The expectation of a Moses-like figure in the end time was common in Judaism (1QS 1.9–11; 4Q175 1.5–8; 1 Macc. 14:41). Josephus (*Ant.* 20.5.1 §97) shows a first-century Jewish figure, Theudas, trying to invoke Moses's parting of the sea to make the case that he is a prophet who could lead Israel (Witherington 1998: 188). The Samaritans pointed to this passage as describing a restorer figure known as the *Taheb* (Memar Marqah 4.3; Teeple 1957: 63–68, 108–9; Polhill 1992: 136; DeWaard 1971; Scobie 1972–73; Jeremias, *TDNT* 4:848–73). This pattern and connection to the Mosaic promise are repeated in Acts 7:22, 25, 30–39 and were alluded to in Luke 9:35 (Pesch 1986a: 157).[11]

3:23 The second OT citation that discusses the promise and the proper response to it comes from a mixture of Deut. 18:19 and Lev. 23:29. Here negative consequences for rejection appear as a prophetic warning. The concept of listening to the prophet is from Deut. 18:19, and the penalty of destruction and separation from God's people comes from Lev. 23:29. The patchwork nature of the citation is not common for Luke (but see Luke 4:16–18 using Isa. 61:1 and 58:6; Acts 7:7 using Gen. 15:13–14 and Exod. 3:12). It suggests the presence of tradition.

The reference to "every soul" (πᾶσα ψυχή, *pasa psychē*) provides the point of contact with Leviticus. Deuteronomy 18:19 appears in various Jewish texts with similar wording (Targum Pseudo-Jonathan on Deut. 18:19b; Codex Neofiti I on Deut. 18:19; 4Q175 6–8 [an eschatological *testimonia* text]). Another point of contact with Leviticus is the strong reference to the penalty of destruction for not listening to the prophet (ἐξολεθρευθήσεται ἐκ τοῦ λαοῦ, *exolethreuthēsetai ek tou laou*, shall be destroyed from the people). The verb depicts utter destruction (BAGD 276; BDAG 351; "completely cut off" in NIV). This is the only use of this verb in the NT. In Leviticus the passage refers to not keeping the atonement, and so there is an interesting parallel here. Failure to listen to (i.e., obey) this prophet and his career of suffering and glorification is like failing to heed the atonement. Given what Jesus went through, the association points to a significant implication of Jesus's death: enabling sin to be blotted out (v. 19; the association of the promise of Gen. 22:18 in Acts 3:25 may also support this allusion; Schneider 1980: 327). The remark warns of total judgment for failing to respond to the person and work of Jesus, who is *the* prophet like Moses. Peter declares that those who fail to respond will have no place among God's people (J. Schneider, *TDNT* 5:171).[12]

3:24 Peter starts by citing Torah texts, the most respected portion of the Hebrew Scripture. But this promise, he argues, runs from Samuel to those

11. Barrett 1994: 207–8 argues against a typological reference to the exodus, but the multiple uses of Deuteronomy in Luke-Acts support such a connection. Barrett is too skeptical of the Jewish roots here. John's Gospel has more of this theme: John 1:21; 6:14; 7:40.

12. In the Mishnah, *Ker.* 1.1 lists thirty-six sins that lead to being cut off from God's people, but nothing on that list is here. Rejecting God's eschatological revelation is present here.

who followed as well. Samuel does not have a specific prophecy about this period, but he is the prophet tied to David, pointing to a messianic allusion as part of a "son of David" Christology (Bruce 1988a: 87; 1 Sam. 13:14; 15:28; 16:13; 28:17). Williams (1990: 73) notes that the Davidic dynastic hope appears in the book that bears Samuel's name. Fitzmyer (1998: 289) distinguishes between messianic hope and the prophet like Moses, but the leader-prophet motif suggests a closer connection in Acts between the two formerly distinct ideas from Judaism. The prophets also "proclaimed these days" (κατήγγειλαν τὰς ἡμέρας ταύτας, *katēngeilan tas hēmeras tautas*). Out of its eighteen NT occurrences, this verb for "proclaim/preach" occurs eleven times in Acts (3:24; 4:1–3; 13:4–5, 38–39; 15:36; 16:17, 19–21; 17:2–3, 13, 23; 26:22–23). Peter says that to speak of the eschaton is to proclaim the days of divinely promised activity. The remark underscores how Peter is treating all aspects of Jesus's career, from death and glorification to return, as a part of this promise.

3:25 Not only is there eschatological and messianic promise, there is also God's covenant commitment stretching all the way back to Genesis. Peter makes the point that his audience consists of descendants (υἱοί, *huioi*) of the prophets and of those who possess the covenant (τῆς διαθήκης, *tēs diathēkēs*, singular) that Abraham originally received.[13] This is one of only four references to covenant in Luke-Acts out of thirty-three NT occurrences of the term (Luke 1:67–75 [Abraham in the context of the Davidic promise]; 22:20 [new]; Acts 3:25; 7:8 [Abraham/circumcision]; mention of seed [descendants] also appears in Luke 1:55). If anyone should be responsive and understand what God is doing, it is those to whom the prophets spoke (Fitzmyer 1998: 290).

The citation points to the basic covenant originally set forth in Gen. 12:1–3, but part of the wording is closer to its repetition in Gen. 22:18, with the use of the key phrase ἐν τῷ σπέρματι (*en tō spermati*) ("in thy/your seed" in KJV, NASB; "offspring" in ESV, NIV; "descendants" in NET, NLT; "posterity" in RSV; Bock 1987: 195–97). One also can note Gen. 26:4c, but that passage is not in view, as Abraham is the specific recipient noted. Through the seed all the families of the earth will be blessed. The Gen. 22 context is in association with Abraham's willingness to sacrifice Jacob, a second sacrificial allusion in the speech alongside the earlier citation to Lev. 23 in Acts 3:23.

The phrase about the seed in Gen. 22:18 is emphatic since it is moved forward in the sentence (in the MT and LXX the verb for blessing is first). This promise of the seed is the topic of detailed exposition by Paul in Gal. 3:8–29, where he plays on the singularity of the seed even while noting its collective force later in his exposition. Here the point is only

---

13. On "sons of the covenant," see Ezek. 30:5. Ps. Sol. 17.15 has the same construction; also 1QM 17.8; 4Q501 1.1.2; 4Q503 7–9.3. It is a genitive of possession (Moulton and Turner 1963: 208).

that God's promises were made to and for Israel first of all (Acts 13:46; Rom. 1:16–17; 2:9–10). Israel's people are thus the natural recipients of this message of hope, a blessing that is not only for them but also for "all the families of the earth" (πᾶσαι αἱ πατριαὶ τῆς γῆς, *pasai hai patriai tēs gēs*).

The reference to families comes neither from Gen. 12:3 LXX nor 22:18 LXX (see Ps. 21:28 LXX [= 22:27 Eng.], a psalm Jesus uttered from the cross). The detail suggests the presence of a traditional source, since φυλαί (*phylai*, tribes) is not used. Families are mentioned, as this says less than the term for "nations" would (ἔθνη, *ethnē*; Haenchen 1987: 208; Williams 1990: 73). The term has ambiguity without yet pointing to the full universality of the message's scope, which clearly is Luke's ultimate intention given the story line of Acts. Peter may be anticipating Israel's vindication as leading to universal kingdom rule and blessing that involves the families of earth as opposed to the direct route to the nations opened up in Acts 10. The term for "bless," ἐνευλογηθήσονται (*eneulogēthēsontai*), is passive here ("will be blessed" by God), whereas in the MT it is reflexive "bless themselves." But since the source of the blessing is God's work and promise, the difference is not great.

The appeal to old promises is important. It shows that although this community is a seemingly new entity, it is rooted in old promises. In the ancient world, for a religion to be old was a virtue because it meant that the religion had the benefit of experience. Peter's appeal to the past is a form of legitimization for the new community.

In verse 26, Peter particularizes the means of blessing and the seed (v. 25) through whom the promise comes. Blessing comes through the servant (v. 13) God raised up (v. 22) to turn (v. 19) each one of them from their acts of wickedness. This ties the speech together and makes the point that one descendant in particular is fundamental to the plan.[14] This servant was sent to those in Israel first of all.

The goal was to bless (εὐλογοῦντα, *eulogounta*; see v. 25 and a word link to it) all of them, each one. Wallace (2000: 278) speaks of a purpose, or telic, participle here. The interplay between the collective (ὑμᾶς, *hymas*, plural you) and the individual need for response (ἕκαστον, *hekaston*, each one) is evident. That blessing is entered into by turning from wickedness (grammatically, the phrase is instrumental, not temporal; Bruce 1990: 146; BDR §404.2n6; Moulton and Turner 1963: 146). So the goal of the promise about the servant is blessing, and it is reached by means of turning. Barrett (1994: 214) argues that the phrase is also intransitive. The servant turns us from our sins (contextually, he blesses and turns). Contending for a transitive use, however, is Schneider (1980: 329n124). He argues that this expression means "in that you turned"

3:26

---

14. The title "servant" was already discussed in v. 13, "turning" in v. 19, and the phrase "to raise up" in v. 22.

and so the audience makes the turn. Schneider appeals to verse 19 and the call to repent (also BDF §404.3). The choice is not a simple one; perhaps a plenary force is in view—God starts the process of turning, but a response is also required. In favor of the intransitive is that God is the one who acts throughout the speech, but speaking for the transitive is that this closes the speech, which usually means an exhortation to response is present. Nonetheless, the fact that blessing is in view that comes from God suggests that the intransitive idea is more prominent, since it is God's act through the servant that has the purpose of blessing by leading us into turning. To bring out this force, the HCSB renders the phrase ambiguously, as we are the objects of blessing, but the blessing is done by God from within us: "to bless you by turning each of you from your evil ways."

The term πονηριῶν (ponērion, evil acts) is plural and probably collective. This is one of only two plural uses of the term in the NT (Mark 7:21–23 is the other; see also Matt. 22:18; Luke 11:39; Rom. 1:28–32; 1 Cor. 5:8; Eph. 6:11–12). In the turning to God, there is a recognition about the need to change direction concerning the sins one commits. Turning to the servant means becoming an ally of the one who provides and seeks righteousness from us (Acts 26:20, 23). To ask Jesus to blot out one's sins is also to make a statement about sin and the need for forgiveness (in v. 19 the reference to sins is also plural, using a synonym, ἁμαρτίας, hamartias; Barrett 1994: 214). So Peter's speech covers Christology with its many titles for Jesus; eschatology by pointing to the basic time frame of suffering, glorification and return; and soteriology by telling how Jesus, and turning to him, deals with sin and righteousness.

In sum, Acts 3 preaches Jesus from the Torah. Here is the promised seed-servant-prophet-leader like Moses who is the Author of life. God both knew he would suffer and exalted him into heaven at God's side until the time of his return, when the rest of God's promise will be completed. To receive the right to participate in this divine refreshment and the realization of all things, one must repent and turn so that sin might be blotted out. But to reject this promise is to guarantee that one will not be among God's people. The opportunity to share in the blessing God gave to Abraham is available only for those who turn to the one whom God sent to them. Blessing is a gift from God, but it requires conscious reception of itself. Everything is at stake, namely, covenant relationship with God and the deliverance it brings. Salvation is not by human right or by ethnic origin; it comes through response to the promise of God (Larkin 1995: 70). This salvation was designed for Peter's listeners, and so they should be encouraged to respond. Williams (1990: 74) argues that the force is that "you of all people" should respond (Acts 2:39). When it comes to salvation, Jesus is not an option but a necessity (4:12). His career is rooted in promises of old. Salvation comes uniquely through him.

Practical points also emerge. This is a team ministry, with Peter and John sharing the message, which is focused on being sure that Jesus holds the attention, not the ministers (Fernando 1998: 141–42). Their ministry is holistic: they preach a message, engage, and minister to a person's needs at the same time. One reinforces the other. To say that God loves you without showing it leaves the message empty. To minister but never point to God leaves the one ministered to without a clue as to what has motivated the love.

Additional Notes

3:16. The odd construction ἡ πίστις ἡ δι' αὐτοῦ (*hē pistis hē di' autou*) with its extra article is probably the result of the prepositional phrase being in a postpositive position (Moulton and Turner 1963: 221). Other scholars speak of the addition being in the second attribute position. The expression means either "faith because of him" or "faith in him" (Moulton and Turner 1963: 267).

3:17. Codex D, Itala, and some Syriac MSS speak of an "evil" (πονηρόν, *ponēron*) act performed here, adding a moral element to the remark, but the attestation is too narrow to be original.

3:22. The best text for this verse is the shortest, merely referring to what Moses said (Barrett 1994: 209). All additions, in their variations referring to the fathers, are poorly attested, and the variations in the addition argue against its originality.

3:24. For the complex syntax here and how the verse is simplified for translation, see Bruce 1990: 146. Literally the verse reads, "And all the prophets from Samuel and his successors who spoke and announced these days," an incomplete sentence or anacoluthon. The sense is made clear by removing the "who."

3:25. There is debate whether the prefix in [ἐν]ευλογηθήσονται ([*en*]*eulogēthēsontai*, shall be blessed) should be read as original. Reading the prefix are 𝔓[74], ℵ, D, E, and Byz. Lacking it are A*, B, and Ψ. The external evidence slightly favors inclusion, but it makes no difference in the text's meaning. Internally the evidence is balanced, as the prefixed form recalls the LXX whereas the nonprefixed form anticipates the word link with verse 26.

3. The Arrest and the Leadership's Deliberation (4:1–22)

This third section, emerging from the healing of the lame man, introduces the first confrontation with the Jewish leadership and its aftermath. Jervell (1998: 175) calls this the first persecution of Christians in Acts. This section includes the arrest (vv. 1–4), the examination of Peter and John and their response (vv. 5–12), and the resolution of their examination by the leadership (vv. 13–22). As in Luke, the major source of rejection of Jesus is the leadership (Luke 22:1–6; 23:1–25). It is common for Luke to leave a speech unfinished and move dramatically to its aftermath (Acts 7:54; 10:44; 17:32; 22:22; 26:24; Stählin 1980: 70). The dialogue makes clear not only that disputes about religious conviction are directing these deliberations but also that sociological factors such as the apostles' political influence, power, and control are being taken into account (vv. 16–17). The introduction of such concerns, realistic as they are, undercuts the picture of the leadership's character and integrity at a literary level. The event is very similar to 5:17–42. In later Judaism, there was a belief that in certain situations one was warned for a first offense and given a minor punishment before a more serious sentence for a second violation was sought (Marshall 1980: 97). Blasphemy and a disobedient son are examples of this (Bock 1998a: 110; *b. Šeb.* 35a, 36a). This may be a part of what is going on in these two arrests.

The passage stresses the "sign" or evidence God has given that he stands behind Jesus (vv. 16, 22). The fact that the healing and its reality are evident and yet rejected reveals the extent of hardheartedness that stands behind rejecting Jesus. That even the obvious is denied gives evidence of a veil over the heart as Luke lays out the response of the leadership. Rejection of Jesus is not rational but is reflective of a refusal to see what God has done.

Whereas God stands behind what the apostles are doing and works with power on their behalf, the leaders are portrayed as maneuvering to undercut God's will and his apostles. Much like Acts 3, the theme at work here is, "God has exalted Jesus, but you killed him," and "God declares the message, but you reject it." The chapter points "to a power struggle for the hearts of the Jewish people" (Witherington 1998: 189). The leadership tries to exercise all the power it can to get rid of the problem. Jesus as the "despised stone" (v. 11) is at the heart of this unit. Nonetheless, God will exalt him no matter what opposition arises (v. 12), for salvation is found in no other. It is here that both the major lesson of this unit and its key literary tension reside. People can reject Jesus and his representatives, but God will still exalt him, and such rejection comes at a cost.

Exegesis and Exposition

¹And while they were speaking to the people, the ⌈priests⌉ and the captain of the temple and the Sadducees approached them, ²annoyed because they were teaching the people and proclaiming in Jesus the resurrection of the dead. ³And they seized them and put them into custody until the next day, for it was already evening. ⁴But many of those who heard the word believed; and the number of men came to around five thousand.

⁵On the next day their rulers, elders, and scribes were gathered together in Jerusalem, ⁶with Annas the high priest and Caiaphas and John and Alexander, and many who were of the high-priestly family. ⁷And setting them in the midst, they inquired, "By what power or by what name did you do this?" ⁸Then Peter, filled with the Holy Spirit, said to them, "Rulers of the people and elders, ⁹if today we are being judged concerning a good work done to a sick man, by what means has this man been saved, ¹⁰be it known to you all and to all the people of Israel that by the name of Jesus the Nazorean, whom you crucified, whom God raised from the dead, by him this man is standing before you healthy. ¹¹This is the stone, the one which was despised by you builders, but the one which has become the head cornerstone. ¹²And there is salvation in no one else, for there is no other name under heaven given among men by which we must be saved."

¹³Now when they observed Peter and John's boldness and perceived that they were untaught, common men, they wondered; indeed, they recognized that they had been with Jesus. ¹⁴But seeing the man that had been healed standing beside the apostles, the leaders had nothing to say in opposition. ¹⁵But commanding them to go outside the council, they conferred with one another ¹⁶saying, "What shall we do to these men? For that a notable sign was made known through them is ⌈obvious⌉ to all those who live in Jerusalem, and we cannot deny it. ¹⁷But in order that it might not spread further among the people, let us warn them not to speak or teach anymore to anyone in this name." ¹⁸And calling them, the leaders charged them not to speak or teach at all in the name of Jesus. ¹⁹But Peter and John answered them, "If it is right in the sight of God to obey you or God, you judge; ²⁰for we are not able not to speak about what we have seen and heard." ²¹And when the leaders had further threatened them, they let them go, finding no way they might punish them, because of the people; for all men were praising God for what had happened. ²²For the man to whom this sign of healing occurred was more than forty years old.

4:1   Peter's declarations of Jesus and God's plan finally trigger a reaction from the officials of Judaism at the temple. As the speech is in progress, the priests, the captain of the temple, and the Sadducees, who run the temple, show up. Literally, "they set upon" (ἐπέστησαν, epestēsan) the apostles. The remark suggests a confrontation as they seek to assert their leadership. Johnson (1992: 76) notes that Luke often uses the verb "to set/come upon" for sudden appearances (Luke 2:9, 38; 4:39; 21:34; Acts 4:1–3; 6:12; 10:17; 11:11; 12:7; 22:13). These officials are responsible for the holy site. Priests are mentioned only three times in Acts (4:1–3; 6:7 [of the priests who come to faith]; 14:13 [the priest of Zeus at Lystra]). The reference to the captain is one of two references in Acts (4:1–3; 5:26), as usually the Greek term refers to magistrates or officials in a city (16:19–23, 35–36, 38 [of Philippi]; Luke 22:4, 52). This captain is the *sāgān* who was in charge of the temple police (Neh. 13:11; 2 Macc. 3:4; Josephus, *Ant.* 20.6.2 §131; *J.W.* 6.5.3 §294; BAGD 770 §2; BDAG 948 §2; Jeremias 1969a: 161, 163). He was a member of the high-priestly family and the number two man at the temple, an elite position among the Levites who made up the temple guard (Bruce 1988a: 89n4; Barrett 1994: 218–19; Le Cornu and Shulam 2003: 216–18). He officiated over the daily whole offering and was captain of the temple police, whose role at the temple was to keep the peace and not allow any messianic expectations that Rome would dislike (John 11:47–48).

The Sadducees were one of the key sects of Judaism. They claimed that their roots went back to Zadok, high priest under Solomon (1 Kings 2:26–27, 35), and even further back to Zadok, elder son of Aaron (1 Chron. 5:30–35 [6:3–9 Eng.]; Sir. 51:12 [Heb.]; Jeremias 1969a: 228–32; Barrett 1994: 219; Fitzmyer 1998: 298). Their name is related to the Hebrew term for "righteousness." From this aristocratic group (of mostly lay nobility) came the high priest. They also were very materialistic in their worldview, cooperative with Rome to maintain their status, and less devoted to detailed questions about the law and piety than the Pharisees. Such political concerns are certainly important to them here (Polhill 1992: 139). They denied the resurrection (Luke 20:27–40; Acts 23:6–10), believing that the soul died with the body, and emphasized the Torah within the OT.[1] They rejected the oral law and the traditions that other sects held. The Sadducees appear occasionally in Acts (4:1–3; 5:17–18; 23:6–8 [3x]; five of the fourteen NT references are in Acts). They react in part because in their view the apostles' teaching could be politically, socially, and religiously destabilizing to their relatively good relationship with Rome.

4:2   The leadership is annoyed (διαπονούμενοι, diaponoumenoi) with Peter for two things: (1) teaching and proclaiming Jesus and (2) teaching

---

1. See Josephus, *Ant.* 13.10.6 §§296–98, noting their lack of popularity with the masses; 18.1.4 §§16–17 describes this important party within Judaism; also *J.W.* 2.8.14 §§164–65. They rejected fate and highlighted free will and human responsibility.

about the resurrection, which they do not accept. The combination of διά (*dia*) plus the infinitives "to teach" (διδάσκειν, *didaskein*) and "to proclaim" (καταγγέλλειν, *katangellein*) points to the cause of their anger (Wallace 1996: 597). These leaders are "greatly disturbed" (NIV) at the proactive preaching of the apostles (BAGD 187; BDAG 235).[2] The expression "proclaim Jesus" is a rare combination in the NT, appearing three times (Acts 4:1–3; 17:3; Rom. 1:8, where faith about Jesus is proclaimed); the verb "proclaim" (καταγγέλλω, *katangellō*) otherwise appears nine times in Acts (3:24 [where prophets spoke and proclaimed these days]; 13:4–5, 38–39; 15:36; 16:17, 19–21; 17:13, 23; 26:22–23). The verb "annoy" (διαπονέω, *diaponeō*) appears only twice in the NT; here and in 16:18, where Paul is annoyed with the spirit-possessed slave girl who follows him. Thus, except for "proclaim," none of the expressions here is common. This could suggest the presence of a church report about this event.

The phrase "in Jesus" (ἐν τῷ 'Ιησοῦ, *en tō Iēsou*) is difficult. It could mean the resurrection that came in Jesus or by Jesus (BDF §219). It could well be the leaders' point also that the apostles were supporting resurrection by means of the Jesus events. So their objections would be twofold: against Jesus and against resurrection. What is clear, however, is that the one resurrection of Jesus is the irritant. Even for Jews who believed in a general resurrection of all at the end, the idea of a singular resurrection of a figure in the midst of history appears to be a new idea. Even more, the idea of a resurrection of such a figure who was a prophet like Moses and a messianic-like figure would make the leaders even more nervous about the crowd's reaction (Polhill 1992: 140). Such an authority figure would undercut the Sadducees' own power and authority. For these Sadducees, it is too much. They move to stop the apostles. The scene indicates that the highest leadership is not responsive to Peter, which makes them subject to the warning just given in 3:22–23. At a literary and theological level, Luke's point is that the leadership does not have the eyes and ears to be responsive to God.

4:3 The Jewish leaders arrest Peter and John. The Greek phrase ἐπέβαλον αὐτοῖς τὰς χεῖρας (*epebalon autois tas cheiras*) means to lay hands on someone (Acts 5:18; 12:1; 21:27; Mark 14:46; Luke 20:19; 21:12 [Jesus predicts this]; Pesch 1986a: 164). It refers here to seizing and arresting them. They are placed in custody (τήρησιν, *tērēsin*) or in "keeping" (Acts 5:18; 1 Cor. 7:19 are the other NT occurrences of the term; Josephus, *Ant.* 16.10.5 §321; Barrett 1994: 221). They are not being punished, just being kept until the leaders can hold a hearing. It is evening, so the hearing will have to wait until the next day (Luke 22:66; Acts 23:20; *m. Sanh.*

---

2. NET's "angry" may give the result of their annoyance. HCSB has "provoked." Barrett 1994: 219 speaks of the leaders being at the end of their tether, that is, at the end of their rope.

4.1; Larkin 1995: 71). The afternoon prayer would have been at three o'clock, so the events have taken most of the remaining daylight time. The grounds for the arrest would have been disturbing the peace in the temple. Where the apostles are taken is not clear. It could be a public prison or a jail located near the temple or a chamber of hewn stone (Le Cornu and Shulam 2003: 220).

4:4 Nevertheless the new community is growing. Many who hear the word believe. This summary is like Acts 2:41 and 47b. The number of five thousand respondents represents significant growth over the less specific "added to their number" of 2:47 and the three thousand of 2:41. In 1:15 they started with 120. Williams (1990: 79) suggests that the total number of believers now is five thousand, as opposed to five thousand converted on this day. This is possible but less likely. Either way, the number of respondents is a source of major concern for the leadership.

Polhill (1992: 140) takes the reference to ἀνδρῶν (andrōn) to mean men and women, which is possible given that the gospel was for everyone and they had left the temple. Witherington (1998: 190) is not certain but seems to see men only, since women are often explicitly noted (5:14; 8:3, 12; 9:2; 17:12; 22:4). Bruce (1990: 148) sees only males noted here, as does Barrett (1994: 222), though he observes that the other meaning is possible. Barrett also claims that no text using ἀνήρ (anēr) can be shown to include women, but this is unlikely given 17:34 and 1:16 (see discussion on 1:16). If only men are meant, then the actual number of respondents could be even larger. It is hard to be certain, however, who is included in the count.

The use of the term "believed" recalls 2:44, where those who responded were called "those who believed." Here it is the word they believe, the first time this verb is used of the response to a message (4:4; 8:12–13; 9:42; 11:21; 13:12, 48–49; 14:1; 15:7; 17:12, 34; 18:8, 27; 19:2, 4). They believe the word when they hear it, a reference to the message of the apostles (6:4; 8:4). Fitzmyer (1998: 299) notes how it was possible for so many to hear Peter (Crisler 1976). The fact that many are responding must be part of what drives the leadership to pressure the new movement. Jesus's crucifixion failed to stop the new community from making its message heard. So something more has to be done. The leaders' initial strategy appears to have been, "If we cut off the head of the snake, the snake will die." But now the head is back and so is the snake in the form of many new preachers.

Schnabel (2004: 420) notes that the growth of the early church came from three different levels of contact: public preaching, preaching in the synagogues, and the attraction of believers gathered in fellowship in homes and caring for each other. This home-based ministry connected with people at the most intimate level of their lives—in the fellowship, hospitality, and worship that pointed to the nature of the newly forming community. This dimension of community life is often the key to a church's vitality.

The Jewish leadership gathers in Jerusalem the next day to hear Peter and John and consider an official response to the apostles' preaching. This is probably an allusion to the Sanhedrin or a significant part of this seventy-one-member tribunal that served as the Jewish supreme court (see v. 15; on its existence this early, see Witherington 1998: 191–92 against E. P. Sanders). **4:5**

The first group noted are the leaders, especially the religious figures or senior priests (ἄρχοντας, archontas; Luke 14:1; 23:13, 35; also 8:41 [of a synagogue]; 11:15; 12:58; 14:1; 18:18; of those who lead to Jesus's death: 24:20; Acts 3:17–18; 4:5–10, 26; 7:27, 35; 13:27–28; 14:5–7; 16:19–21; 23:5). They were referred to in 3:17 as those in part responsible for Jesus's death, looking back to what Luke 22–23 also indicates.

"Elders" (πρεσβυτέρους, presbyterous) points to the civic leaders, the chief tribal and family heads, who often were more senior in age, as the term literally means "old men" (BAGD 700 §2aβ; BDAG 862 §2aβ). In later references Acts' usage of the term splits between describing church elders and describing Jewish leaders who persecute the church.[3]

There are also the scribes (τοὺς γραμματεῖς, tous grammateis), those who studied and interpreted the law. This term is less frequent in Acts, but three of its occurrences look to those opposed to the church (Luke 5:21, 30; 6:7; 11:53; 15:2; 19:47; 20:1; 22:2, 66; 23:10; Acts 4:5–7; 6:12–14; 19:35 [Ephesian town clerk]; 23:9). The entire group examining Peter and John would have been a mixture of Sadducees and Pharisees, with most of the power lying with the Sadducees (Josephus, Ant. 18.1.4 §§16–17) and the scribes being mostly Pharisees. They may have met at the council house that Josephus briefly describes in J.W. 5.4.2 §144, on the west side of the temple (m. Sanh. 11.2; m. Mid. 5.4 has a council meeting location on the south side of the temple; Barrett 1994: 223; Polhill 1992: 141).

The high-priestly family of Annas is listed next. Annas is called high priest but served from AD 6 to 14 (also called Ananus; Josephus, Ant. 18.2.1 §26; 18.2.2 §34; 20.9.1 §198). He was the patriarch of a family that held high-priestly power for several decades, and so he is given the title here (also Luke 3:2). Caiaphas, the current high priest, served as such the entire time that Pilate ruled over Judea, from AD 18 to 36 (Ant. 18.2.2 §35). His ossuary may have been discovered recently (Greenhut 1992; Fitzmyer 1998: 299). He is followed here by John, possibly a reference to Jonathan (so Codex D), who replaced Caiaphas in AD 37 (Ant. 18.4.3 **4:6**

---

3. On the term as meaning Jewish elders, see Luke 7:3; 9:22; 20:1; 22:52, 66. In the Gospel only Luke 15:25 refers to "an elder" in the simple sense of an "older" son. In Acts there are also a variety of meanings: 2:17 (old men); Jewish elders: 4:5–10, 23; 6:12–14 [seize Stephen]; of the church: 11:29–30; 14:23; 15:2, 4, 6, 22–23; 16:4; 20:17; 21:18; Jewish elders: 23:13–14; 24:1; 25:14–15.

§95). If this is not Jonathan, then the figure is not otherwise known. Alexander, the fourth member of the family noted, is otherwise unattested. All the top figures of official Judaism in Jerusalem are gathered to render a judgment about what to do with these two apostles. Information from such a gathering could have come from Paul or from anyone who had been close to him, such as Gamaliel (Stott 1990: 98).

4:7   Like an earlier query to Jesus (Luke 20:2), the leadership asks by what authority or power (δυνάμει, *dynamei*) and by what name (ὀνόματι, *onomati*) they act. The query makes clear that they, the leaders responsible for the temple, have not given the apostles the authority to act, as the question is "what sort of" (ποίᾳ, *poia*) power outside the council gives them this right. The investigation begins with the objection to the preaching of resurrection (v. 2; Marshall 1980: 99). Witherington (1998: 193) argues that the questioning concerns the healing that led to the preaching.

The idea of power or authority looks back, at a literary level, to Acts 3:12. There Peter declares that it is not their own inherent authority that made the healing possible but that Jesus is responsible (v. 16). So the reader of Acts is well aware of the answer even as the question is asked. The query about the name also evokes 3:16 and looks to the source of the apostles' action. In the narrative, the question allows Peter to briefly elaborate on points made in Acts 3.

Josephus notes an examination scene with the Sanhedrin involving Herod (*Ant.* 14.9.4 §§168–76). The participants would have been present in a semicircle around Peter and John (*m. Sanh.* 4.3 notes that the group was organized like "the half round of a threshing floor so they could all see one another"). So the apostles are "in the midst" (ἐν τῷ μέσῳ, *en tō mesō*).

The subject, "you" (ὑμεῖς, *hymeis*), is delayed to the end of the question, making it emphatic. In effect, the emphasis is, "What power or authority gave this right *to you*?" One thing the leadership knows: they did not give them this authority, and in their view, it is theirs to give or withhold. The investigation is also necessary to make sure no sorcery or magic was used (*m. Sanh.* 7.5, 11; 10.1). No one disputes that the man was healed (Le Cornu and Shulam 2003: 234–35).

4:8   Peter begins the response by politely and respectfully addressing his examiners as the rulers of the people and the elders (see v. 5). In Hellenistic rhetoric, such an opening is called a *captatio benevolentiae* (procuring goodwill).

The narrative note describes Peter as filled with the Holy Spirit (πλησθεὶς πνεύματος ἁγίου, *plēstheis pneumatos hagiou*) and points back to Jesus's promise in Luke 21:12–15, where he predicted that his disciples would be held and that wisdom would be given to them (Luke 12:11–12; 1 Pet. 3:15). Here we see the Spirit enabling testimony. They will declare without apology what they have done and by whom it was made possible. Spirit-enabled prophetic work is common in Luke-Acts (Luke 1:15, 41, 67; Acts 2:4; 4:31; 13:9; Schneider 1980: 346; spirit-filled people: Stephen in Acts 6:5; 7:55; Barnabas in 11:24).[4] Peter's remarks will summarize briefly the themes of Acts 2–3.

Peter sees the question as an opportunity to declare Jesus directly to the leaders and to the nation they represent. After all, if these leaders issue a verdict, it will be on behalf of the nation and influence the nation's perception of Jesus.

4:9–10

In using the verb ἀνακρίνω (anakrinō, judge), Peter alludes to the fact that there is a judicial examination taking place. This term often has legal implications (Luke 23:14; Acts 17:11, where it simply means to examine Scripture; 24:8; 28:18; 1 Cor. 9:3; BAGD 56 §1b; BDAG 66 §2). This is why he begins his response by noting the formerly crippled condition of the man. Peter addresses his answer to both the leadership and the people of Israel (τῷ λαῷ Ἰσραήλ, tō laō Israēl; Israel in Acts: 1:6; 2:36; 4:8–10, 27–28; 5:21, 30–31; 7:23, 37, 42; 9:15–16; 10:36–38; 13:17–20, 23–24; 28:20; "all the people," 2:47; 3:9).

The previous condition of this healed man (ἀνθρώπου, anthrōpou) is described literally as "weak," but this refers merely to his former state, when he was begging at the gate.[5] This term ἀσθενής (asthenēs, weak) is found five times in Luke-Acts among its twenty-six NT occurrences (Luke 9:1–3; 10:8–9; Acts 4:8–10; 5:14–16 [2x]). It stands in contrast to the declaration that this man is now "whole" or healthy at the end of v. 10 (ὑγιής, hygiēs). Here may be an allusion from Isa. 35:6 to the work of the new era, as the lame walk. This Greek term for "healthy," placed at the end of verse 10, is emphatic in the Greek. This is the only use of the term in Luke-Acts out of eleven NT occurrences. It is the second "health" term used in the passage, as "perfect health" (ὁλοκληρία, holoklēria) was used in 3:16. The word ὑγιής here refers to physical health, without damage (BAGD 823; BDAG 1023). The term in the LXX is used of an army that returned "safe" (Josh. 10:21; Luck, TDNT 8:311). This healing is the result of the strengthening that took place as described in 3:7 and proclaimed in 3:16.

This whole action is called a "good deed" (εὐεργεσία, euergesia; the only other NT use is 1 Tim. 6:2; conceptually, of Jesus, Acts 10:38–40; Weiser 1981: 127). The Greek term refers to an act of beneficial service

---

4. The terminology used here is significant. Bruce 1988a: 92n18 argues for a distinction between the aorist passive participle (πλησθείς, plēstheis), used here for a moment of inspiration, and the adjective "full [of the Spirit]" (πλήρης, plērēs), used to describe an abiding situation. This reply comes through a special enablement of the Spirit. God is at work in a fresh way.

5. The genitive of "man" here is a good example of an objective genitive (BDF §163): healing for which the man was the object.

that normally was rewarded and well received in the ancient world instead of being made the subject of a judicial inquiry such as the apostles now face (BAGD 319 §2; BDAG 405 and the remark in 66 §2). So there is a touch of irony present in Peter's remark. Why are the apostles here for doing this good deed to "this" man? The term οὗτος (*houtos*) is used twice in these verses and indicates that the man is also present at the examination (see also v. 14). This miracle, like other miracles of Scripture, bothers many modern interpreters, for in their view such miracles do not happen. Stott (1990: 101) cites a wonderful retort from Campbell Morgan: "Granted the truth of the first verse of the Bible, and there is no difficulty with the miracles." God as the Creator is capable of such restorative power.

Who is responsible for this dramatic change in the man's condition? Here ἐν (*en*) is instrumental—By whom is this one healed? None other than Jesus the Nazorean. By his name the man has been "saved" from his condition. The term σέσωται (*sesōtai*) is a perfect passive verb pointing to Jesus doing the saving, by which is meant a deliverance that heals the man, as verse 10 makes clear.[6] With the repetition of the term in its broader sense in verse 12, a wordplay is set up here. The man was saved (i.e., delivered) by Jesus physically (v. 10), but this symbolizes the fact that Jesus saves (v. 12).

Peter does not shy away from making clear that Jesus is the one the leaders crucified and God vindicated by raising him from the dead (Acts 2:22–23, 36; 3:13–15; 4:27–28; 10:39–40; 13:27–37). He speaks like a prophet and confronts them with what he sees as God's revelatory and soteriological work through Jesus. Should the leadership be the ones on trial in God's court? This healing is the work of God's chosen one. If Jesus is healing, then he is alive, vindicated by God, and they are culpable for his death (John 19:11; Bruce 1988a: 93). Jesus is the source of the "power" (δυνάμει, *dynamei*) they asked about in verse 7. So Peter is "guilty" of preaching Jesus. But he is guilty for good, even divine, reasons. The leaders, however, are even more guilty before God, as Scripture warns and verse 11 shows. This is the key implication of the verse. This proclamation of Jesus and the indictment of the leadership are what Peter wants to make known, as the era of ignorance is no longer present (Acts 3:17; Witherington 1998: 194). There is a cost and accountability that come for rejecting God's chosen one.

4:11 Peter makes his point about the divine design of Jesus's rejection and vindication by alluding to Ps. 118:22 (117:22 LXX). He argues that Scripture also indicated that this would come to pass. Psalm 118 is one of the more frequently cited texts in the NT (Matt. 21:42; Mark 12:10;

---

6. On "saved" as physical deliverance, see Luke 7:50; 17:19; 23:35–37; Acts 14:9. Often the term has spiritual overtones: Luke 19:10; Acts 2:21, 40, 47; 4:12; 11:14; 15:11; 16:31; Larkin 1995: 73.

Luke 20:17; 1 Pet. 2:4, 7). The declaration is that the builders rejected the stone that God elevated to be the cornerstone. The expression εἰς (*eis*) plus the accusative functions as the predicate nominative here: the rejected stone has become the chief stone (Wallace 1996: 447). Builders in Judaism were often associated with teaching or leading (Bruce 1990: 152; CD 4.12; with Mic. 7:11; CD 4.19; Ezek. 13:10–16; 1QpHab 10.5–13 on Hab. 2:12). Those close to the stone have failed to appreciate it for what it is.

The wording of this citation differs slightly from the citation in the Gospels and 1 Peter. It is a summary allusion rather than a citation selecting a few key terms from the verse (Bock 1987: 198–201). Additional terms include (1) the direct reference to the rejection of the stone "by all of you" (ὑφ᾽ ὑμῶν, *hyph᾽ hymōn*), which makes the leaders responsible for the rejection of the stone, and (2) the use of the term ἐξουθενηθείς (*exouthenētheis*, literally, scorned) for the rejection rather than a form of ἀποδοκιμάζω (*apodokimazō*), which appears in every other NT use of this psalm (Barrett 1994: 230). This despising describes the attitude behind the rejection of Jesus and mixes the metaphor. The ironic image is of a temple being built as a people of God although the key ingredient for God's presence has been rejected. The different term here suggests that Luke is using a traditional source that differs from the source for Luke 20:17 (Schneider 1980: 348). In the NT, the term ἐξουθενέω (*exoutheneō*) also appears in Luke 18:9–10; 23:11; Acts 4:11; Rom. 14:3, 10; 1 Cor. 1:26–29; 6:4; 16:10–11; 2 Cor. 10:9–10; Gal. 4:12–14; and 1 Thess. 5:19–22. This term may reflect the influence of Isa. 53:3 as seen in translations by Symmachus, Aquila, and Theodotion, but it is more likely that the term simply independently renders the Hebrew מָאַס (*mā᾽as*) in Ps. 118:22.

Peter's point is clear enough. What they rejected God vindicated. God made the rejected stone a key part of the building, an allusion to the cornerstone, the main, oversized stone at the base that holds up two intersecting walls (κεφαλὴν γωνίας, *kephalēn gōnias*; McKelvey 1969: 195–204; not a capstone as Jeremias argues in *TDNT* 1:793; see Luke 20:17 in Bock 1996: 1603–4; 1 Pet. 2:7). The targum to this passage in Ps. 118 also reads it of the Messiah. The remark looks back as well to the speech in Acts 3:18, where Christ's suffering was foretold. The basis of the remark is the righteous, rejected king of Ps. 118. There the enemy would have been the opposing nations. Now the opponent is the Jewish leadership in an ironic and tragic reversal of positions.

The theological conclusion of the speech comes here. Simply put, Peter says that there is nowhere else to turn for salvation. The two uses of ἐν (*en*) to refer to Jesus indicate means (Moule 1959: 77). So salvation comes by means of no one else, nor is there another name by which one can be saved. The remark is significant, for no one had better access to

4:12

God's way and revelation than the Jews to whom Peter speaks. Yet even they need him. Indeed, the phrase "There is in no one else" (οὐκ ... ἐν ἄλλῳ οὐδενί, *ouk ... en allō oudeni*) appears before the subject "salvation" in Greek to make the point emphatically. There is no one else at all other than Jesus who has the means to provide salvation, even for Jews who have access to God's revelation.

Peter goes on to explain (γάρ, *gar*) that no other name exists under heaven by which it is necessary (δεῖ, *dei*) to be saved. Robertson 1934: 749 speaks of how exclusively ἕτερον (*heteron*, other) is used here. All other names cannot save. The phrase ἐν ᾧ (*en hō*) functions as the introduction to a relative clause: "by whom it is necessary to be saved" (BDF §412.4). The expression of necessity in Luke looks to divine design (Luke 2:49; 4:43; 9:21–22; 11:42; 12:11–12; 13:14, 16, 33; 15:31–32; 17:25; 18:1–2; 19:5; 21:9; 22:7–8, 37; 24:6–7, 25–26, 44; Acts 1:15–17, 21–22; 3:19–21; 4:12; 5:29; 9:5–6, 15–16; 14:21–22; 15:5; 16:29–30; 17:2–3; 19:21, 36; 20:35; 23:11; 24:17–19; 25:10, 24; 26:9–10; 27:21, 23–24, 26; thus 40 out of 101 NT occurrences are in Luke-Acts). Jesus is "the" name for salvation. Peter is saying that there is no other person or god to which to turn. Jesus is Savior in a way that no other claimed savior can be.

Eckey (2000: 116) shows how the title "Savior" was applied to a variety of ancient figures, such as Philip of Macedon and Cassander, as well as how this expression echoes a sentence in Josephus about God in the exodus (*Ant.* 3.1.5 §23; Demosthenes, *Orations* 18: *On the Crown* 43; Plutarch, *Lives* 9.26–27). Foerster (*TDNT* 7:1004–12) details a wide range of Hellenistic examples of this title: of the gods, of physicians, of philosophers, of statesmen, and especially in ruler cults and emperor worship for their provision and protection. Foerster also notes, however, that "Savior" was not a technical term during the Roman period, emerging later with Hadrian (*SIG* 3.2.624.4, 16 [Aratus as a statesman]; 3.2.749.B [Pompey]; 3.2.752–54 [Pompey]; 3.2.839.7–9; and *IG* 4.1406 [Hadrian]). The title was more common among the Seleucids, as indicated by a statue of Antiochus I as Soter (Savior) found at Ilium in the temple to Athena. In such contexts, it was physical and political power that had brought deliverance. This verse teaches, however, Jesus's uniqueness when it comes to salvation and spiritual issues such as forgiveness of sins. It is a sphere of activity distinct from those of military emperors. For Peter, Jesus is the only way to salvation. Witherington (1998: 194) correctly observes, "Peter [and/or Luke] is no advocate of modern notions of religious pluralism" (also John 14:6; Heb. 2:3; 1 Tim. 2:5). Marshall (1980: 100) affirms that this is the outgrowth of the idea that Jesus alone was exalted to God's right hand. Pesch (1986a: 167) points out that the remark is exclusive and universal. *Only* Jesus can save, but this declaration is set forth *among men*, that is, to all.

The noun for "salvation" (σωτηρία, *sōtēria*) appears six times in Acts (four times for salvation in 4:12; 13:26, 47; 16:17; twice for rescue in

7:25; 27:34; also Luke 1:69, 71, 77; 19:9; "salvation of God," Acts 28:28; Luke 2:30; 3:6; Fitzmyer 1998: 301). In Acts 4:12 "salvation" is used in its full, spiritual sense, although the imagery is supported by its physical picture of deliverance, as the healing points to this deeper reality. Out of 106 NT occurrences, the verb "save" (σώζω, sōzō) appears 30 times in Luke-Acts (Luke 6:9; 7:50; 8:12, 36, 48, 50; 9:24 [2x]; 13:23; 17:19; 18:26, 42; 19:9–10; 23:35 [2x], 37, 39; Acts 2:21, 40, 47; 4:8–10, 12; 11:13–14; 14:9–10; 15:1, 11; 16:29–31 [2x]; 27:20, 30–31).

Peter's speech produces a response at several levels. The leaders see   **4:13**
and discover certain things. First is the boldness (παρρησίαν, parrēsian) of the apostle and his companion, John. This term appears occasionally in Acts (2:29; 4:13–14, 29–31; 28:30–31; the verb παρρησιάζομαι [parrēsiazomai]: 9:27–28; 13:46; 14:3; 18:26; 19:8; 26:26). In Greek contexts, this term stood for the characteristic of free citizens to speak out (Johnson 1992: 78; Fitzmyer 1998: 302; Euripides, *Hippolytus* 422; in the LXX: Esth. 8:12s [= Add. Esth. 16:19 Eng.]; Job 27:10; Prov. 1:20; 10:10; 13:5). Here the apostles stand before the chief council of Judaism and make clear not only that their authority comes from outside the council but also that the leadership is culpable for what it did to Jesus. There is no attempt to seek favor or to take a poll about how popular what they said would be.

They have spoken out eloquently despite being "uneducated and common men" (ἀγράμματοι . . . ἰδιῶται, agrammatoi . . . idiōtai). The first term has its only use in the NT here. It refers to one who is "without letters"—unschooled or lacking formal education (BDAG 15). It need not mean "unable to read" but simply that the person lacks a certain level of skills. Kraus (1999) has a careful study of both terms in this phrase. In this context, it is religious instruction that is primarily meant. The inference is that much should not be expected from them, although the embarrassing evidence of their handiwork is the healed man standing with them (v. 14).

The second term appears five times in the NT, and this is its only use in Luke-Acts. It refers to one who is untrained, without formal education or formal status, a "private man," in this context a layperson in religious matters (Barrett 1994: 234; BDAG 468 §1; Acts 4:13–14; 1 Cor. 14:16, 23–25; 2 Cor. 11:6). Josephus (*Ant.* 2.12.2 §271) uses the term of one unskilled in speaking. It does not mean "illiterate" here.[7] This lack of educational and theological background leaves the leaders wondering about the apostles' ability to address the issue so effectively, but then the leaders also realize that these men have been with Jesus. Both verbs in this realization expressed in indirect discourse retain progressive tenses, the present and the imperfect—these men are (εἰσιν, eisin) unlettered

---

7. Codex **D** omits this description, probably because its suggests disrespect toward the apostles.

but had been (ἦσαν, *ēsan*) with Jesus all along (Wallace 1996: 539, 553). The recognition here is not that they recognize them only now as his followers but that their association with Jesus explains their ability (Williams 1990: 84; see v. 8). The apostles have received training from outside the official circle, something the reader of Luke-Acts knows the details of because of Luke's Gospel.

4:14   The second reality the leadership has to cope with is the healed man, now standing among them and beside the apostles. No magic has been used. The apostolic claim is that this was the work of the God of the fathers through Jesus (3:13). The healed man's regular begging made him well known to the community. Everyone knew him as a cripple, and now he is healed, standing (ἑστῶτα, *hestōta*) with the apostles like exhibit A in a law court! There is nothing the leaders can say in opposition (ἀντειπεῖν, *anteipein*) to the man's improved condition. The use of this verb here recalls its only other occurrence in the NT, in Luke 21:15, where Jesus predicts that the Spirit will enable the apostles to give a reply to which there is no answer. The remarks are Spirit-inspired speech (Jervell 1998: 180). The theme of not being able to respond will appear again in Acts 6:10. The leadership needs to confer about how to respond. What the apostles have done is obvious. Why it has happened is troublesome. Who did it was being proclaimed. Given that the leaders are not going to embrace the claim, what can and should they do to stop it?

4:15–17   The apostles are excused from the council room so that consultations can take place. Acts uses the term "council" (συνέδριον, *synedrion*) fourteen times (4:15–16; 5:21, 27, 34–35, 41–42; 6:12–15 [2x]; 22:30–23:1 [2x]; 23:6, 15, 20, 28–29; 24:20–21; also Luke 22:66, of the Jewish investigation of Jesus; Bruce 1990: 153–54). The high priest presides over it (1 Macc. 7:33; 11:23; Josephus, *Ant.* 20.10.1 §244, where Hyrcanus in the time of Pompey in 63 BC is called "governor of the nation"). All the NT occurrences of the verb for "consult" (συμβάλλω, *symballō*) are Lukan (Luke 2:18–19; 14:31; Acts 4:15–16; 17:18; 18:27–28; 20:14–15).

     The dilemma is obvious. On the one hand, the leaders wish to stop the apostles from preaching Jesus and the resurrection. On the other hand, the leaders must cope with this "notable sign" (γνωστὸν σημεῖον, *gnōston sēmeion*) that the apostles have performed in front of the citizens of Jerusalem. Of its seventy-seven NT occurrences, the term "sign" appears twenty-four times in Luke-Acts (Luke 2:12, 34–35; 11:15–16, 29 [3x], 30; 21:7, 10–11, 25–26; 23:8; Acts 2:19, 22–24, 43; 4:16–17, 21–22; 29–30; 5:12; 6:8; 7:36; 8:6, 13; 14:3; 15:12). It is also a frequent term in John's Gospel, appearing there seventeen times.

     The term for "notable" (γνωστός, *gnōstos*) is also a Lukan favorite, as ten of its fifteen NT occurrences are in Acts with two more in Luke's Gospel (Luke 2:44–45; 23:49; Acts 1:18–19; 2:14; 4:8–10, 16–17; 9:42; 13:38–39; 15:15–18; 19:17; 28:22, 28). This expression is variously translated here ("notable sign" in ESV, RSV; "outstanding miracle" in NIV; "noteworthy miracle" in NASB; "notable miracle" in KJV). Its basic sense is "pertinent to being familiar, capable of being known," which in this context means it refers to an obvious, unusual event, a manifest miracle (BAGD 164 §1a; BDAG 204 §1a). All this terminology should suggest that the healing points to God's activity. The miracle is undeniable and puts the leadership in an awkward position if it wants to stop the apostles. The fact that the miracle is not responded to in a proper way, given its role as a sign, portrays the leaders as hardhearted. No evidence will count for them or cause them to change their negative response toward those associated with Jesus.

The leaders recognize, however, that they cannot deny the healing, for it is too "obvious" (φανερόν, *phaneron*). The fact that the miracle is obvious is yet a second description, in verse 16, of the miracle's transparent character. Still, their desire is not to respond to the sign but to counter it. There is a sense of helplessness and anxiety, but the leadership will still seek to counter what has taken place. Due to their rejection of God they fail to see and appreciate what has been done. This rejection, however, has begun to fall on hard times because such miraculous acts are difficult to deny.[8]

Who are the potential sources for the information on these deliberations by the leadership, since no disciples would be present?[9] Witherington (1998: 196) suggests that Paul (Acts 22:4–5; 26:9–10) could well have witnessed or known about the deliberations, not to mention the general gossip concerning the Jewish leadership. Williams (1990: 86) notes that Paul was likely not a member of the council but would have known about it. Polhill (1992: 146n55) suggests that the verdict itself gives away aspects of the deliberations. Larkin (1995: 76–77, note on 4:15) names Nicodemus or Joseph of Arimathea as additional potential witnesses.

The beginning of verse 17 gives their clear objective—that the teaching growing out of this miracle about Jesus spread (διανεμηθῇ, *dianemēthē*) no further among the people—the only occurrence of the verb in the NT. So they will warn or threaten (ἀπειλησώμεθα, *apeilēsōmetha*) the apostles not to speak about this name anymore to anyone. The term ἀπειλέω (*apeileō*) is rare, appearing only twice in the NT (Acts 4:16–17; 1 Pet. 2:21–24; Gen. 27:42 LXX). This term is not a "soft" term for warning; it often means to threaten someone with something (BAGD 82–83; BDAG

---

8. They might try to deny that God was at work, but such miracles would affect their credibility in their attempt to stop the preaching of the resurrection. Bruce 1988a: 96 notes another obstacle to their stopping the preaching of the resurrection. Jesus's body was never produced. In fact, the various alternative explanations for the circumstances of the resurrection, such as that the body was stolen or the appearances were hallucinations, basically assume that the body was never produced or discovered.

9. Luke is also surely summarizing here what was a longer deliberation.

100; 4 Macc. 9:5). The related noun ἀπειλή (*apeilē*) means "a threat." A more intensive verb (προσαπειλησάμενοι, *prosapeilēsamenoi*) appears in Acts 4:21. The issue is teaching about the name of Jesus, that is, about his person, his power to heal and save (on the name, see 4:7). The warning is designed to intimidate the apostles with the leadership's priestly authority over Judaism. What Luke is portraying is that the leaders are preventing the people from finding their Messiah and acknowledging him (Jervell 1998: 180). One of the effects of hardheartedness is that it not only blocks the individual from responding to God but also can influence others in the same direction.

4:18   The leaders call the disciples back and carry out their plan. They command (παρήγγειλαν, *parēngeilan*) them not to speak or teach at all in this name. This term for "command" is common in Acts (1:3–5; 4:18; 5:27–28, 39–40; 10:39–42; 15:5; 16:18, 22–23; 17:30–31; 23:22, 30), appearing eleven times there out of thirty-two NT occurrences. The term καθόλου (*katholou*, at all) strengthens the negation, so an absolute prohibition is being called for here. The first term for "speak" (φθέγγεσθαι, *phthengesthai*) is rare in Acts (the first term is only in 2 Pet. 2:16, 18 in the NT; BAGD 857; BDAG 1054). The second (διδάσκειν, *didaskein*, teach) is more frequent, appearing sixteen times in Acts out of ninety-seven NT uses. The first verb refers to proclamation (Wis. 1:8); the second to teaching. The effort is both to silence and control the apostles and to bring any form of testimony about God's work through Jesus to a complete halt. This is damage control. It also sets up the apostles for further punishment if they refuse what is in effect an initial warning that can lead to contempt-of-court charges later (Witherington 1998: 196–97).

4:19–20   The apostles reply that, despite the warnings and threats, they will not stop preaching Jesus. They are called by God to give such a testimony (Acts 1:8, 22), and they must obey God rather than the leadership (5:29; conceptually on obedience: 1 Sam. 15:22–23; Jer. 7:22–23). The term ἤ (*ē*) plus the genitive form of "God" (τοῦ θεοῦ, *tou theou*) points to comparison (Moulton and Turner 1963: 216). Socrates is said to have made a similar response to a call not to teach what he was teaching.[10] The leaders are to judge, that is, understand, that the apostles must follow God rather than a human ruling. The phrase on not speaking appears at the end of the Greek sentence in verse 20 and is emphatic. The apostles cannot do anything other than speak of what they have seen and heard.[11] When this phrase is combined with another negative

10. See Plato, *Apology* 29D; also of Jewish men during the time of the Maccabean War, Josephus, *Ant.* 17.6.3 §159; 2 Macc. 7:2; 4 Macc. 5:16–24; Johnson 1992: 79; Barrett 1994: 237; Eckey 2000: 118–19.

11. On the theological importance that not denying the faith came to have in the church, see Pelikan 2005: 73–75.

at the start of the clause, it creates a double negative (οὐ . . . μή, *ou . . . mē*) and states the refusal to obey most emphatically.

An implication of the reply is that the leadership no longer represents the expression of God's will and way. Their responsibility for Jesus's death, already noted by the apostles (v. 10), is the reason. With the opportunity to respond still available, the leadership is rejecting the chance to come back into God's will. So the apostles will follow God's call over the divergent will of the council.

The reason the apostles give (γάρ, *gar*) for their refusal is that they cannot but proclaim what they have seen and heard. The remark here is broad. The apostles testify to Jesus, his healing, and the teaching and resurrection to which these events point.

Here we see an affirmation of the limits of the power of human institutions. The council is not to be obeyed when it asks the people to do something against God's will (Luke 20:25: rendering to God what is God's). Marshall (1980: 102) speaks of the limits that Rom. 13:1–7 affirms for religious and political systems (also 1 Pet. 2:13–17). Of course, the council would be shocked by such a distinction, but this is the crux of the dispute. Who better represents God? For Luke, the apostles have the healing on their side, as well as God's activity in raising Jesus.

The leaders threaten the apostles further. The expression for "threaten further," προσαπειλησάμενοι (*prosapeilēsamenoi*), is an NT hapax and is not used in the LXX (Josephus, *Ant.* 14.9.4 §170; BDAG 876; the nonprefixed form of the verb appears in Acts 4:17 and 1 Pet. 2:23). This surely includes informing the apostles of the social and legal consequences of their disobedience to the council, but the leaders do nothing more to the apostles at this time because the people know of the healing. How can the leadership punish the apostles for a deed everyone knows was an act of God? The people are grateful to God, giving him praise for his mercy to the man. So for now punishing them (κολάσωνται, *kolasōntai*) is out of the question.[12]   **4:21–22**

The man is healed of a condition he has had from birth (Acts 3:2), for more than forty years. Luke as narrator calls the result "this sign of healing" (τὸ σημεῖον τοῦτο τῆς ἰάσεως, *to sēmeion touto tēs iaseōs*) from God. The phrase appears emphatically at the end of the verse in Greek (Schneider 1980: 352) and is combined with the pluperfect γεγόνει (*gegonei*) to highlight the abiding result (BDF §347.3). It is the final key observation: how could anyone be punished for this? Again, the note is designed to show the council's hardheartedness and its refusal to acknowledge what God has done through the apostles. God is at work, but the leadership is blind to it. In the council's view, the leaders are

---

12. The only other NT occurrence of this term is in 2 Pet. 2:9, for divine punishment.

being gracious, warning the disciples and not doing anything further now. The leaders do not pause to reconsider their position, however, even though Peter has warned them as well (4:10–12).

In sum, this first touch of persecution against the apostles shows that the Jewish leadership's reaction to God's activity is completely inadequate (Pesch 1986a: 170). Here is an obvious healing that even they recognize. Yet they are concerned not about responding to the apostolic message to which the healing points but about trying to silence the apostles with threats and the use of council power. In the face of such pressure, the apostles are courageous and bold, speaking forth Jesus's uniqueness and making clear that they will obey God no matter what the council threatens (Fernando 1998: 155). They are willing to suffer for what they believe and to proclaim Jesus in obedience to God.

Cunningham (1997) gives a full treatment of suffering in Luke-Acts, and Stott (1990: 100–104) has a sober discussion of the role of signs and wonders in Acts and how they are handled by some interpreters today. These first-century Spirit-filled men knew their calling and would not be deterred. They would serve and preach God's way through Jesus, the only one through whom salvation comes. They show that suffering is not to be feared, nor is it necessarily an indication of failure. In fact, it may well come with the territory of sharing the need for Jesus in a world that seeks self-sufficiency (John 15:20). God has not called them to preach a gospel without sacrifice. If Jesus, the servant and example, experienced sacrifice and rejection by many, should those who follow him expect anything different? Those who minister with an appreciation of this truth and let God use his people as his vessels will not fear being poured out in whatever manner God calls for.

There is an exclusiveness to Jesus's work that is not popular today (Fernando 1998: 163–66; Acts 4:12). It is seen in our culture as a blow against religious diversity as well as the cause of great religious and political strife throughout history, especially in European history up to the Enlightenment. But a key point is often missed. It is when religion is imposed that it does damage. Here we see apostles making an appeal and leaving the decision and consequences to individual response. There is no effort to impose the faith, only to inform about it and to stress the responsibility every creature ultimately has to be responsive to the living God. In addition, the offer of Jesus is made to all without discrimination. Thus the exclusiveness of the benefit is directly related to one's willingness or unwillingness to be connected to the benefits. The church's call is to be loyal to God in sharing the message and doing so in such a way that its impact on believers' lives is evident. The call is not to impose the gospel on others. Some will not welcome such a testimony. They are left to go their own way with its tragic consequences. To others, however, the gospel will supply the sweet savor of real life and will open new vistas to how one can live and have fellowship with God.

Additional Notes

4:1. There is a textual problem as to whether "priests" (ἰερεῖς, *hiereis*) or "chief priests" (ἀρχιερεῖς, *archiereis*, in B, C) should be read here. The widest array of MS support is for "priests."

4:16. Codex D strengthens the obvious nature of the sign by using the elative φανερώτερον (*phanerōteron*, all too obvious). This is singularly attested and not original.

4. The Community Reaction: Prayer for Boldness (4:23–31)

This passage, which concludes the scene that began in Acts 3:1, shows the apostles and the church as faithful agents of God (Fitzmyer 1998: 306).[1] How do the members of community react to persecution and the report of the leadership's charge not to preach Christ (v. 23; Witherington 1998: 200)? They do two things (vv. 24–30). First, they pray, neither for judgment on those who are persecuting them nor to avoid persecution but for their own strength and enablement in the midst of persecution. Second, they pray to be able to preach the message boldly, not to cower in fear of the social and political power the leaders possess but to be faithful to God, who is the true Sovereign, following Jesus's instruction in Luke 12:4–7. They depend on God to carry out the mission he has called them to and band together in prayer to show corporately their commitment to proclaim the message.

The early believers also recognize that their rejection was something to be anticipated, and they accept it with praise. God said that there would be people who want nothing to do with his Anointed and would reject him, failing to recognize him. The appeal to Ps. 2 makes this point. In a sense the rulers are insignificant in light of the community's relationship to God and the enablement God can give to them. The prayer has two divisions: its theological underpinnings (vv. 24–28) and the current petition that grows out of that understanding (vv. 29–30).[2] God signals his reception of the prayer in v. 31 as the building shakes and all are filled with the Spirit in a way that has them preach the word boldly. The early church knew that its key priority was the mission of preaching Jesus to a needy world.

This is the second example of corporate prayer in Acts; the first was the appeal for aid in selecting a twelfth apostolic member in 1:24–25. There also is a summary note on community prayer in 2:42. Here we catch a glimpse of the content, focus, and emphasis in their prayers. These prayers are not so much for individual personal needs, as in

1. Schneider 1980: 354–55 highlights all the points of contact with the previous scene and argues for roots in the tradition, though attributing its current style to Luke.

2. On this kind of prayer in Judaism, see Pesch 1986a: 173n2, who notes its early Jewish form: call to God, predication, presentation of historical setting, request, renewed call to God; 1 Chron. 17:16–27; 2 Chron. 20:6–12; Neh. 9:6–37; Tob. 3:2–15; 2 Macc. 15:22–24; Jon. 4:2–3; Dan. 9:9–19. Pesch also says that it is rooted in pre-Lukan tradition, as does Marshall 1980: 104, responding to Haenchen 1987: 228–29.

many locations in the Psalms, but for their needs as a community in terms of their mission; they call on God to support them with spiritual provision for that mission.

Exegesis and Exposition

[23]When they were released, they came to their friends and reported what the chief priests and the elders had said to them. [24]Those who heard it lifted their voices up together to God and said, "Sovereign Lord, who made the heaven and the earth and the sea and everything in them, [25]who by the mouth of our father David, your servant, said through the Holy Spirit, 'Why did the nations rage and people imagine useless things? [26]The kings of the earth set themselves in array and the rulers were gathered together against the Lord and against his anointed.' [27]For truly in this city were gathered together against your holy servant Jesus, whom you anointed, Herod and Pontius Pilate together with the nations and ⌐people⌐ Israel [28]to do all that your hand and ⌐your⌐ will had predestined to occur. [29]And now, Lord, look upon their threats, and grant to your servants all boldness to speak your word, [30]while you stretch out ⌐your⌐ hand to heal, and signs and wonders are performed through the name of the holy servant Jesus." [31]And when they had prayed, the place was shaken in which they were gathered together; and they were all filled with the Holy Spirit and were speaking the word of God with boldness.

The two apostles are released after their warning (v. 21), apparently along with the man. The size and location of the group the apostles return to are not specified. They return to "their own" (τοὺς ἰδίους, *tous idious*), their friends of the community. Acts 21:6 and 24:23 also use this idiom of "their own," meaning their place or their home or their own people (Sir. 11:34 [of one's family]; Philo, *Moses* 1.14 §77 [of one's nation]; 2 Macc. 12:22 [of warrior companions]). Johnson (1992: 83) translates it as "associates" and limits the group to the apostles, but it is unclear if we ever have just that group gathered in these early chapters of Acts (correctly, Polhill 1992: 148). The expression is not accidental, as it presses the point of how the early church saw itself as a community of mutually supportive friends. Their return leads to a report about the warning they have received from the chief priests and elders (vv. 2, 5, 8), how they commanded them not to preach Jesus (vv. 17–18).

4:23

The community members' response to their dilemma is to take it to the Lord in prayer.[3] They speak as one voice (φωνήν, *phonēn*; note the singular noun) in prayer and approach God for God's enablement to perform their task. One person probably prays here with the whole community

4:24

3. On the relationship between worship and doctrine in Luke-Acts and then in the early centuries of the church, see Pelikan 2005: 74–78.

sharing in the spirit and nature of the request. The term for "voice" is singular, and, while the more common term in Acts, ὁμοθυμαδόν (*homothymadon*) underscores the oneness of the effort (for this term, see Acts 1:14; 2:46). The dire situation leads them immediately to express their dependence on God in prayer. They know that God is stronger than their enemy (Jervell 1998: 185) and that without pursuing God's will, their effort will be wasted.

In a situation that includes a power play by the leadership against the community, the prayer begins with an assertion of God's absolute sovereignty. The address of the prayer to God (Δέσποτα, *Despota*) uses a term for lordship that expresses God's sovereign position. The cognate English word "despot" conveys the idea of absolute authority, but the Greek word does not have the negative connotation of the English term. The term appears ten times in the NT, twice in Luke-Acts, which always uses it of God (Luke 2:27–32 [in Simeon's prayer that the Lord can now take him since he has seen the Messiah]; Acts 4:24–25). It often refers to a human ruler, but in the NT it refers to the slave-master relationship, whether involving men or God (1 Tim. 6:1–2 [human ruler who is a master of a slave]; 2 Tim. 2:20–21 [in an illustration about being useful to God, the master in a house]; Titus 2:9–10 [human master]; 1 Pet. 2:18 [human master]; 2 Pet. 2:1 [denying the Master]; Jude 1:4 [denying the Master]; Rev. 6:10 [of God hearing the prayer of the martyrs]). A master is someone who has control or authority (Rengstorf, *TDNT* 2:47–49, who notes that Josephus often uses this term to address God in prayer, *Ant.* 1.18.6 §272; 4.3.2 §46; so NET, "Master of all"). In the OT and Judaism, it is often used of God but with an additional qualifier, as here in Acts, where it is tied to the idea that God is the Creator of everything (of such prayers: Isa. 37:16–20; 2 Kings 19:15–19).[4] It is God's position as Creator that allows him to function as Master over his creatures. There is a corporate humility expressed in turning to the Master.

Some scholars question that the expression of the prayer comes from so early a period in the church's history. The idea that this prayer is late because it uses this terminology fails to take into account the Jewish usage and appeal to the position of the Creator, and so this judgment is misleading (*pace* Barrett 1994: 241–42, who primarily appeals to the lack of such usage in Paul and the appearance of the term δεσπότης later in the early church). Also misleading is the idea that the content of this early portion of the prayer has nothing to do with the situation (Schille 1984: 139). The prayer is not formed merely after the model of

4. In the LXX, God's absolute authority is expressed using κύριος (*kyrios*): Exod. 20:11; Neh. 9:6. For δεσπότης (*despotēs*), see Job 5:8; Isa. 1:24; Jon. 4:3; Sir. 23:1; 34:24 (34:29 Eng.); Wis. 6:7; 8:3; 13:3, 9; 1 Esd. 4:60; 3 Macc. 2:2; Jdt. 9:12; Josephus, *Ant.* 4.2.3 §40; in the NT: Acts 14:15 (conceptually of God as creator); 2 Pet. 2:1 (of Christ); Jude 4 (of Christ); God as "maker" of the creation: Luke 11:40; Acts 17:24; Heb. 3:2; Rev. 14:7; Schneider 1980: 357n24.

Isa. 37:16–20.[5] The early portion of the prayer shows the community thinking theologically about what is taking place. There continues to be a rejection of the Messiah, a response that should not be surprising (Marshall 1980: 103). When Ps. 2 is cited, it may be with a view like that of the Midrash Psalms 2, which taught that this pattern of rejection had been a continuous part of the nation's history, mostly by Israel's enemies' refusal to acknowledge God's messenger (e.g., Pharaoh of Moses). Only in Acts is the nation, ironically, taking part in the rejection along with the nations. A variation of this theme, drawing on ideas reaching back to Deuteronomy, will appear in Stephen's speech in Acts 7. Jews in the midst of rejection would naturally look to such ideas.

The mention of creation underscores the initial address, as this sovereign God is the one who made the heaven, earth, seas, and all that is in them. It is God's creation, and so God's lordship is the highest court of appeal. So the disciples pray for God's aid, not in destroying the enemy but for their own role and mission in his world.

After addressing God as Creator, the prayer lays the theological ground **4:25–26** of the petition by appealing to the language of Ps. 2:1. This psalm is seen as fulfilled by what Herod and Pilate, as well as the Gentiles and Israel, did to Jesus (v. 27). God's plan is being realized (v. 28). The citation begins with an introductory formula whose syntax is less than clear (Bock 1987: 202; Fitzmyer 1998: 308). The phrase τοῦ πατρὸς ἡμῶν (*tou patros hēmōn*, of our father) is placed forward in the formula without a clear connection, and the article ὁ (*ho*, who) would more naturally appear at the end of the formula. That the reference to the mouth of David comes after the reference to the Spirit is also unusual.

A myriad of textual alterations try to fix the word order. Three major variants exist for the formula, and five solutions have been proposed for what happened (Metzger 1971: 321–23 and Bock 1987: 202–5 also defend the citation's traditional roots). Le Cornu and Shulam (2003: 250) suggest a back translation for an original Aramaic or Hebrew version. Bruce (1990: 157) says that the confusion about the text emerged very early. The text as we have it in the current Greek edition is probably the best we can do for the formula's wording, being the best attested reading ($\mathfrak{P}^{74}$, ℵ, A, B, E, Ψ). Fortunately, despite the grammatical anomalies, the basic idea is clear. God spoke through the Spirit by David his servant with the words that are a part of the psalm.[6] When David spoke these words,

---

5. Jervell 1998: 184–85 notes the different views of the origin of the material: (1) Luke's work on the model of Isa. 37, (2) an old community prayer, or (3) a Lukan reworking of traditional material. There is enough syntactical roughness in the way the prayer is introduced to suggest that Luke is using traditional material. Some scholars complain that the interpretive techniques of exposition show that this is not a prayer, but Jervell 1998: 186, 189–90 sees a mixture of Luke's work and traditional material present.

6. See Acts 1:16 for the idea that Scripture is the product of the Spirit speaking through the prophet. On David as God's servant, see Luke 1:69 and Acts 2:30. Jesus was

God's Spirit spoke. Psalm 2:1 is cited in exact agreement with both the LXX and the Hebrew text (Ps. 2:7 appears in Acts 13:33; Heb. 1:5; 5:5; and allusions to Ps. 2:9 appear in Rev. 2:27; 12:5; 19:15). In Judaism the psalm has surfaced in Ps. Sol. 17.24–28 (using Ps. 2:2, 9) and 4Q174 1.10–13 (using vv. 1–2). In the later Jewish midrash, the psalm is read as describing a historical principle of opposition at work from the time of Pharaoh and Aaron to the world of the Messiah to come.

The point of the citation is that the Gentiles and people are arrayed against God and his Messiah. In an original reading of the psalm, most Jews would argue that these opponents are completely Gentile, reading the lines as simple parallelism. The prayer's point, however, is that once one sees who the enemy of God's Messiah is, then one can identify God's enemies, which here explicitly include both Gentiles and Jews. The explanation following the citation makes the application explicit. This hermeneutical key to reading the psalm shows that this is not a misreading of the psalm once it is seen in its canonical role within the Psalter (*pace* Barrett 1994: 246). Also important here may be the thrust of the entire psalm, namely, that opposing this plan is ultimately futile (Bruce 1988a: 99 points to Acts 2:23, 3:18 as speaking about the plan directly; Marshall 1980: 105 says the effort to oppose is "fruitless").

The opposition Jesus faced is now extended to the new community he formed, so they pray. It is often claimed that Luke does not show Roman opposition to Jesus but places blame on the Jews. This text shows this view to be wrong. All ethnic groups in Jerusalem did nothing (Luke 23:1–25) to stop the injustice Jesus experienced, and so they shared in the responsibility for his death.

On the one hand, the "nations raged" (ἐφρύαξαν ἔθνη, *ephryaxan ethnē*). The verb appears only here in the NT. It refers to being insolent. In its everyday use, it refers to "spirited animals," such as snorting horses before a race (BAGD 867; BDAG 1067; 2 Macc. 7:34; 3 Macc. 2:2). The term for "nations/Gentiles" reappears in verse 27 as part of the exposition identifying who is meant in the prayer. The word-link form of explanation in this verse is another example of the Jewish interpretive technique of *gezerah shewa* (Johnson 1992: 85 notes that the technique shows up at Qumran in several texts: 1QpHab; 4QpNah; 4QpPs 37).

On the other hand, "people imagined useless things" (λαοὶ ἐμελέτησαν κενά, *laoi emeletēsan kena*). The imagining here involves the mindless or empty (κενός, *kenos*) attempt to do something to God's Messiah and try to stop God's plan (BAGD 500 §3; BDAG 627 §3). This refers to Israel according to the word linkage with verse 27 (λαοί). If Jesus is the Messiah (Acts 4:18; 10:38) and is opposed, then Ps. 2 applies to his opponents,

---

called God's servant in Acts 3:13, 26. Israel was called God's servant in Luke 1:54. Paul and Barnabas will be presented as the servant in terms of mission in Acts 13:47; on David and the Psalter, see Acts 1:16; 2:25, 30–31.

whoever they may be. It was this combination of kings (Herod) and rulers (Pilate and the council, see Acts 4:5, 8), as well as those they represented, who gathered together (συνήχθησαν, *synēchthēsan*) to oppose God's way. The occurrence of this verb in verse 27 identifies how the prayer reads the psalm and whom it is discussing as sinning against God. Four terms are linked between the citation and the explanation: "nations," "people," "gathered together," and "anointed" (as noun and verb).

Why does this illogical opposition take place? the psalm asks. At one level, it makes no sense. On another it shows how out of tune many are with God's ways. Given the fact that God is working out his plan, the tone of the prayer is very calm, but the implication in the prayer is that many Jews and Gentiles need to see what God is doing and change their approach to Jesus. In the meantime, as the predicted opposition works itself out, the community will seek to be what God has called it to be, faithful and bold.

The theological rationale is now explained (γάρ, *gar*, for) in the word linkages that take place. The use of the phrase "truly" (ἐπ' ἀληθείας, *ep' alētheias*) seems to be Lukan (Luke 4:25; 20:21; 22:59; Acts 10:34; Mark 12:14, 32; LXX: Deut. 22:20; Tob. 8:7; Job 9:2; 19:4; 36:4; Isa. 37:18; Haenchen 1987: 227; Schneider 1980: 358n34). Those gathered together against God's plan through Jesus include Herod, Pilate, the Gentiles, and the people of Israel (on Pilate, see Acts 3:13 and Luke 23:1–25).   4:27–28

Only Luke details a role for Herod Antipas in the trial. Barrett (1994: 247) does not discount the historicity of this detail. Herod is seen as a Jewish leader in Luke 23:6–12, as he is portrayed in his role as a Jewish king, the chief Jewish political ruler. Herod was half Jewish (on Herod's career, Bruce 1990: 158). Pilate is portrayed with a degree of sympathy in Luke 23. He is seen as being pressured by the Jewish leaders. Yet he did succumb to the pressure and allowed the death of an innocent man, according to his own judgment, thus becoming a member of those whose acts opposed Jesus. There is no inconsistency in Luke's portrayal here, just a difference of focus (Weiser 1981: 132 speaks of a tension in the portrayal).

These rulers and others are arrayed against God's set-apart holy servant (τὸν ἅγιον παῖδα, *ton hagion paida*), Jesus, the one "whom you [God] anointed" (ὃν ἔχρισας, *hon echrisas*). This opposition is against the Messiah (on Jesus as servant, see 3:13). Jesus is like the servant David (v. 25). Kilgallen (1998) effectively argues that the unusual phrase "your holy servant Jesus whom you anointed" shows Jesus to be the Messiah, who also is the servant. "Messiah" points to Davidic messianic authority especially as it relates to the arrival in power of the kingdom and the defeat of evil. "Servant" points to one who, like David, obeyed God and was fully at his disposal, and it points to his suffering as well. Just as David had enemies, as Ps. 2 notes, so did Jesus. Both figures, however, were God's chosen and anointed.

This reference to anointing shows that Jesus is the Messiah and is ready to begin his mission. It does not argue that God made Jesus Messiah at some point in time, since the infancy material (Luke 1:31–35) and baptism (Acts 10:38) rule out such a reading for Luke. Barrett (1994: 247), however, suggests this kind of adoptionism in these verses. Fitzmyer (1998: 309) focuses on the terminology only and the baptism; but this is too limited a reading for Luke. An adoptionist reading also is unlikely for the early church view when placed in a context where God is described as having a predestined plan and Jesus is presented as the Lord at God's side. Jesus experienced a call with a symbolic anointing at the baptism but did not become Messiah then. The presence in Luke of an infancy narrative shows that Jesus's status as Messiah was something he possessed before his birth, not something conferred at his baptism or birth. The debate among scholars of early-church Christology is over how far back such a Lukan understanding goes in early-church theology. If Jesus saw his messianic calling in the context of designed suffering, then all the features necessary for this kind of declaration existed by the time such a speech was made. In other words, nothing prevents this declaration from having roots in the church's earliest period.

The human rejection Jesus experienced falls within God's plan and the activity of God's hand (χείρ, *cheir*), that is, God's will and power (Luke 1:66; 23:46; Acts 4:30; 7:25, 50; 11:21; 13:11). Jesus's arrest is expressed as being given over into their hands, viewing the event as it relates to power (in the OT: Exod. 3:20; 13:3, 14, 16; 15:6; Ps. 55:20 [54:21 LXX]; conceptually, Acts 2:23; 3:18). This opposition is not seen as a surprise but as something God had planned and predestined (προώρισεν, *proōrisen*). This verb appears six times in the NT but only here in Luke-Acts (Acts 4:27–28; Rom. 8:29–30 [2x]; 1 Cor. 2:6–8; Eph. 1:3–6, 11–12). Foreknowledge (πρόγνωσις, *prognōsis*; Acts 2:23; 26:5) and foretelling (προκαταγγέλλω, *prokatangellō*; προκηρύσσω, *prokēryssō*; 3:18; 7:52; 13:24) are a part of this understanding as well (Witherington 1998: 203).

The term for God's plan (βουλή, *boulē*) appears twelve times in the NT, with the bulk of occurrences in Luke-Acts (nine times; Luke 7:29–30; 23:50–53; Acts 2:22–24; 4:27–28; 5:38–39; 13:36–37; 20:26–27; 27:12, 42; 1 Cor. 4:5; Eph. 1:11–12; Heb. 6:16–20). Some are going to oppose what God is doing. So the question becomes how members of the new community will face such opposition. They will not obey it or be silent. They seek God's power to be bold in their declarations.

4:29–30   Now the community offers the prayer's request. The phrase καὶ τὰ νῦν (*kai ta nyn*, and now) signals the shift to the request. Luke often uses the term "now" (Acts 5:38; 17:30; 20:32; 24:25; 27:22). The prayer's initial appeal is to the justice of God, who is called to look upon the opponents' threats. God is to take special note of the injustice and act on the community's behalf. This refers to the threats of the Sanhedrin (4:21).

The verb ἐφοράω (*ephoraō*, look upon) is rare, appearing otherwise only in Luke 1:25 in the NT and not at all in the LXX. The request is that God take notice of the situation, as God did of Elizabeth's disgrace when she was childless. The term for "threats" (ἀπειλή, *apeilē*) is also rarely used in the NT (Acts 4:29–30; 9:1–2; Eph. 6:9; also in the LXX: 3 Macc. 2:24; 5:18, 30, 33, 37; 4 Macc. 4:8, 24; 7:2; 8:19; 9:32; 13:6; 14:9; Odes Sol. 4.12; 12.5; Prov. 13:8; 17:10; 19:12; 20:2; Job 23:6; Ps. Sol. 17.25; Hab. 3:12; Zech. 9:14; Isa. 50:2; 54:9). The community leaves to God the moral judgment of the opponents and their actions. It does not pray explicitly for opponents to be crushed, nor does it seek to be spared opposition. It asks to face the opposition and suffering faithfully.

The second request is that God give the community boldness (παρρησίας, *parrēsias*) to speak the word (on this term, see Acts 2:29 and 4:13). The term for "boldness" reappears in verse 31 to show the answer to the prayer. The community's members describe themselves as God's bond servants (δούλοις, *doulois*), a term that fits the address of God as Lord at the prayer's start (Schille 1984: 142) and is Paul's common way to describe himself (Rom. 1:1). There is a cultural irony here, as in the Greek context the right to speak freely was the activity of free men, not slaves (Williams 1990: 89). As God's slaves, the community is free to address God and make requests of him, while submitting to God's leading.

As the community preaches, it is confident that God will show power by means of "your hand" (χεῖρά σου, *cheira sou*). God will heal and perform signs and wonders through the name of Jesus, as God did in Acts 3:1–10 (on signs and wonders, see 2:19 and 43; on the use of ἐν, *en*, plus the dative for means, Wallace 1996: 598). The prayer is not so much a request but an understanding in faith of how God can work (Larkin 1995: 80). The reference to God's hand looks back to verse 28, linking the request to the theological rationale already given. So the prayer is asking for enablement to match God's visible activity and sovereign ability to heal with the proclamation of God's word. God is to show his compassion to the people as the community proclaims the word and faces opposition. The signs serve the sovereign God and God's message (Polhill 1992: 150).

With the prayer complete, three "signs" of divine response follow: (1) the place where they pray shakes, (2) all are filled with the Spirit, and (3) they speak the word with boldness (ἐλάλουν, *elaloun*, were speaking, is imperfect). The shaking of the place of prayer is an unusual sign of confirmation (in the OT: Isa. 6:4; Exod. 19:18 [Sinai quakes at God's presence]; 2 Esd. [4 Ezra] 6:15, 29; T. Levi 3.9; Josephus, *Ant.* 7.4.1 §§76–77). Such confirmation is not always the case (1 Kings 19:11–12; for Greco-Roman examples of divine activity in confirmation, Plutarch, *Vita Publicola* 9.6; Lucian, *Menippus* 9–10; Virgil, *Aeneid* 3.89–90; Conzelmann 1987: 35;

4:31

Bruce 1990: 159; Witherington 1998: 204; van der Horst 1989: 45). In Acts 16:26 an earthquake opens up prison doors and makes the prison shake. Whereas there it shows God's work to free those persecuted, here it shows that God has heard the prayer.

The filling with the Spirit means the enablement to proclaim the word that follows. This is a separate act from the indwelling that appeared in Acts 2. It is specific to the request for boldness, not a "second blessing" or "second Pentecost" (correctly, Polhill 1992: 150: "a fresh filling"; Witherington 1998: 204).

The word is spoken with boldness (μετὰ παρρησίας, meta parrēsias). The community's remarks about God's work through Jesus are the word of God (6:2, 7; 8:14; 11:1; 12:24; 13:5, 7, 44, 46, 49; 16:32; 17:13; 18:11; Fitzmyer 1998: 311). The phrase appears at the end of the verse, making it emphatic. There is an oral message about Jesus that can be called God's word because the message about Jesus is from God, describing God's work. The community's goal to be enabled for mission is met. Action comes with words explaining what God is doing "through the name of Jesus," a theme of this entire literary unit from Acts 3:6, 16; 4:10, 12, 18, 30.

In sum, this prayer is an expression of complete dependence on God, a recognition of his sovereignty, a call for God's justice and oversight in the midst of opposition, for an enablement for mission, and for the working of his power to show that God is behind the preaching of the name of Jesus in healing and signs. The prayer has roots in Hezekiah's prayer in Isa. 37:16–20 (Witherington 1998: 203). It is a mark of success for the community that in preaching the word its members have walked the path of Jesus and have suffered rejection. The reliance on God, the resting in God's justice, the willingness to suffer persecution, the desire to preach Jesus, and the call to God to show himself—all are signs of a healthy community. The presence of rejection and opposition is not a surprise, nor is it sought, but suffering is embraced when it comes from God. Turning to God leads to boldness.

The community's members, as their leaders have done, will obey God and proclaim the name of Jesus. They will not be silent about the unique way God has chosen to save. Their gathering together for prayer is a major expression of their unity. United in one voice before the one God, they seek to do the one thing God has called on them to do, namely, to minister and to proclaim the work of God through Jesus. All of this is rooted in two key convictions: (1) the Lord-servant relationship between God and his followers and (2) the focus on accomplishing a key mission God has called the community to do—to share the name of Jesus and God's work through him. The early believers' self-understanding and dependence on God lead them to face opposition with boldness. They also face it together, not in a series of individual efforts where each acts on one's own. This unity in community gives them added strength to know they are not alone in the cause (Fernando 1998: 173). God responds with enablement for the community. The word is both preached and lived, but most important, the people of God are enabled for the task God calls them to undertake. The best way to face opposition is through what God provides.

Additional Notes

4:27. The plural λαοῖς (*laois*) is better attested than the singular, which appears only in E, Ψ, and Syriac. The plural casts the blame more widely, to many Jews, as do the speeches in Acts 2 and 3, and matches the language of the psalm.

4:28. There is a textual problem about whether the will of God referred to as "your" (σου, *sou*) hand is included in the verse. For the omission are A*, B, E*, 323, and some Vulgate MSS. For inclusion are ℵ, Aᶜ, D, Eᶜ, Ψ, Byz, and Syriac. The external evidence is somewhat divided but favors inclusion of the term. The same term shows up in verse 30 tied to the hand of God, which causes some scholars to suggest that it has been added here on internal grounds. The difference produced a similar textual problem there. The inclusion or lack of it makes little difference to the meaning, as it is clear that the hand is God's, as is the will.

E. Community Life and Problems (4:32–5:11)

This unit reflects a contrast. On the one hand, there is a community that is holding all things in common, with figures such as Barnabas contributing resources to the community (Acts 4:32–37). On the other hand, there are people pretending to give all but who do not, with Ananias and Sapphira experiencing a judgment for claiming to give all while holding back funds (5:1–11). As Luke records the effort at mission, he also takes the community's internal pulse, just as he did after the speech of Pentecost in Acts 2:43–47. For the new community's members, the issue is not only mission but also how they will function together as contributors to the cause and as community. Luke is a realist, for after this unit of individual sacrifice follows a unit where dishonesty surfaces within the community. God deals directly and instantly with dishonesty in this case. They have no doubt that God knows the heart and knows what the individual members of the community are doing. Luke highlights the fact that accountability before God exists within the community. God sees the good, the bad, and the ugly—and will act to deal with it now or later.

1. All Things in Common:
The Example of Barnabas (4:32–37)

This unit is a summary account of the believers' love for their neighbors in the community (Weiser 1981: 136; Jervell 1998: 191). The community continues to form together around God's call, the community's work, and the apostles. Each person in the community voluntarily brings what he or she has in order to hold everything in common (vv. 32–35). The example of Barnabas closes the unit (vv. 36–37). The passage, though largely Lukan in wording, seems to point to underlying tradition (Barrett 1994: 253) with its interweaving of the community and apostolic roles (so also Jervell 1998: 193). Jervell suggests that the relocation of many disciples from Galilee may have created such a need to pool resources.

Exegesis and Exposition

³²Now the company of those who believed was of one heart and soul ⌐ ⌐, and no one said that any of the things he possessed was his own, but they shared everything. ³³And with great power the apostles were giving their testimony to the resurrection of the Lord Jesus, and great grace was upon all of them. ³⁴For no one among them was a needy person, for as many as were possessors of lands or houses sold them, and were bringing the proceeds of what was sold ³⁵and were setting them at the apostles' feet, and it was being distributed to each as one had a need. ³⁶Joseph, the one who was called Barnabas by the apostles, a name that means "son of encouragement," a Levite, a Cypriot by birth, ³⁷having sold a field that belonged to him, brought the money and set it at the apostles' feet.

Community life thrives, as the group is now a "multitude" (πλήθους, *plēthous*; twenty-four of thirty-one NT occurrences are Lukan; Acts 6:2, 5; 15:12, 30; 19:9; 21:36; 23:7). There is unity of heart and soul (καρδία καὶ ψυχὴ μία, *kardia kai psychē mia*; Deut. 6:5; 10:12; 11:13; similar are 1 Chron. 12:39; Jer. 32:39 [39:39 LXX]). Van der Horst (1989: 46) notes that the expression "one soul" was proverbial, equivalent to "one spirit," and pointed to real friendship. As they prayed with one voice in verse 24, so now they are committed to each other in terms of resources. The united rejoicing of one heart is like Acts 2:44–46, where the first mention of common (κοινά, *koina*) possessions appears (on this theme,

4:32

see discussion there). This adjective is part of the series of cognate terms that mean sharing in something with others. The term "fellowship" (κοινωνία, koinōnia) is one of these terms, as is the verb "share" (κοινωνέω, koinōneō) and the noun "partner" (κοινωνός, koinōnos).[1] This sharing of possessions shows how "connected" their mutual participation is. It extends even down to possessions, as verse 34 explains in more detail. Κοινά appears at the end of the sentence here, which makes it emphatic. The expression may be a bit hyperbolic, an example of litotes common in Luke, as Acts 5:4 says that money collected from a sale is at the disposal of Ananias and Sapphira. The point is that many are voluntarily giving over a great deal of their possessions for the use of all. The result is that community members' needs are met.

4:33 Two characteristics reflect the apostles' activity: great power in the ongoing witness to the resurrection, and great grace. The witness to the resurrection surely includes declarations like those seen in Acts 3 and 4. God's presence and the proof of divine enablement for the apostles is also a point. The verb ἀπεδίδουν (apedidoun, were giving) is imperfect, so the ongoing character of the powerful witness is the more dominant point rather than miracles, although miracles may also be in view. It is the resurrection as exaltation that is highlighted, since it shows how God has vindicated Jesus.

The mention of grace is another way to show that the prayer of 4:24–30 has been answered. The context, which highlights what God is doing, favors a reference here to grace from God, not favor from the people as in 2:47 (but so Fitzmyer 1998: 313–14; Le Cornu and Shulam 2003: 254). The apostles as early overseers of this community are at the center of its activity. As the operation grows in complexity and problems arise, a new arrangement for relief will surface (6:1–17). Such sociological flexibility is necessary to manage the community's growth and commitment to each other. By 11:29, this community is receiving help from other communities outside Jerusalem. Everything about the portrayal of this scene is positive in Luke. The type of mutual care and concern it foresees is commended as exemplary and runs through the NT (2:45; 11:27–30; 24:17; Rom. 15:26; Gal. 2:10; 1 Cor. 16:1–4; 2 Cor. 9:11–12).

4:34–35 No needy people (οὐδὲ ... ἐνδεής, oude ... endeēs) are a part of the group, as this pooling of resources meets all needs. Literally, there is no one who "lacked" in the community. This meets a standard God called for in Deut. 15:4, where there are to be no poor because of God's provision in the land for his people (Le Cornu and Shulam 2003: 253; see also Matt. 25:35–40). This OT passage is part of a larger discussion

1. This text portrays the church as introducing a new set of values, which Pelikan (2005: 79–81) connects with the phrase "one, holy, catholic, and apostolic" in the Niceno-Constantinopolitan Creed.

on possessions (Deut. 15:1–18). All of these descriptions of the mutual care within the community are presented positively by Luke. These acts evidence the community's piety and mutual commitment to God and one another. It is a sign that they see each other as family or friends, worthy of compassionate care. Witherington (1998: 162–63) notes that the Qumran Essenes had such a standard—not to show friendship or kinship, however, but for reasons of ritual purity (1QS 5.1–3; 9.3–11; CD 9.1–15). Greek culture also sensed the appeal of such community (Plato, *Republic* 5.449C; *Critias* 110C–D; Aristotle, *Nicomachean Ethics* 1168B: "Friends have one soul between them"). Philo shows that this was evident in Judaism (*Abraham* 40 §235; a major Greek theme, Johnson 1992: 86; Conzelmann 1987: 36; Eckey 2000: 126–27).

The explanation (γάρ, *gar*) for the mechanism of achieving this concrete expression of community follows. Some members own houses and land, part of a very small middle class in this first-century culture, about 10 percent of the population. The upper class was even smaller, constituting 4 to 7 percent. These members of the new movement are selling what they have and bringing the proceeds to the community as represented by the apostles, who oversee the distribution of resources. The imperfect verb ἔφερον (*epheron*, were bringing) and present participle (πωλοῦντες, *pōlountes*, selling) in combination suggest a gradual liquidation of assets, not selling everything all at once (Williams 1990: 93). The Greek verbs for "set" and "distribute" in verse 35 are also imperfect (on the importance of the switch in verb tenses in this unit, see Schneider 1980: 363; Pesch 1986a: 180). Aorists start in verse 36 with the story of Barnabas, the example. The present participle πωλοῦντες in verse 34 has the force of an imperfect because of the verbs surrounding it (BDF §339.3; Moulton and Turner 1963: 67, 81).

That Ananias and Sapphira could have kept some of their proceeds (Acts 5:3–4) supports the idea that such liquidation took place over time, not all at once, as does Mary's owning a home in the city (12:12–13). Such a need to pool resources may well have arisen because many in the new community were poor and, in addition, persecution may well have left others in the community isolated socially. So the response is one that emerges out of concern for fellow members. They are giving without expecting anything back in return, an ethic like that noted in Luke 6:34. The imperfect verb may also suggest that the practice stopped at some point (Polhill 1992: 153), but the fact that we are looking back in the account and that the practice includes an apostolic role makes this conclusion less than certain. What may have changed is how such gifts were handled.

The phrase "the apostles' feet" (τοὺς πόδας τῶν ἀποστόλων, *tous podas tōn apostolōn*) appears three times in Acts, all in this discussion of community activity that extends to 5:11 (4:35, 37; 5:2). Similar phrases in the OT are a way of expressing obedience and submission (Josh. 10:24;

1 Sam. 25:24, 41; 2 Sam. 22:39; Johnson 1992: 87). Here it indicates giving control of resources over to the apostles. The mention of those having need (χρείαν εἶχεν, *chreian eichen*) echoes Acts 2:45, its only other mention in Acts.

4:36–37 An example of such giving is a Hellenistic or Diaspora Jewish believer named Joseph, also known as Barnabas to the apostles. The difference between a Diaspora Jew who has come to Jerusalem and a Hellenistic Jew, a Hebrew who is influenced by Greek culture, is slight. It is debated which category Barnabas fits (Barrett 1994: 258 prefers a Hellenistic Jew). Barnabas's Greek identity emerges from his roots in Cyprus, one of three NT references to this locale (Acts 4:36–37; 11:20; 21:15–16).[2]

The Jews settled the island of Cyprus during the Ptolemaic period (after 330 BC) but were expelled in AD 117 after rebelling. Barnabas most likely was born there or his family came from there. His religious roots are indicated by the fact that he is a Levite, one of only three references to a Levite in the NT (Luke 10:31–32; John 1:19; Acts 4:36–37). Levites were often wealthy and very well educated, but not all were priests. Generally, Levites were not to own land (Num. 18:20; Deut. 10:9). Exceptions, however, existed in the OT, and life for Levites was different by the first century (Jer. 1:1; 32:7–9; Josephus, *Life* 13–15 §§68–83; 76 §§422–30; Bruce 1990: 160). Levites served in the temple, keeping watch over the gates, policing the area, instructing, and copying the Torah (Le Cornu and Shulam 2003: 258).

Joseph is a very common name, which may explain why the apostles called him Barnabas. It is also not unusual for a person to bear two names (e.g., Saul, Paul; Peter, Simon). The meaning of the less-common name, "son of encouragement" (υἱὸς παρακλήσεως, *huios paraklēseōs*) well summarizes the way Barnabas will function in the book, as he will embrace Paul's conversion, minister with him, and be an evangelist (Barrett 1994: 258–59).[3] He is referred to twenty-three times in the book (Acts 4:36–37; 9:27; in Antioch: 11:22, 29–30; 12:25–13:2; in mission with Paul: 13:7, 43, 46, 50; 14:11–12, 14–15, 20; at the Jerusalem Council: 15:2, 12, 22–26, 35–40). Barnabas will be well qualified for a mission to Gentiles, since he came from one of these Gentile areas. Part of the function of the unit is to introduce him to Luke's audience. He surely is one of Luke's heroes.

2. On Jews from that area, see 13:4; 15:39; 21:3; 27:4. On the expression τῷ γένει (*tō genei*, in origin or by descent), see Mark 7:26; Acts 18:2, 24; 2 Macc. 5:22; 3 Macc. 1:3; Josephus, *Ant.* 20.4.2 §81; Schneider 1980: 367n41. On another mention of Jews from Cyprus, see *Ant.* 13.10.4 §287. 1 Macc. 15:23 refers to a large contingent of Jews there; so also Philo, *Embassy* 36 §282.

3. Witherington 1998: 209 notes that Luke uses the term παράκλησις (*paraklēsis*) to refer to speech; conceptual examples of such encouragement include Luke 5:34; 10:6; 16:8; 20:34, 36; and Acts 11:23. The term here is a genitive of quality, given a personal characteristic; Moulton and Turner 1963: 208.

The name may be closer to a nickname. Barnabas can be seen as a "son of a prophet," whose function is to give encouragement (Weiser 1981: 138). The origin of the name is disputed. A literal rendering of the name is said by some to be "son of Nebo" (e.g., Conzelmann 1987: 36, who says Luke is simply incorrect). On the other hand, a popular wordplay can be at work here, as often is the case in the giving of names. Such a nickname rooted in a wordplay on *nabi'* would make the name's sense "son of a prophet" (that is, a prophet, on analogy with the phrase "son of man," meaning a human being). By extension, then, the name refers to what the prophet does by way of encouragement.

Which option is likely? Against "son of Nebo" is the unlikelihood that a Jewish Levite would carry the name of a Babylonian god, which is what Nebo is (Haenchen 1987: 232n2). Haenchen (1987: 232n1) rejects the connection to "son of prophet" as not possible because this expression does not equal "son of consolation." But this ignores the connection between the prophet, what he does, and the likely wordplay nature of the name. Brock (1974) appeals to Syriac and the more direct idea of a "son of comfort," which also is possible although not without linguistic obstacles of its own. Fitzmyer (1998: 321) has a full discussion and rejects any connection to "son of a prophet" or any other alternative, offering no elucidation of the explanation given in 4:36 for the name (also Polhill 1992: 154n80). He regards the connection simply as problematic. One wonders, however, if nicknames hold to firm linguistic rules, so that the etymology may well be a wordplay rooted in Barnabas's prophetic function or in his established role as a comforter. The roots of this knowledge about Barnabas here may well come through several means: (1) Luke's relationship to the Pauline circle and its knowledge of this church, (2) Barnabas's likely association with Antioch, or (3) the possibility that Luke knew Barnabas as a part of the Pauline ministry team.

Barnabas matches the community's description noted in verses 32–35 by selling a piece of land, taking the proceeds, and setting it at the apostles' feet (v. 35). The land's locale and nature are not known. Is it in Cyprus or in Judea? The text does not say.

The verbs in this section are aorist (a summary tense) in contrast to the imperfects (ongoing aspect) of the earlier summary. What is going on in the community as a whole, Barnabas also does.

In sum, this unit testifies to the community's mutual care and the concrete expression of its unity in the voluntary pooling of resources on behalf of the community. These resources are used for the care of those in need (on the social and economic condition of the early community, see Witherington 1998: 210–13). This meeting of needs is a theme that will surface here and there in Acts. The unity of heart and soul in this community is transparent. Not only do its members declare the word of God powerfully; they also make sure that each one in the community has access to everyday needs. Community life means both mission and mutual care. These occur because people care about one another and the cause they share. They see their obligation to God, even their worship, to be reflected in respect for other believers, what 1 John 2 calls a love for the brethren. Unity does not come naturally because we often like to go our own way. But to those who share the goal of reflecting the unity and reconciliation that Jesus brings, there is a desire to be sure that his body, the church, reflects his goals through concrete means.

But communities are often built on the leading example of an important individual. In our account, this is Barnabas. In Acts he cares for the poor, gives of his resources, welcomes Paul when others are skeptical, encourages him in ministering alongside him, leads a mission in a way that takes the initiative of engagement, and testifies about the work of God to those outside and within the community (Dormeyer and Galindo 2003: 83). He is what we call a rounded character in literary terms, as we see him in various situations, almost always in a positive light. It is no wonder this community did so well with the example of servant leadership Barnabas gave. Luke holds him up as a disciple whose example can be followed.

Additional Note

4:32. The MSS D and E add a reference to a lack of division in the body, using different Greek terms to make the point. Such a reading is in tension with 5:1–11 and is not well attested enough to be original.

2. Deceiving the Spirit and Judgment: Ananias and Sapphira (5:1–11)

In contrast to Barnabas stands the deceit of Ananias and Sapphira. This passage includes an instant-judgment miracle that has been the topic of much discussion (see below). Luke is honest that not everyone acted with virtue in the new community. God, however, watches the affairs of this nascent community very closely, even judging its members. Actions of deceit that represent lying to the apostles are presented as acts against God and the Spirit. The passage shows that God knows the hearts of believers. Peter is not the major figure in the text; God is. Luke is teaching about respect for God through one's action. Divine judgment against the act of disrespect produces the fear noted in verses 5 and 11.

There also is a figure lurking behind the scenes. Satan is noted as having influenced Ananias and Sapphira (Gaventa 2003: 99, 105). This does not excuse them. It simply means that cosmic forces are very interested in what happens in God's church, some for ill and others for good. God overcomes this effort of Satan to undercut God's people. Sometimes judgment makes this victory possible.

The passage has a mirror structure as Ananias and then Sapphira are judged: setting, interaction, and judgment followed by burial occur twice in the unit. The setting for Ananias appears in verses 1–2 with the couple's plot. The interaction with Ananias appears in verses 3–4, and the judgment and burial come in verses 5–6. The setting for Sapphira appears in verse 7. The interaction between her and Peter appears in verses 8–9; then her judgment and burial come in verses 10–11. So the structure of the passage is simple and clear.

This is one of two detailed judgment miracles in Acts (see also 13:11). In addition, there is a note of divine judgment on Herod in Acts 12:23 and a severe warning to Simon Magus (8:18–24). The scene has been called a "rule miracle of judgment." Fitzmyer (1998: 316–20) also discusses the likelihood that this account has traditional origins, and surveys the range of views about the text's historicity. He rejects parallelism to the punitive death in Lucian, *The Lover of Lies* 19–20. He also questions the value of other Greco-Roman parallels. Fitzmyer expresses no final judgment on the historicity of the events. Similar kinds of texts appear in the OT: Lev. 10:2 (fire consumes Nadab and Abihu), Josh. 7:1, 19–26 (with Achan, a judgment but no miracle), and 1 Kings 14:1–18 (Abijah's death).[1] The differences between Joshua and this text show that this OT text cannot be the basis for the event here. This event is not an "exact parallel" of Josh. 7, as four differences show (*pace* Haenchen 1987: 239–41): (1) Joshua has no miracle. (2) Here a lie is told to Peter, not a disclosure as with Achan. (3) The community does not suffer any loss. (4) There is no stoning; God acts directly. This kind of instant judgment is unique in the NT, although it is suggested in a text like 1 Cor. 11:30 about how some have died for taking the Lord's Supper inappropriately.

Many critics argue that roots for this event lie in the otherwise unexplainable deaths of community members. But such skeptical analyses of the text, presenting the story as significant embellishment, are really reactions against the possibility of miracles, especially instantaneous-judgment miracles.[2] The very uniqueness of the story argues for its credibility. Peter's remarks and the divine action bringing death are tightly linked as cause and effect (but this is not "magical power," since Peter utters no incantation to call down the judgment; *pace* Conzelmann 1987: 38). This is presented as a unique judgment at a sensitive point in the church's early days. It is not a normal act of God in terms of its instantaneous timing (Polhill 1992: 161). The omniscience of God and the accountability to God the story represents are the key points Luke is making. In addition, the proper and improper handling of resources constitutes another teaching point of the scene, positively by Barnabas and negatively by Ananias and Sapphira (Johnson 1992: 91). God sees and notes it all.

Exegesis and Exposition

[1]But a certain man named Ananias with his wife, Sapphira, sold a field, [2]and he kept back some of the proceeds, with his wife's knowledge, and brought only a part and set it at the apostles' feet. [3]But Peter said, "Ananias, why has Satan ⌐filled⌐ your heart to lie against the Holy Spirit and to keep back some of the proceeds of the land? [4]While it remained unsold, did it not remain yours? After it was sold, was it not in your authority? Why did you devise ⌐this deed⌐ in your heart? You have not lied to men but to God." [5]Hearing these words, Ananias ⌐ ⌐ fell down and died. And great fear came upon all those who heard. [6]And rising ⌐ ⌐, the young men wrapped him up, carried him out, and buried him.

[7]After an interval of about three hours, his wife came in, not aware of what

---

1. For discussion and a brief summary of rabbinic and some Greco-Roman examples, see Weiser 1981: 140–41. Susanna 52–62 also contains a judgment but no miracle; see Pesch 1986a: 196–97.

2. Conzelmann 1987: 37 says that no historical kernel can be extracted, but others argue for some type of death in the background. Weiser 1981: 147–48 rejects any historical connection other than the death of Ananias and possibly his wife, but see Bruce 1990: 164 on v. 5.

had happened. [8]And Peter said to her, "Tell me whether you sold the land for so much." And she said, "Yes, for so much." [9]But Peter said to her, "Why is it that you conspired to test the Spirit of the Lord? Look, the feet of those who buried your husband are at the door and will also carry you out." [10]Immediately she fell down at his feet and died. Coming in, the young men found her dead, and carried her out and buried her beside her husband. [11]And great fear came upon the entire church and upon all who heard of these things.

The first two verses give the setting of this event. This negative example concerns a couple, Ananias and Sapphira, who, like Barnabas, sell a parcel of land but then act in a very different manner. The contrast to Barnabas is a key to this scene and also shows that Luke can discuss problems in the church, in contrast to some who argue that Luke's portrait of the church in Acts is idealized.   **5:1**

Ananias is Hebrew and means "the Lord is gracious," and Sapphira means "beautiful." Κτῆμα (ktēma) is a general term for "possessions" and is rare in the NT (Matt. 19:22; Mark 10:22; Acts 2:44–47; 5:1–2). The term is different from any used in Acts 4:32–37. Here it refers to a field (BDAG 572 §2; Prov. 23:10), as it is reinforced by the term for "field" in Acts 5:3, 8 (χωρίον, chōrion). In the LXX, κτῆμα was sometimes used to refer to vineyards (Prov. 31:16; Hos. 2:17 [2:15 Eng.]), as was χωρίον (1 Chron. 27:27).

This verse plays out the scene of the previous summary, of people bringing the proceeds of their sale to the apostles and setting it at their feet (4:35, 37), but there is one key exception. Although this couple claims that they have set the entire proceeds before the apostles, they have kept back some of the money. The verb for "kept back" (ἐνοσφίσατο, enosphisato) is the same used for Achan's act in holding the spoil in Jericho (Josh. 7:1). It is a verb tied to financial fraud (2 Macc. 4:32; Johnson 1992: 88; Josephus, Ant. 4.8.29 §274). Greek texts use the term in a similar manner (Athenaeus, Deipnosophistae 6.234; Larkin 1995: 84). The middle voice is an indirect reflexive: "He kept it for himself" (Wallace 1996: 421). The term for "proceeds," τιμῆς (timēs), matches Acts 4:34.   **5:2**

The narration makes clear that this is done with joint knowledge (συνειδυίης, syneiduiēs; BAGD 791 §1; BDAG 973 §1). Sapphira is an enabler for Ananias. The only other NT use of συνειδυίης occurs in 1 Cor. 4:4. Later verses (Acts 5:3–4) make clear that they could have honestly kept back these proceeds or a portion of them, but this is not what they have done.

These verses contain Peter's response to Ananias. Peter has the perspective of a prophet who can read another's mind and heart (cf. Luke 7:39 of Jesus). The apostle wastes no time asking why Satan has filled Ananias's heart to lie to the Spirit and keep back the proceeds. With νοσφίσασθαι   **5:3–4** (*nosphisasthai*) Peter repeats the term for financial fraud used in v. 2. References to Satan are rare in Acts (5:3; 26:16–18), but an echo exists here of Judas's sin (Luke 22:2–3) and of a test Peter received from Satan (Luke 22:31–32; Johnson 1992: 88). Satan is present in other texts in Luke's Gospel (10:18; 11:18; 13:16) and in three OT passages (Job 1; Zech. 3:1–2; 1 Chron. 21:1). The devil is noted twice each in Luke and Acts (Luke 4:2, 13; Acts 10:38; 13:10).

The concept of filling (πληρόω, *plēroō*, fill; BAGD 670 §1; BDAG 828 §1) the heart refers to the control Satan has to influence such a decision to lie (ψεύσασθαι, *pseusasthai*; διὰ τί [*dia ti*, why] plus the infinitive ψεύσασθαι points to the result of such filling, the act of lying; BDF §391.4). Satan filled, and the result was the lie. This filling is the opposite of earlier community fillings, of being filled with the Spirit (Acts 2:4; 13:52; 19:21). There is a spiritual element to life in the community alongside the human dimension. Satan is trying to undermine what the community represents. Ananias is accused of being unfaithful in very direct terms. He is to be honest before and to God, but his integrity is severely compromised, and Peter and God know it. Such lying is dangerous to the community and dishonors God (Pesch 1986a: 199; Prov. 26:28 NRSV: "a lying tongue hates its victims").

Fitzmyer (1998: 323) calls it "a lie to *koinōnia*," and thus it is an act against fellowship. As the end of the passage indicates, Ananias has followed man, not God. This final remark makes clear that the responsibility for the act, though influenced by Satan, is Ananias's directly, for it is out of his heart that Ananias has acted, and it is his heart, apart from God, that Ananias has obeyed. The deceit and allegiance represented here reflect the personal characters of Satan and the Spirit respectively, one reflecting deceit and the other honesty and faithfulness to God. Nonetheless, the sin is Ananias's because he left himself open to follow Satan. There are implications here for the person of God, since to act against the Spirit is to act against God.[3] In Luke's view, these are not metaphorical forces but the expression of real, unseen beings.

This is not the only option Ananias possessed. Peter points out that Ananias had control and authority over the land both when it remained unsold (using imperfect tense verbs to stress the duration of the control) and once the proceeds came to him upon its sale (using an aorist to look at the event of the sale). There is nothing required of him by the community. After the sale, the proceeds are still under Ananias's authority (ἐξουσία, *exousia*).

The voluntary nature of this arrangement is different from Qumran, where proceeds were brought provisionally to the treasurer of the com-

---

3. For the development of such ideas in the early centuries of the church, see Pelikan 2005: 82–85.

munity when one wished to be a member of the separated community, as a requirement for prospective membership (1QS 6.18–23; *pace* Capper 1983, who argues that such a giving over of resources was required by the church community in parallel to Qumran). The two questions at the start of verse 4 are controlled by the interrogative particle οὐχί (*ouchi*), which indicates that the questions expect a positive reply. He had the option to keep the proceeds or dispose of only some of it. So the deceitful act was completely premeditated, apparently motivated by the desire of Ananias and Sapphira to appear more generous than they truly are. The desire for human praise is more important to them than being faithful to God.

The blame falls directly on Ananias for the act. He has set or purposed to do this in his heart. The verb τίθημι (*tithēmi*) means to set something or to purpose to accomplish something (Acts 1:7 [of God's timing of the restoration of the end]; 2:35; 3:2; in the LXX at 1 Sam. 21:12–13; 29:10; Jer. 12:11; Hag. 2:18; Mal. 2:2; Dan. 1:8 Theodotion). The question is rhetorical: Why did you do this? The real emotional force of the question is, "How can you do this?" Ananias's action represents a priority to obey man or seek human praise rather than to honor God. It is an act of defiance and disobedience. Verse 4 repeats the verb ψεύδομαι (*pseudomai*) of verse 3, where Satan has led him to lie, the only two occurrences of the verb in Acts. Although some scholars suggest that these verses are in tension with 4:32, 34, where everyone is portrayed as giving to the community (Haenchen 1987: 237), the story of Ananias and Sapphira shows Luke's frankness in that not everything was free of sin in the community. It also indicates that Luke's earlier remarks are hyperbolic. The bulk of the community is generous, but as in many communities, there are tragic exceptions. Luke often points out the danger of not handling possessions well in his Gospel (Luke 6:20, 24; chaps. 12 and 16; 21:1–4). Ananias and Sapphira are caught in this trap as they misrepresent their generosity.

The aftermath of Peter's remarks is a divine judgment against Ananias. As Ananias hears the words (note the present participle denoting simultaneous action), he falls and dies. The term ἐκψύχω (*ekpsychō*) for "die" appears only three times in the NT, all in Acts, with two of the occurrences in this scene (5:5, 10–11; 12:23 [of Herod]; always of a wicked one dying, but the word itself does not carry such a meaning; Barrett 1994: 268). The term is also rare in the LXX, appearing only twice (Judg. 4:21 Alex. [death of Sisera]; Ezek. 21:12). The instant nature of the judgment is shocking, but that is the point. Attempts to explain this on natural terms (a heart attack or something similar) fail to honor the linkage to Sapphira's death. Such a cause might exist with Ananias, but it is less likely for both.

5:5–6

Havelaar (1997: 69–72) notes a few Hellenistic parallels to this judgment.[4] In Greek culture, breaking faith with the gods was seen as a serious error.[5] Havelaar (1997: 73) notes that the parallel of an instant death, however, is rare, appearing in only one example from the Ayazviran inscription (see note 4). Havelaar's (1997: 75–77) attempt to appeal to the Pythagorean example of excommunication (Iamblichus, *Life of Pythagoras* 17.72.8–17.73.3; 17.74.11–16) as a key to understanding the verse, however, is not likely correct in terms of background, as there is far more than an excommunication presented here.

The sense is that however death came, its timing was tied to their sin. This is an exceptional case of instant judgment, but it also indicates that God, as the one who knows and makes assessments, acts in judgment even within God's community. Sin is visible before God. In this case it is removed immediately. The possibility of this kind of judgment is expressed elsewhere (1 Cor. 11:30; James 5:20; 1 John 5:16–17; 1 Cor. 5:5; 1 Tim. 1:20; Bruce 1990: 164). The result is great fear for those who hear about what took place. The phrase φόβος μέγας (*phobos megas*; Mark 4:41; Luke 2:9; 8:37; Acts 5:5, 10–11; Rev. 11:11) appears only in this scene in Acts (for other uses of the term "fear" in Acts, see 2:43; 9:31; 19:17).

In Judaism, burial was done on the same day, but this is an unusually hasty burial (Deut. 21:22–23; Polhill 1992: 158). Derrett (1977) has details about this Jewish practice and argues that a burial without family is an exception (note also Lev. 10:1–7; Josh. 7:25). It indicates one struck down "by the hands of heaven." So here, Ananias is immediately wrapped up and buried. This is the only description of wrapping up a body in the NT that uses συστέλλω (*systellō*; the other occurrence of this term is in 1 Cor. 7:29, but there it simply means that time is "wrapping up"). It is clear, however, that Lazarus also was wrapped up upon his death (John 11:44). The term's occurrence in the LXX is also rare, with none being a reference to a body (1 Macc. 3:6; 5:3; 2 Macc. 6:12; 3 Macc. 5:33; Sir. 4:31 [where a hand closes]). They would have used a shroud to wrap the body. So they dispose of him. The evil one has been cast out from the midst of the people (Deut. 13:5; 17:7, 12; 19:19; 21:21; 24:7; Jervell 1998: 197).

4. Lucian, *The Lover of Lies* 20.1–26; Herodotus, *Hist.* 6.86 (the punishment was the loss of offspring; the crime was "tempting" the god); an Epidaurian miracle from Iamata 47 (a fish carrier promises to give a tenth of his sale to Asclepius but does not; this causes the fish to bite him until he confesses, which he does). In an inscription, *CMRDM* 1.51, from ancient Ayazviran (ancient Koresa in Asia Minor), Apollonius is put to death when he fails to give what he promised to the gods.

5. Virgil, *Aeneid* 6.618–23 ("Learn to be just and not to slight the gods"); Ovid, *Fasti* 2.261 ("You aggravate your fault, by your lies, and dare to aggravate the God of prophecy by your fibs"); Sentences of Sextus 186 ("It is possible to deceive man by words; not so, however, god"); Plato, *Republic* 2.382C ("Essentially falsehood is hated not only by gods but by men as well").

The use of θάπτω (*thaptō*, bury) occurs eleven times in the NT, with three of the occurrences in this scene (Matt. 8:21, 22; 14:12; Luke 9:59, 60; 16:22; Acts 2:29; 5:6, 9–11 [2x]; 1 Cor. 15:3–8). The sin of attempting to deceive God cost Ananias his life. Ananias let Satan enter his heart, and money was involved, as with Judas (Witherington 1998: 217). The abuse of money or material possessions to seek human praise is a real temptation to avoid. It is one thing to have genuine generosity recognized, as with Barnabas, and another to appear to be more generous than one really is, as with Ananias.

Now Sapphira mirrors the earlier scene involving her husband. She arrives after a period of about three hours. This scene has been challenged as not believable because of the three-hour delay, given the death of Ananias. Surely, the argument goes, as a family member, she would have been informed immediately. This criticism ignores the telescoped nature of the narrative, the unusual circumstances of the death, the fact that the timing applies to her arrival before Peter, and the fact that a judgment has taken place where Ananias is treated as an unclean presence in the community because of his act against God's Spirit. As a narrative, it is selective. We do not know if someone was sent to fetch her immediately, whether she had to be found, and how Peter decided to handle a situation in which suspected dishonesty even on her part led Peter to ask her questions. Bruce (1988a: 107) suggests that Peter recognizes the death as a divine judgment and then contemplates how to handle the situation (also Marshall 1980: 112–13). The nature of our literature does not attempt to supply such detail (Polhill 1992: 158–59). The instant judgment by some critical scholars that such a delay is a sign of the scene's legendary character does not sufficiently respect the limits of the narrative genre we may well have before us.

5:7

What the text does tell us is that when she arrives, she does not know Ananias has died. The term εἰδυῖα (*eiduia*, aware) is a perfect participle and may well be concessive in force (Wallace 1996: 635): she arrives, although she does so in a state of ignorance about what has taken place. The kind of questioning that follows also appears in Susannah 44–62, which is a part of Jewish intertestamental literature that discusses how God judges the wicked.

Peter begins to interview her. The question is very simple. Was the land sold for a given amount? The question likely reflects the amount that Ananias brought and claimed was the sale's entire proceeds, given that the charge is that he lied and kept back a portion (vv. 2–3).

5:8

The term τοσούτου (*tosoutou*) appears twice in the verse and simply means "for so much [an amount]." The term is a genitive of price (Bruce 1990: 165; Wallace 1996: 122). Sapphira has the chance to tell the truth and rectify the wrong. But her reply affirms the amount and thereby both the lie and the conspiracy.

5:9   Peter responds and confronts Sapphira (Polhill 1992: 159: Peter confronts; God judges). In terms similar to verses 3–4, Peter asks why Sapphira has conspired to test (πειράσαι, *peirasai*) the Spirit (BAGD 640 §2e; BDAG 793 §2c). Here is the passage's point: the Spirit knows everything that happens in the community. People are accountable. Ananias and Sapphira meet with instant accountability for their agreement to deceive. Similar language of testing the Spirit is found in Exod. 17:2; Num. 20:13, 24; Deut. 6:16; 33:8; and Ps. 106:32 (Fitzmyer 1998: 324). "Tempt" (RSV) is not a good translation of this term in this context. Rather, the query to Sapphira is, "Why do you test [NET, HCSB] the Spirit?" The term is frequent in Acts (5:9; 9:26; 15:10; 16:6–8; 24:5–8). Like Israel, this couple has tested God by rejecting his goodness, denying by their action that righteousness is a virtue to possess in God's community. They took the matter of their reputation into their own hands in their own way.

The test concerns the Spirit's ability to be deceived about what is going on. The Spirit knows, and Peter's remark underscores that the Spirit is quite aware of what has taken place. The Spirit sees sin and deals with it in a timing that the Spirit determines. The question is rhetorical and has a strong force: How could you contemplate and agree to (συνεφωνήθη, *synephōnēthē*) such an act against God? This sin is an act of arrogance, not just avarice. The verb "agree" appears in only one other text in Acts, where it is used positively (Acts 15:15–18, where the words of the prophets agree with Peter's remarks according to James at the Jerusalem Council). The opening words of the remarks (τί ὅτι, *ti hoti*) appear only here and in verse 4 and may point to the use of a source for the story (Barrett 1994: 270). Jervell (1998: 199) also sees tradition used for this scene with only verse 4 coming from Luke. Pesch (1986a: 196), however, is likely more correct when he speaks of tradition being present throughout with only Lukan touches here and there.

Peter announces the presence of the young men who buried Ananias and says that they will do the same to Sapphira. The description of their feet as present is a figure indicating they are ready to act (Isa. 59:7). Money has been laid in dishonesty at the apostles' feet. Now God will judge deceit and strike Sapphira. It is a miracle of judgment, and in an ironic sense the two miscreants are brought to bow to God's power (Johnson 1992: 89). The use of ἰδού (*idou*, look) points to an announcement to be absorbed. The term serves as a dramatic narrative note for the reader, pointing to the importance of what this entire verse says about the consequences of deceiving God.

5:10   This verse echoes verses 5–6. Sapphira's death is immediate (παραχρῆμα, *parachrēma*). This term occurs six times in Acts: 3:7–8; 5:10–11; 12:23; 13:11; 16:26, 33–34. As Peter announced, the young men take her body and bury her beside her husband. This unique divine judgment is complete. Williams (1990: 100) compares this judgment to that of Nadab and Abihu in Lev. 10:3 because both are judgments early in the life of a new community God is forming. The scene is designed to make the point that God's people are called to holiness and are accountable to God for it (Bruce 1990: 165). The absence of wrapping the body may reflect Jewish custom, where men do not wrap a woman's dead body (Semaḥot 12.10).

As in verse 5, great fear is reported for those who hear of these things.   **5:11**
This is not merely respect but a healthy awareness that God is present and can act in judgment (Luke 1:12, 65; 2:9; 7:16; 8:37; Acts 2:43; 19:17). In addition, the church is said to fear.

The term church ἐκκλησία (*ekklēsia*, church) is important in Acts and is used in a variety of ways. This is the first of twenty-three references in Acts (5:10–11; 7:38–40; 8:1, 3; 9:31; 11:22, 26; 12:1, 5; 13:1; 14:23, 27; 15:3, 4, 22–23, 41; 16:5; 18:20–22; 19:32, 39, 40; 20:17, 28). Not all the references are to the church; the term can sometimes refer simply to an assembly of people (Acts 7:38; 19:32, 39–40; Witherington 1998: 219; OT: Deut. 9:10; 18:16; 23:1–2 [23:2–3 LXX]; 31:30; Josh. 8:35 [9:2 LXX]). Such a general usage reflects a rendering of the Hebrew *qāhāl* (Bruce 1990: 166). The other Greek term rendering this Hebrew term is *synagōgē*, but it is used only of the synagogue in the NT. An identifiable religious community is emerging from those who have responded to Jesus, those who earlier were called brethren (1:15) and believers (2:44; 4:32). Later in Acts, members of this group are called disciples (6:1), the saints of the Lord (9:13), and Christians (11:26; Schneider 1980: 377). Ἐκκλησία here refers to the local community of the church as a gathering. The term's use here is not yet a technical, theological one. Later it will be used of the church as a collection of distinct local communities distributed worldwide (20:28). As the church expands, it keeps its sense of connection as a group of communities bound together by Jesus.

In sum, this is a difficult passage because the judgment against Ananias and Sapphira is instantaneous and direct. This judgment indicates, however, how serious sin is to God and how gracious God is in often deferring such judgment. Most sin is not treated so harshly, but at this early stage, such a divine act serves to remind the community of its call to holiness and its loyalty to God. God sees and knows all. Sin is dealt with directly. The resulting fear that the judgment creates is exactly what the passage seeks to engender—respect for God and for righteousness as well as a recognition that sin is destructive and dangerous. There is honesty in this report as well. The church is not a place of perfect people (Fernando 1998: 198).

The sequence of sin is never isolated. The desire for praise and perhaps a desire to hang on to possessions led to lying. Fernando (1998: 201–3) calls the sin of the couple primarily one of pride and deceit. Manipulating their reputation was more important than allegiance to God and

God's reputation. Abuse of possessions can undergird a manipulated reputation. Lying led to deceit and an offense against God. Sin almost never comes in a single package; it begets more sin.

The passage has another lesson: sin will be dealt with. The passage emphasizes a path of honesty and integrity, as Ananias and Sapphira are counterexamples, standing in contrast to the earlier Barnabas (Stott 1990: 109).

Additional Notes

5:3. The verb for what Satan did is disputed. $\mathfrak{P}^{74}$ and the Vulgate read that Satan "tempted" their heart, matching verse 9, but the better-attested reading is that he filled it. Thus do the rest of the MSS read it.

5:4. A few MSS add "to do the evil" or "evil deed" ($\mathfrak{P}^{74}$, D, some Syriac MSS). These readings are not the best attested.

5:5–6. Παραχρῆμα (*parachrēma*, immediately) appears both in verse 5 (D) and in verse 6 (E), but these singular readings attempt to match verse 10 and are not original.

F. Summary: Signs and Wonders (5:12–16)

Signs and ministry are the focus in the summary verses 2:42–47; 4:32–35. This third summary in Acts treats the relationship of apostles to outsiders whereas the community's inner life was highlighted in the earlier summaries. The apostles are at work in Solomon's Portico (v. 12). The healing activities represent an answer to the prayers of 4:24–31, especially verse 30. The reference to "through the hands" (διὰ . . . τῶν χειρῶν, dia . . . tōn cheirōn) is probably figurative for their labor of healing, not for the laying on of hands, as Acts 3:7 concerns simply lifting up the healed, not a formal laying on of hands (plural, "hands," 14:3; 19:6; singular, "hand," 2:23; 7:25; 11:30; 15:23; see 2:43, "through the apostles"; Wis. 12:6). The apostolic ministry is in the midst of the Jewish people, not just in the far corners of their own congregations. On the one hand, fear keeps "the rest" from joining the apostles, even though their ministry is viewed with respect (v. 13; on "the rest," see below). Yet for others, the activity leads them to become believers (v. 14). The tension of expression between these two verses suggests the presence of a combination of sources (Marshall 1980: 114; but Barrett 1994: 273 sees a summary written by Luke here). Peter is healing the sick and exorcising demons (vv. 15–16). New to the summary is the mention of public reaction to the work and of the sick who are healed. Still, most of what is said here reinforces what has been said already in Acts (in an order similar to this Acts 5 text, see 2:43b, 46a, 47 and 4:33; Pesch 1986a: 205). The next passage will make clear that the Jewish leadership sees all of this public attention directed at the new community as dangerous.

Exegesis and Exposition

[12]But through the hands of the apostles there came to pass many signs and wonders among the people. And they [the apostles] were all gathered together at Solomon's Portico. [13]None of the rest [of believers] dared to join them, but the people held them in high honor. [14]And even more believers were added to the Lord, multitudes both of men and women, [15]so that they even carried the sick into the streets and set them on beds and pallets that, as Peter came by, at least his shadow might fall on some of them. [16]The multitude also gathered from the towns around Jerusalem, bringing the sick and those harassed by unclean spirits, and they were all being healed.

5:12   In contrast to the judgment of Ananias and Sapphira (δέ, *de*, but), the work of signs and wonders continues by means of the hands of the apostles, that is, by their mediating labor (see 2:19, 22, 43; on διά, *dia*, indicating means, Moule 1959: 57). The imperfect ἐγίνετο (*egineto*, were taking place, came to pass) highlights the ongoing aspect of this activity. The apostles gather at the temple, at Solomon's Portico, where they have been before (see 3:11). Apparently they gather at a known locale, so that people know where to come. These signs underscore that God is at work (3:16–21; 4:9, 12, 22; Larkin 1995: 88).[1] This description of doing signs and wonders recalls language tied to Moses in the OT (Deut. 34:10–12). Although the reference to "all" in the verse might be to Christians, given the reference to "together" (ὁμοθυμαδόν, *homothymadon*; 1:14; 2:46; 4:24) and verse 13, where "the rest" and "them" are in contrast (Barrett 1994: 274; Polhill 1992: 163), it is more natural to read it as referring to the apostles, whose ministry is the passage's focus of description and reaction (Johnson 1992: 95; Fitzmyer 1998: 328).

5:13–14   These verses reflect an interesting contrast to verse 12, but their meaning is debated. Who are "the rest" (τῶν λοιπῶν, *tōn loipōn*) who do not dare to join (κολλᾶσθαι, *kollasthai*) the group? The term "to join" is not a technical term for conversion but simply for association (Johnson 1992: 95; for NT usage, see Matt. 19:5; Luke 10:11; 15:15; Acts 5:13; 8:29; 9:26; 10:28; 17:34; Rom. 12:9; 1 Cor. 6:16–17; Rev. 18:5). Johnson's sense that "everyone else" other than the apostles do not wish to approach them physically is contradicted by verses 15–16. So something else must be meant. Are "the rest" believers who are hesitant to join the apostles given their earlier arrest? If verse 12b refers to believers, not the apostles, then who else could "the rest" be? Three options are proposed. (1) Are they some remainder of Christians not referred to by the "all" of verse 12? (2) Or does it refer to outsiders to the faith, the rest of the Jews (Jervell 1989: 201)? Haenchen (1987: 242) and Barrett (1994: 274) with Jervell argue for non-Christians and see the remarks in verses 12–14 as confused. In another option, (3) Bruce (1990: 167) argues that those of Jerusalem are scared off by the judgment on Ananias and Sapphira, something Le Cornu and Shulam (2003: 259–66) develop in detail, pointing out numerous later Jewish conceptual parallels to the judgment as "the hand of heaven." This may be a factor but is not the only cause of the fear. Against the apostolic judgment being the major

---

1. On miracles in Acts, see Witherington 1998: 220–24, who names thirteen types of miracles in the book. My list also has thirteen, but distinct contents. They are healing of the crippled, miraculous knowledge, a healing shadow, restoration of sight, healing of a paralytic, raising of the dead, exorcism, healing handkerchiefs, healing from fever, miraculous release, miraculous protection on the sea, protection from a snake bite, and miraculous speech (tongues).

cause of fear is the recognition that *if* one is honest, there is no reason to fear such apostolic judgment.

Those who argue for some remainder of Christians suggest that the timidity of believers in verse 13 is against the tone of Acts 4:24–31 (Polhill 1992: 163). Those who argue against "outsiders" as non-Christians suggest that this makes little sense of v. 14, where many believe (Witherington 1998: 225–26). There is no doubt the verses express somewhat awkwardly, with an imbedded parenthesis, whatever idea is present (BDF §465.1; Robertson 1934: 435). In all likelihood, the rest are believers who recognize the tense environment in which the apostles are working. This represents a fourth option, though a variation of 1, since I see the apostles as the "all" in verse 12b. This option could be viable regardless of whether one interprets the "all" as referring to the apostles (as I do) or to Christians generally. The brackets in my translation of verses 12–13 reflect my interpretive choices. The meaning may well be that these believers hesitate to join with them in this temple ministry given the hostile view and actions of the Jewish leadership, as well as the fear the apostles' access to judgment generated. Perhaps the view is, Why should we place ourselves at unnecessary risk? It is one thing to be an object of persecution and be prepared for it. It is another for a group knowingly to seek it when this is not necessary, as others are successfully performing the ministry of healing.

The populace (ὁ λαός, *ho laos*), however, holds the ministry in high regard (ἐμεγάλυνεν, *emegalynen*). This verb for "praise" or "regard" appears eight times in the NT (Matt. 23:5; Luke 1:46, 58 [both of lifting up God in praise]; Acts 5:13; 10:46 [also praising God]; 19:17 [extolling God]; 2 Cor. 10:15; Phil. 1:20). The apostles' conduct brings them respect from those who watch how they function and minister.

According to verse 14, the result is more faith, as more are added to the Lord.[2] Both men and women came to believe. Luke keeps his eye on both genders as all are offered the message of hope (on this juxtaposition of men and women, Acts 5:1 [Ananias/Sapphira]; 8:3 [persecuted by Paul]; 8:12 [baptized]; 9:2 [persecuted by Paul]; 17:12 [believed]; 17:34 [believed]; 22:4 [persecuted by Paul]).

After the note on the growth in the number of believers comes mention of the resulting response (ὥστε, *hōste*). Perhaps the verse looks back to the whole of verses 12–14 (Barrett 1994: 276) or to verses 12 or 13 (Schneider 1980: 381–82). What is clear is that the healing ministry draws attention to the message. The sick are carried out to the street and placed on beds or pallets in the hope of being healed even by Peter's shadow. This detail indicates the extent of the Lord's power working through him as well as

5:15

---

2. On this use of προσετίθεντο (*prosetithento*, were added), see Acts 2:41, 47; 11:24; on the verb πιστεύοντες (*pisteuontes*, believing) taking a dative, see BDF §187.6; Moulton and Turner 1963: 237.

the perspective of the crowd about how to access that power. The term ἄν (*an*) contained in κἄν (*kan*) may point to an element of contingency or hope in their expectation (Moule 1959: 138; but Robertson 1934: 984 simply sees it as equal to καί, *kai*, meaning "even"). Peter does not even need to touch the sick; his shadow (σκιά, *skia*) is enough (the term for "shadow" is nowhere else used to convey miraculous power: Matt. 4:16; Mark 4:32; Luke 1:76–79; Acts 5:14–15; Col. 2:16–17; Heb. 8:4–6; 10:1–2). Acts 19:12 has Paul working with handkerchiefs, healing from a distance, like Jesus in Luke 7:1–10. There also is healing by touching Jesus's garment (Luke 8:43–44; Johnson 1992: 96).

Van der Horst (1977) observes that a person's shadow was seen as an extension of that individual, and he presents numerous Greco-Roman citations and a smaller number of Jewish references suppporting this idea. Van der Horst notes texts from Ennius, Aelianus, Aristotle, Pausanius, Pliny the Elder, and the later Jewish text *m. ʾAbod. Zar.* 3.8. Pesch (1986a: 207), however, notes that antiquity has yet to attest to an exact parallel to this kind of healing. Does such work represent some of the greater works that Jesus said would come to the apostles through the Spirit (John 14:12)? Popular superstition may also be present here in seeking only to have interaction with the apostle's shadow, but God is gracious in healing anyway. The crowd's expectation shows the attention the apostolic work has drawn and the excitement it has created.

This ministry to the sick and demon-possessed (v. 16) is like the one Jesus exercised (Luke 4:31–44). Κράβαττων (*krabattōn*, pallets) is more common than κλιναρίων (*klinariōn*, cots; the diminutive form of κλίνη, *klinē*, bed). Pallets are referred to eleven times in the NT (Mark 2:4, 9, 11, 12; 6:54–55; John 5:8–11 [4x]; Acts 5:14–15; 9:33), whereas the other term appears only here, although its related term also is common, appearing nine times (κλίνη; Matt. 9:2, 6; Mark 4:21; 7:2–5, 30; Luke 5:18; 8:16; 17:34–35; Rev. 2:22–23). Another related term, κλινίδιον (*klinidion*), appears twice in the NT (Luke 5:19, 24, a parallel to Mark 2:4, 11, where κράβαττος appears). It seems clear that the signs and wonders make a significant impression on those living in Jerusalem.

5:16 Healing comes to the sick as well as to the demon-possessed as the two categories are distinguished here. Unclean spirits (πνευμάτων ἀκαθάρτων, *pneumatōn akathartōn*) are referred to by this combination of terms twenty-three times in the NT (e.g., Matt. 10:1; 12:43; Mark 1:23, 26, 27; 3:11, 30; 5:2, 8, 13; 6:7; 7:25; 9:25; Luke 4:33, 36; 6:18; 8:29; 9:42; 11:24; Acts 5:16; 8:7; Rev. 16:13; 18:2–3). The bulk of the occurrences are in Mark (ten), with Luke's Gospel next (six), followed by Acts (five). This construction does not appear in John's Gospel. The distinction of categories is interesting, given that in some texts sickness is attributed to a demonic cause (also distinguished in Luke 4:40–41; 6:17–18; 7:21; 13:32; contrast Luke 13:11). The idea of being harassed appears only here in the NT (ὀχλουμένους, *ochloumenous*; LXX: Tob. 6:8 [2x]; 3 Macc. 5:41; but Luke 6:18 uses a prefixed form of the verb; 1QapGen 20.16–17; Fitzmyer 1998: 330). These people come from surrounding towns as well, so word is spreading. Luke does not make a distinction between towns and cities in using the word πόλις (*polis*); these are small neighboring communities.

This summary gives a glimpse of the divine power working through the apostles. People are being healed. Outsiders are impressed. People believe. Apparently, the prospect of arrest also keeps some believers from joining the apostles. Nevertheless, the bold apostles engage publicly in their ministry of service to those in need and gain respect and response as a result. They do not cloister themselves away or hide. They continue to serve and reach out in ministry that testifies to their message and God's call for all. The growth of attention demands a renewed response from the Jewish leadership.

II. The Early Church in Jerusalem (1:12–6:7)
    F. Summary: Signs and Wonders (5:12–16)
➤ G. More Persecution (5:17–42)
    H. Community Life: The Appointment of the Seven to Help Hellenist Widows (6:1–6)

G. More Persecution (5:17–42)

With the influence of the new community growing, the Jewish leadership moves to arrest Peter and the apostles. This scene is like 4:1–22 but represents an expansion of the persecution, since all the apostles are at risk. The unit splits cleanly into two subunits: (1) the arrest and divine release, along with a second arrest and confrontation (vv. 17–26), and (2) the aftermath of the rearrest, deliberation of the council, and Gamaliel's advice that leads to the apostles' release (vv. 27–42).

The inroads the apostles make in Jerusalem lead to their arrest (vv. 17–18). It also represents an expansion of God's direction and protection, as there is a miraculous release from the prison with renewed preaching at the temple and a second arrest afterward (vv. 19–26).

The second arrest leads to a confrontation as the leadership reminds the apostles of the earlier instruction that banned preaching about Jesus. However, through Peter the apostles respond with a declaration of what God has called them to do (vv. 27–32). The exchange leads to anger from some of the leaders, which is quelled by a pivotal address by the leading rabbi, Gamaliel. This additional motif points to an intensification of the threat, in contrast to the first arrest, and provides a more complex presentation of persecution (Gaventa 2003: 106). This mature and respected leader cautions the group that rebellions led by those underwritten only by human authority collapse on their own but that if God is at work, they cannot stop what is happening. It is the first speech by a non-Christian in Acts and as such has great significance. It is a speech of warning not to act too fast coming from a seeming opponent. Time will tell, he urges (vv. 33–39). God may be at work. The apostles are released after being beaten, thrilled that they have suffered for the name of Jesus. They promptly resume preaching (vv. 40–42).

This final scene represents a commentary from this wise opponent: the new apostolic movement can be measured by its staying power. Luke is making the point that perceptive opponents are aware of a standard by which the new movement can be assessed. The book of Acts as a whole shows that the new community meets the standard. Gamaliel is a second adversary within Luke-Acts who, when taking a close look at the new movement, does not make a decisive judgment. Pilate saw Jesus as innocent of any crime deserving death (Luke 23:1–25). With juxtaposition of Peter's speech and Gamaliel's reaction, a crossfire of reflection takes place for Luke's reader. Both portraits argue for the new movement's vibrancy.

The apostles represent an emerging new group that is being forced out by Judaism and so is developing its own identity. Although the apostles still preach the God of their fathers, the high-priestly leadership rejects the idea that God is at work and moves to disconnect the apostolic leadership from Judaism. The apostles do not seek this separation; the Jewish leadership does. This leadership rejects fulfillment, a fulfillment underwritten by many diverse divine signs. But some Pharisees may be open to seeing what God is doing. Hope for some Jews exists as long as they are open to God's work. Regardless of the response, God is behind the new way. The work to sustain the movement is in God's hands (Barrett 1994: 281).

1. Arrest, Divine Release, and Rearrest (5:17–26)

This more elaborate scene covers the second arrest of Peter and John (the first was in Acts 4:1–3). It also is the initial arrest of the rest of the apostles. Some see this scene as a doublet of the Acts 4 arrest (Conzelmann 1987: 41). Rather, this is an expansion of the attempt to suppress the influence of the new movement (Pesch 1986a: 213). Polhill (1992: 164) notes that Acts 4 includes a warning and a release whereas this passage includes a beating and a discussion of death, setting up the death of Stephen and the other James in Acts 7 and 12 (Fitzmyer 1998: 332–33).[1] In other words, there is an intensification of the opposition here, not a mere repetition of earlier themes. Jeremias (1937: 208–13) argues that the scene fits the Jewish background for such trials and warnings. This has been debated because of the mishnaic evidence used (Conzelmann 1987: 41), but the leaders' actions do parallel this type of investigation. It suggests that the Jewish leadership is exercising considerable care in challenging the emerging, popular new movement. First, they take on only Jesus. Next, they pressure the lead apostles. Finally, they challenge all the apostles. This gradual intensification fits the setting of dealing with a rising popular movement by not being perceived as overreacting. Responding in steps is a way to create a credible defense that the new movement is being repeatedly warned before persecution intensifies.

Barrett (1994: 281) and Witherington (1998: 228–29) note many differences from Acts 4: (1) all the apostles, not just Peter and John are arrested; (2) teaching is the issue, not miracles; (3) there is no servant language; (4) a miraculous rescue is added; (5) there is a beating; and (6) a Jewish leader gives a speech. Thus a more complicated scene than Acts 4 is presented. In Acts 5 God directly intervenes in the release of the apostolic band (12:6–19; 16:11–40), and so they can renew their preaching at the temple. The act shows which side God is on. The scene is called, in terms of its literary form, a release miracle (Pesch 1986a: 211).

Jesus established the model of innocent suffering (Luke 23:1–25). The apostles are following it, showing in an exemplary manner what

---

1. For the view that this scene is a Lukan formulation, see Weiser 1981: 154–55. The differences in the alleged doublet point to a real and historical escalation of the persecution.

discipleship entails. <mark>God is watching over them in the midst of the suffering.</mark> Victory can come through suffering. Political power will not stop them.

Exegesis and Exposition

[17]But the high priest and all those with him who were of the party of the Sadducees arose. They were filled with jealousy [18]and seized the apostles and placed them in a common prison. [19]But at night an angel of the Lord, ⌜opening⌝ the doors of the prison and leading them out, said, [20]"Go stand in the temple and speak to all the people the words of this life." [21]And when they heard this, they entered the temple at daybreak and were teaching.

The high priest came and those who were with him and ⌜ ⌝ called together the council, that is, all the senate of the sons of Israel, and sent to the prison to have them brought. [22]But when the officers came, ⌜ ⌝ they did not find them in prison, and returning, they reported, [23]"We found the prison standing locked securely and the sentries standing at the doors, but when we opened them, we did not find anyone inside." [24]Now when the captain of the temple and the chief priests heard these words, they were very perplexed about them, wondering what this might be. [25]And someone came and announced to them, "Look, the men whom you placed in prison in the temple are standing and teaching the people." [26]Then the captain with the officers went and ⌜were bringing them⌝ without violence, for they were afraid of being stoned by the people.

Three circumstances evoke the reaction of the high priest and Sad-   **5:17–18**
ducees: the apostles' expanding popularity through preaching, their signs, and the apostles' disobedience to the leadership's prohibition to preach (v. 28). It is the Sadducees' authority that is being challenged (on the Sadducees, see Acts 4:1). Acts 5:34 makes clear that Pharisees also share this reaction.

Luke calls the Sadducees a "party" or "sect" (αἵρεσις, *hairesis*) within Judaism. Josephus (*Ant.* 13.5.9 §171) indicates that this term often has the meaning of a "school" within Judaism (also 20.9.1 §199). The English term "sect" has a connotation the Greek lacks. The term appears several times in Acts to refer to a movement within Judaism or another group and is best rendered "party" (Acts 15:5 [Pharisee party]; 24:5, 14; 26:5; 28:22 [party of Christians]). In Acts 24:5, 14 Paul describes the movement of the Nazoreans, to which he now belongs, as a "school" of Judaism as well, using this term, as he does in Acts 26:5 for the "party" of the Pharisees.

The council members are full of jealousy (ζήλου, *zēlou*; a genitive of content, Wallace 1996: 94). <mark>The Sadducees are often seen as more hostile to the new movement than the Pharisees in Acts, whereas in Luke's Gospel the Pharisees are major opponents of Jesus.</mark> This fits the shift of attention to Jerusalem from the setting of Jesus's ministry outside the city. The Sadducees have more to lose, since they control the council and have worked out a compromise with the Romans to share power. Any destabilizing element in the culture could threaten their control. Acts 13:45 is the only other use of this term for "jealousy" in Acts. In that passage the expression is used of negative Jewish reaction to Paul's preaching. Larkin (1995: 91) correctly describes jealousy as misguided zeal (so Rom. 10:2). The term describes a spiritual vice, appearing sixteen times in the NT (John 2:17; Acts 5:17–18; 13:45; Rom. 10:2–3; 13:13–14; 1 Cor. 3:3; 2 Cor. 7:6–7, 11; 9:1–2; 11:2–3; 12:20–21; Gal. 5:19–21; Phil. 3:4–6; Heb. 10:26–27; James 3:14, 16).[2] The apostles and their message represent a major irritant and a perceived assault on Sadducean authority. They sense a loss of power, which they will seek to reassert. So their reaction is about theology and power politics.

The solution is the arrest, described literally as "setting their hands" (ἐπέβαλον τὰς χεῖρας, *epebalon tas cheiras*) on them (Matt. 26:50; Mark 14:45–46; Acts 5:17–18; BAGD 289–90 §1b; BDAG 367 §1b; Luke 20:19; 21:12; Acts 12:1; 21:27). None of the twelve uses of the phrase in the LXX carry this meaning. They are placed in a public prison. The term δημόσιος (*dēmosios*, public, common) appears only in Acts in the NT (5:17–18; 16:37; 18:28; 20:20; 2 Macc. 6:10; 3 Macc. 2:27). Literally τηρήσει δημοσίᾳ (*tērēsei dēmosia*) refers to "public custody," which alludes to the "public jail." The term for "public" is a Greek loanword that also came into Hebrew rabbinical vocabulary. Barrett (1994: 283) notes a connection to the common Latin idea of "public custody." This arrest is designed to make a visible public point. People are to know that the apostles have been arrested. Despite the public, common holding area, Acts 5:23 makes clear that the apostles are held under special guard. The last and only other reference to a prison in Acts using the term τήρησις is in 4:3. The authorities are doing all in their power to stop the new message from spreading. The hope is that by placing the apostles behind bars, they will silence the message and dissuade others from preaching.

5:19–21a   The release is recounted with maximum brevity. It includes an escape enabled by an angel of the Lord and an instruction to teach in the temple, which the apostles obey. This is the ultimate, cosmic overrule of the Jewish leadership as the sovereign God acts to free the apostles, opening the doors of their prison. This passage shows the leadership's powerlessness before God's action, something that Gamaliel later notes might be possible with this troublesome group (5:39). So, at a literary level as well as at a historical level, the release is God's anticipated an-

2. The term is also found in Judaism: positively, meaning "admiration," Philo, *Hypothetica* 6.4; 11.2; negatively, meaning "jealousy," T. Sim. 2.7 (variant reading). Johnson 1992: 96 notes Greek literature: Plato, *Laws* 869E–870A; Plutarch, *On Brotherly Love* 17.

swer to Gamaliel's options. The plural reference to doors (θύρας, *thyras*) indicates that all the doors necessary for escape are opened (two doors are concerned in 12:10; Polhill 1992: 166).

An angel of the Lord is mentioned here and there in Luke-Acts (Luke 1:11; 2:9; Acts 5:19; 8:26 [to direct Philip]; 12:7, 23 [death of Herod]; in the OT, Gen. 16:7–11; 21:17; 22:10–18; 31:11–13; Exod. 3:2–6; Judg. 2:1–5; and in Matt. 1:20, 24; 2:13, 19; 28:2). This is one of three such escapes in Acts (the others are 12:6–10 [Peter only]; 16:25–26 [Paul and Silas]). Angels are prominent in Luke's two volumes (Luke 2:13; 22:43; 24:23; Acts 10:3, 7, 22; 11:13; 27:23). Johnson (1992: 97) also notes a Greek parallel of this type of account in Euripides' *Bacchanals* 346–640, where Bacchus frees members of his cult from prison. Bruce (1988a: 110) observes that the existence of this kind of story broadly in the culture does not in itself indicate anything about the historicity of each of these accounts (so also Jeremias, *TDNT* 3:175–76). Conzelmann's claim (1987: 41) that this event is artificial tells us more about his worldview of God's activity than about the event or passage. This angel is not to be seen as Jesus, for Acts explicitly mentions him when he is present, as Acts 9 shows. This act results from God's sovereign choice to release these prisoners; later Paul will remain in jail (Acts 21–28).

The angel communicates God's instruction to them. The apostles are told to speak to the people in the temple. Israel is still called the people (τῷ λαῷ, *tō laō*) despite the leadership's disobedience. God is still seeking to reach his wayward people. The message is about "this life" (τῆς ζωῆς ταύτης, *tēs zōēs tautēs*), the unique life God provides through Jesus (13:26 ["words of this salvation"]; 11:18; 13:46, 48; John 6:68). Jesus has already been called the "Author of life" (Acts 3:15). The importance of this message is the reason the angel tells them to disobey the leadership's prohibition on preaching about Jesus (4:17–18).

The apostles instantly obey, preaching in the temple at daybreak (ὄρθρος, *orthros*, the grey of day or dawn; Luke 24:1; John 8:2; and Acts 5:21 are the NT uses).[3] They are teaching (ἐδίδασκον, *edidaskon*, imperfect tense) in the temple. Might the crowd note the apostles' arrest, which was a public act, and see their release, or at least their presence in the temple now, as a picture of God's deliverance? The resurrection, which the Sadducees deny, would certainly be part of the apostles' message (see vv. 30–31). The preaching would have come at dawn, since the temple is closed at night (Witherington 1998: 230; *m. Šeqal.* 5.1; *m. Yoma* 3.1–2 speaks of the morning sacrifice; Josephus, *Ag. Ap.* 2.9 §119; Exod. 29:39; Num. 28:4). Josephus, *Ant.* 18.2.2 §29, speaks of opening the temple at midnight for the Passover sacrifice, but he suggests that this time of opening was exceptional because Passover was an exceptional celebration.

---

3. The phrase ὑπὸ τὸν ὄρθρον (*hypo ton orthron*) is the only case where *hypo* plus the accusative is used with a temporal sense in the NT; BDF §232.1; Moule 1959: 66.

5:21b–23   The escape has gone unnoticed by the leadership. Acts 5:23 explains why: the doors are still locked, and the sentries are still in place, having apparently seen nothing. Marshall (1980: 118) suggests that they were rendered unconscious, appealing to 12:18–19, but such a detail is not explicitly noted there. All that is indicated here is that they did not see anyone escape and thought the apostles were still there. So when morning came, the leadership anticipated interviewing the arrested apostles.

The high priest and his circle call together the leadership (συνέδριον, *synedrion*), that is, the governing council (γερουσίαν, *gerousian*) of Israel. The locale where they gather is not mentioned. Le Cornu and Shulam (2003: 278) suggest that it is the Chamber of Hewn Stone (*b. Sanh.* 88b). Since both terms for the leadership council are used, the point is that every available leader at every level is present (on *synedrion* in Acts: 4:15–16; 5:21, 27, 34–35, 41–42; 6:12–15; 22:30–23:1; 23:6, 15, 20, 28–29; 24:20–21). This is the only use of *gerousia* in the NT.[4] Schneider (1980: 390n38) distinguishes the two expressions, seeing a reference to a senate in the second expression. Haenchen (1987: 250) argues that use of both terms shows that Luke does not know the structure of the leadership, but this is excessively skeptical of an emphatic description. The expression is probably a hendiadys (καί, *kai* before the second term means "even" or "that is"; Jervell 1998: 206). It is emphatic in expressing the scope of those brought in to make a judgment—that is, every available leader (Fitzmyer 1998: 335). The concern is so great over the apostolic preaching that the entire leadership gathers.

They send servants to fetch the apostles. The servants (ὑπηρέται, *hypēretai*, attendants) do not find them and return with the report that they are missing. The term used in verse 21 for "prison" differs from verses 18 and 22 (δεσμωτήριον, *desmōtērion*; Matt. 11:2; Acts 5:21, 23; 16:26 are the NT uses; "place of binding"). These servants would be Levites under the command of the captain (Bruce 1990: 170; *m. Mid.* 1.2 describes the night watchmen; see 4:1). Barrett (1994: 286) discusses a "street ballad" that portrays the violence these guards often utilize. The ballad offers woes for one who experiences the guards' clubs, whisperings, pen, and fists. Whether they use weapons or words, they are to be feared. Beatings are not out of the question. In the current circumstances, the guards could not use any persuasive power. The disappearance has seen to that.

The servants' report is direct and to the point. The prison was found securely locked (κεκλεισμένον, *kekeleismenon*, is a perfect passive participle; literally, the phrase means "being closed with all security"; see also Acts 16:23–24). The prison guards were at their stations. Nothing

---

4. In the LXX, see Exod. 3:16; 12:21, with wording similar to this verse; Jdt. 4:8. On this term in Judaism, see 1 Macc. 12:6; 2 Macc. 1:10; 4:44; 11:27; Josephus, *Ant.* 13.5.8 §166; BAGD 156; BDAG 195; MM 124; Balz, *EDNT* 1:245.

indicated anything unusual about the custody, but when the doors were opened, no one was present.

The situation is perplexing. The term for "perplexed," διαπορέω (*diaporeō*), appears three other times in the NT, all in Luke-Acts (the others are Luke 9:7 [Herod perplexed about reports of Jesus]; Acts 2:12 [the crowd perplexed about the events of Pentecost]; 10:17 [Peter perplexed about his vision]). The verb in the imperfect points to an ongoing perplexity. The captain and chief priests (4:1) cannot figure out what all this might mean. How did the escape take place? Where might the apostles be? They are "at a loss" (BDAG 235; BAGD 187). Translated idiomatically, their reflection is, "What will be the end, or result, of this?" (Barrett 1994: 286).[5] The Sadducees, believing less in divine intervention as a part of their worldview, would be even more perplexed about this situation (Larkin 1995: 92; Josephus, *Ant.* 13.5.9 §173).

5:24

The answer to the question concerning the apostles' whereabouts becomes clear through a report from an unidentified witness. The news is not encouraging for a leadership that wants the message silenced and had acted in a very public manner to stop it. Rather than being silent behind bars, the apostles are back in the temple, teaching the people. The terms "standing," "teaching," and "people" match the angel's instruction given in verse 20. The reference to teaching means that the apostles are disobeying the leadership's instruction. The description parallels Acts 4:18. The apostles do not wish to give up the witness in the temple. An effort to suppress their testimony has failed. The leadership is impotent to stop the spread of the word as the apostles follow the call of God to teach about the way to life.

5:25

The leadership sends the captain with his servants (ὑπηρέταις, *hypēretais*) to bring the apostles back into custody (on these temple police as officials, see John 7:32, 45–46; 18:3, 12; Bruce 1988a: 111n35). Again imperfect tenses are used to portray the process of rearresting the apostles. They were bringing (ἦγεν, *ēgen*) the apostles back but did so without violence, for they were fearing (ἐφοβοῦντο, *ephobounto*) the people. This is like the fear the Jewish leadership had of Jesus in Luke 22:1–6. The fact that a lack of violence is explicitly noted (on Jesus's arrest, contrast Luke 22:50–51) means that often roughhouse tactics were used, as the arrest of Jesus and the way they were prepared to use force also shows. Nothing is done to provoke a reaction on the street. The allusion to stoning (λιθασθῶσιν, *lithasthōsin*) suggests that the people have a better sense of who Jesus is. A public reaction against the high-priestly leadership is feared. Their "blas-

5:26

---

5. On the syntax of the indirect question with the optative, which appears only in Luke-Acts, see Schneider 1980: 392; BDF §385.1, §386.1; Acts 5:24; 8:31; 10:17; 17:18; 21:33; Luke 1:62; 9:46; 15:26; 18:36; Bruce 1990: 171.

phemy" of sorts against God in arresting his messengers could arouse the people if care is not taken during the arrest (Johnson 1992: 97; on λιθάζω, lithazō, in the NT: John 8:3–5; 10:31–33; 11:8; Acts 5:26; 14:19; 2 Cor. 11:24–28; Heb. 11:35–38; a different verb, λιθοβολέω, lithoboleō, appears in Acts 7:58–59; Schneider 1980: 393n64). At the least, the possibility of the people's taking up stones points to the likely unpopularity of the leaders' hostile move. Some fear a public lynching (Barrett 1994: 287).

For their part, the apostles submit obediently to their arrest, returning nonviolently to the council, just as Jesus taught them (Luke 22:50–51; Marshall 1980: 119). The leadership feared the people's reaction also in the case of Jesus (Luke 20:19; 22:2). Luke portrays the populace as seeing the apostles as potentially true prophets. The captain senses that the people might view the arrest with suspicion. The people respect the apostles and do not see them as religious criminals, even if they do not believe them. The term βία (bia, violence) is another Greek term that was picked up by the rabbis and Judaism and is used only in Luke-Acts (Acts 21:35 of a mob; 27:41 [of weather]; LXX: Exod. 1:14; Isa. 52:4; 1 Macc. 6:63; 3 Macc. 2:28; 3:15; 4:7; 4 Macc. 11:26; 17:2, 9; Wis. 4:4 and 19:13 [both of weather]; BDAG 175 §b).

In sum, this unit shows divine support and direction for the apostolic message. It also traces the rise in the leadership's reaction against the apostles. A second arrest leads to a miracle of divine release and an affirmation of the call to preach the message of life. The undercurrent to the passage is that nothing will be able to stop the advance of the gospel message. Divine leading and protection are on the apostles' side. The opposition may persecute them but will never crush them. The application to the readers of Acts is that they can be strong in their support of Jesus. Another note is that the effective preaching of the word brings respect from some, even if it does not always yield faith. This respect can also be a source of protection in the context of persecution. The new community may be under pressure and persecution, but it is to be obedient to God's call and leading. The early church is an example that Luke wishes the church in later times to follow.

Additional Notes

5:19. There is a textual problem over whether "opening" appears as a participle ($\mathfrak{P}^{74}$, ℵ, A, 36, 453, 1175) or a verb (B, [D], E, Ψ, 0189, Byz), but the meaning in either case is the same. The external evidence slightly favors the presence of the participle, as does the parallelism with ἐξαγαγών (exagagōn).

5:21–22. Codex D adds details to both of these verses, speaking of the high-priestly circle arising in the morning and of the servants opening the prison and not finding anyone inside. Neither reading is well enough attested to be original (Metzger 1971: 331).

5:26. In contrast to the ἦγεν (*ēgen*), imperfect for "brought," attested in ℵ and B, two forms of the aorist verb appear in various MSS. "He brought" (ἤγαγεν, *ēgagen*) is read by A, E, Ψ, 33, and Byz; and "they brought" (ἤγαγον, *ēgagon*) is read in D, 2495, and some Syriac MSS. The split in the aorist readings and the Lukan tendency to use the imperfect vividly, along with the presence of the imperfect in the older MSS, favor the reading of the imperfect here.

2. Deliberations and Release (5:27–42)

After rearresting the apostolic band, the leadership reminds the apostles that they were prohibited from preaching in Jesus's name (vv. 27–28). The apostolic response is simple and short. Obedience will be given to God (v. 29). At a narrative level, the reader knows through the release that God is behind the movement. The leadership is portrayed as hardhearted. The apostles are faithful witnesses to what God is doing. All of this is continued evidence of God's exaltation of Jesus, a theme that extends back to Acts 1 and the speech in Acts 2 (vv. 30–32). An opportunity remains to repent and experience forgiveness. The apostles are simply obeying God. The question, then, is what this obedience says about the Jewish leadership's response and persecution.

Many in the leadership are angry with what is perceived as disobedience by the apostles (v. 33). But a leading rabbi, Gamaliel, asks to speak privately to the group and urges caution (v. 34–35). He reviews other troublemakers for the Jews and notes that if the movement is human, it will die out (vv. 36–38). On the other hand, if it is of God, then no opposition will be able to stop it (v. 39). This is a key verse, for if this movement is of God and it is opposed, then the opposition opposes God. Here a wise opponent spots the real options.

The leadership accepts Gamaliel's view and beats the apostles before releasing them (v. 40). The released apostles rejoice that they are worthy to suffer for Jesus (v. 41). They continue their daily trek to the temple to teach and preach Jesus as the Christ (v. 42). The early church has weathered the first wave of persecution with strong faith, a desire to obey God, and bold testimony to Jesus. This material probably reflects tradition, even though Luke has presented it in his own way (Jervell 1998: 213).

Exegesis and Exposition

[27]And when they had brought them, they set them before the council. And the high priest questioned them, [28]saying, "⌜ ⌝ We strictly commanded you not to teach in this name, and look, you have filled Jerusalem with your teaching, and you intend to bring upon us the blood of this man." [29]But Peter and the apostles replied and said, "We must obey God rather than men. [30]The God of our fathers raised Jesus whom you killed by hanging him on a tree. [31]God exalted him to his right hand as Leader and Savior, to give repentance to Israel and forgiveness of

sins. [32]And we are witnesses to these things, and so is the Holy Spirit, whom God has given to those who obey him."

[33]Upon hearing this, they were filled with rage and sought to kill them. [34]But a certain Pharisee named Gamaliel, a teacher of the Law honored among all the people, rose up in the council, urged that the men be put outside for a time, [35]and said ⌜to them⌝, "Men of Israel, be careful what you are about to do with these men, [36]for before these days there arose Theudas, claiming to be someone of significance, and a number of men, about four hundred, joined him; but he was slain and all who followed him were scattered and it came to nothing. [37]After this Judas the Galilean rose up in the days of the census and drew away some of the people after him. That one also perished and all who believed him were scattered. [38]And now I say to you, keep away from these men and let them alone; for if this plan or this work is of men, it will self-destruct; [39]but if it is really of God, you will not be able to destroy them, lest you be found to be opponents of God."

So he persuaded them, [40]and they called in the apostles, and after beating them, they commanded them not to speak in the name of Jesus and released them. [41]Then they were leaving the presence of the council, rejoicing that they were counted worthy to suffer dishonor because of the name. [42]And every day in the temple and house to house they did not cease teaching and preaching the Christ as Jesus.

5:27 The high priest leads the examination of the apostles before the council. The term for "council" (συνεδρίῳ, *synedriō*) also appears in Acts 5:21. It became a loanword in Hebrew and is used in the Mishnah to refer to the high council of Jerusalem (BAGD 786 §2; BDAG 967 §1c). The Sanhedrin governed religious and political issues that Rome did not wish to handle. It was left largely responsible for keeping the peace in the temple environs, which in its view is what it is attempting to do here.

5:28 The high priest reminds the apostles of the council's instruction that prohibits them from preaching (4:17–18). No mention is made of the escape, which is an embarrassment for the leadership. How did they get out? Were the guards irresponsible? The answers to these questions might be too revealing, and so they are not raised (Polhill 1992: 168–69). The use of a verb with a dative of the same lexical root is emphatic, pointing here to the seriousness with which the council has tried to silence the apostles' preaching (παραγγελίᾳ παρηγγείλαμεν, *parangelia parēngeilamen*, strictly commanded; BDF §198.6; Moule 1959: 178; Fitzmyer 1998: 336, imitating a Hebrew infinitive absolute). The apostles have disobeyed strict orders. Their disobedience is blatant. Not only did they continue to preach in this name; they also have filled the city with their teaching and are clearly holding the leadership responsible for Jesus's death. As the high priest puts it, they are seeking "to bring upon us the blood of this man." The expression "His blood be upon us" is an idiom for being responsible for someone's death (Matt. 23:35; 27:25). The leadership could not be placed in a more delicate position. Instead of leading Israel into righteousness, they stand guilty before God of slaying God's chosen one. Luke 11:50–51 is another good example of this expression for being responsible for someone's death, of being held accountable for someone's blood.[1] This charge about the blood under-cuts the leadership's authority to uphold and represent righteousness. Acts 4:10–11; 2:22–23; and 3:13–15 show the charge being raised. The high priest cannot even say Jesus's name, calling him "this man" (τοῦ ἀνθρώπου τούτου, *tou anthrōpou toutou*), a negative, distancing expression also appearing in Luke (23:4, 14; but more positively in 23:47).

The reference to "your" teaching (τῆς διδαχῆς ὑμῶν, *tēs didachēs hymōn*) indicates the separation from the apostles that the leadership senses. They "have filled" (πεπληρώκατε, *peplērōkate*) Jerusalem with this teaching. The perfect tense here is used with an extensive or consum-mative force: Jerusalem is like a cup filled to the full with their teaching (Wallace 1996: 577). From the leadership's point of view, such teaching is unauthorized. The responsibility the apostles place on the leadership makes this more than a dispute about a neutral matter or an issue about theological differences. The leadership is portrayed as opposing God and God's way, something Peter is about to affirm in his response. There is no disagreement about the nature of their dispute. Each group is on trial. The question is simply which of them is on the side of truth.

5:29   Peter replies on behalf of the apostles. He repeats the position he took in Acts 4:19–20.[2] They will obey God, not men.[3] Luke uses another com-parison that expresses exclusion, using ἤ (*ē*; BDF §145a.1; Moulton and Turner 1963: 216). In this case, God has directly instructed them to preach in the temple, and that will continue. The verb for "obey" (πειθαρχέω, *peitharcheō*) appears only four times in the NT (Acts 5:29, 32; 27:21; Titus 3:1–2). The use of δεῖ (*dei*, must) suggests a moral ne-cessity for this obedience. God has the claim on the apostles, and this has priority over any other group.

5:30   Peter repeats a theme of other speeches, namely, that God raised Jesus (Acts 2:24, 32; 3:15; 4:10; 10:40; 22:14). Sometimes the verb for "raise"

1. Other biblical uses of the concept include Acts 18:6; 20:26 (being innocent of the blood); 22:20 (said more indirectly); OT: Gen. 37:22; 42:22; Deut. 19:10; Josh. 2:19; Judg. 9:24 seeks divine vengeance; 2 Sam. 1:16; Hos. 12:14; 1 Kings 2:31–33; Ezek. 18:13; 33:2–4; BAGD 22–23 §2a; BDAG 26 §2a; Jervell 1998: 207n569; the idea is rooted in im-agery from Gen. 4:10.

2. Others note the parallel to Plato, *Apology* 29D, where Socrates also stands up for what he believes to be the truth; Conzelmann 1987: 42.

3. On obeying God rather then men in the Scripture and in the church, see Pelikan 2005: 88–90.

is ἐγείρω (*egeirō*) as here. Sometimes it is ἀνίστημι (*anistēmi*). Reference to "the God of our fathers" shows that Peter still identifies with the Jewish people and faith; thus he appeals to God as the God of promise (see 3:13). Peter and the apostles declare nothing other than what God said long ago when they claim that God raised up Jesus. Some scholars argue, given the parallel in 3:15, that this probably refers to the resurrection and not to arising on the scene of history (Barrett 1994: 289). A case can be made, however, that the resurrection is referred to in 5:31 and so this reference is distinct and means to arise on the scene of history as a Messiah, just as other great figures arose in Israel's past (Judg. 2:18; 3:9, 15). Either sense is possible, as either meaning is logical.

Peter accepts the charge that he blames the leadership for Jesus's death, noting that Jesus is the one "whom you killed" (ὃν ὑμεῖς διεχειρίσασθε, *hon hymeis diecheirisasthe*). This is the only use of this verb to describe the killing of Jesus in Acts, but the charge is a common one (2:23; 3:15; 4:11). The death involved "hanging [Jesus] on a tree" (κρεμάσαντες ἐπὶ ξύλου, *kremasantes epi xylou*), an allusion to Deut. 21:23 (Wilcox 1977; Fitzmyer 1978; 4QpNah 3–4.1.6–8; 11QT 64.10–12; Fitzmyer 1998: 337, where the Qumran texts are connected to crucifixion). This Deuteronomy text makes the point that someone punished in this manner for a sin worthy of death dies a cursed death. Peter is clear that the Jewish charge was that Jesus had done things worthy of a dishonorable death, "cursed of God," as Paul notes in Gal. 3:13 (Acts 10:39; 13:29; 1 Pet. 2:24). The widespread use of this image across many NT writers shows that the idea was a part of Christian tradition.

God's exaltation of Jesus in verse 31 shows an alternative, divine view   **5:31** of who Jesus is. In contrast to the leaders' role in executing Jesus on the tree stands God's exaltation of Jesus to his right hand in heaven. As in Acts 2:33, the exaltation is "to [God's] right hand," as the dative τῇ δεξιᾷ (*tē dexia*) has a local force (BDF §199). This idea is frequent in Luke-Acts (Acts 2:33–34; 7:55–56; Luke 20:42; 22:69).

The move to God's side means that Jesus is Leader (ἀρχηγός, *archēgos*; Acts 3:13–15; 5:30–31; Heb. 2:10; 12:1–2; Judg. 11:6, 11; in the Jewish community prayer of the Eighteen Benedictions 11; Ps. Sol. 17.23–27; Sib. Or. 3.652–56). He also is Savior (σωτήρ, *sōtēr*; Luke 1:47 [of God]; 2:11 [of Jesus]; Acts 5:31; 13:23; see 4:12). Note the unusual word order in Greek: "this one," then "God," then back to the description as Leader and Savior. "This man" of the charge is the figure of deliverance (see v. 28). In answering the second charge, about bringing this man's blood upon the leadership, Peter repeats the charge of the leadership's crime. The boldness prayed for in 4:29 is present.

The term for "Leader" refers to one who is given a preeminent position, a ruler or leader (BAGD 112 §1; BDAG 138 §1). It is variously rendered ("Leader" in ESV, RSV, NET; "Prince" in NIV, NLT, KJV). The title points to the image of shared authority with God. The exaltation also was an opportunity for the nation to receive repentance (see 2:38 for the verb) and forgiveness of sins (ἄφεσιν ἁμαρτιῶν, *aphesin hamartiōn*, which appears four times in Acts, 5:30–31; 10:43; 13:38–39; 26:16–18; also in Luke 1:77; 3:3; 24:47). The exaltation gave evidence of divine support for Jesus, which the leadership has ignored. The word for "repentance" appears six times in Acts (5:30–31; 11:18; 13:23–24; 19:4; 20:18–21; 26:19–20). Whereas 2:32–33 stresses the benefit of the Spirit as a result of exaltation, here it is Jesus's direct role in salvation that is stressed; he is prince, deliverer, and author of salvation (Bertram, *TDNT* 8:609).

Peter is highlighting that instead of the apostolic message about Jesus being a threat to the nation, as the leadership treats it, here is a chance to experience national blessing (Israel in Acts up to this point: 1:6; 2:36; 4:10, 27; 5:21). Jesus's exaltation means that the blood of Jesus need not remain on the leaders' heads. For with repentance and the forgiveness God offers through Jesus, all culpability can be forgiven. That the nation is at risk because of how its leaders have acted is an idea similar to the impact of kings on the nation in Samuel and Kings. The offer is of repentance to Israel so that the nation can be forgiven. This offer of forgiveness that Jesus makes explains why he can also be called Savior. Luke reserves mention of Jesus as savior in contexts where Israel as a nation is being discussed (Luke 1:47; 2:11; Acts 13:23; Jervell 1998: 208n576). In the OT, God is often the savior (Isa. 43:3, 11; 45:15, 21; 49:26; Jer. 14:8; Hos. 13:4; Ps. 24:5 LXX); so also in the NT (1 Tim. 1:1; 2:3; 4:10; Titus 1:3; 2:10; 3:4; Jude 25; Le Cornu and Shulam 2003: 284). God continues to appeal to his obstinate people. He is now saving and cleansing through a mediating savior. Judaism believed that at the end there would be a need to receive cleansing from sin (Ps. Sol. 17.22–29; Jub. 4.26; 50.5; 1 En. 10.22; T. Levi 18.9; T. Jud. 24.1; Jervell 1998: 208n577). This is the apostles' appeal. See what God is doing. It is not the apostles who need to obey God, but the leadership.

5:32   Once again Peter stresses that the apostles are witnesses to Jesus (see Acts 1:8; last used in 3:15). But there is a second divine witness, the Holy Spirit, whom God has given to those who obey God (i.e., not the leadership). Thus the testimony of the human witnesses is actually God's voice and message. The mention of the Spirit means that all three persons of the Trinity are noted in Peter's reply. God raised and exalted Jesus, whom God's Spirit testifies to. The Spirit functions as revealer of the gospel here (John 16:8–12). This is yet another allusion to the Spirit as a key gift of salvation in Acts (see 1:4–5; the gift of the Spirit is sometimes associated with repentance in Luke-Acts: Acts 11:15–18; Luke 24:47–49). The verb for "obey" (πειθαρχέω, *peitharcheō*) appears four times in the NT (Acts 5:29, 32; 27:21; Titus 3:1–2).

Peter's refusal to obey the leadership leads to their intense anger. This **5:33** is one of only two NT uses of the verb διαπρίω (*diapriō*; Acts 5:33; 7:54 [directed at Stephen]). In both cases it is a reaction to a speech by a member of the new community. They are so angry that they desire to kill the apostles (of twenty-four NT occurrences, ἀναιρέω, *anaireō*, kill, appears nineteen times in Acts). It is used of Jesus being killed (Acts 10:39; 13:28), seeking to kill Paul (9:29), James being killed (12:2), and Paul being at Stephen's killing (22:20). Διαπρίω means to be sawn asunder or to be cut to the heart, but here it takes on a negative sense of being infuriated, split open in rage (BAGD 187; BDAG 235). Instead of repentance and response with a pierced heart, the leadership has gone its own way and refused to obey the call of the Spirit through Peter.

The only thing to stop the move toward seeking the apostles' death is a **5:34** speech by a leading rabbinic figure of the Sanhedrin, a member of the Pharisees. This party within Judaism tried to keep the nation faithful to the law but was in the position of being the opposition to the political power in Israel under the Hasmoneans except under Salome Alexandra. That situation prevailed until the Romans came to power (Bruce 1990: 174–75). Under Herod, they came to have more power but still functioned as a minority (Josephus, *Ant.* 18.1.3 §14; 18.1.4 §17). They often were a check against Sadducean power. They believed in oral tradition, the resurrection, the existence of demons, and the sovereignty of God in a manner that contrasted with the Sadducees. Luke tends to treat them more positively in Acts than the Sadducees, because they possess a hope in resurrection and believe in God's active power (Jervell 1998: 212–13).

Gamaliel is the only rabbi named in Acts (also in 22:3 as the teacher of Paul). Luke describes him as held in honor before the people. He also is one of the few rabbis of this period to appear in later Jewish tradition. Mishnah *Soṭah* 9.15 says that when he died "the glory of the law ceased and purity and abstinence died." He was a student of Hillel and was known as Gamaliel the Elder or Gamaliel I.[4] Luke calls him simply a teacher of the law (νομοδιδάσκαλος, *nomodidaskalos*, is used three times in the NT: Luke 5:17; Acts 5:34–35; 1 Tim. 1:5–7). Gamaliel begins his speech by ordering the apostles to be put out of the room so that he can address the group in private. Gamaliel is evidence that cool heads are still present within Judaism. He is a voice of mature, wise reason among the apostles' opponents.

Gamaliel warns the council to take care concerning what they are about **5:35** to do. The verb προσέχω (*prosechō*) appears six times in Acts (5:34–35;

---

4. He is called Gamaliel the Elder nineteen times in the Talmud: *b. ʿErub.* 45a; *b. Roš Haš.* 23b, 29b; *b. Yebam.* 90b, 115a, 122a (3x); *b. Moʿed Qaṭ.* 27a; *b. Ketub.* 10b; *b. Soṭah* 49a; *b. Giṭ.* 32a, 33a, 34b, 35b; *b. ʿAbod. Zar.* 11a; *b. Ber.* 38a; *b. Nid.* 6b. He is referred to as Gamaliel I nine more times: *b. Ber.* 43b; *b. Šabb.* 33a, 136a; *b. Pesaḥ.* 88b; *b. Taʿan.* 30a; *b. Meg.* 18a; *b. Sanh.* 31a, 39a, 48b. On the Pharisees, see additional note on 5:34.

8:6, 9–11; 16:14; 20:28). It means to give attention to something. In this context, it means, "Think before you act on your emotions." A short, recent history lesson follows to justify the warning. The group is addressed as "men of Israel" (the way Peter also addressed his audience, Acts 2:22; 3:12).

5:36 Gamaliel explains (γάρ, *gar*, for) by noting examples of two other "rebel" movements. The first concerns Theudas, who managed to band together four hundred men until he was killed, with the result that his followers were dispersed. This effort self-destructed. Scholars dispute the reference to this figure, who is mentioned only here in the NT. Josephus (*Ant.* 20.5.1 §§97–98) mentions a Theudas revolting during the governorship of Fadus (AD 44–46), but this is too late to fit the timing of Gamaliel's speech, given more than a decade earlier (Barrett 1994: 296 sees Luke erring here). Given the popularity of the name and the turmoil of the period leading to the census and Judas the Galilean, mentioned in verse 37, Gamaliel may well be referring to a Theudas who was earlier than the one Josephus mentions (Witherington 1998: 238–39). This Theudas would have preceded the activity of Judas during the census period. Bruce (1990: 176) argues that this figure may date back to insurgencies that arose in Palestine after the death of Herod the Great in 4 BC, a time that Josephus also mentions as turbulent (*Ant.* 17.10.4 §§269–70; 17.10.8 §285; also Polhill 1992: 172–73).

Gamaliel's point (see vv. 38–39) is that if the movement is of men, it will die out and does not need radical opposition. If the movement is of God, then it would be wrong to oppose it. This reliance on divine sovereignty fits with the belief of the Pharisees.

5:37 Gamaliel's second example concerns a figure whom he places after Theudas, Judas the Galilean (the name appears variously as Theodotus, Theodotion, and Theudion; see Le Cornu and Shulam 2003: 293). This rebel's activity appeared during the time of the census (ca. AD 6; Josephus, *Ant.* 18.1.6 §23 [followers of Judas are part of a politically zealous movement against the taxation of the census]; 20.5.2 §102; *J.W.* 2.8.1 §§117–18 [mentions Coponius as procurator]). Bruce (1990: 177) sees Quirinius as responsible for the census but appointing officers such as Coponius to supervise it in Judea. This Judas also drew an unspecified number of followers. After his death, however, his followers scattered and his movement disappeared.[5] Only Luke mentions his death. Gamaliel's two examples mirror each other. The explanation follows.

5:38 Gamaliel's application and advice are to "keep away" from these men. Luke transitions to this summary with his common expression καὶ τὰ νῦν (*kai ta nyn*, and now) to indicate a conclusion or application. The

---

5. The spirit of Judas's movement continued in the Zealots, but it was not so organized in the period when Gamaliel speaks.

verb for "keep away," ἀφίστημι (*aphistēmi*), appears fourteen times in the NT (Luke 2:36–37; 4:13; 8:13; 13:26–27; Acts 5:37–39 [2x]; 12:10; 15:37–38; 19:9; 22:29; 2 Cor. 12:8; 1 Tim. 4:1–3; 2 Tim. 2:19; Heb. 3:12–15). To make the point emphatically, Gamaliel says that they should leave the men alone or release them. Here the verb for "let [them] alone" is the more common ἀφίημι (*aphiēmi*), which is used 143 times in the NT. Gamaliel's point is simple: if this plan and understanding are of men, it will not succeed. A plan of men would be a human attempt to present God's promise, with a human source for the apostolic message. Gamaliel's point appears in a third-class Greek condition. Rhetorically, Gamaliel does not take a position as to whether a human origin is the case. The verb καταλύω (*kataluō*, destroy) is used only three times in Acts, twice in this passage (5:38–39 [not be able to destroy this movement]; 6:12–14 [destroy the temple]). "Any assembling together that is for the sake of heaven will in the end be established; but any that is not for the sake of heaven will in the end not be established" (*m. 'Abot* 4.11; Polhill 1992: 173).

Gamaliel presents another option, also in a first-class Greek condition but using εἰ (*ei*) so that rhetorically Luke makes clear that this is the more likely option (Moule 1959: 150 notes but does not develop the grammatical contrast in vv. 38–39; see Jervell 1998: 211). If the movement is from God, then opposition is futile, even dangerous. The leadership will not be able to destroy the apostles. The verb καταλύω is used again. The word for "opponent of God" (θεομάχος, *theomachos*) is used only here in the NT and does not appear in the LXX (the cognate verb θεομαχέω, *theomacheō*, is in 2 Macc. 7:19; Hellenistic uses: Epictetus, *Discourses* 3.24.24; Euripides, *Bacchanals* 45; Johnson 1992: 101; Bruce 1990: 178). He is saying, in other words, "Imagine the leadership of the Jewish faith being in opposition to God. It is a prospect that should be avoided." Conceptually, the idea reflects Wis. 12:13–14, where there is a warning not to judge unjustly. In this official setting, Gamaliel would have spoken in a Semitic language, either Aramaic or Hebrew. Such distinctions in expressing a conditional sentence as the Greek text presents likely would not have been made, since these languages did not make such distinctions in their grammar. Thus either Luke is summarizing a longer point Gamaliel made quite vividly (namely, that if the movement should really and truly be of God, there is nothing that can be done to stop it), or Luke has added this Greek touch to Gamaliel's remarks to underscore what is the case among the options Gamaliel raised, as far as Luke is concerned. The rhetorical suggestion is that this movement will not be like Theudas or Judas the Galilean, making the speech ironic. Gamaliel has everything at his disposal to see the truth but, like other Pharisees, refuses to join. Still he sees that to interfere with the apostles will not help (Darr 1998: 134–39).

5:39

Gamaliel's advice is persuasive; the text says simply that the leaders believe him or take his instruction to heart. The verb here is πείθω (*peithō*) and means "persuade" in this context (seventeen uses in Acts: 5:36–37 [2x], 39–40; 12:20; 13:43; 14:19; 17:4; 18:4; 19:8, 24–26; 21:14; 23:21; 26:26, 28; 27:11; 28:23–27 [2x]). The aorist here is consummative in syntactical force: they "were persuaded" (Wallace 1996: 560; HCSB). No reason is given for why the council accepted this course of action, but their motive was probably to avoid inflaming those sympathetic with the apostles and raising Roman concerns about the public peace, as well as accepting Gamaliel's theological point.

5:40   The leaders allow the apostles to return so that they can give them their response. In the midst of the leadership, little has changed as a result of the miraculous work of God. God's work has given them only slight pause, although it may have motivated Gamaliel's remarks and resulted in saving the lives of the apostles. The leaders repeat the command to the apostles not to preach in Jesus's name (4:18; 5:28).

They also punish them physically, beating them before releasing them. Beating (δέρω, *derō*) is mentioned in only three passages in Acts (5:39–40; 16:37; 22:19–20). The flogging looks forward to what Paul will suffer. Such flogging is regulated in *m. Mak.* 3.10–14. It is probably the "forty lashes minus one" (Deut. 25:3; 2 Cor. 11:24; Mark 13:9 is fulfilled; *m. Kil.* 8.3; *m. Mak.* 1.1; Josephus, *Ant.* 4.8.21 §238). The whipping would have been on the back and chest with a three-stranded strap of calf hide (Polhill 1992: 174). This could leave one close to death, if not dead, from loss of blood (Marshall 1980: 124). The hope is that by intensifying the punishment, a deterrent will be established. They are wrong.

5:41–42   These verses summarize the outcome of the apostles' experience: nothing changes in the apostles' activity and attitude. On the one hand, they are rejoicing that they are accounted worthy to suffer dishonor on behalf of Jesus. The terms for "counted worthy" (κατηξιώθησαν, *katēxiōthēsan*) and "suffer dishonor" (ἀτιμασθῆναι, *atimasthēnai*) appear in a few other NT texts (counted worthy, three times: Luke 20:34–36; Acts 5:41–42; 2 Thess. 1:3–10; suffer dishonor, seven times: Mark 12:4; Luke 20:11; John 8:49; Acts 5:41–42; Rom. 1:24–25; 2:23–24; James 2:6). In a strongly shame-honor-oriented society, to be dishonored normally would be considered shameful (BAGD 120; BDAG 148). The phrase "counted worthy to suffer dishonor" is an oxymoron, a dishonor that is a cause for joy. The leaders beat them to produce shame. They hope that the shame might function as a deterrent and stop their preaching or at least persuade others not to heed them.

In the apostles' view, however, being worthy to be a witness to the name of Jesus is a great honor and a cause for rejoicing. As Bauernfeind (1980: 97) notes, "Without joy, no gospel," even though suffering is present. God is using them to present Jesus. Here is the exemplary attitude of the church, willing to preach Jesus and suffer for the honor. This theme is a part of Jesus's teaching and appears in the Epistles.[6]

The result is teaching and preaching every day in the temple and in various homes (κατ᾽ οἶκον, *kat' oikon*, distributive, house to house, as in 2:46; 20:20; BDF §224.3). They do what they said they would: continue to proclaim the name God called them to preach (5:28–29, also 40). This is the first time the verb εὐαγγελίζω (*euangelizō*, to preach good news) appears in Acts with Jesus as the object of the message. The verb is used fifteen times in Acts and is associated with different topics: 5:41–42; 8:4 [the word], 12, 25, 35 [Jesus], 40; 10:36–38; 11:20 [the Lord Jesus]; 13:32–33; 14:5–7, 15–17, 21–22; 15:35 [the word of God]; 16:10; 17:18 [Jesus and the resurrection]; Fitzmyer 1998: 342; Schneider 1980: 404n180).

In sum, the leadership struggles to deal with this new movement. The apostles continue to preach in disobedience to the leadership but in obedience to God (Fernando 1998: 215–16). This type of disobedience means that one serves God before anyone or anything else. Fernando (1998: 220–24) discusses in some detail issues tied to modern civil disobedience. Sometimes one might have to break civil law and suffer the consequences.

Counsel from a wise rabbi tells the leaders (and the readers of Acts) that if the movement is of God, they will not be able to stop it. He advises care in handling the disciples, whose release gives them strength, as they recognize divine support for their call to preach Jesus. The major points of the passage include the note that God is behind the movement and the exemplary way the apostles boldly face persecution, even a beating. All of this fulfills the prayer of 4:24–31. The church will preach Jesus no matter what the cost. The word order of the Greek τὸν χριστὸν Ἰησοῦν (*ton christon Iēsoun*, the Christ as Jesus) emphasizes the identification of the Messiah as Jesus (Johnson 1992: 101). The realization of God's long-established promise is also preached, as is the fulfillment of Jewish expectation in Peter's brief overview of Jesus's exaltation (v. 31). Johnson's conclusion to the unit is well taken: "When Luke shows the apostles triumphantly preaching Jesus as Messiah in the temple (5:42), undaunted by the council's beatings or threats, shown to be empowered and guided by God's Spirit, he has answered for his readers the question concerning leadership over Israel" (Johnson 1992: 103). The apostles and their message, not the Jewish leadership, represent the hope for Israel.

6. Matthew 5:11–12; 10:17–22; Mark 13:9–13; Luke 6:22–23; 12:11–12; 21:12–19; John 15:18–25; 16:2–3; Rom. 5:3–4; 2 Cor. 6:10; Phil. 1:29; Col. 1:24; Heb. 10:34; James 1:2; 1 Pet. 1:6–7; 4:12–16. For the honor/glory contrast, see John 8:49–50; Rom. 1:21, 24; 1 Cor. 15:43; 2 Cor. 6:8; Schneider 1980: 404n175.

This engagement with Judaism stands in contrast to Haenchen's claim that the early Jerusalem church was a quiet, devout community, unlike the more bellicose Hellenistic church, which caused the rise of opposition (Haenchen 1987: 258). This stark contrast has too much of the old Tübingen-Baur school's view of the early church in it, where Jewish Christianity and Hellenistic Christianity are radically different. Something led the church to expand quickly from Jerusalem, and it was not just one wing of the church that set the stage for this expansion. The prominence of Peter and the likely nature of his later death as a martyr indicate that he was an important preacher of the gospel. His leadership may well have motivated others in the cause, just as his example does for Luke in Acts.

Additional Notes

5:27–42. An interesting study of this passage appears in an essay by Lyons (1997). He contrasts two readings of the text, one that sees the remarks of Gamaliel as positive and giving a theological principle to be applied and another that views them as ironic and a failure as advice and therefore of no theological merit. This approach he applies to current debates about certain charismatic phenomena (the "Toronto blessing"). Lyons's essay appears to prefer the negative and "no theological principle" view of Gamaliel's remarks. His assessment measures the remarks, however, against a background of failing Christianity or the closing of churches in modern times. Such an assessment misses Luke's point about the ultimate success of the new faith, which is rooted ultimately not in where the faith stands now but where it is headed eschatologically in Jesus's return and victory. This means that this movement will have staying power, as its content reflects the gospel given from God. Narrow applications to particular phenomena, such as charismatic practice, fail not because Gamaliel's remarks should be read as false and ironic but because the topic that Gamaliel's principle addresses is the Christian faith considered as a whole. In other words, Lyons's reading fails because it does not take the entire Lukan perspective into view as he makes his assessment. Luke sees the gospel as from God. Gamaliel's point is well taken, as both the syntax of Acts 5:39 indicates as well as the Lukan teaching that Jesus will bring victory from God. The speeches of Acts 3 and 10 show this eschatology.

5:28. The particle οὐ (*ou*) before παραγγελία is lacking in several MSS ($\mathfrak{P}^{74}$, א, A, B, 1175) and may not be original to Acts, which is why the Greek text has it in brackets. The MSS D, E, 1739, and Byz contain it and make the sentence a question: "Did we not strictly command you . . . ?" I have omitted the particle and read it as a statement (Metzger 1971: 288). The more difficult reading is the omission of the negative particle. A question would be only rhetorical, in any case, so the force of the options in terms of meaning is the same.

5:34. There is an important debate among NT scholars about the influence of the Pharisees on Judaism in the period of Jesus. E. P. Sanders (1992: 380–412) argues that Josephus has exaggerated the influence of the Pharisees and that this sect was not as powerful as many NT treatments suggest. However, an important review essay by Roland Deines and Martin Hengel (1995) analyzes the key passages and background and contends that the Pharisees were the most important of the sects at a popular level. They worked among the people in the synagogues and were seen as representing the highest level of Jewish piety, a perception that gave them great influence among the populace. A more comprehensive overview of this approach is in Deines's other works on the Pharisees (1997, 2001).

5:35. A variant in D reads that they spoke "to the rulers and the council members," but it is not well enough attested to be original.

H. Community Life: The Appointment of the Seven to Help Hellenist Widows (6:1–6)

Not everything is working smoothly in the church. Luke is a realist. In Acts 5 the issues are the difficulty of persecution and the problem of dishonesty in the church. In Acts 6 we return to internal matters (Fitzmyer 1998: 343). There are ethnic issues to sort out, always a tricky problem in a community that is open to all types of people. The community does, however, work through what is a potentially destructive situation.

The problem is that Hellenist widows are not being as well cared for as the Hebrew widows in the Jerusalem community (v. 1). It is not a problem the Twelve should divert themselves to treat. They should not give up their primary role, to preach about Jesus (v. 2). The decision is that those who raised the problem should provide qualified people to solve it so that the apostles can stay on task (vv. 3–4). Seven men are selected to address the problem (vv. 5–6). As the community grows and becomes more complex, it restructures to meet fresh needs, especially by choosing qualified people closest to a problem to help resolve it. Thus begins a process of socialization that ends in the Jerusalem Council. J. J. Scott (1997) traces this development of socialization in an essay discussing Acts 6–15.

Conzelmann (1987: 44) questions the historical value of this Hebrew-Hellenist construct of the early church. He argues that the portrait of the Seven and the role they play elsewhere in Acts has nothing to do with this conflict, which he argues Luke has artificially constructed. His response errs, however, by failing to note the selectivity of the material we have from Luke. Acts says nothing about how the Hellenists solved the widow problem because once those concerned with the problem were selected, they resolved the issue. Barrett (1994: 306–7) has a better take on matters here and on Luke's selectivity (also Witherington 1998: 243–47). The scene is not "artificially constructed" but does reflect how the early growth of an ethnically diverse church became difficult to manage. Barrett argues that the Seven give care to the poor and preach the gospel. With the selection of them to treat the widows' problem, Luke leaves that issue to tell us about their impact elsewhere in the church. The early Hebrew-Hellenist tension is largely resolved when both parties take responsibility to solve the problem. The material has traditional roots and is historically honest about tension in the church, even if all the details behind how widespread this tension might have been are not presented.

But what caused such tension to arise? Luke does not tell us, but three scenarios exist. (1) The strategy of the Jewish leaders to go hard after Hellenist Christians, as Acts 6–7 might suggest, may well have been an attempt to split the new community along old, established lines. Hebrew Christians would be seen as more law- and temple-sensitive. By pressing one group, one might be able to split the Christians and provoke them to blame each other. (2) Hellenists may have been less attached to Jerusalem and so might leave the city more easily. This would leave Hebrew Christians in control and make the Hellenist Christians a smaller minority in the city. (3) The hypothetical view that Hellenists were targeted may be a critical misreading of Acts, where no distinction of ethnic targeting took place in the Jewish leadership's persecution (so Witherington 1998: 244–46; Hurtado 2003: 206–14, who notes that persecution touches Jewish and Hellenist believers).

Given how little detail we have about this period and how selective Luke is in discussing the situation, it is hard to know which of these scenarios or which combination of them is at work here. Scenarios 1 and 2 could both be at work, but scenario 3 would dissolve the supposed ethnic division problem. Given what Acts does tell us, it seems likely that the critical reading of a persecution against only a segment of the church is overdrawn. But it also is possible that scenario 2 is at work. Those most loyal to the entirety of the law might well be those most likely to remain in Jerusalem and near the temple.

The passage is an "appointment history" (Gen. 41:29–43; Exod. 18:13–26; Num. 11:1–25; 27:12–23; Deut. 1:9–18; Schneider 1980: 422; Talbert 1997: 73–75). It tells how a new structure for community care came to be appointed and developed. The main elements of its structure are problem (v. 1), solution (vv. 2–4), qualifications (vv. 3b, 5), and selection (vv. 5–6). The seven who are chosen could both preach, as Philip and Stephen will show in Acts 7–8, and serve these widows. Luke indicates that preaching will not be limited to the Twelve of Acts 1. This passage is the only direct reference to the Twelve in Acts after 1:26 and 2:14. Others are quite capable of sharing in the mission of the church to preach the word (Marshall 1980: 125). As the church grows, it will need more leaders. The apostles do not hold power to themselves but seek to make sure the church has all the human resources it needs with adequate authority to care for its own.

The unit is an important literary bridge passage in Acts. Luke gives attention to the work of those outside the Twelve, especially Stephen and Philip. Their story is an important component of what Luke will describe in Acts 6–8 before he turns to his key hero figure, Paul. The section makes clear that Paul is not alone. Others also share in the task of taking the gospel out beyond Jerusalem. This concern runs from Acts 6 to 12 (Spencer 2004: 72).

The passage also presents a good method of selection: a popular choice of those close to the ministry with approval by the ministers and then a commissioning so that all can recognize their roles (Barrett 1994: 304). It also is no mistake that those who solve the problem come from within the group whose need is the greatest.

Exegesis and Exposition

[1]Now in these days when disciples were multiplying in numbers, there arose grumbling among the Hellenists against the Hebrews, because their widows were being neglected in the ministry of daily distribution. [2]And the Twelve, summoning the multitude of disciples, said, "It is not appropriate for us to give up the word of God to minister tables. [3]⌜ ⌝Therefore, brothers, ⌜look to select⌝ from among you seven men of good reputation, full of the Spirit and wisdom, whom we may appoint for this duty. [4]But we will devote ourselves to prayer and to the ministry of the word." [5]And the word pleased the entire multitude, and they chose Stephen, a man full of faith and the Holy Spirit, and Philip and Prochorus, and Nicanor, and Timon, and Parmenas, and Nicolaus, a proselyte of Antioch, [6]whom the multitude presented before the apostles, and praying, they laid hands on them.

This verse presents the juxtaposition of two realities in the new community: a growth (πληθυνόντων, *plēthynontōn*, increasing) in the number of disciples and a management problem that this growth is producing among Hellenists and Gentiles (on growth, 6:7; 9:31; 12:24). This is the first appearance in Acts of the noun for "disciples" (μαθητῶν, *mathētōn*; twenty-eight times in Acts: 6:1, 2, 7; 9:1–2, 10, 19–20, 24–26 [3x], 38; 11:26, 29–30; 13:51–52; 14:20–22 [2x], 28; 15:10; 16:1–2; 18:23, 27; 19:1, 9, 30–31; 20:1, 29–30; 21:4, 15–16 [2x]). Fitzmyer (1998: 346) argues that the roots of the concept of disciple are more Greek than Jewish, but this may not be so. Hengel (1981) traces Jewish influences in the rabbi-student relationship and the unique way Jesus used the term. The daily (καθημερινῇ, *kathēmerinē*)[1] distribution or ministry (διακονία, *diakonia*) involves necessary food and probably some clothing and possibly necessary money (Le Cornu and Shulam 2003: 309; see also p. 303 on how widows were cared for). Widows were regarded as needing community care when no family member could care for them. Funds supporting the wife in case of her husband's death were normally built into the wedding contract (*m. Ketub.* 11.1). The current conduct of that ministry engenders complaining or murmuring (γογγυσμός, *gongysmos*)

6:1

---

1. The term for "daily" is an adjective with -ινος (*-inos*) suffix pointing to time, so "each day," BDF §113.3.

between the neglected Hellenists and the Hebrews. Jewish texts indicate that concern for the poor and those in need was common (*m. Pe'ah* 5.4; 8.7; *m. Demai* 3.1; *m. 'Abot* 5.9; Jeremias 1969a: 129–34; Johnson 1992: 106).[2] The practice appears to have been analogous to the Jewish system of once-a-week distribution of food and clothing (*quppah*) and a daily meeting of more urgent needs (*tamhuy*; Polhill 1992: 180).

Γογγυσμός appears four times in the NT (John 7:12; Acts 6:1; Phil. 2:14–16; 1 Pet. 4:9–10) and thirteen times in the LXX (see, e.g., Exod. 16:7–12; Num. 17:25; Wis. 11:1); the generic term for "ministry" (διακονία, *diakonia*) occurs eight times in Acts (1:15–17, 24–25; 6:1, 3–4; 11:29–30; 12:25; 20:24; 21:19). The way the problem is eventually solved indicates that it may well have surfaced not because of ethnic malice but because of a lack of administrative organization caused by the new community's growth across diverse ethnic lines. That the problem broke out along ethnic lines is not surprising, as most relationships would be affected by these distinctions. The community is aware, however, that such distinctions cannot be maintained and supported in a community that confesses a Messiah who has come to give God's grace to all types of people. Something needs to be done to be sure everyone's needs are met.

A key term in the verse is "Hellenists" (Ἑλληνιστῶν, *Hellēnistōn*). This new, emerging group will become important in the story of Acts. This term likely refers to Jews whose primary language was Greek, as distinct from those using a Semitic tongue (BAGD 252; BDAG 319; Barrett 1994: 308–9; Witherington 1998: 240–42). Gutbrod (*TDNT* 3:389) speaks of the difference as between those who are native to Israel and those who come from outside, but it is social and religious practice that seems to be central in the distinction. The linguistic and social differences produced cultural differences that created a division in the church that the community now recognizes and works swiftly to quell. Conzelmann (1987: 45) and Hengel (1979: 1–29), with many other scholars, see both a linguistic distinction (Greek as the mother tongue) and some difference in practice (a less attached approach to the role of the temple). It is unclear if the Hellenists in fact had a looser view of the law in general (Jervell 1998: 216n620 reviews the scholarly debate). Estimates suggest that Hellenists (i.e., those whose primary language was Greek) made up from 10 to 20 percent of the population (Le Cornu and Shulam 2003: 316). Hellenists will be mentioned again later in Acts (9:29; 11:20). It is not clear that the same cultural distinctions are being emphasized in each of these occurrences, as 11:20 seems to be only an ethnic reference.

The NT notes the plight of widows in a few key texts (1 Tim. 5:9–16; James 1:27). This theme also is prominent in the OT (Deut. 14:29; 24:17; 26:12; Isa. 1:17, 23; 10:2; Jer. 7:6; 22:3; Ezek. 22:7; Mal. 3:5; Johnson

---

2. Whether these mishnaic practices were this early is disputed; Fitzmyer 1998: 348.

1992: 105; Fitzmyer 1998: 345). These texts suggest that a community's compassion could and should be measured by how it cares for the poor, the orphaned, and the widowed. So the issue is important to the community's character and credibility as a place where concern is met with action.

The Twelve consider the complaint legitimate but raise the question of the best way to solve it. They prioritize their role and delegate the responsibility, involving more people in the community's work as a result. They observe that it is not appropriate (οὐκ ἀρεστόν ἐστιν, *ouk areston estin*) for them to neglect preaching to take up this problem directly and serve (διακονεῖν, *diakonein*, the verb of the noun in v. 1) tables. The word for "appropriate" is often translated "right" (RSV, ESV, NET, NIV), with the idea that it is not correct for the Twelve to serve tables rather than preach. The nuance of the term, however, is that it is not pleasing (to God; "desirable" in NASB) for them to serve tables. It is a priority choice about observing the call of God versus a moral choice of right, wrong, and sin (BAGD 105; BDAG 130; John 8:29; Isa. 38:3 [to do what is good in God's sight]; also Gen. 16:6; Lev. 10:19; Deut. 6:18; 12:8, 25; Tob. 3:6; Jdt. 12:14; esp. Exod. 18:17–23). They should do what God has called them to do, namely, teach and witness. They cannot and should not do everything in the church, but they should not neglect preaching. Καταλείψαντας (*kataleipsantas*, giving up) means to cease from doing something or neglect one thing for another (BAGD 413 §2c; BDAG 521 §7c). Someone else will be able to do this important ministry so that the apostles are free to keep preaching. In the apostles' view, this ability to prioritize activities and not be responsible to do everything reflects good leadership and stewardship.

6:2

The instruction is to select seven men from among the disciples for this task. The number seven may have some Jewish significance, as Josephus indicates that in Galilee seven judges were appointed to oversee many cities to assess lesser disputes while seventy elders took on more significant issues (*Ant.* 4.8.14 §214; 4.8.38 §287; *J.W.* 2.20.5 §571; Str-B 2:641). This number also shows up in Hellenistic culture to refer to the size of ancient councils (Conzelmann 1987: 45). There is no official or "deacon" office here. These men take on this assignment to make sure that it is dealt with and no longer remains a problem. The idea that some issues should be handled by a group separate from the main teaching leaders is something that emerges in a similar way in later church structure.[3] It is probably rooted in Jewish precedent (Le Cornu and Shulam 2003: 313). Synagogue leaders and leading men of the city are some examples of other "offices," where skill and reputation combine

6:3

---

3. On the development of "faith and order" in the early centuries of the church, see Pelikan 2005: 91–93.

and lead to service (e.g., the seventy elders of Num. 11:16–17). That the selection comes from within the group to the leadership parallels the selection of Judas's replacement in Acts 1:15–26.

The verb ἐπισκέπτομαι (*episkeptomai*) often means "visit" as it does in Acts 15:36, but here it means "select" (for other occurrences, see Luke 1:68, 78; 7:16; Acts 7:23; 15:14 [both meaning "visit"]; Exod. 18:21; Num. 27:16–18). Luke uses the term seven times, and the rest of the NT four times (Matt. 25:36, 43; Heb. 2:6; James 1:27).

Their qualifications have two major components: that they be spiritual men, and that their character be well accepted by others. They are to be "full of the Spirit and wisdom" (πλήρεις πνεύματος καὶ σοφίας, *plēreis pneumatos kai sophias*) and to be men who carry a good reputation (Num. 27:16–20; Acts 7:55; 11:24; 13:50). Spirit and wisdom are genitives of content (Wallace 1996: 93; NET, HCSB). In this context, to be filled with the Spirit means that their lives are directed by God's Spirit so that they are spiritually sensitive, able to make good judgments, a sign of spiritual maturity, as 1 Cor. 2:14–15 and Heb. 5:14 also explain (OT: Gen. 41:33; Exod. 18:21; Num. 27:18; Deut. 1:13, 15; Schneider 1980: 426). The Spirit is so active that they are "full of" the Spirit's power and enablement (BAGD 670 §2; BDAG 827 §1b). This expression is repeated with other characteristics in this passage (v. 5: full of faith and the Spirit; v. 8: full of grace and power). The reference to reputation is a description of men who are "testified to" (μαρτυρουμένους, *martyroumenous*; Acts 16:2; 22:12; 1 Tim. 5:10; 3 John 12). They will have responsibility for caring for the widows, although other texts make clear that this is not the only way they minister for the church. Something has to indicate their spiritual capability and reputation. Apparently their ability to minister is such an indicator. Jervell (1998: 218) says that Luke assumes these men will do more than care for the poor. They will also preach the gospel.

These men will perform their appointed duty, or task. The term for "duty" (χρεία, *chreia*) contains two ideas. It means to deal with a certain task or business that itself reflects a corresponding need (Barrett 1994: 312).

6:4 In contrast, there is another two-pronged ministry (διακονία, *diakonia*) that the apostles will devote (προσκαρτερήσομεν, *proskarterēsomen*) themselves to perform (one of six occurrences of this verb in Acts: also in 1:14; 2:42, 44–47; 8:13; 10:7–8). They will continue to be engaged in prayer and a ministry of the word (on prayer in Acts, see 1:14). Preaching has been noted in verse 2, but here prayer is also seen as an important aspect of what the apostles will do in leading the church and seeking God's will.

6:5 The word (ὁ λόγος, *ho logos*) that the apostles speak on the matter meets with great acceptance, as the word is said to have pleased (ἤρεσεν, *ēresen*) the multitude. This is the only use of this verb in Acts; it appears seventeen times in the NT (see also 2 Sam. 3:36). The list of whom the community chooses (ἐξελέξαντο, *exelexanto*) follows. This is a common use of this verb (Johnson 1992: 107; Luke 6:13; Num. 16:7; Deut. 4:37; 7:7; 10:15; 12:5; Pss. 32:12 [33:12 Eng.]; 77:68 [78:68 Eng.]).

Stephen leads the list and is described as full of faith and the Spirit. The descriptive term πλήρης (*plērēs*) is an indeclinable nominative that serves as an adjective (full of; Bruce 1990: 183; of Barnabas, Acts 11:24). The remark sets the stage for the description of his wider ministry in 6:8–8:1. Philip is next. He will be a key character in Acts 8 (also 21:8). Marshall (1980: 126) distinguishes this Philip from Philip the apostle in 8:5, but the lack of any effort by Luke to distinguish the two makes a distinction unlikely. Polhill (1992: 181n181) argues against a distinction within Acts. The activity of Stephen and Philip probably exemplifies the character of the group as a whole.

We know little about the rest of the group: Prochorus, Nicanor, Timon, Parmenas, and Nicolaus. All the names are Greek (Barrett 1994: 314–15), underscoring the potential and likely Hellenist roots of the group, although by this time such names were common among Jews of Judea (Le Cornu and Shulam 2003: 315–16). Most of the names in question here are not commonly used in Judaism. That one is identified as a proselyte suggests that the others were born Jewish. These men stand alongside a large Hebrew Christian presence in the community, something James's later leadership points to demographically, as does the preference for Hebrew Christian widows in this scene. The fact that so many Hellenist leaders exist points to the early church's multiethnic and multicultural makeup. The adopted solution is also revealing at another level. The disciples do not fragment along ethnic lines or suggest that separate communities be formed along ethnic lines. Rather, they are committed to working together. They may well have recognized that there is strength in numbers, and a powerful testimony is created when different groups can be seen as working together in a world often divided along ethnic lines.

Since the problem involves Hellenists, Hellenists are given responsibility to solve it. Nicolaus is described as a proselyte (προσήλυτον, *prosēlyton*) from Antioch, which means that he joined the new community as a Gentile who had already come to Judaism (Matt. 23:15; Acts 2:9–11; 6:5; 13:43). So Cornelius, technically speaking, is not the first Gentile to become a Christian. Rather, the story of Acts 10 is apparently an initial case of someone coming directly to the new community without having completely connected to Judaism first (but for a discussion of whether "God-fearer" equals "proselyte," see Williams 1990: 122). The story in Acts 10 may well have been told because of Peter's involvement, which led to the recognition of the need to initiate evangelism among Gentiles. Antioch had possessed a large Jewish population since the third century

BC (Josephus, *J.W.* 7.3.3 §§43–45; on the roots of the names, Schneider 1980: 428). The population of Alexandria, Egypt, was at least a third Jewish, according to Philo (*Flaccus* 8 §55). Jewish people from this and other locales may well have returned to the land still influenced by the experience in exile. Luke often points out those who were either God-fearers, such as Cornelius in Acts 10, or proselytes, such as Nicolaus.

Tradition has Prochorus serving as an attendant to John the evangelist and as bishop of Nicomedia. Bruce (1988a: 121) notes his association with the fifth-century Acts of John, and Nicolaus is associated with the Nicolatians of Rev. 2:6, 15 by Irenaeus (*Ag. Her.* 1.23.1). The Nicolatians challenged some of the rulings of the Jerusalem Council. Bruce notes, however, that whether this is the same person is not certain, and Witherington (1998: 250) rejects the connection, noting how far the cities of Ephesus and Pergamum, the key locales of Revelation, are from Syrian Antioch. The unusual nature of the names and the unknown character of the individuals' later work speak to the authenticity of this list of seven and point to roots in tradition.

Antioch will also be an important locale, as Acts 11:19–26 shows. It will be the center for Paul's evangelistic activity (11:19–20, 22, 25–27; 13:1, 14; 14:19, 21–22, 24–26; 15:22–23, 30, 35; 18:20–22). So this passage builds a bridge not only to Acts 8–9 but also to Acts 11 and following.

6:6   These seven stand before the apostles and are commissioned with prayer (1:24–25) and the laying on of hands, which indicates a recognition of God's call for this task.[4] The apostles perform this rite on behalf of the community to underscore God's choice of these men for this task. The laying on of hands is strictly symbolic; formal ordination into ministry is a later practice of the church. These leaders already have the Spirit before hands are laid upon them. This is probably not the origin of the office of deacon. This title is never used of the group, nor is there evidence that these men do all the things that deacons did. However, the principle of designating a set of laborers for this kind of task is probably what led to the creation of this office at a later time.

In sum, this unit shows the community using its own people to solve its own problems. The community hears the complaint, owns up to the problem, allows those closest to it to solve it, delegates the authority to get it done, and then goes to work. The issue is not denied or papered over but confronted directly as a community concern. As the church

---

4. For the laying on of hands, see Acts 13:1–3; Num. 27:18 (of Moses for Joshua); Deut. 34:9 (Moses lays hands on Joshua, who is said to be full of wisdom or "the spirit of understanding" in the LXX); *m. Sanh.* 4.4 (of disciples being ordained for membership in the Sanhedrin); 1 Tim. 4:14; other functions in the OT for the laying on of hands: Gen. 48:13–20 (blessing); Lev. 1:4; 3:2; 4:4; 16:21 (with animals, to picture an association of sin); Num. 8:10 (of priests); in Acts the laying on of hands is tied to baptism in 8:17, 19; 19:6; healings in 9:12, 17; 28:8; Radl, *EDNT* 3:463. On the laying on of hands in the earliest centuries of the church, see Pelikan 2005: 94–96.

was growing, it was encountering natural growing pains. It was adapting to the needs the new situation produced (Gaventa 2003: 116). The needs of the community were being met, as God was already raising up others who were qualified to meet the new challenges. So unity was maintained, and the church did not lose sight of its mission to witness, as the bridge to what follows in Acts 6–8 shows (Talbert 1997: 75). The church continued to affirm and show its multiethnic, multicultural character, one of the potentially powerful elements of its testimony to community (Fernando 1998: 230). Working in the community did not lead to a failure to engage those outside with the gospel, as the Seven both served the church and preached to those outside. The scene also makes clear that to solve the community's problems, ministry must extend beyond those who are called primarily to preach (Stott 1990: 122–23). The solution of the community showed that in the midst of growth, new problems sometimes require fresh structures to cope with them (Fernando 1998: 231–32). The building up of community in unity need not lead to a neglect of evangelism. These are the church's two basic missions. In fact, edification and instruction should support evangelism and lead into it.

Additional Note

6:3. At the start of the verse, D adds a question about what is going on (τί οὖν ἐστιν, ἀδελφοί). The reading is not well attested and shows D's consistent tendency to expand the text. Codex B also has a unique reading, "let us choose," but it is too weakly attested. This variant is an effort to have the Twelve included in the selection process, which is unnecessary in light of the apostolic role in verse 6.

I. Summary of the Jerusalem Community (6:7)

This unit concludes the second major section of Acts and consists of only one verse. In Luke's upbeat style, he notes the growth of the word and the community as he reports that even many priests are coming to believe.

Exegesis and Exposition

⁷And the word of God was growing, and the number of disciples in Jerusalem was multiplying greatly; even a great crowd of ⌜priests⌝ was being obedient to the faith.

6:7   This verse summarizes the new community's growth in Jerusalem with three imperfect verbs to show faith's vibrant and living quality.

First, the word "was growing" (ηὔξανεν, ēuxanen; Acts 6:7; 7:17–18 [the Israelites in Egypt]; 12:24 [the word]; 19:20 [the word]; four of twenty-one NT occurrences are in Acts) as the message is spreading successfully. The word is described in personified terms here, as the word directs its own growth. This depicts God sending forth the word through the apostolic preaching, with the word much like seed growing into fruit or a harvest (Kodell 1974; Larkin 1995: 102; Acts 4:4; 10:36; 11:1; 13:26, 49; 14:3; 16:32; Luke 8:11). There are OT roots about obedience and fruitfulness in this phrasing as well (Lev. 26:9; Jer. 3:16; 23:3; perhaps esp. Isa. 2:3; Johnson 1992: 107).

Second, disciples also "were being multiplied" (ἐπληθύνετο, eplēthyneto; Acts 6:1, 7; 7:17–18; 9:31 [also a summary]; 12:24 [also a summary], five of twelve NT occurrences; OT: Gen. 7:18; 17:2, 20; 34:12; 47:27; Deut. 6:3; Ps. 106:38 [107:38 Eng.]; Schneider 1980: 429n76) greatly as many came to faith. The passive verb probably points to divine work. God is causing the growth.

Third, even a great crowd of priests "was being obedient" (ὑπήκουον, hypēkouon; only two of twenty-one NT occurrences are in Acts; see 12:13) to the faith. This is one of only two direct references to Jewish priests with the term ἱερεύς (hiereus) in Acts (4:1; 14:13 refers to pagan priests). The size of the priesthood for this period has been estimated to be as many as eighteen thousand: eight thousand priests and ten thousand Levites (Jeremias 1969a: 204; Marshall 1980: 128). Josephus (Ag. Ap. 2.8 §108) speaks of twenty thousand, but his numbers are usually high.

Others point to a number as low as two thousand (Le Cornu and Shulam 2003: 322). Johnson (1992: 107) speaks of "many thousands," a vague description but likely the best we can do. They labored in a trade most of the year, except for two weeks when they officiated at the temple. In their hometowns, they could declare lepers cleansed and work in local courts. So a large number from within the priesthood would represent a significant additional number of disciples for the new community. Such conversions would be a cause of alarm for the Jewish leaders. It will not be the first or last time for such concern (Mark 14:57–58; Acts 21:28).

This opening discussion on the Jerusalem community ends with the statement that it is growing, even with many priests coming to obey with faith. Obedience to the faith is yet another way to describe a believer in Acts. This characterization highlights faith's living, responsive, and submissive nature (Rom. 1:5; 10:16). There is a faithful remnant in Israel.

After this summary, Luke shifts his attention to the expansion of the word outside Jerusalem and the persecution that drives that move. He does so after telling the story of the healthy state of affairs in Jerusalem in Acts 1:1–6:7. Growth will lead to concern from opponents and generate increasing persecution from them, as the next section of Acts shows. Success in preaching the gospel may lead not only to popularity, acceptance, and growth. Success can also mean acceptance by some and persecution by others. This means that measuring success and results may need to take into account both those who enter the church and those who react against it, as was the case in Jerusalem.

This is the first of six such summaries in Acts (6:7; 9:31; 12:24; 16:5; 19:20; 28:31; Bruce 1990: 185). I have used these summaries to structure our reading of Acts.

Additional Note

6:7. Codex ℵ and some of the Syriac MSS read "Jews" instead of "priests" here, but it is too poorly attested to be original.

III. Persecution in Jerusalem Moves the Message to Judea and Samaria as a New Witness Emerges (6:8–9:31)

This section shows the church thriving under pressure. Even though some of its leaders give their lives for their testimony (Stephen in Acts 6:8–8:1a) and the church is scattered by Jewish leaders such as Saul (8:1b–4), the word still grows. Philip enjoys a largely successful effort in Samaria, although some will seek to abuse the Spirit's power, treating it as something that can be bought (8:5–25). Philip also has a successful, divinely directed encounter with a eunuch from Ethiopia (8:26–40). Here is an indication that the gospel will spread far beyond the land of Israel. Some efforts involve a region; others work with individuals. Finally, God works to turn a persecutor into a preacher of the gospel as Saul is converted by a vision of the Lord, preaches in Damascus, and is received, after much concern, in Jerusalem (9:1–30). Once again a one-verse summary closes the unit (9:31).

A. The Arrest, Speech, and Martyrdom of Stephen (6:8–8:1a)

The Stephen cycle in Acts comes in three parts. The greatest part by far recounts the speech leading to Stephen's lynching and death. Stephen's witnessing leads to his arrest (6:8–15). A question by the high priest prompts Stephen to review Israel's entire history, a story full of disobedience and hardheartedness against the Spirit's testimony (7:1–53). The speech so angers the authorities that they take matters into their own hands and stone Stephen on the spot for what they perceive to be hostility toward Israel and the temple. However, in death Stephen sees the heavenly welcome of the Son of Man and calls for forgiveness, even as a persecutor named Saul watches all that takes place (7:54–8:1a). The trial also ends a cycle of three trials that appear in the early section of Acts. These trials increase in intensity from warning (4:21) to beating (5:40) to death (7:60; Polhill 1992: 183). With Stephen's martyrdom, many people in Jerusalem finally react by rejecting the message, and Jewish Hellenists join the Jewish leadership in hostile opposition to the new community.

1. The Arrest of Stephen (6:8–15)

The first part of the Stephen cycle summarizes the impact of his ministry, which leads to his arrest. The success of Stephen's work (6:8) leads some in a Hellenist synagogue to rise up against him (6:9). Their failure to overcome him in argument leads them to incite others by charging him with blaspheming Moses and God (6:9–11). Stephen's arrest follows as charges emerge that Jesus will destroy the temple and cancel the law (6:12–14). The three topics, then, are blasphemy, temple in association with law, and Jesus (Fitzmyer 1998: 355). Luke calls the charges false to underscore the injustice of what is about to take place. Nevertheless, as the speech makes clear, Stephen holds views about the temple that, although rooted in the OT, alarm those with authority over this important religious center. Schnabel (2004: 660–67) discusses how Hellenists such as Stephen see the eschatological implications of Jesus's coming for the temple and the law more clearly than many other believers do initially. Jesus also said similar things about the temple (John 2:19; 4:21–24; Mark 13:2; 11:15–19). The temple could be a locale of judgment for unfaithfulness so that loyalty to its sacred space should not replace dedication to God or an awareness that God's presence spread far beyond a single locale. Such statements could have been raised as the basis for the charges against Stephen, even though the leadership misunderstands them. If there are roots to Stephen's view in Hebrew Scripture, as Stephen will argue in Acts 7, then Stephen should not be on trial. In the midst of all this hostility, Stephen bears the face of an angel (6:15). He is an example of Christian self-understanding, preaching, and boldness in the face of opposition. Stephen also is a representative Christian rising up from the ranks. He is a figure whom Luke's readers can respect and emulate, even as Stephen emulates Jesus. Witherington (1998: 253) has a list of ten parallels between Stephen and Jesus. Among them are the following: both appear in a trial-like setting, suffer the testimony of false witnesses, mention the temple's destruction, speak of the temple made with hands, are charged with blasphemy, are asked by the high priest to speak, commit their spirits to God, and ask God to forgive those killing them. The scene prepares for the high priest's query, which leads to a long speech summarizing a history of disobedience in Israel, the topic of the cycle's next section.

Luke appears to be working here with sources whose exact nature is debated and hard to determine (Fitzmyer 1998: 355; Pesch 1986a:

235–36). The account is an arrest narrative, describing the cause of a subsequent trial. The speech that follows allows Luke to begin to articulate the difference between Judaism, as seen in the Jerusalem leadership, and the new community. The basic issue is who is obeying God when it comes to law, temple, and promise. The speech's importance is underscored by two facts: (1) it is by far the longest speech in Acts, and (2) it appears at a point where the focus of the narrative is turning to issues outside Jerusalem.

Exegesis and Exposition

⁸And Stephen, full of ⌐grace¬ and power, was performing great wonders and signs among the people. ⁹Then some of those out of the synagogue of the Freedmen (as it was called), and of the Cyrenians, and of the Alexandrians, and of those of Cilicia and Asia arose, disputing with Stephen, ¹⁰⌐but they were not able to oppose the wisdom and Spirit with which he spoke¬. ¹¹Then they instigated men into saying, "We have heard him speaking blasphemy against Moses and God." ¹²And they stirred up the people and leaders and scribes, and they came upon him, seized him, and brought him to the council. ¹³They set forward false witnesses who said, "This man does not cease speaking words against ⌐the¬ holy place and law; ¹⁴for we have heard him saying, "Jesus, the Nazorean, this one shall destroy this place and shall alter the customs that Moses passed on to us." ¹⁵And all who were seated in the council, gazing intently at him, saw his face like the face of an angel.

Stephen's ministry does not include merely serving tables (6:1–6). He also is effective in preaching and healing, acts that parallel the work of the apostles. He "was performing" (ἐποίει, *epoiei* [imperfect verb again]) great wonders and signs (τέρατα καὶ σημεῖα μεγάλα, *terata kai sēmeia megala*), just as they had (on wonders and signs in Acts: 2:22–24 [Jesus], 43 [apostles]; 7:36 [Moses]; conceptually, 4:30; 5:12). The full phrase describing these wonders as great appears only here in Acts (John 14:12). What empowers this work by Stephen is divine enablement and the character he possesses, described by Luke as being full of grace and power (πλήρης χάριτος καὶ δυνάμεως, *plērēs charitos kai dynameōs*). In Acts, this phrase is used only with reference to Stephen, although the idea of possessing grace or power appears elsewhere (only "grace" in Luke 4:22 [Jesus]; Acts 2:47 [apostles]; 4:33 [the community]; 7:10 [Moses]; 7:46 [David]; Pesch 1986a: 236; only "power" in Acts 4:7, 33). Earlier he was described as full of the Spirit and wisdom (6:3) and full of faith and the Holy Spirit (6:5). The association of Spirit and power as enablement goes back to Luke 24:49 and Acts 1:8. The grace in view here is probably not just a "charm" that Stephen exhibits; more important, he ministers through the enabling power of grace, as the emphasis on his miracles

6:8

here and his speech later show. Stephen is equipped for the unique things God has called him to do. Here is a Hellenist with the enablement that apostles have displayed. God will work through the various ethnic wings of his church. Following the pattern of church activity in Acts, Stephen's work is one of both word and deed.

6:9–10   A movement and reaction against Stephen arise among the Hellenistic Jews. Some of them come from a synagogue composed of freedmen, slaves who now are independent.[1] These slaves may have descended from Jews imprisoned by Pompey in 63 BC and later freed. The synagogue is a place of instruction, worship, prayer, and reading of Scripture. In the Mishnah, tractate *Megillah* describes various rules for reading Scripture in Jewish communities. In many locales, the synagogue became the center of community life. This is the only mention of Alexandrians in the NT apart from a reference to Apollos's hometown (18:24). Others come from a variety of regions outside Israel, unless one assumes that each region had its own synagogue (see note 2 and the discussion below).

The opponents who settled and worshiped in Jerusalem came from a wide range of locations. It is discussed whether this is one synagogue with a variety of nationalities or a group that emerges from several synagogues. Most likely either one or two synagogues are meant.[2] Cyrenians came from northern Africa, and the Alexandrians came from Egypt (Cyrenians: six times in the NT: Matt. 27:32; Mark 15:21; Luke 23:26; Acts 6:9–10; 11:20; 13:1; Alexandrians: Acts 6:9–10; 18:24). Cilicians came from the northeastern Mediterranean and areas such as Tarsus (eight times in the NT: Acts 6:9–10; 15:22–23, 41; 21:39; 22:2–5; 23:34–35; 27:4–5; Gal. 1:21–22). Might Paul have participated? Of those mentioned here, Asia is by far the most discussed region in the NT (eighteen times: Acts 2:9–11;

1. Ethnically, these could include Gentile slaves who had converted to Judaism plus other Jewish free persons. On synagogues in the first century, see Witherington 1998: 253–57, who notes evidence of such synagogues from Masada, Herodium, and Gamala. The Theodotus Inscription of Jerusalem, found in 1913–14, speaks of the reading of the Law and the teaching of the commandments there and of providing accommodations for pilgrims (Strathmann, *TDNT* 4:265–66). Levine (2005: 57–58) cites and discusses the inscription. Some (Kee 1990) have expressed skepticism about the Gospels' testimony to synagogues in Galilee, but the Jewish scholar Levine (2005: 47–48) argues that these sources should not be challenged on this point, since it is unlikely that this detail would have been invented, and there would be no reason to do so if such synagogues did not exist.

2. Bruce 1988a: 124 opts for one synagogue, as does Barrett 1994: 323–25, but Pesch 1986a: 236–37 suggests two, as do Haenchen 1987: 271 and Marshall 1980: 129, with one composed of the freedmen and the Africans and the other of those from Asia Minor and Asia. According to this view, the second occurrence of τῶν (*tōn*) implies a reference to a second synagogue; Jervell 1998: 225. Still others count three or five synagogues (so Larkin 1995: 102–3; Levine 2005: 56), which is less likely, for then one has to assume that each ethnic group had its own synagogue or that the overall community was quite extensive. There is enough unity in the opposition here to suggest that the reaction comes from a lesser number of communities. Schrage, *TDNT* 7:837, notes that it is the community, not the building, that is stressed in the mention of synagogues.

6:9–10; 16:6–8; 19:10, 22, 24–27 [2x]; 20:16, 18–21; 21:27–28; 24:17–19; 27:2; Rom. 16:5; 1 Cor. 16:19; 2 Cor. 1:8–11; 2 Tim. 1:15; 1 Pet. 1:1–2; Rev. 1:4–5). These Jews stand up in opposition to dispute with Stephen. Asian Jews will also form strong opposition to Paul later in Acts.

The verb for "disputing" (συζητέω, *syzēteō*) is also used to describe how Jesus was challenged (Mark 1:27; 8:11; 9:10, 14, 16; 12:28; Luke 22:23; 24:15–16; Acts 6:9–10; 9:28–29). The opposition struggles against Stephen's wisdom and enablement by the Spirit (see v. 8), just as Jesus promised (Luke 21:12–15; also Luke 12:11–12). Jesus said that those who stood against the disciples would not be able to oppose (ἀντιστῆναι, *antistēnai*) those such as Stephen. The situation also presents another answer to the prayer for boldness in 4:29–30. The verb ἴσχυον (*ischyon*, they were . . . [not] able) is imperfect. This trend of being unable to oppose the message will continue in Acts (13:8, of the attempt of Elymas against Paul, and numerous other failed efforts to thwart the word). The idea of resistance or opposition appears in several NT texts (Matt. 5:39–41; Luke 21:14–15; Rom. 9:19; 13:2; Gal. 2:11; Eph. 6:13; 2 Tim. 3:8; 4:14–15; James 4:7–8; 1 Pet. 5:8–9). This opposition is significant because of the range of its geographic scope. The details show that it is not Stephen's Judaism that leads to his controversial stance, that is, Stephen is not opposed because he possesses a Hellenistic Jewish perspective. It is his embrace of Christianity that meets with rejection. It leads him to be critical of the Jewish practices of many around him.

These Hellenists instigate (ὑπέβαλον, *hypebalon*) the people against **6:11** Stephen. This is the only use of this verb in the NT. It often means causing someone to do something by hint or suggestion (BDAG 1036; Barrett 1994: 325; Mart. Pol. 17.2; Josephus, *J.W.* 5.10.4 §439 [of plots made to suborn a false claim]; conceptually, Luke 20:20). The charges are that Stephen has spoken blasphemy, words of insult, against Moses and God (Josephus, *Ant.* 20.9.1 §200, notes Jewish charges of blasphemy against James, the Lord's brother in ca. AD 62; also *J.W.* 2.8.9 §145, where blasphemy against Moses is said to be a capital crime; see Exod. 22:27; Lev. 24:11–16). The order of the blasphemy charge is unusual, with Moses preceding God, but it may point to how important the law is, in their view. The term "blasphemy" is being used in a broader sense than in *m. Sanh.* 7.5, where one has to speak God's name in order to blaspheme (Bock 1998a: 30–112 surveys blasphemy in Judaism). Acts 6:13 gives the topics as the temple and the law.

The elements of the charge appear to contain a serious misrepresentation of Jesus's prediction about the temple as recorded in Luke 21 or Jesus's warnings about the temple in John 2:19–21. Stephen may have suggested that the temple is destined for judgment, as Acts 7 also implies. But the accusers make far more of this than Stephen might be claiming; in 6:14 the Jews argue that Stephen is teaching that Jesus would destroy the temple, charges Luke labels as false in verse 13. Witherington (1998: 258–59) challenges the idea of some critics that the charges might be true or be true to a degree. But his case may be slightly overargued (see vv. 13–14). Many commentators argue that something Stephen is teaching appears to have triggered a hostile reaction and an opportunity to examine him for claiming things the apostles' preaching has not.[3] To act against the holy site or even speak negatively about its potential demise would be seen by zealous Jews as acting against both the law of Moses and God. It also would be a challenge to the leadership, as, according to their theological view, the temple would only be subject to judgment if the nation were in serious sin. Bruce (1988a: 126) suggests that the leadership's economic interests from the temple's activity also might be at work. To suggest one idea about the temple means to assert the other about the leadership theologically. For religious zealots or those in political power, this would be an insult.

6:12   The Hellenists stir up the people and the leaders, namely, the elders and scribes. This is the first time in Acts that people rise up against Christians and not just challenge the Christian leadership. These Hellenists are strongly pro-Jewish, having left the lands of their births to come back to Israel, follow the law, and be in the locale of the temple. They would be especially loyal to the law (Polhill 1992: 185 speaks of religious zealots). The term συγκινέω (synkineō) means arousing or exciting someone emotionally. Idiomatically, it would mean to get them "worked up" (BAGD 773; BDAG 952). This is the only occurrence of the term in the NT, and it does not appear in the LXX.

The people and the leaders "seized" (συνήρπασαν, synērpasan) him and brought him to the council for examination. This term appears four times in the NT and means being pulled or directed against one's will (Luke 8:29 [of a spirit seizing a person]; Acts 6:12–14; 19:29 [dragging two men in persecution]; 27:14–15 [a ship caught by the wind]). So Stephen now finds himself before the Sanhedrin as the Twelve were in 5:27 and as Jesus was in Luke 22:47–71, facing similar charges (Mark 14:57–58; Matt. 26:60–61).[4] A more formal examination is now possible. The passage reflects an air of both popular justice and formal examination, which some critics play against each other (so Schille 1980: 175–76). Here is a tension-filled scene in which both are present. The prospect of blasphemy would have those who are most zealous quite worked up, no matter how formal the process of questioning might be.

6:13–14   Luke underscores the injustice of the examination by describing the witnesses as "false" (ψευδεῖς, pseudeis; the only use of the term in Acts;

3. See Bruce 1988a: 126 and Marshall 1980: 130–31, who challenges Haenchen's more skeptical reading (1987: 274) of this scene with his claim that the scene is completely fabricated.
4. The fact that the charges parallel those of Jesus in Mark and Matthew and not Luke may suggest that Luke has used traditional material here.

Rev. 2:2; 21:8). Bearing false witness is prohibited in the OT (Exod. 20:16; Deut. 19:16–18), so Luke's charge of irregularity in the examination is serious. Such is a common act of the wicked according to the OT (Pss. 27:12; 35:11; Prov. 14:5; 24:28; Haenchen 1987: 271; Barrett 1994: 327). For Luke, it may be that to speak against God's spokesman is automatically to be a false witness. The complainers demean Stephen by referring to him as "this man" (ὁ ἄνθρωπος οὗτος, *ho anthrōpos houtos*; Luke 23:2, 4, 18 refers to Jesus as "this one" or "this man"). This charge is similar to the situation with Jesus in Mark 14:57, where some are said to bear false witness and where the verbal term ψευδομαρτυρέω (*pseudomartyreō*) is used, one of five NT occurrences of that verb (Matt. 19:18–19; Mark 10:19; 14:56–57 [2x]; Luke 18:20). Stephen has supposedly spoken against the temple and the law. These are serious charges, as Josephus in *Ant.* 10.11.2–3 §§233–43 describes Baltasar's (Belshazzar's) use of temple utensils at a pagan party (Dan. 5:2–4) as being blasphemous of things associated with God's presence (also on the law, *J.W.* 2.8.9 §§145–49 [esp. the Sabbath]; *Ant.* 18.2.2 §230 [of the temple]).

Stephen's speech in Acts 7, although citing the OT, will convey the idea that the temple should not be overestimated in its importance. Thus there may be an element of truth in the charge (see v. 11 above), but those making the accusation are pushing it to the limit.

The law is a major concern for Luke in Acts. This is the first of seventeen references to "law" in Acts (6:12–14; 7:52–53; 13:15, 38–39; 15:5; 18:12–15 [2x]; 21:20–21, 24, 27–28; 22:2–5, 12–13; 23:3, 28–29; 24:14–15; 25:7–8; 28:23). In many ways, the disciples respect the law by attending temple and showing concern, at least in Jerusalem, for how the law is observed. How the law is to be treated is a major issue in Acts 11 regarding the question of Gentile belief, in Acts 15 at the Jerusalem Council, and in Acts 21 with the visit of Paul to Jerusalem and James. Paul will say he is on trial for believing in the law and resurrection (24:14–15), a remark that highlights the promise aspects of the law. The claims made against Stephen parallel claims of disrespect about the temple made against Paul. In 25:7–8 Paul will reject the idea that he has acted against the temple. It appears as well that Peter's vision in Acts 10 and the resolution of the law debate in Acts 15 indicate that the way the new community handles the law has changed. The church will argue, however, that this new way is not against the law but represents a realization of it.

The explanation of the charge follows (γάρ, *gar*, for). Here the false nature of the charge becomes more evident. There is an effort to discredit both Stephen and Jesus by noting that Stephen affirmed that Jesus would destroy the temple and change the customs of the law. This would be seen as an attack on the holy place, the law, and God's presence. The temple was frequently a topic of dispute from the time of the northern kingdom to Samaria to Qumran (Johnson 1990: 109). Le

Cornu and Shulam (2003: 331–34) argue in the end that the reaction is against the challenge to the sages' authority, the testimony that was seen to come from Moses to the sages. Mishnah *'Abot* 1.1 speaks of building a fence around Torah as one is faithful to the law that came from Moses to the men of the Great Synagogue. The north and Samaria instituted their own temple locales, and Qumran came to see the current temple as corrupt and lacking validity. For a faith that views the temple as the central location of the activities of the faith, a claim such as Stephen's would be a shock. For example, 7:48 would be a difficult declaration for some Jews. Nowhere does Jesus declare that he will destroy the temple, only that if the temple is destroyed, he will raise it up in three days, which, according to John 2:19–21, is a reference not to the real temple but his body. Jesus's other remarks about the temple concerned God's judgment of the temple as part of Jerusalem being overrun by outsiders. The charge that customs from Moses or of the Jews are not followed by the new community is repeated by opponents throughout Acts (6:12–14; 15:1; 16:19–21; 21:20–21; esp. 21:28 and the charge against Paul) but is denied by Paul at the very end of Acts (28:17–18). Thus Luke introduces an important narrative theme here. He mentions Moses nineteen times in Acts, but almost half of the references appear in Stephen's overview of Israel's history (3:22; 6:11, 14; 7:20, 22, 29, 31, 32, 35, 37, 40, 44; 13:38; 15:1, 5, 21; 21:21; 26:22; 28:23). The phrase "handing down" refers to tradition being passed on (Acts 16:4; 1 Cor. 15:3), and "customs" (τὰ ἔθη, *ta ethē*) refers to Jewish practices (see esp. Luke 23:2 [conceptual, of Jesus]; Josephus, *J.W.* 7.10.2 §424; 2 Macc. 11:25; 4 Macc. 18:5).

6:15 Stephen stands before the council. They are looking intently (ἀτενίσαντες, *atenisantes*) at him. The verb is used of how the Eleven observe Jesus as he ascends into heaven, how Stephen looks into heaven at the end of his speech, how Peter gives careful consideration to the vision he receives, and how Paul looks at the council when testifying (Acts 1:10–11; 3:4, 12; 6:15; 7:55–56; 10:4; 11:6; 13:9–10; 14:9–10; 23:1).

The description of Stephen as having the face of an angel is unique in the NT. It suggests that Stephen has the appearance of one inspired by and in touch with God, reflecting a touch of God's glory (Exod. 34:29–35; Luke 9:29). Other similar descriptions occur elsewhere.[5] It is one of Luke's ways of saying that Stephen is innocent.

In sum, this unit shows the continued escalation of opposition to Christians. Now people on the street oppose the message. Stephen is arrested, charged with blaspheming God as well as speaking against Moses, the law, and the temple. It is hard to imagine a more devastat-

---

5. See Acts of Paul 3 (Paul had a face "like an angel"; Bruce 1990: 189); Dan. 3:92 LXX (3:25 Eng.; seeing an angel with the three young men in the furnace); Esth. 5:2a LXX (= Add. Esth. 15:13 Eng.; where Esther is received by the king); and Mart. Pol. 12.1 (Polycarp filled with grace at his martyrdom).

ing set of Jewish charges against someone. The charges prepare us for Stephen's speech. In Acts, the issue for Luke is who contends for God's truth and gives responsible teaching to the nation. Stephen is portrayed as calm in the midst of the charges, composed, and looking like an angel. The arrest provides the setting for the longest speech in Acts, which surveys Israel's history of poor response to God's revelation and presents a fresh view of the temple. The speech carries forward the debate about religious faith and Israel's God.

Additional Notes

6:8. Byz reads "faith" for "grace," but the reading is not the best attested.

6:10. Two longer renderings about the opposition appear in D and E. Codex D speaks of Stephen's boldness, and E speaks of his rebuking them. Neither reading is well attested or original.

6:13. The addition of τούτου (*toutou*, this) is disputed textually. The MSS B, C, 33, 36, and 323 include it, but $\mathfrak{P}^{74}$, ℵ, A, D, E, Ψ, and Byz lack it. External evidence is against its being original.

2. The Speech of Stephen (7:1–53)

This speech is the longest in Acts and is crucial to the book's development. Two themes are obvious: (1) God has raised up a series of leaders whom the Jews failed to recognize; and (2) they also responded inappropriately to God's presence as reflected in the tabernacle and temple, since they fell into idolatry. All of this comes in defense of the law, Moses, and an appropriate understanding of the temple (*pace* Witherington 1998: 258, who argues that Stephen is on the offensive, not the defensive, in this speech; Stephen is on the offensive but is also answering charges in the process). The temple was never designed to confine God but was intended to be a place of worship to him alone as the one true God. In defending himself and showing how the law truly works, Stephen shows the inadequacy of the Jewish understanding of Christians, God's will, the temple, the law, and God. The speech is one of Acts' two historical overviews of Israel; Paul will also review history as it relates to messianic promise in Acts 13:16–33. Another speech challenging idolatry, this time by Paul to those in Athens, appears in 17:24–31. The text is a historical summary (cf. Deut. 6:20–24; 26:5–9; Josh. 24:2–13; Neh. 9:6–31; Pss. 78; 105; 106; 136; Jdt. 5:6–18; 1 Macc. 2:52–60; Wis. 10; Sir. 44–50; 3 Macc. 2:2–12; 2 Esd. [4 Ezra] 3:4–36; 14:29–31; CD 2.14–3.9; Weiser 1981: 180).

The situation is narratively portrayed as quite dangerous. Those opposed to Stephen have persuaded others to make the charge, incited the people, and brought forward false witnesses (Gaventa 2003: 118). Every effort has been made to put a stop to the preaching. But Stephen faces his opponents directly and uses a most potent weapon in response, the Scripture. Unlike other speeches so far in Acts, this one does not directly preach Christ but works through Israel's history to show why the nation stands in terrible need of God's fresh work. Three audiences are addressed, two in the story and one outside: the opponents, the Jewish leadership, and those reading or hearing the account in Acts (Gaventa 2003: 120–21).

The outline of topics moves in clear steps: a call to hear (vv. 2a), Abraham (vv. 2b–8), Joseph (vv. 9–16), God and Moses (vv. 17–43), tabernacle and temple (vv. 44–50), and application—a history of rejecting the Spirit (vv. 51–53). It is likely that Stephen does not finish his speech. Although Stephen appears to set up a comparison between Moses and Jesus, he never reaches a conclusion or fills out the comparison. The remarks about the temple and disobedience are too much. A lynching follows. Stephen is stoned to death for what his accusers regard as blasphemy. He is put to death, with Saul present as a witness. Jesus stands to receive Stephen; thus Luke makes clear that Stephen speaks for God and is vindicated by him.

The rhetorical outline is also valuable to consider: *exordium* (call to hear; v. 2a), *narratio* (preparatory discourse; vv. 2b–34), *propositio* (proposition; v. 35), *argumentatio* (argument-application; vv. 36–50), and *peroratio* (polemical application; vv. 51–53). The major theme is that Israel has rejected its messengers (as it did Moses) and its proper worship (as it did with the tabernacle and temple). The speech is built around LXX traditions, which fits Stephen's Hellenist background. The critique is rooted in a Deuteronomistic perspective on the nation (2 Kings 17:7–20; Neh. 9:26; 2 Chron. 36:14–16; Witherington 1998: 260–62). God also transcends temples, as Isa. 66:1–2 also argued. There is not as harsh a critique of the temple here as some critics claim, but even the form of Stephen's critique would strike Jewish ears as harsh and controversial. Much in the speech parallels how ancient Greek and Israelite cultures reviewed where they fit in the world; they often recounted their history in this manner (Josephus, *J.W.* 5.9.4 §§376–419; Herodotus, *Hist.* 9.26–27). A full exploration of the speech can be found in Kilgallen (1976).

The debate over sources for this speech is voluminous and complex (Weiser 1981: 180–82; Steck 1967: 266–69; Holtz 1968: 87–109; Wilckens 1974: 208–21). The spectrum of views runs from Luke using a source for the entire speech to Luke creating the speech, with views in between holding that Luke strengthened the polemic against Judaism and or added scriptural references. Schneider (1980: 447), who opts for Luke working over existing tradition, draws on the work of Dibelius (1956: 167–70) and Steck. Schneider (1980: 449–52) also rejects the idea that Samaritan theology has influenced the speech. Dibelius argues that polemic and a real reply do not show up until verse 35, that there is no purpose to the speech until that point, and that the speech does not address the possibility of martyrdom. Dibelius concludes that Luke has inserted a speech from tradition into this scene between 6:15 and 7:55 and has added the more polemical elements.

This reading, however, begs the question whether the reply is not set up by all the preceding history, as the consistent rejection of God's direction and promise is unfolded inductively in the speech. It also overstates the "martyrdom" setting, since it is not clear that Stephen's life is in imminent danger until the crowd reacts. The distinction between martyr scene and historical speech is overplayed. The trial scene becomes a martyr scene as a result of the crowd's overemotional reaction at the end. Thus the speech is not as disconnected as Dibelius suggests. Steck's work was designed to challenge Dibelius by noting the Deuteronomistic critique that belongs to the speech's historical section. Steck sees the hand and perspective of Hellenistic Judaism in this form, one that Hellenist Christians would accept. This is a helpful move but still represents an overreading of opposition to the land and temple in the speech, as early portions of the speech do mention the land in traditional ways (7:3–8) and latter portions declare only that the temple alone cannot contain God (7:48–50). There is nothing here that would be unlikely for someone such as Stephen to say, even if one might see the hand of Luke in streamlining the argument (Jervell 1998: 249–50). Barrett (1994: 335–36) argues that the speech is not as explicitly Christian as it would be if Luke had composed it and that the theology expressed is sufficiently distinct from Luke's in emphasis, suggesting another theology at work. He sees Ezek. 20:30–31 as a close parallel.

Barrett (1994: 337) sees three relevant themes in this material: (1) God is at work in Israel's history, where good comes out of evil; (2) Joseph and Moses are rejected, suffer, and yet are vindicated; and (3) God calls for obedience, not just sacrifices. All these themes are very relevant to Stephen's situation. Of all the charges, only the one concerning the temple might have some merit, but only when the temple is seen in a very fixed and exalted light. Qumran shows that the temple, when seen as corrupt, was not beyond being critiqued. Nonetheless, Barrett (1994: 339) rejects a connection to Stephen, preferring a Hellenist Christian circle such as that in which Stephen functioned. In the end, an excessive skepticism appears in Barrett's approach, since the speech seems to come from the very theological context Stephen represents. It seems that something quite dramatic has taken place with Stephen and that he has a chance to address the charges, something that he takes on with such fervor that he is slain. For Luke to misrepresent this likely well-known scene would have undercut his credibility too greatly. Its roots appear to be very historical, despite many critical claims otherwise.

Fitzmyer (1998: 365–68) calls it "an inherited form of Stephen's speech," ultimately composed by Luke but drawing on Hellenist Christian tradition, possibly from Antioch. Fitzmyer also agrees with Dibelius's analysis that it does not really answer the charges, is not the speech of a likely martyr in defense, is inserted into the account, and is put on Stephen's lips. As already noted, however, Stephen does not speak as one anticipating martyrdom; rather, his death overtakes him suddenly, so seeing the need for a martyr to defend himself here is a misunderstanding of the scene. Again, Fitzmyer's reading is excessively skeptical. Such a dramatic scene with a strong, spontaneous reaction is likely the product of something equally dramatic, a speech in which the leadership's position as representing the truth of God is severely challenged (Simon 1953).[1]

Fitzmyer (1998: 368) highlights another point. The speech recounts the early church's first steps in moving away from Judaism. It was precisely such steps that led to such a hostile reaction to Stephen. In being bold and honest about his position, Stephen lost his life. But this observation should not be overdrawn either. Stephen begins the speech declaring the God of glory and highlighting the promise that God made to "our" forefathers. The promises of Israel are also Stephen's promises to enjoy. Stephen presents himself as faithful to Israel and its God. The dispute is over how God's promises are to be read, understood, and appreciated.

Exegesis and Exposition

[1]And the high priest asked, "Are these things so?" [2]So he replied, "Brothers and fathers, give heed to me. The God of glory appeared to our father Abraham while he was in Mesopotamia before he settled in Haran, [3]⌜ ⌝ and said to him, 'Go out from your land and your relatives, and come to the land which I will show you.' [4]Then going out from the land of the Chaldeans, he lived in Haran. And after his father died, God removed him from there into the land in which you are now living, [5]and gave him no inheritance in it, not even a foot's length, but promised to give it as a possession to him and to his seed after him, though he had no child. [6]And God spoke in this way: that his seed would be foreigners in a land belonging to others who would enslave the descendants and ill-treat them for four hundred years. [7]'But I will judge the nation which they serve,' God said, 'and after these things they shall come out and worship me in this place.' [8]And he gave him a covenant of circumcision. And so Abraham was the father of Isaac and circumcised him on the eighth day; and Isaac became the father of Jacob, and Jacob of the twelve patriarchs.

[9]"And the patriarchs, being jealous of Joseph, sold him into Egypt; but God was with him, [10]and rescued him out of all his afflictions, and gave him acceptance and wisdom before Pharaoh, king of Egypt, and made him governor over Egypt and over all his household. [11]Now a famine came over the whole of Egypt and Canaan, and great suffering, and our fathers could find no food. [12]When Jacob heard there was grain in Egypt, he sent forth our fathers the first time. [13]And at the second visit, Joseph made himself known to his brothers, and Joseph's race became clear to Pharaoh. [14]And Joseph sent and called Jacob, his father, and all his relatives, seventy-five souls. [15]And Jacob went down into Egypt. And he and our fathers died, [16]and they were carried back to Shechem and set in

---

1. Polhill 1992: 187–88 notes the additional theme that God's people are a pilgrim people, not tied to one place. Witherington 1998: 265 suggests Saul as a witness of the speech for Luke.

a tomb that Abraham had bought for a sum of silver from the sons of Hamor in Shechem.

[17]"But as the time of the promise that God had granted to Abraham drew near, the people grew and multiplied in Egypt [18]until there arose another king who had not known Joseph. [19]And he schemed against our race and did evil to our fathers, forcing them to expose their infants so that they might not remain alive. [20]At this time, Moses was born, and he was no ordinary child before God. He was brought up for three months in his father's house; [21]and when he was exposed, Pharaoh's daughter carried him off and cared for him as her own son. [22]And Moses was instructed in all the wisdom of the Egyptians, and he was mighty in his words and deeds.

[23]"When he was forty years old, it entered into his heart to visit his brothers, the sons of Israel. [24]And seeing one of them being wronged, he defended the oppressed man and avenged him by striking the Egyptian. [25]He supposed that his countrymen understood that God was giving them deliverance by his hand, but they did not comprehend. [26]And on the following day he appeared to them as they were quarreling, and he wished to reconcile them, saying, 'Men, you are brothers. Why do you treat each other unrighteously?' [27]But the one who was wronging his neighbor thrust him aside, saying, 'Who made you a ruler and judge over us? [28]Do you want to kill me as you killed the Egyptian yesterday?' [29]Because of this retort, Moses fled and became an exile in the land of Midian, where he became the father of two sons.

[30]"Now when forty years had passed, an angel appeared to him in the wilderness of Mount Sinai in a flame of fire in a bush. [31]When Moses saw it, he wondered at the sight, and as he came near to see it, the voice of the Lord came, [32]'I am the God of your fathers, the God of Abraham and Isaac and Jacob.' And Moses became terrified and did not dare to look. [33]And the Lord said to him, 'Loosen the sandals on your feet, for the place where you stand is holy ground. [34]For I have surely seen the ill treatment of my people in Egypt, and their groanings I have heard, and I have come down to lead them out. And ⌜now⌝ go; I send you into Egypt.' [35]This Moses—whom they rejected saying, 'Who made you ruler and judge?'—God sent this one both as ruler and deliverer together by the hand of the angel who appeared to him in the bush. [36]This one led them out, having performed signs and wonders in Egypt and at the Red Sea and in the wilderness for forty years. [37]This is the Moses who said to the sons of Israel, 'God shall raise up for all of you a prophet from among your brothers like me.' [38]This is he who was in the assembly in the wilderness with the angel who spoke to him at Mount Sinai, and with our fathers; and he received living oracles to give ⌜to us⌝. [39]⌜Our fathers⌝ did not want to obey him but thrust him aside, and in their hearts they turned to Egypt, [40]saying to Aaron, 'Make for us gods to go before us; as for this Moses who led us out of the land of Egypt, we do not know what has happened to him.' [41]And they made a calf in those days and offered a sacrifice to the idol and rejoiced in the works of their hands. [42]But

God turned and gave them over to worship the host of heaven, as it is written in the book of the prophets, 'You did not offer to me slain beasts and sacrifices forty years in the wilderness, did you, O house of Israel? ⁴³But you took up the tent of Moloch and the star of ⌜your⌝ god ⌜Rephan⌝, the images which you made to worship. Therefore I will remove you beyond Babylon.'

⁴⁴"The tent of the meeting was with our fathers in the wilderness, even as the one speaking to Moses commanded him to make it according to the pattern he had seen. ⁴⁵And they also brought it with them when they entered with Joshua to dispossess the nations, whom God thrust out before our fathers until the days of David, ⁴⁶who found acceptance before God and asked permission to find a habitation within the ⌜house⌝ of Jacob. ⁴⁷Solomon built him a house, ⁴⁸but the Most High does not dwell in houses made by human hands, even as the prophet says, ⁴⁹'Heaven is my throne, the earth is the footstool for my feet. What house will you build for me, says the Lord; what is the place of my rest? ⁵⁰Did not my hand make all of these things?'

⁵¹"You stiff-necked people, uncircumcised in heart and ears, you are always resisting the Holy Spirit. As your fathers did, so also do you. ⁵²Which of the prophets did your fathers not persecute? And they killed those who announced beforehand concerning the coming of the Righteous One, whom you have now betrayed and murdered. ⁵³All of you received the law at the direction of angels and did not keep it."

The speech is introduced by a simple question from the high priest, probably Caiaphas, as this is likely still before AD 36. He asks whether the charges of speaking against God, Moses, the law, and the temple (Acts 6:11, 13–14) are true.[2] In effect, the query is whether Stephen is unfaithful to the basic tenets of the faith and is encouraging others in Israel to think likewise. To lead Israel into apostasy is a major crime (Deut. 13:1–5).

7:1

Stephen begins his speech with the rhetorically obligatory call to hear (ἀκούσατε, *akousate*; Acts 2:22; 13:16; 15:13). He addresses his audience by identifying with them as brothers and fathers (22:1), much as Peter has done to both the community and to Jews (1:16; 2:14). The reference to fathers is a respectful way to address Sanhedrin members.

7:2–3

Stephen begins his speech proper with Abraham and the God of glory. Abraham is the topic in verses 2–8. He is a popular figure in Judaism.[3] But the key to Israel's history is not Abraham but the God of glory. In

---

2. In Acts 24:9 Jews claim that the charges against Paul "are so." On εἰ (*ei*) introducing a direct question, see Acts 1:6; 19:2; 21:37; 22:25; and Bruce 1990: 190.

3. See Deut. 6:20–24; 26:5–9; Josh. 24:2–13; Neh. 9:6–31; Pss. 78; 105; Jdt. 5:6–18; 1 Macc. 2:52–60; Wis. 10; Sir. 44–50; 3 Macc. 2:2–12; 2 Esd. (4 Ezra) 3:4–36; 14:29–31; CD 2.14–5.9; Josephus, *Ant.* 1.7.1–15.1 §§154–241; Philo, *Migration* and *Abraham*; Jervell 1998: 232n683.

the phrase ὁ θεὸς τῆς δόξης (*ho theos tēs doxēs*) the genitive τῆς δόξης is one of quality or, perhaps, an attributive genitive (Wallace 1996: 87). The idea is that God possesses glory. This unique reference to God in Acts begins the speech on a note of high respect for the one Stephen is accused of blaspheming. God is unique and is characterized by glory (Ps. 29:3; Exod. 16:10; 24:16–17). God's revelation to Abraham began Israel's saga. God's glory is associated with certain key events for Israel: creation, the giving of Torah, leading Israel during the exodus, and indwelling both the tabernacle and the temple (Le Cornu and Shulam 2003: 341). The speech also will end with the glory of God (v. 55). Stephen's respect for his God and for Israel's roots are evident in his opening remark.

Stephen's reply to the charges he faces will begin more indirectly than through explicit declarations. His reply demands an appreciation of the historical context of God's activity with Israel. He refers to Abraham as "our forefather" (τῷ πατρὶ ἡμῶν, *tō patri hēmōn*), showing Stephen's desire to connect himself with God's promises of the past and the roots of Israel's existence (see also vv. 11–12, 19, 38, 44–45; the switch of pronouns comes in v. 51—"your fathers" always disobey). This is not the language of a break with God, God's promise, and Israel. It is the exact opposite. Stephen contends for the true hope of Israel.

The locale of the promise is Mesopotamia (Gen. 11:27–28) before Abraham moved to Haran, a location in northwest Mesopotamia that was a trade region for caravans. Here God initiated his work with Israel when God "appeared" (ὤφθη, *ōphthē*) to Abraham. The OT does not mention a vision, but this may reflect a deduction from the fact of God's promise. God reveals himself outside Israel and the temple.

Abraham is a major figure for Luke, mentioned twenty-two times (Luke 1:55, 73; 3:8 [2x], 34; 13:16, 28; 16:22–25 [4x], 29–30 [2x]; 19:9–10; 20:37; Acts 3:13–15, 25; 7:2–3, 15–18 [2x], 31–32; 13:26). Stephen says that it is here, before the move to Haran, that Abraham received the call to go to a land that God had promised to him. The allusion seems to be to Gen. 12:1 (1QapGen 22.27 also discusses a vision), but Gen. 11:31–12:4 locates the family in Haran before the call came. The citation is close to the LXX version. God is going to present a land to Abraham, but to receive it, he will have to leave the land he and his relatives are in. How should one regard this difference on the location of the call?

There is an old tradition in Judaism that Abraham's call came in Ur (Gen. 15:7; Neh. 9:6; Philo, *Abraham* 14 §62; Josephus, *Ant.* 1.7.1 §154). Fitzmyer (1998: 369) notes that the detail is not wrong, as Haenchen (1987: 278) claims, but represents the use of another Jewish tradition. Philo knows both traditions, as *Migration* 32 §176 shows. Or we may be dealing with a literary telescope here: the move from Ur to Haran is viewed as God leading Abraham to the land, even though the explicit instruction may have come after Abraham reached Haran. The account simply collapses the travel into one summarized remark. Either possibility or a combination of both appears to be what is taking place. Polhill (1992: 189) suggests that a separate call took place in Ur, and he appeals to Gen. 15:7 for the point (so also Bruce 1988a: 134; Larkin 1995: 106). This third option also is possible.

Abraham leaves in obedience without a land and home, knowing only that God one day will show him where he belongs. This makes him an example of faith, as later texts show (Heb. 11:8). Bruce (1988a: 134) suggests that the speech's opening raises the point that God is not tied to one earthly locale.

The key command (δεῦρο, *deuro*) is a term that normally means "come here," that is, to a place, and so God's direction to a locale is highlighted. Stephen is recounting how God called Israel through promise to make it a nation with a land. That promise started with Abraham (Acts 7:3, 5, 17; also v. 7 speaks of worship in "this place"). In the working out of that promise, it was often the case that the people did not heed those whom God called.

Abraham's journey continued into the promised land after his father,   7:4–5
Terah, died. Abraham left "the land of the Chaldees" (Gen. 11:28, 31; 15:7; Schneider 1980: 454n58). God is said to have resettled (μετῴκισεν, *metōkisen*) Abraham in the land, that is, Canaan. This verb appears only twice in the NT (Acts 7:43), and an explicit subject is lacking in the Greek, but God is clearly in view. Once Abraham arrived in the land where the Jews later lived, no inheritance was given, not even a foot of ground (an allusion to Deut. 2:5 about Mt. Seir of the Edomites). Abraham merely receives a promise that is repeated in different forms from Gen. 12:7; 13:15; 15:2, 18; 17:8; 24:7; and 48:4. The wording of the allusion is closest to Gen. 48; 13; and 17. All this took place before Abraham had any children.

The key to the promise is that it applies to his seed (τῷ σπέρματι αὐτοῦ, *tō spermati autou*), or descendants. It was made before Abraham knew he would have descendants. It required faith for Abraham to go, but Stephen does not note this point. This promise is something Rom. 4:18–22 and Gal. 3–4 discuss in detail as being realized in Jesus, even though there is an awareness of its plural reference to Abraham's descendants in Paul (Gal. 3:28–29). Stephen is using the term in its plural sense as well.

God made a commitment of the land to Abraham's descendants. The land is called "an inheritance" (κληρονομίαν, *klēronomian*), the only such reference in Acts. The fact that they are now in the land indicates that God kept and keeps his promises. This is the only occurrence of the verb ἐπαγγέλλομαι (*epangellomai*, promise) in Acts, but the noun (ἐπαγγελία, *epangelia*) appears eight times in Acts (1:3–5; 2:32–33, 39; 7:17–18; 13:23–24, 32–33; 23:21; 26:6–7). The promise to Abraham is first mentioned here in Acts and appears later in 7:17; 13:32; 26:6 (Fitzmyer

1998: 371). Stephen underscores that God is faithful. Stephen is not a blasphemer.

A problem of chronology arises in these details. Stephen puts the death of Abraham's father before Abraham left Haran. Genesis 12:4 tells us that Abraham was 75 when he left Haran. Terah died at age 205 in Haran (Gen. 11:32). Terah was 70 years old when Abraham was born (Gen. 11:26), so, according to the Hebrew text, Terah apparently was 145 when Abraham departed. This would be 60 years before Terah died, according to the Hebrew text, not after his death as Stephen says here. Philo agrees with Stephen that Terah died at 145. *Migration* 32 §177 has Abraham leave after Terah's death, when Abraham was 75 years old. Also Josephus, *Ant.* 1.6.5–7.1 §§151–54, tells of Terah's death before Abraham departed, although Josephus's ages fit the Hebrew text. Jubilees 12.28–31 has Terah bless Abraham's departure but gives no ages (Weiser 1981: 183; Fitzmyer 1998: 370; Str-B 2:667). There are no variants in the LXX and the MT, although Stephen's version does agree with the Samaritan Pentateuch at Gen. 11:32, which says Terah died at 145.

It is thus likely that Stephen is following a well-known tradition that his audience also knows, a detail that may indicate the use of a source (but Barrett 1994: 342–43 argues for an error of reading here). In the seventeenth century, James Ussher argued that Gen. 11:26 actually discusses the birth of the oldest son, not of Abraham, who was born 60 years later, in which case the ages fit, a solution preferred by Larkin (1995: 106–7, note on Acts 7:4). It is more likely that Stephen is using an old and alternate Jewish tradition here that has left its trace in the LXX and the Samaritan Pentateuch, although the possibility also exists that Gen. 11:26 should be read differently, so that the MT and the LXX are closer than it might appear.

7:6–7 God promised that it would be some time before the nation received the land. In fact, suffering and slavery were predicted for these descendants for a period of 400 years. The language is from Gen. 15:13–14. Exodus 12:40 says that the sojourn was 430 years (Gal. 3:17), whereas rabbinic exegesis of Gen. 15:13 has a figure of 400 years from the birth of Isaac to the exodus (Str-B 2:668–71). Hebrews 11:8–16 looks to the period as one of pilgrimage. The figure in Acts is simply a rounded number, reflecting a simplification like that of the rabbis on Gen. 15:13.

The reference to being foreigners in a land that is not their own indicates that Abraham's sojourn would be matched by the nation.[4] The descendants (αὐτό, *auto*, here refers back to seed or descendants) would be enslaved and treated poorly. The remarks foretell the period when the

---

4. On the word πάροικος (*paroikos*, foreigner or resident alien), see Acts 7:29 (Moses in exile in Midian); Eph. 2:19–22 (Gentiles no longer aliens to the promise and people of God); 1 Pet. 2:11–12 (Christians as aliens); Exod. 2:22; 18:3; Lev. 25:23; Deut. 14:21; 23:7 (23:8 LXX).

nation was plunged into harsh slavery in Egypt only to be delivered by Moses in the exodus as a result of the plagues. In the land they would be able to worship (λατρεύω, *latreuō*, appears five times in Acts: 7:6–7, 42; 24:14–15; 26:6–7; 27:23–24) God. In that land Israel would have a place to worship its God in peace; verse 7 contains a likely paraphrase of Exod. 3:12 and an idea echoed in Luke 1:73–75.

A reference to Mt. Horeb is altered to a more general "in this place," a probable reference to Canaan, the point of arrival after the exodus (Fitzmyer 1998: 372 and Bruce 1990: 194, but Polhill argues that the temple is in view, citing Acts 6:13–14, as does Barrett 1994: 345). Deuteronomy 12:21 and 16:11 speak of "the place" as the locale of the temple (Le Cornu and Shulam 2003: 344). Schneider (1980: 455n74) prefers the temple, arguing that "worship" refers to worship in the temple (other uses of the idea of worship in Acts: 7:42; 24:14; 26:7; 27:23). But at this point in the speech, the issue is primarily the land promised to Abraham, not the temple per se. So a reference to land is more likely, although it could well be that land is noted so that the backdrop for how God came to the temple is made clear. God's presence and activity are not limited to the temple.

Stephen's portrayal shows God's initiative and grace with Israel's people in caring for them and releasing them as well as consistently delivering them and keeping his promises. God has made Israel his people and led them to worship him. Stephen is no blasphemer. He respects God's promise and sovereign leading of his people (Larkin 1995: 108). In addition, Stephen notes that Egypt would be judged for its treatment of them, an allusion to the plagues (Gen. 15:14 promised such judgment, while Exod. 1–12 describes it).

God initiated a special relationship with Abraham that is connected to **7:8** the giving of the covenant of circumcision (Jub. 15.4, 7; Num. 25:12–13; Mal. 2:5; Sir. 47:11). The Greek διαθήκην περιτομῆς (*diathēkēn peritomēs*) means the covenant whose content included and was even characterized by circumcision (for a positive Jewish view of circumcision, see Jub. 15.25–34). Circumcision, the act of removing the foreskin from the male penis on the eighth day after birth, was a sign of the covenant agreement between God and Israel's people. The intimate sign was a reminder of their commitment to God and its connection to life (Gen. 17:1–14; 21:4). This rite is much discussed in the NT, as it was a key indicator that one was Jewish.[5] Tied to the promise to Abraham, circumcision predates the Mosaic law. It was seen as a covenant sign (Gen.

---

5. For the noun (περιτομή, *peritomē*) as here, see John 7:22–23; Acts 7:8; 10:45–46; 11:2–3; Rom. 2:25–3:1; 3:29–30; 4:9–12; 15:8–9; 1 Cor. 7:19; Gal. 2:6–10, 12; 5:6, 11; 6:15; Eph. 2:11–12; Phil. 3:3–6; Col. 2:11–13; 3:7–11; 4:10–11; Titus 1:10–11. For the verb (περιτέμνω, *peritemnō*), see Luke 1:59; 2:21; John 7:22; Acts 7:8; 15:1, 5; 16:3; 21:20–21; 1 Cor. 7:18; Gal. 2:3–5; 5:2–3; 6:12–13; Col. 2:11–13.

17:10–12) and one of the most central indications of being identified with the people of God (Jub. 15.23–24). This is why it was the subject of so much controversy later in Acts (Acts 15) and in Paul's ministry. There was precedent for its importance in the lead up to the defense of Israel's practices during the Maccabean period (1 Macc. 1–2). The eldest patriarchs were obedient in observing this practice (on the term "patriarch," see 4 Macc. 16:25; at that time it was a relatively new term in Judaism; 4 Macc. 7:19; four times in the NT: Acts 2:29; 7:8–9 [2x]; Heb. 7:4). Abraham circumcised Isaac (Gen. 21:4), and then with Jacob came the twelve patriarchs (Gen. 21–36). God had kept his promise of a seed. Abraham had faithfully obeyed God in circumcision (Jervell 1998: 234). Stephen is making the point that he knows and respects the history of the people and the law.

7:9   Stephen moves from Abraham to the twelve patriarchs, especially Joseph in verses 9–16. This scene raised the first hint of trouble, as the brothers were jealous (ζηλώσαντες, zēlōsantes) of Joseph (Gen. 37). The participle is one of cause; they sold Joseph because they were jealous (NET; Wallace 1996: 632; but HCSB reads as a temporal, "became jealous"; RSV reads as descriptive, "patriarchs, jealous of him, sold"). This verb appears eleven times in the NT (Acts 7:9; 17:5–7 [Jews of Paul in Thessalonica]; 1 Cor. 12:31; 13:4–7; 14:1, 39–40; 2 Cor. 11:2–3; Gal. 4:17–18 [3x]; James 4:2–3). Their jealousy led them to sell Joseph into slavery (Gen. 37:2–4, 11–28; 45:4; Josephus, *Ant.* 2.2.1–4 §§7–18, also speaks of the envy of the eleven brothers). Johnson (1992: 117) notes numerous allusions to this scene in the Testaments of the Twelve Patriarchs (T. Gad 3.3; 4.5–6; 5.1; T. Jos. 1.3–4; T. Sim. 2.6–7, 11, 14; 3.2–3; 4.4–9). But God's sovereign protection overruled this evil, malicious act.

    After Joseph came to power alongside Pharaoh, the people of Israel went down into Egypt as "aliens in a strange land" (Gen. 46:1–7; Jub. 39.4; 40.9). The phrase "God was with him" (ἦν ὁ θεὸς μετ' αὐτοῦ, *ēn ho theos met' autou*) means that although Joseph was placed in terrible circumstances, God was protecting him. John 3:2 gives a good sense of the meaning of this phrase. For God to be with someone means that God is present and working through that person in an unusual way. In Joseph's case, it meant protection from harm. Luke in Acts 10:38 states that God was with Jesus as he went about doing good and healing. Acts 14:27, describing the activity of Paul and Barnabas, states that God was "with them" (also 15:4).

    The contrast is important. God was with the one whom the other eleven sons of Jacob rejected, a note introducing the nation's pattern of failure to recognize the one chosen by God. This pattern began even among those who are responsible for Israel's name and for its being known as a people of twelve tribes. The additional note of jealousy as the cause of Joseph's brothers' actions is raised. Is such jealousy implied also here in the reaction against Jesus? One can sense a parallel to Jesus in Stephen's view. Qumran writings also harshly criticize the brothers (CD-A 3.4–6). It says that they strayed and were stubborn of heart. Stephen's version keeps the focus on God and his goal of saving his stubborn people (Le Cornu and Shulam 2003: 346).

Stephen continues to outline the history of Joseph by noting three acts of God: (1) God rescued Joseph from his afflictions, (2) gave him wisdom and favor with Pharaoh, and (3) made him governor over Egypt and Pharaoh's household. Although some translations render the last category as "Pharaoh made him governor" (e.g., RSV), it appears from the syntax of the Greek that God is the subject of all the actions described in the verse (Barrett 1994: 348 notes Gen. 45:8). The grace and favor included the ability to translate dreams, something that shows God's work in his life (Gen. 39:21; 41:38–41, 46; chap. 43; Jub. 40.5, 9; Philo, *Joseph* 20 §106; Josephus, *Ant.* 2.5.7–6.1 §§87–94; of God's favor with Stephen, Acts 6:8, 10; with Jesus, Luke 2:40–52, esp. v. 52). The idea that Joseph had favor with God echoes Acts 6:8 and implies that just as Joseph was treated badly by his own, so will Stephen be (Eckey 2000: 170). Stephen underscores God's sovereign protection and work that proved that God was with Joseph. **7:10**

The situation seemed very dire for the ancestors of Israel when a famine hit both Egypt and Canaan (Gen. 41:54–57; 42:5; Pss. 37:19; 105:16–22). Jacob and his sons had no food. The term χορτάσματα (*chortasmata*) refers to animal fodder or to regular food (Gen. 24:25, 32; 42:27 [of this episode]; 43:24; Judg. 19:19; Sir. 33:25; 38:26; Ps. Sol. 5.10; Luke 6:21; 9:17; 15:16; 16:21). It may suggest that not even the worst kind of food was available. That God had strategically placed Joseph, despite the brothers' earlier rejection of him, shows God's care and faithfulness to the nation. **7:11**

God's divine care extended to Jacob and his sons. Jacob heard that there was grain in Egypt and sent his sons to obtain some (Gen. 41:57; 42:2; 1QapGen 19.10). After the first visit, Joseph recognized his brothers, but they did not recognize him (Gen. 42:8), no doubt assuming Joseph had died. Does this evoke a theme of ignorance in the parallel of Jesus (so Johnson 1992: 118)? On their second visit to Egypt to obtain grain, Joseph made known to them his identity and exalted position, and Pharaoh came to know Joseph's family and race. The term γένος (*genos*) is ambiguous, since it can mean "family" or "race," but the use of this term in verse 19 suggests the broader understanding as race, even though Gen. 41:12 makes clear that Pharaoh knew earlier that Joseph was a Hebrew. This event reinforced the Jewish identity in a very personal manner (Gen. 42:1–45:1; also 45:2, 16). Johnson notes that a "recognition" scene is frequent in Hellenistic romances, but one must not forget that this **7:12–13** story of Joseph is old, predating Hellenism. God protected Jacob and the sons despite the latter's rejecting God's messenger and leaving him for dead. A reconciliation resulted (Bruce 1988a: 137; Larkin 1995: 109). History shows God's grace to Israel and God's constant effort to reach out to the nation. Johnson notes how with Joseph, Moses, and Jesus, there is the theme of two visits, with the second visit for Jesus being tied to Jesus's presence in his current messengers, a list that includes Stephen (Johnson 1992: 118 and Polhill 1992: 192, although others suggest a parallel to Jesus's second coming, which is unlikely, since it is never mentioned in the speech).

7:14–15 The overview of Joseph concludes with his call to bring Jacob and the family to Egypt where they were protected by Joseph's relationship to Pharaoh (Gen. 45:9–11; chap. 46). Seventy-five souls in all came to this alien land.

The tradition has various ways of rendering the exact number, and these differences have apparently existed for a long time, so it is hard to know which number was original. The number seventy-five reflects the LXX in Genesis and Exodus (Gen. 46:27; Exod. 1:5). But Deut. 10:22 has seventy, as does the MT of these passages in Genesis and Exodus.[6] Marshall (1980: 138) says that the seven remaining of Joseph's nine sons are counted along with the sixty-six listed in Gen. 46 to make the number seventy-five. Philo (*Migration* 36 §§198–207) notes both numbers and has a complicated allegorical explanation for the difference, where seventy points to the intellect and five to the senses. Jubilees 44.33 as well shows that the number was uncertain in the tradition from an early point. It has five die in Egypt before seventy successfully reach Joseph. It is in Egypt that all died, Jacob and the twelve patriarchs (Exod. 1:6). At this point in his speech, Stephen still calls them "our" (ἡμῶν, *hēmōn*) fathers; he still identifies himself as part of Israel's history.

7:16 The saga of Jacob and his sons ends with their burial. There is a difference in the burial traditions as well. In Gen. 49:29–32 and 50:13 Jacob was buried at Machpelah near Hebron, a site Abraham had purchased from Ephron the Hittite (Gen. 23). The expression τιμῆς ἀργυρίου (*timēs argyriou*, for a sum of silver) contains a rare genitive of quantity or price (BDF §179.1; Wallace 1996: 122, purchased "for an amount of silver"). Joseph was buried at Shechem (Josh. 24:32) on land purchased by Jacob from the sons of Hamor (Gen. 33:18–20). Josephus has Jacob buried at Hebron, as well as Joseph's brothers (*Ant.* 2.8.2 §199; Jub. 46.8–9, Joseph is buried in Egypt, and Jacob's sons are brought to Machpelah;

---

6. Deuteronomy texts as well as Josephus, *Ant.* 2.7.4 §176, and 4QGen-Exod[a] 17.1–18.2 have seventy-five, as does 4QExod[b] 1.5. Gen. 46:26 LXX has sixty-six plus nine sons of Joseph to make seventy-five, while the MT apparently has only two sons of Joseph plus Jacob and Joseph to make seventy. See discussions in Barrett 1994: 350 and Fitzmyer 1998: 374. Marshall's total (1980: 138) also includes Joseph and Jacob.

T. Reu. 7.2), but a local tradition at Shechem has Jacob's sons buried there (Marshall 1980: 138). Stephen has focused on Shechem. Is this a case of telescoping the details, as may well also have taken place in Acts 7:2 and 7 (so Bruce 1988a: 137n35; Le Cornu and Shulam 2003: 348)? Larkin (1995: 110–11) speaks of a purchase of the original land at Shechem followed by a repurchase by Jacob due to Abraham's travels. Such a purchase is similar to the wells Isaac repurchased (Gen. 21:27–30; 26:26–32). This second solution is possible but is complicated and not explicitly attested. It may be that the "he" who dies in v. 15b refers to Joseph, not Jacob, but that all are alluded to in the burial, and so the issue remains unresolved. Telescoping could involve events (most buried at Shechem) and descendants (Jacob as Abraham's representative). Stephen's key point is that burial took place in the promised land, although in Samaria, and the move was an act of faith that God would keep his word.

The story moves on to Moses by noting the growth of Jacob's descendants   **7:17**
in Egypt (Exod. 1:7) as the arrival of the promise's fulfillment about land drew near (the seed promise was already realized; Gen. 12:7; 13:15; 15:18–20; 17:8; 24:7; 48:4; Luke 1:54–55, 73). The term καθώς (*kathōs*) has a temporal force of "when" (BDAG 494 §4; 2 Macc. 1:31; Neh. 5:6), so: "as the time of the promise . . . drew near."

Stephen recounts events up to the time of Moses until verse 44. Moses is   **7:18–19**
an important figure for Luke, mentioned twenty-nine times out of eighty NT occurrences (Jervell 1998: 236n694; Luke 2:22; 5:14; 9:30, 33; 16:29, 31; 20:28, 37; 24:27, 44; Acts 3:22; 6:11, 14; 7:20, 22, 29, 31–32 [2x], 35, 37, 40, 44; 13:38; 15:1, 5, 21; 21:21; 26:22; 28:23). Nine of the nineteen occurrences in Acts are in Acts 7. Stephen begins citing Exod. 1:8 in a form that follows the LXX. That passage speaks of a pharaoh, a king (βασιλεύς, *basileus*), who did not know Joseph and of Egypt hardening its heart against Israel. This pharaoh did evil (ἐκάκωσεν, *ekakōsen*) to the Jews and devised a crafty plan (κατασοφισάμενος, *katasophisamenos*) to bring the race to an end (Exod. 1:10–11; 1:18, 22 LXX). The "crafty plan" can be viewed as a positive, shrewd plan, as Pharaoh refers to it in Exod. 1:10. The plan is treacherous, however, from the Jewish perspective (Jdt. 5:11 and 10:19 also use the term, which appears only here in the NT). This plan has a nuance of exploitation (Bruce 1990: 197) and fulfills the promise noted in Acts 7:6. Suggested possibilities for the pharaoh who conceived this new policy include Seti I (1308–1290 BC; Fitzmyer 1998: 375), Rameses II (1290–1224 BC; Bruce 1990: 196), and Thutmose I (ca. 1600–1514 BC [Larkin 1995: 111], whose dates are favored by the internal biblical chronology), depending on how the chronology of the OT correlates with Egyptian chronology, an issue that is debated.

Parents were commanded to leave their infants exposed so that they would die. The combination of εἰς (*eis*) and the infinitive points to the purpose of the plan, to separate children from parents and pare down the race (Wallace 1996: 592). This phrase is better read as purpose than result, for the plan ultimately failed thanks in part to what happened with the baby Moses. The adjective ἔκθετα (*ektheta*) is used only here in the NT and means "exposed" or "abandoned" (BAGD 240; BDAG 303; "throw out" in NIV; "abandon" in NLT, NET; the term is not used in the LXX). Since this was an order by Pharaoh, "exposed" is the meaning here and infanticide is the goal, as the final phrase "so they might not survive" (εἰς τὸ μὴ ζῳογονεῖσθαι, *eis to mē zōogoneisthai*) indicates. This verb also appears in Exod. 1:17, 22. In Josephus's version (*Ant.* 2.9.2 §§205–8), Pharaoh had received a prediction of Moses's greatness.

7:20–22   Stephen now relates the story of Exod. 2:2–10. Moses was born as a beautiful child and was exposed after three months (μῆνας τρεῖς, *mēnas treis*) of nursing at home, only to be rescued and carried away (ἀνείλατο, *aneilato*) by Pharaoh's daughter to be a son in her home. The accusative here is one of duration of time (Exod. 2:2; Wallace 1996: 202).

    The term often translated "beautiful" (ἀστεῖος, *asteios*) does not refer so much to looks as to breeding: Moses was well formed or of favored status before God (BAGD 117 §2; BDAG 145).[7] The phrase "before God" (τῷ θεῷ, *tō theō*) makes it even more emphatic (Jon. 3:3; Schneider 1980: 459 and n. 119). This phrase is an ethical dative, which means that it refers to emotions or perceptions (BDF §192.1; Wallace 1996: 147). Perceptions are the point. The verb ἐκτίθημι (*ektithēmi*) means "expose" here, whereas the three other occurrences in the NT refer to making things plain or explaining them (Acts 11:4; 18:26; 28:23). The verb ἀναιρέω (*anaireō*) normally means "kill" or "lift up" but here in the middle voice refers to taking up for oneself (BDAG 64 §3 notes that in this context it means rescue and as a result adoption; Exod. 2:5).[8] Recounting a major figure's birth, upbringing, and education is a frequent way to describe the person's childhood (Acts 22:3).

    Moses received an education that was the best Egypt could offer, including access to all the wisdom of the Egyptians (πάσῃ σοφίᾳ Αἰγυπτίων,

---

7. Various renderings include "beautiful" (RSV) and "no ordinary child" (NIV). Hebrews 11:23 is the other NT occurrence, also of Moses. In the LXX: Exod. 2:2 (of this scene about Moses; the MT has "goodly" [טוֹב, *ṭôb*]; Num. 22:32; Judg. 3:17; Jdt. 11:23; 2 Macc. 6:23; Sus. 7 [= 2 Eng.]). Also with much elaboration in Philo, *Moses* 1.3–5 §§9–18, of his beauty and rescue based on his elegant form. Josephus, *Ant.* 2.9.5–7 §§224–32 (where the name of the daughter is Thermuthis); 2.9.7–10.1 §§236–38 (of Moses's education); 3.1.4 §§13–14 (of his persuasiveness and agreeable presence); *L.A.B.* 9.3–10; and Jub. 47.3–5 (where her name is Tharmuth). Artapanus, *On the Jews*, frg. 3, calls the daughter Meris; Johnson 1992: 125.

8. See Frankemölle, *EDNT* 1:81; Acts 2:22–24; 5:33, 36; 7:20–21, 28; 9:23–25, 28–29; 10:39–42; 12:2; 13:27–28; 16:27; 22:19–20; 23:15, 21, 27; 25:1–3; 26:9–10. Barrett 1994: 354–55 argues for adoption, citing Plutarch, *Antony* 36.3 [= *Moralia* 932] and Epictetus, *Discourses* 1.23.7, who argues against putting away a child or exposing a child as a context for "taking up" a child. See also MM 33–34 with P.Oxy. 1.37.6, which illustrates the use of the term and describes taking up a child from a dung heap.

---

pasē sophia Aigyptiōn). This detail is not in the OT but is in extrabiblical discussion of Moses.[9]

Moses thus became mighty (δυνατός, *dynatos*) in word and deed (δυνατός in Acts: 2:22–24 [of Jesus]; 7:22; 11:17 [Peter's inability to resist God]; 18:24 [Apollos, mighty in Scripture]; 20:16 [able to get to Jerusalem]; 25:4–5 [men of authority]; also Luke 24:19). So Moses providentially was well equipped and trained to be a leader. Exodus 4:10 has Moses claim that he is not eloquent, but this may be a touch of humility on Moses's part as well as hesitation in taking on the assigned task (Marshall 1980: 140; *pace* Barrett 1994: 356, who argues that God's agreement to select Aaron as spokesman agrees with Moses's claim, but this may involve God giving Moses no excuse). The fact that Moses was mighty in word and deed suggests that beyond this education God was working through him.[10] The allusion probably does not include a reference to the plagues, which come later in Stephen's remarks in verse 36 (*pace* Barrett 1994: 356). The account here describes Moses as he was in Pharaoh's house.

Rabbinic tradition divides Moses's life into three forty-year blocks (Str-B 2:679–80; *L.A.B.* 53.2; Sipre §357; 150a; Bruce 1990: 198). In the second block of forty years, Stephen speaks of Moses's visit (ἐπισκέψασθαι, *episkepsasthai*) to his brethren, the sons of Israel (for the idiom "to enter into the heart" in the LXX: 2 Kings 12:5 [12:4 Eng.]; Isa. 65:16; Jer. 3:16). This recalls Exod. 2:11–13. Jervell (1998: 237) notes that the term suggests that God gives a thought to someone. The idea of a visit is important in Luke-Acts, as God visits his people (through a deliverer in Luke 1:68; through a prophet in Luke 7:16; in a missed opportunity for Israel in Luke 19:44; of visiting Gentiles in Acts 15:14; Polhill 1992: 195 and n58).

The incident begins with an Egyptian attacking or striking a Hebrew, what Stephen calls wronging (ἀδικούμενον, *adikoumenon*) and oppressing (καταπονουμένῳ, *kataponoumenō*) him. The verb for "oppress" appears elsewhere in the NT only in 2 Pet. 2:7, of Lot being oppressed by the unrighteous. Philo (*Moses* 1.8 §§40–44) also speaks of an Egyptian beating the slaves. Moses acted in vengeance (ἐκδίκησιν, *ekdikēsin*) on behalf of the Hebrew and came to his defense (ἠμύνατο, *ēmynato*; NT

7:23–25

---

9. Numerous texts make the point: Josephus, *Ant.* 2.9.6 §§229–30 (superior understanding at age three); 2.9.7 §236 (educated with great care); Philo, *Moses* 1.5 §§20–24 (of his royal education and his skill in every area of study); 1.14 §80 (of his exceptional power, which came from God); Artapanus, *On the Jews* 3.6–8 (Moses as a master teacher of Egypt); Pesch 1986a: 252; Johnson 1992: 125; but Jub. 47.9, a work defending Jewish values, speaks of a Jewish education.

10. This theme also receives elaboration in extrabiblical material: Josephus, *Ant.* 2.10.1–2 §§239–53 (defeats the Ethiopians through clever leadership in battle); 2.12.2–3 §§271–72 (turns a rod into a serpent before he meets Pharaoh); and Sir. 45:3 ("by his words he performed swift miracles" [NRSV]).

hapax). The verb is middle voice (BDF §316), although one might have expected it to be active. This means that the point is emphatic—Moses himself provided aid.

The term ἐκδίκησις is common in the NT, appearing nine times (Luke 18:6–8 [2x]; 21:21–22; Acts 7:24; Rom. 12:17–19; 2 Cor. 7:11; 2 Thess. 1:3–10; Heb. 10:30; 1 Pet. 2:13–16). The idea here is that Moses was righting an injustice or exacting retribution (Luke 18:7; Judg. 11:36). Moses struck (πατάξας, pataxas; Exod. 2:12) the Egyptian or smote him (as in the MT) dead. In the MT, Moses killed the man and buried his body in the sand so that the Egyptians might not know about the slaying (Codex D also adds the note about burial here). All these verbs portray Moses as a defender of his brothers.

Stephen's next comment in verse 25 lacks any parallel in the MT. Moses thought that those observing his act would understand that God had given salvation (δίδωσιν σωτηρίαν, didōsin sōterian) through his hands. The idea of salvation given by God is common in Luke-Acts (Luke 1:71–73 [give salvation from enemies], 77 [give knowledge of salvation]; Acts 4:12 [no other name given by which we must be saved]). Josephus has Moses speak of his work as deliverer later, when the Egyptians chase the Israelites to the edge of the sea (Ant. 2.15.5 §331).

The Jews of Moses's time, however, lacked understanding about a divine call to Moses. Here is the beginning of a charge from Luke that the fathers missed their deliverer (7:52) and failed to understand what God was doing in saving. (This idea will be repeated with a double use of the same verb [συνίημι, syniēmi] at the end of Acts [28:26–27], when Paul cites Isa. 6:9.) This second example of rejection of God's messenger expands on the earlier action against Joseph. There they judged wrongly and God delivered. Here they do not even respond to a deliverance. These remarks anticipate 7:33–38 and form a typology to Jesus (also Heb. 11:24–26). Many Jews failed to recognize Jesus as Savior as well.

7:26–29   The attention turns to the events of the day after Moses struck the Egyptian (Exod. 2:13). Two Hebrews were fighting (μαχομένοις, machomenois; NT: John 6:52; Acts 7:26; 2 Tim. 2:23–26; James 4:2–3). Moses sought to reconcile (συνήλλασσεν, synēllassen) them in peace. The contrast with Moses's defense of one Hebrew against an Egyptian in the previous incident is striking. Jews should be reconciled to each other. Such a belief has motivated Stephen to preach Jesus to the nation. This verb for reconcile is an NT hapax and is absent in the LXX (BDAG 964–65). Here the imperfect is conative and speaks to an ongoing attempt to bring a result (Moule 1959: 9; Moulton and Turner 1963: 65; Wallace 1996: 551). He even asked them why they were acting unrighteously (ἀδικεῖτε, adikeite) toward each other, echoing the act of the Egyptian against the Hebrew in 7:24. In the LXX, the question is, "Why do you strike your neighbor?" Moses's effort met with resistance from the man who was wronging (ὁ . . . ἀδικῶν, *ho adikōn*) his brother.

As Luke tells the story, Moses mediates between the two men, although the fact that the unrighteous man addresses Moses shows that Luke is aware that in Exodus one man is the real cause of the dispute. Some critics make more of this difference than is necessary. The repetition of the verb ἀδικέω (*adikeō*, to wrong) emphasizes that the scene involves an injustice that Moses is trying to right; the verb also appears in Exod. 2:13 LXX (Jub. 47.11–12). In Greek culture divine men sought to bring about peace (Lucian, *Demonax* 9; Philostratus, *Life Apoll.* 1.15; Conzelmann 1987: 53). The more important background is Luke's association of peace with Jesus (Luke 1:79; 2:14, 29; Acts 10:36; Johnson 1992: 127).

The unrighteous man rejected or thrust aside (ἀπώσατο, *apōsato*) Moses's attempt with a rebuke (NT occurrences of this verb: Acts 7:27, 39 [points to the theme]; 13:46; Rom. 11:1–2; 1 Tim. 1:18–20; LXX: Judg. 6:13; 1 Sam. 12:22; Ps. 42:2 [43:2 Eng.]; Hos. 4:6). The man asks who appointed Moses a ruler and judge (ἄρχοντα καὶ δικαστήν, *archonta kai dikastēn*). The remark is from Exod. 2:14, the only place using this combination in the LXX. The combination is a way to describe leaders (see the discussion in Acts 5:29–32). Anyone reading Stephen's summary would know that God had protected and prepared Moses (vv. 20, 22), but this man did not see it and reacted against God's chosen one, a pattern of response Stephen is now pointing out. Although not explicitly stated here, these two roles parallel those God had for a later selected leader, Jesus. Acts 7:35–37 suggests this link between Moses and Jesus, as the same combination of ruler and judge appears there with the mention of Moses's promise to raise up a prophet like him. The promise is an allusion to Deut. 18:15 and to Jesus (Acts 3:22). The ruler-and-judge combination in Acts 7:35–37 also refers back to Exod. 2:14. So Moses is a "type" or "pattern" for what Jesus was to do and be. Stephen is tracing what also applies to Jesus, as do other passages in Luke-Acts (Acts 3:17; 4:10–12; 13:27; Weiser 1981: 185). The remark about Moses seeking to kill as he had the Egyptian the day before repeats exactly Exod. 2:14 LXX and shows that Moses's act was known.

The rebuke caused Moses to flee to Midian, probably on the east coast of the Gulf of Aqaba, south of Edom (Barrett 1994: 359). The phrase ἐν τῷ λόγῳ τούτῳ (*en tō logō toutō*) refers to what accompanied the fleeing, namely, the Hebrew's words that Moses took as a rebuke (Moule 1959: 78). The phrase is best read as giving the reason Moses fled (BDF §219.2; "because of this rebuke"). Like his fathers before him, Moses was a sojourner for a time. The locale follows Exod. 2:15, except that in the MT the additional note is made that Pharaoh was seeking to kill Moses, for his act against the Egyptian was known, as Exod. 2:15 also notes. That the Hebrew knew of it suggests that the act had become quite public, as Exod. 2:14 shows. Stephen focuses on the hostility between Hebrews.

Josephus (*Ant.* 2.11.1 §§255–56) elaborates that Pharaoh's envy was motivating his desire to remove Moses. So Moses fled, married, and had two sons. Exodus 2:22 mentions Gershom by name, and Exod. 18:3–4 names Gershom and Eliezer. These remarks point to how Stephen at times telescopes events (Exod. 4:20 speaks of sons in the plural).

7:30–34   Stephen turns next to the appearance of an angel as God's messenger at the burning bush. Here Moses was called and prepared to free the people of Israel (Exod. 3; Jub. 47.12–48.2; Josephus, *Ant.* 2.9.5–6 §§226–29; Philo, *Moses* 1.12–13 §§65–69). The location is Mount Horeb in the MT and the LXX, another name for Mount Sinai, which is the place Stephen names (Exod. 3:12 and Deut. 1:6 compared with Exod. 19:1, 11–25; Josephus, *Ant.* 2.12.1 §264 also speaks of Sinai for this scene). Later the Lord himself will speak (vv. 31, 33), and so God is seen as present in a theophany, namely, a flame of fire (φλογὶ πυρός, *phlogi pyros*; a flame that possessed fire, a genitive of quality; Moulton and Turner 1963: 213; Exod. 3:2). This flame could well be the angel of the Lord (Bruce 1990: 200). The important revelation came in the desert. The rabbis taught that this locale showed that no place was too desolate for God's presence (Exod. Rabbah 2 [68c]; Haenchen 1987: 282; Str-B 2:680). Given the debate about the sacredness of the temple, Stephen appears to make a similar point. Holy ground is where God is (see v. 33).

Once again the 40-year time frame appears (see v. 23). The MT initially mentions simply a long period of time (Exod. 2:23), but Exod. 7:7 has Moses at 80 years when he approaches Pharaoh, and Deut. 34:5–7 has Moses at 120 years when he dies, which may have created the division of his life into periods of 40. The sign of the bush burning without being consumed underscores the call's divine roots.

The unusual scene drew Moses's attention, and as he tried to take a closer look, the Lord spoke. This detail suggests a theophany, an angel-like appearance of God. This passage summarizes Exod. 3:2–6, where God sees Moses and takes notice, identifying himself as the God of the patriarchs Abraham, Isaac, and Jacob, a declaration that causes Moses to fear. The MT in Exod. 3:6 speaks of Moses hiding his face, afraid to look at God. Josephus (*Ant.* 2.12.1 §267) also records Moses's fear. Now God would call Moses to serve his people. The title for God recalls the God of promise Peter describes in Acts 3:13. The Lord then instructed Moses to remove his sandals, for the place where he was standing was holy. This repeats Exod. 3:5 almost word for word. The temple is not the only holy place where God shows himself as holy.

God called Moses to go to Egypt to relieve Israel's affliction (κάκωσιν, *kakōsin*; an NT hapax but used in Exod. 3:7, which is extensively cited here; see also Exod. 3:8, 10). God had heard their groaning (στεναγμοῦ, *stenagmou*; the only other NT occurrence is in Rom. 8:26 [groanings of the Spirit]; see Exod. 2:24; 6:5). God would be faithful to Israel (Bruce

1988a: 141). God's call showed his endorsement of Moses, whom some Jews had already rejected. Stephen now turns to this theme. Witherington (1998: 270) correctly notes the juxtaposition of two themes in the speech: God faithfully sends leaders to the nation, and Israel consistently rejects them. Witherington also correctly observes that Jesus is not merely like these earlier rejected leaders such as Moses but is unique because of the salvation he brings. The array of actions Jesus performed points to the identity of the saving figure. Jesus is like Moses (a deliverer sent to the people) and yet more than him (deliverer into eternal salvation).

The theme of Moses's rejection is now made explicit as Stephen recalls the earlier rejection of Moses noted in verse 27 and cited in Exod. 2:14. The historical overview moves toward historical commentary. Stephen calls Moses a ruler and judge in Acts 7:27 (Philo, *Moses* 1.14 §71 speaks of Moses as a leader). Now he repeats the description and adds a reference to him as a deliverer (λυτρωτήν, *lytrōtēn*) through supernatural means. This is the only use of this noun in the NT. The use of related words is common in the NT (savior: Acts 5:31; redemption: Luke 1:68; 2:38; ransom: Matt. 20:28 = Mark 10:45; "to ransom," Luke 24:21; Titus 2:14; 1 Pet. 1:18). The idea of the noun λύτρωσις (*lytrōsis*) can be release through payment of a ransom, but in its word group as a whole, the emphasis is simply on release (Barrett 1994: 363). The latter idea is what is important here, as Moses did not pay any ransom to gain the release. The contrast is between the Jewish rejection of Moses and God's sending him as both ruler and deliverer. This ongoing, divinely given status of Moses as the sent one is underscored by the use of the perfect-tense verb ἀπέσταλκεν (*apestalken*, I have sent). This point is made more emphatic when one realizes that all the verbs around this perfect tense are aorists.

Once again the presence of the directing angel is noted as a part of the call (see vv. 30–34). The phrase σὺν χειρὶ ἀγγέλου (*syn cheiri angelou*) expresses means: God appointed Moses ruler through the work of the angels. God had sent this one (BDF §217.2). The idea that the law was mediated through angels is Jewish (Jub. 2.1; Josephus, *Ant.* 15.5.3 §136; Eckey 2000: 174; in NT: Gal. 3:19; Heb. 2:2).

In looking at the entire portrait of Moses, one can also sense the potential typology. It suggests that as with Moses, so with the promised prophet to come, Jesus (see v. 37). Barrett (1994: 362–63) notes six themes (the sixth theme repeats the first for emphasis) and a possible hymnic root here: (1) the man rejected by the people becomes a ruler; (2) he is a deliverer through signs and wonders; (3) he is a prophet and prototype of the coming one; (4) he is a mediator between God and humanity; (5) he is a receiver and giver of the words of life, and (6) he is rejected by his people (also Pesch 1986a: 253 speaks of a hymnic character to this section and notes Sir. 44:23b–45:5). Another element

7:35

of the typology is that as Israel was a rejecter in the past, so is Israel currently (vv. 51–53; Jervell 1998: 238, who says the typology revolves around Jesus and the Jews).

7:36–37   Stephen covers the entire deliverance in Exodus in very summary form. He refers to the attestation to Moses in wonders and signs (τέρατα καὶ σημεῖα, *terata kai sēmeia*) in Egypt (Exod. 7:8–11:10), at the Red Sea (Exod. 14–15), and in the wilderness over a forty-year period (Exod. 16–Deut. 34). There is discussion among scholars about the relationship between the Red Sea (LXX: Exod. 13:18; 15:4) and the Sea of Reeds (MT: Exod. 13:18; 15:4; Fitzmyer 1998: 379). Once again Stephen reflects the tradition of his context, speaking of the Red Sea. It is likely that the two may have been considered the same, as the LXX rendering suggests. The language recalls Exod. 7:3 and Num. 14:33 (Ps. 104:27 LXX [105:27 Eng.]; Josephus, *Ant.* 2.12.4 §276; As. Mos. 3.11; Jub. 48.4, 12; Philo, *Moses* 1.14 §77; 1.15 §§90–91). The description of Moses doing signs and wonders recalls that of Jesus earlier in Acts as well as activity in the church (Acts 2:22–24, 43; 6:8). The mention of the duration of divine activity underscores that God consistently showed the nation that Moses was the one he had chosen to deliver Israel. In verses 35–38 there is a fivefold repetition of the term "this one" (οὗτος, *houtos*), as if to emphasize that it was this one whom God had singled out to deliver God's people. Almost like a refrain in a hymn, Stephen speaks of "this one" whom God chose, and prepares a reference to another—Jesus—like him.

This Moses made a promise that there would be another like him (Deut. 18:18; 4Q175 5–8; targum on Exod. 12:42; Ruth Rabbah 5.6; Pesiqta Rabbati 15.10; Larkin 1995: 115; also 4Q158 and 4QExod[a]; 1QS 1.9–11). Josephus (*Ant.* 4.7.2 §165) seems to see Joshua as this prophet, a view that makes sense in terms of the move from Deuteronomy to the book of Joshua. However, there also appears to be the view in Judaism that another like Moses was to come after Joshua, and so the promise took on a typological sense in Judaism. This allusion to a prophet like Moses also recalls a speech of Peter's (Acts 3:22; see discussion there of the Jewish expectation tied to this promise). Another part of the Deut. 18 passage appears at the transfiguration (Luke 9:35). It is a leader-deliverer-prophet whom Stephen seems to have in mind when he speaks about a prophet like Moses. This note about a leader-prophet is important because Moses was more than a prophet. He acted like a delivering king for Israel. The additional difference is what makes Jesus a prophet like Moses. Jesus is all of these things to Stephen. Once again, it is God who directs the activity, as God raised up this prophet onto the stage of history to save. So Moses was not the end of the line of promise, but a beginning. The promised prophet is "for all of you" (ὑμῖν, *hymin*, plural, a clear dative of advantage). Ironically, this promise was for the very ones who slew the sent one. How can Stephen be blaspheming Moses (Acts 6:11) if he respects the role of Moses in the promise (Fitzmyer 1998: 378)? The respect given to Moses and his promise is Stephen's defense against the charges raised against him about Torah and Moses (Le Cornu and Shulam 2003: 357).

Moses delivered. He gave signs. He received living oracles for the people.   **7:38–41**
The allusion is to Exod. 19 and the giving of the commandments and covenant at Sinai (Sinai in the NT: Acts 7:30, 38–40; Gal. 4:24–25). The word ἐκκλησία (*ekklēsia*) appears here, not with its usual NT meaning of "church," but to refer to the gathering of Jews in the wilderness who formed a congregation or an assembly (Deut. 4:10; 9:10; 18:16; 23:2–4, 9; 31:30 often with the phrase "the day of the assembly"). The term will be the one the Christian community chooses to refer to the church.

The law is called the "living oracles" (λόγια ζῶντα, *logia zōnta*), a phrase that appears only here in the NT and is not present in the LXX (Rom. 3:2 has "oracles"; see Lev. 18:5; Deut. 4:1, 33; 5:26; 16:20; 30:15, 19–20; 32:46–47 for images of law and life; life and word: John 6:68; Rom. 7:10; 10:5; Gal. 3:12; Heb. 4:12; 1 Pet. 1:23; Jervell 1998: 241). The law was a crucial element of Jewish faith (Barrett 1994: 366 notes *m. 'Abot* 2.7: "The more study of the Law, the more life").[11] Stephen shows his respect for the law here in light of the charges in Acts 6:13. God spoke to Moses at Sinai and to "our fathers." Stephen still views the Jews as his people.

Moses is seen as the mediator of the law (Philo, *Moses* 2.31 §166, calls Moses a mediator, reconciler, protector, and intercessor; Sipre on Deut. 33:1; Exod. Rabbah, *Ki Thissa* 47.9; Johnson 1992: 130). The association of angels with the moment at Sinai is also in Jewish tradition as well as in the NT (Gal. 3:19, where Paul uses it to express a limitation in the giving of the law).[12]

Stephen says that, despite this divine revelation, "our fathers" refused to give obedience to Moses (referred to in the pronoun ᾧ, *hō*, looking back to "this one" of v. 38). They thrust him aside (Acts 7:27, 39), and in their hearts turned back to Egypt (CD 3.7–11). The term here for "obedient" (ὑπήκοος, *hypēkoos*) is rare in the NT, used only three times (the others are 2 Cor. 2:9 [obedient to the test] and Phil. 2:8 [Jesus was obedient unto death]). Much of the Pentateuch develops this story line around general rebellion (Deut. 32), including figures such as Korah (Num. 16) and the story of the golden calf, which Stephen mentions next as the great example of disobedience extending to idolatry and

---

11. For a careful appraisal of the role of the law across Judaism as its function varied depending on the sect of Judaism involved, see Carson, O'Brien, and Seifrid 2001.

12. See also Heb. 2:2; Deut. 33:2; Isa. 63:9 (angel of the presence saved them); Jub. 1.27; 2.1; *L.A.B.* 11.5; T. Dan 6.2; Pesiqta Rabbati 21.7; "angel of God," Exod. 14:19; 33:14; Bruce 1988a: 143n58; Bruce 1990: 202; Pesch 1986a: 254.

unfaithfulness to God (Exod. 32). Stephen's charge has OT precedent (Neh. 9:17; Ezek. 20:8, 13), and the language is like Exod. 16:3 and Num. 14:3–4. Stephen's point is that Moses as a leader-prophet also received revelation on how Israel should live, a parallel to what God did with Jesus. The latter point is not made explicit because Stephen does not finish his speech, but it is clear that this is where Stephen's review of Israel's history is going.

The forming of the golden calf was the most significant of all the incidents of rebellion against God. Here were an embrace of idolatry and a rejection of the God who made Israel unique. Stephen now recounts the request to Aaron to make this idol. The call to make gods to go before them, the rejection of Moses based on his delay on the mountain, and the nation's not knowing Moses's fate allude to Exod. 32:1, 23 (Pss. 115:4; 135:15). The reference to Moses here is grammatically an example of a nominative pendens, a noun unconnected to the rest of the sentence (Wallace 2000: 35). The plural reference to gods (θεούς, *theous*) makes explicit the participation in polytheism, a fundamental violation of the first commandment (Exod. 20:3–4). The term ἐμοσχοποίησαν (*emoschopoiēsan*) is an NT hapax and does not appear in the LXX. Exodus 32:6 describes the making of the image, the sacrifices, and the "rising up to play." This is one of two references to idols in Acts. In Acts 15:20, involvement with idols is prohibited in the decision of the Jerusalem Council. Josephus omits discussion of the incident of the golden calf in his history of the nation, probably because his primary readers were polytheists.

Stephen also describes the wilderness crowd as rejoicing in the works of their hands. The imperfect tense of the verb εὐφραίνω (*euphrainō*) stands in contrast to the two previous aorist verbs. It highlights the joy of the celebration by portraying it with an ongoing aspect: "they were celebrating" (BDAG 414–15 §§2–3). Usually this verb was used of worship for Yahweh at feasts, so this use is particularly cutting (Lev. 23:40; Deut. 12:7, 12, 18). The association of idols with the work of human hands is also common in the OT and Judaism (Isa. 40:19–20; 44:9–17; Ps. 115:4; Hos. 8:5; Wis. 13:10). Polhill (1992: 200n69) notes that people, left to themselves, take a self-destructive course. Philo (*Moses* 2.31 §165) also speaks of the idol coming from the work of their hands but uses a different verb (also *L.A.B.* 12.1–10; Johnson 1992: 131).

The wilderness period was viewed both positively and negatively in Judaism (Le Cornu and Shulam 2003: 358–59). Israel was devoted to God but also rebelled (Hos. 9:10 and Jer. 2:2–5 reflect both themes).

7:42–43 Citing Amos 5:25–27 LXX (Amos 5:26 is cited in CD 7.14–15), Stephen now quotes the commentary of the prophets about this act of defection. Because Amos is one of the twelve prophets, the citation is described as coming from the book of the Prophets. God turned (used transitively here) them and gave them over (παρέδωκεν, *paredōken*) to their own choice. This language of giving over recalls the repeated verb of Rom. 1:24, 26, 28 regarding God's judgment on the world. God let them go their own way. This is traditional Jewish language for defection into sin (also Jub. 1.13; Wis. 11:15–16).

The worship of the stars is another allusion to idolatry, as the creation is worshiped and not the Creator (Deut. 4:16–19; 17:3; also 2 Kings 17:16 [during Hoshea's reign]; 21:3–5 [during Manasseh's reign]; 23:3 [Josiah's reform destroys this idolatry]; Jer. 7:18; 19:13; Neh. 9:6). The verb λατρεύω (*latreuō*, worship) refers to service given to someone; here it is to the stars of heaven. The verb is a purpose infinitive (Wallace 1996: 592): God gave them over to worship the stars (Rom. 1:18–32). This verb is used five times in Acts (7:7 [serve God], 42; 24:14 [Paul's worship of God]; 26:7 [earnest worship of Israel]; 27:23 [of the God whom Paul worships]), but this is its only negative use as idolatry.

The rebuke from Amos points to the ignominious history of the wilderness wanderings. Sacrifices were not offered to God but to others. This language of rebuke recalls Israel's repeated rejection and unfaithfulness to God's revelation. Here is the ultimate source of Stephen's defense; in the end, Israel's own Scripture condemns Israel. The LXX of Amos is followed here, but its sense brings out the rhetorical force of the Hebrew. It asks, "Did you bring me sacrifices and grain offerings?" The question expects a negative reply. It means that the sacrifices offered went to another, not to God, which is how the LXX reads the citation, or that such sacrifices were brought with less than a pure heart (*pace* Balz, *TDNT* 8:138, who argues that Amos is to be read positively, of no sacrifices being offered in the desert). This reading is reinforced in the next line, where the false objects of worship are specifically named as Moloch and Rephan, as in the LXX. This next line, from Amos 5:26, looks to future idolatry like that of the past in the wilderness. The Hebrew text of Amos has סִכּוּת (*Sikkût*; probably Assyrian Sakkut) and כִּיּוּן (*Kiyyûn*; probably Assyrian Kewan), Mesopotamian gods of the sky, the latter referring to Saturn, also known as Ninib. Moloch is the equivalent of this heavenly sky and sun deity, as represented by either pagan god in the Canaanite-Phoenician context (BDAG 657). Less clear are the roots of Rephan (BDAG 903), but it could be the sun god of Egypt, Repa (Bruce 1988a: 145n70). The reference may well be to the defection to Baal of Peor (Num. 25:1–9; Bruce 1990: 205).

Amos was rebuking the Israel of his time by reminding the people of earlier unfaithfulness that would be replicated in the future as well. Unfaithfulness had taken on a pattern or typology in the nation long before Stephen's time.

There is some question whether Amos 5:25 in the Hebrew says that sacrifices were not important to God or whether the expression is negative: "The sacrifices offered were not for me," reads the LXX. Against the former reading, which is often adopted (e.g., Haenchen 1987: 284; Conzelmann 1987: 55; Bruce 1990: 204), is the fact that sacrifices were commanded in the period for the tabernacle (Exod. 24:4–5). Thus some other meaning is more likely. The point was that God commanded all sacrifices to be offered from the heart (i.e., you are not just to bring me sacrifices but also worship), which also implied that any defection was a perversion of this expectation, according to the LXX. In this light, Amos notes that the sin of idolatry extended itself for generations. Stephen cites Amos from centuries later, knowing the subsequent history as well, and alludes back to the wilderness sin and to the idolatry that followed (now also in the past). Sin led to more sin. It also led to judgment, as seen in the nation's exile. Stephen suggests a similar pattern of disobedience in his own time and possibly hints at judgment. At the least, accountability to God surfaces in this rebuke. In Greek the question begins with μή (mē), so that a negative reply is expected. These sacrifices were not made to God. As Barrett (1994: 367) says, "Never had a people been so privileged or so completely negated their vocation." Ezekiel 20:25–26 possesses a similar rebuke of apostasy into Canaanite idolatry (also 2 Kings 10:29).

As Stephen's speech makes clear, the accusation is that Israel took up idols in the form of Moloch and Rephan, so that divine judgment followed. The MT and LXX tradition referring to Damascus has been updated by Stephen to Babylon to reflect the judgment that God executed on Israel (Le Cornu and Shulam 2003: 360). The point is that such idolatry is a pattern of Israelite behavior and that it results in national judgment. In fact, the change might well suggest that the pattern and consequences continued even beyond what Amos predicted. A similar warning about culpability and judgment came from Peter in Acts 2:16–36 with his reference to the day of the Lord. In the NT such worship is associated with the spiritual battle associated with evil (1 Cor. 10:20; Eph. 6:10–13; Larkin 1995: 116).

7:44   Stephen now mentions the sacred place of worship, the tabernacle, sometimes called the "tent of witness" (Exod. 27:21 LXX for MT's tent of meeting; Johnson 1992: 132; Williams 1990: 141). Stephen has shown his respect for the law as living oracles and pointed out that Israel was disobedient to it as early as the exodus. Now the second topic, the tabernacle-temple, is addressed through verse 50.

The "tent" (σκηνή, skēnē) was also called the tabernacle (NIV, NLT, NET) and housed the ark of the covenant (Exod. 25:21). There is a contrast here between the "tent" of Moloch (v. 43) and the "tent" for God (v. 44). God commanded Moses to make the tabernacle in the wilderness a place to worship God (Exod. 25–27; 33; 36–38; *L.A.B.* 11.15; 13.1). The reference to making it according to "pattern" (τύπον, typon) recalls Exod. 25:40 LXX. Philo makes much of this patterning as parallel to heavenly models, something Hebrews also treats (*Moses* 2.15–17 §§71–88; Heb. 3–10). Once again Stephen speaks of "our" fathers (τοῖς πατράσιν ἡμῶν, *tois patrasin hēmōn*), possessing the tent designed as God had commanded Moses to make it. Again Stephen respects the law and the existence of a place to worship God.

Stephen speaks of the tabernacle as being from the time of Joshua,   **7:45–47** when it was brought into the land (Josh. 3:2–4:18; As. Mos. 1.7–9 recalls Moses's commissioning of Joshua). Luke-Acts refers to the tabernacle five times out of twenty NT occurrences, but only in Acts 7 is the wilderness tabernacle of Israel in view (Luke 9:33 [three tabernacles for a celebration at transfiguration]; 16:9 [eternal tabernacles]; Acts 7:43–44 [2x; Israel's tabernacle]; 15:16 [of David's tabernacle or house]). The tabernacle was in Shiloh (Josh. 18:1) until David brought it to Jerusalem (2 Sam. 6:17). Joshua's name is the Hebrew equivalent of Jesus. Stephen also notes the success in dispossessing the nations (Josh. 3:12–12:24). God was responsible for the victory, as he thrust out (ἐξῶσεν, *exōsen*) the nations before (literally) the "face of our ancestors." The term "face" (προσώπου, *prosōpou*) is singular but distributive in force: "before each face of our ancestors," that is, before all of them as a whole (BDF §140). The verb ἐξῶσεν is strong, as its use in the LXX shows. Second Samuel 14:13–14 uses the term to refer to one who is banished, and 2 Sam. 23:6 uses it of evil people tossed away. Psalm 5:11 (5:10 Eng.) speaks of evil people God is asked to toss away. The implication of the term is that those cast out are evil.

The situation with the tabernacle, the sacred locale of God, until the time of David was this: God was in their midst doing great works of deliverance. In Greek, this time frame appears in the middle part of the sentence, speaking of the time of Joshua, but it appears likely that the sense, expressed in a telescoped manner, is that Israel had the tabernacle in this form until David's time. Translations often break up this sentence into two parts to make this clear. Acts 7:44–45 is really a transition into the time of David, when the next development involving the temple took place.

David found favor with God, an allusion to the unique covenant he had with God pointing to a close relationship with God (1 Sam. 16:13; 18:12, 14). In the context of his special relationship to God and his acceptance before God, David sought to build a habitation, a grand permanent locale of worship (2 Sam. 7:1–17, a text that is the context of the Davidic covenant; 1 Chron. 17:1–15). A textual problem appears at this point: Is it a habitation for Jacob's God or for Jacob's house that David wanted to build? The latter is more likely (see the additional note on 7:46). David wished for God to dwell in support of the house of Jacob and to solidify the relationship between God, land, and dynasty. The goal was for God to have a special, permanent home within his people's home. The term for "habitation" (σκήνωμα, *skēnōma*) is used only here in Acts and refers to a lodging place or dwelling place (BAGD 755 §1; BDAG 929). It refers to the temple that Solomon built to replace the tabernacle (v. 47) and alludes to Ps. 132:5 (see also 2 Sam. 7:11; 1 Kings 5–8; Michaelis, *TDNT* 7:384). As verse 47 makes clear, it was a house (οἶκος) for God (v. 49 also uses this term). The house was built "for him" (αὐτῷ, *autō*). Solomon acknowledged the limitations of the temple (1 Kings 8:27), but a state of mind about it developed that Stephen will criticize (Bruce 1988a: 149). The common term for "temple" (ἱερόν, *hieron*), which most naturally associates it with what is holy, is not used in Acts 7. Yet Luke uses it thirty-nine times, including twenty-five times in Acts. The rare terms σκήνωμα and οἶκος for God's house here may point to tradition.

7:48–50   The principle is noted: God does not dwell in a place made with human hands (χειροποιήτοις, *cheiropoiētois*). The point is that God cannot be confined to such a locale, so they should not give too much importance to the temple. In the Greek sentence, the negative οὐχ (*ouch*) is moved up and away from the verb it qualifies so that the reference to the Most High is emphasized (Moulton and Turner 1963: 287). The term "made with hands" is used in a deprecating way in the NT (Acts 19:26; Eph. 2:11; on these verses, see Sylva 1987). This theme of condemning something so made is common in Judaism (Lev. 26:1; Isa. 2:8; 46:6; Sib. Or. 3.650–51; 4.8–12; in the NT: Heb. 9:11, 24; Williams 1990: 142). One can contrast the following NT texts where reference is made to things "not made with hands": Mark 14:58 (a new temple raised up after three days); 2 Cor. 5:1 (resurrection body); and Col. 2:11 (spiritual circumcision; see Bruce 1990: 207). Rabbinic Judaism also had hints of such a spiritual view of the temple, where God or Messiah is an everlasting light (Le Cornu and Shulam 2003: 364–65; Tanḥuma, *Tetzaveh* 8 [of Messiah]; Gen. Rabbah 59.5 [of God]).

   Bruce (1988a: 149) says that Stephen is not rebuking the temple but the state of mind that tended to emerge about the temple. Jervell (1998: 245) argues that this critique must be set next to positive statements about the temple in Acts (2:46; 3:11; 5:20–21; 21:26; 22:17; 24:18). This point suggests that Bruce's view is correct. The temple is overvalued in Judaism (also Gaventa 2003: 133, who speaks of Luke having a complex view of the temple, with both positive and critical elements). Sweeney (2002) challenges Bruce's claim that the temple is not being critiqued here, but Bruce's view is nuanced. Yes, Stephen criticizes the temple, but not for what it is; rather, he is finding fault with how it is viewed. Sweeney claims that Stephen's remarks are not as negative as some commentators have made them. They do not prove, as those commentators claim, that the charges of Stephen speaking against the temple are somewhat true. Sweeney is correct on this point. Stephen's remarks are not against the concept of the temple. The problem with the temple is not that it exists. Its existence is rooted in God's permission, as Stephen notes.

Part of the problem here is how such remarks may have been heard. Jews sensitive to the temple's unique role would have regarded these remarks, even though they paralleled what was said in the Hebrew Scriptures, as excessively dismissive of the temple and its uniqueness. Christians would have simply claimed, on salvation-historical and scriptural grounds, that they were not saying anything that God had not already promised, warned about, or declared. The difference was part of the religious debate about what Jesus's coming meant for the temple. Here Stephen is simply saying that the temple cannot contain God's presence. There is more to God and God's presence than this one locale. There is a danger in making too much of the temple. The scholarly debate as to whether these remarks about the temple are positive or negative reflect, to a degree, this older debate, with points on each side having merit while neither option is the entire story. Stott (1990: 138–39) seems to have the balance right when he says that the point is not that it was wrong to construct the tabernacle or temple but that "they should never have been regarded as in any literal sense God's home."

The remarks can be seen as very much fitting in with OT teaching (see, conceptually, Isa. 57:15 and Solomon's own words, 1 Kings 8:27 and 2 Chron. 6:18; Josephus, *Ant.* 8.4.2 §107). The divine description "the Most High" (ὕψιστος, *hypsistos*) emphasizes God's sovereignty and uniqueness (Gen. 14:18, 19, 22; Deut. 32:8; Ps. 46:3 LXX [47:2 Eng.]; Luke 1:32, 35, 76). It is a name of high majesty to underscore that humans cannot build something to contain God (BAGD 850 §2; BDAG 1045 §2; Mark 5:6–7; 11:9–10; Luke 8:28; Acts 7:48–49; 16:17; Heb. 7:1–3).

The citation in verse 49 is from Isa. 66:1 in a form very much like the LXX (also used later in Barn. 16.2 and Justin Martyr, *Dial.* 22.11). God spans heaven and earth, with heaven as his throne and the earth as his footstool. The footstool (ὑποπόδιον, *hypopodion*) is another picture of God's sovereignty. The earth is the place where God sets his feet, and heaven is his throne (footstool of God: Matt. 5:34–35 [heaven a throne and earth a footstool]; Luke 20:43; Acts 2:35; Heb. 1:13; 10:13; OT: Pss. 98:5 LXX [99:5 Eng.]; 109:1 LXX [110:1 Eng.]; Isa. 66:1; Lam. 2:1). God dwarfs the earth, so how can a building constructed on it contain him? There is a merism in the reference to heaven and earth, so that God is said to span the entirety of creation. Although there are OT roots for this idea, Stephen states it as emphatically as anywhere in Scripture. Still, this is a prophetic-like critique of a skewed view of the temple, a critique comparable to Jesus's statement in Luke 19:46 (Polhill 1992: 203–4). Stephen's point is that a dwelling place for God made by human hands is not the only place God dwells. Ultimately it is inadequate to contain God, and so to think of the temple as "his house and nowhere else" would be wrong. Witherington (1998: 273) speaks of this as a "God in a box" theology. God is present throughout the creation, as Isa. 66 shows.

Stephen does not cite the positive point in Isa. 66:2b concerning the special favor that God shows to the humble and contrite of heart, what some people call the new temple of God. Does Stephen's text suggest this allusion (so Bruce 1988a: 150, but more circumspect is Marshall 1980: 146)? The absence of a direct reference makes this less than clear, but the main point seems to be that God cannot be confined to a specific locale and perhaps, as an implication, to a specific people. This idea will certainly become Luke's emphasis in Acts 8–15.

The rhetorical question in verse 50 is in fact a statement. God has made all these things, and so a human temple cannot contain God. This is not a statement against the temple; rather, it places the temple in its proper perspective. The God of creation will not find abode or rest in a single locale that is merely a place made by humans. Jewish hearers could understand and appreciate Stephen's point up to here (Schille 1984: 184; *pace* Haenchen 1987: 285, who suggests that Stephen's remarks about the temple would be heard as blasphemy). So far, nothing said about the law or the temple would be objectionable enough to evoke a violent reaction, because the prophets also said what is said up to here. The controversial point comes next.

7:51–53   These verses contain Stephen's application of his survey of Israel's history. This is the key portion of the speech in that it states the main charge against Stephen's audience and produces their hostile reaction. Here Stephen offers his charge of unfaithfulness as an implied call to repent, an idea he is not able to develop because of the crowd's violent reaction to his charge (Polhill 1992: 205). Stephen confronts his audience directly with two charges: they are stiff-necked, and they are uncircumcised of heart and ears. These charges use three terms that appear nowhere else in the NT.

He starts out with a word, σκληροτράχηλοι (*sklērotrachēloi*), that describes people who are stubborn, unable to turn their head to see, the "stiff-necked." The expression looks back to texts such as Exod. 33:3, 5; 34:9; and Deut. 9:6, 13, 27.

To add to the stern rebuke, he calls them uncircumcised of heart and ears. The expression ἀπερίτμητοι (*aperitmētoi*) accuses these Israelites of acting like the uncircumcised (Judg. 14:3; 1 Sam. 14:6; 17:26 Alex.; 2 Chron. 28:3 Alex.; Isa. 52:1; Johnson 1992: 134; 1QS 5.5; 1QpHab 11.13). They are covenantally unfaithful. Both their hearts and their ears are unresponsive. The datives καρδίαις καὶ τοῖς ὠσίν (*kardiais kai tois ōsin*) are datives of respect: uncircumcised with respect to "hearts and ears" (Moulton and Turner 1963: 220). Although this term for "uncircumcised" is used only here in the NT, its roots also go back to the OT (Lev. 26:41; Jer. 4:4; 6:10; 9:26; Ezek. 44:7, 9).

The third hapax in this verse is ἀντιπίπτετε (*antipiptete*). This present-tense verb means to oppose or resist something continually, a point emphasized even more with the adverb ἀεί (*aei*, always). The verb's force here is iterative; they are opposing God again and again (Wallace 1996: 521).

Thus Stephen charges the nation with rejecting the Spirit and being hardhearted (Isa. 63:10 LXX is conceptually similar). These charges, once the audience rejects them as untrue in their view, would be heard as an insult. But the charges made here do not stand alone.

The same point is implied in a key shift of pronouns from elsewhere in the speech. This rejection took place with "your fathers" (οἱ πατέρες ὑμῶν, *hoi pateres hymōn*), a shift from Stephen's consistent use of "our fathers" up to this point. The shift indicates a split within Israel, based upon response to God. There are those who obey God and those who resist him. This charge also has OT roots (1 Kings 19:10, 14; Neh. 9:26; 2 Chron. 36:16; Jer. 26:20; see Luke 6:23, 26; 11:47–50; 13:34). The justification for the charge is in verse 52. One should not forget that Stephen was described as full of the Spirit in Acts 6:3 and 6:5, so the response to his speech is a test of who is responsive to the Spirit.

They (that is, "your fathers") rejected the prophets before. In other words, they rejected those who announced beforehand (προκαταγγείλαντας, *prokatangeilantas*) the coming of the Righteous One (i.e., Jesus; see Acts 3:14 discussion). The only other NT occurrence of this word is in Acts 3:18. The reference to the "coming" (ἐλεύσεως, *eleuseōs*) of the Lord is not to the parousia of the Lord but to his coming in ministry, which already stands rejected (*pace* J. Schneider, *TDNT* 2:675). The previous use of the word προκαταγγέλλω (*prokatangellō*) in Acts 3:18 looks to Jesus's suffering as part of that ministry. The allusion is to prophets who were rejected and slain. Persecution of the prophets is common in the OT, which, although it notes only one example of such rejection to the point of murder, does echo similar complaints (1 Kings 18:4, 13; 19:10, 14; Jer. 2:30; 26:20–24; 2 Chron. 24:20–21 [Zechariah, son of Jehoiada the priest, is stoned]; Fitzmyer 1998: 385; in the NT: 1 Thess. 2:15; Heb. 11:36–38). The Qumran document 4QpHos 2.2–6 says "they cast behind their back all his precepts" (Le Cornu and Shulam 2003: 367). Jewish tradition held that Jeremiah was stoned to death and Isaiah was sawn in two (4 Bar. 9.25–32 [Jeremiah stoned]; 9.22 [alludes to Isaiah's death]; Mart. Ascen. Isa. 5.1–14; Josephus, *Ant.* 9.13.2 §§265–66). The pattern of death moves from the prophets to the murder and betrayal of the Righteous One himself. The idea of betrayal is also rare in the NT, occurring only three times (the others are Luke 6:13–16 [of Judas]; 2 Tim. 3:1–5), and Acts speaks of the murder of Jesus in one other text (3:13–15; 28:4 [of the suspicion Paul was a murderer]). As with the fathers, so it is with the current generation. Nothing has changed.

They should have known better, for these people received the law through the angels. The phrase εἰς διαταγὰς ἀγγέλων (*eis diatagas angelōn*) is one of means, as was the reference to an angel in Acts 7:35 (BDF §206.1). Again it is Jewish tradition that developed the idea that the giving of the law involved the angels, something Paul also notes (Gal. 3:19; Heb. 2:2). A rabbinic midrash on Exodus, Mekilta de Rabbi Ishmael (*Baḥodesh* 9) speaks of angels ministering with God to the people as the commandments were given (Le Cornu and Shulam 2003: 368–69). The term διαταγή refers to a command or direction coming from someone (BDAG 237). So the idea is that the law came "by means of the command or direction of angels." The roots of the idea may go back to Deut. 33:2 LXX, where angels accompany God at Sinai (also Jub. 1.27–29; Polhill 1992: 200; Larkin 1995: 120 sees a possible circumlocution for "God" in the reference to angels). Perhaps the idea that God does not appear to anyone also fueled this idea of angelic mediation. As Paul does in Gal. 3:19, Stephen seems to suggest a less direct involvement by God in the giving of the law. However, the idea is certainly not that God was inactive in the giving of the law. In the NT view, the nation failed to keep the divinely given law (Acts 15:10; Rom. 2:13, 23, 25).

Regarding charges of violating God's will, the roles are reversed, according to Stephen. It is not he who breaks the law, as the Jews have charged. Rather, it is his accusers who have broken the law and covenant by slaying the Righteous One. One could hardly imagine a bolder witness. It has two themes we often see in Acts: (1) the promise of Jesus is in line with the law and hope, and (2) the behavior of Israel has separated it from God's blessing and brought about the distancing of the new community from Judaism (Weiser 1981: 188).

In sum, Stephen defends himself against the charge of being unfaithful to the law and the temple by engaging in a wide-ranging examination of the Jewish Scripture. He is, as he makes his case, a "winsome radical," able to think differently from those around him but engaged as he does so (Fernando 1998: 251–53). Here his citations and allusions to these sacred texts show that (1) the nation looked to the promise of a coming one, (2) it often resisted God's will, (3) it rejected the leaders whom God had chosen, and (4) the temple was never designed to be the single place where God could be found. Deep knowledge of Scripture allows one to have a worldview that differentiates what is in the world from what a child of God should think, be, and do. What Stephen says here, their own Scripture regularly had taught and warned them about much earlier. It is a particularly powerful moment when Scripture is applied in such a way that it exposes what is really going on. Stephen did this in his speech. Such confrontation made his audience quite uncomfortable, even though it was spoken and intended for their benefit. God is far greater than any one building or location. He is the God of the world and should be seen as present throughout it. Stephen's most basic point is that the Creator is the ruler of all creation and is present in all of it. This is the final point Stephen makes as he turns to exhort them to be responsive to God. The speech ends with the question of how they will respond to a history lesson given from their own sacred tradition. In effect, Stephen asks, "Do you appreciate your own history enough not to repeat its mistakes?"

The pericope explains how Judaism and Christianity began to grow apart. The new faith emphasized a view of the law as promise, a view that pointed to one to come, that is, to Jesus. Here was a view that relativized the importance of the temple but along lines already set forth in divine disclosures. God was not limited to one locale. Here was a Jew who saw in Israel's past a great deal of unfaithfulness, which served as a basis for suggesting the need for renewal. The new faith was actually being more faithful to the promise and law than the older faith was! Stephen's audience did not want to hear any of this. They reacted, in all likelihood, before Stephen had any chance to move to a direct discussion of the one to whom this all pointed, Jesus. The martyrdom that emerged out of Stephen's speech was an indicator that the future held a parting of the ways for these two groups. But it was not Jesus's disciples who sought the division. The reaction of most in the nation to the message brought about the separation. The gospel was for all, especially those in Israel, but the rejection by those in the nation made it necessary for the new community to go its own way.

Additional Notes

7:3–51. There are about thirty instances of variants in wording between B and D in this speech; often it is D that has conformed the text more precisely to the LXX (Metzger 1971: 342–43). One exception is in verse 18, where B reads ᾔδει (ēdei). For the most part, we will not trace these variants one at a time, since the conformity to the LXX may well be evidence of the secondary character of the reading, as D often conforms texts to other translations or traditions.

7:34. In $\mathfrak{P}^{45}$ the Greek term νῦν (nyn, now) is omitted.

7:38–39. Whether the pronouns here are second person (v. 38, "to you"; v. 39, "your fathers") or first person (v. 38, "to us"; v. 39, "our fathers") is textually debated. The MSS evidence for "to you" in v. 38 is strong ($\mathfrak{P}^{74}$, ℵ, B), but contextually the evidence favors "to us," given the earlier reference to "our fathers" in the verse, where no textual problem exists. In addition, the evidence for "your fathers" in v. 39 is weak (Ψ, 81). These problems should probably be assessed together. Stephen is still identifying with his audience here. It is "our" fathers, and the law is for "us." The later church's move away from the law might explain the variants.

7:43. In the textual tradition, various spellings for the second figure exist, which are transliterated here for simplicity: Rhompha (ℵ*), Rhomphan (B), Rhemphan (323), Rhempham (D), Rhepha (81). Rhaiphan is best attested ($\mathfrak{P}^{74}$, ℵ², A, 453).

7:43. Another textual problem in the verse is whether Rephan is referred to as "your" (ὑμῶν, hymōn) god. For the omission of ὑμῶν are B, D, 36, 453. For inclusion are $\mathfrak{P}^{74}$, ℵ, A, C, E, Ψ.

The external evidence favors inclusion and represents another jab at the ancestors who made the stars into their gods.

7:46. A textual problem here is whether David wishes to build a habitation for the "God" (θεῳ, *theō*) of Jacob or the "house" (οἴκῳ, *oikō*) of Jacob. Reading "God" are ℵ², A, C, E, Ψ, 33, 1739, and Byz. Reading "house" are 𝔓⁷⁴, ℵ*, B, D, H, and 049. The less "natural" and so more difficult reading is "house," and the distribution also favors this reading. The reading "God" is straightforward and stresses that the temple would be for God (Johnson 1992: 133 opts for this reading). The reading "house" suggests that the building of the temple was designed in part to be an act by the house of Jacob on behalf of God, to give God a permanent locale within the land. "House of Jacob" is the more likely reading here on text-critical grounds. Psalm 132:3–5 seems to be the text at work here: David wished for God to dwell in support of the house of Jacob.

3. The Martyrdom of Stephen (7:54–8:1a)

The Stephen sequence in Acts ends with his lynching and martyrdom, so the form of this passage is a martyrdom account. The crowd reacts angrily to his condemnation of Israel's resistance (v. 54). When Stephen proclaims that he sees the Son of Man, Jesus, standing at the right hand of the Father, it is too much (vv. 55–56). In their view, Stephen is attacking the very uniqueness of God by suggesting that there is one standing next to him in heaven. They see this as a clear act of blasphemy. This difference over Jesus and all that grows out of it is the key to the conflict and parting of the ways between Jews and the new community. Fitzmyer (1998: 389) observes that the vision confirms an important point in Stephen's speech: that God dwells in heaven or in the creation, not in a man-made temple. The stoning for what in their view is blasphemy (Lev. 24:11–16, 23) leads to Stephen's death (vv. 57–60). Stephen dies in a way that parallels Jesus: Stephen makes claims about the Son of Man, utters a final cry, and asks that his opponents be forgiven. The unit ends with the note that Saul, who is watching the Jewish people's cloaks as they kill Stephen, agrees with the action (8:1a). The key figure Saul/Paul is introduced as a willing persecutor of the church.

The issue of sources is complex and much debated (Barrett 1994: 380–82). Most scholars see two accounts woven together here by Luke (Jervell 1998: 256). They argue that one source sees a lynching and another a trial. It is hard to make favorable judgment about the use of two sources, especially by playing the accounts against one another. It is an indication of how uncertain things are that Schneider (1980: 471) argues that Luke has added touches of parallelism to Jesus's death whereas Weiser (1981: 190–91) sees almost the entire unit as Lukan, excepting only 7:58a. In short, we do not know how the sources here work.

The account is an example of mob justice, not a formal legal process. No attempt is made to solicit a verdict. Stoning emerges from the angry crowd's spontaneous reaction. The event's importance and the mark it made on the church is clear from the space Luke devotes to telling the entire story of Stephen's activities and demise. Stephen becomes an exemplary witness who bears his cross on behalf of Jesus.

Exegesis and Exposition

[7:54]When they heard these things, they became furious in their hearts and began to grind their teeth against him. [55]But being full of the Spirit and gazing into heaven, Stephen beheld the glory of God and Jesus standing at the right hand of God [56]and said, "Behold, I see the heavens opening and the ⌜Son of Man⌝ standing at the right hand of God." [57]Crying out in a loud voice, they stopped their ears and rushed together upon him. [58]And casting him out of the city, they stoned him; and the witnesses set their garments at the feet of a young man named Saul. [59]And they were stoning Stephen, while he was calling out, saying, "Lord Jesus, receive my spirit." [60]And kneeling down, he cried out in a loud voice, "Lord, do not hold ⌜this⌝ sin against them." And when he said this, he fell asleep. [8:1a]And Saul was consenting concerning his killing.

7:54 The crowd reacts with anger to Stephen's remarks. Given the timing of the reaction, it is the charge of always resisting the Spirit that has the crowd stirred up. They are "ripped [or sawn through] in their hearts" (διεπρίοντο ταῖς καρδίαις αὐτῶν, *dieprionto tais kardiais autōn*), which describes a visceral, emotional reaction of anger. Acts 5:33 is the only other use of the verb in the NT. They are furious. The grinding of their teeth also reinforces the point (Job 16:9; Pss. 34:16 LXX [35:16 Eng.]; 36:12 LXX [37:12 Eng.]; Lam. 2:16; BAGD 148; BDAG 184). The use of the verb βρύχω (*brychō*, grind) is unique to the NT, but the noun for gnashing (βρυγμός, *brygmos*) appears seven times (Matt. 8:11–12; 13:40–42, 49–50; 22:13; 24:48–51; 25:30; Luke 13:28). Both verbs are imperfects, probably inceptive in force (Barrett 1994: 382, "became enraged" and "began to ground their teeth"). As they heard Stephen chastise Israel, they began the process of becoming more angered.

The reaction breaks into what had been Stephen's defense at what appears to have been a type of legal inquiry or trial. Le Cornu and Shulam (2003: 372) suggest a limited authority to execute, but the evidence here is of a mob response. There is no legal process here. The Sanhedrin may have been gathering evidence against Stephen, but the angry crowd took the verdict into their own hands when Stephen saw Jesus as the Son of Man. In contrast to Le Cornu and Shulam, this is not the end of a capital case legal process but a legal examination gathering evidence that became a mob response to what was perceived to be a blasphemous claim of Jesus's being at God's side. Stephen did not seem headed toward losing his life until the crowd lost its head.

7:55–56 When Luke describes Stephen again as "full of the Spirit" (Acts 6:3, 5), he is clear from his perspective about whose reaction reflects the proper view. Stephen gains a glimpse directly into heaven, as the picture of heaven opening (διηνοιγμένους, *diēnoigmenous*) points to a revelatory experience.[1] Usually διανοίγω (*dianoigō*, open) in the NT means that the perception of a person is opened up, but disclosure is also often an additional point of the verb.[2] God is granting Stephen a glimpse of heaven as an act of vindication for his claims.

Stephen sees God's glory. He also sees the Son of Man standing at the right side of God. God dwells in glory, a glory Jesus shares (Larkin 1995: 121). A preview of this scene was the transfiguration (Luke 9:32; Bruce 1990: 210). Most NT references to the right hand of God allude to being seated at God's right hand, an allusion to Ps. 110:1 (Luke 20:42; see discussion on Acts 2:32–36). Here Jesus stands as if to welcome and receive Stephen and his testimony.

This is one of three occurrences of the term "Son of Man" outside the four Gospels (Rev. 1:13 and 14:14 are the others). It is the only time the exact title shows up outside the Gospels (the Revelation passages refer to one "like a Son of Man," making an allusion to Dan. 7:13). This was Jesus's favorite self-designation. Late in his ministry, he used the title to refer to the one with judgment authority from the right hand of God (Matt. 26:64; Mark 14:62; Luke 22:69; for authenticity, see discussion in Bock 1996: 1796–1801; Bock 1998a: 220–30). So Stephen declares that he sees a judging Jesus standing beside God. The crucified Jesus is both alive and at work.

There is scholarly discussion about why the Son of Man is standing rather than in his normal seated position (Bock 1987: 222–24).

1. Some argue that there is no significance other than the transcendent position of Jesus (Larkin 1995: 120–21). It simply is a way to point to Dan. 7:13 LXX. However, the reference to "right hand" points to the frequently used Ps. 110:1, which mentions sitting. The expression of being seated is too common to ignore. Transcendence is certainly the point, but is that all? Several additional ideas are suggested.

2. Barrett (1994: 383) minimizes any christological significance, since Jesus is not seated, but this ignores the usual backdrop of the reference to the right hand. He says that the act only confirms what Stephen has said, but surely for a raised Jesus to be next to God presents yet another declared vindication of Jesus and has literary echoes of the exaltation in Acts 2 and 3 reverberating in the

---

1. On martyrs, death, and visions, see Mart. Ascen. Isa. 5.9–16 (Isaiah, sawn in two, speaks by the Spirit); Targum Pseudo-Jonathan on Gen. 27:1 (Isaac sees the throne of God's glory as he nears death, but the Isaac passage is not a martyrdom account); Conzelmann 1987: 59.

2. For this verb, see Mark 7:33–34 (eyes); Luke 2:22–24 (womb); 24:30–32 (eyes and Scripture), 45–47 (minds); Acts 7:55–56 (heavens); 16:14 (heart); 17:2–3 (explaining the Christ). In Judaism, for the related term, ἀνοίγω (*anoigō*, to open), see Isa. 63:19 LXX; 3 Macc. 6:18; 2 Bar. 22.1; in the NT, Rev. 4:1; 19:11; Johnson 1992: 140.

background. This is a Jesus whom God has brought into glory at his side. In addition, the conceptual parallels to Jesus's trial scene (see below) also argue for a christological point in the passage. The shock to Jewish ears of the scene as described would be that Jesus is at the side of God.

3. The idea that the figure is angelic is raised as another option, especially given that the vision itself does not name Jesus. Stephen's appeal to forgive sin in 7:59–60, however, does not seek to address an angel.

4. It is possible that the picture of standing indicates Jesus's moving to aid Stephen as he faces rejection, a kind of "individual" parousia of Jesus (Barrett 1963 and Williams 1990: 146 speak of this view as possible). But this also cannot exhaust the imagery.

5. Slightly more likely is that Jesus arises as the judge and receiver of Stephen's testimony. The idea that the exalted Son of Man functions as judge is a key point of the imagery (Luke 12:8; Pesch 1966: 54–58; Polhill 1992: 208; Bruce 1988a: 156). Here Jesus is seen as an advocate for Stephen, a vindicator of his claims (Witherington 1998: 275). This also implies that the Jewish judgment against Stephen will serve to leave the audience subject to the judgment of God and the Son of Man (Schneider 1980: 475). Pesch (1986a: 264) also points to a switch from Jewish to Hellenistic mission and as a result probably overstates the significance of a shift in ethnic focus. Jews continue to be preached to throughout Acts. If Jesus is a judge, then he is Stephen's advocate and witness. The vision means that heaven stands opposed to the Jewish reaction to Stephen.

View 5, the picture of Jesus as vindicating judge, is the most likely force of the image here. Efforts to further distinguish the significance of Jesus's standing—whether he is functioning as judge or advocate or reacting in opposition to the Jewish audience—attempt too fine a set of distinctions. All of these ideas belong together here. Stephen's later appeal in 7:59–60 that his audience be forgiven reinforces this view that judgment is on the horizon and forgiveness is needed. Conzelmann (1987: 60) objects that a judging function is not emphasized in Luke, but this ignores the point of Jesus's reply at his trial: the Son of Man will be the judge on judgment day (see Mark 14:62 and Luke 22:69; Bock 1998a: 231–33). Stephen's vindication by the standing Son of Man implies Jesus's vindication as well because Jesus is functioning in a manner that assumes the previous divine exaltation and vindication of Jesus.

The remarks send the crowd into a frenzy. When Stephen declares that he sees the Son of Man standing at the right hand of God, he is stoned for blasphemy because, in the view of these Jews, no one has the right to be at the side of God's heavenly presence. Bock (1998a: 113–83) discusses the variety of views within Judaism. Many Pharisees appear to have had no place for the possibility of God sharing his glory (see the punishment of Metatron in 3 Enoch, a work that challenges such a shared glory option). Since Son of Man was Jesus's favorite self-designation and Stephen, as a believer in Jesus, was preaching about the one to come, the crowd may well have perceived a reference to Jesus in the remark. In effect, Stephen is declaring that he sees God's vindication on behalf of Jesus, matching Jesus's controversial claim at his trial in Luke 22:69 that "from now on" the Son of Man would be at God's right hand (Bruce 1988a: 154 develops this point nicely).

For the careful reader of Luke-Acts, Stephen's testimony is of Jesus's complete vindication by God. This claim leads to Stephen's martyrdom. So the issue that led to Jesus's execution, his claim to be able to sit at God's right hand (Luke 22:69), also leads to Stephen's death. This christological point and belief, embedded in the allusion to the Son of Man and to Jesus's trial scene, reflect the difference between the new community and the Jews who stone Stephen. The parting of the ways between Judaism and what became Christianity centered on the status the believers in the new faith assigned to Jesus.[3] Stephen's vision and the crowd's violent reaction exemplify this difference.

The mention of the Son of Man at the side of God intensifies the reaction. Crying out in a loud voice and stopping the ears are indications that, for the crowd, blasphemy has taken place. Philo in *Decalogue* 13 §63 explains that blasphemy reflects such an insult to the pious that they feel an "indescribable and irreconcilable affliction, which enters in at their ears and pervades the whole soul." In the later Talmud, *b. Ketub.* 5a says that when people hear a word that is not seemly, they are to stop up their ears (Str-B 2:684). Thus the covering of the ears symbolizes the desire not to hear what has been uttered. Johnson (1992: 140) notes the irony of Stephen having called them uncircumcised in ears, so that when the report of the vision of the risen, vindicated Jesus comes, they choose not to hear it. The crowd rushes Stephen to remove him from the city, yet another indication that they regard Stephen's remarks as blasphemy (Lev. 24:14; Num. 15:35; *m. Sanh.* 6.1–4).

7:57–58

Some controversy surrounds the fact that this execution takes place as capital punishment. Such punishment was a prerogative of Rome (John 18:31; for how this debate relates to the parallel execution of Jesus, see Bock 1998a: 7–12). Those who see a trial here sense a problem in the portrayal, which allows the crowd to execute Stephen. The account suggests, however, the reaction of a mob and the equivalent of a lynching, since there is no formal verdict (Pesch 1986a: 264; Bruce 1988a: 157–59; Polhill 1992: 208–9; Jervell 1998: 252; differences with a formal verdict and trial, as Haenchen 1987: 296 outlines, do not indicate that Luke

---

3. Hurtado (2003) shows how this honor worked in the early centuries of the church.

lacks knowledge about such a procedure but that this process was not a normal one). Barrett (1994: 386) argues that the lynching scene takes away any strength to the argument that the execution is for blasphemy, as no formal rationale is necessary. Barrett's argument, however, ignores the earlier stopping of the ears and Stephen's removal from the city, which point to a stoning for blasphemy. Eckey (2000: 181) simply refers to these verses as "lynch justice" (*Lynchjustiz*). This kind of paralegal zeal against "blasphemy" had precedent in other acts noted in the OT and Jewish literature (apostasy in a mixed marriage [Num. 25:6–15]; sacrificing a pig on an independent altar in obedience to Antiochus IV [1 Macc. 2:23–28]).

Nonetheless, the crowd carries out the execution in traditional Jewish fashion by stoning Stephen (*m. Sanh.* 7.4)[4] and doing so outside the city (Lev. 24:14; *m. Sanh.* 6.1). Bruce also suggests that the fact that the temple was included in the charges might have allowed for a Jewish execution, as the Romans left administration of the temple mostly in Jewish hands. Bruce also correctly rejects the idea that Rome was in an interregnum, with Pilate in the midst of being replaced, as some have suggested (Larkin 1995: 122 agrees about the temple jurisdiction issue). The point about the temple is not, however, so clear in this scene. Furthermore, Josephus (*Ant.* 20.9.1 §200) later shows that the unauthorized execution of Jesus's brother James by Jews on a nontemple matter made some of the Jews nervous about usurping Roman authority. The controversial execution of James took place during an interregnum, so that an interregnum explanation for Stephen's death does not seem plausible, given how nervous Jews were when James was independently executed. Witherington (1998: 276) is right that debates over whether a legal action was permitted here are moot, for this is a crowd action, not a complete legal process. The crowd acts out of what it thinks is a moral duty.

The witnesses to what Stephen said lay their garments at the feet of a young man named Saul. Luke introduces the hero of the second half of Acts by noting that he observes and shares in the persecution and rejection of Christians. He is an eyewitness to the nature of the dispute between many Jews in Jerusalem and the new community (Acts 22:20). Acts 8:1a notes that Saul approves of what is happening to Stephen, something Luke would know as a companion of Paul. Suggestions that the remark is redactional and that Saul was not present are simply

---

4. Fitzmyer 1998: 393 notes different reasons for stoning: Deut. 17:2–7 (worship of alien gods); Lev. 20:2–5 (sacrifice of children to Molech); Deut. 13:2–6 (prophesying in the name of a false god); Lev. 20:27 (divination); 24:14–16 (blasphemy); Num. 15:32–36 (Sabbath labor); Deut. 22:22 (adultery); 21:18–21 (filial insubordination); Josh. 7:25 (violating the *ḥerem* by taking the spoils of war). Le Cornu and Shulam (2003: 379) note that in the Pentateuch, eighteen offenses are punishable by stoning, including incest and other prohibited sexual relations, blasphemy, idolatry, divination, sorcery, soothsaying, profaning the Sabbath, and a rebellious son.

skeptical speculation. That witnesses have a key role in the execution is also according to Jewish custom (Deut. 17:7; 13:9–10). Those who will cast stones shed their garments, no doubt to be able to cast those stones more effectively. In *m. Sanh.* 6.3 it is the victim whose clothes are shed, but there is no confusion about the law here, merely a practical description of how much the crowd wants to stone Stephen. Saul's name points to the king of the tribe of Benjamin, to which Paul belongs (Rom. 11:1; Phil. 3:5).

When Stephen is stoned, his actions echo that of Jesus but with one   7:59
major difference. He "calls out" to heaven. The term here, ἐπικαλούμενον (*epikaloumenon*), is no accident. It recalls the exhortation of Peter that to receive salvation one must call out to the Lord (Acts 2:21). Thus in the moment when Stephen is truly alone and his life is at an end, he turns to God and asks that his spirit be received. Given the vision of 7:55–56, he is asking the standing Son of Man and the Father to receive him. In a manner very similar to Jesus's call to the Father, "Into your hands I commit my spirit," Stephen prepares to die (Luke 23:46; Ps. 31:5). There is one major difference: as he cries to heaven, he explicitly addresses his mediator, the Lord Jesus (κύριε Ἰησοῦ, *kyrie Iēsou*), to receive him. The work in heaven is now shared between God and the one at his right hand. Here is evidence of a high Christology. Prayer is now made to Jesus, and requests to heaven go through him.

Stephen ends up on his knees in prayer (on this posture: Luke 22:41;   7:60–8:1a
Acts 9:40; 20:36; 21:5). He cries out to the Lord (probably to Jesus, see v. 59) for the forgiveness of those stoning him, thereby recalling Jesus's words to pray for those who abuse you (Luke 6:27–28) and emulating Jesus's act on the cross (Luke 23:34, which is textually disputed but likely original, given that Jesus's saying does not match this one in wording; Bock 1996: 1867–68). According to Eusebius, *Eccl. Hist.* 2.23.36, James uttered a prayer similar in spirit, and Stephen's prayer appears in *Eccl. Hist.* 5.2.5 (contrast the call for revenge from Zechariah, which is really a call for justice, 2 Chron. 24:22; Bruce 1990: 213). Following the Mishnah, Haenchen (1987: 293n7) maintains that such a prayer could not happen, but this is overly skeptical. The event is too spontaneous to be subject to such an evaluation. It is not certain that this event followed mishnaic procedure, and prayer for one's own sin and forgiveness was allowed (*m. Sanh.* 6.2); therefore Stephen could offer a prayer, given it was an appeal for compassion from God.

The request is that their sin not count against his Jewish executioners. The text for the request uses the verb ἵστημι (*histēmi*, hold; LXX; Gen. 6:18; 9:11; 17:7; 26:3). The loud cry also recalls the crucifixion (Matt. 27:46 = Mark 15:34 with Ps. 22:1; Luke 23:46 with Ps. 31:5). With forgiveness on his lips, Stephen dies. Despite the earlier denunciation of sin, Stephen still cares for those he addressed, despite their rejection of him (Marshall 1980: 150). Some say that the conversion of Paul was God's answer to the prayer (Larkin 1995: 123). Another benefit of the persecution that emerges after this event (Acts 8:1b–4) is that the gospel is preached outside Jerusalem. Opportunity remains for Israel to respond, as Paul's ministry makes clear. To describe the death, Luke uses the euphemism that he "fell asleep," which according to later NT teaching will result in a resurrection (Polhill 1992: 210; John 11:11; 1 Cor. 11:30; 15:6, 18, 20; 1 Thess. 4:13–15; 2 Pet. 3:4; sleep as death in the OT: Gen. 47:30; Deut. 31:16; 1 Kings 2:10; Isa. 14:18; Fitzmyer 1998: 394).

A final note concludes the scene: it is the attitude of Saul. He consents to the death. The verb συνευδοκέω (*syneudokeō*) speaks of agreement (BDAG 970; Luke 11:48; Acts 8:1; 22:20; Rom. 1:32; 1 Cor. 7:12–13). The imperfect periphrastic construction highlights the duration of Saul's consent. Saul is agreeing to the action as it proceeds. The noun for Stephen's death (ἀναίρεσις, *anairesis*) appears only here in the NT; it is a strong term that refers to "killing" (BDAG 84; the cognate verb form is in Acts 22:20; 26:10). Saul may well have been a significant help to the pressure against Stephen, considering that he was from Cilicia, the place from which the attacks on Stephen originate (Acts 6:9; Johnson 1992: 141). He also leads the later persecution (8:3). Only a later appearance of Jesus will change his mind. In Acts 22:20, the apostle Paul later notes the effect of Stephen's death. Acts 8:1a is a bridge into the next short section, where persecution sends many in the church out beyond Jerusalem.

In sum, this unit looks at someone who paid the ultimate price for faith: martyrdom. Stephen dies not only seeing Jesus standing in heaven to receive him but also praying for those who killed him. Stephen dies as Jesus did and follows his example. Death is frightening, but martyrdom for Jesus, though not sought, is an honorable death. Other believers can draw strength from the way in which Stephen bears his cross.

The scene also portrays what is dividing the new faith from Judaism: the honor Jesus receives. What is glorious to Stephen is blasphemy to his audience. The two views cannot be more divergent. The vision of God's glory reinforces the conclusion that Stephen's view of things is the truth. A second appearance by Jesus to Saul will convince the model persecutor of the church that Stephen is right about Jesus.

Additional Notes

7:56. Instead of "Son of Man," "Son of God" (τὸν υἱὸν τοῦ θεοῦ, *ton huion tou theou*) is read here by 𝔓[74vid], 614, and some Bohairic MSS. But this is not well enough attested to be original.

7:60. An issue of word order in the verse does not affect its meaning. In some MSS "this" (ταύτην) comes after the reference to sin (𝔓[74], ℵ, E, Ψ, 33, Byz). The best MSS evidence, however, has "this" coming first (𝔓[45vid], A, B, C, D).

B. Saul the Persecutor and the Spread of the Word (8:1b–4)

This short unit serves as a transition to Philip's work (Acts 8:5–40), which comes as a result of the persecution that falls especially on the Hellenist church in Jerusalem. The persecution arises in reaction to Stephen's work. The clue that the Hellenists are targeted is the fact that the apostles don't depart and a vibrant Jewish believing church exists in Jerusalem later in Acts. The unit has four parts: (1) the persecution leading to scattering (v. 1b); (2) the burial of Stephen (v. 2); (3) the work of Saul the persecutor (v. 3); and (4) the effect of the persecution in spreading the word (v. 4). The order reflects some rearrangement, as Stephen would have been buried almost immediately after his death. This rearrangement allows Stephen to appear in the middle of the unit and reminds us that his death plays a key role in the persecution (Polhill 1992: 210–11). The unit shows that persecution faced faithfully can have positive results for the church (see also Acts 11:19–30 for more results from this dispersion). It also prepares for the amazing transformation of Saul the persecutor into Paul the apostle, which comes as a result of Jesus's appearance to him in Acts 9.

The geographical movement in Acts shifts as attention moves from the Jerusalem church to what is happening outside Jerusalem. The main characters in Acts 8–12 are the scattered church, Philip, Paul, Peter with Cornelius, the unknown Hellenists, and Peter again. Movement beyond Peter and the Twelve continues to expand.

Exegesis and Exposition

[1b]And on that day a great persecution arose against the church in Jerusalem; and they were all scattered throughout the region of Judea and Samaria, except the apostles. [2]Pious men buried Stephen and made a great lament over him. [3]But Saul was ravaging the church, and entering house after house, he dragged off men and women and committed them to prison. [4]Now those who were scattered went about preaching the word ⌜ ⌝.

A great persecution arises against the church (on the term ἐκκλησία, *ekklēsia*, church, see 5:11). This is the first use of the noun διωγμός (*diōgmos*, persecution) in Acts (Marshall 1980: 151; Matt. 13:20–21; Mark 4:16–17; 10:29–30; Acts 8:1; 13:50; Rom. 8:35; 2 Cor. 12:10; 2 Thess. 1:3–10; 2 Tim. 3:10–11; 2 Macc. 12:23). We have moved from a warn-

8:1b

ing (4:21) to a flogging (5:40) to martyrdom (7:58–60) to persecution (Polhill 1992: 211). In Judaism, the view was sometimes expressed that scattering is a good event. Second Baruch 1.4 speaks of God scattering Jews among the Gentiles so they can do good among them. A similar positive result emerges from this persecution, as Acts 8:4 and the Philip episode show.

Why do only the apostles stay? The fact that the apostles remain may well mean that the persecution is directed primarily against the Hellenist believers Stephen represented (Schneider 1980: 479; Bruce 1988a: 162). The fact that the next unit is about Philip outside the region and that a vibrant Jewish believing church appears later in Acts also suggests this Hellenist focus of the persecution (on the early Hebrew church in Jerusalem, see Eusebius, *Eccl. Hist.* 5.18.4; Clement of Alexandria, *Stromata* 6.5).

The church is scattered (διεσπάρησαν, *diesparēsan*) into Judea, Samaria, and beyond (Acts 1:8) and (according to 11:19–20) to Phoenicia, Cyprus, and Antioch. This is one of three occurrences of this verb, all in Acts (8:4; 11:19). The term "Diaspora" is derived from this word (Josephus, *Ant.* 12.6.2 §278). The reference to "all" the church being scattered is probably hyperbolic (Williams 1990: 151), but it shows that when a significant portion of the church is persecuted, the whole is attacked and affected. Williams notes that Luke sometimes uses "all" to mean "many" (Acts 9:35; Barrett 1994: 391 notes that Calvin also saw hyperbole here). Still, one must distinguish between a possible focus on the Hellenists and the idea that others in the church are completely exempt. The latter is unlikely. The result of the pressure is that the church in Jerusalem scatters out like seed into the neighboring regions, although the bulk of the opposition may well be directed against the Hellenists. Jervell (1998: 254) regards the idea of an ethnically focused persecution as unlikely given the unity of the church. He sees Luke as in error here in having the apostles left behind. However, that a community of believers is still present in Jerusalem (8:26; 9:26, 28, 31; 11:22) means that Luke is using hyperbole here and that one wing of the church likely feels the most pressure. Out of this scattering emerge major outreaches, as the events surrounding Philip later in the chapter indicate. No matter where members of the new community are, mission follows.

The apostles remain behind. Why they would have been safe is not entirely clear, but it could be that they are too well known to be persecuted or that they took the risk, feeling it their duty to remain (Bruce 1990: 215). Eusebius (*Eccl. Hist.* 3.5.2) says that they were harassed until they finally left to engage in wider mission after James's death (Acts 12). It might also have been the Jewish hope that by pressuring a key wing of the church, the situation might settle down. If such was the goal, future events show that it failed. Bruce (1988a: 162–63) suggests that the Hellenists are the object of the brunt of popular resentment against the believers, and Polhill (1992: 211) argues that the Hellenist believers' view of an "unbounded God" is particularly offensive to those who are devoted to the temple. Stephen's role as a prominent Hellenist Christian may have had consequences for his community. Nevertheless, it is not clear that only the Hellenists were persecuted. It could well be that the Hebrew Christians felt a greater loyalty to Jerusalem.

An unspecified number of pious men take care of Stephen's burial and **8:2** make a great lament (κοπετὸν μέγαν, *kopeton megan*) over him. The term for "lament" appears only here in the NT (BAGD 443; BDAG 558). Usually such mourning entailed beating one's breast and weeping. They are honoring Stephen, as *m. Sanh.* 6.5–6 permits burial of one who was stoned but no lamentation. Their act is both defiant and a statement of their perception that Stephen was righteous (Le Cornu and Shulam 2003: 386; on mourning and wailing, see Exod. 12:30; Mic. 1:8). Such mourning often lasted from thirty to seventy days (Gen. 50:3 [seventy days]; Deut. 34:8 [thirty days]).

In the meantime, Saul begins continually to persecute the church se- **8:3** verely. In the NT, much is made of Saul the persecutor (Acts 22:4–5; 26:10–11; 1 Cor. 15:9; Gal. 1:13, 22–23; Phil. 3:5–6; 1 Tim. 1:13).[1] He watched Stephen die (7:58), agreed with the death (8:1a), and now takes action against the church. Haenchen (1987: 294–95) is skeptical of such a quick transformation of Saul into a persecutor and sees only a Lukan literary move, but again Haenchen is too skeptical of these accounts. It may well be, however, that a significant event such as Stephen's speech and death leads Saul to see a need to act against this vocal but lesser-known part of the church. He may sense that things are becoming serious, as Jews of all kinds are responding to the gospel and speaking up for Jesus while challenging Israel's need to come to faith. Fitzmyer (1998: 397) addresses Haenchen's view, noting that Paul himself speaks of his fierce persecution of the church (Gal. 1:13). Schneider (1980: 480) complains that Paul says he was not known to the churches in Judea, according to Gal. 1:22, but Paul seems to mean it in terms of careful acquaintance, especially since his conversion. Barrett (1994: 390) also defends the essential historicity of this verse and argues that it is based on traditional material, although Luke has reworked it.

The term used for Saul's work is λυμαίνω (*lymainō*). This word describes someone who damages or spoils something (BAGD 481; BDAG 604).[2] The imperfect tense again highlights Saul's ongoing act, possibly

1. On such violent divisions within Judaism, see Le Cornu and Shulam 2003: 388–91, who note (1) civil war among the Pharisees during the time of Alexander Jannaeus (102–76 BC); (2) Qumran's reaction to Jerusalem; (3) tensions between the schools of Hillel and Shammai before AD 70; and (4) sicarii, or zealot, violence during the same period.
2. The active form of the verb is used in the LXX and often means "oppress" or "subvert"; see Exod. 23:8; 2 Chron. 16:10; Prov. 18:9; 19:3; Isa. 65:8. But Ps. 80:13 (79:14

carrying an ingressive force. Saul either is "trying to destroy" (conative force, NET) or beginning to seek to damage the church (ingressive force). This is the only time the term is used in the NT. According to later texts in Acts (9:1–2; 26:10–11), Saul works with the approval of local Sanhedrin officials.

Saul's dragging people to prison parallels what will happen later in other locales. The participle σύρων (syrōn, dragging) can either indicate the means by which imprisonment takes place or be rendered as a finite verb. In Thessalonica, Jason and some believers are dragged into the amphitheater (17:6). At Lystra, crowds drag Paul out of the city after stoning him (14:19). John 21:8 uses the verb σύρω (syrō) of dragging fish in a net (Rev. 12:4 has the final NT use, where the dragon's tail sweeps away a third of the earth; in the OT: 2 Sam. 17:13; Isa. 28:2; 4 Macc. 6:1; Johnson 1992: 142). The house-to-house nature of his search underscores the seriousness of his quest.

8:4   This verse is a bridge and could well be connected with the next unit. The use of οὖν (oun, now) points to a fresh discussion (Acts 1:6, 18; 5:41; and twenty-four more times), but the verse also connects back to the "dispersed" of verse 1b, so here it is noted as a transition verse and is kept with the earlier unit.

The church is "those who are dispersed" (οἱ διασπαρέντες, hoi diasparentes). The verb appears only three times in the NT, all in Acts (8:1, 4; 11:19). The result of dispersion is not disappointing because it leads to a widened preaching of the word (5:42), which is detailed with Philip's work in Samaria. Acts 11:19–20 reports work even farther away. Ironically, it is persecution that helps the church carry out the commission Jesus gave them (Acts 1:8; Matt. 28:18–20). Marshall (1980: 154) observes that it is a natural thing for wandering Christians to spread the word of the gospel. Stott (1990: 146) notes that the persecution has the exact opposite effect of its intention—it does not stop the spread of the gospel but contributes to it. Persecution correctly handled by the church can do that.

In sum, this brief unit prepares us for Philip and the positive effects of persecution. Faithfully, the persecuted church disperses and preaches the word of the gospel. Luke notes the principle and then gives an example in Philip.

Additional Note

8:4. Codex E and a few other MSS of the Vulgate, Syriac, and Bohairic traditions add τοῦ θεοῦ (tou theou): the church preaches the "word of God." The point is correct in that the gospel is intended, but the wording is not original, lacking broad attestation.

LXX) uses the word for a boar that rips up a vineyard, and Isa. 65:25 speaks of a lion who no longer destroys his prey.

C. Philip in Samaria and with a Eunuch from Ethiopia (8:5–40)

The Philip cycle has two parts linked by a summary. First are his work in Samaria and the encounter Peter and John have with the magician Simon Magus (8:5–24). Then comes a summary verse of activity in Samaria (8:25), followed by Philip's meeting with the Ethiopian eunuch, where Isa. 53 is the basis for preaching Jesus (Acts 8:26–40). Success in preaching the gospel is not limited to the apostles. Many are spreading the word. When the report of the Samaritan response reaches the apostles, Peter and John go to investigate the results. The Spirit is responsible for the second encounter. As soon as Philip's work is done, he disappears. The scene continues to underscore how God is leading the mission, whether through persecution or by direct guidance. Philip is God's faithful messenger, and divine providence drives the mission. What seemed a disaster, the scattering of the church, has resulted in a successful mission that was not the result of human planning (Johnson 1992: 150). Sometimes God puts us in places we do not plan on to further his work.

There is a second important dimension to this section. Those who respond are not Jews but those on the edge of Judaism, namely, Samaritans and an Ethiopian (Schneider 1980: 480; Witherington 1998: 279–80). The reach of the gospel is moving toward those beyond the center of Judaism in fulfillment of Jesus's postresurrection commission (Acts 1:8), on its initial journey "for all who are far away" (Gaventa 2003: 134). By use of a bridge that involves those on the periphery of Judaism, the unit sets the stage for the outreach to the Gentiles.

1. Philip in Samaria (8:5–25)

There are two major elements to Philip's work in Samaria. First is the successful expansion of the spread of the word as Philip's ministry of word and deed makes a significant impression on the Samaritans. Luke earlier placed the Samaritans in a positive light (Luke 10:29–37). Now the first significant expansion he records involves them as well. Second is the encounter with a magician named Simon Magus, who is impressed by Philip's power (or, better, God's power through Philip and the apostles). Simon mistakenly wants to buy access to this power. The work of the Spirit is not for sale, so Peter challenges him. Rather, the Spirit is a gift from God, bestowed when and where God wishes. The scene is important, for Simon, wielding the greatest magical power in the world, recognizes God's greater power operating in Philip (Schneider 1980: 484). Johnson (1992: 152) also compares the encounter to the case of Ananias and Sapphira in terms of integrity. Later texts in Acts will renew this confrontation between magical or hostile supernatural forces and those who have the Spirit (13:6–11; 16:16–18; 19:11–20; 28:3–6). The scene also shows the church by God's direction growing outside Jerusalem and this growth being accepted in Jerusalem.

The unit's structure, which is straightforward, contains three basic parts: the summary of Philip's ministry (vv. 5–8), the introduction of Simon (vv. 9–13), and the confirming work of Peter and John in giving the Spirit, along with Peter's rebuke of Simon (vv. 14–24). A transition verse on the preaching of the gospel to Samaria closes the unit (v. 25). There is some verbal repetition in the account (compare v. 6 with vv. 10–11; v. 9 with v. 11; v. 9 with v. 10; v. 12 with v. 13; Barrett 1994: 398). This may well suggest that Luke had access to multiple sources about Simon. Schneider (1980: 484) suggests three sources for the chapter: (1) a Philip history with both a Simon episode and the eunuch account, (2) a Simon tradition, and (3) a tradition on Peter and John in Samaria. He acknowledges some overlap in the sources. It is hard to be certain about such details.[1]

---

1. See Witherington's dissent about the supposed long histories of transmission for these events. Witherington 1998: 280 notes that Luke may well have had direct contact with Philip and/or his daughters (Acts 21:8–10). He regards the lack of editing in the story as evidence of Luke's direct handling of the story through such sources rather than the assembling of distinct traditions without editorial attention to the combining of these sources.

The source debate is complex, with multiple options suggested. Dickerson (1997a) has a detailed treatment of the question and notes six general approaches. His own solution is that there were at least two sources, possibly three, and that Philip and Simon were connected in the tradition (Barrett 1979 argues for three sources as well). Most views see a major break in the passage at 8:14. Most modern source theories, however, underestimate the possibility of oral tradition or the use of personal sources to which the author had access, including Philip himself (21:8). For example, Haenchen (1987: 307) argues that the accounts of Philip and Simon were originally completely separate, which is very unlikely given the probable personal roots of this account.

The passage's form combines a summary narrative of Philip's ministry with narrative focused on the Spirit. The section on the apostolic confirmation with the Spirit presents a confrontation account (Fitzmyer 1998: 401 notes only the narrative about the Spirit). Hengel (1979: 77–79) sees a two-stage mission to Samaria, the first by Philip and the second by Peter, perhaps to see what the Hellenists have done. In his view, it is possible that Luke connects the two for the first time. The fact that in the passage Philip disappears when Peter is present could well point to two sources about two missions.

Exegesis and Exposition

[5]And going down into ⌜the⌝ city of Samaria, Philip began proclaiming to them the Christ. [6]And the crowds with one accord gave heed to the things being said by Philip, when they heard him and saw the signs that he performed. [7]For many unclean spirits came out of those who were possessed, crying out in a loud voice; and many who were paralyzed or lame were healed. [8]So there was much joy in that city.

[9]But there was a man named Simon who previously practiced magic in the city and amazed the nation of Samaria, saying that he was someone great. [10]They all gave heed to him, from the least to the greatest, saying, "This is the power of God that is called Great." [11]And they gave heed to him because for a long time he had amazed them with his magic. [12]But when they believed Philip as he was preaching the good news of the kingdom of God and the name of Jesus Christ, they began to be baptized, both men and women. [13]Even Simon himself believed, and being baptized, he continued with Philip. And seeing great signs and miracles performed, he was amazed.

[14]When the apostles in Jerusalem heard that Samaria had received the word of God, they sent to them Peter and John, [15]who, coming down, prayed concerning them that they might receive the Holy Spirit, [16]for it had not yet fallen on any of them, but they had only been baptized into the name of the Lord Jesus. [17]Then they laid hands on them, and they received the Holy Spirit. [18]But seeing that

through the laying on of hands of the apostles the ⌜ ⌝ Spirit was given, Simon offered them money, [19]saying, "Give also to me this authority so that anyone on whom I lay hands may receive the Holy Spirit." [20]But Peter said to him, "May your silver go with you into destruction because you thought you could obtain the gift of God with money! [21]There is for you neither part nor portion in this matter, for your heart is not right before God. [22]Repent, therefore, from this wickedness of yours and pray to the Lord that, if possible, the intent of your heart may be forgiven you. [23]For I see that you are in the gall of bitterness and the bond of iniquity." [24]And Simon answered, ⌜ ⌝ "Pray on my behalf to the Lord that nothing that you say may come upon me."

[25]Having testified and spoken the word ⌜of the Lord⌝, they returned to Jerusalem, preaching the gospel to many villages of the Samaritans.

8:5   Philip goes to an unspecified city in Samaria and begins preaching the Christ, an elaboration on the preaching of the word in verse 4 (on the Christ: 3:20; 9:22; 17:3; 26:23). The imperfect verb ἐκήρυσσεν (*ekēryssen*, began proclaiming) probably has an ingressive force, pointing to Philip's entry into his mission. The idea of evangelizing appears in verses 4, 12, and 25, linking the unit. The Samaritans were not popular among the Jews, as they were despised for being unfaithful and of mixed ancestry, and they were treated as defecting half-breeds (Bock 1996: 1031; 2 Kings 17:24–41; to eat with a Samaritan was said to be like eating pork, Jeremias, *TDNT* 7:88–92; their daughters were seen as unclean, *m. Nid.* 4.1; *m. Ṭohar.* 5.8; they were accused of aborting fetuses, *m. Nid.* 7.4; Le Cornu and Shulam 2003: 402–3; Josephus, *Ant.* 11.8.6 §§340–41; *m. Šeb.* 8.10; *b. Sanh.* 57a). Luke 17:18 has Jesus speak of them as "another" race, a description that reflects a Jewish perspective. But the gospel was meant also for them. Ironically, they are responsive, which is somewhat surprising, as they did not share the predominant Jewish view of the Messiah but expected a "prophet like Moses," or "the coming/returning one" (known as the *Taheb*; Deut. 18:15–18; Fitzmyer 1998: 402). This figure was expected to perform miracles, restore the law, renew worship, and bring knowledge to other nations (Le Cornu and Shulam 2003: 399). In Samaritan belief, this figure was simply a herald of the end's arrival. They also worshiped at the rival site of Mt. Gerizim.

There is discussion whether, in Acts, Samaria should be viewed (1) as "Jewish," (2) as a "halfway" step toward Gentiles, or (3) as part of the nations (Le Cornu and Shulam 2003: 395–96 favor the last option). It seems clear that Samaritans cannot be seen as Jewish. It is harder to choose between the other two options. Those who view the Samaritans as connected with Gentiles argue that the expansion of the gospel out from Jerusalem parallels the "table of nations" (cf. Gen. 10). Against this is the emphasis Luke places on the Cornelius episode as "groundbreaking." Though boundaries are certainly being pushed in Acts 8–9, these expansions do not seem to have the same epochal character as Peter's encounter with Cornelius in Acts 10. This leaves option 2, placing Samaritans halfway between Jews and Gentiles, as the most likely. Le Cornu and Shulam appear to offer some support for option 2 by arguing that the Samaritans were viewed as "sons of Shem" and as Semites were more closely related to the Jews than other Gentiles.

The Samaritan city is unknown (see textual problem below), but its identity is not important in Luke. That Samaria is the location is all Luke wishes to note. Justin Martyr (*1 Apol.* 26.2) suggests Gitta, home of Simon Magus. Bruce (1990: 216) suggests Shechem, a key city, or the ancient Nablus as potential locales (as does Pesch 1986a: 272; Shechem is the religious center of Samaria). It could be Sebaste, named by Herod the Great in honor of Augustus but also known as Samaria (Barrett 1994: 402, apparently; Schille 1984: 201 thinks it is the only option). Against this choice is that Sebaste was strongly Gentile and not a Samaritan religious center. Simon's presence as a magician, however, might be evidence in its favor. Hengel and Schwemer (1997: 80–81) opt for the Samaritan capital, Sychar (i.e., in the environs of Shechem), along with Ashdod and Caesarea on the premise that this is where Philip is active later. In the end, we cannot make a clear identification of the exact locale, although Shechem is the best candidate.

Church fathers identify Simon Magus as the first source of heresy, especially Gnosticism (Bruce 1988a: 166n30; Polhill 1992: 216; Justin Martyr, *1 Apol.* 26.3 and 56.2, calls him a magician). Justin presents many details about him: Simon was called by many a first god, was from Gitta in Samaria, ended up in Rome, and traveled with a woman named Helena, a former prostitute, who was the "first idea" generated by him.[2] Justin was from Shechem and so might have access to key traditions (Le Cornu and Shulam 2003: 399; Klauck 2003: 17). Acts, however, lacks any of these details (Barrett 1994: 396–97). One cannot establish that all of what the later fathers say of Simon is true, although it is likely that his reputation had its roots in his being iconoclastic and syncretistic in his attempt to connect to Christianity (R. Wilson 1979: 485–91). According to traditions, Samaria did have some fascination with the magical arts at certain times (see Mart. Ascen. Isa. 2.12–3.12 about Belkira of Samaria).

The crowd is said to pay heed to Philip. The verb προσέχω (*prosechō*) reappears two more times in the passage as Simon also pays heed in   8:6–8

---

2. See also Justin Martyr, *Dial.* 120.6, which names him as a magician and god but does not call him a Gnostic. Irenaeus (*Ag. Her.* 1.16.2–3) connects him to Gnosticism. Hippolytus (*Refutation of All Heresies* 6.2–20) says that Simon failed to rise from the dead after making such a prediction (other texts: Pseudo-Clement, *Homilies* 2.22, 24; 18.12, 14; Epiphanius, *Refutation of All Heresies* 21; Origen, *Against Celsus* 1.57; Acts of Peter 4–32, where Simon is bested by Peter; for more of the views of Ignatius, Justin Martyr, and Irenaeus, see discussion in vv. 9–11).

8:10–11. Half of the six uses of this word in Acts appear in this unit (5:34–35; 8:6, 10–11 [2x]; 16:14; 20:28). The term means paying careful attention (BAGD 714 §1αβ; BDAG 880 §2b). Two items garner their attention (note the explanatory use of γάρ, *gar*, for): his preaching and the signs (see 2:22) he performed. The explanation is that exorcisms and healings of the paralyzed draw them to Philip's message. Miracles, for Luke, draw people into considering the message. Philip's actions recall the ministries of Jesus and Peter (Luke 7:22–23: signs of the arrival of the age). Luke refers to unclean spirits in Acts 5:16, calling them "immoral or evil spirits" in 19:12–16. That demons cry out is seen in Luke 4:41 and Acts 16:17, and such spirits coming out of people are noted in Luke 4:35 and Acts 16:18–19 (exorcisms in Luke: 4:33, 36; 6:18; 8:2, 29; 9:1, 6, 42; 11:24). The paralyzed are healed in Luke 5:18 and Acts 9:33, and the lame appear in Acts 3:2 and 14:8. The Acts 14 and 16 passages show that Paul will also exercise such power. The kingdom of God is moving out and overcoming forces opposed to it (Johnson 1992: 151). People other than the Twelve are exercising God's power and gifts.

God's work through Philip fills the city with joy (χαρά, *chara*). Luke's Gospel often mentions joy, but this is its first mention in Acts (Luke 1:14; 2:10; 8:13; 10:17; 15:7, 10; 24:41, 52–53; Acts 8:7–8; 12:13–14; 13:51–52; 15:3).

8:9–11   Luke provides a flashback of another man, Simon Magus, who enjoyed the attention of the Samaritans before Philip came to them. He is the topic of verses 9–13. Luke sees him as either a Jew (Jervell 1998: 261n795) or at least a Samaritan (Klauck 2003: 15–17), for Gentiles are not the topic until Acts 10. This type of syncretism in not unprecedented in Judaism; Jewish inscriptions exist that have magical formulas. However, this association especially fits Samaritans since they were a mixed race and had a mixed cultural heritage that included non-Jewish influences. Philo (*Spec. Laws* 3.18 §§100–101) notes two types of magic: (1) a respectable science of discernment tied to Persian magi and kings and (2) an "adulterated" species full of quacks, charms, and incantations (Eckey 2000: 190–92). The Samaritan city was accustomed to unusual displays of power, as Simon practiced magic (μαγεύων, *mageuōn*) there. This is the only use of this verb in the NT; the noun μαγεία (*mageia*, magic) sees its only occurrence in verse 11, although in 13:6–11 we meet Elymas (Bar-Jesus), who also is a magician (μάγος, *magos*, in 13:6, 8; similarly 19:13–20; Delling, *TDNT* 4:356–59). Although the term is always negative in Luke-Acts, it can have a more neutral use, such as "wise men" in Matt. 2 (Grundmann, *TDNT* 4:540–41, says that the expression comes from the "world of Hellenistic magic piety" and notes several examples). The name explains why Simon is better known as Simon Magus, which means "Simon the magician/ sorcerer" (on stories about Simon in patristic sources, see comments on v. 5 above; Bruce 1988a: 166). His magic would have involved charms and incantations (on magic among the Greeks, Johnson 1992: 147, who notes the Great Magical Papyrus, a book of magical "recipes"; numerous examples can be found in H. Betz 1992).

Originally, such magi would have been Median priests or Zoroastrians, but the term came to mean any who practiced magic. Williams (1990: 159) notes several references in Strabo, Plutarch, Juvenal, Horace, Philo, and Josephus. In Josephus, *Ant.* 20.7.2 §142, it is clear that the term has moved beyond describing those from Persia, as a Jew is a magician in this text. Luke does not portray Simon as a Gnostic (Witherington 1998: 283; Barrett 1994: 406; Weiser 1981: 202; against Haenchen 1987: 307, who argues that Luke downgraded Simon from Gnostic to magician). The point is important because Simon's status became elevated in the early church to the point of being "the Father of all Heretics" (Eckey 2000: 192).[3] It was Simon's equating himself with God, or permitting this, that evoked the reaction of the church fathers (Irenaeus, *Ag. Her.* 3.12). Justin Martyr (*1 Apol.* 26) and Irenaeus discredit him by noting his moral failure and saying that he went around with a prostitute named Helena (for more on Justin Martyr's view, see comments on v. 5 above). Luke mentions none of this.

Simon's acts of magic amaze the crowd throughout the nation of Samaria (on the expression "amaze," see Acts 2:7, 12). In this event, we have Philip exorcising demons (v. 7), healing (v. 7), and facing off against one who practices magic.

Simon calls himself great, drawing attention to himself and his own work. This seems to suggest that he portrays himself as some type of heavenly power, possibly even divine (Marshall 1980: 155). It seems likely that the claim to being "the great power" means being divine (Haacker, *NIDNTT* 3:456–58; Pesch 1986a: 274; Jervell 1998: 261n799: "an incarnation of the highest God"). This claim is not explicitly gnostic (Weiser 1981: 202). *PGM* 4.1225–29 speaks of one with "Great Power" who is not the supreme god but is very powerful. The Samaritan targums speak of "the great power" as a divine designation (Bruce 1990: 219; Spencer 1992: 92–93). Barrett (1994: 407) notes that the title is not a claim to be the supreme being, just one of God's great powers. This stands in contrast to Philip, who points to Jesus as the Christ, not to himself. And the crowd, both the least and the great, accept Simon's claim, pay heed to his self-exaltation, and give him their own adulation. So the crowd sees Simon as the bearer of God's power (ἡ δύναμις τοῦ θεοῦ, *hē dynamis tou theou*) and describes that power as great.

---

3. See Irenaeus, *Ag. Her.* 1.23.2 ("from whom all sorts of heresies derive their origin"); 1.27.4 (refutes the school of Valentinus, a "successor to Simon Magus"); 2.preface.1 (denounces the doctrine of the pleroma and the demiurge as "declaring at the same time the doctrine of Simon Magus of Samaria, their progenitor, and of all those who succeeded him").

The grammatical construction about great power using "this" (οὗτος, *houtos*) is an example of a *constructio ad sensum*; it refers to this man by the context (Wallace 2000: 147). The expression for "great" (ἡ καλουμένη μεγάλη, *hē kaloumenē megalē*) with the article, when placed next to another articular phrase, functions like an adjective ("the power of God that is called Great" in NET). Luke quotes this saying of the Samaritans that shows they "give heed" to Simon, just as they have to Philip (Acts 8:6). Luke repeats the note about the crowd's taking heed of Simon in verse 11 (see v. 10), noting that he has worked in Samaria for a long time and amazed them with his "magic arts" (μαγείαις, *mageiais*, an NT hapax; the amazement repeats v. 9). Barrett (1994: 408) calls the verse "curiously repetitive." The repetition might point to a mixing of sources or to Luke's own stitching together of oral reports. This description of Simon as connected to God sets up a contrast between Simon's power and that of Philip and Peter in verses 15–18. The crowd believes Simon has supernatural powers, and so his face-to-face encounter with Philip is portrayed as raising the question of who really speaks and works for God. It also will show that what the church brings is distinct from the magic practiced in the world (Jervell 1998: 262).

8:12   The message about the Christ (v. 5) is now called the message about the kingdom, showing the relationship between the two ideas (Acts 3:6; Grundmann, *TDNT* 9:535). The mention of believing in the name of Jesus refers to responding to his power and occurs several times in Acts (2:38; 3:6; 4:8–10; 8:12; 10:48; 16:18). The kingdom (βασιλεία, *basileia*) was one of Jesus's favorite topics in his teaching (Bock 2002a: 565–93). This is one of eight uses of the term "kingdom" in Acts but is the first since Jesus spoke to the disciples about it during his forty days with them after the resurrection (Acts 1:3–6 [2x]; 8:12; 14:21–22; 19:8; 20:25; 28:23, 30–31). God's rule appears in what Philip is doing. Those who believe the message are baptized, both men and women. Here ἐπίστευσαν (*episteusan*) is aorist and refers to the moment of faith that leads each one into the community. It contrasts with the imperfect tense for "taking heed," which means that they listen for a while and then respond. This response leads immediately to baptism (ἐβαπτίζοντο, *ebaptizonto*), also probably an ingressive imperfect verb to suggest that people are beginning to be baptized when they respond ("began to be baptized" in NET), given that one scene is in view when Philip impresses the crowd, in contrast to Simon.

8:13   Simon is among those responding and being baptized. He follows Philip. There is much discussion about whether Simon truly believes here, given that he is initially described like the others who respond with faith and baptism (ἐπίστευσεν καὶ βαπτισθείς, *episteusen kai baptistheis*, he believed and was baptized) and yet later wants to barter concerning the gift of the faith. Is this a superficial faith made evident in the larger context?

The answer depends on how one reads Peter's rebuke and Simon's response in 8:20–24. Barrett (1994: 409) says that nothing in the verse suggests that Simon's faith is less sincere or less satisfactory than anyone else's (so also Pesch 1986a: 275; Schneider 1980: 491; Fitzmyer 1998: 405). Barrett notes that Calvin saw this as somewhere between faith and pretense. Views vary considerably. Haenchen (1987: 303) calls this not the "soundest" faith. Williams (1990: 155) says that Simon professes faith. Marshall (1980: 156) suggests that overall nothing suggests a superficial faith but that it is too early in the narrative to know where Simon stands. Bruce (1988a: 167) calls the nature of his faith uncertain but counts the faith as sincere, superficial, and inadequate. In his later commentary (1990: 220), however, Bruce cites Drane's view that his faith is sincere but confused. Stählin (1980: 121) argues that this is not true faith or conversion but that he remains a magician. The decision about the genuineness of Simon's faith is not strictly a lexical issue, nor is it an easy decision, but some point out that whereas the Samaritans are said specifically to believe Philip's message, Simon's belief is stated with no explicit object (Witherington 1998: 288; see discussion in Acts 8:20, 21, and 24; Marshall 1980: 156 correctly suggests these early verses alone do not settle the matter).

Simon continues on (ἦν προσκαρτερῶν, *ēn proskarterōn*; note the periphrasis) with Philip (Witherington 1998: 285 compares this to one following a rock star). This is not the normal way of describing discipleship. The verb appears only once in the Gospels, where it refers to a boat being ready (Mark 3:9–10; Acts 1:14; 2:42, 44–47; 6:3–4; 8:13; 10:7–8; Rom. 12:9–13; 13:6; Col. 4:2–4). It normally means "persist in" something or "stick to it" (Acts 1:14; 2:42), but here lexicons give it a separate sense of attaching oneself to another, being faithful to or serving another (BDAG 881; Acts 10:7, of those who wait on Cornelius; *EDNT* 3:172).

Simon is amazed (ἐξίστατο, *existato*; the imperfect points to an ongoing amazement). This verb also appeared in verse 11 to describe how the crowds react to Simon. Now the magician is amazed while beholding Philip's signs and "great" miracles. The participle θεωρῶν (*theōrōn*, beholding) explains what motivates the amazement, as it looks back syntactically to that idea. This is what causes Polhill (1992: 217) to question the sincerity of Simon's faith (so also Jervell 1998: 262). The term "great" is ironic in light of what Simon is calling himself (vv. 9–10). This points to the superior power Philip has, so superior that Simon, the "great divine power," wishes to buy it in verses 18–19. The evangelist has greater power than the magician. Jervell (1998: 262n806) points out the parallel to Moses's power, which is greater than that of Pharaoh's magicians. Is the attachment Simon has to Philip a sincere attachment to the gift of God or a quest to enhance his personal power? The next part of the event will elaborate that question.

8:14–17   Philip now bows out of the scene. The attention turns to the work of Peter and John through verse 24. They appear in Samaria to investigate what has been reported to the apostles in Jerusalem (Acts 8:1; John's last action in Acts). The apostles also go to Antioch later (11:22). Barrett (1994: 410) gives several reasons why they might appear there but notes that none of these are specified in the text. They include: to convey the gift of the Spirit that Philip could not, to inspect (Bruce 1990: 220), and to share in and identify with what has been accepted (Polhill 1002: 217).

The first reason is unlikely because the apostles do not control the Spirit. Bruce (1988a: 169) argues against an apostolic "confirmation," noting that Paul does not connect the Spirit to apostolic confirmation work in his epistles and is not confirmed in such a manner in Acts. Nor does this act "minimize" Philip's success, as Haenchen (1987: 304) tries to argue. Most especially against this option is how Luke has Philip parallel the way John the Baptist is viewed in comparison to Jesus: just as Jesus affirmed John the Baptist's ministry but carried it further, so Philip's work is carried further by the apostles (cf. also Apollos with Paul in Acts 18–19; Spencer 1992: 188–92).

The apostles' presence and response are an endorsement of Philip's work, elevating him as also being an instrument of God. Jervell (1998: 263) argues that this mission serves to unite the people of God. This is certainly a result of the apostles' action. It is probable that the apostles appear in Samaria to conduct an inspection but with the expectation that they will endorse the work there. Pesch (1986a: 275) speaks of legitimizing Philip's mission. The prayer of the apostles allows God to show his acceptance of the Samaritans so that the entire church can see it. Bruce suggests that the theological and social controversy over Samaritans within Judaism requires special evidence that God is directing matters here (see discussion above on Acts 8:5; also Larkin 1995: 128). The laying on of hands and confirmation of the Spirit are actions that indicate fellowship and identification with these new believers. The result is the unity of the church as all participate in the expansion to Samaria. The text is neither hierarchical, by teaching that the Spirit comes only through the apostles, nor "early catholic," as some imply.[4] The two stages to the Spirit's appearance are part of the scene's unusual context, where church practice is breaking new ground, so that a confirmation and an affirmation are noted in a way that is not a paradigm for later practice, as Stott (1990: 151–59) also argues in detail.

---

4. This is correctly noted by Jervell 1998: 263, *pace* Fitzmyer 1998: 400, who argues for evidence of the influence of the institutional church here, seeing hierarchy in this act. Weiser 1981: 203 is somewhere in between, noting that this is not evidence of full hierarchical control over the sacraments but of grounding and acceptance within the hierarchical apostolic community. Weiser's view is more likely. The apostolic role, however, is simply confirming what God has already done independently of the apostles, an important qualification against any claim that "early catholicism" is evidenced in this account.

Some scholars note this sudden turn in character focus from Philip to the apostles to argue that the scene is not historical (Conzelmann 1987: 64, even suggesting that if a Philip tradition is present, then its form is secondary). This is an excessively skeptical reading for an account that is summarizing events. It is not surprising that the church in Jerusalem and the apostles in particular would have interest in a Samaritan response. Once Peter arrives, his reaction to events is an important barometer. After all, Peter has been the key character up to this point and was important in the early church, frequently representing the view of the apostles.

The entire region of Samaria is said to have received (δέδεκται, *dedektai*) the word of God (word of God in Acts: 4:31; 6:2, 7; 8:14–16; 11:1; 12:24; 13:4–5, 7, 46; 17:13; 18:11). This expression "receive the word" occurs two other times in Acts (11:1; 17:11) out of seven NT occurrences (also Luke 8:13; 1 Thess. 1:6; 2:13; James 1:21). A prefixed form of the verb appears in Acts 2:41. Here is yet another term for accepting the gospel.

The reason for praying for the Spirit is that the Spirit has not yet fallen on the Samaritans, as they have been baptized only into the name of the Lord Jesus (on baptism in the name of Jesus taking place side by side with the coming of the Spirit through the laying on of hands, see Acts 19:5–6). Baptism with a later coming of the Spirit is exceptional and not normative (Williams 1990: 157). Being baptized "into" (εἰς, *eis*) the name denotes incorporation into the Lord and his community, declaring one's allegiance and implying the Lord's ownership (Bruce 1990: 221; like Acts 19:5). Marshall (1980: 157–58) notes that there is no indication of a defective faith in the group as a whole nor do the apostles preach to them.

There is no delay in baptizing a believer in these early days. Apparently the church is taking the reception of the Spirit as a clear indication that people have truly believed, as God's sanction of them as a group. This special dispensing of the Spirit comes as a new region or recognized group receives the gospel (Samaria here; Gentiles in Acts 10; John's disciples in Acts 19). The dispensing of the Spirit is an event awaited in Acts 2 but comes automatically with faith in Acts 10. Here it is the result of prayer and the laying on of hands, as also in Acts 19 with Paul's ministry. There is no set pattern to dispensing the Spirit in Acts. At various junctures God acts in different ways for different purposes. The reason for the delay here may well be to make clear to the apostles, as the witnesses, that God has acted. The one constant in the first three bestowals of the Spirit is the presence of an apostle (on the importance of the Spirit, see Acts 10:44–48; 11:15–17). Normally the Spirit comes with faith in the NT (Acts 2:38; 1 Cor. 12:3, 13), but these are special circumstances that make a break in the pattern to underscore a fresh move of God (on giving the Spirit, see Luke 11:13; Acts 5:32; 11:17; 15:8; in all the other passages in Acts, it is God who gives the Spirit; Schneider 1980: 493n91). Jervell (1998: 264) speaks correctly of a "special legitimization" taking place here because of the potential controversy of Samaritan inclusion. The Spirit is described as a gift in 2:38; 10:45; and 11:17 as well as by Peter in verse 20. The description here makes clear that the coming of the Spirit is God's work.

The laying on of hands leads to the reception of the Spirit, an act made evident to all. As with the coming of the Spirit with the apostles' ministry, so the addition of the laying on of hands with the coming of the Spirit here points to a special situation. Acts 8:38 and 10:44 show that baptism and the Spirit do not require an apostle or the laying on of hands (Barrett 1994: 412). Exactly how this manifestation of the Spirit is recognized is not indicated. Do they speak in tongues (so Jervell 1998: 264 with most), or is it through some other unspecified indicator? Although this text is not explicit, an experience like Acts 2 and 10 is likely (Pesch 1986a: 276; Acts 2:4; 10:46; 19:6; but Polhill 1992: 218 is not certain, arguing that nothing is said about anything audible). Polhill also suggests that Simon Magus does not receive what is given, since Simon asks to be able to give it. There is, however, a difference between receiving the Spirit and asking to give it, so Polhill's point is not persuasive. Bruce (1990: 222) correctly speaks of tongues or a comparable manifestation. It obviously is something visible because Simon reacts when he sees its effect.

8:18 The apostolic laying on of hands has an impact on Simon Magus. Here the apostolic role (δία ... τῶν χειρῶν τῶν ἀποστόλων, *dia ... tōn cheirōn tōn apostolōn*, through the apostles' hands) is designed to help the Jerusalem church accept what is happening outside its home, in a land that might not be seen as a beneficiary of grace. Paul will lay on hands in 19:6 for some of John the Baptist's disciples. Ananias, a non-apostle, does likewise so that Paul can receive the Spirit (9:17). These are the only three places the Spirit is bestowed through the laying on of hands. Each is a case where doubts might exist about the experience's authenticity. It is an exceptional activity, as there are many places where people believe, and the laying on of hands is not described. Acts 2:38–39 declares the normative pattern. Marshall (1980: 158) notes that on other occasions joy accompanies the Spirit, not charismatic experience (13:52; 16:34; 1 Thess. 1:6).

Haenchen (1987: 304) argues that Simon's question reveals a clumsy narrative seam, since there is no reason for Simon to be excluded from having received this gift. This ignores two points. Simon may have received the Spirit but is asking to be able to give it, or he may be asking for this when his turn comes to receive the Spirit. Either is possible and removes the reason to argue for a bad seam.

8:19 Simon Magus asks to have this power or authority, that is, the right to give the Spirit. The expression "this authority" (τὴν ἐξουσίαν ταύτην, *tēn* *exousian tautēn*) points to a right, an assigned enablement (BAGD 278 §2; BDAG 352 §2; "power" in NLT, KJV, ESV, NET, RSV; "ability" in NIV; "authority" in NASB). Simon requests such authority to distribute the Spirit by offering to pay for it. Simon does not understand or appreciate that the Spirit's distribution is a result of God's sovereign work that is a gift from God (v. 20). This may well suggest a lack of understanding about the gospel and the promise of the Spirit.

The English term "simony" derives from this event. Simon's proposal is a "syncretizing" request (Larkin 1995: 129). It was not unknown to pay for a priestly office, but it was less than honorable. For example, 2 Macc. 4:7–8 and 4 Macc. 4:17–18 refer to Jason's purchase of the high priesthood from Antiochus of the Seleucids. Such a payment was something a Gentile leader like Antiochus might expect and accept. Also one could buy magical secrets (Acts 19:19), and so Simon is thinking in his old and more Gentile ways here (Williams 1990: 157; Derrett 1982 details this background). Barrett (1979: 289–91) shows how Luke makes a theme out of connecting a magical worldview with the desire to minister for money, something Christian ministers in Acts do not do (13:6–8; 16:18–19; 19:14–19). Luke makes a distinction between divine provision and magic. The gift of the Spirit is not magic, nor is it like it. Conzelmann (1987: 65–66) says that the distinction is between miracle and magic and sees the original story lying here, but the distinction is between the manifestation of the Spirit and magic. There is no reason to change the account. The passage warns how a desire for power and the misuse of material goods can lead to a spiritual fall, a common Lukan point (Weiser 1981: 205; Luke 12:13–21; 16:14–15; Acts 5:1–11).

Peter is clear that the work of the Spirit does not come by purchase. His rebuke is severe. In sense it reads, "May destruction take your money with you" (τὸ ἀργύριόν σου σὺν σοὶ εἴη εἰς ἀπώλειαν, *to argyrion sou syn soi eiē eis apōleian*, may your silver together with you be into destruction). This is the only use of a present optative in the NT (BDF §384). It states a wish that also is a rebuke and warning. J. B. Phillip's paraphrase is, "To hell with you and your money!" This rebuke is why some scholars see Simon not as a genuine believer but as only associated with the community for superficial reasons.

Marshall (1980: 159) equates the rebuke to excommunication and a curse; at best, it is a solemn warning he must heed to avoid this fate (on the expression "to be into destruction," see Dan. 2:5 and 3:96 Theodotion [3:29 MT]; Johnson 1992: 148–49). Proverbs 27:20 uses the phrase with reference to hades. The expression refers to judgment (also in Greek sources, *PGM* 4.1247–48; Schille 1984: 206). Derrett (1982: 64–65) speaks of a curse. This is a most severe rebuke because it makes an explicit reference to destruction (ἀπώλειαν; BAGD 103; BDAG 127 §2). Barrett (1994: 414) argues that this is not a curse but the threat of one.

8:20–24

Barrett appears to be on the right track. Note how the effect of the remark here differs from Ananias and his immediate death in Acts 5, as the optative εἴη expresses a wish and is followed by a call for repentance. Forgiveness could then follow. This final point is expressed inferentially as part of a condition (εἰ ἄρα, *ei ara*, if perhaps) that is in doubt, given what Simon must do (Moule 1959: 158). Peter is testing Simon's heart with this rebuke. Simon's response indicates where he is in relationship to God. Peter warns that this judgment could happen and places responsibility on Simon Magus to respond actively. How does Simon respond?

The nature of Simon's response is debated. Weiser (1981: 205) argues that Simon's response in verse 24 is as sincere as in verses 12–13, and so argues that Luke sees Simon as responsive to the call (so also Schneider 1980: 495). Schille (1884: 207) argues the exact opposite because Simon refuses to act himself. Bruce (1990: 223) says of verse 23, "It is clear that, in Peter's judgment, Simon was still unregenerate." (See also Bruce 1988a: 171–72: "Canonical literature bids farewell to Simon with this entreaty on his lips that by the apostle's intercession he may escape the judgment pronounced on his crooked heart.") Witherington summarizes by giving six reasons Simon's response should not be seen positively: (1) the negative description in verses 9–11; (2) the fact that there is no object for his belief in verse 13; (3) his separate treatment from the Samaritans, including the motive of what drew him; (4) the desire to buy the gift in verses 18–19; (5) the negative description in verse 23; and (6) his failure to pray for himself as Peter recommends.

How verse 24 is read determines in the end whether one thinks Luke is portraying Simon as responsive. His fate seems bound up ultimately with his response. That it does not match what Peter requests does not point to an obedience that does as commanded. Still, that there is some debate shows the uncertainty about how Luke resolves the issue (Williams 1990: 158 expresses similar negative leanings and cites 1 Sam. 24:16 with 26:21; Gaventa 2003: 139 calls the attempt to resolve the question "futile").

Peter equates the gift of God with the distribution of the Spirit. The Spirit is not for sale, nor is it like magic. It is received as a benevolent and gracious act of God, as Acts 2:38–39 already stated (10:45; 11:17).

Peter issues a second rebuke when he says that Simon has no "part or portion" (οὐκ ἔστιν σοι μερὶς οὐδὲ κλῆρος, *ouk estin soi meris oude klēros*) in this matter (v. 21; 1:25–26 has a positive use of "portion/lot") unless his attitude changes by repentance (v. 22). The dative σοι, which opens the phrase in verse 21, is a possessive dative, meaning that these things do not belong to Simon (Wallace 1996: 149). This is a way of saying that there is no blessing for him (Deut. 12:12; 14:27; 18:1; Josh. 18:7; *m. Sanh.* 10.1–4). Polhill (1992: 220) agrees and interprets the remark to mean that Simon has no share with God's people (also Barrett 1994: 414). This word combination also suggests that Simon's faith is deficient at the time when Peter addresses him. To have a "portion" is to have a share of something (BAGD 435 §2; BDAG 548). The term "part" has the same meaning (BAGD 505 §2; BDAG 632–33 §2). Using two terms for the idea makes the point emphatic ("part nor lot" in ESV; "share or part" in NET; "part or share" in NIV, HCSB; "part or portion" in NASB; also present together in Col. 1:12: "the share of the lot of the saints"). Peter goes on to say that Simon's heart is not right before God (Ps. 78:37 [77:37 LXX]; not morally right, Luke 3:3–4; Acts 13:10; Judg. 17:6; 21:25; 2 Sam. 19:6). Jervell (1998: 265) says that Simon's faith at this point is not genuine.

Peter thus places the spiritual onus on Simon to set things right. Peter tells him to repent and pray that the thought of his heart might be forgiven if possible (the condition here is incomplete and so is presented as a possibility). The remark echoes Acts 2:38 and may suggest that Simon needs to enter truly into the trust of God's grace, as often the term "intent" (ἐπίνοια, epinoia) of heart is negative (Wis. 9:14; 14:12; 15:4; Johnson 1992: 149), meaning wickedness, something that verse 22 already indicates with the use of the term "wickedness" (κακίας, kakias). So there are many suggestions in these verses that things are very wrong with Simon and that doom awaits if he does not respond.

Besides being in the "bond of iniquity" (σύνδεσμον ἀδικίας, syndesmon adikias; Isa. 58:6), Simon is in the "bitter poison," or "gall of bitterness" (χολὴν πικρίας, cholēn pikrias; BAGD 883 §2; BDAG 1086 §2; Deut. 29:18 [29:17 LXX]; 1QS 2.11–17), which means being a reprehensible person ("bitter," BAGD 657 §1; BDAG 813 §1). The NET renders this in terms of a concrete emotion, "bitterly envious," which certainly describes Simon's motive, since he is envious of what the apostles have (so also NIV, NLT: "full of bitterness"). The phrase, however, is more about Simon's condition and position. It points more to the risk it entails than the attitude that has brought him there (so "gall of bitterness" in ESV, RSV, NASB, KJV; a genitive of quality, see Moulton and Turner 1963: 213). Simon's attitude is a poison of bitterness that risks missing God's blessing. Simon's response in verse 24 that what Peter says may not happen to him shows that his condition and its great risk are in view.

The question of the quality of Simon's response also is debated (see discussion just above). Does his request to Peter indicate sincerity and remorse (Schneider 1980: 495; Barrett 1994: 418; Fitzmyer 1998: 407; Jervell 1998: 266)? Jervell argues that Simon views Peter's prayer as more powerful than his own, and so repentance is what motivates his request to Peter. Others take a different view. Does Simon's failure to obey the request to pray for himself show that he has not responded personally (Pesch 1986a: 277)?

It is a difficult choice, but the overall impression is that Simon does not completely embrace Peter's instruction and warning. If Simon were obedient, he would pray for himself and ask Peter to pray for him. Read in this light, his request to Peter is seen as dismissive. Peter can pray, but Simon will not. Perhaps the account concludes in an open-ended manner to allow the reader to ponder the proper response. The key to the text is the warning that Simon has been headed in a wrong direction, and so his example is primarily negative, no matter how the question of Simon's fate in Acts is ultimately resolved.

In sum, Luke has shown that Christianity has nothing to do with magic. Even more, those engaged in magic can see the divine power residing among the apostles. In addition, the Spirit cannot be bought. The gospel moves out of Jerusalem, but there are obstacles of misunderstanding to overcome. Anyone who accepts the gift of God can come into salvation. The Spirit is neither controllable nor subject to purchase; the Spirit comes by God's direction, as a gift, and is to be received as such.

8:25   The unit closes with a short note that the apostles continue the mission to the Samaritans. They testify to and speak the word from the Lord to the group (the aorist participles here probably look at previous action, preaching to the villages). The antecedent to "they" is unclear but is most likely the apostles Peter and John, given the previous unit. Philip may be with them, as the next scene (vv. 26–27) has Philip and the eunuch both coming from Jerusalem. The verb διαμαρτύρομαι (*diamartyromai*, testify) has ten of its fifteen NT occurrences in Luke-Acts (Luke 16:28; Acts 2:40; 8:25; 10:42; 18:5; 20:21, 23–24 [2x]; 23:11; 28:23).

Once their work in the city of Samaria was done, the apostles were preaching (imperfect) the gospel throughout the villages of Samaria. This Lukan summary echoes verse 4 with the preaching of the word. The verb εὐαγγελίζω (*euangelizō*, preach the gospel) is also frequent in Luke-Acts (fifteen times in Acts: 5:42; 8:4, 12, 25, 35, 40; 10:36; 11:20; 13:32; 14:7, 15, 21; 15:35; 16:10; 17:18; ten times in Luke; twenty-nine more times in the rest of the NT). Their mission done, the apostles return to Jerusalem. The note shows that the apostles fully endorse and extend the Samaritan mission. Now Luke's story returns to Philip. We do not see Peter again until Acts 9:32, and John does not take part in the action again in Acts, although he is named in 12:2.

In sum, this unit shows the gospel as it begins to move away from an exclusive concern for Israel. The gospel is for every person, for each one to consider, it is hoped, with ears and a heart that responds. This is as true today as it was then. Here we see Jews moving out to engage marginal Jews with the gospel. Crossing racial and ethnic lines with the message of hope and taking the initiative to do so are part of the church's calling.

In Simon Magus we also see the idea that not all spiritual power is positive. Simon can do wondrous things, and yet they are not of God. There is false as well as true spiritual power, what Fernando (1998: 276) calls "miraculous but wrong." Pointing out false spirituality is not an act of hostility, as our diverse culture often wants to suggest. It is a warning that not all spiritual activity is beneficial. To point out such error is an act of love for one's neighbor.

The blindness that money and power bring are also evident in this text. Simon Magus is corrupted by both as he pursues a reputation that aggrandizes himself.

Additional Notes

8:5. There is debate whether the text refers to "the" (τήν, *tēn*) city of Samaria or lacks the article and refers to "a" city of Samaria. Reading the article are $\mathfrak{P}^{74}$, ℵ, A, B, 1175. Lacking the article are C, D, E, Ψ, 33 1739, Byz. External evidence slightly favors inclusion, but the sense favors its absence (Metzger 1971: 355–56). Given that Samaria is a district in the NT, the verse may mean that the city of the district is meant, which would point to a major Samaritan locale, either political (Sebaste) or religious (Shechem or its environs).

8:18. The shorter reading "the Spirit" (ℵ, A^c, B) is also the more difficult reading here (why omit τὸ ἅγιον if it were present?). "Holy Spirit" is, however, more widely attested ($\mathfrak{P}^{45}$, $\mathfrak{P}^{74}$, A*, C, D, E, Ψ, 33, 1739, Byz), but it also is more likely to have been added later (Metzger 1971: 358). The correct original reading is a difficult determination given the MSS distribution. It makes no difference to the meaning of the text. It is slightly more likely that "the Spirit" is the original reading.

8:24. Codex D views Simon's actions here positively, speaking of his "weeping copious tears." The reading is not original but does show that one could read Simon's response positively in contrast to the way suggested here that the verse be read. Bruce (1990: 223) notes that this reading does not accord with later views of Simon in the tradition (see vv. 9–11 above).

8:25. There is textual uncertainty whether to read "word of the Lord" (κυρίου; so ℵ, B, C, D, E, 33, 1739, Byz) or "word of God" (θεοῦ; $\mathfrak{P}^{74}$, A, Ψ, 326) here. Both phrases are frequent in Acts, with "word of the Lord" appearing eight times besides here and "word of God" appearing eleven times. External evidence favors "word of the Lord."

2. Philip and the Eunuch (8:26–40)

The second incident in the Philip cycle sends us south of Jerusalem, toward Gaza (v. 26). A eunuch and servant of the queen of Ethiopia, a treasurer, is reading Isaiah (vv. 27–28). Philip is guided by the Spirit to him (vv. 29–30a) and leads him to understand how the text describes Jesus (vv. 30b–35). The Ethiopian believes and is baptized (vv. 36, 38–39a). Philip departs and passes through Azotas on the way to Caesarea (vv. 39b–40).

This unit distinguishes itself from what we have seen up to this point in Acts (Jervell 1998: 269). Whereas up to now mass conversion has been in view, our next three scenes contain individual conversions (the eunuch, Saul, Cornelius). This is the more personal side of evangelism.

How is the Ethiopian to be understood ethnically? Is he a Gentile? This has long been suggested and is held today (Eusebius, *Eccl. Hist.* 2.1.13; Conzelmann 1987: 67; Schneider 1980: 498; Marshall 1980: 160, who also notes that since no real church is raised up, no real issues emerge for the church to consider, as this conversion lacked a corporate or ethnic impact; Barrett 1994: 426–26; Polhill 1992: 222; Gaventa 2003: 143). It is, however, unlikely that the Ethiopian is a pure Gentile, given the emphasis that the conversion of Cornelius receives as a breakthrough to Gentiles and the fact that Paul's mission to the nations is set up by his conversion in Acts 9 (Fitzmyer 1999: 410; Pesch 1986a: 288; Johnson 1992: 159—part of the ingathering of the scattered people of Israel). Jervell (1998: 271) notes the remaining options: Diaspora Jew, proselyte, or God-fearer. More likely the Ethiopian is a Diaspora Jew or a Gentile who is already tied to Judaism, as his coming to Jerusalem and reading Isaiah suggest. This option is sometimes challenged on the premise that as a eunuch he could not be a proselyte (Barrett 1994: 420), but all he needs to be is one who has embraced Judaism, not a full proselyte (Pesch 1986a: 289; so Schnabel 2004: 685 says his being a proselyte is "plausible"). This would put him somewhere between one who has been merely exposed to Israel's God and may have respect for this deity and one who is fully circumcised. In sum, we cannot be sure of his exact status, but it is quite likely that he has been significantly touched by Judaism, since he is reading Isaiah and coming from Jerusalem. As such, he would not be seen as a pure Gentile.

Witherington (1998: 290) argues that the ancients regarded Ethiopia as "the end of the earth," so the gospel reaching this goal announced in Acts 1:8 is foreshadowed here (Herodotus, *Hist.* 3.25.114; Strabo, *Geogr.* 1.1.6; 1.2.24; Philostratus, *Life Apoll.* 3.20; 6.1; Heliodorus, *Aethiopica*; Homer, *Od.* 1.23 ["the last men"]). The gospel not only reaches the end of the earth but also includes those located on the margins of, or excluded from full rights in, Judaism, that is, the God-fearers (Johnson 1992: 158; Witherington 1998: 296; Isa. 11:11; 56:3–5; Zeph. 3:9–10; Ps. 67:32 [68:31 Eng.] refers to Ethiopians turning to God). The region known as Ethiopia in ancient times is probably not the same as today but was located south of Egypt in ancient Cush, in the central part of modern Sudan, at a location known as Meroë (also known as Nubia; Yamauchi 2006). It was one thousand miles north to the Mediterranean.

The nature of Luke's source is not entirely clear. It may be the same as what lies behind Acts 8:5–25 and involve a Philip history of some kind. Luke's own contact with Philip also may be at work (Acts 21:8; on a Philip history source, see above on 8:5–25).

In form, the account is another narrative story of conversion, showing the word slowly but inexorably moving out into the world, a movement directed by God's Spirit. It shows some parallelism to Luke 24 and the Emmaus road (Witherington 1998: 292). It takes place on the way out of Jerusalem. As in Luke 24, a question initiates the encounter, and Scripture is central, Jesus becomes the key topic, and realization of who Jesus is leads to disappearance of the messenger. The account also sets up the next phase of outreach to the Gentiles, acting as a bridge to the larger world and showing Philip as a type of forerunner to Peter in going to the Gentile world, even if the figure in question is tied also to Judaism (*pace* Spencer 1992: 220–41, who overplays the connection to Luke 4 to make Philip the inaugurator of the Gentile mission). The person that the eunuch and Philip discuss is Jesus, who suffered as the servant, dying the death of an innocent, like a lamb going to slaughter. Still, God was active in Jesus's death, as the Ethiopian comes to see and believe. Other scholars highlight parallels to Elijah and Elisha (Brodie 1986), even suggesting that these parallels are rhetorical, not historical, but this ignores vast differences in the accounts (Witherington 1998: 292).

Exegesis and Exposition

[26]But an angel of the Lord said to Philip, "Rise and go toward the south to the road that goes from Jerusalem to Gaza." This is a desert road. [27]And he arose and departed. And behold, an Ethiopian, a eunuch, a minister of Candace, queen of the Ethiopians, who was in charge of all of her treasure, had come to Jerusalem to worship [28]and was returning, seated in his chariot, reading the

prophet Isaiah. ²⁹And the Spirit said to Philip, "Go and join this chariot." ³⁰So Philip ran and heard him reading Isaiah the prophet and said, "Now indeed, do you understand what you are reading?" ³¹And he said, "How am I able unless someone ⌜guides⌝ me?" And he invited Philip to come and sit with him. ³²Now this was the passage of the Scripture he was reading: "As a sheep led to the slaughter or a lamb before its shearers is dumb, so he opens not his mouth. ³³In ⌜his⌝ humiliation justice was denied him. Who can describe this generation? For his life was taken up from the earth." ³⁴And the eunuch said to Philip, "I ask you, about whom does the prophet say this: concerning himself or concerning someone else?" ³⁵Then Philip opened his mouth, and beginning with this Scripture, he proclaimed to him the good news of Jesus. ³⁶And as they went along the road, they came to some water, and the eunuch said, "See, here is water! What is to prevent me from being baptized?" ⌜ ⌝ ³⁸And he commanded the chariot to stop and both descended into the water, both Philip and the eunuch, and he baptized him. ³⁹And when they came up out of the water, the Spirit ⌜ ⌝ of the Lord caught up Philip; and the eunuch saw him no more, for he was proceeding on his way rejoicing. ⁴⁰But Philip was found at Azotus, and passing on, he proclaimed the gospel to all the towns until he came to Caesarea.

8:26 An angel of the Lord instructs Philip to head south (κατὰ μεσημβρίαν, *kata mesēmbrian*) for Gaza on a road that is located in a desolate area (ἔρημος, *erēmos*). The preposition κατά points to direction, so "to the south." The alternative and normal classical understanding of the term μεσημβρία, "noon," is often rejected by appeal to the fact that travel did not take place in the heat of midday, although Barrett (1994: 422–23) defends it as an unusual act that shows God is behind the request, and Strelan (2001: 33–34) sees noon as the time of revelation (Acts 22:6; 26:13 [both are instances of Paul's vision of Jesus]; 10:9 [Peter]). Despite claims that an exception is possible here, direction is still more likely than time for this reference (Lake and Cadbury 1933: 95; Horton and Blakely 2000: 59–61; BDF §253.5; BDAG 634 is undecided; RSV, HCSB, and NET argue contextually that direction is more needed than time here). That a revelation is occurring is obvious from the angelic guidance. Either way the phrase is taken, God directs the expansion through one of his agents. The angel of the Lord is prominent in Acts (5:19; 10:3, 7, 22; 12:7–15, 23; 27:23; angel in 7:30, 35, 38, 53; also in Luke: 1:11, 13, 26, 28; 2:9–10, 13; Johnson 1992: 154). In verse 29, the Spirit speaks to Philip. Witherington (1998: 294) comments that Luke often has angels working in concert with the Spirit (Luke 1:26–35) and that Luke does not think that the angel of the Lord is Jesus. A similar interchange that includes giving directions takes place in Acts 10. God is directing this event. Philip's movements are like those of Elijah in the OT (1 Kings 18:12; 2 Kings 1:3; 2:16).

Gaza was the last water stop in southwestern Israel before entering the desert on the way to Egypt and was 2,400 feet lower than Jerusalem (on this city, Josephus, *J.W.* 1.4.2 §87; 2.6.3 §97; 2.18.1 §460; *Ant.* 14.5.3 §88; 15.7.3 §217 [a "maritime" city]; 17.11.4 §320; Strabo, *Geogr.* 16.2.30 [refers to the destroyed old city as "remaining desolate"]). It is not clear whether old Gaza, destroyed in 98–96 BC by Alexander Jannaeus, is meant or the new Gaza, rebuilt by the Romans and just to the south. The deserted nature of the locale and a reference to the wilderness road may favor old Gaza or, better, a part of the road very close to there, since most of this road was not desolate (Barrett 1994: 424). Αὕτη (*hautē*, this) refers to the road, not to Gaza (Horton and Blakely 2000: 61; BDF §290.1). Horton and Blakely (2000) have made a strong case that the locale is the area around Tell el-Hesi, which has a spring that likely has existed for centuries. This is more likely than the more traditional site near Hebron at ʿAin ed-Dirweh. The suggestion goes back to E. Robinson in 1838 (E. Robinson and E. Smith 1856: 47). This is the only place Gaza is mentioned in the NT.

The second sentence of verse 27 <mark>opens with "behold" (ἰδού, *idou*) to note a surprise on this remote road.</mark> There is another traveler, a eunuch who is treasurer to the queen of Ethiopia, called Candace, a term used as a hereditary dynastic title (Pliny the Elder, *Nat.* 6.186; Pseudo-Callisthenes, *Life of Alexander of Macedon* 3.18; on Ethiopia, see Ps. 68:31; Zeph. 3:10). Ethiopia is to the south of Egypt (Ezek. 29:10) and is known as Cush in the earlier books of the OT (Gen. 2:13). It is in what today is known as the Sudan, and it was in the Nubian kingdom, whose capital was Meroë. As an Ethiopian, the eunuch probably is black (Witherington 1998: 295), and so the gospel is expanding to a new ethnic group. He went to Jerusalem in order to worship. The future participle (προσκυνήσων, *proskynēsōn*) with the pluperfect verb (ἐληλύθει, *elēlythei*) serves adverbially to indicate the purpose of the just-completed trip (Moulton and Turner 1963: 157; BDF §418.4). <mark>He is now on his return journey.</mark>

8:27–28

Eunuchs were castrated men who often served as keepers of harems (BAGD 323 §1; BDAG 409; in the NT, they appear only in this scene and in Matt. 19:12; Philostratus, *Life Apoll.* 1.33–36; Jer. 48:16 LXX; Esth. 2:14). They often served as treasurers (Polhill 1992: 223). His condition would not allow him full participation in Jewish worship (Deut. 23:1; also 1QSa 2.5–6). In the eschaton, eunuchs will be restored to full worship (Isa. 56:3b–5). He is an important person, a powerful man (δυνάστης, *dynastēs*, minister) from a faraway place who hears the gospel. Jervell (1998: 270–71) questions whether this man in a high office should be seen as literally a eunuch. He suggests that the Ethiopian is one who by his position functions as a celibate and thus symbolically a "eunuch." In this case, however, there would be no need to call him a eunuch, as verse 27 does. <mark>So a literal eunuch is likely in view</mark> (Petzke, *EDNT* 2:81).

Since he is reading Isaiah from the OT (v. 28), he is most likely an adherent of Judaism, probably a Diaspora God-fearer (a non-Jew who worships the Jewish God). He would be limited to the Court of the Gentiles at the temple or perhaps just to a synagogue (but in the future, this would change to access, as Isa. 56:3–5 [noted above] shows; *m. Yebam.* 8.2 and 8.4 discuss the limits of eunuchs). The mishnaic texts distinguish between those who are so by birth and those who become eunuchs later. Those who become eunuchs later in life have more rights in some forms of worship. For Luke, this story likely is an indication that the hope of worship expressed in Isa. 56 is beginning to take place, but there is no such explicit note.

The eunuch is reading Isaiah, probably aloud as was ancient custom to help the memory (*m. 'Abot* 6.5). He is wealthy enough to have his own copy of Isaiah. This would likely be a scroll (about 8 inches x 12 inches and anywhere from 16.5 to 145 feet long), written in square Assyrian Hebrew script or in Greek (Le Cornu and Shulam 2003: 419). The chariot he rides in is not a military carriage but simply a traveling vehicle (ἅρμα, *harma*) that could hold at least three people (v. 31; the driver, the eunuch, and Philip when he is invited in). This is "little more than a flatboard on wheels" and "not the most luxurious kind of vehicle" (Barrett 1994: 426; BDAG 132 §a; LXX: Gen. 41:43; 46:29 [not always a war chariot]; in the NT: Acts 8:28–29, 38; Rev. 9:9 [a war chariot]; Le Cornu and Shulam 2003: 421 suggest a more regal-like chariot, with sides, a roof, and a curtain). It is hard to know how luxurious the chariot was for a trip that took five months each way.

8:29–31 The Spirit, not the angel of verse 26, now directs Philip to go and join (κολλήθητι, *kollētheti*) the man in the chariot. The Spirit frequently directs in Acts (10:19; 11:12; 13:2, 4; 16:6–7). Running to the man, Philip hears the eunuch reading Isaiah. Strelan (2001) points out that running is often tied to prophets or priests.[1] Philip asks the man if he comprehends what he is reading. The phrase ἆρά γε (*ara ge*) is somewhat emphatic, thus the translation "now indeed." The interplay between knowing and understanding (γινώσκεις ἃ ἀναγινώσκεις, *ginōskeis ha anaginōskeis*) makes for paronomasia, adding elegance to an account that itself would often have been read aloud. The eunuch humbly asks to be led in a discussion about understanding what Isaiah is saying. The question is introduced by γάρ (*gar*), which goes untranslated in an unusual use of this term, where it has the force of "then" (BDF §452.1). The term ὁδηγέω (*hodēgeō*, guide) refers in everyday usage to someone guiding someone to another place, such as guiding a blind person, the guidance Moses or God gave the Jews, or being led into wisdom (BAGD

---

1. See Elijah in 1 Kings 18:46, noted by Josephus, *Ant.* 8.13.6 §346; false prophets in Jer. 23:21; an angelic messenger in Zech. 2:4 (2:8 LXX); the word runs swiftly in Ps. 147:15; Aaron in Num. 16:47; David in 1 Sam. 20:6.

553 §2; BDAG 690; Johnson 1992: 157; Matt. 15:14; Luke 6:39; Exod. 15:13; 32:34; Pss. 5:9 LXX [5:8 Eng.]; 22:3 LXX [23:3 Eng.]; Wis. 9:11; 10:10). When the Ethiopian says that he needs a guide, it becomes clear why Philip is here, especially when the man invites him into the chariot. Philip the evangelist is ready to explain the text to his inquirer and even hurries to do so. Philip serves as an interpretive guide to God's wisdom, both to Scripture and to God's plan in Jesus. He fulfills the mission to which God has called this member of the church.

The passage (περιοχή, *periochē*) being read is Isa. 53:7b–8a. It is cited   **8:32–34** in a form like the LXX, but the sense reflects the MT.[2] Williams (1990: 162) suggests that the LXX is the likely version this official would be reading. The differences in citation between the LXX and the MT are not crucial because the issue is not the details but the identity of the figure described. Περιοχή is an NT hapax. In the LXX it often refers to an enclosure such as a stronghold or fortress (1 Sam. 22:4–5; 2 Sam. 5:7, 9, 17), so in a literary context it refers to a defined text. Barrett (1994: 428) plausibly suggests that in a discussion taking place during a journey, the six lines cited would not be the only topic (v. 35—"beginning with this Scripture"—says as much).

Isaiah 53:7 looks at the innocent, silent suffering of the servant and compares the figure to a sacrificial lamb, unjustly slain as verse 33 makes clear ("justice was denied him"). The term for "lamb" (ἀμνός, *amnos*) is relatively rare in the NT, appearing four times (John 1:29, 35–36; Acts 8:32; 1 Pet. 1:17–21). This suggests a traditional source, since the NT use of this term is relatively restrained and not limited to one writer. Philip will compare this description to Jesus (v. 35). The comparison to a lamb might suggest atonement, but this is not the most emphasized idea. Luke makes such a point more clearly elsewhere in Luke-Acts (the substitution with Barabbas, Luke 23:18–19; Acts 20:28).

The death is described as being taken up from the earth (αἴρεται ἀπὸ τῆς γῆς, *airetai apo tēs gēs*). It also is called humbling (ταπεινώσει, *tapeinōsei*). The Greek term is relatively rare in the NT, appearing four times (Luke 1:46–48; Acts 8:33; Phil. 3:20–21; James 1:9–10). In its context, the Isaian passage refers to both submission and the idea of injustice. The text asks what kind of generation can take a life like this (v. 33). The implied suggestion is that only a wicked generation can do so (Isa. 53:8–9; views that see this as a reference to the innumerable followers of Jesus are unlikely, but so Schneider 1980: 505). The verb αἴρω (*airō*) in a context such as this means "to remove" something or "to take it out of the way" (BAGD 24 §4; BDAG 28–29 §3). Here it is justice that is removed, as the unjust death of an innocent takes place. This was the

2. See Bock 1987: 226–27 and the textual discussion for details. The only portion often debated here is the very difficult Hebrew of v. 8—does it refer to a lack of posterity for the servant or to his death? Either way an untimely death is suggested.

major element of Jesus's death in Luke 23, and Isa. 53:12 is used also in Luke 22:37, where Jesus is reckoned with the criminals. Bruce (1988a: 176) suggests that Jesus alluded to the servant as well, as in Mark 10:45. He also notes that the voice at the baptism pointed to Isa. 42, another servant passage. Johnson (1992: 156) notes the use of portions of Isa. 52:1–53:12 in John 12:38; 1 Pet. 2:21–25; and Rom. 10:16.

The reading that justice was removed by an unjust death is more likely than the idea of a vindication, that his judgment was removed, as some suggest. The issue of injustice fits with the Lukan portrait of Jesus's death. He died unjustly because he was who he claimed to be, the promised one of Israel. But there is irony here: in the generation's act of taking Jesus's life from earth, there is also, for Jesus, God's vindication of that death. This, in effect, nullified the judgment of Jesus on earth. If there is a positive viewpoint in the reading, it is one of irony involving the vindication that the servant eventually experienced. This combination of the innocent person suffering and being taken from the earth is probably what Philip eventually explains about Jesus, with an elucidation of what this death now means in light of God's vindication. In my view, it is the failure to work with the irony of the original passage, seen now in Christian terms, that leads interpreters to speak of a positive reading. But an exclusively positive reading undercuts the very irony and reversal that stand at the core of the experience of the cross. This tragic, unjust death, which looked as if it had resulted in all being lost, in fact resulted in everything being gained.

The Acts text, however, develops only one issue: Who is the text describing? This is the focus of the eunuch's question. The eunuch asks if the passage is about Isaiah or another. At the time, Jews may well have considered three candidates for the subject of the text: (1) the prophet, (2) Israel, and (3) another individual, such as an Elijah revived or a Messiah, but not one who suffered (Fitzmyer 1998: 414; Jeremias, *TDNT* 5:684–89). In asking the question this way, the eunuch may think that the passage is about Isaiah. Philip will explain that the passage is about Jesus, who is that servant who suffered unjustly (v. 35).

8:35   The query from the eunuch leads Philip to preach the gospel from the Scripture. The expression "open the mouth" is in Acts 10:34 and 18:14 and often means lecturing on Scripture in Judaism (Barrett 1994: 431). Simply put, Philip "gospeled" Jesus (εὐηγγελίσατο . . . τὸν Ἰησοῦν, *euēngelisato . . . ton Iēsoun*). The phrase in this form is unique, but variations exist in Acts (5:42 [preach the Christ Jesus]; 10:36 [peace through Jesus Christ]; 11:20 [preached the Lord Jesus]; 17:18 [preached Jesus and the resurrection]). Philip begins from this Scripture in Isaiah and moves on. This kind of generalized reference to Scripture, Jesus, or the Christ recalls Luke 24:44–47 (also 24:27). No other details of the conversation appear, although many have been suggested, such as developing Isa. 53, pointing to the new era of Isa. 56 and the full access of eunuchs, or explaining that the righteous Jesus suffered as the text describes (Larkin 1995: 135).

The discussion takes place as they travel. As they come to some water, the eunuch asks what might prevent him from being baptized. The following possible locales are discussed among scholars: (1) Wadi el-Hasi, located north of Gaza and a traditional locale for the event; (2) 'Ain ed-Dirweh near Beth Zur, north of Hebron; (3) 'Ain Yael, five miles south of Jerusalem; and (4) 'Ain Hanniya, one mile west of 'Ain Yael (Larkin 1995: 135, note on 8:36; Polhill 1992: 226). No clear candidate exists because the text provides no detail to help pinpoint the locale.   **8:36**

The verb "prevent" (κωλύω, *kōluō*) appears six times in Acts.[3] How the eunuch knows about baptism is not made clear. Has Philip explained it to him (so Fitzmyer 1998: 414), or has he heard about it in Jerusalem? His willingness to receive baptism means that he is responsive to the gospel. All the barriers are down, and so a eunuch, a black, God-fearing Gentile, is baptized (Polhill 1992: 226).

A confession appears in Acts 8:37, but this verse is not original to Acts (see additional note).   **8:37**

The eunuch commands the chariot to stop. Philip baptizes the eunuch after they enter the water. The verse suggests some type of immersion, since the baptism follows going into the water, although pouring is also possible.[4] That baptism was undertaken immediately in the early days also follows from the call of Acts 2:38, as well as the scene with Cornelius in 10:47–48. The verb "baptize" is frequent in Acts, appearing twenty-one times, almost always of water baptism.[5] In the early church immersion seems to have been the preferred but not the exclusive mode for baptism, as baptisteries show that effusion was also used (Marshall 2002: 18–23). Here is a baptism performed by a non-apostle.   **8:38**

With the baptism complete, so is Philip's mission. The Spirit takes Philip away. The verb here for being caught up, ἁρπάζω (*harpazō*), appears   **8:39**

---

3. See Acts 8:36; 10:46–47 (of not hindering baptism to Cornelius's house); 11:17 (Who could hinder God from giving Cornelius's faith?); 16:6–8 (hindered going to Asia); 24:22–23 (not hinder Paul seeing friends); 27:43–44 (prevented a plan to kill prisoners on the ship voyage). The adverb (ἀκωλύτως, *akōlytōs*) appears in the final verse of Acts in 28:31, where Paul preaches the gospel of the kingdom unhindered.

4. Would one have to go into the water to pour it? There is the parallel with John's baptism in the Jordan River as well. In second-century Christian texts, there is the note about using running water when possible, as in Did. 7.1; Bruce 1990: 229. Still, Did. 7.3 says that immersion is not necessary. Such water was seen as "living."

5. See Acts 1:3–5 (2x; John's baptism); 2:38 (related to the gift of the Spirit but "in the name of Jesus"); also 2:41; 8:12–16 (3x), 36, 38; 9:18–19; 10:46–48 (2x); 11:16 (2x); 16:15, 33–34; 18:8; 19:3–6 (3x; discusses and distinguishes between John's and Jesus's baptisms); 22:16.

twice in Acts (in 23:10 Paul is taken away from a scene to protect him) and twelve other times in the NT (Matt. 11:12; 12:29; 13:19; John 6:15; 10:11–13, 27–29 [2x]; 2 Cor. 12:2–4 [2x; Paul caught up into the third heaven]; 1 Thess. 4:15–17 [saints being caught up in the air]; Jude 22–23; Rev. 12:5). His instant removal makes clearer still that God is at work. It recalls Jesus's removal in Luke 24:31. Like Elisha, Philip is directed in ministry (1 Kings 18:12, 46; 2 Kings 2:16 [a similar taking up]; similarly, Ezek. 11:24). There is no opportunity for the eunuch to develop a personal attachment to Philip. Nonetheless, the eunuch moves on, rejoicing at his newfound relationship to God. Acts notes such rejoicing seven times with the verb χαίρω (chairō; 5:41–42; 8:39; 11:23–24; 13:48–49; 15:22–23, 31; 23:23–26; note also Rom. 14:17; Ps. 68:31).[6]

8:40   The unit ends with a summary verse much like 8:25. Philip finds himself at Azotus, the OT site of Ashdod (Isa. 20:1). This city was restored by the Romans and given to Herod. It was located just off the coast of southern Palestine about twenty miles north of Gaza, thirty-five miles west of Jerusalem, and three miles inland (Josephus, J.W. 1.7.7 §156; 1.8.4 §166; Ant. 13.15.4 §395; 14.4.4 §75; 14.5.3 §88; Bruce 1990: 230). It is mentioned only here in the NT.

Philip does not stay still. He preaches the gospel to all the towns, as the apostles did in Acts 8:25 in Samaria, until he reaches Caesarea, a major city by the sea, located south of Mt. Carmel, fifty-five miles up the coast (BDAG 499 §2; Acts 9:30; 10:1, 24; 11:11; 12:19; 18:22; 21:8, 16; 23:23, 33; 25:1, 4, 6, 13; Fitzmyer 1998: 415). Caesarea, named after Augustus Caesar, was the home of the Roman procurators, the Roman capital of Judea (Josephus, J.W. 1.21.5–8 §§408–15; Ant. 15.9.6 §§331–41; 16.5.1 §§136–41). Two Roman legions were there (Josephus, Ant. 3.9.1 §§409–13). The famous inscription naming the prefect Pilate was found here. So Philip engaged in ministry up the coast and finally reached a major center as he was preaching (imperfect tense again) to the towns in the area. Philip is still here in Acts 21:8, twenty years later. Lydda and Joppa of Acts 9 were also in the area between these two locales, as were other key sites such as Jamnia and Antipatris (Williams 1990: 164). In effect, Philip's work helps open up activity along the entire coast.

In sum, this unit shows the continued expansive activity of one outside the Twelve, but the real focus is the momentum of God's leading and direction through the Spirit for the church's mission. Philip is faithful, going wherever the Lord calls, ready to explain Jesus and the gospel to whoever might hear the message. The eunuch represents the expansion pushing in a direction toward the end of the earth and toward Africa.

---

6. For a summary of the Ethiopian's career among the church fathers, see Irenaeus, *Ag. Her.* 3.12.10, where he is said to have proclaimed the message in Ethiopia, but clear evidence of a vibrant church there does not appear until the fourth century.

Haenchen (1987: 314–16) complains that the account's historicity is in doubt in part because of how the story sets up the later conversion of Gentiles (Acts 10), while the conversion of a Jew seems of no real interest. In fact, it is the supernatural activity that is Haenchen's greatest objection to the text. He also fails to see how the "fringe" character of this Jew makes a point about the social scope of God's salvation. He sees the account as the Hellenistic rival to Peter's outreach to Cornelius, noting that the only other account where God is so active is in the conversion of Cornelius through Peter. But there is no rivalry here, only a gradual expansion of outreach, which God is directing in many places virtually simultaneously (one senses here the shadow of F. C. Baur's push for competition among Christians). There is parallelism between the two accounts, which simply underscores how active God is in the process. Here Haenchen is too wedded to the old Tübingen school's view of early-church conflict. The Acts of the Apostles could just as well be named the Acts of God. This event is an important intermediate stop in the journey to Gentile inclusion (so correctly Pesch 1986a: 295). Jervell (1998: 275) sees a Hellenist Christian tradition legitimizing the conversion of Gentiles with an almost Jew being converted first. The event is rooted in history for him.

Nor should one downplay the importance of Philip's convert, as Haenchen does. The eunuch is not just any person associated with Judaism. He is a eunuch, which restricts him from Jewish worship. And as one who respects the God of Israel from a faraway land, his exposure to the gospel shows that even a brief encounter in the midst of travel can allow the gospel to spread. In all likelihood, he is another example of a God-fearer and a significant government official responding to Jesus, just what someone such as Theophilus, to whom Acts is addressed, needs to hear. Acts 8 is full of contrasts showing the expansion of the mission: there is work in the north (Samaria) and the south (Gaza on the coast); a magician and a government figure are exposed to the message, as are Samaritans and God-fearers from Africa. God is mightily at work with a wide array of people. Skeptical judgments about the account relate to what the interpreter sees as possible for God, not to problems with the account itself.

The key characters are also important to the teaching of the narrative. The eunuch is an example of someone with an open heart before God, asking questions and ready to learn. Philip is the faithful and obedient evangelist, ready to move at a moment's notice to share the word, even across cultural lines. Fernando (1998: 287–92) points to these elements of good evangelism: it reflects faithful obedience, is ready to cross cultural lines, is sensitive to hearts prepared by God, often starts with the other person's questions, is rooted in scriptural teaching, and has Jesus as the theme. In Acts 8 we see Philip in two modes. In the first he evangelizes large groups in a public context. In this final passage, he shares the gospel one-on-one. Both styles and capabilities are important to possess in the church. He serves in Acts as a "model of a Christian missionary" (Dormeyer and Galindo 2003: 125).

Additional Notes

8:31. There is divided external evidence whether to read the aorist subjunctive ὁδηγήσῃ (*hodēgēsē*; $\mathfrak{P}^{74}$, A, B², Ψ, 1739, Byz) or the future indicative ὁδηγήσει (*hodēgēsei*; $\mathfrak{P}^{50}$, ℵ, B*, C, E, L), both of which carry the same force, "shall guide." The future indicative is the more difficult reading with ἐάν (*ean*), being more classical in style. The confusion could well be rooted in the fact that these two words were pronounced the same.

8:32. There is a difference between the present tense of the LXX's κείροντος (*keirontos*, shearing) and the aorist reading κείραντος (*keirantos*) of the Acts text. Here Luke is assimilating the text to the past setting that Isaiah represents.

8:33. The first use of αὐτοῦ (*autou*, his) is disputed, with $\mathfrak{P}^{74}$, ℵ, A, B, and 1739 omitting the term whereas C, E, Ψ, 33, and Byz include it. The exclusion matches the LXX, and external evidence favors exclusion as well, so inclusion is the more difficult reading. Inclusion emphasizes slightly more the personal nature of the suffering. Whether it is original is not clear. I slightly favor exclusion, following the MS evidence.

8:37. Acts 8:37 appears only in MSS of the Western family. It is not in $\mathfrak{P}^{45,74}$, ℵ, A, B, C, 33, 81, 614, or many Vulgate texts. It is in E, several minuscules, a few versions of the Itala, and some Vulgate texts (Metzger 1971: 359–60). It appears to have been added because there is no mention of a confession of faith by the eunuch. The text reads, "And Philip said, 'If you believe with all your heart, you may.' And he answered and said, 'I believe that Jesus Christ is the Son of God.'" The call to believe with all one's heart in a confession is unusual. The verse was not in the original version of Acts and so is omitted in the translation. Barrett (1994: 433) has a full discussion and notes that "believe" is used in two distinct ways within the verse. He goes on to say that although the verse is not original, it is one of the earliest witnesses for how confession took place in the church, being written sometime just after the composition of Acts. It is probably a second-century addition that reflects practice at that time (Bruce 1988a: 178).

8:39. In a few later MSS, the eunuch is said to have the Spirit fall upon him, and the angel of the Lord removes Philip (Aᶜ, 36, 323, 453, 945, 1739, 1891). Despite being a difficult reading (which might suggest authenticity), this longer text is not well enough attested to be original.

D. The Conversion and Early Reception of Saul (9:1–30)

God directs the conversion of Saul from start to finish, involving both Saul and a figure named Ananias. The term "conversion" is chosen consciously, as Saul after his encounter with the Lord is not the same person. Having had his own theology challenged by the Lord, Saul sees the light and has time to reflect on it. Kern (2003) works through this portrayal of Saul/Paul from a narrative standpoint and rejects the view that there is no conversion here or any break with the past. Saul still seeks the God of Israel, but now Saul views this God as working through the promise of Jesus with those in Judaism also in need of responding to their Messiah. Kern is reacting to claims by Stendahl (1976: 7–23) and Gaventa (1986) that diminish the idea of conversion for Paul, mostly on the basis that his God has not changed. The object of worship does not change for Saul, but the way this God is understood changes significantly as a result of this experience. As a result, Saul also changes.

Jesus appears to Saul as he heads to Damascus to continue the persecution of the church. This persecution represents an expansion of his earlier activity noted in Acts 8:3 (9:1–9). Jesus also appears to Ananias to prepare him to help Saul and explain Saul's calling to him (9:10–19a). The first place Saul preaches is Damascus, the ultimate irony: the place where Saul intended to arrest Christians becomes the place where he preaches to people to become Christians (9:19b–22). Even more ironic is the result: Saul has to escape to avoid persecution himself (9:23–25). The unit ends with Barnabas taking Saul back to Jerusalem, where Saul engages the Hellenists who had earlier slain Stephen. Saul escapes to Caesarea and then to Tarsus (9:26–30).

Detailed discussion about this period in Paul's life can be found in Hengel and Schwemer (1997: 24–90; see more discussion at 9:1–2). They place this conversion within three years of Jesus's death whereas Riesner (1998: 64–74, esp. 73) sees an even tighter chronology of about a year. Paul's conversion likely falls somewhere between these two estimates. Hengel and Schwemer (1997: 39–40) also note how the accounts in Acts and Paul's own statements complement each other, both emphasizing God's election, the appearing of God's glory, and a call to the Gentiles. What Paul sees is the glory of the risen Lord in a manner somewhat distinct from, and more intense than, the resurrection appearances and the appearance to Stephen.

God is raising a new curtain for the progress of mission by reconstructing the old manner of doing things. Saul is the ultimate example of God's initiative to save the enemy, who, more importantly, is still a sinner who is loved and in need of salvation. God's rescue of Saul replaces some of what was seemingly lost with Stephen's death. Saul's mission will move far beyond Jerusalem. The church is being built up, and new witnesses are being sent forth to new places, sometimes showing up in surprising ways through unexpected opportunities and encounters.

This conversion is surely one of the major events in Acts, as it is told three different times, each time with fresh detail (Acts 9 in the third person; 22:3–16 and 26:4–18, both in the first person; Hedrick 1981). Fitzmyer (1998: 420) correctly argues that this is a commission account in the mold of the OT prophets.[1]

Witherington (1998: 303–15) has a full discussion of the relationship of these three accounts. He stresses that all of them are summaries. He also (1998: 307–8) enters the debate about the Paul of Acts and that of his epistles; many scholars view these Pauls as being in conflict. Witherington argues that Paul's letters treat his biography in a somewhat selective manner, since they are occasional letters to other communities, whereas Acts has a more direct treatment of the roots of Paul's ministry and its larger context. Thus both sources are valuable in gaining insight about Paul. This is especially the case with Luke, since he was a traveling companion of Paul's. Marshall (1980: 167) views the ultimate sources of these conversion events as Paul and Ananias, and Schneider (1982: 23) speaks of Paul, Ananias, and possibly a legendary church tradition as the sources. Because of the differences with details from Paul, Jervell (1998: 289–90) sees Luke using various church traditions about the conversion, but he also notes some overlaps (Gal. 1:13–17, 22–23; Phil. 3:4–6; 1 Cor. 15:9; 2 Cor. 11:22–25). Surely Paul's account and trusted church sources would have been the most influential for Luke. However, the description of such traditional sources as legendary is itself an exaggeration, probably reacting to the supernatural elements in the account. The larger context of Acts also explains why Paul's letters are not mentioned. Luke's focus is the church as a whole and not so much the individual concerns of specific communities. These communities are seen in the light of their comprehensive mission or for what they can teach about such a mission. Acts is not a digest of local church politics or issues.

The accounts of Paul's conversion in Acts all share the same basic facts. Saul is on his way to gather up Christians for the Jews. He sees a great light. The Lord asks why Saul is persecuting him. Saul asks who the speaker is. Jesus reveals that it is he. This is the core of the ac-

---

1. *Pace* Hedrick 1981, who sees a miracle account transformed into a commission account.

counts. It also can fit with Paul's claim in Gal. 1:11–23 that he received the gospel by revelation, for here the point is not conversion but an understanding of what he is to preach. Acts, in turn, highlights the receiving of a commission from Ananias, who does not instruct Paul at all on how to preach. Acts 26 shows evidence of being a telescoped summary, as Ananias does not appear at all. This may be in part the result of the fact that he has already been mentioned in detail twice in the book, in Acts 9 and 22.

The biggest difference in the accounts has led to a dispute over whether the companions see the light and hear nothing (22:9) or stand speechless, hearing the voice but seeing no one (9:7). The elements at play here can be reconciled (Witherington 1998: 312–13). The larger group hears sound but nothing intelligible, while also seeing a light but not Jesus himself. Only Saul sees someone and hears in an understandable form what is said. His colleagues experience something less than the full event, which means that the appearance is neither a private vision nor merely an "inner crisis" but a public event.[2] This is a special postresurrection appearance of Jesus, a revelatory Christophany. Fitzmyer (1998: 420–21) correctly speaks of earlier commentators exaggerating the differences in these accounts both in Acts and in Paul's letters. This appearance is also different from other resurrection appearances, however, because Saul sees Jesus's full revelatory glory, unlike those who saw Jesus earlier.

The second, key difference is the lack of a direct mention by Saul of his Gentile call in the appearance of Acts 9, whereas it is present in Acts 22 and 26. This call is, however, noted to Ananias in 9:15, so we probably have another example of telescoping. Another possibility is that Luke chose not to note this detail in his third-person narrative because the Gentile mission had not yet taken place, but this argument is somewhat weakened by the mention of the mission to Ananias.

In many ways, Acts is a defense, not so much of Paul but of what his mission to the Gentiles represents. This is the story of how a man's conversion gives additional impetus to a movement that seeks to restructure formal Judaism, a goal advocated by John the Baptist, Jesus, and the Qumran community in different ways. Considering the controversies Jesus's own ministry engendered over issues such as Torah, purity, and Sabbath, as well as what the church is preaching about the uniqueness and divine vindication of Jesus, it is no wonder that Saul, as a representative of official Judaism, initially reacts against the church. This makes his conversion into a preacher for the community all the more amazing, a change of worldview that only the Lord could work. Fitzmyer (1998: 420) is correct that this story is "not an account of his

---

2. So correctly Williams 1990: 166, who notes and rejects other naturalistic explanations such as epilepsy, some type of ecstatic trance, or a mere legend, the option for which Conzelmann 1987: 72–73 argues.

psychological 'conversion,' as it is often characterized, but the story of how divine grace transforms even the life of a persecutor."

The account also shows how the Lord identifies with the church and considers its suffering as an attack against himself. The Lord not only protects his church in this case but gives it a powerful new ally. Saul's conversion is one of the great testimonies to the risen Jesus. To explain how Saul became Paul the apostle is to describe how the early church preached and saw Jesus—and how Jesus directly guided the early church. This is why Paul's own works are such a major witness to the character of the earliest Christianity. He understood both the position of the church and that of its opposition, having been a key opponent himself. Paul understood well the church's message and theology as well as what it was facing in the opposition. Paul's emphasis on the resurrection is one of the great testimonies that such an event of vindication did take place. The reason Saul reacted when the Lord appeared to him must rest in part on the preparation God had engaged in when faithful people such as Stephen preached to Saul even though he opposed the church. One never knows when God may open a heart to hear God's message and see how God acts in history.

1. The Conversion of Saul (9:1–19a)

Saul's conversion brings his persecution program (9:1–2) to a fast end. The roadblock is the appearance of the risen Lord himself and his inquiry as to what Saul is doing by persecuting him through persecuting his followers. The query shows the Lord's solidarity with his followers and their suffering (9:3–5). Instructed to go into the city, Saul has to be led there, as the appearance leads to temporary blindness and to Saul's fasting as he prepares for his calling (9:6–9).

The church also needs preparation, however, for this startling turn of events. Such preparation on each side of a great event will repeat itself in Acts 10 with Peter and Cornelius. The Lord directs a nervous Ananias to receive Saul (9:10–12). Ananias replies that he knows that this man has done evil to the saints (9:13–14). Jesus replies that this man is a chosen instrument to take Jesus's name before Gentiles, kings, and Israel (9:15–16). So Ananias obeys, meets Saul, and lays hands on him to fill him with the Spirit, ending Saul's blindness and leading him to take food (9:17–19a). Ananias shows how one should welcome an enemy who comes to faith. He also gains insight and strength from what the Lord reveals to him. Everything about Saul's conversion is of the Lord.

The story is a calling account, which has roots in the OT and Judaism (Barrett 1994: 441–42; Witherington 1998: 304n10; Marshall 1980: 167; see Samuel, in 1 Sam. 3:2–18; the prophets, Isa. 6:1–13; Jer. 1:4–10; Jos. Asen. 14.6–8; and the vision to Heliodorus in 2 Macc. 3). The genre of Joseph and Aseneth is romance and its story is about marriage, not mission as in the OT examples and Acts. A major difference in the account about Heliodorus is that this event of protection came as a result of intense intercession and was a judgment, not a conversion (Weiser 1981: 217–18; Pesch 1986a: 300). Saul's story is distinct not only because Saul is called to change sides in a dispute (in addition to being commissioned for a mission) but also because his conversion appears unexpectedly with no long intercessory introduction by the persecuted. Gaventa (2003: 155) calls it a "reversal of an enemy" account. God simply takes the initiative here.

Exegesis and Exposition

[1]But Saul, still breathing threats and murder against the Lord's disciples, came to the high priest [2]and asked for letters to the synagogues of Damascus, so that

if he found anyone belonging to the Way, men and also women, he might bring them bound to Jerusalem. [3]Now as he journeyed, he approached Damascus, and suddenly a light from heaven flashed around him. [4]And falling to the ground, he heard a voice saying to him, "Saul, Saul, why are you persecuting me? ⌜ ⌝" [5]And he said, "Who are you, Lord?" And he said, "I am Jesus ⌜ ⌝, whom you are persecuting; [6]⌜ ⌝ but rise and enter the city, and it will be told to you what you are to do." [7]The men who were traveling with him stood speechless, on the one hand, hearing the voice but, on the other, seeing no one. [8]Saul arose from the ground, but opening his eyes, he could not see anything. Leading him by the hand, they brought him to Damascus. [9]And for three days he could not see and did not eat or drink.

[10]Now there was in Damascus a certain disciple named Ananias, and the Lord said to him in a vision, "Ananias." And he said, "Here I am, Lord." [11]And the Lord said to him, "Rise and go to the street named 'Straight,' and inquire in the house of Judas for a man of Tarsus named Saul; for, look, he is praying [12]and he has seen a man named Ananias coming in and laying on hands so he might see." [13]But Ananias answered, "Lord, I have heard from many about this man, how much evil he has done to your saints at Jerusalem; [14]and here he has authority from the chief priests to bind all those who call upon your name." [15]But the Lord said to him, "Go, for this one is my chosen vessel to carry my name before even Gentiles, kings, and the sons of Israel; [16]for I will show him how much he must suffer because of my name." [17]So Ananias departed and entered into the house and, laying hands upon him, said, "Brother Saul, the Lord Jesus, the one appearing to you on the way by which you came, has sent me so that you might see and be filled with the Holy Spirit." [18]And immediately something like scales fell from his eyes, and he had sight and, arising, was baptized, [19a]and, taking food, was strengthened.

9:1–2　Saul is still (ἔτι, *eti*) at work against the church (Acts 8:3), breathing threats and murder against its members. This is the only NT use of the term ἐμπνέω (*empneō*) for "breathe." It is part of an idiom about breathing out threats and murder (BAGD 256 §1; BDAG 324 §1).[1] The expression reflects Saul's highly hostile attitude toward believers. It may not mean that he seeks to murder them himself, given that execution remains in Roman hands, but it expresses what he hopes will be the result of his arrests (22:4; 26:10; Marshall 1980: 168; Weiser 1981: 222–23). If (ἐάν, *ean*) he should find them, Saul would deliver them to prison, from where they could be sent to Roman authorities. The conditional clause is third class and is presented with a touch of uncer-

---

1. For conceptual parallels, see Acts 22:4, 26:10; OT: Ps. 18:15 (17:16 LXX). In classical literature, Euripides, *Bacchanals* 620, also uses it of a persecutor; Conzelmann 1987: 71. In Jewish literature, see 4 Macc. 4:8 (of Apollonius threatening to seize funds from the temple).

tainty (Culy and Parsons 2003: 170). It may also be that Rome already has not decided to give the Jews such authority to imprison, given the scope of the perceived problem. Saul has consented to Stephen's death already, which indicates that he is accepting of such an outcome for Jesus's followers (8:1).

Saul pursues the disciples even beyond Jerusalem and obtains authority for doing so (probably from Caiaphas; 22:5; 26:10). Bruce (1988a: 180) suggests that Saul models his zeal after Phinehas (Num. 25:7–13; Ps. 106:30–31), Elijah (1 Kings 18:40; 19:10, 14), and Mattathias (1 Macc. 2:23–28). The Maccabean period makes clear that religious zeal often did work its way into Jewish practice. Witherington (1998: 302–3) notes the later activism that led Rome to destroy Jerusalem in AD 70. Paul himself confesses that he was a persecutor of the church (1 Cor. 15:9; Gal. 1:13–14; Phil. 3:6; 1 Tim. 1:13).

The letters that Paul asks for concern the right of extradition, if 1 Macc. 15:21 applies. Conzelmann (1987: 71) disputes the genuineness and the relevance of the letter in 1 Macc. 15:16–21, noting that it is too far removed in time to be relevant, even if it were genuine. Barrett (1994: 446–47) has a full discussion and concludes that the more important issue is how the Sanhedrin is related to outside synagogues. Haenchen (1987: 320n2) is also skeptical of such extradition authority. Even though the Maccabean letter is old, however, it might reflect Jewish beliefs and Roman practice that continued into Paul's time regarding religious issues. Josephus in *Ant.* 14.10.2 §§192–95 describes a later, parallel letter of authorization. Thus the practice appears to span Paul's time period.

Conzelmann argues that Josephus, *J.W.* 1.24.2 §474, does not agree with this right of extradition, since it makes a unique claim for such authority for Herod. Conzelmann does not note, however, the *Ant.* 14 text, which indicates the possibility of such authorization to a Jew. Haenchen calls the *Ant.* 14 text irrelevant, but it does show the potential for a close relationship like the one Caiaphas had with Pilate. In addition, the subject at hand is the authority over the synagogues of Judaism, a religious-oversight issue. Since this is not so much a matter of legal execution as imprisonment, it is quite likely that the high priest and Sanhedrin had such authority and that with a letter the synagogues of the Diaspora might cooperate if it were a question of the presence of heterodoxy. That the governor under king Aretas sought to arrest Saul in Damascus (2 Cor. 11:32) is not surprising, given Saul's turn in allegiance and the public destabilization it may well have brought (but Schille 1984: 219 is skeptical); this detail does not indicate a lack of authority of Jews over their faith in Syria (Acts 26:12; 2 Cor. 11:32–33). As a whole, then, the scenario involving letters for Paul seems credible.

Christianity has already spread as far as Damascus, an important city 135 miles north-northeast of Jerusalem. This is the first city outside the land of Israel to be noted as having Christians. Hengel and Schwemer

(1997: 80–90) see it as a small community, something Saul's own letters in verse 2 suggest by the words "might find" Christians there. They also propose that it was fleeing Jewish Christian Hellenists from Jerusalem who helped found the community, something the juxtaposition of this event with Acts 7 suggests (given that Peter and Philip went in the other direction). These Hellenists may well have pushed steadily north and shared the gospel. If so, Saul is sent to block the advance of the message.

Damascus was a commercial center on the way between Egypt and Mesopotamia. It had a substantial Jewish population.[2] The mention of Damascus is significant, for Luke has not told us anything about this church yet. In Acts the church has now moved north to Samaria (Acts 8), west and south to the coast, and east to Syria (Acts 9).

"The Way" is the early name for Christians (19:9, 23; 24:14, 22), sometimes referred to as "the way of the Lord" or "the way of God" (18:25–26).[3] It appears to point to the way of salvation as a way of and to life. Later Christian works such as Did. 1–6 may well have borrowed this metaphor in speaking of the two ways, one leading to life, the other to death. Haenchen (1987: 319n2) discusses the various names given to Christians in Acts 9: disciples, those of the Way, saints, those who call on the name of the Lord, brothers, and witnesses. Each name points out a distinct feature of what being a believer means or entails.

Saul will apprehend both men and women, as he must know that the faith is spreading among both genders (Jervell 1998: 279).

9:3　This is the first of three descriptions of Paul's conversion (the others are 22:3–16; 26:4–18). It also is the last major Christophany in Acts (Jervell 1998: 278). The description of the vision covers verses 3–9.

Two of the three versions of this event use the verb περιαστράπτω (*periastraptō*, to flash around) to describe Jesus's initial appearance to Saul. They are the only two occurrences of the word in the NT (Acts 9:3; 22:6). The term refers to something shining all around an area. So the appearance of Jesus lights up all that Saul sees.

A flashing light suggests a glorious epiphany (Acts 26:13, "brighter than the sun"; 12:7; Matt. 17:5; Gal. 1:16; 1 Cor. 9:1).[4] The instantaneous nature of the event also gives the scene supernatural features, like apoca-

---

2. Josephus, *J.W.* 2.20.2 §561, speaks of at least ten thousand being massacred there, but 7.8.7 §368 speaks of more than eighteen thousand killed. Both are estimates and point to a large Jewish population. On the city's history, see Fitzmyer 1998: 423; details in Hengel and Schwemer 1997: 55–61.

3. For a similar description at Qumran, see 1QS 9.17–18; 10.21; 11.13; CD 1.13; 2.6; 20.18. In Judaism, see 1 En. 91.18; 2 En. 30.15; T. Ash. 3.1–6.5; Ebel, *NIDNTT* 3:935–43; Johnson 1992: 162; Fitzmyer 1998: 424 notes multiple references at Qumran. It is also present in the OT: Pss. 1:1, 6; 2:12.

4. Contrast the descriptions of Jesus in Acts of Thomas 34; Acts of John 97, where Paul sees the Lord. For other presentations of such a vision, see 4 Macc. 4:10; in the OT: Exod. 19:16 (light flashes like lightning); 2 Sam. 22:15; Ezek. 1:28; Schille 1984: 220.

lyptic events or the transfiguration (Mark 13:36; Luke 2:3; 9:39; Acts 9:3; 22:6 are all the NT uses of ἐξαίφνης, *exaiphnēs*, suddenly). Acts 22:6 and 26:13 say that the appearance takes place at about noon.

The light is so intense that Saul falls to the ground (Ezek. 1:28; 3:23–24; 43:3; Dan. 8:17; Josephus, *Ant.* 10.11.7 §269 describes Daniel's experience of falling to the ground; Rev. 1:17). This Acts 9 account initially focuses on Saul's experience, with the experience of his companions not noted until verse 7.

   9:4

The double calling out of the name of Saul indicates intense emotion (Luke 10:41 [Martha]; 22:31; Gen. 22:11 [Abraham]; 46:2 [Jacob]; Exod. 3:4 [Moses]; 1 Sam. 3:4, 6 LXX [Samuel]; 2 Sam. 19:4 [Absalom]; 2 Bar. 22.2 [Baruch]; Weiser 1981: 224). The event appears in a manner similar to ones described in 2 Macc. 3:13–40 and 4 Macc. 4:8–14, but many of the details are different. In the 2 Maccabees passage, a rider on horseback and two angelic beings strike down Heliodorus as an act of divine judgment for his attempting to steal money from the Jerusalem temple treasury. In 4 Macc. 4:10, Apollonius's attempt to gain access to the temple treasury is stopped by angels on horseback and flashes of lightning. Appeals to 2 or 4 Maccabees as the basis for the scene are therefore not credible (see introduction to 9:1–19a above). The encounter between Saul and Jesus is a rescue not a judgment, and there is no raiding of the temple. Also, the 4 Maccabees passage uses lightning to depict heavenly glory, not light as in Acts. In the 2 Maccabees passage, Heliodorus is physically struck down rather than being startled by the light and falling as Saul does in Acts.

Jesus asks why Saul persecutes him, although Saul does not yet know who is speaking. This curious remark is unexplained at first but points to Jesus's corporate solidarity with the church. To persecute the Way is to persecute Jesus. Jesus closely identifies with his own (Matt. 25:35–40, 42–45). The roots of the concept of the "body of Christ" are here, although this does not dawn on Paul immediately.[5] Schneider (1982: 26) rejects such a vision-body connection, seeing only the kind of connection expressed in Matt. 25, but the two ideas are not unrelated. Pesch (1986a: 304) says that the concept is not directly behind the remark but is close to it. Certainly the solidarity expressed here suggests an intense form of identification between Jesus and his followers and, at the least, implies the idea of the body of Christ.

Conzelmann (1987: 71) speaks of a theophonic dialogue here and cites examples from the OT and Judaism (Exod. 3:4–10; Gen. 46:2–3; 31:11–13; Jub. 44.5; and Jos. Asen. 14.6–8). Such heavenly voices also appear in Acts 7:31; 10:13; Luke 3:22; 9:35; and John 12:28 (Bruce 1990: 234). Heaven has reached down to call someone on the earth.

---

5. Kim 1981 details the influence of this event on Paul's Christology; Acts 22:7; 26:14; Col. 1:18; Eph. 1:22–23; 4:15–16. This view goes back to Augustine, *Sermons* 361.14.

9:5–6 Saul, although he does not yet realize it, is seeing the full glory of the risen Jesus. Saul asks who is speaking. His use of "Lord" in his question here is not a christological confession but indicates his high respect for the heavenly one in the vision, whose identity he does not yet know (more than "sir" but less than an expression of a christological understanding; Johnson 1992: 163; Witherington 1998: 317). Saul's question leads Jesus to identify himself. Jesus tells Saul that the persecution is really directed against himself, who is appearing to Saul as a heavenly glorious figure. Luke 10:16 indicates how serious a charge persecuting Jesus is. It means to be against God. Would Saul really want to challenge heaven? Larkin (1995: 139) sees a reminder of Gamaliel's remarks in Acts 5:39 about which side God is on (also Williams 1990: 169). If God is granting Saul such a vision and warning, what does it mean?

The verb διώκω (diōkō, persecute) appears twice in verses 4–5. What Paul does against the church represents an attack against Jesus, who here appears as the exalted Lord. This verb appears nine times in Acts (7:52; 9:4–5 [2x]; 22:4, 7, 8; 26:11, 14–15 [2x]). Six of the occurrences are in the three descriptions of this event. Two of the others appear in Paul's description of his early work against the church. In 26:11 Paul alludes to chasing believers down in foreign cities, just as he is doing here in Acts 9. The dialogue of verse 5 is in all three appearance accounts (22:7–8; 26:14–15).

Jesus directs Saul to arise and go to Damascus to receive instructions on what he "must" (δεῖ, dei) do. Luke uses δεῖ to note the "divine necessity" inherent in the calling (twenty-two times in Acts alone out of forty in Luke-Acts: Acts 1:15–17, 21–22; 3:19–21; 4:12; 5:29; 9:5–6, 15–16; 14:21–22; 15:5; 16:29–30; 17:2–3; 19:21, 36; 20:35; 23:11; 24:17–19; 25:10, 24; 26:9–10; 27:21, 23–24, 26). "From this moment on he is a new man" (so Williams 1990: 169; 2 Cor. 5:17; Phil. 3:4–8). In one of the parallel accounts, Saul is told a little about his mission during this vision (Acts 26:16–18), but this may reflect literary telescoping, since Ananias is not mentioned in this later version and Ananias delivers the Lord's directive in Acts 9 and 22. Saul goes to Damascus as a chosen witness. Saul the persecutor with a letter from the high priest now is Saul the witness with a commission from Jesus. The heavenly calling has trumped the original earthly mission.

9:7 Luke now describes the bystanders' experience, which is different from Saul's. Those around Paul hear the voice but do not see anything; this excludes a merely private vision. The μὲν . . . δέ (men . . . de, on the one hand . . . on the other hand) construction here rules out the conclusion that it was Saul's voice the men are said to have heard (Bruce 1988a: 185 argues against John Chrysostom, Hom. Acts 47). A voice is heard but no one is seen. There is something public about what takes place, even though Paul alone receives the event's full impact. This is in contrast to the Lord's appearance to Ananias in a vision in 9:10. Acts 22:9 has Paul report that they saw the light but did not hear the voice, by which is probably meant that they did not understand the voice and that they did not recognize anyone in the light. Acts 9:7 highlights the fact that no one (μηδένα, mēdena) is seen, not that there is no light. Acts 26:13–14 has them see the light and fall to the ground as Paul did in 9:4. There is no value in appealing to the distinction between hearing and understanding, with the genitive case, and hearing and not understanding, with the accusative, for the distinction does not work in Acts (Bratcher 1959–60: 243–45; Wallace 1996: 133–34; Polhill 1992: 235n15). The accusative is used of understanding in verse 4 (note also 10:46; 11:7; 14:9; 15:12; 22:7; Fitzmyer 1998: 426). The idea that some see such an event while others do not has precedent in Judaism. In 3 Macc. 6:18, angels appear to all "but the Jews" to frighten away their enemies.

When Saul arises from the ground, he cannot see. The sign of blindness **9:8–9** for Saul is like the sign of deafness for Zechariah in Luke 1:22, although it is not as long a punishment. It is an outcome of having seen such glory and shows Saul reduced to powerlessness and helplessness before the Lord (Conzelmann 1987: 72).

Saul is led by the hand to Damascus. The note about being guided by hand will mark a judgment in Acts 13:11 against Elymas the magician, who is blinded by God through Paul, but this is not the point here. There is precedent for this kind of action in the OT and in Judaism (Gen. 19:11; Exod. 4:11; Deut. 28:28; 2 Kings 6:18–20; Zech. 12:4; Let. Aris. 315–16; Le Cornu and Shulam 2003: 492). However, this act is not so much a judgment as it is a time for Saul to pause and reflect as his eyes have reacted to the strength of God's glory. For three days he sits in darkness and probably fasts by having no food or drink, processing what has taken place (on fasting, see Bock 1996: 1463). There is no specific reference to fasting, but it seems implied, since no physical impairment prevents Saul from taking sustenance. Marshall (1980: 170) speaks of Saul's penitence here at realizing what has happened, as does Haenchen (1987: 323; Jos. Asen. 10.2). He may be preparing for baptism (Did. 7.4; Justin Martyr, *1 Apol.* 61; Tertullian, *On Baptism* 20), but he certainly is preparing for his commission. Pesch (1986a: 305) rejects the idea that preparation for baptism is in view, but does see repentance at work in the radical, no-food-or-drink fast. Acts 9:12 makes clear that Saul is praying and receives yet another indication of what will happen during this three-day period. Saul, now blind, is also now seeing (Fitzmyer 1998: 426). Meanwhile God also is preparing Ananias to receive him.

A disciple named Ananias receives a vision from the Lord, who is iden- **9:10–12** tified as the Lord Jesus in verse 17. The account of the Lord preparing him for Saul continues to verse 16. Acts 22:12 tells us Ananias is a Jewish believer. How Christianity reached Damascus is not noted, showing

Luke's selectivity. The new faith is present and active there; that is all we are told.

Visions expressed with the term ὅραμα (*horama*) appear here and there in the NT, but are prevalent in Acts (Matt. 17:9; Acts 7:31–32 [Moses]; 9:10–12; 10:1–3 [Cornelius], 19 [Peter]; 11:5 [Peter]; 12:9 [Peter, mistakenly thinking he had a vision]; 16:9–10 [Paul]; 18:9–10 [Paul]). Another term, ἔκστασις (*ekstasis*), is also used for such events (10:10 [Peter]; 11:5 [Peter]; 22:17 [Paul]). When Ananias is addressed, he responds with "Here I am," an indication he is ready to obey (Gen. 22:1–2, 11–12; 1 Sam. 3:4–14; Isa. 6:8; Jub. 44.5; 2 Esd. [4 Ezra] 14:1–2; Pesch 1986a: 305). Double visions mean that an event is fixed by God (Gen. 41:32).

The vision is very specific, naming Saul of Tarsus as the one being sought, giving Saul's locale (at Judas's home on Straight Street), and noting what Saul himself saw as he was praying (Ananias coming to him to lay hands on him to restore his sight). Paul's praying underscores the importance of prayer throughout Acts (1:14, 24; 2:42; 3:1; 6:4, 6; 8:15; 10:2, 4, 9, 31; 12:5; 13:2–3; 14:23; 16:13, 16, 25; 20:36; 21:5; 22:17–21; 27:35; 28:8; Williams 1990: 170). Prayer and vision together are also common in Luke (Luke 1:10–11; 3:21; 9:28–29; 22:41–43; Acts 10:3–4, 30; 22:17–18; Weiser 1981: 225).[6]

Tarsus was the major city of Cilicia Pedeias (Acts 6:9; 9:30; 21:39; 22:3). It was a great commercial and educational center. The detail makes clear that Saul is a Jew of the Diaspora. Tarsus was a seat for the Roman governor. Many who lived there were granted Roman citizenship, an important detail later when Paul is in prison.

The locale of the meeting is a bit ironic, as usually in Acts the term used for "straight" (εὐθεῖαν, *eutheian*) means to be ethically straight (8:21; 13:10). This street is still a major road in the city (Bruce 1990: 237). It runs east and west in the eastern portion of the old city and is known today as Derb el-Mustaqim, although its direction has changed slightly since that time. It was known to have had major halls with colonnades and two great city gates at each end, making it a "fashionable" street (Haenchen 1987: 323). It was fifty feet wide (Le Cornu and Shulam 2003: 497). Ananias's laying on of hands is one of many instances of this practice in Acts. All uses point to a type of association or commission (6:6 [apostles of the commissioning of the Seven]; 8:17–19 [Peter to give the Holy Spirit]; 9:12 [Ananias to restore sight]; 13:3 [church to commission for a missionary journey]; 28:8 [Paul in healing someone]). The note does not make the account a miracle story because the account's major focus is not the healing but the meeting itself. Everything indicates that

6. Wikenhauser 1948 discusses examples in Greek and Latin works, as does Conzelmann 1987: 72. In Judaism, see Josephus, *Ant.* 11.8.4–5 §§325–35, the high priest Jaddua's meeting with Alexander the Great.

the Lord is behind all that is taking place. In the full sense of the term, Jesus is directing events and setting things in the "right" direction.

Ananias balks a little. He has heard from many about Saul's activities   **9:13–14** in Jerusalem and ostensibly knows why he is in Damascus: to persecute Christians at the behest of the priests (note the plural "priests" in contrast to just the high priest in 9:1). Paul's action is on behalf of the leadership. The Christians are described as "those who call upon your name" (τοὺς ἐπικαλουμένους τὸ ὄνομά σου, *tous epikaloumenous to onoma sou*). Here is another ancient way to describe believers: those who call upon the name of the Lord for salvation (2:21; 22:16; Rom. 10:13–14; 1 Cor. 1:2). Ananias also calls believers saints (ἁγίοις, *hagiois*), the first time this designation appears for Christians in Acts (9:32, 41; 26:10; 3:14 [of Christ]; 3:21 [of the prophets]; 6:13 [of the temple]; 7:33 [of the ground at the bush]). Barrett (1994: 455) notes that Paul uses the term often in his letters. Saul has been trying to stop such faith. Ananias knows his reputation. The issue of the "name" will be noted in verses 15–16, 21 and especially in verse 27, where Jesus is mentioned specifically. "Evil" (κακά, *kaka*) refers to the persecution and imprisonment that Saul has participated in as he gathered up and pursued believers.

The Lord replies that he knows the situation and has changed Saul's   **9:15–16** vocation, a marvelous fact unknown to Ananias. Now Saul is the Lord's chosen instrument (σκεῦος ἐκλογῆς, *skeuos eklogēs*). The genitive here is one of quality: a vessel that is selected (BDF §165). Saul now possesses a new calling that has him finally working for God's cause. His ministry will include taking the name of Jesus (see v. 14) to Gentiles, kings, and Israel. These three groups are tightly bound together in a τε καὶ . . . τε construction (*te kai . . . te*, a closely connecting idiom for items in a series). Saul will take the Lord's name to all. The translation highlights this emphasis with a periphrastic "even."

His ministry will reflect the ultimate intent of Jesus's work: ministry to all people, both Jews and Gentiles. The term for "vessel" (σκεῦος) here refers to someone who has a certain function or role to perform (BAGD 754 §2; BDAG 927 §3; Jer. 27:25 LXX [50:25 Eng.]; 2 Tim. 2:20–21; Rom. 9:20–24 [of peoples as vessels]; 2 Cor. 4:7 [we carry a treasure in earthen vessels]; similarly Rom. 1:1, 5 [Paul of his ministry]; 2 Cor. 11:23–30; Gal. 1:15–16; Eph. 3:7–13). The note of being chosen for this task underscores this point. Saul shall also suffer in bearing Christ. In fact, it "must" be so, as verse 16 explains (using δεῖ, *dei*; see 9:6; 2 Cor. 11:30, noted just above, lists the suffering Paul experienced by the time he wrote that epistle). According to church tradition, the Romans martyred Paul (1 Clem. 5.5–7 [departed an "example of patient endurance"]; Eusebius, *Eccl. Hist.* 3.1.2 [said to suffer martyrdom under Nero according to Origen]). The use of γάρ (*gar*) in verse 16 shows that this verse explains the chosen-instrument and bearing-the-name remark of verse 15. Witnessing to Jesus can be costly, and ironically, Saul will receive as much as he gave. Johnson (1992: 165) correctly calls this a "programmatic prophecy for Paul's career" (Acts 13:47; Isa. 49:6).

9:17 Ananias is obedient and has absorbed what the Lord said. Dutifully Ananias goes and addresses Saul as "brother" (ἀδελφέ, *adelphe*), something impossible to consider just moments earlier. Ananias tells Saul that the Lord has commanded him to lay hands on Saul. Ananias will be the mediator of the restoration of Saul's sight and of the Spirit's filling. At Qumran, 1QapGen 20.28–29 mentions the laying on of hands to drive a demon away from Pharaoh, but this Qumranic text is not technically an exorcism, as there is no possession here, only oppression and demonic presence (Fitzmyer 1998: 429). What Ananias does is not designed to send a force away but to associate Saul with God. It is significant that here a non-apostle is the mediator of the Spirit. The church's ministry is expanding in ways that mean that non-apostles will do important work. In Acts 8 it was baptism by Philip. Here it is laying hands on Saul so that the Spirit may come. Three times in Acts the laying on of hands is tied to the Spirit. The other two scenes are in 8:17–18, through Peter and John to the Samaritans, and in 19:6, through Paul to John the Baptist's disciples.

The purpose of laying on hands in this scene is obvious. The Spirit is connecting Saul to his brothers, as Ananias's opening address affirms. He also is empowered for witness, a Pauline "Pentecost" (Larkin 1995: 143; see v. 15). This meeting is covered in more detail in 22:14–16, while 26:16–18 describes Saul's commission in more detail and connects it to Jesus's vision in what is probably a telescoped account, given that Ananias is not mentioned in Acts 26 at all. This is the first time that Luke will indicate the Spirit's coming outside the land of Israel; the spread of the Spirit in faraway locales is a mirror of the worldwide focus of Saul's ministry.

9:18–19a The response is immediate as every limitation Saul experiences in 9:9 is reversed. He can see. He takes food and drink. Something like scales (ὡς λεπίδες, *hōs lepides*) fall from his eyes. The term for "scales" is an NT hapax. It is some type of flaky substance. The cognate verb appears in Tob. 3:17 and 11:13—both about the end of blindness (in everyday use, the scales on a fish or a dragon; BDAG 592; Deut. 14:9–10; T. Job 43.8). Now liberated and prepared for his mission, Saul is baptized immediately, as the eunuch was. Next he will go out into Damascus and preach Jesus.

Additional Note

9:4–6. Several textual variants in these verses are not well attested. They represent attempts to bring agreement between the account here and those in Acts 22 or 26. Variants in 9:4, 6 add references to the kicking-against-the-goads remark that appears in 26:14. A variant in 9:5 identifies Jesus as the Nazorean, as appears in 22:8. The variant in 9:6 also adds from 22:10 Saul's question about what he should do. None of these is original.

2. Saul Preaches in Damascus (9:19b–25)

This short unit shows Saul immediately undertaking his calling to preach Jesus as Son of God in Damascus (9:19b–20). The preaching produces shock in the city, since people recognize him as a former persecutor (9:21). But Saul continues to preach Jesus as the Christ (v. 22). When a plot to kill him arises, Saul escapes the city at night in a basket (9:22–25). It does not take long for Paul's work to become controversial and produce opposition. Paul's work also parallels that of Jesus: in a synagogue, with an astonished audience that questions his past (Jesus because of his family roots, Paul because of his past as persecutor). Rejection is the result (Witherington 1998: 320).

One of the more discussed problems is the correlation between this unit, Gal. 1, and 2 Cor. 11:32–33. Paul says that after his conversion he went to Arabia, not to Jerusalem (Gal. 1:17). He also connects his escape in a basket with a threat from King Aretas, whereas Acts blames the Jews. For Barrett (1994: 460–62, 466), these differences are irreconcilable. Others are not so sure. They argue that there may well be truth in each of the perspectives offered, especially when one recalls that Luke is not tracing Paul's entire career but the points where it affects the church in a major way.[1] Why, then, would a three-year retreat to Arabia be of any interest to his account, even if Luke knew about it? Or could it be that the ministry in Damascus occurred, like bookends, at both ends of this three-year sojourn in Arabia? Williams (1990: 175) sees in these verses Saul returning to Damascus after Arabia. Marshall (1980: 174) and Hengel and Schwemer argue for an eighteen-month to two-year stay in Damascus in ministry rather than in silence.

Luke is interested in activity across the expanse of the church, not meditation (Witherington 1998: 323, but a time of meditation is not necessarily all Paul does). Luke may well have known about the short time in Arabia but not deemed it important enough to mention in his big sweep of events. It may also be that the journey did not enter into the larger church tradition and so Luke did not know about it or mention it. We simply do not know. And if Paul did disappear from Jerusalem's sight for three years, might not some Christians have been suspicious again when he did show up? There is no indication

---

1. See Hengel and Schwemer 1997: 127–32, where Paul's portrait is preferred but "here we cannot exclude the possibility Paul *and* Acts are right." They refer to attempts by both Jews and the Nabateans to do away with Paul.

of how long a period passed from the time in Damascus until the time in Jerusalem. In addition, if Saul's preaching caused a stir, there is no reason to exclude the possibility that a regional leader such as King Aretas might be concerned for the public peace (Hengel and Schwemer 1997: 131). After all, Pilate in the end executed Jesus, but Pilate's primary concern was for the public peace, an issue raised by many of the important Jews in Jerusalem. Fitzmyer (1998: 434) notes that even though Luke and Paul give different reasons, they are not incompatible. He notes also Pesch's suggestion (1986a: 315) that the Jews denounced Saul to the ethnarch. Fitzmyer (1998: 439) also appears to suggest that the arrival in Jerusalem in 9:26 seems to be three years after conversion. None of this can be considered proved, but neither is it improbable.

Ironically, the overlap of distinct details gives us some chronological pegs for Paul's ministry. Since Aretas died in AD 39, the beginning of Paul's ministry falls before this date. In addition, Aretas came to full power in the region after Tiberius died, sometime in AD 37, but he may well have had some significant influence before then. So an AD 36–39 time frame fits for 9:1–26.

The unit shows a powerful Saul who also is growing in rhetorical effect as he works through the aid of the Spirit. He becomes the persecuted, but he does so as he is faithful to his call. Saul suffers for Jesus, but he is clear that Jesus is the Christ. Once again, as in Acts 7–8, the word is victorious even in rejection as the church grows in its dependence on God's protection and direction. Success is defined not by numbers but by faithfulness in giving out the gospel.

Exegesis and Exposition

[19b]For several days he was with ⌜the⌝ disciples in Damascus. [20]And in the synagogues immediately he proclaimed Jesus, saying, "He is the Son of God." [21]And all who heard him were amazed and were saying, "Is this not the one who made havoc in Jerusalem on those who called on this name? And he has come here for this purpose, to bring them bound before the chief priests." [22]But Saul increased even more in strength and confounded the Jews who lived in Damascus by proving that this one is the Christ.

[23]When many days had passed, the Jews plotted to kill him, [24]but their plot became known to Saul. They were watching the gates day and night to kill him; [25]but his disciples took him by night and let him down through the wall, lowering him by a basket.

9:19b–20   Saul spends a little time in Damascus. Bruce (1988a: 190) discusses how this relates to Paul's own discussion in Gal. 1:15–17, which says that Paul went away to Arabia. Bruce argues that a short period in Damascus is not precluded as related to such a journey because Paul is summarizing major points of time (see also the discussion of the relationship between Acts 9, Gal. 1, and 2 Cor. 11 in the overview to this unit).

Saul preaches in the synagogue that Jesus is the Son of God (ὁ υἱὸς τοῦ θεοῦ, *ho huios tou theou*; the ὅτι (*hoti*) clause reflects direct discourse). Perhaps surprisingly, this is the only occurrence of this full phrase in Acts ("Son" appears in Acts 13:33; see also Luke 1:32; 3:22; "Son of God" appears in Luke 1:35; 4:3, 9, 41; 22:70). Other titles, such as "Christ" (see v. 22), "Lord," "Righteous One," and "Judge," are more prevalent. What Saul's sermon was like is suggested by his sermon on a later occasion in Acts 13:16–41. The title "Son of God" is probably meant in terms of full "sonship," given its outgrowth from Saul's vision in seeing a glorified Jesus whom he had heard preached as the Son of Man at God's right hand in Acts 7:56. However, the title also has a messianic thrust if 9:22 and the speech of chapter 13 are guides. Romans 1:1–4 shows how Paul confessed Jesus as Son of God (Rom. 8:3; Gal. 4:4; Col. 1:15–20; 1 Thess. 1:10). "Son of God" in the OT refers to Israel as a people (Exod. 4:22), the king of Israel (2 Sam. 7:14; Ps. 89:26–27), and to the king of the future (Ps. 2:7 [seen as the covenantal ideal]; 1 En. 105.2; 2 Esd. [4 Ezra] 7:28–29; 13:32, 37, 52; 14:9; 4Q174 1.10–11; Bruce 1988a: 190). Jesus is preached as the unique promised one of God; he is certainly seen in a glorified state, given Saul's experience of him. Paul often goes to the synagogue to preach in Acts (13:5, 13–16; 14:1; 16:13, 16; 17:1; 18:4; 19:8). He goes to more than one synagogue in Damascus to make his case.

The crowd is amazed and perplexed and asks if this is not the persecutor   **9:21**
from Jerusalem (ἐξίστημι, *existēmi*, to amaze: Luke 2:47; 8:56; Acts 2:7, 12; 8:13; 10:45; 12:16). The negative interrogative οὐχ (*ouch*) means that the question expects a positive reply. This man now preaching Jesus as the Son of God is the one who was trying to destroy believers, creating havoc among them. Saul is described as one who was pillaging (ὁ πορθήσας, *ho porthēsas*) believers or seeking their complete destruction (BAGD 693; BDAG 853). The Greek term appears only here and in Gal. 1:13, 23. Paul uses it in Galatians to describe his own persecution of the church. In the LXX it is used of Antiochus against Jerusalem and of the murderers of Jewish martyrs (4 Macc. 4:23; 11:4; MM 529; Johnson 1992: 171).

The reaction is amazement that a persecutor who was going to arrest believers is now preaching Jesus in the synagogue. The pluperfect "has come" (ἐληλύθει, *elēlythei*) makes the point that persecution is no longer Saul's goal. Either news of Saul's mission for the Jewish leadership had reached Damascus before he arrived, or his reputation as a persecutor was well established and preceded him. It is as if a member of the Anti-Defamation League were now preaching Jesus.

9:22   Saul continues to preach Jesus, growing stronger and confounding the Jews by proving that Jesus is the Christ. The description of Saul becoming stronger (ἐνεδυναμοῦτο, *enedynamouto*) is in the imperfect and is not so much physical in force as conceptual. The prefixed form of the verb expresses the idea with a touch of emphasis. Saul is becoming stronger in his ability to preach Jesus. The term συμβιβάζω (*symbibazō*) often means to "unite" something. But since here a proposition is being defended, it has the sense of "proving" something to be so, combining the facts, if you will, to show something is the case (BAGD 777 §3; BDAG 956–57 §3; Acts 9:22; 16:10; 19:33; 1 Cor. 2:16; Eph. 4:11–16; Col. 2:1–3, 18–19). The participle is one of means here. So the force is that Saul "confounded them by proving" his claims about Jesus (Wallace 2000: 275). Paul is an effective preacher of Jesus from the start, becoming more effective as he continues. The idea of confounding (συγχέω, *syncheō*) appears in the LXX, where God confounds people by introducing various languages (Gen. 11:7, 9; also Acts 2:6; 19:32; 21:27, 31). "The Jews" (Ἰουδαίους, *Ioudaious*) as a group separate from Christians appear here for the first time in Acts.

9:23–25   The Jews take counsel to kill Saul, as they had concerning Jesus in Luke 11:53–54. The blame is placed on the nation as they now move to act with full hostility against him. Saul escapes a Jewish plot against his life with the disciples' help. Saul apparently ministers long enough to have his own band of disciples. The Jews constantly watch the city gates to try to catch him, but Saul hides in a basket and is covertly lowered to safety. The term for "watch" (παρατηρέω, *paratēreō*) often refers to hostile observance in Luke (Luke 6:7; 14:1; 20:20). The summary is Lukan, with many terms he alone uses or uses frequently. The verb for "kill" (ἀναιρέω, *anaireō*) is used twenty-one times in Luke-Acts out of twenty-four NT occurrences; nineteen of them are in Acts. This is the first of several plots (ἐπιβουλή, *epiboulē*) noted in Acts (9:23–24; 20:3, 19; 23:30 [all against Paul by Jews]), the only NT occurrences of the term (also 23:21; 25:3 conceptually).

     The term for "basket" (σπυρίς, *spyris*) describes a container often used to collect excess food, such as at the feeding of the multitudes (Matt. 15:37; 16:10; Mark 8:8, 20; Acts 9:24–25). It is like a hamper basket. Such escapes are not unusual (Josh. 2:15 [Jewish spies escape by being lowered by a rope]; 1 Sam. 19:12 [David lowered through a window]). Saul is lowered, possibly "along" a wall, an unusual use of διά (*dia*) plus the genitive (BDF §223.5, although HCSB has "through [an opening] in the wall"; Le Cornu and Shulam 2003: 509 suggest plausibly that windows in the gates were large enough for Paul to be let down through them). Second Corinthians 11:33 refers to this incident and speaks of his going through an opening in the wall, but Acts lacks the detail, although its language could reflect reminiscence of it. The action indicates that on some occasions Christians did not wait to be martyred but moved on to preach another day. The relationship of this escape to 2 Cor. 11:32–33 was treated in the introduction to this unit.

In sum, in this passage Saul has now been introduced as a bold preacher for the Lord by Jesus's own initiative and election. An important point emerges here. The dramatic nature of Saul's conversion indicates that many of the historical factors and claims about Jesus lying at the root of the faith must have been present and at work. Only their existence could explain how Saul the persecutor could have become Paul the apostle. Disciples must have been preaching the resurrection of Jesus with accompanying facts that could support the claim in order for Saul to even consider a conversion. In other words, when Jesus appeared to him, there must have been enough factual evidence to make such an appearance persuasive and plausible. In addition, although the final step of Saul's conversion was quick and dramatic, in fact much had led up to it, including the planting of seed by people such as Stephen. The visible presence of the church and its message also must have made an impression. Even if at first his response to Christian preaching was negative, it still had an impact on Saul. His lips and actions reflected rejection, but God was at work opening his mind and heart until finally the light broke through.

Conversion is an interesting phenomenon. For Saul, it was instant and dramatic; for others, especially those growing up in a Christian context, it might be very gradual. Saul's experience with a direct appearance of the Lord is the exception (Stott 1990: 165–66), but many do experience a kind of instant transformation where God opens the heart to receive the message. Fernando (1998: 302–4) highlights some features of conversion: God's initiative, a personal encounter with Jesus that leads to allegiance to him, a sense of connection to his community, and finally a sense of commission and belonging to him. Fortunately, after Saul's conversion, believers embraced Saul at God's directive and connected him to the community, another important dimension of the church's work in building community. New believers need special nurture. Saul experienced this.

Yet in another very important sense, Saul's transformation was not rooted in his conversion in the sense that Saul did something. It was, rather, that he was overwhelmed by God's grace and initiative as God called him to faith (Gal. 1:15; Hengel and Schwemer 1997: 101). As in the rest of the book of Acts, the main character is God and his work through Jesus.

Additional Note

9:25. The reading "his disciples" (i.e., Saul's disciples) is the more difficult reading and is likely original, as disciples are usually tied to Jesus. Luke is making a point here: Saul's ministry is effective. This is the reading of $\mathfrak{P}^{74}$, ℵ, A, B, C, and 81ᶜ. Given the normal usage, the deletion of αὐτοῦ (*autou*, his) was natural, resulting in "the disciples."

3. Saul in Jerusalem (9:26–30)

This unit is an extension of the previous two units on Saul. It describes how the community in Jerusalem receives him initially with uncertainty. Indeed, the pattern of events in Damascus almost repeats itself in Jerusalem. Saul's preaching leads to opposition and a plot that requires his departure. The new element in the account is that the church also needs to come to trust that Saul is a believer. It is Barnabas who enables those in Jerusalem to appreciate what the Lord has done for Saul. Not only is Barnabas generous with resources, but he also is gracious toward people.

The unit is a summary account. The initial fear is described in verse 26 with Barnabas's successful intervention in verse 27. Saul's preaching of Jesus leads to another plot against his life in verses 28–29, so that Saul is taken to Tarsus in verse 30. The unit shows the church acclimating to the new instrument God has chosen. Saul also continues to deal with the prospect of persecution unto death. Sources here would be Paul, Barnabas, and the Jerusalem community (Fitzmyer 1998: 438 speaks of a Pauline source only). Barrett (1994: 467) treats the unit with the same type of skepticism he did the previous passage (so also Haenchen 1987: 332–33, 335, who argues that if three years have passed, Jerusalem would know about Saul; Conzelmann 1987: 75). It seems better, however, to regard the uncertainty over Saul as fueled by his past and perhaps by the delay in his coming back to Jerusalem if he has been away for three years during his time in Damascus and Arabia. His work for the church, followed by a period of silence, might have caused uncertainty about him upon his return. It would be one thing to have heard about Saul, another for him to minister, disappear, and then reappear.

Exegesis and Exposition

[26]And when he had come to Jerusalem, he tried to join the disciples; and they were all afraid of him, for they did not believe he was a disciple. [27]But being concerned for him, Barnabas brought him to the apostles and explained to them how on the road he had seen the Lord, who spoke to him, and how at Damascus he had preached boldly in the name of Jesus. [28]So he went in and out among them at Jerusalem, preaching boldly in the name of the Lord, [29]and he was speaking and was disputing with the Hellenists, but they were seeking

to kill him. ³⁰And when the brethren discovered it, they brought him down to Caesarea and sent him off to Tarsus.

In Jerusalem, Saul's conversion meets with skepticism when he tries to join the disciples. It is not clear whether the report about Saul has not made it back to Jerusalem or whether once the report is received it is viewed with skepticism, especially if this Jerusalem visit is delayed by several years. Should not the real, converted Saul be expected to have come back immediately? Thus the delay, instead of being a problem historically, may well have created an uncertain climate in an already tense atmosphere of persecution (Larkin 1995: 146 note on 9:26–27; Fitzmyer 1998: 438). At any rate, the Christians of Jerusalem are afraid of him when he first arrives. They remember what he did earlier.

9:26

Barnabas speaks up for Saul before the apostles, explaining Saul's vision and bold preaching for Jesus. The expression is "taking him, he brought him" (ἐπιλαβόμενος αὐτὸν ἤγαγεν, *epilabomenos auton ēgagen*) to the apostles. The idea of "taking him" here has the force of "taking him under his wing" (Le Cornu and Shulam 2003: 516). There is debate about the subject of the verb here, but that Barnabas speaks up for Saul is the most natural way to read the passage. Who and how many apostles are present is not stated. Galatians 1:18–19 mentions Paul seeing only Peter (and James), but this might mean in an extended private conversation. Another, more likely, option is that Peter represents all the apostles in this discussion, and thus to see him is to see the group (Bruce 1990: 243 speaks of a generalizing plural). Hengel and Schwemer (1997: 133–50) lay out a plausible scenario for the core of this account that includes some care to protect Paul initially. Galatians 1:18 puts this visit at fifteen days in duration. Hengel and Schwemer (1997: 205–21) also discuss Barnabas's relationship to Paul and challenge skeptics of Luke's account who question whether Barnabas was connected to the Jerusalem community at all. Hengel and Schwemer point out how Paul's account of resurrection and the core of the gospel points to Jerusalem as the roots of the tradition, given the list of appearances in 1 Cor. 15. They note that (1) Barnabas is a Semitic name; (2) his relatives are in Jerusalem, as John Mark's locale indicates; (3) levitical property would likely be in the area; and (4) Barnabas's lapse toward Judaism in Gal. 2:13 also suggests a tie to Jerusalem. About such skepticism they say, "Isn't this completely unrestrained criticism of Luke just a pretext for developing one's own creative imagination as freely as possible?" (1997: 212). Later they add, "The questionable separation of Barnabas from Jerusalem, in analogy to that of Paul, is caused by the ahistorical tendency, in the footsteps of F. C. Baur, to make the gulf between Jerusalem and Antioch as wide as possible from the beginning. Behind this lies a latent aversion to the Judaism of the mother country" (Hengel and Schwemer

9:27

1997: 214). Finally, one of the authors concludes, "I believe that Paul's sparse but at the same time illuminating information about Barnabas will be understood better if we trust Luke's accounts rather more than is usual today" (1997: 216).

The verb used for Saul's preaching is παρρησιάζομαι (*parrēsiazomai*, speak freely, openly, or fearlessly; BAGD 631 §1; BDAG 782 §1; see also v. 28b). Acts uses this verb often (18:26; 19:8; 13:46; 26:26; 14:3). It is one of two defenses Barnabas uses for Saul. Barnabas also explains how the Lord called Saul. Only someone of Barnabas's stature and respect could bring the church to lay aside its fears. Barnabas will be a key companion of Saul later in Acts (11:25–30; 12:25; chaps. 13–14) but will separate from him in 15:37–40 over John Mark. He is an example of someone who works for the church's unity and reconciliation.

9:28–29   Saul is ministering in Jerusalem, again boldly contending for the gospel, taking on the Hellenistic Jews who executed Stephen and now seek to kill him. Saul addresses people in the name of the Lord. Saul and the Jerusalem church, including the apostles, are working together. The verbs for speaking and contending are part of a periphrastic imperfect. The picture is of an ongoing campaign of bold evangelism. Saul apparently ministers only in the city, as Gal. 1:22 says. He is not known personally by the church of Judea, which may well mean the church of the larger region (Fitzmyer 1998: 440).

9:30   When danger to Saul's life becomes clear, he is taken to Caesarea and Tarsus. Acts 22:17–21 notes direction from the Lord for this move. Since Caesarea is a port town, he may well have sailed to Tarsus (on Tarsus, see comments on 9:10–12). Caesarea was a key city, possibly the fifth largest in the empire, and home to a large Jewish community, possibly as large as half the city (Le Cornu and Shulam 2003: 519–20). It was the principal port city of the Herodian kingdom. After his escape, Saul is absent from the story of Acts until 11:25. Why does he go to Tarsus? We do not know, but, given Paul's later travels and the possible locale of Tarsus in Jewish understanding, Tarsus being his former home may not be the only reason. Apparently there is a safe community there to care for him. Hengel and Schwemer (1997: 171–77) suggest it is because, in terms of Jewish salvation history, Tarsus was on the edge of the land of Japheth, and so Saul is doing the opposite of Jonah. We cannot be sure this is right, but neither can it be ruled out.

In sum, Saul/Paul begins his ministry. His conversion leads to an immediate desire to serve. The Gentile mission awaits. But that breakthrough will require the Lord's direct intervention and leading. God will use no one other than Peter, whose credibility will help the church to cross over this difficult ethnic bridge. Saul's work of evangelism shows how the Lord can lead even the most hostile into conversion. The church's faithful witness in the midst of suffering lays the groundwork for Saul's response. Stott (1990: 178–79) summarizes Saul's early ministry this way: it was Christ-centered, driven by the Spirit, courageous, and costly. We would note that the church's members also nurtured it, as they encouraged his calling and cared for him when persecution grew to dangerous levels.

E. Closing Summary (9:31)

This third large unit closes as the last one did in 6:7, with a simple summary of the church's growth. These summaries function like triumphant choral refrains in the book, as they ring out with joy over what God is doing.

Exegesis and Exposition

[31]So the church throughout all Judea and Galilee and Samaria was experiencing peace. Being built up and proceeding in the fear of the Lord and in the comfort of the Holy Spirit, it was being multiplied.

9:31   The term ἐκκλησία (*ekklēsia*, church) carries its technical, theological meaning of the community of believers, but with a new twist (earlier 5:11; 8:1, 3). The term here is singular; it is one community in three regions that is in view. This sense of the church in many locales appears only here and in 20:28. Usually the word refers to a specific local gathering (13:1; 14:23, 27; 15:3; 16:5; 18:22; 19:32, 39, 40; 20:17; Jervell 1998: 294).

    The church now has spread to Galilee and Samaria, moving well outside Jerusalem. In this context, it is not a building or place but a group of people who share a faith in Jesus. The threefold grouping may well indicate that all the native Jewish areas have been covered by the gospel (Barrett 1994: 472). Luke has said nothing to us about the church in Galilee until here (also only in 10:37; 13:31). But the key area of Jesus's earthly ministry has responded to him. This new detail indicates that Luke's account is selective in what it mentions. Samaria has been noted with more detail, but Galilee too has a community.

    The peace and growth the church experiences are part of the support the Spirit gives to the community even in the midst of persecution. This support is called "comfort" or "encouragement" (παρακλήσει, *paraklēsei*), one of four occurrences of this term in Acts (4:36–37 [of Barnabas]; 9:31; 13:15; 15:31; but see the description of the Spirit with this concept in John 14–16). The term has a broad meaning, and to choose between comfort and encouragement here seems to narrow the word too much.

    Both comfort and encouragement yield peace. Peace (εἰρήνη, *eirēnē*) appears seven times in Acts (7:26; 9:31; 10:36–38; 12:20; 15:32–33; 16:36; 24:2–3). Acts 4:17–32 already described how this combination of peace and persecution worked. It is important to note that although there is pressure from persecution all around, the church itself is at peace. The result is edification or strengthening (οἰκοδομουμένη, *oikodomoumenē*, being built). This participle almost has the force of a result, so that peace leads to strength ("experienced peace and thus was strengthened" in NET; note our translation). This strength is rooted in the support of the Spirit and an attitude that fears the Lord. They fear the Lord, which increases their ability to cope with the circumstances. The phrase τὸν φόβον τοῦ κυρίου (*ton phobon tou kyriou*, the fear of the Lord) last appears in the NT in 2 Cor. 5:11.

Several things contribute to the church's health and sense of peace: it is a community that (1) is being strengthened, (2) lives in the fear of the Lord, and (3) is receiving the comfort that the Spirit of God is able to supply. With these unusual ingredients and despite the presence of persecution and rejection by others, the church "was being multiplied" (ἐπληθύνετο, *eplēthyneto*). The passive probably points to God's growing the church in the midst of all of these factors.

IV. The Gospel to the Gentiles and More Persecution in Jerusalem (9:32–12:25)

This section of Acts transitions from Peter to Paul, from Jerusalem to Antioch, from outreach to Jews to Gentile inclusion. Peter begins the unit, still active in healing and raising people from the dead (9:32–43). Next comes the section's dominant unit, the conversion of Cornelius's house, an event that requires visions from God on both sides to bring things together. It also includes one of the main speeches in Acts, where Scripture recedes from being cited but the theology of what God is doing through Jesus is fully expressed (10:1–43). The reaction to Gentile inclusion is not automatic, so Peter must explain to Jerusalem how it happened. The short answer is that God brought about this inclusion (11:1–18). We also obtain a glimpse of the church in Antioch, to which Barnabas brings Saul from Tarsus, and Agabus leads the church through a prophetic word to provide famine relief for Jerusalem (11:19–30). The church outside Israel is caring for the church there. Finally, during the persecution in Jerusalem, James, not the Lord's brother but the brother of John, is slain. Peter is also arrested, but the apostle is spared through a miraculous release by God. God rescues Peter from Herod, whose arrogant speech leads to God's judgment against him (12:1–23). A summary about the church's health closes the unit, as is always the case in Acts (12:24). God is protecting as the church is suffering but growing.

A. Peter Performs Two Miracles at Lydda and Joppa (9:32–43)

Peter continues his apostolic work in Lydda and Joppa as Luke presents two brief miracle accounts, one of a paralytic and another of resuscitation from the dead. Pesch (1986a: 317–18, 321–22) describes six elements in the healing account and fifteen elements in the resuscitation event to show how the second account is far more detailed and brings the paired accounts to a climax.

This is our first glimpse of Peter since Acts 8:25. It is often suggested that these miracles are here because they explain Peter's presence in the area of Caesarea, where Cornelius lives. It is also argued that they were attached to the Cornelius account in the tradition (Marshall 1980: 177; Pesch 1986a: 317). Fitzmyer (1998: 443), however, suggests that the accounts may have been independent. There is no way to know.

In Lydda, Peter heals a paralyzed man named Aeneas (9:32–35), and in Joppa he raises Dorcas from the dead (9:36–43). Peter has done miracles earlier, so the question is, Why have more miracles here? The answer seems to be that Luke is setting up the next event, where Cornelius is the first full Gentile to come to the Lord. The point is that God is still working quite powerfully through this apostle, as he becomes God's instrument to make this breakthrough. Whether it is the power to walk or the power to restore life, Peter is still blessed of God. His ministry parallels Jesus's healings and the work of the prophets, especially Elijah and Elisha (Weiser 1981: 238; 1 Kings 17:17–24; 2 Kings 4:32–37). Stipp (1999: 71–73) notes parallels in 1 Kings 17 with an upper room, the removal of witnesses, prayer, and the opening of the eyes. He also points to the fulfillment again of words uttered in Acts 4:10: healing has taken place in the name of Jesus. Johnson (1992: 179) also points out that the juxtaposition of Peter and Saul shows how God is using a variety of people to accomplish his task.

Peter also ministers to a variety of people, as we have a pair, a man and a woman, who benefit from this divine work. Luke favors gender pairing, which is evidenced as far back as the infancy narrative in his Gospel, with Simeon and Anna.

Exegesis and Exposition

³²Now as Peter went through the area among them all [to visit them], he came down also to the saints who lived at Lydda. ³³There he found a certain man with

the name of Aeneas, who had been confined to a bed for eight years because he was paralyzed. ³⁴And Peter said to him, "Aeneas, Jesus Christ heals you; rise up and make your bed." And immediately he arose. ³⁵And all who lived in Lydda and Sharon who saw him turned to the Lord.

³⁶Now there was in Joppa a certain female disciple named Tabitha, which means Dorcas. She was full of good works and acts of mercy. ³⁷In those days, she became sick and died. And washing her, they laid her in an upper room. ³⁸Since Lydda was near Joppa, the disciples, hearing that Peter was in the city, sent two men to him, entreating him, "Please do not delay to come to us." ³⁹So Peter rose and went with them. And when he had come, they took him to the upper room. All the widows stood there with him, weeping and showing tunics and other garments that Dorcas made while she was with them. ⁴⁰But Peter sent them all outside and knelt down and prayed; then, turning to the body, he said, "Tabitha, rise." And she opened her eyes, and seeing Peter, she sat up. ⁴¹And giving her his hand, Peter lifted her up. Then, calling the saints and the widows, he presented her alive. ⁴²And it became known throughout all Joppa, and many believed in the Lord. ⁴³And he stayed in Joppa for many days with one Simon, a tanner.

9:32   Peter is traveling through the region, apparently on a church preaching and visitation tour. He visits the saints at Lydda. The city of Lydda (= OT Lod, 1 Chron. 8:12; 1 Macc. 11:34) is on the road from Jerusalem to Joppa, about a day's journey by foot from Joppa and twenty-five miles northwest of Jerusalem (Josephus, *J.W.* 3.9.3 §§419–20; *Ant.* 20.6.2 §130). It was the center of a toparchy, one of ten administrative districts in Judea (Josephus, *J.W.* 3.3.5 §§52–56; Johnson 1992: 177). It was a predominantly Jewish town of mixed population. Commerce revolved around pottery making, wine, figs, and linen work (Le Cornu and Shulam 2003: 527). The origin of the church here is not discussed, but Barrett (1994: 477) suggests that it might be the result of Philip's ministry.

9:33–34   Luke introduces us to Aeneas with little detail other than his malady. Is he a believer? We are not told, but it is likely that if he were not, then the healing might well have led to a remark about his conversion, as Luke indicates in verse 35 for the town's other residents (Barrett 1994: 480). He is paralyzed and has been confined to bed for eight years. The idea is expressed in an adjectival participle, followed by a relative clause that has almost the force of a causal idea (κατακείμενον ἐπὶ κραβάττου, ὃς ἦν παραλελυμένος, *katakeimenon epi krabattou, hos ēn paralelymenos*: "Aeneas, who had been confined to a mattress for eight years because he was paralyzed" [NET]).

Peter heals him in the name of Jesus Christ and tells him to arise. Peter makes a declaration of healing instead of calling on Jesus to heal. He already knows what the Lord has done and tells Aeneas the good news. To mediate healing is an ability Peter received during Jesus's ministry (Luke 9:1, 6; 10:9).

This is one of four occurrences of the verb ἰάομαι (*iaomai*, heal) in Acts (the others are 10:38, where it describes what Jesus did; 28:8, where Paul performs a healing; and 28:27, where Isa. 6:10 LXX is cited and the prospect of God healing is challenged because the people are resistant to him). The tense here is an aoristic present, simply summarizing the fact that healing takes place (Robertson 1934: 866; BDF §320). Here the healing is explicitly associated with the risen Jesus, just as it was in Acts 4:1–12. The Jesus focus parallels in form the healing of 3:1–10, which Acts 4 explains.

The healing is immediate. Aeneas is told, "Make your bed." The phrase στρῶσον σεαυτῷ (*strōson seautō*) means "spread for yourself," which could mean "set the table" or "make your bed" (BDAG 949; BAGD 771). Given the situation, a command to make the bed is more natural. The instruction means that he can now care for himself, since he is restored. Other similar healings involve Jesus, Peter, and Paul (Luke 5:12–17; Acts 3:1–10; 14:8–12; in a summary, 8:7). This tradition of apostolic healing was well known (2 Cor. 12:12; Rom. 15:18–19; Weiser 1981: 241).

The healing lays the groundwork for conversions to the Lord in Lydda and the Sharon region. Joppa (v. 36) is about twelve miles from Lydda and on the coast (on Joppa, Josephus, *J.W.* 3.9.3 §§419–20, describes a rough shore with precipices into the sea). Lydda and Sharon respond, and those who dwell there are said "to turn" to the Lord. This is one of two occurrences of the phrase "turn to the Lord" (ἐπέστρεψαν ἐπὶ τὸν κύριον, *epestrepsan epi ton kyrion*; Acts 11:21). The region was partly Gentile, as Sharon comprised the coastal plain extending from Joppa to Carmel and to Caesarea. Joppa was a far more Gentile city than Lydda (Barrett 1994: 482) and was involved in battles during the Maccabean war (Josephus, *Ant.* 13.5.10 §180; 13.6.4 §202; 13.6.7 §215). The reference to all being converted is a Lukan hyperbole for a significant number coming to the Lord.

9:35

A woman, Tabitha, is introduced in a manner that underscores her character. She is "full of good works and acts of mercy." This is the only reference to a female "disciple" with the term μαθήτρια (*mathētria*) in the NT. "Acts of charity" (ἐλεημοσυνῶν, *eleēmosynōn*) refers to providing alms—acts of mercy through charitable giving. Almsgiving was highly regarded in Judaism (Tob. 1:3, 16; 3:2; 4:7–8; Sir. 7:10). The detail suggests that she is wealthy and generous. The alms may involve widows if verse 39 points in this direction. Her name means "gazelle" or "deer" in Aramaic. Translated into Greek, her name is Dorcas. "Gazelle" was the metaphor for "beloved" in Song 2:9 and 8:14 (Johnson 1992: 177). In this case, the name fits her character.

9:36–37

Dorcas becomes sick and dies. The care for her includes washing her body in preparation for burial (*m. Šabb.* 23.5; Semaḥot 11.2; Homer, *Il.*

18.350), but the placing of her body in an upper room is unusual. This action may well express the faith and hope that she can be raised from the dead, as usually burial took place before sunset in Judaism. Her being kept may also indicate a more Hellenistic Jewish approach to burial, as Joppa was a heavily Hellenistic city. She may well have been anointed, as this was common. In this case, "washing" is shorthand for the entire preparation procedure. In the OT, bodies in an upper room were often noted in resuscitation accounts (1 Kings 17:19; 2 Kings 4:10, 21; Marshall 1980: 179). Luke's Gospel has two such accounts (Luke 7:11–17; 8:49–56). When a body was kept, it was kept for three days because there was the belief that after three days the soul had departed (John 11:17; m. Yebam. 16.3; Lev. Rabbah 18.1; Eccles. Rabbah 12.6).

9:38–40 Those in Joppa, knowing Peter is near, send two emissaries to bring him to Dorcas (on two messengers: Acts 8:14; 11:30; 13:3; 15:27; 19:22; 23:23). They ask him not to delay in coming to them. The phrase μὴ ὀκνήσῃς (mē oknēsēs) is an NT hapax; the subjunctive indicates a formal request (Num. 22:16; Sir. 7:35). Barrett (1994: 484) argues that the wording expresses the concern that such a request might be refused either because Peter is on tour or because Joppa is a Hellenistic city. But Peter's immediate response makes it likely that they sensed he would come. The formal request simply reflects respect.

Peter meets the weeping widows and is shown tunics and cloths that Dorcas had made. The middle voice ἐπιδεικνύμεναι (epideiknymenai) perhaps indicates that what is shown is what they are wearing. Barrett (1994: 485) suggests that the expression indicates only that they own what is shown. Either sense is possible. Widows are mentioned only three times in Acts, twice in this passage (6:1; 9:41; cf. 1 Tim. 5:9–10; 16). Peter asks them to leave the room (2 Kings 4:33) as he prays and calls her back to life with the command to rise, in language very similar to Mark 5:41.[1] Luke underscores again the power of prayer as Peter intercedes for the woman. The goal appears to be not to draw excessive attention to himself as the healer (Pesch 1986a: 324). She opens her eyes and rises up to recognize Peter (2 Kings 4:35; Luke 7:15).[2] Peter's prayer mediates life to Dorcas, as the Lord hears his appeal. The mood of the passage is much like Luke 8:54–55. The parallel is no accident. Peter's ministry shows that Jesus is still at work.

9:41–42 Peter presents her alive (ζῶσαν, zōsan) to the saints, including the widows (Mark 5:40–42; 2 Kings 4:33–36; also using a form of ζάω [zaō, live] for the resurrected Jesus, Acts 1:3). Her healing becomes well known

---

1. Jesus also performed such a healing after asking others to leave the room (Mark 5:40; Luke 8:51).

2. There is significant parallel wording between this account and 1 Kings 17:17–24 and 2 Kings 4:19–37.

in Joppa and leads many "to believe in the Lord" (Acts 11:17), just as the healing of Aeneas caused many "to turn to the Lord" in Lydda and Sharon (9:35). The two summaries show the synonymous character of these expressions for coming to faith (Williams 1990: 182).

Peter stays in Joppa for a few days with Simon, a tanner. The reference to Simon almost treats his vocation as a surname (BDAG 185; BAGD 148; MM 118). A tanner would work with dead animals' carcasses, an unclean occupation (*m. Ketub.* 7.10; *m. B. Bat.* 2.9; Le Cornu and Shulam 2003: 542–43 describe it as a "despised" trade). We should not make too much of this, however, given that Peter is not a Pharisee, who would be sensitive about such scruples, but a fisherman-apostle (Marshall 1980: 180). Still, that Peter would house himself in such an unclean place shows that some in the church's leadership are not overly sensitive about all aspects of Jewish purity laws.

9:43

In sum, the Lord is still powerful and active in his work through Peter as we approach the breakthrough of reaching out directly to Gentiles. Peter is the picture of the faithful servant as his healing power brings people back to life and usefulness. These miracles frame the important events that follow. God uses an authenticated, trustworthy minister to take the gospel to the Gentiles, an action that will prove to be controversial.

Peter is an example in ministry, but so is Tabitha. She illustrates someone who ministers to needs, showing mercy to others (Fernando 1998: 311).

The role of hospitality in Acts receives little attention. Wherever Peter, and later Paul, went, people were ready to host them, an important ministry to those who serve the Lord on the road.

B. Peter and Cornelius: The Gospel to the Gentiles (10:1–11:18)

This section is one of the most important units in Acts. Here the gospel goes out directly to a Gentile and his household for the first time. Everything is coordinated by God, as was the case with Saul's conversion. The Spirit's coming upon the group independently of any action by Peter also confirms God's direction in what takes place, a point Peter makes very clearly when the controversial inclusion of the Gentiles is discussed in 11:15–18. In a sense this scene is the book's turning point, as from here the gospel will fan out in all directions to people across a vast array of geographical regions, something Paul's three missionary journeys will underscore.

The section comes in two segments: (1) the divine direction of Cornelius and Peter that leads to Peter's speech and Cornelius's household coming to faith (10:1–48) and (2) the report to Jerusalem about the event, a report that is required because some Jewish believers are concerned about Gentiles being included in the promised plan of God for Israel (11:1–18). In the end, the dispute's resolution comes with the recognition that God has given the same Holy Spirit to the Gentiles that the believing community received at the beginning, an allusion back to Acts 2. So, if one asks how it is that Gentiles came to be a part of the people of God, the answer is that God directed it, not that anyone among the Twelve decided it would be so.

That this event would have been controversial is not surprising, given the past history of problematic relationships between Jews and Gentiles, not to mention the hope held by many in Judaism that the end of the age would bring vindication against Gentiles. Everything about this event shows that God's way includes reconciliation and compassion offered to all who will respond. God is not about achieving revenge, although justice will come one day. Though overplaying the language of myth and legend, Walker (2001) indicates that the manner in which Luke tells this story has points of contact with Greco-Roman accounts of the origins of communities and what he terms "guestfriendship." As such, this section is a key element in Luke's legitimization of the church as a thriving institution that was designed for Jews and Gentiles by God's plan and direction.

1. Peter and Cornelius (10:1–48)

This unit is nicely structured. Its importance is indicated by how it dominates the central portion of Acts. The event portrayed here is the major topic of Acts 10–11 as well as an important element in Acts 15. Cornelius is directed to send emissaries to fetch Peter in 10:1–8. Then God directs Peter through a vision in 10:9–16. The meeting of Cornelius's emissaries with Peter follows in 10:17–23a. Next is the journey to Cornelius's home in 10:23b–33, followed by Peter's speech in 10:34–43. The major new theme in the speech is the ethnic impartiality of God (vv. 34–35). In addition, an old christological theme, "Christ is Lord of all," finds new depth (v. 36). If Jesus is Lord of all, then the gospel can go to all. Finally, the unit's climactic and decisive event is the surprising divine bestowal of the Spirit in 10:44–48.

Gaventa (2003: 163) shows the unit's balance, resulting from eight scenes in four parts: two visions (Cornelius: 10:1–8; Peter: 10:9–16), the journey and welcome (Cornelius: 10:17–23a; 23b–29); speeches (Cornelius: 10:30–33; Peter: 10:34–43); confirmation (the Holy Spirit: 10:44–48; the community: 11:1–18).

The hand of God appears throughout, directing the main characters. God's independent action in giving the Spirit makes clear that these Gentiles are welcome among the people of God. This theme has been prepared for throughout Luke-Acts (Luke 2:32; 3:6; 24:47; Acts 1:4–8). The key to the passage is the way it stretches the old view of who counts among God's people. Nothing sets forth the theme of the passage more clearly than the opening of Peter's speech: "Truly I perceive that God shows no partiality, but in every nation anyone who fears him and does what is right is acceptable to him" (Acts 10:34–35). The speech goes on to show that to fear God is to embrace Jesus and his promise of forgiveness.

The source of the account is ultimately Peter and perhaps some of those who were with him. Hengel and Schwemer (1997: 154) speak of a Jerusalem source and a Lukan exaggeration that Cornelius is the first converted non-Jew. They argue that disciples such as Philip would have inevitably preached to non-Jews in their Diaspora mission. It is also likely that Luke has stylized the scene, and it is possible that a tradition about Cornelius existed in a place such as Caesarea or Jerusalem. This may have been the first conversion with an explicit supportive sign from the Spirit. This would explain why Luke has presented the event as epoch-making: it functioned as confirmation of the direction things were going. Kurz (1997) studies the narration of the passage and its repetitions from a narrative perspective. He points out a mixture of a dominating third-person narration, which makes use of an "omniscient" narrator, and some first-person narration that only observes what a character could see. Dickerson (1997b) speaks of a "New Character" narrative formula with the introduction of Cornelius. It is what Cornelius represents as a Gentile that makes his character so important to Acts. Soon there will be many Corneliuses. Luke employs his common style of introduction, describing the figure and then telling a story about him.

There is also scholarly discussion of the scene's historical elements. Some express skepticism about the vision because it deals with food, not fellowship and conversion (Haenchen 1987: 356–63; Conzelmann 1987: 80 says that it has only a historical kernel—that Peter had a mission to such locales). Barrett (1994: 492–98) notes three important issues: (1) the breakthrough, although Cornelius is really close to Judaism; (2) Peter's vision and the scene's tension with Mark 7; and (3) the tension between this account and Acts 15. He opts, it seems, for a possible Caesarean source in which these themes were present, but Luke has heightened their importance. The roots of the view splitting Cornelius's conversion from Peter's vision go back to Dibelius (1956: 107–22).

Such objections to this scene, however, lack merit. The debate about whether the vision's topic is food fails to see the cultural and symbolic nature built into the associations made in the vision between food, fellowship, and thus acceptance. Marshall (1980: 181–82) cogently argues for the scene's essential historicity. To have fellowship with Gentiles and receive them as equals means that Gentile food and Jewish purity laws are not going to be issues for the church or a cause for separation between the ethnic groups that Jesus will reconcile.

Witherington (1998: 344–45) notes how central Peter's vision is to the development of the entire scene, so that it is not easily separated out from the account as a distinct incident (also S. Wilson 1973: 171–78; Löning 1974; Haacker 1980; Schneider 1982: 61–63).

Regarding the tensions with Mark 7, it can be said that the implications of what Jesus taught in Mark 7 were slow to penetrate the church and that the key point Mark makes about clean and unclean foods is his later editorial comment after that understanding had been achieved.

Regarding Acts 15, the issue here was not whether Gentiles should be included but how and what they should be asked to do and not do. This is merely a further step toward assimilating the new group smoothly into the church. The Jerusalem Council reviews what took place with Cornelius to consider the implications of God placing no conditions on the Spirit's reception by Gentiles. This tension, then, is overstated as well. The event is well rooted in history and also makes sense of what takes place later.

The speech's source is debated, with many simply arguing that it is a Lukan composition (Wilckens 1974: 50–56). Fitzmyer (1998: 459), however, contends that it contains traces of source material from tradition, citing especially the remarks of verses 36–37. He also notes how those verses are tied together and the use of allusions to Isa. 52:7 and 61:1.

The significance of this scene is that what began as a Jewish movement struggling for acceptance within Judaism has now expanded to become a movement to reach all people. God directs and confirms this expansion. Theophilus may well have been a "God-fearer" who was struggling with his choice to be part of this Jesus movement. After all, many of the original Jewish recipients of the kingdom promise were hesitant to join. In addition, the God-fearers and Gentiles to whom the movement expanded later were controversial members. Did Theophilus really belong here? Was this really God's movement, given the persecution it was facing? Should he stay in or be a part of it? Luke's answer is that God designed all of this, namely, Jesus's rejection, the church's suffering, and, especially, Gentile inclusion.

Exegesis and Exposition

¹At Caesarea there was a certain man named Cornelius, a centurion out of what was known as the Italian Cohort, ²a pious man, who was fearing God together with his household, giving many alms to the people and always praying to God. ³About the ninth hour of the day, he clearly beheld in a vision an angel of God coming to him and saying, "Cornelius." ⁴And staring at him and being terrified, he said, "What is it, Lord?" And he said to him, "Your prayers and your alms have ascended as a tribute before God. ⁵And now send men to Joppa, and bring one Simon who is called Peter; ⁶this one is staying with Simon a tanner, whose house is by the seaside." ⁷When the angel who was speaking to him departed, he called for two of his servants and a pious soldier from among those who waited on him, ⁸and having told them everything, he sent them to Joppa.

⁹The next day, as they were on their journey and coming near the city, Peter went up on the housetop to pray about the ⌐sixth⌐ hour. ¹⁰And he became hungry and desired something to eat; but while they were preparing it, he fell into a trance ¹¹and saw the heaven opened and a vessel descending, like a great sheet, let down by four corners upon the earth. ¹²In it were all kinds of four-footed creatures and reptiles of the earth and birds of the sky. ¹³And there came a voice to him, "Rise, Peter, sacrifice and eat." ¹⁴But Peter said, "No way, Lord; for I have never eaten anything common or unclean." ¹⁵And the voice came to him again a second time, "What God has cleansed, you shall not regard as

common." ¹⁶This happened three times, and the thing was taken up ⌜at once⌝ to heaven.

¹⁷Now while Peter was inwardly perplexed as to what the vision that he had seen might mean, behold, the men sent by Cornelius, having sought out Simon's house, stood before the gate ¹⁸and, calling out, inquired whether Simon who was called Peter was lodging there. ¹⁹And while Peter was pondering the vision, the Spirit said to him, "Behold, ⌜three⌝ men are looking for you. ²⁰Rise and go down, and accompany them without concern; for I have sent them." ²¹And Peter, going down to the men, said, "I am the one you are looking for; what is the reason for your coming?" ²²And they said, "Cornelius, a centurion, a righteous and God-fearing man, holding a good reputation according to the entire nation of the Jews, was instructed in an appearance by a holy angel to send for you to come to his house and to hear what you have to say." ²³So he called them in to be his guests.

The next day Peter arose and went off with them, and some of the brethren from Joppa accompanied them. ²⁴And on the following day they entered Caesarea. Cornelius, expecting them, had invited his kinsmen and close friends. ²⁵As Peter entered, Cornelius, meeting him and falling down at his feet, gave him homage. ²⁶But Peter lifted him up, saying, "⌜ ⌝ Stand up; I too am a man ⌜ ⌝." ²⁷And as he was talking with him, Peter went in and found many people gathered; ²⁸and he said to them, "You yourselves know how it is unlawful for a Jew to associate with or visit any one of another nation; but God has shown me that I should not regard any person common or unclean. ²⁹So when I was sent for, I came without objection. I ask, then, why you sent for me."

³⁰And Cornelius said, "Four days ago, I was ⌜ ⌝ praying in my house ⌜at about the ninth hour⌝; and behold, a man stood before me in bright apparel, ³¹saying, 'Cornelius, Your prayers have been heard and your alms have been remembered before God. ³²Send therefore to Joppa and seek out Simon who is called Peter; he is lodging at the house of Simon, a tanner, by the seaside.' ³³So I sent to you at once, and you have been kind enough to come. Now therefore we are here in God's presence to hear all the things that you have been commanded ⌜by⌝ the Lord."

³⁴And Peter, opening his mouth, said, "Truly I perceive that God shows no partiality, ³⁵but in every nation anyone who fears him and does what is right is acceptable to him. ³⁶The word you know ⌜that⌝ he sent to the children of Israel, preaching peace through Jesus Christ (this one is Lord of all). ³⁷You know what took place through all Judea, beginning from Galilee after the baptism that John preached: ³⁸the discussion about Jesus of Nazareth, how God anointed him with the Holy Spirit and with power. Jesus went about doing good and healing all who were oppressed by the devil, for God was with him. ³⁹And we are witnesses to all that he did both in the country of the Jews and in Jerusalem. They also killed him by hanging him on a tree. ⁴⁰God raised this one on the third day and caused him to be visible, ⁴¹not to all the people but to us, witnesses, who were

chosen beforehand by God. We ate and drank with him after he rose from the dead. [42]And he commanded us to preach to the people and testify that this one is ordained by God to be judge of the living and the dead. [43]To this one all the prophets testify that forgiveness of sins through his name is received by everyone who believes in him."

[44]While Peter was still speaking these words, the Holy Spirit fell on all who heard the message. [45]And the believers from among the circumcised who had come with Peter were astonished because the gift of the Holy Spirit had been poured out even on the Gentiles. [46]For they heard them speaking in tongues and magnifying God. Then Peter declared, [47]"Can any forbid water for baptizing these who received the Spirit even as we did?" [48]And he commanded them in the name of Jesus Christ to be baptized. Then they asked him to remain for some days.

This key scene begins in Caesarea, an important town already noted in Acts 9:30. It is where the Roman prefect lives, and thus it has a heavy Roman presence. Josephus (*Ant.* 15.9.6 §§331–41) describes Herod's building up of Caesarea into a major administrative and harbor city. In *J.W.* 3.9.1 §409 Josephus notes that mostly Gentiles inhabited it. The city was formerly known as Strato's Tower. It had an amphitheater, a hippodrome, and a temple dedicated to Caesar. Its role as the Roman provincial capital is why Cornelius is there.

10:1–2

Cornelius is a centurion, a commander of one of the six units of one hundred men within a cohort (σπείρης, *speirēs*). A cohort would have had about six hundred members and would have been part of a legion of about six thousand men, which was the main division in the Roman army. He would have served under a tribune (BAGD 237; BDAG 298–99). Acts frequently notes such military figures (10:22; 21:32; 22:26; 24:23; 27:1, 6, 11, 43). Luke 7:1–10 has a key account of a centurion who is likewise portrayed positively. Centurions were to be men who were "good leaders, of steady and prudent mind" (Polybius, *Hist.* 6.24.8; Bruce 1990: 252). Cornelius's unit has a name, the Italian Cohort, and is probably an auxiliary force, not part of the regular army. An inscription found in Austria documents its presence in Palestine as late as AD 69 (*ILS* 9168; Polhill 1992: 251n69).[1] The event here in Acts is probably still before AD 41 (Fitzmyer 1998: 449).

Cornelius is introduced with a series of four positive descriptions (other such descriptions: Acts 13:16, 26, 50, 16:14, 17:4, 17; 18:7):

1. He is devout (εὐσεβής, *eusebēs*). This means that he fears God and leads his entire household in such devotion. His devotion shows

1. On the debate about whether the cohort was stationed here during the time of Herod, see Bruce 1988a: 214–15. Another inscription about this unit, in *CIL* 11.6117, is hard to date; Witherington 1998: 346; Barrett 1994: 499.

itself in his generous giving of alms and in his praying always to God. The occurrence of εὐσεβής is rare in the NT, appearing here twice (v. 7) and in 2 Pet. 2:9 (related terms are in Acts 3:12; 13:43, 50; 16:14; 17:4, 17, 23; 18:7, 13; 19:27).

2. References to fearing God, as Cornelius is described, are slightly more common, appearing five times in the NT (Acts 10:1–3, 22; 13:16, 26; Rev. 14:6–7; Did. 15.4). As a "God-fearer" (Acts 13:16, 26; in the LXX: 2 Chron. 5:6; Pss. 113:17–19 [115:9–11 Eng.]; 117:2–4 [118:2–4 Eng.]; 134:19–20 [135:19–20 Eng.]; Mal. 3:16), Cornelius has not become a full Jewish proselyte but as a Gentile has been exposed to the God of Israel. The description means that he has responded positively to this exposure without embracing in any detailed way elements of Jewish legal practice (Kuhn, *TDNT* 6:741; Sir. 11:17; 27:11; 39:27; Kraabel 1981; Finn 1985; Fuks 1985; Levinskaya 1995: 51–126). An inscription at Aphrodisias clearly distinguishes between Jews and God-worshipers, who all have Greek names (Witherington 1998: 341–44). For Luke, it is probably not a technical term for some special class of Gentile believer in Israel's God. Cornelius would not have been circumcised, as the later questions about Gentiles and circumcision make clear. He is different, however, than the eunuch in that there is no mention of his engagement yet in worship tied to Judaism. He apparently has engaged only in acts of piety, such as almsgiving and prayer, although this may suggest some exposure to the synagogue (so Jervell 1998: 303). Against heavy involvement with the synagogue is that if the centurion were virtually Jewish, then Peter's move would not be seen as so unusual. Schneider (1982: 65) describes him as a Gentile sympathizer with Judaism who has adopted its piety. This openness to Judaism would be rare among such soldiers (Le Cornu and Shulam 2003: 548).

3. Alms is a more frequent topic still, being noted thirteen times in the NT (Matt. 6:2–4 [3x]; Luke 11:41; 12:33–34; Acts 3:2–3 [2x], 9–10; 9:36; 10:1–4 [2x], 30–31; 24:17–19; see also Sir. 7:10; Tob. 12:8). It is included in the descriptions of Tabitha in the previous healing account and of Paul in Acts 24:17, where he is recounting how he was arrested. Cornelius gives generously.

4. One of Luke's most important ways to show someone's piety is to say that the person prays often, although Luke's description of Cornelius as a "prayer warrior" (δεόμενος τοῦ θεοῦ διὰ παντός, *deomenos tou theou dia pantos*, praying to God at all times) is unique.

Cornelius would likely be a freedman. More than ten thousand former slaves took this name when Cornelius Sulla freed them in 82 BC (Appian, *Civil Wars* 1.100), and so the name was quite common. As a Roman officer, he would have had social status. This is reinforced by the fact that only his Gentile first name is used by Luke, something he does with

only two characters of Gentile origin (Julius in Acts 27:1 is the other;
Le Cornu and Shulam 2003: 245–46). To the Jewish mind, Cornelius
would be a real threat if he were to come to the newly emerging faith.
It would make Jews who feared close relations with Gentiles nervous if
Christianity gained support among some Gentiles of high social standing
and pulled them away from their leanings toward Judaism, for it would
tighten Gentile-Christian links and give stability and social credibility
to the new movement (Witherington 1998: 344). Cornelius would have
been a key tactical officer and probably an older man (Le Cornu and
Shulam 2003: 247).

Cornelius is engaged in his daily prayer time at three in the afternoon,   **10:3–6**
also known as the ninth hour, when he has a vision (ἐν ὁράματι, *en
horamati*; eleven of the twelve NT occurrences of this term are in Acts:
7:31–32; 9:10–12 [2x]; 10:1–3, 17–20 [2x]; 11:4–5; 12:9; 16:9–10 [2x];
18:9–10; Matt. 17:9). This is the same time as the afternoon offering at
the temple in Jerusalem. The coordination of prayer and spiritual events
is common in Luke (Luke 3:21–22; 6:12–16; 9:18–22, 28–31; 22:39–46;
Acts 1:14; 13:1–3). An angel calls out to him by name, an act that initially terrifies him, as is often the case when an angel appears (Luke
1:12). Cornelius finds himself gazing intently at what is before him, a
description Luke often uses (Luke 4:20; 22:56; Acts 1:10; 3:4, 12; 6:15;
7:55; see Acts 1:10 discussion). The term ἔμφοβος (*emphobos*) refers to
fear or terror: startled and caught by surprise (BAGD 257; BDAG 326).
The term also appears in Luke 24:5, 37; Acts 24:25; and Rev. 11:13.

When Cornelius respectfully inquires as to the angel's intent, he is
told that his prayers have been heard along with his alms, which have
ascended to God as a memorial or tribute (μνημόσυνον, *mnēmosynon*).
This is the only occurrence of this term in the NT (conceptually, Mark
14:8). Its roots go back to language in the OT (Exod. 17:14; Lev. 2:2, 9,
16; 5:12) and Judaism (Sir. 38:11; 45:16; 50:16; Tob. 12:12; 1QS 8.1–9).
It is an offering made in commemoration to God that God accepts as
pleasing (Rom. 12:1–2; Phil. 4:18; Heb. 13:15–16). Cornelius's prayer is
described like a sacrifice (Ps. 141:2). The picture is of God responding to
Cornelius's effort to know him, granting him "more light" (Larkin 1995:
154). Witherington (1998: 348) speaks of Cornelius giving a sacrifice
that God honors outside the temple.

Cornelius is to send his men the thirty-one miles to Joppa. There they
should fetch Simon Peter at the house of Simon the tanner (9:43). This
is a full day's journey, probably traveling with horses. Simon is noted as
being called Peter to distinguish him from his Joppan host. Again the
instructions are detailed, just as they were when Ananias was told to
meet Saul. God ensures that they will know where to go, but they are
not told why they are summoned. That remains a mystery and sustains
the suspense.

10:7–8 Cornelius, in immediate obedience, sends two servants and a devout military orderly to Joppa to collect Peter. The description of the military man as pious (εὐσεβῆ, *eusebē*) matches verse 2. The reference is "to those attending him." In a military context, however, the phrase could mean "from his staff" (Johnson 1992: 183). He explains to (ἐξηγησάμενος, *exēgēsamenos*) his emissaries what has taken place so that they know exactly whom to get and where (on this term, see Luke 24:35; Acts 10:8; 15:12, 14; 21:9; John 1:18).

10:9 The verse begins the treatment of Peter's vision, which runs to verse 16. At the precise time that Cornelius's men draw near, Peter goes up to the rooftop to pray at the sixth hour, or noon. Another midday vision is described in 22:6.[2] An outside stairway would lead to the roof, where he could pray undisturbed.[3] As in 10:3, the vision takes place during the time of prayer, but this is not a normal prayer time, which would be around either 9 a.m. or 3 p.m. (Jervell 1998: 305).

10:10–12 Peter is hungry and food is being prepared for him. Usually Jews had a midmorning meal and then a late-afternoon main meal.[4] The term πρόσπεινος (*prospeinos*, hungry) is exceedingly rare, with only one extant occurrence in Greek (Demosthenes Ophthalmicus, *Aëtius* 7.33) outside its appearance here.

As the food is being prepared, Peter falls into a trance (ἔκστασις, *ekstasis*), another expression for "vision" (10:17). The term with this sense refers to a trance where God communicates directly with someone. Such a meaning appears only in Acts (11:5; 22:17; Gen. 15:12 LXX). Its other uses refer to being amazed or distracted (Mark 5:42; Luke 5:26; Mark 16:8; Acts 3:10). Peter sees an object like a sheet of linen (ὀθόνην, *othonēn*) with four corners descend from heaven. This refers to cloth or to material like that used in a sail (BAGD 555; BDAG 693). Its only two NT occurrences are in this vision. The description of heaven opening also points to a disclosure, recalling what was said at Jesus's baptism (Luke 3:21–22; Acts 7:56). Within the sheet are all kinds of unclean animals, reptiles, and birds.[5] We know that these are unclean creatures because of Peter's response in verse 14. This is especially the case for the

---

2. For rooftop prayers in the OT and Judaism, see 2 Kings 23:12; Neh. 8:16; Jer. 19:13; 32:29; Zeph. 1:5; Dan. 6:10; Tob. 3:17.

3. On the daily schedule of prayer, see Dan. 6:10; Ps. 55:17; Did. 8.3. In this Cornelius narrative, prayers take place at noon and 3 p.m. Another popular time to pray was 9 a.m. Again 9 a.m. and 3 p.m. are the times of prayer at the temple. A later text (*b. Šabb.* 9b) places a key afternoon prayer time at around 12:30 p.m. (Le Cornu and Shulam 2003: 558).

4. In the Talmud, *b. Šabb.* 10a says that men had their meal at the fourth hour (10 a.m.), workmen at the fifth (11 a.m.), students of Torah at the sixth (12 p.m.); Barrett 1994: 505.

5. See Gen. 1:20, 24 where birds are noted; 6:20 LXX for these three basic categories in slightly different terms. On the Jewish law concerning unclean creatures, see Lev. 11:2–47, esp. 46–47; 20:25; Deut. 14:3–21; Acts 11:6; Rom. 1:23; Wenham 1981.

"crawling creatures." In the OT, there are a few places where someone is asked to do something offensive or illegal (Gen. 22:1–2 [Abraham to sacrifice Isaac]; Hos. 1:2–3 [Hosea to marry a harlot]; Isa. 20:2–3 [Isaiah to go naked for three years]). Note that in each case the person is to do what is presented. This observation will become important in sorting out the vision's point.

The instruction comes from a voice out of heaven. The command is to **10:13–15** rise, sacrifice (θῦσον, *thyson*), and eat (φάγε, *phage*) what is displayed, something that shocks Peter because the food includes the common or unclean. Barrett (1994: 507) argues that the term "sacrifice" almost makes the action a religious act. Initially, Peter absolutely refuses. Luke's use of two negatives (μηδαμῶς, *mēdamōs*, with οὐδέποτε, *oudepote*) points to an emphatic rejection of the suggestion (in the NT, the first term is used only here and in the parallel 11:8). He eats nothing common or unclean (κοινὸν καὶ ἀκάθαρτον, *koinon kai akatharton*). This is the only place in the NT where this expression appears, although the expression appears two more times with "or" (ἤ, *ē*) instead of "and" (καί; Acts 10:28; 11:8). The term for "common" appears five times in Acts, three of those times tied to this incident (2:44; 4:32 [of possessions in common]; 10:14, 28; 11:8 [all of common food]). The term for "unclean" also appears five times in Acts (of spirits in 5:16; 8:7; of food in 10:14, 28; 11:8).

By rejecting this call to eat, Peter believes he is being obedient to God. Peter responds as a faithful Jew and notes that to agree to eat all these unclean things would be a violation of the law (Lev. 10:10; 20:25; Ezek. 4:14; Dan. 1:8–12; 2 Macc. 5:27; 6:18–25 [a rather vivid account of a Jew refusing to eat pork]; Tob. 1:10–11; Jdt. 10:5; 12:2; Hauck, *TDNT* 3:790–91; Gaventa 2003; 166). Peter would never eat such food. The heavenly reply makes clear, however, that God has cleansed the food so that it is not common anymore (Rom. 14:14 gives Paul's view, as does 1 Tim. 4:3–4; also 1 Cor. 10:19). That God has the right to declare food clean is the vision's fundamental premise, functioning much like a pronouncement in a pronouncement story (i.e., a Gospel account, such as Luke 20:20–26, whose focus is a solemn declaration by Jesus). The reply's point is emphatically made with a pronoun plus a negative (σὺ μή, *sy me*) that matches Peter's earlier refusal. The present imperative (κοίνου, *koinou*, regard as common) means not to go on doing what he has been doing, that is, calling common such things that God has cleansed (Bruce 1990: 256; Wallace 1996: 487). The threefold presentation reinforces that God is speaking and is to be believed (Ps.-Philo, *L.A.B.* 53.6; Le Cornu and Shulam 2003: 568).

The vision, whether a parable or a command about food, shows the arrival of a new era and is not just about diet (Acts 10:28–29). Midrash Psalms 146 §4 (268) says that in the future (i.e., in the days of Messiah) God will declare clean all the animals that in this world are declared unclean (Str-B 2:702; Barrett 1994: 509). Barrett rejects the view that the vision suggests a change into a new era; instead he thinks that this lack of distinction was always in the mind of God. A lack of distinction seems unlikely, however, given the food distinctions in the Torah.

The two concepts of food and of table fellowship as signs of accepting Gentiles are related, for associating with Gentiles and eating what they may have prepared as hosts would in normal Jewish thinking entail the probable risk of uncleanness. In addition, the two ideas are closely tied together in the law (Lev. 20:24b–26). Indeed, Polhill (1992: 255) argues that "purity distinctions and human discrimination are of a single piece." The food laws underscore Israel's separation from the nations. By making unclean food clean, God is showing how table fellowship and acceptance of Gentiles are more easily accomplished in the new era. The vision symbolizes that what separated Jews from Gentiles is now removed, as Peter will explain in Acts 10:28. It "frees Peter from any scruples about going to a Gentile home and eating whatever might be set before him" (so Marshall 1980: 186; also Bruce 1990: 256; a similar idea is expressed by Paul in 1 Cor. 10:27). God uses the picture of unclean food now made clean to portray unclean Gentiles now made clean.[6] That such previous lawbreaking visions point to the act being carried out also shows that food and people are in view here.

Jervell (1998: 306) challenges this view, saying that the decree is only about people, not food. He argues that food distinctions are still in place in Acts 15. What we have in Acts 15, however, is a declaration about what Gentiles are wise to do out of consideration for the Jews they are trying to reach. Had the law been the basis for such restrictions, it would have been appealed to. Instead the point is not that God commands this dietary restriction but that Moses is read in the synagogues (15:21). The difference is slight but significant. The point concerns how Jews view such matters, not that God has commanded it for the church.

Acts 10 is the strongest passage in Acts indicating the removal of food laws that have social implications. The vision also has implications for how the law should be viewed. Peter is portrayed as a faithful Jewish believer who protests the move until he is convinced that God is speaking and means what he says. God directs and confirms this effort to expand the gospel.

6. For Jesus's teaching on clean and unclean, see Mark 7:1–23, esp. Mark's own comment in 7:19b about food now declared clean, which the remark to Peter (Acts 10:15) also indicates. Rather than appealing to Jewish law, Paul speaks of food practices in terms of conscience (Rom. 14–15; 1 Cor. 10:25, 27) and regards circumcision as of no consequence (1 Cor. 7:17–24), in both cases showing that the era and role of the law has changed because of Christ's coming. In Gal. 3, Paul portrays the law as a pedagogue, as a temporary instructor and guide until Christ comes.

The importance of the message requires three repetitions to convince   **10:16**
Peter. As subsequent events show, Peter does respond to the divine message as he journeys to Cornelius and welcomes the opportunity to present the gospel. Once the vision is successfully communicated, the sheet
with the animals is removed back to heaven. The fact that the vision is
from heaven is stated at its beginning (v. 11) and end. The verb for its
ascending to heaven also matches the verb of the ascension in 1:11.

The vision leaves Peter at a loss to know what is happening (literally   **10:17–18**
in an indirect question, "what the vision that he had seen might be").
The arrival of men from Cornelius, the word of the Spirit, and their
explanation (vv. 17–22; 11:12) help Peter sort out what is taking place.
By the time he speaks to Cornelius, Peter has figured out what God is
doing. The term for "perplexed" or "puzzled over" (διηπόρει, *diēporei*)
is present only in Luke-Acts (Luke 9:7 [of Herod's view of Jesus]; Acts
2:12 [at Pentecost]; 5:24 [the prison guards about how Peter was able to
get out of prison]). It is in the imperfect tense, so Peter is seen lingering
over what might be going on. As he is trying to figure it out, the emissaries arrive at the gate of Simon the tanner's house (9:43; 10:6). They
ask about Simon Peter, just as Cornelius instructed them in verses 5
and 8. The "whether" clause (v. 18) introduces a direct question about
whether Peter is staying here. The timing and direction are part of what
God uses to help Peter understand why the vision took place and what
its implications are.

The Spirit now informs Peter about the three men who seek him. So   **10:19–20**
the reader has been presented with an angel (v. 3), a heavenly voice (vv.
13–15), and now the Spirit. For Luke, they all speak for God (and thus
for the Spirit). The references allude back to the earlier communication.
Weiser (1981: 265) suggests that the fact that the vision is not alluded to
shows that it was originally independent of this account, but this is not
at all certain. The information, given in a compact manner, probably
assumes the vision already told. The Spirit does not need to reiterate
what is puzzling Peter. The most important point the Spirit tells him is
to go without trying to discern or discriminate (μηδὲν διακρινόμενος,
mēden diakrinomenos) about what is going on (so the RSV and NET
translate "without hesitation"). In fact, the use of ἀλλά (*alla*) at the beginning of the sentence may suggest, "You may object, *but* go without
refusing" (Barrett 1994: 511). The phrase "without discriminating" occurs only here and in Acts 11:12, also about this incident. Even though
the Greek middle voice is used in 10:20 and normally means "without
doubting," the repetition of the idea in 11:12 in the active voice, with
a sense of "discriminate," gives the likely force here as well. A similar
phrase using ἀνακρινόμενος (*anakrinomenos*) appears in 1 Cor. 10:25,
27 to discuss buying meat in the marketplace that may have been offered to idols. This is technical language about not raising questions of

conscience (v. 29 says, "without objection"). So Peter is to go with the men because the Spirit has sent them.

10:21–22 Peter goes down to meet them. He asks why they have come and pieces together the reason for the vision in light of the men's appearance. Here is another example where reflection on experience, focused by a divine comment, helps to define what a revelation from God means (e.g., Jesus's ascension and the angelic remarks in Acts 1:9–11 lead to an understanding of Jesus's return in 3:18–22). The men explain that Cornelius, a centurion, a righteous and God-fearing man, has sent them. In a verse that largely repeats what 10:2 said about Cornelius, the new element is that the entire nation of Jews "testify to" (μαρτυρούμενος, *martyroumenos*) Cornelius, which means that they speak well of him (BAGD 493 §2b; BDAG 618 §2b; Acts 16:2, 22:12; "well spoken of" in NET, RSV; "is respected by" in NIV). The reference to the entire nation is almost a technical phrase and shows that Cornelius is well known among the Jews (1 Macc. 10:25; 11:30, 33; Josephus, *Ant.* 12.3.3 §135; 14.10.22 §248; Fitzmyer 1998: 457).

The men go on to explain that an angel appeared to Cornelius and sent them to bring Peter back to Caesarea. The verb ἐχρηματίσθη (*echrēmatisthē*) refers to a divine disclosure (Matt. 2:12, 22–23; Luke 2:25–26; Acts 10:22; 11:26; Rom. 7:3; Heb. 8:4–6; 11:7; 12:25–26; OT: Jer. 32:30 LXX [25:30 Eng.]; 36:23 LXX [29:23 Eng.]; Stählin, *TDNT* 9:450–52; Bruce 1990: 257). The explanation, given in some detail, shows how carefully Cornelius has informed his messengers about their role, including emphasizing the divine initiative (Polhill 1992: 257). The one added fact is that they wish to bring him to Cornelius to hear what Peter has to say. For Peter to enter a Gentile home would be defiling according to strict Judaism; as *m. 'Ohol.* 18.7 reads, "The dwelling places of Gentiles are unclean." Nevertheless, Peter has been told that they are sent by the Lord, and he has been instructed to go without hesitation.

10:23 Peter hosts them overnight before the trip back the next day. Already the idea of fellowship is implied. This would not be viewed as containing as much risk of uncleanness as a Jew going to a Gentile home, but it is still a significant step. It probably would be regarded as risking potential exposure to uncleanness by the more scrupulous observers of law. Jubilees 22.16 reads, "Separate yourself from the nations, And eat not with them: And do not according to their works, And become not their associate; For their works are unclean, And all their ways are a pollution and an abomination and uncleanness" (see also Jos. Asen. 7.1; Le Cornu and Shulam 2003: 573–75 have a full discussion of impurity and food issues in Judaism). Food was often tied to idol worship, and various trades brought Gentiles into contact with unclean animals (see Jdt. 10:5; 12:1–4; Tob. 1:11). Peter goes ahead without hesitation (v. 20; Fitzmyer 1998: 457). He hosts them overnight because the journey will take more than the day remaining, and they have already made a full journey to reach him. On the next day, Peter leaves, with some from Joppa joining him. Acts 11:12 says the number from Joppa is six, making seven the total plus the three emissaries. So there would be multiple witnesses at this event.

As the emissaries collect Peter to bring him to Caesarea, Cornelius prepares for his arrival by inviting close friends (ἀναγκαίους φίλους, *anankaious philous*, close intimates) and kinsmen to hear him (BDAG 60 §2; BDAG 52 §2). The term for "close" has a meaning similar to the Latin *necessarius*. The narrative builds with a sense of expectation about what Peter will say. Four days after Cornelius's vision, the apostle Peter stands before them.

10:24

Cornelius greets Peter with great respect, falling down before him and offering some form of homage. Bruce (1990: 259) argues that the term προσεκύνησεν (*prosekynēsen*) means to pay homage to someone of whom a favor is asked (Matt. 8:2; 9:18; 15:25; 18:26; 20:20), along with a second meaning, "worship." Peter's response indicates that he sees in this act more of the second sense. Cornelius is receiving Peter as a heavenly messenger. In verse 26, Peter refuses this act of respect, which suggests that he regards Cornelius's act as showing too much deference (Deut. 6:13; Wis. 7:1; Luke 4:8; Rev. 19:10; 22:9; contrast Acts 12:22–23; Polhill 1992: 258; on the Greco-Roman belief in divine men, see Le Cornu and Shulam 2003: 580–81 and their citing of Cicero, *De natura deorum* 3.2.5, where respect for "the immortal gods who have come down to us" is affirmed). A similar incident appears in Acts 14:13–15, but the term for "worship" is not used there; only the wish to offer sacrifices for Paul and Barnabas is refused. Peter makes clear that he is but a creation of God (ἄνθρωπός εἰμι, *anthrōpos eimi*, I am a man), one no different from Cornelius and those he is about to address. The NET renders this as "I too am a mere mortal," because the point is not Peter as a male but Peter as a human. Peter is not a "divine man" in the Greek sense of the term. As he enters the house to address them, he sees that many are gathered to hear him.

10:25–27

Peter explains how unusual this situation is for a Jew. The expression ὡς (*hōs*) introduces an indirect discourse clause like ὅτι (*hoti*; BDAG 1105 §5: "you know *that*"). They know that the common practice is that a Jew should not associate in this manner with someone from another nation. Such an act is regarded as "unlawful" (ἀθέμιτον, *athemiton*). This term means that something is not permitted or allowed (BAGD 20; BDAG 24; in another context in 1 Pet. 4:3, it means to do something indecent; these are the only two NT occurrences). The idea of indecency shows the term's emotive implication. Here it is open association with Gentiles that is prohibited because of fear that Gentiles are unclean.

10:28–29

The first verb means "to associate or join to" on intimate terms (κολλάω, *kollaō*; BDAG 556 §2b; BAGD 441 §2b; Acts 5:13; 9:26; Luke 15:15; 1 Cor. 6:16–17; Matt. 19:5). This is a "taboo" (Bruce 1990: 259). The concern was that a Jewish person would become unclean during the visit with a Gentile who had contact with unclean food and other types of uncleanness from the viewpoint of the Torah. Some contact was allowed, but to eat and visit, as Peter does here, was prohibited, although how this worked and how restrictive this practice was are debated by scholars.[7] John 18:28 shows that visiting a Gentile house renders one unclean. Josephus (*Life* 3 §14) has the example of imprisoned Jews in Rome eating only figs and nuts to protect themselves from being unclean (Leviticus Rabbah on Lev. 20). But God has shown Peter in the vision that he should not call (λέγειν, *legein*) people of different nations common or unclean (κοινὸν ἢ ἀκάθαρτον, *koinon ē akatharton*). These two terms appear in Acts 10:14 to describe Peter's commitment, which God reversed, not to eat unclean food. The vision God shows Peter tells him this is now permitted. Peter interprets the vision's provision to eat food as freeing him to associate with Gentiles, since their dietary habits would be one of the Jewish concerns about purity, especially being hosted in a Gentile home (see comments above on 10:13–15). So Peter comes without objection (ἀναντιρρήτως, *anantirrētos*) and asks what they desire from him (v. 29). This term is an NT hapax (BAGD 58; BDAG 69; the adjective in Acts 19:36 means "incontestable").

10:30–32   Cornelius reviews the sequence of events beginning four days ago, counting inclusively; it was three days ago by our counting of elapsed time. The chronology is this (our way of counting is in parentheses): day 1 (start), he sees the angel; day 2 (day 1), the emissaries arrive in Joppa; day 3 (day 2), they set out for Caesarea; day 4 (day 3), they arrive. God is directing the events all along the way, beginning with the angel who appears to Cornelius during prayer at the ninth hour (v. 3; see comments on 3:1). Cornelius basically repeats the account for the third time in the passage with some slight variation, a repetition that underscores the divine direction behind what is taking place. The threefold telling says that this definitely took place (see comments above on 10:13–15 and the threefold repetition of the vision). What Cornelius refers to as a man here is called an angel in 10:3. The combination of terms ἐν ἐσθῆτι

---

7. Was table fellowship common between Jews and Gentiles in this period (Jervell 1998: 308n160)? Dunn 1983: 3–57 sees it as possible in cases where God-fearing Gentiles or less scrupulous Jews were concerned. He also notes that strict Jews would have avoided table fellowship as much as possible. Esler 1987: 73–86 says that such table fellowship is hard to imagine in a Jewish home and going to a Gentile home would be even less likely. Peter's presence in a Gentile home is the issue here. This is the less common practice for certain. Jervell 1998: 309 argues that it is because Cornelius is a God-fearer that Peter feels comfortable doing this, but this seems to understate the vision, which makes no distinctions.

λαμπρᾷ (*en esthēti lampra*) and similar combinations refer to bright apparel and often describe angels, as here (Luke 24:4, "dazzling apparel"; Acts 1:10, "white robes"). The syntax of verse 30 is not entirely clear, as the phrase "until this hour" does not go well with "at the ninth hour." The sense seems to be that it was about the same time four days ago that everything began. It is possible, however, that the "until this hour" phrase is an ancient addition to the text (Marshall 1980: 188).[8] A few textual variants also raise the question about the text's exact wording.

God tells Cornelius that his prayers have been heard and his alms remembered. This recalls Acts 10:4, where his prayers ascend as a tribute before God. In 10:31 it is his alms that are welcomed by God. Acts 10:4 had the noun μνημόσυνον (*mnēmosynon*, tribute). Here we have the verb ἐμνήσθησαν (*emnēsthēsan*). Because God welcomes Cornelius's act, God will send a messenger to him. Cornelius is to send for Simon Peter at the seaside house of Simon, a tanner.

10:33

Cornelius is immediately obedient, and now Peter, in his kindness, has come. The new detail here is that Cornelius has responded immediately (ἐξαυτῆς, *exautēs*). The note about Peter's kindness (καλῶς, *kalōs*) recognizes that Peter has deviated from normal Jewish practice, as the aorist participle παραγενόμενος (*paragenomenos*, coming) is simultaneous in temporal force to the idea of sending. They all gather to hear what the Lord has commanded Peter to say. They are gathered in the sight of the Lord (ἐνώπιον τοῦ θεοῦ, *enōpion tou theou*); they know God is responsible for their being together. God also is a witness to what is taking place. The commandment turns out to be the preaching of the gospel. Peter has a crowd whose hearts are prepared to hear what he will say.

10:34–35

Peter now addresses the audience (vv. 34–43). Jervell (1998: 309n168) suggests that this is not a missionary speech, because there is no call to repent; it is merely that Cornelius recognizes his access to God as one who fears God. But this understates the speech's thrust. First, Peter does not finish his address, since the Spirit's coming interrupts it, and so we do not know how Peter would have concluded. More important, he does mention the work of Jesus with reference to forgiveness of sins (vv. 42–43), and so groundwork for a call to turn is present in the speech. Finally, Jews also need to turn to God in Jesus, not just recognize what God has done. So an embrace of the new program is necessary for anyone now that Jesus has come.

The beginning of the speech has Peter open his mouth, a solemn expression with biblical roots (Job 3:1; Matt. 5:2; Acts 8:35; 18:14). Peter begins with his new theological insight—God shows no partiality (προσωπολήμπτης, *prosōpolēmptēs*). This term has been found only in

8. Barrett 1994: 517 suggests a still unknown idiom, noting that few copyists seemed troubled by the expression.

Christian works and appears only here in the NT (BAGD 720; BDAG 887; Kuhn, *TDNT* 6:741).[9] Paul's usage emphasizes that Jews are as accountable to God for sin as Gentiles, and so there is no distinction (Barrett 1994: 519). The roots for this term go back to the LXX and Judaism (Lev. 19:15; Deut. 10:17; 2 Chron. 19:7; Ps. 82:2; Mal. 2:9; Sir. 4:22; 35:12–13; Ps. Sol. 2.18–19). The word conveys the idea that God "receives faces" or "lifts up the face" that bows to him in acceptance. The point is that he makes no distinction in how he reacts to people. All have the same potential access to God. In every nation, those who fear him and perform righteousness are acceptable to him. The phrase "in every nation" is placed forward in the Greek sentence for emphasis (Rom. 3:29).

Peter highlights two characteristics of the person whom God regards as acceptable (δεκτός, *dektos*) from any nation (Lev. 19:5; Isa. 56:7). The first is that the person fears God, which Prov. 1:7 calls the beginning of wisdom (Deut. 10:12–13; Rom. 1:21). Cornelius has this characteristic, and so God has extended God's revelation to him. The second characteristic is that the person does right, or "performs righteousness" (ἐργαζόμενος δικαιοσύνην, *ergazomenos dikaiosynēn*; Ps. 14:2 LXX [15:2 Eng.]; Heb. 11:33; James 1:20; conceptually, Matt. 7:23; Rom. 2:10; 13:10; Gal. 6:10). In Judaism, Philo (*Spec. Laws* 2.15 §§62–63) speaks of duty to God in piety and holiness and of duty to people shown in humanity and justice. The idea is like Mic. 6:8 (also Gen. 4:7; Rev. 22:12). Again the commendations that Cornelius possesses were presented in Acts 10:2, 4, 22. The point is not that Cornelius earned righteousness as his due (Rom. 4:5) but that his responsiveness leads God to send Peter to reveal more of God's way to him, as the rest of the speech points the way to what Cornelius now must do. The effect is that Cornelius enters into the peace of God and can now serve God in a way that honors him.

10:36–37 Peter now reviews the gospel: God sent the word to Israel, offering peace through Jesus Christ. The syntax is complex. The term "word" is placed forward in the Greek sentence for emphasis (so in our translation). It also is assimilated to the accusative relative pronoun that follows, which in turn is in apposition to the thought of verses 34–35 and expresses what Peter realizes. The point is that the extension of the word of this salvation to Gentiles is something that Peter knows is taking place (Fitzmyer 1998: 463; BDF §295). The word here refers to the apostolic, preached message about Jesus and the gospel (Kittel, *TDNT* 4:120). The gospel message contains an opportunity for peace (εἰρήνην, *eirēnēn*). This is the concept of shalom from the OT (Pss. 29:11; 72:7; 85:8–10; Prov. 3:17; Isa. 48:18; 54:10; Ezek. 34:25–29), a well-being of relationship between

9. See James 2:9, which has a variation of this term. Romans 2:11 has the idea; conceptually, other Christian texts: Eph. 6:9; Col. 3:25; James 2:1; 1 Pet. 1:17; 1 Clem. 1.3; Barn. 4.12; Pol. *Phil.* 6.1; Bruce 1990: 260; Bassler 1985.

the person and God, which now seems to express itself in peace between people as well (Eph. 2:11–22). The idea of preaching peace recalls OT ideas (Isa. 52:7; Nah. 1:15).

When Peter says "you know" about these things, he suggests that Cornelius is likely to be aware of this ministry. Indeed, such a report went about the region of Judea from the time of John's baptism. It was a spreading verbal communication (ῥῆμα, *rhēma*) of what God did through Jesus, as verses 38–41 show (see our translation). This term is distinct from the earlier term for "word" in v. 36 (λόγον, *logon*). So Jesus was a topic of public discourse.

What made Jesus important is what God was doing through him. God brought peace through what Jesus did, and this Jesus is described as Lord of all (Rom. 10:12; Acts 2:36). This title presents the christological theme of the speech. Jesus is exalted and is Lord over all people. Since he is Lord of all, the gospel can go to all, including people of the nations (the Gentiles) such as Cornelius. Jesus's authority is described in the next few verses as a function of his work that came through God's anointing him with the Spirit and power so that he could do good and heal those oppressed by the devil. Even though the remark is parenthetical grammatically, it is the theme of the speech conceptually. Jesus is the one with authority to deliver the peace that comes from God to those of every nation. His activity and God's vindication of him show this. God takes the initiative here, as is always the case in Acts. The message comes from God.

Peter now traces the major steps of God's activity through Jesus after **10:38–41** his baptism by John the Baptist, which also included the Spirit. This ministry was a part of the public record circulating about Jesus across Judea.

John's baptism is linked to the plan, as also in Luke 1–3. Acts 18:24– 19:10 will show a distinction between John's baptism and what Jesus did, indicating a break between eras and demonstrating John's role, in Luke-Acts, of serving as a bridge between the eras. A similar break is evident here. John set the table for God's major work through Jesus. That is where the real story of God's new work begins. The outline of Peter's summary very much parallels Mark's presentation of Jesus's ministry: John the Baptist, the Galilean ministry, and then Jesus meeting his fate in Jerusalem. Luke's Gospel follows this outline as well. God's anointing with the Spirit gave Jesus power to do good (Ps. 107:20) and to heal those oppressed by the devil (Isa. 61:1–2; Luke 4:16–18, looking back to 3:21–22; Luke 7:22–23 with its link to Isa. 35:5–6; Luke 11:17–23; 13:16).[10]

The idea of doing good (εὐεργετῶν, *euergetōn*) is a powerful one in a Greek context, pointing to a benefactor, someone who does good

---

10. On sin seen as captivity to the devil, from which exorcism frees, see Pelikan 2005: 133–35.

for society (Eckey 2000: 245; Bertram, *TDNT* 2:654–55). The term was applied to gods, heroes (e.g., Heracles), kings (e.g., Ptolemy IV), statesmen, philosophers (e.g., Socrates), inventors, and physicians (Euripides, *Heracles* 1252; Plato, *Apology* 36D [Socrates referring to himself in his defense]; 3 Macc. 6:24). Such activity calls for gratitude from the beneficiaries. Although in the OT it is God who performs such a role, the LXX often avoids using the term. The NT uses various forms of the word four times (Acts 4:9; 1 Tim. 6:2; Luke 22:25, where the title is applied to kings and other patrons in contrast to how Jesus's activity is described verbally here in Acts 10). Jesus's good work of healing and ministry was that of one who served and benefited humanity.

The healing ministry of Jesus was a confrontation with evil and suffering and the devil. The prepositional phrase ὑπὸ τοῦ διαβόλου (*hypo tou diabolou*, by the devil) follows a passive participle and looks to the devil as the ultimate agent behind the suffering Jesus confronted and treated (Wallace 1996: 433). The term καταδυναστευομένους (*katadynasteuomenous*, oppressed) occurs only here and in James 2:6. In James it refers to what the rich do to the poor. This enablement to reverse oppression was fundamental to Jesus's divine calling (Luke 4:18–19). It showed that God was with Jesus in a special way (ὁ θεὸς ἦν μετ' αὐτοῦ, *ho theos ēn met' autou*, God was with him), an expression also used of Joseph in Acts 7:9 (Ps. Sol. 17.37–38, of the Messiah). Indeed, the ὅτι (*hoti*) clause gives the reason Jesus worked with such power (Wallace 1996: 460). It was the presence of God through him enabling him to counter the devil. Here is evidence of the kingdom, since the battle is with the spiritual forces that stand opposed to humanity (Luke 4:31–44; 11:14–23). This preaching took place throughout Judea, so that both Galilee and the south are included in the reference to Judea.

The reference to Jesus in verse 38 is placed at the beginning of the clause, making it emphatic. Peter notes that those of the apostolic circle are witnesses (μάρτυρες, *martyres*) to what God did (v. 39), repeating a key idea that goes back to Acts 1:8 and 22. The term μάρτυρες is also somewhat emphatic, as it occurs next to the subject in the sentence in a construction that lacks a verbal connective. Peter will emphasize the witness theme by repeating it in verse 41 when the resurrection is affirmed. The events involve both Judea in the broad sense and Jerusalem in particular, since the city is where the key final events took place. The review in these verses is regarded as the essence of early preaching about Jesus's ministry and is very similar in perspective to Mark (Bruce 1990: 261, on v. 36; Dodd 1936).[11]

---

11. See esp. Stanton 1974: 67–85, who notes that the speech alludes to Ps. 107:20 (106:20 LXX); Isa. 52:7; 61:1; and Deut. 21:22. He sees Luke using early-church exegetical tradition here.

Finally, Peter turns to Jesus's death and resurrection. His death is described as "hanging him on a tree" (κρεμάσαντες ἐπὶ ξύλου, *kremasantes epi xylou*), an allusion to Deut. 21:22–23 and the cursed death that Jesus experienced from the Jewish point of view (Acts 5:30 and Gal. 3:13 are other uses of this phrase). Death was not the end of the story, but the beginning, as God raised Jesus from the dead on the third day and had him appear to the apostles as preappointed (προκεχειροτονημένοις, *prokecheirotonēmenois*) witnesses (Luke 24:13–52, esp. v. 48; Acts 1:1–11). This term is in the perfect tense, underscoring the appointment to a fixed role. It is the only NT use of this prefixed verb (variations are in 3:20; 14:23). This is one of two references outside the Gospels to the third day, with 1 Cor. 15:4 being the other. Jesus's resurrection is also noted in Acts 3:15; 4:10; 5:30, but this is the first note of the third day in Acts (Barrett 1994: 526). The third day is counted inclusively (Friday = day 1; Saturday = day 2; Sunday = day 3). Peter says that Jesus made himself manifest (ἐμφανῆ, *emphanē*), a term used only here and in Rom. 10:20 in the NT, which refers to a person appearing in the open. They saw him eat and drink after his death (Luke 24:27–42), which was a proof of his resurrection (Ign. *Smyrn.* 3.3; Bruce 1990: 263). Thus Peter's message is not only a declaration but also his recounting of an experience he participated in directly. Peter makes this point by noting that the appearances were only to those chosen by God as witnesses.

The apostles were commanded to preach to the people about God's work **10:42–43** through Jesus. Scholars dispute whether God or Jesus gave the command. Jervell (1998: 312) argues that it is God, since God is the subject of all the actions from verse 36 on. The reference to Jesus eating and drinking with them is, however, the closest reference in the context, and the command to preach the gospel to the world was given by Jesus at one of these appearances in Luke (Luke 24:36–49). So Jesus is the likely subject, especially since the reference to God is part of a passive construction in verse 42.

The apostles were also to warn the people or testify solemnly (διαμαρτύρασθαι, *diamartyrasthai*) about this message. The term τούτῳ (*toutō*) in verse 43 is probably neuter here, not masculine, as that is Luke's usual preference in such contexts. So the idea is that to this fact or message the prophets testify (Barrett 1994: 528; Luke 24:47–48). The reference to "people" (λαῷ, *laō*) is important, for the term refers normally to Israel as the people of God (Luke 2:32), but here it has a general sense of people of all nations (Acts 15:14 as well). This message is for all nations, as the speech itself shows.

Most important to realize is the role God has given to Jesus before all humanity. Jesus is the one decreed (ὁ ὡρισμένος, *ho hōrismenos*) to be the judge of the living and the dead (κριτὴς ζώντων καὶ νεκρῶν, *kritēs zōntōn kai nekrōn*), or of all people. That Jesus is judge is what his resurrection attests to. This role partially explains why he is called Lord (Fitzmyer 1998: 466; John 5:22, 27; Rom. 14:9; 2 Tim. 4:1; 1 Pet. 4:5; 2 Clem. 1.1). He is the ultimate eschatological judge, possessing full authority over life and death. In Judaism the Son of Man had such an exalted role (1 En. 38–71, drawn from Dan. 7:9–14). This title was Jesus's favorite self-designation. In Greek his judging role as Lord (Acts 10:36) expresses the same idea. This idea will appear again in Acts 17:31.

Peter goes on to note (v. 43) that all the prophets testified to the message about Jesus; he uses the term μαρτυροῦσιν (martyrousin), the verbal form of the noun that appears in verses 39 and 41. Jesus offers forgiveness of sins (2:38) through his name (3:16). Barrett (1994: 528) suggests that the allusion here is to the new covenant (Jer. 38:34 LXX [31:34 MT and Eng.]), whereas Fitzmyer (1998: 466) thinks that this is another example of Luke's general appeal to the OT (Luke 24:25–27, 44; Acts 8:35). Marshall (1980: 193) speaks of allusions to Isa. 33:24; 53:4; Jer. 31:34; and Dan. 9:24. Here Peter underscores that it is faith in the Jesus he has just described that brings the forgiveness. So the way of salvation is through the judge of the living and the dead, by appealing to him to forgive sin, which leads into the way of peace through the gospel (v. 35). Everyone who believes in this forgiveness receives this salvation. Christians are described as "those who believe," a key response in Acts (passages referring to those who believe: Acts 14:23; 19:4; 9:42; 11:17; 16:31; use of the verb "to believe," 5:14; 8:12; 16:34; 18:8; 24:14; 26:27; 27:25).

10:44–46a God confirms the speech with the dispersal of the Spirit upon the Gentiles who are listening to Peter. The Jews are amazed that "the gift" is poured out on Gentiles as well (Joel 2:28–32; Acts 2:17–21). The Spirit "fell" (ἐπέπεσεν, epepesen) on them (Acts 8:16; 11:15). God is leaving no doubt that this initiative is his (11:15–17). The event has correctly been called the "Pentecost of the Gentile world" (v. 47; Bruce 1990: 264). The Spirit's arrival is the sign of the new age (Luke 3:15–17). The arrival of promise confirms that Gentiles can be saved, as verse 45 also suggests. In recording the amazement of the Jews that the Spirit has fallen on Gentiles, a promise traced throughout Luke-Acts reappears (Luke 3:15–17; 24:49; Acts 1:8; 2:16–41; 11:15–17; 15:8).

The presence of tongues and the praise of God make it obvious that the Spirit is present (v. 46). The verb ἐξέστησαν (exestēsan, were astonished) describes the surprise the Jews have that the Spirit is given to Gentiles. This term appears in several key passages to denote a reaction to what is taking place (Acts 2:7, 12 [to the coming of tongues]; 8:9, 11, 13 [to the work of Philip and Simon]; 9:21 [to Paul's preaching Christ after having persecuted the church]; 12:16 [to Peter's escape from prison]). The 2:12 text is important, for the description in 10:45 matches the reaction that took place at the original Pentecost.

The Jews, called literally the "believers out of circumcision" (οἱ ἐκ περιτομῆς πιστοί, *hoi ek peritomēs pistoi*), are amazed that this gift of the Spirit, which is so fundamentally tied to salvation, can be given to Gentiles. This phrase referring to circumcision appears occasionally: sometimes it refers to Jews and other times to Jewish Christians (Acts 11:2; Col. 4:11) or to a portion of them (the circumcision party, where the phrase may lack a reference to believers in Gal. 2:12; Titus 1:10).

It is not clear if the manifestation of the Spirit's outpouring in tongues entailed other languages or is simply praise of God, as in 1 Cor. 12–14, as the need for other human languages with this singular audience of Gentiles is not self-evident. Regardless, God is working directly to make the point. There is no apostolic intermediary on earth who helps with the distribution. Those present immediately understand the importance of what has taken place, appreciating the divine initiative.

What they hear are Gentiles speaking in tongues and "magnifying God" (μεγαλυνόντων τὸν θεόν, *megalynontōn ton theon*). The term μεγαλύνω (*megalynō*) appears eight times in the NT (Matt. 23:5–7; Luke 1:46–48, 58; Acts 5:12–13; 10:45–46; 19:17; 2 Cor. 10:14–16; Phil. 1:18–20; OT: Ps. 34:3 [33:4 LXX]). The remarks are similar to Acts 2:11 as well, where the mighty works of God were declared.

Peter is led to comment on what should be done next. He calls for im- **10:46b–48** mediate baptism, since the Gentiles have received the Spirit just as those present at Pentecost had in Acts 2 (also 11:15, 17; 15:8, 11). Peter understands the significance of the Spirit's distribution. The Spirit is the sign of the eschaton's presence and shows that God is blessing Gentiles directly. Peter asks if there is anything to prevent their being baptized. The interrogative particle μήτι (*mēti*) tells us the expected answer: "No, nothing should prevent this" (Culy and Parsons 2003: 216). So baptism follows in the name of Jesus Christ (8:36), and Peter stays with Cornelius for several days, implying that he sees these Gentiles now as "clean." As with the Ethiopian eunuch, there is nothing to hinder baptism or fellowship. It appears that Peter does not perform the baptism but those with him, since he commands the new believers to be baptized (Polhill 1992: 264).

In sum, God directs an epoch-making event in which Gentiles are accepted in fellowship and receive the gospel. Their faith leads to the gift of the Spirit, the sign that the new era has arrived. In addition, they are not circumcised and yet table fellowship and full hospitality between Jews and Gentiles ensues.

The Trinity is quite active here (Gaventa 2003: 173–74). God takes the initiative. Jesus Christ is at the center of the plan. The Spirit confirms that all of this is God's work. The actions that take place represent the act and will of God working in harmony. The church does not lead here but follows God's leading, thereby learning a great deal about how God views people.

Jews and Gentiles are equal in Christ (Eph. 2:11–22). Their need and the answer to that need are the same. This is why judgment and accountability before God are keys to Peter's speech.

As creatures, we are all responsible to the Creator. This theme will become more prominent as Paul preaches to Gentiles (Acts 17). It is a theme that is foundational to any proclamation of the gospel. Pluralism desires to wash away this theme and reality, rendering the pursuit of the Creator optional, but every person's responsibility to the Creator is one of the most important ideas that the Scripture and the church teach.

Also key to the speech are Jesus's life, death, and resurrection. That resurrection explains the heavenly position and role Jesus now has. Without the person of Jesus and the work he has done on our behalf, there is no gospel (Stott 1990: 190–91). In Acts the gospel is now ready to go into all the world, but not without more theological reflection later in Acts 15 about how this should be done.

The case of Cornelius raises an interesting question, given that he was respectful of God but had not yet responded to Jesus. Luke is aware that there are people who show respect for God, and Luke's account of them is respectful. This does not mean, however, that Luke ignores that their spiritual state still leaves them in need of salvation. Their pursuit of God by itself does not exempt them or inoculate them from needing the forgiveness Jesus has obtained (Fernando 1998: 339–40). There is a difference between seeking and entering into fellowship with God. God directs Peter to complete Cornelius's journey back to God. Cornelius's heart has been well prepared for the gospel. His conversion in many ways stands in contrast to Paul's. Where Paul went from enemy to believer by a dramatic appearance, Cornelius went from an open seeker to a believer through the preached gospel. The contrast reveals the variety of ways in which God can work.

Additional Notes

10:9. The "sixth" hour is the preferred rendering here, as the "ninth" hour is too poorly attested (only $\aleph^c$, 225) and the hour to become hungry would be midday. The variant is probably meant to point to a normal hour for prayer.

10:16. The reading "immediately" (εὐθύς, *euthys*) is original here ($\mathfrak{P}^{74}$, $\aleph$, A, B, C, E, 81) over "again" (πάλιν, *palin*; D, Ψ, 33^vid, 1739, Byz) or over the absence of any reference ($\mathfrak{P}^{45}$, 36, 453, 1175). It has the better attestation.

10:19. External evidence favors "three" men ($\mathfrak{P}^{74}$, $\aleph$, A, C, E, 33, 81, 323, 453, 945, 1739) seeking Peter, not "two" (B) or simply "men" (D, Ψ, Byz), although "two" is the more difficult reading. The expression "two men" is too poorly attested to be original. It may be that B relied on the normal two-witness motif and excluded the military protector as a witness.

10:26. Codex D intensifies Peter's rejection of Cornelius's homage, adding a phrase at the beginning and the end. Its reading translates as, "What are you doing? Arise, I myself am a man just like you."

10:30. Codex D^1 has Greek that means fasting "from the third day until the present hour," counting elapsed time, and D speaks of fasting from the ninth hour. Codex E has Cornelius fasting and praying from the sixth to the ninth hour. Many other texts have Cornelius fasting and at the ninth hour praying ($\mathfrak{P}^{50}$, A^c, D*, Ψ, Byz). The addition of fasting makes Cornelius look even more pious.

10:33. The reading here may be, "to hear all that you have been commanded from [ἀπό, *apo*] the Lord," rather than "by [ὑπό, *hypo*] the Lord." The first reading is in $\mathfrak{P}^{45, 74}$, $\aleph^2$, A, C, and D, whereas the second, which is in the Greek text of NA^{27}, is present in $\aleph$*, B, Ψ, 1739, and Byz. Both readings are well attested, and so the choice here is difficult.

10:36. The relative pronoun ὅν (*hon*) should be retained, as its inclusion makes the verse's reading more difficult and the inclusion is well attested ($\mathfrak{P}^{74}$, $\aleph$*, C, D, E, Ψ, and Byz; omitting it are $\aleph^1$, A, B, 81, 614, 1739). For the resultant meaning, see the discussion of the verse. If the pronoun is omitted, then the verse looks ahead to verse 37. If not, it connects back to verses 34–35.

2. Peter Reports to Jerusalem about Gentiles (11:1–18)

The divine initiative meets with criticism from the circumcision party (v. 2), so that a review of what has taken place is required to resolve the dispute. The account treats the effect of the inclusion of Gentiles in the church and shows that this new emphasis did not go without objection or reflection. The complaint is registered in verses 1–3, and Peter retells the story of his vision and that of Cornelius in verses 4–10 and 11–14 respectively. Peter then recounts in verses 15–17 the events that followed his speech of Acts 10:34–43. Peter's point is that God directed the entire event and that this divine blessing has come to the Gentiles without their being circumcised (esp. vv. 12, 17). The conclusion emerges in verse 18: God also has granted to the Gentiles repentance unto life, something that also leads to praise of God.

What bothers those who object the most is that Peter and company have gone in and eaten with uncircumcised men (v. 3). That such a level of table fellowship has taken place is quite likely, given that Peter and his group stayed with Cornelius for days and would have received the food of their host. The question that is less than clear is whether Cornelius would have been sensitive enough not to insult his Jewish guests with unclean food (Barrett 1994: 533). The nature of Peter's vision in verses 4–10, however, which is the key to his initial reply, seems to make the debate moot. If God calls this "unclean" food clean, then God has made it clean and opened the door to table fellowship. Such a direct connection between food and table fellowship is the only way to make sense of the later dispute between Paul and Peter over Peter's withdrawal from associating with Gentiles in Gal. 2:11–12. It also fits the way that miracles, which would include divinely given visions, conveyed two levels of meaning, physical and spiritual (Luke 5:1–11, 17–26), not to mention how God's commands to break the law were to be followed (noted above in comments on 10:13–15).

The account is a recapitulatory speech and a defense speech (Fitzmyer 1998: 470). It is a second retelling of events, given that Cornelius retold the story in Acts 10:30–33 from his point of view. Peter's main point is that what God has declared clean is not unclean (11:9). Peter's account also highlights again how the Spirit is the fundamental sign of the new era and of God's activity. The scene also lays groundwork for the debate in Acts 15, where the issue of

Gentile involvement surfaces again, this time concerning whether Gentiles would have to observe any Jewish legal requirements in the new interracial context. Although the account may well be stylized by Luke to show the parallelism to Acts 10, its ultimate source would be either Peter, a tradition formed by those who accompanied him, or those who were present at this initial dispute. There is little question that the church would have found such a revolutionary move initially controversial, which would require a defense of its legitimacy and a justification for this new avenue of ministry.

Exegesis and Exposition

¹Now the apostles and brothers in Judea heard that the Gentiles also had received the word of God. ²So when Peter went up to Jerusalem, those from the circumcision complained to him, ³saying, "You came to uncircumcised men and ate with them."

⁴But Peter began to set out in an orderly sequence an explanation for them, saying, ⁵"I was in the city of Joppa praying; and in a trance I saw a vision, a vessel descending, like a great sheet, let down from heaven by four corners; and it came down to me. ⁶Gazing at it closely, I observed animals and beasts of prey and reptiles and birds of the air. ⁷And I heard a voice saying to me, 'Rise, Peter, sacrifice and eat.' ⁸But I said, 'No way, Lord, for nothing common or unclean has ever come into my mouth.' ⁹But the voice answered ⌜a second time⌝ from heaven, 'What God has made clean you shall not regard as common.' ¹⁰This took place three times, and all was taken up again into heaven. ¹¹And at that very moment three men came upon the house where we were staying, sent to me from Caesarea. ¹²And the Spirit said to me to go with them, making no hesitation. These six brethren also came together with me, and we went into the man's house. ¹³And he related to us how he had seen ⌜the⌝ angel standing in his house and saying, 'Send to Joppa and bring Simon called Peter, ¹⁴who will declare to you a message by which you will be saved, you and all your household.' ¹⁵As I began to speak, the Holy Spirit fell on them just as on us in the beginning. ¹⁶And I remembered the word of the Lord, how he said, 'John baptized with water, but you shall be baptized by the Holy Spirit.' ¹⁷If therefore God gave the identical gift to them as he gave to us when we believed in the Lord Jesus Christ, who was I that I could hinder God?" ¹⁸Hearing this, they were silenced. And they glorified God, saying, "Then to the Gentiles also God has granted repentance unto life."

The report of the reception of the word reaches the apostles and brethren in Judea—in other words, all the church. The idea of "receiving the word of God" (ἐδέξαντο τὸν λόγον τοῦ θεοῦ, *edexanto ton logon tou theou*) describes a positive response to the gospel. To receive the word of God is to welcome the gospel message with one's heart (Luke 8:13 [an initial

11:1–3

positive response that is reversed later]; Acts 8:14; 11:1; 17:11; 1 Thess. 1:6–7). Those of Jewish background, or of the "circumcision" (οἱ ἐκ περιτομῆς, *hoi ek peritomēs*) in Jerusalem, however, not having been at Cornelius's conversion, criticize Peter for being so receptive of Gentiles and having table fellowship with them (on this Greek phrase, see Acts 10:45–46; 11:2–3; Gal. 2:12). "Those of the circumcision" must refer to the more conscientious of the Hebrew Christians, for most believers at this time were Jews and circumcised.[1] Those so described argued for being careful about how Jews related to Gentiles in terms of purity and diet. This was Peter's view before he had the vision in Acts 10, as he explains in verses 4–10.

Those verses are his reply to the complaints of these Jewish Christians who have responded instinctively with doubt. Peter's retelling of the vision of 10:9–16 shows the event's importance. Marshall (1980: 195) is right that the RSV's rendering, "circumcision party," is not correct (see the same phrase in 10:45 merely of Jewish Christians). The NET renders this "circumcised believers." These sensitive Jewish Christians are not organized but react out of an instinctive concern for the law and covenant. Marshall notes that the problem is one of both food and fellowship (also Bruce 1990: 267).

The circumcision group's understanding would be that Gentiles need to observe the law, keep away from unclean food, and be circumcised to show their participation in the covenant (Gen. 17:9–14; on clean and unclean, see the discussion of Acts 10:13–15). In their view, Peter should have been assured that the Gentiles were clean before associating with them. For these Jewish believers, the likelihood of Peter contracting uncleanness was almost certain. This follows the general Jewish view that Gentiles were inherently likely to be unclean (expressed in Josephus, *Ant.* 14.11.5 §285 about Hyrcanus asking Herod not to bring his troops into Jerusalem; at Qumran, according to CD 11.14–15, there was to be no contact with Gentiles on the Sabbath). How much contact Jews could have with Gentiles was debated; scrupulous Jews were concerned about such issues. This problem with circumcision and table fellowship will persist across the church and be discussed again in Acts 15. Some old ways die hard in the new era.

The complaint is expressed more likely as a statement rather than as a question (Barrett 1994: 537–38). It almost has the force of "You went in and ate with Gentiles, so what about it! Explain yourself." Thus verse 2 says that they criticized (διεκρίνοντο, *diekrinonto*) him. Perhaps their

---

1. Jervell 1998: 314 sees it as a reference to all Christians, but this comprehensive sense is unlikely here. The description has the feel of a group within a larger group. He also argues that table fellowship seems to be the primary complaint, not the effort to bring them salvation. Peter's reply, however, esp. in vv. 15–18, treats the coming of salvation and baptism to Gentiles, and so salvation appears to be the point as well.

view matches Jub. 22.16: "Separate thyself from the nations, and eat not with them: and do not according to their works, and become not their associate; for their works are unclean, and all their ways are a pollution and an abomination and uncleanness" (see comments above on 10:13–15). In their view, if Gentiles are to join the believing community, they must become like Jews.

Peter's explanation retells the story about the trance, which in this new summary he also calls a vision (ὅραμα, *horama*). The account is told "in an orderly sequence" (11:4), an expression that recalls Luke 1:3, and Peter starts from the beginning of events as he experienced them. Peter does not know what version of events his audience has heard, so he goes through the events again. The key fact is that in a vision Peter sees the sheet descend with food. He also notes four categories of creatures, as opposed to three in 10:12 (so Ps. 148:10). The fourth category includes beasts of prey (τὰ θηρία, *ta thēria*). The rest of the retelling is virtually a word-for-word repetition of the earlier Acts 10 account with some abbreviation and a first-person (versus third-person) narration. Peter's point of view is presented directly here (Marshall 1980: 196). In contrast to Acts 10, which starts with Cornelius's vision and then tells about Peter, the account here starts with Peter, since it comes from his point of view. The conversation is also virtually word for word. In the most direct witness form possible, Peter makes the decisive case for what God has done.

     11:4–10

In this version, Peter says that nothing common or unclean has ever entered his mouth. The expression "has come into [my] mouth" (εἰσῆλθεν εἰς τὸ στόμα, *eisēlthen eis to stoma*) is like Ezek. 4:14 (also Matt. 15:11, 17). In Acts 10:14 he simply said that he had not eaten anything common or unclean. It makes the point with emphasis. This slight variation of wording where the point is basically the same is frequent when Luke retells an event. Peter closes his review of the vision by noting that the vision repeated itself three times before being drawn back up into heaven. The expression "taken up" (ἀνεσπάσθη, *anespasthē*) appears only here and in Luke 14:5 in the NT.

As the vision ended, the three men sent to Caesarea by Cornelius arrived at the home where Peter was staying. The Spirit had told Peter to go with them, without hesitation, a point also made in Acts 10:20 with the description of going without doubting. The expression literally "without discriminating" (μηδὲν διακρίναντα, *mēden diakrinanta*) means that no partiality should be exercised against them because they are Gentiles (10:34; 15:9). So with six Jewish Christian brothers Peter went to Cornelius's home. He does not mention that he hosted the Gentiles overnight. The six men apparently are present to corroborate what Peter says. There are seven witnesses in total, far beyond the normal two required. The number of men Peter took is another detail not supplied in 10:23. Seven seals were often attached to a will in Roman law

     11:11–12

for witness purposes (Rev. 5:1; Bruce 1990: 269). Peter and his group entered the Gentile's home without hesitation, just as the Spirit commanded. They were simply being obedient to God.

11:13–14 Peter relates how the man inviting him, whom he never names or describes in this review, told of the angel commanding him to send for Peter in Joppa, a review of Acts 10:30–33. Nor does Peter mention here the compliment of Cornelius's prayers and alms that appeared in the earlier version. Peter also introduces the angel's declaration that Peter's message would contain an offer of salvation for the man and his household. Acts 10:22 and 33 simply indicated they were to hear what Peter had to say. That the gospel be preached to Gentiles was a command of heaven. Thus the new details in retelling the account include the identification of the topic as salvation and the fact that the audience included the entire household (16:31). This would include slaves and attendants beyond family relatives. If salvation includes Gentiles, then fellowship with them is also implied (Fitzmyer 1998: 471).

The failure to name Cornelius is not a case of a story told poorly (so Barrett 1994: 540) but rather reflects the likelihood that everyone already knows the identity of the man (or else why have the discussion?). It also makes the story one of principle. The issue is not Cornelius but what Cornelius represents: a Gentile saved directly by the act of God. The concern is about establishing a bad halakic precedent.

11:15–18 When Peter began to speak, the Spirit came upon (ἐπέπεσεν, *epepesen*) the group of Gentiles. Peter is indicating here that the Spirit came before he finished speaking and without any initiative on his part, such as laying on of hands. This observation calls into question Dibelius's claim that the remarks are poorly written. Dibelius argues that the text says that the Spirit came when Peter began his speech rather than when he was done. Peter may well have said much more, however, had the Spirit not interrupted the proceedings (Fitzmyer 1998: 472 and Marshall 1980: 197; *pace* Dibelius 1956: 110). Nonetheless, the Spirit comes after Peter has made key points about the availability of Jesus to all, so the scene is not poorly written by not getting to a key theological point and a clear gospel presentation.

So the Spirit fell on the group as it had on the believers at Pentecost, what Peter calls "in the beginning" (ἐν ἀρχῇ, *en archē*), a reference back to Acts 2. Since the Spirit is the sign of the eschaton promised by John the Baptist in Luke 3:16 and also by the Lord in Acts 1:5, Peter understood immediately what this meant. The wording is close to Acts 10:44 and 47.

The new note is the reference to "the beginning," the beginning of distribution of the promise. This distribution means that key blessings of the new era have come (Luke 24:49; Acts 1:4–5; 2:14–21). The Lord has shown that these Gentiles are also a part of the plan of salvation. The reference to Gentiles is emphatic in the Greek, as it is placed forward in the sentence. The argument is that if God can sovereignly distribute to the Gentiles the same promised Spirit of the new era that Jews received, then how could Peter hinder (κωλῦσαι, *kōlysai*) their inclusion in the blessings of the people of God (see Acts 10:47)? So the implication here is that Peter allowed them to be baptized in water as a confirmation of their faith and presence in the new community (on water and Spirit, John 3:5; Ezek. 36:25–27; Bruce 1990: 269). Peter remembers this teaching of Jesus about the Spirit as the sign of promise and repeats it here in verse 16. The roots of the teaching are found in John the Baptist's remarks in Luke 3:16 in preparing the way for the new era. The "identical [ἴσην, *isēn*] gift" of the Spirit given by God means that these people are cleansed and indwelt by the divine sacred presence. Thus no one can or should resist their inclusion. God is the one who orchestrated this "halakic" move.

The complaints of the objecting group are silenced. They glorify God for his initiative in giving repentance unto life to the Gentiles (Acts 4:21; 21:20). God is now seen as the one who brought this about, so they rejoice. The expression "repentance unto life" (τὴν μετάνοιαν εἰς ζωήν, *tēn metanoian eis zōēn*) represents another summary phrase for the response to the gospel. God has given repentance unto life to the Gentiles. In Judaism, repentance was seen as a divine gift (Wis. 12:10, 19, "You give repentance for sins"; Jervell 1998: 316). Life here equals salvation (Barrett 1994: 543; Luke 10:25; Acts 5:20; 13:46, 48). God took the initiative for this new work. God's action has resulted in (1) repentance as the response and (2) life as the gift. Gentiles now are included in the offer of the gospel. The remaining questions will be about the law and circumcision, which are treated in Acts 15.

As just noted, two elements are highlighted in the outcome: the human response (repentance) and the divine provision (the Spirit who gives life). These associations run deep in the NT. The role of the Spirit as life-giver is little different from John 4 and 7 (living water) and, in a more ethically emphasized way, Rom. 8 (resurrection power). The link between the gift of the Spirit and possession of life is the link between soteriology and sanctification (Acts 2:38; 3:19; 5:31; 20:21; 26:20). In all of this, a response of faith by the Gentiles is assumed, as they were ready to hear what Peter had to say (10:33; Marshall 1980: 197–98).

In sum, this passage confirms the divine initiative in the outreach to Gentiles. Stott (1990: 194–96) notes that in this case it was a series of divine acts that produced the breakthrough: there was a vision, a command, preparation, and, finally, action. God had prepared the hearts of the recipients in a way that did not involve Peter or anyone else connected to him. Sometimes God works alone, behind the scenes, before the gospel is brought to someone. Yet Peter came to see the fruit of these labors.

God brings various ethnic groups into one in Christ. This message is important in Acts. Jesus brings reconciliation not only with God but also between people. The new community will be diverse in makeup, equal in status, and called to reflect peace with one another (Eph. 2:11–22). Peter is the example of one who understands and actively pursues this fresh opportunity that is opened up to all people. Indeed, he defends it vigorously as the will of God. God had opened up a new way to himself through Jesus. Now Peter understands the importance of pursuing the full vision God has directed to be put in place. For the most part, it is a lesson he would not forget. Galatians 2:11–14 shows a lapse, but one he recognized when it was pointed out to him. This is another feature of learning a new lesson. Sometimes old habits return, but they are also not treated as acceptable when pointed out.

This reconciliation worked itself out with cultural sensitivity. Gentiles did not need to become Jews, nor Jews Gentiles, apparently. According to Paul's letters and some of the differences he tried to arbitrate, Paul's position was this: if the issue did not touch on the core of the gospel, then let each do what was appropriate for their own conscience. Some would eat only certain foods, others would eat anything. Some would set apart certain days; others would treat all days the same (Rom. 14:1–5). This approach reflected a respect for cultural roots that did not seek to make everyone in the church exactly the same when it came to practices that were not of essential importance. Today such issues surface when the gospel enters a new culture or when one looks at messianic Jewish congregations. For example, care must be exercised not to invert the mistake of the first century by insisting that Jewish believers become like Gentiles. This is a decision of the believer's conscience with regard to practice once one has responded in faith to the gospel. Similarly one should be sure that when one ministers cross-culturally, practices that are Western but not necessarily specifically Christian are not imposed on others, and vice versa. Perhaps in our culture the choice of where and how to educate children is a similar kind of decision. Not everyone needs to do the same thing in this matter.

Additional Notes

11:9. Codex D has simply "a voice came out of heaven to me," apparently reading the reference to the "second time" in the bulk of MSS as odd.

11:13. The MSS D, Ψ, and 𝔓⁴⁵ omit the article with "angel." It should be included, however, even though it is awkward because there has been no mention of this angel since Acts 10:3. The article's inclusion is better attested.

C. The Church at Antioch: Barnabas, Saul, and Agabus (11:19–30)

Luke's next topic is the church's expansion as a result of persecution, which prepares for the reintroduction of Paul and the work of a major church outside Jerusalem, the community at Antioch. This is a community full of Hellenistic Jews. Acts 11:19–21 discusses the successful mission to Greeks in this community. Acts 11:22–26 tells how Barnabas comes from Jerusalem to look over the new work and how he goes to get Saul to help him. The church grows to the point where believers became known as "Christians" for the first time. Acts 11:27–30 shows God's protection of the Jerusalem community through the prophet Agabus and the believers in Antioch. They make provision for the Jewish brethren in view of a predicted famine. The Jews brought salvation to the Gentiles, and the Gentiles reciprocate by bringing material support to the Jews. Reconciliation is evident not just in word but also in deed.

The account is a simple narrative and is probably rooted in traditions emerging from Antioch (Fitzmyer 1998: 474, 480; Barrett 1994: 546 sees Luke "editing a tradition"; see also Barrett 1994: 559 for his comments on vv. 27–30). There is scholarly discussion as to whether this is the Paul-Barnabas visit of Gal. 2:1–10, a point to be discussed when the other option of Acts 15 is introduced (Marshall 1980: 200 does equate Gal. 2 with Acts 11).

B. Longenecker (2004) notes that this unit is a "chain-link interlock," an ancient rhetorical device that links separate units to each other. Other examples include how Luke links his Gospel to Acts, Acts 8:1–2, and 19:21–41. The accounts are linked by an overlap between separate units (Lucian, *How to Write History* 55; Quintilian, *Institutio oratoria* 9.4.29). The link in Acts 11 sets up the transition from Peter to Paul as the key figure of the book. Longenecker goes on to note that the section has been seen as either temporally contemporaneous or a flashback where the events of Acts 11 came after those of Acts 12. He discusses the flashback option in detail and notes that the dating scheme of Riesner (1998: 118–22, 134–36) and Hengel and Schwemer (1997: 243, 257) make sense out of the data. This puts Agrippa's persecution at AD 41–43 and the Antiochene collection at AD 42–45. Riesner's dates are generally a year earlier than those of Hengel and Schwemer (for these kinds of fluctuation in dating, see the introductory discussion on chronology). Longenecker suggests that when the section is read in this way, the indication is that leadership in Jerusalem changed with the death of James (not the Lord's brother) and Peter's departure. In the end, however, he hesitates to adopt the flashback option as a part of Luke's intention to make a conscious historical point, saying only that Luke placed the events as part of the same broad sweep of time. The "chain-link interlock" is interested only in a literary transition and not a specific temporal link. The literary point may be true, but the observations about the cogency of the chronology seen in such a light mean that Luke must be appreciated for the skilled and careful writer that he is.

Exegesis and Exposition

[19]Now those who were scattered because of the persecution that came about with respect to Stephen traveled as far as Phoenicia and Cyprus and Antioch, speaking the word to none except Jews alone. [20]But there were some of them, men of Cyprus and Cyrene, who on coming to Antioch were speaking also to the ⌜Greeks⌝, proclaiming the good news of the Lord Jesus. [21]And the hand of the Lord was with them, and a great number who believed turned to the Lord. [22]Word about such things came to the ears of the church in Jerusalem, and they sent Barnabas to go as far as Antioch, [23]who, coming and seeing the grace ⌐ ⌐ of God, was glad; and he exhorted them all to remain faithful to the Lord with steadfast purpose of heart, [24]for he was a good man, full of the Holy Spirit and of faith. And a large crowd was added to the Lord. [25]So Barnabas went to Tarsus to look for Saul; [26]and when he had found him, he brought him to Antioch. For an entire year they met with the church and taught a large crowd of people; and in Antioch the disciples were for the first time called Christians.

[27]Now in those days prophets came down from Jerusalem to Antioch. [28]And standing up, one of them named Agabus foretold by the Spirit that there would be great famine all over the world, which took place in the days of Claudius. [29]And some of the disciples, even as each one purposed, determined, each according to his ability, to send relief to the brothers who lived in Judea; [30]and they did so, sending it to the elders by the hand of Barnabas and Saul.

11:19–21   Luke looks at the ministry of those scattered in Acts 8:1b, 4 as a result of persecution, or more precisely "hardship" or "tribulation" (θλίψεως, *thlipseōs*; Acts 7:9–11; 11:19; 14:21–22; 20:22–23). Some of the scattered believers go only to Jews while others minister also to Greeks. And the word has now spread beyond Samaria to Phoenicia, Cyprus, and Antioch. These locales had important Jewish communities.

Phoenicia was the Mediterranean seacoast area of Syria, with Tyre and Sidon as its main cities. It was one hundred miles long and normally fifteen miles wide (Bruce 1990: 271; Le Cornu and Shulam 2003: 613 note that its widest point extends thirty miles). Cyprus, an island to the south of Asia Minor, was one hundred miles west of northwestern Syria (13:4–12). It was the original home of Barnabas (4:36) and had a large Jewish colony (1 Macc. 15:23; Philo, *Embassy* 36 §282; Josephus, *Ant.* 13.10.4 §§284–87; Fitzmyer 1998: 475).

Antioch is the second key church that Luke discusses. Its ministry becomes a point of focus for Acts. Antioch is on the Orontes River and located in what is now southeastern Turkey. It was the seat of Syria during the Seleucid reign and was the third largest city in the Greco-Roman world, with as high as six hundred thousand inhabitants (of which perhaps twenty-five thousand were Jews), but possibly a few hundred thousand less.[1] Founded in about 300 BC by Seleucus I Nicator and named in honor of his father, Antiochus, it was the capital of the Seleucid Empire. Only Alexandria and Rome were larger. Within five miles was the city of Daphne, known for worship of the gods Artemis, Apollos, and Astarte, and so the area was known for its moral laxity. Astarte worship included cultic prostitution. It was known for immorality (Juvenal, *Satires* 3.62; Polhill 1992: 269). Josephus calls it "the principal city of Syria" and notes that it had a famous street cutting through it (*Ant.* 16.5.3 §148; on their privileges, see *Ant.* 12.3.1 §119).

Antioch reflected a marriage of oriental and Hellenistic life with Greeks, Syrians, Phoenicians, Jews, Arabs, Persians, Egyptians, and Indians making up the population. The church with its practice and doctrine represented a distinctly countercultural way of life. Libanius (*Orations* 11.15) in AD 350 wrote that the city was "the abode of the gods." Zeus, Apollos, Poseidon, Adonis, and Tyche were worshiped there. It was a city full of religious activity and presence. So Antioch was a cosmopolitan city full of gods, where Judaism functioned as an exception in clinging to the one true God. In this context, the church in Antioch emerged and reached out into the larger world with its own mission. Antioch was also a commercial hub, tied as it was to a fertile plain. The river led to a port fifteen to eighteen miles away.

Hengel and Schwemer (1997: 270) fully treat the significant influence of the local god Tyche. They also discuss the history of the city and note among the Jews the absence of evidence of syncretism with Syrian gods (1997: 268–79). Most important, they also challenge the existence of any "pan-Antiochenism," as the history-of-religions school and many NT theologians today claim (1997: 279–86). For Hengel and Schwemer, the exaltation Christology that is central to orthodox Christianity has its roots in Jerusalem and is clearly in place by AD 36. This Christology is

1. See Josephus, *Ant.* 12.3.1 §§119–20; *J.W.* 3.2.4 §29; 7.3.3 §§43–45; 2 Macc. 4; Pliny the Elder, *Nat.* 6.122, states six hundred thousand in the first century; Eckey 2000: 254–55 thinks this number is too high and speaks of two hundred fifty thousand, and Hengel and Schwemer 1997: 186 suggest three hundred thousand; Le Cornu and Shulam 2003: 615 speak of one hundred thousand.

something the Christians in Jerusalem and Antioch share, and its roots are also found in Jewish thinking, not Hellenistic religion.

Cyprus was an island in the Mediterranean Sea with a sizable Jewish community (1 Macc. 15:23). Cyrene was the capital of the Roman province of Cyrenaica (= Libya) in North Africa. It was an intellectual center, home to a medical school and a classical academy (Le Cornu and Shulam 2003: 617). Josephus (*Ant.* 14.7.2 §§114–15) notes a significant Jewish presence there. Simon, Alexander, and Rufus were from there (Luke 23:26; Mark 15:21; Matt. 27:32), and it is included in the list of regions from which Jewish pilgrims had come for the Passover in Jerusalem (Acts 2:10).

All of these locales (Phoenicia, Cyprus, Antioch plus Cyrene) were heavily Hellenistic in character. It is possible that the churches there were rooted in earlier work. In Acts 15:41, Paul visits these churches at the start of his second journey. This may point to Paul's role earlier in these communities, as one of their founders or an important early leader, perhaps during his so-called silent years.[2]

There is scholarly discussion as to who the Hellenists/Greeks are. Are they pure Greeks or Hellenistic Jews? Following the work of Peter, it would seem that the term "Hellenist," if original, does not mean Hellenist Christians but possesses a largely racial, cultural sense, equal to "Gentiles." The reading "Greeks" says this more directly and is probably the best reading (see the additional note on 11:20). This is a mission independent of Jerusalem and shows the vibrancy of the church in Antioch. The mission meets with success because "the hand of the Lord was with them" (cf. Exod. 9:3; 1 Sam. 5:6; 6:9; 1 Chron. 28:19; Isa. 59:1; 66:2, 14; Ezek. 1:3; Luke 1:66; Acts 4:30; 13:11; Polhill 1992: 271). God's "hand" refers to his power. Enablement comes from God. Significant numbers respond. The Hellenists turn and believe; 11:21 is the only verse to use both verbs to summarize a response of faith. Thus faith entails turning to the Lord Jesus. In the Greek context, the title "Lord" makes sense as the key concept to associate with Jesus, for reasons of authority that 10:36 has made clear.

11:22–24 When the church in Jerusalem hears about the growth in Antioch, it sends Barnabas to investigate. The church's reception of the news about Antioch is expressed by an idiom that literally reads, "was heard . . . in the ears" (ἠκούσθη εἰς τὰ ὦτα, *ēkousthē eis ta hōta*; Culy and Parsons 2003: 226). The Jerusalem church has sent emissaries to Antioch before in 8:14 and 9:30. They harbor some concerns about Gentile expansion in 11:1–18 that are not completely resolved until Acts 15. Nevertheless, in each case, the expansion is welcomed. Here the emissary is not an apostle but one whom Jerusalem trusts.

---

2. See Schwemer 1998; M. Wilson 2003. Schwemer's burden is to suggest that Gal. 2:11–14 should be tied to Acts 18:21–23, as Antioch drops out of Acts at that point.

That the Jerusalem community is called the church (ἐκκλησία, *ekklēsia*) testifies to a growing self-identity as a community, as the term has not been used since Acts 9:31 and now becomes more frequent (11:26; 12:1, 5; 13:1; 14:23, 27; 15:3, 4, 22, 41; 16:5; 18:22; 20:17, 28; Barrett 1994: 552).

Barnabas observes the "grace of God" (τὴν χάριν τὴν τοῦ θεοῦ, *tēn charin tēn tou theou*) and rejoices (ἐχάρη, *echarē*; note the wordplay on "grace" and "rejoice"; grace of God: 13:43; 14:24–26; 20:24). He encourages the community to be steadfast in purpose of heart and remain in the Lord (τῇ προθέσει τῆς καρδίας προσμένειν τῷ κυρίῳ, *tē prothesei tēs kardias prosmenein tō kyriō*). This expression has two important parts. In the first part, steadfastness is the main idea, as the term προθέσει refers to having a purpose or resolve about something (BAGD 706 §2a; BDAG 869 §2a renders προθέσει as devotion because it is connected to the heart; Acts 11:23–24; 27:13; 2 Tim. 3:10). Acts 27:13 is a more everyday use of the term. The English versions render this with some variation ("with steadfast purpose" in RSV; "devoted hearts" in NET; "with all their hearts" in NIV). The second part is the idea of remaining or abiding in the Lord, a call to remain true to the Lord (BAGD 717 §1aα; BDAG 883 §1aβ; Matt. 15:32; Mark 8:1–3; Acts 11:23–24; 13:43; 18:18; 1 Tim. 1:3–4; 5:5–6). The NET combines all of this well in the phrase "to remain true to the Lord with devoted hearts."

Barnabas is commended as a messenger who is a "good man" full of the Spirit and faith. The full description is unique in the NT, but the expression "be full of the Spirit" appears in a few texts (Luke 4:1 [of Jesus]; Acts 7:55 [of Stephen]; see also 6:5). No one else is called "good" in Acts (Marshall 1980: 202; on the adjective "good," Acts 9:36; 23:1; Luke 23:50 [of Joseph of Arimathea]). Barnabas gave his goods to help the Jerusalem church in Acts 4:36–37 and supported Saul in 9:27. Now he encourages the new saints in Antioch (4:36 calls him the "son of encouragement"). The church needs people like him, since they often can do delicate jobs of mending and reconciliation. Luke's descriptions of Barnabas support the portrait of him as a person of maturity, promoting maturity in others and unity in the church. Since Barnabas was from Cyprus, he was ethnically suited for the task in this area (Le Cornu and Shulam 2003: 619).

In the meantime, the church is growing, as a sizeable crowd (ὄχλος ἱκανός, *ochlos hikanos*) is added to the Lord, making the development of disciples a major concern. It is not clear if the Father or Jesus is meant by "Lord," but verse 23 may well suggest a reference to Jesus as the one to whom they should remain faithful (see also vv. 20–21, where Jesus seems to be in view). Of course, to turn to the one is to embrace the other.

Now Barnabas seeks help to build up the church. He brings back Saul from Tarsus, where Saul went in Acts 9:30. So this resumes the Pauline **11:25–26** strand of Luke's story. Barnabas and Saul remain in Antioch for a year to teach this church. Antioch is a vibrant community in the Acts account (11:27; 13:1; 14:26; 15:22, 23, 30, 35; 18:22). This church will send Barnabas and Saul out for a more extensive outreach in Acts 13. Later the issue of the Gentiles will become a momentary bone of contention between Paul and Barnabas (Gal. 2:13), when Barnabas sides for a time with those who are concerned about Jewish scruples. But for now the relationship is smooth.

In Antioch the testimony to Jesus as the Christ is so strong that community members are called Christians (Χριστιανούς, *Christianous*) for the first time. Hengel and Schwemer (1997: 225–30) discuss the roots and legends associated with this name in the early centuries but defend its roots as coming from those outside the community. The suffixes *-ianos/-ianus* indicate Greek/Latin sources and are tied to the title Messiah, or Christ, in Greek. The importance of Jesus as the Christ early in the church's history is highlighted by the rise of this name. The term appears only three times in the NT (Acts 11:26; 26:28 [of Agrippa almost being persuaded by Paul to become a Christian]; 1 Pet. 4:16 [of suffering as a Christian]; Schneider, *EDNT* 3:477–78). The name is significant because it shows that it was the identification with Jesus as the Christ, as the Messiah, that people noticed. It also suggests that a separate identity is emerging for this group, which earlier was appealing to Jews only (Grundmann, *TDNT* 9:536–37). It may well be that the mixed ethnicity is now forcing the issue of self-identification alongside the believers' messianic declarations about Jesus. Fitzmyer (1998: 478) notes other early uses of the term in Josephus, *Ant.* 18.3.3 §64; Pliny the Younger, *Ep.* 10.96–97; Tacitus, *Ann.* 15.44; and Lucian, *Alexander the False Prophet* 25, 38. These texts show the spread of Christians to Rome and Bithynia in the first and second centuries, respectively, as well as the stir Christians caused in Judea by the time of Josephus.

The probably intransitive passive expression "be called" (χρηματίσαι, *chrēmatisai*) suggests that the name was given to believers by others. It may well have been derisive or used to mark them out as distinct (Fitzmyer 1998: 478 has a more complete discussion; Grundmann, *TDNT* 9:536–37; Schnabel 2004: 792–96). Polhill (1992: 273) notes that Ignatius is the first Christian to use the term extensively of other believers, and Barrett (1994: 557) cites other references in the second-century church (Ign. *Eph.* 11.2; *Rom.* 3.2; *Magn.* 10.3; Pol. *Phil.* 7.3). The term mixes the Greek for "Christ" with the Latin ending for a group, *-ianus*. It is formed in the same way as the reference to Herodians or Augustinians is (Barrett 1994: 556). Bruce (1990: 274) notes that sometimes "Christ" was misunderstood as the Greek term for "useful" (χρηστός, *chrēstos*; possibly Suetonius, *Claudius* 25.4; *NewDocs* 2 no. 102; 3 no. 98). Christians in Acts are also called saints (9:13), disciples (6:2), believers (4:32), the church (8:1), brothers (1:15), and Nazoreans (24:5). It appears that this Gentile mission in Antioch is the first major successful, extensive effort directed toward that group, and this is why Luke notes it. It sets the stage for even more extensive efforts by this community later.

The sending of Barnabas is not the only contact Jerusalem develops **11:27–30** with Antioch. Prophets also come and go.[3] This is the first note about prophets in Acts (13:1; 15:32; 21:10; 1 Cor. 12:28–29; 14:29, 32, 37; Eph. 2:20; 3:5; 4:11). Fitzmyer suggests that NT prophets were somewhat distinct from the OT term and served more as "inspired or gifted preachers," a real possibility in a few texts, given its usage in the NT, but this is not certain. On occasion, they could read the hearts of others as well (1 Cor. 14:24–25; Did. 11.7–12).

A particularly significant incident concerns Agabus, who helps relieve the pressure of a famine by leading the church in Antioch to provide aid to those in Jerusalem. Agabus shows another characteristic of a prophet: he is able to predict what is coming, the foretelling often associated with prophetic activity such as that in the OT. A NT prophet appears to have these various abilities, which place him in a category separate from a mere preacher or proclaimer of the gospel. Such prophets seem to have moved from church to church, if the Didache is any indicator of their ministry style. The itinerant nature of the prophets described in Acts is consistent with the Didache.

Agabus predicts that an extensive famine will affect the empire, which is probably what the reference to the whole world in the verse implies. Agabus indicates (ἐσήμανεν, *esēmanen*) through the Spirit that this famine will take place (other occurrences of the verb σημαίνω [*sēmainō*, indicate, signify] in the NT: John 12:33; 18:32; 21:19; Acts 11:28; 25:27; Rev. 1:1–2; Rengstorf, *TDNT* 7:264). The verb points to the giving of oracles (Barrett 1994: 562–63; Josephus, *Ant.* 6.4.1 §50; 8.15.4 §409).

This famine came during the days of Claudius, who was Caesar of Rome from AD 41 to 54 and the nephew of Tiberius Caesar. Claudius reluctantly succeeded another Tiberian nephew, Gaius, upon his murder. At the time of Gaius's murder, Claudius hid behind a curtain, fearing his own demise. He was an able administrator but had to deal with a series of natural disasters in his empire. So Agabus's prediction of the famine points to one of the prominent events in his reign.

Famine hit in the first, second, fourth, ninth, and eleventh years of Claudius's reign.[4] One inscription from Asia Minor (*CIG* 3973.5–6) speaks

3. Hengel and Schwemer 1997: 239 argue that multiple visits have been combined into one by Luke, but the rationale for this opinion is not clear beyond some question expressed about the collection and the silence regarding it in Gal. 2:1. Josephus (*J.W.* 2.8.12 §159) mentions prophets at Qumran who foretold and were seldom wrong.

4. See Suetonius, *Claudius* 18.2; Tacitus, *Ann.* 12.43; Dio Cassius, *Rom. Hist.* 40.11; Bruce 1990: 276 has a full list of Greco-Roman discussions. Riesner 1998: 127–36 argues that local famines are in view.

of a famine that gripped the whole world. Fitzmyer (1998: 481–82) provides extensive discussion of how widespread these famines were. They struck Egypt (at the beginning of Claudius's rule), Greece (eighth to ninth years), and Rome (ninth to eleventh years) as well as Judea. We have notes about this famine concerning its presence in AD 40–41 and 46–47 (Talbert 1997: 117; Josephus, *Ant.* 3.15.3 §§320–21; 20.2.5 §§51–53; 20.5.2 §101). This was a sporadic, empirewide famine, but the final Josephus reference speaks of a famine in Judea in AD 44–48 (Riesner 1998: 132, 135, placing this prediction in AD 39–42).

The prediction of the famine precedes the death of Herod in Acts 12, which was some years earlier than the later Judean famine. If this famine tied especially to Judea is intended, as is quite possible, then plenty of warning was provided.

In Acts 21:10–11 Agabus will return with another prediction, concerning Paul's arrest. Some scholars take the name Agabus as coming from the Greek form of the names Hagab and Hagaba (Ezra 2:46; Neh. 7:48; Bruce 1990: 275), but Fitzmyer (1998: 481) prefers a parallel to a woman's name from Syria meaning "love" or "lover."

Significantly, the Gentile church moves to help its Judean and predominantly Jewish brethren. Literally the phrase is "to send service," as from διακονία (*diakonia*) comes our term "deacon," one who serves. Here it means something like sending "support" or "aid" (BAGD 184 §4; BDAG 230 §4; Acts 6:1 of the aid to widows; 12:25). Each person sets apart what seems appropriate, a point parallel to 2 Cor. 9:7 (also 1 Cor. 16:1–4). Barrett (1994: 565) notes that the community is not pooling its resources as Jerusalem had but now seems to live with each person conducting his or her own business. The aid is delivered to Jerusalem, about 310 miles away, and then Saul and Barnabas return to Antioch.

They bring the aid to the elders at Jerusalem, the first mention of such a group in the church community in Acts. Of its sixty-six NT occurrences, the term πρεσβύτερος (*presbyteros*, elder) appears eighteen times in this book.[5] These Jerusalem elders appear to function alongside the apostles there and take care of administrative and daily matters (Marshall 1980: 204). A structure including elders parallels Judaism and thus need not be a late development in the church (Hengel and Schwemer 1997: 254–55, who see their main role as supervising membership).

The famine relief indicates a complete reconciliation as needs are met across geographical and ethnic boundaries. The relief portrays the oneness and caring of the community, as did Acts 4 in Jerusalem, where goods were shared. Racial harmony and caring are possible. The church is one despite being in different locales. Whether this is the visit

---

5. Acts 2:17; 4:5, 8, 23; 6:12; 11:30; 14:23; 15:2, 4, 6, 22–23 [2x]; 16:4; 20:17; 21:18; 23:14; 24:1; 25:15. Other, earlier uses refer to the mature leaders of a Jewish group, a usage that reappears in Acts 23–25, or to older people, as in 2:17.

Gal. 2:1–10 also mentions awaits the discussion below of Acts 15, but Marshall (1980: 205) equates this relief visit with that text, as do Bruce (1990: 278) and Schnabel (2004: 987–92).

In sum, we see the emergence of another key community, engaged in mission, instruction, discipleship, and caring for other communities in need. Word and deed again are side by side. The summary could hardly do a better job of showing a vibrant church at work, performing the essential tasks of a community so visibly that outsiders note who its members are. As always, it is responsiveness to divine direction and vision that leads to this effective ministry.

An interesting feature is that these laborers are unnamed. As Fernando (1998: 353) says, "Some of the most significant work for the kingdom has been done by unknown witnesses who are obedient to Christ right where they are and where they do not attract much attention." He calls them "unnamed pioneers" (1998: 351), a very apt description, and Stott (1990: 201) speaks of "daring spirits." The key to any effective community is that it has vibrant and exemplary people throughout.

We also see Barnabas, the encourager, at his best. He encourages the grace of God to be manifest in himself and others. He knows that this will require perseverance and solid character as well as a willingness to go the extra mile for others, as he does with Saul. Indeed, character is more important in a believer than anything else, including "getting results" (Fernando 1998: 355–57). Character and encouragement also have the capacity to bring others on board and let them serve because there is no jealousy, again pictured by how Barnabas works with Saul. In this it is Barnabas's humility that stands out (Stott 1990: 204).

A final note concerns how one church came to the aid of another here. Today many churches are interested only in their own ministry or in using their facilities and resources only for their own efforts. It is sad to see large-budget churches that give very little to missions or do very little for other believing communities in need in their own area when they easily could. We must be careful that the desired pursuit of excellence in ministry to our own does not leave us neglecting others whom we could help with a little more self-sacrifice. Other churches, reflecting the character of this Acts 11 community, are engaged in actively helping others as they are able, as part of the perspective of their own ministry. In a world where everyone looks out for number one, this kind of selflessness is itself a great testimony to the power and witness of the gospel to change people.

Additional Notes

11:20. NA[27] reads Ἑλληνιστάς (*Hellēnistas*), or Hellenists, with B, D[2], E, Ψ, 33, 81, 614, 1739, and Byz. This could refer to Greek-speaking Jews, but such a ministry would hardly be noted in contrast to Jews only, so if this is original, it should mean Greeks. Barrett (1994: 551) sees this reading as the original and more difficult reading. Ἕλληνας (*Hellēnas*), or Greeks, is a key variant that refers to ministry to Gentiles. It is supported by $\mathfrak{P}^{74}$, $\aleph^2$, A, D*, and 1518. This is likely to be the original reading (Fitzmyer 1998: 476; Bruce 1990: 272).

11:23. The inclusion of the extra article τήν between "grace" and "of God" is supported by $\aleph$, A, and B. It is more grammatically correct, but its absence could also be original, as the omission is well attested ($\mathfrak{P}^{74}$, D, E, Ψ, and Byz).

D. Persecution in Jerusalem (12:1–23)

The final major discussion of the church in Jerusalem has three parts: (1) the martyrdom of James, brother of John, along with the arrest of Peter (12:1–5); (2) Peter's miraculous delivery from prison (12:6–19); and (3) Herod's arrogance and judgment (12:20–23). The delivery from prison is told vividly in two parts: the escape (vv. 6–11) and then the surprising arrival at the home of John Mark's mother (vv. 12–19a). As the persecution intensifies in Jerusalem, God's protection is still at work. Acts 12:11 gives the assurance that the passage intends: the Lord has rescued Peter. This act, in turn, seems rooted in the church's earnest prayer, noted in verse 5. On the other hand, the result for one who does not give God the glory is a terrifying judgment, as worms in verse 23 consume Herod. So contrast drives the unit. Herod found "himself fighting against God and suffered the consequences" (so Polhill 1992: 276).

The character of the Jerusalem church emerges from this account (Witherington 1998: 383). It obviously operates on the fringe of Judaism at this time and is still being rejected by the Jewish authorities. Some converts still have social means and status, as evidenced by the home of John Mark's mother, which is large enough for meetings and has servants. Whatever the result of the pooling of resources in Acts 4, the church still has some members who have property and financial means. The church seems to have maintained multiple meeting places in Jerusalem, since differing locations for gatherings are noted (compare 12:12 with v. 17). The account also serves as a "recapitulation" that lets the story in Jerusalem catch up with the story elsewhere and explains why Peter no longer heads the church in Jerusalem, since the persecution and arrest drive him away (Hengel and Schwemer 1997: 245–46).

The account is a combination of narrative and miracle. Other divine rescues appear in 5:18–20; 16:23–29; and chapter 27. The divine-rescue form abounds also in Greco-Roman accounts.[1] Johnson notes the historical core of this account with the parallel in Josephus of Herod's gruesome death in *Ant.* 19.8.2 §§343–52. Barrett (1994: 580) discusses a difference with many of the form parallels, which contain a self-release. Such a self-release does not occur with Peter, since an angel

---

1. See Johnson 1992: 217; Lucian, *Toxaris* 28–33; Achilles Tatius, *Leuc. Cleit.* 3.9–11; Ovid, *Metam.* 3.690–700; Artapanus, *On the Jews*, frg. 3; Euripides, *Bacchanals* 346–57, 434–50, 510–643.

is responsible for the liberation. This account may well be rooted in Judean sources.

Fitzmyer (1998: 486) notes that no effort is made to reconstitute the Twelve after James's death, a point with implications about the view of a permanent role for the Twelve. In other words, Judas was replaced as the twelfth member, and then no replacement was made after James's death here, probably on the belief that the Twelve would be reestablished in the resurrection.

Witherington (1998: 376–81) speaks of the last use of Luke's Petrine source here and challenges Pervo's (1987) claim that this text is evidence that Acts is a classical romance. The story may be included either to suggest how James, the brother of the Lord, came to a key position in Jerusalem as outside pressure mounted on Peter, or to show how Peter's discipleship paralleled that of Jesus and would parallel that of Paul. Marshall (1980: 206–7) also affirms its core historicity.

Johnson (1992: 21) mentions numerous parallels to Jesus's suffering and that of Stephen. This is the first appearance in Acts of James, brother of the Lord. Barrett (1994: 569) suggests that the detail about persecution and meeting suffering directly might be Luke's point in presenting this text. Fitzmyer (1998: 486) sees a parallel between the account of Herod's death in this text and the lament for the king of Tyre in Ezek. 28:17–20. Witherington (1998: 383) adds that this persecution in Jerusalem might explain why missionary activity became focused in Antioch as Jerusalem became even more dangerous. None of these choices rules out the others as possibilities, for this passage may well be doing several things at the same time. At any rate, the account differs from the first prison escape in that the concern now is with Peter and the growing distance between the church and Judaism as the persecution continues (Pesch 1986a: 369). The church is giving witness at any cost and is establishing its identity while God is protecting it, whether in death leading to glory (Stephen) or in miraculous escape (Peter).

Exegesis and Exposition

[1]About that time Herod the king laid violent hands on some from the church. [2]He killed James, the brother of John, by the sword. [3]Seeing that it pleased the Jews, he proceeded to arrest Peter also. (It was during the days of Unleavened Bread.) [4]And having seized him, Herod put him in prison and delivered him to four squads of soldiers to guard him, intending after the Passover to bring him out to the people. [5]So Peter was being kept in prison; but earnest prayer for him was coming to God by the church.

[6]The very night when Herod was about to bring him out, Peter was sleeping between two soldiers, bound with two chains, and sentries before the door

were guarding the prison; ⁷and behold, an angel of the Lord stood by, and a light lit up the cell; and striking Peter on the side, he woke him, saying, "Get up quickly." And the chains fell off his hands. ⁸And the angel said to him, "Dress yourself and put on your sandals." And he did so. And the angel said to him, "Wrap your mantle and follow me." ⁹And Peter went out and was following him; he did not know that what was done by the angel was real, but he was thinking that he was seeing a vision. ¹⁰Having passed the first and second guards, they came to the iron gate leading into the city. It opened to them automatically, and going out ⌜ ⌝, they passed on through one street; and immediately the angel left him. ¹¹And Peter came to himself and said, "Now I am sure that the Lord has sent his angel and delivered me from the hand of Herod and all that the Jewish people were expecting."

¹²Realizing this, he went to the house of Mary, the mother of John, whose name was Mark, where many were gathered together and praying. ¹³And as he was knocking at the door of the gateway, a maid named Rhoda came to answer. ¹⁴Recognizing Peter's voice, in her joy she did not open the gate but, running in, announced that Peter was standing at the gate. ¹⁵They said to her, "You are mad." But she was insisting that this was so. But they were saying, "It is his angel." ¹⁶But Peter remained knocking; and opening the gate, they saw him and were amazed. ¹⁷But motioning to them with his hand to be silent, he described to them how the Lord had brought him out of the prison. And he said, "Go tell these things to James and to the brothers." Then he departed and went to another locale.

¹⁸Now when day came, there was no small disturbance among the soldiers over what had come about with Peter. ¹⁹And seeking him but not finding him, Herod examined the sentries and ordered that they should be led away ⌜(for execution)⌝. Then he went down from Judea into Caesarea and remained there.

²⁰Now Herod was angry with the people of Tyre and Sidon, and they came to him as a group, and having persuaded Blastus, the king's chamberlain, they asked for peace because their land was fed by the king. ²¹On an appointed day, Herod, putting on his royal robes and taking his seat upon the throne, made a speech to them. ²²And the people were shouting, "The voice of a god, and not a man." ²³Immediately an angel of the Lord struck him down because he did not give God the glory; and being eaten by worms, he died.

Persecution becomes more intense for the Jerusalem church during the reign of Herod Agrippa I (ca. 9 BC–AD 44), grandson of Herod the Great. This ruler had been educated and raised in Rome. He reigned over Judea for several years. In AD 37 Caligula had allocated to him the territory that had been held by Philip and Lysanius (Luke 3:1). He did not, however, assume control over the entire old empire of Herod the Great until AD 41 because he had to compete with Herod Antipas for the authority. Full affirmation of his rule came from Caligula and

12:1–2

in AD 41 was expanded to its maximum extent under Claudius, who had been a classmate of his. He ruled until AD 44. Herod Agrippa was imprisoned at one time by Tiberius, but he had better relations with Rome's other Caesars and was very close to the Pharisees (Josephus, *Ant.* 18.5.3 §126; 18.6.1–5 §§143–69; 18.6.6–7 §§179–204; 18.6.10–18.8.8 §§228–301; 19.4.1 §§236–44; 19.4.5 §265; 19.5.1 §§274–77; 19.5.3 §288; 19.6.1–19.9.1 §§292–354; *m. Soṭah* 7.8). He was especially pious, at least when he was in Jerusalem (*Ant.* 19.6.1 §293; 19.7.3 §331). Polhill (1992: 278) describes his Roman lifestyle when he was in Rome. Eckey (2000: 266–67) has a nice summary of his career. Given that Herod was in Rome in AD 41 and died before Passover in 44, the events described in Acts 11 should be dated to either 42 or 43.

Agrippa I was quite popular with the Jews, as this excerpt from Josephus, *Ant.* 19.7.3 §§328–31 shows:

> Now, this king was by nature very beneficent, and liberal in his gifts, and very ambitious to oblige people with such large donations; and he made himself very illustrious by the many chargeable [expensive] presents he made them. He took delight in giving, and rejoiced in living with good reputation. He was not at all like that Herod who reigned before him; for that Herod was ill-natured, and severe in his punishments, and had no mercy on them that he hated; and everyone perceived that he was more friendly to the Greeks than to the Jews; for he adorned foreign cities with large presents in money; with building them baths and theatres besides: nay, in some of those places, he erected temples, and porticoes in others; but he did not vouchsafe to raise one of the least edifices in any Jewish city, or make them any donation that was worth mentioning. But Agrippa's temper was mild, and equally liberal to all men. He was humane to foreigners, and made them sensible of his liberality. He was in like manner rather of a gentle and compassionate temper. Accordingly, he loved to live continually at Jerusalem, and was exactly careful in the observance of the laws of his country. He therefore kept himself entirely pure: nor did any day pass over his head without its appointed sacrifice. (Whiston 1987: 522)

His popularity among the Jews may well explain his hostility to the new movement that the Jewish leadership so opposed, especially as he sought to stay in the good graces of the ruling Sadducean party (Hengel and Schwemer 1997: 247–50). He died suddenly in early AD 44.

At some point in this reign, he decides to go after the church more aggressively and executes James, the brother of John. The text speaks of his use of violent hands (τὰς χεῖρας κακῶσαι, *tas cheiras kakōsai*; for a similar expression, see 1 Esd. 9:20). The verb κακόω (*kakoō*) means "do evil" and appears six times in the NT, all but one of them in Acts (7:6–7, 19; 12:1; 14:2; 18:10; 1 Pet. 3:13). The infinitive, which syntactically points to purpose, is an epexegetical infinitive: he lays violent hands on them in order to do evil (Culy and Parsons 2003: 231).

The next verse (v. 2) describes the murder of James (not the Lord's brother but John's brother) by the sword (μαχαίρῃ, *machairē*; a dative of instrument, Wallace 1996: 163). Acts 16:27 has the only other use of this term in Acts. The "laying on of hands" appears here and there in Acts for arrests or hostile action (4:3; 5:18; 21:27; Bruce 1990: 279). It is clear that this evil is particularly violent. James, son of Zebedee, is probably beheaded as John the Baptist was, although, if some Jewish sensibilities are maintained, he may have been run through with a sword (Deut. 13:15 [13:16 LXX]; 1 Sam. 22:18–19; 2 Sam. 1:13, 15; Jer. 26:23; beheading as part of execution, 1 Sam. 17:46, 51; 2 Kings 10:6–8). On the other hand, *m. Sanh.* 7.3 allows beheading, among the most shameful of deaths, in the Roman manner, and so this is the likely form of execution. Indeed, *m. Sanh.* 9.1 suggests that an apostate can be beheaded, and 10.4 says that such have no share in the world to come (Johnson 1992: 211). It is possible that this is seen as a political execution as well (Barrett 1994: 574–75). Such an act would be done with Roman understanding and support.

James is the first apostle to suffer martyrdom. He is the second martyr in Acts, after Stephen (Dormeyer and Galindo 2003: 190). There is no reason given for the act other than that it pleased the Jews. Hengel and Schwemer (1997: 247) call the execution a use of the royal *ius gladii* ("the right of the sword" given to a Roman governor). The execution is dealt with in a legal context and Roman manner to show Herod Agrippa's own authority (also Riesner 1998: 119n75, who places this event in either AD 41 or 42). Mark 10:39 predicts the possibility of death for the sons of Zebedee (on this event in church tradition, see Eusebius, *Eccl. Hist.* 2.9.2–3; John, his brother, was not martyred, in all likelihood, Bruce 1990: 280).

12:3–5 Ingratiating himself to the Jews, by which is surely meant the Jewish leadership, Herod Agrippa arrests Peter during the Feast of Unleavened Bread (14 to 21 Nisan) and keeps him under guard (ἐτηρεῖτο, *etēreito*; note the imperfect tense, stressing the ongoing duration of the arrest). The timing is indicated in a parenthesis beginning with ἦσαν δέ (*ēsan de*; BDF §447.7, §465; NET). It is the very same season of the year during which Jesus was executed (Luke 22:1). So the note sets an ominous tone. This is the first time in Acts that the term "Jews" is used negatively (Jervell 1998: 332). The leadership's hardening and persistent use of violent tactics is creating distance between Israel and those calling the nation to respond to the promised Messiah.

Four squads of soldiers guard Peter. Such custody is described in various texts (Philo, *Flaccus* 13 §111; Vegetius, *On Military Affairs* 3.8; Philostratus, *Life Apoll.* 7.31; Fitzmyer 1998: 487). In a procedure like that in Luke 23:1–5, the plan probably is to bring Peter before the people after the holiday to face judgment and be executed (Bruce 1990: 282 cites

MM 32 and *SIG* 366.24 as showing that the phrase "to bring up" means to come for sentencing in such a context). This squad of four soldiers (BAGD 813; BDAG 1001) consists of sixteen soldiers in total, as a squad was a group of four. Their watch would change every three hours in the night to guarantee they were alert (Josephus, *Ant.* 18.6.7 §196). They are guarding Peter until Passover is completed, as an execution during this time normally would have offended the Jews. If he is held at the same locale as Paul later in Acts 21:34–23:30, then he is at the Antonia at the northwest edge of the temple complex, although Herod's palace near the Jaffa Gate (= Joppa of OT) is also possible (Barrett 1994: 577). Acts 12:6 tells us that two are chained to Peter and two act as sentries. Witherington (1998: 385) suggests that this points to some Roman involvement as well, since this practice is Roman (Haenchen 1987: 382), so that the Romans also are a part of this entire process. But these guards are not able to see or stop the escape the angel facilitates in 12:7–11.

While he is held, the church is praying for him earnestly (ἐκτενῶς, *ektenōs*; BAGD 245; BDAG 310). This is the only use of this term in Acts, but variations appear in Luke 22:44 (Jesus at Gethsemane) and Acts 26:7 (Schneider 1982: 103n21). Prayer is to be seen as a catalyst for the escape and is expressed with an imperfect (ἦν . . . γινομένη, *ēn . . . ginomenē*) to show its ongoing character. Marshall notes that the prayer would also have sought God's will in all of this (Luke 22:42). Acts 12:14–15 shows they are not anticipating an escape, and so the prayer must be for God's protection and strength in some other way, either in a positive verdict or in some type of lesser punishment.

12:6–10   At the last moment, the night before Peter is to appear for judgment, God acts with the help of an angel from the Lord (see vv. 7–11, esp. v. 11; Gen. 16:7; Acts 8:26). Stott (1990: 209) points out that some commentators who accept the event but find the miracle difficult argue that this was some type of inside job, with the "angel" being a human who opposed what was taking place (Hengel and Schwemer 1997: 251–52 speak of "legendary" elements in the account). Stott goes on to observe, however, that the description of the angel from the Lord almost certainly looks at a supernatural deliverance for which the Lord is ultimately responsible (v. 17). Angels are quite active in Acts, part of the theme of God's activity in the book (directing in 8:26; 10:3–6; helping in 5:19–20; 12:7–10; 27:23; agents of judgment in 12:23; Fernando 1998: 366).

Peter is asleep, amazing in itself given what the next day may bring. He is between two soldiers to whom he is chained, and the other two sentries guard the door. There would be one soldier chained to each arm (Seneca, *Moral Ep.* 5.7; Schneider 1982: 104n28). Herod has done a great deal to make sure that Peter is secure and well guarded. Is he aware of a previous escape, and/or does this represent his special carefulness with a key leader?

An angel appears in a bright light, stands over (aorist tense) Peter, wakes him up, and instructs him in steps to get up, dress, put on his sandals, wrap himself in his cloak, and follow him, all of which Peter does. The contrast between the aorist imperative for "putting on" the cloak (περιβαλοῦ, *peribalou*) and the present imperative (ἀκολούθει, *akolouthei*) for "follow" is a good example of the difference in the tenses: "Put on your cloak, and keep following me" (Moulton and Turner 1963: 77). Dressing would include putting on his belt. The mention of light points to a heavenly visit (Luke 2:9; Acts 9:3; 22:11). The verb for "strike" (πατάσσω, *patassō*, v. 7) is usually negative, meaning "smite," as in the approaching scene containing Herod's death in verse 23, but here it bears the lighter meaning "strike hard" (Johnson 1992: 212; Exod. 2:12; Judg. 1:5; Pss. 3:8 [3:7 Eng.]; 77:66 [78:66 Eng.]; Matt. 26:31, 51; Mark 14:27; Luke 22:49–50; Acts 7:24; 12:7, 23; Rev. 11:6; 19:15–16).

The text is clear that Peter thinks he is having a vision, not a "real" or "true" (ἀληθές, *alēthes*) experience (BAGD 36–37 §3; BDAG 43 §3). Nor is he expecting to escape. This is one of three prison rescues in Acts (5:18–20; 16:23–29). The two imperfect-tense verbs in verse 9 continue the sense of vivid detail and ongoing action: he was following the angel and supposing that he was experiencing a vision. The account seems to assume that the guards are asleep, as they pass the first two guards, who are not chained to Peter (Haenchen 1987: 384n3; the term for "first," πρῶτος, *prōtos*, is used as πρότερος, *proteros*, would be; BDF §62). Then it seems that the various gates or doors open automatically, something explicitly said of the third gate they pass in verse 10 (Polhill 1992: 281).[2] With the gate to the city opened, they are out on the street. Having Peter free, the angel departs.

Peter's commentary on the event is also the scene's point. Peter recognizes that the rescue is the Lord's protection of him from Herod and all the expectations of the Jewish people. The phrase πάσης τῆς προσδοκίας τοῦ λαοῦ τῶν Ἰουδαίων (*pasēs tēs prosdokias tou laou tōn Ioudaiōn*) has the term "Jews" functioning as a subjective genitive, and προσδοκίας refers to the full expectation Jews have of Herod (Moulton and Turner 1963: 200; Wallace 1996: 114). The apostle is confident that they want him dead, and the rescue has prevented that result. The term for "rescue" (ἐξαιρέω, *exaireō*) also appears in Acts 7:10, 34; 23:27; and 26:17. Both political and religious leaders are singled out as Peter's opponents. The idea recalls Exod. 18:1–4 (Moses's deliverance by God); Dan. 3:28; and

12:11

---

2. See Josephus, *J.W.* 6.5.3 §293 (not of a prison escape but of an evil portent to the Jews); Euripides, *Bacchanals* 443–48 (Bacchus frees himself); Ovid, *Metam.* 3.696–700 (an escape also involves a self-escape and the handcuffs falling away). Barrett 1994: 581 calls the parallels superficial, as self-escape is not the same; Schneider 1982: 105n39; Eckey 2000: 270.

Luke 22:47–54. Peter has recognized that many Jewish people are against him. They are opposed to him and what he represents.

12:12–15 Peter heads for Mary's house.[3] She is the mother of John Mark and likely is a widow, as her husband is not noted. She is obviously a woman of some means if the church can gather in her home. This is yet another confirmation that in Acts 4 the giving over of material goods was voluntary and did not involve every single possession. The community is praying, not knowing that God has already answered their prayers. Peter seems to know the location where the church is meeting, suggesting that this is a house church locale. Not the entire Jerusalem church is present, however, as James and other brethren are at another location, according to verse 17. John Mark appears several times more in Acts (12:25; 13:5, 13; 15:37, 39; Col. 4:10; 2 Tim. 4:11; Philem. 24; 1 Pet. 5:13; Eusebius, *Eccl. Hist.* 2.15.1–2.16.2; 3.39.14–16; 5.8.3; 6.14.6).

Peter knocks at the gate of the house and is heard by a maid (παιδίσκη, *paidiskē*) named Rhoda (Acts 16:16 is the only other use of the term for "maid" in Acts; Luke 12:45; 22:56). The fact that a slave girl would answer the door is one of those little details that points to authenticity (Hengel and Schwemer 1997: 447n1113). Her name is a common one and means "rosebud" or "little Rose" (Haenchen 1987: 385).

Rhoda recognizes his voice and, full of joy (ἀπὸ τῆς χαρᾶς, *apo tēs charas*), forgets to let him in. Luke 24:41 is another case where joy overwhelms, a theme that occurs occasionally in Greco-Roman literature (Johnson 1992: 213; Longus, *Daphne and Chloe* 2.30; Achilles Tatius, *Leuc. Cleit.* 1.3; 2.23). Rather, she runs to announce his presence, an announcement that those inside reject as the hope of a girl gone crazy (μαίνῃ, *mainē*, you are mad). Festus will call Paul mad at his examination, using this term (Acts 26:25; John 10:20; 1 Cor. 14:23; Schneider 1982: 106n57). In their view, Rhoda is not rational, a response similar to that given the announcement of Jesus's resurrection (Luke 24:10–11) where another report by women is rejected. Rhoda, however, is insistent (note the imperfect διϊσχυρίζετο, *diischyrizeto*; Luke 22:59 also contains the expression). Dormeyer and Galindo (2003: 189) point out the comedy of the scene. Peter is left behind at the door while everyone tries to sort things out. The varied reactions and emotions to such a surprising event are quite normal.

Some take Rhoda's announcement more seriously and suggest another alternative: that "his angel" is present. Tobit 5:4–16 records an angelic visit by Raphael to heal a blind man but lacks the idea of his being a particular person's angel. Tobit 5:22 has a specific angel accompany a person (on angels, Gen. 48:16; Ps. 91:11; Dan. 3:28; 6:22; Matt. 18:10; Heb. 1:14; Rev. 2–3 has an angel associated with a church). The later

---

3. In the sixth century, this locale became linked to the events of the Last Supper and an anointing by the Spirit (Jervell 1998: 334n329).

rabbinic text Gen. Rabbah 78 [50a] on Gen. 33:10 has a specific personal angel whose look matches that of the person he protects (Str-B 2:707–8; *L.A.B.* 59.4; T. Jac. 1.10; in early Christian literature, Herm. *Mand.* 6.2.2; Johnson 1992: 213). It may be that this alternative is seen as indicating that, in the view of some, Peter is already dead and his angel is now present, having appeared after his death (Polhill 1992: 282n155). Polhill's comment, however, does not cite evidence for such a view. The suggestion seems to assume that they simply refuse to accept the possibility that Peter has escaped. Those inside the room do seem to have rejected the idea that God would spare Peter with a miraculous escape. They have been praying for some other outcome (see v. 5). Thus the idea of a communication from beyond becomes an option, although it is not clear that they think Peter is already dead. Again God works beyond their expectation, just as Peter thought he was only experiencing a vision.

12:16–17 In another dramatic detail, Peter keeps knocking (ἐπέμενεν κρούων, *epemenen krouōn*), and finally the door is opened for him. The reference to knocking is a good example of a complementary participle (Wallace 1996: 646). While Rhoda went to tell the gathered believers who was at the door, Peter simply wanted in. When the group realizes it is Peter, they are completely amazed (ἐξέστησαν, *exestēsan*). This word for "amaze" is frequent in descriptions of surprising events in Acts (2:7, 12; 8:9, 11, 13; 9:21; 10:45; 12:16). Peter enters, motions them together, and asks for silence, no doubt because of the reaction his arrival has caused. He reports to them (διηγήσατο, *diēgēsato*) how the Lord accomplished the rescue. This verb is used eight times in the NT, with five in Luke-Acts (Mark 5:16; 9:9; Luke 8:39; 9:10; Acts 8:33; 9:27; 12:17; Heb. 11:32). An angel led him out, but the Lord is responsible (ὁ κύριος αὐτὸν ἐξήγαγεν, *ho kyrios auton exēgagen*). Peter instructs them to tell James and other brethren in the area before he departs to another place. This locale is not given. Peter moves out of Jerusalem to avoid danger.

Where Peter goes is debated by scholars; Rome and Antioch are among the possibilities (Polhill 1992: 283). Peter does not reappear until Acts 15, when he is back in Jerusalem. This makes Rome unlikely, but the lack of reference to Antioch also argues against his staying there for any significant time, although Gal. 2:14 lets us know that he was there at least briefly. Corinth is also an option (1 Cor. 1:12; 9:5). In short, where he went is not clear, and an itinerant ministry is quite likely (Barrett 1994: 587; Fitzmyer 1998: 489).

Here also is the first important mention of James, the Lord's brother (Acts 1:14; 15:13; 21:18; also Mark 6:3; Matt. 13:55; Gal. 1:19; 2:9 ["pillar of the church" with Peter and John]; 2:12–13; 1 Cor. 15:7). He would be martyred in AD 62, slain by Annas II in an act that made other Jews nervous that the high priest had overstepped his authority by executing someone when only Rome had that authority. The act cost Annas II the office of high priest, since Rome removed him as a result (Josephus, *Ant.* 20.9.1 §§197–203). Eusebius (*Eccl. Hist.* 2.23.11–18; 2.23.1) calls James a bishop of Jerusalem, but this title is used there anachronistically. It is clear, however, that by the time of Acts 12, James is a major figure in the Jerusalem church.

12:18–19   The narrative has been quite vivid with the comical details of Rhoda's response, leaving Peter stranded at the gate of the home. It now turns to a scene that has the modern feel of "meanwhile back at the ranch" in a television show.

The fact that Peter is missing causes no small stir (τάραχος οὐκ ὀλίγος, *tarachos ouk oligos*) among the soldiers as they seek to figure out how he escaped and who is responsible. Acts 19:23 is the only other occurrence of τάραχος in the NT, where it refers to a civil disturbance, the term's more common use. In Acts 5, however, a scene like this points to mental agitation, and so the scene suggests being frantic (BAGD 805; BDAG 991; Acts 5 uses διηπόρουν [*diēporoun*], which means to be at a loss about something). The commotion in 12:18–19 is like 5:21–26. The reference to "no small" stir is litotes, a rhetorical device Luke favors but reserves for the latter parts of Acts (14:28; 15:2; 17:4, 12, 19:23–24).

Herod inquires or cross-examines (ἀνακρίνας, *anakrinas*) the guarding soldiers as to the circumstances and their culpability. Apparently, they were asleep (Pesch 1986a: 366) or are suspected of aiding in the escape (Williams 1990: 215). Such an examination of guards could include torture (Johnson 1992: 214; Chariton of Aphrodisias, *Chaer.* 5.1–2; Pliny the Younger, *Ep.* 10.96.8). The guards are "led away" (ἀπαχθῆναι, *apachthēnai*). In this context this verb is a euphemism for being led away to execution (BAGD 79 §2c; BDAG 95 §2c). This was frequently the cost for letting an important prisoner get away (the later Code of Justinian 9.4.4 formalized this approach; also noted in Chariton, *Chaer.* 3.4.18). Acts 16:27 and 27:42 show that guards would kill prisoners to prevent their own lives from being lost. Sometimes they would kill themselves to escape the execution. Herod then returns to his home in Caesarea on the coast, the region's administrative hub. The scene ends with the apostle free and the ruler punishing those he thinks are at fault.

12:20–23   The scene now turns to consider the fate of this ruler who has tried to eliminate Peter. Now Herod is caught in a dispute with Tyre and Sidon over the provision of food. These two Phoenician cities need food and commerce from the region and have engaged in trade over a long period (1 Kings 5:10–12; Ezek. 27:17; Fitzmyer 1998: 490). Herod can control where the commerce goes, and so, if he uses another port, such as Berytus (Beirut) or Caesarea, it could hurt Tyre and Sidon financially and possibly in terms of provision as well. The text says that Herod is furious (θυμομαχῶν, *thymomachōn*) with them over this issue. This term is an NT hapax and is absent from the LXX. There probably is an embargo in place (Jervell 1998: 336). So the cities seek reconciliation and convince Blastus, Herod's chamberlain, of their case. This Blastus is otherwise unattested, although the name is not rare. A chamberlain was like a personal chief of staff (Le Cornu and Shulam 2003: 661; Josephus, *Life* 68 §§381–82). Sometimes this role also involved being chief of the guard (Philo, *Embassy* 27 §175). The two regions reach an agreement. Herod gives a public speech (ἐδημηγόρει, *edēmēgorei*) to commemorate the new arrangement. This term is another NT hapax.

This is a speech that Josephus also recounts, noting that the crowd attested to Herod being more than a mere mortal (*Ant.* 19.8.2 §§343–50 recounts the praise and Herod's immediate painful death, signaled by the portent of an owl seated on a rope, a death that had been announced in *Ant.* 18.6.7 §200).[4] Marshall (1980: 212) argues that there is no reason for Luke to invent the detail about Tyre and Sidon, and takes the account as reliable. Herod speaks to them from his "royal" throne, dressed in royal robes, which Josephus describes as made of silver and glistening in the sun (*Ant.* 19.8.2 §344).

Neither Luke nor Josephus gives the speech's content, only the crowd's praise in response. The crowd exalts Herod, comparing him to a god (Acts: "the voice of a god"; Josephus: "superior to mortal nature"). The term for "god" in Greek is in a slightly emphatic location, preceding its noun (θεοῦ φωνή, *theou phōnē*). Fitzmyer (1998: 491) calls it a royal acclamation (Dio Cassius, *Rom. Hist.* 62.5, is another example). The occasion may be the quinquennial games at Caesarea, held in March, or Claudius's birthday in August if it is not a special convocation.[5] The likely date of his death is March, AD 44, making this one of the key dates by which we can determine the chronology of events in Acts.[6] The verb for "die" (ἐκψύχω, *ekpsychō*) appears also in Acts 5:5 and 10, its only other NT occurrences. After the death the area returned to full Roman oversight under a legate stationed in Syria, although Herod's descendants still were in the region and sometimes were consulted (Acts 24:24; 25:13; Schneider 1982: 109).

According to both Luke and Josephus, Herod accepts the praise, which is his downfall. Luke says that Herod does not give God the glory, and Josephus notes that he does not rebuke them or reject their "impious flattery." Josephus describes the death as the result of a painful stomach condition, which lasted for five days, because he did not react to the impious remarks. Accepting this kind of praise is rebuked in the Tosefta

---

4. Other Herod references from Josephus include *Ant.* 18.6.2 §150, 18.6.7 §§195–201 (a prediction that his earlier imprisonment would end, but if he saw an owl again, it would be a bad sign); *J.W.* 2.11.6 §219 (a shorter reference to his death).

5. The games are discussed in Josephus, *J.W.* 1.21.8 §415; *Ant.* 16.5.1 §§136–41, but not this particular occasion; Bruce 1990: 288; Marshall 1980: 212.

6. See Pesch 1986a: 368, opting for March 10; Barrett 1994: 592, opting for March 5 while noting that August, AD 44, is also possible.

(*t. Soṭah* 7.16), the Talmud (*b. Soṭah* 41b), and the OT (Ezek. 28:2, 6, 9; esp. v. 9, "You are of man, not God" [to the prince of Tyre]). So his demise is typical for an enemy of God (Jervell 1998: 337; cf. 2 Macc. 8:4–10 [Antiochus Epiphanes]; Josephus, *Ant.* 17.6.5 §§168–79 [Herod the Great]; *b. Giṭ.* 56b Emperor Titus]; Le Cornu and Shulam 2003: 665). When Herod reports that he will die, in the next portion of the scene in Josephus, it is because of the crowd's "lying words." Paul's and Barnabas's immediate response to being called a god in Acts 14:11–15 stands in stark contrast to Herod's nonreaction in Acts and his delayed reaction and understanding in Josephus.

Luke says Herod was struck down by an angel of the Lord ("smote" in KJV, RSV; "struck" in NASB, NIV, NLT; "struck down" in NET). The term πατάσσω (*patassō*, strike down) is occasionally used to describe a judgment and has OT roots (Gen. 8:21; Exod. 9:15; 12:23; Num. 14:12; Deut. 28:22; Rev. 11:6; 19:15; BAGD 634 §2; BDAG 786 §2). Angels smite in the OT frequently (2 Sam. 12:15; 2 Kings 19:35; Bruce 1990: 289; Fitzmyer 1998: 491), although the Lord can also strike down (1 Sam. 25:38; 2 Chron. 13:20).[7] The result is that Herod's body is "consumed by worms" (σκωληκόβρωτος, *skōlēkobrōtos*), that is, the severe disease leads to his painful death (Jdt. 16:17, of the Lord's enemies as a group).[8] This term is yet another NT hapax in this account. The exact disease remains unknown. By placing the account here, Luke is suggesting that Herod also dies for persecuting Peter.

In sum, an opponent of the gospel is judged while Peter is freed. Mercy and judgment appear side by side (Polhill 1992: 285). God is active on behalf of the church. We see a contrast between those God protects and those he judges. Peter is protected at this point by a deliverance even the disciples find hard to believe, whereas Herod is struck down for opposing the people of God and for his arrogance in allowing himself to be declared equal to God. And yet James is not delivered but suffers a martyr's death. Thus the contrast of the text is threefold (Peter-Herod and James-Peter; Fernando 1998: 364, who calls the theme "rescue, no rescue"). This points to how God works in different ways with different people. As the church expands, the persecution continues with differing consequences for the church's members.

In the midst of all this uncertainty, we see a church in fervent prayer. This kind of faithfulness is precisely what allows the word to increase, as the passage notes in the closing summary that follows. It also serves as a warning to those who rule not to take their power too seriously or

7. In the Apocrypha, see 2 Macc. 9:5–28 (about the death of Antiochus IV Epiphanes), and in the NT, Acts 23:3. Greco-Roman accounts of severe death include Herodotus, *Hist.* 4.205 (of Pheretime); and Pausanius, *Descr.* 9.7.2 (of Cassander).

8. Bruce 1990: 289; Johnson 1992: 216; and Barrett 1994: 591–92 have a complete listing of parallels with gruesome deaths, not just "by worms." Lang, *TDNT* 7:456.

to have too elevated a view of who they are. Their call is to serve people in the corporate best interest and not to take glory to themselves, something that was common for rulers and patrons of that time (Dormeyer and Galindo 2003: 196). The risk today is that rulers and the prominent may do the same (this reminds one of the comment by John Lennon that the Beatles were more popular than Jesus Christ).

Additional Notes

12:10. Codex D adds a reference to the "seven steps," a colorful detail that is not likely to be original (Metzger 1971: 394).

12:19. That the soldiers were led away (ἀπαχθῆναι) to be executed can be inferred from the use of the verb in this context. Codex D has an explicit reference to being put to death (ἀποκτανθῆναι), which, though correct, is not original in Acts.

E. Summary (12:24–25)

This brief unit performs three roles as a summary. First, it concludes Luke's focus on the church in Jerusalem, setting up the transition to the church in Antioch, which is the key mission church in Acts 13 and in the second part of Acts. Second, it connects us back to the mission that concluded Acts 11, which is the link between Jerusalem and Antioch. Third, it shifts attention from Peter to Barnabas and Saul. So this brief account is a bridge working both backward and forward in Acts. Its source, in terms of information about timing, is likely the same as 11:19–30, although, as a summary, Luke composed it as a narrative seam (see 11:19–30 introduction).

The unit is like the summary in 6:7, where the growth of the word is highlighted, by which is meant the spread of the gospel.

Exegesis and Exposition

²⁴But the word of ⌜God⌝ grew and multiplied. ²⁵And Barnabas and Saul returned when they had fulfilled their mission in Jerusalem, bringing with them John, the one called Mark.

12:24–25   The word about the good news and Jesus continues to expand, even amid pressure against it (Acts 6:7; 9:31; 19:20). Barnabas and Saul return from taking the collection to Jerusalem and bring John Mark with them (11:30). Luke changes main characters as he notes this movement. Barnabas and Saul now are the focus of his attention, as is the mission from Antioch. Intense persecution, including martyrdom, cannot stop the growth and penetration of God's word through faithful witnesses.

John Mark is the son of the Mary in whose house the Jerusalem church met (Acts 12:12). He goes on the first of Paul's missionary journeys (13:5) but does not make it to the end of that mission (13:13). Later, when Barnabas wishes to take him, Paul and Barnabas split their efforts so that John Mark can go with Barnabas (15:37–39). Interestingly, in Acts John Mark is sometimes called John (a Jewish name; 13:5, 13), sometimes Mark (a Roman name; 12:25; 15:39; Bruce 1988a: 238), and sometimes John Mark (specifically, "John, the one called Mark," 12:12; 15:37).

There is the combination of a textual and a syntactical problem in the verse. Many read the phrase εἰς Ἰερουσαλήμ (*eis Ierousalēm*) with the verb "returned" and see a return to Jerusalem here (א, B, 81, Byz, and some Syriac MSS). This is problematic because of Paul's list of trips to

Jerusalem and the fact that Barnabas and Paul are in Jerusalem already in 11:30, when we last saw them (but NET adopts this reading). This issue led to two variants reading "from." One used ἐξ (*ex*), as in 𝔓⁷⁴, A, 33, 945, and 1739, while the other reads ἀπό (*apo*), as in D, E, Ψ, 36, 323, 453, and 614. The fact that two variants have the same meaning and the other reading is more difficult makes it unlikely that either of them is original (but apparently the NIV accepts one of these variants). Some of these MSS even make the text clearer by speaking of a return "to Antioch" (E, 104, 323, 945, 1175, 1739; note how these contain a mixture of the other variants).

A syntactical solution looks more promising (Haenchen 1987: 387; Fitzmyer 1998: 493; Schneider 1982: 109; Barrett 1994: 595–96; discussed in Metzger 1971: 398–400 with the problem rated as "D," indicating its difficulty [upgraded to "C" in UBS⁴]). This solution also removes any need to take the reference to John Mark "being taken along" as a futuristic aorist, which also is an unusual force in this context. The syntactical solution ties the phrase "to Jerusalem" to the completion of the mission, which makes good sense (so "had fulfilled their mission in Jerusalem"). The translation reflects this choice. Now Luke can give renewed attention to what the church in Antioch is doing.

Additional Note

12:24. A variant reading appears in B, as it has "word of the Lord," but this is not well enough attested to be original.

V. The Mission from Antioch and the Full Incorporation of Gentiles (13:1–15:35)

Attention turns to Antioch and beyond as the first missionary journey (13:1–14:28) and the Jerusalem Council (15:1–35) are the key elements of this unit. The move to go to the end of the earth has started in earnest. Cyprus and Galatia receive visits. Saul becomes Paul and emerges as the key figure of the expansion for Luke. One of the results of the council is the central role Paul will play in the Gentile mission. Antioch is a church full of teachers and prophets who sense the direction of the Spirit to engage in organized mission. For the first time in Luke's account, a church other than the one in Jerusalem is the center for a major divine initiative. Luke sees the act as important and symbolic. The church can be active in places outside Jerusalem, as God directs through the Spirit. In modern terms, a church plant has taken up the call. More than that, the center of the church's activity is no longer limited to Jerusalem. In fact, many centers of activity are emerging. The scope of the task requires this. This expansion into the Gentile world extends as far as Acts 21:36, where Paul's arrest then dominates the account (Spencer 2004: 140).[1]

---

1. Spencer's case for a literary break of only two expeditions to seas in the East (the Mediterranean and the Aegean), though interesting, is less compelling when one keeps in mind the role of Jerusalem in Acts. More interesting is his observation that the ministry involves four social groups: Jews, Greco-Romans, Christians, and charismatic groups, by which he means magicians and beneficiaries of miracles, who probably are better seen as two distinct classes, one containing those being challenged in terms of their associations to supernatural power and the other containing positive beneficiaries of ministry.

A. The First Missionary Journey
(13:1–14:28)

This subsection finds Barnabas and Paul on the move, primarily to Cyprus and Galatia. They visit Cyprus (13:4–12), Pisidian Antioch (13:13–52), Iconium (14:1–7), Lystra (14:8–20), and then return to Syria (14:21–28; Schnabel 2004: 1074–1124). The journey covers about 895 miles (Schnabel 2004: 1076). The account of the visit to Pisidian Antioch includes an example of how Paul preaches in the synagogue, and Lystra gives a sense of what preaching in a Gentile-dominated context is like. Themes arising from a Gentile context will be developed in more detail in Acts 17 at Athens. This is a "journey" in the real sense, as the missionaries move from place to place very quickly (Marshall 1980: 214). Schnabel (2004: 1076) estimates that they cover about 15 miles a day by foot. Later "journeys" involve longer stays in specific places to solidify the results. The account describes the first step in "missions" as the called-out and divinely directed activity of a group organized for this specific goal. This contrasts with the less-systematic work of individuals, which we have seen earlier. The church is becoming more organized and intentional about outreach.

1. Barnabas and Saul Commissioned (13:1–3)

The call of Barnabas and Paul takes place in the context of worship led by teachers and prophets who have been fasting. Everything about the event argues that mission is grounded in God's command and the response of a church engaged in devotion. The Spirit directs that the two be sent out, and the church is obedient to the call. The listing of prophets and teachers is probably rooted in some source within the Antioch church (Haenchen 1987: 394; Barrett 1994: 599–600). Jervell (1998: 342) and especially Fitzmyer (1998: 495) note that Paul could have been a source. Paul emerges to fulfill his calling by the Spirit, which he received in Acts 9:15–16, here first with Barnabas and later on his own, as the name change to Paul in 13:9 also indicates. This is the end of spontaneous ministry to Gentiles. Now this Gentile outreach is planned and directed by God in a fuller, more intentional manner. Barrett (1994: 599–601) notes that Barnabas and Paul become "apostles" in the generic sense of this term, those sent by others in their stead. This is a commission account in form. Fitzmyer (1998: 136–37, 495) notes that this form is no reason to question the historicity of this mission, which also is alluded to in Gal. 1:21–23 and Phil. 4:15 (also Jervell 1998: 342–44, who observes that it is not right to pit Gal. 1:21–23 against such a mission, since it is concerned with the limited issue of how Paul related to Jerusalem, not his full missionary history).

Exegesis and Exposition

¹There were in the church in Antioch prophets and teachers: Barnabas; Simeon who was called Niger; Lucius of Cyrene; Manean, a member of the court of Herod the tetrarch; and Saul. ²As they were worshiping the Lord and fasting, the Holy Spirit said, "Set apart for me Barnabas and Saul for the task to which I have called them." ³Then after fasting and praying and laying their hands on them, they sent them off.

13:1–3   Returning to discuss the church at Antioch, Luke notes the presence of teachers and prophets there, engaged in worship and fasting. So the call takes place during a time of spiritual focus on God. This is the only occurrence of a form of διδάσκαλος (didaskalos, teacher) in Acts. The verb "teach," however, appears sixteen times, and a reference to teaching four times, but only using διδαχή (*didachē*), not διδασκαλία (*didaskalia*), which is never used in Luke-Acts (Barrett 1994: 602). A teacher's ministry would involve a less-spontaneous declaration and preaching than that of the prophets, including instruction and the passing on to others of the received apostolic teaching (Williams 1990: 223; 1 Cor. 12:28–29; Eph. 4:11). This was how the church taught its doctrine before the use of the books that later became a part of the NT. Short doctrinal summaries, hymns, and rites like baptism as well as the Lord's Table taught people the core doctrine (1 Cor. 8:4–6; 11:23–26; 15:1–3; Rom. 1:2–4; Phil. 2:5–11; Col. 1:15–20).

In this case, there appears to be an overlap between the two roles of prophet and teacher for these five; it is not clear if there is any distinction made here in the lists as to who did what. Of the thirty occurrences of the word προφήτης (*prophētēs*, prophet) in Acts, this is one of the few times that specific prophets in the church are named. There is Agabus (Acts 11:28; 21:10), the combination of Judas and Silas sent to deliver the letter of the Jerusalem Council with Barnabas and Paul (15:32), and the prophetess daughters of Philip (21:9; on prophets, see 11:27).

The Greek names of many of these prophets in Acts 13 are significant. God is gifting the church without ethnic distinctions. Not much is known about these five men except for Barnabas and Saul. It is thought that Niger and Lucius may be from north Africa (Jervell 1998: 340–41), and Niger may be black, considering that this is what his name means in Latin. Lucius is sometimes confused with Luke as one and the same person, but without good reason. Manean is described as one raised with Herod, as the term σύντροφος (*syntrophos*) means one who eats together or nurses together with someone else, but it can mean "courtier" (MM 615). He would have had high social standing through this connection. Williams (1990: 221) suggests that he is Luke's source on Herod Antipas. Some are left to minister in Antioch, but now God will call out Barnabas and Saul for another task.

The Spirit calls Barnabas and Saul to be separated out for him (ἀφορίσατε δή μοι, *aphorisate dē moi*) for a special work (τὸ ἔργον, *to ergon*) in the context of what is likely congregational worship. God calls those among the most gifted out from the larger community (Bruce 1990: 294). These two are an integral part of the community, having ministered there for at least a year. Those sent are qualified to plant new works on the basis of their previous contribution to the church. God's leading takes place here in the context of worship and fasting. The reference to this special work will reappear at the end of the unit, in 14:26.

The Spirit does not yet reveal the exact nature of this labor. The particle δή here is emphatic, and its usage is rare in the NT (Matt. 13:23; Luke 2:15; Acts 13:2; 15:36; 1 Cor. 6:20). The verb ἀφορίζω (*aphorizō*) basically means "separate" someone or something out. It can mean to appoint someone to something, as here (BAGD 127 §2; BDAG 158 §2;

Exod. 13:12 Alex.; 29:26–27; Gal. 1:15; Rom. 1:1; "set apart" in NIV, RSV, NASB, NET; "dedicate" in NLT).

Note how the Spirit is directing this call (see also v. 4). The work is for the Spirit and represents God. Here the Spirit is directing the mission. Earlier Jesus did so in calling Saul. God also has been active, and so the unity of God in his activity is seen in this variety.

After more fasting and prayer (Acts 14:23) and laying on of hands (6:6; 8:17, 19; 9:12, 17; 19:6; 28:8), they are sent out or released to the task (ἀπέλυσαν, apelysan). The combination of fasting and prayer appears here and there in Scripture (Jer. 14:12; Neh. 1:4; Matt. 6:5, 16; Johnson 1992: 221). As noted in earlier verses, the laying on of hands points to the establishing of connection and is used in commissioning and in healing. This is not a call into a new office, as their role was already defined before the call. Rather it is an identification with this specific "work" to which God has called them. The only two occurrences of the verb νηστεύω (nēsteuō, fast) in Acts are in these verses; the noun form appears in Acts 14:23; 27:9. The only occurrence of the verb λειτουργέω (leitourgeō, worship) in Acts also appears here (NT: Rom. 15:27; Heb. 10:11; the cognate noun is in Luke 1:23). In the OT, it is mostly used for priestly service at the temple (Exod. 28:35; 38:27; Num. 1:50; in the Greek context of public festivals, see Johnson 1992: 221; Aristotle, Politics 1291A; 1335B). Luke uses it here to indicate prayer, a key ministry of believer-priests (Strathmann, TDNT 4:226–28). Here is a church that has seen the need to reach out to the world as its members draw near to God. Their heart has become wedded to God's calling as a result. They commission their messengers to their work for the world. They are acting as believer-priests on behalf of God. Worship and mission appear side by side as key tasks of the church.

In sum, as always, prayer and spiritual forces work together in this text and play a role in guiding the church. These are realities the modern world tends to shun but are foundations of a Christian worldview. Particularly unspecified is exactly how the Spirit initiated this mission (Stott 1990: 217). There was some type of clear indication that this was to be done among the group. Often God directs in ways that are spiritual and mysterious. In this case, the community, sensing God's clear direction, put its weight behind an outreach far beyond its own walls. God loves churches that look beyond their own needs. One wonders where the church today would be if Antioch had not been led to look beyond its own community and city limits to do evangelism. Everything about Acts shows us that its impetus is toward the church's call in mission. We build churches not just to go in for worship but also to go out with God's heart for people.

As the missionary team is sent out, it reflects a diversity of backgrounds, something that, if appreciated, can make a team stronger by providing variety in perspective.

2. Barnabas and Saul's Mission in Cyprus (13:4–12)

With this event in Cyprus, Saul becomes Paul (13:9) and emerges as the key figure of the journey. Barrett (1994: 609) theorizes that Saul was the name in the Antiochene source whereas the name Paul was better known to most, but the change is a conscious literary move, given that it appears consistently once the change is made. From this point on, Saul is Paul except where he recounts how he was addressed during his vision of Jesus.

In form, this is a confrontational miracle account between Paul and Bar-Jesus, a Jewish false prophet and magician who tries to thwart the mission in Paphos. The account contains one of the few judgment miracles in Acts. This miracle is like the earlier one that Peter performed regarding Ananias and Sapphira (5:1–11). The parallelism is intentional to show that Paul has gifts equal to Peter and that both, given the Acts 8 parallel, oppose magic. But there also is a contrast. Acts 5 was discipline exercised within the church's community whereas here Paul is a mediator of divine discipline with someone outside the church. There also is the conversion of the proconsul Sergius Paulus, indicating that success among the Gentiles, even prominent ones, will continue.

The account contains (1) the journey to Cyprus (v. 4), (2) the preaching throughout Cyprus in the synagogues (vv. 5–6a), and (3) the encounter with Bar-Jesus and the meeting with Sergius Paulus (vv. 6b–12). It is the judgment miracle of Paul that draws Sergius to believe. Luke again highlights the effective combination of word and deed in ministry. The account also shows the superiority of divine power to that of the magicians. Likely sources include Paul, Barnabas, and/or Mark, but Luke tells the story in his own language in verses 8–11. In favor of the historicity of the first journey as a whole is the embarrassing note of John Mark's failure, something unlikely to be present if the scene were invented and idealized (Williams 1990: 224). Williams also notes that some locations are either obscure or nothing happens at them. They add nothing to the account and seem merely to be part of the journey's itinerary.

Exegesis and Exposition

⁴Therefore, being sent out by the Holy Spirit, they went down to Seleucia; and

from there they sailed to Cyprus. ⁵Upon arriving at Salamis, they proclaimed the word of God in the Jewish synagogues. And they had John to assist them. ⁶And going through the whole island as far as Paphos, they came upon a certain magician, a Jewish false prophet, named Bar-Jesus, ⁷who was with the proconsul, Sergius Paulus, a man of intelligence. Summoning Barnabas and Saul, he sought to hear the word of God. ⁸But ⌜Elymas⌝ the magician (for that is the meaning of his name) opposed them, seeking to turn away the proconsul from the faith. ⁹But Saul, who is also called Paul, filled with the Holy Spirit, staring at him, ¹⁰said, "Oh, you, full of deceit and villainy, son of the devil, enemy of all righteousness, will you not stop making crooked the straight paths of the Lord? ¹¹And now, behold, the hand of the Lord is upon you, and you shall be blind and unable to see the sun for a time." Immediately mist and darkness fell upon him, and he was going about seeking people to lead him by the hand. ¹²Then the proconsul believed, seeing what had occurred, for he was amazed at the teaching of the Lord.

13:4 The journey to Cyprus by way of Seleucia is sixty miles; this port was sixteen miles from Antioch and five miles from where the Orontes River meets the Mediterranean (Polhill 1992: 291). Schnabel (2004: 1078–79) presents a short history of the locale and of Jewish settlement there starting in the second century BC. Cyprus had been a senatorial province since 22 BC with a proconsul, who in this case is Sergius Paulus, as we see in verse 7. During its history, the island had been inhabited by a wide array of people groups, including Egyptians, Phoenicians, Greeks, Assyrians, Persians, and Ptolemies, making it a microcosm of the entire Mediterranean. It exported wood and copper, was relatively dry in climate, and is the third largest island in the Mediterranean. It is 140 miles long and 60 miles wide.

The verse makes clear that this mission is initiated and directed by the Spirit of God, something Luke often notes in Acts (4:31; 8:29, 39; 10:44; 16:6; Johnson 1992: 221). It is not indicated, however, that this is the first evangelistic effort in the area. There was previous activity from either Jerusalem or Antioch (11:19; Schnabel 2004: 1079). The Spirit again appears in the scene when Paul judges the magician in verse 9.

13:5–6a Barnabas and Saul reach Salamis, on the east coast of the island (on this city, see Schnabel 2004: 1079–80). After an earthquake in AD 15, it was rebuilt by Augustus and was the island's major city. Salamis was a commercial and Jewish center on the island (1 Macc. 15:23; Philo, *Embassy* 36 §282; Josephus, *Ant.* 13.10.4 §§284–87).

As will be Paul's custom throughout Acts, the preaching begins in Jewish synagogues (synagogues in Acts: 6:9; 9:2, 20; 13:5, 14, 43; 14:1; 15:21; 17:1, 10, 17; 18:4, 7, 19, 26; 19:8; 22:19; 24:12; 26:11; for Paul's approach, see Rom. 1:16, "to the Jew first and also the Greek"). Synagogues were gathering places of teaching and prayer, as well as of worship and Scripture reading (Le Cornu and Shulam 2003: 686–93 detail the structure and organization of the synagogue, at the core of which was the "Ark," which contained the scroll of the Pentateuch). The inclusion of Gentiles does not mean the exclusion of Jews from the gospel message.

John Mark is their assistant or helper, perhaps even an apprentice (ὑπηρέτην, *hypēretēn*; Acts 5:22, 26; 13:5; 26:16 [Paul as a witness]; Rengstorf, *TDNT* 8:541). Besides its appearances in Acts, this term describes the servants of the word in Luke 1:2 and the synagogue worship leader in Luke 4:20. The key idea in the term is the service rendered to another. What he does is not specified. This description does not suggest that John Mark should not be part of the mission because the Spirit has not called him, as some argue. Such assistance is not unusual, and other missions will have such figures (Marshall 1980: 218). The Spirit's call concerned who would lead the mission. Bruce (1990: 296) notes that Mark is likely an eyewitness to Jesus's ministry, something Barnabas and Saul may not have been.

According to Acts 11:19, the church has already been planted in Cyprus, but there is no indication that the effort in this journey focuses on the church. Evangelism is the main concern. Luke simply mentions that they journey through Cyprus and does not describe any activity along the way. His focus is on the two major cities of the island.

On the southwest coast of the island, about ninety miles from Salamis, lies Paphos. The locale is probably New Paphos, a stopping point for those associated with the cult of the Syrian goddess Paphia, equivalent to Aphrodite. This was but one of many cults located there (Artemis, Leto, Zeus). It was built after an earthquake destroyed the older city in 15 BC. The older city was ten miles away. The new city was Roman in style and layout. It replaced Salamis as the capital after the earthquake (Schnabel 2004: 1082).

13:6b–7

There the missionaries meet a Jewish false prophet (ψευδοπροφήτην, *pseudoprophētēn*) and magician (μάγον, *magon*) named Bar-Jesus. The text's description of Bar-Jesus adds a note of irony, as the first opponent of Paul and Barnabas is a false prophet named "son of Jesus/Joshua." His other name, Elymas (v. 8), means "wise." As with Simon Magus in Acts 8, this is the confrontation between a magician and a gifted worker of the church. A spiritual battle is pictured (Delling, *TDNT* 4:358–59; on magicians, see the discussion on Acts 16:16–18, 19–21). Witherington (1998: 397–98) has a discussion of how Christianity viewed magicians, who functioned as part of popular folk religion of the time. Christians opposed such activity, an opposition that was matched by other religions (also Nock 1933).

This is the only text in Acts that calls someone a false prophet, although the term is common elsewhere in the NT (Matt. 7:15; 24:11, 24; Mark

13:22; Luke 6:26; Acts 13:6–7; 2 Pet. 2:1; 1 John 4:1; Rev. 16:13; 19:20; 20:10). The references to magicians are rare, with only two occurrences of this term in Acts (Matt. 2:1, 7, 16 [more neutral in force, of the magi who visit Jesus]; Acts 13:6, 8; but conceptually in 8:9, 11; 19:19). Bar-Jesus may well be a court astrologer (Haenchen 1987: 398). The rabbis argued that Jews should not practice magic, but some did (Str-B 1:76). The power they exercised was real and needed to be opposed. Josephus tells the story of another infamous Jewish sorcerer during a slightly later period, the time of Felix (*Ant.* 20.7.2 §§142–43).

In contrast to the Jewish false prophet stood the proconsul, Sergius Paulus, who is called an intelligent man, possibly because he is open to hearing about the faith. Proconsuls are rarely named in Acts (13:8, 12 [looking back to this verse]; 18:12 [Gallio]; 19:38 [unnamed]). They were Roman magistrates who headed the government in a senatorial province where no troops were required (BAGD 69; BDAG 82). By contrast, Judea was an imperial province and required a significant number of troops.

Three inscriptions bearing a similar name have been found, two in Greek and one in Latin, in addition to one that refers to a Lucias Sergius Paullus near Pisidian Antioch.[1] It is not clear, however, that any of these refer to this particular proconsul (Williams 1990: 227–28; Van Elderen 1970: 151–56 is skeptical of connections). Bruce (1990: 297) thinks a connection may exist with an inscription found in northern Cyprus (*IGRR* 3.935) and is less confident of one from Soloi, also in northern Cyprus (*IGRR* 3.930). Witherington (1998: 399–400 and n. 158) rejects the connection to a third northern Greece inscription and thinks the inscription found near Pisidian Antioch (discussed by Ramsey) gives evidence of the influence of the family. Witherington also thinks this Latin inscription from Greece, which refers to Paullus as a curator of the river Tiber (*CIL* 6.4.2 and no. 31545), could mean the same person. Barrett (1994: 613–14) also holds this as possible. Marshall (1980: 219), however, feels that the evidence for a connection is weak, holding the northern Cyprus inscription as possible, whereas Barrett (1994: 614) rejects it in favor of the Latin inscription. In sum, the inscriptions may allude to this figure, but we are not sure if they do or, if so, which one does.

13:8   The magician Elymas opposes the missionary effort, possibly out of fear for his own position. He tries to keep Sergius from the faith. "Faith" here is probably the body of belief that the missionaries preach, although it might refer to one's personal response as well, since the preaching of the faith calls for response. Διαστρέφω (*diastrephō*, turn away) is often used of preventing someone from embracing the truth (Num. 15:39; 32:7; Ezek. 13:18; Luke 23:2; and esp. Paul's countercharge in v. 10). This is

---

1. Paullus is the Latin spelling.

the first example of opposition from forms of magic or idolatrous worship in Acts, Ephesus (Acts 19) among the most notable.

How the name Elymas means "wise" is debated (Luke is not discussing the meaning of the name Bar-Jesus with this remark). Two options are possible (Polhill 1992: 293; Witherington 1998: 401). Either the name is a variation of the Arabic root *alim*, which means "sage" (Bruce 1990: 297; Haenchen 1987: 398–99n2), or the name is derived from the Aramaic *haloma*, which means "interpreter of dreams" (Schneider 1982: 122), a vocation that in popular thought implied wisdom. Barrett (1994: 616) objects to both options, rejecting the influence of an Arabic nickname. Still, the Jewish magician is already engaged in somewhat syncretistic activity that might engender a cross-cultural connection. That a proconsul has such a figure in his entourage is not surprising (Johnson 1992: 223; Philo, *Spec. Laws* 3.18 §100; Pseudo-Callisthenes, *Life of Alexander of Macedon* 1.1–12). Le Cornu and Shulam (2003: 701–2) detail the syncretism of the period. The magician's work would involve healing and looking for signs using formulas, incantations, amulets, and other forms of inducing discernment.

As Saul takes the lead in this challenge, Luke notes Paul as the other, well-known name of Saul. Paul is his Roman name, and Saul is his Jewish name (Bruce 1990: 298; Haenchen 1987: 399–400n3). The change indicates that Paul is becoming the prominent and leading member of the group. He also is functioning in a new Gentile context, so the name shift makes sense. He confronts the magician directly under the Spirit's guidance, since Paul speaks while being filled with the Spirit (πλησθεὶς πνεύματος ἁγίου, *plēstheis pneumatos hagiou*) and functions exclusively as a true prophet in contrast to the magician. Paul looks intently at his opponent as he speaks and addresses the magician. For the use of the verb ἀτενίζω (*atenizō*, look intently), see Luke 22:56; Acts 3:4; 10:4; and 14:9–10, all involving speech. Barrett (1994: 616) notes a later rabbinic saying from the Talmud that wherever the wise direct their eyes, there is death or misery (Str-B 2:714; *b. Moʿed Qaṭ.* 17b; *b. Ḥag.* 5b; *b. Soṭah* 46b; *b. Ned.* 7b). Whether this idea is being alluded to here is unclear, since the tradition is late.

13:9–11

Paul delivers a strong judgment against the magician, rendering him temporarily blind, a judgment designed to have him reflect on where God's power and truth reside. Darkness of mind leads to darkness of sight, one picturing the other (Le Cornu and Shulam 2003: 705–6). This is one of a few judgment miracles. The others are Ananias and Sapphira in Acts 5 and the judgment against Herod in Acts 12. In this case, however, the judgment is temporary. There is important symbolism here. The false prophet sits in darkness as Paul works.[2] The temporary

2. On how a text such as this evokes a theme popular later in the church of *Christus Victor* (Christ the Victor), see Pelikan 2005: 154–55.

nature of the judgment is like that which fell on Zechariah in Luke 1, a judgment from which Zechariah learned to believe God. Paul accuses the magician of being full of deceit and villainy as well as being opposed to righteousness.

The interjection ὦ (ō) is emphatic, coming as it does at the beginning of Paul's address to the magician (BDF §146; Wallace 2000: 39–40). The judgment also cuts Bar-Jesus off from being able to practice all of his craft, as astrology might well be a part of his repertoire (Klauck 2003: 48). Even more, he is a son of the devil, an irony in light of his name as "son of Jesus." The reference to "villainy" (ῥᾳδιουργίας, rhadiourgias) is unique in the NT. It means "unscrupulousness" (BAGD 733; BDAG 902) and usually refers to someone who wishes to gain through some means of trickery, a con artist. It is a term used in Hellenistic moral teaching (Johnson 1990: 224; Plutarch, *On the Malice of Herodotus* 23 [= *Moralia* 860D]; Philo, *Cherubim* 24 §80). Elymas's work makes crooked what should be straight paths from the Lord. The imagery of the crooked path or ill-gotten gain has OT roots (ill-gotten gain: Jer. 5:27; crooked path: Prov. 10:9; Hos. 14:10, esp. Isa. 40:3; 59:8). So Elymas's opposition goes against God's plan and perverts the truth (Michaelis, *TDNT* 5:87). He is to stop making the Lord's path crooked, which is a way of saying that he is to stop resisting the truth and the straight path.

Elymas is where Saul was years earlier, and the difference is obvious. Paul is now full of the truth and the Spirit whereas Elymas is full of deceit and villainy. The reference to deceit may suggest the financial gain he seeks from his work. Witherington (1998: 402) calls this judgment "an oath curse," and Barrett (1994: 617) says he is "roundly cursed." The "hand of the Lord" is against him (Judg. 2:15; 1 Sam. 12:15). This is judgment on a corrupt religious figure who is associated with magic. Elymas is also a prophet, and so this is also a battle of the prophets. Whatever power he has fails in the face of God's presence in Paul, and his claims are shown to be false. This judgment, however, comes with mercy, for it is not permanent. This also parallels what happened to Saul when he was called, except that here the judgment gives an opportunity for Bar-Jesus to respond. We are not told what he does, although every reader of Acts knows what he should do.

Luke's major point is the superiority of Paul's access to God and truth. Paul's call for judgment works. Mist (ἀχλύς, achlys) and darkness follow for Elymas, so that others must lead him by the hand, a confirmation of his condition. This is the only occurrence of ἀχλύς in the NT; in Greek contexts it is often associated with loss of sight (Barrett 1994: 618; Homer, *Il.* 5.696; 20.321; *Od.* 22.88; Josephus, *Ant.* 9.4.3 §56). The prophet has a punishment much like what Saul faced. In a sense, Paul judges his former self here (Klauck 2003: 55). As the magician is led away, one can imagine Paul recalling that he himself was led away after seeing the Lord and being rendered temporarily blind. This judgment also teaches the rejection of any form of syncretism, something Elymas's vocation reflects.

Paul's authority is also like Peter's action in Acts 5:1–11. The act-preaching sequence recalls Luke 4:16–44 and Acts 2, but as in Acts 2 we have the act first and then the preaching.

Sergius responds with faith as a result of Paul's work. The teaching   **13:12**
of the Lord astonishes him. This is the only occurrence of the verb ἐκπλήσσομαι (*ekplēssomai*, be amazed) in Acts (in Luke: 2:48; 4:32; 9:43). In this context, the word describes the reaction to the combination of word and deed, as in Mark 1:27, although it is the word that is decisive over the miracle, clinching the deal (Klauck 2003: 53). Witherington (1998: 402–3) expresses uncertainty about whether Sergius is converted, but all the contrast in the passage and the implication of Pauline success suggest that Sergius did respond (correctly, Fitzmyer 1998: 504). Without a conversion, there is not complete success here. A Roman Gentile responds whereas a Jew with supposed religious connections rejects the message. The contrast is intentional. In addition, one of high social class is responsive.

In sum, this passage is built around the character contrasts it presents. We see Paul being very forceful in his confrontation with someone who utterly denies what he represents (Fernando 1998: 377). Sometimes evangelism will require such confrontation with one who is preventing another from hearing the message. Sergius represents the person who has no background to appreciate the message and to whom Paul appeals to consider the gospel. Thus Bar-Jesus and Sergius serve as contrasting characters in the passage. They are two kinds of people who are outside the faith: one strenuously objected to it, and one is more neutral or open and needs to learn the first things about the faith. Paul adopts two different styles to suit the two types.

Additional Note

13:8. The Western text (D) reads a name here that means "ready" (ἑτοίμας, *hetoimas*), which might be equated with Atomos, a textual variant for the name of a Jewish magician (also called Simon) mentioned by Josephus in *Ant.* 20.7.2 §142. This is not well enough attested to be likely. The addition might seek to make a parallel with Simon Magus in Acts 8.

3. Paul and Barnabas in Pisidian Antioch (13:13–52)

This scene contains the most developed Pauline synagogue speech in Acts along with the reaction it generates. In Pisidian Antioch of Asia Minor, Paul addresses the Jews about God's promise. The address rehearses the history of Israel from its origin to David and then leaps over a thousand years to John the Baptist and Jesus.

The setting of the speech comes first (vv. 13–15), and then the survey of Israel's history to the time of John (vv. 16–25). Next are the declaration about Jesus (vv. 26–37) and the application (vv. 38–41). So the speech itself has three basic sections, once the setting appears.

A second way to outline the speech is grounded in the kind of material being presented and divides it into five parts. The history (vv. 16–25) leads to the basic kerygma (vv. 26–30), as attested by witnesses (v. 31) and scriptural proof (vv. 32–37), so that a response of conversion is in order (vv. 38–41; Schneider 1982: 128–29).

The aftermath includes a follow-up speech on the next Sabbath in verses 42–47. The unit ends in vv. 48–52 with the impact of the speeches and the largely negative Jewish reaction, which leads to the missionary party's departure from the city.

The major point of the progress of Paul's ministry appears in verses 46–47: that Jewish rejection will not stop the mission as the message proceeds to the Gentiles, even though the promise was originally "for us" (so vv. 26, 30–33a).

The purpose is to declare how Jesus fulfilled promises made to David long ago, by giving a sample of Paul's message in a synagogue. Thus the narrative is a speech in form and rooted in a Pauline source (Fitzmyer 1998: 507). This speech, Peter's opening addresses in Acts 2–3, and Stephen's speech in Acts 7 are the key speeches in Acts on Jewish promise. Paul's speech here parallels another synagogue speech that Jesus gave in Luke 4:16–30, declaring fulfillment, after which he confronted the force of evil in the same chapter (Luke 4:16–44, but in reverse order, since Paul confronts in Acts 13:1–12 and then preaches here whereas Jesus preached in Luke 4:16–30 and then confronted in 4:31–44). The ministry of Jesus continues through Paul. Rejection also continues, but it will not stop the impact of this ministry, which is rooted in divine work and power. Witherington (1998: 403–4) suggests that Sergius Paulus may have suggested Pisidian Antioch as the next place to visit, given that he had family connections there.

Exegesis and Exposition

[13]Setting sail from Paphos, Paul and his company came to Perga in Pamphylia. And John left then and returned to Jerusalem; [14]but they passed on from Perga and came to Antioch of Pisidia. And on the Sabbath day they went into the synagogue and sat down. [15]After the reading of the Law and the Prophets, the rulers of the synagogue sent to them, saying, "Brothers, if you have any word of exhortation for the people, say it."

[16]So rising up and motioning with his hand, Paul said, "Men of Israel and you that fear God, listen. [17]The God of this people Israel elected our fathers and lifted up the people during their stay in the land of Egypt, and with uplifted arm he led them out of it. [18]And for about forty years he ⌜bore with⌝ them in the wilderness. [19]And destroying seven nations in the land of Canaan, God gave them their land as an inheritance [20]⌜for about four hundred and fifty years. And after those things⌝ he gave them judges until Samuel the prophet. [21]Then they asked for a king; and God gave them Saul the son of Kish, a man of the tribe of Benjamin, for forty years. [22]And removing him, God raised up David to be their king; of whom also he said testifying, 'I have found in David the son of Jesse a man after my own heart, who will do all my will.' [23]From this man's seed God has brought to Israel, according to promise, a Savior, Jesus. [24]Before his coming, John had preached a baptism of repentance to all the people of Israel. [25]And as John was finishing his course, he said, 'What do you suppose that I am? I am not he. No, but after me one is coming, the sandals of whose feet I am not worthy to untie.'

[26]"Brothers, sons of the family of Abraham, and those among you who fear God, ⌜to us⌝ has been sent the message of this salvation. [27]For those who live in Jerusalem and their rulers, not recognizing this one nor understanding the utterances of the prophets that are read every Sabbath, fulfilled these by condemning him. [28]Though finding no charge against him deserving death, yet they asked Pilate to have him killed. [29]And when they had fulfilled all that was written about him, taking him down from the tree, they laid him in a tomb. [30]But God raised him from the dead; [31]and for many days he appeared to those who came up with him from Galilee to Jerusalem, who are now his witnesses to the people. [32]And we proclaim to you the good news that what God promised to the fathers [33]he has fulfilled to us ⌜their children⌝ by raising Jesus; as also it is written in the ⌜second⌝ psalm, 'You are my Son, today I have begotten you.' [34]For of the fact that he raised him from the dead, no more to return to corruption, he spoke in this way, 'I will give you the holy and sure blessings of David.' [35]Therefore he says also in another psalm, 'You will not let your Holy One see corruption.' [36]For David, after he served the counsel of God in his own generation, fell asleep, and was laid with his fathers, and saw corruption; [37]but he whom God raised up saw no corruption. [38]Let it be known to you therefore, brothers, that to you through this man forgiveness of sins is proclaimed, [39]and

by this one everyone who believes is justified [freed] from everything from which you could not be justified [freed] by the law of Moses. ⁴⁰Beware, therefore, lest there come upon you what is said in the prophets: ⁴¹'Behold, you scoffers, and wonder, and perish; for I do a deed in your days, a deed you will never believe if one declares it to you.'"

⁴²As they went out, the people were begging that these things might be told them the next Sabbath. ⁴³And when the meeting of the synagogue broke up, many Jews and devout converts to Judaism followed Paul and Barnabas, who spoke to them and urged them to remain in the grace of God. ⁴⁴The next Sabbath almost the entire city gathered together to hear ⌜the word of the Lord⌝. ⁴⁵But when the Jews saw the multitudes, they were filled with jealousy and contradicted by slander what was spoken by Paul. ⁴⁶And Paul and Barnabas spoke out boldly, saying, "To you it was necessary that the word of God should be spoken first. Since you reject it and judge yourselves unworthy of eternal life, behold, we turn to the Gentiles. ⁴⁷For so the Lord has commanded us, saying, 'I have set you to be a light for the Gentiles, that you may bring salvation to the uttermost parts of the earth.'"

⁴⁸Hearing this, the Gentiles were rejoicing and glorifying the word of the Lord; and as many as were ordained to eternal life believed. ⁴⁹And the word of the Lord was spreading throughout the entire region. ⁵⁰But the Jews incited the devout women of high standing and the leading men of the city, and stirred up persecution against Paul and Barnabas, and cast them out of their district. ⁵¹But shaking off the dust from their feet against the city, Paul and Barnabas went to Iconium. ⁵²And the disciples were being filled with joy and with the Holy Spirit.

13:13–14a As the group travels to Perga in Pamphylia, Mark, that is, John Mark, who has traveled with them up to this point (Acts 12:25; 13:5), departs. The reason for his departure is not noted, but later it will be a source of irritation between Paul and Barnabas (15:37–38). Pamphylia is in southern Asia Minor, about four hundred miles from Jerusalem (Schnabel 2004: 1089–90). The trip to Perga was a 112-mile journey, and the city was located twelve miles inland. The major deity was Vanassa Preiia, hellenized as Artemis (Cicero, *In Verrem* 1.20[54]).

They reach Antioch of Pisidia (on the city, see Strabo, *Geogr.* 12.3.31; 6.4; 8.14). Located in Phrygia Galatica, it was a civil and military center for the province and so the leading city of the region and a Roman colony (Schnabel 2004: 1098–1103). Situated in the highlands 3,600 feet above sea level, it faced Pisidia, and so it was associated with that area. Its name also distinguishes it from Phrygian Antioch on the Meander River (one of sixteen such Antiochs in the ancient world that were established by Seleucus Nikator to honor his father, Antiochus; Polhill 1992: 297). The chief god was Men Askaenos. The distance from Perga to Pisidian Antioch was a hundred miles as the crow flies. It had a large Jewish population (Josephus, *Ant.* 12.3.4 §§147–53, notes two thousand Jewish families in the region). Schnabel (2004: 1103–4) points out that the missionaries encounter seven different social levels of people: synagogue officials, Jews, proselytes, God-fearers, devout women of high standing, Gentiles, and leading men of the city. Their message penetrates all levels of the society.

The synagogue service follows the normal order of reading from the   **13:14b–15**
Law and the Prophets, followed by a word of exhortation from one of the attending men. Often along with the reading of Scripture in the synagogue came a homily or brief exposition that here is called a word of encouragement. The reading would include a portion from the Torah and one from the Prophets (*m. Meg.* 4.1–5 discusses this order of service in outline form: Shema, prayer, Torah reading, prophet's reading, priestly blessing, exposition; Str-B 4:153–88). Here the visitors are asked if they wish to encourage those attending. The plural reference to synagogue rulers may suggest a large community, or it may suggest that some members keep the designation as an honor for their previous service (*CII* 2.803; Marshall 1980: 223; Barrett 1994: 629).

Paul probably stands up to speak. After motioning for attention, Paul   **13:16–18**
reviews Israel's history to the Jews and God-fearers who are present in the synagogue. Bruce (1988a: 254) observes that the list of events corresponds to what the nation would confess in its liturgy (Deut. 26:5–10; Josh. 24:2–13, 17–18; Pss. 78:67–72; 89:3–4).[1] According to Bowker 1967–68, this is like a proem homily, with word links presenting, he suggests, Deut. 4:25–46 (*seder*), 2 Sam. 7:6–16 (*haftorah*), and 1 Sam. 13:14 LXX (proem text). A proem homily contains an introductory text that links the other two liturgical readings into a sermon. The homily with its application extends to verse 41.

The reference to God-fearers (οἱ φοβούμενοι τὸν θεόν, *hoi phoboumenoi ton theon*) probably refers to Greeks in the audience who respect the God of Israel, as distinguished from children of Israel (Barrett 1994: 630; Jervell 1998: 353). This twofold audience is reaffirmed in 13:26 as sons of the family of Abraham and those who fear God (note also v. 43). Paul outlines how God chose Israel through "our" fathers, identifying with those he addresses. A special covenant relationship exists between God and Israel at God's initiative (Deut. 4:37; 7:7; 10:15). God supported the people in Egypt, lifted them up, and protected them with an uplifted arm (μετὰ βραχίονος ὑψηλοῦ, *meta brachionos hypsēlou*) to deliver Israel during the exodus (Exod. 6:1, 6; 32:11; Deut. 3:24; 4:34; Ps. 136:11–12). The NIV renders, "with mighty power." This is the only reference to God's arm in Acts. All three NT occurrences of this term refer to God's arm (Acts 13:17; Luke 1:51; John 12:38). God is the subject of all the actions

---

1. On the worship form of speeches in the synagogue, see Bowker 1967–68; *b. Meg.* 29b; Philo, *Spec. Laws* 2.15 §62; Str-B 1:997.

in verses 17–22. God also tolerated or "bore with" them for forty years of inconsistent belief in the wilderness (Exod. 16:35; Num. 14:33–34). The verb τροποφορέω (*tropophoreō*) means to put up with someone's manners or moods (BAGD 827; BDAG 1017), and so it alludes to God's faithfulness despite Israel's lack of faith. This is the term's only NT occurrence. The phrase ὡς τεσσερακονταετῆ χρόνον (*hōs tesserakontaetē chronon*) is an accusative of time, which also appears in verse 21 (BDF §201). God put up with them for forty years, just as Saul was king for forty years.

13:19–21 Next, Paul mentions the conquest (Deut. 7:1), the period of the judges (Judg. 2:16), and the request for a king (1 Sam. 8:5–10, 22). The verb κατεκληρονόμησεν (*kateklēronomēsen*) has a causative force even though it is an intransitive verb: God brought about the inheritance of the land (Moulton and Turner 1963: 53). The people's request for a king resulted in the selection of Saul from the tribe of Benjamin (1 Sam. 9:1–2; 10:1, 20–21, 24; 11:15; 13:1; also Paul's tribe, Phil. 3:5). This was after Samuel initially refused to have anything to do with the request. The time of the sojourn in Egypt, the wilderness wanderings, and the conquest totals 450 years (Josh. 14:10 [some of the wandering years plus conquest years equals 45, plus 400 years in Egypt. These figures likely are rounded off]; Deut. 29:5 [40 years in the desert]; Marshall 1980: 223; Polhill 1992: 300n29; Witherington 1998: 410; Fitzmyer 1998: 511; Schneider 1982: 132). The phrase ὡς ἔτεσιν τετρακοσίοις καὶ πεντήκοντα (*hōs etesin tetrakosiois kai pentēkonta*) is a dative of duration of time (BDF §201; Moulton and Turner 1963: 243). Deuteronomy 7:1 names the Hittites, Girgashites, Amorites, Canaanites, Perizzites, Hivites, and Jebusites as the seven nations the Israelites encounter in the promised land. Marshall notes that other scholars (such as Conzelmann 1987: 104) connect it to the rest of verse 20 and make it the period of the judges, but this seems to pose problems with 1 Kings 6:1. Saul's rule for forty years is a traditional figure (Josephus, *Ant.* 6.14.9 §378; but 10.8.4 §143 reports a twenty-year reign; 1 Sam. 13:1 has a reign of two years, but the number is likely corrupt).

13:22–23 After removing Saul (1 Sam. 13:13–14), God "raised up" (ἤγειρεν, *ēgeiren*) David onto the scene of history as king (1 Sam. 16:12–13; ἤγειρεν is one of the link words in this passage, see vv. 30, 37). This verb has a different meaning in verses 30 and 37, where God raises up Jesus from the dead. Thus a wordplay is present in the speech.

God spoke of David as a man after his heart who would perform God's will. The description comes from 1 Sam. 13:14 (Ps. 89:19–29, esp. v. 21). First Samuel 13:14 is like Isa. 44:28, where the phrase applies to Cyrus (see also the targum on Ps. 89:21; Marshall 1980: 224; Johnson 1992: 232 notes Ps. 88:21 LXX [88:20 Eng.]; 4Q174 1.10; 1 Clem. 18.1). God's promise to David about the everlasting character of his dynasty and seed (σπέρματος, *spermatos*) produced a hope that spoke of a great descendant in this family (2 Sam. 7:6–16; Pss. 89:29, 36–37; 132:11–12, 17; Isa. 9–11; Jer. 23:5; 33:14–22; Ezek. 21:27; 34:23; Ps. Sol. 17.4, 21–34). This promised Savior Paul now identifies as Jesus (on Jesus as a son of David, see Rom. 1:3; 2 Tim. 2:8; Matt. 1:1; Luke 3:23, 31; Mark 12:35; Fitzmyer 1998: 512; the idea is developed in Luke: 1:31–35; 18:38–39; 20:41). Peter made much of this point in Acts 2:30–36.

The title "Savior" (σωτήρ, *sōtēr*) appears in only two texts in Acts (5:31; 13:23). It also appears at the announcement of Jesus's birth in Luke 2:11. John 4:42 is its only other use in reference to Jesus in the Gospels (God is Savior in Luke 1:47). The term describes Jesus's role as deliverer (BAGD 801 §2; BDAG 985 §b). In the LXX, this is a common description of God (Ps. 26:1 LXX [27:1 Eng.]), but in Jesus's time it was also used as a title of honor for prominent people, ranging from physicians to rulers. In the NT, however, this term never describes a political ruler. It is used only of God and Jesus.

This speech develops Israel's history in detail, phase by phase, until it reaches David. It then leaps over one thousand years of Israel's history to go directly to the promise of a son of David who will deliver the nation. This is Paul's point in the speech.

John the Baptist pointed the way to this Jesus, first by preparing for **13:24–25** the Lord's coming with a baptism of repentance. Luke 3:3 tells us it was for the forgiveness of sins.[2] This ministry was to Israel, called the "people" (τῷ λαῷ, *tō laō*; another link word in the speech: vv. 24, 31). He was the bridge between the promise and realization of the promise, the last link in Israel's history before the Messiah came (Jervell 1998: 256; Luke 16:16).

As he was completing (ἐπλήρου, *eplērou*) his course, John the Baptist also declared, in response to a question, that he was not the one to come (John 1:20; 3:28) but that there would be one coming later whose sandals John would not be worthy to untie (Matt. 3:11; Mark 1:7; Luke 3:16).[3]

John preached about the Messiah as he finished his "course." The term δρόμος (*dromos*) refers to John's mission and is used of an athletic contest or of the course on which it is held. The term often was a metaphor for a course taken (Johnson 1992: 233; Epictetus, *Discourses* 3.14.11–14; Eccles. 9:11; Wis. 17:19 [17:18 LXX]; Jer. 8:6; 2 Macc. 14:45; 2 Tim. 4:7). Fitzmyer (1998: 513) notes that John is pictured as running ahead on the course to herald Jesus's coming. The verb for "completing" the course is imperfect (ἐπλήρου, *eplērou*).

---

2. On John the Baptist in Luke-Acts, see Luke 1:17, 76–77; 3:1–17; 5:33; 7:18–33; 9:7–9, 19; 16:16; 20:4–6; Acts 1:5, 22; 10:37; 11:16; 18:25; 19:3–4; and parallels in Matt. 3:1–17 and Mark 1:2–11; also John 1:19–27; Josephus, *Ant.* 18.5.2 §§116–17.

3. On τί (*ti*) functioning as a question and not a relative clause, see Moule 1959: 124, 132; BDF §298.4, §299.2; "What do you think I am?" (NET); "Who do you think I am?" (HCSB).

That Jewish slaves were not supposed to untie the thongs of sandals was treated in the discussion of Luke 3:16 (Bock 1994: 320–24; *b. Ketub.* 96a; Le Cornu and Shulam 2003: 728). John does not feel worthy of doing even the most menial task of a slave. More significant, however, is that this saying introduced John's remark about Jesus bringing the baptism of the Spirit in Luke 3:16, pointing to Jesus's work, which signals the new era. The humility and submission of John are highlighted here in part to make the point that John is not the center of the story of God's activity but, rather, Jesus is (Acts 19:1–6).

13:26–29   Paul now addresses the sons of Abraham as well as proselytes, described as those who fear God. The promise is now preached to Israel as realized. He presents the salvation message, the kerygma (vv. 26–31). He notes that this message (see v. 23) is "for us." This phrase is placed forward in the Greek sentence for emphasis. The message of salvation is a message of deliverance and enablement, as 13:23, 34–39 shows. The term σωτηρία (*sōteria*) was discussed in Acts 4:12. The phrase "message of salvation" may allude to Ps. 118:22 and Isa. 53:3 (Marshall 1980: 225). Paul summarizes the circumstances that led to Jesus's death and resurrection, the core events of the kerygma.

Paul makes the point that the prophets' message was not understood even though it was read each Sabbath (Acts 15:21). The Jewish leadership had two failures: (1) it did not recognize Jesus and his work, and (2) it failed to understand the prophets read in the synagogue each Sabbath (on such blame, see 2:22–24; 3:17; 4:26–28). And so they condemned their Savior as Scripture predicted. A note of fulfillment runs through the entire speech (vv. 27, 29, and the scriptural citations).

Paul reaffirms that Jesus's death took place despite his innocence, which was the point of the account in Luke 23:1–25, 47 (esp. vv. 4, 14–15, 22; also John 18:38; 19:4, 6). Pilate had him killed, despite declarations that Jesus had done nothing worthy of death, because of the Jewish leadership's demands (Luke 23:2, 21–23). Pilate was a part of the conspiracy against Jesus because he helped to underwrite the injustice against Jesus by sentencing him to death, as Acts 4:25–27 also states. Preachers in Acts also will be called innocent (16:35–39; 18:14–16; 19:31, 37; 23:29; 25:14–19; 26:31–32).

The scriptural predictions about Jesus's suffering have been fulfilled (3:18). They took him down from the "tree" (ξύλου, *xylou*), an allusion to Deut. 21:22 (Acts 5:30; Gal. 3:13; on who killed Jesus, see Acts 2:23; 3:13; 4:26–28; 5:30–31; 10:39–40). The texts in mind here would include Isa. 52:13–53:12; Pss. 22; 69; and 118. They buried him in a tomb. The reference to "they" is generic, an allusion to Joseph of Arimathea and probably to Pilate's permission that allowed Jesus to be buried and the opposition that caused his death (Luke 23:25–26, 53; John 19:16–17, 38). This "they," then, includes those who rejected Jesus (Jewish leaders and Pilate) and those who respected Jesus (Joseph of Arimathea with Pilate's permission), depending on the act in view. The details show that there is no doubt that Jesus died on the cross.

The Jewish leadership, citizens in Jerusalem, and Pilate led Jesus to his death, but God raised Jesus from the dead. This is the key "contrastive act" of the kerygma (Jervell 1998: 358). It was also the central divine act of vindication, showing where God stood. The shift of subject here is important. The Jewish leaders and Pilate had handled Jesus up to this point, but now God acted on his behalf (Acts 2:24; 3:15; 4:10; 5:30; 10:39–40; 17:31; also 1 Thess. 1:10; Gal. 1:1; 1 Cor. 6:14; 15:4–20; 2 Cor. 4:14; Rom. 4:24–25; 6:4, 9; 7:4; 8:11, 34; 10:9; Col. 2:12; Eph. 1:20; Fitzmyer 1998: 515). **13:30**

Next, Paul mentions Jesus's numerous appearances over many (πλείους, *pleious*) days to the disciples who had been with him, both in Galilee and now in Jerusalem (Acts 1:3). The number of days for these appearances is expressed by a comparative that functions as an elative (thus "many" days; Wallace 2000: 133). **13:31**

The appearances made these apostles witnesses (Luke 24:48; Acts 1:8) of the resurrection on behalf of Israel, called "the people" here (on the term "people," see Acts 2:47; 3:9). Here is personal proof that these events took place. These witnesses proclaim what God did through Jesus. They guarantee the truth of the message (Jervell 1998: 358). Acts 1:3 tells us that the appearances lasted for forty days. Jesus's ministry spanned the area from Galilee to Jerusalem, and this makes the point that these witnesses were with him throughout his work (1:22). There is no effort to downgrade Jesus's appearance to Paul here, only to note that the core of the gospel goes back to witnesses who were there and who had walked with Jesus.

Not only do witnesses testify to the resurrection; so does Scripture, indicating that the promise has come in Jesus through God's vindication. Thus Paul preaches the promise (the word is singular) made to the fathers (on the fathers, see 3:13). This is the promise made to David in verse 23 (Schneider 1982: 516). Once again the note of fulfillment appears, as it will in the next several verses (also earlier, vv. 27 and 29). But other Scripture tells us more about this promised program of God and the work of the Son. Three OT citations follow in verses 33–35: Ps. 2:7; Isa. 55:3; and Ps. 16:10. **13:32–33**

The introductory formula of Acts 13:32–33 for Ps. 2:7 has three points: the coming of the promise, its fulfillment for the Jews, and the "raising of Jesus." The term ἐπαγγελίαν (*epangelian*, promise) is accusative in anticipation of the object (BDF §476.3). Paul says that the promise has come "to us their children," a reference to the descendants of the promise, especially to the current generation of Jews. The perfect-tense verb ἐκπεπλήρωκεν (*ekpeplērōken*) means that the promise stands fulfilled. The idea of "to you" is taken up again and emphasized in verse 34 with respect to the sure blessings of David. The phrase "to you" is placed forward in the citation in the Greek to underscore the declaration and is plural: "for all of you." This fulfillment has come through the resurrection of Jesus to God's right hand into an active role as Son of God, as Ps. 2 declares. Paul cites the text exactly as it appears in the LXX. The offer of the promise is for them all. The key is to respond.

The psalm, as a royal psalm, is ultimately about the Messiah. It points out that his relationship to God is one of intimate sonship (Ps. Sol. 17.21–26; Marshall 1980: 226; on the use of this psalm, see O'Toole 1979; Goldsmith 1968; Lovestam 1961). Jesus now functions as the Promised One installed to carry out his divinely appointed role. This is one of the few uses of the title "Son" for Jesus in Acts (see discussion of 9:19b–20). Psalm 2 is also cited in Heb. 1:5 and 5:5 (Luke 3:22; Acts 4:26 also uses Ps. 2 but cites vv. 1–2). Luke here uses a different verb for "raise up" (ἀναστήσας, *anastēsas*) Jesus from the word used in Acts 13:30 (ἤγειρεν, *ēgeiren*).

There is scholarly discussion about whether ἀναστήσας means "raise up" onto the stage of history (so 3:22, 26; 7:37). This is what Barrett (1994: 645–46) argues when he sees the resurrection in verse 34 and views Ps. 2 as referring to Jesus's ministry. This could well be correct. Most scholars think that it is slightly more likely that the reference is to the resurrection, since the immediate context in which the term appears is surrounded by references to the resurrection (see esp. v. 34). This is also possible. One could make the case that with the resurrection already noted in verse 30, a more generic reference to being on the scene of history is intended here with the different term. Other occurrences of this verb in Acts, however, refer to the resurrection (2:24, 32; 10:41; 17:3, 31). So a reference to the resurrection is slightly more likely. Sonship was vindicated and made evident by the resurrection (Rom. 1:1–4). This is not Jesus becoming Son or being adopted as Son, as some argue, but being made evident as Son (correctly, Marshall 1980: 22 versus Barrett 1994: 646 and Schweizer, *TDNT* 8:367). By this time, Jesus had established his sonship by the character of his ministry.

13:34   Paul now remarks, appealing to the promise of Isa. 55:3, that the resurrection means that the Promised One would not see corruption as part of God's promise to David. Again Paul uses the term ἀνέστησεν (*anestēsen*) to make the point about the resurrection. The discussion of Jesus not seeing the corruption of decay after death also appeared in Acts 2:25–30 (see the discussion on 2:27). God brought Jesus back to life before he decayed. Here the reference to the resurrection leads to the citation of Isa. 55:3 LXX to make the point that the resurrection was the means by which God distributed the promised blessings that were given to David for the people.

That the promise is for the people is a major theme in the speech, as it appears again in verses 38–39. Isaiah 55:3 taught that the promises once given to David are going to be made available to God's people (ὑμῖν, *hymin*, to you) in the deliverance.

There is a difference here between the MT and the LXX, which is the form Paul cites, except that he simplifies the LXX verb "I shall covenant" (διαθήσομαι, *diathēsomai*) to "I shall give" (δώσω, *dōsō*). The LXX reads, "I will make with you an everlasting covenant, my steadfast, sure love for David." The Greek translation differs from the Hebrew in reading "holy things" (τὰ ὅσια, *ta hosia*) instead of a Hebrew term meaning "faithful love" or "mercy" (חֲסָדִים, *ḥăsādîm*). The Greek OT has a paraphrastic rendering, for it makes concrete (the holy [and sure] things of the promises of David) what God's love and mercy expressed (Johnson 1992: 235). Fitzmyer (1998: 517) calls the LXX translation a fairly accurate rendering of Isa. 55:3, which is also reflected in 1QIsaᵃ 45.22–23. It is often said that Luke's version lacks a reference to the covenant, but this overstates the difference. Any Jew would be aware that the "holy things of David" alludes to the covenant. The change only makes the idea of covenant less explicit. This covenant promise comes from 2 Sam. 7:13–16. Some extend the idea of "holy things" specifically to "divine assurances or decrees," which would point also to the covenant (BDAG 728.3). This more concrete rendering is the direction of the language but is not the best translation of the term here, for "assurance" makes explicit what is stated more implicitly here.

These promises are faithful or sure (God keeps his word) and holy (sacred, set apart). Now they are made available to Paul's hearers. "Holy things" (τὰ ὅσια) and "Holy One" (τὸν ὅσιον, *ton hosion*) are the link words between Isa. 55:3 and Ps. 16:10 as Paul employs *gezerah shewa*, one of Hillel's rabbinic rules of interpretation,[4] where two texts can be exposited together if they share a term or a related form of a word. We saw this technique in Acts 2 as well. Paul's exposition is also linked to Ps. 16:10, cited in the next verse through the term "corruption" (διαφθοράν, *diaphthoran*). Yet a third link between the verses is "I will give" (δώσω) in verse 34 and "you will not let" in verse 35 (δώσεις, *dōseis*). This argument reflects rabbinic technique. The "you" in the verse is primarily Jews but includes the proselytes who now are a part of the people and promise (v. 26). They are the beneficiaries of God's completion of his promise if they respond to the offer Paul makes. Indeed, whoever responds to the promise, including Gentiles, will be its beneficiary, as events later in the chapter show (see vv. 42–48).

Next Paul cites Ps. 16:10 to show how the resurrection was predicted.   **13:35**
This psalm was also used in Acts 2:25–28 (see those verses for the her-

---

4. On holy things as things said, see Wis. 6:10 and Josephus, *Ant.* 8.4.3 §115. In Josephus the expression refers to "holy laws"; Witherington 1998: 412; Dupont 1961.

meneutic used in citing the psalm). "Holy One" is another title applied to Jesus in this speech alongside "Savior" and "Son" (for "Holy One," see the discussion on 2:27 and 3:14).

13:36–37   Paul's point is that Jesus did not see corruption in contrast to David, who served his generation, died, and remains buried. The phrase ἰδίᾳ γενεᾷ (*idia genea*) is a dative of time (BDF §200.4; Moulton and Turner 1963: 243). The most natural reading here is that the text notes how David, having served during the time of his generation by the will of God, fell asleep (on the multiple syntactical options here, see Barrett 1994: 648; for this reading, Rengstorf, *TDNT* 8:540). His mission done, David fell asleep and went to be with the fathers (on "sleep" for death, see Acts 7:60; on "with the fathers," Judg. 2:10; 1 Kings 2:10; 1 Macc. 2:69). So the psalm, pressed in its understanding in light of its language of hope, ultimately cannot be about David. It must be about someone else. The one whom God raised, understood to be Jesus, is the one who did not see corruption and is the one who fulfills the promise. In this passage the other verb for "raised" (ἤγειρεν, *ēgeiren*) appears, as does the link word "corruption" (διαφθοράν; vv. 34–35). Paul argues that all of these texts are connected and lead to this conclusion.

13:38–39   Paul applies the lesson from his survey of history. This portion of the speech is the word of exhortation, also called the *peroratio* (Witherington 1998: 413). There is a "call to repent" put in Pauline terms of justification (Schneider 1982: 139). It is through the raised and living Jesus that forgiveness of sins is made available "to [all of] you" (ὑμῖν). The speech has already called him Savior, Son, and Holy One. He is to be accepted, not rejected. "To you" is yet another verbal link back to verse 34 and the promises of David given to all those who respond ("you" is plural here as in v. 34). Deliverance is declared in terms of forgiveness of sins (Acts 2:38; 3:19; 5:31; 10:43; 26:18; Rom. 4:7; Eph. 1:7; Col. 1:14) and justification (as part of Davidic realization, due to the link). This forgiveness comes "through this man" (διὰ τούτου, *dia toutou*), a good example of διά with the genitive referring to the means by which something is done (Moule 1959: 58). The key to everything offered here is Jesus. There is a change in the pronoun from "to us" (v. 33) to "to you" (here and in v. 34) to press the point that the offer is being made to those who have yet to respond. The new phrase is also placed forward in the Greek sentence for emphasis. The history is "for us," but the offer is "to you" because Paul's audience still stands outside the blessing. They need to respond so that they can receive what Paul and his group already possess.

Paul also notes that Jesus can provide what Moses and the law could not, namely, justification (v. 39). The law might be able, in the view of Jews, to deal with some sin through sacrifice, but it could not bring complete forgiveness and thus is for Paul completely inadequate. Witherington (1998: 413) argues for an intended nuance here of the law being able to forgive some but not all sin, but Bruce (1990: 311) and Fitzmyer (1998: 518–19) argue persuasively that there is no such implied comparison with sacrifices here or in Paul. The law is utterly inadequate (Johnson 1992: 236 is uncertain whether there is comparison or full contrast). Paul's concern is not the intermediate way of picturing forgiveness in the law or sacrifices but the extension of full forgiveness in Christ. This is total forgiveness that the law of Moses could not give.

Justification is what Jesus brings. Paul twice uses the verb δικαιόω (*dikaioō*). This is a favorite term of Paul and means "declare [someone] righteous." This happens in Jesus and not by the law because the law could not justify and make one righteous. The allusion here is to the declaration of righteousness and the provision of the Spirit that justification enables (Rom. 3:21–8:39). These two benefits are the core of the gospel and bring righteousness (Acts 2:39). This verb is often used to speak of God's declaring us righteous: to justify or render a favorable verdict (Gal. 2:16; 3:11, 24; Rom. 2:13; 3:20, 24, 28; 4:2, 5; 5:1, 9; 8:30, 33; 1 Cor. 6:11). A passage such as Acts 13 shows that the verb can also mean "be set free" from a claim (BAGD 197 §3a; BDAG 249 §3). So here it is rendered, "Everyone who believes is freed (from all things) from which you could not be freed by the law of Moses" (the RSV adds the parenthetical phrase; the ESV and NASB also use "freed"). The NET renders the verse thus: "By this one everyone who believes is justified from everything from which the law of Moses could not justify you." It is the awkwardness of the English in using "justified" that leads to the other rendering. The NLT rendering uses both ideas: "Everyone who believes in him is freed from all guilt and declared right with God." Fitzmyer (1998: 518) says a good alternative rendering is simply "is acquitted." This usage is very close to Rom. 6:7 in what it says (also 1 Cor. 6:11; Schneider 1982: 140). To seek forgiveness is to repent, because it recognizes wrongs committed. To seek forgiveness is also to exercise faith in what God has done through Jesus.

Some scholars argue that Luke views justification in an entirely negative way here and that this is not Paul's view (Vielhauer 1966). However, with Paul Luke sees justification for one's sins as clearing the way for the Spirit—not as synonymous with forgiveness but providing for it (Acts 19:1–7; Rom. 3:21–8:39), and so it is not as entirely negative as is suggested. Others (Barrett 1994: 650–51) argue that the expression does not have its full Pauline forensic sense, but this may be nothing more that a Lukan telescoping of Paul's view. The legal declaration of forgiveness, which is Paul's emphasis, leads to a release from sin, which is highlighted here.

The forgiveness Jesus gives sets believers free from the legal obligations that sin brought against them (Rom. 6:7) and leads into fellowship with God by giving them the Spirit (Rom. 6–8). The language has OT roots (Johnson 1992: 236; Exod. 23:7 LXX; Deut. 25:1; 1 Sam. 12:7; 2 Sam.

15:4; Pss. 18:9; 50:4; 81:3; 142:2 LXX [19:8; 51:2; 82:3; 143:2 Eng.]; Isa. 5:23; 45:24–25; 50:8; 53:11; also Sir. 7:5; 10:29; 18:2).

It is "through this man" (διὰ τούτου; v. 38) and "by this one" (ἐν τούτῳ, en toutō; v. 39) that justification takes place. Both of these phrases are also placed forward in the Greek sentence for emphasis. The phrase "by this one" points to the means by which one is freed or justified from what one could not be freed by through the law. The one who brings release is the person of Jesus through his work. This liberation before God with reference to sin comes for all who believe in him and this work. Belief or faith is the core response that one must have to experience the blessings of salvation. Those blessings God promised to his people, to the fathers, and to David long ago. They are reserved for "everyone who believes" (πᾶς ὁ πιστεύων, pas ho pisteuōn; Acts 10:43; Rom. 1:16; 3:22; 4:11; 10:4, 11).

13:40–41 Paul calls on his audience to watch carefully (βλέπετε, blepete), that is, to pay attention lest they fall into judgment as the prophets warned. Failure to respond will mean judgment. Luke 21:8 uses this term to tell disciples to beware of being misled about events of the end, as do the parallels, Matt. 24:4 and Mark 13:5. Such warnings are common in the NT: 1 Cor. 8:9; Gal. 5:15; Eph. 5:15; Col. 2:8; Heb. 3:12; 12:25 (Schneider 1982: 141).

Next, Paul cites as a warning a passage from the prophet Habakkuk (1:5 LXX). He tells his listeners to watch out lest judgment come for not heeding or believing God when he acts. The prophet calls the nation to see the rise of Babylon and the judgment intended for Israel. Fitzmyer (1998: 519) notes that the text follows the LXX and 1QpHab 2.1–2 in including the word "scoffers" to describe those who have not believed God. The citation is a shortened version of the LXX, which reads, "Look, you scoffers, observe closely and be amazed at wondrous deeds, and then disappear! For I am doing a deed in your days that you would not believe if someone told you." The MT differs in that where "scoffers" appears, the term "among the nations" appears, so that the beginning reads, "Look among the nations and see." The point being highlighted in the speech is the same: failure to embrace what God is doing leads to judgment. The warning also refers to God's work twice. The response of amazement rather than faith is negative. The audience risks failing to respond properly. The LXX includes the word "scoffers" because it is a description of what the verse in the MT describes. God acts; they look but they do not believe. Wall (2000) traces the use of the book of Habakkuk in Acts, treating its appearance here and as an echo in Acts 15:5, where some believers question what is taking place with the Gentiles.

Paul uses Hab. 1:5 analogously to Israel's situation with Babylon in the past. His hearers are to see what God is doing in Jesus and respect God's work. He warns them not to be scoffers (οἱ καταφρονηταί, hoi *kataphronētai*) of God as the earlier generation was. This is the only occurrence of this term in the NT. It refers to someone who despises or has contempt for something (BAGD 420; BDAG 529). Rejecting God's work in Christ puts one in this category. The citation speaks of a "deed" or "work" twice in the singular, the second occurrence being an addition to the citation for emphasis. Does this work refer to the resurrection (Pillai 1980: 72–73), the work of God in Christ (Barrett 1994: 652), the preaching of the message (Fitzmyer 1998: 519), or the church's turning to Gentiles (Schneider 1982: 141)? A combination of God's work in Christ and the message about it is most likely, since the message is about God's work in Christ. The resurrection itself is too narrow a referent because, although it serves to vindicate God's work through Jesus, the vindication of what God did in Jesus extends into the rationale for why the church preaches good news, which is what Paul is doing here. So a broader reference, including the message, makes better contextual sense.

There is also another turn in God's plan: the missionaries will actively evangelize Gentiles, but this is not the exclusive point of the text, as the speech has already made clear. Gentile inclusion is an implication that emerges alongside Israel's lack of response and is not explicitly present until verse 46 (Polhill 1992: 305; Moessner 1988). For Paul, this message summarizes Christ's entire work, which has not been believed up to now (ἔργον ὃ οὐ μὴ πιστεύσητε, *ergon ho ou mē pisteusēte*). The scoffer does not respond even if told what is taking place. The singular reference to "work" is a collective term pointing to the ministry of Jesus as a whole. The message of the church is about that work.

So those who fail to heed the prophet's word are destroyed for their lack of faith. This is the only use of the verb ἀφανίζω (*aphanizō*, perish) in Luke-Acts. Here it is passive, giving the sense of being destroyed or perishing in judgment (Matt. 6:19–20 speaks of the moth destroying earthly treasure but unable to destroy heavenly treasure). Josephus (*Ant.* 1.3.2 §76) applies this term to the destruction of sinners in the flood. This theme of rejection will reappear in Acts (13:46; 18:6; 28:28).

The people are urging (παρεκάλουν, *parekaloun*) Paul and Barnabas **13:42–43** to come back and preach more about this on the next Sabbath. Some, then, are interested in hearing more about Jesus. This Greek verb is in the imperfect, portraying the requesting in a vivid, ongoing manner.

Many in the crowd are uncommitted at this point, but the next verse indicates that many others respond. These include both Jews and "converts," or those outside Judaism who now worship at the synagogue. The phrase describing this second group is τῶν σεβομένων προσηλύτων (*tōn sebomenōn prosēlytōn*, [God-]fearing proselytes). This probably combines a reference to two groups normally distinguished, as verses 16b and 26a refer to God-fearers. Schneider (1982: 142n141) prefers to limit the reference to God-fearers. There is a difference between the two. God-fearers worship Israel's God but do not become circumcised, receive baptism, or offer a sacrifice, whereas proselytes take the final step. Luke appears to speak of the combination of both groups here, although Barrett (1994: 654) suggests that only devout proselytes are meant (also Marshall 1980: 229, who, like Barrett, relies on the presence of the noun "proselytes" as key). These non-Jews have embraced the God of Israel. Now they are responding to the message of God's grace. Paul urges them to remain faithful in that grace (see the discussion on Acts 11:22–24; on Luke's use of grace, see Luke 1:30; 2:40, 52; 4:22; Acts 2:47; 4:33; 11:23).

13:44–45 The next Sabbath the whole city gathers to hear Paul preach the word of the Lord about God's work through Jesus. The reading "word of the Lord" is preferred to "word of God" on the basis of better MSS ($\mathfrak{P}^{74}$, $\aleph$, A, B², 33, 81, and 1739). Johnson (1992: 240) notes that this theme of the whole city responding is common in Hellenistic literature (Chariton of Aphrodisias, *Chaer.* 3.4.18; Heliodorus, *Aethiopica* 4.9.15).

The positive reception causes some in the Jewish leadership to oppose Paul and "slander" (βλασφημοῦντες, *blasphēmountes*) him. This is a strong term. When it refers to God, it means "blaspheme" (2 Kings 19:6, 22 LXX; Luke 12:10). Johnson (1992: 240) argues that near blasphemy is meant here because it is the word of God that is being rejected (v. 44; on slander/blasphemy in Luke, see Luke 5:21; 22:65; 23:39; Acts 18:6; 26:11). Luke 22:65 reports a similar response to Jesus, showing that Paul's experience as a follower is like his teacher's. He is being hated for the sake of the name of Jesus (Luke 21:17). It is also the jealousy (ζήλου, *zēlou*) of the Jews that leads them to contradict Paul and strongly oppose him (see 14:2 for a parallel reaction). This suggests a struggle for power and control of the people, as some are jealous of the drawing in of the Gentiles to a distinct expression of promise rooted in Judaism.

Kilgallen (2003a) details how the opposition to the word is directed especially at the claim that every person who believes in the Lord will be justified, a move beyond God-fearers to include all Gentiles. Kilgallen also shows how ζῆλος (*zēlos*, zeal) and related forms in the LXX indicate a positive zeal for covenant, a religiously directed zeal in defense of the law (1 Kings 19:10, 14 [Elijah, affirmed in Sir. 48:2]; Num. 25:11, 13 [Phinehas]; Ps. 106:30; Sir. 45:23 [against false idols]; 1 Macc. 2:26, 54 with 2:42, 48 [the Maccabees against Antiochus]; 4 Macc. 18:12). This jealousy parallels the reaction to Peter in Acts 5:17. Witherington (1998: 415 and n. 236) posits that the backdrop is of some in Judaism engaged in gaining proselytes, but it is more likely that they object to the way Gentiles are being connected to Israel's God, not that they hope for such a response from Gentiles (Polhill 1992: 307; note the reaction in Acts 13:50 to Gentile inclusion, an issue that also surfaced in Jesus's speech at Capernaum in Luke 4:25–28). In other words, zeal for covenant has blinded them from seeing the breakthrough of God's promise, with the result that positive zeal has become negative by cutting short the ultimate promise intended in the law. This reaction also shows that those rejecting Jesus and the message about him are the "scoffers" Paul mentioned earlier at the synagogue (v. 41). As such, they are subject to judgment.

Paul boldly (παρρησιασάμενοι, *parrēsiasamenoi*) declares that "to [all of]   **13:46–47** you" (ὑμῖν, *hymin*) the word has come first. Of its nine NT occurrences, παρρησιάζομαι appears seven times in Acts (9:27–29 [2x]; 13:46; 14:3; 18:25–26; 19:8; 26:26; Eph. 6:20; 1 Thess. 2:2). All the occurrences concern Paul (Schneider 1982: 145). This is a fulfillment of Luke 21:13–15, as Paul is given utterance to preach the word (Polhill 1992: 307). The phrase "to you" is placed forward in the Greek sentence for emphasis. Paul sees going to the Jews first as "necessary" (ἀναγκαῖον, *anankaion*), one of only two occurrences of this term in Acts (in 10:24 it has a different meaning; to the Jew first: Acts 13:26, 32–33; 14:1; 16:13; 17:1, 10, 17; 18:4; 19:8; Rom. 1:16; 2:9–10; Jervell 1998: 363). This is only proper because it is Israel's history that holds the promise.

Three points dominate the verse: (1) there is rejection; (2) the result is that they judge themselves unworthy of life, as the explanation using "since" (ἐπειδή, *epeidē*) indicates; and so (3) Paul and company will turn to the Gentiles.

First, they have rejected the message, a point expressed as having thrust it out (ἀπωθεῖσθε, *apōtheisthe*, you thrust out). This is another graphic term for rejection. As a group, the Jews have taken God's word and have pushed it aside or repudiated it (BAGD 103 §2; BDAG 126 §2; 1 Sam. 12:22; Pss. 61:5; 76:8; 77:60, 67 LXX [62:4; 77:7; 78:60, 67 Eng.]; Jer. 23:17; Acts 7:27, 39). The term refers to pushing something away forcefully.

Second, they have judged themselves not to be worthy of eternal life, another way to describe what salvation is by highlighting its content. So rejection and lack of salvation are their responsibility. This is one of the few references to eternal life in Acts. This passage (here and in v. 48) is the only place in Acts that this term appears. Acts 11:18 and 5:20 are close with references to "life" (Luke 10:25; 18:18, 30; Gal. 6:8; 1 Tim. 6:12; in the OT and Judaism: Dan. 12:2; Sir. 37:26; 4Q181 1.4, 6; 1QS 4.7; CD 3.20; 4Q511 2.1.4; 6Q18 2.2; Fitzmyer 1998: 521). The message of salvation is now equated with the hope of eternal life.

So, finally, Paul turns to the Gentiles. This is the first of several places in Acts where Paul goes to the Gentiles after being rejected by most Jews (18:6; 28:28). This turning away is not absolute, however, as in each place Paul goes, he again starts by preaching to Jews (14:1; 18:4–6, 19; 19:8–9; 28:28; explained in Rom. 9–11). Paul repeatedly faced violent resistance in many synagogues (2 Cor. 11:24) but continued to preach to Jews. In this he turned the other cheek, as Jesus had commanded in the Sermon on the Mount (Matt. 5:39).

In verse 47 Paul turns to Scripture, explaining how the Lord commands the missionaries' response. This is an allusion to the commission noted in Acts 9:15 and what is reported in 22:18, that Paul would be called to the Gentiles. The entire series of connections to things said earlier in Acts along with parallels to Luke's Gospel show how important this chapter is to the book. Paul's ministry mirrors that of Jesus and the apostles. He also is obedient to the commission God has given him at great cost. He perseveres, modeling what the commitment of the church is to all people.

Paul cites Isa. 49:6, a passage that defines the servant's role in Isaiah (on the servant as light, see Isa. 42:6; 9:2). The citation is closer to the MT than to the LXX, which mentions the servant being set up as a covenant for the people, an allusion to the covenant for the Jews (Fitzmyer 1998: 521). Paul says that the Lord has commanded Barnabas and Paul to undertake this role of being a guide to the nations concerning the way to God. This task is much like the way a light illumines a path.

What is surprising is that Paul and Barnabas are now cast in the role of the servant of Israel. The servant was normally an image tied to Jesus in the NT. Now they are the light (describing Jesus in Luke 1:78–79; 2:29–32, using Isa. 49:6; 2 Cor. 4:3–6; servant and Jesus: Isa. 42:1–4 in Matt. 12:17–21; Isa. 53:12 in Luke 22:37; Isa. 53:7–8 in Acts 8:32–35; Marshall 1980: 230). They bring salvation to the "end of the earth" (cf. Luke 3:6). So Paul and Barnabas are now seen as an extension of the work of the Servant of the Lord, who was Jesus.

The hermeneutic used here is the "one in the many," which is a basic way of connecting themes between the testaments. One can compare the use of "servant" in Luke-Acts to the use of "seed" in Gen. 12:3 and Gal. 3, where it is about both Jesus and those incorporated into him. The task of Jesus continues in his commissioned servants. Their call is to be a light to the Gentiles and go to the end of the earth. This verse echoes Acts 1:8, which alludes to Isa. 49:6 as well. The goal of God's plan of salvation is to take the message to the end of the earth, to extend it to all nations in every part of the world.

13:48   The Gentiles who hear this message begin rejoicing and glorifying the word of the Lord (on joy, see Luke 1:14, 28; 2:10; Acts 5:41; on glory, Luke 2:20; 7:16; Acts 4:21; 11:18). The reading "word of the Lord" rather than "word of God" is adopted here because the best MSS support it ($\mathfrak{P}^{45, 74}$, ℵ, A, C, Ψ, 33, 1739, and Byz). Again imperfect verbs (ἔχαιρον . . . ἐδόξαζον, *echairon . . . edoxazon*) are used to indicate the ongoing nature of the reaction.

Those who have been ordained to eternal life believe. The word τάσσω (*tassō*, ordain) appears four times in Acts (13:48; 15:2; 22:10; 28:23; in the rest of the NT: Matt. 28:16–17; Luke 7:8; Rom. 13:1; 1 Cor. 16:15–16). In the other contexts of Acts, it means "appoint" or "assign" to something.

Here it refers to God's sovereign work over salvation, where God has assigned those who come to eternal life (BAGD 806 §1b; BDAG 991 §1b). The passive voice indicates that God does the assigning. It is as strong a passage on God's sovereignty as anywhere in Luke-Acts and has OT and Jewish roots (Witherington 1998: 416n242; on the "book of life," see Exod. 32:32–33; Ps. 69:28; Dan. 12:1; 1 En. 47.3; 104.1; 108.3; Jub. 30.20, 22; *b. Ber.* 61b; CD 3.20; 1QS 3.18–4.1; Str-B 2:726–27). Just as God was the major active agent in the events of Israel's history earlier in the speech, so he is the active agent in bringing Gentiles to himself. Repentance leads to eternal life not only because sins are forgiven but also because the Spirit is given (Acts 11:15–18). Barrett (1994: 658) argues that the Spirit is not present in a text such as Acts 10:35, but 11:15–18 shows the connection between life and the Spirit.

This campaign meets with both success and opposition, as the final verses   **13:49**
in the chapter indicate. The word is spreading through the region. Luke often notes the progress of the word or the growth of the community (2:41, 47; 9:31; 11:24b; 12:24). The verb διαφέρω (*diapherō*, spread) appears in Luke-Acts four times out of thirteen NT occurrences (Matt. 6:26; 10:31; 12:12; Mark 11:15–16; Luke 12:7, 24; Acts 13:48–49; 27:27; Rom. 2:17–21; 1 Cor. 15:41; Gal. 2:6–10; 4:1–2; Phil. 1:9–11).

The Jewish leadership incites pious women and leading men to react   **13:50–51**
against Paul and Barnabas and drive them from the city. In the case of the women, these upper classes would be Gentiles who also frequent the synagogue. Josephus tells of many Gentile women being attracted to Judaism in Damascus (*J.W.* 2.20.2 §§559–61). Epigraphic evidence tells us that women often were the most responsive, composing 50 percent of the proselytes but 80 percent of the God-fearers (Le Cornu and Shulam 2003: 756). The contacts these Antiochene women have with other prominent Greeks help to heighten the pressure against Paul and Barnabas.

Thus there is a chain reaction: the Jewish leadership moves the women, who move the city's Greek leadership. The verb παρώτρυναν (*parōtrynan*) means "stir up" someone's emotion against someone else (BAGD 629; BDAG 780). It is the only occurrence of this word in the NT. The noun διωγμός (*diōgmos*, persecution) shows up only here and in Acts 8:1. The reaction, given where it appears in the account, seems to be directed against the outreach to the Gentiles as much as, or more than, it is against the preached message of fulfilled promise. This recalls a similar reaction in Luke 4:25–28 (see Acts 13:44–45). That the reaction comes from the upper classes that control the Jewish community in the city is not entirely surprising, as a mass conversion would leave them with the most to lose (Witherington 1998: 417). The leading men would have included the *duoviri*, the local government's highest representatives, who would have been tied to the cult of the moon god Men as well as the imperial cult. A response to Jesus would imperil such worship (Schnabel 2004: 1107–9 notes the remains of three church buildings in Pisidian Antioch).

Paul and Barnabas leave the city, shaking the dust from their feet, a symbolic act against those who oppose them (Mark 6:11 = Luke 9:5; Luke 10:10–11 = Matt. 10:14). This custom is a way of signaling that responsibility for an action is with the people or town (Str-B 1:571; Cadbury 1933). It portrays leaving defilement behind and moving on. In other words, no trace of their presence is left, even on their feet. This response was also commanded by Jesus in Luke 9:5. Other texts where Paul notes the judgment for rejection are Acts 18:6; 28:25–27.

They move on to Iconium (ninety miles southeast of Pisidian Antioch; on the city, see Pliny the Elder, *Nat.* 5.25.95; Strabo, *Geogr.* 12.6.1; Xenophon, *Anabasis* 1.2.19; Fitzmyer 1998: 522).[5] It is in Galatia, or the old district of Phrygia. The quick movement from city to city helps the gospel spread more rapidly across the world (Schneider 1982: 148). Ironically, sometimes it is persecution that drives the movement and expansion (Acts 8).

13:52 The disciples are filled (ἐπληροῦντο, *eplērounto*) with joy and with the Holy Spirit (Luke 6:23; Acts 5:41; Gal. 5:22; 1 Thess. 1:6). The verb here is imperfect, depicting an ongoing joy and full involvement with the Spirit. Even rejection and persecution do not stop the gospel's progress, nor does such pressure discourage the disciples. This is part of what indicates that they are filled and controlled by the Spirit (Delling, *TDNT* 6:291). The theme is common in Acts (2:4–10; 4:31; 8:17; 9:31; 10:44; 13:2).

In sum, this unit gives the first detailed missionary speech Paul made to Jews and God-fearers (Jervell 1998: 366). The scene also depicts what Paul typically faced as he preached the realization of Jewish promise in the synagogue and to others who would listen. It also indicates a turn to the Gentiles because, when opposition mounted, the Gentiles became the audience.

At the center of the message were the person, promise, and provision of Jesus as the Christ, who came according to the promise of God focused in David's line. There is nothing here a Jew or a Gentile could not appreciate once the outline of the program became clear. God's promise was triggered by Jesus's work. With forgiveness of sins came the Spirit (vv. 38, 52). The life of the church was about the life God gave by grace. The gospel was offered to all, but only by a response of belief does one receive the benefits. Paul and Barnabas warned that judgment awaits scoffers and others who do not respond.

We also see how Barnabas and Paul worked together. Barnabas was able to share the stage with Paul and eventually trained him to be able

---

5. This is modern-day Konya in Turkey.

to step ahead. Good leadership can often be measured by whether it leaves a trail of successors behind it. Barnabas not only encouraged Paul; he also enabled him. Barnabas did not feel the need to be always the front man. So, although Paul is the focus in this text, in many ways Barnabas is a hero in the passage because of the way he teamed with his partner. As Fernando (1998: 390) notes, "Encouragers hand over leadership." In addition, leaders lead by replicating.

Additional Notes

13:18. A difficult textual problem arises here; there is only a one-letter difference in the variants, and both readings are also attested in LXX MSS in the verse that is alluded to (Deut. 1:31). We read that God bore with Israel (ἐτροποφόρησεν, *etropophorēsen*; ℵ, B, C², D, Byz). The variant (ἐτροφοφόρησεν, *etrophophorēsen*) is more positive, meaning "care for" someone, as a nurse for a child ($\mathfrak{P}^{74}$, A, C*, E, Ψ, 33). This second reading has clearer support in Deut. 1:31 LXX. If this were the reading, the meaning would be that God fed them for forty years in the desert (Deut. 1:31; Exod. 16:35; Num. 14:34). But it is slightly more difficult to explain the reading that does not match the LXX than the one that does, so "bore with them" is the slightly more likely reading (Metzger 1971: 405–6; Fitzmyer 1998: 510–11). Barrett (1994: 632) with R. Gordon (1974) and Witherington (1998: 409–10) prefers the more positive reading on the premise that God's positive activity is underscored (Deut. 2:7; 32:10; Hos. 13:5; Zech. 9:11), but God's patience is also a positive feature of God's work for Israel, so that the reading "bore with them" also carries a positive sense.

13:20. The Western text reverses the order of the clauses, assigning the 450 years to the period of the judges.

13:26. The variant here "to you" (ὑμῖν, *hymin*) is found in $\mathfrak{P}^{45}$, C, E, 36, 181, 1175, 1739, and Byz, whereas "to us" (ἡμῖν, *hēmin*) is read in $\mathfrak{P}^{74}$, ℵ, A, B, D, Ψ, 33, 81, and 614. The latter reading has the better MSS distribution and is likely the original.

13:27–29. There are several differences in the Western text from the original text of Acts in these verses. There are even differences between the various witnesses to the Western text, but none of these differences is a part of the original Acts (for details, see Barrett 1994: 642–43). Most of these additions either make additional reference to Scripture or discuss the handing over to Pilate.

13:33. The best reading here is τοῖς τέκνοις αὐτῶν (*tois teknois autōn*, their children), since it makes the best sense (C³, E, Byz, Syriac). This is not a very well attested reading, but the alternative τοῖς τέκνοις ἡμῶν (*tois teknois hēmōn*, our children) does not make good sense (attested by $\mathfrak{P}^{74}$, ℵ, A, B, C*, D). The reading may have resulted from the combination of pronouns juxtaposed to each other in the verse. It is possible that the original had no qualifying pronoun and simply read "children," and then differing clarifying pronouns were added (Barrett 1994: 645).

13:33. A second variant in the verse has D refer to the "first" (πρώτῳ, *prōtō*) psalm, an unlikely reading that is poorly attested.

13:44–45. Codex D has numerous small differences here, showing how free its text of Acts is (Fitzmyer 1998: 520; Barrett 1994: 655–56). The most important, in verse 44, has Paul make "many an address about the Lord." These additions are poorly attested and not original.

4. In Iconium (14:1–7)

Paul and Barnabas move to a city on a high plateau over the plains, Iconium (v. 1a), sitting at an altitude of 3,370 feet. It was a culturally mixed city. The missionaries are traveling the well-known Roman commercial road known as the Via Sebaste or Royal Road (Witherington 1998: 418). Here the typical preaching pattern emerges. They preach, and many Jews and Gentiles respond (v. 1b). Opposition surfaces, however, despite the work of word and act that the missionaries perform (vv. 2–3). The city is divided, and violence ensues against the missionary effort (vv. 4–5). The preachers are forced to flee to Lystra and Derbe, where they continue to preach in a new setting (vv. 6–7).

The account is a narrative summary that Luke would know about from Paul and/or Barnabas (Fitzmyer 1998: 525 speaks of a Pauline source). It has a solid claim to be summarizing real events versus being a creation of Luke (so correctly Marshall 1980: 232 versus Haenchen 1987: 421–23). Barrett (1994: 664) argues that 14:1–23 preserves a basic tradition from Antioch that has been overlaid with typical Lukan themes that were also in his sources. Barrett seems more skeptical, however, about the Iconium information for reasons that are not all that clear, other than that the Iconium account is more general, lacking detail. This difference in detail, however, may reflect three elements: (1) Luke will focus on opposition, with details later in Acts, and so he is brief here; (2) often Luke handles a theme briefly and chooses to fill it out with more detail in another locale; and (3) the previous account in Pisidian Antioch is very similar in its reception-opposition theme. The Lystra-Derbe encounter in the next scene will be filled out by a very similar, detailed account of ministry in Athens in Acts 17. It may be that, planning to give one locale with detail, Luke simply makes his point briefly here, showing that the response at Iconium is the first of a pattern. The presence of literary choice does not indicate a lack of historicity. Some scholars think that verse 3 is out of place in the story, but it indicates that initially even opposition did not preclude Paul and Barnabas from being bold in their outreach.

Exegesis and Exposition

¹It came to pass at Iconium that they entered, as was their custom, into the Jewish synagogue and so spoke that a great company believed, both of Jews and Greeks. ²But the ⌜unbelieving Jews stirred up⌝ the Gentiles and

led their souls to do evil against the brothers. ⌐ ¬ ³Still, they remained for some time, speaking boldly for the Lord, who testified to the word of his grace by giving signs and wonders through their hands. ⁴But the people of the city were split; some sided with the Jews, and some with the apostles. ⁵When an attempt was made by both Gentiles and Jews, with their rulers, to harass and stone them, ⁶they learned of it and fled to Lystra and Derbe, cities of Lycaonia, and to the surrounding country; ⁷and there they were preaching the gospel ⌐ ¬.

Iconium was in the central part of what is now Konya province in Tur- **14:1**
key, a rugged, somewhat isolated location on a plateau in the steppes of central Turkey. It was a ruling center in the region (Schnabel 2004: 1111). Strabo (*Geogr.* 12.6.1) describes the region aptly as cold, bare of trees, with scarcity of water, while the town is well settled. Le Cornu and Shulam (2003: 765) note that little else is known about the Jewish community there.

Barnabas and Paul go to the synagogue, after their pattern (κατὰ τὸ αὐτό, *kata to auto*, after the same manner). This is a reference to their custom of initially going to the synagogue (Barrett 1994: 667). So they begin with the Jews, and they meet with some success. A large multitude (πολὺ πλῆθος, *poly plēthos*) of both Jews and Greeks believe. This is the only time this phrase appears in Acts out of three NT occurrences (Mark 3:7; Luke 23:27). Here the response is described in terms of belief, not repentance or turning (on this verb πιστεύω, *pisteuō*, see Acts 2:44–45). The Greeks here are likely God-fearers and/or proselytes, since they respond at the synagogue (Schneider 1982: 150).

In contrast stands the reaction of unbelieving Jews. The expression οἱ **14:2**
ἀπειθήσαντες (*hoi apeithēsantes*) can mean "the disobedient." In the LXX, it is often used of rebellion (Lev. 26:15; Num. 11:20; Deut. 1:26; 9:7, 23–24; 32:51; Isa. 30:12; Johnson 1992: 246). That is probably too strong a meaning here, given the simple contrast with verse 1 (Acts 19:9; John 3:36; Rom. 2:8; 1 Pet. 3:1). So lack of belief is the point, which is disobedience to God. They work against the effort of Paul and Barnabas to reach Gentiles. The verb κακόω (*kakoō*) in this context means to make "someone think badly about another" (BDAG 502 §2) or "poison the minds of some persons" (BAGD 398 §2). Some translations adopt this more graphic rendering, to "poison" the minds of the Gentiles (RSV, NIV, NET, NLT ["stirred up distrust"]; Ps. 105:32 LXX [106:32 Eng.]; 1 Pet. 3:13; Josephus, *Ant.* 16.7.3 §205; 16.8.6 §262). Our translation opts for "led their souls to do evil." The verb is used of acts of oppression in Acts 7:6, 19 and of Herod's wicked acts in 12:1. The term that is often rendered "mind" here is ψυχή (*psychē*), which can refer to the feelings, emotions, and judgments of a person, so that it matches the idea of how the soul controls the thinking of a person (BAGD 893 §1aγ; BDAG 1099

§2c). In other words, not only did the Jews stir up Gentiles against Paul and Barnabas, they so stirred them that they acted out their feelings in persecution. This is an interesting move, since often Jews and Gentiles were corporately distinct. Gentiles viewed Jews with suspicion, holding that the Jews "profane all we hold sacred," and their Sabbath custom was seen as "the charms of indolence" (Tacitus, *Hist.* 5.4.1, 3). That opposing Jews would seek Gentile support shows how seriously they took the threat of the preaching of the gospel (Le Cornu and Shulam 2003: 767). The tone here is similar to Acts 3–4 with both success and opposition. It also parallels the reaction at Pisidian Antioch in Acts 13. A pattern of varied response is emerging.

14:3 Whatever the opposition, Paul and Barnabas decide to stay and continue the effort. Some scholars see this verse as out of sequence, but in fact it indicates resolve in the face of opposition (Witherington 1998: 419). Moulton and Turner (1963: 337) suggest translating the μὲν οὖν (*men oun*) construction at the start of the verse as "nay rather," to show the contrast between the opposition and the response. In my translation, I opt for a term with an equivalent force: "Still." Despite the opposition, they remain for a long time and speak boldly for the Lord (Acts 4:13; 9:27), who in turn witnesses to them through signs and wonders. Their ministry is a combination of word and action. The message is a word of grace (20:32). God's gracious act in forgiveness and provision of life is the topic, like what we saw detailed in Acts 13. The combination of signs and wonders appeared in 2:19 (see the discussion there; also 2:22, 43; 5:12; 6:8; 8:6; 15:12; 19:11; 28:9; Jervell 1998: 370). The order of these two terms varies, with σημεῖον (*sēmeion*) first, as here, in 4:30; 5:12; and 15:12. This is the consistent order in the epistles as well (Rom. 15:19; 2 Cor. 12:12; 2 Thess. 2:9; Heb. 2:4). The other term, τέρας (*teras*), never appears in the NT without the mention of σημεῖον, and it is used sixteen times. The Lord is the key source of the activity. It is he who "bore witness" (Acts 13:22; 15:8; 20:23). He supports the work of preaching the gospel.

14:4 The city is split (ἐσχίσθη, *eschisthē*). This verb is at the root of the English word "schism." It vividly describes a division in the city. Some are for "the Jews." Others favor "the apostles." This incident is described in Acts of Paul 3.3 with additional detail that includes a famous traditional description of Paul: "And he saw Paul coming, a man small in size, bald-headed, bandy-legged, well-built, with eyebrows meeting, rather long-nosed, full of grace. For sometimes he seemed like a man, and sometimes he had the countenance of an angel." We do not know if this description is accurate, but the citation is often noted.

Acts 14:4, 14 contains the only use of the term "apostles" for Paul and Barnabas. Since Barnabas is included, this is a slightly broader use of the term than a technical reference to the Twelve. It is like the usage in

1 Cor. 9:4–6, where it refers to a commissioned messenger, one sent out by the church into missionary work (2 Cor. 8:23; Phil. 2:25; Fitzmyer 1998: 526; Barrett 1994: 671–72).[1] Elsewhere the term is reserved for the eleven listed in Acts 1:13 and for Matthias (Acts 1:26).

An effort is made to physically assault and stone them. The term ὑβρίσαι   **14:5–7**
(*hybrisai*) refers to mistreating someone in an insolent manner (BAGD 831; BDAG 1022; cf. Matt. 22:6, of abused servants in the parable of the wicked tenants; Luke 18:32, of Jesus's suffering; 1 Thess. 2:2). "Harass," "molest," or "physically intimidate" gives a good sense of this term. There is a desire to stone them either as false teachers or for teaching blasphemy, since that is what stoning indicated in a Jewish context. The plot comes from both Jews and Gentiles. Such variation in terms of the opponents occurs throughout the book. Though Jews are often most responsible, in other settings Gentiles join the opposition. On a few occasions Gentiles alone are responsible for opposition (as in Ephesus in Acts 18–19). Both populace and rulers are involved, so the opposition spans the whole society. It has the feel of mob violence, as in Acts 13:50 (Polhill 1992: 312). The cooperation of Jews and Gentiles shows that the threat is seen as socially serious (see comments above on 14:2).

The plot is discovered, and so they flee to Lystra and Derbe, eighteen miles south and fifty-five miles south-southwest of Iconium respectively. These two cities were part of Lycaonia. An important part of this area had been united with Phrygia, Pisidia, Pamphylia, and old Galatia to create a province in 25 BC. It lay on the Imperial Road connecting Antioch and Laranda (Barrett 1994: 673). Lystra was Timothy's home. This area had a reputation for being somewhat "rustic," where the people were not very learned (Béchard 2001). These people were regarded as militant, intractable, and "non-Roman" in their lifestyle (Strabo, *Geogr.* 12.6.2–5 [described as having little regard for civil law, being full of robbers, a source of much trouble to the Romans, and living among the mountain caves that protected them]; 14.5.24 [living on food unmixed with salt and were either Greek or barbarians]). Hemer (1989: 110) calls it a "less developed part of Anatolia." If so, the two scenes appearing early in Acts 14 and involving exclusively Gentile audiences cover both the most civilized (Iconium) and the more rustic (Lystra, Derbe) parts of Gentile culture, a type of geographical *inclusio* that shows the gospel's universality. At Lystra and Derbe they continue to evangelize.

In sum, the pattern of preaching, acceptance, and rejection continues. Persecution again causes them to move on. Sometimes a ministry that is not accepted must do the same.

---

1. But see Marshall 1980: 234, who seems to prefer the explanation that apostleship extended beyond the Twelve and included Barnabas.

Additional Notes

14:2. Codex D makes an explicit reference to the "chiefs of the synagogues of the Jews and the rulers of the synagogues" and to the "persecution of the righteous." At the end of the verse, it adds, "But the Lord soon gave peace," making a cleaner transition to v. 3. Neither addition is original.

14:7. Codex D again expands the original text, adding, "The whole of the multitude was moved by the teaching. But Paul and Barnabas remained in Lystra."

5. In Lystra and Derbe (14:8–20)

The ministry in Lystra begins with the healing of a lame man (vv. 8–10). This is a simply told miracle story. The miracle leads the people to hail the preachers as gods (vv. 11–13). That Greeks might understand such an event this way is seen in Ovid, *Metam.* 8.611–724, where Jupiter and Mercury visit in the form of the mortals Philemon and Baucis (Schneider 1982: 156).[1] Marshall (1980: 237) also notes an inscription to Zeus and Hermes dated about AD 250, found in the area just outside the city, as well as a stone altar.[2] It would be wrong, however, to view this as simply a literary creation, as it has the feel of a historical event and these details fit the locale, as the archaeology suggests (Marshall 1980: 232–33 against Haenchen 1987: 429–34).

The two messengers react, remarking that the town's acclamation of them as gods is blasphemy, tearing their garments, and addressing the populace regarding God's gracious care for the citizens through God's creation (vv. 14–17). This theme of God's care functions as a preamble to the gospel, expressing a natural theology about God's treatment of all people (Williams 1990: 247). The people are barely restrained from offering sacrifices to them (v. 18). But then, under pressure from Jews pursuing Paul from Antioch and Iconium, the people stone Paul and leave him for dead; he survives, however, and goes to Derbe (vv. 19–20). There is a rhetorical chiasm in the passage (Schnabel 2004: 1114).[3]

The narrative is a combination of a miracle account and short summary that includes a very brief speech. The likely source is again the Pauline circle. Again the key theme is that Paul's work leads to opposition, even to the point of his being stoned and left for dead. Opposition is intensifying, including an act of violence, though those opposing Paul think they are acting against a false prophet.

1. Witherington 1998: 421–22 cites the text, and D. W. Gill 1994b: 81–85 discusses the civic cult of Zeus and Hermes located there.
2. See also Bruce 1988a: 274–75; Calder 1910a; 1910b; 1925–26; Hemer 1989: 111; *MAMA* 8 §1 (a triad of gods: *Epēkoos* [= Zeus], Hermes, and the goddess *Gē*).
3. The A element is the crippled man's illness and Paul's survival (vv. 8 and 20a). The B element is the healing through Paul and the stoning of Paul (vv. 9–10 and 19). The C element is the desire to honor Paul and Barnabas and their stopping such honoring (vv. 11–13 and 18b). The D element is the protest of the missionaries (vv. 14–15a and 18a). The central E element is the proclamation (vv. 15b–17). Schnabel 2004: 1115 also correctly questions the reading of the text offered by Fournier 1997: 81–84, who argues that to the Gentiles Paul preached God and declared a salvation that was possible outside Christ.

Unlike most other accounts in Acts, however, there is no mention of a synagogue, as the ministry begins with this healing (Marshall 1980: 234) and focuses on a purely Gentile audience. The scene is a precursor to the visit to Athens in Acts 17. The account also shows the missionaries refusing to allow divine honor to come to them. They are simply servants of God. The healing account has parallels in Luke 5:18–26 and Acts 3:1–10; 9:32–35.

Exegesis and Exposition

[8]There was in Lystra a certain man sitting, who could not use his feet. He had been a cripple from the womb, who had never walked. [9]This one listened to Paul speaking; and Paul, looking intently at him and seeing that he had faith to be delivered, [10]said in a loud voice, "Stand upright on your feet." And he sprang up and walked. [11]And the crowd, seeing what Paul had done, lifted up their voices, saying in Lycaonian, "The gods in the likeness of men have come down to us!" [12]Barnabas they were calling Zeus, and Paul, because he was the chief speaker, they called Hermes. [13]And the priest of Zeus, whose temple was in front of the city, brought oxen and garlands to the gates and wanted to offer sacrifice together with the people. [14]⌜But hearing of it, the apostles⌝ Barnabas and Paul tore their garments and rushed out among the multitude, crying, [15]"Men, why are you doing these things? We also are men, of like nature with you, and proclaim to you the good news, that you should turn from these vain things to the living God who made the heaven and the earth and the sea and all that is in them. [16]In past generations he allowed all the nations to go their own ways; [17]yet he did not leave himself without witness, for he did good and gave you rains and fruitful seasons from heaven, filling your hearts with food and gladness." [18]With these words they barely restrained the people from offering sacrifice to them.

[19]But Jews came from Antioch and Iconium; and having persuaded the people and stoning Paul, they dragged him out of the city, supposing that he was dead. [20]But when the disciples gathered about him, ⌜ ⌝ arising ⌜ ⌝, he entered the city; and on the next day he went out together with Barnabas to Derbe.

14:8–10 Luke begins the ministry in Lystra, a town made a Roman colony in 6 BC and founded twenty years earlier (Schnabel 2004: 1112–13 notes the significance of the city and its wealth).[4] The healing of a lame man recalls Jesus's act in Luke 5:17–26 and Peter's in Acts 3:1–10. This man has had the condition since birth and has never walked. Paul observes him intently and sees that he has faith. In contrast, in Acts 3:5 the lame man gazes at Peter and John. That the scene takes place in the open

---

4. For more on how many outsiders would have viewed the region, see comments on 14:5–7.

points to the lack of a synagogue here and also reflects the Greek practice of public oratory that was common among Greek philosophers (Le Cornu and Shulam 2003: 774).

What Paul as a prophet realizes is that the man wants to be healed. The phrase ἔχει πίστιν τοῦ σωθῆναι (*echei pistin tou sōthēnai*) should be rendered "faith necessary for the purpose of saving" (i.e., to be physically delivered, the common non-theological use of the term "salvation"). Here the genitive and the articular infinitive point to purpose (BDF §400.2; Moulton and Turner 1963: 141). What is likely meant here is faith to be delivered from his crippled condition, as the infinitive σωθῆναι points to some form of deliverance (BAGD 798 §1c; BDAG 982 §1c). Paul does not speak directly of spiritual salvation here. The picture of the miracle, however, moves in this more spiritual direction because the scene typifies the signs and wonders Paul and Barnabas have done (v. 3; Jervell 1998: 374; Luke 7:50; 8:12, 48, 50; 17:19; 18:42; Acts 4:9–12; 16:31). In addition, the spiritual remarks Paul makes when the crowd reacts to the healing point in this direction (vv. 15–17). Paul commands the man to stand, which leads him to spring up (ἥλατο, *hēlato*; aorist of ἅλλομαι, *hallomai*, leap, spring up; cf. Acts 3:8) and proceed to walk (imperfect tense). This is Paul's first public miracle in Acts.

This is a crisply told miracle account. Two details are important. The stare (ἀτενίσας, *atenisas*) and the loud voice (μεγάλη φωνῇ, *megalē phōnē*) were often used in Greco-Roman stories about the coming of the gods (Strelan 2000). These details suggest in part why the crowd reacts as it does. So does the description of Paul as a stranger, as often gods were said to appear unknown.[5] Of course, Luke denies this view about Paul and Barnabas, but the way the story is told places the impression of a supernatural source for their power.

The sacrifices would be offered on the terrain of a pagan temple (Béchard 2000: 411; Schnabel 2004: 1116). The idea of the gods healing would not be foreign to Greeks who had made the association with figures like Aesclepius, who was seen as a god at Epidaurus in Greece during the fifth century BC (Le Cornu and Shulam 2003: 776). The site is a monument to his claims. Numerous stele (tablets), seventy of which survive, record the claim of miracles (Charitonidou 1978:14). The gates

---

5. Deities posing as strangers and mingling with mortals are common in the literature: Ovid, *Metam.* 8.611–725 (tells of such a visit); Homer, *Od.* 17.485–86 (a request that such a visit might take place). On the stare, see Heliodorus, *Aethiopica* 3.13.2–3, although this is a late text; PGM 7.768; 13.946. On the loud voice, see Origen, *Against Celsus* 6.75 (where Celsus argues that if Jesus had been a god, he would have been different and had a different voice); Homer, *Il.* 20.375–80 (Apollo's voice identified as one of a god that causes fear); *Od.* 24.529–35 (Athena's voice produces fear and respect for instruction); Apollonius of Rhodes, *Argonautica* 4.640–42 (Hera's voice produces fear). This is also said of God in OT and Jewish texts: 1 Sam. 7:10; Ezek. 9:1; Deut. 4:11–12; 5:22; 3 Bar. 11.1–5.

mentioned in verse 13 are likely the gates of the temple (though city gates are also possible).

14:11–13 The Gentile crowd, seeing the creative power in the crippled man's healing, believes that Barnabas and Paul are gods. This is expressed with a summary aorist tense as they lift their voices (ἐπῆραν, *epēran*) to make the declaration that they are acclaiming them (with an imperfect tense, ἐκάλουν, *ekaloun*) as gods. Paul is compared to the god of interpretation, Hermes, and Barnabas, as the leader, is compared to Zeus, chief of the pantheon (v. 12). This detail suggests that Barnabas is the elder of the two. They are likely seen as "divine" men or sharing in a divine visitation.[6] Acts 28:6 describes a similar reaction to Paul. Barrett (1994: 676) suggests that they may be using local names of gods (Pappas and Men perhaps), which Luke translated into their equivalents; this is possible.

At first the missionaries do not understand what is being contemplated because the people speak in their local dialect of Lycaonian. The priest of the temple of Zeus is prepared to offer a celebratory and commemorative sacrifice of thanksgiving, parading the oxen, dressed for the offering with garlands, that would have accompanied the crowd to the temple.[7] The relatively small temple by Greek standards would probably be located just outside the city or by the city gates and may have only one priest (Béchard 2001: 91nn22–23). Béchard contrasts the "enthusiasm" of this Greek scene to the intellectual climate of the other Greek scene at Athens in Acts 17.

Barnabas and Paul want to be sure the right God receives the honor. Béchard (2001: 99–101) argues that Luke presents Paul and Barnabas as "self-authenticating" sages but in a Jewish light. This means that the language of turning (v. 15) evokes a sense of the presence of prophetic call from divinely sent messengers. Gentiles might have mistaken this call as coming from a sage. The goal of this reading is to distinguish between the Lycaonians, regarded as rustic in their response, and Paul and Barnabas as prophets who do not take advantage of the Lycaonians' gullibility. Taking advantage of gullibility may have been an accusation made by some more elite people in the culture against the early church's success among poorer people. Paul and Barnabas, however, are actually trying to enhance the people's understanding. They are not taking advantage of them but are taking the people's correct sense that the supernatural is present and pointing them in the right direction. These "rustic" people have a better intuition of what is going on than the elite, who simply want nothing to do with anything

---

6. See Chariton of Aphrodisias, *Chaer.* 1.1.16; 1.14.1; 3.2.15–17; Xenophon of Ephesus, *Eph. Tale* 1.12.1; Heliodorus, *Aethiopica* 1.2.1; Johnson 1992: 248. For such accounts, see Ovid, *Metam.* 1.390–779; 2.466–95; D. W. Gill 1994b: 79–92; Winter 1994: 93–103.

7. See Ovid, *Metam.* 4.755; Persius, *Satires* 2.44; Virgil, *Aeneid* 5.366; Euripides, *Heracles* 529; Williams 1990: 249.

supernatural and tend to deny its presence in any kind of powerful or demonstrative way.

In all of this, the power of the apostles is evident. This power must come from above; that much the crowd understands. These are not divine men, however, but simply servants of the one true and living God who works through them and authenticates what they are claiming.

The apostles (see v. 4) try to stop the procession by tearing their clothes **14:14** and addressing the crowd. In the OT and Judaism, the tearing of garments indicated that a blasphemy had been uttered against God (cf. Gen. 37:29, 34; Num. 14:6; Josh. 7:6; Judg. 11:35; 2 Sam. 1:2, 11; 1 Macc. 2:14; 3:47; Mark 14:63–64; Matt. 26:65; *m. Sanh.* 7.5; Johnson 1992: 248). Their act would have gotten the crowd's attention. Unlike most references to the two during the journey, Barnabas appears first, possibly because the crowd connects him with the higher god Zeus.

Paul asks why (τί, *ti*) the crowd seeks to offer sacrifices when Paul and **14:15–18** Barnabas are mere mortals (ὁμοιοπαθεῖς, *homoiopatheis*, literally, of like passions; James 5:17; similarly, Acts 10:26). They are no different from anyone in the crowd, simply being creatures of the Creator God.

The question "Why are you doing these things?" is really a request to stop (Haenchen 1987: 428; on τί, BDF §299.1). Their only goal is to bring the good news to the crowd that they should turn from vain idols (Rom. 1:21) to the living Creator God. This is classic prophetic Jewish natural theology like that seen in Isa. 40–41 (Bruce 1990: 323; Acts 17:24).[8] This also is the first speech to purely pagan Gentiles in Acts, as Cornelius had an acquaintance with the God of Israel as a God-fearer (Gärtner 1962; Downing 1982). It is a speech summary (Witherington 1998: 426).

To this audience, Paul's message is that they are to change orientation (ἐπιστρέφειν, *epistrephein*, turn) from vain and dead idols to the God who lives and is the creator of heaven and earth and everything in them (Luke 1:16–17; Acts 3:19; 17:25–26). It is God as Creator who makes his creatures accountable to him. This point is the foundation stone of Jewish thought about the relationship between God and God's creatures and is a classic way to address Gentiles.

Beyond this there is something new in God's relationship to Gentiles. In the past, God let the nations go their own way, but not so anymore. That former time is what Acts 17:30 will call "the times of ignorance." In other OT and Jewish texts, such vain pursuit is called foolishness (Isa. 2:20 LXX; 30:7; 31:2; Ezek. 8:10; Wis. 13:1; 3 Macc. 6:11). In Rom.

8. See also Exod. 20:11–12; 1 Kings 16:2, 13, 26; 2 Kings 17:15; Esth. 4:17 LXX [Add. Esth. 13:8–14 Eng.]; Ps. 145:6 LXX [146:6 Eng.]; Jer. 2:5; 8:19; Neh. 9:6; 3 Macc. 6:11 (addressed to the living Creator God); 4Q521 2.2.2; in the NT: 1 Thess. 1:9–10, but the 1 Thess. 1:10 point is not in Acts; Johnson 1992: 249.

1:20 Paul goes on to suggest that the nature of this revelation among the Gentiles leaves them without excuse for not responding to the Creator God, a point Paul is now trying to drive home but with a more gentle emphasis (Polhill 1992: 316; Bruce 1990: 324; Rom. 2:14–16; 1 Cor. 1:20–21; against Haenchen 1987: 428).

The absence of any mention of Jesus is striking but not surprising, as first there needs to be established that there is only one God (Deut. 6:4), to whom all are responsible and whose will stands revealed. The "living" God stands in contrast to and implies "dead" idols (Fitzmyer 1998: 532; Isa. 37:4, 17; Hos. 2:1 LXX [1:10 Eng.]; 4:15; Dan. 5:23; 6:27). God is the creator, who shows mercy and yet reveals much kindness in the creation. Polhill (1992: 316) argues that the message is cut short; this is possible. Jervell (1998: 376–78) calls the unit not a full missionary speech of the kerygma, but simply a polemical response to stop the sacrifice; this also is a quite likely reading of the unit. The chaotic nature of the scene may prevent a full missionary speech. Paul rejects polytheism here (Klauck 2003: 60), especially an effort to worship mere mortals. He holds to one God and one message of salvation. So that is what Paul preaches because he believes that the view is rooted in the activity and revelation of God. One cannot discuss Jesus without first establishing that God is one.[9]

Paul declares that God is now more actively engaged with the nations than in years past. The dative ταῖς παρῳχημέναις γενεαῖς (*tais parōchēmenais geneais*, in past generations) is temporal here (BDF §200.4). During past generations he allowed the nations to walk in their own way, but this is no longer the case. The verb εἴασεν (*eiasen*, permitted) speaks of God's lack of direct, active spiritual engagement with the nations. God allowed them to go "according to their own way," where ταῖς ὁδοῖς (*tais hodois*) is a dative of rule, indicating a standard of orientation (BAGD 212 §1; BDAG 269 §1; Wallace 1996: 158). The verb ἐάω (*eaō*, permit) can mean "leave [someone] alone." There was no special revelation for the nations as Paul is giving now, although there were general revelation and care, as Paul notes in verse 17. God gives the rain, the seasons, and "food for the joys" of life.[10] This is the only reference to God's not lacking witness (ἀμάρτυρον, *amartyron*) in the NT. God provided enough food and joy to satisfy them (ἐμπιπλῶν, *empiplōn*). This verb means "fill" to the full (BAGD 256 §1; BDAG 323; Luke 1:53; 6:25; John 6:12; Rom. 15:24 are the other NT uses). The grace of the care of creation in rain, seasons, and fruit is also a prevalent idea in the OT: Gen. 8:22; Pss. 4:7; 145:15–16; 147:8–9; Isa. 25:6; Jer. 5:24;

9. That the early church worshiped Jesus in light of such feelings about the worship of humans is significant, for it shows that Jesus clearly was seen as more than a mere mortal.

10. BDF §442.16 discusses the hendiadys reflected in the last phrase of this list.

Eccles. 9:7 (also Luke 12:22–34). The term ἀγαθοεργέω (*agathoergeō*, do good) is also rare in the NT (1 Tim. 6:18 is the only other NT occurrence). This may be a polemical and contextualized response to the idea of Zeus being *kalakagathios*, or "the one who does good and is fruitful," a description of Zeus that has been uncovered in Phrygia and Pisidia (Schnabel 2004: 1118, who notes how well the speech fits the setting, which points to its credibility). God gives abundant care to all.

Paul's speech barely restrains the crowd from sacrificing to the apostolic messengers, as verse 18 notes. This is the only occurrence of the verb καταπαύω (*katapauō*, restrain or bring to rest) in Acts; μόλις (*molis*, scarcely) appears four times (14:18; 27:7–8 [2x], 16).

Some time now has passed since verse 18. From nearby Antioch (13:50) **14:19–20** and Iconium (14:5), the Jews who are keeping track of Paul show up and speak out against him. These Jews who are pursuing Paul ironically parallel the actions of Saul going to Damascus to take Christians into custody (9:1–2). These are religious zealots. Despite the healing miracle Paul performed and their initial excitement, the militant Jews stone Paul as a false prophet and leave him for dead (2 Cor. 11:25; Gal. 6:17; 2 Tim. 3:11; fulfills Acts 9:16). This is a mob action. The quick reversal is not entirely surprising: if Barnabas and Paul had not brought the gospel, the crowd would have regarded them as Jews, but in Jewish eyes these two bring a false message and are a threat to Jewish faith. Perhaps the Jews emphasize the threat they represent to the Gentiles' forms of worship, since some Jews are not interested in bringing Gentiles to faith.

Barnabas is absent because he is not the speaker before the crowd and may not be present on this occasion. The disciples, probably from Lystra, surround Paul and help him to gain his feet and enter the city. Opposition again comes and intensifies in the Gentile context, but by God's grace Paul survives (Weiser 1985: 353).

The next day Paul leaves for Derbe. Derbe is a little more than thirty-five miles southeast of Lystra and so a few days' journey by foot. It is on the frontier with Galatia (Strabo, *Geogr.* 12.6.3), the site today of Devri Şehr (Schnabel 2004: 1121). It is not entirely clear whether it was seen as a part of Galatia at this time. It was a stop on the road from Iconium to Laranda. This is the easternmost point of the journey, located right on the edge of the province of Galatia. Derbe, Lystra, and Iconium make a triangle in the central portion of Asia Minor.

In sum, an effort to share the gospel divides a community. In Gentile areas, idolatry will be a powerful force against embracing the gospel. The way of life ingrained by idolatry will be hard to reverse in some areas. So reception and intense opposition exist side by side. Sensing the danger, Barnabas and Paul flee. Sometimes the nature of opposition means that it is time to move on and trust that those ministered to and responding will have the strength to remain faithful. As the next passage shows, however, they will do what they can by coming back and strengthening the believers, despite the danger. They will exhort them to continue in the faith and will teach them that opposition will be part of the believers' experience. They will also appoint leadership and leave in an atmosphere of spiritual dependence on God through prayer and fasting.

Additional Notes

14:14. Codex D has a shorter text here, simply reading the singular ἀκούσας δέ (*akousas de*, having heard) and dropping the term "the apostles." There is a false concord here, as a singular form of the participle is linked to a plural subject. It is the more difficult reading but too poorly attested to be original.

14:20. At various points, Western witnesses fill in gaps and expand the text, noting the crowd leaving the scene at evening, in darkness, and having Paul get up with difficulty (Metzger 1971: 425).

6. Return to Antioch (14:21–28)

In the conclusion of the first journey, Paul and Barnabas return to Lystra, Iconium, and Pisidian Antioch, encouraging these new communities to continue in the faith and warning them that tribulation may well come in the future (vv. 21–22). They also appoint elders for these communities, appointments that come with prayer and fasting (v. 23). They return to Pisidia, Pamphylia, and Perga before returning to Antioch (vv. 24–26). Here they report on what the Lord has done, especially in opening a door among the Gentiles. They remain in Antioch for a time (vv. 27–28). Now that Gentiles are entering the church in large numbers, how they should do so becomes an important issue. This will be the topic of Acts 15; the first journey is a bridge to that section of the book.

In form, the account is a simple summary narrative with little detail about what takes place at each stop. There may be elements of church tradition and exhortation reflected in verses 22–23 (Schneider 1982: 164). Its roots are in the Antiochene church and/or the Pauline sources. Paul and Barnabas remain concerned about and in touch with these communities after their ministry to them. Their primary goal is to ensure that solid leadership is put in place and that all understand what the walk of faith entails. This is shown in part by the missionary team's choosing not to take the shortest route home, which would have been to continue east from Derbe through Tarsus. Instead, they purposely retrace their steps (Witherington 1998: 428). Follow-up and nurture are a priority for them (Polhill 1992: 318).

Exegesis and Exposition

[21]After preaching the gospel to that city and making many disciples, they returned to Lystra and to Iconium and to Antioch, [22]strengthening the souls of the disciples, exhorting them to remain in the faith, and declaring, "Through many tribulations we must enter the kingdom of God." [23]Appointing elders for them in every church and praying with fasting, Paul and Barnabas committed them to the Lord in whom they had believed.

[24]Then they passed through Pisidia, and came to Pamphylia. [25]And speaking the word ⌐ ¬ in Perga, they went down to Attalia [26]and from there they sailed to Antioch, where they had been commended to the grace of God for the work that they had fulfilled. [27]And arriving and gathering the church together, they were declaring all that God had done with them, and that he had opened a

door of faith to the Gentiles. [28]And they remained no little time together with the disciples.

14:21–23 The two men preach the gospel in Derbe but meet no opposition, a point unique in Luke's description of this journey. Instead they are engaged in the task of "making disciples" (μαθητεύσαντες, *mathēteusantes*), an example of an intransitive verb having causative force even as a participle (Moulton and Turner 1963: 52–53).

Next they bravely go back through Lystra, Iconium, and Antioch. There they encourage the believers in three ways: encouraging or strengthening their souls (Acts 15:32, 41; 18:23), exhorting their continued faith (11:23; 13:43), and warning them about continuing tribulation. Souls can be induced to evil (14:2), and so they need strengthening (Schweizer, *TDNT* 9:640). This is Paul's characteristic call and encouragement to believers who have embraced the gospel, so that they continue in the faith (see discussion on 11:23 and 13:43; 15:32; 16:40; 20:1–2; Rom. 1:11; 16:25; 1 Thess. 3:2, 13; 2 Thess. 2:17; 3:3; Johnson 1992: 254). They are to "remain" (ἐμμένειν, *emmenein*) solid with respect to the faith (τῇ πίστει, *tē pistei*), an expression close to the idea of abiding that one sees in John 15:1–7. This is a dative of reference or respect syntactically (Wallace 1996: 146). The verb appears only four times in the NT (Acts 14:22; 28:30; Gal. 3:10; Heb. 8:9). Such perseverance, however, will not come easily. It will entail tribulation (Phil. 1:28–30; 1 Thess. 3:3; 2 Thess. 1:5; Rom. 8:17; 2 Tim. 2:11; Bruce 1990: 326, "no cross, no crown"; Schneider 1982: 166, "suffering before glory" in Luke 24:26). Sufferings and persecution will precede the full arrival into the kingdom.[1]

Unlike other texts in Acts, where "kingdom" refers to God's entire program, here the term refers to the moment of final vindication that one enters after death (Barrett 1994: 686; 2 Tim. 4:18). Jesus addressed this issue in the Olivet Discourse (Luke 21:5–36, esp. 12–19). "Tribulations" could well be a reference to messianic woes that precede the end (on entering the kingdom, see Luke 18:25; John 3:5; Mark 9:47; 10:23–25). Haenchen (1987: 436) rejects this eschatological association, seeing the suffering as long past. Paul, however, sees all the events from the time of Jesus's first coming to the end as eschatological and as part of birth pangs (Rom. 8:12–25: creatures and believers long for redemption in the midst of suffering). The great example of such a reassuring speech is the one Paul gives to the Ephesian elders in Acts 20. Christianity is now called "the faith," pointing to the dynamic that drives the community.

Paul and Barnabas appoint leadership for the churches and leave elders behind to oversee the congregations. They do so in each church, as the preposition κατά (*kata*) is used distributively (BDAG 512 §B.1.d).

---

1. On the implications of such a passage for the "imitation of Christ" in the teaching of the church through the centuries, see Pelikan 2005: 167–69.

The verb χειροτονέω (*cheirotoneō*) means "select [someone] by raising hands" but came to mean "choose, elect, or appoint," which is the
meaning here (2 Cor. 8:19 is the only other NT occurrence, where Titus
is appointed; Josephus, *Ant.* 6.13.9 §312; Philo, *Rewards* 9 §54; *EDNT*
3:464–65). Paul notes such leadership in his letters.[2] Thus it is an exaggeration to suggest that these positions are a reflection of the post-
Pauline church, although Paul does not use the term "elders" outside
the Pastoral Epistles (see the discussion of Acts 11:27–30). Perhaps Luke
applies a later, equivalent term to this function, but the role is surely
likely to have already been present, based upon the analogy with Jewish
leadership structures (Marshall 1980: 241). Later churches appointed
their own elders (Ign. *Phld.* 10.1; *Smyrn.* 11.2; Pol. *Phil.* 7.2). There was
more than one elder per community. Elders are mentioned in Acts 11:30
as those who receive the offering to relieve the famine in Jerusalem. Up
to that point in Acts, "elders" referred to Jewish town leaders. Here we
have the appointment of elders to lead a Christian community. This is
the first mention that Paul and Barnabas appoint such leaders as they
establish new believing communities.

They commit them—and probably the church as a whole—to the
Lord's service. The verb παρατίθημι (*paratithēmi*) means "set [some-
one] before another" (in Acts this verb appears four times: 14:23; 16:34;
17:3; 20:32). It is into the Lord's care and safekeeping that Barnabas
and Paul place these leaders in a context of prayer and fasting (BAGD
623 §2bβ; BDAG 772 §3b). This is not a mere administrative exercise
but a spiritual one, with prayer and fasting (13:2–3). Παρατίθημι also
describes Paul's action regarding the Ephesian elders in 20:32 (the other
occurrences of the verb in Acts are non-theological: to bring someone
to a house [16:34] and to set forth the content of something [17:3]). The
faith of the community is expressed with a pluperfect (πεπιστεύκεισαν,
pepisteukeisan, had believed) in verse 23, making a point about the
ongoing nature of faith.

Paul and Barnabas now return to the earlier churches to which they   **14:24–26**
ministered in Pisidia and Pamphylia, including Perga, and also visit
Attalia, the port near Perga. Located on the gulf of the same name, Attalia was the chief port of Pamphylia. Perga was already mentioned in
13:13, but now it is reported that evangelism takes place there. They
have journeyed through the mountain paths of Pisidia to the lowlands
of Pamphylia (Polhill 1992: 320). Then they return to the site of their
commissioning in Antioch of Syria, where they were called and commended "by the grace of God" to this journey. The reference to the grace
of God (τῇ χάριτι τοῦ θεοῦ, *tē chariti tou theou*) is yet another way to

---

2. 1 Cor. 16:15–18; 1 Thess. 5:12; Phil. 1:1, referring to overseers (ἐπίσκοποι, *episkopoi*);
Bruce 1990: 326; 1 Tim. 5:17; Titus 1:5; also 1 Pet. 5:1–2; 2 John 1; 3 John 1.

speak of God's care in their safe return within the mission (15:40). The expression serves as a reminder that God's grace has directed them and cared for them in their travels, even in the face of persecution. This passage looks back to 13:1–2.

14:27–28 Now back at their sending church, they were reporting (ἀνήγγελλον, *anēngellon*, imperfect tense) to the gathered community all God had done in opening a door to the Gentiles, a topic still to be developed and in fulfillment of Paul's call (15:4, 9, 11–12; 9:15–16). Antioch is described as a church that "commended" (παραδεδομένοι, *paradedomenoi*, v. 26) them to God's grace (BDAG 762). The expression could also be translated "committed," to stress God's care. The point is that they were handed over to God. It is the Gentile mission that is the focus of the report, as God has given access to faith for the Gentiles, much as one can come through a door into a new place. The point of the metaphor here is access to God. The image of the door (θύρα, *thyra*) for evangelism is common in Paul (1 Cor. 16:9; 2 Cor. 12:2; Col. 4:3; Witherington 1998: 429). As always, God is the primary agent and initiator in the account. "Faith" has been a major theme in this journey (Acts 13:8, 12, 39, 41, 48; 14:1, 9, 22–23; Johnson 1992: 255 notes that this prepares for 15:9, 11). The church is described in the singular here (τὴν ἐκκλησίαν, *tēn ekklēsian*), pointing to its larger unity and how the entire community shared in the sending. They stay in Antioch for an unspecified time. "No little time" is Lukan litotes (other examples: 12:18; 15:2; 17:4, 12; 19:23–24; 27:20; Schneider 1982: 168n41).

In sum, this passage completes the first mission, but it shows a sense of ongoing pastoral care. Above all, they have left leadership behind to continue the work. This is why Paul and Barnabas make sure elders are in place. What this does not mean is that now that others are in place, Paul and Barnabas are no longer concerned for the community that has been planted. Communities formed are not ignored once their founders move on. Rather, there is an abiding connection that also means that return visits can take place. Too many communities lose track of those they send out into ministry or of those who have ministered to them in the past. In addition, many ministers leave a community and then are never heard from again. But the attitude here is not "gone and forgotten." It is of a family that is left behind for other responsibilities but that is still precious enough to care for when possible.

Another way this connection is maintained is by the reports about what God is doing elsewhere. Here it is the sending church that is the beneficiary of hearing what God is doing. Missionaries are also not to be sent, gone, and forgotten; a line of communication is to remain so that both communities can be connected and blessed by seeing how God is working and binding them together.

Paul's First Missionary Journey

City	Region
Antioch	Syria
Salamis	Cyprus
Paphos	Cyprus
Perga	Pamphylia
Antioch	Pisidia
Iconium	Lycaonia
Lystra	Lycaonia
Derbe	Lycaonia
Lystra	Lycaonia
Derbe	Lycaonia
Iconium	Lycaonia
Antioch	Pisidia
Perga	Pamphylia
Attalia	Pamphylia
Antioch	Syria

Additional Note

14:25. The MSS B, D, and Byz read "speaking the word" (λαλήσαντες ... τὸν λόγον, *lalēsantes ... ton logon*; Acts 11:19; 16:6). Other MSS add at the end either τοῦ θεοῦ (*tou theou*, of God; 𝔓⁷⁴, E) or τοῦ κυρίου (*tou kyriou*; of the Lord; א, A, C, Ψ, 33, 81, 326, 614). The variation among the additions and the shorter text support the originality of "speaking the word."

V. The Mission from Antioch and the Full Incorporation of Gentiles (13:1–15:35)
   A. The First Missionary Journey (13:1–14:28)
➤ B. Consultation at Jerusalem (15:1–35)

B. Consultation at Jerusalem (15:1–35)

Acts 15 is a central chapter in terms of both its location in Acts and the theological issue it presents. Fitzmyer (1998: 538) notes that Acts 1–14 has about 12,385 words in English translation and Acts 15–28 has about 12,502 words. So we are right in the middle of the book. This passage shows the church decisively addressing the question of Gentile involvement in the new community. What should be the basis of their inclusion? This is a major point of concern in Acts. The resolution issuing from the consultation at Jerusalem is an affirmation of Gentile inclusion and equality with Jews. The hope that Jesus represents is designed to bring reconciliation between people as well as between people and God. After this chapter, the role of the Jerusalem church recedes into the background until Acts 21. For example, Peter's last appearance in the book is in this chapter. From here on, the main theme is the gospel going out into all the world.

We call this meeting a consultation. It is not a council in the later technical ecclesiastical sense (so correctly Jervell 1998: 403n741).[1] It includes more than the apostles and engages the Jerusalem congregation in a major way.

This chapter has been the object of much scholarly discussion as to its timing and authenticity. We will consider these issues before examining its structure and potential sources. It might seem odd that such a conference is necessary given what took place in Acts 10 and the discussion in Acts 11. But the size of the Gentile response and the passing of time leads to reflection on, and perhaps reconsideration of, how Gentiles should be received into the church. The debate now is not whether Gentiles should be included but on what basis they should enter the community (J. J. Scott 1997).

For Jews to whom the law has been important, how to relate all of this to the law is a crucial question (Williams 1990: 256). The question is, How can Gentiles ignore God's covenant law? Also, How can fellowship occur if Jewish Christians keep the law, especially dietary practices as a rule, but Gentiles do not (Marshall 1980: 242–43)? Does the issue of uncleanness emerge if Gentiles ignore the law? Both Gal. 2:11–14 and Acts 15:20 show that table fellowship and issues of uncleanness are major issues in the discussion. Such issues and their implications

---

1. For variety, I will still occasionally use the traditional term "council" to refer to this meeting, but I use the word in a nontechnical sense.

need to be sorted out. How can law-observing Jewish Christians and law-ignoring Gentile Christians coexist?[2]

The solution some propose is to make Gentiles respect the law and at least be circumcised. This view is like that espoused by Philo, a Diaspora Jew (*Migration* 16 §§89–94; Bruce 1990: 329; such a dispute is noted in Josephus, *Ant.* 20.2.4 §§38–46; *b. Sanh.* 56b). First Maccabees 1:11–15 shows the importance of such issues to Jews. Circumcision was a covenant sign that predated the Mosaic law in the tradition (Gen. 17:9–10). So the argument surely was that to be among the people of God one has to partake of the sign of the Abrahamic covenant and be tied to promises God made to him. If anything in the law should be followed, it should be the covenantal sign that reaches back to Abraham. Of course, the NT never tells us the detailed argument from the other side, but surely it was something close to this.[3]

Paul and Barnabas take another view. Let the Gentiles in without circumcision. Gentiles do not need to become Jews in order to be Christians. As Paul argues in Galatians, salvation is by faith by means of grace through Christ's work, not by works of the law. The problem is significant enough that one community alone should not resolve it. On this, all agree. So a meeting is called.

The scholarly debate over the event's timing concerns this event's relationship to Gal. 2 and the connection of Gal. 2 to Acts 11:30. For those who think a choice is possible, two views exist. (1) Acts 15 could equal Gal. 2:1–10 (Gutbrod, *TDNT* 4:1065–67, "certainly no invention of Ac[ts]"; Williams 1990: 257–59; Polhill 1992: 321–22; Fitzmyer 1998: 539–40; Jervell 1998: 404n745), or (2) Acts 11:30 equals Gal. 2 (Bruce 1990: 330–31; Marshall 1980: 244–25; Witherington 1998: 440–42; Schnabel 2004: 987–90). Johnson (1992: 270) appears to make no choice in the historical debate over the timing, apparently regarding it as unresolvable. Part of the question is how to relate Paul's two visits to Jerusalem and how Paul's notes in Gal. 1:18–19 and 2:1–10 fit into this scheme. Normally, Acts 9:26–30 is seen as matching the first visit. It is the second visit that is a matter of discussion for those who see historical merit in this material.

Other scholars question the entire scene, representing a third approach to the issue. For example, Haenchen (1987: 457–58, esp. 463,

---

2. Exactly how to describe the issue beyond this is much discussed by scholars. Details include (1) the issue of table fellowship; (2) freedom from the law; (3) setting aside part of the law; (4) showing continuity with God's people; (5) making concessions for Gentile Christians; and (6) making concessions for Jewish Christians (Jervell 1998: 403n742). Circumcision and the law seem to be the key issues requiring treatment in a way that allows for unencumbered fellowship between Jews and Gentiles as well as the evangelizing of Gentiles. A key obstacle to fellowship is Gentile association with idolatry, something that also surfaces in Paul's letters (Rom. 1:18–32; 1 Cor. 8–10).

3. For other key Jewish texts on circumcision, see Lev. 12:3; Jub. 15.28; Exod. Rabbah 15.7; *m. Ned.* 3.11; Le Cornu and Shulam 2003: 802–4.

where he calls it intrinsically impossible), building on Dibelius (1956: 93–101, originally published in 1947), distinguishes Luke's literary work from his historical work and questions the historicity of this meeting and the production of a decree. This view is followed by Bornkamm in *TDNT* 6:663, who sees the authority over the entire church of the Jerusalem elders in the council as not historically credible. This overarching role for the Jerusalem elders, however, exaggerates their function, since representatives of other churches are present. Dibelius (1956: 100) says, "Luke's treatment of the event is only literary-historical and can make no claim to historical worth." For Haenchen (1987: 458), the goal is to create an impressive, animated scene to make an imprint on the mind.

This is far too skeptical a reading of Luke's work. There is little doubt that such debate existed in the early church. We should not confuse selectivity with creativity and overplay the differences in the account. There is enough overlap in what we shall trace to suggest that this skeptical reading is overdrawn.

A fourth view exists that sees historical roots without being clear about timing issues. Barrett (1998: xli) argues more subtly that Luke reflects the compromising views of his own time and projects them back into the past. His explanation is that "this makes better sense than to suppose that he [Luke] invented a fictitious story to conceal the horrid truth about the church's past." He goes on to say that this use of "controlled imagination" Luke did not achieve with "complete success." In this, Barrett accepts the observations of F. C. Baur, but in a tighter time frame.

Yet even this reading is too skeptical. Yes, tension and conflict existed before the council, but this meeting went a long way toward resolving many of these matters. Yet, Luke is clear that this meeting did not solve everything, as James's request to Paul in Acts 21 shows. So we get not "perfect peace" here but only a basic solution. As such, the scene has more credibility than Barrett allows. The first two options open up the likelihood that Luke has well summarized a complex debate.

Marshall (1980: 244–45) opts for Acts 11:30 equaling Gal. 2. Against an equation of Acts 15 and Gal. 2, he notes the following points: (1) Galatians 2:2 is a private meeting, not a public one as in Acts 15. (2) Galatians 2 lacks any mention of the conditions of Acts 15. (3) How could Gal. 2:11–14 happen after a decree like that in Acts 15? (4) Galatians 2 is Paul's second post-conversion visit to Jerusalem, and Acts 15 is his third. (5) How can one accept the silence of the council when the letter of Acts 15 is to the Galatian region? The strength of this view is that it argues that the decree came after Galatians was written, explaining its silence on this major meeting.

Another variation argues that the basic agreement was made in Acts 11:30 but the formal agreement occurred in Acts 15, without Paul present (Catchpole 1976–77), but this view also has problems. It is argued that the supposed fusion of Acts 15 and Acts 11 is required because Paul would not have accepted a compromise like that presented in Acts 15. This ignores, however, that Paul himself said he was a "Jew to Jews and a Gentile to Gentiles" (1 Cor. 9:19–20), showing flexibility in his own approach. Marshall (1980: 246) argues that Paul opposed unchastity (1 Cor. 6:9) and eating meat clearly offered to idols (1 Cor. 10:25–28), two of the items specified at Jerusalem in Acts 15. The debate in Rom. 14, he continues, may well have included food with blood in it. So three of the four recommended prohibitions made to Gentiles make appearances in Paul's letters. This shows that Paul could well have accepted such a compromise, although he preferred to make an independent argument for such points. Marshall (1980: 244) notes how similar the restrictions are to Lev. 17–18, a point this exegesis will detail later, so that there is OT precedent for such limits. As long as such issues were seen as related not to salvation but to community peace, Paul could have lived with such advice. Bruce (1988a: 285) seems to suggest that Paul may have tolerated this ruling but really preferred a more open policy, which is what his letters reflect. This may be the case.

Schnabel (2004: 988–89) makes the following points in supporting the Acts 11 visit equaling Gal. 2: (1) Galatians 2:1 speaks of Paul's second visit to Jerusalem, which equals Acts 11. (2) The visit was the result of a revelation, which connects to the revelation to Agabus about the famine in Acts 11:27–28. (3) Both texts mention material needs in Judea. (4) Contrary to the claims of some scholars, the Gentile mission is noted in the visit at Acts 11:19–26. (5) The absence of any mention of Peter is a difficulty but is solved by noting that the leadership in Jerusalem had already changed by this time, and the famine relief was brought to these "elders" of the church. Schnabel goes on to suggest that the leaders discussed some issues here related to Gentile mission, but circumcision, a key topic of Acts 15, was not one of them. Another study by Zeigan (2005: 463–84) also goes this way, with three of his four reasons largely parallel to Schnabel. He also notes that it is a (1) second visit (2) with a similar context and (3) a collection as a key part. The new feature Zeigan adds is the harmony that resulted from the event, at least for the short term.

Williams objects to connecting Acts 11:30 with Gal. 2 for the following reasons: (1) The apostles are not mentioned in Acts 11:30 but are in Galatians. (2) How could Titus be present in Acts 11, given that he is mentioned in Gal. 2 but not in Acts 11? (3) Why did the Gal. 2:11–14 controversy concern dietary practice and not circumcision? (4) Can one place the Galatian commendation of Paul and Barnabas's work among the Gentiles this early, before the first missionary journey, rather than after it? He goes on to add that a commendation assuming a Gentile mission this early makes Acts 13–14 appear to be unnecessary. (5) Can Acts 11:30 fit the chronology, since AD 46 is the latest this event could take place and Paul mentions both three- and fourteen-year periods preceding this time in Gal. 1:18 and 2:1? (6) Paul is subordinate to Barnabas in Acts 11:30 but does not seem to be so in Gal. 2. On the issue of Paul's not mentioning the decrees and the continued trouble, Williams simply says that not all easily accepted the decision. Peter's inconsistency in Gal. 2:11–14 is explained because dietary issues are raised, which is a different area. The difference in count in the enumeration of the visits is attributed by Williams to the fact that Paul numbers only important visits in Galatians. Since the famine visit recorded in Acts 11 was not relevant to this debate, it was not counted in Galatians.

The objections Williams raises can be answered, for the most part, by the fact that Luke chose to discuss the Gentile problem in detail in Acts 15, where it was decisively resolved. This could well mean that not all the details of the Acts 11 visit are noted by Luke. He simply reports the relief effort. The advantage of Acts 11:30 equaling Gal. 2:1–10 is that then the rationale for why Galatians does not mention the decree becomes transparent: it had not yet taken place. The "fight and dissension" in the community that Acts 15:2 notes are still in process when Paul writes to the Galatians, as both 2:1–10 and 2:11–14 show.

A decision on the issue is not straightforward or clear. It seems, however, that an identification of Acts 11:30 with Gal. 2:1–10 has fewer problems, although it is the less common view. The major problem with the view is that it collapses Pauline chronology into a very tight package. But it also more clearly explains why Paul did not mention this decree in Galatians. All the other differences may well reflect different concerns and choices of the biblical writers. Luke saves the discussion of the resolution of the Gentile problem until the big meeting. Paul, in defending his understanding of the gospel, highlights his more independent defense of his views and thus notes in more detail his own involvements.

The authenticity of the contents of this meeting is also disputed. Barrett (1998: xxxvii–xxxviii) lists seven points of tension within Acts that this chapter raises. They are as follows: (1) Acts 15:1–2, 5, 7a speak of a violent debate, but the overall tone of the chapter reflects only agreement. (2) Acts 11:18 appears to settle this issue, yet here we are again in debate in Acts 15. (3) What Peter says about the law being a burden says too much against the law in light of the rest of the book of Acts. (4) Paul and Barnabas say too little, given their importance in the dispute. (5) James's use of the LXX does not fit one who represents the Hebrew community (see below). (6) The prominence of the decree here stands in contrast to how little is said of it elsewhere (see below). (7) What was the issue of the council, salvation only or more?

Most of these issues are simply cases of authorial selection or simply require not overreading the account. For example, that the full debate is not laid out in Acts 15 reflects Luke's choice not to drag the reader through everything that took place but to focus on the factors that led to resolution. The fact that the topic of how Gentiles are related to the law came up again after Acts 11:18 was already treated above. In Acts 11 Luke is concentrating on famine relief and notes the acceptance of Gentiles but not the details that became more sensitive concerns as time passed. The possibility that some wished to revisit the initial solution also cannot be ruled out. Anyone who has worked with controversial matters knows that revisiting a controversial decision reflects human nature. Peter's remarks about the burden of the law need to be seen in light of a debate over salvation, not its function as guiding some practice. The minor role of Paul and Barnabas simply reflects the situation of a council engaging the entire church. It leaves the resolution outside the hands of the key protagonists who created the need for the meeting. The goal is a churchwide solution, and so it is not surprising that there are other major players. After the basic decision was made, the council then in its communication to the churches treated the implications beyond salvation that also needed addressing.

Barrett (1998: xxxviii–xxxix) goes on to note four issues that arise between the Acts account and the Pauline Epistles: (1) There is the relationship already noted between Gal. 2:1–10 and Acts 15, with Barrett concluding that these are the same event. (2) A reference to a decree is absent in Galatians. (3) The Acts council comes as a result of a visit of Judean Christians to Antioch whereas in Galatians it is a visit of people from James who create a division between Peter, Barnabas, and others from the Christians in Antioch (this difference can be explained if Acts 15 does not equal Gal. 2). (4) Differing portraits of Paul are presented in the two accounts. The tension is that Paul compromises in Acts 15 whereas he seems to refuse to do so in Galatians.

Two important issues in Barrett's list remain: issue 5 and issue 6 in combination with Pauline issues 2 and 4 noted just above.

Issue 5 concerns James's use of a Greek version of Amos 9:11–12 to make his argument, a point that seems initially surprising for one who represents the Jewish Christian position. But this would have been a regionwide discussion, and the use of Greek here would not be unlikely. If James were conciliatory, then his use of a Greek rendering would only solidify the point.

Issue 6 is the absence of reference to the decrees in Paul's letters. He does not mention them even in Rom. 14 and 1 Cor. 8–10, where they seem relevant. This also raises questions about the different portraits of Paul's strength of reaction in Acts versus Galatians. The contrast and silence do seem odd. This silence can be tempered, however, by the fact that Paul desires to make his own case for how to handle such questions. This Pauline independence may be present because the decrees were not as effective in squelching dissent as the leadership may have initially hoped. Paul's own position of being sensitive to the "weaker" brother is a general reflection of the decision made here.

Johnson (1992: 270) provides valuable remarks about how the general portrait of this event and its essential conclusion reflect this debate's historical resolution in the church's early decades. God's mission to the Gentiles was a gift and calling of God, with Paul's work being legitimized in the process. Johnson, however, overplays the literary role of Luke being less concerned with what happened than with what should have happened. This distinguishes narrative truth from referential truth too greatly for a writer such as Luke, but Johnson's basic point that Paul and the council run the same track is on the mark. It is more precise to say that both Paul's letters and Acts cover the topic with a selectivity that makes bringing all the details together difficult, not because either played fast and loose with the facts but because they made different choices and had different concerns and emphases.

The passage has three key units. The problem is presented in 15:1–5. The discussion and decision emerge in 15:6–21, with the key speakers being Peter, recounting his experience with Cornelius, Paul and Barnabas relating what God did in the journey, and James speaking in support of them, using Scripture. This effectively reviews the content and significance of Acts 10–14 and fits rhetorical style in Greco-Roman contexts (Chariton of Aphrodisias, *Chaer.* 3.4.4–18; 8.7.1–16; Johnson 1992: 268). It is likely that Luke has taken a longer deliberation and boiled it down to core elements that relate to his own account (Jervell 1998: 404–5). What Luke recounts are the key events that led the church to discern as a community what God desires. In the discussion is an interesting interaction between what God clearly has done and what Scripture says, and these come together into a solution. James makes clear that it is more than what Amos alone says that makes James's point, as the prophets (plural) agree with his argument. The final major unit is 15:22–35, where the letter is both composed and sent with commissioned messengers. The result is a compromise sensitive to Jewish conscience. The letter reports a fourfold recommendation for Gentiles to abstain from things sacrificed to idols, food placed in blood, food that has been strangled, and immorality. The decision reflects a cross-cultural concern and sensitivity for the conscience of some whose sense of freedom does not match the rest of the community. This is the only official formal decree in Acts (Johnson 1992: 268).

The issue of sources is also debated by scholars, depending on how one views the historicity of the account. Barrett (1998: 710) has a nice summary of the various options and combinations proposed. He proposes that Acts 15 and Gal. 2 match, that James and Paul did not agree with each other, and that Paul did not agree with the decree (1998: 710–12). This solution looks too much like the old Tübingen school, which placed Paul and James in irreconcilable tension with each other. It also opts to accept Paul's account over that of Luke. But it is better to see Gal. 2 as a different event and to see Acts 15 as a solution that set the basic outline for resolving the problem. It may well be that Paul was not entirely happy with the outcome—which might explain why he never mentioned it—but, for the sake of community unity, accepted it as a workable, if not ideal, solution.

Schneider (1982: 176–77) discusses the theory that some material came from Antioch (15:1–4 and 12b) and another, possibly Jerusalem, source utilized by Luke dealt with the decree (15:5–12a, 13–33; also Weiser 1985: 376; Pesch 1986b: 72, 74, who also suggests what came from where; Jervell 1998: 404–5 is for multiple traditions at work). Schneider also considers the possibility that two separate ideas were combined: the Antiochene conflict and a later compromise solution. This view is common among commentators. Fitzmyer (1998: 540) prefers a combination of Pauline source material and Antiochene sources.

The origin of the sources is not clear, and the possibility of a multitude of sources for this event is likely. Luke's summarizing narrative and condensed account of what was a much longer deliberation make precise delineation of sources difficult.

In sum, the scene is important because it completely legitimates the Gentile mission. It also establishes faith alone rooted in the grace of God through Christ alone as the principle of inclusion, and it does so by showing continuity with the promises of old. The new faith and practice are actually rooted in old promises, making the faith an old one in its roots. The idea that circumcision is necessary is emphatically refuted in the chapter. Peter calls that idea "testing God" (v. 10). James tells the brothers to stop bothering the Gentiles (v. 19). God's initiative must be appreciated for what it is: a full inclusion of Gentiles without making them Jews. Galatians 2 and Acts 15 will not be compared to each other in the exposition of the chapter, since the view here is that the two scenes are distinct. One thing that is not made clear from the chapter is how Jewish believers are to view the practice of keeping the law. On this point, if Paul is a guide, there are two options: (1) keep the law scrupulously for the sake of evangelizing Jews, or (2) be less scrupulous for the sake of Gentiles (1 Cor. 9:19–22; Rom. 14–15). Each person is to do what conscience permits without imposing a requirement on someone who has different convictions.

1. The Problem (15:1–5)

Most of the major issues tied to this paragraph were discussed in the preceding section. This unit introduces the problem that leads to the meeting, with verses 1–2 and 4–5 greatly overlapping. The difference is that verses 1–2 cover the situation in Antioch whereas verses 4–5 treat the situation when the emissaries arrive in Jerusalem. The two locales mirror each other in their concern. In the middle stands verse 3, where Luke summarizes the response to Gentile inclusion and notes how God has acted. It hints at the rationale for welcoming the Gentiles in without additional restrictions.

Exegesis and Exposition

¹But some men ⌜ ⌝ coming down from Judea were teaching the brothers and sisters, "If you are not circumcised ⌜ ⌝ according to the custom of Moses, you cannot be saved." ²And when Paul and Barnabas had no small tension and debate with them⌜ ⌝, Paul and Barnabas and some of the others were appointed to go up to Jerusalem to the apostles and the elders ⌜ ⌝ about this question. ³So, being sent on their way by the church, they came through both Phoenicia and Samaria, reporting the conversion of the Gentiles, and they were giving great joy to all the brethren. ⁴Coming to Jerusalem, they were welcomed by the church and the apostles and the elders, and declared all that God had done with them. ⁵⌜But some⌝ believers who belonged to the party of the Pharisees arose, saying, "It is necessary to circumcise them and to command them to keep the law of Moses."

15:1–2   Some Jewish believers from Judea raise the question of Gentiles following the law. Also mentioned is "the custom of Moses" (τῷ ἔθει τῷ Μωϋσέως, *tō ethei tō Mōuseōs*; Acts 6:14). This is a dative of cause or rule, "because of the custom of Moses" or "according to the custom of Moses" (BDF §196; Moulton and Turner 1963: 242; Wallace 1996: 155). This phrase may refer to Jewish tradition, but this is uncertain since the command to be circumcised comes directly from the Law itself, issued in connection with the patriarch Abraham (Gen. 17:10–14). On the other hand, verse 5 suggests that it is not circumcision alone but keeping the law that is the issue. In addition, the decree covers more than circumcision, suggesting that the discussion is wide-ranging, with circumcision the most sensitive question.

The question is introduced as a third-class condition, showing an element of openness to the matter as Luke states it (Wallace 1996: 699). In particular, the concern is the command to be circumcised, the roots of which go back to God's command about the "sign" of belonging to God's people, a fundamental association independent of the laws given by Moses to Israel.

Who are these brothers from Judea? Two plausible views exist: (1) they may be messengers from James (Gal. 2:12) who exceed their authority by insisting on circumcision, or (2) they may be "false brothers secretly brought in" (Gal. 2:4) to spy out Paul and company. (Nowhere is it clear that they hold the view of James; they are merely associated with him and his congregation.) Either way, they clearly are zealots when it comes to keeping the law, although there is a logical consistency in their view that had some appeal. In their view, without such covenantal faithfulness, salvation is not possible. This would be an issue only for Gentiles having just come to faith because Jewish Christians would have already been circumcised. So must a Gentile become like a Jew to be a genuine Christian? This is a key question at this important Jerusalem Council.

The question is logical, but it produces tension and debate (στάσεως καὶ ζητήσεως, *staseōs kai zētēseōs*), especially given what has already been done. Paul and Barnabas are on the side of the issue opposite these Judeans. The term "tension" or "dissension" indicates that the division of opinion runs deep; it refers to a serious lack of agreement (BAGD 764 §3; BDAG 940 §3; Acts 23:7, 10; Josephus, *Ant.* 18.9.9 §374). In other contexts, the term can refer to a riot or revolt (Acts 19:40; Luke 23:19, 25), showing the intensity of the term's force. They decide to go to Jerusalem to meet over the question. The issue is too important to be left to a local decision. It is clear from the way Luke presents the council that the answer will not come from Paul, Barnabas, or those opposed to them but that the apostles and elders (ἀποστόλους καὶ πρεσβυτέρους, *apostolous kai presbyterous*) will adjudicate this crucial question in Jew-Gentile relations (ζήτημα, *zētēma*, question, issue; all five NT occurrences are in Acts: 15:2; 18:15; 23:29; 25:19; 26:3).

As they were journeying (διήρχοντο, *diērchonto*, imperfect tense) the **15:3** 250 miles to the council through Phoenicia and Samaria, Barnabas and Paul are reporting (ἐκδιηγούμενοι, *ekdiēgoumenoi*) on Gentile conversions, a topic of joy to all of them (14:27). The term for "report" (ἐκδιηγέομαι, *ekdiēgeomai*) appears only here and in 13:41 in the NT (OT occurrences include Ps. 117:17 LXX [118:17 Eng.]; Hab. 1:5; Sir. 34:9; Johnson 1992: 260). It refers to a full report that sets the tone for the council to follow. Gentile conversion is a positive thing that God is doing. The term ἐπιστροφή (*epistrophē*) refers to a change of thinking, a "turn" in orientation, and so a conversion; this is the noun form of the verb ἐπιστρέφω (*epistrephō*, turn). It is the only place the noun is used in the NT, although the verb is frequent in Acts (3:19; 9:35, 40; 11:21; 14:15; 15:19, 36; 16:18; 26:18, 20; 28:27). Polhill (1992: 324) calls this journey almost a "campaign trip," which overstates the matter slightly, but there is no doubt that there is wide enthusiasm for what God is doing through them.

15:4–5   Their arrival is welcomed or received (παρεδέχθησαν, paredechthēsan) by the church, apostles, and elders. The use of ἀπό (apo) here indicates means: reception is by means of the church (Moule 1959: 73). They report (ἀνήγγειλαν, anēngeilan, aorist) what God has been doing through them. As Luke quickly notes, the positive reception is from most of the church, even as others rise up (ἐξανέστησαν, exanestēsan) in contention against them. The complaining party is a group of Jewish believers of Pharisaic background. Paul has similar roots but does not share their view of how Gentiles should relate to the law.

Marshall (1980: 248) suggests that this is not the table fellowship issue raised by the men sent by James, mentioned in Gal. 2:12, but involves a more conservative group taking a more radical position, which explains why James speaks against them later. This is one of the reasons Marshall does not equate Gal. 2 and Acts 15. The group may also have some members who went to Antioch, as noted in verse 1, but this point is not explicitly made. The term "party" (αἱρέσεως, haireseōs) refers to a distinct subgroup that has distinct beliefs (BAGD 23 §1a; BDAG 27–28 §1a). It is not a pejorative term here equal to our sense of heresy (correctly, Witherington 1998: 453n381). The term is used descriptively of the Sadducees in Acts 5:17, of the Pharisees in 26:5, and of the Christians in 24:5, 14 and 28:22. All of this suggests that Luke presents Christianity as a natural extension of Judaism because promises given originally to the Jews are now offered in the new community formed by Jesus the Messiah. There also are different views among the earliest Christians that now will begin to be sorted out. The church is not a "monolithic block" (correctly, Williams 1990: 267), nor is the portrayal as ideal and absent of tension as some critics of Acts suggest. Luke is honest about debated points in this early period.

This group makes two demands: Gentiles are (1) to keep circumcision, as also noted in verse 1, and (2) to keep the law. Luke uses the term δεῖ (dei, it is necessary) to make the point, and so they are arguing that such compliance is a divine necessity. These believers, who are also Pharisees, think that Gentiles should live like Jews, but this would make the inclusion of Gentile believers awkward by requiring them to become like those of Israel. The position is similar to making them Jewish proselytes, but the council deliberations suggest that a new era with new means of administration has come.

Acts 15:5 restates the problem introduced in 15:1 but with more detail (also Gal. 5:2–3, where Paul argues that circumcision, if it is observed as part of the law, requires that all the law be observed for salvation). Circumcision is a key part of the law but is not all of it for Pharisees. The necessity of circumcision includes the importance of the law for this viewpoint. The view probably is rooted in claims made from texts such as Gen. 17:10–14 and Deut. 5:28–33 (Fitzmyer 1998: 546). Williams (1990: 262) appeals to Exod. 12:48–49 and Isa. 56:6.

In sum, ever since the Maccabean period (1 Macc. 1:10–15), Jews anxious to remain faithful to God were sensitive toward the keeping of Jewish legal distinctives in order to continue to affirm Judaism, but now the question is whether Gentiles affirming faith in Jesus should also observe such practices for salvation.[1] The issue is not whether Gentiles should be included in the community but the specific requirements for their inclusion. This is the crucial issue introduced in this section of Acts. The resolution follows in the deliberations of verses 6–21.

Additional Notes

15:1. The issue comes from those of the Pharisee sect, according to Ψ, 614, and 1799 (see v. 5, where Pharisees are noted). In a separate addition, D says that the issue is not just circumcision but also not walking according to the custom of Moses, which is noted in verse 5. Neither of these readings is original.

15:2. Codex D has Paul arguing that converted Gentiles should stay as they are when converted (i.e., uncircumcised). In a separate addition, it argues that the Jerusalem group orders them to go to Jerusalem to be judged. One can sense in these additions in D that the reaction against Judaism is stronger in this MSS tradition. These poorly attested additions are not original.

15:5. Codex D sees this party as including those who originally went down from Judea and complained in Antioch, as noted in 15:1. The repetition between verses 1–2 and verses 4–5 in the original text leads some to suggest that Luke is combining sources here that had very similar facts (Bruce 1990: 334).

---

1. Other "law of Moses" texts in the NT include Luke 2:22; 24:44; John 7:23; Acts 13:39; 28:23; 1 Cor. 9:9; and Heb. 10:28; Schneider 1982: 179n39. Other texts refer to a "law of Christ" or a "royal law," 1 Cor. 9:21; Gal. 6:2; James 2:8. The law of Christ is tied to the law of love or of freedom from requirements of the law, a theme at work in all three passages where the expressions appear.

2. The Discussion and Decision (15:6–21)

Luke summarizes what is certainly a much longer discussion. That there is much debate is indicated in 15:6–7a, but then we see a series of three key speakers: Peter (15:7b–11), Barnabas and Paul (15:12), and James, whose remarks resolve the matter (15:13–21). His views are expressed in verses 13–18, and his solution, which is adopted, appears in verses 19–21. This leads to the composition of a letter and the sending of messengers (15:22–35). Peter sets the stage by detailing what God originally did. Barnabas and Paul underscore it with a word about the recent activity. James says that Scripture parallels and explains what has been described. The three together summarize what Acts 10–14 has already presented in detail, with the missionaries' remarks along with the teaching of Peter and James serving as theological commentary.

The likely sources for such an event include those rooted in Jerusalem and in Antioch, although Fitzmyer (1998: 544, 552–53) sees two distinct sources from Antioch telescoping two somewhat distinct events. What may well suggest Antioch for some of the source material is that Barnabas is listed before Paul in 15:12, a perspective like what appears in the text before the first missionary journey. It is not clear why two distinct events are suggested. The idea that the injection of dietary matters reflects another setting fails to see the unity of perspective from a Jewish point of view, where issues of circumcision and law are often closely connected to each other. James is simply making explicit what also needs to be settled when a cross-cultural topic is raised. Such moves in expanding the topic are common in NT discussions of this type (Acts 10, visions; Mark 7:1–23; Luke 11:37–54).

The passage is a combination of narrative summary and short addresses. As Barrett (1998: 709–10) notes, the extensive spread of the gospel into the world among Gentiles is the result of this decision and is the central concern of Luke in Acts from this point on.

Exegesis and Exposition

⁶The apostles and the elders were gathered together to take a look at this matter. ⁷And after there had been much debate, rising up ⌜ ⌝, Peter said to them, "Brothers, you know that from the very start God chose from among you that by my mouth the Gentiles should hear the word of the gospel and believe. ⁸And God who knows the heart gave witness to them by giving them the Holy Spirit just as he did to us; ⁹and he made no distinction between us and them,

having cleansed their hearts through faith. [10]Now therefore why do you test God by placing a yoke upon the neck of the disciples that neither our fathers nor we have been able to bear? [11]But through the grace of the Lord Jesus we believe that we are saved, just as they are."

[12]And ⌜ ⌝ all the assembly became silent; and they listened to Barnabas and Paul relate what signs and wonders God had done through them among the Gentiles. [13]After they finished speaking, James replied, "Brothers, listen to me. [14]Simeon has related how God first visited the Gentiles, to receive a people for his name. [15]And with this the words of the prophets fit together, as it is written, [16]'After these things I will return, and I will rebuild the dwelling of David, which has fallen; I will rebuild its ruins, and I will set it up, [17]that the rest of men may seek the Lord, and all the Gentiles who are called by my name, [18]says the Lord, who has made these things known from of old.' [19]Therefore I judge that we should not trouble those of the Gentiles who turn to God, [20]but should write to them to abstain from the pollutions of idols ⌜and from unchastity⌝ and from ⌜what is strangled⌝ and from blood ⌜ ⌝. [21]For from early generations Moses has had in every city those who preach him, being read every Sabbath in the synagogues."

The apostles and elders gather to discuss the question. Literally, the text speaks of "looking at this matter" (ἰδεῖν περὶ τοῦ λόγου τούτου, *idein peri tou logou toutou*). The entire community's involvement is similar to Acts 6:1–2, but there is one difference. Here it is the apostles and elders who deliberate, whereas in Acts 6 only the apostles are involved.

15:6

After much debate (ζητήσεως, *zēteseōs*), Peter makes a key address with a review of his experience with Cornelius, the third time Luke has recounted this event, indicating its importance (Acts 10; 11:1–18). The detail tells us that Luke is summarizing, as none of the debate of the various sides is laid out for the reader.

15:7–9

Peter goes back to the "days of the beginning" (ἀφ᾽ ἡμερῶν ἀρχαίων, *aph' hēmerōn archaiōn*), or the start of these recent events concerning Gentiles. He has gone back as much as a decade in time.[1] God chose from "among you" (the leaders who are being addressed and are deliberating) through "my mouth" (that is, Peter) to present the gospel to Gentiles. Williams (1990: 263) notes how the expression of "through the mouth" appears in Acts only when Peter speaks (1:16; 3:18, 21; 4:25). Peter starts with God's initiative and keeps the emphasis there.

God chose (ἐξελέξατο, *exelexato*) Peter to give the word of the gospel to Gentiles. The idea of God's choice occurs a few times in Acts. God chose to work through the patriarchs (13:17), and chose the one to replace Judas (1:24).[2] In effect, Peter is the apostle for the breaking of

---

1. If this event dates to AD 48–49, then we are looking back about a decade.
2. In the OT, see Num. 16:5; Deut. 4:37; 7:7; 21:5; Josh. 24:15; 1 Sam. 16:9–10 LXX; 1 Kings 8:16, 44 LXX; 1 Chron. 28:4–5; Neh. 9:7; Bruce 1990: 336.

the good news to the Gentiles. The key fact is that as Peter presented the word of the gospel and called Gentiles to faith, the Spirit was given to them just as it had been given to Jewish believers at the beginning, an allusion to Acts 2 (11:17). This gift comes from God, who knows the heart. It was an act by which God bore witness to their genuine response and God's acceptance of them. What is important here is that God gave the Spirit without any circumcision being done. God accepted Gentiles as they were when the Spirit came. The theological implication here is that the Spirit would not have come to indwell Gentiles unless they are completely accepted and cleansed.

Peter's description of God's initiative and understanding in acting is the key to the argument. Also crucial is the presence of the divine gift of the Spirit identifying the arrival of the new era of promise in Acts 2 and 10 (2:4; 10:44–47; 11:15–17). Peter had nothing to do with how Gentiles were to be included. God has acted and shown the way. If anyone should be blamed for this new departure, it is God (Bruce 1988a: 290). Does Peter see this as an internal circumcision of the heart (Jer. 4:4; 9:26; Rom. 2:29; Polhill 1992: 326)? If so, he does not say so, referring rather to the related idea of cleansing the heart, a connection that shows how baptism represents new life (Ezek. 36:24–26). Peter is more interested in God's taking the lead in disclosing his approval and its timing. God does the work of washing their hearts clean. This divine washing takes place in the context of faith. So the entire work reflects God's directive.

The noun εὐαγγέλιον (euangelion, gospel) appears here for the first time in Acts and is used only one more time (20:24). Here Peter summarizes the proper response to the gospel as faith, a key term for response in Acts 13–14 (13:8, 12, 39, 41, 48; 14:1, 9, 22, 27).

The first conclusion Peter makes is that God equally receives both Jews and Gentiles, a point he made in his speech to Cornelius in 10:34–35. There is no distinction between them when it comes to access to salvation (10:20, 34; 11:12; Eph. 2:11–22).

15:10–11   Peter now strengthens his point and asks rhetorically, "Why do you test [τί πειράζετε, ti peirazete] God?" This is really a declaration not to test God. God has revealed himself and shown how Gentile hearts are now cleansed without circumcision. The idea of testing God is a strong warning, as it is used in Exod. 17:2 (Barrett 1998: 717; also Exod. 15:22–27; Num. 14:22; Fitzmyer 1998: 547; in Luke-Acts: Luke 4:2; 11:16; Acts 5:9). Those who are complaining cannot trust God and follow God's way. So they will test God's goodness. In fact, the yoke of doing every aspect of the law should not be placed (ἐπιθεῖναι, epitheinai) upon the Gentiles at all, since this is a burden no one, not even Jews, have been able to bear. This infinitive gives the means by which God is being tested inappropriately (Moule 1959: 127). Even though the action involves people, it is God and God's way that is being challenged. Here is the only use of the term yoke (ζυγός, *zygos*) in Acts. It refers to a frame placed around an animal's neck to restrict its movement (BAGD 339 §1; BDAG 429).[3]

Le Cornu and Shulam (2003: 823–26) have a long treatment of "yoke," viewing its use in Judaism as positive, so they conclude that Peter cannot be criticizing the law here. They think Peter's point is that the law is yoked together as one (to keep it, one must keep it all). The point is that Jews and Gentiles both benefit from God's grace equally. However, one should see here not a point about the unity of the law or a problem with it as law but an inability that the law fosters. As Paul explains in Rom. 7, the law is holy, but its demands cannot be met; it cannot be kept by people who sin in reaction to it.

Gaventa (2003: 216) sees the term as positive, so that Luke's view is not a problem with the law but with Israel's ability to keep it (also Jervell 1998: 392–93; Acts 7:53). Peter is arguing that these requirements place more restrictions on Gentiles than God has done by his act of saving Cornelius and create a weight that does not allow one to complete a task, just as Israel has failed. The topic here is Gentile salvation and the law, not the value of the law in witness to the Jews.

This does not mean that there is no value in practicing the law in order to reach out to Jews, as the decree itself will show. Barrett (1998: 719) overplays the differences here and argues that this remark cannot be anything that reflects Peter's real view, as it sounds too Pauline. There is a shadow of the old Tübingen critical view here (see Polhill 1992: 327; Acts 13:38–39; 1 Pet. 1:8–12; Bruce 1990: 337; Witherington 1998: 454–55). Other occurrences of ζυγός in the NT are also figurative (Gal. 5:1; 1 Tim. 6:1; Matt. 11:29–30 in contrast to Matt. 23:4, which is like Luke 11:46).

Peter gives his theological conclusion in verse 11. It reads almost like a confession of faith. Salvation is through grace by the work of Jesus. What this implies is that salvation is not through works of the law, as the complaining group from the Pharisees would require. The reference to the grace or gift of God is placed forward in the Greek construction for emphasis. God's grace as it relates to the Lord Jesus has opened the way for both Jews and Gentiles to experience God's blessing. This comment gives no place to the law in terms of salvation (Gal. 5:6). God is now doing his work through what he is doing through Jesus. Peter also emphasizes and underscores the theological equality of Jew and Gentile when it comes to matters of salvation, for what he says about grace applies to both groups. This is the last we see of Peter in Acts.

---

3. On the term "yoke" applied to the keeping of commandments in Judaism, see *m. Ber.* 2.2, where it is seen positively; also *m. 'Abot* 1.19; 3.5; Sir. 51:26; Ps. Sol. 7.9; 17.30; Josephus, *Ag. Ap.* 2.37 §§271–80; and contrast Philo, *Rewards* 14 §80: "For the commandments are not burdensome or too weighty for the ability of you who are to live by them to obey."

15:12 The assembly became silent (ἐσίγησεν, *esigēsen*) as a result of Peter's remarks (an ingressive aorist, Moulton and Turner 1963: 71). It is here that Barnabas and Paul make their only remarks at the meeting as Luke summarizes it. They recount how God worked with signs and wonders (Acts 2:22, 43) among the nations. That God would work miracles in the midst of the Gentiles is another divine indicator for Gentile inclusion ("it shows divine approval"; Barrett 1998: 721). After 13:2, it is only here and in 15:25 that Barnabas is named first.[4]

15:13–14 James, who represents the Jewish Christian contingent in Jerusalem (12:17; 21:18–24), now speaks in support of Peter, calling on his audience to listen (2:22; 7:2; 13:16; 22:1; 24:4; 26:3). The use of μετά (*meta*) plus the infinitive places the timing of James's remarks after Peter's (Moulton and Turner 1963: 143; Wallace 1996: 595). James refers to Peter using his Jewish name, Simeon. Fitzmyer (1998: 552–53) suggests that in the original source this was Simeon Niger of Acts 13:1, but such a connection is not at all transparent. James's note about Peter's recounting of events uses a verb (ἐξηγέομαι, *exēgeomai*, narrate) similar to the noun Luke uses in Luke 1:1 (διήγησις, *diēgēsis*, narrative), where tradition about Jesus is discussed. James concludes that what God has done is receive a people from among the Gentiles (λαβεῖν ἐξ ἐθνῶν, *labein ex ethnōn*) who will represent God and bear God's name in the world.

The term "people" (λαός, *laos*) is significant because it often refers to the people of God (Acts 7:34; 13:17), as it does here. In the OT, this term refers to Israel (Deut. 26:18–19; 32:8–9; Ps. 134:12 LXX [135:12 Eng.]), although Zech. 2:11 (2:15 LXX) uses it to refer to Gentiles as a part of renewed Israel (Polhill 1992: 329). Another allusion is also possible: it may parallel Deut. 14:2 and/or 26:18–19 and picture a call to Gentiles similar to the one Israel experienced (Schneider 1982: 182; Barrett 1998: 724). The phrase "people for my name" is not in the LXX but is common in the Palestinian Targum, so there may be traces of an idiom common in Jewish contexts, although its application to Gentiles is surprising (Codex Neofiti I on Exod. 19:5–6 and 22:30; Dahl 1957–58). Even a committed Jewish believer such as James can see and affirm that Gentiles can be included among believers directly without having to become Jews. This is an innovation of the new era that Jesus and the distribution of the Spirit on Gentiles have brought. Bruce (1990: 339) notes that these Gentiles are sheep not of this fold (John 10:16). Also significant is the term ἐπισκέπτομαι (*episkeptomai*, visit), for it refers to a miraculous or a messianic visitation that God has directed (Luke 1:68, 78; 7:16; 19:44; T. Levi 16.5; 1 En. 25.3; Larkin 1995: 222). Luke's

---

4. This might point to the influence of a traditional source (see the introduction to this unit).

uses suggest a messianic visitation (only 7:16 might be an exception). James's remarks are full of theological terms and ideas.

The people of God are now found in the new entity God has formed in the church. The passage is not entirely about Israel (*pace* Jervell 1998: 394). It addresses the rebuilt Davidic house and the new kingdom work Jesus started with the Spirit at a point Peter earlier called the beginning, in Acts 11:15–18 (cf. 1:3–5 about Acts 2). This new community is in continuity with the promise made to Israel of the past but is a fresh work of God (Matt. 16:16–20) and results in a new work and institution.

James now notes how the teaching of the prophets matches or agrees   **15:15–18** with the inclusion of the Gentiles. The verb συμφωνοῦσιν (*symphōnousin*) literally means "share the same sound," and thus "match" or "agree" (BAGD 780 §1a; BDAG 960–61 §1). The only other occurrence in Acts is when Ananias and Sapphira agree to deceive the church (5:9; other NT occurrences: Matt. 18:19; 20:2, 13; Luke 5:36). The reference to the prophets is important. James's point is not just about this one passage from Amos; rather, this passage reflects what the prophets teach in general, or what the book of the Prophets as a whole teaches. Other texts could be noted (Zech. 2:11; 8:22; Isa. 2:2; 45:20–23; Hos. 3:4–5; Jer. 12:15–16). James is stressing fulfillment, for the prophets agree with what Peter has described. This is not an affirmation of analogous fulfillment but a declaration that this is now taking place. God had promised Gentile inclusion; now he is performing it. Paul cites a string of OT texts on this theme in Rom. 15:7–13.

James's quotation matches Amos 9:11–12 LXX with material in verse 18 from Isa. 45:21. Jeremiah 12:15 may be the source for the opening "After these things I will return," but this is less than clear, since the phrases may be only a transition into the citation that shows how James sees the timing. Amos 9:12 MT refers to Edom and looks to its judgment as well as its inclusion during the rule of David's restored dynasty. As Fitzmyer (1998: 555) says, "Yahweh promises the prophet that the Davidic line will be restored, and God's people will inherit what is left of Edom and other nations that will be called God's people." In the LXX all the peoples seek the rebuilt kingdom that comes from the restored Davidic line. Edom now refers to all humanity. The key difference is that in the MT a people group is conquered and incorporated whereas in the LXX all people seek incorporation. Ådna (Ådna and Kvalbein 2000: 125–44) argues that the text has Hebrew roots, and he defends the authenticity of its use in this scene.

Whether there is a wordplay here between Edom and Adam, given their similar sounds, could be discussed. Bruce (1988a: 293–94) and Witherington (1998: 459) note that two changes in the Hebrew make the shift. One comes from changing the verb "possess" (*yāraš*) to the verb "seek" (*dāraš*). The other involves a shift from *Edom* to *Adam*. This kind of wordplay is known as "al tikri" (Le Cornu and Shulam 2003: 833). They see James adopting the LXX view, which has recast the MT. Larkin (1995: 223) defends the idea that the LXX is closer to the original Hebrew whereas the MT reflects a corruption, but this, though possible, is less than clear (Witherington 1998: 459). James uses a shortened version of the LXX and follows the common Jewish practice of not always citing the MT but making use of a respected alternate text. Witherington (1998: 456–57) calls the form deliberative rhetoric. Bauckham (1996: 160–61) also accepts the adoption of the LXX against Haenchen (1987: 448), who argues that a Jewish Christian would never use such a text. Barrett (1998: 726–28) takes Luke as the source of the citation in this form, not James, because of the deviation, making too much of it. Bruce (1990: 341) notes that the MT can also be read in a way that agrees with James, since the new community could be seen as having a claim of possession on Gentiles, and so the difference in rendering is not significant, moving in an explicitly positive direction. Polhill (1992: 329) notes that the key idea of Gentiles "called by my name" is in both versions of the citation.

James shows deference and sensitivity in the debate by citing the Greek version of the OT text, which the Gentiles would recognize. The passage declares the rebuilding of the dynasty of David, fulfilled here in Jesus's messianic arrival, along with the current inclusion of Gentiles. God is acting to perform his work of restoration through Jesus, much as Acts 3 declared. The reconstructed booth of David, for James, portrays the place of the rule and benefits that come through the Messiah, Jesus. The current community now preaches about these benefits to Gentiles, who can also be included among God's people (Acts 2:30–36; 13:32–39). The rebuilding of the dynasty does not refer just to the resurrection (but so Schneider 1982: 182–83; Haenchen 1987: 448). God's hope does not call for proselytes to Judaism but for a fresh work in Jesus (Larkin 1995: 224). The reference to "nations" agrees with verse 14, so that the Jewish link-word technique *gezerah shewa* appears again (on this Amos text, see CD 7.16; 4Q174 1.12–13). Gentiles are also "called by my name," as God is now actively including them in the call to faith (Acts 2:21, 32–36; 9:14; conceptually, 13:48).

The goal of this rebuilding work is to allow the rest of humanity, not just Jews, to seek God. This fulfills not only the promise to David about his line but also a commitment to Abraham that through his seed the world would experience blessing (Gen. 12:3; Acts 3:25–26; Gal. 3). Thus James argues that this Gentile inclusion is part of the plan of Davidic restoration that God through the prophets said he would do. The prophets affirm what is taking place now. So both divine events and Scripture sustain the church's inclusion of Gentiles. This is the only occurrence of the verb ἐκζητέω (*ekzēteō*) for "seeking" in Acts (the use in Heb. 11:6 is like its use here, describing those who seek God as men of faith).

The remark that God has made these things known from of old is a way to say that these things were revealed and form a part of God's plan. The new way was revealed and is really an old promise. The phrase "known from of old" (γνωστὰ ἀπ' αἰῶνος, gnōsta ap' aiōnos) recalls Isa. 45:21. Bruce (1990: 341) cites the OT texts about Gentile inclusion that Paul quotes in Rom. 15:8–12, to show that the church had a collection of such inclusion texts that reflected its understanding of God's plan.

James argues that the Gentiles who turn with faith to God should not   **15:19–20** be burdened with issues of the law. Luke's description of the response as turning is consistent with other texts in Acts (3:19; 11:21; esp. 14:15 and 26:18). No obstacle should be put before them. The verb παρενοχλέω (parenochleō) means "cause unnecessary trouble or difficulty" (BAGD 625; BDAG 775; EDNT 3:38). This is the term's only occurrence in the NT. It appears in the LXX in Judg. 14:17, where it refers to Samson being bothered by Delilah, and in 1 Macc. 10:35, where it describes the pestering of Jews during feasts. In effect, James agrees with Peter's point in 15:10.

The council asks Gentiles to be sensitive about four matters and to refrain from them. The verb ἀπέχω (apechō) means "avoid contact" with something (BAGD 85 §3; BDAG 103 §5). To be avoided are (1) the pollution that comes from idols (ἀλισγημάτων τῶν εἰδώλων, alisgēmatōn tōn eidōlōn; Mal. 1:7); (2) immorality, probably associated with pagan rites and temple prostitution (πορνείας, porneias); (3) strangled things (πνικτοῦ, pniktou); and (4) blood matters (αἵματος, haimatos; for the Jewish background, Str-B 2:729–39). This list reappears with slight variation in Acts 15:29 and 21:25. The only two occurrences of ἀπέχω in Acts concern this decree (vv. 20, 29).

The word ἀλίσγημα (alisgēma, pollution) appears only in this verse and is not repeated in the NT, not even in 15:29 or 21:25, where the limitations reappear. Nor does the term appear in the LXX. The verb form appears in Dan. 1:8; Mal. 1:7, 12; and Sir. 40:29, where it concerns the eating of food and suggests a kind of desecration (see 4 Macc. 5:1–2 for a conceptual parallel using terminology that appears in 15:29; also Lev. 17:7; Exod. 20:4). It seems that pollution associated with idols and their rituals is in view.

The association with sexual immorality appears also to have a cultic dimension. The only three occurrences of πορνεία in Acts are in contexts where these limitations on behavior are in view (15:20, 29; 21:25). A similar use may appear in Rev. 2:21, and the occurrences in Rev. 14:8; 17:2, 4; 18:3; and 19:2 show its cultic leanings. Fitzmyer (1998: 557–58) sees a connection to various intrafamilial relationships like those that appear in CD 4.12–5.14a, a view that is possible, as it is connected to Lev. 17–18.

The reference to things strangled is also rare, being absent in the LXX. The verb πνίγω (pnigō, strangle) appears in Matt. 13:7; 18:28;

and Mark 5:13, where it refers to plants choking other plants or to pigs drowning. This likely is a description of what happens with sacrifices or meals among Gentiles. The result of this form of death is that blood often is not drained from the animal (Gaventa 2003: 222). Philo (*Spec. Laws* 4.23 §§122–23) describes such a practice.

The reference to blood appears to be drawn from Lev. 17:10–14 (Bietenhard, *TDNT* 6:457–58; also Gen. 9:4; Lev. 3:17; 7:26–27; 19:26; Deut. 12:16, 23, 25, 27; 15:23; 1 Sam. 14:32–34; Ezek. 33:25; Wis. 12:2–5). The key here is the association of life and blood. Leviticus prohibits eating blood or meat that has not been properly drained of blood. This reflects a Jewish concern over the sacred nature of life as possessed in the blood (1 En. 7.5; 15.4; 98.11; Jub. 6.7–16; 7.28–29; *m. Ker.* 1.1; 5.1), but this does not extend to the kinds of restrictions the rabbis imposed (Bietenhard, *TDNT* 6:457). Still, the term is not a secondary addition to the text as Bietenhard suggests. It is too well attested and yet too rare a term with this cultic force to have been added in several places later (only Hebrews uses the term frequently with a cultic force). What may have been particularly offensive was the Gentile priest tasting the blood of the sacrifice (Witherington 1998: 464). The expression that Gentiles have turned from idols to the living God may well have such idolatrously connected practices in mind and may well serve as more than an abstract statement about conversion (1 Thess. 1:9–10). Witherington (1998: 465–66) also points to 1 Thess. 4:1–9 as the ethical dimension of the decree in Paul (other traces include longer discussions of idols or morals and Christians in 1 Cor. 5–6; 8–10).

In all likelihood, this is a request to be faithful to the one true God, to be moral in worship, and to have sensitivity to issues of unclean animals and eating strangled animals without draining the blood, as Lev. 17:13–14 and 18:6–30 suggest. The limitations are probably to keep relations from becoming strained in a mixed community of Jews and Gentiles as well as to warn about association with idolatry. It is quite likely that the prohibition relates especially to attending pagan temples and what goes with them. Witherington (1998: 462–65) argues for this background exclusively but may go a step too far. He also argues that this is not an appeal to Noahic law from Gen. 9:3–4, where no issues of meat are mentioned (also rejected as the single explanation by Barrett 1998: 734). He notes that the limitations are not an attempt merely to invoke Lev. 17–18 (but so Conzelmann 1987: 118–19 and Jervell 1998: 397). Rather the issue is the burden of adding the law to Gentiles, an idea that has been specifically excluded by the argumentation already made at the council by Peter.

Barrett (1998: 734) shows how Lev. 17–18 cannot explain all the topics noted here. Key ideas present in the limitations (things strangled and the pollution of idols) are not present in these OT texts. It is also clear that this list deals with more than table fellowship although that is part of the concern (Conzelmann 1987: 118; Williams 1990: 266; Bruce 1990: 342).

The list seems to reflect an ethos instead of being the invocation of a specific text. In Judaism this ethos is summarized in a text such as *b. Šeb.* 7b, where idolatry and the shedding of blood are prohibited and chastity is urged. As such, the list is not so much about the law as having a spirit of sensitivity about that which may cause offense. The reason some texts seem prominent is that they contributed to the overall ethos that the limitations seek to represent. There is good evidence that such limitations were observed in the church for some time (Williams 1990: 268; Rev. 2:14, 22; Justin Martyr, *Dial.* 34.8; Eusebius, *Eccl. Hist.* 5.1.26; Tertullian, *Apology* 9.13). There is a cultural sensitivity here where the issue is not establishing a fixed set of practices but respecting the practices of others and not forcing oneself on another because of such views (Larkin 1995: 225). In German, these limitations are called the *Jakobsklauseln*, or "James clauses," which is a good description of them (Wikenhauser 1961: 173). They display a cross-cultural concern that leads to harmony. Nonetheless, Paul in Rom. 14–15 expresses a similar type of cross-cultural concern, so that the spirit of what is invoked here can be seen in the self-styled apostle to the Gentiles as well.

James refers to the fact that Moses is read each week in the synagogue, **15:21** to indicate the need for sensitivity. The note about the reading of Moses shows a missionary concern. The point is that the law is read each week to Jews, and so one should be sensitive to Jewish concerns (see 1 Cor. 9:19–23 for the practical principle explained).[5] Johnson (1992: 267) notes that the practice of reading Moses is long-standing ("from ages past"), widespread ("in every city"), and regular ("every Sabbath"). The remark makes one of two points: (1) Moses is read every week, so be sensitive to those who read him; or (2) as a Gentile, if you need more guidance as to Jewish concerns, these can be determined by hearing Moses, who is read regularly in the synagogue (Marshall 1980: 254). It is not entirely clear which meaning is intended, but the point either way is that Gentiles should show sensitivity to Jewish concerns. A third sense, looking back to verse 19, is that Moses still has a great following (noted by Bruce 1988a: 296). This is less than likely, as it really does not contribute to James's rationale and verses 20–25 point in the direction of the other explanations.

In sum, we see the church in deliberation about a disagreement whose resolution paved the way for the church's future. Several points emerge. First, however deep the original disagreement, the meeting allowed both sides to speak and relied on what God had done, as well as what Scripture teaches. The result, a compromise, led to an understanding

---

5. In Judaism see Philo, *Spec. Laws* 2.15 §§61–64, for a description of how people learn from Moses each "seventh" day; *Creation* 43 §128; also Josephus, *Ant.* 16.2.3 §43; *Ag. Ap.* 2.17 §175.

that may not have completely satisfied anyone. Nevertheless, each side agreed that it could live with this agreement and that it would be wise to be sensitive to all the groups, given the differences in the cultures that made up the new church.

Stott (1990: 255–57) summarizes two additional, complementary lessons. On the one hand, salvation by grace is an issue of Christian truth that is not to be compromised. No particular work of the law was added as a requirement for salvation or membership in the new community. Salvation cannot be a matter of human works. It is about receiving God's grace from start to finish. Faith means relying only on what God has provided in terms of forgiveness and the benefits of salvation that come with it. On the other hand, Christian fellowship means that grace should be shown for differences that are not central to the truth of salvation, as an expression of love. This deference preserves the church and protects it from fragmentation. In his discussion, Stott notes that Luther spoke of Paul as being hard, even adamant, on the gospel but soft and flexible when it comes to love—or, as Stott notes that John Newton said, an iron pillar in essentials and a reed in nonessentials.

In terms of character, we see in both Peter and James figures who trust each other enough to engage each other and listen to each other as they frame a solution by the leading of the Spirit. Part of what drives them is a mutual love that is "sensitive to the scruples of others" (Fernando 1998: 425). James takes the lead in seeking harmony with a point of view his instincts may have originally sought to oppose. As long as the gospel is not compromised, then diversity of expression can be tolerated. We see Paul discuss this principle elsewhere, as in Rom. 14–15, where nonessential issues of food and days are left to each person's conscience instead of Paul imposing one approach on everyone.

Another implication emerges here: Jewish believers are free to practice the faith in their way, just as Gentiles are not required to come under the law. The principle is that neither side sees salvation as the issue in following these practices.

A final consideration, which the next passage makes clear, is that interpreting the results of such meetings for the rest of the community is also an important practice. What is communicated is an agreement by the entire church, not a rehashing of what the original sides may have held.

Additional Notes

15:7. Codex D and 614 add a reference to Peter rising up "in the Spirit" (see 15:29 and 32 for similar additions that make clear the source of the actions).

15:12. The Western text expands by referring to the elders agreeing with Peter and becoming silent along with the whole assembly, probably a reference to no more debate from the opposition.

15:20. Codex D lacks the reference to things strangled, possibly because it was redundant to a degree with animals not drained of blood. Codex D also adds a negatively expressed version of the Golden Rule—"Whatsoever things they do not wish for themselves, do not do to others" (in Judaism, *b. Šabb.* 31a and Tob. 4:15). This move to have the decree be more ethical than ritual may reflect a shift of concern at the time of the Western text (Bruce 1988a: 296). Yet another, earlier MS, $\mathfrak{P}^{45}$, lacks any reference to immorality, making the decree almost exclusively ritualistic.

3. The Reply and Messengers (15:22–35)

The final section of the council passage contains two steps: the writing of the letter (vv. 22–29) and the sending of the emissaries bearing it (vv. 30–35). The letter basically repeats the decision made by the Spirit and the leaders (vv. 25, 28–29). The emissaries are to read the letter, which encourages the church and exhorts it to faithfulness (vv. 31–32). Paul and Barnabas remain in Antioch and instruct the church there. A parallelism of structure exists between verses 22 and 25. Fitzmyer (1998: 562–63) sees the Antiochene source as behind Luke's information about the letter but argues that the decision was from the Jerusalem church and James, not the apostles and elders. This view relies on the known theological emphasis of the Jerusalem church. His rationale for splitting the decision into two steps relies significantly on identifying Acts 15 with Gal. 2, but this identification has already been questioned above. What speaks in part for authenticity here is the central role given to the Jerusalem church at the council, when the rest of the book mostly ignores that congregation. It is not clear, however, what would motivate a "created" story or detail to place the apostles and elders there and leave them in a minor role. This has the look of a unique event, where the dynamics were such that the surprising argument from the most theologically conservative element sealed the agreement. The letter does not represent a pattern of activity between the churches but is a specific letter for this specific issue. Once this decision is made, local implementation is assumed. These actions are taken for the unity of the church. It shows not only how the interrelationships among early church communities function but also how they are to handle their diversity with discernment and deference. Furthermore, it also evidences the mutual respect that the various communities have for each other.

Exegesis and Exposition

²²Then it seemed good to the apostles and the elders together with the whole church to choose men from among them and send them to Antioch with Paul and Barnabas. They sent Judas called Barsabbas, and Silas, leading men among the brothers, ²³writing the following letter: "The apostles and the elders to the brethren who are of the Gentiles in Antioch and Syria and Cilicia, greetings. ²⁴Having heard that some persons from us have troubled you with

words, unsettling your souls, although we gave them no instructions, [25]it has seemed good to us, having come to one accord, to choose men and send them to you with our beloved Barnabas and Paul, [26]who have dedicated their souls for the name of our Lord Jesus Christ ⌜ ⌝. [27]We have therefore sent Judas and Silas, who themselves will tell you the same things through the spoken word. [28]For it has seemed good to the Holy Spirit and to us to lay upon you no greater burden than these necessary things: [29]that you abstain from what has been sacrificed to idols and from blood ⌜and from what is strangled⌝ and from unchastity ⌜ ⌝. If you keep yourselves from these, you will do well. Farewell."

[30]So when they were sent off, they came down to Antioch; and having gathered the multitude together, they delivered the letter. [31]And reading it, they rejoiced at the word of comfort. [32]And Judas and Silas, who were themselves prophets ⌜ ⌝, with a long address exhorted the brethren and strengthened them. [33]And after they had spent some time, they were sent off in peace by the brethren to those who had sent them. ⌜ ⌝ [35]But Paul and Barnabas remained in Antioch, teaching and preaching with many others the word of the Lord.

The apostles and elders select some men, leaders, to accompany Paul   **15:22–24** and Barnabas to Antioch. They are to report on the consultation and represent Jerusalem on the journey.[1] This is Judas's only appearance in Acts. He is not mentioned anywhere else in the NT. His surname, Barsabbas, means "son of the Sabbath." Better known is Silas (probably = Silvanus of 2 Cor. 1:19; 1 Thess. 1:1; 2 Thess. 1:1; 1 Pet. 5:12), who ends up traveling with Paul to Philippi, Thessalonica, and Corinth (Acts 15:27, 32, 34, 40; 16:19, 25, 29; 17:4, 10, 14–15; 18:5). So a Jerusalem presence on Paul's journeys from Jerusalem also exists (Polhill 1992: 333). They are called prophets in verse 32. In effect, two communities serve as witnesses to the letter, a version of the two-witness motif of the OT (Deut. 19:15).

The letter carries a regional address, as it is sent to Antioch, Syria (Acts 15:41; 18:18; 20:3; 21:3), and Cilicia. But this is not only a local problem and decision. The problem arose in Antioch, but communities in Syria and Cilicia are informed, showing the desire to prevent the problem from appearing elsewhere. Acts 16:4 suggests that other communities are informed as well. That these additional communities should be included is not surprising, as Antioch is the hub for this double province of Syria and eastern Cilicia. The point made would be relevant wherever Jewish evangelism takes place.

The letter fits the style of an official document, an encyclical letter.[2] The apostles and elders write the letter. It represents a brother-to-brother or

---

1. On the role of councils in church history, see Pelikan 2005: 175–77.
2. See Witherington 1998: 467; Winter and Clarke 1993: 305–36, although Winter does not mention this passage; and *NewDocs* 1:78 no. 26. On encyclicals in Judaism, see Le Cornu and Shulam 2003: 843–45. Second Macc. 1:1 is an opening to such a letter.

community-to-community correspondence.[3] After its standard greeting, it reviews the problem (v. 24) and explains the resolution (vv. 25–29). It is one long periodic sentence in Greek, one of only two in Luke-Acts (Luke 1:1–4 is the other). The key term in the letter is the repeated expression "it seemed good" (ἔδοξε, edoxe, vv. 22, 25, and 28), pointing to the judgment they have all reached. The expression often appears in official Greek (Barrett 1998: 738, 742; Thucydides, *Pel. War* 4.118.7; Josephus, *Ant.* 16.6.2 §163).

The letter outlines the problem that led to the decision. Some have "disturbed" the letter recipients without being instructed to do so by the leaders. The verb ἐτάραξαν (etaraxan) here means "shake up" or "disturb" someone (BAGD 805 §2; BDAG 990). It is used of agitating a crowd in Acts 17:8 (also Gal. 1:7). The result is an "unsettling" (ἀνασκευάζοντες, anaskeuazontes) of their souls. The term ταράσσω (tarassō) can be translated "dismantle" or "tear down," so that when it refers to someone's mental condition, it means "cause inward distress" (BAGD 60; BDAG 71). Bruce (1990: 345) speaks of a military metaphor for plundering a town. Here is the only occurrence of the term in the NT (Josephus, *Ant.* 14.15.3 §406). The group that caused the problem overstepped their authority, as they had been given no instructions (οὐ διεστειλάμεθα, ou diesteilametha) on the topic that caused the trouble (Rengstorf, *TDNT* 7:592) for the letter recipients' souls, which are capable of being disturbed by outside forces (Schweizer, *TDNT* 9:640). The leaders accept that they sent the troublemakers but not that those who disturbed them acted by their instruction. They did so in a private, unauthorized manner. What is to be done?

15:25–29   The apostles and elders agree on a solution (ὁμοθυμαδόν, homothymadon, of one accord) and choose representatives to accompany the "beloved" (ἀγαπητοῖς, agapetois) Barnabas and Paul (note the order of the names again) and inform the Gentile churches. The commendation of these two as beloved underscores the support for their position. In turn, the character of these two men emerges from the fact that they risked their lives for the church. The verb παραδίδωμι (paradidōmi) means "give over," so in this context it refers to those willing to lose their lives or dedicate their lives for the sake of the Lord Jesus Christ (Barrett 1998: 742). Barnabas and Paul were almost killed in sharing their faith. Polhill (1992: 334) correctly comments that a distinction between risk and dedication in this context is slim, as the two are virtually synonymous (see Rom. 16:4; Gal. 2:20). The letter commends the men from Jerusalem as worthy witnesses on behalf of the council. They can trust what these men report, an important point to make in

3. Note the double use of ἀδελφοί (adelphoi, brethren) and ἀδελφοῖς (adelphois) to introduce the letter. This is the first time this title is used primarily of Gentiles in Acts (Jervell 1998: 400).

the face of a controversy where positions are strongly held and in light of the activity of the previous delegation Jerusalem sent. Judas and Silas will give the report to confirm the letter's contents and instruction (other bearers of letters: Eph. 6:21–22; Col. 4:7–8; 1 Macc. 12:23; Johnson 1992: 277). The claim that such a note fits a fictitious letter better than a real one is unsustainable (Conzelmann 1987: 120). This is excessive skepticism. Live witnesses in a controversy are important, and witnesses from a church that might be expected to have concluded otherwise makes consummate sense.

The Holy Spirit also has a role in this instruction: to lay no greater burden on the Gentiles than the four limitations the council affirmed through James in verse 20 (on a decision by Augustus communicated by decree, see Josephus, *Ant.* 16.6.2 §163, "by me and my council"; Fitzmyer 1998: 566). Repeating in verse 29 the four items that were noted in verse 20, the letter tells the Gentiles that no greater burden or weight (BAGD 133–34 §1; BDAG 167 §1) is to be borne by them other than to be sensitive to these four items because of their association with idolatry. This is the only instance of βάρος (*baros*, burden) in Acts (2 Macc. 9:10; Matt. 20:12; 2 Cor. 4:17; Gal. 6:2; 1 Thess. 2:7; Rev. 2:24). The only difference in the list of four items from verse 20 is a reference to sacrifice offered to idols (εἰδωλοθύτων, *eidōlothytōn*) rather than the more cumbersome reference to the pollutions of idols (ἀλισγημάτων τῶν εἰδώλων, *alisgēmatōn tōn eidōlōn*, v. 20). Εἰδωλοθύτων highlights the connection to idol worship and the sacrifices tied to it (Jervell 1998: 401). The list is in a distinct order as well, since the reference to immorality comes at the end, with things strangled and blood in the middle. Ἀπέχεσθαι (*apechesthai*, abstain) in each of the four restrictions takes the genitive—a good example of genitives of separation; they should be separated from these things (Moule 1963: 41; Wallace 1996: 108). The more cultic elements all come first in the letter. The list matches 21:25.

The adverb ἐπάναγκες (*epanankes*, v. 28) refers to things of a necessary nature or that are compulsory (BAGD 282; BDAG 358). The prohibitions are designed not only to prevent offense to the Jews but also, if they are tied to worship, to prevent offense to God. This is the sole occurrence of this term in the NT. So they are asked in v. 29 to avoid these necessary items. In doing so, they do well, that is, they perform what is right (Schneider 1982: 187n123). This is not about salvation but about what is necessary to maintain positive fellowship with each other. With a fond farewell, the letter closes (2 Macc. 11:21, 33; 3 Macc. 7:9; Josephus, *Life* 44 §227).

The emissaries arrive in Antioch and share the letter with the multitude (πλῆθος, *plēthos*) of believers (for this use of the term, see Acts 15:12). The letter would be "read aloud" (ἀναγνόντες, *anagnontes*; NET). There is joy all around (13:48), and they are comforted. The term παρακλήσει (*paraklēsei*) can mean "comfort" or "encouragement," but given the

15:30–32

past conflict, "comfort" is slightly better, as the decision is a comfort to them. The matter is resolved (Barrett 1998: 749: "Luke is claiming that Gentile Christianity is free from the Law and that the unity of the church had been preserved").

Jervell (1998: 402) overstates the cause of joy when he limits it to the announcement of the duties noted in the decree and the conditions for Gentile incorporation. Jervell excludes the issue of circumcision as relevant on the premise that the letter says nothing about it. But everyone knows the council has gathered to rule on the circumcision question, so its absence in the letter does not mean that the missionaries do not address the matter.

Judas and Silas are called prophets (11:27) and exhort the congregation to strengthen its resolve (11:23; 1 Cor. 14:3). They do so through a long word (διὰ λόγου πολλοῦ, *dia logou pollou*), or "long speech" (NET). The verb ἐπιστηρίζω (*epistērizō*) is used four times in the NT, all in Acts (14:22; 15:32, 41; 18:23; see Luke 22:32, with a related verb). It refers to strengthening something or someone. In Acts 14:22 it is part of an exhortation to remain in the faith. Here it is the result of Judas and Silas's exhortation. In verse 41 Paul and Silas will travel through the churches of Syria and Cilicia to strengthen those communities. In 18:23 it is the churches in Galatia and Phrygia that are strengthened.

15:33–35 Judas and Silas stay for an unspecified short time. They are sent back with a traditional commendation of peace to those who sent them (Gen. 26:29 LXX; Mark 5:34; Luke 7:50; 8:48; 10:5–6; 24:36; Acts 16:36; Rom. 1:7; 1 Cor. 1:3). There are cordial relations between groups of mixed origin. The scene ends on a note of joy and peace. This commentary's exclusion of verse 34 is treated below in the additional note, but the key point is that the verse is not well attested in a variety of MSS. Paul and Barnabas remain in Antioch and continue to preach and teach (Acts 5:42) with many others (11:26; 13:1; 14:28). As often is the case, the topic is the "word of the Lord" (8:25; 13:44, 48–49; 15:35–36; 16:32; 19:10; 20:35).

In sum, the resolution of this problem did not result in a secret solution. The result and, to a degree, its rationale were made public. The emphasis was on producing a church that was not monochromatic in its practice. Jewish believers, such as those in Jerusalem, would continue their practices, but Gentile believers were not to be forced to live like Jews. There was to be unity on the essential centrality of Jesus, God's grace, and on the uniqueness of salvation in that grace by faith alone.

Additional Notes

15:26. Again D adds and intensifies the reference by speaking of their risking "at every trial."

15:29. Again D drops the reference to things strangled and adds a variation on the Golden Rule, as it did in 15:20.

15:32. Codex D adds a reference to Judas and Silas being "full of the Holy Spirit."

15:34. This verse is not well attested, and so it is omitted from the translation. It says that "it seemed good to Silas to remain there." The variations in how this is stated also argue against its originality in Acts (D adds, "that they remain, and Judas journeyed alone"). Lacking the verse are $\mathfrak{P}^{74}$, ℵ, A, B, E, Ψ, and Byz (Metzger 1971: 439). The reason for the addition is likely verse 40, where Paul chooses Silas to accompany him on the next journey. The verse makes an effort to have Silas in Antioch. It ignores the fact, however, that some time has passed and Silas could well have returned after reporting to Jerusalem (Witherington 1998: 470 against Barrett 1998: 750, who sees the plurals in v. 33 as a mistake since they suggest that both Silas and Judas departed). In fact, the addition creates a problem with verse 33 that is lacking without it.

VI. The Second and Third Missionary Journeys: Expansion to Greece and Consolidation amid Opposition (15:36–21:16)

This sizable unit comprises Paul's remaining missionary journeys. The second journey appears in 15:36–18:23. A short aside about Ephesus and Apollos follows in 18:24–28 before the story picks up again with Paul in Ephesus and his travels to Macedonia, Greece, Troas, and Miletus before returning to Jerusalem. These travels make up his third journey (19:1–21:16). Here we see the expansion of the mission to the Gentiles, stretching out into the world. Opposition dogs Paul the whole way as both Jews and Gentiles oppose him. Jews oppose his beliefs about Jesus, and Gentiles sense the threat to the economic benefits derived from their idolatrous cults. The battle is for theological truth as well as the souls of people, but in the background hover sociological elements that involve money and/or power. Part of what creates the tension is Paul's success as he makes inroads in many of the locales with a significant number of people.

A. The Second Missionary Journey (15:36–18:23)

The second journey includes Derbe, Lystra, Phrygia, and Galatia, sites visited on the first journey. In addition, God leads Paul to Macedonia, starting from Troas. He goes to Philippi, Thessalonica, Berea, Athens, and finally Corinth before returning to Antioch. Here we see the mix of success and opposition that is a part of the entire larger unit of the last two journeys.

1. Paul and Barnabas Split Up (15:36–41)

Paul launches an initiative to visit the churches planted on the first journey. He initially asks Barnabas to come along (v. 36). When Barnabas wishes to take John Mark, however, Paul hesitates because of Mark's departure at Pamphylia (vv. 37–38). The contention created over the difference of opinion leads Barnabas and Mark to go to Cyprus and Paul to take Silas to Syria and Cilicia on the way to Derbe and Lystra (vv. 39–41). From here on Acts is a Pauline historical account (Jervell 1998: 408).

This summary account would have been rooted in Pauline sources (Fitzmyer 1998: 571) and/or in Barnabas (but Weiser 1985: 395 prefers a Lukan composition, as does Haenchen 1987: 477). The account contains an embarrassing detail about tension among the leaders, a detail unlikely to have been created (Barrett 1998: 756, although Barrett is not clear whether the tension may also have been fueled by the incident of Gal. 2:11–14). Many scholars connect the tension here to the residue of the earlier confrontation described in Gal. 2:11–14 that Luke does not detail. Haenchen (1987: 475–77) see problems here in the Lukan portrayal. Conzelmann (1987: 123) argues that Paul could not have successfully opposed Peter and Barnabas and so he left, but this reading is too skeptical of the ability of these leaders to arrive at a solution (see Fitzmyer 1998: 572). Philemon 24 shows that Paul did not hold a grudge against John Mark over this experience. In fact, 1 Cor. 9:6 shows his continued respect for Barnabas. Johnson (1992: 287–88) takes the scene as credible because the estrangement is set forth so clearly.

Exegesis and Exposition

[36]And after some days Paul said to Barnabas, "Come, let us visit the brethren in every city where we proclaimed the word of the Lord, and see how they are." [37]And Barnabas wanted to take with them John called Mark. [38]But Paul thought it best not to be taking with them one who had withdrawn from them in Pamphylia and had not gone with them into the work ⌜ ⌝. [39]And there arose a sharp disagreement, so that they separated from each other; Barnabas took Mark with him and sailed away to Cyprus, [40]but Paul chose Silas and departed, being commended by the brethren to the grace of the Lord. [41]And he went through Syria and Cilicia, strengthening the churches.

After an unspecified number of days in Antioch, Paul wishes to return **15:36**
and proclaim the word of the Lord again to those in the communities of
the first journey. Paul wants to go to "every city" (κατὰ πόλιν πᾶσαν, *kata
polin pasan*, distributive use of *kata*) where they had converts and desires
to see how they are doing. This is a follow-up to their earlier efforts,
and so he proposes to Barnabas a joint oversight visit (ἐπισκεψώμεθα,
episkepsōmetha; Ps. 26:4 LXX [27:4 Eng.]; Zech. 11:16; 2 Macc. 11:36; Acts
6:3; see Num. 14:34 for a similar verb; Johnson 1992: 282). The request
comes with some intensity, as the particle δή (*dē*) suggests. God will do
far more than Paul plans, as a new journey is launched at Acts 16:6.

A dispute arises between them (v. 39), however, over whether to take **15:37–38**
John Mark, who earlier withdrew (ἀποστάντα, *apostanta*) from them
in Pamphylia (13:13). Luke seems to share Paul's question about John
Mark in noting how he left them. Barnabas wants him along, but Paul
does not count (ἠξίου, *ēxiou*) it wise, given Mark's past track record. This
word appears rarely in the NT (28:22; Luke 7:7; 2 Thess. 1:11; 1 Tim.
5:17; Heb. 3:3; 10:29; 2 Macc. 4:19; 4 Macc. 5:17). The idea is to count
something worthy. There is a variation in tense here. Barnabas wants
to take (συμπαραλαβεῖν, *symparalabein*, aorist) along John Mark, but
Paul does not want him to be along (συμπαραλαμβάνειν, *symparalam-
banein*, continuous present). John Mark is Barnabas's cousin (Col. 4:10),
a detail Luke does not note. Philemon 24 suggests that Paul and John
Mark reconciled later (2 Tim. 4:11; 1 Pet. 5:13).

There arises a major contention between Paul and Barnabas about what **15:39**
to do with John Mark. The term παροξυσμός (*paroxysmos*), when used
negatively, describes anger, irritation, or exasperation in a disagreement
(BAGD 629 §2; BDAG 780 §2). In Heb. 10:24 it is used positively of
stimulating or stirring someone to love, but it is also used of God's wrath
and of how Paul was provoked at seeing idols.[1] The uses for God's wrath
show how strong in force the term can be—this is a major disagreement.
They reach a solid compromise and create two missions instead of one.
Barnabas takes John Mark with him to Cyprus, his home (Acts 4:36),
while Paul takes Silas with him. Luke will follow Paul's path from here
on. Barnabas seems to have opted to take a family member on a less
perilous assignment where home was not far away.

   Some scholars argue that the real point of contention was that Barnabas preferred a Jewish Christian style of mission to Gentiles, as did
Antioch, whereas Paul wanted a law-free effort (Roloff 1988: 122; Jervell
1998: 410–11). This is most unlikely (Schnabel 2004: 1126–27). There is

---

1. See Deut. 29:27 LXX (29:28 Eng.) and Jer. 39:37 LXX (32:37 Eng.), where it refers
to God's wrath; these are the two occurrences in the LXX; for the verb, see Num. 14:11;
15:30; Deut. 1:34; 9:19; Ps. 9:34 (10:13 Eng.); Johnson 1992: 282; also Acts 17:16, where
the presence of idols provokes Paul.

no indication that Barnabas held to such a view; Paul challenged him not for a theological failure but for hypocrisy (Gal. 2:13). Paul is still associating with Antioch later in Acts (18:22). Acts 16:3, where Paul has Timothy circumcised, shows that he is concerned to be careful about how ministry to the Jews takes place. The reading of an abiding theological conflict seems to be the result of connecting Acts 15 to Gal. 2 and a residue of the old Tübingen school's reading of major ongoing tension in the early church, a view rooted in the work of F. C. Baur, who argues for a gulf between Jewish and Gentile Christianity. The view is dying a very slow death despite problems pointed out by J. B. Lightfoot in the late nineteenth century (Kümmel 1972: 174; Baird 2003: 71).

15:40–41   Paul journeys out with Silas (15:22), a Roman citizen (16:37–38). They go with a commendation from those in the church (14:26): Jerusalem and Antioch work together. There is no blame apportioned, and Luke's realism is to be noted. Paul and Silas journey to Syria and Cilicia, strengthening the churches (15:32), on the way to southern Galatia, the locale of the first journey, as the next unit shows. In going this way, Paul takes an overland route, which he often prefers (Bruce 1990: 351). There they will also share the results of the Jerusalem meeting (16:4). For Paul to include one who has been in Jerusalem shows that the breach is not a matter of "schools" having separate views (Witherington 1998: 473; Jervell 1998: 409). Paul's concern here is not about a theological difference with Barnabas or John Mark but whether John Mark will persevere when the pressure becomes strong. This is the start of Paul's second journey.

In sum, here is an example where a disagreement was so great that the ability to work side by side was affected. What resulted was a solution that allowed the advance of the gospel to continue, but in a way that recognized a need for distinct ministries. Sometimes this is the best solution.

Additional Note

15:38. Codex D adds to John Mark's failure by noting that he departed from the work "for which they had been sent."

2. Timothy Joins Paul and Silas in Lystra (16:1–5)

Paul and Silas travel to Derbe and Lystra, where Timothy joins them (vv. 1–2). Paul wishes Timothy to accompany them, and so he circumcises him out of sensitivity to the Jews because Timothy has a Jewish mother and a Greek father (v. 3). This way there will be no side debates about Timothy when they share the gospel. As the three travel, they report on the council decision (v. 4). Their ministry strengthens the churches, which are growing (v. 5).

This narrative summary would have sources like those of the previous account, coming out of either the Pauline group (Fitzmyer 1998: 574) or from Antioch or Jerusalem, given Paul and Silas's connections. Barrett (1998: 758) argues that some detail is the result of local knowledge, and Haenchen (1987: 482) argues that Luke is the victim of an unreliable tradition (but see the cultural background discussions challenging this claim of inaccuracy on both vv. 2 and 3).

Exegesis and Exposition

[1]And he came also to Derbe and to Lystra. A disciple was there, named Timothy, the son of a Jewish woman who was a believer; but the father was a Greek. [2]He was well spoken of by the believers at Lystra and Iconium. [3]Paul wanted Timothy to accompany him; and he took him and circumcised him because of the Jews that were in those places, for they all knew that his father was a Greek. [4]As they were passing through the cities, they passed on to them for observance the decisions that had been reached by the apostles and elders who were at Jerusalem. [5]So the churches were strengthened in the faith, and they grew in numbers daily.

16:1–2 Paul and Silas travel to Derbe and Lystra in southeast Galatia, revisiting sites noted in Acts 14:8–20. There they meet Timothy, who has a good reputation in Lystra and Iconium (on the theme of good reputations, 6:3; 10:22; 22:12). The nature and scope of Timothy's reputation show that adjoining communities may well have been in contact with each other.

Timothy poses a special problem because he is the child of a mixed marriage. His mother, Eunice, is a Jewish believer (2 Tim. 1:5) whereas his father is Greek. His grandmother Lois also is Jewish (2 Tim. 1:5).

Paul takes him on the journey but circumcises him first (v. 3). This act prevents Timothy from becoming an issue to the Jews to whom he would minister. Even though Paul holds a view of freedom regarding the law (Gal. 5:2; 1 Cor. 7:18), he is sensitive to how it works in a mixed community and in the context of the gospel (1 Cor. 9:19–23). So, out of respect for the customs of his prospective evangelistic audience, he acts to render moot any debate over Timothy's lineage.

Some scholars see this text as differing so markedly from Galatians that Luke cannot have this scenario right (Barrett 1998: 760–61, although he notes [762] that there is a slight possibility that Luke does have this right; Haenchen 1987: 480–82). The issue here, however, concerns what to do with someone of a mixed Jewish-Gentile background, not a Gentile of unmixed ancestry as in the debate in Acts 15. Paul's action indicates support for the attitude of sensitivity shown in the council of Acts 15 (Marshall 1980: 260; Witherington 1998: 474–75).[1] Timothy will not become a matter for debate. Paul may be pragmatic here, as he will be in Acts 21:21. Having just gone through one council, why immediately head into another major dispute? If Timothy honors his Jewish background, then there is no question.

The issue is not that of taking an uncircumcised Gentile into a synagogue, since this could be done, as Barrett (1998: 761) correctly notes. It is whether Paul regards Gentile perspectives as being more important than Jewish ones. Paul is already pushing the boundaries, in the view of some, by being so aggressive in how Gentiles should be included. Would he want to negate the Jewish identity of a person of mixed background in the process? Does Jewish heritage mean so little to him? That is the problem Paul's solution avoids (Hengel 1979: 64). Paul is not standing up for the law, as many claim, but is affirming Jewish heritage alongside Gentile heritage (Jervell 1998: 412). Here Paul is being faithful to the promise for Israel (Jervell 1998: 414, who sees the act as historical).

Timothy is a major figure in the Pauline circle (16:1; 17:14–15; 18:5; 19:22; 20:4; Rom. 16:21; 1 Cor. 4:17; 16:10; 2 Cor. 1:1, 19; Phil. 1:1; 2:19; Col. 1:1; 1 Thess. 1:1; 3:2, 6; 2 Thess. 1:1; 1 Tim. 1:2, 18; 6:20; 2 Tim. 1:2; Philem. 1; Heb. 13:23).

16:3   If Paul is going to work in the synagogue, circumcision will ensure Timothy's credibility. Mixed marriages were forbidden in Judaism, but when they occurred, children were still to be raised as Jews. A later text, *b. Yebam.* 45b, makes the mother's nationality determinative for the children: "And the law is that if an idolater or a slave cohabited with the daughter of an Israelite, the child [born from such a union] is legitimate, both in the case of a married, and in that of an unmarried

---

1. The relevant OT texts Neh. 13:23; Ezra 9:2; 10:2, 10; Mal. 2:10–16 show sensitivity to the question of mixed marriage; Fitzmyer 1998: 576. Schneider 1982: 200–201 calls it an exceptional situation; also Jub. 30.7–17.

woman" (also *y. Yebam.* 2.6). According to *m. Qidd.* 3.12, the child has the status of the parent of the lower status, and this applies to a woman who has a relationship to a *mamzer* or *natin*. A *mamzer* is a child of a couple that could not be legally married. A *natin/netin* is a descendant of the Gibeonites, who were made temple slaves (Josh. 9:27). Both would have low social status. Timothy's father and mother would fit this example (Witherington 1998: 475–76). The mother is also determinative in some Greco-Roman cultures (Cicero, *De natura deorum* 3.18[45]).

Scholars debate how far back this view of the importance of the maternal line goes. Cohen (1986) says that Timothy would not be seen as Jewish, as the tradition of the mother's line is late, but Witherington (1998: 475) rejects Cohen's contentions (see Bryan 1988) and has the better of the argument, noting that the text from *m. Qidd.* 3.12 is an early-second-century text at the latest and is most likely earlier, given the conservative nature of such tradition. First Corinthians 7:14 shows that spiritual benefits can flow to the child through either the father or the mother, whichever one is "closer" to God. Galatians 5:11 shows how Paul can speak positively of circumcision, and Gal. 5:6 and 6:15 state that it is an indifferent matter. Johnson (1992: 284) says that the priority of the mother's ethnicity seems to be assumed here. In addition, an uncircumcised son of a Jewish mother was regarded in Judaism as an apostate Jew, a violator of the covenant.

Paul's action shows his desire to continue to reach out to Jews and affirm the new faith's link to the promises of the past in Judaism. Although it is an issue of indifference, Paul has Timothy circumcised out of respect, since a Jewish person is involved (Gal. 5:6; 6:15; 1 Cor. 9:16–23; D. Wenham in Winter and Clarke 1993: 254–55). But Titus, who is Gentile, is a different case and principle. He is not to be circumcised (Gal. 2:3–5; 1 Cor. 7:17–24); there is no mixed-ancestry question, so there is no circumcision. This principle of sensitivity reflects what we see Paul say elsewhere about food practices (Rom. 14–15; 1 Cor. 10:23–30).

The decisions of the Jerusalem Council are delivered to Lystra and Derbe. **16:4–5**
Paul's decision to circumcise Timothy is in line with the sensitivity these instructions request (BAGD 201 §1; BDAG 254 §1). This is one of two occurrences in Acts of the term δόγματα (*dogmata*, decisions). In Acts 17:7 it refers to a decree of Caesar (Eph. 2:15 and Col. 2:14 use it to refer to the law of Moses). As Luke often notes, such communication serves to strengthen the church or bring joy to the church (Acts 14:28; 15:32, 35, 41), with growth following. The dative τῇ πίστει (*tē pistei*) is syntactically a dative of reference: they are strengthened with respect to their faith (Moulton and Turner 1963: 239; Wallace 1996: 146). This is the only use of the verb στερεόω (*stereoō*, strengthen) in Acts in this way (otherwise of healings, 3:7, 16). The language of handing over (παρεδίδοσαν, *paredidosan*) the decrees refers to passing on tradition, a

more technical use than other instances in Acts (15:26, 40; 1 Cor. 11:2, 23; 15:3; Johnson 1992: 284).

Barrett (1998: 763) does not see how this account can fit with Galatians. It has already been shown above, however, that Paul can agree with these practices by noting that the decree deals with noncircumcision of Gentiles as the key principle and sensitivity to Jews as a corollary. These ideas are sufficiently parallel to Paul elsewhere (noncircumcision of Gentiles in Galatians and sensitivity in Romans). These churches fall outside the addressed areas of the decree in the letters. Reading the letters to them shows that the intention was to issue a decision that extends beyond the original region of the dispute. This is another summary in Acts (2:41, 47b; 4:4; 5:14; 6:1, 7; 8:25, 40; 9:31; 11:24–25; 12:24; 14:21–23).

In sum, what is seen here is Paul's cultural sensitivity. Instead of making Timothy a sideshow to the gospel in terms of whether he was a Jew or not, Paul permitted circumcision so that the gospel would remain the main topic. Knowing which principles are worth standing up for and which ideas are not worth elevating to an importance they do not deserve is a sign of discernment and leadership. Not every issue is worth starting a war over when it comes to the gospel and the ethnic unity of the church.

3. The Vision of the Macedonian Man (16:6–10)

Paul gradually journeys to Troas after being blocked by the Spirit in an unspecified way from preaching in Asia or going to Bithynia (vv. 6–8). In Troas he is given a vision to go to Macedonia, where he arrives in Philippi (vv. 9–10). The unit shows Paul continuing to extend the gospel's proclamation under the Spirit's direction into locales where Gentiles are prevalent (vv. 6–7, 10 repeat references to the Spirit and to God). The gospel is on its way in Europe, although this designation for the region was not used in the first century. For Luke, this represents further ethnic expansion of the gospel's outreach.

This account is another narrative summary, but here the use of "we" suggests that Luke has joined the scene. This raises the question of the "we" sections (16:10–17; 20:5–15; 21:1–18; 27:1–28:16). Is this an independent itinerary source that represents only a Lukan literary move (Haenchen 1987: 491), or is it a reflection of where Luke accompanied Paul? Against a literary source are the random points at which the "we" appears. There is nothing strategic, in terms of the events covered, about the timing of its appearance. This suggests the likelihood that Luke is indicating where he was involved (Fitzmyer 1998: 98–103; Hengel 1979: 66; Witherington 1998: 480–86). Barrett (1998: xxv–xxx, also 773) appears to prefer a traveling companion who is not necessarily Luke (Johnson 1992: 296–97 is undecided). That this source is left significantly unredacted and appears at this minor point speaks against his merely incorporating a source.

Witherington (1998: 481–83) notes that Luke intrudes into his account very rarely (Acts 17:18, 21). Witherington also makes clear that "we" passages were not automatically a part of sea voyage accounts nor was there a literary convention that sea voyages were rendered in the first person (also Praeder 1987). Praeder (1987: 215) notes that the idea that this source is not Luke has the problem of explaining why he would use first-person sources from someone else and yet not identify them as eyewitnesses. Conzelmann (1987: 126) sees the scene as too rushed in its narration to be authentic, but this simply fails to appreciate the selective nature of Luke's presentation and to take into account that this scene is a transition setting up the details about Philippi. In sum, the "we" is Luke's way of suggesting his own presence.

At a more synthetic and literary level, Spencer (2004: 170) identifies five "major public accusation type scenes" between here and 21:36—Philippi, Thessalonica, Corinth, Ephesus, and Jerusalem—with three main elements each: seizure, charges, reaction. Another important scene in the same unit occurs in Athens, but there is no accusation in Athens that leads to seizure, only debate about what Paul claims.

Exegesis and Exposition

[6]And they went through ⌜the region of Phrygia and Galatia⌝, having been prevented by the Holy Spirit from speaking the word in Asia. [7]And coming opposite Mysia, they attempted to go into Bithynia, but the Spirit of Jesus did not allow them; [8]so, passing through Mysia, they went down to Troas. [9]And ⌜ ⌝ a vision appeared to Paul in the night: ⌜ ⌝ a certain man of Macedonia was standing ⌜ ⌝ and beseeching him, saying, "Come over to Macedonia and help us." [10]⌜And when he had seen the vision, immediately we sought to go into Macedonia, concluding⌝ that God had called us to proclaim the gospel to them.

16:6   Paul heads to Macedonia because some type of direction by the Spirit has prevented (κωλυθέντες, *kōlythentes*) him preaching the gospel in Asia. The participle here is causal, telling us why Asia is not the target (Moule 1959: 100). There are no details as to how the Spirit prevents this work from going on in Asia. Κωλυθέντες is one of two terms describing the Spirit's action (the other is in v. 7 and is discussed there). Acts 27:43 shows an everyday use of the verb κωλύω (*kōluō*) for "preventing" an action (also 8:36; 10:47; 11:17; 24:23; BAGD 461 §1; BDAG 580). What is meant by Asia here is not clear: Is it the Roman province, ancient Asia, or simply cities on the Aegean coast? Whatever the locale, the Spirit prevents them from speaking there. In verses 9–10 a divine vision will direct Paul to Philippi in Macedonia. The direction of the Spirit is common in Acts (4:31; 8:29, 39; 10:44; 13:2, 4). Here, as in the case of Peter with Cornelius and of Philip with the Ethiopian eunuch, the Spirit leads the outreach (Schneider 1982: 204). There are OT precedents for such a call as well (Isa. 6:8; Jer. 1:5–10; Fitzmyer 1998: 578).

The regions of Phrygia and Galatia can mean one of two areas: ethnic territories, in which case Galatia is to the north (Fitzmyer 1998: 578; Barrett 1998: 766–69), or Roman divisions, where Phrygia is part of the larger province of Galatia, all lying to the south (for details, Bruce 1990: 353–54).[1] Larkin (1995: 232–33) with Marshall (1980: 261–62) holds the

---

1. See Hemer 1989: 280–99 for detailed source and inscription data that show the adjectival use of Phrygia; Witherington 1998: 477–78; also *NewDocs* 3:174 no. 90 with arguments against the northern Galatian view summarized by Haenchen 1987: 483–84n2; Jewett 1997: 1–22 presents a proposed itinerary based on the northern Galatian theory, the view Hemer vigorously challenges. Schnabel 2004: 1132–34 has a full treatment and

southern view as more likely whereas Polhill (1992: 345) prefers the northern option.

Which choice is correct is not entirely clear, but 18:23 seems to lean in the direction of a reference to one area in the south whereas the route in 15:41–16:5 may well suggest the northern Galatian view, as the south has already been visited (in Barrett's view, this is the key argument). A textual problem in this verse also figures significantly into the discussion (see details in the additional note below). A reference to a combined Phrygian-Galatian region, which is the likely original reading for 16:6, favors the southern Galatian view. In the southern Galatian view, Galatia then would include Derbe and Lystra, and Phrygia would allude to Iconium and Antioch. I have a slight preference for the southern Galatian view, seeing 18:23 as making clear that Luke is here referring to a single region, a view that assumes a consistency in Luke's references and is favored text-critically.

As they near the northern edge of Asia, opposite Mysia, they have planned to go to Bithynia, which is north and east of Mysia and often associated with the region of Pontus in northwestern Asia Minor. At this point, they are either at Dorlaeum or at Cotiaeum on the border of Mysia. It is about the Christians in Bithynia, worshipers of Jesus as divine, that the Roman Pliny the Younger writes in the early second century (*Ep.* 10.96; Johnson 1992: 285). The major cities there included Nicea and Byzantium (previously called Constantinople and subsequently Istanbul), which became important for the church in the fourth century and beyond, especially in the East. **16:7–8**

The Spirit of Jesus prevents Paul and his company from going to Bithynia. Mysia is the northern and western portion of the Roman province of Asia (Strabo, *Geogr.* 12.564–65, 571; Schnabel 2004: 1144–45). This description of the Spirit's preventive action uses a second expression (v. 6 has the first) indicating yet again how the Spirit directs Paul not to go somewhere (οὐκ εἴασεν, *ouk eiasen*; "did/would not allow" in NET, RSV, NIV; "did not permit" in NASB; "suffered them not" in KJV). The expression "Spirit of Jesus" is unusual (Phil. 1:19 has "Spirit of Jesus Christ," which is its only other NT occurrence; but see Rom. 8:9; Gal. 4:6; 1 Pet. 1:11 for variations). Bruce (1988a: 355) suggests that this prophecy may have come through a directly expressed instruction in the name of Jesus, but Witherington (1998: 478) allows that it might also have involved internal leading. We are not given the specifics.

They reach Troas, a coastal city (Schnabel 2004: 1145), probably after traversing (παρελθόντες, *parelthontes*) Mysia (on "passing through," not "passing by," 1 Macc. 5:48). The NET notes that the most likely route would take them through Mysia. This means that they do not stop and

---

opts for the southern Galatian theory. He notes that there is no evidence of Jewish presence in northern Galatia until the third century.

preach there. Troas was located on the northwestern tip of Asia Minor, near ancient Troy, which was about twenty-five miles to the north (2 Cor. 2:12–13; Pliny the Elder, *Nat.* 5.124; Fitzmyer 1998: 579). It was often used as a port of embarkation for Greece. It was about 585 miles from Antioch in Syria. They are now heading west.

16:9 One night, in a vision of a man from Macedonia, Paul is asked for help. A call to help is often a cry to save in the Bible (Gen. 49:25; Exod. 18:4; Deut. 33:26; Ps. 9:35 LXX [10:14 Eng.]; Isa. 41:10; Johnson 1992: 286). If so, it would mean to bring the message of salvation. Macedonia, located in northern Greece, was bordered by the Illyria and Nestos rivers. Macedonia had been a world power under Philip of Macedonia and Alexander the Great four centuries earlier. Since 168 BC it had been a Roman province. The Greeks regarded the Macedonians as barbarians, except for the royal family, but they shared the same gods as the Greeks. Philippi became its principal city during the Roman period (Fitzmyer 1998: 579; Schnabel 2004: 1150–51).

This is another indication of God's direction. It comes in a vision (on visions, using ὅραμα, *horama*: Acts 7:31; 9:10, 12; 10:3, 17, 19; 11:5; 12:9; 16:9, 10; 18:9). Visions are also often mentioned in Greek contexts.[2] This might suggest that the earlier prevention by the Spirit came not by a vision but by some other means. The multiple instances of direction by God underscore divine involvement in the journey's itinerary.

16:10 They immediately obey the vision, perceiving it as God's call (προσκέκληται, *proskeklētai*) to evangelize (Delling, *TDNT* 7:765). References to "we" now enter the narrative (see the discussion in the unit introduction). They occur until 16:17 and then resume in 20:5. Luke has now joined the group.

In sum, here it is not human planning but what God wills that drives the response. Paul may well have had a plan to go to Asia, to take the gospel to the end of the earth. Stott (1990: 261) speaks of the elements that often characterize divine guidance here: God's use of a period of time, the circumstances of open and closed doors, pondering what was taking place, and seeking response and input from others in pursuit of a kind of corporate wisdom. In this situation, God made it evident to Paul that another ministerial itinerary was desired. To this there was only one response: obedience.

Additional Notes

16:6. A textual issue is part of the geographical discussion. Byz with E, H, L, and P points to two distinct regions and reads τὴν Φρυγίαν καὶ τὴν Γαλατικὴν χώραν (*tēn Phrygian kai tēn*

---

2. Herodotus, *Hist.* 7.12; Philostratus, *Life Apoll.* 4.34; Pseudo-Callisthenes, *Life of Alexander of Macedon* 1.35; Conzelmann 1987: 127; Johnson 1992: 286. Weiser 1985: 412–15 notes eight examples from Greek and Jewish writers extending into the second century AD.

Galatikēn chōran). This reading would favor the north Galatian view. The better MSS indicate a combined region: τὴν Φρυγίαν καὶ Γαλατικὴν χώραν (*tēn Phrygian kai Galatikēn chōran*). In the latter reading, the second definite article is missing before Galatia, pointing to a combined Phrygian-Galatian region. In favor of this reading are 𝔓⁷⁴, ℵ, A, B, C, and D. The older hesitation for accepting this reading concerned the long-unattested use of Phrygia as an adjective (noted in Metzger 1971: 441). Hemer (1989: 280–99), however, extensively documents this use, citing about thirty examples (Bruce 1988a: 306 and n18).

16:9. Again D expands the verse with numerous small additions so that the verse reads thus (additions noted in italics): "And *in* a vision in the night there appeared to Paul, *as it were* a man of Macedonia, standing *before his face*, beseeching and saying" (Metzger 1971: 443).

16:10. Again D adds, "When therefore he had risen up, he related to us the vision."

4. In Philippi (16:11–40)

The visit to Philippi has four subunits: the journey to Philippi and the meeting with Lydia (vv. 11–15), the possessed servant girl (vv. 16–24), the conversion of the Philippian jailer (vv. 25–34), and a scene involving Paul and the city magistrates (vv. 35–40). Rapske (1994b: 115–34) covers the general historical veracity of this unit in detail, and Sterck-Degueldre (2004) presents a detailed treatment of Lydia that also sees Luke working with solid historical sources to show her as an exemplary woman of piety. She is a pious Jew who is open to the Gentiles and whose support and hospitality permit effective ministry in a Gentile context.

This composite of events uses the "we" source for the first portion, at least through the scene concerning the possessed girl, and other Pauline sources for the rest (Fitzmyer 1998: 583). Witherington (1998: 487) notes that one woman and one man are the main examples of conversion in this section, showing Luke's tendency to tell accounts in gender pairs: Simeon and Anna (Luke 2); raised boy and girl (Luke 7:11–17; 8:40–56); Spirit poured out on all (Acts 2); miracles for Aeneas and Dorcas (Acts 9:32–43). This unit also is an example of the new faith meeting the full array of competing religious elements of the first century: the synagogue, the Roman religious beliefs, and the spirit world. The new faith can stand up to these opponents.

Here Paul encounters his first major legal trouble with the Romans. Acts 13:4–12 has an earlier encounter but no legal issue. We see Rome struggling about what to do with this new faith. The trials of missionary work are set forth.

The issue of the historicity of Paul's encounters with Rome has been the subject of scholarly debate that mirrors the general debate on historicity, with scholars' conclusions spanning the spectrum from truthfulness to full skepticism. The introductions to this and subsequent units of this commentary will trace this debate in some detail because here is one of four places that we can carefully check Luke against the cultural backdrop to assess his historical reliability instead of merely theorizing about it positively or negatively. Recent assessments have generally rated Luke favorably (e.g., Sherwin-White 1963; the series launched by Winter and Clarke 1993). Omerzu (2002) traces the background in detail related to the rights of Roman citizens and the appeal to Caesar, before working through the scenes at Philippi, Thessalonica, Corinth, Jerusalem, and Paul's arrest and appearance before the Sanhedrin,

Felix, and Festus. He concludes that the material accurately reflects these legal relationships and that the scenes draw from sources that have a historical core going back not to official court records but to oral traditions about Paul (Omerzu 2002: 506, 507–8). This suggests that Luke is a credible ancient historian who needs to be taken seriously, as also his recent treatment by classical historians shows (Nobbs 2006).

The two parts of this unit where the biggest historical questions are raised are the section on the exorcised slave girl and the earthquake (Marshall 1980: 265 discusses these, interacting with Haenchen's skepticism [1987: 499–504]). Haenchen argues that the earthquake scene has too many inconsistencies and fits Hellenistic motifs, but Jervell (1998: 429–30) sees the earthquake as a part of the traditional account. Such details will be covered in the treatment of the verses (vv. 25–27), which defends the historical worth of the account. Exorcism was a part of this world and its worldview, and earthquakes are common to the area. Jervell (1998: 431) also notes that the Roman citizenship of Paul is also historical and sees the entire scene deeply rooted in tradition. For Jervell, the entire scene is a "very good historical recollection." The account shows that God not only directs this journey but also offers protection during it.

Exegesis and Exposition

[11]Setting sail from Troas, we made a direct voyage to Samothrace, and the following day to Neapolis, [12]and from there to Philippi, which is ⌜a leading city of the district of Macedonia⌝ and a Roman colony. We remained in this city some days; [13]and on the Sabbath day we went outside the gate by the river, where ⌜we thought there was a place of prayer⌝; and sitting down, we were speaking to the women who had come together. [14]A certain one who heard us was a woman named Lydia, from the city of Thyatira, a seller of purple goods and a worshiper of God. The Lord opened her heart to accept what Paul said. [15]And when she was baptized with her household, she invited us, saying, "If you have judged me to be faithful to the Lord, come to my house and stay." And she convinced us.

[16]As we were going to the place of prayer, we were met by a slave girl who had a spirit of divination and brought her owners much profit by soothsaying. [17]She followed Paul and us, crying, "These men are servants of the Most High God, who proclaim to you a way of salvation." [18]And this she was doing for many days. But being annoyed and turning, Paul said to the spirit, "I charge you in the name of Jesus Christ to come out of her." And it came out that very hour.

[19]Seeing ⌜that their hope of profit was gone⌝, they seized Paul and Silas and dragged them into the marketplace before the rulers; [20]and bringing them to the magistrates, they said, "These men are disturbing our city, being Jews. [21]They

advocate customs that it is not lawful for us to accept or practice, as we are Romans." [22]The crowd joined in attacking them; and the magistrates tore the garments off them and gave orders to beat them with rods. [23]And having inflicted many blows upon them, they threw them into prison, charging the jailer to keep them safely. [24]Having received this charge, he put them in the inner prison and fastened their feet in the stocks.

[25]But about midnight Paul and Silas were praying and singing hymns to God, and the prisoners were listening to them, [26]and suddenly there was a great earthquake, so that the foundations of the prison were shaken; and immediately all the doors were opened and the fetters of all were unfastened. [27]And the jailer, awakening and seeing that the prison doors were open, drew his sword and was about to kill himself, supposing that the prisoners had escaped. [28]But Paul cried with a loud voice, "Do not do anything evil to yourself, for we are all here." [29]And calling for lights, he rushed in, and trembling with fear, he fell down before Paul and Silas, [30]and ⌜ ⌝ bringing them out, he said, "Sirs, what must I do to be saved?" [31]And they said, "Believe in the Lord Jesus ⌜ ⌝, and you will be saved, you and your household." [32]And they spoke the word of the Lord to him and to all who were in his house. [33]And taking them at the same hour of the night, he washed their wounds, and he was baptized at once with all his family. [34]Then bringing them up into his house, he set food before them and rejoiced with his entire household because he had believed in God.

[35]But when it became day, ⌜the magistrates sent⌝ the police, saying, "Let those men go." [36]And the jailer reported the words to Paul, saying, "The magistrates have sent to release you; now therefore, going out, leave in peace." [37]But Paul said to them, "Beating us publicly, uncondemned, men who are Roman citizens, they have thrown us into prison; and do they now cast us out secretly? No! Let them come themselves and take us out." [38]The police reported these words to the magistrates, and they were afraid, hearing that they were Roman citizens. [39]So ⌜coming, they came to appease them. And leading them out, they asked them to leave the city⌝. [40]So coming out of the prison, they visited Lydia; and seeing the brethren, they ⌜ ⌝ exhorted them and departed.

16:11–12 They sail into Samothrace, the site of a mystery religion worshiping the twin fertility gods, the Cabiri. Samothrace is an island with a 5,577-foot mountain peak (Mt. Fengari, from which Poseidon was said to watch over Troy; Strabo, *Geogr.* 2.5.1; frg. 7.47). This is a midway point, and then they journey to Neapolis, 10 miles away from Philippi and its port (Schnabel 2004: 1149 notes that it was a naval base in 42 BC). This journey covers 125 miles in total. It is a journey with favorable winds, as the return trip in 20:5 takes five days, not two as here. The last 10 miles would involve traveling on the Via Egnatia. This road ran from Dyrrhachium on the Adriatic Sea eastward through Macedonia and thus through Thessalonica, Amphipolis, and Philippi to Neapolis (Polhill 1992: 347).

They arrive in Philippi, a principal city of Macedonia (πρώτη τῆς μερίδος, *prōtē tēs meridos*) and a Roman colony (Livy, *Hist. Rom.* 45.29; Strabo, *Geogr.* frg. 7.34, 41; Schnabel 2004: 1151–53). Besides observing the imperial cult, the city was home to the worship of many gods. It was neither a capital nor the largest city in the region; the phrase πρώτη πόλις (*prōtē polis*) means "a leading city" (on this Greek phrase, see the additional note on 16:12). Moule (1959: 111) thinks that the expression here means that it is the primary city of "that" division of Macedonia, with the article working like a relative pronoun. Witherington (1998: 489) suggests that this is Luke's hometown. The area was rich with copper, silver, and gold deposits and was part of a fertile plain, tucked as it was against the hills of the area. So it was a wealthy city. The Roman influence was strong here because of Philippi's status as a Roman colony, which made it legally like a Roman city. It had an autonomous government, freedom from tribute and taxation, and legal-ownership rights like those in Italy (Larkin 1995: 235). This was the highest status a provincial city could have. It may well have seemed like a "little Rome." Other colonies in Acts are Pisidian Antioch, Lystra, Troas, Corinth, and Ptolemais (Bruce 1990: 357). Witherington (1998: 488) notes that the Roman character of the city is indicated by the fact that 80 percent of the inscriptions found here are in Latin, compared with 40 percent in Antioch. The Jewish presence seems relatively minor, given the way Lydia is introduced as the key figure among the Jews of the city gathered for prayer. They stay for "some days" (ἡμέρας τινάς, *hēmeras tinas*).

These verses tell the story of Lydia, a woman from Thyatira living in prayer before God in Philippi. Paul's group goes outside the city, by the river where women are gathered for prayer. This would be the Gangites River, also known as the Angites, or a closer creek known as Crenides. They may well be meeting by the river in order to be able to fulfill purity requirements (Rengstorf, *TDNT* 6:602–3). An interpretive dispute turns on the question of how far a journey Jews would take on a Sabbath for prayer and how scrupulous these Jewish worshipers are (Fitzmyer 1998: 585). It is a little more than a mile west of the city (Conzelmann 1987: 130). The city may have too small a Jewish population for a synagogue, which requires ten men (Jervell 1998: 421; *m. 'Abot* 3.7). It is more likely, however, that this place of prayer is a synagogue, as elsewhere the locale for prayer is always a synagogue when the term προσευχήν (*proseuchēn*, a place of prayer) is used (Schnabel 2004: 1153; Le Cornu and Shulam 2003: 879–81). **16:13–15**

These women gather on the Sabbath to worship God. Williams (1990: 282) thinks that they may be meeting beyond the *pomerium*, a line encircling an empty space outside the city, with no buildings and where no burials could take place or strange cults meet (McDonald 1940). If the locale is a synagogue, then they do not meet in such a location. Barrett

(1998: 781) notes that Josephus (*Ant.* 14.10.23 §258) mentions a decree that legally allows Jews to gather near the sea for prayers. The locale allows for ceremonial washings as well as prayer. All "seas" were valid as immersion pools (*m. Miqw.* 5.4; Le Cornu and Shulam 2003: 880).

Women participated in the prayers and worship but otherwise appear to have been very restricted, so Paul's engagement of them directly reflects a less strict approach toward women (for the role of women in the synagogue, see Le Cornu and Shulam 2003: 881). That only women are mentioned here may suggest that a small Jewish community was present and leads also to the suggestion that this locale may not have been a synagogue. They meet Lydia, a worker with "purple goods" (πορφυρόπωλις, *porphyropōlis*). This term, used only here in the NT, describes her as a "merchant dealing in purple cloth" (BAGD 694; BDAG 855). This is an indication that she works in fine cloths for the wealthy (Luke 16:19; 1 Macc. 10:62; Josephus, *J.W.* 6.8.3 §390; on the significance of such women of status, Witherington 1998: 492–93). Thyatira was known for this skill (BAGD 364; BDAG 460; the city is noted in Rev. 2:18–29).[1] The noun "purple" (πορφύρα, *porphyra*) is also the name for a shellfish from which one form of purple dye is derived (BAGD 694; BDAG 855; Fitzmyer 1998a: 585). Another way to gather the dye was from the madder plant (Bruce 1988a: 311; *NewDocs* 3:53–55). The wealth of the area fits the later description of the Philippian church as giving major monetary support to Paul (Phil. 1:5; 4:15–18). Women often have a key role in Paul's work (Acts 17:4, 12, 34; 18:2; Polhill 1992: 349).

Lydia is also a pious woman (σεβομένη τὸν θεόν, *sebomenē ton theon*). This phrase often describes former polytheists who become worshipers of the God of Israel, adopt monotheism, and attend the synagogue but do not keep the entire law (Acts 13:43). Josephus, *Ant.* 14.7.2 §110, describes some worshipers who contribute to the temple (BAGD 746 §2a; BDAG 918 §1b). This may well be the case here.

She was "hearing" them. The imperfect verb here (ἤκουεν, *ēkouen*) may suggest more than one meeting (Williams 1990: 282), or it may simply be a vivid way of summarizing the discussion, a conclusion that seems more likely given the overall context (Johnson 1992: 293). "The Lord opened her heart to accept" Paul's message (on the expression ὁ κύριος διήνοιξεν τὴν καρδίαν, *ho kyrios diēnoixen tēn kardian*, see 2 Macc. 1:4; Luke 24:32). This is yet another way to describe that she comes to faith, a point made clear in verse 15 when she and her house are baptized (Acts 10:48; 16:33). God creates the initiative to faith from within. She invites them to stay with her if Paul should judge her to be faithful to the Lord (πιστὴν τῷ κυρίῳ, *pistēn tō kyriō*). The request contains a first-class condition, signaling that she will likely be found faithful (Wallace 1996:

---

1. *CIL* 3.664 contains a damaged inscription with "purple" noted; Conzelmann 1987: 130; *CIG* 3496–98; Fitzmyer 1998: 585.

451, 694). So they stay in Philippi. Jewish believers reside with the new Gentile converts who have come to faith after first being associated with Judaism. Peter made a similar ethnic move in receiving hospitality in Acts 10. She responds in a manner the epistles encourage (Rom. 12:13; 1 Tim. 3:2; Marshall 1980: 268). Her home becomes a center for the new faith in the city (16:40). She appears as the head of her household, so she likely is either single or widowed (Bruce 1990: 359).

Paul now encounters a slave girl (παιδίσκη, *paidiskē*) with a spirit of divination who harasses God's messenger by announcing his proclamation in a manner that disturbs him. The phrase πνεῦμα πύθωνα (*pneuma pythōna*) means either a "spirit, namely, a Python" or "a Pythonian spirit." Either way, a spirit of divination is intended. Here social status is made clear by the fact that she serves masters. This woman is portrayed as inspired by the Pythian god, Apollo. Soothsaying was a lucrative religious art of the period, a detail Luke notes. As with Acts 13 and Bar-Jesus, Paul is now face-to-face with one who is directed by a hostile spirit. Unlike that text, where there is judgment upon a magician clearly hostile to the gospel, here Paul, by exorcising the demon, liberates the woman being abused by her masters.

16:16–18

"Python" is a reference to the soothsaying divinity, originally conceived of as a snake or dragon that inhabited Delphi, which was originally known as Pythia (Barrett 1998: 785; BAGD 728–29; BDAG 896–97). This spirit was defeated and slain by Apollo (Ovid, *Metam.* 1.438–47; Johnson 1992: 293). Priestesses at Delphi were called Πυθίαι (*Pythiai*). This spirit was said to direct women by overpowering them and allowing them to foretell the future—soothsaying (μαντευομένη, *manteuomenē*), as here. Witherington (1998: 494) challenges the idea that ecstatic possession is involved, in contrast to Johnson (1992: 294). The term often pointed to ventriloquism.[2] Foerster (*TDNT* 6:920) is too skeptical in simply saying that ventriloquism was a matter of a person's will and so there is no exorcism here. The ability to predict is the heart of the woman's vocation and is not a matter of one's will. Klauck (2000: 11) speaks of a "spirit of augury" here to stress the function of the girl.

In the ancient world, magic and oracles were often combined and were used (1) to protect a person from misfortune, (2) to attack another or issue curses, (3) to win others over, and (4) to secure oracular utterances (Klauck 2000: 211 [see also 209–31] makes a useful distinction by noting that magic seeks to coerce the gods whereas prayer petitions them). Pliny the Elder (*Nat.* 28.19) said, "There is in fact no one who is not afraid of being cursed by terrible imprecations," while alluding to tablets on which curses were recorded. Philo (*Spec. Laws* 3.18 §§100–101) speaks against

---

2. See Plutarch, *De defectu oraculorum* 9.414E [= *Moralia* 414E]. The association with ventriloquism evokes 1 Sam. 28:8 LXX with the witch of Endor, and *m. Sanh.* 7.7 notes a rabbinic condemnation of python spirits; Str-B 2:743; Larkin 1995: 237.

magic that seeks to change another's emotion. Often such magicians were young, beautiful girls or older witches, with Circe as the prototype (Homer, *Od.* 10.234–40). Some saw magic as engaging the sympathetic powers of the universe (so Plotinus, *Enneads* 4.4.40–45). To most readers from highly modernized cultures, all of this is very foreign. But in the ancient world, when this slave girl is called a magician, it conjures up this kind of background and association. This helps to explain Paul's nervousness and reaction to her declarations about him.

This is the only occurrence of the term for soothsaying in the NT. It refers to the practice of divination (BAGD 491 §1; BDAG 616). The scene will lead to a confrontation like that in Luke 4:33–35 and 8:28–35. The challenge from non-Jewish faith is also paralleled in Acts 8:4–25 and 19:11–41. There is a financial element (ἐργασία, *ergasia*, "business" and by synecdoche "profit") to this work as well that also parallels Acts 19 and was critiqued in Greco-Roman works (Acts 16:19; 19:24; Lucian, *Alexander the False Prophet*; Apuleius, *The Golden Ass* 8.26–30; Witherington 1998: 494).

Bruce (1988a: 312) notes that in Philippi three very different kinds of individuals are singled out: religious women, a possessed woman from the "dark side" (Deut. 18:10–12; 1 Sam. 28:8; Ezek. 13:6; 21:29; Mic. 3:11), and a simple "secular soldier." Williams (1990: 280) argues that they are the three groups held in contempt by Jews: women, slaves, and Gentiles—so all gender, ethnic, and social barriers are crossed.

For many days "she was crying out" (ἔκραζεν, *ekrazen*, imperfect tense). She describes Paul's group as bond servants (δοῦλοι, *douloi*) of God, an expression Paul also uses of himself (Rom. 1:1). They serve "the Most High God" (τοῦ θεοῦ τοῦ ὑψίστου, *tou theou tou hypsistou*), a key description of God in a polytheistic environment but one that could be misunderstood because non-Jewish religions also used the expression for pagan gods (Barrett 1998: 786; Witherington 1998: 494; Trebilco 1989: 58–62; Schnabel 2004: 1154–55). This title for Paul's God appears to highlight God's uniqueness by proclaiming him as the one true God, but it also could have struck the non-Jewish ears of the Philippians as a reference to God as a great one (used of Zeus in Aeschylus, *Eumenides* 28–29). Le Cornu and Shulam (2003: 893–94) seem to read the scene too much in terms of a Jewish versus Greco-Roman audience when they prefer to explain Paul's reaction as less about what is said or heard and more about its simply coming from a pythonic source. In other words, she could have been understood as saying that Paul's God was the highest among many gods, because the expression is not necessarily a reference to Yahweh but simply to a supreme god of one's preference. Although what the woman is saying could be construed as ironically true, the fact that she represents many gods makes her testimony less than welcome and, ultimately, potentially misleading. The title is rare in the NT, although Luke's Gospel uses it often (Luke 1:32, 35, 76; 6:35;

8:28; Acts 7:48) as does the LXX but in a decidedly unnatural way. Only Heb. 7:1 has the full phrase "Most High God" as here. Finally, the phrase ὁδὸν σωτηρίας (*hodon sōtērias*) may mean only "a" way of salvation, adding to the confusion of what she is saying.

The girl's declaration annoys (διαπονηθείς, *diaponētheis*) Paul. This verb means "be disturbed" or "be burdened" by something (BAGD 187; BDAG 235; Acts 4:2 is the only other NT occurrence of the verb, which is also not used in the LXX). So Paul moves to stop the woman's actions. By stopping her, he shows his divine power over such forces. This is part of the significance of Paul's speaking in Jesus's name. It is Jesus's authority that is at work in this exorcism. The God Paul proclaims is specifically tied to the divine work through Jesus. The exorcism is immediate, taking place "at that very hour." The specification of Jesus here is important in identifying the God whom Paul preaches. Paul's exorcism is not well received by those who are earning money from the woman's activity. Here, the reaction is as important to the account as the miracle.

The girl's masters are not happy, as their means of profit has disap-   **16:19–21** peared. Money is more important to them than salvation (Luke 12:21; 18:18–30; Mark 5:16–17; Acts 19:24–29), not to mention the woman's welfare and dignity. They seize Paul and Silas and bring them into the marketplace (ἀγοράν, *agoran*) to the magistrate, complaining that they are "disturbing our city" and "advocating customs that it is not lawful [for Romans] to accept or practice." What this could mean culturally is much discussed by scholars. Paul and Silas have done nothing to disturb the peace other than to liberate the slave girl, which costs the owners some of their livelihood, but this could well be the point. The owners ironically could perceive Paul's act as magic that also brings harm, something outlawed in Rome (de Vos 1999). The charge is really a microcosm of what will erupt later as a full-blown conflict in Ephesus. The pattern of a simple account followed later by a more developed one is a stylistic feature of Luke's writing (compare Iconium [Acts 14] with Athens [Acts 17] that is similar in development).

The marketplace would have a raised judgment seat, the *bēma*, where the magistrate sits to render judgment (Witherington 1998: 496). This site in Philippi has been excavated, with a second-century level now uncovered. The magistrates would be known as *praetores* or, better, as *duoviri* (for these titles, *CIL* 3.633, 650, 654, 7339; Josephus, *Ant.* 14.10.22 §247; 20.6.2 §131 notes such an office; Barrett 1998: 789). Luke uses two general Greek terms for this office in verses 19–20 (ἄρχοντας, *archontas*, rulers; στρατηγοῖς, *stratēgois*, magistrates).

The two-part charge makes clear that Paul and Silas have focused on the Gentiles in their work. They bring a foreign religion, in their accusers' view, or, perhaps more accurately, a destructive foreign cult, given that the Roman policy was one of religious tolerance unless a religion was seen to be destructive to others (Pliny the Elder, *Nat.* 30.11; Apuleius, *Apology* 47, mentions laws against using spells to harm crops). This is the first formal indictment against Paul in Acts (Le Cornu and Shulam 2003: 902).

The ethnic perspective present in this charge is that these men are Jews who advocate customs or undertake practices that are not what Romans espouse or practice. The Roman pride of Philippi is a point of focus here, as Artemis will be for Ephesus in Acts 19. Since the Romans emphasized tolerance of such differences and allowed each ethnic and religious group to observe their own customs, the charge of trying to get Romans to do what they do not normally do is serious, since Paul would be seen as challenging a person's livelihood and the economic well-being of the city. The complaint is probably that if Romans are encouraged to become Christians, their new loyalties will direct them away from Caesar and faithful citizenship to Rome, since Christians do not worship the emperor as Roman law instructs (see Acts 17:7). The fear may also be that if this religion is adopted, with acts similar to the one Paul performed, anyone could be at risk of losing their livelihood, not to mention the effect on commerce involving the gods. Thus the charge may also be that Paul and Silas practice an "unsanctioned" religion or threaten the stability of the colony by promoting revolution (Schnabel 2004: 1155).

This is similar to the Roman view that feared Judaism, which, although it was tolerated as a sanctioned religion, was not held in high esteem because it promoted practices regarded as drawing allegiance from Rome and its myriad religions (Tacitus, *Hist.* 5.5; Cicero, *Pro Flacco* 28; Juvenal, *Satires* 14.96–106). Sherwin-White (1963: 78–83) notes that proselytizing was not illegal but was discouraged. It was preferred that religions be officially recognized. Probably because this is a new teaching, there is a call for a hearing (Cicero, *De legibus* 2.8.19; Fitzmyer 1998: 587). Barrett (1998: 790) suggests that Luke sees Christianity as a form of true Judaism here, against Conzelmann (1987: 131). It is hard to be sure, but portraying this as the early Roman and Pauline view of Christianity fits with other texts in Acts (23:29; Acts 24 defense speech). Paul and Silas are portrayed as Jews who appeal across ethnic lines to Romans (21:39; 26:4–5). Only the Jews are referred to. There is no mention of Timothy or Luke. They may well have been spared because they were Gentiles or because they were not in as visible a role.

In a sense, the reaction here is like that of another city's to the Gerasene demoniac (Mark 5:1–20). Despite the man's healing, the townspeople ask Jesus to leave because of the disturbing loss of pigs that resulted from the exorcism. In both cases, the point is that larger monetary interests outweigh concerns for the person benefited. It also illustrates a point Luke often makes that material concerns can distort perception.

The charge of "disturbing our city [i.e., the peace]" (ἐκταράσσουσιν ἡμῶν τὴν πόλιν, *ektarassousin hēmōn tēn polin*) crosses directly into the magistrate's authority (on disturbing a city, see Josephus, *J.W.* 7.3.2 §41; *Ant.* 17.10.1 §253). This is what he cannot allow. The charge is not unlike what was said of Jesus in Luke 23:2, 5.

The accusers try to make the issue an ethnic one. Although Paul's message   **16:22–24** transcends ethnic distinctions, the local magistrate is ignorant of this. He is a product of local (mis)information. Here is a picture of Roman justice at the most local level. Paul's group has no chance to defend itself from the charges. What now follows is either the allowance of a mass riot and beating (2 Cor. 11:25; 1 Thess. 2:2) or the carrying out of a judgment against Paul by the citizens (on the scholarly discussion, see Schnabel 2004: 1156).[3] The magistrates command them to be whipped (ῥαβδίζειν, *rhabdizein*; the only other NT instance of this verb is in 2 Cor. 11:25). The whipping will later become a point of consternation when Paul's Roman citizenship emerges in verse 37, because Roman citizens are not to be whipped (Cicero, *In Verrem* 5.62; Williams 1990: 288). This punishment would take place at the hands of the *lictores*, "rod-bearers," who keep bundled rods as the symbol of Roman justice to inflict lighter punishments. This in effect is a caning designed to discourage Paul's group from continuing to preach. In Latin, this punishment was called an *admonitio*, from which is derived the word "admonition." The term indicates the "warning" element in the punishment. This kind of beating was also called the *fustigatio* (BAGD 733; BDAG 902). They remove their garments and beat them. This would take place in public (C. Schneider, *TDNT* 6:971). Other forms of beating included a lashing with cords or leather strips (*castigatio*) and a flogging with chains (*verberatio*).

With the completion of the beating, they are tossed into the "inner" prison and fastened to stocks. The first meaning of the term τὸ ξύλον (*to xylon*) is "wood" (Herodotus, *Hist.* 9.37). The stocks are made of wood and designed to prevent escape. They can be tight and painful, with holes to push the legs apart (Bruce 1988a: 315), but Luke does not mention torture here. This is the only occurrence of this term in the NT with this meaning. The magistrate probably wants to make an example of them, so he holds them for a time. Nothing about such confinement was pleasant. Prisoners slept seated or on the hard floor and were seen as deserving harsh treatment (Le Cornu and Shulam 2003: 905; esp. Rapske 1994b: 123–27; Lucian, *Toxaris* 150–51). These details prepare for the miracle of the deliverance to come.

3. It is often asked why Paul does not here defend and protect himself by mentioning his citizenship. But for Paul to opt for a Roman emphasis here when the connections to Judaism are being challenged might send the wrong message about where Paul's cultural and religious loyalties lie. See Schnabel 2004: 1156–57. It is a considered choice, as Rapske 1994b: 121–34 argues in detail.

16:25–27 Divine deliverance takes place in the context of Paul and Silas singing and praising God near midnight (κατὰ δὲ τὸ μεσονύκτιον, *kata de to mesonyktion*, literally, "about midnight"). The other prisoners hear the praise. Tertullian says of this event, "The legs feel nothing in the stocks when the heart is in heaven" (*To the Martyrs* 2; joy amid suffering: Rom. 5:3; James 1:2; 1 Pet. 1:6; T. Jos. 8.5; "hymning," Eph. 5:19; Col. 3:16). Prayer is common in Acts at difficult moments (1:14; 4:23–31; 6:4; 7:60; 9:11; in the OT, Dan. 3:24 LXX, prayer of the three men in the oven [= Prayer of Azariah 1 Eng.]). Prayer and singing also were a common response of those in prison (Epictetus, *Discourses* 2.6.26 [emulating Socrates, there is singing by the imprisoned Bacchae]; Conzelmann 1987: 132; Barrett 1998: 793; Lake and Cadbury 1933: 197). An earthquake shakes the prison, so that the doors open and the fetters (δεσμά, *desma*) come free from the walls (on divine shaking: Exod. 19:18; Pss. 17:8; 47:6; 81:5; 96:4; 98:1 LXX [18:7; 48:5; 82:5; 97:4; 99:1 Eng.]; Matt. 28:2; Acts 4:31; 12:6–11).[4] Earthquakes in this region are common. Fitzmyer (1998: 588) notes that the timing of this event is key in pointing to God's work. In Hellenism, an earthquake points to a theophany (Ovid, *Metam.* 9.782–83; 15.669–78; Johnson 1992: 300). In a few passages in Acts, the term δεσμά refers to one who is imprisoned (the "chained") by a kind of metonymy (20:23; 23:29; 26:31). In other passages, it refers to the chains directly (26:29). God is still the primary agent in these events, and special providence is at work as these chains come loose (ἀνέθη, *anethē*; used of loosening linkages on a boat in 27:40).

When the jailer awakes, he decides that the escape means that he is a dead man anyway, as the penalty for allowing an escape is often death (12:19; 27:42; Justinian, *Code* 9.4.4, over a third of Justinian's legal compilation is older, going back to Ulpian in the third century AD). This is another common theme that mirrors Hellenistic life (Chariton of Aphrodisias, *Chaer.* 3.1.1; 1.5.2; 5.9.9–10; Xenophon of Ephesus, *Eph. Tale* 2.4.6). Schnabel (2004: 1157) challenges this on the premise that the situation does not change after the jailer is saved, but fails to note that with the prisoners being present, there is no escape and thus no risk. Schnabel prefers the explanation that the jailer's religious sensitivities are upset as he realizes that punishing them was wrong. This may be a factor at work here, but it is not the only one.

Haenchen (1987: 500–501) finds the entire scene unbelievable. Would the mere loosing of the chains have let the prisoners be at risk to flee? Would the jailer have sought to kill himself without checking first? How did Paul know what the jailer was about to do? The jailer's reaction, however, reflects ancient values of shame and honor, since the jailer and

---

4. Origen, *Against Celsus* 2.34, compares this event to the one, described by Euripides, of the deliverance of the Bacchanals and Dionysius in *Bacchanals* 443–50, 586–602; Bruce 1990: 363.

his superiors might see the incident as a dereliction of duty. The severity
of the quake may have led him to assume that they have escaped, given
that it shook the chains loose. There is no indication that the jailer is
completely rational and thinking clearly in his response (Marshall 1980:
272), because an earthquake might be seen as a legitimate excuse and thus
lessen his punishment for allowing prisoners to escape (Justinian, *Digest*
48.3.12; Barrett 1998: 795). The earthquake, especially if severe enough
to loosen chains, may also have made the jailer nervous about who was
imprisoned and why the gods have acted in this way. He decides that it
will be better for him to take his own life, since his fear of his superiors
is great. Only Paul stops him by telling the jailer that they are all still
present in the prison (v. 28). The miracle is different from Acts 5 and 12,
as here there are no angels and no escape. Paul will trust in God's care
and stay where he is in this case (at other times he seeks to escape).

What happens next changes the jailer's life. Paul calls out to the jailer not   **16:28–30**
to do anything bad (μηδὲν πράξῃς σεαυτῷ κακόν, *mēden praxēs seautō
kakon*; i.e., commit suicide), for all the prisoners remain. Conzelmann's
claim (1987: 132) that Paul's knowledge here shows the legendary character of the scene is excessively skeptical (also Haenchen 1987: 501).
There is nothing that prevents Paul from seeing what the jailer is about
to do (Bruce 1990: 364). Witherington (1998: 498) notes that Luke does
not tell us whether there is enough light to see or whether this is a
prophetic insight. Marshall (1980: 272) suggests that Paul might have
heard the reaction or seen it. He also reminds the reader of Acts that as
a condensed account, it does not give us every imaginable detail of the
scene. When the jailer comes in and sees them all there, he falls before
Paul and Silas, trembling out of respect, not worship (for trembling,
Acts 7:32; Heb. 12:21). Luke sometimes notes this kind of behavior (Acts
10:25–26; 14:11–13). The jailer does seem to sense that some divine
force has been at work.

The jailer leads them out of the prison and asks what he must do to
be saved. The use of ἵνα (*hina*) indicates purpose (Wallace 1996: 472).
Luke again uses the divine "must" (δεῖ, *dei*) here. Acts 2:37 and Luke 3:10
record similar questions without the divine "must." In the logic of the
narrative, the jailer surely knows why the men are there. Their religious
claims must have registered with him when the quake came and they
preserved his life by staying. He in effect asks to share in their deliverance, which the earthquake has symbolized (for this kind of question,
see Aelius Aristides, *Orations* 70; Bruce 1990: 364). This is more than a
request to save his life, as that has already taken place (Acts 13:47 and
16:17 set up the heightened sense here; Johnson 1992: 301). The earthquake has presented him with irrefutable evidence that God is at work
with Paul's group. He wants to know whatever more Paul can offer. Is
there a way to escape God's reaction to the injustice in which the jailer

has played a role? In the face of this evidence, the jailer does not want to be found on the opposing side.

16:31 Paul explains that faith in the Lord Jesus will save the jailer and his household. This brief confession expresses the core of what saving response is—to trust in Jesus's salvation authority and work. "Lord" is the title chosen here to summarize that authority (κύριος, *kyrios*; see Acts 2:36). The use of this title reflects tradition (Rom. 10:9; Phil. 2:11; Barrett 1998: 797; Acts 5:14; 9:42; 11:17). Clearly, Luke is summarizing here. The jailer would have the meaning of such a confession explained to him (v. 32 says as much). The theme of Jesus's authority is what was highlighted in a first-century Gentile context in the church's preaching (Acts 10:42; 17:30–31). At a literary level in the unit, faith in Jesus is the answer to the way of salvation (16:17; Fitzmyer 1998: 589). It is the theological point as well, being the core of the kerygma.

16:32–34 Paul's group speaks the word about the Lord to the jailer and his household. Luke gives no details in this case. This summary is all he presents.

In a response filled with gratitude, the jailer takes them and washes their wounds from the earlier beating. His household is baptized immediately, as was the case in Acts 2, 8, 10, and 16 (Pentecost, the Ethiopian eunuch, Cornelius, and Lydia, respectively).[5] The involvement of the household is stressed, as it is noted three times in the unit (vv. 31, 32, 33; Jervell 1998: 426). Household responses appear also in 11:14 and 16:15 with Cornelius and Lydia. As with the Ethiopian eunuch and with Cornelius's family (8:38; 10:48), baptism follows immediately upon faith to symbolize the washing that is associated with their response of faith. The jailer may have washed the prisoners' wounds, but he himself received a better washing. "He washed and was washed; he washed them from their stripes, and was himself washed from his sins" (John Chrysostom, *Hom. Acts* 36.2).

The jailer takes them to his home and feeds them. Although some suggest it, this is not a eucharistic meal. Schneider (1982: 218) correctly rejects this association, as Luke would have been clearer if this were meant. The verse uses the Greek idiom παρέθηκεν τράπεζαν (*paretheken trapezan*, he set a table), which means that he prepared a meal for them (Homer, *Od.* 5.92; Josephus, *Ant.* 6.14.3 §338). Another issue is whether such food would have been unclean from a Jewish perspective. Le Cornu and Shulam (2003: 914–18) think it is quite possible that it was clean, either in what was offered or what they chose to eat. However, if 1 Cor.

---

5. Numerous commentaries enter into discussions about infant baptism because of such verses, but there is no point here to be made about what later became a distinct, important question. This washing of baptism may have come from the well used for the prison (see Le Cornu and Shulam 2003: 913; Rapske 1994b: 253–54 for this scene).

10:23–30 is any guide, Paul would not have been too concerned with questions of kosher meals and kashrut laws (the Hebrew name for laws about unclean or, better, "worthy" food).

The verse ends with a summary note that there is joy that the household has believed in God. Once again Luke links God with the unique work of Jesus. There is joy that faith has come to the household (Luke 1:14, 44, 47; 10:21; Acts 2:26, 46). Their faith is summarized in a causal perfect participle (πεπιστευκώς, *pepisteukōs*) to suggest its enduring quality (Wallace 1996: 632). Given the near midnight occurence of the earthquake, it is now surely deep in the night. Sometimes joy loses track of time.

The give-and-take of the scene portrays the new fellowship that the bonds of Christ have formed (on hospitality, Acts 2:42, 46; 16:15; 17:5; 18:7; Larkin 1995: 242). Now that they are no longer in prison, God has brought about a different kind of connection between them. Those who were enemies and separated are immediately brought together. Thus the scene also illustrates the reconciliation that the gospel brings at the human level. It shows faith through the reception of the word about Jesus, leading to baptism and joy followed by the service of meeting the needs of others in care and hospitality. To know God means that others are treated with care.

The magistrates decide to let Paul and Silas go, seemingly the end of **16:35–36** the matter. They send the "police" to inform the jailer of what has been decided. These could be the men who beat them, because the term τοὺς ῥαβδούχους (*tous rhabdouchous*) refers to those who are carriers of wooden rods, called *fasces* in Latin. These men function as constables or police (BAGD 733; BDAG 902). This and Acts 16:38 are the only occurrences of the noun in the NT. They tell Paul and Silas that they are free to go.

At this point, Paul reports that he and (apparently) Silas are Roman **16:37–39** citizens (22:25–29), although why he waited so long to mention this is not clear and is much discussed, as noted above (see the discussion of 16:22–24). Josephus tells a story about Jews who have Roman citizenship (*Ant.* 14.10.13 §228; Schille 1984: 349). Had Paul tried to make the point but been unable to obtain the attention of the magistrate over the crowd's reaction? The text does not indicate this at all, although the crowd's spontaneous reaction might make it so. More likely is that Paul made a strategic decision not to mention it during the judgment because it would confuse the understanding of his loyalties.

The text does indicate that the stealthy manner of the release leaves Paul less than pleased because the issue of his (and especially his new faith's) innocence would be left publicly unresolved. The use of γάρ (*gar*) here reinforces the remark that the release should not be done secretly (BDF §452.2). Paul is not a troublemaker, and his Christian cohorts will not be either (the view of Le Cornu and Shulam 2003: 920 that Paul is concerned here about affirming and vindicating his Jewish identity misses the point that Paul in particular represents the Christian presence). Arbitrary treatment should not be allowed (Marshall 1980: 274). In Rome, fair trials are advised (Barrett 1998: 802). Paul's caning has been public shame for him, but the release is to keep the magistrates from shame (Johnson 1992: 301). This would not be a good result for others in Philippi who also might be subject to persecution for their faith.

In addition, if Paul avoided persecution by his Roman citizenship and left his Philippian brethren exposed to it, then this would be a violation of his solidarity and oneness with them in being willing to share in Christ's sufferings. So he presses the matter, noting that the Romans have beaten him without a verdict of guilt, so that the issue of the injustice of his suffering will be public (Rapske 1994b: 129–34). When Paul claims Roman citizenship in Jerusalem in 22:25, the situation is different, since there is no doubt as to Paul's oneness with the community in boldly testifying to Jesus, and the scourge to be faced is more severe.

This detail about the release is important because it is against Roman law to cane a Roman citizen, and so Paul is owed an apology at the least. Paul's rights, established by ancient law codes, have been violated. The Valerian (509 BC), Porcian (248 BC), and Julian law codes (ca. 23 BC) affirmed such protections (Conzelmann 1987: 133; Bruce 1990: 366).[6] Livy (*Hist. Rom.* 10.9.4) notes the heavy penalty for flogging or killing a Roman citizen, according to the Porcian Law (Barrett 1998: 801). Some exceptions allowed Roman citizens to be beaten, but it was never without a full hearing (Williams 1990: 291; Sherwin-White 1963: 72–76). The risk to the magistrates is significant, for part of their role is to protect Romans from injustice. If they fail in giving such protection, they might never serve in such a role again (Dio Cassius, *Rom. Hist.* 60.24.4).

Paul therefore refuses simply to go free, given that as a Roman citizen he has been beaten without a formal charge being proved against him and without receiving a formal hearing. He wishes to make his innocence a matter of record to those in charge and to be publicly escorted out of prison, an act showing his innocence. A false claim of such citizenship could mean execution, so that is not likely here (Witherington 1998: 499–502; Suetonius, *Claudius* 25.3).

As proof of such citizenship, individuals might carry a *professio* with them, or birth certificate indicating their status. These were small wooden

---

6. See Cicero, *Pro Rabirio* 4.12, although such rights were not always honored. Cicero (*In Verrem* 2.5.62 §§161–62) tells of one who is beaten protesting his citizenship as the beating goes on inappropriately, in Cicero's view (see *In Verrem* 2.5.66 §170: "To bind a Roman citizen is a crime, to flog him is an abomination, to slay him is almost an act of murder; to crucify him is—what? There is no fitting word that can possibly describe so horrible a deed" [Greenwood 1935: 655, 657]).

diptychs (Williams 1990: 292; Sherwin-White 1963: 148–49). Normally, however, people did not carry such important documents. It may well be that the officials accepted Paul's claim because the legal risk to Paul for lying made it unlikely that he would do so. Paul's public release constituted an added element of protection for the local community. The magistrates would be more careful in the future.

The magistrates come, address the concern, and ask (ἠρώτων, *ērōtōn*) Paul's group to leave the city,[7] probably to guarantee the peace. Paul and Silas graciously accept. The imperfect tense of ἠρώτων is probably iterative, given the progressive nature of the tense in this context: they "repeatedly asked" them to leave as they discussed the matter. Although the RSV, NET, and NLT translate the aorist verb παρεκάλεσαν (*parekalesan*) as "apologized," this rendering may be too strong. The term simply indicates an effort at exhortation and comfort, a conciliation (BAGD 617 §5; BDAG 765 §5), much as the father does with the elder son in the parable of the prodigal, where this term also appears (Luke 15:28). "Appealed to them" (NASB) and "came to appease them" (NIV) are better renderings.

A pattern will emerge in Acts 16–18: Christians are brought before officials, are accused, and are told to stop preaching or face a reaction that seeks to curb their mission, but the mission continues. The mission is shaking the pagan culture, but justice shows that it should not be stopped. Paul notes his suffering here in 1 Thess. 2:2 and in 2 Cor. 11:25. These events remain with him.

16:40 Peter and Silas go to Lydia's house to see her and the other believers. After giving their exhortations (11:23; 14:22; 15:31–32) to the brethren, they depart.

In sum, this text provides a clear glimpse of the impact of Paul's ministry as an example for our own. Paul challenged things that were destructive to people's well-being and liberated a woman from a vocation that was taking advantage of her. His challenge of the servant girl and what she represented was part of the battle for the presence of the kingdom. The real problem was not the girl but the demonic forces and the desire for greed that drove her vocation. Fernando (1998: 453–54) speaks of how reluctant we are today to see anything as demonic or as being influenced by malevolent spiritual forces. We ignore such destructiveness to our peril. What Paul pushed for here was not a political or legal change but a personal change. If the way in which people lead their lives is changed, then the practice around them changes, even to the dislike of others who wish to continue such destructive practices. Such work some will not accept.

We also see Paul faithful in prison. The impact of God's actions around him lead to change for a Philippian jailer, who himself remains

7. The preposition ἀπό (*apo*) has locational force (BDF §209.1).

open to what God may be doing, even keeping an eye on the circumstances around him. Key characters in this unit are revealed through two conversions: Lydia and the jailer. In one case, a pious woman related to the God of Israel responds. She provides a strategic base of operation for Paul through her supportive hospitality, an act that Acts records as an example to others (Sterck-Degueldre 2004: 248–49). In the other case, a pure Gentile responds and opens his home to Paul as a grateful expression for the gospel's reception. The one might well represent someone of religious background whereas the other is truly the first-century equivalent of an unchurched person. What both together show is the scope of Paul's ministry and what can happen if someone remains open to what God has done through Jesus. The third key figure of the unit is the liberated girl. Nothing more is said about her after the exorcism, but she also is the beneficiary of an act of God's liberating grace. As Stott (1990: 268) observes, there were few people more diverse ethnically, socially, psychologically, and culturally than Lydia, the girl, and the jailer, and yet Paul engaged them all with a gospel intended for all.

Additional Notes

16:12. A complex textual problem here has led to a conjecture in NA[27] about what the reading should be. Bruce (1990: 357) supports this conjecture when he reads the description as πρώτης μερίδος τῆς Μακεδονίας πόλις (*prōtēs meridos tēs Makedonias polis*, a city of the first division of Macedonia) on the basis that the region had four subdistricts. What precipitated the issue is that Philippi is not the chief city of Macedonia, as the text might suggest, because Thessalonica was the capital and Amphipolis was a larger city. The reading found in 𝔓[74], ℵ, A, C, Ψ, and 81 is opted for here: πρώτη τῆς μερίδος Μακεδονίας πόλις (*prōtē tēs meridos Makedonias polis*, a leading city of the district of Macedonia). Two points favor this reading. First, there is attestation for it. Second, such a description can be read as an expression of civic pride, as Ascough (1998) shows in discussing the problem in detail. His article demonstrates that civic pride often meant ascribing titles to a city to lift it up. He notes various inscriptions and texts showing that Ephesus often made such claims, as did Pergamum, Miletus, Smyrna, Athens, Sepphoris, and Thessalonica. The term "district" is being used in a colloquial, not a technical, sense, and so there is no error here. The problem also is discussed in detail in Metzger (1971: 444–46). Their solution (also the NET note on Acts 16:12; HCSB) is accepted here.

16:13. This verse also has a difficult textual problem. The oldest MSS (𝔓[74], ℵ) read ἐνόμιζεν προσευχή (*enomizen proseuchē*; ℵ has the accusative form, προσευχήν), which raises a couple of issues. Oddly, the normal first-person plural (we) of two other verbs in verse 13 shifts to a third-person singular at this one point in some MSS, and the noun is a nominative where an accusative would be expected. The result is that a host of variant readings exist for both the verb and the noun. The critical edition of the Greek text reads ἐνομίζομεν προσευχήν (*enomizomen proseuchēn*), following A[2], C, and Ψ: "we supposed a place of prayer." This looks like the "least unsatisfactory solution" (so Metzger 1971: 447).

16:19. Codex D has a variant reading: "that they had been deprived of the moneymaking they had through her."

16:30. Here D and the Syriac add τοὺς λοιποὺς ἀσφαλισάμενος (*tous loipous asphalisamenos*, having secured the rest).

16:31. Some MSS add "Christ" to the title for Jesus in this verse (C, D, E, Ψ, Byz), but the addition does not qualify as the more difficult reading because Christ is a common title.

16:35. Here D has another major expansion. It notes that the magistrates came together in the agora and that they remembered that the earthquake had occurred and were frightened.

16:39. Again D adds to the text, as friends of the magistrates are present, the innocence of Paul and Silas is stated explicitly, and a rationale for their departure is given: "lest they gather against us, crying out against us." This worry about immediate retribution is not a Lukan theme.

16:40. Codex D expands by noting, "They narrated the things the Lord had done for them."

5. In Thessalonica (17:1–9)

This unit recounts Paul's work in the capital of Macedonia. After traveling (v. 1), Paul makes the case for Jesus as fulfilling the divine plan of Scripture. He teaches for three weeks at the synagogue (vv. 2–3). Some Jews are persuaded along with many Greeks and prominent women (v. 4). This arouses the reaction of other Jews, who attack the home of Jason. They also charge him and those who are hosting the preachers with acting against Caesar and declaring Jesus to be another king (vv. 5–7). Only after Jason pays security is he released (vv. 8–9). The section is tightly bound with the following scene, as Acts 17:11 and 13 look back to Thessalonica, one verse making a comparison and the other telling of persecution (Schneider 1982: 222). It also repeats the pattern of opposition and the kind of charge that surfaced at Philippi.

The unit is a Lukan narrative summary and could have its roots in Pauline sources (Fitzmyer 1998: 593), although Schneider (1982: 222) speaks more generally of news from the tradition. Barrett (1998: 807) suggests local tradition perhaps even from Jason of Thessalonica, and Jervell (1998: 435) speaks of solid mission and community traditions. Paul's preaching meets with both success and persecution, a consistent pattern in the book. Johnson (1992: 308–9) notes parallels between Acts and Paul's summaries in 1 Thess. 1:6; 2:2, 16; and 3:1–2. These include Paul's humiliation in Philippi before arriving at the city, the opposition in Thessalonica by Jews and Gentiles, the receiving of the word with affliction, his going to Athens afterward, and his sending of Timothy to them. Marshall (1980: 275–76) is right to point out against Haenchen (1987: 513) that Paul describes his suffering at the hands of both ethnic groups in 1 Thess. 2:14–16, a point Haenchen notes but dismisses. Where sources overlap enough to be compared, Luke's description appears accurate. This can speak well for his general method and his treatment in passages where corroboration is not available.

Paul preaches to Jews and Gentiles here and does so with an argument that almost looks syllogistic: Scripture said that the Messiah would suffer and be raised. Jesus experienced this. Therefore Jesus is the promised Messiah. The idea of the Messiah for Greek minds involved a claim of kingship, something Jesus possessed but not in the merely political sense the Greeks associated with the concept. All of this leads to the mixed and culturally debated reception Paul receives.

This mixed reaction is the way the world responds to the gospel. In this case, the situation is stirred up in part by Jews who reject Paul's message and the Gentiles' reaction who see Jesus as directly challenging Caesar. A different reaction by another group of Jews awaits in Beroea. Luke is clear that the gospel meets with different reactions within Judaism. Witherington (1998: 502) notes that accusations against Paul in this journey are raised twice by Jews, in Acts 17:5–7 and 18:12–13, and twice by Gentiles, in 16:19–21 and 19:24–27. Two times the charges are believed (16:22–24; 17:8–9), and twice they are dismissed (18:14–17; 19:35–40). The world's jury is still out on the new faith, but it is not the clear threat some make it out to be.

Exegesis and Exposition

[1]Passing through Amphipolis and Apollonia, they came to Thessalonica, where there was a synagogue of the Jews. [2]And Paul went in, as was his custom, and for three Sabbaths he argued with them from the Scriptures, [3]explaining and proving that it was necessary for the Christ to suffer and to rise from the dead, and saying, "This one is the Christ, Jesus, whom I proclaim to you." [4]And some of them were persuaded, and joined Paul and Silas, as did a great many of the worshiping Greeks and not a few of the leading women. [5]But being jealous and taking some wicked fellows of the rabble and gathering a crowd, the ⌜ ⌝ Jews set the city in an uproar; and attacking the house of Jason, they were seeking to bring them out to the people. [6]And not finding them, they dragged Jason and some of the brothers before the city authorities, crying, "These men who have turned the world upside down have come here also, [7]whom Jason has received; and they are all acting against the decrees of Caesar, saying that there is another king, Jesus." [8]And the people and the city authorities were disturbed upon hearing this. [9]And taking a security for peace from Jason and the rest, they let them go.

Paul and Silas travel to Thessalonica by way of Amphipolis and Apollonia.   **17:1–3**
Amphipolis was capital of one of the four subdistricts (the first district) in Macedonia (Livy, *Hist. Rom.* 45.29; Barrett 1998: 808; Schnabel 2004: 1149). The Strymon River surrounded it on three sides. Much of the Macedonian leadership of Philip of Macedon and Alexander the Great came from this area. Amphipolis also was a major city under Augustus. It was thirty-three miles south-southwest of Philippi, and Apollonia was twenty-seven miles west-southwest of Amphipolis.

Thessalonica, thirty-five miles west of Apollonia, was the capital city of the second district of Macedonia (Marshall 1980: 276) and also served as capital of the whole region and home of the proconsul from 148 BC (Schnabel 2004: 1160–63). Strabo (*Geogr.* 7.7.21) called it "the metropolis of Macedonia." The road used by Paul and Silas was the Via Egnatia, which took them along the eastern Macedonian coast and then west into Thessalonica. This city was located a little more than seventy miles southwest of Philippi, but the journey was longer because the route wove around the rugged Greek coast, which went from shore to hills almost immediately. It was a three-day trip if they had horses but would take a few days longer if they traveled on foot. Thessalonica was a vital link to the Balkans with routes by land and sea (Rom. 15:19; 1 Thess. 1:7–8; Larkin 1995: 245). As a "free city," it had the right to self-government on a Greek model (Sherwin-White 1963: 95–98). The poet Antipater of Thessalonica called it "the mother of all Macedonia" (*Palatine Anthology* 4.228). It had a major harbor and was a key link to the Bosporus and the Black Sea. Its population has been estimated between twenty and a hundred thousand (Schnabel 2004: 1162). As a senatorial province, it was very loyal to Rome, a point that will be important in the events to come. As Luke notes in verse 6, provincial governors ran the city. Its location on the coast made it ideal for commerce.

As is Paul's custom (Acts 13:5, 14; 14:1; 18:4; 19:8), he goes to the synagogue and presents the case for Jesus from the Scriptures on three Sabbaths (1 Thess. 1:5–2:16 gives Paul's account of this event). Whether these are three consecutive Sabbaths, and so in three weeks, is not clear.

His explanation and apologetic are described as revealing (διανοίγων, *dianoigōn*) and setting before (παρατιθέμενος, *paratithemenos*) them a case. The opening of Scripture recalls Luke 24:31–32, 45, where Jesus opened both the Scripture and the eyes of his followers after his resurrection. The second participle carries the idea of commending something or someone (Acts 14:23; 20:32). Here Paul makes the case that God is at work through Jesus (Josephus, *Life* 1 §6, has a similar use of the verb). Paul's two-part argument in the synagogue begins with the idea that Scripture predicts two things: the Christ would suffer (Luke 22:15; 24:26, 46; Acts 1:3; 2:23; 3:18; 26:22–23) and be raised (by God) from the dead (the passive construction makes God the provider of resurrection; Luke 24:46; Acts 2:22–24; 10:41; 13:32–36). Wright (2003) shows how rooted the resurrection of Jesus was in early Christian thinking and how a resurrection within history for an individual lacked precedent in Judaism, which expected a resurrection only at the consummation. Jesus's suffering followed by resurrection was a necessity of divine design (ἔδει, *edei*), but no details about how the argument was made are given. Luke's readers can think back to Acts 13 as a possible example. Part two of the argument is that Jesus fulfilled this plan (Acts 18:28). The use of the verb καταγγέλλω (*katangellō*, proclaim) is frequent in Acts (3:24; 4:2; 13:5, 38; 15:36; 16:17, 21; 17:13, 23; 26:23).

17:4   Paul persuades both Jews and Greeks. Among the responders are devout Greeks and prominent women, so that the message runs across social classes. The reference to prominent women could be translated as a reference to the wives of prominent men, a reading Codex D makes explicit by mentioning the women "of the prominent." The response among Jews, however, is not great, as only some (τινες, *tines*) are persuaded (ἐπείσθησαν, *epeisthēsan*). Luke often uses this verb, especially about Paul (Acts 13:37; 14:19; 18:4; 19:8, 26; 26:28; 28:23–24). Those who respond identify with Paul and Silas's message and are joined (προσεκληρώθησαν, *proseklērōthēsan*) to them, which may well suggest that they are meeting separately from the Jews now. The passive verb may again suggest God's work in making them a part of the new community. If the verb has a middle force, then they are throwing in their lot with the missionaries (Williams 1990: 295). The verb is rare, an NT hapax, and does not appear in the LXX (Johnson 1992: 306). The major success is with the Gentiles.

There also is opposition. Jealous Jews gather some of the "rabble" and   **17:5–7**
stir up the city, attacking the house of Jason in hopes of finding Paul and his coworkers. The active voice of the participle ζηλώσαντες (*zēlōsantes*) speaks to a state of jealousy in this context (Wallace 1996: 413). The expression ἀγοραίων ἄνδρας (*agoraiōn andras*) refers to men who hang around the marketplace and is often translated "market people" (BAGD 13; BDAG 14–15). When the term is associated with the idea of evil (πονηρούς, *ponērous*), however, then a reference to the "rabble" is appropriate (on this adjective for "evil" or "immoral," see Luke 3:19; 7:21). Johnson (1992: 306) suggests they could be called "low lifes."[1] The verb ἐθορύβουν (*ethoryboun*, stir up) is imperfect, and so the meaning is that jealous (or perhaps zealous) Jews are going along and stirring up the crowd. Larkin (1995: 246) prefers a reference to Jews zealous for God's glory and the law, which is likely the motivation for at least some. The verb θορυβέω (*thorybeō*) means "stir up a riot" or "agitate" (BAGD 362 §1; BDAG 458; Josephus, *Ant.* 18.3.4 §65). It often entails shouting and frightening others (Johnson 1992: 306; Nah. 2:4 LXX [2:3 Eng.]; Dan. 8:17; Plato, *Phaedrus* 245B; Acts 20:10; the noun is used in 20:1; 21:34; 24:18). They go to Jason's home, hoping to find Paul and Silas. Jason is not identified beyond being a host to Paul and Silas. He may be the person mentioned in Rom. 16:21, but this is not certain. Fitzmyer (1998: 595) rejects the connection. Since Jason is a common name, the connection cannot be established.

When they cannot find Paul and Silas, they drag Jason and other believers in front of the people. The reference to people uses the Greek term δῆμος (*dēmos*), which can refer to a public assembly of citizens responsible for judicial matters (Larkin 1995: 247). It is unclear whether the term has this technical sense here, as it is the authorities who are

---

1. See Aristotle, *Politics* 1291A; Plato, *Protagoras* 347C; Herodotus, *Hist.* 2.141; Bruce 1990: 370; on agora-led riots, see Plutarch, *Aemilius Paullus* 38.3.

asked to act. It is possible that the assembly is called together to persuade the leaders.

Next, the Jews who instigated these events bring them to the city authorities (πολιτάρχας, *politarchas*). This office is well attested in inscriptions.[2] The city would have had five such leaders when Augustus ruled, but now may have six (Barrett 1998: 814).

The first charge noted in verse 6b is that they have disrupted civil peace and now bring this practice to Thessalonica. In this description of Paul and his company, ἀναστατώσαντες (*anastatōsantes*) means literally "subvert" or "overthrow" the world, to "cause trouble everywhere" (NEB; Marshall 1980: 279). They are accused of stirring things up, as was the case in Philippi (Acts 16:20; BAGD 61; BDAG 72, to upset the stability of something; Gal. 5:12 and Acts 21:38 are the other NT occurrences). It is an old charge that goes back to Jesus's examination before Pilate (Luke 23:2). The Jews in Thessalonica seem to have been informed about Paul and Silas's activity elsewhere. Haenchen's claim (1987: 508) that the description is a bad fit, given the faith's newness, is another example of his more skeptical take on Acts and an overly literal reading of an idiom that means "cause widespread trouble." Schnabel (2004: 1165–66) argues that the charge is purposefully exaggerated by those accusing Paul in order to try to get a response and has good historical credibility. Bruce (1990: 371) notes the idiom in P.Lond. 1912, lines 96–100, where Claudius writes the Alexandrines about the trouble some Jews from Syria and Egypt cause "the world" (οἰκουμένη, *oikoumenē*), the same term as used here. Conzelmann (1987: 135) finds it strange that the prominent women cannot stop these events, but it is not clear if these women are among the leaders or other prominent Gentiles. The remark also ignores the spontaneous nature of these uprisings. Paul summarizes this event in 1 Thess. 2:14–16. The "shock" is now that these men "have come" here to spread their views. The use of πάρεισιν (*pareisin*) is an example of a present tense use with the force of a perfect tense (BDF §322; Moulton and Turner 1963: 62).

The second charge, noted in verse 7, is more serious: sedition (Latin, *maiestas*). It also is an old charge (Luke 23:2–4; John 19:12, 15; Polhill 1992: 362). Fitzmyer (1998: 596) suggests three charges, with inciting against Caesar and proclaiming another king being distinct charges, but the two are related, as we argue below.[3] Jason and those he hosts are acting against the decrees of Caesar, saying that Jesus is another king. There is a touch of truth to the charge about Jesus and kingship, but the accusation is not entirely truthful, since there is no effort to overthrow

---

2. Bruce 1988a: 324n8 mentions thirty-two inscriptions from the second century BC to the third century AD; *NewDocs* 2 no. 5; G. Horsley 1994.

3. The third charge is that of turning the world upside down, that is, disturbing the peace (v. 6).

Caesar (see 1 Pet. 2:17, where the instruction is to honor the emperor). The missionaries may well have been heard to be predicting a change of rulers rather than fomenting outright rebellion. This would also be against Caesar's decrees (Marshall 1980: 279; Judge 1971). Roman texts indicate sensitivity to astrological predictions and other projected future occurrences (Dio Cassius, *Rom. Hist.* 56.25.5–6; 57.15.8; Tacitus, *Ann.* 6.20; 12.52; Larkin 1995: 248; Bruce 1990: 371; Chilton 1955).

Fitzmyer (1998: 596) notes this in an oath from the Augustan period, where loyalty was sworn to the emperor with the promise that one would report sedition. Witherington (1998: 508) suggests that Paul urges turning from idols (1 Thess. 1:9), speaks of the coming of Jesus as God's Son (1 Thess. 4:15; 1:10), teaches about a kingdom (1 Thess. 2:12), and questions if peace would come throughout the world (1 Thess. 5:3; 2 Thess. 2). Listeners could understand all of this in the wrong way. The suggestion of sedition heightens and expands the detail on the charge raised in Philippi. Those in charge of the city have a political duty to make sure that Caesar's place is not challenged (references to Caesar in Luke-Acts: Luke 2:1; 3:1; 20:22, 24–25; 23:2; Acts 25:8, 10–12, 21; 26:32; 27:24; 28:19; Schneider 1982: 225). The charge is important because it shows that Paul preaches a messianic Jesus, one who was proclaimed to be a king, although not in the sense the charge suggests. Those who see what Christians are doing in Acts should appreciate that the charge is false.

The charges disturb the leaders, and so they secure an agreement with Jason and take a security from him, probably to guarantee the peace. Their solution is moderate, for they do not succumb to the crowd's desire to punish the men (Johnson 1992: 307). In this context, the term ἱκανός (*hikanos*) refers to the taking of "legal security" or bail, something to guarantee that this missionary group will not break the Roman law (BAGD 374 §1c; BDAG 472 §1). This act in Latin is called *satis accipere* and is well attested (Schneider 1982: 225n42; *OGIS* 484.50–51; 629.100–101).

Does Jason agree to send Paul and Silas away? This seems quite probable in light of Paul's remarks in 1 Thess. 2:14–18 suggesting that he would like to have remained (Bruce 1990: 372). With this commitment in place, Jason and the others are let go. The believers in Thessalonica send Paul and Silas away, no doubt to calm the city's nerves. The believers agree that the only way to guarantee the peace and for Paul to be safe is for Paul to leave.

In sum, the scene in Thessalonica shows how the arrival of the gospel continued to produce mixed results and reactions. We also know that the church held strong in the face of such pressure, as Paul's later letters to the church there show (Bruce 1988a: 326). Fernando (1998: 460–61) observes that six verbs in this passage summarize the evangelistic effort.

Paul "reasoned," "explained," "proved," and "proclaimed." The response was that some were "persuaded" and "joined." Evangelism is about an exchange in which the evangelist sets forth the gospel, both affirming and defending it. This entails neither imposition nor manipulation but a straightforward setting forth of what God has done in Jesus (Fernando 1998: 468).

Additional Note

17:5. Once again D expands and makes things clear by referring to disbelieving Jews.

6. In Beroea (17:10–15)

Paul now travels to Beroea, where he meets with a positive welcome (vv. 10–12). The account serves to show that not all locales are as contentious as Philippi and Thessalonica. Indeed, an explicit comparison with Thessalonica appears in verse 11. But another fact also remains: Paul is being pursued by those opposed to him, as the Jews of Thessalonica come and stir up trouble in Beroea as well (v. 13). Paul is sent away, but Silas and Timothy remain there until Paul reaches Athens and calls for them to join him (vv. 14–15).

This narrative summary account would also be rooted in Luke's Pauline sources or other community traditions, as in other scenes.

Exegesis and Exposition

¹⁰The brothers immediately sent Paul and Silas away by night to Beroea, where, arriving, they went into the Jewish synagogue. ¹¹These Jews were more noble than those in Thessalonica because they received the word with all eagerness, daily examining the Scriptures to see if these things might be so. ¹²Therefore many of them believed ⌜with not a few Greek women of high standing as well as men⌝. ¹³But when the Jews of Thessalonica learned that the word of God also was proclaimed by Paul at Beroea, they came there too, stirring up and inciting the crowds. ¹⁴Then the brothers immediately sent Paul off on his way ⌜ ⌝ to the sea, but Silas and Timothy remained there. ¹⁵Those who escorted Paul brought him as far as Athens; ⌜ ⌝ and receiving a command for Silas and Timothy to come to him as soon as possible, they departed.

Paul is sent to Beroea by night, indicating perhaps a hasty exit and concern for safety (Jervell 1998: 437). This terraced Macedonian town was located about forty-five miles west-southwest of Thessalonica, off the main road and to the south of the Via Egnatia (Lake and Cadbury 1933: 206 say about fifty miles; Schnabel 2004: 1168). It sat on a slope overlooking the Haliacmon River on the southernmost pass to Mount Bermion. Today it is known as Veria (or Veroia). A traveler going to Athens would pass through this town. It is also often spelled Berea. Cicero, *In Pisonem* 36.89, calls it an "out of the way" town, a way of indicating that it was not on the main road. Livy calls it a "noble" town (Bruce 1988a: 327; Williams 1990: 298). It had been under Roman control since 168 BC. Again the preaching starts in the synagogue. Inscriptions confirm the existence of Jews there (Barrett 1998: 817; Schürer 1973–87: 3.67,

17:10

68). Today a colorful monument to Paul marks the spot where he was said to have preached. Silas is explicitly said to be with Paul; Timothy is noted in verse 14, so he also came along or followed later.

17:11–12   Luke describes the Beroean Jews as more noble (εὐγενέστεροι, *eugenesteroi*) than those in Thessalonica because they receive the word eagerly, examining the Scriptures (ἀνακρίνοντες τὰς γραφάς, *anakrinontes tas graphas*) daily to see if these things might be so (note the use of the optative ἔχοι, *echoi*, here). The relative pronoun οἵτινες (*hoitines*) describes the Beroeans, but its semantic force is almost one of "because," explaining why the Beroeans are better (Moulton and Turner 1963: 48 says that the relative should be rendered "who," but the implied causal idea is contextually present; NET: "for they eagerly received"; HCSB: "since they welcomed"). This stands in contrast to the meetings held each Sabbath in Thessalonica. The depiction of the Beroeans as eager or zealous (προθυμίας, *prothymias*) is the only place such a description appears in Acts (Rengstorf, *TDNT* 6:699). The expression for "examining" (ἀνακρίνω, *anakrinō*) is graphic, for it refers to a legal process, such as a trial. The expression "more noble" can also mean "more generous" or "of a more noble attitude," and it likely does so here, since a character quality is in view (Bruce 1990: 373; Polhill 1992: 363; 4 Macc. 6:5; 9:13; 10:3). "These things" that they examined surely include Christ's suffering, his being raised, and his "kingship," since this was the issue in Thessalonica to which the Beroeans are compared.

As in Thessalonica (Acts 17:4) and Philippi (16:13–15), Luke notes the response of prominent women to the gospel alongside Jews and Greeks. In Thessalonica the women were called prominent (πρώτων, *prōtōn*), and here their high social standing (εὐσχημόνων, *euschēmonōn*, respected) is highlighted. "Not a few" (οὐκ ὀλίγοι, *ouk oligoi*) of these respected men and women respond. One of the converts, Sopater, son of Pyrrhus, will be with Paul later (Acts 20:4).

17:13   Upon hearing that Paul is proclaiming the word of God in Beroea, the zealous Jews of Thessalonica incite and stir up the crowd there as well. Since there is no connection between jurisdictions in this area, the judgments made at Thessalonica would need to be repeated (Sherwin-White 1963: 98). Luke again equates the "word of God" with the gospel message about Jesus (4:29–31; 13:5; 16:32). The verbs used here are different from those in the description of stirring up the crowds in 17:5. Here the first, σαλεύω (*saleuō*), means "shake" or "disturb" (BAGD 740 §2; BDAG 911; Acts 2:25; 4:31; 16:26; 17:13). The second verb, ταράσσω (*tarassō*), appeared in 15:24 regarding what the false teachers were doing in inciting people against the gospel (see the discussion of 15:22–24) and in 17:8 regarding the rise of persecution. Luke uses a variety of terms to describe how the Jews stir up a reaction to Paul. In other settings, such as Ephesus, the reaction will come from Gentiles. The action in

Beroea is like that in Lystra, when Jews from Antioch and Iconium pursued Paul (14:19).

Paul is sent away and heads for Athens. To reach there, one usually goes   **17:14–15**
to the coast and travels by sea, as Mount Olympus blocked the way by land. Bruce (1988a: 328) notes that Methone or Dium would be the port used; Barrett (1998: 820) adds Pydna as a possibility. Some scholars suggest that the lack of reference to a port of embarkation means that he went by land, since Luke normally indicates the means of Paul's travels. Perhaps Paul goes by land to throw off those following him (Larkin 1995: 250–51). It is not clear, however, which route Paul takes.

Silas and Timothy remain behind until Paul calls for them. Athens, the intellectual capital of the Greek world, was 195 miles south-southeast of Beroea (Schnabel 2004: 1170–74). Examples of such commands are prevalent in Paul's letters (Titus 3:12–13; 2 Tim. 4:21; 1 Tim. 1:3; Col. 4:10; Phil. 2:19; 1 Cor. 16:10–11; Johnson 1992: 308). Acts parallels descriptions in 1 Thess. 3:1–6 at this point. Silas and Timothy apparently arrive in Athens, although Acts does not note this; then Paul sends them back to Macedonia and does not meet up with them again until he is in Corinth (Acts 18:5). Timothy goes to Thessalonica (1 Thess. 3:2) and Silas probably to Philippi, although that is less certain. The Acts account is selective here (Polhill 1992: 364; Conzelmann 1987: 136 says that Luke's description is "simplified").

In sum, the pattern of preaching to mixed reaction and opposition continues, as does each local congregation's concern that Paul not be put at risk by too much controversy. The additional note here is the character of the Beroeans as willing to seek out what the Scripture teaches. The Christian life is an examined life, where one employs the Scripture like an X-ray to ascertain the nature of religious truth, life, and one's heart.

Additional Notes

17:12. The Western text improves the syntax: "and of the Greeks and of those of good position many men and women believed." By leveling out the reference to women, D continues its pattern of not giving women a high profile. It also adds a note that some of the Jews do not believe, thus emphasizing unbelief among the Jews.

17:14. The Byz MSS see Paul going by land to Athens yet "as if" by sea to throw off his pursuers.

17:15. Again D expands, noting that Paul passes by Thessaly, thus making clear that no new work takes place until Athens.

7. In Athens (17:16–34)

Paul reaches Athens alone. This scene presents one of the more developed speeches of Acts. It is the most complete example of how Paul addresses a purely Gentile audience. Fitzmyer (1998: 600) rightly calls it the most important episode of Paul's second journey. From the starting point of the one true God, Paul's speech moves on to present Jesus's uniqueness. But Paul does not complete his discourse. When Paul mentions the resurrection, the speech comes to a halt. Resurrection would have been difficult for Greeks to accept, since they did not have such a category of teaching. For Greeks, death meant the soul became a shade going to hades, with no possibility of coming back to life (Homer, *Od.* 11.160–225). Wright (2003: 32–84) has an entire opening section devoted to Greco-Roman views of the afterlife, explaining how revolutionary a bodily resurrection was for Greeks.

The tone of this speech is so different from Rom. 1 that some have argued that Paul cannot be the source of these remarks (Vielhauer 1966). This conclusion fails, however, to appreciate Paul's ability to contextualize. How Paul reached out with the hope of the gospel and how he theologically viewed the culture is an important distinction to maintain. Kilgallen (2003b) argues that the speech deals with issues arising from Paul's earlier preaching in Acts and focuses on how Jesus could be the judge of the world in a divine plan. Acts is clear that Paul is vexed by the idolatry (v. 16), but he finds it important to graciously show the way to the one God.

The passage has a simple structure. The introduction to the speech appears in verses 16–21, where Paul is disturbed at the number of idols, and the Athenians are portrayed as being open to hearing about any new thing. Paul's speech, which covers vv. 22–31, moves from the "unknown god" to the Creator to the one whom God has appointed to judge the world. At Paul's mention of the resurrection, discussion and confusion ensue. The speech has a rhetorical structure: *captatio benevolentiae* (vv. 22–23), *narratio* (vv. 24–26), *argumentatio* (vv. 27–28a), *reprehensio* (v. 29b; Weiser 1985: 457). Witherington (1998: 518) has a slightly different outline: *exordium* (vv. 22–23a), *propositio* (v. 23b), *probatio* (vv. 24–29), *peroratio* (vv. 30–31). The second outline focuses the argument a little more clearly on knowing God. The reaction appears in verses 32–34, which describe a varied response: rejection, a desire to hear more, and acceptance.

Luke again would be relying on his Pauline sources for this material, which contains the final major missionary speech of the book. Conzelmann (1987: 138–39) prefers to see Luke composing the scene to carry out the Lukan schema, citing a lack of concrete material, as does Haenchen (1987: 529). The speech alone is not enough to suggest a source to them. The tone of the speech, so conciliatory to the culture, is also unlike Paul in their view, citing Rom. 1:18–32 as an example. Barrett (1998: 825–26) also sees Luke responsible for the speech, as does Johnson (1992: 318). It is a fuller version of what has been hinted at in Lystra in Acts 14:15–17. The parallel indicates the general direction Paul took in addressing a polytheistic context and need not be seen as merely a Lukan schema. Luke would have been aware of how Paul addressed such a context, even if he is summarizing.

However, Fitzmyer (1998: 602) suggests that Paul could have spoken as Luke depicts him here (also Nauck 1956). The speech shows how Christianity encountered paganism. It starts with natural theology, or revealed theology, and then moves to God's plan (Williams 1990: 301). Schneider (1982: 235) prefers to speak of creation theology, which is more technically precise. There is a call to repentance, which here means turning to the one true God. The passage also shows the Greeks' initial confusion over the message, since the gospel was foolishness to the Greeks (1 Cor. 1:22–24; Marshall 1980: 281). As we shall see, the ideas of how to address the Gentile religious context have roots in Jewish thought and expression (Gärtner 1955), not Hellenistic Stoic philosophy (*pace* Dibelius 1956: 63). In favor of the speech's authenticity are the lack of an express christological focus and the lack of results (Williams 1990: 301; Bruce 1988a: 334 has a survey of views). In these details, it does not seem like a scene someone would create. Wikenhauser (1961: 200) says the speech is not a free creation of Luke but reflects the essential content of Paul, truly rendered. The tone distinct from Rom. 1 is the difference between Paul addressing Christians about the fallenness of the culture as a ground for the gospel in Romans and the attempt to make a bridge to the culture in presenting the gospel in Acts (Witherington 1998: 533–35).

Exegesis and Exposition

[16]Now while Paul was waiting for them at Athens, his spirit was provoked within him when he saw that the city was full of idols. [17]So he was arguing in the synagogue with the Jews and the devout persons, and in the marketplace every day with those who happened to be there. [18]Some also of the Epicurean and Stoic philosophers met him. And some were saying, "What would this idle babbler say?" Others said, "He seems to be a preacher of foreign divinities"— ⌐because he proclaimed Jesus and the resurrection⌐. [19]And taking hold of him

⌐ ¬, they brought him to the Areopagus, ⌐saying,¬ "Are we able to know what this new teaching is that you present? ²⁰For you bring some strange things to our ears; we wish to know therefore what these things are." ²¹Now all the Athenians and the foreigners who lived there spent their time in nothing except telling or hearing something new.

²²So Paul, standing in the middle of the Areopagus, said: "Men of Athens, I perceive that in every way you are very religious. ²³For passing along and observing the objects of your worship, I found also an altar with this inscription, 'To an unknown god.' What therefore you worship as unknown, this I proclaim to you. ²⁴God, the one who made the world and everything in it, being Lord of heaven and earth, does not live in shrines made by man, ²⁵nor is he served by human hands, as if needing anything, since he himself gives to all men life and breath and everything. ²⁶And he made from one ⌐ ¬ every nation of men to live on all the face of the earth, having determined allotted epochs and the boundaries of their habitation, ²⁷that they should ⌐seek God¬, in the hope that they might feel after him and might find him. And indeed he is not far from each one of us, ²⁸for 'By him we live and move and have our being'; as even some of ⌐your¬ poets have said, 'For we are indeed his offspring.' ²⁹Being then God's offspring, we ought not to think that the Deity is like gold, or silver, or stone, a representation by the art and imagination of man. ³⁰On the one hand, therefore, the times of ignorance God overlooked, but now he ⌐commands¬ all men everywhere to repent, ³¹because he has fixed a day on which he is about to judge the world in righteousness through a man ⌐ ¬ whom he has appointed, and of this he has given assurance to all men by raising him from the dead."

³²On hearing of the resurrection of the dead, some mocked; but others said, "We will hear you again about this." ³³So Paul went out from among them. ³⁴But some people believed, joining him, among them Dionysius the Areopagite ⌐and a woman named Damaris¬ and others with them.

17:16–17 Athens was a famous city, the capital of ancient Attica and located in the Roman province of Achaia (see D. W. Gill 1994a: 441–48 for the relevant cultural background). Cicero describes it as singularly upholding the reputation of Greece (*Pro Flacco* 26.62); Ovid simply calls it "learned Athens" (*Heroides* 2.83; Conzelmann 1987: 138). As a city full of idols, it arouses Paul to react with inner anger. Such a description of Athens is well attested, as Livy, *Hist. Rom.* 45.27, speaks of statues of men and gods (also Strabo, *Geogr.* 9.396; Pausanius, *Descr.* 1.17.1). The many relics housed today at the magnificent Archaeological Museum of Athens also testify to this. The verb παροξύνω (*paroxynō*) means "provoke" (Deut. 9:7–8 LXX; Ezra 9:14 LXX) or "despise" or "revile" something (Deut. 31:20 LXX; Ps. 73:10 LXX [74:10 Eng.]). It is used of God's anger at idolatry (Isa. 65:3; Hos. 8:5; Witherington 1998: 512). The verb is only used here and in 1 Cor. 13:5 in the NT. Paul is very disturbed by

what he sees. A Jewish text that expresses this attitude toward idols is
Wis. 14:11–12, which speaks of idols as an "abomination, to make men
stumble and to catch the feet of fools" (see also Isa. 44:9–20). This reaction is rooted in belief in the one true God and the refusal to worship
idols (Exod. 20:2–5; Deut. 5:6–9).

As is Paul's custom, he takes his message to the synagogues and to
the pious (σεβομένοις, sebomenois). Luke uses this term often in Acts
(13:43, 50; 16:14; 17:4; 18:7, 13; 19:27), generally regarding God-fearers
(19:27 is the exception, where it has its general meaning of "worship"
of a goddess). At the synagogue Paul is arguing the case for Jesus with
them (the verb διελέγετο, dielegeto, is imperfect). He also makes his case
in the marketplace (ἀγορᾷ, agora), which was north of the Acropolis
(Schnabel 2004: 1175–76 describes how littered with idols this entire
area was, honoring Themis [Justice], Eueteria [Prosperity, or Good Harvest, related to Demeter], Apollo Agyieus, Hekate, and Hermes among
the more popular gods). Zeus and Athena also were well represented
on the famous Acropolis. Here in Acts Paul first encounters the more
philosophical Greeks. Paul could well have been in the northwest corner of the agora, where such idols were located. Here also were lines
of idols, especially in an area where a series of square pillars, phallic
symbols, and a bust of Hermes were placed. This collection of statues
was located in an area known as the Stoa Basileios.

Paul meets with Epicureans and Stoics, followers of two of the best-   **17:18**
known philosophical schools of the period, though the Stoics were more
numerous (Polhill 1992: 366–67). The Epicureans were followers of
Epicurus (341–270 BC) and were indifferent to gods, viewing them as
too removed to be objects of concern (Diogenes Laertius, Lives 10.1–21).
They were like agnostic secularists. Diogenes summarizes their view of
life: "Nothing to fear in God; Nothing to feel in death; Good [pleasure]
can be attained; Evil [pain] can be endured" (Witherington 1998: 514).
The Stoics followed the teaching of Zeno (340–265 BC). Their name came
from the Stoa where he would teach (Fitzmyer 1998: 605). They were
pantheists who argued for the unity of humanity and kinship with the
divine (Diogenes Laertius, Lives 7.1–160). Reason, the world-state, and
the "cosmopolis" (or community as the great city) were major themes,
along with self-sufficiency and obedience (Bruce 1988a: 330). So in
orientation they were very different from the Epicureans, something
also noted by Michel (TDNT 9:187).

Luke summarizes their reaction to Paul in two ways. Some see him
as a "babbler" (ὁ σπερμολόγος, ho spermologos). This term literally refers to birds that pick up seeds, and so it often means "scavenger" or
"scrapmonger" (BAGD 762; BDAG 937; Philo, Embassy 30 §203). The
more traditional rendering is "babbler" (RSV, NET, NIV, NLT), but the
term has the connotation of a person who picks up bits of information

and passes them off as if he knows what he is talking about (Barrett 1998: 830: "third rate journalist"). Some translations therefore render it as "foolish babbler" or "show off" (NASB: "idle babbler"; L&N 33.381 and 27.19). The intellectual arrogance of the Athenians may be alluded to in this reaction. The topics of Jesus and the resurrection elicit this judgment from the Epicurean and Stoic philosophers.

A second reaction is that he is a teacher of foreign deities. This is a philosophical description of the subject of Paul's teaching. The idea is part of an incomplete fourth-class conditional sentence that would say, "What would this babbler say, if he could say anything that made sense!" (Wallace 1996: 484, 701; Moule 1959: 151). The term δαιμόνιον (*daimonion*) can refer to a demon or to any kind of deity. In a pagan context, it would be a reference to a god. Socrates likewise was said to be guilty of promoting new and strange gods (Xenophon, *Memorabilia* 1.1.2 [uses the same term, δαιμόνιον]; Plato, *Apology* 24B; Barrett 1998: 830). Josephus notes a similar description of an Athenian reaction to gods (*Ag. Ap.* 2.37 §267). The philosophers realize that Paul is discussing some new god and his divine activity that they do not recognize.

The expression ἀνάστασιν (*anastasin*) probably is not a reference to "Resurrection" as the name of a goddess, as some scholars suggest (against Kistemaker 1990: 627; see also Bruce 1990: 377; R. Longenecker 1981: 474). Paul would not be that unclear about a reference to a goddess, although it may well be that Luke ironically wants to indicate that some have no clue about what Paul is saying. Rather, Paul preaches a new religion with new ideas like resurrection and so in the listeners' view discusses "foreign divinities."

Paul is described as a "proclaimer" (καταγγελεύς, *katangeleus*) of strange gods. To the Greeks, this term refers to a herald, a messenger sent by the gods, rather than a teacher (Schniewind, *TDNT* 1:73; *IG* 12.8.190.39–40 [of the heralds of Augustus]). In verse 20 his interlocutors will speak of his addressing "strange things" (ξενίζοντα, *xenizonta*), using a verbal variation of the term for "foreign" (ξένος, *xenos*). Again it is especially the resurrection that is confusing, as verse 32 indicates.

17:19–20   Paul is brought to the Areopagus to speak. Two interpretive issues arise from the verse. (1) Is Paul arrested or merely brought to the Areopagus? The term ἐπιλαμβάνομαι (*epilambanomai*) can refer to being arrested (16:19; 18:17) or simply to being brought somewhere (9:27; 23:19). (2) Is he simply brought to the locale, or is he brought before the council that meets there, as Aristotle (*Politics* 1273B–74A) and Pausanius were (*Descr.* 1.285; Johnson 1992: 314)? The Greek is ambiguous, especially on the second point, although it is unlikely that Paul was arrested, since no description in the outcome of the scene really points to that kind of an event. Had Paul been arrested, would he remain in custody? However, the description of Paul standing in the middle of the Areopagus in verse 22 may well suggest that he is before the council. It had great power, trying crimes and regulating, for example, city life, education, philosophical lectures, public morality, and foreign cults (Barrett 1998: 832). This location was used by the Athenians to discuss various matters of mutual interest and curiosity (v. 21). So Paul may well have been invited to speak more formally to many about his "new ideas." The locale's Latin name was Mars Hill. A plaque marks the traditional site today, which can almost be missed, located just to the side of and under the Acropolis, which bears the towering Parthenon on the vast area that served as a major forum for Athens. It was a location at the hub of the city's activity.

The crowd seeks to hear Paul on his "new teaching" and "strange things." This second phrase refers to foreign things (ξενίζοντα), which is what the resurrection would be for Greeks. So they ask to hear more. The combination of the new and the unknown sparks curiosity. In this context, a charge is probably not being leveled against Paul. The scene has the feel of a discussion, not a legal proceeding, unlike later scenes in Acts (for an Athenian trial, see Diogenes Laertius, *Lives* 7.168–69). Paul is not under arrest, nor is he under some type of legal proceeding (but Witherington 1998: 515 sees the scene as concerning a legal matter). Polhill (1992: 368) argues that it is not a formal trial but more like a parallel to the story of Socrates and to Paul's pattern of being brought before city leaders. Bruce (1988a: 331–32) sees Paul being led before this council to obtain their expert reaction, not to be designated a lecturer as others suggest. Whether the council is included among those who hear Paul is not certain, but their presence seems likely for such a new topic. If so, Paul could be making a case to be a legal lecturer before the council (Larkin 1995: 253; on analogy with Plutarch, *Cicero* 24.5). Winter (1996) claims that Paul is simply arguing that the God he discusses is not "new." The lack of any formal judgment at the end, however, makes it unlikely that this is a legal setting or a speech to give him a designation of lecturer. Luke is usually clear about the legal implications of Paul's discussions where they are present. Paul could well be sharing the new thought of the day on the hill with those who are there, including council members (Marshall 1980: 285).

The narrative remark in this verse is a critique of the Athenians' interest **17:21** in wanting to hear anything new. It is almost as if they waste their time on the latest philosophical fad. This Athenian tendency is described as well by Chariton of Aphrodisias (*Chaer.* 1.11.6–7; also Demosthenes, *1 Philippic* 4 10[43]; Thucydides, *Pel. War* 3.38.5; Fitzmyer 1998: 606). Luke is having some fun here, as he portrays the intellectual Athenians as the "seed pickers" they suggested Paul was.

Paul begins his speech while standing in the middle of the council, in **17:22–23** all likelihood. This reading is better than seeing him standing in the middle of the hill, since the location of such meetings would not be the central part of the hill. He begins with a seeming compliment, although the term used has the potential for a double meaning, so that a pure *captatio benevolentiae* may not be present.

The term δεισιδαιμονεστέρους (*deisidaimonesterous*) is a comparative adjective being used as a superlative (Wallace 2000: 133; Moulton and Turner 1963: 30). It is difficult to translate. Renderings include "very religious" (RSV, NET, NLT, NIV, NASB, NKJV) and "too superstitious" (KJV; Acts 25:19 has this force). The range reveals the issue. Barrett (1998: 835) prefers the neutral "religious" as the rendering, but this is ambiguous. It portrays Paul as respecting the Athenians' groping for God but still believing it to be done in ignorance. Romans 1:20–23 reflects a harsher tone and less generous assessment of the spiritual ignorance of the pagan world when Paul speaks directly to the church. The term can have a positive or negative sense, referring to either a sincere pursuit of the divine transcendent being (whether a true pursuit or not) or an embracing of superstition (BDAG 216). Jews often spoke of Greek spirituality this way (Josephus, *Ag. Ap.* 2.11 §130, called the Athenians the most pious of Greeks, using this term). Since this is an introduction where Paul is trying to gain his audience, the dominant idea is probably this positive sense (BAGD 173). Later, he will tell them that their religiosity is wrongheaded (vv. 23 [unknown god], 24–27 [grope after God but do not find him], 30 [times of ignorance]).

Even in their use of idols, Paul recognizes an attempt to grope after God. He hopes to help the Athenians by what he says. Their idol to the "unknown god" allows Paul to open the door for discussing the one true God of creation. Paul is not equating the god worshiped here by the Greeks and the God he will preach, but the altar is a segue into discussing the one true God. What they cannot name and seek to worship he will explain to them (1 Thess. 4:5; Gal. 4:9; Wikenhauser 1960: 201). Pausanius describes such altars to unknown gods in his works; *Descr.* 1.1.4 and 1.17.1 speak of the Athenian religiosity and their veneration of the gods (also Philostratus, *Life Apoll.* 6.3; Diogenes Laertius, *Lives* 1.110; Williams 1990: 311; Bruce 1990: 380–81). Haenchen (1987: 520–21) is excessively skeptical again, stressing no parallel to Paul's reference to the singular unknown god (see esp. Witherington 1998: 521–23; Schnabel 2004: 1176–77, who argues that the ancient evidence does show such a reference to be possible).[1] Either Paul made the reference singular (Jerome, *Commentary on Titus* 1.12), or an altar existed that expressed the name in the singular. Given that many such altars of this class did exist, it is likely that one addressed such a category in the singular. The

1. References to unknown gods in the plural are attested: the above-mentioned Pausanius and Philostratus, *Life Apoll.* 6.3, speak of altars erected to unknown gods.

term for "objects of worship" (σέβασμα, *sebasma*) is used in a critical sense in Wis. 14:20 and 15:17 (Marshall 1980: 285).

Barrett (1998: 838) observes that what was a monument to polytheism, being one statue among many, Paul has turned in a monotheistic direction. Paul's speech is confrontational, but in a gentle manner. Turning ignorance about spirituality and God into knowledge is Paul's goal.

Paul begins with the God of creation (Gen. 1–2; Isa. 42:5), who cannot   **17:24–25**
be contained in handmade (χειροποιήτοις, *cheiropoiētois*) shrines. Acts 14:15 begins in the same way. The reference to being made with hands is a way to belittle something (Mark 14:58; Acts 7:48; Heb. 9:11, 24; Eph. 2:11), although some translations give the resultant force, which is "made by man" (RSV; "man-made temples" in NLT). The term describes something man does in contrast to what God does. Acts 17:25 continues the theme by noting that human hands do not serve God with things the Deity needs because God is the source of all life, suggesting that God needs nothing from anyone else.

Thus God is defined in a twofold way. The first is as Creator of all.[2] Larkin (1995: 257) notes that the Epicureans had similar views. The second idea is that God is not contained in a temple and, by implication, is not reflected by an idol. This second remark recalls Stephen's view and the basic view of Judaism (1 Kings 8:27; Isa. 66:1–2; Acts 7:47–50; on this use of "world" in relation to creation, see Wis. 9:9; 11:17; 2 Macc. 7:23; Josephus, *Ant.* preface 4 §21). The idea that a temple cannot contain the gods is something some other Greeks also recognized, as Euripides, frg. 968, expresses the idea that a house built by craftsmen could not enclose the divine form (Bruce 1988a: 336n65).

Paul's emphasis is on God as Sustainer and Creator, along with the idea that God does not need humans for anything.[3] The Greeks shared this idea of deity as independent (Aristobulus, frg. 4; Euripides, *Heracles* 1345–46, "God . . . is in need of nothing"; Fitzmyer 1998: 608). Wikenhauser (1961: 203–5) has several citations for verses 25–27 from Jewish and Greco-Roman sources and notes that the themes Paul uses in describing God do not reflect the silent divinity of the Stoics. The ideas are rooted in Judaism, even as they touch on ideas that were also expressed in some circles of Greek culture. Polhill (1992: 373) argues that "every statement Paul made was rooted in Old Testament thought" and that this is not the immanent God of philosophy but a God who works

2. See Acts 4:24; 14:15; Exod. 20:11; Neh. 9:6; Ps. 74:17; Isa. 45:7; Wis. 9:1, 9; 11:17; 2 Macc. 7:23, 28; 4 Macc. 5:25; Epictetus, *Discourses* 4.7.6; Zeno, founder of the Stoics, was against building temples to the gods (Plutarch, *Moralia* 1034B).

3. See 1 Chron. 29:14; Ps. 50:9–12; Amos 5:12–23; 2 Macc. 14:35; 3 Macc. 2:9; Philo, *Spec. Laws* 1.53 §291; Josephus, *Ant.* 8.4.3 §111; giver of life, Isa. 42:5; Gen. 2:7; Wis. 1:7, 14. The numerous references to the themes in this speech show how basic and Jewish the theology is that Paul expresses here.

in creation (also Williams 1990: 307). The verb θεραπεύω (*therapeuō*) here means "give service to" Deity (Herodotus, *Hist.* 2.37; Isa. 54:17 LXX; Johnson 1992: 315). Human hands do not serve God, since God needs nothing from humanity and gives to humanity life, breath, and all the things needed for life. God's grace in creation on behalf of all people is the point (Luke 6:35).

17:26–27 God is seen as the Creator of the nations from one man (Adam) and as setting the times and limits of the earth.[4] It is uncertain whether Paul alludes here to seasons of the various nations' dominance (Williams 1990: 306), seasons of divine provision of food, national boundaries, land boundaries between land and sea, or some combination (Marshall 1980: 288; Barrett 1998: 84; and Delling, *TDNT* 8:38–39, list the options). The basic choice is between seasons or years, which look to God's care, and epochs, which look to God's ordering the nations. Bruce (1988a: 337–38) opts for food and boundaries, citing Acts 14:17 and Deut. 32:8. Marshall and Witherington (1998: 527) slightly prefer national dominance and boundaries, that is, epochs, given the context of this speech. Witherington appeals to Deut. 32:8 and rightly argues that it is affirming monotheism in the face of polytheism. He also notes Gen. 10–11 as the remote background. It is difficult to be at all certain here, but the context's emphasis on how God is handling the nations may well favor a choice for national dominance and boundaries. Regardless, the point is God's sovereignty.

The reference to Adam is intended to show that all people have their roots in the Creator God. Indeed, humanity is to seek God.[5] Johnson (1992: 315–16) notes a similar argument in Philo, *Spec. Laws* 1.6–7 §§32–40, especially 1.7 §36: "Nothing is better than to seek the true God." This affirmation would be hard for the Athenians, who prided themselves in being a superior people, calling others barbarians. Even as they grope for God, people should know that the Divinity is not far away (Deut. 4:7 [near to his nation]; Pss. 14:1–2; 145:18 [God is close]; Prov. 8:17; Isa. 55:6; 65:1; Jer. 23:13, 23–24). God's closeness in the OT is sometimes a product of people's knowing his revelation and sometimes a part of their being a part of his creation. How these two ideas relate to each other Paul saves for later in the speech.

If they seek God, they just might find him. The two verbs for seeking, "grope" (ψηλαφήσειαν, *psēlaphēseian*) and "find" (εὕροιεν, *heuroien*), are optative, expressing a possibility of finding God. The term ψηλαφάω (*psēlaphaō*) is used only four times in the NT (BAGD 892; BDAG 1098–99; Acts 17:27; Luke 24:39; 1 John 1:1; Heb. 12:18; LXX: Gen. 27:12; Isa.

4. See Gen. 1:24; 10:1–32; Deut. 32:8; Pss. 74:17; 104:5–9; Job 12:23; 38:8–11; Dan. 2:21; Wis. 7:17–19; 1QM 10.12–15; Acts 14:17.
5. See Deut. 4:28–29; Pss. 26:8 LXX [27:8 Eng.]; 104:4 LXX [105:4 Eng.]; Prov. 16:8 LXX; 28:5; Wis. 13:6; Jer. 27:4; 29:12–14; Isa. 31:1; 51:1; 55:6.

59:10). It normally means "touch" or "handle" something, as it does in the other NT verses. For example, in Luke and 1 John a point is made about handling Jesus. In Acts the expression refers to a spiritual groping after God, to looking for something in an uncertain way. But the term in nonbiblical Greek and LXX usage is negative, of a blind person or a person walking in the dark (Witherington 1998: 528; Plato, *Phaedo* 99B; Isa. 59:10; Deut. 28:29; Judg. 16:26; Job 5:13–14; 12:25). Paul describes the Greeks as humans seeking God in their own imperfect way in the hope that they may "get a hold" of God—and this goal is attainable because God is close (Deut. 30:11; Josephus, *Ant.* 8.4.2 §108 [God is close to his own]; among the Greeks, Seneca, *Moral Ep.* 41.1, "God is near you, with you, within you"). Although the Greeks had similar expressions, this is not a mere intellectual attainment, which the Greeks tended to emphasize. Rather, there is a personal dimension that leads to serving and honoring God in truth, as verses 30–31 will show (Marshall 1980: 288; Larkin 1995: 257, "a gracious, personal Creator, Ruler and Sustainer of all"). In effect, Paul is saying that the Greeks' effort proceeds with uncertainty until they understand what God has revealed.

Paul appeals to the appreciation of God through the creation as a bridge to the idea of looking for the expression of God's will and plan, an idea Paul will now develop. God will not be discovered through nature alone, even though nature does at least show us that God is not like humanity (vv. 28–29). One must come to grips with God's revelation, as Paul will emphasize in verses 30–31 (Polhill 1992: 375). Barrett (1998: 845) and Weiser (1985: 472–73) are too optimistic that the search from creation is able to be successful by itself. Creation reveals God in his glory, power, care, and attributes but does not speak to God's plan to deliver humanity (Rom. 1:18–32).

Haenchen (1987: 523–24) rejects an appeal to the OT background because that background is rooted in covenant and revelation and is not to all men as Paul says here. The point he makes is correct, but the deduction he makes from it is not. God's action in Jesus has now brought fresh revelation to all and the covenant near to those who had not had access to it (Eph. 2:11–22). Paul will turn to understanding the plan now revealed to all as the way to come to an understanding of what God asks of those he creates. God is near to all those he has created, and has acted on their behalf. Without an appreciation of God's plan and action, God will not be found, according to Paul in this speech.

Conzelmann (1987: 144) is wrong to suggest that Luke does not address the method of seeking. The speech proceeds inductively and in verses 30–31 does raise what God has said as the key to finding him. Paul is speaking to make known the unknown God, but God is known to a degree in creation, as Paul is showing. What is needed to know God better is an understanding of what God asks from people and what God has done for humanity. Such knowledge is not far removed from "each one" (ἑνὸς ἑκάστου, *henos hekastou*), and so it is the individual response that Paul also highlights, pointing to the intimate knowledge about God that is now available. The "each one" here connects to the "all people everywhere" (τοῖς ἀνθρώποις πάντας πανταχοῦ, *tois anthrōpois pantas pantachou*) in verse 30. To miss this point about how revelation completes understanding is to miss the key, final point of the entire speech.

Witherington (1998: 529) is right to contrast what is happening here with a famous speech of Dio Chrysostom, *Man's First Conception of God* (*Olympic Discourse* 12.28), to which Paul's remarks are often compared. There Stoic ideas are used positively to declare how people have innate conceptions of God and all are kin to God. Paul says that there is a kinship at creation but that this is not enough. Fellowship requires that one respond to God as God's creature, as one accountable to the Creator and his divine revelation.

17:28 This text about living, moving, and having our being in the Deity appears to allude to pagan ideas (BAGD 432 §3; BDAG 545 §3). Polhill (1992: 375–76) discusses the debate over whether this statement is rooted in a specific passage in Epimenides of Crete (ca. 600 BC), a point that is unlikely given the frequency of the thought in ancient thinking. An association with Epimenides goes back to Clement of Alexandria (*Stromata* 1.14.59; among the Greeks, a citation from Isho'dad of Merv is also known; Bruce 1990: 384; Williams 1990: 308; Barrett 1998: 847). These citations suggest a widespread belief that people exist by God's creation and sustenance, so that God is not far off.

In addition, "we are his offspring" (γένος ἐσμέν, *genos esmen*). The expression that we are God's offspring comes from another pagan poet, Aratus (ca. 315–240 BC), *Phaenomena* 5 (some scholars also note Cleanthes, *Hymn to Zeus*; Marshall 1980: 289; but Fitzmyer 1998: 611 rejects a connection to Cleanthes). Paul explicitly notes this connection in introducing the citation as coming from "some of your poets." Paul is working with ideas in the Greek world that are familiar to the Athenians and only alludes to Scripture in his speech instead of quoting it directly. The text from Aratus, as Paul uses it, recognizes the shared relationship all people have to God. It also makes a more subtle point when the remark about being God's children is repeated in verse 29: we are God's creation; we do not create him by making images of the gods (Witherington 1998: 530). Thus the remark does express Paul's view in this limited sense (*pace* J. Schneider, *TDNT* 3:718–19, who argues that this is not Paul's view but a mere missionary accommodation). Paul contextualizes the citation and presents it in a fresh light, setting up his critique. He takes a Greek idea of the "spark of the divine being" in us as tied to Zeus and speaks of being made as God's children by the Creator, alluding to our being made in God's image.

In fact, creation should teach us that temples and idols are inadequate   **17:29**
representations of God or his dwelling place. We are God's children, and
so the Creator should not be thought of as a piece of gold, stone, or silver,
a product of human skill and imagination. This is a biblical critique of
idolatry.[6] The theology behind this idea is that humanity is made in the
divine image, which means that human beings are living, animated,
conscious beings, not objects like idols. So God must be the same and
more (Conzelmann 1987: 145). Paul identifies with his audience when
he says that "we" should not conceive of God in this way.

Paul now turns to the key part of the speech and its application (οὖν,   **17:30–31**
oun). So, what should one do? Formerly "times of ignorance" (χρόνους
τῆς ἀγνοίας, *chronous tēs agnoias*) existed, but now God commands all
people everywhere to repent.[7] God's overlooking those times of ignorance
includes his not judging idolatry as severely as he might have (Rom. 3:25;
Acts 14:16; Larkin 1995: 259; but see Rom. 1:18–32, where a price is paid
for idolatry). God "overlooked" the situation at one time but no longer.
The verb ὑπεροράω (*hyperoraō*) is an NT hapax. It means "overlook,"
"ignore," or, negatively, "scorn," as it often does in the LXX (Nah. 3:11;
Ezek. 7:19). The expression "times of ignorance" underscores the fact that
the Greeks' view of the divine is not according to knowledge. To charge
the Athenians with ignorance is a bold move and critique, given their
intellectual history. The remark also links the conclusion to the speech's
opening, where ignorance is also noted about the unknown god (v. 23).
Paul will make clear that ignorance is no excuse for not responding to
God, since God now commands all to repent, as the end of the verse
affirms (on ignorance as not an excuse, see Acts 3:17; 13:27).

There is a turning that God calls for and holds people responsible for
undertaking. Repentance is a category Luke often notes as the proper
response to God's message (Luke 3:7–9; see Acts 2:38; 3:19–21; in Paul:
1 Thess. 1:9–10). In this case, it appears that Paul is saying that God
did little to remedy the direction of the nations as a whole in the past
(besides issuing prophetic warnings and calling Israel to be a light to
the nations). Acts 14:16 says that God let them go their own way. He
largely ignored them. Now, however, God has acted. God calls to all
people everywhere to repent. The call to repent matches Acts 14:15 with
its call to turn from idols.

6. See Exod. 20:4; Deut. 4:28; 5:8; Ps. 115:4–8; Isa. 37:19; 40:18–20; 44:9–20; 46:5–11;
in Judaism: Wis. 13:10; 15:7–17; Philo, *Decalogue* 14 §66; *m. 'Abodah Zarah* shows the
rabbinic view.
7. On the role of divine economies or dispensations in the program of God, see Pelikan
2005: 173–75 as he discusses Acts 15:8–9 and what has now come with Christ. Jewish
texts express the idea that God's judgment is slow in order to allow time for repentance
(Wis. 11:23). Other Jewish texts suggest that God lets sinners go their own way (2 Esd.
[4 Ezra] 3:8; Le Cornu and Shulam 2003: 970).

In verse 31 Paul alludes to Jesus, the man through whom God has fixed a day for judgment of the living and the dead (Rom. 14:9; 2 Tim. 4:1). The prepositional phrase ἐν ἀνδρί (*en andri*) is instrumental and means "by/through a man" (BDF §219.1; Moule 1959: 77). Jesus was named in verse 18 as the subject of Paul's message. Paul leaves the timing of the judgment unspecified. God confirmed this position for Jesus by the attestation of the resurrection. These two ideas are the christological elements in the speech's conclusion. This judgment will be done justly or in a sphere of righteousness. The phrase ἐν δικαιοσύνῃ (*en dikaiosynē*) is adverbial (BDF §219.4).

The idea that Jesus is the judge of all the living and dead was expressed in Acts 10:40–42 (John 5:27). The roots of this may well be in Son of Man Christology with the idea that the Son of Man receives judgment and dominion authority (Dan. 7:13–14; Bruce 1990: 386). The idea of a righteous judgment runs through the Bible (Pss. 9:8; 67:4; 96:13; 98:9; Amos 5:18; Isa. 2:12; Rom. 2:5, 16; 1 Cor. 1:8; Phil. 1:6, 10; 1 Thess. 5:2, 4; 2 Thess. 1:10; 2:2; 2 Tim. 1:18; Heb. 6:11; 2 Pet. 3:10). Paul is turning to his major point, but once he mentions the resurrection, the speech is interrupted by the Athenians' reaction.

The resurrection (Acts 2:24, 32; 13:33–34) is God's attestation about Jesus to all people. The phrase pointing to confirmation is πίστιν παρασχών πᾶσιν (*pistin paraschōn pasin*). This combination of terms means "show or grant proof [to all]" (BAGD 662, 626 §1b; BDAG 818 §1c, 776 §2; note the paranomasia in the phrase; Josephus, *Ant.* 2.9.4 §218; 15.3.6 §69; Acts 1:3 conceptually). The resurrection was a universal demonstration and proof of God's call to Jesus to be judge. Acts 2:32–36 explained this to the readers of Acts, as did 10:40–42.

17:32–34   A mixed reaction follows mention of the resurrection. Greeks believed dead people remained dead and had no resurrection hope (Homer, *Od.* 11.160–225; *Il.* 24.551; Wright 2003: 32–38). The Greek tragedian Aeschylus has Apollo state, "When the dust has soaked up the blood of a man, once he has died, there is no resurrection" (*Eumenides* 647–48; Conzelmann 1987: 146; Fitzmyer 1998: 612). Some mock Paul, following the beliefs of their culture. The verb χλευάζω (*chleuazō*) means "mock" or "sneer" (BAGD 882 §1; BDAG 1085; 2 Macc. 7:27; 4 Macc. 5:22; Wis. 11:14). It suggests rejection of Paul's message. This is the only use of this term in the NT. The cross and the things tied to it, such as the resurrection, are a "folly to the Gentiles" (1 Cor. 1:23) when viewed by the standards of cultural wisdom.[8]

Others say they are willing to hear Paul again, keeping an open mind. That this middle reaction is not negative is indicated by the contrastive μὲν . . . δέ (*men . . . de*) construction (correctly, Croy 1997: 21–39, esp.

---

8. Many of the ideas expressed in this speech parallel what Paul says in his letters.

26–28; *pace* Haenchen 1963: 526, who sees this as a polite dismissal as
opposed to an open mind). Croy notes that Greeks believed either in
a complete extinction of body and soul (Epicureans; Pliny the Elder,
Nat. 7.189–90), in an afterlife in hades, or in the limited immortality of
the soul (as opposed to an eternal immortality; Eusebius, *Preparation
for the Gospel* 15.20.6 summarizes Stoic views similarly). For example,
Pliny the Elder, speaking of views that discuss some type of life after
death, says that "these are fictions of childish absurdity, and belong to
a mortality greedy for life unceasing" (*Nat.* 7.189). Pliny goes on to say
"a plague on this mad idea that life is renewed by death." It is a "sweet
but naïve view" (*Nat.* 7.190). The options for this view he notes include
soul immortality (what he calls a change of shape), giving feeling to
those below, and worshiping spirits and deifying a man (*Nat.* 7.188).
He notes cynically that man's breath is not different from that of the
animals, yet there is no immortality for them.

None of these Greek views represented a resurrection back into this
world. For Croy, what Paul teaches is precisely the opposite of Epicurean
teaching. Stoics had a variety of views on the afterlife, but a limited immortality of the soul was common. Cicero in *Tusculanae disputationes*
1.31.7 says, "The Stoics say that souls will endure for awhile; they deny
that they will endure forever" (similar is Diogenes Laertius, *Lives* 7.156,
who tells of views holding that the soul survives death yet is perishable).
Cicero notes this Stoic view in contrast to the Epicureans, who believed
that the soul is mortal. Stoics too would struggle with Paul's declaration
but might be able to entertain it. One point all these Greek views shared
is that the body is not restored in any form.[9] So some mock, but on the
other hand, others say they will hear more. Before discussing one more
category of response, Luke notes Paul's withdrawal. Croy takes the scene
and the varying reactions as plausible in a first-century context.

A third group believes. Some are named in verse 34 (the Areopagite
Dionysius, the woman Damaris). We know nothing more with certainty
about these believers, but the description of Dionysius as the Aeropagite
(ὁ Ἀρεοπαγίτης, *ho Areopagitēs*) means that he is a member of the council
and has significant social standing. The reference to Damaris continues Luke's focus on the response of women (Acts 16:15; 17:4, 12). She
may be a foreigner, since women of Athens would not likely have been
present (Witherington 1998: 533). Eusebius (*Eccl. Hist.* 3.4.10; 4.23.3)
describes Dionysius as a shepherd at Corinth and bishop of Athens.
Paul's address thus meets with a full array of reactions. D. H. Gill's (1999)
attempt to argue that these believing figures are fabricated in order to
produce ideals in line with the rest of the scene fails (1) by assuming
the ideal nature of the scene to begin with and (2) by suggesting that

9. Later gnostic Christianity, which was syncretistic with the Greek culture, also
denied a bodily resurrection and was seen as heretical for holding such a view.

the presence of a common name (Dionysius) and a rare one (Damaris) is enough to discredit the reference and reveal the scene's ideal nature. He also sees problems with the Areopagus setting and argues that other names in Acts likely work the same way. The reading is far too skeptical (see the critique of Gill by Schnabel 2004: 1179). In fact, as Gill notes, Damaris as a name is unattested, but this argues against its being an ideal name. Why mention a name no one ever uses? The disjunction here is for authenticity, not against it. Another question arises. If Luke invented this scene, then why is the success of the preaching so meager? Such a lack of success makes it the exception to the rule in Acts. The very honesty that Paul did not have a great deal of success here speaks for the scene's authenticity.

There is a point to note, given discussions on gender. The summary of verse 34 refers to "men" (ἄνδρες, *andres*) joining and believing. The inclusion of a woman in the list, however, shows that ἄνδρες can be used generically of humans. This stands against the claim that the Greek term must refer only to males (Polhill 1992: 378n100). The contention that the word refers only to males here (Dionysius and others) because Damaris is designated a female (γυνή, *gynē*) fails to note that she is placed in the middle of this listing headed by the term ἄνδρες and that unnamed others are mentioned with Dionysius and Damaris in the same list. These others thus belong to the group called ἄνδρες. The additional argument that the term γυνή is employed to show that Damaris is a woman and is not referred to by ἀνήρ says too much. The normal use of ἀνήρ (*anēr*) as meaning "male" means that she has to be identified as a woman in order to make clear that she, as a woman, is in the larger group. The argument that γυνή shows the normal use in this verse fails to account for the bracketing of the entire grouping in this context. This use of the term ἄνδρες to include women is exceptional. In one sense, it is the exception that proves what the normal rule is in most other texts. Efforts to reject it as an exception show how difficult it is to discuss the topic without emotion these days.[10]

Luke's summary of Paul's time in Athens ends with this note of some positive response. While certainly not an overwhelming success, nothing

10. The issue of gender has become so contentious that it is hard to make a linguistic argument such as this on one side or the other without being accused of having ulterior motives. This kind of charge does not advance the discussion. That some do have an agenda for or against the question may certainly be the case, but those wishing to lay out the data pro and con in a balanced way should be able to do so without their motives being impugned. In other words, there are protagonists on each side of this discussion, but also many others are simply trying to lay out the data. The debate over the linguistic force of ἀνήρ is an example of a point that is not as clear as some claim. The controversy over certain renderings in the Today's New International Version is another example of such a discussion, where each side has impugned the integrity of the other side by suggesting hidden motives for their translation choices. This is not the way to advance understanding.

about what Paul does or says is viewed negatively or as a failure (Weiser 1985: 477; Polhill 1992: 379). Rather, Luke seeks to make the point that Paul fully engages the culture in its intellectual capital.

In sum, Paul directly engages the current culture. He does so with the attitude that although his argument challenges the way people are living, his message stresses the gospel as an invitation into a new life and seeks points of contact with such desires as already exist in the culture. Paul knows his own message and the mentality of the people he evangelizes. Too many Christians know their own message but understand far too little about how and why others think as they do. As Stott (1990: 281) points out, one can admire how Paul could speak to people in the synagogue, to those in the city square, and to the highly sophisticated. This ability to adapt made him very effective. Whether in informal conversation or in formal settings, the ability to set forth the faith at a level appropriate to the setting is a valuable talent.

Key to all of these presentations of the gospel is a theology that sees God in his most basic roles as Paul proclaims here (Stott 1990: 285–87). He is creator, sustainer of life, and thus sovereign over the nations and the Father of us all. For all the disputation over creation and how it took place, the most fundamental truth is that God is the creator of life and we are God's creatures, responsible to him. This means that God is, and has the right to be, our judge, something our world seeks to avoid acknowledging.

Another important observation is that despite being aggravated by all the idolatry he sees around him in Athens, Paul manages to share the gospel with a generous but honest spirit. The Paul of Rom. 1 who speaks of the sad state of society is still able to love and connect with that society in Acts 17. This also is an important lesson; sometimes we Christians are so angry at the state of our society that all that comes through is the anger and not the love we are to have for our neighbor in need. Those who see this anger and want to represent the faith differently can overreact the other way, almost pretending as if there is no idolatry as long as the religious search is sincerely motivated. Paul avoids both of these extremes. He knows how to confront but does so honestly and graciously. Both message and tone are important in sharing the gospel. Here Paul is an example of both.

Additional Notes

17:18. Codex D and the Itala omit the explanation about Paul preaching Jesus and the resurrection, perhaps to avoid associating Jesus with what Paul's hearers may have regarded as a female deity (i.e., Ἀνάστασις; see Metzger 1971: 455).

17:19. Codex D has a few minor additions to the verse by having Paul seized "after a few days" and adding the verb "inquiring" to characterize the question they ask Paul (Metzger 1971: 456).

17:26. The Western text says "from one blood" rather than "from one." This reading also appears in Byz and so is in the KJV. Irenaeus also has the reading. Thus it is more widespread than other Western readings. It means that from one race or stock God created all humanity (Fitzmyer 1998: 609). What might make it original is that it is not a normal term to add to the context and it does not match the reference to dust in Gen. 2:7, which is the passage behind the remark. It also could have been skipped by copyists, given that it ends with sigma (αἵματος, *haimatos*) as does ἑνός (*henos*). Nevertheless, the attestation is not so widespread as to assure confidence about the term's originality (Metzger 1971: 456). The difference does not impact the passage's meaning, which still alludes to Adam.

17:27. The problem here concerns a probable confusion of the abbreviation for "God" with that for "Lord," a difference of a capital theta (Θ) for a capital kappa (Κ̄). The result was that "seek God" is read as "seek the Lord" in E and Byz. The second alternate reading in D adds a term (μάλιστα, *malista*) and mentions seeking divinity (θεῖον, *theion*), possibly influenced by Acts 17:29. The change in D also requires changing the syntax of the rest of the sentence, so it is an unlikely original reading. "Seek God" is the more difficult reading and is widely attested ($\mathfrak{P}^{74}$, ℵ, B, Ψ, 33, 81, 1739).

17:28. Some MSS read "our poets" ($\mathfrak{P}^{74}$, B, 33, 326, 614) instead of "your poets," possibly because Paul is about to cite a fellow Cilician, Aratus. This reading has good attestation, but a copyist also might have been hesitant to have Paul cite a pagan poet. It is also unlikely that Paul would have made such an explicit comparison between himself and a pagan poet (Metzger 1971: 458).

17:30. Some MSS have "announce," using the verb ἀπαγγέλλει (*apangellei*; ℵ*, B). But most MSS read "command" (παραγγέλλει, *parangellei*; $\mathfrak{P}^{41, 74}$, ℵ², A, D, E, Ψ, 1739, Byz).

17:31. Several Western witnesses (D, some MSS of the Vulgate, Irenaeus) add the name Jesus, so that the verse reads, "by a man Jesus."

17:34. The reference to Damaris is missing in D, replaced by an emphasis on the high standing of Dionysius. This is not the first time we have seen D reduce a reference to women (see the additional note on 17:12).

8. In Corinth (18:1–17)

Paul moves on to Corinth, another major city of Achaia (v. 1). Here he works alongside Priscilla and Aquila. They came from Rome as a result of a decree from Claudius expelling them along with other Jews (vv. 2–3). Paul argues the case for Jesus in the synagogue (v. 4). Meeting a mostly hostile reaction (vv. 5–6), Paul turns his attention to the Gentiles, where he has success. He also converts a few Jews, such as Crispus, a synagogue ruler (vv. 7–8). Paul stays there for a year and a half after receiving a vision (vv. 9–11). While Gallio is proconsul, zealous Jews make a case against Paul that he is teaching worship contrary to the law (vv. 12–13). Gallio responds that he will not judge an internal Jewish religious dispute (vv. 14–16). This leads to the beating of another believer who is a synagogue ruler, Sosthenes, an act Gallio does not stop (v. 17). Once again, success and persecution occur as the gospel goes forth. Rome judges Christianity not to be a threat to the state but stands to the side when persecution arises.

The narrative summary must be rooted again in Pauline sources. Barrett (1998: 858) sees too many non-Lukan details for there not to be a Pauline source. Jervell (1998: 463–64) speaks simply of a mission account, while noting that historically we are on firm ground. Conzelmann (1987: 151) also appears grudgingly to see source material here but still insists on Lukan stylizing, as does Haenchen (1987: 537, 541). Haenchen, usually skeptical of Luke's accounts, believes this account gives the gist of what took place (also Fitzmyer 1998: 623, but he attributes the remarks of Gallio mainly to Lukan composition; Schneider 1982: 247). The pattern Luke has noted elsewhere appears here; it is the Jewish community's reaction that drives the persecution.

The mention of Gallio and the expulsion decree of Claudius allow us to date the scene to after about AD 49–50 (D. W. Gill 1994a: 449–50). Fitzmyer (1998: 621–22) discusses various pieces of inscriptional evidence dating Gallio's proconsulship to Claudius's twelfth regnal year, AD 52.[1] Gallio's service was cut short by a fever, and so he did not serve there long.

Many of those living in Corinth had Latin names, an indication of the Roman influence. Paul probably wrote 1 Thessalonians here.

---

1. One is an inscription found at a temple to Apollo in Delphi; the other, from Kys in Caria, is found in *CIL* 6.1256 and 8.14727 and is often not included in discussions of Pauline chronology, according to Fitzmyer.

Johnson (1992: 324–25) notes six details of overlap between this section and 1 Corinthians: (1) Paul working with Priscilla and Aquila (Acts 18:2; 1 Cor. 16:19); (2) his practicing a trade (Acts 18:3; 1 Cor. 9:12, 15–18); (3) his converting and baptizing Crispus (Acts 18:8; 1 Cor. 1:14); (4) his association with Sosthenes (Acts 18:17; 1 Cor. 1:1); (5) his experiencing fear (Acts 18:9; 1 Cor. 2:3); and (6) the role of Timothy (Acts 18:5; 1 Cor. 4:17; 16:10–11). This suggests the trustworthiness of the section. Johnson suggests Priscilla and Aquila as Luke's source here. The unit has the common themes of the journey: to the Jew first and then to the Gentiles, divine direction and strength in the face of persecution, and the continued expansion of God's people. One final point is especially important: when Rome examines Paul's activity, it finds him breaking no Roman law. Rather, Gallio sees only an internal theological dispute among Jews. As such, the matter pertains to a faith already recognized and tolerated by the Romans.

Nothing more graphically illustrates Luke's selectivity than a comparison of Athens with Corinth in Acts (Polhill 1992: 379). Paul is in Athens a few weeks whereas he is in Corinth more than a year and a half, yet the accounts are about the same length. Luke is not telling us everything he might be aware of, but crafts a selective account where each scene adds to the overall portrait. In Athens it is engagement with the philosophers. In Corinth it is a legal encounter and judgment by a proconsul.

Exegesis and Exposition

[1]After these things, leaving Athens, he came to Corinth. [2]And finding a Jew named Aquila, a native of Pontus, lately come from Italy with his wife, Priscilla, because Claudius had commanded all the Jews to leave Rome, ⌜ ⌝ he went to see them; [3]and because he was of the same trade, he stayed with them, and he worked, for by trade they were tentmakers. [4]⌜ ⌝ And he was arguing in the synagogue every Sabbath and tried to persuade both Jews and Greeks.

[5]When Silas and Timothy arrived from Macedonia, Paul began to be devoted to preaching, testifying to the Jews that the Christ was Jesus. [6]⌜ ⌝ And when they opposed and reviled him, he, shaking out his garments, said to them, "Your blood be upon your heads! I am innocent. From now on I will go to the Gentiles." [7]And going out from there, he went to the house of a man named ⌜Titius⌝ Justus, a worshiper of God, whose house was next door to the synagogue. [8]Crispus, the ruler of the synagogue, believed in the Lord, together with his entire household; and many of the Corinthians, upon hearing Paul, believed and were baptized. [9]And the Lord said to Paul one night in a vision, "Do not be afraid, but keep speaking and do not be silent; [10]for I am with you, and no man shall attack you to harm you; for I have many people in this city." [11]And he remained a year and six months, teaching the word of God among them.

¹²But when Gallio was proconsul of Achaia, the Jews made a united attack ⌜upon Paul and⌝ brought him before the tribunal, ¹³saying, "Contrary to the law this man is persuading men to worship God." ¹⁴But when Paul was about to open his mouth, Gallio said to the Jews, "If it were a matter of wrongdoing or vicious crime, then I would have reason to bear with you, O Jews; ¹⁵but since it is a dispute of questions about words and names and your own law, see to it yourselves; I refuse to be a judge of these things." ¹⁶And he drove them from the tribunal. ¹⁷And seizing Sosthenes, the ruler of the synagogue, ⌜they⌝ all beat him in front of the tribunal. But Gallio showed no concern for these things.

Paul goes from Athens to Corinth (for relevant cultural background about Corinth, see Schnabel 2004: 1181–86; D. W. Gill 1994a: 448–53; Murphy-O'Connor 1983). Corinth is located a little more than forty miles west of Athens. It was a day's sail away or else took a few days by foot. It was a key and prosperous city of Greece (Pausanius, *Descr.* 2.1–5; Strabo, *Geogr.* 8.6.20–23). It was a major port, at the crossroads of east and west for the Mediterranean Sea, located under Acrocorinth, a significant mountain in the region and today dominated by the remains of a Byzantine fort. Corinth had served as the administrative center for the province since 27 BC. This made it a strategic location for planting the faith. The Isthmian Games were held near here as well, once every two years. It was a new city with no major building more than one hundred years old, as it was refounded by Caesar in 44 BC after the old city was destroyed in 146 BC by the Roman general Mummius for a civil revolt. A temple to Aphrodite sat in the city, which itself was perched at the top of a 1,900-foot hill. A synagogue has been excavated at a locale near the agora, but its Jewish population seems to have been modest in size (Polhill 1992: 381; Le Cornu and Shulam 2003: 979–80). Its population is estimated to have been about two hundred thousand, a significant size for an ancient city and larger than Athens (Larkin 1995: 262); the population estimate by Le Cornu and Shulam (2003: 978) of three hundred thousand plus four hundred sixty thousand slaves is much too high. It had a reputation for prosperity and licentiousness. Horace (*Ep.* 1.17.36) calls it a town where only the tough survive. It was the Las Vegas of its time.

18:1

Luke introduces Priscilla and Aquila, tentmakers and/or leatherworkers from Rome (on such practices in Judaism, see Le Cornu and Shulam 2003: 982–83). They left Rome because of the edict of Claudius. This probably alludes to the decree in AD 49 that expelled Jews who created civil disturbances at the instigation of Chrestus (either a misspelled reference to Christ or an alternate spelling based on Latin pronunciation). The debate over Jesus had caused riots in the city, probably about whether Jesus was the Christ (Suetonius, *Claudius* 25).[2] Paulus Orosius,

18:2–3

2. Witherington 1998: 539–44 has a full discussion of the background of the decree. Fitzmyer 1998: 619 explains that Suetonius misunderstood *Christus* for *Chrestus* as the latter was the more common name.

a Christian writer of the fifth century, places the edict in the ninth year of Claudius's reign, giving us the date AD 49, a point most scholars accept (*Historiae adversum paganos* 7.6.15–16; Fitzmyer 1998: 620). Those who wish to place this decree in AD 41 on the basis of remarks by Dio Cassius (*Rom. Hist.* 60.6.6) fail to observe that the decree of AD 41 only prohibited Jews from gathering for meetings and explicitly said there was no expulsion. The decree of expulsion and the fact that they had to leave Rome may well suggest that the two were Christians while in Rome. They would have been among the estimated fifty thousand Jews living in Rome (Polhill 1992: 383). Aquila originally came from Pontus, near the Black Sea (on this couple, see Rom. 16:3–4; 1 Cor. 16:19; 2 Tim. 4:19). Priscilla was also known as Prisca. Luke uses Priscilla, the diminutive form of her name.

Paul and these two make an immediate connection because they share the same trade (τέχνη, *technē*). First Corinthians 4:12 refers to how Paul labored with his hands to earn a living (also 1 Thess. 2:9). They are tentmakers, which likely included working with leather in general, so that they can be considered leatherworkers (Michaelis, *TDNT* 7:393–94, speaks of primarily leatherwork, which also could include tents; Jervell 1998: 458). They are not weavers of goat hair as some suggest (correctly, Schneider 1982: 249; Larkin 1995: 262–63n). There was precedent for having such a trade among rabbis (*m. 'Abot* 2.2). Rabbis were not to profit from the study of Torah, nor were they to sit idle.

18:4   As is his pattern, Paul heads for the synagogue to debate and try to persuade Jews and Greeks on the Sabbath about Jesus. The imperfect ἔπειθεν (*epeithen*) is probably conative in force: "tried to persuade" (Moulton and Turner 1963: 65; HCSB). Philo mentions Jews in Corinth (*Embassy* 36 §281), and an inscription testifying to the presence of a synagogue survives (Weiser 1985: 490; *CII* §718). The inscription was found on the Lechaion Road, leading into the agora (Fitzmyer 1998: 626). It comes from a time just after that of Paul. The verb διαλέγομαι (*dialegomai*, debate) is common in the second part of Acts, where it refers either to giving a discourse or to debating, depending on the context (17:2, 17; 18:4, 19; 19:8–9; 20:7, 9; 24:12, 25). Its combination with the next verb suggests debate in the synagogue. The verb πείθω (*peithō*, persuade) is common in Acts, appearing seventeen times, but this is one of the few instances where it is used in an evangelistic context (17:4; 19:8, 26; 26:28; 28:23–24). Both verbs are in the imperfect, and so the discussion is portrayed as ongoing.

18:5–6   Silas and Timothy arrive from Macedonia as Paul begins to devote himself to preaching to the Jews that Jesus is the Christ. He may well have received support from Macedonia (2 Cor. 11:9; Phil. 4:15; Conzelmann 1987: 152). The verb συνείχετο (*syneicheto*) is imperfect and has an ingressive force (became "absorbed in" or "devoted to"). The verb can have the meaning of being "constrained" or "compelled" to do something (BDAG 971 §§6–7). The dative τῷ λόγῳ (*tō logō*) has the syntactical force of reference or respect: Paul devoted himself "with respect to" the word (Moulton and Turner 1963: 220).

The result is substantial opposition. The verb ἀντιτάσσομαι, *antitas-somai*) is used only here in Acts and can suggest organized opposition (Herodotus, *Hist.* 4.134). The reviling could refer either to Paul or to the subject of his message, Jesus. The word used here (βλασφημούντων, *blasphēmountōn*) can mean "blaspheme," "slander verbally." It appears sporadically in Acts (13:45; 18:6; 19:37; 26:11).

In a symbolic gesture, Paul shakes dust off his garments (Luke 10:11; Acts 13:51; Neh. 5:13). He also declares his opponents responsible and culpable for their actions: "Your blood be upon your heads!" (Josh. 2:19; Judg. 9:24; 2 Sam. 1:16; 1 Kings 2:33, 37; Ezek. 33:4–6; on blood guilt in the NT: Matt. 23:35; 27:25; Acts 5:28). His action depicts a break in fellowship and means that Paul is innocent of anything that takes place, which is why he says that he is clean, a remark suggesting that he is free to share with others since he has fulfilled his call to the nation (Acts 20:26). He has gone to the Jew first (Rom. 1:16). Paul then affirms that he will turn to the Gentiles, as he has earlier, in 13:47. This is not a complete abandonment of the Jews (18:19; 19:8; 28:17–24) but means that his efforts in Corinth will concentrate elsewhere.

18:7–8 Luke notes only two converts, Titius Justus, a God-fearer who lives next to the synagogue, and Crispus, a synagogue ruler who comes to faith with his entire household and was a man of some means. They are but two of many who believe and are baptized. The imperfects referring to believing and baptizing are iterative in force, so the two people mentioned are only a sample of the many who respond (Moulton and Turner 1963: 67). Crispus is noted in 1 Cor. 1:14 as one whom Paul baptized. Some scholars connect Titius to Gaius of Rom. 16:23 (Bruce 1988a: 350). This connection is not at all certain. His name does seem to indicate that he is a Roman citizen, in which case we have an exemplary Gentile and an exemplary Jew noted in these verses. The mention of Titius is the last mention of a God-fearer in Acts.

18:9–10 A vision from the Lord Jesus instructs Paul to stay and continue to preach, since the Lord will protect him from harm (Jervell 1998: 460). Some scholars question whether "the Lord" is a reference to God or to Jesus (Le Cornu and Shulam 2003: 1000), but in Acts such contact usually involves Jesus (Acts 9), and in the previous verse (v. 8) "the Lord" clearly refers to Jesus. So it is assumed that Jesus is in view here as well. The direction not to fear echoes numerous OT texts (Deut. 31:6; Josh. 1:6, 9; Isa. 41:10; 43:5; Jer. 1:8). He can go on proclaiming (present imperative) the word without concern for his safety. Three promises are made: (1) "I am with you," and (2) "no man shall harm you, for (3) I have many people in this city." So there will be pressure but also success in terms of response. The two uses of διότι (*dioti*) in verse 10 have a weak causal force (Moulton and Turner 1963: 318; BDF §400.8). The theme of God having a special people occurs in Acts 13:48 and 15:13–14. When Paul appears before Gallio, God is seen to have directed the events. Such reassurance appears elsewhere in Acts (23:11; 27:23–24).

18:11 Paul teaches the word of God in Corinth for eighteen months in response to the vision. Here the word of God again would be the gospel and all it entails.

18:12 While Gallio is proconsul, the Jews launch a united (ὁμοθυμαδόν, *homothymadon*) attack against Paul and bring him before the βῆμα (*bēma*) for judgment. This elevated judgment seat (some 7.5 feet high) was located on the south side of the agora. Scholars discuss whether the examination would take place here or whether the *bēma* refers to an unspecified private place of judgment (Williams 1990: 318; Barrett 1998: 871). Luke does not record any such detail, but a public meeting seems suggested by his description. Josephus (*Ant.* 19.5.3 §290) spells out Jewish privileges as set forth by an edict from Claudius. These included the right to observe ancestral customs and to worship their own God (Fitzmyer 1998: 629). The examination that follows is according to Roman procedure (Sherwin-White 1963: 99–107).

Gallio is a Roman proconsul about whom we have much information. He was a son of the orator Seneca the Elder (ca. 50 BC–ca. AD 40) and the elder brother of the Stoic philosopher Seneca the Younger (4 BC–AD 65). Although popular, he was also known to be anti-Semitic (Seneca, *Natural Questions* 4a.preface.11; Dio Cassius, *Rom. Hist.* 61.35; Tacitus, *Ann.* 15.73). Witherington (1998: 551) cites Seneca the Younger as describing the Jews as an "accursed race" (cited by Augustine, *City of God* 6.11; Le Cornu and Shulam 2003: 1010). Cicero (*Pro Flacco* 280.67–69) saw Jews as holding to a "barbaric superstition." So Rome tended to be anti-Semitic. He was not proconsul for long in Corinth; a fever forced him to leave early (Seneca, *Moral Ep.* 104.1). We can date his time there to AD 51–52, and so this incident in Acts is to be dated during this time period. It is one of the most solid dates in Acts. Winter has taken a careful look at Seneca's career and says that ancient sources show him to be a meticulous lawyer; so his legal judgment would be made with care.

18:13 The charge is that Paul is persuading men to worship against the law. The verb ἀναπείθω (*anapeithō*, persuade) is an NT hapax. It can refer to evil persuasion (Bruce 1990: 396; Jer. 29:8 [36:8 LXX]; 1 Macc. 1:11;

Herodotus, *Hist.* 3.148).[3] Paul's opponents are requesting Gallio to force Paul to leave the Jews alone. God is referred to in the singular. This may show that the concern is Jewish practice. Some scholars question the accuracy of the remarks because of this detail. They expect a plural reference about gods in speaking to a pagan ruler, since the topic is about what Paul is saying to all men, including Gentiles. But Jews are making the complaint, so a singular is appropriate.

Less clear is whether the reference to law is to Jewish law or to Roman civil law. It is unclear why the complaint would be about Jewish law, as this would not concern Gallio, and so the appeal may be that this new faith is not one Rome recognizes (Schneider 1982: 252n54). Witherington (1998: 552), however, sees Jewish law in view in light of Paul's activity and Gallio's response. Even with this sense, Witherington sees the possibility that to Roman ears the charge is about a legitimate faith. Williams (1990: 318) and Barrett (1998: 872) see the charge as similar to that in Philippi, trying to proselytize Romans, but this does not seem to be the concern, given Gallio's response. Either sense shows that the charge appears to be slightly different from other contexts in Acts. It accuses the new faith of not being a *collegium licitum*, or a legitimately recognized religion, without raising the issue of proselytes. Josephus discusses the acceptance Judaism enjoyed from the time of Alexander to Julius Caesar in *Ag. Ap.* 2.4 §§35–47, and an edict from Claudius allowed the Jews to worship (*Ant.* 19.5.3 §290). If the Jews have the right to worship but they complain that Paul's teaching is not their faith, then this faith must be illegitimate. This disturbance of the peace might therefore be something the proconsul wants to take care of, in the Jewish view. After all, it is his duty to keep the peace. Seen in this light, a reference to Jewish practice and law could be in view, as Witherington suggests. Luke raised the issue of new teaching in the account in Athens. Luke appears to follow up that point here with a challenge to the "new" faith, which a Roman ruler refuses to rule out of bounds.

Gallio does not let Paul speak but instead renders a verdict. In his judgment, there is no wrongdoing (ἀδίκημα, *adikēma*) or vicious, fraudulent crime (ῥᾳδιούργημα πονηρόν, *rhadiourgēma ponēron*). This is just a dispute about words, names, and Jewish law that he will let them settle, refusing to make a judgment. Both expressions for wrongdoing are rare in the NT (ἀδίκημα: Acts 18:14; 24:20; Rev. 18:5). The reference to "vicious" is a hapax and does not appear in the LXX, although a related term appears in Acts 13:10 (Harder, *TDNT* 6:558). The reference to names or titles may well allude to the claim that Jesus is the Christ. Fitzmyer (1998: 630) argues that the perspective is pre-Neronian, since

18:14–15

---

3. MM 37 quotes a papyrus from 200 BC (P.Magd. 14.3–4) in which a father complains that a courtesan induced his son to sign a bill for one thousand drachmas.

Nero distinguished Christians from Jews, a time frame that is consistent with Gallio's rule.

There is no judgment. It is outside the scope of the court, an examination or investigation "outside the rules" (*cognitio extra ordinem*, literally, "inquiry outside the order," a phrase that is rare in the actual documents), being only a debate over concepts (Sherwin-White 1963: 14, 102 has remarks about this category; Le Cornu and Shulam 2003: 1004–5). The Greek of verse 14 has a contrary-to-fact condition open the remark about whether there is a crime present (εἰ + ἦν, *ei* + *ēn*; BDF §360.4). So the text underscores that no crime has been committed. Luke is making clear that Christians are not a legal threat to Rome. Rome, as a matter of state policy, will not meddle in matters of religious practice by a particular group other than to determine whether a religion is legitimate and not contrary to state interests. The debate is over issues that reach back into Judaism and the Hebrew Scriptures. Gallio is seen as a fair, impartial judge of the matter, although his later indifference to Sosthenes' beating makes Luke's portrait more complex. There is an element of indifference and hastiness in Gallio that will be unlike later investigations, but the instinct that this new faith is not a threat to Rome and is about Jewish issues is correct, in Luke's view.

18:16 Gallio dismisses the accusers from the court, driving them out of the tribunal. This is an issue the Jews and the Christians must settle among themselves.

18:17 Some take matters into their own hands, however, seizing Sosthenes and beating him in front of the tribunal. Who is involved is not clear. This is vigilantism, about which Gallio does nothing. This is not a flattering picture of Roman rule.

Sosthenes is a ruler of a synagogue. If 1 Cor. 1:1 points to the same person, then this indicates Paul's effectiveness in Corinth (but Fitzmyer 1998: 630 sees Sosthenes as converted later). Others simply view this as Greeks seizing the accuser of Paul in an act of anti-Semitism (Schneider 1982: 253; Fitzmyer 1998: 633; Winter 2006: 304 as a likely scenario; also Hubbard 2005). In this case, Sosthenes is a Jew, not a believer, who tried to slander Paul. Sosthenes is a common name, so the name does not solve the problem or reveal the identity of who is beaten. Nowhere else in Acts do we have Luke concerned about strictly Jew-Gentile relations, which suggests that Sosthenes is a believer, but the choice is not clear (as Witherington 1998: 555 notes). Le Cornu and Shulam (2003: 1012) suggest an "internal Jewish affair, most likely connected with some form of 'Christian' involvement, with vital details missing which would help clarify the picture." So Sosthenes is likely either a believer or one who sympathized with or attempted to protect Christians. When the crowd breaks up after Gallio's ruling, Sosthenes is manhandled because of anti-Semitic feelings in the crowd, who would not distinguish between Jews and Christians. Regardless, Gallio shows his total indifference and does nothing. The ambivalence is not unlike the way Pilate handled Jesus. The account as a whole shows that Rome is going to stay out of the dispute, if possible. It will not rule for Christianity or against it. There is no real interest in Jewish affairs. Luke shows that the Roman government is not overly concerned about the situation.

In sum, this is another glimpse of Paul engaged in mission, making clear that Christianity is not a threat to the state, for it operates at a level of human promise, touching areas that a government cannot possibly meet. In a secular world where life is often viewed in terms of things and politics, this is an important reminder. There are issues of the heart that cannot be touched by legislation or government programs. As important as it is that our society operate in ways that lift up humanity, nothing lifts up society more than a community filled with people whose hearts are right before God. The irony is that the Roman rulers seem to sense the difference by refusing to take on Christianity as a legal matter or problem. They place it where it belongs, as an expression of faith that can be tolerated because it is not overtly political in its goals. Rome changed its view later and persecuted Christians, not because they were a real threat to the state but because their allegiance to God was seen as a competitor to allegiance to Caesar and the state. This also is a lesson for today. One should not confuse congregation and country. They are not the same. Christianity transcends the state because Christians come from every state and society and, most especially, because God is the Father of all of us, no matter which country we live in or what a country's style of government is.

Additional Notes

18:2–4, 6. There are numerous small variations in the Western text for these verses. Verse 2 contains a slightly different way of introducing Aquila and Priscilla as Priscilla comes *with* (σύν, *syn*) Aquila from Italy. There is the added note that they settle in Greece and become known to Paul. In verse 3, Aquila is said to be of the same tribe as Paul. In verse 4 they enter into the synagogue, where, in a discussion, Paul inserts the name of the Lord Jesus, persuading not only Jews but also Greeks. Some of this may be an effort to smooth out the original text (Metzger 1971: 460–61, who notes that some of these differences are part of a reconstruction by Ropes [1926] based on a version of the Itala and Syriac). In verse 6, opposition arises after much discussion and after interpretations of the Scriptures have been given. This is yet another clarifying addition.

Finally, more difficult to decide is the verb in verse 3. Is it ἠργάζετο (he worked) or ἠργάζοντο (they worked)? The first reading is found in $\mathfrak{P}^{74}$, ℵ^c, A, D, E, Ψ, 33, 1739, Byz, Lat, and Syr, while the second is found in ℵ*, B^c, and some Sahidic Coptic MSS (Barrett 1998: 864). The singular form is better attested.

18:7. Readings of Titus instead of Titius seem to be cases of using a more familiar name (Metzger 1971: 462–63).

18:12. The Western text expands, noting that the Jews talk among themselves, lay hands on Paul, and, crying out, bring him to the governor.

18:17. Many MSS (D, E, Ψ, 33, 1739, Byz) make clear that Greeks are responsible for this reaction to Sosthenes. Other MSS do not specify who is responsible; this is the more difficult reading ($\mathfrak{P}^{74}$, ℵ, A, B, Vulgate).

9. Back to Antioch and through the Region (18:18–23)

This summary narrative completes the second journey as Paul returns to Antioch after taking a vow (v. 18). A stop in Ephesus brings a request to stay, but he refuses, only promising to return if God permits (vv. 19–21). His return to Antioch is only for a time, before he heads out again to Galatia and Phrygia (vv. 22–23). Pauline sources would note such an itinerary (Fitzmyer 1998: 633).

Exegesis and Exposition

[18]After this Paul stayed many days longer, and then, taking leave of the brethren, he sailed for Syria with Priscilla and Aquila. At Cenchreae he cut his hair, for he had a vow. [19]And ⌜they⌝ came to Ephesus. And leaving them ⌜there⌝, he himself, coming into the synagogue, argued with the Jews. [20]When they asked him to stay for a longer period, he declined; [21]but taking leave of them, he said, "⌜ ⌝ I will return to you if God wills," and he set sail from Ephesus.

[22]And landing at Caesarea, going up and greeting the church, he then went down to Antioch. [23]After spending some time there, he departed and went from place to place through the region of Galatia and Phrygia, strengthening all the disciples.

18:18 With persecution again at work, Paul heads back to Syria by way of the Corinthian port, Cenchreae, which was located seven miles southeast of Corinth. A shrine to Isis was located there (Pausanius, *Descr.* 2.2.3; Schnabel 2004: 1197 estimates the population at 4,400). There he undertakes a vow and, as he moves to complete it, cuts his hair. It is not certain what kind of vow this is. Four views are prevalent. Two of them assume a Jewish background. (1) Plausibly, it may be a Nazirite vow (Num. 6:1–21). Or (2) it may be a mere vow of thanksgiving for preservation as God promised in verse 10 (Witherington 1998: 557; Bruce 1988a: 355 opts for a private vow). If this vow were Nazirite, then Paul for the duration would abstain from alcohol and uncleanness, such as touching a corpse. In addition, he would need to complete this vow by offering a sacrifice in Jerusalem, assuming that he is following the law and tradition on this matter (Jervell 1998: 465–66). It is also possible to cut the hair before offering the sacrifice to denote the vow's end (*m. Naz.* 3.6; 5.4; Josephus, *J.W.* 2.15.1 §§309–14 relates a vow made in Jerusalem; Marshall 1980: 300; Polhill 1992: 390; Johnson 1992: 330).

(3) A third option assumes a Greek background. Barrett (1998: 877–78) notes that sailors sometimes shaved after surviving a tough journey (citing Juvenal, *Satires* 12.81–82). (4) A fourth option argues that this is a Lukan insertion, rejecting the historicity of the act. This view thinks it unlikely that Paul would have agreed to such a vow and argues that the practice of cutting the hair outside Jerusalem for a Nazirite vow was not possible (Weiser 1985: 497–98; Schneider 1982: 255). Since, however, 1 Cor. 9:20 explains that Paul was a Jew to the Jews, such a vow, if a Jewish practice, was not out of character for him in certain circumstances. In addition, the Mishnah, as already noted, allows the hair to be cut before the sacrifice is made. It seems more likely that Paul acts out of his Jewish heritage rather than following Greek practice. So probably a private vow is more likely than a Nazirite vow. At any rate, whether a Jewish or a Greek practice, the act is not at all unlikely.

18:19–21 Paul then travels to Ephesus and the synagogue, arguing his case for Jesus (on διαλέγομαι, *dialegomai*, argue, see 18:4). Ephesus was an important city, as it had long been the home of the shrine of Artemis, one of the major pagan goddesses. It also was a great commercial city. The shrine was one of the seven wonders of the world. Ephesus sat at the mouth of the Cayster River and was on the main trade route east from Rome; it was the major trade center in Asia Minor north and west of the Taurus Range (Strabo, *Geogr.* 14.1.24; see Levinskaya 1995: 137–52 for a host of inscriptions found there; Schnabel 2004: 1206–11). The city was strategically located: one could hardly see it from any angle until arriving there, because the local hills shielded it from view. Today it constitutes the largest "outside ancient museum" in Turkey, with a full layout of the ancient city and theater. Trebilco (1994: 302–57) has a detailed discussion of Ephesus, including its history, its strategic role, and the lecture hall there as well as its reputation for healing, magic, the Artemis cult with its temple and influence, the role of silversmiths, the Romans in the city, their attitude toward riots, the theater, the town clerk, the myth of the falling stone, and the role of the courts. Trebilco (1994: 332, 342) notes how the townspeople's zeal for Artemis's honor in Acts 19 is in keeping with this background, as is the scene of the silversmiths' defense of the goddess. A free city, Ephesus had its own senate and assembly. It was the capital of the Roman province of Asia. Many Jews lived there, in part because of legal privileges defending Jewish rights granted by a partisan of Julius Caesar in 44 BC and confirmed by Augustus (Josephus, *Ant.* 14.10.12 §§225–27; 16.6.2–4 §§162–68; 16.6.7 §§172–73). Its population was estimated at the time to be a quarter of a million, one of the largest cities of the empire. It will be Paul's missionary center for his third journey. The Artemis cult, which had its center here, was an "expansionist" religion (Trebilco 1994: 336).

Paul will not remain long in Ephesus (v. 20), as he wishes to return to Antioch and visit the churches he has ministered to earlier (vv. 22–23). His haste is probably due to a wish to reach Jerusalem for the Passover festival, as some MSS explicitly indicate (see additional note on 18:21), before the sea traffic stops for the winter. If Paul waited until after winter, the window for travel to reach Jerusalem for Passover would be short. Only a handful of days in March were open for sailing on this route, since sailing did not start until March 10 and Passover was in early April (Vegetius, *On Military Affairs* 4.39; Bruce 1990: 399; Witherington 1998: 558). Thus Paul refuses to stay on in Ephesus, though promising to return "if God wills" (τοῦ θεοῦ θέλοντος, *tou theou thelontos*; James 4:15; an expression among Greeks as well, Plato, *Phaedo* 80D; MM 286; Johnson 1992: 330). The remark about Paul leaving Priscilla and Aquila alludes to his departing Ephesus and leaving them behind to watch over the new labor there, as Acts 18:24–28 shows. The church meets in their home (1 Cor. 16:19). Luke will have Paul return to Ephesus in Acts 19:1.

Paul returns briefly to Antioch in Syria besides making a few other   **18:22-23** stops. In this compact text, he goes down to Caesarea and then goes up and greets the church (τὴν ἐκκλησίαν, *tēn ekklēsian*), which suggests a trip to Jerusalem (Fitzmyer 1998: 635). Next he goes down to Antioch. Then Paul leaves on what will be his third missionary journey, starting in Galatia and Phrygia, where his first or second journey took him. Luke summarizes a fifteen-hundred-mile journey here. Which locale is meant depends on which Galatia is referred to, as was noted earlier. I prefer a trip to the first missionary journey's region, described in Acts 13–14 (Marshall 1980: 302; see discussion at 16:6). As is his custom (14:22), Paul returns to strengthen the disciples.

In sum, Paul continues to be directed by God's will as he makes his plans, remaining flexible in how he will proceed, depending on that leading. As he travels, he also continues to minister with a concern for those he has served.

Paul's Second Missionary Journey

City	Region
Antioch	Syria
unnamed cities	Cilicia
Derbe	Lycaonia
Lystra	Lycaonia
unnamed city	opposite Mysia
Troas	Mysia
unnamed city	Samothrace
Neapolis	Macedonia
Philippi	Macedonia
Amphipolis	Macedonia
Apollonia	Macedonia

City	Region
Thessalonica	Macedonia
Beroea	Macedonia
Athens	Achaia
Corinth	Achaia
Cenchreae	Achaia
Ephesus	Lydia
Caesarea	Judea
Jerusalem (probably)	Judea
Antioch	Syria

Additional Notes

18:19. To conform to the other singular verbs in the context, $\mathfrak{P}^{74}$, Ψ, and Byz read a singular "he" coming to Ephesus, not the plural "they," which is the harder reading and likely original here. The issue of the more difficult reading also applies to the use of ἐκεῖ (*ekei*) rather than αὐτοῦ (*autou*) as an adverb in the verse, since the adverbial use of the latter term is rare. The more common ἐκεῖ is attested in $\mathfrak{P}^{74}$, ℵ, A, D, and 33.

18:21. The Western text adds Paul's rationale, namely, that he must keep the feast in Jerusalem, as he says also in 20:16 and, in the Western tradition, as recorded in 19:1.

B. The Third Missionary Journey, Ending in Jerusalem (18:24–21:16)

Paul launches out on what is often called his third journey, which would take place in the mid-50s. He revisits sites associated with his initial journey. In a sense, however, this is not a journey: once Paul reaches Ephesus, he stays there for some time. Paul works long and hard to plant a solid community there. He will stay for more than two years. The unit's major incident occurs here as the Ephesians react when the commerce associated with the goddess Artemis is affected and magic books are burned. Also an exorcism makes a deep impression. Toward the end of the unit, Paul directs the Ephesian elders to exercise careful oversight of their community. Then he returns to Jerusalem, where he will be arrested and begin his long trip to Rome. Paul is warned of what he will face there and goes nevertheless (Acts 20:22–23; 21:4, 11–14). Paul will trust in the Lord in the midst of his suffering. Gaventa (2003: 262) discusses the reemerging themes of the journey: concern for believers already visited, preaching in the synagogues and the resulting conflict, miracles, and confrontation with magic.

1. Backdrop to Ephesus: Apollos (18:24–28)

Luke sets the stage for Paul's trip to Ephesus with a cameo scene including Apollos, Priscilla, and Aquila. Apollos preaches in the synagogue with only knowledge of John's baptism (vv. 24–25). Priscilla and Aquila correct him, bringing him up to date (v. 26). Apollos moves on to Achaia, bringing with him a letter of commendation. There he strengthens the believers and presents Jesus as the Christ to the Jews (vv. 27–28). The scene shows how Priscilla and Aquila help in Ephesus and that solid work is being done by others beyond Paul. In addition, some minister but need more instruction about details of the new faith. Instruction about the Spirit and the work of indwelling is still needed for some. This reference to the Spirit links this account to Acts 19:1–7, where the disciples of John the Baptist face the same problem. The promise is about Jesus and the Spirit he makes available.

The narrative summary may well reflect tradition from Priscilla and Aquila or from other Ephesian sources (Barrett 1998: 886; Witherington 1998: 562; Jervell 1998: 472), although Fitzmyer (1998: 637) speaks of Pauline sources, which are also possible and may also include Priscilla and Aquila. Trebilco (2004: 121) argues that local sources were also used and that the story is credible, being confirmed by affirmations of Apollos in Pauline passages, such as 1 Cor. 3:6–9; 16:12, making clear that he is not an opponent (contra Käsemann 1964a: 136–48 and Haenchen 1963: 566, "Apollos was, therefore, no Paulinist"). Haenchen's claim that 1 Corinthians gives no support or affirmation to Apollos ignores the fact that the epistle has both Apollos and Paul build on the same foundation. Here is no sense of separation but rather identification. Trebilco refutes the "Apollos as opponent" view in detail.

Exegesis and Exposition

[24]Now a certain Jew named Apollos, a native of Alexandria, came to Ephesus. He was an eloquent man, well versed in the Scriptures. [25]He was instructing in the way of the Lord; and being fervent in spirit, he was speaking and teaching accurately the things concerning Jesus, though he knew only the baptism of John. [26]He began to speak boldly in the synagogue; but ⌜Priscilla and Aquila⌝, upon hearing him, took him and expounded to him the way of God more accurately. [27]⌜ ⌝ And when he wished to cross to Achaia, the brethren encouraged him and

wrote to the disciples to receive him. Upon arriving, he greatly helped those who through grace had believed, ²⁸for he powerfully confuted the Jews in public, demonstrating by the Scriptures that the Christ was Jesus.

The scene shifts back to Ephesus and to an insightful preacher, born   **18:24–25**
in Alexandria, named Apollos (1 Cor. 1:12; 3:4–6, 22; 4:6; 16:12). Paul uses the short form of his name, which would have been Apollonius. Literally, the phrase "a learned man" (ἀνὴρ λόγιος, *anēr logios*) refers to someone who is eloquent or well educated. Alexandria was the Roman seat in Egypt. It was one of the larger cities of the empire and had a large Jewish population, occupying all of one of the five districts of the city and the majority of a second district (Philo, *Flaccus* 8 §55; Josephus, *Ant.* 14.7.2 §117; Le Cornu and Shulam 2003: 1027–30 have a full discussion of the city and the relationship of its Jews with Jerusalem). It was also well known for its educational opportunities and as a place of philosophical reflection (Let. Arist. 301–21; Johnson 1992: 331). The Jewish philosopher Philo was from there. Apollos is well versed in the Scriptures, which probably means that he understands how the Scriptures make promises about the Christ (vv. 25, 28).

Apollos is instructed in the way of the Lord (τὴν ὁδὸν τοῦ κυρίου, *tēn hodon tou kyriou*). This is probably a reference to his knowing the way to God and doing God's will (Exod. 32:8; Deut. 5:33; Jer. 7:23; 1QS 8.13; Jervell 1998: 470). He knows about God's work of salvation through Jesus and God's plan tied to it.

He also is "fervent in spirit" (ζέων τῷ πνεύματι, *zeōn tō pneumati*). Τῷ πνεύματι is syntactically a dative of reference or respect: Apollos is fervent with respect to the Spirit/spirit (Moulton and Turner 1963: 220). The description of someone as fervent means that the person is enthusiastic, excited, or "on fire" (BAGD 337; BDAG 426; "talked . . . with great enthusiasm," NLT). The term literally means "boiling" or "seething" (Josephus, *Ant.* 13.12.6 §345). It is often used in a positive context about emotions, as here. The only two NT uses are here and in Rom. 12:11.

There are two views on the meaning of the reference to Apollos being fervent in "Spirit/spirit." The options reflect the ambiguity of the term πνεῦμα (*pneuma*). (1) Is this a reference only to Apollos's emotions? So argues Larkin (1995: 270–71), who also sees him as unregenerate at this point. Schneider (1982: 261) likewise sees him as a Jewish follower of Jesus but not yet a Christian. If the term has this sense, then Apollos preaches with "great enthusiasm" (NET). The idea that Apollos is not a believer is not tied to this reading, however. If he is not portrayed as a believer, then this is how the expression should be read, but the expression in this sense also simply could describe the emotion Apollos brings to his message, without questioning his spiritual status. (2) Or should we see it as an allusion to the work of the Spirit in Apollos's life? Against this is his lack of knowledge of the baptism of the Spirit, but in favor of it is the fact that the expression includes the article, so that the description can be read as "fervent in the Spirit." The expression is parallel in wording to Rom. 12:11, where it clearly describes Christians. Marshall (1980: 303–4) notes a variety of reasons why Apollos would not yet know about the Spirit's baptism, as he refutes Käsemann's view (1964a) that Apollos is seen as dangerous because of his lack of instruction. If the phrase means "fervent in the Spirit," then Luke would be indicating that Apollos is gifted by the Spirit in his ability to preach effectively (Bruce 1990: 402; Barrett 1998: 888).

Regardless of how one interprets the phrase, Larkin's view of an unregenerate Apollos does not seem to square with the other description of Apollos as one who teaches accurately the things concerning Jesus. Nothing about the way Priscilla and Aquila instruct Apollos gives one the sense that he has yet to believe or repent, which is how Luke describes conversion. Especially important here is that there is no mention of baptism for Apollos, which Luke often mentions when one comes into the community. In all likelihood, given Apollos's lack of awareness of the Spirit, the expression is not a technical term but refers to Apollos as an effective preacher. If the Spirit is referred to, then the description would also be ironic, as Apollos would be seen as directed by God's Spirit, concerning whom he also needs instruction. This is possible but not likely. So "fervent in spirit" is the more likely reading here (Jervell 1998: 470). What is also clear is that Apollos speaks as a believer.

Apollos teaches about Jesus accurately but knows only of John's baptism. This lack of knowledge has created much discussion among commentators. Is Apollos really a Christian at this point (Witherington 1998: 564–66 has a full discussion)? The likely answer, as already suggested, is yes, despite the gap in his knowledge. At the least, the expression "fervent in spirit/the Spirit," even if it points only to enthusiasm, is positive. The fact that he speaks about Jesus accurately is unlikely to be said of a non-Christian who preaches. Apollos is a figure caught in transition who ministers in the Diaspora and thus needs to be brought up to date. His preaching is not inaccurate, merely incomplete (Williams 1990: 324 describes him as a "Christian of sorts"). Acts 10:45–46 shows that one can have the Spirit without being baptized, since God sovereignly distributes the Spirit in response to faith. Apollos is easily brought up to date when Priscilla and Aquila speak with him. They inform him of the Way "more accurately," where ἀκριβέστερον (akribesteron, v. 26) is a comparative used as an elative with an adverbial force (Moulton and Turner 1963: 30; Culy and Parsons 2003: 357). Apollos now understands better than before the full benefits offered in salvation, especially as it relates to the Spirit of God. Certainly the commendation of him to Achaia tells us that the church does not have any concerns after the time of additional instruction.

The action begins with Apollos speaking boldly in the synagogue, a description echoing an earlier one of Paul's preaching (9:27–28). Priscilla and Aquila take him aside and explain to him the way of God more accurately. The verb used here (ἐκτίθημι, *ektithēmi*) means "explain carefully," "fill someone in on something" (BAGD 245 §2; BDAG 310 §2). This verb appears only in Acts, where three of the occurrences have this sense (18:26; 28:23; 11:4; 7:21 has the verb's other sense of "abandon" or "expose" something [in this case, children in the exodus]). Here both Priscilla and Aquila update Apollos on baptism, moving him beyond John's baptism, probably to the gift of the Spirit, telling Apollos that the Spirit has come and acquainting him with the importance of the arrival of this eschatological promise (see 2:16–36; 19:2). Apollos now has a more accurate understanding of the gospel than before. Priscilla and Aquila must teach him but do so sensitively in private. The unit shows that not all who ministered in this early period had the full story of what God had done and yet they were effective as well as open to instruction.

18:26

Apollos desires to minister in Achaia and is encouraged to do so. This region was to the west, across the Aegean Sea (Schnabel 2004: 1169). It became a senatorial province in AD 44. Corinth and Athens were located there, in what is now southern Greece. It included cities such as Sparta and Delphi as well. Given that Paul left there long before, Apollos would be of benefit to the church there. Thus the church writes to commend him to the believers there. Romans 16:1–2 is an example of such a commendation, and the letter of Acts 15:23–29 serves a similar function (also 2 Cor. 3 alludes to such a letter). Once Apollos arrives there, he benefits and encourages those who believe, for he also goes to the synagogue and argues that the Christ is Jesus. Indeed, Luke points to his effectiveness by saying that Apollos "refuted" (διακατηλέγχετο, *diakatēlencheto*) the Jews in public. This compares favorably with Paul's public ministry as noted in 20:20. This strong verb appears only here in the NT. It means "overwhelm" someone in argument (BAGD 184; BDAG 229). Scholars discuss whether the reference to God's grace refers to those who believe through grace (so RSV) or means that Apollos helps through God's grace, which is grammatically possible. The position of grace at the end of verse 27, next to the mention of belief, slightly favors the first option (Barrett 1998: 890).

18:27–28

This brief portrait helps us to appreciate why Paul sees Apollos as a colleague in 1 Cor. 1–4 (esp. 3:9, they are fellow workers of God). They will also cross paths in Ephesus, according to 1 Cor. 16:12, where Paul reports he has urged him to come to Corinth later.

In sum, this unit shows how growth can occur in the church. Priscilla and Aquila minister to and encourage Apollos in his new ministry. They instruct him. Apollos, for his part, is open to their instruction. Thus these ministers encourage each other in a task they know they share. They are aware that it is a task bigger than any one of them. This encouragement even extends to letters of recommendation so that people will be more likely to receive what he is saying. This kind of mutual cooperation and encouragement in pursuit of a theologically faithful ministry enables the church to carry out its mission. Apollos ministers even though he has more to learn. On the other hand, Priscilla and Aquila encourage him to grow even as they recognize that he is an effective minister.

Additional Notes

18:26. The Western text and numerous other later MSS shift the order of Priscilla and Aquila, so that he is first. The older MSS read the reverse order ($\mathfrak{P}^{74}$, ℵ, A, B, E, 33).

18:27. The Western text is expanded, reporting that the Corinthians persuade Apollos to come to Achaia.

2. In Ephesus (19:1–41)

This scene recounts Paul's final missionary swing through the Greco-Roman world. In Ephesus Paul has a face-to-face encounter with Greco-Roman religion. The scene begins with him bringing some believers from John the Baptist into a full knowledge of the work of the Spirit and baptizing them. Paul's work is confirmed by their speaking in tongues and giving prophecy (vv. 1–7). Next, Paul goes to the synagogue, as is his custom. There he makes the case for the kingdom of God over a three-month period. He also meets with strong rejection and so moves to the hall of Tyrannus to make his case to the city. He remains in the city for two years (vv. 8–11). During this time, the sons of Sceva, itinerant Jewish exorcists, try to invoke Jesus's name in their exorcisms, only to be rebuked by an evil spirit and attacked. The event makes a deep impression on those in Ephesus (vv. 12–17). In addition, many who come to faith burn their books on the magic arts (vv. 18–20). Luke is showing the great impact of faith on the lifestyle of those who believe. Paul is planning to move on to Jerusalem and Rome, and so he sends for Timothy and Erastus (vv. 21–22). Before he leaves, however, the city reacts. Many Ephesians become concerned about the economic impact of "the Way" and the affront to Artemis, the goddess of the city. Demetrius, who makes silver shrines to the goddess, tells the city that the tradesmen may lose their livelihood if things continue like this. His action stirs up a crowd and leads those present to praise the goddess. Only the town clerk's insistence that they should bring their complaints legally or else face Roman reaction brings calm to the crowd (vv. 23–41).

The entire scene powerfully presents the impact of the new faith when fully embraced. For believers, lives are transformed. Societal structures are challenged through those changed lives, not by force on others, but by their own personal lifestyle changes. The reaction is negative, however, among many of those who do not embrace it. Here it is Greeks, not Jews, who react negatively to the threat to their religious practice. The commerce that goes with their Greco-Roman faith is seen to be especially at risk. So we have, in effect, four scenes: Paul with the disciples of the Baptist (vv. 1–7), Paul's ministry and the confrontation with the Jewish exorcists (vv. 8–20), Paul's travel plans (vv. 21–22), and the demonstration by the Ephesians on behalf of Artemis (vv. 23–41). Bruce (1988a: 373) compares the scenes to a lecture with slides, moving from one vivid event to another.

Luke's choice of material is again selective. We know that there was much suffering in Ephesus (1 Cor. 15:32 [Paul speaks of fighting wild animals in Ephesus; that is, he fought for his life there]; 2 Cor. 1:8; 4:9–12; 6:4–10), possibly an imprisonment (2 Cor. 11:23; Williams 1990: 328), and that Paul also made a quick trip to Corinth (2 Cor. 12:14; 13:1).

The event, told in rich detail, is rooted in Pauline (Fitzmyer 1998: 641, 646, 655) or local Ephesian sources (Pesch 1986b: 178; Barrett 1998: 886, 901, 917; Jervell 1998: 878, 485). Schille (1983: 376) sees it as a Lukan formulation, as does Johnson (1992: 342–43), on the basis that these "typical" events are not sufficiently unique or specific to be authentic. But Luke often notes patterns of reaction and moves to a scene that details what has been portrayed in more general terms elsewhere. So the typical nature of these events does not speak against their historicity. The appeal to typical events also fails to note that here the key reaction is from Gentiles on their own, not from Jews or from Gentiles incited by Jews. The sources are more likely local and Pauline. Trebilco (2004: 130–32) shows that the scene involving John the Baptist's disciples is credible in terms of its background (also see mention in our introduction to 18:24–28 of Trebilco defending the credibility of the accounts). Trebilco (2004: 104–96) has a detailed treatment of the entire Ephesian cycle in Acts and defends its fundamental historical credibility.[1] Schnabel (2004: 1121–1231), who considers about eight different theories that question Luke's presentation in this chapter, finds them all wanting.

The passage shows how the Pauline mission worked to include those who have responded but still have something to learn. Luke also reinforces the idea that John the Baptist prepared the way for Jesus. The baptism that counts is the one based on the name of Jesus and representing the Spirit's coming. The washing pictures new life that comes from the Spirit (vv. 4–5). The scene further legitimates Paul as God's servant and the faith he proclaims in the face of opposition from Jewish (sons of Sceva) and Greco-Roman (conflict over Artemis) worldviews. The section also represents Paul's longest sustained ministry in one area in Acts, showing what a mission in a given locale might look like (Witherington 1998: 572–73). In this sense, it is not a typical Lukan scene with respect to Luke's portrait of Paul, because of the variety of detail presented. Only the scene in Philippi, with its multiple events (exorcism plus the prison episode and the conversion

---

1. See Trebilco 2004: 152 ("A strong case can be put that there is an historical basis for Luke's account of Paul's success in Ephesus"), 157 (studies argue for the credibility of the local coloring of the riot scene; especially important here is the marginal role of Paul in the story, something unlikely if the story were invented), 163 (speaking of the riot scene, he says, "We conclude that objections to the historicity of the event are unconvincing").

of the jailer's family) is similar in detail. Trebilco (2004: 155–56) notes these key Lukan themes: (1) the success of Paul's work in Ephesus in the context of Artemis worship portrays the superiority of Christianity over cultic worship; (2) Christianity is not a threat to the Roman order; (3) Paul has some friends in high social places who are not Christians (part of the "no threat" argument); and (4) Christianity's superiority to paganism leads to opposition to Paul that is weak and confused. The net result is that Christianity is superior to paganism and will prove victorious in the end.

Exegesis and Exposition

¹⌐While Apollos was at Corinth,⌐ Paul passed through the upper country and came to Ephesus and found some disciples. ²And he said to them, "Did you receive the Holy Spirit when you believed?" And they said, "No, we have never even heard that ⌐there is⌐ a Holy Spirit." ³And he said, "Into what, then, were you baptized?" They said, "Into John's baptism." ⁴And Paul said, "John baptized with the baptism of repentance, saying to the people to believe in the one who was to come after him, that is, Jesus." ⁵On hearing this, they were baptized in the name of the Lord Jesus. ⁶And when Paul had laid his hands upon them, the Holy Spirit came on them; and they began speaking with tongues and prophesied. ⁷There were about twelve of them in all.

⁸And entering the synagogue, over a period of three months ⌐ ⌐ he spoke boldly, arguing and persuading about the kingdom of God. ⁹But some hardened themselves and disbelieved, speaking evil of the Way before the congregation. So, withdrawing from them, he took the disciples with him, each day arguing in the hall of Tyrannus. ¹⁰This continued for two years, so that all the residents of Asia heard the word of the Lord, both Jews and Greeks.

¹¹And God did extraordinary miracles by the hands of Paul, ¹²so that handkerchiefs or aprons were carried away from his body to the sick, and diseases left them and the evil spirits came out of them. ¹³Then some of the itinerant Jewish exorcists undertook to pronounce the name of the Lord Jesus over those who had evil spirits, saying, "I adjure you by the Jesus whom Paul preaches." ¹⁴There were seven sons of a Jewish chief priest named Sceva ⌐doing this⌐. ¹⁵But the evil spirit answered them, "Jesus ⌐ ⌐ I know, and Paul I am acquainted with; but who are you?" ¹⁶And leaping on them and mastering ⌐all of them⌐, the man with the evil spirit overpowered them, so that they fled out of that house naked and wounded. ¹⁷And this became known to all residents of Ephesus, both Jews and Greeks; and fear fell upon them all; and the name of the Lord Jesus was extolled. ¹⁸Many also of those who were now believers came, confessing and divulging their magic spells. ¹⁹And a number of those who practiced magic arts, bringing their books together, burned them in the sight of all; and they counted the value of them and found it came to

fifty thousand pieces of silver. [20]So ⌜the word of the Lord mightily grew and became strong⌝.

[21]Now after these events Paul resolved in the Spirit to pass through Macedonia and Achaia and go to Jerusalem, saying, "After I have been there, I must also see Rome." [22]And having sent into Macedonia two of his helpers, Timothy and Erastus, he himself stayed in Asia for a while.

[23]About that time there arose no little stir concerning the Way. [24]For a man named Demetrius, a silversmith, making replica silver temples to Artemis, brought no little business to the craftsmen. [25]Gathering together with the workmen of like occupation, he said, "Men, you know that from this business we have our wealth. [26]And you see and hear that not only at Ephesus but almost throughout all Asia this Paul has persuaded and turned away a considerable company of people, saying that the gods made with hands are not gods. [27]And there is danger not only that this trade of ours may come into disrepute but also that the temple of the great goddess Artemis may be reckoned for nothing, and that she may even be deposed from her magnificence, she whom all Asia and the world worship."

[28]Upon hearing this, they became full of rage and cried out, "Great is Artemis of the Ephesians!" [29]So the city was filled with confusion; and they rushed together into the theater, dragging with them Gaius and Aristarchus, Macedonians who were Paul's companions in travel. [30]Paul was desiring to go in among the crowd, but the disciples were not letting him; [31]some of the Asiarchs also, who were friends of his, sending to him, were urging him not to venture into the theater. [32]Now some cried one thing, some another; for the assembly was in chaos, and most of them did not know why they had come together. [33]Some of the crowd prompted Alexander, whom the Jews had put forward. And Alexander, motioning with his hand, wished to make a defense to the people.[34]But when the crowd recognized that he was a Jew, for about two hours they all with one voice cried out, "Great is Artemis of the Ephesians!" [35]And quieting the crowd, the town clerk said, "Men of Ephesus, what man is there who does not know that the city of the Ephesians is temple keeper of the great Artemis and of the sacred stone that fell from the sky? [36]Seeing, then, that these things cannot be contradicted, you ought to be quiet and do nothing rash.[37]For you have brought these men here who are neither sacrilegious nor blasphemers of our goddess. [38]If therefore Demetrius and the craftsmen with him have a complaint against anyone, the courts are open, and there are proconsuls; let them bring charges against one another. [39]But if you seek anything further, it shall be settled in the regular assembly. [40]For we are risking being charged with rioting today, ⌜there being no cause that we can give⌝ to justify this commotion." [41]And when he had said this, he dismissed the assembly.

19:1–5   While Apollos is in Corinth, Paul takes the upper-country route westward to Ephesus, a probable reference to traveling through the Cayster River valley rather than by way of Colossae and Laodicea (on Ephesus, see the discussion on 18:19–21). Paul comes to Ephesus and meets some disciples who do not know that the Spirit has come and who have only had John's baptism. There is scholarly debate about whether these are believers. Most commentators understand disciples as being disciples of Jesus here, but Witherington (1998: 570) argues that they are not believers, given their lack of the Spirit, just as he argued in the case of Apollos. Witherington argues that for Luke, if one is without the Spirit, then one is not a Christian (so also Marshall 1980: 305, citing John 3:5; Acts 11:17; Rom. 8:9; 1 Cor. 12:3; Gal. 3:2; 1 Thess. 1:5–6; Titus 3:5; Heb. 6:4; 1 Pet. 1:2; 1 John 3:24; 4:13; Schneider 1982: 263). Polhill (1992: 399) notes that "disciples" can refer to John's followers (Luke 5:33; 7:18–19). Witherington's option could well be right.

The impression of verse 2 and its mention of their believing, however, is that their instruction is incomplete, not that Jesus is not a part of it at all. We are caught in the special situation of a transition here. Larkin (1995: 273) summarizes well—they are "at best nominal Christians and at worst simply disciples of John." These disciples need "finishing" in their understanding but have embraced Jesus, or else belief likely would not be mentioned. Paul discovers their situation when he inquires about whether they received the Spirit when they believed. The text seems clear they have come to faith in Jesus (πιστεύσαντες, *pisteusantes*), so their problem is like that of Apollos, knowing about Jesus but not the work of the Spirit that is also a part of the promise. Those who see unbelievers here maintain that Paul is using the language of appearances in speaking about belief.

The text says that these disciples have never heard of the Spirit. This probably does not mean that the disciples of John do not know that the Spirit exists, since this is a common Jewish concept and John the Baptist discussed the coming of the Spirit (Luke 3:15–16). Rather, it means that they have not heard that the Spirit of God has come (Williams 1990: 330). Fitzmyer (1998: 643) argues for a reference to Gentile followers of John the Baptist who may not know about the Spirit at all, but it is not clear how any follower of John would not know about the Spirit, given the eschatological nature of John's message. In fact, in verse 4, Paul makes the point that John the Baptist told his disciples to look for Jesus, the very point Luke 3:15–16 suggests, without naming Jesus, by saying that the Messiah will baptize with the Spirit. That the Messiah brings the Spirit is a point Luke often makes (Luke 24:49; Acts 1:4–5; 2:16–36; 11:15–16; 13:25 alludes to the start of John's saying; 15:8 alludes back to 11:15–16).

Paul indicates the close connection between the Spirit and baptism by asking what baptism they experienced. They have had only the baptism of John. Paul explains that since John performed a baptism of repentance (Mark 1:4; Luke 3:3, 8; Acts 10:37; 13:24–25), he told his disciples to believe in the one who was to come after him (Luke 3:15–17;

7:18–23). In the Synoptics John the Baptist described only what would point to the Messiah, but in John's Gospel he testifies that Jesus is the one (John 1:29–34; Bruce 1990: 407). The disciples are baptized in the name of Jesus after hearing this message about the Spirit (Acts 2:38–39; 22:16). In Acts, this is the only case of a second baptism, where Christian baptism follows John's baptism.

19:6–7 Paul lays hands on them after their baptism with the result that the Spirit descends, so that they began to prophesy and speak in tongues (2:4; 8:17; 10:45–46; the imperfects here are inceptive). This is the final mention of tongues in Acts (2:2–4, 9–11, 26–27; 10:45–46; 19:5–6). The association of tongues and prophecy is like Acts 2. This special distribution confirms that the Spirit has come and shows how John's disciples are completed in their faith, pointing to the fact that John did point to Jesus. This is the one locale where Paul bestows the Spirit in a manner much as the apostles have done in Acts 8. This action indicates the importance of Paul's work by paralleling it to that of Peter and John. This scene together with the last one shows how Paul and those tied to him instruct the church more deeply in the way of God. In this way, it legitimates his mission and teaching (Gaventa 2003: 266).

There is no pattern in how the Spirit comes in Acts. The Spirit can come before or after baptism, as Acts 10 shows.

About twelve disciples are baptized. There is no symbolism in the number, especially given the estimation (correctly, Williams 1990: 331; Jervell 1998: 477). Johnson (1992: 338) sees it as pointing to Israel. It is the twelve apostles, however, who point to Israel.

19:8–10 Paul spends three months in the synagogue, arguing and persuading about the kingdom of God (8:12; 20:25; 28:23, 31; persuade, 17:4; 18:4; argue, 17:2, 17; 18:4, 19). As Luke often notes, Paul speaks boldly (2:29; 4:13, 29, 31; 9:27–28; 13:46; 14:3; 18:26). The term "kingdom of God" is another way that Luke presents Paul's case for Jesus as the Messiah who fulfills promise (18:5, 19). Marshall (1980: 309) says that Paul preaches Jesus and the kingdom. For Paul, the two are bound up together in the gospel.

Paul finds the audience stubborn and disbelieving, speaking evil of the Way (13:45; 18:6; on the expression "the Way," see 9:1–2). The verb σκληρύνω (sklērynō), often rendered "stubborn," actually means "be hardened" to something; it speaks of stubbornness when it comes to emotions (BAGD 756 §2; BDAG 930). The expression appears in the OT regarding Pharaoh (Exod. 8:15; 9:35) and of the people in the wilderness (Deut. 2:30). It is rarely used in the NT but always with this same force (Heb. 3:8, 13, 15; 4:7; Rom. 9:18). In this scene the verb is in the middle voice (ἐσκληρύνοντο, esklērynonto), "they hardened themselves." The term κακολογέω (kakologeō, revile) is a general one for speaking evil of someone. It is the only instance of this term in Acts (in the NT:

Matt. 15:4; Mark 7:10; 9:39–40; Acts 19:9). The threefold response of hardening, unbelief, and speaking evil indicates complete rejection of Paul's message.

So Paul withdraws with his disciples. The reference to disciples indicates that there has been some success in the synagogue, but the rise of strong opposition (perhaps because of this limited success?) means that it is time to move on, so Paul takes his case to the hall of Tyrannus. This is either a lecture hall or a school building, as the term σχολῇ (*scholē*) indicates (Fitzmyer 1998: 648; Plutarch, *Alexander* 7.3; Epictetus, *Discourses* 3.21.11; Johnson 1992: 339). Tyrannus would likely be the owner or teacher. Marshall (1980: 309) contends in detail with the skepticism of Haenchen (1987: 560–61), who rejects the idea that Paul could work in the morning, preach in the afternoon, and make a sufficient supporting wage. Barrett (1998: 902) also challenges Haenchen's skepticism on a variety of points but leaves the issue of historicity open. The scene is credible for a dedicated, hard worker, as Paul obviously was.

The Western text places the hours of Paul's speaking as from the fifth to tenth hour (11 a.m. to 4 p.m.). Metzger (1971: 470) suggests that this may be an accurate piece of oral tradition, but it is not original to Luke, as there would have been no reason to remove it from the text if it had been present. If this is the correct time, then it would be during the afternoon break or siesta time (Williams 1990: 331; Martial, *Epigrams* 4.8). As Lake says in Lake and Cadbury 1933: 239, at "1 p.m. there were probably more people asleep than at 1 a.m." If correct, then Paul meets in an off-peak time but also when people would be free to hear him. Although the Western text is not original, the timing is likely. Larkin (1995: 275) speaks of the example of a tireless Paul who works in the morning and preaches in the afternoon. This pattern continues for two years with the result that Jews and Greeks hear the word of the Lord. Paul's ministry in Ephesus runs into its third year (Acts 20:31). Out of Ephesus came a ministry that impacted the entire Lycus valley, planting churches that received the letters later recorded in Rev. 2–3. Workers such as Epaphras were key in this expanding church work (Philem. 23; Col. 1:7; 2:1; 4:12–13; 1 Cor. 16:19).

A new scene focuses on God's miraculous work through Paul, even to the point that handkerchiefs and aprons that touched Paul's body are given to the sick and bring healing. The handkerchiefs (σουδάρια, *soudaria*) are probably sweat rags that wrapped around the head (Polhill 1992: 401; John 11:44; 20:7). The aprons (σιμικίνθια, *simikinthia*) may be "belts" or sweat towels tied around the waist, but this is not certain (Leary 1990; Larkin 1995: 276; Martial, *Epigrams* 14.153; Petronius, *Satyricon* 94.8). Barrett (1998: 907) argues against the idea of a belt, contending that contact with Paul's skin is necessary, but the meaning may be a sweat towel tied around the waist. A precedent with Jesus

19:11–12

and the woman with the hemorrhage suggests that only a garment needed touching (Luke 8:44). Williams (1990: 332) suggests that the unusual character of these people and their beliefs about magic leads to the unusual form of the miracles. Paul also notes such mighty works (2 Cor. 12:12; Rom. 15:18–19). That God is the source of these works is important to Luke. Paul is but a mediator of God's power, which attests to God's approval of Paul.

The emphasis on magic and power in Ephesus as shown in 19:18–19 may also explain the emphasis on "rulers and authorities" in the epistle to this region (Eph. 1:15–23; 3:10; 6:12). It certainly indicates why such unusual miracles take place here. God is shown to be gracious in the face of the people's misunderstanding (Williams 1990: 333, "meeting the needs of these people at their own level of understanding"). The statue of Artemis had certain symbols that were used as magical formulas (Larkin 1995: 276; Plutarch, *Moralia* 706E; 85B; Arnold 1989: 15–16). Larkin relates the reaction of modern discussions representing two ends of the spectrum—those who deny these events took place and modern imitations of these events by media evangelists. Haenchen (1987: 563) claims that such glorification of Paul is against Paul's own idea that his strength is shown through weakness. This ignores the fact, however, that God works in such ways to show support for his workers, as Paul even argues in 2 Cor. 12:12. Polhill (1992: 402) notes how conversion leads to a distancing from such "magical" responses. Indeed, Luke senses the unusual nature of some of these healings, describing them as "extraordinary" (οὐ τὰς τυχούσας, *ou tas tychousas*; literally, "no ordinary [powerful deeds]," an example of litotes; v. 11). Τυγχάνω (*tynchanō*) normally means to experience something or for something to happen (BAGD 829 §2d; BDAG 1019). But it sometimes means to have an out-of-the-ordinary experience, something very unusual, which is its meaning here (Conzelmann 1987: 163; Bruce 1990: 410; Barrett 1998: 906; Vettius Valens, *Anthologiae* 43.29, 32; 60.20; see also Acts 28:2).

Paul is shown to be more than equal to anything Ephesus can offer. Witherington (1998: 577–79) distinguishes miracle from magic in that magic seeks to manipulate the gods, expecting formulaic results, whereas miracle is God's sovereign act through someone (also Arnold 1989: 18–19). Magic includes rituals, spells, the use of names, and coercion. The collection of texts in *PGM* richly documents such incantations. The failure of the sons of Sceva shows the distinction between miracle and magic.

Both healings of disease and exorcisms are performed. The verb ἀπαλλάσσω (*apallassō*), used for the departing of disease, appears only here in the NT with this sense (Luke 12:58 and Heb. 2:15 use it in the sense of "reconcile" and "free" respectively). The idea is that of being released from something. This summary of Paul's miraculous work sounds like the summaries in the Gospels about Jesus (Luke 4:40–41;

Mark 5:27–34; 6:56) and a summary in Acts about Peter (Acts 5:15). Such encounters with magic have been part of several scenes in Acts (5:16; 8:7; 16:16–18).

Some Jewish exorcists, the seven sons of Sceva, try to perform an ex-   **19:13–16** orcism in the name of the Lord Jesus, adjuring the spirits (note the plural) by the name of the Jesus whom Paul preaches (Mastin 1976: 405–12). There is a textual problem here regarding whether one of them speaks, using the singular (ὁρκίζω, *horkizō*, I adjure; so most MSS), or all of them speak, using the plural ([ἐξ]ορκίζομεν, [*ex*]*orkizomen*, we adjure; $\mathfrak{P}^{38}$, 36, 453, 614, 1739, Byz). Either way, they are seen as acting as a group, given the way the demons reply in verse 15. So the scene is seven exorcists in contrast to one Paul, one minister of the gospel versus one set of demons. They are sons of a chief priest (not "high" priest).[2] Fitzmyer (1998: 649–50) discusses the historical issue raised by the term, rejecting Conzelmann's view (1987: 163–64) that a legend is present. Some see the description as a false claim by the exorcists. Bruce (1990: 411) calls it "an advertisement" claiming chief-priest or high-priestly family connections (also Mastin 1976; Witherington 1998: 581n92). Jervell (1998: 482) speaks of a claim of association with the high priests in Jerusalem, which is also possible.

In exorcistic practice, the use of a correct or powerful name is impor-tant. This is what these exorcists are attempting to do by using Jesus's name. Their ministry stands in contrast to that of Apollos, who lacked certain knowledge but knew Jesus (Gaventa 2003: 267). To use Jesus's name fraudulently leaves one culpable before God. So the attempt fails completely.

Their effort shows the syncretism present in Ephesus.[3] There is irony here: they do not believe Paul's gospel, yet they seek to tap into his power. The verb ὁρκίζω (*horkizō*), describing their attempt, is rare in the NT (Mark 5:7; Acts 19:13), and Jesus never uses it for exorcism. The term ἐξορκιστής (*exorkistēs*, exorcist) is an NT hapax, but references to exorcists do appear elsewhere (Matt. 12:27; Luke 11:19; Josephus, *Ant.* 8.2.5 §§45–49; Justin Martyr, *Dial.* 85.3; Lucian, *The Lover of Lies* 16). Old Testament names show up in some magical papyri, and Polhill (1992: 403) notes a formula reading, "Hail, God of Abraham, hail, God of Isaac, hail, God of Jacob, Jesus Chrestus, Holy Spirit, Son of the Father." Schneider (1982: 269) cites another formula: "I adjure you by the God

2. The problem is raised because the term used here, ἀρχιερεύς (*archiereus*), normally means high priest, but it is unlikely that these figures, so far away from Jerusalem and associated with magic, are relatives of the high-priestly family in Jerusalem.

3. Jervell 1998: 481–82 argues that a boundary between magic and syncretism is not the point here but showing on whose side God stands, whether with the Jewish ex-orcists or with Paul. Jervell's point of emphasis is correct, but part of the problem is the syncretistic approach of these exorcists. In this case, the point is not a matter of either/or but of both/and (see esp. vv. 18–19 below).

of the Hebrews, Jesus . . ." (magical papyri known as Paris papyri 4, in *PGM* 4.3019–20; written in the third century AD; Johnson 1992: 340).

The evil spirit responds critically, saying that it knows Jesus and Paul but does not recognize these imposters. The different verbs for knowing Jesus and being acquainted with Paul probably suggest a different level of knowledge between them. Schneider (1982: 270) speaks of knowing Jesus and respecting Paul, to indicate the difference, but others see them as synonyms (Bruce 1988a: 369n36; on demons recognizing Jesus, see Luke 4:41; 8:28; James 2:19). God performs the healing through Paul, who uses the name of Jesus. In no way is this simply a matter of the magic of naming and manipulation (J. Schneider, *TDNT* 5:463). Evidence of attempts to use Jesus's name in such a manner does exist (*NewDocs* 1 nos. 8, 79; *PGM* 1; Clement of Alexandria, *Stromata* 5.8.46; forbidden by the Jews, *t. Ḥul.* 2.22–23; *y. Šabb.* 14.4.14d; *b. ʿAbod. Zar.* 27b; Metzger 1944). The rejection is an indictment of Jewish exorcism that attempts in a magical way to use the name of Jesus.

The man with the spirit also attacks. The strength supplied by the demon is evident in the overcoming of the itinerant exorcists, as indicated by "leaping upon" to overpower (ἐφαλόμενος, *ephalomenos*; an NT hapax; 1 Sam. 10:6; 11:6; 16:13; MM 269). The shame of their resultant condition, fleeing naked and wounded, underscores their complete lack of success.

19:17   The report of this event circulates among both Jews and Greeks in Ephesus. The result is a reverent fear (2:43; 3:10; 5:11) and a magnifying of the name of the Lord Jesus as the source of such power (on extolling the name, BAGD 497 §2; BDAG 623 §2; Acts 10:46; 5:13; Luke 1:46). The scene speaks powerfully to those conditioned in such an environment. This is not so much mass conversion, however, as an awareness of the power tied to this new faith, similar to the remarks of Acts 5:12–13. Luke often notes the public nature of such events (Acts 1:19; 4:16; 9:42), setting up the climatic remark in 26:26. Johnson (1992: 341) observes that the verse combines an array of summaries also seen in Luke's Gospel (Luke 4:37; 5:26; 7:16–17; 8:35–39).

19:18–19   The believers recognize that syncretism with magic is not a good thing, and so they confess and divulge their practices, turning from their past ways. In this context, the term πράξεις (*praxeis*) means "magic spells" or "magical acts"; normally it simply means "deeds" (MM 533; *PGM* 4.1227; Maurer, *TDNT* 6:644; Barrett 1998: 912). Their divulging of spells is important, as one of the keys to magic is the secrecy and mystery behind the spells. Once made public, the spell is perceived to be impotent. The fact that this becomes evident to those who already believe shows their growing maturity in the faith. They did not appreciate this when they initially responded to Jesus, but now they see it. So they did not give up the practice first and then become Christians. Rather, in their maturing walk with God, they came to renounce the practice, no doubt through the spiritual guidance and enablement that the gift of the Spirit brought. These believers are described through the use of a perfect-tense participle here (τῶν πεπιστευκότων, *tōn pepisteukotōn*, those who have believed), highlighting the enduring nature of their faith (Bruce 1990: 412).

The second step is the public burning of magic books worth a large sum of money, fifty thousand pieces of silver. This rejection of magic and the burning of these manuals of magic are a major public statement about a change of direction in life. If the silver refers to denarii, then fifty thousand of them would equal a single worker's wages for 137 years without a day off, since a denarius was an average worker's wage for a day (so BDAG 128 §2c; BAGD 105 §2c, but counting denarii, not drachmas, which the BDAG note mentions). Ehling (2003) argues that denarii were more common in Ephesus than drachmas, noting that we have forty-seven inscriptions of the former but only six of the latter. She places the sum at equal to eight hundred thousand small pieces of bread, or enough to allow one hundred families to live for five hundred days. It is a large sum of money and reflects the city's commercial commitment to such trade and practice, as this is only a portion of the community's holdings of such material. The act is not so much a protest against others as a public renunciation of the believer's former practice, since books are not seized but voluntarily destroyed (on the practice of burning books, see Jer. 36:20–27; 1 Macc. 1:56; Suetonius, *Augustus* 31; Livy, *Hist. Rom.* 40.29; Diogenes Laertius, *Lives* 9.52; Lucian, *Alexander the False Prophet* 47; on the expression "Ephesian writings" for such works, see Plutarch, *Symposium* 7.5.4 [= *Moralia* 706E]; Witherington 1998: 582; esp. Arnold 1989).

19:20 The encounter with the sons of Sceva and the reaction of believers to magic result in the growth of the word of the Lord (2:47; 6:7; 9:31; 12:24; 16:5) and its prevailing mightily. The allusion to power (κράτος, *kratos*) here is no accident, given the battle with magic.

19:21–22 Once again Paul receives divine direction. He resolves in the Spirit to go through Macedonia, Achaia, and on to Jerusalem and Rome. Romans 15:23–25 is Paul's own description of these plans, where taking the collection for Jerusalem is a major motive for the trip (1 Cor. 16:1–4; 2 Cor. 8–9; Bruce 1988a: 371–72). The middle voice, ἔθετο (*etheto*), suggests that Paul's own resolve plays a role in the decision. The reference to πνεύματι (*pneumati*) is ambiguous, referring either to Paul's spirit or to the Holy Spirit. The term δεῖ (*dei*) indicates the divinely directed necessity of traveling to Rome. The word is placed forward in the Greek word order for emphasis. The divine sense of "must" in the verse suggests a combination of wills. It appears that Paul has a resolve that he lays before God to see if it is from the Spirit (Larkin 1995: 279). Paul has the sense that he must ultimately go to Rome. In going through

Macedonia and Achaia, Paul will be returning to strengthen churches he has already visited.

Paul will soon have spent two and a half years in Ephesus and written to the Corinthians from there. This is the beginning of a sequence of texts indicating that going to Rome is a part of Paul's divine destiny (Acts 20:23; 21:11, 13; 23:11; 27:23–25). It may be connected to the itinerary sources that Luke used (Schneider 1982: 273; Barrett 1998: 918). The scene also parallels Jesus's having to go to Jerusalem in Luke's Gospel (9:51; 13:33–34). Paul's plans come before the riot in Ephesus that Luke reports next. The riot will not cause him to leave, although it may confirm that it is time to move on.

With forthcoming travel in mind, Paul sends Timothy (1 Cor. 4:17; 16:10–11) and Erastus ahead of him into Macedonia (on Timothy, see Acts 16:1). Sending two on a mission is common (Acts 9:38; 11:30; 15:27, 39–40; Bruce 1990: 414). Timothy and Erastus are described as ministering (διακονούντων, diakonountōn) to Paul. The same Erastus may or may not be mentioned in Rom. 16:23, as the name is common, but in 2 Tim. 4:20 it is likely the same person. The same uncertainty of identification applies to an inscription found in Corinth with this name (Le Cornu and Shulam 2003: 1070). A minister is one who helps or serves (BAGD 184 §2; BDAG 229–30). Luke and Paul also use a related term (διακονία, diakonia) regarding those who help to take up the collection for Jerusalem (Acts 11:29; 12:25; Rom. 15:31; 2 Cor. 8:4; 9:1), something that also is a part of their labor (Johnson 1992: 346).

19:23–24 The response of the Christians causes the other Ephesians to become nervous about their trade on behalf of the gods and goddesses, such as Artemis. The Christians have created a "stir." Here the term τάραχος (tarachos), also used in Acts 12:18, refers to a civil disturbance. These are the only two NT instances of the term (1 Sam. 5:9 is an example from the LXX).

This is the second and last direct confrontation between Paul and Greco-Roman religion in Acts (16:16–18 is the other; the event in Lystra [Acts 14] is not a confrontation but more a correction of a misperception about Paul and Barnabas). Paul is not really the subject of the passage; rather, the movement he represents and the power of God associated with it are. Witherington (1998: 584–88), Stoops (1989), and Marshall (1980: 315–17) critique Haenchen's claim (1987: 576–79) that a rescue miracle takes place and that the scene is not plausible (Marshall's evaluation is especially full). The observation that "the Way" is the issue indicates that it is the Christians who cause the stir. A wise city official provides the proper analysis at the end of the scene and calms the crowd.

Several details reflect solid local knowledge: the reference to the temple keeper (v. 35), the commerce surrounding silver shrines (v. 24), the reference to Asiarchs (v. 31), and the role of the scribe of the people, or town clerk (an elected official, v. 35). Thus Luke has solid sources for this event (Sherwin-White 1963: 81–92). Sherwin-White shows that the way the people function, the appeal to the town clerk, and the march to the theater all fit a first-century setting. Yamauchi (1980: 81) notes a parallel scene in Dio Chrysostom from the second half of the first century AD in *The Hunter* (*Euboean Discourse*) 25–26, where an angry mob gathers in a theater to hear the case of a hunter. Sherwin-White (1963: 92) concludes that "Acts does not show such detailed knowledge of any other city as of Ephesus." Yamauchi (1980: 79–114) summarizes well what is known about the site today through archaeology. The scene is not invented as skeptical scholars claim. Even Conzelmann (1987: 165) lacks his usual skepticism here, citing the "intermezzo" with Alexander as evidence, since this detail has no clear literary motive in advancing the story (also Fitzmyer 1998: 655).

Other points also support a genuine account: Paul is not really central to the scene, the Ephesian audience has trouble distinguishing Christianity from Judaism, and the concern about peace and order at the end of the scene reflects official concerns. The incident may be alluded to in 2 Cor. 1:8–10 and divides nicely into three parts: (1) Demetrius's speech sets the scene (vv. 24–28); (2) he stirs up the populace (vv. 29–34); and (3) the town clerk calms the crowd (vv. 35–40).

A silversmith named Demetrius takes things into his own hands (Crocker 1987). He has a lucrative trade of making silver shrines, actually temple replicas (ναοὺς ἀργυροῦς, *naous argyrous*), honoring the goddess Artemis (Trebilco 1994: 336–37). Such shrines have been found in terra-cotta and marble but not in silver. Molds in which such material could be formed have been found, however, as have coins with temple images (Reeder 1987; Kreitzer 1987; Polhill 1992: 408; Larkin 1995: 280). We also have inscriptions about such silver materials (Bruce 1988a: 374n63; BMI 3.481 = *Inschr. Eph.* 1.27). Demetrius may well be a leader among the silversmiths.

Artemis, Ephesus's major goddess, was known as a goddess of fertility and as "mistress of the wild beasts," a daughter of Zeus and Leto, and a sister of Apollo. In Roman religion she was known as Diana. In this cult she was a virgin who helped women in childbirth, a huntress with bow and arrow, and the goddess of death. Her role in Ephesus paralleled the role of the great Anatolian mother goddess Cybele, since Artemis had become the product of syncretism (Arnold 1989: 25–26; Fitzmyer 1998: 657; Barrett 1998: 922–23).

As the text suggests, there was a whole array of commerce built around her. She was worshiped in many locales, since we know of thirty-three shrines to her, but the major site for her worship in Asia Minor was at Ephesus. Here the temple to her was four times the size of the Parthenon. It had pillars 60 feet high and was about 425 feet by 225 feet, much larger than a football field (Larkin 1995: 282). Le Cornu and Shulam (2003: 1072) place the dimensions at 377 feet by 197 feet, or 130 meters by 70 meters. Pesch (1986b: 180) has the dimensions as 120 meters by 70 meters. It was the largest building in the Greek world. The temple was a mile and a half northeast of the city. Eunuchs and female cultic slaves served it. The cult of Artemis was one of the most widely followed in the Greco-Roman world. Statues depict her as wearing a zodiac necklace, showing her authority over the stars and events. A weeklong festival to her, known as Artemision, took place each spring. Her shrine in Ephesus was a major site, one of the seven wonders of the ancient world.[4] She was a major attraction for the city (BAGD 110; BDAG 135).

It is the protection of such religious commerce that motivates the silversmith Demetrius. Again the issue of idolatry is a theme in Acts (v. 26). The key term is ἐργασία (ergasia), which appears in verses 24–25 and in this context refers to profit. For the roots of this attraction to Artemis, see verse 35 below, where the legend of the stone falling from the sky on Ephesus is mentioned. Luke often notes how material concerns get in the way of responding properly to God (Luke 16:1–14; Acts 1:17–20; 5:1–11; 8:20–22; 16:16–18).

The charges here recall texts such as Acts 16:20–21; 17:6–7; and 18:13. The scene also compares with 21:27–36, where Jews form the opposition. For Fitzmyer (1998: 656), the scene has three points: (1) Christianity now reacts against a pagan cult, as it critiqued aspects of the Jewish cult in Acts 7; (2) having claimed the Creator God to be close to the Greeks in Acts 17, "the Way" does not insult other gods or their temple; and (3) there is an implication that Christianity has the right to exist. The second point is subtle. It is an attack on polytheism, but only out of a respect for the one true God. Any act against gods that are not the true God is not an insult (1 Cor. 8:4–6 balanced by 10:19–21). On the last point, the stir Christians cause does not lead to their disturbing the peace but to others potentially doing so. Christianity is not the disturber of the peace that some claim it to be. Any persecution of it is unjust.

19:25–27   Demetrius gathers together his fellow workmen and spells out his concerns. First, there is the issue of profit (ἐργασίας, ergasias), since the cult business gives them their wealth. Second, there is the danger Paul poses because he teaches that gods made with hands are not gods and many are turning away. The verb here for "turning" is the not-so-common μεθίστημι (methistēmi; Luke 16:4; Acts 13:22; 19:26; 1 Cor. 13:2; Col. 1:13, "turned us to the kingdom of his beloved Son"). The issue of gods made with hands (idols) not really being deities is a major subject of dispute (Isa. 44:9–20; 46:1–7; Rom. 1:18–32; 1 Cor. 8:4–6; 10:20; Larkin 1995: 282; see Acts 17:28–29 for similar views among some Gentiles). Paul's point would be not only that idols are empty of any power but

---

4. See Strabo, *Geogr.* 14.1.22–23; Pliny the Elder, *Nat.* 16.213; 36.95–97, 179; Dio Cassius, *Rom. Hist.* 39.20, speaks of such trade in Ephesus, as does Ammianus Marcellinus, *Res gestae* 22.13; Xenophon of Ephesus, *Eph. Tale* 2.2–3.3; Oster 1976; Knibbe 1995.

also that the one true God must be worshiped. Paul has influenced many Greeks, for whom idolatry had been a way of life, to leave their idolatry behind. The impact on pagan religious commerce is significant enough for Demetrius to attempt to rally support from those who benefit from the commerce idolatry provides. The influence of Paul's preaching has extended far beyond Ephesus as well, a matter of even additional concern.

The perspective here is clear. The turning away from idols is the concern in the two points above (1 Thess. 1:9–10). Third, and most ominous, are the potential results for Artemis herself, as described in three distinct ways: (1) The temple of Artemis may be "reckoned as nothing" (εἰς οὐθὲν λογισθῆναι, *eis outhen logisthēnai*; Isa. 40:17 LXX; Wis. 3:17; 9:6; note Paul's frequent use of λογίζομαι [*logizomai*] in Rom. 4). (2) The silversmiths' trade could fall into "disrepute" (ἀπελεγμόν, *apelegmon*, an NT hapax). The verb form of this word means "discredit," so the noun points to a lowering of respect for the goddess.[5] (3) She might even be deposed, this one whom all Asia and the world worship. This fear shows that the threat is seen as powerful. Artemis's greatness may well be destroyed. The verb καθαιρέω (*kathaireō*) means "bring [something] down" or "destroy" (BAGD 386 §2b; BDAG 488 §2b; Deut. 28:52; 1 Kings 19:14; Sir. 10:14; Luke 1:52; Acts 13:19). Artemis's divine honor is at stake for the silversmith as he piles up the consequences of her fall (on the construction using θεά, *thea*, goddess, see BDF §44.2).

So profit, turning from gods, and the fall of Artemis are all put forward as reasons for concern. The city's chant for her appears in verses 28 and 34 and affirms her greatness in their view. For Demetrius, the threat is economic, cultural, and religious (Roloff 1988: 291 speaks of a combination of religious, patriotic, and business interests). For Luke, the battle Paul wages is not a political one with Rome but with a worldview that takes people captive into empty idolatry. The battle is real, as Pliny the Younger (*Ep.* 10.96) in about AD 112 records how Rome's strong suppression of Christianity in another part of the empire (Bithynia) led to the reoccupation of abandoned temples and to the revival of participation in festivals (Conzelmann 1987: 165). Both sides see the Way as part of a cultural and religious war about divinity.

19:28–29 The city, full of anger and civic pride to defend its goddess, responds with praise to Artemis's greatness. Such acclamations for gods are not uncommon (Xenophon of Ephesus, *Eph. Tale* 1.11.5, "our ancestral goddess, the great Artemis of the Ephesians"; Bel and the Dragon 18, "Great are you, Bel"; 41, "Great are you, Lord, God of Daniel"). The city also is full of confusion, the tumult of a civic disturbance (συγχύσεως,

---

5. On the reputation of Artemis, see Pausanius, *Descr.* 4.31.8, who notes that all cities recognize her and treat her as the greatest of gods; also Livy, *Hist. Rom.* 1.45.2; Barrett 1998: 927.

synchyseōs; an NT hapax; BAGD 775; BDAG 954; LXX: Gen. 11:9, as the name for Babel; 1 Sam. 14:20).

There seems to be a procession from the guild hall to the theater. By the time they reach the theater, they have dragged along with them Paul's two Macedonian traveling partners (συνεκδήμους, *synekdēmous*), Gaius and Aristarchus. This Greek term is used only twice in the NT (Acts 19:29; 2 Cor. 8:19). Scholars discuss whether this Gaius is the same as the one named in Acts 20:4, since there Gaius is said to be from Derbe, which is not in Macedonia (Witherington 1998: 594–95; Fitzmyer 1998: 659 views it as possible but not certain). Aristarchus is named in Acts 20:4 and 27:2 (also Col. 4:10; Philem. 24).

The theater at Ephesus eventually came to have a capacity of twenty-four thousand people, and huge civic assemblies were held there three times a year (Bruce 1988a: 376; on such meetings, Josephus, *J.W.* 7.3.3 §§47–49 [in Antioch after Paul's time]; Tacitus, *Hist.* 2.80). It underwent expansion from the time of Claudius to Trajan so that it could handle many thousands (Schneider 1982: 276n28). The theater is cut impressively into the western slope of Mount Pion (Panayir), facing west toward the harbor. Still beautifully preserved, it reaches a height today of 100 feet into the mountain and is the most impressive of the wonderful collection of remains at Ephesus (Le Cornu and Shulam 2003: 1076–77). At this location all who want to know what is happening can see what is taking place, so the populace is referred to as δῆμον (*dēmon*) in verse 30. This term can refer to a town meeting, but the impression is that the situation is so chaotic that this is not such a meeting. It is more of an ad hoc gathering with little legal status, as the town clerk's remarks at the end of the scene suggest. The scene is similar to the end of Acts 7 but is less violent, and here it is Gentiles who react against the new movement.

19:30–31 Paul desires to go into the gathering (δῆμον) and do something, but the disciples are not permitting (εἴων, *eiōn*) him to go to the theater. The verb is vivid, being rendered in the imperfect. The suggestion is they have to persuade Paul about this. Paul's peripheral role speaks for the authenticity of the scene. Would Paul be absent from the central action if Luke had created the scene?

The disciples are not alone in persuading Paul not to enter the fray. Asiarchs (Ἀσιαρχῶν, *Asiarchōn*) also advise him against it. The Asiarchs would likely be civic rulers or leading men of Ephesus from the upper class rather than merely cultic figures (Sherwin-White 1963: 90; Strabo, *Geogr.* 14.649–65; Johnson 1992: 349). They proposed motions to the civic council and distributed undertakings to them in line with needs for the city's administration (Le Cornu and Shulam 2003: 1079, who note that we possess some sixty inscriptions from Ephesus alone). Fitzmyer (1998: 660) rejects Haenchen's (1987: 574n1) claim that their concern is highly improbable. They were elected for one-year terms, though some could keep the title thereafter. That Paul has such friends shows his influence and impact. That they would be urging (παρεκάλουν, *parekaloun*) him to avoid the danger shows these leaders' concern or at least that they are less easily upset than the larger crowds (Bruce 1990: 418). At the least, they recognize that if Paul dives in, then the situation could become even more chaotic. The remark fits the setting. The imperfect verb—they "were urging" (παρεκάλουν) him not to go—points to the ongoing nature of the appeal. This is the last we see of Paul in this scene.

Confusion abounds as some cry out for one solution, others for another.   **19:32–34**
Still others do not know what is going on. The crowd is called the "assembly" (ἡ ἐκκλησία, *hē ekklēsia*), showing a common, everyday use of what is normally a term for "church" in the NT (see also v. 39 below, where it is used of the formal assembly). The term συγκεχυμένη (*synkechymenē*, confusion) differs from verse 29 and can be rendered "chaos" given the differing views being shouted out. It refers to being "mixed up" or "confounded" (BAGD 775; BDAG 953). They do not know which way to go with all the views being expressed. The Greek verb also shows up in the discussion of Babel in Gen. 11:7, 9 (also 2 Macc. 10:30).

The meaning of verse 33 because of the compressed expression about Alexander's being put forward is not clear. However, the idea seems to be that some instruct Alexander about what is going on and he goes forward. Do Gentiles or Jews begin to involve Alexander? This is unclear from the sentence, and it could be either group. In all likelihood, because of the context, eventually some Jews put a man named Alexander forward to give a defense (ἀπολογεῖσθαι, *apologeisthai*) to the assembly (δήμῳ, *dēmō*) once it becomes clear what is causing the chaos (Larkin 1995: 284–85n; NIV; the Western text modifies the verse in this direction by speaking of Alexander's being "pulled down," which suggests that he had mounted a platform to speak). The crowd has no desire, however, to hear his views and for two hours shouts him down with fresh cries of Artemis's greatness (cf. v. 28), since he would not support the goddess. The confusion is evident: the crowd sees the Jews as associated with the problem even though Alexander's defense likely makes a distinction between members of this new movement and Jews (Pesch 1986b: 181). Le Cornu and Shulam (2003: 1081) have another take on the scene, arguing that Alexander wants to quell the reaction against Paul, fearing that it will spill over into a blaming of all Jews. Either option is possible. In fact, this second view is even likely, given that Jews also would have found Artemis worship objectionable. Paul's presence seems to have disturbed an uneasy civil tolerance between Jews and Greeks and their religious views. Roloff (1988: 293) suggests that Alexander might be an elder of the Jewish community. As was the case earlier (18:14–15), the

Gentiles have trouble separating the new movement from Judaism. Only the intervention of a town clerk will bring calm.

19:35–37 A town clerk (ὁ γραμματεύς, *ho grammateus*) arises to address the crowd and comments on the circumstances in an effort to quell or pacify (καταστείλας, *katasteilas*) a situation that is getting out of hand. Verses 35–36 have the only two instances of this Greek term in the NT (Rengstorf, *TDNT* 7:595). The town clerk is a keeper of records, registrar, and accountant for temple funds (Sherwin-White 1963: 86–87; Apollonius of Tyana, *Letters* 32). He is the highest civic official in the city, operating much like a powerful city manager, and serves as the city's liaison to Roman authorities (Le Cornu and Shulam 2003: 1083). Elected locally, this town clerk would be aware that the temple has been radically impacted by what is happening in the city. His voice would count for a great deal on this matter, especially given that he represents the city that is seen as the keeper of the temple.

His speech comes in a typical rhetorical form with a review (v. 35), the proposition (v. 36), the arguments (vv. 37–39), and the appeal (v. 40; Witherington 1998: 598). He addresses the city as one who shares its temple interests, as his affirmation of Ephesus as the "temple keeper" (νεωκόρος, *neōkoros*) of Artemis shows.[6] His view is that everyone knows about Artemis, her power and the key Ephesian relationship to her, so why overreact? He alludes to the legend of the sacred stone falling from the sky as proof beyond contradiction. The phrase translated "the sacred stone that fell from the sky" literally means simply "that which fell" from Zeus (τοῦ διοπετοῦς, *tou diopetous*) and alludes to a divine sign that apparently involved a meteorite. The claim of such a miraculous event would explain why Artemis was so revered in Ephesus. A similar story appears in Euripides, *Iphigenia at Tauris* 87–88, 1384–85, where the story is tied to Artemis in Taurus (BAGD 199; BDAG 250–51; Weiser 1985: 554; but we have no example of such a story associated with Ephesus beyond this remark).

In an argument that might parallel how Christians argued for the resurrection, the clerk believes that what the Ephesians believe happened shows Artemis's power and is indication enough of her honor. For him, she is not merely a lifeless idol. He goes on to note that no physical act has been done against the goddess by these men and that they have not blasphemed her. There was no explicit sacrilege or blasphemy to justify any action. (Jews were prohibited from striking against temples, robbing shrines, or blaspheming other gods.[7]) In effect, he says, "Why get so worked up?"

---

6. *NewDocs* 6 no. 30 shows that the term was used of the temple cult as well as the cult surrounding the emperor; *CIG* 2972.

7. See Jewish tradition on Exod. 22:28a; Josephus, *Ant.* 4.8.10 §207; *Ag. Ap.* 2.34 §237; Philo, *Spec. Laws* 1.9 §53; *Moses* 2.38 §205; on such acts, Plato, *Republic* 1.344B; 2 Macc.

The argument is the kind of levelheaded statement that we hear from Gamaliel in Acts 5:33–39. If Artemis is really a goddess, then we do not need to worry about her demise. Of course, the key issue is whether the "if" premise is correct. If goddesses and idols are really powerless, then his argument fails. For those who embrace Artemis, however, the argument on the surface would be persuasive. The clerk is progressing toward the argument that civil law must be followed and order kept. At this point, ironically, if a law is being broken, it is the Ephesians who risk committing a crime.

The clerk completes his argument by observing that if a legal complaint **19:38–40** exists, the courts are open and proconsuls can hear the case. The plural reference to proconsuls is generic, since there was only one proconsul at a time: there are people such as proconsuls to appeal to for justice. These matters should be settled legally there. Here the term λόγος (*logos*) is used in its technical legal sense of a legal complaint against someone, a lawsuit. Ephesus was a capital for such courts (ἀγοραῖοι, *agoraioi*) or assize districts (Hemer 1989: 123; on the term "courts," see Josephus, *Ant.* 14.10.21 §245; Pliny the Elder, *Nat.* 5.105–26). The term ἀγοραῖοι primarily means "market days" but in a legal context was used of legal business (Bruce 1990: 421). The clerk then notes that if they wish to go beyond a personal case, then there is the assembly (ἐκκλησία, *ekklēsia*), which met as often as three times a month by the fourth century, in the time of John Chrysostom (*Hom. Acts* 42.2; Sherwin-White 1963: 87; see vv. 32–34 above for "assembly"). So two legal options exist.

The clerk's request to bring a formal charge at the open courts and not riot is heeded (vv. 40–41). The danger is that the city may be charged with rioting and for no legal cause. The phrase ἐγκαλεῖσθαι στάσεως (*enkaleisthai staseōs*) contains a genitive after an infinitive of accusation (BDF §178, so "to be accused of a riot"). The term "we are risking" (κινδυνεύομεν, *kindyneuomen*) is used here in contrast to v. 27, where the silversmiths' income and the honor of Artemis are at risk. The risk is that the crowd will be the danger, not Paul. The clerk includes himself in the group. He fears that the rabble will be arrested by the Romans for causing a disturbance (στάσεως, *staseōs*) without any direct evidence that Paul and the others have acted directly or physically against the goddess in such a way that they could be charged with a crime (v. 37; Polhill 1992: 413; Stoops 1989; Johnson 1992: 350; on this term, see Luke 23:19, 25). Johnson notes that both terms used for the riot can have the nuance of sedition (on συστροφή, *systrophē*, with this meaning, see 1 Macc. 14:44; Josephus, *J.W.* 4.10.4 §601). The implication is that Romans might be forced to step in and limit Ephesus's privileges as a free city (Fitzmyer 1998: 662). So the clerk warns of dire consequences for civic freedom,

4:42; Josephus, *J.W.* 1.33.4 §654; *Ant.* 4.8.10 §207; *Ag. Ap.* 1.26 §249; 1.34 §310; Rom. 2:22; Johnson 1992: 350; Fitzmyer 1998: 661.

appeals for calm, and is successful. The scene's irony is that the law-breakers may well be those who persecute the new movement.

19:41 The clerk completes his remarks and dismisses the crowd. A riot is avoided. The scene depicts a levelheaded ruler who senses that Christians are not breaking any laws. This kind of assessment by neutral yet interested authorities is common in Acts. Fitzmyer (1998: 662) notes that the tumult is "ingloriously ineffective" and Christianity is "seen to triumph" in the scene. At the least, it is justified as not being the cause of a disturbance of law and order.

The Christians' sense of triumph has been short-lived, as the established Ephesian culture has moved to stop their progress (Gaventa 2003: 274–75). Luke relates both the initial success and the reaction of the opposition. He is a realist and knows that some will not take well to growth of the gospel.

In sum, this is the major unit in Acts showing how the transformation of a community affects the culture at large, making it so nervous that it reacts to stop the progress. Luke does not speak of a campaign against others but of the presence of effective internal reform. What affects the commerce of idolatry in Ephesus is apparently not a program to stamp out magic but the change of lifestyle among the believers, which entails separating themselves from such practices. The prospect that others would be so influenced is what causes the Ephesian community to react in fear and hostility.

The second lesson of the unit is that those who do not wish to be transformed will often react with hostility to the evidence of a lifestyle that challenges their own. Once again, however, the believers are not on a campaign against others. They allow the difference in lifestyle to speak for itself, and they trust in God's protection in the midst of the testimony. This protection comes in part from outsiders who also have a sense of justice and fairness. When those who desire fairness speak up, the church is protected.

A look back at the incident involving John the Baptist's disciples proves to be a review of the key elements of the Christian faith. They include baptism, repentance, faith in Jesus, and the gift of the Spirit. Turning, trust, and an acceptance of God's provision for ministry and righteousness are at the core of the gospel (Stott 1990: 305).

What created the environment for such effective ministry? It was Paul's example. He sought a ministry that engaged the community at large. He engaged in homes, in public places, and in contexts where the city as a whole might hear about it, always in the form of persuasive discussion, not imposition. He argued his case, even going into contexts that allowed for debate and expressions of contrary opinion, as when he went to the synagogue or to Mars Hill. He often stayed long enough to have an impact. Stott (1990: 311–14) contrasts this to (1) the often isolationist form of our evangelism, where we bring people to church rather than take the initiative to engage in their context; (2) the emotional emphasis of our appeals in contrast to the attempt to gain a real appreciation for the gospel; and (3) the pursuit of quick encounters and decisions instead of taking the time to relate to someone so that personal follow-up is possible. In the end effective evangelism is rarely done in the context of a guerilla-like encounter but usually requires a sustained effort over time.

Additional Notes

19:1. The MSS D and $\mathfrak{P}^{38\text{vid}}$ lack the reference to Apollos going to Corinth. Instead they have a sentence about the Spirit directing Paul to Asia instead of to Jerusalem. This would have left Paul's vow uncompleted and is out of character for Luke's description of Paul as always seeking the Lord's direction (Metzger 1971: 468–69).

19:2. The MSS D and $\mathfrak{P}^{38,\,41}$ change the difficult reference to not knowing that there is a Spirit into a reference to not knowing that the Spirit has been received. If this were the original reading, it would be hard to explain the existence of the other, which is the more difficult reading. Interestingly, it does explain the likely meaning of the original.

19:8. The Western tradition adds a reference to speaking "with great power" alongside Paul's boldness.

19:14. Again the Western text (D and for the most part, $\mathfrak{P}^{38}$) expands the discussion. It explains that the sons of Sceva are accustomed to exorcising such people; they began invoking the name and commanding the demon by Jesus to come out.

19:15. The use of μέν (*men*) is probably to be omitted, given that $\mathfrak{P}^{38\text{vid},\,74}$, ℵ*, A, D, 33, 1739, and Byz lack it. So there is no "on the one hand . . . on the other hand" contrast here.

19:16. The reference to the demon leaping on them "both" (ἀμφοτέρων, *amphoterōn*) has led to a revision in verse 14 of the number seven to two in one MS (Codex Gigas) and to the omission of the number of exorcists in others (D, Itala). But the term can mean "all," which is its force here (MM 28; Bruce 1990: 411).

19:20. Codex D and some Syriac MSS read here, "The faith of God grew and multiplied."

19:40. There is a double issue in the verse regarding syntax. To what does οὗ (*hou*) refer? And how does οὐ (*ou*) fit? The force of the relative pronoun is not at all clear and has led to suggestions of emendations. The possibility of dittography here must also be considered, given the similarity of the two words. It appears that the best way to answer the first question is to understand αἰτίου (*aitiou*, cause) as the antecedent of the relative pronoun (οὗ), so that the force is, "If we do not disperse quietly, we shall not have grounds by which we can justify this commotion." The answer to the second question is clear enough in this reading. The οὐ negates δυνησόμεθα (*dynēsometha*, we will be able). They will not be able to justify the commotion legally. The city will be exposed to having acted unjustly and thus dishonorably (Barrett 1998: 939–40).

3. From Macedonia and Greece Back to Miletus (20:1–16)

Paul now leaves the tense situation in Ephesus and travels through various locations to strengthen the churches. Greece and Macedonia are visited after a plot is uncovered against Paul as he seeks to go to Syria. He reaches Troas with several co-laborers (vv. 1–6). In Troas Paul speaks past midnight, causing a listener, Eutychus, to fall from a high window. That fall appears to lead to a tragic death. Paul, however, raises him from the dead (vv. 7–12). From there Paul sails back toward the Ephesian region but avoids the city, stopping in Miletus briefly as he seeks to reach Jerusalem by Pentecost (vv. 13–16).

This travel summary indicates the concern to keep Paul effective and out of harm's way. The summary is rooted in Pauline sources (Schneider 1982: 279; Fitzmyer 1998: 664, 671), if not in the itinerary notes (Witherington 1998: 600). These notes show up here and there in Acts, given the reappearance of the "we" sections in 20:5–15, last seen in 16:17. There is some debate as to whether this is the same "we" material as in Acts 16 (Conzelmann 1987: 167), but this is hard to establish (Roloff 1988: 294–95; Barrett 1998: 944–45 is for it, noting that 16:17 ends in Philippi). The narrative about Eutychus in Troas is a miracle account (Fitzmyer 1998: 668). Pesch (1986b: 193) sees the concrete details as supporting its historicity. The scene serves to show Paul's power as he prepares to enter into his suffering.

Exegesis and Exposition

[1]After the uproar ceased, Paul, sending for the disciples and exhorting them, took leave of them to go to Macedonia. [2]And going through these parts and having encouraged them with many words, he came to Greece, [3]spending three months. And when a plot was made against him by the Jews ⌜as he was about to set sail for Syria⌝, he determined to return through Macedonia. [4]Sopater of Beroea, ⌜the son of Pyrrhus⌝, accompanied him; and of the Thessalonians, Aristarchus and Secundus; and Gaius of Derbe, and Timothy; and the Asians, Tychicus and Trophimus. [5]These, going ahead, were waiting for us at Troas, [6]but we sailed away from Philippi after the days of Unleavened Bread, and in five days we came to them at Troas, where we stayed for seven days.

[7]On the first day of the week, when we were gathered together to break bread, Paul talked with them, intending to depart on the morrow; and he prolonged the

speech until midnight. [8]There were many lights in the upper chamber where we were gathered. [9]And a certain young man named Eutychus was sitting in the window. Sinking into a deep sleep as Paul was talking still longer, and being overcome by sleep, he fell down from the third story and was taken up dead. [10]But going down, Paul bent over him and, embracing him, said, "Do not be alarmed, for his soul is in him." [11]And going up and breaking bread and eating and conversing with them a long while, until daybreak, he departed. [12]⌜And they took the lad away alive⌝ and were very comforted.

[13]But going ahead to the ship, we set sail for ⌜Assos⌝, intending to take Paul aboard there; for so he had arranged, intending himself to go by land. [14]And when he met us at ⌜Assos⌝, taking him on board, we came to Mitylene. [15]And sailing from there, we came the following day opposite Chios; the next day we touched at Samos; ⌜ ⌝ and the day after that we came to Miletus. [16]For Paul had decided to sail past Ephesus so that he might not have to spend time in Asia; for he was hastening, if possible, to be at Jerusalem on the day of Pentecost.

Paul leaves Ephesus after the uproar has ceased and travels, as he has planned, through Macedonia, stopping in Greece, which here probably refers to Achaia and the Aegean coast (Bruce 1990: 423; on Achaia, see Acts 18:27–28).[1] He stays for the three months of winter to encourage (παρακαλέω, *parakaleō*) the saints (either AD 55–56 or 56–57); this would entail a return to Corinth. This verb is used in both verse 1 and verse 2 for Paul's activity with the Ephesian and Greek saints (also in 11:23; 14:22; 15:32; 16:40). The uproar is not the reason for Paul's departure, since he has already planned the trip through Macedonia (19:21), meaning Philippi, Thessalonica, and Beroea (16:12–17:10).

20:1–3

Second Corinthians 1–9 tell us that Titus earlier made a journey to Greece and Corinth, probably with the no-longer-extant "epistle of tears," to confront the church in Corinth (2 Cor. 2:4). Paul hoped to meet Titus at Troas. Titus's delay appears to cause Paul to move on, and he finally meets Titus in Macedonia (2 Cor. 2:12–13). Titus has news about Corinth (2 Cor. 2:5–11; 7:5–13). Paul continues to gather the collection for Jerusalem as he travels (Rom. 15:25–26; 2 Cor. 8:16–24), something Luke does not mention here but does so in 24:17. It is not clear why Luke does not mention the collection here, and all answers to this question are arguments from silence (correctly, Polhill 1992: 417). What Luke is indicating is that Paul has his own journey of divine destiny to Jerusalem and then to Rome, as Jesus had in Luke 9–19, when he went to Jerusalem.

Paul also probably ministers to Illyricum during this time (Rom. 15:19; Marshall 1980: 323). Luke never mentions Titus in Acts. It is not

---

1. On the option that Achaia and Macedonia should be distinguished, see Le Cornu and Shulam (2003: 1091), who argue that Paul distinguishes Macedonia from Corinth in his second letter to Corinth. Of course, we are dealing with Lukan usage in Acts, and in 18:27–28 the two areas are treated synonymously.

clear why, but it may simply be that he did not encounter his work for Paul or know about it (Witherington 1998: 601). Another suggestion is that he joins the group by another route.

There arises a Jewish plot against Paul as he seeks to go to Syria. The plot leads him to return through Macedonia rather than by sea. The word ἐπιβουλῆς (*epiboulēs*, plot) highlights another form of "persecution," a plan to do harm to someone (BAGD 290; BDAG 368; 2 Macc. 5:7; 3 Macc. 1:2, 6; Acts 9:24; 20:19; 23:30; Johnson 1992: 355). The term's use in the NT is limited to Acts (9:24 [the first plot against Paul]; 20:19 [the plots of the Jews]; 23:30 [Paul's nephew reports a plot]). As verse 4 indicates by the names, most of those accompanying Paul would be Hellenistic believers. Second Corinthians (from Macedonia) and Romans (from Greece) may have been written at this time (Rom. 16:1, 21–23), and the total time covered by this traveling could have been as long as a year and a half to two years (Le Cornu and Shulam 2003: 1093).

20:4–6   Paul lists seven coworkers traveling with him. As noted above, they are mostly of Greek origin. These saints represent his success from a wide-ranging mission. Macedonia, Asia, and Galatia are mentioned. Sopater may well be a shortened from of Sosipater of Rom. 16:21. Aristarchus is noted in Acts 19:29 (see also 27:2). Timothy was last mentioned in 19:22 (see 16:1–3). Tychicus is noted in several NT passages (Eph. 6:21–22; Col. 4:7–8; 2 Tim. 4:12; Titus 3:12). Trophimus is in Acts 21:29 (also 2 Tim. 4:20). The absence of anyone from Corinth and Philippi is surprising, but Pesch (1986b: 186) suggests that they reach there by a different route with Titus. Marshall (1980: 324) sees Paul as representing Corinth, and Luke as representing Philippi. Bruce (1988a: 382–83) notes the option of Luke representing Corinth if the unnamed Titus does not. Williams (1990: 346) sees Luke tied to Philippi, and Titus to Corinth. In sum, it is not clear how Corinth and Philippi are represented, but that they are represented seems evident. There is a Gaius mentioned in 19:29, but he is from Macedonia, which again could simply be a note that they are from the general region of Greece. This has led to a variety of suggestions and textual variants here, since this text has Gaius from Derbe. One suggestion is to accept a variant reading at 19:29 (Μακεδόνα, *Makedona* [sg.] instead of Μακεδόνας, *Makedonas* [pl.]) so that only Aristarchus is said to be from Macedonia. An alternative approach is to accept a variant reading for Derbe at 20:4 (Δοβήριος, *Dobērios* [also spelled Δουβ(έ)ριος, *Doub(e)rios*] instead of Δερβαῖος, *Derbaios*), a reading found in Codex D, which makes Gaius hail from a town in Macedonia. This latter option is not well attested, and the former one is awkward as well as being poorly attested. So neither of these suggestions is likely. Another suggestion is to see the Gaius in 20:4 as different from the person in 19:29 (Metzger 1971: 475–76). Roloff (1988: 296) notes that the frequency of the name Gaius makes an alternate person quite possible here. So the list has one from Beroea, two from Thessalonica, two from Lycaonia, and two from Asia, showing the scope of Paul's work.

These men likely represent the churches giving to the collection (1 Cor. 16:3–4). This collection is for the church in Jerusalem and not for general temple funds or for the Jewish poor as Le Cornu and Shulam (2003: 1095) suggest. It was the spiritual support of the church that made it appropriate for the Gentile church to return needed material support (Rom. 15:27). Some of them go ahead to Troas, probably by sea, while Paul and some of the others join them there, sailing from Philippi after Paul arrives in that city by land, taking five days for the trip (the trip earlier took two days [see Acts 16:11] but winds are responsible for the difference).

Who of the seven men travel with Paul to Troas is not entirely clear. The last two probably go ahead by ship (Lake and Cadbury 1933: 253; Schneider 1982: 282; Barrett 1998: 947 sees only one unnamed from the seven traveling with Paul).

Here the "we" section resumes. They are in Troas for a week. This site is located along the rugged eastern Aegean coast about 150 miles north and slightly west of Ephesus. The writer of the "we" source, probably Luke (Fitzmyer 1998: 665), apparently joins Paul in Philippi and goes on to Troas. There Paul observes the Feast of Unleavened Bread as he continues to keep Jewish feasts. The season here is the spring, and there are seven weeks remaining until the arrival in Jerusalem in 21:17 (note also 20:16, which places the arrival by Pentecost). The following incident involving Eutychus takes place in Troas.

At Troas, Paul speaks on the first day of the week at a special meeting to break bread, the first mention of such a gathering on a Sunday (1 Cor. 16:2; Rev. 1:10; Did. 14; Gospel of Peter 35; 50). Llewelyn (2001) discusses the reference to Sunday in the NT texts and argues that they show the early importance of this day for Christians. Mark 16:2 and Matt. 28:1 indicate that this first day of the week was the day of the resurrection. The meeting includes a community meal (Acts 2:42, 46; 1 Cor. 10:16; 11:24). Since he is leaving the next day, Paul spends much time addressing the Christians. With an extended sermonic exhortation, he speaks until midnight (see Acts 20:17–35 for a farewell speech in its brief form).

20:7–8

Polhill (1992: 418) discusses whether this is a Saturday evening, reckoning in a Jewish manner the new day from sunset to sunset, or a Sunday evening, reckoning in a Roman manner the new day from sunrise to sunrise. A Roman reckoning seems likely here, though not certain.[2] Marshall (1980: 326) notes a Roman reckoning of days in Acts 3:1 (also 2:15). Luke appears to refer to days by Roman reckoning but

2. Rordorf 1977 opts for a Roman reckoning. Fitzmyer 1998: 668 sees a Jewish reckoning, as does Staats 1975.

uses the Jewish religious calendar—a foot in both camps (Witherington 1998: 606).

There are many lights, probably torches, in the upper chamber so that Paul can continue to speak. They may well have helped to contribute to what is about to happen, by affecting the air quality (Fitzmyer 1998: 669) and/or creating a hypnotic atmosphere (Larkin 1995: 290), but the text says nothing about this.

20:9–10 A young man, Eutychus, falls asleep in the window and then plunges three stories as Paul continues to speak. The size of the building could suggest a well-to-do host (noted by Witherington 1998: 607) or a tenement building (*insula*) for the poor (Williams 1990: 348; Martial, *Epigrams* 1.117.7). The exact setting is unclear.

The shift from the present participle "falling asleep" (καταφερόμενος, *katapheromenos*) to the aorist "was overcome" (κατενεχθείς, *katenechtheis*) because of sleep vividly shows the movement to the apparent tragedy. The phrase "because of sleep" (ἀπὸ τοῦ ὕπνου, *apo tou hypnou*) is causal, explaining the reason for the accident (on this use of ἀπό, see Moulton and Turner 1963: 258). As a lad or young man (παῖς, *pais*, v. 12), he would likely be between eight and fourteen years old (Philo, *Creation* 36 §105). Witherington (1998: 607) notes that the term παῖς can mean "slave" and thus refer to a man, but there is nothing in the context to relate the slave to anyone, so "lad" is a more natural rendering. The fall seems to have killed him, since he is taken up dead. But Paul goes over to him, bends down, and announces that they should not be troubled, for life (ἡ ψυχή, *hē psychē*) is in him. Μὴ θορυβεῖσθε (*mē thorybeisthe*) does not mean "stop being troubled" merely because it is a present imperative. The exact meaning must be determined from the context (Culy and Parsons 2003: 387).

Here is another case where the term "soul" refers to the person as a whole and his being alive. The point is not that life is still in him as if nothing significant has taken place as a result of the fall (Conzelmann 1987: 169, "a real raising of the dead is meant"). This resuscitation from death recalls deeds by Jesus (Luke 7:11–15 [widow of Nain's son]; 8:49–56 [Jairus's daughter]; John 11:38–44 [Lazarus]), Elijah and Elisha (1 Kings 17:19–22; 2 Kings 4:34–35), and Peter (Acts 9:36–41 [Dorcas]). The parallel with Elijah and Elisha is strong, with Paul bending over the boy's body. It is clear in verse 9 that a miracle is intended, as the remark that the boy is "taken up dead" shows. The boy's name means "lucky one" (Fitzmyer 1998: 668). This is the final miracle that Acts notes about Paul in his missionary endeavors. The power of God over life is reaffirmed.

20:11–12 Afterward Paul breaks bread with them and visits until daybreak and his departure. Meanwhile the boy is taken away alive to the comfort of all. Luke again uses litotes, saying that they are "not a little comforted" (παρεκλήθησαν οὐ μετρίως, *pareklēthēsan ou metriōs*). Paul spends every last minute he can with them.

Paul's coworkers, including the writer of the "we" source, head for Assos by boat. Paul goes by land to meet them there. This is no easy trek, since the land here is quite rugged and mountainous. No reason is given for his choosing a route by land, but previously such separation and Pauline travel by land were for safety reasons (20:3). Witherington (1998: 608) and Polhill (1992: 420) suggest that this plan allows him a little more time to stay in Troas in order to see how the boy is doing and to address the believers. A boat ride is long and potentially dangerous, given its route around Cape Lectum (see Bruce 1990: 427 on the ship route). We do not know, however, why the different route is taken. **20:13–15**

Assos was a port city, about twenty miles southwest of Troas (Schnabel 2004: 1260). It stood on a seven-hundred-foot-high volcanic hill and faced south toward the island of Lesbos. Assos today is a beautiful little coastal town tucked on the edge of a rapidly rising coastline off the Aegean. Lesbos can be seen from its shore on a clear day, and the site is full of wonderful vistas. From Assos, Paul and his coworkers sail to Mitylene, the main city of Lesbos, a distance of about forty-four miles, then the next day to the island of Chios, which is opposite Smyrna. One more day, they sail briefly to the island of Samos. Finally, after a third day, they go to Miletus. Samos is thirty miles south of Ephesus, and the trip from Chios to Samos would pass by Ephesus. These short one-day trips from port to port are typical of ancient sea trips. They proceed carefully because of the combination of winds and rocky coasts tricky to navigate. Chios was the birthplace of Homer, and Samos was the birthplace of Pythagoras (Witherington 1998: 609; on Samos, Assos, and Mitylene, see Schnabel 2004: 1260–61; on Chios, see Le Cornu and Shulam 2003: 1117).

Paul is trying to get to Jerusalem by Pentecost, if possible (εἰ δυνατὸν εἴη, *ei dynaton eiē*; expressed with a conditional optative; Wallace 1996: 484; see 20:6). He is now less than five weeks away from that holiday, and so he does not wish to stop in Ephesus and risk being delayed, probably because of visits and/or security reasons. The pluperfect verb (κεκρίκει, *kekrikei*) points to a resolved decision to avoid Ephesus. The distance from Miletus to Jerusalem is about 610 miles. Miletus is 30 miles south of Ephesus, and so a stay in Miletus to say farewell to the Ephesian elders will take a couple of days. This apparently is better for Paul than going to Ephesus and then having to return and board a ship in Miletus to continue the trip.[3] **20:16**

---

3. On Miletus, see Schnabel 2004: 1231–33. The city at one time had four ports; it founded many cities on the Black Sea coast in the seventh century BC. The philosopher Thales was from here.

In sum, this unit gives us a sense of Paul the pastor. Here he seeks to instruct his people as he departs. One of the highest priorities for Paul in ministry is that his people will be equipped theologically and spiritually to persevere after he is gone. In a sense this is the Pauline legacy, to ensure that he leaves behind not a monument to himself, but Christians who are a monument to God in their faithfulness. It is also clear that part of what makes this ministry possible is the commitment of time that people give to hearing the word. Paul can spend a long evening with people on this special occasion. No one seems to be watching the clock, as it were. They are eager to hear what is being taught, all except a boy who grows weary and yet experiences God's grace in an unusual way.

We also see Paul as one who is committed to team ministry. He understands that team ministry builds experience for the future and allows those ministering to share the burden and accomplish far more as a group than one individual can.

Additional Notes

20:3. Codex D and some Syriac MSS add an explicit reference to the direction of the Spirit and suggest that the wish to go to Syria is motivated by this plot, ignoring 19:21.

20:4. Pyrrhus is omitted in some MSS (Byz, Syriac), but it is hard to explain its presence in so much of the textual tradition if it originally had been absent. Its omission is probably a copyist's error.

20:12. Codex D makes a smoother transition and reads, "As they were bidding farewell, he brought the boy alive."

20:13–14. The reading of the island Thassos as the locale in several MSS (among them $\mathfrak{P}^{41}$, L, P, 614 in v. 13 and P and 614 in v. 14) is regarded as too difficult given its location east of Amphipolis (Metzger 1971: 478).

20:15. The MSS D and Byz add one more stop in Trogyllium, a promontory south of Samos (Johnson 1992: 356; Metzger 1971: 478). Such a visit was customary and may explain why it was added. But the text without this stop has better attestation.

4. The Farewell Speech to the Ephesian Elders at Miletus (20:17–38)

This scene records Paul's only speech made exclusively to Christians and his third major public speech (Antioch: 13:16–41 [to Jews]; Athens: 17:22–31 [to Gentiles]). It also is the speech that is most conceptually similar to his letters, which is not surprising, since this audience is most like the audience for his letters. Gaventa (2003: 281) correctly notes that with this event attention turns to the impending separation of Paul from the churches and his approaching suffering for his faith. In his journey to Jerusalem and Rome, Paul mirrors Jesus's journey to Jerusalem and the way he prepared the disciples for his absence in Luke 9–19. Paul likewise is preparing the churches for his absence. What he says to the community of Ephesus could be said to any of the communities to which he has a ministry. Indeed, this is how the passage functions in Acts. It tells churches how to carry on now that they will minister without figures such as Paul present. Paul is concerned with more than evangelism. He seeks healthy churches.

Commentators have different views about the roots of the speech.

Witherington (1998: 610–16) includes a chart that shows numerous parallels to the undisputed Pauline Epistles and argues that this is neither a "last will and testament" farewell speech (as Fitzmyer 1998: 674 suggests) nor an example of epideictic (or merely emotional) rhetoric. He sees it as a deliberative speech, which makes it an exhortation in the fullest sense. Witherington also defends the authenticity of the speech as rooted in a Pauline address, even if Luke summarizes it. Marshall (1980: 329–30) also defends its essential authenticity.

Weiser (1985: 571–72) sees it as a Lukan creation, appealing to both its style and its thought, but influenced by pieces of tradition associated with Paul. We shall review the parallels between Paul's ideas and the speech in defense of its authenticity. Against Weiser, Luke is aware of the speech's content and setting. The content reflects Pauline concerns and ideas. There is no reason to create a Miletus scene to deliver such content if this had been Luke's only goal. The speech is too scene specific and echoes Pauline concerns too well to doubt its core authenticity.

Fitzmyer contends that it is a departure farewell speech that covers past service, in addition to being an exhortation. As a farewell, the speech notes that the hearers may not see him again (Gen. 49:1–27; Josh. 23–24; 1 Sam. 12; Jub. 20.1–10; also Pesch 1986b: 199).

Roloff (1988: 301) sees a Lukan hand because of traces of a later situation in terms of church order, but this assumes that we can be sure of the history of such structures and ideas when we have only limited texts for this very early period. It also questions the use of such categories in the texts we do have.

Jervell (1998: 515–16) sees a speech composed by Luke that might contain recollections of the type of things Paul said in it, although if and what Paul said at Miletus has been lost. He thinks the speech betrays too much knowledge of the entire career of Paul, even presupposing his death. Paul, however, has been left on the edge of death so often in persecution that it is likely that he thought he could die for his faith. Philippians 1:19–26 says as much, as he considers the prospect of his dying.

Johnson (1992: 367) calls the speech "in character" and different from Peter or Stephen speaking, which seems to suggest that, despite Lukan stylizing, there is a discernibly different character to the speeches. This is the character of Paul, as the contacts to his thought, noted in the exegesis, show.

In sum, Fitzmyer's case for a farewell genre seems to have merit despite Witherington's objections, even though this is a decisive departure, not a death. Fitzmyer also recognizes the speech's hortatory character. So the speech is deliberative and at the same time expresses a farewell.

Trebilco (2004: 172–95) defends the traditional character of the speech against the idea that it is invented, and notes numerous points of contact with what we know of Paul (Paul's tears and trials in Ephesus, house-to-house teaching, working with his hands, elders appointed, Jew and Gentile ministry, the threat of wolves, three years). In making these points, however, he notes that none of them can be tied specifically to Ephesus, but they all fit well with that setting. Trebilco (2004: 182) points out how the basis for challenging the speech has problems. This skepticism was rooted in Walter Bauer's suggestion that Gnosticism had already made an impact in Ephesus and that, as Haenchen (1963: 596) puts it, western Asia Minor was "largely lost to the Gnostic heresy." Historians have now set aside this view, however, as erroneous (T. Robinson 1988: 204). Trebilco concludes (2004: 195), "We can put a strong case that Luke was either dependent on Ephesian tradition, or has applied general Pauline tradition to the Ephesian Christian community appropriately and with good reason."

The speech can also be viewed from another angle. It is not related primarily to Paul but to God's plan for the church and its sense of community. Gaventa (2004) has shown how the speech turns the church's focus toward God. Christians are to rely on God for their future well-being. The nature of God's plan, the provision of the Spirit, and the presence of Jesus all lead the church in this direction. No matter how difficult things get, they can rely on God. In a sense, Paul edifies the church when he points them in this direction.

The speech has a clear structure. The setting appears in verses 17–18a. Paul reviews his faithfulness in ministry at the beginning (vv. 18b–21). Next, he reveals his plans and the likelihood that they will not see him again (vv. 22–25). He then declares his innocence of any guilt, having carried out his responsibilities faithfully (vv. 26–27). The exhortation proper begins in verse 28. The elders are to take care of the flock because of the dangers that lurk from fierce wolves emerging from within the community (vv. 28–30). Therefore they must be alert (v. 31). He next commends them to God's grace and again declares his faithful service in not having taken advantage of them and in following the Lord's teaching to give and not receive (vv. 32–35). The scene concludes with prayer and tears as he boards the ship to depart (vv. 36–38). Thus verses 18b–27 look at Paul's role, and verses 28–35 address the Ephesians' situation.

Some scholars speak of how difficult the speech is to outline, given its many repetitions (Barrett 1998: 963), but this is an indication of the emotion behind what was surely a difficult speech for Paul because of his pending departure. Here we see a pastoral Paul passing the torch to the leaders of a community he has nurtured. In a sense, the speech has the same function for readers of Acts, who should look for communities that are diligent about faithfulness and truth. In the Pauline Letters, 1 Tim. 4:1–16 and 2 Tim. 3:1–4:8 have the same character (Polhill 1992: 423; Barrett 1998: 965, but with a less-than-likely suggestion that the Acts material is as late as the Pastorals; refuted by Trebilco 2004: 174–75). It is not "an enigma" that Paul would speak of himself in such terms (but so Haenchen 1987: 588; 1 Cor. 11:1). Paul also often calls for people to remember (Phil. 1:5; 4:15; Col. 1:6; 1 Thess. 2:1–2; 5:10–12; Williams 1990: 352). This is not a response to enemies but a reminder of how he has prepared them to take charge once he has to leave them because of circumstances they all understand. Perhaps Schneider's suggestion that this is a "pastoral testament" or a "testament for the church" is the best way to characterize the speech (Schneider 1982: 293; Johnson 1992: 362; farewell, last-testament speeches: Gen. 48:21; T. Reu. 1.4–5; T. Dan 2.1; T. Naph. 1.3; T. Job 1.4).

Exegesis and Exposition

[17]From Miletus, Paul sent to Ephesus and called to him the elders of the church. [18]And when they came to him, he said to them: "You yourselves know from the first day that I set foot in Asia how I lived among you all the time, [19]serving the

Lord with all humility and with tears and with trials that befell me through the plots of the Jews; [20]how I did not shrink from declaring to you anything that was profitable and teaching you in public and from house to house, [21]testifying both to Jews and to Greeks of repentance to God and of faith in our Lord Jesus Christ. [22]And now, look, I am going to Jerusalem, bound in the Spirit, not knowing what shall meet me there, [23]except that the Holy Spirit testifies in every city to me that imprisonment and afflictions await me. [24]But I do not account my soul of any value or as precious to myself, if only I may accomplish my course and the ministry that I received from the Lord Jesus, by testifying to the gospel of the grace of God. [25]And now, behold, I know that all you among whom I have gone preaching the kingdom ⌜ ⌝ will see my face no more. [26]Therefore I testify to you this day that I am clean of all bloodguilt, [27]for I did not shrink from declaring to you the whole counsel of God. [28]Take heed to yourselves and to all the flock, in which the Holy Spirit has made you overseers, to shepherd the church ⌜of God⌝, which he obtained with the blood of his own [Son]. [29]I know that after my departure fierce wolves will come in among you, not sparing the flock; [30]and from among your own selves will arise men speaking perverse things, to draw away the disciples after them. [31]Therefore be alert, remembering that for three years I did not cease with tears night and day to admonish each one. [32]And now I commend you to God and to the word of his grace, which is able to build you up and to give you the inheritance among all those who are sanctified. [33]No one's silver or gold or apparel I coveted. [34]You yourselves know that these hands ministered to my necessities and to those who were with me. [35]In all things I have shown you that, by so toiling, one must help the weak, remembering the words of the Lord Jesus, how he said, 'It is more blessed to give than to receive.'"

[36]And when he had spoken thus, kneeling down, he prayed with them all. [37]And there came many tears for all, and embracing Paul, they kissed him, [38]sorrowing most of all because of the word he had spoken, that they should see his face no more. And they brought him to the ship.

20:17–18a The setting of the speech is Miletus, as Paul calls the elders of Ephesus to come to him. There is a Jewish community here as well (Le Cornu and Shulam 2003: 1118). The presence of elders in Ephesus shows that Paul structured the church and its leadership before departing (see Acts 11:30; 14:23). These elders would be responsible for shepherding the church and guiding it, as Paul's speech itself indicates. Summoning them to Miletus would take two to four days, since the trip was a one-day journey each way and we do not know how long it took to gather the elders. Once they arrive, he addresses them.

20:18b–21 Paul will open and close the speech in the same manner, declaring the faithfulness of his ministry to them (1 Thess. 1:5c). He has been a model for them (Jervell 1998: 509). The Ephesians both remember and know that Paul's life has been an example. This is how a minister should serve the Lord. He notes that from his first day in Asia, he served the Lord with all humility, tears, and trials arising from the plots of the Jews (serving the Lord: Rom. 12:11, 16; 14:18; 16:18; Acts 19:9; 2 Cor. 7:6; 10:1; 11:7; 12:21; Phil. 2:3, 8; 3:21; 4:12; 1 Thess. 2:6). "Trials" (πειρασμῶν, *peirasmōn*) is a summary term for all the persecution Paul experienced (Acts 19:9; 20:3; 1 Thess. 2:14–15; 2 Cor. 2:4; Phil. 3:18) as the Lord's bond servant (δουλεύων, *douleumōn*). Paul often refers to himself as a bond servant in his letters (Rom. 1:1). Paul has already warned a church that tribulation accompanies believing in Jesus (Acts 14:22). He has risked much for them but has simply been carrying out his duty before the Lord he serves. Paul's primary obligation is to the Lord. So his message also is faithful, as he did not shrink from declaring to them what is profitable, both in public and from house to house.

Neyrey (2003) discusses the cultural background of references to speaking in public and house to house. He argues that in Acts the public places are in cities of significant social status whereas the private places are places of assembly. The fact that Paul speaks openly in such places shows his own high cultural status. In such places Paul is not timid about what he teaches the church, nor does he draw back in fear (ὑπεστειλάμην, *hypesteilamēn*; v. 20; BAGD 847 §2c; BDAG 1041 §2b); the context is about facing persecution. This verb "to shrink back" reappears in 20:27, where Paul does not shrink from declaring the whole counsel of God (Rengstorf, *TDNT* 7:598). He speaks about both encouraging and challenging things. Paul covers the full scope of what the gospel means. He wants the church to be prepared for the persecution coming as a result of preaching the gospel. So he teaches the elders what is profitable, what will edify. The word συμφέρω (*sympherō*) means that which is for the better or confers benefit, and so is "profitable" (BAGD 780 §2b; BDAG 960 §2b).

The beneficial message is the same to Jews and Greeks: repentance to God and faith in our Lord Jesus Christ (1 Thess. 1:9–10; 1 Cor. 9:20–23; 10:32–33). This combination is an excellent summary of Paul's mission. Repentance and faith are two sides of the same coin (repentance for Paul: Acts 17:30; 26:18, 20; faith: 11:17; 14:23; 16:31; 20:21; 24:24; Gal. 2:16; 3:26; Phil. 1:29; Fitzmyer 1998: 677; OT roots: Jer. 34:15; 26:3–5; Hos. 6:1–3; Larkin 1995: 294). This view is defended grammatically by Wallace (1996: 289), who argues that this is not a chiasm, where faith is what Jews do and repentance is the response of Gentiles. Repentance to God represents a change of direction in how one relates to God. It entails faith in Jesus, so that the turning results in one placing trust in what God did through Jesus as one embraces his person and work. This is a message for both Jews and Greeks, considering that both need to hear the same thing. Paul also makes this point in his letter to the Romans (3:19–4:25; 10:8–13). So, according to Acts 20:18–21, Paul's ministry has three characteristics: faithfulness, direct preaching of all that is necessary, and testimony about Jesus to all people without distinction, including a call to have faith in God's work through Jesus.

20:22–24 Paul announces that the Spirit is leading him to Jerusalem. This will be confirmed in 21:4, 11. Indeed, the Spirit has taken Paul "captive" (δεδεμένος, *dedemenos*) in this figurative expression about divine constraint. The participle in the perfect tense suggests that this understanding has been fixed for some time (see 19:21; for other occurrences of this verb in Luke-Acts: Luke 13:16; 19:30; Acts 9:2, 14, 21; 12:6; 21:11 [2x], 13, 33; 22:5, 29; 24:27). The reference to the Holy Spirit in verse 23 suggests that the same Spirit is intended in verse 22, not a reference to a mere inner conviction of Paul's human spirit. The announcement has a sense of the ominous: Jerusalem will be the place where Paul's arrest sends him on his final journey in Acts, the journey to Rome. Acts 20:23 makes clearer that the Spirit has told Paul that imprisonment and afflictions (note the plural) await him there. He does not know exactly what will follow other than that imprisonment and affliction will come (literally, "chains and tribulation"). In Rom. 15:30–31 Paul requests prayer for the same situation with the same tone.

Whatever he may face, Paul does not regard his life as being of ultimate value (2 Cor. 4:7–12; 6:4–10; 12:9–10; Phil. 2:17; 3:8; 2 Tim. 4:7; Bruce 1988a: 390). In fact, he says he does not account his soul as precious in itself, where "soul" stands for a person in this life. The language reflects business accounting or reckoning, where his soul has its only worth in its service to God. Paul could lose his life, but it would not matter if it were done for God as the gospel is preached. His only desire is to accomplish the course to which the Lord Jesus has called him as he testifies to the content of God's grace and the gospel (a genitive of content is here in the reference to God's grace; 1 Cor. 9:15–27; Gal. 1:15–16; 2:2; Phil. 2:16). He compares his ministry (διακονίαν, *diakonian*) to a race (δρόμον, *dromon*) with a course to be completed or accomplished (τελειῶσαι, *teleiōsai*). Luke expresses this with a rare use of ὡς (*hōs*) to introduce a final clause: "I do not consider my life worth anything, so as [ὡς] to complete my course." This commission to minister was given in Acts 9:15 (Fitzmyer 1998: 677). This term for "race" appears three times in the NT (Acts 13:25; 20:24; 2 Tim. 4:7 [where Paul speaks of successfully finishing the race]; Bauernfeind, *TDNT* 8:234). Paul is faithfully walking with God, wherever it may take him. He does not need to be certain where he is going or what he shall face to be faithful to God. He need only carry out his ministry.

20:25–27 Paul looks to the future and the expectation he has that he will never see them again. As it turned out, however, Paul apparently did return to the area later in his life, as the Pastorals indicate, but at the time, his sense was that a later visit was not likely. This detail might suggest that when Luke wrote, Paul had not yet died in Rome and a trip back to Ephesus had not yet taken place. Some scholars, however, suggest that Luke wrote later but did not know that Paul ever returned. Barrett (1998: 972) says that drawing inferences about the date of Acts is impossible from the verse, but this seems too strong a conclusion. The problem is that the possible implication is not certain. The idea that the verse presupposes that Paul's death has taken place is wrong (*pace* Conzelmann 1987: 174; Jervell 1998: 515; see Bruce 1988a: 391–92). This makes the verse say too much, since Paul has already indicated that he does not know what will happen. To this degree, this speech is not like a final will and testament that knows death is coming. Instead he is closing up a ministry that on and off has spanned seven to eight years. The remarks are more like a farewell, given without certain knowledge that he will return again.

Paul is innocent of any responsibility should the Ephesians fail, as he has told them all they need to know to walk well with God, for he declared to them the entire counsel of God. What Paul says here is that he is "clean" or "pure" (καθαρός, *katharos*) with respect to any guilt regarding people's lives. The word αἷμα (*haima*, blood), like the term καθαρός, is a cultic word referring to a pure offering or an act of worship done in cultic purity (Ezek. 3:15–21; 33:4 [he has been a successful "watchman"]; Witherington 1998: 622). The result is his claim of innocence, since he has carried out his calling (1 Sam. 12:2–5; 1 Chron. 29:2–5, 17; Jub. 21.2–3; T. Sim. 6.1; T. Levi 10.1; Roloff 1988: 304; Johnson 1992: 362). Thus the translation reads, "clean of all blood guilt." The language of purity and worship is important, for Paul sees his mission as tied to a proper response to God and to faithfulness in his relationship to others. His ministry is an act of worship, to be carried out faithfully. In referring to "the whole counsel of God," Paul appears to have in mind all that is a part of God's plan as it is tied to the preaching of the gospel (1 Thess. 4:3; 1 Cor. 1:1; Gal. 1:4; Squires 1993). The beauty of grace and the prospect of persecution are laid before the church. The term βουλή (*boulē*) refers to the divine will and is common in Acts (2:23; 4:28; 13:36; also Heb. 6:17; Eph. 1:11; Luke 7:30).

The key exhortation to the elders is that they should take constant heed   **20:28–30** (προσέχετε, *prosechete*, present imperative) to themselves, fulfilling their overseer (ἐπίσκοπος, *episkopos*) role (Gen. 24:6; Exod. 10:28; Deut. 4:9; Sir. 13:8; Hos. 5:1; Luke 12:1; 17:3; 20:46; Johnson 1992: 362). The idea of an overseer was often associated with the idea of being a guardian and protector (Phil. 1:1; 1 Tim. 3:2; and Titus 1:7 are other important occurrences; BAGD 299 §2; BDAG 379 §2). It is not the idea of a single presiding bishop, which emerged in the second century with Ignatius and Irenaeus (Ign. *Eph.* 6; *Magn.* 2, 7; *Trall.* 2–3; *Smyrn.* 8; Irenaeus, *Ag. Her.* 3.2.2; 3.3.1–2; 4.26.2). This oversight responsibility is a part of their role to shepherd (ποιμαίνειν, *poimainein*) the flock.[1] The present-tense infinitive means to shepherd continually and in this context also indicates the purpose of being an overseer (Moulton and Turner 1963: 78, 135; BDF §390.3). The elder is to protect, rule, and foster care (Acts 11:22–26; 13:2–3; Eph. 4:11–12; BAGD 683 §2aβ; BDAG 842 §2). A negative example is set forth in Ezek. 34. Explanations about how to accomplish this are set forth in Paul's Pastoral Epistles (1–2 Timothy and Titus). The role as overseer came from appointment by the Spirit, either by prophetic naming and/or recognition by the church. The overseer became an office with qualifications that the Pastorals set forth. Polhill (1992: 426–27) notes the functional stress rooted in the term "overseer" as one who has oversight care.

The flock is in danger of being exposed to false teaching, and Paul compares false teachers to fierce wolves who devour and destroy (Ezek. 22:27; Zeph. 3:3; 2 Esd. [4 Ezra] 5:18; 1 En. 89.13–27; Matt. 7:15; Luke 10:3; 2 Cor. 10–13). To use the imagery of wolves together with the imagery of the church as a flock is natural (Gaventa 2003: 289). This imagery is like John 10, where the shepherd protects against the thieves. These false teachers are a serious moral threat to the flock (Bornkamm, *TDNT* 4:310). The Pastorals and the letter to Ephesus in Revelation show that Paul's concern is valid (1 Tim. 1:3; 2 Tim. 1:15; Rev. 2:1–7; Bruce 1988a: 393; in the later church: Did. 16.3; Ign. *Phld.* 2.1–2; 2 Clem. 5.2–4; Haenchen 1987: 593n4). Their goal will be to draw people away from the church that Jesus obtained by his blood.

This is one of two direct references to Jesus's sacrificial work in Luke-Acts. Luke 22:19–22 is the other. That Jesus purchased the church with his blood underscores the cost that God incurred to establish the church. Jesus "purchased" (περιεποιήσατο, *periepoiēsato*) it with his own life (literally, αἵματος, *haimatos*, blood; Eph. 1:7, 14; Heb. 9:12; 1 Pet. 1:2, 19; Rev. 1:5; 5:9–10). The verse does not explicitly mention the title "Son" but rather speaks of God's giving his own to gain the church. The image implies sonship. The picture is like what Abraham had been willing to do with Isaac (Gen. 22), only here God does carry out the offering so that others can benefit from the sacrifice ("purchased" in Isa. 43:21; Ps. 74:2). Thus the acquiring of the church had as its basis a substitution of God's own for those God would bring to eternal life. Such a sacred form of down payment for the church makes the responsibility of the elders sacred. It is clear that the death of Jesus, God's own Son, is described here.[2] Behind the action stands the loving commitment of God

---

1. See Ps. 100:3; Isa. 40:11; Jer. 13:17; 23:2; Ezek. 34:12; Zech. 10:3; 11:16; NT: Luke 12:32; 15:3–7; 19:10; John 10; 21:15–17; 1 Pet. 5:2; church father: 1 Clem. 44.3; 54.2; 57.2; Schneider 1982: 296.

2. On the use of the imagery of blood in the history of the church as related to the work of the person of Christ as God, see Pelikan 2005: 221–22.

to take the initiative and suffer sacrifice in order to restore a broken relationship with humanity. Wolves will deny this work in one way or another, challenging the work or denying the uniqueness of the one through whom it is done.

The danger is that these wolves will emerge from among them after Paul departs. It is not clear if the danger comes from the elders or the Ephesian membership, although the latter is more likely, given the scope of the potential threat (Rom. 16:17–18; Col. 2:8; 2–3 John).

Such fear need not be limited to the "late" church (against Conzelmann 1987: 174–75, who argues that the presence of an office is also late). The roots of the idea of eldership already existed in Judaism (Barrett 1998: 975). Synagogue rulers played a similar role. Such concern for potential unfaithfulness was common in a departure setting (T. Levi 4.1; 10.2–5; 14.1–3; T. Iss. 6.1–4; T. Jud. 18.1–6; T. Naph. 4.1–5; 2 Tim. 3:1–5; 4:3–4; 2 Pet. 2:1–3; 3:3–4; Johnson 1992: 363).

These false teachers will pervert (διεστραμμένα, *diestrammena*) things. This term means "to twist" something (BAGD 189 §1b; BDAG 237 §2; Acts 13:10; Phil. 2:15; Prov. 10:9; 11:20). Its result stands in contrast to something that is straight and true. The threat is of teaching that takes one off the "straight" path and draws disciples away (ἀποσπᾶν, *apospan*) from God's direction and leading. This verb means "draw away" from a place (BAGD 98 §2; BDAG 120 §2). The image is of pulling someone in a direction that the person should not go, as here, or of leaving a former location (Luke 22:41; Acts 21:1). The elders should prevent false teaching at all costs. They are "guardians of the tradition of the apostles" and are entrusted with the guidance of the community (Bornkamm, *TDNT* 6:665).

Paul calls on the elders to be constantly alert (present imperative; 1 Cor. 16:13; Col. 4:2; for Christ's return in Mark 13:35, 37; 1 Thess. 5:6). Paul returns to his own example in ministry. He has admonished them over the past three years of ministry, with tears day and night. His constant goal was to urge faithfulness to the living God (νουθετέω, *noutheteō*, admonish: Rom. 15:14; 1 Cor. 4:14; 1 Thess. 5:12, 14). **20:31**

He commends (παρατίθεμαι, *paratithemai*) them to God and offers them a word of grace (v. 24; Acts 14:23; 2 Tim. 1:12). The verb παρατίθημι (*paratithēmi*) means "set [someone] before" something (BAGD 623 §2bβ; BDAG 772). In the middle voice, when this concerns God, it is to commend someone to divine care and protection (Rom. 8:17; Eph. 1:14; Col. 1:12; Deut. 33:3–4; Ps. 16:5; Wis. 5:5). They are not alone or left without provision for the call. This word of grace can build them up (Acts 9:31; Rom. 16:25; 1 Cor. 8:1; 10:1, 23; 14:4, 17; 1 Thess. 5:11; Eph. 1:18; 4:12–16, 29) and give them the inheritance that is the heritage of all who are sanctified (Acts 26:18; 1 Cor. 1:2; 6:11; 1 Thess. 5:23). The phrase ἐν τοῖς ἡγιασμένοις (*en tois hēgiasmenois*) stresses their corporate **20:32** unity by indicating that saints share "among" each other God's benefits (Moulton and Turner 1963: 264 speaks of a dative of advantage here). The "inheritance" (κληρονομίαν, *klēronomian*) in this context refers to the "transcendent salvation" that stands as the center of the gospel rooted in grace (BAGD 435 §3; BDAG 548 §3; Acts 26:18; 1 Cor. 6:9–10; 15:50; Gal. 3:18; 5:21; Eph. 1:14; 5:5; Col. 3:24; 1 Pet. 1:4).

20:33–35 Paul concludes his speech by underscoring his faithfulness again (1 Cor. 9:4–12, 15; 2 Cor. 7:2; 11:8–9; Phil. 4:10–11). He has provided an example (ὑπέδειξα, *hypedeixa*, v. 35) by showing them how to minister (so Johnson 1992: 365). He did not covet anyone's money or clothes (Exod. 20:17; Rom. 7:7; 1 Cor. 10:6; Gal. 5:17; 1 Thess. 2:5). The reference is to seeking personal status (1 Macc. 11:24; James 5:2–3; Williams 1990: 357). At Corinth and Thessalonica, he worked for his own support (Acts 18:2–3; 1 Cor. 4:12; 9:12, 15; 2 Cor. 11:7; 12:13; Eph. 4:28; 1 Thess. 2:9; 2 Thess. 3:7–8; Polhill 1992: 429). He did likewise in Ephesus. Samuel spoke similarly of his faithfulness at the end of his ministry (1 Sam. 12:3). Paul was not greedy but "served" (ὑπηρέτησαν, *hypēretēsan*, v. 34) and took care of himself. This verb means "render service" and appears in the NT only in Acts (13:36; 24:23; BAGD 842; BDAG 1035). In his labor Paul was an example of caring for the weak. He was following the Lord's instruction that it is more blessed to give than to receive. The term for "blessed" (μακάριον, *makarion*), or "happy," is used as a comparative even though it is grammatically a positive form (Moulton and Turner 1963: 31). Paul is saying that blessing, even happiness, comes from giving. Using the term "must" (δεῖ, *dei*), Paul raises a moral obligation. It is a moral imperative to help the weak and be generous to them (Sir. 4:31 [stated negatively]; Luke 6:35–38; 1 Clem. 2.1; Did. 1.5; Barrett 1998: 983).

This is one of the few places outside the Gospels where Jesus is directly quoted. There are numerous conceptual Greek parallels to this saying.[3] It was a familiar idea in antiquity, but Jesus's affirmation of it is what is important to Paul. Love of money is something leaders should avoid (1 Tim. 3:3, 8; 6:3–10; Titus 1:7, 11; Polhill 1992: 429). The saying seems well known in church tradition, as Paul calls on them to remember (μνημονεύειν, *mnēmoneuein*) what the Lord said, an expression that points to oral tradition. Suggestions that an outside saying has been put into Jesus's mouth ignore the fact that the emphasis is on not only the origin of what is said but also the affirmation of its content, which is what Paul is pointing to here.

20:36–38 Paul concludes and prays with them while kneeling, an indication of the solemn nature of the moment (9:40; 21:5; Luke 22:41). The emo-

---

3. See Seneca, *Moral Ep.* 81.17; Plutarch, *Sayings of Kings and Commanders* (= *Moralia* 173D [Artaxerxes I] and 181F [Ptolemy Son of Lagus]); Thucydides, *Pel. War* 2.97.4; Johnson 1992: 365.

tion of the departure overflows in tears (Gen. 33:4; 45:14; 46:29), hugs (Luke 15:20b), and kisses (Luke 7:38; 45; 15:20b) as the elders respond to Paul's announcement that they will see him no more (Tob. 7:6–7; 11:9, 13). The kissing is culturally appropriate. A later midrash teaches that "all kissing is indecent, save in three cases: the kiss of high office, the kiss of reunion, and the kiss of parting" (Gen. Rabbah 70.12). The word ὀδυνώμενοι (*odynōmenoi*, sorrowing) is very graphic. It primarily means "experience pain" (BAGD 555 §2; BDAG 692; Isa. 53:4; Luke 2:48 [of Mary and Joseph's pain as they looked for a missing Jesus in Jerusalem]; 16:24 [of the rich man's torment in hades]). In this context, emotional pain is meant. Paul's remark that he will not see them again leaves the elders in emotional distress, even though they understand it to be God's will. There is no assumption here that Paul is dead as Luke writes, as some claim (but so Conzelmann 1987: 176; Pesch 1986b: 208, because of the farewell testament form, but this ignores the possibility of a simple farewell/departure speech). It is their sense that they will not see him again, underscored by Paul's words, that makes them so sad. With this they bring him to the ship.

In sum, this text makes a major statement about the responsibility of shepherding that is to be the task of God's leaders. When Paul prepares the communities to function in his absence, he notes that his responsibility was to equip them both positively and negatively. Positively, they are to develop a theological understanding that reflects exposure to the entire counsel and program of God and that gives them a mind-set that can discern what is taking place. This is equipping in the most positive sense. Out of genuine understanding comes discernment. Negatively, it means being on guard for the deception and distortion that the world often offers and that can seep into the church, undermining its call, testimony, and mission. Protecting from the undercutting of God's unique saving work in and through Christ is what Paul is most concerned about. This is what he preached as God's word about God's plan.

The key to all of this is found in what Paul commends to them as he departs: God's grace and God's word. Both the attitude and tone of grace and the content of the word serve as protections for the church. In fact, in many ways the subject of the speech is not so much Paul as what God has done through him (Gaventa 2003: 290–91). If one is open to God, then such ministry is possible, even though it can be fraught with danger.

None of this can take place, however, if these leaders do not keep an eye on themselves to be sure that their guidance has integrity. Successful shepherding can take place only when the shepherd is equipped to protect the sheep and steer away the wolves. The shepherds' main task is to ensure that the sheep are fed and protected (Stott 1990: 328). When a shepherd sleeps either spiritually or through theological negligence, the wolves can gain access to the flock. The flock needs shepherds who guard the sheep by keeping a watch for wolves as well as for what can distract the shepherd from the task. All of this is grounded in a purchase of great price, that of the Son, Jesus, for the flock. Ministers can be good shepherds, and they should be so because of the cost paid for the sheep. If the blood of God's Son is good enough for the sheep, so is the faithful labor of his steward-shepherds for the flock God has bought.

Additional Notes

20:25. Western texts add "of Jesus" to "the kingdom"; E and Byz add "of God."

20:28. There is uncertainty whether the best reading here is "church of God" or "church of the Lord." Because of how the sacred names "God" and "Lord" were abbreviated, the difference is one letter in the text ($\bar{\Theta}$ versus $\bar{K}$). This is a case where the more common reading "church of God" is also the most difficult because the church was obtained with "his own blood" or "blood of his own" (Metzger 1971: 480–81). This makes "church of God" the more likely reading.

5. Paul's Journey to Jerusalem (21:1–16)

In another "we" section, Acts now outlines Paul's trip to Jerusalem. The unit presents the itinerary with brief notes about visits to Tyre and Caesarea. The travel in the first section of the trip is quickly covered in verses 1–6; the scene in Caesarea is longer (vv. 7–14). The arrival in Jerusalem is noted in verses 15–16. In Caesarea, Philip and his four unmarried daughters, who are prophets, appear. Here Paul is warned about the dangers he will face in Jerusalem, dangers he is ready to face (vv. 4b, 11–15). Thus the unit prepares for the final section of Acts, where Paul is arrested in Jerusalem and taken to Rome. Paul is ready for what lies ahead. As Jesus resolved to go to Jerusalem (Luke 9:51–53), so Paul has resolved to go to Rome.

The unit is a travel log with a few glimpses of local tradition about Paul. Marshall (1980: 337) suggests a diary by one of Paul's companions, which is likely given the "we" section (so even the normally skeptical Weiser 1985: 588; also Roloff 1988: 308; Fitzmyer 1998: 686). Barrett (1998: 987) seems to be correct in seeing a combination of itinerary and local incidents all woven together with a theological perspective.

Exegesis and Exposition

[1]And when we had torn ourselves away from them, setting sail and making a straight course, we came to Cos, and the next day to Rhodes, and from there to Patara ⌐ ⌐. [2]And having found a ship crossing to Phoenicia, we went aboard and set sail. [3]Coming in sight of Cyprus and leaving it on the left, we sailed to Syria and landed at Tyre; for there the ship was to unload its cargo. [4]And seeking out the disciples, we stayed there for seven days. Through the Spirit they were telling Paul not to go on to Jerusalem. [5]And when our days there were ended, departing, we went on our journey; and they all, with wives and children, brought us on our way till we were outside the city; and kneeling down on the beach, we prayed [6]and bade one another farewell. Then we went on board the ship, but they returned home.

[7]Finishing the voyage from Tyre, we arrived at Ptolemais; greeting the brothers, we stayed with them for one day. [8]On the morrow departing, we came to Caesarea, entering the house of Philip the evangelist, who was one of the Seven, and stayed with him. [9]And he had four unmarried daughters, who prophesied. [10]While we were staying for some days, a prophet named Agabus came down from Judea. [11]And coming to us, he took Paul's belt, and binding his own feet and hands,

he said, "Thus says the Holy Spirit, 'The man who owns this belt, thus shall the Jews in Jerusalem bind and deliver him into the hands of the Gentiles.'" [12]And when we heard this, we and the people there were begging him not to go up to Jerusalem. [13]Then Paul answered, "What are you doing, weeping and breaking my heart? For I am ready not only to be in bonds but even to die at Jerusalem for the name of the Lord Jesus." [14]And when he would not be persuaded, we ceased and said, "The will of the Lord be done."

[15]After these days, making ready, we went up to Jerusalem. [16]And some of the disciples from Caesarea went with us, bringing us to the house of Mnason of Cyprus, one of the original disciples, with whom we should lodge.

21:1–3 Paul and company now head to Jerusalem after tearing themselves away from their friends. The term ἀποσπασθέντας (*apospasthentas*) indicates the emotional difficulty of the departure (Luke 22:41). The first half of this paragraph quickly runs through a series of one-day stops: the island of Cos (about forty miles), the island of Rhodes (about ninety miles), and then Patara (just over sixty miles). Cos had a famous medical school founded by Hippocrates and was the home of a Jewish community (1 Macc. 15:23; Tacitus, *Ann.* 22.61; Strabo, *Geogr.* 14.2; Horace, *Odes* 4.13.13; Schnabel 2004: 800; Le Cornu and Shulam 2003: 147–48). An early mention of this locale shows Roman sensitivity to Jewish practice (Josephus, *Ant.* 14.10.15 §233). Rhodes was a trading port, a locale for education, and a free city that had a Jewish population (Pliny the Elder, *Nat.* 5.132–34; 1 Macc. 15:23; Schnabel 2004: 800). The mentor of Cicero and Caesar, Apollonius Molon, taught there (Le Cornu and Shulam 2003: 1149). Patara in western Lycia was the site of a famous oracle of Apollo (Bruce 1990: 438; Horace, *Odes* 3.4.64; Schnabel 2004: 1261). They then board another, larger ship sailing toward Phoenicia on the open sea instead of hugging the coast, traveling within sight of Cyprus. They come next to the major commercial city of Tyre in Syria. Patara to Tyre is a trip of more than four hundred miles (Williams 1990: 359; Xenophon of Ephesus, *Eph. Tale* 1.11–12 and 1.14.6, says that it is a three-day trip; John Chrysostom, *Hom. Acts* 45 says that the trip takes five days). The arrival in Tyre allows the ship to unload some cargo and load fresh freight. Paul visits disciples there for a week, since the direct trip from Patara allows them to get there quickly (Bruce 1988a: 398). Tyre was on the Mediterranean east coast, a hundred miles north of Jerusalem (Schnabel 2004: 775). It was a center for crafts, purple production, and trade. Phoenicia is the coastal strip in this area, and Syria is the larger region. Both Syria and Phoenicia had a significant Jewish presence and had possessed a Christian presence for about twenty years by this point (Acts 11:19; Le Cornu and Shulam 2003: 1153). The "we" section that starts here runs through verse 18.

21:4–6 Paul and his companions stay in Tyre seven days and visit with disciples there. These disciples become very concerned for Paul. Through the

Spirit, they warn him not to go on to Jerusalem. As the parallel warning in Caesarea shows in 21:11–15, the Spirit seems to have revealed what Paul would face, and the warning comes out of the resultant worry about Paul's well-being, what Le Cornu and Shulam (2003: 1154) call "an inference" from the message (Rapske 1994b: 408). He is ready to risk his life for the gospel, however, and is determined to move ahead (19:21; 20:21–22; for the result, see 21:33, 28:17; Pesch 1986b: 210–11; Polhill 1992: 433). Paul and his companions depart, having prayed together on what was a well-known, smooth beach. This is a shorter version of a farewell such as that described at Miletus (20:36). Paul has formed a solid bond with them during the week. Paul's company journeys on, leaving the disciples at Tyre to return home.

Paul's company sails to Ptolemais and stays for a day. This seaport was located about twenty-five miles south of Tyre on the Mediterranean's southern Phoenician coast. It was almost eighty miles north of Jerusalem and the population included both Jews and Christians. We are not told how the church came to be there, but obviously other missionary activity has brought the gospel there. It was previously known as Acco (Judg. 1:31; medieval Acre). Then they go on to Caesarea, known as Caesarea Maritima, about another forty miles south (Schnabel 2004: 688–90). This was a major port south of Mt. Carmel, with four harbors in the complex. Almost all the gods are represented here. Herod the Great founded Caesarea (BAGD 396 §2; BDAG 499 §2). Luke mentions it frequently (Acts 8:40; 9:30; 10:1, 24; 11:11; 12:19; 18:22; 21:16; 23:23; 25:1, 4, 6, 13). There is some scholarly discussion as to whether they sail on to Caesarea or travel there by foot, because the verb here (διανύω, *dianyō*, v. 7) can mean "complete" or "continue" a voyage (Bruce 1990: 440 favors having the voyage end in Ptolemais; the verb is an NT hapax; on Ptolemais, see Schnabel 2004: 690–91). It is likely that they sail on, since one-day ship stops are so common in Acts and it is unlikely that Paul waited a week in Tyre simply to take a ship for a one-day trip (Marshall 1980: 339).

Paul stays in Caesarea with Philip and his four unmarried daughters, who also are women who give prophecy (προφητεύουσαι, *prophēteuousai*), which would seem to make them prophetesses. Acts 2:17–18 shows that such gifts come on both men and women. First Corinthians 11:5 indicates how a woman should give prophecy in the church. Luke mentions Anna in his Gospel (2:36–38). The daughters' pious social status is noted by calling them virgins (BAGD 627; BDAG 777). The fact that these are women and that little detail is given about them, as they are mentioned in passing, speaks to the remark's authenticity. Despite the mention of their gift, it is another prophet, Agabus, who gives the warning to Paul at Caesarea. Philip became known as "the evangelist" (Eph. 4:11 [of the gift]; 2 Tim. 4:5 [of Timothy]), for reasons Acts 8 makes clear (Eusebius, *Eccl. Hist.* 3.39.9; 5.17.3). He was also one of the Seven

21:7–9

chosen in Acts 6:5. The entire family reflects a deep piety. It is debated whether this Philip is the same person as the apostle (Acts 1:13), since the later church identified the two (Eusebius, *Eccl. Hist.* 3.31.2–5; Bruce 1990: 441 notes the discussion and suggests that one person could be meant; Hengel 1983: 14 also holds this as a possibility). In line with most commentators, however, it is better to see a confusion between the two in this identification as more likely because, if Philip had been an apostle, then he would not have been one of the Seven in Acts 6:5 and primarily identified with this second, lesser group. It also makes it harder to explain why Peter would need to come to Samaria in Acts 8 if Philip were an apostle. The family later traveled to Asia, according to Eusebius, with most ending up in Hierapolis.

21:10–12   Agabus, a prophet from Judea, appears in Caesarea and issues a vivid prophecy. The use of τάδε (*tade*) "Thus," adds solemnity to the prophecy (Wallace 1996: 328; Culy and Parsons 2003: 405). Agabus has spoken already in 11:27–30. The prophecy is acted out, as he takes Paul's waistband (ζώνη, *zōnē*). This was a long band, wrapped around the waist, in which money could be placed (BAGD 341; BDAG 431). The translation refers to a "belt," which may well be a money belt. Paul may well have kept in it some of the Jerusalem collection money he was gathering. Agabus wraps it around his own hands and feet. Then he declares that the Holy Spirit says that in this manner the Jews in Jerusalem "shall bind" (δήσουσιν, *dēsousin*) the waistband's owner and deliver him to the Gentiles.[1] The reference to Jewish involvement in the binding here is "causative" in force: the Jews will not physically bind Paul but will be responsible for his being arrested (21:27, 30, 33; Wallace 1996: 412). The prophecy is accurate in this sense and is not to be pressed too literally. Agabus does not tell Paul not to go to Jerusalem. He only declares what he will face there. Gaventa (2003: 292–93) is right to defend the idea that Agabus lays out what will happen and those around are to draw their conclusion. There is no tension between the groups in this account, only a request out of concern. The crowd reacts to the declaration by begging Paul not to go to Jerusalem. The imperfect verb παρεκαλοῦμεν (*parekaloumen*, were urging) also makes the pleas vivid. This pleading includes tears (v. 13). The reaction is similar to 21:4. The language of the prophet's declaration recalls the prediction about Jesus in Luke 18:32 (Matt. 20:18–19).

21:13–14   The reaction of Paul and the others makes clear that he has a choice here. Stott (1990: 333) argues a distinction between a prediction and a prohibition in the various messages referring to utterances through the Spirit in this chapter. Agabus has predicted what will take place, and the believers urge Paul not to go to Jerusalem. He is not, however, pro-

---

1. For other such symbolic prophetic acts, see 1 Kings 11:29–31; Isa. 8:1–4; 20:2–4; Jer. 13:1–11; 19:1, 13; 27:1–22; Ezek. 4:1–8; Hos. 1:2; Polhill 1992: 435.

hibited from doing so. He will go to Jerusalem and face his persecution and arrest. Paul tells them he is ready to face imprisonment and even death for the sake of the name of the Lord Jesus, and so they do not need to weep and break his heart. The verb for "breaking" (συνθρύπτοντες, *synthryptontes*) the heart is vivid, as it is often used of beating clothes to clean them (Polhill 1992: 436): they are pounding on Paul's emotions. They accept his response, however, and cease their pleading with the remark "The will of the Lord be done." This ministry everyone takes to be the Lord's will (Conzelmann 1987: 178). The wording is like Jesus's remarks in Gethsemane (Luke 22:42; Marshall 1980: 341; also Paul, Rom. 15:30–31 [stated positively as acceptable service]; 1 Pet. 4:14). There is no indication in Luke's narrative that Paul is disobedient here, as the Spirit has told Paul what he will be facing (Acts 20:22–23).

Paul and his companions travel toward Jerusalem, probably by horse, given the participle "making ready" (ἐπισκευασάμενοι, *episkeuasamenoi*; Xenophon, *Hellenica* 5.3.1; Bruce 1990: 442). Witherington (1998: 636–41) notes the hazards of travel in this period, and 2 Cor. 11:23–29 details the dangers Paul faces from opposition that seeks to stop him. They stay with Mnason of Cyprus. The distance from Caesarea to Jerusalem is slightly more than sixty miles, more than one day's trip, and so there is scholarly discussion whether the stop at Mnason's is on the way (so Codex D in an expansion) or in Jerusalem. It may be an in-between stop, since the arrival in Jerusalem is noted again in verse 17, but this is not clear. More likely, Bruce (1990: 443) sees Mnason as being in Jerusalem and serving as a well-known, sensitive, Hellenist host there for a group that includes Gentiles.[2] Paul has repeatedly heard from the Spirit what will happen in Jerusalem. He is ready for what is to come. Boldly Paul will testify to Jesus, whatever the result. With this note, Paul's third journey in Acts ends.

In sum, this passage shows us a community in deliberation in the midst of a situation where the stakes are high. The interaction between the believers and Paul about whether he should face suffering is significant because it shows that sometimes well-intentioned people can be wrong about what God desires. There is no doubt that those who warn Paul have his best interests at heart and are trying to protect him. It also is clear, however, that Paul has a real sense of what God is calling him to do and that he has prepared himself to pay the human price to do it. What is so instructive about the scene is that once it becomes clear that Paul is being driven by the Spirit to face what is ahead, the believers who love him and God's will embrace the path and support him. As this scene and the next with James show, good arguments can often be assembled for a variety of options in life's direction, but sometimes

21:15–16

---

2. So also Marshall 1980: 341 argues, asking why the host of the intermediate stop would be noted. Barrett 1998: 1004 also strongly defends the Jerusalem option, even though he notes that the wording here is clumsy.

flexibility in seeing what God desires allows for support and unity to form a bond of cohesion that makes the spiritual community stronger. In one case, it is believers who are asked to be flexible. In another, it is Paul who shows cultural sensitivity. In both cases, it is a willingness to minister in an engaging manner and tone with some sensitivity to others that makes a healthy change of mind possible. Fernando (1998: 555) speaks of examples of community life and love in this passage. Part of this includes a genuine interaction and not a mere digging in to defend a position. If all believers possess God's Spirit, we must be willing to learn from each other and hear each other.

Another point Fernando (1998: 556) correctly makes is that sometimes what may not be necessary for us personally may be what is required for the sake of the community or in order to help maintain unity. Such is the case in both this scene and the next one with James. This may even be the case when some might not understand why the hard path chosen is being taken, especially when it seems that such a difficult path could be avoided. Sometimes the easy way out is not the right path to take. Only discernment, engagement, and prayer, however, can determine when the hard path is to be taken and when an easier escape should be sought. In Acts we have seen both routes followed at different times.

Paul's Third Missionary Journey

City	Region
unnamed cities	Galatia
unnamed cities	Phrygia
Ephesus	Lydia
unnamed cities	Macedonia and Greece
Philippi	Macedonia
Troas	Mysia
Assos	Mysia
Mitylene	Lesbos
unnamed city	Chios
unnamed city	Samos
Miletus	Ionia
Cos	Cos
Rhodes	Rhodes
Patara	Lycia
Tyre	Phoenicia
Ptolemais	Phoenicia
Caesarea	Judea
Jerusalem (probably)	Judea

Additional Note

21:1. Codex D adds a stop at Myra. This may reflect assimilation to 27:5 or harmonization with the second-century Acts of Thecla, a popular text about Paul and an Iconian follower (Metzger 1971: 482).

VII. The Arrest: The Message Is Defended and Reaches Rome (21:17–28:31)

This section closes the book of Acts. Paul's trip to Jerusalem leads to his arrest and several legal hearings in the city (21:17–23:30). He is moved to Caesarea to face more examination before Felix and Festus (23:31–26:32). Paul's appeal to Caesar sends him on to Rome, where, after a long sea journey and a visit to Malta, he awaits his imperial trial at the book's end (27:1–28:31). This section is dominated by Paul's defense speeches, where he explains and defends his ministry as being faithful to God's call and plan.

A. In Jerusalem (21:17–23:35)

After going to the temple in Jerusalem to show his faithfulness to the law (21:17–26), Paul is arrested, as the Jews accuse him falsely of bringing Gentiles into the temple (21:27–35). Paul defends himself before the crowd and the arresting tribune until the crowd reacts (21:36–22:21). The tribune withdraws with Paul to the barracks and suggests scourging Paul. It is then that Paul discloses his Roman citizenship (22:22–29). He is next brought before the entire Jewish council, where he again defends himself (22:30–23:10). At this point the Lord tells Paul that he will defend himself in Rome (23:11). Paul's nephew discovers and reveals a Jewish plot to seize Paul (23:12–22). This leads Claudius, the commanding officer, to send Paul out of the city to Felix in Caesarea (23:23–35). As the overview shows, the bulk of this section covers Paul's defense.

1. Paul and James (21:17–26)

This scene is significant because of the discussion between Paul and James. After Paul's arrival and the recounting of God's work among the Gentiles through Paul (vv. 17–19), the Jews in Jerusalem introduce the issue of Jewish believers and concerns, including a report that Paul tells the Jews among the Gentiles to forsake Moses (vv. 20–21). Paul is asked to take a vow with four men at the temple, while James also notes that the issue of the law and Gentile practice was decided earlier at the Jerusalem Council with the letter with the four recommendations (vv. 22–25). James is not asking Paul to revisit old decisions but to be sensitive to Jewish concerns about Jewish practice among Jewish believers. Paul agrees and goes to the temple to make the vow the next day (v. 26).

The scene is significant for Luke, as Acts 21:17–23:35 (with 24:11) covers twelve days whereas 24:24–26:32 covers more than two years (Bruce 1990: 444; Polhill 1992: 445; Witherington 1998: 642). Paul's arrival can be dated to a period around AD 57, when Jerusalem is tense with rising Jewish nationalism, political unrest, and the presence of Rome in a ruler, Felix, who was said to have the "instincts of a slave" (Tacitus, *Hist.* 5.9). Most loyal Jews would have viewed Gentiles and the Gentile mission with suspicion. The church in Jerusalem was caught in the middle, wanting to preach to the Jews but supporting the outreach to Gentiles. How to address both sets of concerns was a major issue (Polhill 1992: 447). Witherington (1998: 644) argues that the portrait is "quite believable, and easily understandable," including Luke's silence about the collection that brought them to Jerusalem. Witherington (1998: 646) goes on to suggest that the collection met with only a mixed reception because of these concerns.

So Paul will make the case that he is a loyal Jew and that outreach to Gentiles is not anti-Jewish. Paul is still defending his relationship to Judaism. The passage reflects the fact that the church's relationship to Judaism was still a concern at the time Luke wrote. The scene reinforces and deepens the development of Acts 15, as here Jewish concerns are met without compromising the soteriology established for Gentiles at the council. Paul is also portrayed as being concerned about Jewish issues and the new faith's relationship to Judaism. Paul does not accept the entire approach of the Judaism of the time but makes a distinction between receiving the promise of the new covenant and honoring current Jewish practice. In all of this, we see Paul committed to the unity of the Christian body as he honors the request of his Jerusalemite hosts. He is willing to do this provided nothing central to salvation is compromised. This means that Jewish believers can continue to live by Jewish practice provided it does not compromise either salvation or association and outreach to Gentiles.

The passage raises important and hotly debated questions about Paul and the law. Many scholars think it theologically impossible (Conzelmann 1987: 180) or at least problematic for the Paul of the epistles to act in a way that suggests support for the law. Johnson (1992: 377–79) has a summary of the elements of the argument that deal with the absence of mention of the collection and the lack of specific indication of the Jerusalem community's support for him after his arrest. Others such as Roloff (1988: 315), however, do not see anything inconsistent with the ideas expressed in 1 Cor. 9:20 that Paul is willing to be a Jew to the Jews. Fitzmyer (1998: 692), making the same point, adds 1 Cor. 9:22. Readers should not forget that Paul made a vow earlier—but not noted here—that probably shows some traces of Jewish practice (Acts 18:18). Roloff (1988: 313) also argues that James is tactical here, "trying to build a golden bridge on both sides." It is not clear that Paul tells Jews to disobey the law. He did, however, stress being sensitive to Gentiles and to Jews in outreach, a position with inherent tension that Paul left to conscience (Rom. 14–15).

Barrett (1998: 1000) suggests that Paul may have accepted James's advice and come to see its "sham" character from the results. Barrett (1998: 1013) rejects an appeal to 1 Cor. 9, as the claim in Acts is that Paul is a regularly observant Jew. The issue is more complicated for the church, however, which has already made clear that certain practices of the law do not need to be followed when mixed fellowship with Gentiles is involved. Paul may well be an observant Jew in Jewish contexts, which is what he faces in Jerusalem. After all, why is he so anxious to reach Jerusalem by Pentecost? It is because he keeps the feasts. Barrett's reading is too harsh on James's proposal and seems to understate the new reality in the church that the presence of Gentiles raises for issues of law. The church is in the process of hammering out an understanding and is in transition on the question. Nothing in Paul's defense speeches indicates his rejection of this effort at harmony, and 1 Cor. 9 looks as though it applies from the epistles. Paul does not try to persuade Jewish believers to live like Gentiles, only to be sensitive to issues related to them. This means that table fellowship, food laws, and issues tied to ceremonial purity may be handled differently when Gentiles are involved, but Paul probably does not see this as encouraging Jewish believers to ignore the law.

The presence of the "we" source is evident in verses 17–18, and the account is a narrative (Fitzmyer 1998: 691). Even those who see a heavy Lukan hand in the account see some tradition behind it (Weiser 1985: 595).

Exegesis and Exposition

[17]When we had come to Jerusalem, the brothers received us gladly. [18]On the following day Paul went in with us to James; and all the elders were present. [19]After greeting them, he related one by one everything that God had done among the Gentiles through his ministry. [20]And those who heard it were glorifying God. And they said to him, "You see, brother, how many thousands there are among the Jews of those who have believed; they are all zealous of the law, [21]and they have been told about you that you teach all the Jews who are among the Gentiles to forsake Moses, telling them not to circumcise their children or follow the customs. [22]What, then, is to be done? They will certainly hear that you have come. [23]Do therefore what we tell you. We have four men who are under a vow ⌐ ⌐; [24]taking these men, purify yourself along with them and pay their expenses, so that they may shave their heads. Thus all will know that there is nothing in what they have been taught about you but that you yourself live keeping the law. [25]But as for the Gentiles who have believed, we have sent a letter ⌐judging what they are to keep⌐: to abstain from what has been sacrificed to idols and from blood and from what is strangled and from unchastity." [26]Then Paul, taking the men and the next day purifying himself with them, went into the temple, giving notice when the days of purification would be fulfilled after which the offering would be presented for every one of them.

Paul arrives in Jerusalem to a warm welcome, possibly a reference only to his Hellenist hosts at this point (Marshall 1980: 342) or perhaps to a representative delegation of the church (Larkin 1995: 307).[1] On the following day, Paul and his entourage meet with James and the elders (on elders, see Acts 11:27–30). It is clear that James functions as the leader of this community. The description suggests a formal meeting (Roloff 1988: 314). Apostles, such as Peter and John, are no longer in the city. Paul tells his hosts of all that has happened with the Gentiles in his ministry. Such summaries appear elsewhere in Acts (14:27; 15:3–4, 12). **21:17–19**

Citing Rom. 15:30–31, Barrett (1998: 1005) suggests that Luke understates the problem here. Although Luke is positive and diplomatic, on the basis of what Luke goes on to say it is clear that tensions do exist. The clearest indication of tension is that the elders with James make a suggestion about Paul making a vow, that he should do this out of concern for Jews zealous about the law (vv. 20–24). This will indicate Paul's respect for the law when it comes to Jewish practice. Paul is not alone in hearing this discussion, as the "we" source is still present, although after verse 18 the reference to "we" is lacking until Acts 27.

1. Bruce 1990: 444 is uncertain which is meant.

The report about what God has done with the Gentiles is well known to readers of Acts at this point, so Luke does not go into detail. The point, however, shows that Paul does represent the divine ministry for the Gentiles to the Jerusalem church. Once again, as always in Acts, God is responsible for the outreach (esp. 15:12, 14; also 14:27; 20:24). It may be that the reference to "ministry" (διακονίας, *diakonias*) alludes to the collection here, as this is the term used in Rom. 15:30–31 (also 2 Cor. 8:4; 9:1, 12–13). More likely, however, it is a reference to the ministry in general, since God is said to direct it. Luke seems to know about the collection (Acts 24:17) but chooses not to note it here.

21:20–21 The news about the Gentiles leads to God being glorified (note ἐδόξαζον, *edoxazon*, which is in the imperfect tense, ongoing glorification). But there is a concern. A strong contingent of thousands (μυριάδες, *myriades*) of Jewish believers also respect the law, being zealous for it. This is probably hyperbole for a significant response. The phrase "zealous of the law" (ζηλωταὶ τοῦ νόμου, *zēlōtai tou nomou*) has a rich background, as it was used in 1 Maccabees of faithful Jews who stood up against the increasing hellenization of Judaism (1 Macc. 2:42; 2 Macc. 4:2; 1QS 1.7; 6.13–14; Fitzmyer 1998: 693).

The Jewish population in the Jerusalem church is significant. Acts 2–6 records thousands of Jews responding (2:41; 4:4; 6:7). In other words, the church has made inroads in the city, whose population is estimated to have been about thirty to fifty thousand.

They have been told that Paul teaches Jews living among the Gentiles to forsake Moses by not having children circumcised and by not observing customs (also raised in 24:5–6, 13–21; 25:8). The language is of "defection" (ἀποστασίαν, *apostasian*) from Moses. The term is often used of religious apostasy (Josh. 22:22; 2 Chron. 29:19; 1 Macc. 2:15; Barrett 1998: 1008). The tractate *m. 'Abot* 3.12, condemning someone who gives such an instruction, declares that such a person has no place in the world to come. Philo, as a Diaspora Jew, calls for respect toward the law and explicitly mentions the Sabbath and feasts (*Migration* 16 §§87–92). The issue here is not what Gentiles do, since Acts 15 took care of how to treat Gentiles. The question is what Jews should do. In Jerusalem there is concern that respect should be shown for the law.

This follows what Paul taught, as 1 Cor. 7:18 has Paul teach Jews not to undo their circumcision, although verse 19 notes that circumcision is nothing ultimately (cf. Gal. 6:15). Paul's remarks about the law look to downplay the law, deal with soteriology, or treat relations with Gentiles (Gal. 2:1–14; 3:10–25; Rom. 3:19–20, 31; Marshall 1980: 344). Thus practices tied to the law are probably a "weak" thing without being prohibited (Rom. 14:15; 1 Cor. 8:10). Justin Martyr (*Dial.* 47) describes Jews who keep the law without having a problem from their Gentile brothers. On the other hand, on matters where Gentiles are involved, freedom seems to be advised (Gal. 2:12–14; 1 Cor. 10:25, 27). So the likelihood is that Paul does not teach nonobservance, but neither does he insist on observance where Gentiles are involved. But Paul also understands context, as the way Paul handled Timothy's religious status in Acts 16:3 shows. The way this charge is presented suggests that it is a rumor that needs to be dealt with wisely, as the passive "they were told" (κατηχήθησαν, *katēchēthēsan*) leaves the informants unidentified. Jervell (1998: 529) argues that this event is historical and reflects where Paul's thinking ends up, in contrast to the views expressed in Galatians and 1 Thessalonians. The differing context, however, may be more relevant to its historicity.

Paul's presence in Jerusalem means that something needs to be done,   21:22–24
since the Jews will know he is in the city. The church therefore asks him to take a vow and pay for four others so that all may know he respects the law. Paul has already been described as having taken a vow himself (18:18), and so this is not something Paul opposes doing. Four options for this vow exist (Marshall 1980: 345 has three):

1. The purification for Paul is to restore purity after he has traveled in Gentile areas; for the others, it is an affirmation of their Nazirite vow of at least thirty days (*m. Naz.* 6.3). In this view, the payment for sacrifices (see v. 26) and the shaving of the head are part of the observance of the law. The OT and Jewish roots here include the Nazirite vow (Num. 6:2–21) and restoring purity generally (Num. 6:9–10; 19:12; *m. 'Ohol.* 2.3). Fitzmyer (1998: 694) and Schneider (1982: 310) note that this might be what is taking place. Also, Str-B 2:759 has a discussion of the Jewish background and takes this view (*m. Naz.* 6.5–8.2). Larkin (1995: 308–9) sees it as the solution.
2. Haenchen (1987: 610n3, 611) rejects this option and prefers the idea that Paul shares in the end of their vow for its remaining duration of a week (also Marshall 1980: 345; Witherington 1998: 649).
3. Bruce (1988a: 407) suggests that the four men have contracted uncleanness themselves during their vow and need to restore their purity as well.
4. Paul's cleansing is not for having been in Gentile territory but is tied to the completion of his own vow, noted in 18:18, along with four men who are also from overseas. Jervell (1998: 526) considers the possibility that this is what Paul's vow is about whereas the four men are undertaking Nazirite vows.

The last view is difficult given the years that have passed since Paul made his vow and the lack of a mention that the four men are from overseas. Barrett (1998: 1011) says that no option is entirely satisfactory, but it should be noted that any of these first three options is possible.

Le Cornu and Shulam (2003: 1186, 1190–91) see the men as completing a Nazirite vow (see also my comments above on 18:18), while Paul is dealing with general uncleanness. We simply lack enough detail and Luke's account is so compact that we cannot know which scenario is correct. Gaventa (2003: 299–300) says that we simply do not know what is meant. The shaving of heads does point to a Nazirite vow somewhere in the action (Josephus, *J.W.* 2.15.1 §313; *Ant.* 19.6.1 §§293–94). This leans in the direction of the first option. Acts 21:27 tells us that Paul's vow is for a week, probably for Gentile uncleanness as he approaches the temple (see Num. 19:11–13 on analogy with cleansing for touching a dead body; also see *m. Naz.* 7.3 for various causes of uncleanness). The hope is that by his acting in accordance with the law, the remarks made that Paul has taught against the law will be refuted. There is no ambush of Paul here as some more skeptical readings about James's request suggest. This view is discussed and rightly rejected by Bruce (1990: 446). Nor is it likely that the collection money is used for this, as Haenchen (1987: 614) suggests. There is no clear evidence for either of these suggestions. Paul's reaction does not fit with the "ambush" theory, and the collection money goes to the Jerusalem church as intended.

21:25   The distinction between practice for Jews and Gentiles is made clear. With respect to the Gentiles, the church's position is established, as the letter tied to the Jerusalem Council showed (15:22–29). The four prohibitions noted there are repeated (they should not be involved with sacrifices to idols, blood, that which is strangled, and immorality). What James is asking for here does not change that earlier decision. Paul is not hearing this for the first time here, but James is making clear the distinction. The remark also follows Luke's tendency to repeat key points in his book.

21:26   The next day Paul carries out the initiation of the vow in the temple as they all purify themselves and give notice of the length of the vow. They also bring the appropriate sacrifices. For the four men, for whose sacrifices Paul pays, this would involve a male and female lamb, a ram, and cereal and drink offerings (Num. 6:14–15; Polhill 1992: 448–49). Unlike the completion of the vow, the initiation of it apparently brought no controversy—at least Luke mentions none. Paul is sensitive to Jewish Christian concerns, especially in Jerusalem.

In sum, what we see here is Paul being asked to act with cultural sensitivity to the Jewish context he now finds himself in, without compromising the gospel. He is quite willing to do so for the sake of the unity it may create. Oftentimes we may be asked, in ministry or in a given community, to engage in neutral practices that are culturally driven, not because we have to but because it may prevent unnecessary static from getting in the way of sharing the gospel or doing damage to the unity of the church. This represents a curb of freedoms. Still, it can be well advised, especially when one is visiting another context. Stott (1990: 342) cites a remark by F. F. Bruce: "A truly emancipated spirit like Paul's is not in bondage to its own emancipation." Liberty is a great thing, but sometimes the expression of liberty can be counterproductive. Paul sensed that James's request made sense, so he willingly restricted his freedom. Paul taught this in other areas as well, as Rom. 14–15 also indicates. Both men show a generous spirit in interacting with each other, which is always an indication of a healthy relationship. Neither is making a power play against the other.

Additional Notes

21:23. Some Alexandrian texts (ℵ, B) have the phrase "on their own" to describe the four men's initiative in taking a vow.

21:25. The Western text (D) and Byz have a more paraphrastic reading of the introduction to the prohibition ("judging nothing of these to keep themselves from except"), which is distinct from the wording of Acts 15:28. Although some scholars argue that the phrase was deleted because of the difference, it fits with an expansion earlier in the verse and so seems to be a variant rather than original (Metzger 1971: 485).

2. The Riot and the Arrest at the Temple (21:27–36)

When Paul returns to complete the vow a week later, a riot ensues around the false claim that he has brought a Gentile into the temple area (vv. 27–29). Paul is seized and dragged out of the temple, where he is beaten (v. 30). The tribune, seeing the chaos, enters the scene, so that those beating Paul stop (vv. 31–32). The tribune arrests Paul and, as the crowd shouts, takes Paul to the barracks (vv. 33–34). As they reach the barracks, the crowd is still crying that he be taken away (vv. 35–36). The scene becomes the occasion for the first defense speech of Paul (21:37–22:21). It shows that Paul is not the problem, and that zealous Jews unjustly disturbed the peace. A pious Paul has ended up in prison. A faithful, worshiping Jewish believer is falsely seen as disobedient.

The vivid narrative is likely rooted in local sources, as such an event would be well known. Fitzmyer (1998: 696) simply calls this a Pauline source. Roloff (1988: 316) calls them "good, trustworthy sources." Béchard (2003: 233) speaks of traditional sources in this passage and the others running through Acts 22:29, arguing for a mix of tradition and redaction in these texts (tradition in 21:27–29, 31b–33, 34c–35, 37–39a; 22:1, 22–29). The details of his reconstruction, however, assume too much confidence in being able to tell where ideas break and largely leave the following speech out of such consideration, which is unlikely.

Exegesis and Exposition

[27]When the seven days were almost completed, the Jews from Asia, seeing him in the temple, stirred up all the crowd and laid hands on him, [28]crying out, "Men of Israel, help! This is the man who is teaching men everywhere against the people and the law and this place; moreover he also brought Greeks into the temple and has defiled this holy place." [29]For they had previously seen Trophimus the Ephesian with him in the city, whom they supposed Paul had brought into the temple. [30]Then the whole city was aroused, and the people ran together; seizing Paul, they were dragging him out of the temple, and immediately shut the gates. [31]And as they were trying to kill him, word came to the tribune of the cohort that all Jerusalem was in confusion. [32]At once taking soldiers and centurions, he ran down to them; and seeing the tribune and the soldiers, the people stopped beating Paul. [33]Then the tribune, drawing near,

arrested him and ordered him to be bound with two chains. He was inquiring who he might be and what he had done. ³⁴Some in the crowd shouted one thing, some another; and not learning the facts because of the uproar, he ordered him to be brought into the barracks. ³⁵And when he came to the steps, he was actually carried by the soldiers because of the violence of the crowd; ³⁶for the multitude of people followed, crying, "Away with him!"

Paul's attempt to complete his vow runs into extreme danger. Cleansing **21:27–30** tied to the vow would be required on days three and seven (Num. 19:12). It is day seven that is now in view. Jews from Asia recognize him and stir up a crowd by making two sets of claims.

The first charge is that Paul teaches against the people, the law, and the temple. This charge is like that made against Stephen in Acts 6:11–14 (Köster, *TDNT* 8:204–5). Köster's claim that this charge is not based in tradition is misguided. It is quite unlikely that the church would not know why Paul had been arrested.

The second charge is that Paul has brought Greeks into the temple area and has defiled it. The reference to defiling is intensive, as a perfect tense (κεκοίνωκεν, *kekoinōken*) is used; the effect of his action is that the sacred space stands desecrated (BDF §342.4). Paul's view of his relationship to Judaism appears in 24:14–16. The irony is that as Paul seeks to support his Jewish roots, he is accused of not caring about them (Larkin 1995: 312). The charge against "this man" is like other charges in Luke, where the man in question is not named (Luke 23:4, 14; Acts 4:16; 5:28; Pesch 1986b: 225).

Gentiles were not allowed into the main temple area (*m. Mid.* 2.3; Josephus, *Ant.* 15.11.5 §417 [notes that a Gentile who entered was subject to death]; *J.W.* 5.5.2 §§193–94; 6.2.4 §§124–25; *m. Kelim* 1.8; *b. 'Erub.* 104b). Four-and-a-half-foot tall stone markers inscribed in Greek and Latin in the outer court that surrounded the Court of Women announced to foreigners that they were prohibited from entering the sanctuary (Wikenhauser 1961: 242). Two of these notices have been found. They read, "No foreigner may enter within the barricade which surrounds the temple and enclosure. Anyone who is caught trespassing will bear personal responsibility for his ensuing death" (Bruce 1988a: 409). Four concentric rectangular inner courts of the temple precincts were for Jews, with restriction tightened as one moved inward. Gentiles were permitted in an outer court, outside the fourth court, the one for women. The four inner courts were the courts of women, then men, then the holy place for priests, and finally the holy of holies, where access was most restricted: only the high priest could enter just once a year, on the Day of Atonement (Polhill 1992: 452). In the Mishnah, there is a text that speaks of ten ascending degrees of holiness within Israel's land: (1) a walled city, (2) within the walls of Jerusalem, (3) the temple mount, (4) the rampart,

(5) the court of women, (6) the court of the Israelites, (7) the court of the priests, (8) the area between the porch and altar, (9) the sanctuary, and (10) the holy of holies (*m. Kelim* 1.6–9; Le Cornu and Shulam 2003: 1194–95). The inner court (item 6) is the issue here.

The issue is racial and concerns the temple's sanctity. The charge also confirms in the eyes of those who make it that Paul does not care to follow the law. The accusers mistakenly suppose that Paul has brought Trophimus of Ephesus (Acts 20:4) into the temple area. As Jews from Asia, and so possibly from Ephesus, they may well have recognized Trophimus and thought that one of the men with Paul is he.

The city is stirred up. It is a common Lukan hyperbole to refer to the entire city as a way of saying a disturbance is widespread. Sometimes the verb κινέω (*kineō*) means "shake," but here, where it refers to a crowd, it means "be emotionally aroused" or "agitated" (BAGD 432 §2b; BDAG 545 §2b). They seize Paul, take him outside the temple, and, dragging him outside the inner court, shut the gates and begin to beat him, possibly in the court of the Gentiles if not further outside the temple. The verb εἷλκον (*heilkon*, drag) is imperfect, vividly depicting the step-by-step process: "They were dragging him out of the temple." It is here, in an area where the tribune could go, that the Roman officer tries to deal with the situation. This is the last scene dealing with the temple in Acts. It pictures rejection of the one bringing God's message.

21:31–33   A report of the situation quickly reaches the Roman garrison, which is stationed adjacent to the premises. Recognizing a dangerous situation, the tribune, in charge of a cohort of a thousand men, makes an appearance to calm things. A cohort consists of about three-quarters infantry and one-quarter cavalry (760 troops and the remainder on horse; Wikenhauser 1961: 243). The troops likely come from the fortress known as Antonia, located on a hill on the northwest corner of the temple. Josephus, *J.W.* 5.5.8 §§238–47, describes it in some detail (also *Ant.* 5.11.4 §§403–8; 18.4.3 §92). The location allows them to keep an eye on the potentially volatile temple without violating its sanctity, from one of the turrets just over a hundred feet high. If a problem arises, they can react quickly, using two sets of stairs running from the fortress into the outer court. The tribune appears, probably with a significant contingent of his forces, since at least two centurions are with him (note the plural ἑκατοντάρχας, *hekatontarchas*). This suggests a force of at least two hundred men. The tribune's presence indicates the situation's potential seriousness. The beating of Paul stops. Acts 23:26 and 24:22 tell us that the tribune's name is Claudius Lysias. He arrests Paul and binds him with two chains, probably to a soldier on each side (12:6). He has not come to rescue Paul but to stop a potential riot. The effect of his action is that Paul's life likely is saved from the very zealous Jews who seek to kill him. Paul is also under Roman authority. His legal fate is in their hands. Roman presence has proved to be a protection.

As predicted in general terms in 21:11, a Jewish reaction has led to Paul being bound. The tribune "was inquiring" about what has happened. The verb ἐπυνθάνετο (*epynthaneto*) is in the imperfect tense. He was seeking to determine the cause of the chaos. The mood of the scene is much like the riot in Ephesus in 19:21–40.

The effort to determine what has occurred also meets with confusion. **21:34–36** People in the crowd are shouting different things. Agitation and clamor rule in the crowd, making an "uproar" (θόρυβος, *thorybos*; BAGD 363 §1; BDAG 458 §1; Philo, *Flaccus* 14 §120; 3 Macc. 5:48; Josephus, *J.W.* 1.10.4 §201; 2.21.5 §611). This leaves the tribune unable to obtain certainty about the facts, and so he withdraws to the barracks. Paul has to be carried there by the soldiers because of the crowd's violence. This likely is for his protection rather than because of any serious injuries, as he will speak shortly. His being bound would limit his ability to defend himself. In the NT, only Luke uses the term βίαν (*bian*, violence; Acts 5:26; 21:35; 27:41 [of the violent surf of the sea]). The scene ends with the people following the soldiers, crying out at the same time that Paul be taken away. In effect they are saying, "Good riddance, judge him!" (see 22:22). The mood is like the choice to free Barabbas and execute Jesus (Luke 23:18; John 19:15). The bulk of Jerusalem has reacted now against Jesus, Peter, John, Stephen, and Paul. For Acts, this is a final, key rejection of the gospel (Roloff 1988: 318, who sees the city left behind, as no more mention of it takes place; Pesch 1986b: 227).

In sum, this passage introduces us to a journey of suffering and injustice that Paul will experience as an innocent man arrested for his commitment to the gospel. In the chapters that follow, we will see him trust God and yet argue his case, never losing sight of the fact that the proper representation of the gospel is of more importance than his own freedom. In addition, nothing Paul does evidences a threat to the state even though his opponents claimed this about Paul's teaching. Paul works within the legal system of Rome to the best of his ability. He does not try to undercut the rule of law, attempting to let justice, which sometimes can be very slow, play itself out. At the same time, he will utilize what is available to him within the law to do as much as he can to defend himself. By this manner of defense, he enhances the gospel's credibility, for he does not look like many others who might do whatever it takes to escape. The difference and the patience shown are a part of the testimony to those who do not yet appreciate the gospel.

3. Paul Defends Himself (21:37–22:29)

This scene has three parts. First, in a short exchange between Paul and the tribune, Paul is able to identify himself and explain that he is not an Egyptian rebel (21:37–39). Second, there is Paul's first defense speech in Acts (21:40–22:21). All of Paul's speeches from this point on concern his defense. The themes are that he is a faithful Jew, responding to the promise of God at God's direct leading. God has brought him from persecutor to believer. In this first speech, Paul highlights his conversion at Damascus (22:6–11) after reviewing his Jewish past as a persecutor (22:1–5). He reviews his calling (22:12–16). He also tells of the Lord leading him to leave Jerusalem because of the danger facing him there (22:17–21). The mention of being sent to Gentiles brings the speech to a halt. These remarks and reactions parallel an earlier reaction to Jesus in Luke 4:16–30. Third, the crowd reacts, causing the tribune to take Paul into the barracks, where Paul's Roman citizenship is revealed (22:22–29).

This scene begins Paul's defense and journey to Rome. It marks the end of missionary travel. Now Paul is under arrest. Spencer (2004: 212) calls the unit from here to the end of Acts "Prisoner's Progress." It is a mixture of travel narratives and defense speeches and it covers a full quarter of Acts, indicating its importance. Paul and the ministry to the Gentiles that he has just narrated and represents are being defended here as a fulfillment of the original call of God to Israel. This call is a part of the hope that came with Jesus, along with resurrection to life. This is the gospel: the offer of unbroken life with God to people of every nation through Jesus the Christ. The apologetic here is more about the promise of God than about defending oneself before Rome. This is the first of three major defense speeches (24:10–21; 26:2–23 are the others). These speeches likely are summaries of what Paul said on such occasions. Witherington (1998: 660–61) notes that the speeches from this point on are forensic, not deliberative, in their rhetorical form. A characteristic of such speeches is to defend the character of the accused (Witherington 1998: 665). Carrying out God's call with character is a core element of Paul's defense.

The bulk of this section presents a brief biographical review of Paul in speech form. It begins and ends with Paul noting that he used to persecute Jesus's followers. The central portion of the speech reviews his experience on the Damascus road. Weiser (1985: 607) argues, with almost all others, that the scene is entirely a construction of Luke

(Haenchen 1987: 620–21 ["unhistorical"]; but see evaluation of Weiser by Barrett 1998: 1032–33). This skeptical view sees particular difficulty at several points: (1) the tumultuous crowd suddenly becomes quiet for Paul, (2) the tribune agrees to let him address them, (3) the speech does not address the temple circumstances at all but recounts Paul's past, and (4) there are other stylistic parallels. Roloff (1988: 319–20) states that the speech is aimed at Luke's readers. Marshall (1980: 352–53) notes these points and argues for a Lukan compactness in the scene, presenting the essence of Paul's witness on such an occasion. Marshall's take may be correct, but it also may give too much credence to the questions raised about the scene. It may well be that the tribune, thinking that others have made the same misidentification as he has, allows Paul the chance to set his identity straight, in hopes that this might calm things, especially given the social status Paul has. Witherington (1998: 664) focuses on this point. Although the claim is that Paul's speech does not address the current temple circumstance, the speech does present Paul as a faithful Jew following God's call. His speech is also interrupted with the mention of the Gentiles, which is the issue of the setting, so that he never reaches the temple situation. It is not unusual for speakers in Acts not to make it to the conclusion of their speech (e.g., Stephen, Peter at Cornelius's, Paul in Athens).

This interruption also speaks to the speech's essential authenticity. Fitzmyer (1998: 703) says that it may be derived from Luke's Pauline source. Barrett (1998: 1031) also questions if this speech is merely literary. Why would Luke invent a speech that does not address the situation as directly as it could? It is quite likely that the presentation does summarize well what has taken place (Williams 1990: 372–73; Polhill 1992: 456). Witherington (1998: 667–68) notes that the speech does not have the opportunity to present proofs but does contain an *exordium* in vv. 1–2 and a *narratio* in vv. 3–21. The complaints about the scene, then, are exaggerated.

All agree that one point of the speech is to distinguish the Christians from violent, politically motivated movements. In other words, this "new" faith is no political risk to Rome. Paul also is not anti-Jewish. His work is in line with promise, so the "new" faith has "old" roots. Luke spends more time on the defense speeches than he does on the missionary addresses. There are 97 verses of defense speech, which represent 39 percent of the prison-defense section. This compares with 47 verses of Pauline missionary speech, or 21 percent of the missionary section. There are 239 prison verses and 226 missionary verses. This shows that Paul the defender of the faith is as important as, if not more important than, Paul the preacher of the faith. This fits with Luke's goal. Part of what Theophilus needs is the reassurance Paul gives about the roots of the faith. The Way is rooted in God's promise and is moved by God's direction. Paul's defense speeches speak not only for Paul but also for the Way, since he represents the natural extension of what the promise calls for, the taking of the message to all people (Luke 24:47).

Exegesis and Exposition

21:37As Paul was about to be brought into the barracks, he said to the tribune, "Is it proper for me to say something to you?" And he said, "Do you know Greek? 38Are you not the Egyptian who recently rose up in a revolt by leading the four thousand men of the Assassins out into the wilderness?" 39Paul replied, "I am a Jew, from Tarsus in Cilicia, a citizen of no mean city; I beg you, permit me to speak to the people." 40And when he had given him leave, Paul, standing on the steps, motioned with his hand to the people; and when there was a great hush, he spoke to them in the language used by the Hebrews, saying:

22:1"Brothers and fathers, hear the defense which I now make before you."

2And hearing that he addressed them in the Hebrew language, they were the more quiet. And he said:

3"I am a Jew, born at Tarsus in Cilicia but brought up in this city at the feet of Gamaliel, being educated according to the strict manner of the law of our fathers, a zealot for God as you all are this day. 4I persecuted this Way to the death, binding and delivering to prison both men and women, 5even as the high priest bears me witness along with the whole council of elders. From them I received letters for the [Jewish] brethren, and I journeyed to Damascus, intending to take those also who were there, bringing those [believers] there in bonds to Jerusalem to be punished.

6"As I made my journey and drew near to Damascus, about noon a great light from heaven suddenly shone about me. 7And falling to the ground, I heard a voice saying to me, 'Saul, Saul, why are you persecuting me?' 8And I answered, 'Who are you, Lord?' And he said to me, 'I am Jesus the Nazorean, whom you are persecuting.' 9Now those who were with me saw the light ⌜ ⌝ but did not hear the voice of the one who was speaking to me.

10"And I said, 'What shall I do, Lord?' And the Lord said to me, 'Get up, and go into Damascus, and there you will be told all that stands appointed for you to do.' 11And when I could not see because of the brightness of that light, I was led by the hand by those who were with me, and came into Damascus.

12"And a certain Ananias, a pious man according to the law, being testified to by all the Jews who lived ⌜there⌝, 13coming to me and standing, said to me, 'Brother Saul, receive your sight.' And in that very hour I received my sight and saw him. 14And he said, 'The God of our fathers appointed you to know his will, to see the Just One and to hear an utterance from his mouth; 15for you will be a witness for him to all men of what you have seen and heard. 16And now why do you wait? Get up and be baptized, and wash away your sins, calling on his name.'

17"When I had returned to Jerusalem and was praying in the temple, I fell into a trance ¹⁸and saw him saying to me, 'Make haste and get quickly out of Jerusalem, because they will not accept your testimony about me.' ¹⁹And I said, 'Lord, they themselves know that in one synagogue after another I was imprisoning and beating those who believed in you. ²⁰And when the blood of Stephen your witness was shed, I also was standing by and approving, and keeping the garments of those who killed him.' ²¹And he said to me, 'Depart; for I will send you far away to the Gentiles.'"

²²Up to this word they listened to him; then they lifted up their voices saying, "Away with such a fellow from the earth! For he ought not to live." ²³And as they were crying out and throwing off their garments and throwing dust into the air, ²⁴the tribune commanded him to be brought into the barracks and ordered him to be examined by scourging to find out why they shouted thus against him. ²⁵But when they had stretched him out for the thongs, Paul said to the centurion who was standing by, "Is it lawful for you to scourge a Roman citizen uncondemned?" ²⁶The centurion, hearing that and going to the tribune, said to him, "What are you about to do? For this man is a Roman citizen." ²⁷So, coming, the tribune said to him, "Tell me, are you a Roman citizen?" And he said, "Yes." ²⁸The tribune answered, "I bought this citizenship for a large sum." Paul said, "But I was born a citizen." ²⁹So those who were about to interrogate him withdrew from him instantly; and the tribune also was afraid, for he realized that Paul was a Roman citizen and that he had bound him.

21:37–39 Paul asks for permission to address the tribune in Greek. This move causes the tribune to think that Paul is an Egyptian rebel who led four thousand men into the desert. Marshall (1980: 352) notes that the question "Are you not the Egyptian?" expects a positive answer. The use of οὐκ (*ouk*) indicates this expectation, and when combined with ἄρα (*ara*), it indicates astonishment that this is who may be present (BDF §440.2). Paul's Greek and the tumult that has taken place lead the man to this conclusion. Greek was widely spoken in Egypt, the lingua franca of the age, and it was not unknown in Israel (Gaventa 2003: 305). Paul's origin from Tarsus, however, would make him a Greek speaker from a young age.

The activities of this Egyptian rebel are summarized in Josephus (*J.W.* 2.13.5 §§261–63 [he gathered thirty thousand in the wilderness]; *Ant.* 20.8.6 §§169–72; Barnett 1981: 681–83). He attracted followers during the time of Felix and said he would bring down the walls of Jerusalem, much like Jericho. When the Romans attacked as he approached the Mount of Olives, he escaped and never appeared again, although four hundred died and two hundred were captured. These attack numbers from the *Antiquities* are more likely closer to being correct than the numbers in the *Jewish War* (Bruce 1990: 452).[1] Bruce places this attack

1. On Jewish prophetic pretenders in the period, who often claimed to reproduce signs of the exodus, see Barnett 1981. He also notes that among the six named sign prophets of the period, only the Egyptian presented himself as a king-prophet.

about three years earlier than the current scene. Apparently, the tribune thinks that Paul is that insurrectionist. The description of the Egyptian's men as σικαρίων (*sikariōn*) identifies them as political troublemakers. This term, which means "dagger men," became a reference to other political revolutionaries of the 60s in Israel, also known as assassins, who caused Rome to overrun the nation in AD 70. Josephus (*J. W.* 2.13.3 §§254–57; *Ant.* 20.8.5 §§164–65; 20.8.10 §§185–87) clearly distinguishes between the Egyptian and the group known as the *sicarii*, as his separate discussion indicates (Foakes-Jackson and Lake 1920–33: 1.421–25; M. Smith 1971: 3). Luke uses the term generically (Fitzmyer 1998: 700; for the view that *sicarii* might be at work in the plot to kill Paul in Acts 23:12–15, see, O. Betz, *TDNT* 7:281).

Paul corrects the tribune, identifying himself as a Jew from Tarsus (Acts 9:11, 30; 11:25) and asking to speak to the people. Paul's hometown was known as a cultural center of Hellenism, rhetoric, and Stoic philosophy (Strabo, *Geogr.* 14.4.12–15; 14.5.13–15; Witherington 1998: 662–63; Schnabel 2004: 1056–58). It had several hundred thousand inhabitants. Noted for its textile industry, it was a center for trade and possessed a lively literary and philosophical tradition (Larkin 1995: 316). With Ephesus and Smyrna, it was furthest east of the key cities running along the edge of the coast of Asia Minor.

Paul is portrayed as a cultured man. The expression "no mean city" (οὐκ ἀσήμου πόλεως, *ouk asēmou poleōs*) is a litotes for a city of significance (Euripides, *Ion* 8 [of Athens]; Strabo, *Geogr.* 8.6.15). Paul is seeking to make his significant background clear to the soldier (Rengstorf, *TDNT* 7:267). One thing Paul is not is a political threat to Rome (Jervell 1998: 539).

21:40 The tribune grants the request, which Conzelmann (1987: 184) sees as "inconceivable," but given that Paul is a Jew, perhaps the tribune thinks that the crowd can be quelled by noting a crucial misidentification like the one the tribune has made. So Paul motions to the people and addresses them in a "Hebrew" dialect, a likely reference to Aramaic (Ἑβραΐδι, *Hebraidi*; BAGD 213; BDAG 270; Acts 22:2; 26:14; but Larkin 1995: 316 sees Hebrew being used). Fitzmyer (1998: 701) notes that when this term is used elsewhere in the NT, the transcriptions reveal that Aramaic was spoken (John 5:2; 19:13, 17, 20; 20:16; Rev. 9:11; 16:16). This was the most common lingua franca for Jews of the time. If Paul wished to be understood by most Jews, he would use Aramaic. Philostratus, *Life Apoll.* 6.34, shows that it was possible for Paul as a Jew to be a citizen of a Hellenistic city (Johnson 1992: 383).

22:1 Paul now makes his defense before the crowd. Because it is delivered in Aramaic, it is not a defense to and for Rome but for the faith in which Jews should also share (Jervell 1998: 539). The noun ἀπολογία (*apologia*) identifies the speech as a defense (the verb ἀπολογέομαι, *apologeomai*, speak in one's defense, 24:10; 25:8, 16; 26:1–2, 24). An ἀπολογία is a defense speech in which one makes the case for what one is doing or believing.[2] Such speeches dominate the closing section of Acts. Paul argues that he is being faithful to God in preaching about Jesus as the divine promise. Although this is a "new" faith, it has old roots. Establishing this fact is important in a culture where a religion is valued for its age. This cultural defense of Christianity is one of the major points of the book of Acts. Paul opens by addressing "brothers and fathers," suggesting that some of the leaders of the nation are present (7:2).

As Paul uses the "Hebrew dialect" (see 21:40), the crowd becomes quieter. With the Romans protecting him, the people seem to deem it wise to let him speak. **22:2**

Paul summarizes his autobiography in verses 3–5. He begins with his roots: a Jew, born in Tarsus of Cilicia (9:11; 21:39). After coming to Jerusalem, he was educated under the respected teacher Gamaliel (5:34; *m. 'Abot* 1.4) according to the strict order of the law. Although scholars debate whether "this city" is Tarsus or Jerusalem, it is more likely that instruction by a rabbi took place in Jerusalem (Barrett 1998: 1035–36; Jeremias 1969b). Thus Paul is a Pharisee in terms of education, a law-abiding Jew (Gal. 1:14; Rom. 10:2; Phil. 3:6). This point touches directly on the charge that he does not have regard for the law. He even notes that his zeal for the law is like that of the crowd, implying that he understands what is motivating them (zeal: Ps. 69:9; 1 Macc. 2:26–27, 58; Jdt. 9:4). By noting his own respect for and understanding of the law, Paul's opening remarks provide important background to help calm the crowd. Three standard themes in the Pauline biography are highlighted: (1) born in the cultured city of Tarsus, (2) raised there, and (3) instructed as a good Pharisee by Gamaliel (Bertram, *TDNT* 5:619). This is the first of a three-part argument in the speech: "I was where you were" (vv. 3–5), "I was called by God" (vv. 6–14), and "I was called to be a witness to the nations" (vv. 15–21). **22:3**

Paul was a persecutor who even delivered men and women of the Way (Acts 9:2) to prison (8:3). The persecution extended to supporting the death of some, a likely allusion to Stephen and another parallel to Acts 9, where he "breathed murder." He went from threat to act (26:10; 1 Cor. 15:9; Gal. 1:13; Phil. 3:6; 1 Tim. 1:13). He knows that the high priest and other leaders can testify to this. He even had letters from the high priest and elders with authority to go to the Damascus brethren, that is, the Jews there, and bring some members of the Way **22:4–5**

2. See Johnson 1992: 392; Plato, *Apology* 28A; Thucydides, *Pel. War* 3.52–60 is an example; Wis. 6:10; Josephus, *Ant.* 16.4.3 §§105–20. On its structure, see Quintilian, *Institutio oratoria* 3.9.1; Cicero, *De inventione rhetorica* 1.14.19.

back to Jerusalem in bonds (Acts 9:1–2). The elders' presence behind the letters is another increase in detail over the Acts 9 account and refers to the Sanhedrin. The high priest then was Caiaphas, but now it is Ananias (23:2). The irony of Paul saying this while in bonds himself should not be missed. He was a zealot for God, but not according to knowledge (Rom. 10:2). God would change this. God can turn the persecutor into the pious.

22:6–8   Once again Paul recounts the appearance of Jesus that was narrated in Acts 9, but here, as in Acts 26, the account is in the first person instead of the third person of Acts 9. The appearance began with a great heavenly light appearing about noon (26:13). Acts 22:11 speaks of the blindness that emerged in the day, a possible allusion to Deut. 28:28–29 and a sign that disobedience is now being addressed. No time for the appearance was given in Acts 9, so this is a new detail in verse 6. In addition, the reference to the greatness of the light intensifies the account of Acts 9. Here we learn that the light was brighter than the midday sun. This was no dream or vision. A different term to describe the "glory" (δόξης, doxēs) of the risen Jesus is used in Acts 9:3 (φῶς, phōs, light). The reference to glory or light explains the source of Paul's blindness as an external, not an internal, event. Much of Acts 22:6–11 repeats 9:3–8. With Saul prostrate on the ground, a voice asked why Saul persecuted him. This led to the disclosure that the heavenly voice addressing Saul belonged to "Jesus the Nazorean, whom you are persecuting." The addition of a reference to Nazareth intensifies the remark by highlighting Jesus's earthly roots.

22:9–11   Those present at the incident on the Damascus road saw a light but heard no voice, a probable reference to not comprehending rather than not hearing the voice, since 9:7 indicates that a voice, or at least sound, was heard. Wallace (1996: 133–34) notes that an attempt to argue for a distinction in meaning based on a difference in case for φωνή (phōnē, voice; here accusative but genitive in 9:7) does not work because there are too many exceptions to the rule (Matt. 2:9; Acts 3:23; Matt. 13:19; Acts 5:24, to name but a few). It is overinterpretation to suggest that Acts 9:7 says that they did not see the light whereas here it says they did. All that is said here is that they did not see anyone. For those with Saul, there was neither an appearance nor revelation. The point is that the others knew something happened and that Saul did not have a merely inner, psychological experience. Those with Paul, however, did not know exactly what took place.

Saul responded with a question about what he should do. This adds to what Acts 9 relates. In addressing Jesus as Lord, he was indicating his respect for Jesus; here he is not concerned with how his Jewish audience will take this, since in this context its meaning is ambiguous as an address of respect to a superior. Jesus told Saul what would happen. In

Damascus Saul would hear about what he stood appointed (τέτακται, *tetaktai*) to do. The perfect-tense verb indicates that Paul is part of an established divine plan. In the later account at 26:16, Saul is given a commission at this point.

Next Paul relates that he was blind from the brightness of the glory of the light. This refers to the Shechinah (2 Cor. 4:4–6). Those who were with him led Saul to Damascus. This is another intensified description, as Acts 9 implied but did not directly state that brightness was the cause of Saul's blindness.

Paul then speaks about the role of Ananias (9:13–14), a devout man   **22:12–16** according to the law and well spoken of by the Jews. He was the one through whom the Lord restored his sight. It may well be that the mention of Ananias the believer here is why the high priest Ananias was not named earlier, so that no confusion would result. The note about Ananias's character shows that others who respected the law were responsive to Jesus. In 9:10 Ananias was described as a believer. Acts 22 lacks any mention of a vision to Ananias.

Ananias called Saul a brother and told him to receive his sight. The verb ἀναβλέπω (*anablepō*) can mean either "look up" or "see again." Saul now could see. Ananias then gave him a commission from the "God of our fathers," yet another tie to the Jewish roots of the promise (3:13; 5:30; 7:32; Exod. 3:13, 15–16; Deut. 1:11, 21). God had appointed (προεχειρίσατο, *proecheirisato*) Saul to know God's will, see the Just One, and hear from him (Exod. 4:13; Josh. 3:12; 2 Macc. 3:7; 8:9; Acts 3:20; 26:16; Williams 1990: 376; Michaelis, *TDNT* 6:863). This detail is lacking in Acts 9, but 9:15 states that Saul is a chosen instrument of God, which is a similar idea. The Greek term for "appointed" in 22:14 (προεχειρίσατο) is different from that used in 22:10 (τέτακται, *tetaktai*). A key point in Paul's defense is that his calling came directly from God.

The reference to Jesus as the Just One (τὸν δίκαιον, *ton dikaion*) points to his exalted position and to the vindication of his innocence that Luke 23 highlighted (for this title, see Acts 3:14; Jer. 23:5–6; 33:15; Zech. 9:9). Saul would now be a witness (μάρτυς, *martys*) to the Just One before all men (Luke 24:48; Acts 9:15; 22:20; 26:16; Gal. 1:16; Eph. 3:7–9). The role of witness takes us back to Acts 1:8. Saul could testify to what he specifically had seen and heard, which is what his speech is now doing. The perfect tense for "see" and "hear" stresses the abiding effect of what has happened to him directly as a key to the witness (BDF §342.2). Jesus's appearing to Saul allowed him to have this role of being a witness to the resurrection.

The instruction was given for Saul to rise, to allow himself to be baptized so that his sins could be washed away. This language mirrors Peter's call in Acts 2:38. The response of faith is described as calling on the name of the Lord (ἐπικαλεσάμενος τὸ ὄνομα αὐτοῦ, *epikalesa-*

menos to onoma autou), an expression initially presented at 2:21 (see the discussion there; Rom. 10:12–13; 1 Cor. 1:2). This means that Paul will call on Jesus's name, an expression pointing to salvation. Such a faith invocation of God washes away sin with the cleansing symbolized in water baptism (Rom. 6:3–11; 1 Cor. 6:11; Gal. 3:27). The call to be baptized is in the middle voice, which is not a reference to baptizing oneself but certainly to having himself baptized, that is, a "causative" middle (Polhill 1992: 461n39). Paul's actions will lead to his baptism, but he does not baptize himself. More precisely, the middle voices βάπτισαι (*baptisai*) and ἀπόλουσαι (*apolousai*) are permissive in force (Wallace 2000: 185; BDF §317). Saul was to allow the baptism and washing to take place.[3]

22:17–18 From Damascus Paul returned to Jerusalem and went into the temple, again showing his piety and practice of following the law. There he was praying when he was directed by the Lord in a trance or vision (ἐν ἐκστάσει, *en ekstasei*) to leave Jerusalem quickly, for the people would not accept his testimony about Jesus. Like Peter's experience in 10:10, when he saw the vision of the sheets (also noted in 11:5), Paul was directed by the Lord, although this vision was not mentioned in Acts 9.

Is the reference to the Lord a reference to God or Jesus? Jervell (1998: 544) argues that God, as the highest authority, is meant, but the narrative flow suggests that the exalted Jesus was directing him. That is, the one speaking seems to be the same one who spoke in verses 13–16. Also in favor of Jesus is that the title "Lord" in verses 10 and 17 seems to point to the same speaker. This fits the pattern in Acts that Jesus or the Spirit guides people, not the Father directly (e.g., 23:11; the vision of Acts 9; Stephen's vision of Jesus in Acts 7). In favor of God the Father would be that Paul was called to be God's witness in verse 15 and Stephen was given the same description ("your witness") in verse 20. Regardless, Paul sees this as a divine command. The ambiguity of the source of the utterance is no accident. In some passages, it is very difficult to ascertain who is speaking for God, whether it be the Father or the Son. Paul's state of consciousness was focused as God spoke directly to him (BAGD 245 §2; BDAG 309). The passage may contain an allusion to Isa. 6:1–13 (O. Betz 1970).

The comment from God about a plot and the need for a hasty escape adds a new detail compared with Acts 9. In 9:29–30, it is the Jerusalem believers who surface a plot and have Paul slip away. However, in Acts 22 Paul is warned by the Lord that such danger will come. Paul apparently was prepared when word of a plot came, or else Luke is telescoping the timing of these events. So again the description here intensifies the experience of Acts 9. This event took place so fast that in Gal. 1:17–18

---

3. On the role of baptism in the early church, see Pelikan 2005: 236–41.

Paul does not count it as a real visit. The Lord protected him from the start.

Paul initially questioned the call to leave Jerusalem, since he thought **22:19–20**
he had credibility, given that he persecuted the new community by imprisonment and beating, including his support for the death of Stephen, another witness of the Lord (8:1). This is something those in Jerusalem know (10:28; 15:7; 20:18). The reference to the blood of Stephen refers to his martyrdom (shed blood: Exod. 24:6; Num. 35:33; Johnson 1992: 391; Witherington 1998: 675). This statement also is new, not appearing in Acts 9.

The Lord told Paul that he had another calling ("I will send you"; Isa. **22:21**
6:9). It was to be sent far away to the Gentiles (13:46; 18:6; Rom. 11:13; Gal. 2:2, 7). This is the second mention that Paul would take the message to all, but here it is the distance he would travel to do it that is highlighted. Paul is claiming a new zeal for God, one rooted in revelation and knowledge.

Paul's defense is that he was where the crowd is now, a persecutor and a faithful Jew; only God's direction has made him otherwise. If there is a complaint to be made about Gentiles being included in God's promise and message, Paul is not to blame. God is responsible for these events. Paul also identifies with the Jews in several verses (vv. 1, 2, 3, 5, 7, 12–13). Paul's speech and faithfulness to the Jews show that he is living out what Jesus called for in the Sermon on the Plain (Luke 6:27–36), namely, to love one's enemies.

With the mention that Israel's God has called him to invite the Gentiles **22:22–24**
into blessing, the crowd reacts, no doubt feeling somewhat confirmed in its suspicions about Paul's pro-Gentile attitudes. As in 21:36, the people cry that Paul should be taken away and does not deserve to live (also Luke 23:18; Acts 8:33; Barrett 1998: 1046). The imperfect verb καθῆκεν (*kathēken*, ought [not to live]) suggests that this has been their ongoing, settled view. The irony is that this is said in front of Gentiles, the Roman soldiers. The reaction is like that against Jesus in Luke 4:24–30, when he spoke of Gentiles being blessed, and that against Paul in Acts 13:48–50. The Jews throw their garments in the air along with dust to indicate that something offensive has been said. It is not entirely clear what this garment-waving gesture is. Do they shake out their garments, take the outer garment off in a mock preparation for stoning, or wave them in the air? Either shaking them out (Witherington 1998: 675) or taking them off (BAGD 736 §1; BDAG 906 §1) is possible. The verb ῥίπτω/ῥιπτέω (*rhiptō/rhipteō*) normally means "throw [something] away" (Exod. 32:19; Deut. 9:17). Throwing dust is a sign of grieving at what has been said (forms of πάσσω, *passō*, sprinkle: 2 Sam. 16:13; Job 2:12), suggesting that they have heard something almost blasphemous

(ἐντινάσσω, *entinassō*, hurl against: 2 Macc. 4:41). In Acts 14:14 garments were torn away at words of offense. It symbolizes waving away the sound of the words, rejecting them.

The tribune has had enough. He orders Paul to be brought into the barracks and prepares to scourge him in order to beat the truth out of him. He would use a whip consisting of a wooden handle with leather thongs attached, to which are tied metal or bone chips (Josephus, *Ant.* 15.8.4 §§289–90; 16.8.1 §232; 16.8.4 §245). In contrast to Acts 16, the beating in Acts 22 is known as a *flagellatio*, since whips (*flagella*) would be used (Polhill 1992: 464). The word Luke uses is μάστιξ (*mastix*, whip; BAGD 495 §1; BDAG 620 §1). The *flagella* were used on noncitizens and slaves. Paul has been speaking in Aramaic, and so the tribune likely would not know what Paul has been saying. If there were a translator, the tribune might be perplexed at the reaction Paul's words provoke.

22:25–29 As in Acts 16, Paul notes that, as a Roman citizen, he should not be treated this way. He is not to be scourged, and there has been no trial to condemn him. He is innocent and yet faces a beating. Paul raises the issue as they stretch him out for the scourging. Barrett (1998: 1048) says that "stretched out for the thongs" is a more likely reading of the Greek than "stretched out by thongs," which would mean that Paul is tied to the whipping frame with thongs.

The area was probably the Gabbatha, a stone pavement in the fortress that also served as a central courtyard. Williams (1990: 381) notes that Jesus was probably scourged here as well.

The centurion decides to report Paul's comment to the tribune to avoid violating Paul's rights as a Roman citizen (v. 26). "To bind a Roman citizen is a crime, to flog him an abomination, to slay him is almost an act of murder" (Cicero, *In Verrem* 2.5.66). Paul's identity as a Roman citizen is the topic of the next several verses.

The centurion informs the tribune of Paul's claim to citizenship. He raises the question in an idiom τί μέλλεις ποιεῖν (*ti melleis poiein*), the force of which is, "Do you know what you are about to do?" (Culy and Parsons 2003: 435). The tribune confirms Paul's citizenship by asking him directly and receiving an affirmative reply. Paul must be able to prove his status because a false claim is also a crime (Suetonius, *Claudius* 25.3; Barrett 1998: 1048). Perhaps he carries his *diploma*, a wooden diptych containing his registration as a citizen (Suetonius, *Nero* 12; Sherwin-White 1963: 146–49). The Valerian and the Porcian Laws prohibited beating a Roman in this way (see Acts 16:37). The Julian Laws allowed appeal to Rome (Sherwin-White 1963: 57–59, 71–76). Any officer who violated these limits would be guilty of a crime (Polhill 1992: 464).

The officer notes that acquiring his own Roman citizenship cost him a great deal of money. The term κεφάλαιον (*kephalaion*) means "capital" or "sum of money" (BAGD 429–30 §2; BDAG 541). This is the only place in the NT where the term has this force. The only other occurrence of this term in the NT is in Heb. 8:1, where it refers to the "sum" of an argument, the main point. This money may well have been a bribe for an offer of citizenship. Such bribes were frequent during the time of Claudius's reign, as the goal was to appear on a list that the emperor would approve (Dio Cassius, *Rom. Hist.* 60.17; Sherwin-White 1939: 237–50; Tajra 1989: 76–89). Paul says that his citizenship came with his birth. This may suggest that his father had some social status that was passed on to the son. The information brings an immediate end to the plan to scourge Paul. They all withdraw, nervous about how they have treated Paul, just as in Acts 16:38. The Roman legal system now protects Paul. He is under arrest unjustly but not physically abused.

Witherington (1998: 679–84) defends Paul's use of citizenship in the scene against the objections of Haenchen (1987: 639; also *pace* Lentz 1993: 21–61, who argues that Luke's desire to portray Paul as having high status and being a man of virtue has nothing to do with Paul's real life). Sherwin-White (1963: 48–75) defends Paul's citizenship in detail (also Rapske 1994b: 72–149; Schnabel 2004: 924, esp. n. 5). In particular, Witherington notes that Paul waited to reveal his Roman citizenship in a setting where Jews were not present, since it was his Gentile-like behavior that the Jews objected to. His appeal to Roman citizenship might not sit well with Jews who refused to compromise with Rome. In addition, it was the tribune's responsibility to determine the status of his prisoner.

In sum, this passage shows us how focused Paul is on representing the gospel even while he also defends himself. The unit also shows how, in an ironic way, the legal system of Rome has nothing to fear from Christianity (and so neither does any other present political state). The passage also indicates that sometimes God can use the governmental systems devised by men to protect Christians. Christians have nothing to fear from systems that seek justice; for, if a Christian has integrity, then the state has nothing to fear from the believer and the believer can make the case that nothing that has been done is designed to undercut the state's right to both exist and create a society of law, order, and peace.

Finally, we see in the opposition to Paul a traditionalism that ends up distorting the genuine tradition. Part of Paul's defense is that he is defending hopes the Jews have held for a long time. His claim is that the faith he possesses is the natural outcome of genuine Jewish tradition, not the distortion of it that has come to deny the messianic hope that God has confirmed through Jesus's resurrection. One danger of a longtime practice or belief that has established itself as a tradition is that it can undercut the faith it is supposed to support. The unwillingness of Paul's opponents to consider how God's recent activity relates to God's promise and program has made them unwilling and unable to respond to a hope designed for them. This is tradition gone bad. It creates blindness and stubbornness, a deadly combination.

Additional Notes

22:9. The phrase "and they became afraid" is another expansion of the Western text and other MSS (D, E, Ψ, Byz).

22:12. The reference to Jews who lived there produced two sets of expansions, neither of which is original. One reads "in Damascus" ($\mathfrak{P}^{41}$, Ψ, 33, 1739, Byz), and the other simply adds the word for "there" (some Itala and Syriac MSS), the latter supplied for the sake of the English but not present in the Greek.

4. Paul before the Jewish Council (22:30–23:11)

Paul gives another defense speech here. The setting is briefly covered in 22:30. Paul has hardly begun, claiming that his conscience is clear, when he is slapped by order of the high priest, and a short exchange takes place about Paul insulting the Jewish leader (23:1–5). Paul then launches into his defense, stating that he is a Pharisee and is being tried because he believes in hope and resurrection, doctrines to which the Pharisees hold (23:6). This leads to a discussion and debate between the Pharisees and Sadducees, since the latter do not hold to resurrection. Some Pharisees even contend that Paul is innocent (23:7–9). The clamor is so great that the tribune ends the meeting (23:10). The scene ends with the Lord appearing to Paul and telling him to take courage because Paul will be the Lord's witness in Rome (23:11). The scene argues again that the new faith is but a natural extension of Judaism (Fitzmyer 1998: 715).

The narrative is rooted in Pauline sources. Fitzmyer (1998: 715) defends the scene against claims of many historical improbabilities and argues that the dialogue is not pure fabrication. Three issues are often raised in objection to the scene: (1) that a tribune could summon the Sanhedrin, (2) that Paul would use the Greek OT in verse 5, and (3) that the issue is not the temple dispute but resurrection. Weiser (1985: 615) has a full list of noted problems (the high-priest incident will be discussed in the exposition), as does Haenchen (1987: 639–42). Roloff (1988: 326–27) also questions the Lord's appearance in verse 11, but this sems to reflect a bias against the supernatural.

None of these three elements is improbable. The Sanhedrin, as adviser to the tribune, may well have come to the inquiry with the hope of finally ridding itself of Paul and placing him in "Roman care" (Sherwin-White 1963: 54; Marshall 1980: 361–62; Pesch 1986b: 240–42; Fitzmyer 1998: 716). There is nothing conceptually in the LXX citation in verse 5 that does not reflect the MT. Paul begins his defense with the resurrection as background to the current dispute and does not succeed in bringing up the temple topic because of the debate over resurrection that emerges between Sadducees and Pharisees. So it is not at all clear that the inquiry is intended to look at the temple issue. Even more, Paul is trying to convince Claudius Lysias of his circumstances. If Paul can convince the tribune that this is but a religious dispute, the Romans will stay out of it. An additional benefit of Paul's approach is that the gospel can be set forth as well (Witherington 1998: 685). The scene is credible. Barrett (1998: 1054–55) discusses the objections one at a time and shows that none is persuasive. Instead he argues that Luke has formed a scene out of traditional material, as does Jervell (1998: 558).

Exegesis and Exposition

²²:³⁰But on the following day, desiring to know the real reason he was accused by the Jews, the tribune unbound him and commanded the chief priests and all the council to meet, and he brought Paul down and set him before them. ²³:¹And Paul, looking intently at the council, said, "Brothers, I have conducted myself before God in all good conscience up to this day." ²And the high priest Ananias commanded those who stood by him to strike him on the mouth. ³Then Paul said to him, "God shall strike you, you whitewashed wall! Are you sitting to judge me according to the law, and yet contrary to the law you order me to be struck?" ⁴Those who stood by said, "Would you revile God's high priest?" ⁵And Paul said, "I did not know, brothers, that he is the high priest; for it is written, 'You shall not speak evil of a ruler of your people.'"

⁶But perceiving that one part was Sadducees and the other Pharisees, Paul cried out in the council, "Brothers, I am a Pharisee, a son of Pharisees; concerning the hope and the resurrection of the dead I am on trial." ⁷And when he had said this, a dissension arose between the Pharisees and the Sadducees; and the assembly was divided. ⁸For the Sadducees say that there is no resurrection, or angel, or spirit; but the Pharisees acknowledge them all. ⁹Then a great clamor arose; and rising up, some of the scribes of the Pharisees' party were contending, "We find nothing wrong in this man. ⌜What if a spirit or an angel spoke to him?⌝" ¹⁰And when the dissension became violent, the tribune, fearing that they would tear Paul in pieces, commanded the soldiers to go down and take him by force from among them to bring him into the barracks.

¹¹The following night the Lord, standing by him, said, "Take courage, for as you have testified about me at Jerusalem, so you must bear witness also at Rome."

22:30 The tribune is still determined to discover why there was so much re-action to Paul. He calls what, in effect, is a pretrial hearing to gather information. Jervell (1998: 553) notes the dispute over whether a Roman ruler could call such a meeting of the Jewish leaders. It does not seem farfetched to recognize, however, that if the Roman tribune wants the leaders' input on Paul, they would welcome the opportunity to give it (see overview to this unit).

The expression γνῶναι τὸ ἀσφαλές (gnōnai to asphales, to know with certainty) refers to the tribune's goal of obtaining the real facts in the matter (BAGD 119 §1b; BDAG 147 §2). The other occurrences of this term in Acts are negative, pointing to an inability to figure out the facts (21:34 [the crowd's shouting out various views about Paul makes it impossible to determine what has caused the riot]; 25:26 [Festus is unable to determine what is going on with Paul and his imprisonment]). Often this term appears in a context where something has to be ferreted out with difficulty. The next day the tribune calls a meeting of the chief priests and council to ascertain the reasons for the chaos. Paul is brought in as well. He is now unbound, no longer held in chains, probably out of respect for his Roman citizenship. The tribune is trying to get to the bottom of this, as in his view he cannot release Paul until he figures out what has caused the disturbance.

In what is surely a condensed account of the scene (Marshall 1980: 362), Paul addresses his audience, since it is Paul's perspective that Luke undertakes to present. Paul opens by declaring that he has a clear conscience, a remark similar in tone to how he addressed the Ephesian elders (20:18–20, 33–35). He has lived as a good citizen before God; this is the force of the perfect-tense verb (πεπολίτευμαι, *pepoliteumai*; 3 Macc. 3:4; 4 Macc. 5:16; Phil. 1:27; Larkin 1995: 326; Barrett 1998: 1057–58; Strathmann, *TDNT* 6:534). Paul will appeal to conscience again in another defense speech, when he says that he takes pains to have a blameless conscience before God (Acts 24:16). Johnson (1992: 396) calls "conscience" (συνείδησις, *syneidēsis*) a thoroughly Pauline word (Rom. 2:15; 9:1; 13:5; 1 Cor. 8:7, 10, 12; 10:25–29; 2 Cor. 1:12; 4:2; 5:11). These are the only two occurrences of the term in Acts. Paul mentions a good conscience in 1 Tim. 1:5, 19 (conceptually, 1 Cor. 4:4). When the high priest hears this, he orders Paul struck for an offensive utterance (Stählin, *TDNT* 8:267–68). According to later tradition, one could strike a Jew only in order to defend God's honor (*b. Sanh.* 85a; Le Cornu and Shulam 2003: 1243). The high priest Ananias served from about AD 47 to AD 58 or 59 (Josephus, *Ant.* 20.5.2 §103). He had a reputation for being insolent and quick-tempered (Josephus, *Ant.* 20.9.1 §199; on his death in AD 66, see *J.W.* 2.17.9 §§441–42, which tells us that his pro-Roman position caused him to be slain by the zealot leader Menahem; on his handling of tensions while in office, see *Ant.* 20.9.2–3 §§205–9; Le Cornu and Shulam 2003: 1238–40). Did he order this verbally or by a signal? The text does not say.

Paul's response to being struck is firm. It may even reflect that he loses his own temper here, as he steps back in verse 5 from his verbal attack. He calls Ananias, the one responsible, a "whitewashed wall" (τοῖχε κεκονιαμένε, *toiche kekoniamene*) and warns that God will strike him for ordering that Paul be struck contrary to the Jewish law. The allusion may well be a curse (Deut. 28:22; *m. Šeb.* 4.13; Str-B 2:766). The phrase "whitewashed wall" is unique in the NT, but a similar expression, "whitewashed tomb," appears in Matt. 23:27 (Ezek. 13:10–16; CD 8.12).

The description is an insult, as it says that although the person appears clean, there is no depth to the person (BAGD 443; BDAG 558). In the background may be the idea of painting a washed wall with ashes to warn of the defilement a seemingly clean appearance hides (*m. Šeqal.* 1.1; *m. Maʿaś. Š.* 5.1; Le Cornu and Shulam 2003: 1243). Such a person is like a clean and sturdy wall only on the surface and is actually unclean and insecure. Paul goes on to accuse Ananias of hypocrisy, violating the law he claims to defend, because Paul is presumed innocent until proved guilty (Lev. 19:15; Bruce 1988a: 425).

23:4–5   Those present with the high priest rebuke Paul for insulting him. To revile the high priest is against the law (Exod. 22:28 [22:27 LXX]; revile: BAGD 479; BDAG 602), as Paul's reply explains. This is the only occurrence of the verb (λοιδορέω, *loidoreō*, revile) in Acts. It is a common term for religious disputes but appears in only three other places in the NT (John 9:28 [Jews reacting to Jesus]; 1 Cor. 4:12 [when reviled, we bless]; 1 Pet. 2:23 [of Jesus reviled at his death]).

Paul says that he did not know it was the high priest giving the order. His address of the audience as "brothers" as in verse 1 shows Paul again identifying with his audience. This remark has produced much discussion. How can Paul fail to recognize the high priest? Gaventa (2003: 314) sees none of these five proposed options as satisfying: (1) Paul does not hear the order for him to be struck. (2) His eyesight, which is not good, does not allow him to see that it is the high priest who gives the order. This second view may assume that a sign is given to strike Paul. (3) Fitzmyer (1998: 717) argues that Paul's long absence from Jerusalem means that he no longer knows the high priest (Bruce 1988a: 427 notes this option). (4) The remark is ironic in the sense that Paul is trying to show that the high priest is not really the representative of the people and of God's way, but because the high priest is so perceived by the people, Paul retracts his words (Marshall 1980: 364; Williams 1990: 385; Culy and Parsons 2003: 440 note this view and read the verse with this ironic force: "Oh, I did not know he was the high priest"). (5) Paul reacts without considering the man's position (Polhill 1992: 469n68; Larkin 1995: 328). Any of these options is possible, although either of the latter two is more likely, as the first two are difficult to accept as probable and the third also seems uncertain given Paul's past relationships with Jews in Jerusalem. Barrett (1998: 1061–62) makes no choice but sees historical roots in the remark. A key point is that Paul ultimately submits himself to the law here.

23:6–9   The scene now turns to Paul's key remarks. Paul knows that he has Pharisees and Sadducees in the audience, and so he begins by appealing to his roots as a Pharisee (Phil. 3:5) and his belief in hope and resurrection (Acts 13:32–33), two themes Pharisees emphasize in contrast to Sadducees, who tend to shun eschatology and to deny resurrection (Josephus, *Ant.*

18.1.2–3 §§12–17; *J.W.* 2.8.14 §§163–65; Mark 12:18–27). Eckey (2000: 515–16) notes that Luke is less harsh on the Pharisees than the other evangelists. This is truer of Acts than of the Gospel of Luke, but it makes an important point. Even opponents of Jesus and the gospel may have the ability to appreciate and respond to the message. It is certainly true that Pharisees, as believers in resurrection, had less mental distance to overcome than the Sadducees did, who denied resurrection as part of their own doctrine. Some opponents of the gospel are in a better position to respond to the message than others are because of what they do believe (on the Pharisees, see Meyer and H. Weiss, *TDNT* 9:11–48, esp. 45–46; on the Sadducees, Meyer, *TDNT* 7:35–54). "Ac[ts] 23:6–9 is important in the history of primitive Christianity to the degree that in the tradition which Luke uses there is still a lively sense that for all the differences which the kerygmatic content of the gospel necessarily entails, the preaching of the apostles is closer to the world of popular belief and thought, in which Pharisaism is very largely rooted, than it is to the priestly theology of Jerusalem, which is regarded as Sadducean in the pejorative sense and hence essentially alien" (*TDNT* 7:54).

No extrabiblical text speaks of such a complete denial of angels and spirits by the Sadducees. In fact, the Pentateuch, which the Sadducees held as authoritative, affirms the existence of such beings. Parker (2003) notes and evaluates four views on this expression of doctrinal denial by the Sadducees, noting that almost everyone recognizes that Luke's description of the Sadducees in verse 8 must be qualified or is not intended to be universal in scope (see also Meier 2001: 406–8). There are a total of six possible explanations for Luke's claim:

1. The Sadducees rejected angels and spirits altogether (Str-B 2:767). This view sometimes includes appeals to *b. Sanh.* 38b, where Rabbi Idith contends that in Exod. 24:1 the prayer is to God, not an angel Metatron. This angel was sometimes seen in Judaism as the angel of the Lord. But this tractate passage only presents one Sadducee's view about not praying to an angel, not a denial of their existence. So it does not offer unqualified support for Luke's statement.
2. They rejected excessive speculation about angels and spirits (Manson 1938; Bruce 1990: 466).
3. They rejected that the righteous dead came back in the form of spirits between death and resurrection. This view argues that "angel" and "spirit" mean the same thing in verses 8 and 9 (Daube 1990; Gaventa 2003: 315). It is unlikely, however, that these two terms should be taken as synonymous. Parker (2003: 351) notes how Luke's use of "neither . . . nor" (μήτε, *mēte* [2x]) in verse 8 rules this out.
4. They denied that resurrection included coming back in the form of an angel or spirit (so Lachs 1977; Viviano and Taylor 1992). Parker (2003: 353–59), however, argues that the Pharisees likewise would

not have been open to a resurrection within history before the end, which is what Paul's argument along the lines of view 4 would also require.

5. They rejected the idea that an angel or spirit can speak through a human being as an agent of revelation (Bamberger 1963). This view, however, does not seem relevant to Acts 23, as the issue is not about an angel speaking through a human being but a "raised from the dead" human speaking.

6. Many think that what Luke describes here is a belief in a full hierarchy of angels and their role in eschatology (Polhill 1992: 470). A variation of this is the idea that the Sadducees' rejection of Fate included a rejection of the belief that angels are "agents of Fate" (Le Cornu and Shulam 2003: 1250). The Greek has a reference to the Pharisees confessing "both" (τὰ ἀμφότερα, *ta amphotera*), although three things are discussed (resurrection, angels, and spirits). Either this is an expression that collapses angels and spirits into one theme (Fitzmyer 1998: 719), or Luke is using the term loosely to refer to three things (Polhill 1992: 470), which sometimes happens (Acts 19:16; Johnson 1992: 398).

There is almost a choral-like mention of this issue in the text, as 23:6, 8, and 9 show. The dispute, to Paul's Jewish listeners, is focused on two points: (1) the possibility of resurrection and (2) that some particular supernatural force addressed Paul.

Which of the six views is most likely? In Parker's view, a concern about how a spirit could communicate with Paul explains the singular reference to an angel or a spirit in verses 8 and 9 and may imply the Sadducees' rejection of such communication. So Parker (2003: 360–65) opts for view 6, which sees angels or spirits as agents of the outworking of God's sovereignty and the fate of humanity, another concept the Sadducees reject by emphasizing free will. This best combines the data and so could well be the point of the verse. The remark about denying an afterlife may well mean any "positive form of afterlife," as some Sadducees held to a shadowy existence in Sheol (Witherington 1998: 692). Also note how often angels are invoked as present when they are not (Luke 24:36–43; Acts 12:15; 23:9).

The reference to hope and resurrection is probably a hendiadys: it is hope rooted in resurrection. The OT and Jewish roots of the concept point to the hope of life after death (Dan. 12:2; 2 Macc. 7:14; 1 En. 51.1–5; Ps. Sol. 3.11–12). The term "hope" appears eight times in Acts.[1] These uses are more frequent at the end of the book as Paul explains his message.

---

1. Acts 2:26 (from the promise of protection through resurrection); 16:19 (hope of gain was gone when the slave girl was exorcised by Paul); 24:15 (hope of resurrection); 26:5–7 ([2x]; hope of the promise made to the fathers); 27:20 (a secular use: no hope of

His hope is to induce them to debate with each other. He also is making the point that he is on trial for holding a Jewish teaching.

The theme of the law pointing to promise and hope is frequent in Acts (24:15, 20–21; 26:6–7, 26–29; 28:20). We see the law treated in a variety of ways in Luke-Acts. Jesus generally handles law as commandments, especially when asked theological questions by others, because this is how Jesus's audience related to law. But law can also be seen as being about promise (Luke 16:16; the patch and wine passages in Luke 5:33–39; Luke 6:1–11), and this is how Paul addresses it here. Being a believing Jew means having hope, including hope in resurrection. In the Mishnah, denial of the afterlife leads to a strong rebuke, as *m. Sanh.* 10.1 reads, "He that says there is no resurrection of the dead prescribed in the law" has no share in the life to come. The theme of hope just noted is associated with this point in Acts 2:26; 24:15; 26:6–7; and 28:20.

The proximity between the Pharisees' belief in resurrection and Christian faith leads to a discussion and split in the assembly, as the Pharisees accept Paul's view of the possibility of resurrection whereas the Sadducees do not (Luke 20:27). The text points to dissension by using the term στάσις (*stasis*) in verses 7 and 10 and calling the disagreement a great "clamor" (κραυγή, *kraugē*) in verse 9. The term στάσις has often been used in Acts to express division, such as the one that launched the Jerusalem Council (15:2). Five of the nine NT occurrences appear in Acts (15:2; 19:40; 23:7, 10; 24:5). Here is the only instance of κραυγή in Acts among six occurrences in the NT (the others are Matt. 25:6; Luke 1:42; Eph. 4:31; Heb. 5:7; Rev. 21:4). It refers to an outcry (Luke 1:42) or, in this case, a series of verbal exchanges. They "were contending" (διεμάχοντο, *diemachonto*) with each other back and forth. This is the only instance of this verb in the NT. It means "vie for" something, "fight for" something verbally (BAGD 186; BDAG 233).

In a narrative aside, Luke notes that the Pharisees also accept the idea of another form of existence, as their acceptance of angels and spirits shows, in contrast to the Sadducees, who accept no angel or spirit (μήτε ἄγγελον μήτε πνεῦμα, *mēte angelon mēte pneuma*). This remark may suggest a condensed account because the idea of Jesus raised could evoke for Pharisees either the idea of an intermediate state (Lachs 1977; Barrett 1998: 1065; Daube 1990) or an angelic type of form. On the other hand, Sadducees believed death brought either a complete end to life or a shadowy existence in Sheol apart from the angels and God. So this denial of angel or spirit may mean that they held to no positive form of afterlife (Witherington 1998: 692). This remark might also represent an allusion to the announcement at the tomb or, more likely, to the Lord's spiritual appearance to Paul. It also shows that the readers

being rescued from the ship); 28:20 (because of the hope of Israel, Paul has been bound); in Paul: 1 Cor. 15:19; Col. 1:5; 1 Thess. 4:13; Titus 1:2; 3:7; Johnson 1992: 398.

of Acts include Gentiles, since Jews would know these details about the Pharisees and Sadducees. Some Pharisees defend Paul explicitly, saying there is nothing wrong with his views and that he might have seen an angel or a spirit. Here BDF §482 sees the remark as an example of speech that cuts short its idea because of emotion. The full idea would be, "If an angel or spirit spoke to him, then what point would there be in opposition?" This reaction defends Paul's experience as possible, but does not affirm Jesus's authority, something possible for these Pharisees. In their view, Paul cannot be challenged for the mere claim of such an experience. Hence, their conclusion, "There is nothing wrong with this man." Paul's innocence is something consistently affirmed from here on (Acts 23:29; 25:18–20, 25; 26:31–32).

23:10   The dissension continues to have the potential to become violent, and the tribune fears that Paul might be torn in two. The only other NT occurrence of the verb διασπάω (diaspaō) is in Mark 5:4, where the demon-possessed man tears apart his chains as he wanders among the tombs. Judges 14:6 LXX (Alexandrinus text) uses it to describe how Samson tore apart a lion. The tribune commands the soldiers to take Paul back to the barracks to protect Paul.

23:11   That night the Lord reappears to Paul (cf. Luke 2:9 [angel of the Lord]; 24:4 [two men (angels) appear]; Acts 12:7 [angel of the Lord]; 16:9 [vision]; 18:9 [Lord in a vision]; 22:17 [Lord in a trance]; 27:23–24 [angel of the Lord]), an act confirming his claims. He tells Paul to take courage, for Paul will be a witness in Rome as he has been in Jerusalem (take courage: Matt. 9:2, 22; 14:27; Mark 6:50; 10:49; John 16:33; to Rome: Acts 19:21; 22:21). As uncertain as things appear to the tribune and others, this appearance indicates that the Lord has a plan that Paul will carry out.

In sum, we see here that Paul defends his faith both with an understanding of what he believes and an ability to express it in relationship to those hearing him. When Paul mentions the hope of resurrection, he is speaking to Jews about a doctrine the Jews have discussed. Paul's ability to think from a variety of perspectives, even perspectives he does not share, is part of what makes him so effective. This connection with his Jewish hearers is rooted in the fact that Christianity sees itself as the natural and promised extension of Jewish hope, but this principle of connecting with an audience is also seen in Acts 17, when Paul addresses non-Jewish hearers and seeks to connect with them through the idea of God as Creator of all, even citing ideas from the Greeks' own poetry to make his point.

There is another application here. It is that despite the opposition, there is a respect that Paul seeks to embody as he communicates, and when it is pointed out that he has crossed that line into disrespect, he acknowledges it (Stott 1990: 352). We see this tone in all of Paul's evangelistic and defense speeches. Even when Paul is direct and has to confront, he does so in a tone of respect.

Additional Note

23:9. Byz completes the "if" clause with an apodosis: "If a spirit or an angel spoke to him, let us not fight against God."

5. The Plot against Paul Uncovered (23:12–22)

This scene reconfirms that Paul is in considerable danger. His nephew uncovers the fact that more than forty Jews have taken a vow to murder the apostle. The plan is to intercept Paul when he is brought down for another hearing (vv. 12–15). Paul's nephew tells the apostle, who sends his nephew to the tribune by way of a centurion (vv. 16–18). The nephew reports the plot to the tribune (vv. 19–21), who tells the nephew not to let anyone know that he has informed the Romans of the plot (v. 22). God's sovereign care for Paul is underscored in this discovery. The movement to Rome begins. Paul now departs Jerusalem for the final time in Acts with the Roman tribune as his unwitting, just protector. The divine plan has some surprising twists (Roloff 1988: 330–31).

This is not the first plot against Paul in Acts (9:23–25, 29–30; 20:3), but it is presented with the most detail (Gaventa 2003: 317–18). The scene adds a note of drama as it details the real threat to Paul. Intrigue and conspiracy surround Paul's efforts. His mission has much at stake, so people react.

This narrative section is rooted in Luke's Pauline source (Fitzmyer 1998: 722). Barrett (1998: 1070–71) even notes the possibility of family memories here. Paul is brought to Caesarea, where official Roman examinations occur. This is not an independent anecdote that knows nothing about an examination by the Jewish Council (but so Conzelmann 1987: 194). It is only natural that the tribune would want to move Paul out of Jerusalem once violence becomes possible. This is the third Roman rescue of Paul (21:32–36; 23:10).

Exegesis and Exposition

[12]When it became day, the Jews, making a plot, bound themselves by an oath neither to eat nor drink till they had killed Paul. [13]There were more than forty who formed this conspiracy. [14]And going to the chief priests and elders, they said, "We have strictly bound ourselves by an oath to taste no food till we have killed Paul. [15]You therefore give notice now to the tribune to bring him down to you along with the council, as though you were going to determine his case more exactly. And we are ready to kill him before he comes near ⌜ ⌝."

[16]Now the son of Paul's sister, hearing of their ambush, going and entering the barracks, told Paul. [17]And calling one of the centurions, Paul said, "Take this

young man to the tribune; because he has something to tell him." [18]So taking him, the centurion brought him to the tribune and said, "Paul the prisoner, calling me, asked me to bring this young man to you because he has something to say to you." [19]Taking him by the hand and going aside, the tribune asked him privately, "What is it that you have to tell me?" [20]And he said, "The Jews have agreed to ask you to bring Paul down to the council tomorrow, as though they were going to inquire somewhat more closely concerning him. [21]But do not yield to them; for more than forty of their men lie in ambush for him, having bound themselves by an oath to neither eat nor drink till they have killed him; and now they are ready, waiting for the consent from you." [22]So the tribune dismissed the young man, commanding him, "Tell no one that you have informed me of these things."

Justice is moving too slowly for some, so they seek to take matters into their own hands. More than forty Jews swear an oath during a conspiracy meeting, as the term "plot" (συστροφήν, *systrophēn*) indicates (Acts 19:40 is the only other NT use of this term; Polybius, *Hist.* 4.34.6; 1 Macc. 14:44; BAGD 795; BDAG 979; Johnson 1992: 403). They swear to take neither food nor drink until Paul has been killed. This oath is a commitment to swear to do something or to underwrite a statement by placing oneself under a curse if it fails (BAGD 54 §1; BDAG 63; 1 En. 6.4–5). The verb ἀναθεματίζω (*anathematizō*, bind with an oath) is used only four times in the NT, three of them in this passage (vv. 14, 21). In Mark 14:71, it refers to the oath Peter invoked to deny that he knew Jesus. One could escape from such a vow if it became unfulfillable (*m. Ned.* 3.1, 3; Bruce 1988a: 431). Although the reference to "Jews" is vague, the point is that some but not all Jews are very hostile toward Paul and are trying to do something to remove him from the scene.

From a narrative standpoint, the effort to take matters into their own hands flies in the face of God's program as revealed in Acts 23:11. Those who seek to take events into their own hands do not have as much control as they think (Gaventa 2003: 322). And in seeking to take matters into their own hands, they also overstep the divine law they think they are defending, by agreeing to lie and murder. The irony is that they take an oath before God that actually violates God's standards and will.

The forty report their plan to the chief priests and elders and implore them to cooperate by asking the tribune to bring Paul in for another examination where they can "determine more exactly" (διαγινώσκειν ἀκριβέστερον, *diaginōskein akribesteron*) what has taken place. The comparative ἀκριβέστερον is used with elative force, something repeated in verse 20 with the claim that the Jewish group wishes to examine Paul "more closely" (Moulton and Turner 1963: 30). The ruse is to promise to make a judgment about Paul to the tribune. This is more than a simple request by the forty, as the verb ἐμφανίσατε (*emphanisate*, give notice)

23:12–13

23:14–15

is in the imperative mood. The verb is repeated in verse 22. The whole exercise is a pretense. When they bring him in, the plotters will seize Paul. At a narrative level, the high priest's involvement in this conspiracy shows the truth of Paul's insult in verse 3 that the priest is a whitewashed wall. This is because the priest agrees to deception and violates the law he is supposed to defend. His undercutting of a legal process entails injustice and potential murder. The entire group has contemplated violating one of the Ten Commandments. We are not told that the leaders agreed, but such agreement is implied by the reaction of the nephew, who hears about the plot and advises the tribune of it.

23:16–21   Paul's nephew gets wind of the plan and tells Paul, who in turn asks the centurion to take the nephew to the tribune so that the Roman leader can be informed of the plot (ἐνέδραν, *enedran*, ambush, v. 16). This term appears only twice in the NT (the other instance is 25:3, where a plot is attempted before Festus; see also Josh. 8:7, 9 LXX). The verb for this idea (ἐνεδρεύουσιν, *enedreuousin*) appears in 23:21. The centurion reports to the tribune that Paul sent his nephew "because he has" something to tell you; ἔχοντα (*echonta*, having) in verse 18 is a causal participle in force (Moulton and Turner 1963: 157; NET; HCSB). The nephew reports the plot in detail, including the idea that the request for a further inquiry includes an ambush involving more than forty men who have taken an oath. The nephew tells the tribune that they are ready to act if the tribune promises them an inquiry. Roloff (1988: 331) thinks that the nephew has circulated in Zealot circles, but we in fact know nothing more about him.

   The presence of the nephew means that Paul has family in the Jerusalem region. The nephew is described in a manner that makes him either a teenager (νεανίσκον, *neaniskon*, v. 18; Williams 1990: 389) or in his twenties (νεανίαν, *neanian*, v. 17; Witherington 1998: 695; Philo, *Creation* 36 §105). The visit to Paul is not problematic, considering that Paul is not convicted of a crime and is a Roman citizen. There is other evidence of such visits (Lucian, *The Passing of Peregrinus* 12–13; Phil. 2:25; 2 Tim. 1:16–17; Passion of Saints Perpetua and Felicity 3; Johnson 1992: 404; contra Haenchen 1987: 646). Some scholars suggest that there was too much tumult around Paul to allow visitors (Gaventa 2003: 320), but it may be that one's family may have had access, though with visitation limited. The fact that the tribune thinks that Paul is innocent may also mean that Paul is given access to others. Acts 23:18 is the first mention that Paul is prisoner (δέσμιος, *desmios*).

23:22   The tribune prepares to act, telling the nephew to let no one know that they have discussed the matter.

   In sum, this passage is rooted in God's providence, which moves to protect God's children, although the means are not always known as they are here. God works behind-the-scenes here. Stephen's martyrdom shows that providence also does not always mean physical rescue as here with Paul. Paul is assured that he will reach Rome (23:11). It is ironic that Roman justice will bring him there as a prisoner so that Paul will arrive safely and immediately be speaking to the highest levels of Roman society. It is unlikely that if Paul had journeyed as part of a missionary outreach to Rome on his own, such a high-level audience would be possible. It is one of the mysteries of God and his providence that many times we cannot see why things are happening as they are. Yet God is surely at work in ways we could not have planned for ourselves.

Additional Note

23:15. The Western text adds a note that the plotters will kill Paul even if they also are killed for seizing him. Although this point is not in the original wording, it is a likely outcome for the plot.

6. Paul Is Sent to Caesarea and to Felix (23:23–35)

The tribune, Claudius Lysias, acts to protect Paul from ambush and to move him overnight to Caesarea. He commissions two hundred soldiers, seventy horsemen, and two hundred spearmen to serve as an escort. Paul and his guards will go by horse (vv. 23–24). In addition, the tribune supplies an explanatory letter to Felix, the governor, that indicates the cause of the arrest and that he is not able to determine much beyond the fact that it is a dispute over Jewish law. His conclusion is that nothing here deserves imprisonment or death. In addition, he tells of the plot as the reason Paul is sent on, with any further trial to be called by Felix (vv. 25–30). The military escorts Paul to Caesarea, where Felix says that he will schedule a hearing when the accusers arrive (vv. 31–35).

The account is a narrative rooted in Pauline sources. Jervell (1998: 565) attributes 23:12–35 to multiple sources, even possibly some eyewitnesses. He argues that the unit is in Lukan style, and attributes the letter to Luke (on the letter, see vv. 26–30). The letter states what is obvious about why Paul is being held as the object of a necessary examination.

Exegesis and Exposition

[23]Then calling two of the centurions, the tribune said, "At the third hour of the night get ready two hundred soldiers with seventy horsemen and two hundred spearmen to go as far as Caesarea. [24]Also provide mounts for Paul to ride, and bring him safely to Felix the governor." [25]⌜ ⌝ And he wrote a letter that went like this:

[26]"Claudius Lysias to His Excellency the governor Felix, greetings. [27]This man was seized by the Jews, and was about to be killed by them, when I came upon them with the soldiers and rescued him, having learned that he was a Roman citizen. [28]And desiring to know the charge because of which they accused him, I brought him down to their council. [29]I found that he was accused about disputes over their law, but charged with nothing deserving death or imprisonment. [30]And when it was disclosed to me that there was a plot against the man, I sent him to you at once, ordering his accusers also to state before you the things they have against him."

[31]So the soldiers, according to their instructions taking Paul, brought him by night to Antipatris. [32]And the next day they returned to the barracks, leaving the

horsemen to go on with him. ³³And coming to Caesarea and delivering the letter to the governor, they presented Paul also before him. ³⁴On reading the letter, asking to what province Paul belonged, the governor learned that he was from Cilicia. ³⁵He said, "I will schedule a hearing when your accusers arrive." And he commanded him to be guarded in Herod's praetorium.

The tribune calls two of his centurions and orders that a force of 470 soldiers be gathered to escort Paul to Caesarea. This is Caesarea Maritima, the Roman governor's seat in Judea (see the discussion on Acts 21:7–9 about this city). The soldiers will leave at the third hour of the evening (9 p.m.) and ride with Paul to the governor, Felix.[1] He was a favored freed slave, appointed by the emperor Claudius. Felix's rule began in AD 52 or 53 and likely ended in AD 59 or 60, when he was recalled for his failure to deal well with Jewish violence. His third wife was Drusilla, daughter of Herod Agrippa I, and his first was the granddaughter (or great-granddaughter) of Antony and Cleopatra. Felix's rule was violent and chaotic, as the Zealots began to emerge during his time. In defense of Roman authority, he ruthlessly tried to put them down, only heightening the violence.

Paul is allowed to ride the distance, giving him added mobility in case of attack. The term κτήνη (*ktēnē*) is a general word for an animal that can be ridden; it might not be a horse but a mule or donkey (BAGD 455; BDAG 572). The journey covers about sixty miles. The over ten-to-one ratio of soldiers to plotters will guarantee that they reach Caesarea. The 470 make up half the garrison, but the entire escort goes only part of the way (v. 32). The reference to δεξιολάβους (*dexiolabous*) is probably to spearmen; it means "taking something in the right hand." Barrett (1998: 1077–78) notes another possible meaning for the rarely used term, that is, lead horses by the right hand as replacements to ride on the journey. In this case, the force would be halved. This would seem to limit the responsiveness of the escort, however, if there were trouble. The number seems large, but the extent of the threat is something the tribune does not know, and the trip to Caesarea is filled with the possibility of attacks from other Zealots (Pesch 1986b: 249–50n10; Williams 1990: 390; Witherington 1998: 696–97). Perhaps the tribune is using the occasion as an exercise for troops whose job might otherwise be rather tedious. It may also be that such displays of troop power serve as a reminder of a powerful Roman presence, especially in a rule that

---

1. On Felix, see Josephus, *Ant.* 20.7.1 §§137–38 (appointed by Claudius, he persuaded the beautiful Drusilla to divorce her husband and marry him); 20.8.9 §182 (not popular with the Jews, who accused him of not being a just governor); *J. W.* 2.12.8 §247; Suetonius, *Claudius* 28; Tacitus, *Hist.* 5.9 (portrays him as an evil man who wielded power insensitively, like a slave); *Annals* 12.54. For issues tied to the name and wives of Felix, see Brenk and Canali de Rossi 2001; Jervell 1998: 562n171; and the additional note on 23:24.

has dealt with numerous incidents (Jervell 1998: 562). This is the last time in Acts that we see Paul in Jerusalem.

23:25   Claudius Lysias pens a letter of explanation that comes with Paul to the governor. Such a letter was common in this situation. It was known as a *litterae dimissoriae*, a letter sent in case of an appeal (*provocatio*; Justinian, *Digest* 49.6.1; Fitzmyer 1998: 726). There is no appeal yet here, but the circumstances are similar, as it is not yet clear to the tribune what took place. The letter that accompanies the transfer will lead to a trial that follows Roman custom in the case of a *cognitio extra ordinem*, an inquiry outside the order (Sherwin-White 1963: 48). The nature of the charge, disturbing the peace in a major way, also means that the governor needs to handle the case (Polhill 1992: 474). The remark "of this type" (ἔχουσαν τὸν τύπον τοῦτον, *echousan ton typon touton*) may indicate that Luke is not quoting the letter but summarizing its content in typical form (Marshall 1980: 370), but Bruce (1990: 471) suggests that the expression could point to a verbatim copy, in which case the phrase would refer to a letter "that went like this" (*NewDocs* 1 no. 26; 2 no. 27; 1 Macc. 11:29; 15:2; 3 Macc. 3:30; Let. Aris. 34; Bruce 1978 [on Felix's name]; Hemer 1987). Interestingly, Bruce (1988a: 434) earlier preferred the general-purport view. This is possibly the sense, as such letters were normally not made public, but in this case its basic contents may have been revealed at the hearing, given the uncertainty of the situation. Our translation reflects the verbatim view. Witherington (1998: 698) argues correctly that a decision on the sense and force of the phrase is not clear, since we do not have enough information to decide. At the least, we have a translation, since the letter most likely would be in Latin. Other works also quote official records like this (see Josephus, books of Maccabees, and Letter of Aristeas; Le Cornu and Shulam 2003: 1273–74; see also the introduction to 24:1–27 below).

23:26–30   The letter begins with a standard greeting of respect for Felix as His Excellency (of Theophilus in Luke 1:3). The letter has five parts: introduction (v. 26); Paul's arrest (v. 27); the investigation (v. 28); the conclusion (v. 29); and the reason Paul is now in Caesarea (v. 30; Fitzmyer 1998: 726). The tribune's first name, Claudius, is a Roman name this Gentile took when he became a Roman citizen. Claudius explains the circumstances of Paul's confinement but with an exaggeration of Felix's role, a way of ingratiating himself to Felix, despite Barrett's (1998: 1083) note that there is a possibility that Luke himself supplied this feature. Part of a decision here is dependent on one's opinion of the letter's authenticity (discussed above). Claudius explains that the Jews were about to kill Paul, a Roman citizen, when Claudius rescued him. Actually, the discovery of Paul's social status came after the seizing of Paul, although it is true that Claudius's act did save the apostle. The concise nature of the report also allows Claudius to ignore that he almost flogged a Roman citizen (Johnson 1992: 405). The Greek in verse 30 moves from a genitive absolute into an indirect statement that closes with the normal farewell. Conzelmann (1987: 195) notes the many juristic terms in verses 27–35 as this transfer sets up the examination in 24:1–23.

Claudius explains that he held a council meeting to determine the cause of the disturbance but was unable to reach any conclusion except that there was a dispute about Jewish law, nothing that should result in Paul's death or imprisonment. Statements about Paul's innocence appear repeatedly in Acts (24:19–20; 25:25; 26:31; 28:18). Gallio draws a similar conclusion earlier in Acts (18:15). This detail is important to Luke: a "neutral" outside party assesses the issue and determines that there is no real threat to Rome, only an internal Jewish religious debate. The term for "disputes" (ζητημάτων, zētēmatōn) appears only five times in the NT, all of which are in Acts (the others are 15:2 [the Jerusalem Council dispute]; 18:15 [another Roman judges the disputes to be about Jewish issues]; 25:19 [yet another legal report that the dispute is about Jewish issues]; 26:3 [Paul looks forward to Agrippa judging such disputes with knowledge]). The judgment that Paul has done nothing worthy of death is like Pilate's judgment about Jesus in Luke 23:14–15, using the same terms. Jesus and Paul are on parallel tracks in this respect. The portrait is not entirely flattering to the Romans as some claim, given that the tribune thinks that Paul is innocent but still holds him in custody.

The soldiers escort Paul to Antipatris before the horsemen take the **23:31–35** apostle the rest of the way. Antipatris was thirty-seven miles northwest of Jerusalem, roughly halfway to Caesarea, which was not quite twenty-five miles more to the north, northwest of Antipatris (Josephus, *Ant.* 1.21.9 §417). It was built by Herod the Great, was located in Samaria, but had a mixed Samaritan and Jewish population that ran to the coast (Le Cornu and Shulam 2003: 1277). Reaching Antipatris completes the dangerous part of the trip by getting away from the plotters. They also have traversed the locales most likely to be used in an ambush (Dar and Applebaum 1973, although there is discussion on the exact location of Antipatris). The area between Antipatris and Caesarea is predominantly Gentile and so less dangerous for Roman troops. Some scholars complain that the trip to Antipatris is too long for one night, given that infantry could cover only about twenty miles in an evening. However, once the escort reaches Antipatris, the footmen return to Jerusalem. So "by night" may well mean "overnight," reaching into the next day.

When Paul arrives, the letter is presented to the governor. Felix asks Paul where he is from, and Paul tells him Cilicia. Still, Felix decides to try the case in the locale of the offense rather than in the accused's home province. To try the case in the locale of the crime is known as the *forum delicti* (Sherwin-White 1963: 55–57; Marshall 1980: 373; *forum domicilii* is to try the case in the accused's hometown province). Such information about a defendant's home is typical in a Roman legal process that includes something like a pretrial hearing. Felix commits to have a hearing when Paul's accusers arrive. He would not want to send Paul to the Syrian legate, since the case is too small and Paul's accusers would have to travel too far, a point that would annoy them (Le Cornu and Shulam 2003: 1279). Until Paul's accusers can arrive, he is held in Herod's praetorium (Josephus, *Ant.* 15.9.6 §331). Paul spends two years in prison here. Ironically, Paul is under both Roman custody and protection.

In sum, this passage continues to develop how God has providentially made it possible for Paul to travel to Rome to witness to the empire's highest levels. We also obtain a glimpse of human nature through Claudius Lysias. He takes credit for more than he was really responsible for in protecting Paul, making it sound as if he stepped in and provided the appropriate protection from the start. This tendency to self-exaltation, common as it is, still is not exemplary. It is one of the very human touches Luke gives to Acts.

When we combine this section with the previous one, we see an array of characters reflecting diverse responses to the gospel. The Jewish leadership is mostly hostile, though some are willing to entertain the ideas Paul sets forth. For the most part, the Romans are strictly functional in their reaction. They are more interested in living through and carrying out the duties of their everyday lives than seriously engaging what Paul is setting forth. Many people go through life just pursuing their own goals or seeking to survive rather than engaging in a serious way with what God has for them. Whether this is the result of their own background and training about life or is motivated by the self-focus our culture tends to generate, it is a major distraction from the reason we were created by God. The Creator deserves more than a patronizing recognition in our lives. As throughout this section of Acts, Paul is the exemplary figure. He acknowledges God not only in his words but also by the very manner he faces this diversity of response. He also uses the opportunities he has to be a testimony to God.

Additional Notes

23:24. The full name of Felix is debated and has received much discussion because Josephus and Tacitus do not agree about it. Tacitus in *Hist.* 5.9 (and implied in *Ann.* 12.54) calls him Marcus Antonius Felix whereas Josephus calls him Tiberius Claudius Felix in *Ant.* 20.7.1 §137 (Tajra 1989: 109–10). Bruce (1978) argues that his name was Tiberius Claudius Felix, on the basis of an inscription from Bir el Malik known as the Clemens epitaph. Hemer (1987), however, says that later discussion shows this inscription not to be about Felix. He notes that evidence from other inscriptions is ambiguous and so the issue is still not resolved (on the inscription, see *Année épigraphique* 1967: no. 535:166–68 and Robert and Robert 1970: no. 633). Bruce later (1990: 436n64) also leaves the question open.

More important for us is the wide power a governor possessed in such cases, a power limited only by the Roman citizen's right to appeal. Tajra (1989: 112–16) notes the likely procedure in cases that were *extra ordinem* (see the discussion on 18:14–15): the case was heard in person, a formal act of accusation came from formal accusers, the defendant confronted his accusers face-to-face, the magistrate could weigh the charges, and governors could make an immediate decision. Tajra (1989: 115) concludes, "Paul's appearances before Governors Felix and Festus are very good examples of working *extra ordinem* procedure in the provincial court of an imperial province" because these hearings follow this outline of procedure.

23:25. The Western text has an extensive expansion of these verses. The most important gives an explanation for the transfer: the tribune is afraid that the Jews would seize Paul and kill him and that afterward the tribune would incur the accusation of having taken money (to allow the lynching). Such explanation is typical of the Western text.

B. In Caesarea (24:1–26:32)

In this important section, Paul gives repeated defense speeches before the governors of Rome, Felix (24:1–21) and Festus (25:1–12), and various Jewish leaders, including Agrippa II (25:23–26:29). Paul's appeal to Caesar results in his going to Rome. Here Luke reveals how Paul views his mission and its relationship to God's program and hope. Paul has done nothing worthy of arrest and is on trial for holding to Jewish hope.

1. Paul's First Defense and Custody before Felix (24:1–27)

Paul gives his initial defense before the Roman governor here. This section contains a full examination, with representation by both the Jewish accusers and Paul. The scene begins with the setting (vv. 1–2a). Then Tertullus makes the case against Paul (vv. 2b–8). He begins with praise of the ruler, a *captatio benevolentiae* (vv. 3–4). Then Tertullus raises charges: Paul is a public nuisance and agitator, a ringleader of the Nazoreans, and a temple desecrator (vv. 5–6, 8).[1] Paul then gives his defense (vv. 9–21). Paul says that there is no proof of the charges and that he was the cause of no disturbance at the temple. The Way is merely the completion of Judaism (vv. 9–14), and resurrection is a hope of Judaism (vv. 15–21). In Paul's portrayal to the Roman leadership, this, in effect, is an in-house Jewish religious dispute (Pesch 1986b: 255). Paul gives a spirited defense through the work of the Spirit, as Jesus promised (Luke 21:13–15). In vv. 22–23 Felix decides to give a verdict later, when Claudius Lysias comes to Caesarea. This means that Paul is held in custody even beyond Felix's rule (vv. 24–27). Much in Paul's speech tells the reader of Acts what the narrative has already shown; it acts as a review and summary of Luke's argument in the book (Schneider 1982: 343). The trial fits the Roman procedure (Sherwin-White 1963: 49). Such a trial is open to the public (Witherington 1998: 703; Tajra 1989: 114–16).

These summaries of the trial, especially the speech of Tertullus, would be rooted in Pauline sources (Pesch 1986b: 254–55; Fitzmyer 1998: 732, in contrast to Weiser 1985: 626–27, who sees Luke responsible for the scene, although Weiser seems to be aware of some historical roots in Tertullus's remarks, namely, the allusion to alms and the accusation of temple desecration). Witherington (1998: 702) notes that it also is possible that Luke had access to notes of this trial (see esp. Winter and Clarke 1993: 307–9).[2] Winter (1993: 305–36) shows in more detail how the Greco-Roman background and the form and

---

1. It is likely that v. 7 was not an original part of Acts; so, among others, Larkin 1995: 338. This is part of an addition that also includes sections of v. 6 and v. 8. The addition is poorly attested (see the additional note on 24:6–8a). It argues that the Jews would have judged Paul according to their law if Lysias had not come and seized Paul from their hands.

2. Jervell 1998: 573–74 sees sources but is uncertain about a trial source. Luke has presented this in his own style.

availability of such legal sources help to illumine the court proceedings in Acts 24–26 and argues that Lukan access to official sources is a good possibility. He suggests that the printing of Lysias's letter is an indication to Luke's readers of access to such sources.

Hemer (1989: 129) observes that both Sherwin-White (1963: 48) and Mommsen (1901), experts in ancient Roman legal practices, view the account as "an exemplary account of provincial penal procedure *extra ordinem*." These two experts compare the scene to that in Apuleius, *Apology*. Again Luke has helped give the material its final shaping as a summary, but the scene is well rooted in a historical event.

The material in verses 24–27 is also from traditional sources. Some argue that verses 24–25 are too positive to be from sources (Roloff 1988: 339). Weiser (1985: 63) contends that the whole unit of verses 24–26 reflects Lukan themes, including a person's fear when faced with a man of God, the elevation of women, and Christianity exposed to people in high places—points Fitzmyer (1998: 738–39) also regards as possible. Felix's alarm at the raising of moral questions, however, is not positive, and the note that he understood the Way more accurately may only indicate that having a Jewish wife gave him an advantage in understanding certain issues and that he sought her opinion. Marshall (1980: 381) and Williams (1990: 402) note that the inclusion of Drusilla serves no clear purpose, as nothing came of this meeting, and so the scene is not invented. As for the Lukan character of the themes, Luke is the only writer to detail Christianity's interaction with political forces; thus the prominence of such themes in Acts is not surprising. One also must distinguish between Luke expressing himself in his own language as a writer and the likelihood that he did so with access to sources, which the background shows is both possible and likely.

Exegesis and Exposition

¹And after five days the high priest Ananias came down with some elders and a legal advocate, a certain Tertullus. They laid before the governor their case against Paul; ²and being called, Tertullus began to accuse him, saying: "Because through you we enjoy much peace, and since by your provision, most excellent Felix, reforms are being introduced on behalf of this nation, ³in every way and everywhere we accept this with all gratitude. ⁴But, to detain you no further, I beg you in your kindness to hear us briefly. ⁵For we have found this man a plague, an agitator among all the Jews throughout the world, and a ringleader of the sect of the Nazoreans, ⁶who even tried to profane the temple, but we seized him. ⌜ ⌝ ⁸By examining him yourself, you will be able to learn from him about everything of which we accuse him."

⁹The Jews also were joining in the charge, affirming that these things were so. ¹⁰And when the governor had motioned to him to speak, Paul replied: "Realizing

that for many years you have been judge over this nation, I cheerfully make my defense. ¹¹As you may ascertain, it is not more than twelve days since I went up to worship at Jerusalem; ¹²and they did not find me disputing with any one or stirring up a crowd, neither in the temple nor in the synagogues nor in the city. ¹³Neither can they prove to you that of which they currently accuse me. ¹⁴But this I admit to you, that according to the Way, which they call a sect, I worship the God of our fathers, believing everything laid down by the law or being written in the prophets, ¹⁵having a hope in God that these themselves accept, that there will be a resurrection of both the just and the unjust. ¹⁶So I take pains to have a clear conscience toward God and toward men always. ¹⁷Now after some years I came to my nation making alms and offerings. ¹⁸While I was doing this, they found me engaging in a rite of purification in the temple without any crowd or tumult. But some Jews from Asia—¹⁹who ought to be here before you and to make an accusation if they have anything against me. ²⁰Or else let these men themselves say what wrongdoing they found when I stood before the council, ²¹except this one thing which I cried out while standing among them, 'Concerning the resurrection of the dead I am on trial before you this day.'"

²²But Felix, having a rather accurate knowledge of the Way, put them off, saying, "When Lysias the tribune comes down, I will decide your case." ²³Then he gave orders to the centurion that Paul should be kept in custody but should have some liberty and that none of his friends should be prevented from attending to his needs.

²⁴After some days Felix came with his wife, Drusilla, who was a Jewess ⌐ ¬; and he sent for Paul and heard him speak upon faith in Christ Jesus. ²⁵And as he was arguing about righteousness and self-control and future judgment, Felix, being alarmed, said, "Go away for the present; when I have an opportunity, I will summon you." ²⁶At the same time he hoped that money would be given him by Paul. So sending for him often, Felix conversed with him. ²⁷But when two years had elapsed, Felix was succeeded by Porcius Festus; and desiring to do the Jews a favor, Felix left Paul in prison.

Five days later the high priest Ananias, the elders, and a lawyer, Tertul-**24:1–2a** lus, arrive to conduct the Jewish leadership's case against Paul before Felix. Tertullus makes the opening speech as the "rhetorician" (ῥήτορος, *rhētoros*) or, better, "legal advocate" (so our translation; Rapske 1994b: 159). He is a hired pleader, a legal gun, if you will, whose ethnicity is not clear. His job is to inform the governor of the case against Paul. The verb ἐμφανίζω (*emphanizō*, inform) occurs fives times in these scenes (23:15, 22; 24:1; 25:2, 15). The plaintiffs are the Jewish leadership.[3] Tertullus brings a formal legal complaint.

3. On Jewish views of being in Gentile courts, see Le Cornu and Shulam 2003: 1286–87. It generally was not viewed positively, but in this case there is no other option (*m. Giṭ.* 9.8; *b. Giṭ.* 88b).

24:2b–3 Tertullus begins the speech by praising Felix, a typical move to ingratiate the ruler (2 Macc. 4:6) but one that is not entirely sincere given what we know about how the Jewish leadership viewed him (Lösch 1931). Nonetheless, there is praise of Felix's ability to bring peace and of his vision in bringing reforms or improvements to the region, something the leadership sees and welcomes. They want him to do the same here (Gaventa 2003: 325). He is also addressed as "most excellent" Felix, as is common, to recognize his social status (23:26). Josephus (*J. W.* 2.13.2 §252) credits Felix with putting down the Zealots for a time (also *Ant.* 20.8.5 §§160–61, where he also notes that the situation became worse under Felix). The speech contains this note of praise, a narration of facts as Tertullus sees them (vv. 5–6), and then an appeal that the governor act. The praise prepares for Tertullus's request because he wants the ruler to exercise vision and do what makes for peace here. Alliteration greets us in verse 3 with the phrase "in every way and everywhere" (πάντῃ τε καὶ πανταχοῦ, *pantē te kai pantachou*).

24:4–6 As Tertullus asks the governor to hear the Jewish leaders' charges, he notes, as is also typical in such speeches, that he will not delay in getting to his point. The call to hear the charges may be a recognition that really hard evidence is lacking, so that Tertullus asks Felix to listen with care.

    Paul is a "pest" or "plague" (λοιμόν, *loimon*). He is like a pestilence or plague that infects the people (BAGD 479 §II; BDAG 602 §II, a person dangerous to the public). In Luke 21:11, the only other NT occurrence of this word, it refers to a time of pestilence. It is as if someone said today that a given person is a cancer that needs to be checked. The charge is conceptually like that made against Paul in Thessalonica in Acts 17:6–7. Paul is also an "agitator" (κινοῦντα στάσεις, *kinounta staseis*; on στάσις, 15:2; 19:40; 23:7, 10). This charge makes Paul a danger to civic peace. He disturbs Jews throughout the world (a hyperbole) and is a ringleader (πρωτοστάτην, *prōtostatēn*) of the Nazoreans, that is, the dangerous leader of a sect (αἵρεσις, *hairesis*).[4]

    A sect is a recognized group with identifiable beliefs. The term is used five other times in Acts (5:17 [of the Sadducees]; 15:5 [of the Pharisees]; 24:14 [of the Way]; 26:5 [of the Pharisees]; 28:22 [of reports to Roman Jews about Christians]). The name "Nazoreans" is no accident. It identifies the regional origin of the group and falls short of making any messianic claims (John 1:46). By being called a sect, the "Nazoreans" are still seen as Jewish in origin. This charge is more political than that in Acts 21:28: it is a charge of sedition (Jervell 1998: 568). No witnesses are brought forward. It is framed in a way that connects this case with Felix's chief area of responsibility, keeping the peace.

---

    4. On this description of the new movement, see Jervell 1998: 568 and Justin Martyr, *Dial.* 17.1; 108.2. On this term, see Kuhli, *EDNT* 2:454–56.

The proof of the danger is in Paul's profanation of the temple, which is why the Jews seized him. This charge of defiling the temple is false but is raised again here because it was the cause of the original disturbance (BAGD 138; BDAG 173; the original charge is in 21:28). The term βεβηλόω (*bebēloō*, profane) appears only twice in the NT. Matthew 12:5, the other occurrence, records Jesus's example of the temple being profaned without anyone experiencing judgment when the priests labor there on the Sabbath. In the original scene, it is not a charge that Paul came to the temple defiled but that he brought a Gentile there that evokes the reaction. The charge here either omits the ethnic element because of the audience or is stated in a very collapsed form. A papyrus (P.Lond. 1912, line 99 = *CPJ* 153) has the emperor Claudius warning Alexandrian Jews who engage in suspicious activity that they will be avenged if they infect the world.

In sum, four elements are present in the charges: Paul is (1) a pest, (2) a political agitator, (3) the leader of a sectarian movement, and (4) one who tried to be disruptive at the temple. This can be reduced to the statement that Paul disturbs the peace as a seditious member of a dangerous sect. The evidence is his act in the temple. He should be stopped. Such charges are serious. The rising foment among politically oriented Jews, who eventually produced the troublesome Zealot movement, may serve as background to the charge. Christians were being compared to others who would cause Rome headaches, although it should be noted that the temple charge does not fit the political picture of Zealots campaigning for Israel, since their enemy was Rome. Here the "Zealot" was Paul, who was sympathetic to Gentiles, although this detail is not raised here. The implication is that Paul, as a violator of Jewish law, was disturbing the peace in a way that was socially disruptive, and the Romans did try to enforce public peace in Jewish regions (Gaventa 2003: 326; Rapske 1994b: 162). The lack of a direct danger to Rome, however, is evident. The most they could charge Paul with was being allegedly disruptive.

See the additional note on 24:6–8a.   24:7

Tertullus claims that an examination (4:9) of Paul will confirm all of   24:8–9
these allegations. The Jews, that is, the high priest and elders (v. 1), join in agreement with his argument, but Luke makes the point in an interesting manner. The verb φάσκω (*phaskō*, allege) appears only three times in the NT, two of them in Acts (24:9; 25:19; Rom. 1:22). The word refers to a claim that is uncertain as to its truth. For example, in Acts 25:19, there is a report about Paul's belief of resurrection, but by using this term, the indication is that the one making the report is not sure if it is true. So the term points only to a claim. Here the Jews are claiming that Tertullus's report is accurate, but the use of the word expresses Luke's doubt. Romans 1:22 has the same force. In that passage, men,

claiming to be wise, are actually foolish in responding to God with the practice of idolatry.

The verb συνεπέθεντο (*synepethento*, joined in the attack) in verse 9 is a military term, here suggesting that Paul is a public enemy (Josephus, *Ant.* 10.7.4 §116; Barrett 1998: 1100). It is an NT hapax.

24:10   Paul is invited to speak by Felix's nod to him. Paul has a shorter *captatio benevolentiae*, simply recognizing Felix's role for many years as judge and expressing appreciation for an opportunity to defend himself. Felix would have been a judge for about five years at this point (ca. AD 57), unless one includes his being an aide to Cumanus, in which case his experience is longer. The implication is that the governor will be able to weigh and discern the lack of evidence against Paul. Paul lays out his remarks as a defense, to give an *apologia* to declare his innocence (other occurrences of ἀπολογέομαι: Luke 12:11–12; 21:14; Acts 19:33; 24:10; 25:8; 26:1–2, 24; Rom. 2:15; 2 Cor. 12:19). As verse 12 says, he was not disputing with anyone, nor was he causing any stir with anyone, in either the synagogues or the city. In short, he was minding his own business.

The structure of his reply is that he did not make a disturbance (vv. 11–13), his relationship to the Way is not a violation of Judaism (vv. 14–16), there was no temple desecration (vv. 17–19), and there is no proof for the charges, as even the previous examination showed (vv. 20–21).

24:11–13   Paul begins his formal defense with a declaration of innocence. It has been debated how twelve days are reckoned here. (1) Is it twelve days since the incident, counting to the day he was taken to Caesarea (Bruce 1988a: 443)? (2) Is the statement merely adding Acts 21:27 and 24:1 (Marshall 1980: 376)? Or (3) is it simply saying that twelve whole days had gone by without trouble emerging (Barrett 1998: 1102; Witherington 1998: 710)? Either the first or the last option is possible, as 24:1 and those five days are irrelevant with Paul in custody. He was not the cause of any disturbance anywhere in either the synagogues, the temple, or the city. He did not even dispute with anyone while there, something he could have done. He was there merely to worship. In fact, Paul claims that they cannot prove any of their charges. Literally, they cannot "stand by," "show," or "present" what they are charging Paul with (παραστῆσαι, *parastēsai*; BAGD 627–28 §1f; BDAG 778 §1f; Acts 4:10, 26; 9:41).

24:14–16   Paul does admit to certain things, none of them crimes. He makes a confession of faith, not of guilt (Gaventa 2003: 327). He is a member of the Way (ὁδός, *hodos*, 9:2), the way to God and salvation. Others call it a "sect," but it is not a "heretical" movement (on the contrast between "sect" in 24:5 and "Way" in 24:14, see Michaelis, *TDNT* 5:88–89). The Jews claim that this is a minority sect and is disturbing the peace, whereas Paul claims it is the "Way."

Those in this movement of God believe what the law and prophets teach and in the hope of the resurrection of the just and the unjust (Acts 10:42; 17:31; 23:6; Matt. 25:31–34; Luke 10:12; John 5:28–29; Rom. 2:5; 2 Cor. 5:10; 2 Tim. 4:1; Rev. 20:12–15; OT: Dan. 12:2–3; Judaism: Ps. Sol. 3.13; 1 En. 41.1–2; 51.1–2; 54.1–6; Josephus, *Ant.* 18.1.3 §14). Barrett (1998: 1105) suggests that many NT texts leave unclear the role of the unrighteous as it relates to resurrection. The reason is that only the righteous are seen to benefit from resurrection in a positive manner, and so it is their resurrection as hope that is often noted alone. Acts speaks of the resurrection of the living and the dead because the Jewish view is of an end-time judgment that all are to face (Bruce 1988a: 444). Paul believes this Jewish hope. Resurrection is also important because it indicates who Jesus is (Acts 2:24, 32; 3:15; 4:10; 10:40; 13:30; 17:3), but Paul does not develop this point here.

The law here is seen in terms of redemption, salvation, and promise, that is, in terms of eschatological deliverance. It is hope (24:15). The "new" movement is actually rooted in old promises (13:15; 22:3; 28:17, 23), a sign that it should be respected as an appropriate reflection of Jewish hope. It is no subversive movement (Roloff 1988: 337).

As his personal practice Paul tries to have a "clear conscience" (ἀπρόσκοπον συνείδησιν, *aproskopon syneidēsin*) before God and others (20:20, 27, 33; 23:1; Stählin, *TDNT* 6:756, speaks of a "quiet" conscience). The term ἀσκέω (*askeō*, do one's best, attempt) is rare, an NT hapax; it appears in 2 Macc. 15:4, where it means "practice" or "observe with care" the seventh day (the Sabbath). In sum, Paul believes the God of "our" fathers and is "guilty" only of being religiously faithful, a good Jew. This has been Paul's consistent defense in Acts.

Now Paul turns to what has brought him in front of the governor, the **24:17–21** tumult in Jerusalem. He was simply bringing alms and offerings to Jerusalem. He begins by noting that it has been many years since he was in Jerusalem, by which he means an extended time; about five years have passed. The reference to alms is the one clear remark in Acts confirming the fact that Paul had brought a collection for the church in Jerusalem (Gal. 2:10; Rom. 15:26; 2 Cor. 8–9). For Paul, this offering was appropriate as a reflection of the church's unity and the contribution Jerusalem has made to the Gentiles' faith. It also was for "my nation"; here Paul is supportive of Judaism and the nation of Israel and identifies with it.

Haenchen (1987: 655) complains that this is misleading historically, but in fact it is Paul's point (Fitzmyer 1998: 736). In Paul's view, to contribute to Jews who believe in the hope of resurrection and the Messiah is to support Israel. That is the irony of the charge—Paul is on trial for supporting Israel and its faith.

He was giving thanks in the temple. There they found Paul in an appropriate purified state, not causing any trouble as he worshiped. Paul claims that it was the Jews from Asia who caused his arrest and the disturbance. They should be brought before the governor to make the accusation if there is anything against Paul. He may be suggesting that they have nothing of substance or that those who were eyewitnesses have not bothered even to make an appearance. Sherwin-White (1963: 52–53) notes that the Romans thought little of people who abandoned their legal charges.[5] An abandonment of a charge was called a *destitutio* (Barrett 1998: 1109). This reference to the Asian Jews breaks off before being completed in the Greek.

Paul is saying that his Jewish accusers simply disturbed someone engaged in genuine worship. The Jewish leadership can testify to the fact that he has done nothing worthy of punishment except for crying out to the people that he was being examined because he believed in the resurrection from the dead (23:6–10). There has already been an examination of the facts, which the governor can check (22:30–23:9). There resurrection was a key issue. Like Tertullus in verse 8, Paul asks Felix to examine his opponents. He thereby confidently claims that the charges are false. He closes his remarks as they began: the only thing he is guilty of is having certain religious beliefs. These are issues that the Romans do not regard as illegal, nor do Jews view these beliefs as worthy of a civil sanction. As Fitzmyer (1998: 737) notes, "'The resurrection of the dead' thus echoes like a refrain in these latter chapters of Acts." Claudius Lysias has already declared that the issue is really a religious dispute (23:28–29). Paul's basic defense is that he is orthodox in his belief about Jewish hope (Schneider 1982: 349).

24:22–23 Felix decides to put off a decision and wait for Claudius Lysias to come to Caesarea. To use Roman legal terminology, he "reserves judgment" (*amplius*) until he can gather more data. This nonresolution is summarized in the term ἀναβάλλω (*anaballō*, bring a hearing to a close), an NT hapax. He probably wants to hear from someone who, in his view, is nonpartisan. Paul is to remain in custody, but with some freedom (ἄνεσιν, *anesin*), as visitors can come and go (Rapske 1994b: 171–72). Felix is described as one who has a rather accurate knowledge of the Way. This is the last of six occurrences of some form of the word ἀκριβῶς (*akribōs*, accurately) in Acts (18:25–26 [2x; helping Apollos's understanding]; 23:15, 20 [sorting out Paul's case]; 24:22; 26:5). Luke does not indicate whether Lysias ever appears before them. Luke later notes that Felix kept Paul in jail as a favor to the leadership of the Jews (v. 27), even though the end of Felix's rule resulted from his insensitivity to them (Josephus, *J.W.* 2.13.7 §270; *Ant.* 20.8.9 §182). The impression is that Felix is saying one thing but doing another (Polhill 1992: 485).

5. See Witherington 1998: 712–13; Appian, *Civil Wars* 3.54; Dio Cassius, *Rom. Hist.* 60.28.6; Suetonius, *Claudius* 15.2.

While Felix keeps Paul in prison, he holds a private audience with Paul   24:24–26
before Felix's Jewess wife, Drusilla. The impression of the narrative is
that Felix is seeking input from someone who is distant from the dispute
but may offer her expertise. Her Jewish connections may have given her
some knowledge about the new movement. Paul's testimony reaches the
nation's highest social levels. Born in AD 38, she is not yet twenty years
old, the youngest daughter of Herod Agrippa I and sister to Agrippa II.
This is her second marriage. She left her first husband, whom she had
married in a customary, arranged marriage at fourteen. She is Felix's
third wife. Josephus (*Ant.* 20.7.2 §§141–44) notes that she was beautiful
and was persuaded by Felix to leave her first husband (also *Ant.* 19.9.1
§354; *J.W.* 2.1.6 §220; Suetonius, *Claudius* 28; Tacitus, *Hist.* 5.9).

Paul covers the topic of faith in Jesus, identifying who the Messiah is.
Paul also covers issues of morality, namely, righteousness (δικαιοσύνης,
dikaiosynēs), self-control (ἐγκρατείας, *enkrateias*), and future judgment
(τοῦ κρίματος τοῦ μέλλοντος, *tou krimatos tou mellontos*). Some scholars might wish to translate the first of these terms "justice," but there
seems to be a personal moral dimension raised by the mention of the
next term, "self-control," that makes the discussion one that includes
personal ethics. The term "self-control" also raises an ethical element,
as the moral environment of Greek culture is the likely subject (BAGD
216; BDAG 274). This is the only occurrence of ἐγκρατεία in Acts; it
appears four times in the NT (the others are Gal. 5:23 [one of the fruits
of the Spirit]; 1 Pet. 1:6 [2x; one of the virtues leading to patience]). As
often in Greek contexts within Acts, God's judgment is also a major point
here (10:42; 17:29–30). The issue of final judgment would be familiar
to Drusilla but mostly new for a Roman like Felix (Larkin 1995: 343).
One's moral responsibility before God seems to be the topic, in addition to what verse 24 notes, faith in Christ Jesus. Jesus's role as exalted
judge is apparently a major point. As Bruce (1990: 483) observes, righteousness, self-control, and the coming judgment are "three subjects
Felix and Drusilla certainly needed to hear about."

The personal circumstances of Felix's marriage to Drusilla seem to
be alluded to here, since the discussion makes Felix nervous. The term
ἔμφοβος (*emphobos*; Luke 24:5, 37; Acts 10:4; 24:25; Rev. 11:13) reflects
emotions that are more intense than those indicated by the Greek word
φόβος (*phobos*, fear). The ethical discussion recalls John the Baptist's
preaching about Herod (Luke 3:19–20), except that here Paul does it
face-to-face.

Felix sends Paul away for future meetings, but his motives are not
entirely pure. The term πυκνότερον (*pyknoteron*) in verse 26 refers to his
meeting "often" or "as much as possible" (on this term, see BDF §244.1).
He desires a bribe, an irony in light of the topics Paul is addressing and
an indication of why Felix is portrayed as a Roman ruler in a less than
favorable light by those who wrote about him. Although the term χρήματα

(*chrēmata*) generally refers to possessions, in this context it means a bribe (BAGD 885 §2a; BDAG 1089; Mark 10:23; Luke 18:24; Acts 4:37). The term appeared earlier in Acts when Simon tried to offer money to Peter to gain the right to distribute the Spirit (8:18). Felix knows from Paul's remarks about alms and offerings that Paul has access to large amounts of money, and he may assume that Paul can get more.

Taking bribes was illegal in principle (*Lex Julia de repetundis*; Bruce 1990: 483; Tajra 1989: 330–31), but the restriction often was not heeded. Sometimes the powerful seek favors for their acts of benevolence. Not long after Felix, there is the example of Albinus, who succeeded Festus in AD 61.[6] Despite the many claims that Luke portrays Rome positively, this is not a flattering portrait of a ruler (correctly, Witherington 1998: 716–17, who notes that Felix never issues a judgment about Paul). There is no discrepancy in the mixed portrait of Felix as curious about the Way and yet seeking bribes (but so Haenchen 1987: 662; correctly assessed by Barrett 1998: 1116, who notes that people are quite capable of mixed motives).

24:27   Paul is still in prison two years later when Felix is replaced by Porcius Festus in about AD 59–60 (Porcius is the clan to which Festus belongs [BAGD 693]). Scholars debate the chronology here because of the influence of Felix's brother Pallas on Felix's situation, an influence that could suggest a date as early as AD 55 given that Nero diminished Pallas's status, but the bulk of the evidence is for the later date (Barrett 1998: 1117–18 does not rule out an earlier date). The debate turns in part on whether Pallas maintained some influence after losing his office. We lack explicit information on this point.

Festus, as new governor of Palestine, had a better reputation for fairness than Felix did (BAGD 856; BDAG 1053). Josephus (*J.W.* 2.14.1 §271) says that he sought to prevent disturbances in the country, and *Ant.* 20.8.9 §182 and 20.8.10 §§185–88 have him deal with the *sicarii*, or Zealots; *Ant.* 20.8.11 §§193–95 has him agree to let some Jews go to Nero to make a case for leaving up a wall they had built to prevent Agrippa from seeing what went on inside important parts of the temple with respect to worship, something Nero agreed to allow. All we know of Festus comes from Acts and Josephus. These details indicate how sensitive the issues were in the early sixties.

As a favor to the Jewish leadership, Felix refuses to release Paul. The understanding seems to be that Paul cannot do major harm if he remains in custody. All of this is taking place in a context of fulfilling what Jesus said would happen both to his followers and to Paul specifically when he appeared to him (Luke 21:12–15; Acts 9:15–16; Gaventa 2003: 330).

---

6. Josephus (*J.W.* 2.14.1 §§272–76) describes Albinus as a ruler of complete wickedness (*Ant.* 20.9.2 §205; 20.9.5 §215). James, the Lord's brother, was slain in the interim between Festus and Albinus, when no Roman governor was present to stop the high priest from acting against James (*Ant.* 20.9.1 §200).

It is plausibly suggested that Luke may well have done his initial research for his Gospel and Acts in this two-year period (Witherington 1998: 717). At this location he had access to multiple witnesses of such events.

In sum, Paul makes an exemplary case for why Christianity is a threat neither to Rome nor to any state. In his case, he could say he did not break any laws, so that a look at the evidence of any alleged charges would be shown to lack merit. In particular, by being blameless before God, Paul also left himself in a position where he also had not broken any laws of the state. Today this cannot always be the case, as some governments outlaw seeking conversion. What should be made clear, however, is that such actions represent no threat to the state's well-being. In fact, to bring people to faith should result in more law-abiding citizens who have a moral compass and do not harm others but seek what is best for them. In today's world, where the moral compass has lost its magnetism, such a life stands in contrast to that of many. This contrast, if lived out in an effective, engaging manner, can be attractive when people sense the chaos of the alternative lifestyle that a lack of morals produces (Fernando 1998: 583–85). No state should fear this, unless an ideological or religious agenda blinds it. Of course, all of this assumes that God's people live in a manner in accordance with what they claim and that they evidence the faithfulness to God and the love and concern for others that they profess God has called them to reflect.

We also see a directness in Paul's engagement with Felix. He does not say merely what Felix might wish to hear, even though he does communicate respect for Felix's work as a public servant. When Paul speaks to Felix of "righteousness, self-control, and the judgment to come," he is preaching what he himself is seeking to live, because Paul's major goal is to live in a manner that honors God, not just to talk about God. Paul challenges a common core value among many who have power: the idea that they are self-made people in control of their lives and need no one. Indeed, power often expresses itself in a desire to control or gain access to resources that can abuse others in the process. It can care little for others except in ways that use people to reach its own gain. Paul's directness here, borne out by Felix's own personal history, points to a need of Felix's that parallels what many need and need to hear. Paul's defense is that he is a citizen guilty of nothing but living out his faith and experiencing God's promise. His offense is to challenge others to see the benefit of responding to God's leading and direction as he has. Whether Paul's offensive for the gospel is a cause for offense or is met with a recognition of the need to acknowledge God depends on the heart of the listener. Paul has met his responsibility by sharing. He is not responsible for the result or the response. The same is true today for those who spread God's message, reflecting Paul's example.

Additional Notes

24:6–8a. The Western text has an additional explanation after the mention of the Jews' seizure of Paul. It is that the Romans take Paul from Jewish hands. The legal advocate's point would be that the Jews had the right to judge the case, since they had seized him in the temple area. The remark is not true, but scholars question whether the original version of Acts made this additional point. It is possible that this is original because it states an objection to the Roman initiative, but the better MSS evidence is for the shorter reading ($\mathfrak{P}^{74}$, ℵ, A, B, H, L, P; Polhill 1992: 481; Witherington 1998: 709). It is likely that the Western text added the expression because the copyist, failing to recognize the original remark's rhetorical dimension, found it hard to accept that Tertullus would commend Paul's testimony.

24:24. In an addition by the Western text, it is Drusilla who wants to hear Paul.

2. Paul's Appeal to Caesar before Festus (25:1–12)

This scene has two main parts. In verses 1–5 Festus informs the Jewish leaders in Jerusalem that he will hear the case in Caesarea after they ask for a trial in Jerusalem. Their desire is to ambush Paul, as had been intended earlier. Festus's hearing in Caesarea unknowingly prevents this possibility, another example of divine protection for Paul, unwittingly aided by the Romans. In verses 6–12 the hearing takes place, with Paul giving a brief defense and ending his examination by making an appeal to be heard by Caesar. In this second portion, the setting of the hearing appears in verses 6–7. Paul declares himself innocent with respect to both Jewish faith and Roman law in verse 8. When Festus offers a trial in Jerusalem to Paul in verse 9, the apostle replies with his appeal to Caesar in verses 10–11 and again asserts his innocence. Festus agrees to give him the appeal in verse 12.

The scene is a narrative and is rooted in Pauline sources (Pesch 1986b: 264; Roloff 1988: 341). Weiser (1985: 638–39) argues for a heavy Lukan hand in the scene mainly because it parallels Luke 23. Many of these points, however, reflect a general Roman procedure in examinations, and no explicit effort is made in Acts to point out a parallelism, showing that the connection is less important than Weiser suggests (Barrett 1998: 1122).

The scene paints Festus as competent and engaged in his role, and Paul as innocent. Still, again against the tenor of the examination, Paul continues to be held in custody. Barrett (1998: 1121) counters objections about the scene by Haenchen (1987: 668–69), who suggests that it is incomprehensible that there is no verdict, that Paul does not wish to simply remain in Caesarea, and that Festus does not want to resolve the case. Barrett hesitates on making a final historical judgment. Paul, however, has been led by the Spirit to seek to travel to Rome and has appealed to go there. Festus is pleased to have the examination move on. None of this is too difficult to appreciate either in the first-century context or as a matter of Pauline strategy. The scene is important because it explains how Paul ultimately heads for Rome.

Exegesis and Exposition

[1]Now when Festus had come into his province, after three days he went up to Jerusalem from Caesarea. [2]And the chief priests and the principal men of

the Jews informed him against Paul; and they were urging him, ³asking a favor to have the man sent to Jerusalem, planning an ambush to kill him on the way. ⁴Now Festus replied that Paul was to be kept at Caesarea and that he himself intended to go there shortly. ⁵"So," said he, "let the men of authority among you go down, and if there is anything wrong about the man, let them accuse him."

⁶Staying among them not more than eight or ten days, Festus went down to Caesarea; and the next day taking his seat on the tribunal, he ordered Paul to be brought. ⁷And when he had come, the Jews who had gone down from Jerusalem stood about him, bringing against him many serious charges that they could not demonstrate. ⁸Paul said in his defense, "Neither against the law of the Jews, nor against the temple, nor against Caesar have I sinned in any way." ⁹But Festus, wishing to do the Jews a favor, said to Paul, "Do you wish to go up to Jerusalem to be tried on these charges before me?" ¹⁰But Paul said, "I am standing before Caesar's tribunal, where I ought to be tried; to the Jews I have done no wrong, as you know very well. ¹¹If, then, I am guilty and have committed anything for which I deserve to die, I do not seek to escape death; but if there is nothing in their charges against me, no one can give me up to them. I appeal to Caesar." ¹²Then Festus, after conferring with his council, answered, "You have appealed to Caesar; to Caesar you shall go."

25:1–3 Festus, as governor, goes to Jerusalem three days after his arrival in Judea to meet with the Jewish chief priests and leaders (literally, οἱ πρῶτοι, *hoi prōtoi*, the first men; Luke 19:47). The Jewish leadership discusses Paul's case with him and urges that Paul be brought to Jerusalem for a legal examination. The Jews present this proposal to Festus as a favor to them, something a new ruler might be inclined to do. Luke says that the real motive is an ambush (ἐνέδραν, *enedran*) against Paul with the stated goal to kill him (ἀνελεῖν, *anelein*), as had been planned earlier (Acts 23:12–22, esp. v. 16). The imperfect tense in the request (παρεκάλουν, *parekaloun*) presents it as an ongoing request and may suggest an element of pressure (Williams 1990: 406).

During this time, the high priest was Ishmael ben Phiabi. There was much infighting for power within the leadership in this period (Josephus, *Ant.* 20.8.8–9 §§179–82; 20.8.11 §§194–96).

25:4–5 Festus says that Paul is in Caesarea and will be examined there. If the Jewish "men of authority" (δυνατοί, *dynatoi*) want him to conduct a hearing, they must come back to Caesarea. Those of authority are synonymous with the "first men" of verse 2. If there is anything amiss or wrong legally (ἄτοπον, *atopon*, literally, "out of place"), they must accuse him there. The term ἄτοπον here suggests that Festus is not going to commit himself to anything until a trial is held. This term is a soft legal expression and is put in a conditional construction (Barrett 1998: 1125). By requiring a trial in Caesarea, Festus unknowingly protects Paul. His decision seems to be for strictly pragmatic reasons. The onus is on the leadership to press the case.

Festus is efficient. He stays in Jerusalem for eight to ten days and then **25:6** returns to Caesarea, where he convenes a meeting over Paul the next day. He sits on the raised judgment seat known as the βῆμα (*bēma*; 18:12, 16–17). Le Cornu and Shulam (2003: 1359) discuss the question of whether Luke had access to the archives Romans kept with care. There is no way to know, but it is quite possible. Winter (1993: 306–9) notes that over two hundred fifty papyri of official court proceedings have been found. He says that shorthand was used as early as AD 50, although what was present were accurate summaries of such speeches. Copies would be available to a defendant. Winter also points out that the speeches are about the length of those in Acts 24. This stands against Haenchen's (1987: 656) claim that the speeches are too short to be authentic.

The leadership surrounds Paul and accuses him of many serious crimes. **25:7** The description sets a tone of confrontation. The nature of these "heavy" or "serious" (βαρέα, *barea*) charges is not specified (Matt. 23:4, 23; Acts 20:29; 25:7; 2 Cor. 10:10; 1 John 5:3). Luke simply summarizes here that they cannot prove their charges. The charges likely parallel what Acts 24:5–6 noted, especially given the categories Paul mentions in verse 8 (also Luke 23:2; Acts 17:6–7).

Paul's reply is also summarized as a claim to be innocent, not having **25:8** done anything against the law of the Jews (24:14–16), the temple (21:28; 24:18–19), or Caesar. Paul includes both Jewish and Roman legal concerns, since his point is that the dispute is over Jewish religious beliefs. He has not "sinned," or transgressed (ἥμαρτον, *hēmarton*), against any of these. This list suggests that the charges are about Paul's allegedly acting against Jewish custom at the temple and perhaps contending for Jesus as another king. The issue regarding Caesar is important because if Paul is viewed as seditious, then the governor would be obligated to judge him. Paul is protecting himself from the political dimension of the Jewish leadership's challenge. He is a good Jew and a good citizen (Fitzmyer 1998: 744). There is no treason (*maiestas*) present (Le Cornu and Shulam 2003: 1361).

Festus asks Paul if he wishes to be tried in Jerusalem. Festus is still **25:9** trying to do the Jews a favor (24:27) early in his rule but does not simply accede to their request. The narrative makes clear that there is no reason for Paul to be tried, but he is still in custody. Also unclear is whether Festus is suggesting that he preside over such a trial to review at closer hand the facts of the case (Marshall 1980: 384) or whether the Sanhedrin would have authority in such an examination and then the favor would be to allow them to look at the religious charge. This scholarly discussion emerges because the phrase ἐπ' ἐμοῦ (*ep' emou*, before me) is in an unusual position in the sentence. The expression suggests Festus presiding over a Jewish proceeding in Jerusalem, given that the only reason to move the hearing is to allow for full participation of the leadership. Festus can fulfill his legal responsibility in Caesarea. Acts 25:11 suggests that Paul thinks something is not quite right about the option.

25:10–11   Paul's defense is that he is charged with Roman violations and wishes nothing more than to be tried in a Roman court, as this is only appropriate under the circumstances. He reaffirms his innocence but restates that if he has done wrong or anything worthy of death, then he does not wish to escape such a penalty. If he did the crime, then he will do the time. But Paul says that the Roman court knows "very well" (κάλλιον, *kallion*) that he has done nothing wrong; here Luke uses a comparative as an elative (Moulton and Turner 1963: 30). Literally, Paul says that he will not beg off (οὐ παραιτοῦμαι, *ou paraitoumai*) from death (Barrett 1998: 1130; Josephus, *Life* 29 §141) if he has done wrong. If he is innocent, then his appeal to Caesar should be accepted. Both conditional clauses are stated as first-class conditions, and so each option is presented with equal likelihood. Here Rome is seen as a potential puppet for Israel's leadership. Rome should not be a tool in this unrighteous pursuit of Paul. One senses Paul's desire that justice be done. There is implicit criticism of Festus here, since a verdict of innocent should be given. Nonetheless, Roman protection is better than a return to the hands of the Jewish leadership. In a sense, the new movement is severing itself formally from Jewish judicial care and seeking the protection of the state (Pesch 1986b: 267).

25:12   After consultation with his advisers, Festus accepts the appeal to Caesar. Paul will go to Rome. These advisers were known as the *consilium* (συμβούλιον, *symboulion*; Schneider 1982: 360; Tajra 1989: 148–49; 4 Macc. 17:17; Josephus, *Ant.* 16.6.2 §163).

    Paul's appeal to Caesar is known as the *provocatio*, an appeal of a citizen for Caesar's judgment before a judgment has been rendered (BAGD 294 §2aβ; BDAG 373; Reese 1975).[1] Originally, this was the right of appeal to have the people, not a ruling official, decide a case. By the first century, the appeal was to have the highest official make the decision (Conzelmann 1987: 203–4). The case is *extra ordinem* (outside the order or code of law), which means that there is some freedom in how it is being handled. This secular use of *provocatio* (a calling upon) is a nice parallel to "calling upon the name of the Lord" in other texts in Acts (2:21, rendered *invocatio* in the Vulgate). This

---

1. An *appelatio* is the appeal after a verdict and is a distinct legal category; Roloff 1988: 344.

type of appeal is one of the oldest Roman ancient rights, dating back to 509 BC.[2]

Bruce (1990: 488–89) details this arrangement and also discusses how such an appeal made sense before the great persecutions of AD 64–65. Paul probably suspects a problem here in the Jewish proposal to return to Jerusalem and in how Festus might respond because of politics, something that might be confirmed in verses 19–20. So Paul makes a legal maneuver around Festus, who allows the move and takes himself out of the line of fire because it does fit Roman custom. Suetonius notes the procedure by which Nero would hear such a case (*Nero* 15.1; Eckey 2000: 537). The judgment would not be rendered on the same day as the trial and would be given in writing. Acts, however, never brings us as far as this point.

Numerous issues regarding Paul's appeal to Caesar are discussed among scholars: whether this right is limited to Roman citizens and capital cases, whether it can be made during a trial instead of after, and whether, once made, it prevents release (Garnsey 1966, who opts for appeals only after a trial). Paul is exercising his right not to be tried before an incompetent tribunal (Fitzmyer 1998: 745). The final movement to Rome can now proceed (Acts 19:21; 23:11). The Caesar here is Nero, whose early reign, advised by Seneca and Afranius Burrus, enjoyed a relatively tranquil period (Suetonius, *Nero* 9–10) before, however, attaining a different kind of infamous notoriety.

In sum, this exchange with Festus is a short outline of events, much like the scene with Felix, except that Paul's appeal to Caesar serves as protection for Paul the Roman citizen. Once again God's sovereignty has protected Paul through the means of the state's law. And once again Paul's key point of appeal, as he is tried, is that he has done nothing against the state, something that Festus recognizes is true. There is also irony here. Even though Festus senses Paul's innocence, he cannot release him because of Paul's appeal to Caesar. But he also is not sure what to write to Caesar, given the circumstances.

In a sense, Paul sends himself to Rome through his own actions in appealing Roman law. It is not clear whether Paul's appeal is done for apologetic purposes, to argue that Christianity should be recognized by Rome, or because Paul desires to share the gospel in Rome. Against the former idea is that nowhere is there an indication that Paul expects justice in Rome (Jervell 1998: 582, also n. 297). The sometimes critical portrait of Roman justice is also against this. But Roman justice is better than the expectation Paul would have with the Jewish leadership. So he seeks Rome's protection while telling the Romans that there is nothing to fear from him in terms of disturbing the peace. If there is

---

2. Justinian, *Code* 1.19.1; *Digest* 48.6.7, notes the roots in Ulpian; Mommsen 1901; Sherwin-White 1963: 58, 68–70; Dio Cassius, *Rom. Hist.* 51.19; Tajra 1989: 144–47.

an apologetic to Rome, here it is indirect. Paul's greater concern is to take the gospel to Rome, and this appeal is an easy way to do so. Paul has a sense of his priorities as a servant of the gospel. Again we see how sometimes God's plan works in unusual ways, ways where our own actions can move the plan forward.

Luke's concern is to show that this new faith of the Way is rooted in God's ancient promises, is committed to hope, and is not a public threat to peace for anyone.

3. Before Agrippa and Bernice (25:13–26:32)

This important passage has the fullest discussion in Acts of Paul's situation. It begins with Festus reviewing for Agrippa and Bernice what has taken place (25:14–21). He recounts the situation (25:14–16) and then the examination he has already held, which ended with Paul's appeal to Caesar (25:17–21). Agrippa asks to hear Paul, and so with much pomp, a meeting is held (25:22–27). Festus publicly explains his rationale for the hearing in such a way that Luke could then likely reconstruct the earlier conversation (25:24–27). Festus wishes to have an explanation that he can give to Rome (25:26). He believes Paul is innocent (25:18, 25), and he hopes that these rulers, who are Jewish but also faithful vassals to Rome, will be of help. The pomp of the scene fits with first-century Judea (Johnson 1992: 428 calls it a "show trial"; Josephus, *Ant.* 17.5.3 §93; *J.W.* 1.32.1 §620 [both Varus and Herod]; *Ant.* 16.2.3 §30 [Marcus Agrippa]).

Paul's formal defense (26:1–32) both reviews and adds to various themes that have run throughout the trial. It is Paul's last major discourse as well as his longest and most stylized. Witherington (1998: 737) notes nine elements of Greek rhetorical style. At a literary level, it ties together the entire cycle of events surrounding Paul. Two themes dominate: the declaration of the cross and the insistence that this new faith is actually an extension of Judaism. The charges are not as directly engaged. However, numerous witnesses to his testimony are appealed to: (1) Paul's companions on the way to Damascus, (2) the Jews of Jerusalem, (3) Agrippa's knowledge of Judaism, (4) the Scriptures, (5) a heavenly revelation, (6) Paul's own testimony, and (7) Paul's presence before the dignitaries as evidence of God's protection (Witherington 1998: 737). These themes and the multiple lines of support give the motivation for his actions and the official Jewish reaction. It is a defense of his life mission, more for Agrippa than Festus, which makes it a speech addressing Jewish concerns (Witherington 1998: 735). Paul, very much the witness to the faith, is still reaching out to Jews. The speech has the following structure: Paul gives a generous remark about Agrippa (26:2–3), discusses his own Jewish life (26:4–8), speaks of his persecution of Christians and his conversion (26:9–18), and closes with his theology and hope rooted in the suffering Messiah (26:19–23).

Paul reviews his life as a persecutor (26:4–11). He is on trial for the promise of the fathers (26:6). He also reviews his conversion and divine calling (26:12–18), to which he was not disobedient (26:19–23). His summary defense is that he does nothing but what Moses and the prophets have revealed (26:22); he thereby keeps the religious dimension at the forefront. The hope is that the Romans will sense that no civil issues exist for them to adjudicate. In one sense, this speech summarizes many of the key theological points about the new faith and how those in leadership and representing world power have trouble grasping it. Paul even appeals to Agrippa to believe (26:24–29), showing himself the exemplary witness who calls for a response. The entire defense obtains a verdict that Paul has done nothing worthy of death or prison. His appeal means, however, that he must be sent to Rome (26:30–32).

O'Toole (1978: 156–60) sees the Pauline defense focused on Christology as the main point, with the resurrection at the core. God's promise points to resurrection. Hope is a key idea in the speech, appearing three times. Agrippa's reaction is also important. It shows that Paul's testimony registers with some force, although Agrippa does not come to believe. Paul testifies to kings as Jesus predicted of him (Acts 9:15). The speech is an apologetic for the resurrection but also a presentation of the gospel. There is proclamation as well as apologetic here.

This material is rooted in Pauline sources, like the other defense speeches. The discussion between Festus, Agrippa, and Bernice is harder to trace, but Fitzmyer (1998: 748) speaks of Pauline sources here also. This discussion may pull together issues raised at Paul's examination or perhaps Festus explained the other ruler's presence at the hearing. Festus has the appearance of being a ruler in search of the facts. Official trial sources are also possible (Winter 1993: 306–9, 333). Winter also argues that Lukan redaction does not preclude his working with forensic sources. The use of such sources "cannot be ruled out" (Winter 1993: 334).

The origin of the scene is debated among commentators. Weiser (1985: 644) argues that it is simply to create a parallel between Paul and Jesus when Jesus was examined by Herod Antipas in Luke 23:6–12, but Barrett (1998: 1333–34) notes that this scene is much longer and that Bernice is present throughout, so that this explanation of mere paralleling is not enough. Pesch (1986b: 266–67) argues against a completely freely constructed scene by Luke. Roloff (1988: 345) argues for a freely constructed scene to give vividness, as is common in ancient history writing, and Conzelmann (1987: 206) calls it a free literary composition. Williams (1990: 410), however, suggests that the scene accords with ancient practice (Fitzmyer 1998: 748, it is "far from certain the whole scene is 'a free literary composition'").

Haenchen (1987: 678) doubts that a Roman ruler would have held a hearing that in effect admits his inability to make a decision. He also thinks Festus's search for something to write to Rome is artificial ("anything but a realistic description"; so also Conzelmann 1987: 207). However, this conclusion ignores the fact of Paul's appeal and the sense Festus has from the history of the case that the charge is without real substance, which he knows could be a problem. The insistence of the Jewish leadership against Paul is also a concern. A decision from Festus is not required, but he should supply important information to Rome without revealing his own incompetence (Marshall 1980: 387, 390).[1] Paul has now appeared before a synagogue, a governor, and a king (Luke 21:12–15; Acts 9:15).

Exegesis and Exposition

25:13Now when some days had passed, Agrippa the king and Bernice arrived at Caesarea, welcoming Festus. 14And as they stayed there many days, Festus laid Paul's case before the king, saying, "There is a man left prisoner by Felix; 15and when I was at Jerusalem, the chief priests and the elders of the Jews gave information about him, asking for judgment against him. 16I answered them that it was not the custom of the Romans to give up anyone before the accused met the accusers face-to-face and had opportunity to make his defense concerning the charge laid against him. 17When therefore they came together here, I made no delay but on the next day took my seat on the tribunal and ordered the man to be brought in. 18Standing up, the accusers brought no charge, in his case, of such evils as I supposed; 19but they had certain points of dispute with him about their own religious beliefs and about a certain Jesus, who was dead but whom Paul asserted to be alive. 20Being at a loss how to investigate these disputes, I asked whether he wished to go to Jerusalem and be tried there regarding them. 21But when Paul had appealed to be kept in custody for the decision of the emperor, I commanded him to be held until I could send him to Caesar." 22And Agrippa said to Festus, "I should like to hear the man myself." "Tomorrow," said he, "you shall hear him."

23So the following day, coming with great pomp, Agrippa and Bernice entered the audience hall with the military tribunes and the prominent men of the city. Then, by command of Festus, Paul was brought in. 24And Festus said, "King Agrippa and all who are present with us, you see this man about whom the whole Jewish multitude petitioned me both at Jerusalem and here, ⌜shouting that he ought not to live any longer. 25But I found that he had done nothing deserving death; when he himself appealed to the emperor,⌝ I decided to send him. 26But

---

1. Sherwin-White 1963: 51, 68 says that the delay in holding Paul is also a problem and that the account is accurate. Fitzmyer 1998: 752 argues that this is "hardly a blatant contradiction" as Conzelmann claimed.

I have nothing definite to write to my lord about him. Therefore I have brought him before you and especially before you, King Agrippa, that, after we have examined him, I may have something to write. [27]For it seems to me unreasonable, in sending a prisoner, not also to indicate the charges against him."

[26:1]Agrippa said to Paul, "You have permission to speak for yourself." Then Paul, stretching out his hand, made his defense:

[2]"Concerning all the accusations of the Jews, I think myself fortunate that it is before you, King Agrippa, I am to make my defense today, [3]because you are especially familiar with all customs and disputes of the Jews; therefore I beg you to listen to me patiently.

[4]"Now, my manner of life from my youth, spent from the beginning among my own nation and at Jerusalem, is known by all the Jews. [5]They have known for a long time, if they are willing to testify, that according to the strictest party of our religion, I have lived as a Pharisee. [6]And now I stand here being judged for the hope of the promise made by God to our fathers, [7]to which our twelve tribes hope to attain, as they earnestly worship night and day. And for this hope I am accused by Jews, O king! [8]Why is it thought unbelievable by any of you that God raises the dead?

[9]"I myself was convinced that I ought to do many things in opposing the name of Jesus the Nazorean. [10]And I did so in Jerusalem; I not only shut up many of the saints in prison, by authority from the chief priests, but when they were put to death, I cast my vote against them. [11]And punishing them often in all the synagogues, I tried to force them to blaspheme; and in raging fury against them, I persecuted them even to foreign cities. [12]"Thus I was journeying to Damascus with the authority and commission of the chief priests. [13]At midday, O king, I saw on the way a light from heaven, brighter than the sun, shining round me and those who journeyed with me. [14]And when we had all fallen to the ground, I heard a voice saying to me in the Hebrew language, 'Saul, Saul, why are you persecuting me? It hurts you to kick against the goads.' [15]And I said, 'Who are you, Lord?' And the Lord said, 'I am Jesus whom you are persecuting. [16]But rise and stand upon your feet; for I have appeared to you for this purpose, to appoint you servant and witness to the things in which you have seen me and to those in which I will appear to you, [17]delivering you from the people and from the Gentiles—to whom I send you [18]to open their eyes, that they may turn from darkness to light and from the power of Satan to God, that they may receive forgiveness of sins and a place among those who are sanctified by faith in me.'

[19]"Wherefore, O King Agrippa, I was not disobedient to the heavenly vision [20]but declared first to those at Damascus, then at Jerusalem and throughout all the country of Judea, and also to the Gentiles, that they should repent and turn to God, performing deeds worthy of repentance. [21]For this reason the Jews seized me in the temple and tried to kill me. [22]To this day I, having the help that comes from God, stand here testifying both to small and great, saying nothing but what the prophets along with Moses said would come to pass: [23]that the

Christ must suffer and that, by being the first to rise from the dead, he comes to proclaim light both to the people and to the Gentiles."

24And as he thus made his defense, Festus said with a loud voice, "Paul, you are mad; your great learning is turning you mad." 25But Paul said, "I am not mad, most excellent Festus, but I am speaking the sober truth. 26For the king knows about these things, and to him I speak openly; for I am persuaded that none of these things has escaped his notice, for this was not done in a corner. 27King Agrippa, do you believe the prophets? I know that you believe." 28And Agrippa said to Paul, "In a little while you ⌜try with persuasion⌝ to make me a Christian!" 29And Paul said, "Whether short or long, I would to God that not only you but also all who hear me this day might become such as I am—except for these chains."

30Then, the king, the governor, and Bernice and those who were sitting with them arose; 31and when they had withdrawn, they said to one another, "This man is doing nothing to deserve death or imprisonment." 32And Agrippa said to Festus, "This man could have been set free if he had not appealed to Caesar."

Festus seeks help and advice from two important people close to Judaism: Agrippa and Bernice, his sister. This would be Herod Agrippa II (AD 28–100), also known as Marcus Julius Agrippa. He was the only surviving son of Herod Agrippa I, whose death is recorded in Acts 12:23, and great-grandson of Herod the Great, ruler of the region at Jesus's birth. He ruled over the territory Philip originally received from Herod the Great, and in AD 56 he received even more territory, so that he ruled over the northeastern portion of Herod the Great's empire (Lebanon and to the east, in modern terms, and over parts of Galilee and some areas east of the Jordan River). Judea, Samaria, and large parts of Galilee, however, remained in Roman control. The Romans did allow him to appoint the high priest, and this shows that they trusted him. He was called king in some inscriptions (*OGIS* 419; Fitzmyer 1998: 749). Agrippa II was part Jewish, and so the Roman governor was seeking his help as one with some knowledge about these matters. Agrippa had a reputation of being very pious in religious matters and expert in Jewish issues. He also was a faithful vassal: later he would side with Rome in the war that led to Jerusalem's defeat in AD 70 (Photius, *Bibliotheca* 33). One of his sisters, Drusilla, was the wife of the previous Roman governor, Felix. Agrippa's appointment appears in Josephus (*J.W.* 2.12.1 §223; *Ant.* 19.9.2 §§360–62, and several paragraphs in *Life*; also *Ant.* 20.6.3 §135; 20.7.1 §138; *J.W.* 2.16.4 §§235–401 [a long speech about not going to war]; Bruce 1990: 490–91). The very fact that his opinion is sought shows Festus's suspicion that the debate is over Judaism.

Bernice (Julia Bernice), his sister, lived in the palace with Agrippa, after having been a wife to Herod of Chalcis (in Lebanon), who was also her uncle, and to King Polemon of Cilicia (Barrett 1998: 1135;

25:13–16

Josephus, *Ant.* 20.7.3 §§145–46; *J.W.* 2.11.6 §220; 2.17.6 §426; Tacitus, *Hist.* 2.81; Suetonius, *Titus* 7; Dio Cassius, *Rom. Hist.* 66.15; Juvenal, *Satires* 6.156–60). She was a year younger than her brother (Le Cornu and Shulam 2003: 1369). It was rumored that she was his incestuous partner (Gaventa 2003: 335–36). The Juvenal text cited above shows that this was a matter of gossip in Rome. Later she was mistress to Vespasian and especially to Titus, who desired to marry her but did not because of Roman antipathy to Jews. There is irony in having such a couple sit in judgment on Paul, who, as Luke makes clear, is innocent. This is a world turned upside down.

After an unspecified number of days, Herod and Bernice have come to Caesarea to greet the new ruler. Festus uses the opportunity to allow them to hear Paul. The aorist participle ἀσπασάμενοι (*aspasamenoi*, greeting) expresses an element of purpose and is presented as coincident in time, working without a time marker (Conzelmann 1987: 206; Fitzmyer 1998: 749; BDF §339.1).

Luke has Festus explain the situation. Festus has to present an explanation of Paul's appeal to the emperor (Justinian, *Digest* 49.6.1; Fitzmyer 1998: 748). This scene functions as a narrative review (vv. 14–21). Paul is a prisoner under Felix and is still being held. Festus notes that the Jewish chief priests and elders want a judgment against Paul. In v. 15 the term καταδίκην (*katadikēn*) means "sentence of condemnation" or "conviction" (BAGD 410; BDAG 516). This is the only instance of the term in the NT.

Festus reports that Roman custom requires that a man meet his accusers face-to-face (Justinian, *Digest* 48.17.1 reads, "And we employ this right lest those who are absent be condemned, for the concept of equity does not allow anyone to be condemned without his case being heard"; Tacitus, *Hist.* 1.6). Appian, *Civil Wars* 3.54.222 reads, "Our law, Senators, requires that the accused shall himself hear the charge preferred against him and shall be judged after he makes his own defense" (Conzelmann 1987: 206). This is the recognition that *aequitas romana* (Roman fairness) has been followed (Fitzmyer 1998: 750).

There is subtle polemic here, since a pagan state's procedure is protecting Paul from the murderous plots coming from God's nation and those who claim to walk after the law. But Festus, despite recognizing his innocence, does not free Paul, showing that he lacks nerve.

25:17–19   Festus explains that he brought Paul to trial as soon as he could with no delays. This is in contrast to 24:22 and the process under Felix. The concern for a fair trial is slightly different from the portrait of 25:1–12, where Festus was considering handing Paul over to the Jewish leadership. This account may make Festus look more honorable than initially. At least it makes clear that he does not succumb to the pressure to do otherwise.

Festus has ended up with charges that he has not anticipated. In the end, "they brought no charge" (οὐδεμίαν αἰτίαν ἔφερον, *oudemian aitian epheron*) against him involving evils or illegalities a Roman judge normally handles. This remark is like that in 23:29, where Claudius Lysias said that he found no cause for charges against Paul. Festus finds himself dealing with religious accusations and disputes, not matters of civil law. It also is similar to 25:7, where the charges are said not to be provable. The dispute at the temple has disappeared, probably because, in listening to Paul, the emperor realized that the temple dispute was only the surface issue for more basic differences (24:15, 21)—at least that is how Luke wants us to see Festus. This has been a point of Paul's throughout the dispute (22:7–10, 14–15, 17–21; 23:6). The difference between the charges not being proved and the dispute over religious matters is more apparent than real. To show no violations of Roman law is to leave the charges unproved and raise questions about what the real subject of the dispute is. To this extent, Festus's report does identify the true point of contention.

The dispute centers on Jewish superstition or, better, religious beliefs (δεισιδαιμονίας, *deisidaimonias*). Johnson (1992: 426) prefers the rendering "superstition," seeing Agrippa treated as an outsider, but this view is in the minority. This term previously appeared in 17:22, where Paul used it of idolaters. It was a common Roman term to describe the religion of those with whom one does not agree (Polybius, *Hist.* 12.24.5; Staudinger, *EDNT* 1:282; Josephus, *J.W.* 2.9.3 §174; *Ant.* 10.3.2 §42 [with a more neutral sense]). Here the term is probably more neutral, since Festus is speaking to Jews. Specifically, the issue is Jesus, a man who died and now is claimed to have come back to life. The Romans did not believe in resurrection, so this would be a foreign religious concept for them. So Paul is being charged with believing in the resurrection, something that Rome cannot judge and that is not a civil matter anyway. As often in these Pauline defense speeches, it is the authority Paul claims for this risen Jesus and the salvation he brings that is at the center of the dispute. In Festus's internal report, Paul's innocence is again asserted with regard to Roman law. The central role of Jesus in the dispute is also clear. In Festus's view, this is purely an internal Jewish dispute, and it leaves him uncertain what to tell Caesar, as verse 27 indicates. Festus does not say anything about doing the Jews a favor, but he need not here, as he is speaking with Jews and so is carrying out his desire to be sensitive to them.

25:20–21 Festus states that he gave Paul the opportunity to go to Jerusalem and be tried by the Jews, on the logic that this was a strictly Jewish dispute. Festus himself says that he was at a loss on how to deal with the situation, although this is probably not an admission of his lack of competence but more a plea for understanding the complexity of his dilemma (Witherington 1998: 729).

Paul's appeal to be heard by the emperor means that Paul will need to be sent to the ruler. Festus reports that he is keeping Paul until Paul can be sent to Caesar (Σεβαστοῦ, *Sebastou*), since the appeal is for a decision by the emperor. This term literally means "worthy of reverence" or "august" (BAGD 745; BDAG 917). Our equivalent is "His Majesty." It is the official Greek equivalent of the Latin *Augustus* (worthy to be worshiped; MM 570). Its use for emperors dates back to Octavian in 27 BC (Suetonius, *Augustus* 7; Dio Cassius, *Rom. Hist.* 53.16.18; Williams 1990: 413).

The term ἀναπέμπω (*anapempō*, send up) is a technical term for remitting a case to a higher court (Barrett 1998: 1140; Larkin 1995: 352; Fitzmyer 1998: 751; Josephus, *J.W.* 2.20.5 §571). There was precedent for this type of judgment and understanding based on religious grounds: Josephus tells of how Hyrcanus II was comfortable leaving his fate in the hands of Julius Caesar (*Ant.* 14.10.2 §195; Fitzmyer 1998: 751).

25:22 Agrippa asks to hear the case. This may indicate that he has longed to hear him, since ἐβουλόμην (*eboulomēn*, I was wanting) is in the imperfect. Another option is that this is a desiderative imperfect (so Williams 1990: 413: "was desiring" to hear him). Festus agrees that he will do so the very next day. Like Herod Antipas with Jesus (Luke 23:6–12), Agrippa wants to hear about the movement. There are two differences. Pilate initiated the contact with Herod, but here Agrippa steps forward. Jesus was silent, but Paul will give a full defense.

25:23 The audience takes place with great pomp (φαντασίας, *phantasias*; BAGD 853; BDAG 1049). Here is the only instance of this term in the NT. The inquiry is held before the prominent people of the city and military leaders (χιλιάρχοις, *chiliarchois*; 21:31–33, 37; 22:24, 26–29; 23:10, 15, 17–19, 22; 24:22; 25:23). These are probably the five tribunes, officers commanding over one thousand men each, stationed in Caesarea (Weiser 1985: 649). It is a grand occasion, a meeting of "royals" with the Romans. Luke 21:12 is fulfilled, as is Acts 9:15.

25:24–27 Festus explains to Agrippa and the other dignitaries that Paul is someone whom the Jewish people have asked him to judge. In making this point, Festus no doubt is reading the leadership as the people's representatives; their role did share some popular support (21:36; 22:22). Those in Jerusalem and Caesarea have argued that Paul should not be allowed to live (ζῆν μηκέτι, *zēn mēketi*). Is this an exaggerated charge? If Paul is seen as a social and political threat to stability, then the claim is not exaggerated.

Festus does not see anything worthy of death (23:29). He notes, however, that he must explain to the emperor, Nero, Paul's appeal to Caesar. This is the second of three declarations of innocence for Paul (23:29; 25:25; 26:31). Caesar is called lord (κυρίῳ, *kyriō*) here in a typical secular use (Fitzmyer 1998: 752; P.Oxy. 1143.4 [Augustus]; 37.6 [Claudius]; 246.30, 34, 37 [Nero]). Festus admits that he has nothing certain (ἀσφαλές, *asphales*) to write. This explains why he has assembled them together: perhaps they can help him know what to say, given that it is unreasonable (ἄλογον, *alogon*) to send a prisoner without charges against him. This Greek term describes something that does not make sense or lacks cause, that is absurd (BAGD 41 §2; BDAG 48). It appears only three times in the NT (2 Pet. 2:12; Jude 10). Festus had to submit such a report, since it was required, and it had to be his own report (Conzelmann 1987: 207; Polhill 1992: 496; Witherington 1998: 733; Justinian, *Digest* 49.5–6).

Again the question is raised why Paul has not been released if this is how Festus feels. The appeal is the reason Paul continues to be held. In effect, Festus says that Paul remains a prisoner because of his own demand. There is irony here as well. Festus has nothing to write because Paul is innocent, as he already knows. The scene shows him fishing for a credible charge. Luke does not come back to the letter or note what Festus wrote. More important is that the major figures express exasperation at not being able to articulate a charge (21:34; 22:30). Jervell (1998: 590) calls it an "absurd" situation for Festus (not to mention Paul).

The hearing proper begins with Agrippa's invitation to Paul to speak. **26:1** Agrippa may well have been placed in charge of the meeting, since it is his help that is being sought. Paul begins his ἀπολογία (*apologia*), that is, his defense. This is not a legal defense, however, since Paul's innocence has been acknowledged. Rather, Paul takes this hearing as an opportunity to explain the motivation for his life and ministry. Paul stretches out his hand not to ask for silence, as in 21:40, but as a greeting to the king (Bruce 1990: 496). The imperfect verb ἀπελογεῖτο (*apelogeito*, made defense) is inceptive. He begins his defense in this way.

Paul begins with a compliment to Agrippa for his familiarity with Jew- **26:2–3** ish practice. This *captatio benevolentiae* is common in rhetorical settings (see 24:2–3). The rest of the speech proceeds according to typical rhetorical form: *exordium* (vv. 2–3), *narratio* (vv. 4–18), *confirmatio* (vv. 19–20), *refutatio* (v. 21), and *peroratio* (vv. 22–23; Winter 1993: 329–31). These elements are the prologue, narration, confirmation, refutation, and concluding appeal. Agrippa was known for being pious, so the compliment fits. The apostle feels fortunate (μακάριον, *makarion*) to have such a knowledgeable person hear his case. Paul asks to be heard with patience, since Agrippa is well equipped to appreciate the situation and Paul's address will go into some detail. He may well be suggesting that Agrippa is better qualified to hear the case than the Sanhedrin. Luke reports Paul's speech in a formal style of long sentences unlike other speeches, a style that fits the occasion. Josephus notes that Bernice could be very devout when a crisis emerged (*J.W.* 2.15.1 §§313–14 [a vow she made in the midst of danger from the plundering by Florus]).

26:4–8 Paul sets forth his life story, his resume, if you will (Le Cornu and Shulam 2003: 1385). He begins by making two points: (1) All his life he has been a Jew (Gal. 1:13–14). He grew up in Jerusalem as a Jew. (2) He was a pious Pharisee, a group known for its strictness (often called "the strictest party" as here; Acts 22:3; 23:6; Phil. 3:4b–6; Josephus, *J.W.* 2.8.14 §162). Paul describes the Pharisees as a sect of a faith Paul's Christianity shares because the Pharisees belong to "our religion" (ἡμετέρας θρησκείας, *hēmeteras thrēskeias*). The Greek term refers especially to religious practice (James 1:26–27). Those present can testify to these facts (Acts 22:5). He is on trial for having a hope in the promise made to "our" fathers (v. 6, also 7; 23:6; 24:15; 25:19; 28:20). Paul thoroughly identifies with being Jewish, and his faith is not a violation of this heritage. He is faithful to "our" religion and "our" fathers. In defending himself, Paul is also explaining that the roots of this new faith are in fact old, reaching into Jewish promise. This is one of the most important statements in Acts about the relationship of Jesus to Jewish promise. It ties in to verses 8, 22–23 in the speech. It is Jesus's suffering and resurrection that are alluded to here in line with Jewish messianic hope (for messianic hope in Judaism, see Isa. 25:6–12; 51:5 LXX; 2 Macc. 2:18; 1 En. 40.9; T. Benj. 10.11; 2 Bar. 30.1; 4Q521 2.2.1–13; Larkin 1995: 356; Le Cornu and Shulam 2003: 1388). "The true Jew must become a Christian in order to remain a Jew" (so Conzelmann 1987: 210).

This section of Paul's speech is laid out in a chiasm of three parts (Gaventa 2003: 339): Paul is faithful to the tradition (vv. 6–8, 22–23); Paul persecuted Christians and was persecuted (vv. 9–11, 21); and Paul was commissioned as a witness and serves as a witness (vv. 12–18, 19–20).

Paul refers to all of Israel as "the twelve tribes" (cf. Luke 22:30). Note again Paul's identification with Israel. These are "our" twelve tribes. Agrippa is still the focus in the speech and is addressed with respect as king. There is no sense that Israel or anyone who belongs to it is disqualified from hope or the plan of God as Paul preaches it (Rom. 9–11 holds out hope for Israel, including ethnic Israel).

The tribes give constant worship to God for the hope of resurrection. Anna in Luke 2:37b was an example of this hope. Paul asks rhetorically whether it is unbelievable (ἄπιστον, *apiston*) that God can raise someone from the dead. He is really saying that such a thing is not incredible. Central to the hope is that God gives life to the dead. Central to the resurrection is the raising of Jesus. This act showed that God can perform resurrection (Paul calls Jesus's resurrection the "firstfruits" in 1 Cor. 15:20). Through this resurrection Jesus was elevated to a position of authority at God's side. From this position Jesus offers salvation or judgment, with all people accountable to him (Acts 2:30–36; 10:40–43).

All these ideas are wrapped up in Paul's defense of the resurrection. This hope centers on resurrection and what it can accomplish.

Nothing should hinder his audience from faith, although each group would have to make adjustments to its current view. The Gentiles would have to adjust the most, as they do not believe or generally even discuss resurrection. The Pharisees need only accept that Jesus was raised for their sins in order to receive the Spirit (2:30–38). The Sadducees would have to reverse their view that resurrection does not take place. Jews who believed in resurrection saw it as a doctrine that was to come in the end, but Paul is declaring that the first realities of this end have already come (Roloff 1988: 351). Here is the irony. The coming and preaching of the very resurrection hope that Jews should respond to as the goal of their worship is why they charge Paul with sedition. Sadly, they could not be more blind.

Paul then turns to describe his persecution of Christians, what he calls his opposition to the name of Jesus of Nazareth (2:22). In using Jesus's simple name, he refers to him as he would have as a persecutor: no Christ or Lord here. Only the direct intervention of the risen Jesus brought him to appreciate who Jesus is. Paul, as Saul, busied himself in locking up "the saints" (τῶν ἁγίων, *tōn hagiōn*) in prison with the approval of the chief priests (8:3; 9:13; 22:5). **26:9–11**

Saul also voted for their death. Is this a reference to many dying, in which case the Romans would have intervened, since the Jewish leadership did not have the right to execute, or is the remark somewhat rhetorical and generalizing, indicating what he would have liked to see? Literally, the phrase καταφέρω ψῆφον (*katapherō psēphon*, cast a vote) means "set down a stone" or "pebble," which is how votes were cast in the ancient world (Philo, *Unchangeable* 16 §75; *m. Sanh.* 5.5; Le Cornu and Shulam 2003: 1397). Some commentators discuss whether Paul is suggesting that he was a member of the Sanhedrin. This is unlikely. More probable is an allusion to his support of what happened to people such as Stephen in Acts 7 (Witherington 1998: 742). Paul's repeated references to the plural "them" show that many suffered such a fate and suggest that he and the Jewish leadership were breaking the law.

As a persecutor, Saul also tried to compel these Christians to blaspheme. The imperfect ἠνάγκαζον (*ēnankazon*, I compelled) here is conative (Wallace 1996: 551; BDF §326); it suggests a consistent effort that did not succeed: "I tried to force." The reference to blasphemy probably means denying who Jesus really is or even cursing him (*m. Mak.* 3.10–15). Pliny the Younger (*Ep.* 10.96.5) shows a Roman attempt to make Christians deny Jesus in Bithynia during the early second century. The mention of synagogues is a new detail. The remark about blaspheming is made from the perspective of his now appreciating who Jesus is, as is the reference to Christians as "saints." Saul's persecution extended to cities outside Israel as he raged in anger (ἐμμαινόμενος, *emmainomenos*) against them. Here is the only instance of this verb in the NT. The adjective (ἐμμανής, *emmanēs*, frenzied, frantic) appears only in Wis. 14:23. Paul details his persecution with more intensity than in Acts 22:3–4.

26:12–15   Saul was on such a mission when he was headed to Damascus (9:1–2, 14, 21; 22:14–21). The chief priests had commissioned him. He therefore has been on the other side of this dispute. At midday a bright light shone around Saul's group on the road to Damascus (9:7; 22:6, 9; an appearance from heaven, Exod. 20:18; Deut. 4:12; Isa. 60:1–3; Larkin 1995: 359). It was brighter than the sun. All fell down, but only Saul heard the voice. Only this version notes that all fell to the ground. This shows that it was a real, external event, not merely an internal vision of Jesus. Only Saul, however, understood the exchange. A voice spoke to Paul in a Hebrew dialect and asked why he was engaged in persecution.[2] Saul was addressed with his Semitic name, Σαούλ (*Saoul*). Elsewhere Luke uses the Greek form of the name, Σαῦλος (*Saulos*; Acts 9:1; Marshall 1980: 395). The double naming, "Saul, Saul," points to a theophany (Gen. 22:11; 46:2; 1 Sam. 3:4; 2 Esd. [4 Ezra] 14:1; 2 Bar. 22.2; Johnson 1992: 435).

Why was Saul kicking against the goads? The reference to goads is a new detail for this scene. A goad is a stick that serves the same purpose as a whip and is used to prod and direct an animal. So in the appearance Jesus was asking why Saul is kicking against God's discipline and direction. The word often occurs when speaking of a horse that was not to kick against the goad (κέντρον, *kentron*; BAGD 428 §2; BDAG 539–40). Saul was being told not to resist the divine call and to stop persecuting God's people. The "kicking against the goads" pictures his being pricked and his reaction against them. The pricks are not just his conscience but also the new forces crowding in around him, fighting his sense of divine destiny. To kick against the goads is part of a Greek proverbial idiom, although a general reference simply to the goads is common in Greek literature.[3] Paul cannot and should not fight against Jesus. Paul himself speaks of compulsion in his ministry (1 Cor. 9:15–18; Fitzmyer 1998: 759).

The account launches into a commission narrative (Hedrick 1981). The scene is focused on Jesus's call. There is no mention of Saul's blindness or of Ananias as in the other accounts. The variation is part of Luke's

---

2. Jervell 1998: 593 argues that it was Hebrew, the language of Scripture and heaven, which is possible since Paul is a rabbi (so also Le Cornu and Shulam 2003: 1398–99). It could also have been the common language of the time, Aramaic. Later Jewish tradition argued that the angels did not know Aramaic (*b. Šabb.* 12b).

3. See Ps. Sol. 16.4; Philo, *Decalogue* 17 §87; Euripides, *Bacchanals* 794–95; Aeschylus, *Agamemnon* 1624; Pindar, *Pythian Odes* 2.173; Terence, *Phormio* 1.2.27; Eccles. 12:11; Schmid, *TDNT* 3:666–67; Vogeli 1953; Polhill 1992: 502; Stendahl 1963; Bruce 1990: 501; Gaventa 2003: 343.

skill in telling the event three times (Acts 9, 22). Each time additional angles are given as to what took place.

When Saul asked who was speaking to him (Acts 9:5; 22:8), the reply came, "I am Jesus whom you are persecuting." The Lord who appeared to Saul is the risen Jesus who is being persecuted when his people are persecuted. Jesus identifies closely with the believers' suffering. This scene convinced Saul that Jesus was raised, that God had done this, and that Jesus had authority even as Jesus's lead in Saul's calling shows. Paul came to believe the apostles' message as the word of God. The living Lord was defending his followers.

The event has key implications. If Paul came to faith in the mid-30s, then the core theology about which he wrote was clearly in place by then. In other words, the only way Paul could process this vision and understand it as he did was by having heard and now believed the apostolic message from figures like Peter or Stephen. Even though Paul argues in Gal. 1 that he received the gospel by revelation, his ability to understand that appearance of Jesus assumes a preunderstanding that the apostolic preaching would have supplied. Thus, the event shows how old the core theology of Christianity is; it goes back to the earliest days of the apostles' preaching.

In the commission proper, Saul was told to rise to his feet. He was appointed (1) to serve God and (2) to bear witness to the things associated with Jesus. The concept of servants and witnesses for those who proclaim is common in Luke (Luke 1:2; 24:48; Acts 1:8, 22; 2:32; 3:15; 5:32; 10:39, 41). It may well be that Paul's service is primarily as a witness, and so the two ideas are placed next to each other so that the second term explains the first (Rengstorf, *TDNT* 8:542–43). The allusion to language such as in Luke 1:2 and Acts 1:8 may suggest the elevation of Saul to a witness of first rank. There is no meeting with Ananias, as Paul's account is condensed in its recounting of events (Wikenhauser 1961: 271; Marshall 1980: 395 ["telescoped"]). Such telescoping, however, does not suggest that Jesus did not commission Saul in this vision. Witherington (1998: 743) rightly notes that Paul attributes his commission to the Damascus road experience (Gal. 1:1, 15–16), and argues that Ananias does not give a commission to Paul but confirms this call. We should see this detailed commission, then, as supplied here for its dramatic effect and giving details held back until now. Paul's speech to Agrippa is exactly such a testimony by a witness, where Paul serves God by giving the message.

26:16–18

In addition, Jesus would appear to him in the future as the Lord delivered (ἐξαιρούμενος, *exairoumenos*) Saul from the "people," that is, the Jews, and the Gentiles, to whom Saul was being sent. The verb could mean "choose" or "rescue," but here deliverance is the point, as this is often its force in Acts (Johnson 1992: 436; Acts 7:10, 34; 12:11; 23:27; also Exod. 3:8; 18:4; Deut. 32:39; Pss. 36:40; 58:1 [37:40; 59:1 Eng.]). A clue is that the language here parallels Jer. 1:5–8 (note also Ezek. 34:10; 1 Chron. 16:35). Perhaps a scene such as the rescue of Acts 27, which is yet to come, is foreshadowed, or even Paul's protection up to this point, since the Lord has assured Paul that he will travel to Rome. Paul is sent to preach this Jesus. The message is to both groups, as the relative pronoun in verse 17, οὕς (*hous*, those whom), probably refers back to both the Jewish people and the Gentiles, since verse 20 makes clear that both audiences are in view (Luke 2:32). Schneider (1982: 374) sees the pronoun as referring only to Gentiles, but verse 20 argues otherwise, as does the idea that Jews need their eyes opened as well (Luke 1:16, 78–79; 4:18). Witherington (1998: 744) points to the picture of blindness in Bar-Jesus at Acts 13:4–12 (the gospel to Gentiles: 9:15; 13:47; 22:21). Such guidance by Jesus also has been repeatedly described; 16:9, 18:9, 22:17–21, and 23:11 are key examples.

Paul's task is described in three infinitives: to open (ἀνοῖξαι, *anoixai*), to turn (ἐπιστρέψαι, *epistrepsai*), and to receive (λαβεῖν, *labein*; Barrett 1998: 1161). Paul is to open the eyes of people and turn them from darkness to light (Col. 1:13; 1 Thess. 1:9–10; T. Levi 19.1; Jos. Asen. 8.9), from Satan to God. Cosmic conflict has been a theme of Acts (8:11, 20–23; 13:10; 19:13–19). It is a part of Jewish thinking about God's work in the world (1QS 1.9–10, 18, 23; 2.19; 1QM 1.1; 2.2–5; 14.9; Fitzmyer 1998: 760). The image of a ministry of light is like Isa. 42:7, 16. With the opening of people's eyes and their turning in response comes receiving the gift, the reception of forgiveness of sins (Luke 1:77; 3:3; 4:18; 5:20–21; 7:47–49; 11:4; 17:3–4; 24:47; Acts 2:38; 5:31; 10:43; 13:38), giving those who respond a place among those sanctified (i.e., set apart) by faith in Jesus (Acts 20:32; 1 Cor. 1:2; Titus 2:11–14). So the gift of the gospel has two prime elements: (1) the forgiveness of sins and (2) the reception of a place with God and the saints.

To have a place among the sanctified is to have fellowship with God. Light is a frequent Pauline image (Rom. 2:19; 13:12; 2 Cor. 4:6; 6:14; Eph. 5:8; Col. 1:12; 1 Thess. 5:5). This "place" (κλῆρον, *klēron*) means a portion of an inheritance (Ps. 77:55 LXX [78:55 Eng.]; Larkin 1995: 361). Light is also a messianic image in the OT. It describes what the Messiah is as he leads God's way in—an image of the morning star and of the Messiah as light in Isaiah (Luke 1:79; see v. 23 below). The language of Saul's commission reflects typical Christian language (Eph. 5:8; 6:12; 1 Pet. 2:9). His mission is an extension of Jesus's work as the servant.

Inheritance is linked to sanctification as the natural extension of justification. The categories are distinguishable but not separable. So three parts of the process appear in response to the message: understanding, change of direction, and the reception of gift. The result of response is that one receives an inheritance among those who believe in Jesus. The issue of faith in Jesus follows as the climax of the saying; πίστει (*pistei*, through faith) gives the means by which these benefits come (Culy and Parsons 2003: 497, an instrumental dative). This is all triggered by faith as it grows out of conviction and repentance. For both Paul and Luke, "opening eyes" and "turning" are other ways to speak of faith.[4] Polhill (1992: 504) correctly says, "One could hardly give a more succinct presentation of the gospel." One also could hardly find a text that better summarizes the major theological concerns of Luke-Acts when it comes to mission.

Paul says that his arrest is the result of obeying God and the heavenly   **26:19–21** vision (ὀπτασία, *optasia*). Paul's experience was both an event that others sensed and a vision that was his uniquely in terms of its instruction. He was "not disobedient," a description that reflects litotes; he was fully obedient (Rom. 1:16). He declared to Jews and Gentiles the need to repent, turn to God, and perform deeds that reflected such repentance. Paul's message was for all types of people. Note the link between response and the concrete expression of change (Acts 15:9, 11; on repentance, 2:38; on turning, 3:19; "evidence of genuineness," Gal. 5:22–23; 2 Cor. 13:5–7).

Verse 20 is a key verse telling what Paul asked for when he preached. He asked the same from both Jews and Gentiles, namely, that they repent (i.e., change their minds) and turn (i.e., change the direction of the orientation of their life). These responses can also be called faith directed toward Jesus, the idea mentioned at the end of verse 18. So all these ideas are related to each other. Faith in Jesus is where the process ends, but to get there, a person changes his or her mind about sin and God and turns to God to receive the offer of salvation through Jesus. So each of these terms ("repent," "turn," "believe") is adequate for expressing the offer of the gospel, since Paul used each of them.[5]

Paul was not an antinomian. He did not believe that someone who had faith could do whatever one wished without concern for God's moral standards. So here he also exhorts his audience to live, in response to grace, in a way that produces fruit reflecting the change of direction called for by forgiveness. This is not a third responsibility, since the term πράσσοντας (*prassontas*, performing) is a present participle, making the performing of deeds something that happens alongside, and simultaneously with, the other elements, in dependence upon repenting and turning (Luke 3:8; Eph. 2:8–10; Titus 2:14; 3:8; Gal. 5:22–23; 2 Cor. 13:5–7). This response is wrapped up in the ideas of repenting and turning, just as here repenting and turning are wrapped up in faith. One who turns to God follows in God's way and produces fruit. To trust God is to be responsive to God. John's Gospel calls this loving God, knowing God, or

---

4. On the difference between faith as belief and the faith as doctrine delivered to the saints, see Pelikan 2005: 271–73.

5. For more on repentance, see the discussion of Acts 2:38. For more on turning, see the discussion of 3:19, which shares the verbs "repent" and "turn."

abiding in God (John 14–16). Polhill (1992: 505) summarizes, "Works can never be the basis of salvation. They are, however, the inevitable result of a genuine experience of turning to God in Christ."

In verse 20, there is an odd geographical link between Judea and the Gentiles and difficult syntax (Barrett 1998: 1163; πᾶσάν τε τὴν χώραν τῆς Ἰουδαίας καὶ τοῖς ἔθνεσιν, *pasan te tēn chōran tēs Ioudaias kai tois ethnesin*). The accusative among datives is odd. Some scholars suggest that an εἰς (*eis*) has dropped out before the accusative clause; Bruce (1990: 503), Marshall (1980: 397), and Haenchen (1987: 686–87) note the possibility of an early gloss (a later scribal addition); but there is no MS evidence for either of these ideas. Some complain that the account is in contradiction to Gal. 1:22 and to the narrative of Acts 9, since in those passages no one in Judea knows Paul and he has no ministry in Judea, at least for a time (Acts 15:3–4; 18:22; and 21:7–16 are later examples; Witherington 1998: 746). The remarks, however, may well be a compression of events over a long period (Rom. 15:19). Williams (1990: 420) notes that the syntactical issue distinguishes between preaching in Damascus and Jerusalem (in synagogues) and among the Gentiles elsewhere if one sees an accusative of extent (also Larkin 1995: 362). Fitzmyer (1998: 760) simply calls the reference a Lukan hyperbole, meaning that Paul preached everywhere to anyone. It might be best to see an ellipse, so that the verb "I evangelized" is missing before the accusative. Then the point is that Paul evangelized everywhere: "I preached repentance and turning to God to those in Damascus and Jerusalem—I evangelized Judea—and to the nations."

Paul's obedience to God began immediately in Damascus. Paul's message, especially in including Gentiles, is why he was seized in the temple (Acts 21:27–29) and why the Jews wanted him dead, a repeated effort that failed, as the imperfect (ἐπειρῶντο, *epeirōnto*, were trying) suggests. This Greek verb is an NT hapax. Texts such as Ps. Sol. 17.22–23 and 2 Bar. 72 show that for many Jews, there was no possibility that Gentiles could share in divine eschatological blessing.[6] The Jewish leaders may also be upset that Paul claims to represent true Judaism. Here is Paul's only direct reference to the formal charge against which he must defend himself. He is not responsible for the civil disruption. A religious difference is the cause of the charge; this is why no Roman role is described in this section. Paul's defense is, "I have a divine calling through Jesus. It was the risen Jesus who gave me this call and made me do it. I was directed from heaven to do so." It is likely that the inclusion of Gentiles in this message was a major irritant and not just the preaching about Jesus, because the temple complaint was that Paul had brought Gentiles

---

6. Some OT texts, however, look to Gentile blessing: Gen. 12:1–3; Isa. 2:1–4; and the OT texts Paul notes in Rom. 15:7–13. The difficult relations with Gentiles in the intertestamental period hardened attitudes about the Gentiles and their gods among some Jews.

into the temple area and defiled it. Luke 4:25–30 shows how some Jews reacted to the inclusion of Gentiles into promised blessing.

Paul says that he has survived all this because God has helped him. The $\quad$ **26:22–23** term ἐπικουρία (*epikouria*, help) is an NT hapax. It is used only of supplication in the LXX (Wis. 13:18). Josephus (*Ant.* 1.19.2 §281) has the term in its sense of "aid" or "help." Philo (*Spec. Laws* 1.54 §298) uses the term where God helps people by giving them sleep for rest.

Paul gives testimony to all kinds of people, great and small, about nothing other than what Moses and the prophets said would take place (Josephus, *Ant.* 2.6.1 §94, uses the idiom regarding how Joseph of the book of Genesis helped great and small overcome the famine).

This kind of summary appeal to Scripture recalls Luke 24:44–47, where the appeal is to the faithfulness of the crucifixion and resurrection to Israel's hope.[7] Such a claim of faithfulness is also common in this section of Acts (22:14, 18; 23:6, 29; 24:15, 21, 25; 25:19; 26:6–7). Paul is a preacher of Jewish promise and hope. Here the claim is that although the preaching of Christ seems new, it is in fact very old, rooted in the Hebrew Scriptures, already ancient in Paul's time. So Paul is not a religious innovator and perverter of the truth; he is merely preaching what God promised from long ago.

The content of his message is that the Messiah must suffer and be the first to rise from the dead. The remark here triggered by εἰ (*ei*) in verse 23 has the force of indirect discourse, giving the content of an utterance. The idea of fulfillment looks back to verses 6–8. This message would free Paul to preach "light" to both the people (Jews) and Gentiles (Isa. 49:6; Luke 2:32 has the parallel image). Three ideas are key: suffering, resurrection, and the proclamation of light.

The term παθητός (*pathētos*, suffering) is an adjective and describes the Christ as one who would undergo rejection (Acts 2:23; 13:29; 17:3; esp. 8:32–36, where Isa. 53 is cited; also Luke 22:37 and Isa. 53:12). Texts such as Isa. 53 and Pss. 2 and 118 are probably alluded to here (see Acts 8:32–33; 4:25–26; 4:11). Jesus must undergo this suffering; it is a part of the divine plan. Luke notes this concept often (Luke 24:26, 46; Acts 3:18; 17:3; van der Woude, *TDNT* 9:524).

The second major teaching in Scripture is the resurrection from the dead. Paul in his epistles adds the note that Jesus was the first to experience this, as he says here (1 Cor. 15:20; Col. 1:15–20; Rev. 1:5). Texts in mind here include Pss. 16:8–11 and 110:1 (Acts 2:22–36).

Finally, the gospel here is portrayed as a light that guides. Jesus is the light shining out of darkness (Luke 1:78–79; 2 Cor. 4:6). This light is proclaimed to both Jews ("the people") and Gentiles. The two groups are tightly linked by the conjunction *te*, meaning "both" Jews and Gen-

---

7. On Scripture, see Luke 16:29–31; 24:25, 27; Acts 2:16; 3:18, 24; 10:43; 13:15, 27, 40; 15:15; 24:14; Johnson 1992: 438.

tiles. The Scripture always looked to include both Jews and Gentiles in divine blessing (Gen. 12:3). Through Jesus the opportunity comes to both groups, which is part of what may well have been upsetting some of the Jewish audience.

26:24 Festus responds loudly (μεγάλη τῇ φωνῇ, *megalē tē phōnē*, in a loud voice) that Paul's declaration means that the preacher is mad as a result of his learning (on the expression without the article, see Acts 14:10; 16:28). His interruption might seem somewhat rude if it were not for his status. One is reminded of how supreme court justices today cut off lawyers' arguments with questions or observations. Although Paul is really speaking to Agrippa, it is Festus, the Gentile, who interrupts. Festus has heard enough and declares that Paul has lost his mind; he is "mad" (μαίνῃ, *mainē*; BAGD 486; BDAG 610; Acts 12:15) in the sense that his learning has driven him to embrace insane things (εἰς μανίαν περιτρέπει, *eis manian peritrepei*). Insanity is what resurrection would have seemed like to a Roman, who might have believed only in the immortality of the soul (Acts 17:32; 25:19). For Festus, such a doctrine is learned speculation, having the sound of wisdom but not believable (Roloff 1988: 355). The gospel is, as Paul says elsewhere, foolishness to the Gentiles (1 Cor. 1:23). As Polhill (1992: 507) paraphrases, "All your learning . . . has lifted you out of the real world." It is possible that a parallel blessing to Jews and Gentiles also is a difficult thought for the ruler (Le Cornu and Shulam 2003: 1412). Reconciliation of the races before God is a struggle for some people to accept. The reaction is like the one to Paul's speech in Acts 17:18, 32.

26:25–27 Respectfully addressing Festus as His Excellency (cf. Luke 1:3), Paul defends the sanity of his thinking and turns to Agrippa, a Jew who might understand. Perhaps the Jewish ruler has an appreciation of the truth of these ideas, which were not "done in a corner." Without missing a beat, Paul appeals to the Jewish representative who may appreciate his argument and who has been his key audience from the start of his speech.

   Paul has not lost his mind but speaks "true and prudent words" (ἀληθείας καὶ σωφροσύνης ῥήματα, *alētheias kai sōphrosynēs rhēmata*), or "the sober truth." The combination of "true" and "prudent" is common in Greek, as is a contrast between "prudent" and "mad" (Lucian, *Timon* 55; Xenophon, *Memorabilia* 1.1.16; P.Oxy. 1.33; Plato, *Phaedrus* 244D; Barrett 1998: 1168). In this context, where Paul has been accused of being crazy, his reply is that his words are truth. He has not lost control of his thoughts; they are quite sober and thought through. The metaphor of things not being done in a corner refers to no hidden events tucked away somewhere in the corner out of public sight (BAGD 168; BDAG 209; Malherbe 1985–86; Epictetus, *Discourses* 2.12.17; Plutarch, *Moralia* 777B; Fitzmyer 1998: 764). The idiom means not doing one's philosophical reflection in a way that is disengaged from the public.

Paul can speak boldly and say that these events were public enough that anyone paying attention could appreciate them. Paul asks the king if he believes the prophets, who declare that such things are possible and a part of God's plan. The issue Paul wants to focus on is God's teaching as set forth in the prophets. Paul is a model witness and evangelist here. Agrippa is capable of understanding and appreciating what Paul claims (Acts 26:2–3).

Agrippa senses the pressure of Paul's remark about the prophets and ap- **26:28–29** pears to marvel that in such a short time Paul would think or try to make him a Christian. The present tense πείθεις (*peitheis*, you [try to] persuade) here is conative (Wallace 1996: 534): Paul is attempting to make Agrippa into a Christian, something the king will not accept. The king is backed into a public corner before Festus and wants out. This is the second and final occurrence of the term "Christian" in Acts; the term was used derisively in 11:26, and so Agrippa is probably not serious here. The other NT occurrence is in 1 Pet. 4:16, which teaches that if one suffers as a Christian, then one is to glorify God. It may be that the force of the reply is, "With such few arguments you seek to make me a Christian" (Witherington 1998: 751; Larkin 1995: 364–65n). Another option is that Agrippa replies rhetorically, "With such little argument you make me play the role of the Christian" (Johnson 1992: 439–40; 1 Kings 20:7 LXX B [1 Kings 21:7 Eng.] has an expression close to the one in Acts using the verb ποιέω, *poieō*, to do or make). Fitzmyer (1998: 764) and Barrett (1998: 1171), however, reject this understanding, arguing that such an idiom is later, and Marshall 1980: 400 notes that the 1 Kings idiom requires a present tense, not an aorist, infinitive as appears in Acts 26:28. Barrett (1998: 1170) notes that any debate over whether the point in verse 28 is the short time or the little argument does not make sense, as one idea implies the other ("a short time would not permit a long argument"). In light of the appearance of a similar phrase in verse 29, he opts for the idea of "with little trouble." The reply falls somewhere between earnestness and irony, rather than being sarcastic. Agrippa recognizes what Paul is trying to do (Weiser 1985: 655).

In verse 29 Paul's reply is that whether it takes a short or a long time (ἐν ὀλίγῳ καὶ ἐν μεγάλῳ, *en oligō kai en megalō*), he would pray that all who are listening to him might become a Christian as he is, with one exception, namely, that they not share his chains of imprisonment. The reference to prayer indicates that Paul desires to intercede on behalf of all the audience to become Christians. Paul's desire is expressed with the potential optative (εὐξαίμην, *euxaimēn*), rarely used in the NT. This makes the point gently (BDF §359.2, §385.1; "I would pray"). The reply clearly expresses his heart (BAGD 329 §1; BDAG 417 §1). The verb εὔχομαι (*euchomai*) reappears in 27:29. The reference to a short or long time is slightly more likely than reading the phrase as another reference to small and great as in verse 22, given that the remark in verse 28 (ἐν ὀλίγῳ, *en oligō*) is about time as well.

26:30–32 Festus, Agrippa, and Bernice then arise and meet with other prominent people. They privately make a judgment that Paul has done nothing worthy of death or prison. This is the third such declaration in this sequence (the others are 25:19–20, 25, as was the case with Jesus: Luke 23:4, 14, 22). It is the fifth such remark in Acts (also 23:9, 29). The scope of Paul's innocence has grown since 25:25: now he is innocent even of grounds for imprisonment. The socially highest people to hear the case declare that Paul is without guilt in this matter. The speech is a legal success but changes nothing. Agrippa concludes the deliberations by noting that if there not been an appeal to Caesar (25:5, 11, 21), then Paul could have been set free. Nothing, however, will short-circuit the appeal to Caesar. It is now a matter of honoring Caesar's prestige or *auctoritas* to render a decision he has been asked to make (Sherwin-White 1963: 65).

Some scholars challenge this part of the passage and its credibility. How could this conversation be known? The results of the hearing would have made the view of the governor, Agrippa, and Bernice evident. It is possible that this result and explanation would have been communicated to Paul, possibly even as "You could have been freed if you had not appealed to Caesar." So it is off to Rome for Paul. The injustice—but providence—of his situation continues.

In sum, we see an overview of Paul's defense that also allows him to present the gospel. The personal nature of his testimony is an important element of his message. This is not an abstract presentation of theology; rather, it focuses attention on how Paul knows that God is at work in his life through the gospel. This personal element is part of what makes testimonies to the gospel so powerful. Many churches are now incorporating into their services a time for personal testimony from members. When this is done well, in crisp, personal, and anecdotal style, it is a very effective means of presenting the gospel. Some shy away from such appeals to experience, noting that there are a variety of experiences out there in our culture, some authentic and others not reflective of truth, but the point is that God in a genuine experience does work through the everyday events of our lives, and such accounts do connect with people and cause them to reflect. Paul's basic appeals are that he is innocent of anything destructive and that his faith is in line with promises God made long ago. These actions of realized promise God has performed through Jesus.

We also see a summary of how evangelism takes place (Fernando 1998: 598–605). God calls and enables, both through circumstances and through faithful witnesses. These witnesses speak to anyone, great or small, about Jesus. The message is focused on what God has done with and through Jesus on behalf of others. Christianity is neither merely an ethic nor a culturally grounded faith that has contributed to Western culture; it is a divinely revealed relationship to God that God initiates through the work and provision he graciously provides through Jesus, an obstacle-free way into fellowship with him. It is rooted in teaching that God has revealed in words of promise, in Scripture, and through attested events. This message is for anyone, east or west, north or south, rich or poor, slave or free. It is presented with persuasion and invitation but not coercion. Agrippa senses this "pressure" to believe. Paul acknowledges it but also acts in such a way that it is clear that God must work in the heart of the person responding. Paul was a faithful witness at his trial not because everyone he witnessed to became Christians as he stood in the dock. That was not success in his view. He was faithful because they all heard how central Jesus was to life as Paul defended his own actions.

Paul the defendant teaches us that evangelism is not about results but about faithfully delivering the message. It is like being a paperboy. The paper arrives at the front door because the witness brings it. But to enjoy the benefit of the paper, the person at home must open the door, read the news, and understand it. Paul shows us that the message can be naturally brought forth in a variety of settings and circumstances. He also demonstrates that the personal nature of that story is often the most compelling. Paul makes clear that the results are God's business; we are merely the means of delivery.

Additional Notes

25:24–25. An expansion of these verses appears in the Western text. Festus says that he would not hand Paul over without any defense. In fact, he could not do this because of the emperor's orders, and so he ordered the Jewish leaders to Caesarea. Festus also notes that he asked Paul if he wished to be judged by them in Jerusalem. All these details have already been alluded to in the account.

26:15. The Western text adds a reference to the "Nazorean," making the remark parallel to 22:8.

26:28. The reading πείθεις (*peitheis*) appears to be the original here (‍‍ℵ, B, 33, 18), since it explains the reading of A (πείθῃ, *peithē*) and fits the rhetorical setting.

C. The Long Sea Journey to Rome (27:1–28:16)

Luke makes use of a common motif in this section of Acts, the long sea voyage. One need only think of Homer's epic the *Odyssey* to know how popular such accounts were.[1] To survive a test of life at sea was to be portrayed as righteous (Williams 1990: 426). Readers who know the OT will think of the story of Jonah or texts in the Psalter (Pss. 42:7; 66:12; 69:2–3, 15; also Isa. 43:2; Roloff 1988: 360).

The earlier segment of the journey has two parts. First they take a ship of Adramyttium from Caesarea to Myra (27:1–5). Then they sail on an Alexandrian ship from Myra until the shipwreck in Malta (27:6–44). Gaventa (2003: 350) speaks of seven scenes to the journey in chapter 27: the initial phase and difficulties (vv. 1–8), Paul's failed intervention (vv. 9–12), the storm and loss of hope (vv. 13–20), Paul's intervention and prophecy (vv. 21–26), the ship drifting and the loss of hope (vv. 27–32), Paul's intervention with a meal (vv. 33–38), and the shipwreck (vv. 39–44).

The storm at sea dominates the early part of this account (vv. 13–38), and verses 39–44 depict the shipwreck and Paul's survival. One of the main themes of the account, beyond God's sovereign protection, is that Paul can influence events even as a prisoner.

The trip from Malta to Rome completes the unit. In 28:1–10 Paul's surviving a venomous bite in Malta underscores God's protection and Paul's righteousness. The final steps to Rome appear in 28:11–16. They take another Alexandrian ship from Malta to Puteoli (28:11–13) and go by foot the rest of the way to Rome (28:14–16). Gentiles saw Rome as the center of the earth. In this journey, however, starting as it does in Judea, Rome is a long way off, on the edges of the earth for one starting from Caesarea. With Paul's arrival in Rome, the gospel can go out to all people, since everything comes to and from Rome. Paul notes his travels in a general way in 2 Cor. 11:25–26.

Paul speaks four times in this material: 27:10 (his warning); 27:21–26 (an angel tells him that the ship will be destroyed but all will be rescued); 27:31 (he gives counsel as sailors try to escape); and 27:33–34 (he urges passengers to eat and says they will be rescued; Schneider

---

1. Homer, *Od.* 5.291–332, has a storm. Weiser 1985: 660 lists eleven such sea accounts from the ancient world. Examples include Josephus, *Life* 3 §§13–16; T. Naph. 6.2–10; Lucian, *The Ship* 7–10; Johnson 1992: 450–51.

1982: 379). Schneider also notes that three life-threatening situations dominate the scene: the sea storm, the shipwreck, and the snakebite. Paul survives all three. Deliverance is key to the passage, and many variations of the Greek verb σῴζω (sōzō, deliver) occur here.

The journey is rooted in the "we" source and is told with vivid detail. Conzelmann (1987: 215) sees a literary device here. His view is rooted in the position of Dibelius (1956: 204–6). Hanson (1985) has challenged this approach by a comparison with such sea voyage accounts in Thucydides that no one questions historically (*Pel. War* 6.1–61).

Roloff (1988: 358) also challenges the scene's trustworthiness. He argues that the picture of Paul's treatment does not fit the way prisoners traveled. He also questions the way in which the scene of Paul's intervention is in tension with the flow of the account. Finally, he sees as strained the manner in which the "we" portions are noted. He has in mind here the speeches in 27:9–11 and 21–26, which, he argues, are not consistent. Fitzmyer (1998: 774) also sees the Pauline portions as insertions into the sea voyage account, with verses 21–26 perhaps having roots in the Pauline source. Roloff, however, does see some elements of authentic material behind the chapter, into which the Pauline scenes are inserted, which makes his position different from that of Conzelmann. This is a position close to that of Haenchen (1987: 709–10).

Pesch (1986b: 286) challenges the view that Luke formed the material completely, but agrees with Roloff about insertions of scenes about Paul. Pesch defends the core of the account by pointing to details about the name of the cohort and the presence of Aristarchus that point to a nonliterary origin. The noting of a change of ships is another such detail.

A variation of the "literary" explanation is found in Robbins (1978). He argues that the sea voyage genre is normally written in the first person plural. This approach has been examined by C. J. Hemer (1985), however, and found wanting. There is no first-person-plural sea voyage genre (Bruce 1990: 509).

The account in 28:1–10 is also a piece of tradition that Luke has worked over (Schneider 1982: 401; Pesch 1986b: 296). It includes two miracle accounts: Paul's survival of the snakebite and a Pauline healing of Publius's father, who had fever.

The entire unit does give the sense of a genuine event to which the "we" source was a witness. Also, the idea that the Pauline scenes have been inserted is questionable. Jervell (1998: 612–14) speaks of the nautical details being unlike the voyage scenes in romances and sees an event with a high degree of historical probability. To survive such an event would leave a clear impression (J. Smith 1880; Rapske 1994a: 1–47). There is detail in this story that is unlike its parallels. The difference in the way the prediction is handled by Luke in 27:9–11 and 21–26 also suggests a source where Paul's view of things is altered slightly by a vision of the Lord. If verses 9–11 and 21–26 are created pieces, the author has not remembered how he created one differently from the other. This is an unlikely scenario. It is clear that Paul was not a normal prisoner, as he seemed to have unusual freedom, with his Roman citizenship being an element in the equation (Witherington 1998: 759), not to mention the peaceful nature of his long incarceration up to this point. From two millennia away, one should not underestimate the power or effect of what was clearly a significant personality (Marshall 1980: 402–3 and esp. Barrett 1998: 1178–80, who sees in the account the "actual experience of Paul and his friends," though acknowledging some literary coloring). Under stress to preserve his own life, the centurion may well have come to engage Paul, who would be seen as a religious figure in touch with the divine. Determining interruptions in a narrative is subjective.

The account does have a few major narrative themes. Whereas Rome's leaders earlier pointed to Paul's innocence, now God and the creation speak to it by having him survive a life-threatening test (Miles and Trompf 1976, although their emphasis on judgment for the Jewish leadership is less than likely; Talbert and Hayes 1995; see Fitzmyer 1998: 767–68). Paul's stature as a figure thereby grows, for his survival indicates that God has marked him out as an unusual man, a hero in the best sense of the term. Finally, those who listen and follow the message of Paul experience deliverance, a symbol of what his real message also brings. Paul is the exemplary witness and epitome of faithfulness. He is one who trusts in God. It also is important to recognize that the Pauline parts of the account bear the narrative burden of the story (27:9c–11, 21–26, 31, 33–36), although the theme may well be found in 27:24.

Why does Luke give such detail to this journey? Witherington (1998: 755) suggests that part of the reason was the eyewitness character of the scene, which was a part of Greek historical writing. We should add that the risk of the journey allows Luke to show how far away Rome was and how God protected Paul in every way to assure his arrival there. Rome has the feel of being at the "end" of the earth as viewed from the land of Israel.

Exegesis and Exposition

²⁷:¹And when it was decided that we should sail for Italy, they delivered Paul and some other prisoners to a centurion of the Augustan Cohort, named Julius. ²And embarking in a ship of Adramyttium, which was about to sail to the ports along the coast of Asia, we put to sea, being accompanied by Aristarchus, a Macedonian from Thessalonica. ³The next day we put in at Sidon; and Julius

treated Paul kindly and permitted him to go to his friends and be cared for. ⁴And putting to sea from there, we sailed under the lee of Cyprus because the winds were against us. ⁵And sailing across the sea that is off Cilicia and Pamphylia ⌜ ⌝, we came to Myra in Lycia. ⁶There finding a ship of Alexandria sailing for Italy, the centurion put us on board. ⁷Sailing slowly for a number of days and arriving with difficulty off Cnidus, as the wind was not allowing us to go on, we sailed under the lee of Crete off Salmone. ⁸Coasting along it with difficulty, we came to a place called Fair Havens, near which was the city of Lasea.

⁹As much time had been lost and the voyage was already dangerous because the fast had already gone by, Paul advised them, ¹⁰saying, "Men, I perceive that the voyage will be with injury and much loss not only of the cargo and the ship but also of our souls." ¹¹But the centurion paid more attention to the captain and to the owner of the ship than to what Paul said. ¹²And because the harbor was not suitable to winter in, the majority gave counsel to put to sea from there, on the chance that somehow they could reach Phoenix, a harbor of Crete, looking southwest and northwest, and winter there.

¹³And when the south wind blew gently, supposing that they had obtained their purpose, they weighed anchor and sailed along Crete, close inshore. ¹⁴But after a little time a tempestuous wind, called the ⌜northeaster⌝, struck down from the land. ¹⁵And when the ship was caught and unable to face the wind, we gave way to it ⌜ ⌝ and were driven. ¹⁶And running under the lee of a small island called ⌜Cauda⌝, we managed with difficulty to secure the boat, ¹⁷after which, hoisting it up, they took measures to undergird the ship; then, fearing that they would run on the Syrtis and lowering the gear, so they were driven. ¹⁸As we were violently storm-tossed, they began next day to throw the cargo overboard; ¹⁹and the third day, with their own hands, they cast out the tackle of the ship. ²⁰And when neither sun nor stars were appearing for many a day and no small tempest was pressing upon us, at last all hope of our being saved was abandoned.

²¹As they had been long without food, Paul then, standing among them, said, "Men, you ought to have listened to me and not set sail from Crete to incur this injury and loss. ²²I now bid you take heart; for there will be no loss of souls among you, but only of the ship. ²³For this very night there stood by me an angel of the God to whom I belong and whom I worship, ²⁴and he said, 'Do not be afraid, Paul; you must stand before Caesar; and look, God has granted you all those who sail with you.' ²⁵So take heart, men, for I have faith in God that it will be exactly as I have been told. ²⁶But it is necessary to run aground on some island."

²⁷When the fourteenth night had come, as we were drifting across the sea of Adria, about midnight the sailors suspected that ⌜they were nearing⌝ land. ²⁸So taking sounding, they found twenty fathoms; a little farther on they sounded again and found fifteen fathoms. ²⁹And fearing that we might run on the rocks, letting out four anchors from the stern, they prayed for day to come. ³⁰And as

the sailors were seeking to escape from the ship and had lowered the boat into the sea under pretense of laying out anchors from the bow, [31]Paul said to the centurion and the soldiers, "Unless these men stay in the ship, you will not be able to be saved." [32]Then the soldiers cut away the ropes of the boat and let it go.

[33]As day was about to dawn, Paul urged them all to take some food, saying, "Today is the fourteenth day that you have continued in suspense and without food, having taken nothing. [34]Therefore I urge you to take some food; it will give you strength, for no one of you shall lose a hair from your head." [35]And when he had said this, taking bread and giving thanks to God in the presence of all, he broke it and began to eat. [36]Then being encouraged, they ate some food themselves. [37](We were in all ⌜two hundred and seventy-six⌝ persons in the ship.) [38]And having eaten enough, they lightened the ship, throwing out the wheat into the sea.

[39]Now when it was day, they did not recognize the land, but they noticed a bay with a beach, on which they planned if possible to bring the ship ashore. [40]So they cast off the anchors and left them in the sea, at the same time loosening the ropes that tied the rudders; then hoisting the foresail to the wind, they made for the beach. [41]But striking a shoal, they ran the vessel aground; the bow, becoming stuck, remained immovable, and the stern was being broken up by the surf. [42]The soldiers' plan was to kill the prisoners lest any should swim away and escape; [43]but the centurion, wishing to save Paul, kept them from carrying out their purpose. He ordered those who could swim to throw themselves overboard first and make for the land, [44]and the rest on planks or on pieces of the ship. And so it came about that all escaped to land.

[28:1]After escaping, we learned that the island was called ⌜Malta⌝. [2]And the natives showed us unusual kindness. Kindling a fire, they welcomed us all because it had begun to rain and was cold. [3]When Paul had gathered a bundle of sticks and put them on the fire, a viper came out because of the heat and fastened on his hand. [4]When the natives saw the creature hanging from his hand, they were saying to one another, "No doubt this man is a murderer. Though he has escaped from the sea, justice has not allowed him to live." [5]He, however, shaking off the creature into the fire, suffered no harm. [6]They waited, expecting him to swell up or suddenly fall down dead; but when they had been waiting a long time, and seeing that no misfortune came to him, they ended up changing their minds, saying that he was a god.

[7]Now in the neighborhood of that place were lands belonging to the chief man of the island, named Publius, who received us and entertained us hospitably for three days. [8]It happened that the father of Publius lay sick with fever and dysentery; and Paul, visiting him and praying and laying his hands on him, healed him. [9]And when this had taken place, the rest of the people on the island who had diseases also came and were cured. [10]They honored us with many gifts; and when we sailed, they put on board what we needed.

[11]After three months we set sail in a ship that had wintered in the island, a ship of Alexandria, with the Twin Brothers as figurehead. [12]Putting in at Syracuse, we stayed there for three days. [13]And from there weighing anchor, we arrived at Rhegium; and after one day a south wind sprang up, and on the second day we came to Puteoli, [14]where, finding brethren, we were prevailed upon to stay with them for seven days. And so we came to Rome. [15]And the brethren there, when they heard of us, came as far as the Forum of Appius and Three Taverns to meet us. On seeing them, Paul, thanking God, took courage. [16]And when we came into Rome, ⌜Paul was permitted to stay by himself with the soldier who guarded him⌝.

Once the trip to Italy is imminent, Paul is handed over to an imperial **27:1–3** military unit called the Augustan Cohort and to the centurion Julius. Such a journey, under the best of conditions and sailing straight to Rome, would take about five weeks (Bruce 1990: 511; Casson 1951). It is likely autumn leading into AD 60. Julius is probably not a member of Agrippa II's garrison referred to by Josephus (*Ant.* 19.9.2 §§364–65; but so Larkin 1995: 366–67). He probably is a centurion in the auxiliaries' army of Syria and Judea (*OGIS* 421; *ILS* 1.2683). The latter group was more likely to handle prisoners (Witherington 1998: 758) and would have been composed of mostly Syrians, not Romans. The term Σεβαστῆς (*Sebastēs*, Augustan) points to an imperial-army figure, as it refers to Caesar and in this context to his army (Acts 25:21). The detailed sea journey is designed to show God's determination to bring Paul to Rome. It may also suggest that Rome is on the road to the "end of the earth" in terms of distance from Jerusalem, although this is more disputed.

The "we" section appears again as Paul and those with him board a private ship from Adramyttium, a seaport of Mysia, opposite the isle of Lesbos, 110 miles north of Ephesus and a day's journey east of Troas (on Mysia, see Schnabel 2004: 1144–45; on Adramyttium, Schnabel 2004: 1147; a port that was near silver mines). The "we" is prominent in the account (vv. 1a, 2, 3a, 4–8, 15–16, 18, 20c, 27a, 29a, 37; Pesch 1986b: 284). They will journey along the ports of Asia once they depart from Caesarea. Most ships were cargo ships. People who wished to travel by sea went to the dock to find a ship heading where they wanted to go. Sailing was dependent on favorable winds and religious superstitions about the seas. Inauspicious days such as August 24, October 5, and November 8[2] were avoided as well as the end of the month (Le Cornu and Shulam 2003: 1422–23).

The more common route was by way of Alexandria. Paul travels with at least two companions: Aristarchus, a Macedonian from Thessalonica

2. The three days of *Mundus Patet,* the Roman festival on which the door of the underworld was believed to be opened and the spirits of the dead were allowed to walk among the living.

(20:4), and Luke. Aristarchus is possibly the same figure noted in Col. 4:10 and Philem. 24. No one senses Paul as dangerous. At one port of call, Sidon, Julius allows Paul to visit "the friends" (τοὺς φίλους, *tous philous*) there and receive care. Sidon is sixty-nine miles north of Caesarea and would take a full day and night to reach. It was known as the "mother city of the Phoenicians" (Achilles Tatius, *Leuc. Cleit.* 1.1) and had a double harbor (Bruce 1990: 512; Schnabel 2004: 776). Glass, the purple industry, and its port drove its commerce. Luke notes it elsewhere (Luke 4:26; 6:17; 10:13–14; Jervell 1998: 604). The ship likely stops to unload or pick up cargo. Prisoners would be responsible for their own supplies.

Paul is allowed to see his friends. In the ancient world, friendship was greatly valued. Friends demonstrated their loyalty, transcended disagreement, grieved over parting, and cherished mementos of their relationship. Among believers, friendship was grounded in Christ and a modeling of divine fellowship with humanity and the Son (Pelikan 2005: 284–86). Soldiers no doubt accompany Paul, but their permitting this visit indicates their trust of him. Paul is not seen as a security risk. Paul may well have picked up support and supplies here.

27:4–6 The ship next sails under the lee of Cyprus. This is sailing in such a way that the island protects the ship from the westerly and northwesterly winds of summer and autumn (BAGD 846; BDAG 1040). They would be sailing east and north of the island. Here they can also take advantage of the currents running along the coast. Sailing in the reverse direction would call for a route in the open sea to take advantage of these winds, as in 21:1–3. The verb ὑποπλέω (*hypopleō*, sail under shelter) appears only twice in the NT, and both occurrences are in this chapter (vv. 4, 7). After they pass Cilicia and Pamphylia, the next destination is Myra, a town of Lycia, about fifteen-days' journey by ship and more than five hundred miles (Schnabel 2004: 1266). A temple to Eleuthera has been found at Myra. Its port, called Andriace, was three miles west and south of the city. It lay due north of Alexandria, on the other side of the Mediterranean. Lucian (*The Ship* 7) records a nine-day journey on this route. The Western text is explicit in giving the length of the voyage. On the southern tip of Asia Minor, this seaport was 108 miles southeast of Colossae.

Here a private ship from Alexandria is found that is heading for Rome, so they board it. This is likely part of a grain fleet, given the mention that it is carrying wheat (v. 38). Egypt was the chief source of grain for Rome (Suetonius, *Claudius* 18–19; Josephus, *J.W.* 2.16.4 §§385–86; Seneca, *Moral Ep.* 77.1–2; Barrett 1998: 1185). Such ships were often used by Rome with its protection. The empire also offered insurance in case of damage at sea because of the importance of the food trade (Haenchen 1987: 699n2). It is late in the sailing season, so rapid progress is advised. These ships were large; a ship called *Isis* was estimated to weigh anywhere from 1,200 to 2,900 gross registered tons (Conzelmann 1987: 215–16; Casson 1950). Lucian (*The Ship* 1–9, esp. 5) describes a ship 120 by 30 by 29 cubits, or 180 by 45 by 43.5 feet (also Johnson 1992: 446; Barrett 1998: 1185; Eckey 2000: 559–60).

The voyage continues but with lack of progress because of the wind. **27:7–8** It appears that they are sailing into the wind. They come to Cnidus, a trip of 130 miles (Thucydides, *Pel. War* 8.24.35). This trip should have taken only a couple of days, given the average speed of such ships at six miles an hour, but it took more. In adverse conditions, the speed could reduce to two knots, or two miles an hour (Le Cornu and Shulam 2003: 1432). The trip from Alexandria to Rome normally took ten to thirteen days, but adverse conditions could slow the trip to as much as forty-five days. Cnidus was on Asia Minor's southwestern coast, 108 miles south of Ephesus.

They then proceed under the shelter of Crete, just off from Salmone on the northeast point of the island. The wind prevents them from taking the more normal route across to the island of Cythera, north of Crete. The island of Crete is located in the northern Mediterranean Sea, about 130 miles southwest of Cnidus. They eventually land at Fair Havens, that is, "Good Harbor," near the city of Lasea. It was located on the south-central coast of Crete. It is not attested elsewhere. The normal route would have been Myra, Rhodes, and then south to and past Crete (Haenchen 1987: 699; Marshall 1980: 405). This harbor may well have been too small to leave the boat safely in port for the three weather-beaten months of winter. Its bay was half open to the sea and so did not provide much protection (Bruce 1990: 514). This may be why debate swirls about whether to press the journey forward.

The lack of progress puts the crew under more pressure, as the favorable **27:9–10** time to travel is passing away. The timing is indicated by the reference to the fast, which would be tied to the Day of Atonement (Josephus, *Ant.* 14.4.3 §66; 18.4.3 §94). So we are in the fall of late September and October, just before the winter months (v. 12), when sea travel would be especially perilous (Suetonius, *Claudius* 18; Pliny the Elder, *Nat.* 2.122). If the year is AD 59, we are reaching mid-October, since the fast would have started on October 5. Sea travel was normally not undertaken after mid-September and was avoided from November 11 to mid-March (Vegetius, *On Military Affairs* 4.39). The expression *mare clausum* (the sea is closed) marked this period (Roloff 1988: 361). Pliny the Elder (*Nat.* 2.122) places the resumption of sailing a little earlier, but the point is that November to mid-February were months to be avoided for sailing. When Luke has a three-month pause in 28:11, he is referring to this period and is using schematic language as opposed to precise days. Jewish views were even more cautious, as Gen. Rabbah 6.5b advises avoiding the sea from mid-October to mid-May (Larkin 1995: 368). In winter, the scant daylight, long nights, cloud cover, poor visibility, raging winds, rain, and snow were problems.

With danger lurking, Paul is ready to advise them. Second Corinthians 11:25–26 tells us that he was an experienced passenger at sea and knew its dangers. Paul is not treated like a mere, normal prisoner. The verb παραινέω (paraineō) in verse 9 means "strongly recommend" or "urge" (BAGD 616; BDAG 764). The only other instance of this verb in the NT is in verse 22. It may be that the sense of danger leads people to hear out a "religious" man. It is not inconceivable (against Conzelmann 1987: 216). Barrett (1998: 1187) notes that Paul is not guilty, has the privilege of being transported to be heard by the emperor, and is deemed innocent by some of the leaders. Paul senses the danger of the trip and suggests waiting before moving on. He participates in what seems to be a shipwide meeting about what to do.

He tells them of great danger (ὕβρεως, hybreōs), including potentially much loss (πολλῆς ζημίας, pollēs zēmias) of cargo, the ship, and even lives. The combination of danger and loss will be noted by Paul again in verse 21 (Bertram, TDNT 8:305). This prediction, expressed in the dire manner that it is, will be altered later by the Lord's direction to indicate that life will not be lost. The story has the ring of truth about it, given that a composed story might well have had Paul make a prediction that is accurate in every detail from the start. As it is, the account has Paul make a judgment based on his experience now, with the Lord giving insight later (see v. 23). This appears to be a more satisfactory view than to see Paul making a prophecy from the start (with Bruce 1990: 516; Witherington 1998: 763; Barrett 1998: 1189).

27:11–12   In the end, the advice of the captain and the shipowner, or perhaps his representative (τῷ κυβερνήτῃ καὶ τῷ ναυκλήρῳ, tō kybernētē kai tō nauklērō), prevail with the centurion. The meaning of ναύκληρος (nauklēros) is not entirely certain, but it is likely that the owner is meant (Barrett 1998: 1190; Plutarch, Moralia 162A; for the first term, Moralia 807B). The majority seem to agree. The expression οἱ πλείονες (hoi pleiones) is a comparative used as a pronoun and with a positive sense: "the majority" (Moule 1959: 95; Moulton and Turner 1963: 30). The ship will press on with the goal of wintering at Phoenix, a harbor in Crete. The goal is to stay protected by sailing as close as possible (ἆσσον, asson) next to Crete, as the description in verse 13 indicates. The term ἆσσον is a comparative being used with an elative sense (Moulton and Turner 1963: 30; BDF §244.2). It is not a long trip.

Phoenix was up the coast only, at the most, fifty miles west of Fair Havens. Its exact location is not certain, although some ancient texts describe it (Strabo, Geogr. 10.4; Ptolemy, Geogr. 3.17; Ogilvie 1958). The Cape Mouros area of southern Crete is the locale commonly noted.

Some scholars suggest Lutro on the east side whereas others argue that the description "looking southwest and northwest" (κατὰ λίβα καὶ κατὰ χῶρον, *kata liba kai kata chōron*) does not fit this site well. An alternate site is Phinika, a site across this peninsula to the west from Lutro (Williams 1990: 430; Hemer 1985: 97–98). The topography of the area has been altered since the first century by earthquakes and silting, so that it may well be that the first site gave more protection than it does now. Nevertheless, the second site, Phinika, is maybe slightly more likely as the intended locale, given the work by Ogilvie and the textual evidence he cites (Hemer 1989: 139–40). Still, it is not certain which site is meant. It does not matter much, since the locale is not reached. This trip normally was quite practicable in a day, even a half day. So this appears to be a prudent plan not to push too hard.

27:13–17 They set out with the support of a gentle south wind, using Crete as shelter in case there is trouble (see the remarks about ἆσσον above in 27:11–12). Their sailing so close to the coast might suggest that there is some difficulty, but it is the crossing from Cape Matala to Phoenix in the Gulf of Messara where things change. Cape Matala was six miles west of Fair Havens. Phoenix was another thirty-five miles or more away. Indeed, trouble does arise in the form of tempestuous winds that were nicknamed with a hybrid Greek-Latin term, "the Northeaster" (Εὐρακύλων, *Eurakylōn*). It leaves them no longer in control of the ship (Hemer 1975). Acworth (1973), taking a different reading, *Euroklydon* (cf. KJV), opts for the ship being driven into the Adriatic and not to Malta (but see Polhill 1992: 520n22; *CIL* 8.26652 attests to the term in its full Latin form). The noun form of the Greek term τυφωνικός (*typhōnikos*) is the origin of our word "typhoon." In Greek it refers to a severe windstorm that now takes hold of the ship (v. 15), with winds coming out of the northeast, driving the ship southward, away from the island and its protection. Such winds come off Mt. Ida, a major, eight-thousand-foot-high peak on the island. They are unable to turn the bow of the boat into the wind, or "face the wind eye to eye" (ἀντοφθαλμεῖν τῷ ἀνέμῳ, *antophthalmein tō anemō*). They are driven by the wind and not able to control the ship. To be at the sea's mercy was not unusual (Homer, *Od.* 9.82–84; Lucian, *The Ship* 7; Heliodorus, *Aethiopica* 5.27.2; Johnson 1992: 448).

They are driven to sea and secure the dinghy with difficulty, as it is probably full of water. They move past a small island known as Cauda, about twenty-three miles from where they started. This island sometimes carries the spelling "Clauda" and is known today as Gozzo (Polhill 1992: 521; Pliny the Elder, *Nat.* 4.61). This secures short-term shelter and allows them to take emergency measures. They struggle to bring stability to the boat so as not to hit the Syrtis. This is a combination of sandbars and shoals off the North African coast. It is about four hundred miles from where they started. The site was known as a graveyard for vessels, equal in fame to the often catastrophic journey between Scylla and Charybdis (Praeder 1984: 692). It is located at the Gulf of Sidra (Josephus, *J.W.* 2.16.4 §381; Pliny the Elder, *Nat.* 5.26–27; Strabo, *Geogr.* 17.3.20; Polybius, *Hist.* 1.39.2–4).

Several desperate measures are taken. Scholars discuss what these would have been. They probably shorten the sail and bring the lifeboat on board. They use what are likely cables (βοηθείαις, *boētheiais*, helps) to undergird the ship lest they drift into land. This method of securing the ship with rope cables (ὑποζωννύντες, *hypozōnnyntes*) is not clearly understood. It could entail (1) running cables under the ship a few times to secure the ship in a process known as frapping, (2) running cables longitudinally along the ship's hull, known as hogging, (3) running ropes along the deck from one side to another, or (4) running them inside the hold (Conzelmann 1987: 218 lists these four options). The cables ensure that the timber hull stays together. "Lowering the vessel" may refer to lowering the main yard, which carried the mainsail (χαλάσαντες τὸ σκεῦος, *chalasantes to skeuos*; Plutarch, *Moralia* 507A; Lucian, *Toxaris* 19). Otherwise it may refer to setting a loose anchor. If a loose anchor is intended, then the goal is to create drag for the ship.

27:18–20 After a day they begin to toss cargo (Jon. 1:5; Josephus, *Ant.* 9.10.2 §§209–10; Achilles Tatius, *Leuc. Cleit.* 3.2.9; Jervell 1998: 606n456, "the ship's heavy equipment"). Obviously everything is not tossed, as in verse 38 more cargo goes. The targum on Eccles. 3:6 says, "There is a time for throwing a thing into the sea—namely the time of a tempest" (Barrett 1998: 1197). On the third day at sea, they begin to toss the tackle of the ship, a common practice in dire circumstances (T. Job 18.7; Aristotle, *Nicomachean Ethics* 1110A; Juvenal, *Satires* 12.29–50; Achilles Tatius, *Leuc. Cleit.* 3.2; Heliodorus, *Aethiopica* 5.27.7; Josephus, *J.W.* 1.14.3 §280; Johnson 1992: 448). This is because they are continuing to take in water, and by making the boat lighter, they are hoping that the boat will sit higher over the water. The tackle would be all the spare gear and might even include the mainsail and main yard. They are that desperate. This work they do with "their own hands" (αὐτόχειρες, *autocheires*), a point that may mean either that they lack any lifting gear or that all are required to help lift the load, including the prisoners and those associated with them, as Luke would have been. They then fall under darkness with no sun or stars for many days. Without the stars and sun, they have no way of determining their location—no gear, no sun, no stars, no hope. The tempest continues and things are quite bad. The term ἐπίκειμαι (*epikeimai*), when it refers to an impersonal force, means "confront" or "attack." In this context, it refers to the attack of a storm (BAGD 294 §2a [the storm "pressed upon" them]; BDAG 373 §2b). All hope of being saved (σῴζεσθαι, *sōzesthai*) has been given up (Homer,

Od. 5.297–304; Lucian, *Toxaris* 20; Thucydides, *Pel. War* 1.2.65; Achilles Tatius, *Leuc. Cleit.* 3.2). Here is a good secular use of this Greek verb; its basic meaning is "deliver" or "rescue."

Those on board lack an appetite. It may be that the ship's tossing and turning prevents them from eating and keeping food down and/or that they have no appetite through sheer anxiety, although there is food on board. This indicates how serious the situation has become. Paul now speaks in their midst (ἐν μέσῳ, *en mesō*), reminding them of his advice not to sail because of potential danger and loss. That advice was turned down (vv. 10–11). Paul is not trying to make them feel worse here, but he is making an appeal to be heard now as a credible speaker. **27:21–22**

The scene is not "completely unreal," as Conzelmann claims (also Haenchen 1987: 709 is skeptical). Part of the problem is the attempt to portray the scene as a stand-up oration as if it were taking place in a calm setting. Other than the fact that Paul speaks in their midst, no such details are present. We should not think of Paul speaking on the deck in the midst of the storm. Instead they are in a place where they all can gather. The remark is an attempt to lift spirits in a difficult time, which surely would be undertaken by someone at some point. The presence of such speeches in sea voyage accounts is common (Praeder 1984: 695–96; Homer, *Od.* 5.299–312; Virgil, *Aeneid* 1.92–101; Lucan, *Civil War* 5.653–71). Literary practice here might well echo real practice, where major figures address everyone and assess the scene. In contrast, however, to such literary scene messages, which tended to be about impending doom, this speech is positive (Witherington 1998: 767, who defends the speech's basic integrity). Paul's standing position while speaking recalls other places where prophetic words are spoken (2:14; 17:22).

Paul addresses the situation. Injury and loss (τὴν ὕβριν ταύτην καὶ τὴν ζημίαν, *tēn hybrin tautēn kai tēn zēmian*) have occurred. Paul uses irony here: the choice to sail and not heed Paul "gained" (κερδῆσαι, *kerdēsai*) injury and loss. The terms "injury" and "loss" are repeated from verse 10. But now Paul will encourage them. Injury and loss will take place, but only for the ship. No one will lose his life. Paul is not a miracle-worker here who can command nature. He will ride out the storm with everyone else. Would this be so if the scene were made up by a church that believed in miracles? There is no "divine-man" motif here (contra Conzelmann 1987: 219; with Barrett 1998: 1201, who notes that the speech has Paul only as God's servant). Paul does nothing but announce God's plan.

An angelic visit is the reason for Paul's confidence that life will be spared (18:9–10; 23:11). The message received is said to be from "the God . . . [Paul] worships." This roundabout way of describing God underscores the pagan context, in which Paul's fellow sailors can invoke many gods. This communication is not an appearance of Jesus but of an angelic messenger. **27:23–26**

The assurance is that Paul will stand before Caesar. Such divine rescues were understood by the culture (Lucian, *The Ship* 9; Plutarch, *Moralia* 161F; Achilles Tatius, *Leuc. Cleit.* 3.4–5; T. Naph. 6.8–9; Aelius Aristides, *Sacred Tales* 2.12–13; Homer, *Od.* 5.300–302; Pokorny 1973; Johnson 1992: 449). The angel reminds Paul that he *must* (δεῖ, *dei*) appear before Caesar and that all who travel with him will be spared. The reason is that God has favored (κεχάρισται, *kecharistai*) him and all who are with him. Acts 19:21 made the original promise that this would occur as a part of God's plan (also 23:11). Genesis 18:26–32 shows how the presence of good people can protect a community. Indeed, because of Paul's presence, all with him will survive. This is a slight modification of Paul's earlier warning that life could be lost. The difference is simply that now God has revealed what will take place, whereas before Paul issued a warning rooted in his own wisdom. Such a deliverance suggests that divine justice will show Paul to be an innocent man, not guilty of anything, and not deserving of being a prisoner (Miles and Trompf 1976; Ladouceur 1980).

So Paul tells them to take heart (εὐθυμεῖτε, *euthymeite*), as Paul has faith in this word from God (Acts 27:22, 25 [both in this scene] and James 5:13 are the other NT occurrences of this term). Paul is a figure very much like Elizabeth and Mary in Luke 1–2. Paul trusts God's word.

Paul has one final point: he assures them that the ship will be lost. This also is an event marked by necessity, as (δεῖ, *dei*, v. 24) is used here. It is debated whether this is a part of the revelation or Paul's deduction, but being part of the revelation seems likely given how Paul is being guided by God in this scene and because of the use of the divine δεῖ. Shipwrecks are a common ancient theme (Lucian, *Salaried Posts in Great Houses* 2; *A True Story* 1.6; Dio Chrysostom, *The Hunter* [*Euboean Discourse*] 2; Johnson 1992: 449–50). The trip will be tough but survivable. It also is amazing that the only island for them to hit, given where they are and where they are headed, is Malta. It would be like finding a needle in a haystack. This detail, of where they will land, they do not yet know, but the story will make it clear later.

The scene is a symbol of how Paul's message saves because of the connection to Paul's God. This is not allegory; it is good literary style to have one event also symbolize another reality. That historical reality is a point of the narrative. Paul shows his superior grasp of the events in comparison to the other human figures present. Actually, it is God working through Paul that is the point here. There is no indication whether they believe Paul or respond to his speech.

27:27–29   On the fourteenth night of the journey, they find themselves in the Sea of Adria, in the central Mediterranean. This was a larger area than what is called the Adriatic Sea today (Barrett 1998: 1202; Ptolemy, *Geogr.* 3.4.1; 3.15.1; 3.17.1 [Crete to Silicia]; Strabo, *Geogr.* 2.5.20; Pausanius,

Descr. 5.25.3; Josephus, *Life* 3 §15 speak of sailing in the Sea of Adria to Rome; Bruce 1990: 522). It included what is today called the Ionian Sea and the northeastern Mediterranean (Polhill 1992: 525). They have gone 475 miles. About midnight the sailors think they are near land. They may have heard breakers or an echo from the area where land is. So they take a series of soundings. This would involve throwing a line overboard with a lead weight attached. This action indicates that they are in waters twenty fathoms deep (ca. 120 feet), then fifteen fathoms (ca. 90 feet) deep. A fathom is 1.85 meters or just short of six feet, being the width of a man's arms outstretched (BAGD 579; BDAG 721). They fear running aground, and so four anchors are lowered from the stern in the hope that morning light will show their location. Anchors usually were lowered at the bow, but the ship is not facing the proper direction for this.[3] The site is often regarded by scholars as Point Koura and St. Paul's Bay, where one can hear the approach of the land (Williams 1990: 437), but the locale is not certain. For this entire sea voyage, and especially for this portion, the classic work by J. Smith (1880) is worth consulting.

Other sailors are nervous and are lowering the lifeboat into the sea to escape, although they try to make it look as if they are laying out anchors from under the bow. The winds may well have calmed to a degree at this point if the approach of land can be heard. Some scholars complain (Haenchen 1987: 706) that such an escape at night is unrealistic and too dangerous, but this may well show how desperate things are. Marshall (1980: 412) suggests a mood of desperation ("men will do foolish things") or that their motives are misread by other passengers. People are doing things that they normally would not do.   **27:30–32**

Paul is now directing events (so also vv. 33–34). He again intervenes with the centurion and soldiers, warning that only if the men stay with the ship will they remain safe (σωθῆναι, *sōthēnai*, be saved). So the soldiers cut away the ropes of the boat and let it drift to sea, an act done in difficult situations (Heliodorus, *Aethiopica* 5.27.6; Achilles Tatius, *Leuc. Cleit.* 3.3). There will be no escaping the boat by the lifeboat. This move does add to the danger of the situation, for if they are really close to land, the only way in now is to maneuver the boat in or wait for better conditions. It shows how trusted Paul has become.

On what is now the fourteenth day, Paul urges everyone to take food. The remark should not be overread to argue that they have had nothing at all to eat for this time. Luke's point in this hyperbole is that it has been long since they have had much to eat (note a parallel theme in Aelius Aristides, *Sacred Tales* 2.68). He argues that it will give them strength   **27:33–34**

---

3. Anchors weighing about 1,320 pounds were found off Campo Morino near Taranto (Le Cornu and Shulam 2003: 1464).

and will be all right to do, since all of them will survive. Paul makes the point with an idiom: "No one of you shall lose a hair from your head" (οὐδενὸς γὰρ ὑμῶν θρὶξ ἀπὸ τῆς κεφαλῆς ἀπολεῖται, *oudenos gar hymōn thrix apo tēs kephalēs apoleitai*; 1 Sam. 14:45; 2 Sam. 14:11; 1 Kings 1:52; Luke 12:7; 21:18). No physical harm will come to them at all. Paul is portrayed as a competent philosopher in Greek eyes (philosopher–sea voyage stories: Diogenes Laertius, *Lives* 2.71; Lucian, *The Passing of Peregrinus* 43–44). In this intervention, he again assures and strengthens the sailors.

27:35–38 Paul breaks bread in their midst and begins to eat. It is debated whether an allusion to the Lord's Supper is here. The language is like Luke 9:16 and 22:15–19.[4] A connection to the meal is unlikely, given the unbelieving audience present, but there are echoes of such a meal and a sense that this is a sacred moment because God will deliver them as Paul said God would. This is not a normal meal because under normal circumstances they would all die at sea. Paul's act encourages all 276 present with his example of eating. The theme of encouragement runs throughout the passage (vv. 22, 25, 36). Some scholars want to make the number merely symbolic, but it is not the triangulation of counting from one to twenty-three (discussed in Bruce 1988a: 493n87). Jervell (1998: 610n484) observes that such ships could hold up to six hundred people (Josephus, *Life* 3 §15, mentions a ship holding six hundred).

They are now taking Paul's advice fully. The participle ἐκβαλλόμενοι (*ekballomenoi*) is a participle of means telling how the boat is lightened (Wallace 1996: 630). They lighten the ship by casting over the wheat, indicating their confidence that they will obtain access to food again soon. This also will lift the boat higher out of the water so that the vessel can come closer to shore (1 En. 104.4–5). They probably do not toss over all the wheat so that some will remain for ballast.

27:39–44 The day brings the sight of land and a bay with a beach. Literally, what is described here is a "fold" (κόλπον, *kolpon*) with a beach, which would describe a bay. The sailors do not know where they are, but they know that they want to guide the ship to the beach on the bay if they are able. This indicates that the effort might be tricky.

Sailors would not normally know this part of Malta (28:1) because it was not on the normal sea route. The traditional site is said to be St. Paul's Bay on the northeast coast, which today lacks a beach but whose topography would have been different many centuries ago. Nevertheless,

---

4. Witherington 1998: 772–73 gives seven reasons an allusion to the Lord's Supper is not intended. Barrett 1998: 1208 shows five points of connection with the supper in Luke 22:15–19, and also canvasses the various views, most of which fall short of a full identification with the meal in this scene; Reicke 1948. Gaventa 2003: 355 notes that the lack of wine, no mention of a distribution of food, and the presence of unbelievers are all against an allusion to the meal.

the exact site is not certain (for alternatives: Mellieha, see Heuger 1984; Polhill 1992: 529n49; or St. Thomas Bay, Cornuke 2003).

Luke describes the shipwreck next. The sailors, in their effort to make land, cast off the anchors, leaving them at sea. They also loosen the ropes of the rudders and hoist the foresail to make for land. The front sail on the boat has been saved for such a moment. This is the only instance of the term ἀρτέμων (artemōn, foresail) in the NT (BAGD 110; BDAG 135). This would allow them to steer. The rudder on a boat allowed it to be directed. By freeing the ropes that secured it, they could try to direct the boat landward. The term πηδάλιον (pēdalion, rudder) is used only twice in the NT. Most ships had two rudders connected by a crossbar operated by one sailor (BAGD 656; BDAG 811). James 3:4 refers to the rudder as a metaphor for the tongue. In the present scene, the steering plan fails as they strike a shoal (εἰς τόπον διθάλασσον, eis topon dithalasson, a place of two seas). This term describes a locale that sits up in the water between two seas, thus the rendering "shoal," "sandbank," or "a point" (BAGD 195; BDAG 245; Strabo, Geogr. 1.1.8; 2.5.22). It could also refer to a narrow channel where the bay and the sea meet (Witherington 1998: 774; Fitzmyer 1998: 780). A reference to "a point" is more likely, as something causes the ship to stay put, which is why the text says that the ship runs aground "into" this place. The ship runs aground as the bow becomes stuck, and the stern begins to break up (ἐλύετο, elueto, an ingressive imperfect: began to break up). This is the shipwreck. The destruction could be the result of the initial impact; or it could result from the ship's inability to give ground to the pressure from the crashing waves. The language of verse 41 appears to favor the waves being the cause of the breakup. The sea bottom would be of hard clay and lock the ship in place.

The soldiers desire to kill the prisoners, since the soldiers would be liable for allowing them to escape (12:19; 16:27). This is one of the few places in Acts where the term βουλή (boulē, will or plan) refers to a human plan (5:38; 27:12). Most occurrences refer to God's will (2:23; 4:28; 13:36; 20:27). Seven of the term's twelve NT occurrences are in Acts, with Luke using the term twice in his Gospel (Luke 7:30; 23:51; 1 Cor. 4:5; Eph. 1:11; Heb. 6:17).

The centurion desires to save Paul, however, and does not allow the soldiers to carry out their execution plan. Syntactically, the verb ἐκώλυσεν (ekōlysen, hinder) expresses the idea that the centurion not only hinders the plan but also succeeds in preventing the plan from being executed, because of a perfective use of the aorist tense in this context (Moulton and Turner 1963: 72; Wallace 1996: 561). Those who can swim are ordered to make an effort to reach the coast. The rest either are given wooden planks from the broken ship to float their way to land (reading the terms τινων τῶν in the phrase ἐπί τινων τῶν ἀπὸ τοῦ πλοίου, epi tinōn tōn apo tou ploiou, as neuter) or used the backs of the swimmers like planks to make it inland (reading the phrase as masculine; Barrett 1998: 1214 sees both methods used). Planks are more likely (T. Naph. 6.6; Xenophon of Ephesus, *Eph. Tale* 2.11.10, describes a similar rescue; Conzelmann 1987: 221). All of them, both swimmers and floaters, make it safely. God has sovereignly protected them all. Paul's prediction is fulfilled.

28:1 They learn that the island they are on is called Μελίτη (*Melitē*), now known as Malta (Strabo, *Geogr.* 6.2.11; 17.3.15–16). It is located about 58 miles south of Sicily and 180 miles northeast of Africa, with a length of 18 miles and a width of 8 miles (Williams 1990: 442). The island's ancient name means "refuge," but Luke makes nothing of the etymology. They remain here for the three months of winter. There is a recent revival of a tenth-century view that this was Mljet, off the coast of Dubrovnik, but this depends on reading the Sea of Adria in 27:27 as the Adriatic Sea, which is a mistake (Witherington 1998: 775 notes that a northeaster would not blow the ship there; see comments above on 27:27–29 and the Adriatic Sea). Also unlikely is the locale of Kephallenia, five hundred miles south of Mljet.[5]

28:2 The natives are very friendly. They would be Phoenician in origin and speak mostly Punic (Marshall 1980: 415).[6] Some may know Greek, as inscriptions found there are bilingual. Luke describes them as βάρβαροι (*barbaroi*, barbarians), which means that they are ignorant of Greek and Latin or lack such a cultured background (Herodotus, *Hist.* 2.57; Johnson 1992: 461). The name βάρβαροι sounds like the gibberish Greeks and Latins did not understand. They are kind and kindle a fire to keep the newly arrived guests warm in the cold. Such themes with shipwrecks are common (Xenophon of Ephesus, *Eph. Tale* 2.2.4; Lucian, *A True Story* 1.28–29; 2.46; Johnson 1992: 461). It is not clear whether this one fire warms all 276 or that there are many small fires and Luke discusses only the relevant one. This is likely a smaller fire. The term φιλανθρωπία (*philanthrōpia*) refers to the benevolence of unconditional kindness, a love for humanity (BAGD 858; BDAG 1055–56). The term is used only twice in the NT (the other instance is Titus 3:4).

28:3–6 Paul places a bundle of sticks in the fire. It is probably around fifty degrees Fahrenheit, but the wet conditions make it feel cooler. One of the sticks turns out to be a viper (ἔχιδνα, *echidna*, snake, BAGD 331; BDAG 419; Foerster, *TDNT* 2:815), which bites him. It either leaps out of the fire or bites as Paul approaches the fire. How ironic to survive a

---

5. Warnecke 1987 suggests the latter option, but Larkin 1995: 378 correctly rejects both of these options. See also Polhill 1992: 531; Hemer 1975; Schwank 1990; and Wehnert 1990 for a more complete analysis of these other views.

6. Phoenician presence dates back to the tenth century BC (Le Cornu and Shulam 2003: 1476). The island came into Roman hands in 218 BC. The area was also full of pirates, so the kind treatment is further evidence of divine protection.

shipwreck only to be killed by a poisonous bite! Such a story is recounted in the *Palatine Anthology* 7.290 with the same touch of irony: "Why did he struggle with the waves in vain, escaping then the fate that was his lot on the land?"

Conzelmann's view (1987: 223) of the scene is too skeptical in doubting whether a poisonous snake would bite so and in questioning the allusion to the goddess Justice (ἡ δίκη, *hē dikē*). It is possible that Luke merely translated the natives' allusion to a goddess into terms Greeks could understand. Some deny that the island had poisonous snakes (Barrett 1998: 1222 discusses the issue but reaches no clear conclusion; for a discussion of Maltese snakes, see Le Cornu and Shulam 2003: 1479). Bruce (1990: 531), commenting on the possibility of poisonous snakes at that time, cites the analogy of Ireland, which had poisonous snakes at one time but no longer does (for ancient texts on snakes: Pliny the Elder, *Nat.* 8.85–86 [all poisonous and seek vengeance]; Lucian, *Alexander the False Prophet* 10; Johnson 1992: 462 contends that such views were popular and widespread).

The judgment is made that Paul must be a guilty murderer, for he has lived through a shipwreck but "justice" is not going to allow him to live (Wis. 1:8; 4 Macc. 18:22; Hesiod, *Works and Days* 239, 256; *Theogony* 902; Plutarch, *Moralia* 161F; Arrian, *Anabasis* 4.9.7; Larkin 1995: 380n). This is the personification of justice as a goddess, a reference to fate directing events (BAGD 198 §2; BDAG 250). She was seen as the daughter of Zeus and Themis. Of the three NT occurrences of this word, this is the only one with this sense (2 Thess. 1:9; Jude 7).

As for the serpent, the creature is characterized as a "wild beast" (θηρίον, *thērion*) here, a term often used of dangerous snakes (Acts 11:6; Mark 1:13; Rev. 13:1). To everyone's amazement, Paul merely shakes the creature off his hand and suffers no harm (Luke 10:19; Mark 16:17–18). The situation appears not to concern Paul because he has been assured that he will reach Rome (Acts 27:24). Polhill (1992: 532) relates a story that circulated about Rabbi Hanina ben Dosa in *y. Ber.* 5.1. The rabbi grabbed a snake in a hole, which bit him, only for the snake to be found dead later. The refrain went, "Woe to the man whom the snake meets; woe to the snake Hanina ben Dosa meets."

When Paul is left unharmed, the attitude changes. The term ἄτοπον (*atopon*) in verse 6 means "abnormal" or "surprising" (BAGD 120 §1; BDAG 149). Nothing abnormal happens. So no "misfortune" comes (so the translation). There is no swelling on Paul, nor does he die. Πίμπρημι (*pimprēmi*, swell up), an NT hapax, is a medical term for inflammation. Now they change their mind and begin to speak of Paul as a god (Acts 14:11–19; ἔλεγον, *elegon*, is the imperfect tense). Μεταβάλλω (*metaballō*, change one's mind) is an NT hapax. The entire story is told from a Maltese perspective, which means that not everything believed is what Luke believes. This detail makes that point the clearest.

Paul is not seen as a "divine man" here but as one whom even pagans recognize as being in close contact with God. The next scene, with Paul seeking God's help by praying for the healing of others, shows that Paul is not portrayed as a divine man (Pesch 1986b: 299 and Barrett 1998: 1226 against Haenchen 1987: 716 and Conzelmann 1987: 223). Polhill (1992: 532–33) notes earlier corrections of this divine-man idea in Acts (10:25–26; 14:11–15).

28:7–10 The chief man (τῷ πρώτῳ, tō prōtō) of the island hosts them for three days. Publius may well be a procurator, if not merely the chief landowner (*IG* 14.601 confirms the use of this term for a ruler as it speaks of the "chief of Malta"; also *CIL* 10.7494; Bruce 1990: 532; Barrett 1998: 1224). The use of only his Roman forename is unusual (Williams 1990: 444). Paul often establishes a relationship with leading figures in a locale (Acts 13:7; 16:22; 17:19; 18:12; 19:31; Johnson 1992: 462).

His father is suffering from fever and dysentery (πυρετοῖς καὶ δυσεντερίῳ, pyretois kai dysenteriō). This is the only mention of dysentery in the NT (K. Weiss, *TDNT* 6:958 ["a medically sound definition of feverish dysentery"]). A microbe found in goat's milk was often the cause of such fever on Malta. This fever could last for months or even for a few years (Larkin 1995: 381). Paul prays over him and lays hands on him (Mark 5:23; 6:5; 8:23, 25; 16:18; Acts 9:12, 17; James 5:13–14; 1QapGen 20; Weiser 1985: 670; Pesch 1986b: 299). This the only place where prayer and the laying on of hands are combined for healing in Acts (cf. Luke 4:40). No such activity occurs in the OT or in the rabbinic literature (Fitzmyer 1998: 784; 1QapGen 20.21–29 does have such a combination; Le Cornu and Shulam 2003: 1487–88). Paul the prisoner is still a blessing to those around him, even as he is held unjustly.

Apparently, Publius's father is cured, although the text does not explicitly say so, for many on the island who have diseases are then cured by Paul. This kind of healing summary recalls descriptions of Jesus (Luke 4:38–44). This is the fifth occurrence of the verb θεραπεύω (therapeuō) in Acts (4:14; 5:16; 8:7; 17:25). Peter, John, and Philip are the others who heal in Acts. The medical terms in these verses are general and cannot be used to suggest that Luke was a doctor.

The Maltese are grateful, so that when the group launches out again months later, the travelers are given gifts and all they need for the trip to Rome. The term τιμαῖς (timais, gifts) literally means "honors." Luke often uses this term for material benefits (Acts 4:34; 5:2–3; 7:16; 19:19; for the meaning of payment for medical services, see Sir. 38:1–2).

28:11–16 After three months, they set out again for Rome. It is February of AD 60 (Witherington 1998: 781n138) and the earliest time of the year one would resume sailing (Pliny the Elder, *Nat.* 2.122). The critical part of the journey is the sixty miles to Sicily in open seas and then a largely protected sail along the eastern coast of Sicily and up the southwestern coast of Italy. It is a 210-mile journey to Rome from where they are starting out.

They use another ship from Alexandria that is "marked" (παρασήμῳ, parasēmō) by the Twin Brothers (Διοσκούροις, Dioskourois) as figure-heads at the front of the ship. These are Castor and Pollux, sons of Zeus and Leda, the "savior gods" (BAGD 199; BDAG 251; Epictetus, Discourses 2.18.29; Lucian, The Ship 5, 9; Dölger 1950). Many statues of these gods still exist, on display in Rome. Leda was queen of Sparta and married to Tyndareus, the king, but their children were connected by legend to Zeus. They sailed with Jason and the Argonauts (Le Cornu and Shulam 2003: 1490). Castor was said to be an excellent horseman, and Pollux could box. Their astral sign was Gemini. The pair were especially popular in Egypt (Haenchen 1987: 717). Euripides (Electra 1342–55) saw them as guarding the truth and punishing perjurers, and so their mention may again underscore Paul's innocence. They were seen as protectors of good fortune on the seas, being said to rid the seas of pirates and buccaneers. This journey has an added symbol of protection for the Gentile travelers that has nothing to do with the gods: the Lord will deliver Paul to his destination.

The sail is fairly uneventful. For three days they stay at Syracuse, on the eastern coast of Sicily (Cicero, In Verrem 2.4.117–19; Strabo, Geogr. 6.2.4). It was about sixty miles from Malta (so Le Cornu and Shulam 2003: 1492; Larkin 1995: 383; Polhill 1992: 535 gives a figure of ninety miles). During Roman rule, it was the capital of Sicily and a center of Greek culture, a natural stop on a journey through the Straits of Messina. Cicero describes it as very prosperous, possessing two harbors, and very lovely. It had been in Roman hands since 212 BC (Le Cornu and Shulam 2003: 1491).

They then travel on, apparently with some difficulty, to Rhegium, located on the toe of Italy and seventy-four miles from Syracuse (Strabo, Geogr. 6.1.6). This segment of the trip is described oddly. They are said either to have "weighed anchor" or to have "gone around," so that less than favorable winds guided them. The former is more likely if the term here is περιελόντες (perielontes, casting loose, א*, B) rather than περιελθόντες (perielthontes, going around), which is not as well attested (𝔓74, א2, A, Byz), but Conzelmann (1987: 224) claims that the other reading makes no sense without an object to refer to (cf. Metzger 1971: 501).

Leaving Rhegium, after two more days with a favorable south wind, they arrive at Puteoli (modern Pozzuoli), a port just over 200 miles northwest of Rhegium in the Bay of Naples, 8 miles northwest of Neapolis (Naples) and about 130 miles south of Rome.[7] This was the main port

7. See Strabo, Geogr. 5.4.6; 17.1.7, where it is called Dikaiarchia; Seneca, Moral Ep. 77.1–2; Suetonius, Titus 5.3; Josephus, Life 3 §16; Fitzmyer 1998: 787; Eckey 2000: 582. The name comes from the volcanic dust of the northern shore of the Gulf of Naples on

for grain in the country. Later this port was overtaken in importance by the recently built Ostia, although often passengers still disembarked here first (Barrett 1998: 1229). Josephus knew of Jews who lived in Puteoli (*J.W.* 2.7.1 §104; *Ant.* 17.12.1 §328). Paul is not intended to be seen as the founder of these Christian communities (against Conzelmann 1987: 224), and so the fact that Christians are present is not surprising. There they stay for a week with brethren after being invited, that is, exhorted to stay, or perhaps better, "prevailed upon" to remain, reading παρεκλήθημεν (*pareklēthēmen*) as a perfective aorist (Moulton and Turner 1963: 72). Perhaps Aristarchus and Luke mediated this request, which may have allowed the gathering of fresh provisions. Witherington (1998: 786) suggests that they rested before undertaking the long last leg by foot. Fitzmyer (1998: 787) suggests that simply the end of the sea voyage explains the delay. He suggests that having reached the end of a long, arduous trip, they simply took the time to rest, especially given the trip by foot to come (see next paragraph and the discussion in Le Cornu and Shulam 2003: 1496–97, who see a variety of factors at work, including organizing for this final leg by foot).

Scholars sometimes discuss how Paul could stop in the midst of a journey as a prisoner. By the time the journey has progressed this far, however, Paul has achieved a level of respect with those who hold him. The church is already established in the area, something Paul's letter to the Romans, written years before this trip, also shows. They are now a five-day walk from Rome by means of two well-traveled roads, the Campanian Way and the Appian Way. The latter route, which entered Rome from the south next to the Circus Maximus, was where many Jews lived in ancient Rome (Juvenal, *Satires* 3.10–16). Known as an area of light forest, the end of this route later became the location of the Christian catacombs, where persecuted Christians were buried in underground graves.

The trip from Malta has taken three weeks. The total journey has taken well over four months. God's word has come to pass: Paul has made it to Rome. Themes extending back to Luke 1–2 about God's word being realized are affirmed in Paul's overcoming storms and snakes to reach Rome. When other believers hear that Paul is there, they travel from the Forum of Appius and Three Taverns to meet him. The Forum of Appius on the Appian Way was about forty-three miles south of Rome, and Three Taverns was ninety-one miles north of Puteoli and twenty-one miles south of Rome. Paul is grateful to God for the meeting and takes courage from it. The Forum of Appius had a reputation; Horace describes it as "full of boatmen and stingy tavern keepers" (*Satires* 1.5.3–6; Plümacher,

---

which it lies (Le Cornu and Shulam 2003: 1493; *puteolanum*). It had a significant Jewish population and strong economic links to Alexandria since the end of the Punic War (201 BC).

EDNT 1:147). Cicero often mentions Three Taverns, showing that it was a common stop in the area (*Epistulae ad Atticum* 1.13.1; 2.12.2; 2.13.1; Johnson 1992: 465). In Rome, Paul is allowed to stay by himself under the guard of one soldier instead of the normal two. This means that in all likelihood he stays in rented quarters (v. 30). The monetary support for this would be borne by the Christians. There is no worry that he will try to escape or that he represents any danger to others. On this note, Luke ends his description of Paul the prisoner and turns to a final set of meetings. Thus also ends the final "we" section of Acts.

The book of Acts ends without telling us how the hearing before Nero turned out. Good evidence exists for the fact that Paul was released at this point and headed west. Eusebius (*Eccl. Hist.* 2.22.1–7) says that Paul was twice imprisoned in Rome and was martyred after the second imprisonment (1 Clem. 5.5–7). This may have included an "exile" to the west (Witherington 1998: 792).

In sum, this passage is about the details of a long journey undertaken by someone who is obeying God's will and is being protected by divine providence. In effect, Luke is indicating that God knew what he was doing with Paul even though everything about the circumstances looked problematic. We see the Maltese people as good hosts who care for those who have suffered, a reminder that people are capable of showing kindness in the hardest of times. We also see Paul, certain of his call, continuing to trust God and bear witness about God to those who might hear. The impact is that others come to appreciate him as well. This does not always take place for someone obeying God's will, but sometimes it does. Fernando (1998: 618–22) speaks of Paul's leadership in a secular circumstance here: Paul as an agent of hope, his use of human wisdom in the positive sense of that phrase, as the provider of a clear testimony, his servant attitude—all of which become an encouragement as well as an example for Luke's readers.

The most important theme of the passage is that God can be taken at his word. God told Paul that he, the messenger, would reach Rome, and Paul did. God told Paul that no lives would be lost, and none were. And God told Paul that the ship would run aground, and it did. God's word can be trusted because God can be trusted. The only thing one does not know is when God will accomplish his will.

Additional Notes

27:5. The Western text (614, 1518, Vulgate, Itala, and Syriac witnesses) has an addition that places the voyage's length at fifteen days.

27:14. The term for the type of storm, εὐρακύλων (*eurakylōn*), is a hybrid word, combining Greek (*euros*, east wind) and Latin (*aquilo*, north wind). This led to many variations in copying the term, including εὐροκλύδων (*euroklydōn*; B² [ευρυ-], Ψ, 33, 1739, Byz), which is read in the KJV and means a southeast wind. This reading would suggest that the boat was driven in a different direction (see the discussion between Acworth 1973 and Hemer 1975). The "northeaster" reading is likely correct, being better attested ($\mathfrak{P}^{74}$, $\aleph$, A, B*).

27:15. The Western text adds references to blowing wind and furling sails.

27:16. The variant spelling of the island includes a lambda—*Klauda*, which Byz uses, altering the case to the accusative (H, L, P).

27:27. Discussion about the verb concerns the sailors' sense that land is close. Codex B* reads προσαχεῖν (*prosachein*), which is Doric Greek and is unattested elsewhere in the NT. It speaks of the land "resounding." Better attested is προσάγειν (*prosagein*), which simply means that land "was approaching" them, looking at the matter from the perspective of how it felt to the sailors. This is likely the original reading.

27:37. The Western text and B read that only "about seventy-six" people made the trip rather than the 276 of the other MSS.

28:1. The reading of B* is Μελιτήνη (*Melitēnē*). Several Latin witnesses have an underlying reading of Μυτιλήνη (*Mytilēnē*). Neither of these readings is well enough attested to be original.

28:16. The Western text, expanding the verse, refers to Paul being handed over to a garrison commander of the guard, a stratopedarch (Sherwin-White 1963: 108–11). Some scholars think that the text may be a later expansion but still reflects the true situation. Barrett (1998: 1233) prefers a reference to the chief administrative officer of the Praetorian Guard.

D. Visitors in Rome: The Gospel Preached (28:17–31)

This final unit depicts Paul receiving Jewish visitors on two occasions (vv. 17–22, 23–28) and others to whom he sets forth the gospel message (vv. 30–31). The Jews as a group are not receptive (vv. 24–28), but at the end of the unit, Paul is proclaiming to all about the Lord Jesus. In each scene with the Jews, Paul speaks (vv. 17–20, 23) and then there is a Jewish reaction (vv. 21–22; 24–25a). A summary reaction from Paul concludes the second Jewish meeting (vv. 25b–28). Still, Acts ends on a note of triumph (vv. 30–31), but also with a note of regret at the lack of Jewish response, as the final citation of the OT comes from Isa. 6:9–10. Paul will turn to the Gentiles, though not giving up hope on what has proved to be a mostly stubborn Israel.

The first scene makes four points, and the second makes three (Fitzmyer 1998: 790). (1) Paul has done nothing against his people or customs. (2) The Romans wished to free him. (3) The Jewish opposition led to his appeal to Caesar. (4) He is a prisoner for believing in the hope of Israel. (5) He is a witness to the Jews of Rome. (6) He sees their rejection as a realization of what Scripture has said, as Isa. 6 shows. (7) The message is going out to the Gentiles now.

The scene recapitulates many elements in Luke-Acts (Weiser 1985: 677–79). God has led the way to Rome (Acts 1:8; 19:21; 23:11; 25:10–12; 27:24). The experience with the Jews in Rome reflects the experience with Jews in the rest of the book: much rejection. The passage contains a summary of the entire trial sequence with Paul (Acts 21–26). Paul's innocence and suffering are like those of Jesus (Luke 23). The kingdom of God as fulfilled in Jesus according to the word of Scripture is the center of the proclamation. The call to all people to hear the message echoes themes in Luke 1–2. Paul's attitude fits with Rom. 1:16 and his larger treatment in Rom. 9–11.

The account lacks mention of two points one might expect: the outcome of the appeal and a meeting with the church in Rome (Marshall 1980: 420; Witherington 1998: 793). The selectivity makes clear that Luke has another point he wishes to make at the end of his two volumes: the relationship between Israel and the new belief, together with the Way's move toward the Gentiles. The book opens and closes on this same theme. The new faith is intended for everyone but continues to make the effort to reach Israel because the faith is the culmination of Israel's hope. This is not to be seen as the end of Jewish mission (against Pesch 1986b: 306 and Roloff 1988: 370–71); it is simply the repetition of the pattern of Pauline proclamation (Acts 13:42–48; 18:5–7; 19:8–10; Polhill 1992: 538 notes the study of Hauser 1979 on the structure of the unit). The Jews need to embrace the fulfillment of their hope as much as anyone. The commission is to take the gospel into all the world (Luke 24:47) and to the end of the earth (Acts 1:8). Fitzmyer (1998: 791) notes that the Jewish people's stubborn refusal to accept matches a pattern in the nation's history according to the prophet Isaiah. Other portions of the OT also make the point, much as Stephen's speech in Acts 7 did. The point in the passage is not the fate of Paul or a biographical interest in him but the advance of the word through Paul to Rome, as Acts 1:8 makes clear (Schneider 1982: 413).

It seems curious that the story ends without mention of Paul's fate. There is no evidence that Luke intended to write a third volume or that Luke died before he finished. The account comes to a rounded-off ending. Some scholars argue that he wrote before the trial of Paul had met in the early sixties, but this also seems unlikely given the probable origin and dating of the Gospels. Simply put, Luke's story is that the gospel reaches Rome and is carried on the start of its journey to "the end of the earth" (so correctly, in our view, Fitzmyer 1998: 791–92). God sovereignly and powerfully brings the word to the capital of the world on a long and arduous journey from Jerusalem. This journey has been coupled with unjust suffering and bold witness. As ironic as this combination may sound, it means triumph for the message of the kingdom and the Lord Jesus (28:30–31).

Pauline or Roman sources would stand behind this summary, as tradition about Paul's stay in Rome would certainly have circulated through the church. Pesch (1986b: 307) notes that the use of Isa. 6:9–10 is traditional (also Barrett 1998: 1237; Jervell 1998: 631 sees the core elements as historical). This is in contrast to Roloff (1988: 370), who sees Luke as responsible for the unit.

Exegesis and Exposition

[17]After three days he called together the local leaders of the Jews; and when they had gathered, he said to them, "Brothers, though I had done nothing against the people or the customs of our fathers, yet I was delivered prisoner from Jerusalem into the hands of the Romans, [18]who, examining me ⌜ ⌝, wished to set me at liberty because there was no reason for the death penalty in my case. [19]But when the Jews objected ⌜ ⌝, I was compelled to appeal to Caesar—though I had no charge to bring against my nation ⌜ ⌝. [20]For this reason therefore I have asked to see you and speak to you, since it is because of the hope of Israel that I am bound with this chain." [21]And they said to him, "We have received no letters

from Judea about you, and none of the brothers coming here has reported or spoken any evil about you. ²²But we desire to hear from you what you think; for with regard to this sect we know that everywhere it is spoken against."

²³Appointing a day for him, they came to him at his lodging in great numbers. He expounded the matter to them, testifying to the kingdom of God and trying to convince them about Jesus both from the Law of Moses and from the Prophets, from morning till evening. ²⁴And some were convinced by the things he said, while others disbelieved. ²⁵So, as they were disagreeing among themselves, they departed after Paul had made one statement: "The Holy Spirit spoke correctly in saying to your fathers through Isaiah the prophet: ²⁶'Go to this people, and say, You shall indeed hear but never understand, and you shall indeed see but never perceive. ²⁷For this people's heart has grown dull, and their ears are heavy of hearing, and their eyes they have closed, lest they should perceive with their eyes, and hear with their ears, and understand with their heart, and turn that I might heal them.' ²⁸Let it be known to you then that to the Gentiles this salvation has been sent; they will listen." ⌐ ⌐

³⁰And he lived there two whole years at his own expense and welcomed all who came to him, ³¹preaching the kingdom of God and teaching about the Lord Jesus Christ quite openly and unhindered.

These verses allow Paul to review his situation with the local Jews now **28:17–20** gathered around him. The Jewish presence in the city is well attested, especially around the edges of the city (Schürer 1973–87: 3.95–100; Wikenhauser 1961: 287). Leon (1960: 136–37) places the bulk of Jews in a region known as Trans Tiberim (Augustus's fourteenth region), the chief foreign quarter of the city, which was full of narrow streets, tenements, and crowded conditions. The region was known to be full of unsavory characters, vendors, and peddlers, as well as the poor and unassimilated. Rents were said to be four times the cost of other Italian locales (Le Cornu and Shulam 2003: 1505–12). Another prominent Jewish area was the Subura.

Barrett (1998: 1238) notes eleven synagogues named in the sources, apparently drawn from Leon's study (1960: 140–66). The first mention of Jews in Rome dates to about 139 BC. Valerius Maximus (*Facta et dicta memorabilia* 1.3.3) refers to Gnaeus Cornelius Hispalus's interaction with Jews who were accused of a form of syncretism (Fitzmyer 1998: 792 discusses the text in some detail). First Maccabees 14:16–18 and 15:15–24 note contact with Rome during the Maccabean period. Jewish population numbers are placed at anywhere from twenty to fifty thousand, with Rome's total population at about one million (Larkin 1995: 386; Witherington 1998: 795; Philo, *Embassy* 23 §§155–58). Josephus (*Ant.* 18.3.5 §§81–83) shows that the authorities did not like Jews proselytizing in Rome; he reports an expulsion under Tiberius (Dio Cassius, *Rom. Hist.* 60.6.6; Johnson 1992: 468). The Jews were seemingly not well organized but simply belonged to a conglomeration of independent synagogues (Polhill 1992: 539). This may be the result of the various expulsions they had experienced. Their checkered experience with Rome may have made them cautious about being too aggressive in certain situations.

Paul has invited the prominent Jews of first social rank (πρώτους, *prōtous*) to hear him. He took only three days to invite them. Once again the pattern of "to the Jew first" (Rom. 1:16) begins the activity in a city. This speech is a short example of forensic rhetoric with a brief *apologia* (Witherington 1998: 796). Luke's summary here assumes that readers are aware of the earlier details. This speech has the Jewish leadership's role in primary view. Paul is honest about their opposition to him.

He addresses them as "brothers" (ἀδελφοί, *adelphoi*). He still sees himself as a part of the Jewish community. Despite Paul's call to minister to all men, he continues to seek out the Jews, even given their previous rejection. Paul claims to have done nothing against "the people" or the Jewish customs (Acts 24:12–21; 25:8) yet was made a prisoner in Jerusalem (21:11, 31–33). This may have been a point the Jews would have disputed, as in other places it seems clear that Paul was not as scrupulous or as completely law affirming as other Jews might be (1 Cor. 9–10; Gal. 1:1–4:6). The issue may have been whether Paul cared about the traditions attached to the law and only acted otherwise when engaged with Gentiles. Paul sees his innocence in terms of how God has advanced the promise as it is tied to the new era. He is on trial for the hope of Israel (Acts 23:6; 24:15; 26:6–8; longer Pauline defenses of this idea appear in 22:1–21 and 26:2–23). So Paul's innocence is emphasized. This theme matches his formal defense speeches when he was delivered over to Caesar (21:11; this is like Jesus: Luke 9:44; 18:32–33a).

The Romans examined (ἀνακρίναντες, *anakrinantes*) him and found him guilty of nothing (Luke 23:14; Acts 4:9; 12:19; of Paul: Acts 17:11; 23:29; 24:8; 25:18, 25; 26:31–32; 28:18). He certainly is not guilty of anything worthy of death, just as Jesus was innocent in Luke 23. The irony of the events, which Luke only implies, is that Paul is still being held, and so Paul's explanation continues. Agrippa made his innocence clear in front of Festus (Acts 26:32). When the Jews, by which Paul means the leadership, objected to the claim that he was innocent, Paul appealed to Caesar (25:2–7). Paul wanted to prevent Festus from doing the Jews a favor (25:9). Rome has not really opposed him, but the Jewish leadership has. Paul has no desire, however, to charge his own nation with anything, only to be declared innocent. He has no ill intent toward his nation. The Jews should not see Paul as not caring about the nation or its promise; nor should they suspect that he is some type of informer. He is a faithful Jew. The term κατηγορεῖν (*katēgorein*) at the end of verse 19 means "have a legal cause" against someone (BAGD 423 §1; BDAG 533 §1a). Paul has no such issue with the Jews. They are pressing him, not the other way around. There is more irony: Paul seeks only justice, but here the pagan state protects him from those who are supposed to pursue justice and honor God. Paul has asked to speak with these local Jewish leaders because he is in chains for the hope of Israel, something Paul also has claimed earlier, in 23:6; 24:15; and 26:6–7. He may literally be chained to an armed guard. Paul's letters often allude to his life in prison (Phil. 1:7, 13; Col. 4:18; Eph. 6:20; 2 Tim. 1:16; 2:9; Philem. 10, 13; Johnson 1992: 470).

The Jews respond that they have not received any letters about Paul nor **28:21–22** has anything evil about Paul reached them from other Jews. Although some scholars question the remark's believability, it is not surprising that they have not heard about Paul, for the following reasons: (1) Paul's case was long delayed and has only recently been moved along to Rome. Any communication to Rome may well have been delayed as well. (2) Paul's journey was very difficult but was attempted with as much haste as could be mustered (Polhill 1992: 540). At the end of winter, Paul's journey resumed very early in the travel season and so reached Rome before most others would have arrived (Witherington 1998: 799). Thus it may well be that news about Paul's situation has not yet reached Rome. (3) Haenchen (1987: 727–28) reads the remark too literally, that they have heard nothing about Paul at all, not just nothing evil about him, and that they know of Christians only through hearsay. The remark in verse 22 appears to argue that these Jews do know that Christians are opposed almost unanimously, as the reaction against them comes from "everywhere" (πανταχοῦ, *pantachou*). What these Roman Jews have not heard is anything specifically negative about Paul, which may mean that they do not know specifically why he is being brought to Rome. (4) It might also be that with the case moved to Rome, the Jews in Jerusalem were relieved that Paul was no longer a matter of concern for them, so they made no effort to say anything to Jews in Rome. The remark does imply that Roman Jews did seek input from other Jews in other locales, likely including Jerusalem, on such matters, but nothing yet has reached them.

There is a final implication to note. Luke is capable of noting a Jewish conspiracy when one exists (21:27). That there is nothing known yet may indicate the authenticity of Luke's account. Why not further the "conspiracy," if details are simply being created by Luke? So the lack of hostility toward Paul among the Roman Jews speaks for the authenticity of the scene.

The result of the lack of information is that the Jewish leaders desire to hear from Paul, although they know that the sect is rejected by all the reports they receive. Luke portrays the new movement as an internal sect (αἱρέσεως, *haireseōs*) of Judaism in the eyes of the local Jewish leadership (5:17 [of Sadducees]; 24:5 [of Christians]). Although they have not heard about Paul, they have heard about this new teaching. Word about the Christians is out. The Roman Jews' own experience is likely also to be at work here, as the trouble noted in 18:2 suggests a struggle between Jews and Christians in Rome. Here they stress that knowledge of this new movement is well known. It stands opposed by Jews elsewhere. They could be curious to hear the other side. The reaction tells us that they will listen, but with skepticism.

The division of this scene into two meetings is like 13:14–50, where Paul first meets Jews in the synagogue. Here a second meeting follows the first, with rejection being the keynote as one moves into a second meeting. In Acts 13 the turning to Gentiles is stressed. Here the culpability of the rejecting Jews is highlighted (Polhill 1992: 541).

28:23–24   The appointed day for the second meeting arrives, and a great number show up to hear Paul at his lodging (ξενίαν, *xenian*; see Philem. 22). All day he speaks to them about the kingdom and Jesus. One of Paul's topics is the rule of God that arrives through Jesus. This major theme of Jesus appears twice in the climactic scene (see v. 31). Although it is rare elsewhere in Acts (1:3; 8:12; 14:22; 19:8; see the discussion at 1:3), the idea is a part of key speeches throughout Acts (2:17–36; 3:12–26; 13:32–39). The fact that the idea begins and ends the book is also important; this is a literary *inclusio* that underscores the idea's associations and significance. Paul uses the Law of Moses and the Prophets (Luke 24:27, 44; Acts 17:2–3; 18:5). The theme recalls Luke 16:16. At the center of the kingdom promise stand Jesus and the promise of the whole of the Hebrew Scriptures. Paul tries to show them from their sacred texts that Jesus and the kingdom promise belong together (ἐξετίθετο, *exetitheto*, is a conative imperfect, "he was trying to convince them"). He is "witnessing" or "testifying" (διαμαρτυρόμενος, *diamartyromenos*) to them. Some are convinced (ἐπείθοντο, *epeithonto*) but a great many must not have been (ἠπίστουν, *ēpistoun*, they disbelieved) because Paul's reaction cites Isaiah's prediction of rejection. The division of Israel that Jesus causes reflects Luke 2:34, where Simeon predicted that Jesus would bring a division within Israel. In Acts 28:24, the contrast between the groups, pointing to division, is indicated by a classic use of a μὲν . . . δέ (*men . . . de*) contrast. Such a division recalls other texts in Acts where a Jewish audience is present (14:1–2; 18:6–8; conceptually, 17:32–34; such division of response is common in Acts: 2:12–13; 4:1–4; 5:12–17; 6:8–14; 9:21–25; 13:42–45; 17:1–5; 18:4, 12–17; 19:8–10; Johnson 1992: 471). The few who respond positively remind us that God always keeps a remnant. The term for "were convinced" in verse 24 is also positive elsewhere in Acts (13:43; 17:4; 19:8–9).

28:25–28   The leaders depart, disagreeing (ἀσύμφωνοι, *asymphōnoi*) among themselves. This adjective is an NT hapax. Paul then comments, using the words of Isa. 6:9–10, which Paul attributes ultimately to the Holy Spirit, who originally addressed them to an earlier generation that Paul calls "your fathers" (Acts 3:25; 7:51–52; cf. 13:32–33; 26:6). Paul now separates himself from those who reject the way of God, since it was "your" fathers who were warned originally by Isaiah. Now this generation risks repetition of their error. Paul speaks like a prophet here, warning them about their rejection. The cited passage agrees with the LXX with these exceptions: (1) In Acts the phrase "to the people" goes with "go," rather than with "say" as in Isaiah. This difference, however, does not affect the meaning at all, since the audience is the same in both cases. (2) Also, Acts has finite verbs instead of imperatives for "make dull," "blind," and "closed." It presents the passage as describing something that has occurred instead of as a strict prediction, because this is how the matter has in fact turned out. The alterations make the application clearer. Isaiah 6:9–10 is a traditional Christian text, used in Matt. 13:14–15; Mark 4:12; Luke 8:10; John 12:39–40; and Rom. 11:8 (also Justin Martyr, *Dial.* 12.2; 33.1; 69.4). The form of the citation matches Matthew's version.

Israel's heart, mind, and eyes are closed to the proclamation of God coming from his prophet. Israel's problem is a dull heart. The verb ἐπαχύνθη (*epachynthē*) in verse 27 literally means "has grown fat" or "thick" and pictures a heart so full that it is unresponsive (BAGD 638 §2; BDAG 790). Nothing can penetrate it to its core. Their ears falter as well, since hearing has become difficult. The term βαρέως (*bareōs*, heavy) is used only twice in the NT (Matt. 13:15, where Isa. 6 is cited as well). The ears are pictured as tired and too weighed down to function. Paul also notes closed eyes. No sensory part of the person is responding. The dullness of the people has prevented their being responsive and turning to God for healing. Turning to God (ἐπιστρέψωσιν, *epistrepsōsin*) is the response that is lacking (see the discussion of Acts 3:19). Such turning would heal them, but they refuse to do so.

God was predicting their response here in Isaiah. He told the fathers through the picture of Isaiah's call and ministry that they were stubborn, hearing a divine report but not understanding, seeing but not really perceiving. The pair of negative particles (οὐ μή, *ou mē*) appears twice in verse 26. They are emphatic in force. Paul cites the passage to warn the audience that the nation of Israel is falling into the national pattern of not believing and of reflecting hardheartedness. Paul is like Isaiah, and the present Jewish community is like the ancient nation. This warning fits the pattern of Acts 13, where Paul is associated with Isaiah's servant, but it is not a permanent rejection of the nation. Paul still preaches to anyone who might hear (vv. 30–31). In addition, the rebuke is much like that in 13:41, which cites Hab. 1:5. It is a prophetic warning (cf. Tannehill 1985; Moessner 1988; Moessner 1989) that to refuse to hear the word is to risk reaching a point where it will never be heard (Marshall 1980: 425).

The result is expressed with a solemn call (v. 28) to understand what is taking place: "Let this be known to you" (Acts 2:14; 4:10; 13:38). Salvation goes to the Gentiles (Isa. 40:5; Pss. 67:2 [66:3 LXX]; 98:3 [97:3 LXX]; Acts 1:8; 10:1–11:18; 13:46–47; 18:6). They will hear the message and respond. Here Paul appears to be baiting Israel's people with this prophetic warning in the hope of making them jealous (Rom. 11:11–12, 25–32) or prodding them not to be disobedient to God.

Roloff (1988: 375) argues that Luke's view differs from Paul's and sees no hope for Israel as a nation here. This thesis is the burden of an entire work by J. Sanders (1987) arguing that Luke-Acts is anti-Semitic. This message of Jesus and the kingdom, however, is the message of salvation for anyone. This is what Scripture promised and God brought in Jesus. The message will go out even if most in Israel do not want anything to do with it. Everywhere Luke presents the gospel in Acts, Jews are included, even in the face of consistent rejection. The fact that Paul will see everyone who comes to him argues for Paul continuing to hope for the Jewish nation. The fact that Luke records all of this shows that his view parallels Paul's. Nothing precludes his going to Gentiles now, but Jews are not shut out.

How Acts ends and the role of the Jews in it have been debated among students of this book. Larkin (1995: 390n) presents a variety of views: (1) replacement of Israel by Gentiles (many, as just noted above; among them, Jervell 1998: 628);[1] (2) remnant Jews with Gentiles make the mission a success (Jervell 1972; Moessner 1988; Ravens 1995);[2] (3) official Judaism rejected the gospel, but individual Jews did not (Polhill 1992: 545); and (4) God continues to preach to rebellious Israel. Everything we know about Paul tells us that the fourth view is the most likely, as Paul continues to hold out hope for ethnic Israel and its response to Jesus (Rom. 11:25–32, where "Israel" must refer to ethnic Israel). Jesus's own teaching also appears to go in this direction, as Luke 13:31–35 indicates a judgment until Israel says, "Blessed is the one who comes in the name of the Lord." Finally, Acts 28:28 makes no mention of turning from anyone. There is no remark that Jews have been excluded, only that the gospel will be preached to Gentiles, and

1. Jervell 1998: 629 does not make a conclusion about the conversion of individual Jews, since the church is made up of Jews and Gentiles. The rationale for this view includes the idea that the proclamation, in reaching Rome, has fulfilled Acts 1:8 and the city represents the world. It is not clear, however, that the scene in Rome means all of this, especially if the ending of Acts is open-ended, as shall be argued below: there is still more of the mission story to come.

2. Ravens's study presents in detail a future for Israel but plays Luke too much against Matthew, Paul, and Hebrews, mostly by denying an atoning view of soteriology to Luke. This understates Luke's soteriology. Luke argues that the church was purchased with the Son's blood and the Last Supper meal is a new covenant that comes through Jesus's sacrifice (Acts 20:28; Luke 22:20; for text-critical issues tied to these texts, see the additional note on 20:28 above and Bock 1996: 1721–22).

they will respond (Brawley 1998: 296 suggests that as Acts ends, it is still reaching out to the Jews).

See the additional note for why this text is unlikely to have been originally in Acts.

The book of Acts ends on a note of triumph. It is a final summary like the closing of earlier units (6:7; 9:31; 12:24; 16:5; 19:20). Paul, even though imprisoned, lives at his own expense and receives any who would visit him. The aorist verb ἐνέμεινεν (*enemeinen*, he remained, lived) is a constative aorist, viewing the two years as a summarized and completed whole (BDF §332.1). Mealand (1990) discusses the reference to μισθώματι (*misthōmati*, rent, expense) here; its force is much debated. On the one hand, the term is an NT hapax, and its etymology suggests something earned, not a reference to a locale. The preposition ἐν (*en*), however, can suggest a locale, as does the verb ἐμμένω (*emmenō*, dwell). The debate yields two possible meanings: Paul stays where he does either *"at* his own expense" (i.e., with his own payment) or *"in* his own rented quarters" (so NET; key inscriptions: *SIG* 1024, 1200; P.Mich. 9.563.19). The implication is that Paul has his own quarters, which means that he likely pays for it or, if not, his support by Christians does, as a letter such as Philippians might suggest. The verse points to a locale, but one for which expenses are paid rather than a prison cell.

Luke does not divulge what eventually happened to Paul. He likely writes after the results were known, but Luke does not recount any of this. Witherington (1998: 807–9) treats the various views and specifically rejects the idea that Luke writes in about AD 62. If Luke did write later, then the reason Luke did not tell us about Paul's fate, or even what it was, cannot be conclusively answered, but possibilities of how the imprisonment turned out and what Luke did can be explored:

1. The idea that Luke contemplated a third volume has much against it, as nothing earlier in the two volumes gives any indication of a story beyond Rome. In this view, the open ending looked to more of the story, which Luke never came to write. The nature of Acts does not look to future events, as the predictions of persecution in Luke 21:12–19 appear to do for Acts.
2. The idea that Paul was released after a few years because his accusers failed to appear is unlikely, since this view is based on the improper dating of papyri that supposedly describe such a legal situation. Bruce (1990: 541) covers the discussion, as does Sherwin-White (1963: 112–19). Fitzmyer (1998: 796–97) appears to hold out for this option in the mention of the two-year stay, citing Claudius's example in Dio Cassius, *Rom. Hist.* 60.28.6. The later examples appear in Pliny the Younger, *Ep.* 10.56.4 and 10.57.2, and Philo, *Flaccus* 16 §128. Johnson (1992: 473) notes the same texts but argues that they

cannot support the point. What would this option mean for Luke? The inquiry died for lack of interest, and so Luke did not mention it. It seems, however, that if this happened, Luke would have had a great closing argument. In the end, no one made an appearance to support a decisive case against Paul.

3. Did Paul die during this imprisonment? Was he martyred during this time? In this view, the outcome was too negative for Luke to mention. Evidence from 1 Clem. 5.5–7 and Eusebius (*Eccl. Hist.* 2.22), however, suggests that Paul did not die as a result of this inquiry. Paul lived through this imprisonment and was executed in the late sixties about the same time as Peter. This view stands against that of Haenchen (1987: 732), who argues that Luke's ending for Acts presupposes Paul's martyrdom but Luke did not wish to end on a note about martyrdom. Conzelmann (1987: 228) agrees with Haenchen, citing the farewell speech at Miletus. Acts 7, however, shows how Luke can exalt a martyred figure, and so Haenchen's premise seems unlikely. Acts 27:24 suggests that Paul would appear before Caesar, but the outcome is not relevant to Luke. This is especially the case if Luke knew that Paul was released in this inquiry but eventually was martyred by Rome. He could have ended saying Rome released him, but the argument has little force if some are aware that Rome eventually did bring Paul's life to an end.

4. Luke chose to end his book here because his point was the arrival of the word to the highest levels of Rome. The book's ending is open-ended with respect to the future of the Jewish nation because the church is still preaching the word to whoever will hear it (Witherington 1998: 809). This was Luke's key point, even if Luke knew of Paul's eventual demise. This is the best explanation for the ending of Acts.

To all who come to him, Paul does the same thing: preach the kingdom and teach about the Lord Jesus Christ. His imprisonment cannot chain the word of God (2 Tim. 2:9). He speaks openly and unhindered. The second term, "unhindered" (ἀκωλύτως, *akōlytōs*), concludes the book on an emphatic note in closing the sentence. It is an NT hapax (Delling 1973). The kingdom is the delivering promise of the rule of God among people found through Jesus. As the first speech of Acts 2 told us, with it come forgiveness and the provision of the enabling Spirit for the mission to which believers are called. In Acts we have bookends in the use of the concepts of the kingdom and Jesus (1:1–3; 28:23, 31). The kingdom is restored to all who respond to Jesus Christ, as the contrast to Jewish rejection shows. At whatever point God decides, the kingdom will be restored to Israel (1:6), and this also will happen through Jesus (3:14–26). It will be a time when judgment takes place through this one whom God has appointed judge of the living and the dead (10:40–42;

17:30–31). As with the earlier messengers, at the center of Paul's discussion is Jesus, the one who was exalted to be Lord and who serves as the Anointed One of God, the Christ. Paul emphasizes the combination of Jesus's authority and his right to rule over God's promised kingdom. It is to Jesus that people must come because they are accountable to the one whom God has shown to be the Messiah. It is on this positive note that Acts ends. This message of salvation is beginning to reach the "end of the earth" as it comes to the Gentile capital of Rome (1:8), a long, perilous journey from Jerusalem (Acts 27). The gospel is spreading to the entire world. Even if Paul later died for this testimony, the fact that God's word is preached and people make their choice about the message is the point.

In sum, the book of Acts, a book of witnesses to the risen Jesus, ends with one of the key witnesses living out his calling despite having suffered unjustly. We see the continued tragic nature of Jewish unbelief, yet Paul continues to keep an open door to anyone who will listen to him and consider his message. Paul loves his enemies, whom he views as brothers who have lost their way. We see what makes for good evangelism: (1) a confidence and readiness to share because God is sovereign, (2) a focus on God and God's kingdom program through Jesus, (3) an open door to any who will hear, and (4) a recognition that evangelism and mission are a priority, even the most fundamental calling of the church in the world (Fernando 1998: 628–32). Nothing, including prison, persecution, or possible death, has hindered Paul's ability to minister and preach the message. We are to marvel at how God has protected Paul and accomplished his word (Stott 1990: 402). We also can see in this book that Paul suffered well. He kept the faith and continued to serve, living out his call.

The book also has an open ending, with the word still being preached. In fact, the Great Commission anticipated in Luke 24 is realized here as the word goes out. The Spirit of God has directed the operation, and the Spirit has been a Spirit of enabling boldness. The word spreads even when some try to keep it from doing so. Faithful witnesses make sure that this happens. Faithful witnesses understand God's calling and support, just as Paul did.

All of this is the work of an active God. God has been directing events throughout the book. God set forth the call for the mission. God gave the Spirit. God directed the church to the Gentiles. God called out Paul with Barnabas and then sent Paul to Jerusalem and Rome. God protected Paul as he brought the word there as God's faithful witness. God can be trusted, and his calling is to be followed. Paul shows us that the combination of divine aid and humans' faithfulness to God's calling is powerful.

The theological premise of Acts is that Jesus is Lord of all, and so the gospel can go to all. Luke's message is this: be reassured; the unhindered progress of God's word about salvation to all people is occurring by God's direction, fulfilled in the Lord Jesus Christ, according to the long-revealed promise of Scripture to Israel—and despite opposition. The new religion is really an old one, rooted in God's promise and direction. The word will get out. In fact, despite all the obstacles we see in Acts, the book ends with the gospel going out unhindered, for wherever the gospel is shared, there is offered an open door to the presence of God, no matter how tension-filled or restricted life is. God is the hero of Acts, and the plot line is how he reveals his word through Jesus and a faithful church. God will make sure it happens, and so will a faithful church.

Additional Notes

28:18. The Western text adds "concerning many things" as the topic of the legal examination.

28:19. The Western text adds an exclamation to the Jewish rejection of Paul: "and they cried out, 'Take away our enemy!'" This addition shows the prejudice and hostility of the Western text to Jews. The Western text also has Paul explain why he appeals to Caesar: "that I might redeem my life from death."

28:29. This verse is not well attested for the original text of Acts. It is missing in $\mathfrak{P}^{74}$, ℵ, A, B, E, and Ψ, and so it is excluded from the translation. It has the Jews disputing among themselves as they depart from Paul's place. The reading is in Byz and in the Itala MSS.

Works Cited

Acworth, A.
1973 "Where Was St. Paul Shipwrecked? A Re-examination of the Evidence." *Journal of Theological Studies*, n.s., 24:190–93.

Ådna, J.
2000 "James' Position at the Summit Meeting of the Apostles and the Elders in Jerusalem (Acts 15)." Pp. 127–61 in *The Mission of the Early Church to Jews and Gentiles*. Edited by J. Ådna and H. Kvalbein. Wissenschaftliche Untersuchungen zum Neuen Testament 127. Tübingen: Mohr.

Ådna, J., and H. Kvalbein (eds.)
2000 *The Mission of the Early Church to Jews and Gentiles*. Wissenschaftliche Untersuchungen zum Neuen Testament 127. Tübingen: Mohr.

Alexander, L. C. A.
1996 "The Preface of Acts and the Historians." Pp. 73–103 in *History, Literature, and Society in the Book of Acts*. Edited by B. Witherington III. Cambridge: Cambridge University Press.

Arnold, C.
1989 *Ephesians—Power and Magic: The Concept of Power in Ephesians in the Light of Its Historical Setting*. Cambridge: Cambridge University Press.

Ascough, R.
1998 "Civic Pride at Philippi: The Textual Problem of Acts 16.12." *New Testament Studies* 44:93–103.

Avemarie, F.
2002 *Die Tauferzählungen der Apostelgeschichte*. Wissenschaftliche Untersuchungen zum Neuen Testament 139. Tübingen: Mohr.

Avigad, N.
1984 *Discovering Jerusalem*. 2nd edition. Oxford: Blackwell.

BAGD *A Greek-English Lexicon of the New Testament and Other Early Christian Literature*. By W. Bauer, W. F. Arndt, F. W. Gingrich, and F. W. Danker. 2nd edition. Chicago: University of Chicago Press, 1979.

Baird, W.
2003 *History of New Testament Research: From Jonathan Edwards to Rudolf Bultmann*. Minneapolis: Augsburg Fortress.

Bamberger, B. J.
1963 "The Sadducees and the Belief in Angels." *Journal of Biblical Literature* 82:433–35.

Barnett, P. W.
1981 "The Jewish Sign Prophets, AD 40–70—Their Intentions and Origin." *New Testament Studies* 27:679–97.

Barrett, C. K.
1963 "Stephen and the Son of Man." Pp. 31–38 in *Apophoreta: Festschrift für Ernst Haenchen*. Beihefte zur Zeitschrift für die neutestamentliche Wissenschaft 30. Berlin: Töpelmann.
1979 "Light on the Holy Spirit from Simon Magus (Acts 8:4–25)." Pp. 281–95 in *Les Actes des apôtres: Traditions, redaction, théologie*. Edited by J. Kremer. Bibliotheca ephemeridum theologicarum loveniensium 48. Louvain: Leuven University Press.
1994 *A Critical and Exegetical Commentary on the Acts of the Apostles*, vol. 1: *Preliminary Introduction and Commentary on Acts I–XIV*. International Critical Commentary. Edinburgh: T&T Clark.
1998 *A Critical and Exegetical Commentary on the Acts of the Apostles*, vol. 2: *Introduction and Commentary on Acts XV–XXVIII*. International Critical Commentary. Edinburgh: T&T Clark.

Bassler, J. M.
1985 "Luke and Paul on Impartiality." *Biblica* 66:546–52.

Bauckham, R.
1996 "James and the Gentiles (Acts 15,13–21)." Pp. 154–84 in *History, Literature, and Society in the Book of Acts*. Edited by B. Witherington III. Cambridge: Cambridge University Press.
2006 *Jesus and the Eyewitnesses*. Grand Rapids: Eerdmans.

Bauernfeind, O.
1980 *Kommentar und Studien zur Apostelgeschichte*. Wissenschaftliche Untersuchungen zum Neuen Testament 22. Tübingen: Mohr.

BDAG *A Greek-English Lexicon of the New Testament and Other Early Christian Literature*. By W. Bauer, F. W. Danker, W. F. Arndt, and F. W. Gingrich. 3rd edition. Chicago: University of Chicago Press, 2000.

BDF *A Greek Grammar of the New Testament and Other Early Christian Literature*. By F. Blass, A. Debrunner, and R. W. Funk. Chicago: University of Chicago Press, 1961.

BDR *Grammatik des neutestamentlichen Griechisch*. By F. Blass, A. Debrunner, and F. Rehkopf. Göttingen: Vandenhoeck & Ruprecht, 1984.

Beardslee, W. A.
1960 "The Casting of Lots at Qumran and in the Book of Acts." *Novum Testamentum* 4:245–52.

Béchard, D.
2000 *Paul outside the Walls: A Study of Luke's Socio-Geographical Universalism in Acts 14:8–20*. Analecta biblica 143. Rome: Pontifical Biblical Institute Press.
2001 "Paul among the Rustics: The Lystran Episode and the Lucan Apologetic." *Catholic Biblical Quarterly* 63:84–101.
2003 "The Disputed Case against Paul: A Redaction Critical Analysis of Acts 21:27–22:29." *Catholic Biblical Quarterly* 65:232–50.

Betz, H. D.
1992 *The Greek Magical Papyri in Translation, Including the Demonic Spells*. 2nd edition. Chicago: University of Chicago Press.

Betz, O.
1970 "Die Vision des Paulus im Tempel von Jerusalem: Apg 22,17–21 als Beitrag zur Deutung des Damaskuserlebnisses." Pp. 113–23 in *Verborum veritas*. Edited by O. Böcher and K. Haacker. Wuppertal: Brockhaus.

Blomberg, C.
1984 "The Law in Luke-Acts." *Journal for the Study of the New Testament* 22:53–80.
1998 "The Christian and the Law of Moses." Pp. 397–416 in *Witness to the Gospel: The Theology of Acts*. Edited by I. H. Marshall and D. Peterson. Grand Rapids: Eerdmans.

Bock, D. L.
1987 *Proclamation from Prophecy and Pattern: Lucan Old Testament Christology*. Journal for the Study of the New Testament: Supplement Series 12. Sheffield: JSOT Press.
1994a *Luke 1:1–9:50*. Baker Exegetical Commentary on the New Testament 3A. Grand Rapids: Baker Academic.
1994b "A Theology of Luke-Acts." Pp. 87–166 in *A Biblical Theology of the New Testament*. Edited by R. B. Zuck and D. L. Bock. Chicago: Moody.
1996 *Luke 9:51–24:53*. Baker Exegetical Commentary on the New Testament 3B. Grand Rapids: Baker Academic.
1998a *Blasphemy and Exaltation in Judaism and the Final Examination of Jesus*. Wissenschaftliche Untersuchungen zum Neuen Testament 2.106. Tübingen: Mohr. Reprinted as *Blasphemy and Exaltation in Judaism: The Charge against Jesus in Mark 14:53–65*. Grand Rapids: Baker Academic, 2000.
1998b "Scripture and the Realization of God's Promises." Pp. 41–62 in *Witness to the Gospel: The Theology of Acts*. Edited by I. H. Marshall and D. Peterson. Grand Rapids: Eerdmans.
2002a *Jesus according to Scripture: Restoring the Portrait from the Gospels*. Grand Rapids: Baker Academic.
2002b *Studying the Historical Jesus: A Guide to Sources and Methods*. Grand Rapids: Baker Academic.

2006   *The Missing Gospels: Unearthing the Truth about Alternative Christianities.* Nashville: Nelson.

Boismard, M. E., and A. Lamouille
1984   *Le texte occidental des Actes des apôtres.* 2 vols. Paris: ERC.

Bolt, P.
1998   "Mission and Witness." Pp. 169–90 in *Witness to the Gospel: The Theology of Acts.* Edited by I. H. Marshall and D. Peterson. Grand Rapids: Eerdmans.

Bonz, M. P.
2000   *The Past as Legacy: Luke-Acts and Ancient Epic.* Minneapolis: Fortress.

Bowker, J.
1967–68 "Speeches in Acts: A Study in Proem and Yelammedenu Form." *New Testament Studies* 14:96–111.

Bratcher, R.
1959   "Having Loosed the Pangs of Death." *Bible Translator* 10:18–20.
1959–60 "Ἀκούω in Acts ix.7 and xxii.9." *Expository Times* 71:243–45.

Brawley, R. L.
1987   *Luke-Acts and the Jews: Conflict, Apology, and Conciliation.* Society of Biblical Literature Monograph Series 33. Atlanta: Scholars Press.
1990   *Centering on God: Method and Message in Luke-Acts.* Literary Currents in Biblical Interpretation. Louisville: Westminster/John Knox.
1998   "The God of Promises and the Jews in Luke-Acts." Pp. 279–96 in *Literary Studies in Luke-Acts: Essays in Honor of Joseph B. Tyson.* Edited by R. P. Thompson and T. E. Phillips. Macon, GA: Mercer University Press.
2005   "Social Identity and the Aim of Accomplished Life in Acts 2." Pp. 16–33 in *Acts and Ethics.* Edited by T. E. Phillips. New Testament Monographs 9. Sheffield: Sheffield Academic Press.

Brenk, F. E., and F. Canali de Rossi
2001   "The 'Notorious' Felix, Procurator of Judaea, and His Many Wives (Acts 23–24)." *Biblica* 82:410–17.

Brock, S.
1974   "ΒΑΡΝΑΒΑΣ ΥΙΟΣ ΠΑΡΑΚΛΗΣΕΩΣ." *Journal of Theological Studies*, n.s., 25:93–98.

Brodie, T. L.
1986   "Toward Unraveling the Rhetorical Imitation of Sources in Acts: 2 Kings 5 as One Component of Acts 8,9–40." *Biblica* 67:41–67.

Bruce, F. F.
1942   *The Speeches in the Acts of the Apostles.* London: Tyndale.
1954   *Commentary on the Book of Acts.* New International Commentary on the New Testament. Grand Rapids: Eerdmans.
1974   "The Speeches in Acts—Thirty Years After." Pp. 53–68 in *Reconciliation and Hope: New Testament Essays on Atonement and Eschatology Presented to L. L. Morris on His 60th Birthday.* Edited by R. Banks. Grand Rapids: Eerdmans.
1976   "Is the Paul of Acts the Real Paul?" *Bulletin of the John Rylands Library* 58:282–305.
1978   "The Full Name of the Procurator Felix." *Journal for the Study of the New Testament* 1:33–36.
1988a   *The Book of the Acts.* Revised edition. New International Commentary on the New Testament. Grand Rapids: Eerdmans.
1988b   *The Canon of Scripture.* Downers Grove, IL: InterVarsity.
1990   *The Acts of the Apostles: Greek Text with Introduction and Commentary.* 3rd edition. Grand Rapids: Eerdmans.

Bryan, C.
1988   "A Further Look at Acts 16.1–3." *Journal of Biblical Literature* 107:292–94.

Buckwalter, H. D.
1996   *The Character and Purpose of Luke's Christology.* Society for New Testament Studies Monograph Series 89. Cambridge: Cambridge University Press.
1998   "The Divine Saviour." Pp. 107–23 in *Witness to the Gospel: The Theology of Acts.* Edited by I. H. Marshall and D. Peterson. Grand Rapids: Eerdmans.

Byington, S.
1957   "יהוה and אדני." *Journal of Biblical Literature* 76:58–59.

Cadbury, H. J.
1922   "The Tradition." Pp. 209–64 in *The Acts of the Apostles*, vol. 2: *Prolegomena II: Criticism.* Edited by F. J. Foakes-Jackson and K. Lake. London: Macmillan.

1933   "Note XXIV: Dust and Garments."
          Pp. 269–77 in *The Acts of the
          Apostles*, vol. 5: *Additional Notes
          to the Commentary*. Edited by
          F. J. Foakes-Jackson and K. Lake.
          London: Macmillan.
1958   *The Making of Luke-Acts*. 2nd
          edition. London: SPCK.

Calder, W. M.
1910a   "A Cult of Homonades." *Classical
          Review* 24:76–81.
1910b   "Zeus and Hermes at Lystra."
          Expositor 7:1–6.
1925–26   "Acts 14^{12}." *Expository Times* 37:528.

Capper, B.
1983   "The Interpretation of Acts 5.4."
          *Journal for the Study of the New
          Testament* 19:117–31.
1998   "Reciprocity and Ethics." Pp.
          499–518 in *Witness to the Gospel:
          The Theology of Acts*. Edited by I. H.
          Marshall and D. Peterson. Grand
          Rapids: Eerdmans.

Carroll, J. T.
1988   *Response to the End of History:
          Eschatology and Situation in Luke-
          Acts*. Society of Biblical Literature
          Dissertation Series 92. Atlanta:
          Scholars Press.

Carson, D. A., P. T. O'Brien, and M. A.
Seifrid (eds.)
2001   *Justification and Variegated Nomism*,
          vol. 1: *The Complexities of Second
          Temple Judaism*. Wissenschaftliche
          Untersuchungen zum Neuen
          Testament 2/140. Tübingen: Mohr
          Siebeck/Grand Rapids: Baker
          Academic.

Casson, L.
1950   "The Isis and Her Voyage."
          *Transactions of the American
          Philological Association* 81:43–56.
1951   "Speed under Sail of Ancient
          Ships." *Transactions of the American
          Philological Association* 82:136–48.

Catchpole, D.
1976–77   "Paul, James and the Apostolic
          Decree." *New Testament Studies*
          23:428–44.

Charitonidou, A.
1978   *Epidaurus*. Monuments and
          Museums of Greece. Athens: Clio.

Chilton, C. W.
1955   "The Roman Law of Treason under
          the Early Principate." *Journal of
          Roman Studies* 45:73–81.

CIG   *Corpus inscriptionum graecarum*.
          Edited by A. Boeckh. 4 vols. Berlin:
          Ex Officina Academica, 1828–77.
CII   *Corpus inscriptionum iudaicarum*.
          Edited by J. B. Frey. 2 vols. Rome:
          Pontificio Istituto di Archeologia
          Cristiana, 1936–52.
CIL   *Corpus inscriptionum latinarum*.
          Berlin: Reimer, 1862–.

Clark, E. A.
2005   *History, Theory, Text: Historians and
          the Linguistic Turn*. Cambridge:
          Harvard University Press.

Clarke, W. K. L.
1922   "The Use of the Septuagint in
          Acts." Pp. 66–105 in *The Acts of the
          Apostles*, vol. 2: *Prolegomena II:
          Criticism*. Edited by F. J. Foakes-
          Jackson and K. Lake. London:
          Macmillan.

CMRDM   *Corpus monumentorum religionis
          dei Menis*. Edited by Eugene Lane. 4
          vols. Leiden: Brill, 1971–78.

Cohen, S. J. D.
1986   "Was Timothy Jewish? Patristic
          Exegesis, Rabbinic Law, and
          Matrilineal Descent." *Journal of
          Biblical Literature* 105:151–68.

Conzelmann, H.
1960   *The Theology of St. Luke*. New York:
          Harper & Row.
1987   *The Acts of the Apostles*. Translated
          by J. Limburg, A. T. Kraabel, and
          D. H. Juel. Edited by E. J. Epp
          with C. R. Matthews. Hermeneia.
          Philadelphia: Fortress.

Cornuke, R.
2003   *The Lost Shipwreck of Paul*. Bend,
          OR: Global.

Cosgrove, C. H.
1984   "The Divine *dei* in Luke-Acts:
          Investigations into Lukan
          Understanding of God's Providence."
          Novum Testamentum 26:168–90.

CPJ   *Corpus papyrorum judaicarum*.
          Edited by V. Tcherikover. 3 vols.
          Cambridge: Harvard University
          Press, 1957–64.

Crisler, B. C.
1976   "The Acoustics and Crowd Capacity
          of Natural Theaters in Palestine."
          Biblical Archaeologist 39:128–41.

Crocker, P. T.
1987   "Ephesus: Its Silversmiths, Its
          Tradesmen and Its Riots." *Buried
          History* 23:76–78.

Croy, N. C.
1997 "Hellenistic Philosophies and the Preaching of Resurrection." *Novum Testamentum* 39:21–39.

Culy, M. M., and M. C. Parsons
2003 *Acts: A Handbook on the Greek Text.* Waco: Baylor University Press.

Cunningham, S.
1997 *"Through Many Tribulations": The Theology of Persecution in Luke-Acts.* Journal for the Study of the New Testament: Supplement Series 142. Sheffield: Sheffield Academic Press.

Dahl, N. A.
1957–58 "A People for His Name." *New Testament Studies* 4:319–27.

Dar, S., and S. Applebaum
1973 "The Roman Road from Antipatris to Caesarea." *Palestinian Exploration Quarterly* 105:91–99.

Darr, J. A.
1998 "Irenic or Ironic? Another Look at Gamaliel before the Sanhedrin (Acts 5:33–42)." Pp. 121–39 in *Literary Studies in Luke-Acts: Essays in Honor of Joseph B. Tyson.* Edited by R. P. Thompson and T. E. Phillips. Macon, GA: Mercer University Press.

Daube, D.
1990 "On Acts 23: Sadducees and Angels." *Journal of Biblical Literature* 109:493–97.

Deines, R.
1997 *Die Pharisäer: Ihr Verständnis im Spiegel der christlichen und jüdischen Forschung seit Wellhausen und Graetz.* Wissenschaftliche Untersuchungen zum Neuen Testament 1/101. Tübingen: Mohr Siebeck.
2001 "The Pharisees between 'Judaisms' and 'Common Judaism.'" Pp. 443–504 in *Justification and Variegated Nomism,* vol. 1: *The Complexities of Second Temple Judaism.* Edited by D. A. Carson, P. T. O'Brien, and M. A. Seifrid. Wissenschaftliche Untersuchungen zum Neuen Testament 2/140. Tübingen: Mohr Siebeck/Grand Rapids: Baker Academic.

Deines, R., and M. Hengel
1995 "E. P. Sanders' 'Common Judaism,' Jesus and the Pharisees: A Review Article." *Journal of Theological Studies* 46:1–70.

Delling, G.
1973 "Das letzte Wort der Apostelgeschichte." *Novum Testamentum* 15:191–204.

Derrett, J. D. M.
1977 "Ananias, Sapphira and the Right of Property." Pp. 93–100 in *Studies in the New Testament,* vol. 1: *Glimpses of the Legal and Social Presuppositions of the Authors.* Leiden: Brill.
1982 "Simon Magus (Acts 8:9–24)." *Zeitschrift für die neutestamentliche Wissenschaft* 73:52–68.

DeWaard, J.
1971 "The Quotation from Deuteronomy in Acts 3,22, 23 and the Palestinian Text: Additional Arguments." *Biblica* 52:537–40.

Dibelius, M.
1949 *Die Reden der Apostelgeschichte und die antike Geschichtsschreibung.* Sitzungsberichte der heidelberger Akademie der Wissenschaften, philosophisch-historische Klasse. Heidelberg: Winter.
1956 *Studies in the Acts of the Apostles.* London: SCM.

Dickerson, P. L.
1997a "The Sources of the Account of the Mission to Samaria in Acts 8:5–25." *Novum Testamentum* 39:210–34.
1997b "The New Character Narrative in Luke-Acts and the Synoptic Problem." *Journal of Biblical Literature* 116:291–312.

Dodd, C. H.
1936 *The Apostolic Preaching and Its Development.* London: Hodder & Stoughton.
1953 *According to the Scriptures.* New York: Scribner.

Dölger, F. G.
1950 "Dioskuroi: Das Reiseschiff des Apostels Paulus und seine Schutzgötter: Kult- und Kulturgeschichtliches zu Apg 28,11." Vol. 6 / pp. 276–85 in *Reallexikon für Antike und Christentum.* Edited by T. Klauser et al. Münster: Aschendorff.

Dormeyer, D., and F. Galindo
2003 *Die Apostelgeschichte: Ein Kommentar für die Praxis.* Stuttgart: Katholisches Bibelwerk.

Downing, F. G.
1982   "Common Ground with Paganism in Luke and Josephus." *New Testament Studies* 28:546–59.

Dunn, J. D. G.
1970   *Baptism in the Holy Spirit: A Re-examination of the New Testament Teaching on the Gift of the Spirit in Relation to Pentecostalism Today.* London: SCM.
1975   *Jesus and the Spirit.* London: SCM.
1983   "The Incident at Antioch." *Journal for the Study of the New Testament* 18:3–57.

Dupont, J.
1961   "*Ta hosia ta pista* (Ac xiii 34 = Is lv 3)." *Revue biblique* 68:91–114.

Eckey, W.
2000   *Die Apostelgeschichte: Der Weg des Evangeliums von Jerusalem nach Rom.* Neukirchen-Vluyn: Neukirchener Verlag.

EDNT   *Exegetical Dictionary of the New Testament.* Edited by H. Balz and G. Schneider. 3 vols. Grand Rapids: Eerdmans, 1990–93.

Ehling, K.
2003   "Zwei Anmerkungen zum ἀργύριον in Apg 19,19." *Zeitschrift für die neutestamentliche Wissenschaft* 94:269–75.

Ehrhardt, A.
1958   "The Construction and Purpose of the Acts of the Apostles." *Studia theologica* 12:45–79.

Ellis, E. E.
1974   *The Gospel of Luke.* Revised edition. New Centruy Bible. Greenwood, SC: Attic.

Epp, E. J.
1966   *The Theological Tendency of Codex Bezae Cantabrigiensis in Acts.* Society for New Testament Studies Monograph Series 3. Cambridge: Cambridge University Press.

Esler, P.
1987   *Community and Gospel in Luke-Acts: The Social and Political Motivations of Lucan Theology.* Society for New Testament Studies Monograph Series 57. Cambridge: Cambridge University Press.

Evans, C. A., and J. A. Sanders (eds.)
1993   *Luke and Scripture: The Function of Sacred Tradition in Luke-Acts.* Minneapolis: Fortress.

Ferguson, E.
1982   "Canon Muratori: Date and Provenance." Vol. 17 / pt. 2 / pp. 677–83 in *Studia patristica.* Edited by E. A. Livingstone. Elmsford, NY: Pergamon.

Fernando, A.
1998   *Acts.* NIV Application Commentary. Grand Rapids: Zondervan.

Finegan, J.
1998   *Handbook of Biblical Chronology: Principles of Time Reckoning in the Ancient World and Problems of Chronology in the Bible.* Revised edition. Peabody, MA: Hendrickson.

Finn, T. M.
1985   "The God-Fearers Reconsidered." *Catholic Biblical Quarterly* 47:75–84.

Fitzmyer, J. A.
1972   "David, 'Being Therefore a Prophet . . .' (Acts 2:30)." *Catholic Biblical Quarterly* 43:332–39.
1978   "Crucifixion in Ancient Palestine, Qumran Literature, and the New Testament." *Catholic Biblical Quarterly* 40:493–513.
1979   *A Wandering Aramean: Collected Aramaic Essays.* Society of Biblical Literature Monograph Series 25. Missoula, MT: Scholars Press.
1998   *The Acts of the Apostles: A New Translation with Introduction and Commentary.* Anchor Bible 31. New York: Doubleday.

Foakes-Jackson, F. J.
1951   *The Acts of the Apostles.* Moffatt New Testament Commentary. London: Hodder & Stoughton.

Foakes-Jackson, F. J., and K. Lake (eds.)
1920–33   *The Acts of the Apostles.* 5 vols. London: Macmillan.

Fornara, C. H.
1983   *The Nature of History in Ancient Greece and Rome.* Berkeley: University of California Press.

Fournier, M.
1997   *The Episode at Lystra: A Rhetorical and Semiotic Analysis of Acts 14:7–20a.* American University Studies, Series 7: Theology and Religion 197. New York: Lang.

Fuks, G.
1985   "Where Have All the Freedmen Gone? On an Anomaly in the Jewish Grave Inscriptions from Rome." *Journal for Jewish Studies* 36:25–32.

Fuller, M. E.
2006   *The Restoration of Israel: Israel's Re-
        gathering and the Fate of the Nations
        in Early Jewish Literature and Luke-
        Acts.* Beihefte zur Zeitschrift für die
        neutestamentliche Wissenschaft 138.
        Berlin: de Gruyter.

Gaebelein, A. C.
1912   *The Acts of the Apostles: An
        Exposition.* New York: Our Hope.

Garnsey, P.
1966   "The *Lex Julia* and Appeal under the
        Empire." *Journal of Roman Studies*
        56:167–89.

Gärtner, B.
1955   *The Areopagus Speech and Natural
        Revelation.* Lund, Sweden: Gleerup.
1962   "Paulus und Barnabas in Lystra:
        Zu Apg. 14,8–15." *Svensk exegetisk
        årsbok* 27:83–88.

Gasque, W. W.
1989   *A History of the Interpretation of the
        Acts of the Apostles.* Peabody, MA:
        Hendrickson.

Gathercole, S. J.
2006   *The Preexistent Son: Recovering the
        Christologies of Matthew, Mark, and
        Luke.* Grand Rapids: Eerdmans.

Gaventa, B. R.
1986   *From Darkness to Light: Aspects of
        Conversion in the New Testament.*
        Philadelphia: Fortress.
2003   *Acts.* Abingdon New Testament
        Commentaries. Nashville: Abingdon.
2004   "Theology and Ecclesiology in
        the Miletus Speech: Reflections
        on Content and Context." *New
        Testament Studies* 50:36–50.

Gehring, R.
2004   *House Church and Mission: The
        Importance of Household Structures
        in Early Christianity.* Peabody, MA:
        Hendrickson.

Gilbert, G.
2002   "The List of Nations in Acts 2:
        Roman Propaganda and the Lukan
        Response." *Journal of Biblical
        Literature* 121:497–529.

Gill, D. H.
1999   "Dionysios and Damaris: A Note
        on Acts 17:34." *Catholic Biblical
        Quarterly* 61:483–90.

Gill, D. W. J.
1994a   "Achaia." Pp. 433–53 in *The Book of
        Acts in Its Graeco-Roman Setting.*
        Edited by D. W. J. Gill and C. Gempf.

The Book of Acts in Its First Century
Setting 2. Grand Rapids: Eerdmans.
1994b   "Acts and Roman Religion, A:
        Religion in a Local Setting." Pp. 79–
        92 in *The Book of Acts in Its Graeco-
        Roman Setting.* Edited by D. W. J.
        Gill and C. Gempf. The Book of Acts
        in Its First Century Setting 2. Grand
        Rapids: Eerdmans.

Goldsmith, D.
1968   "Acts 13,33–37: A Pesher on
        2 Samuel 7." *Journal of Biblical
        Literature* 87:321–24.

Gordon, A.
1971   "The Fate of Judas according to Acts
        1:18." *Evangelical Quarterly* 44:97–
        100.

Gordon, R. P.
1974   "Targumic Parallels to Acts xiii,18
        and Didache xiv,3." *Novum
        Testamentum* 16:285–89.

Green, J.
1998   "Salvation to the Ends of the Earth:
        God as the Saviour in the Acts of
        the Apostles." Pp. 83–106 in *Witness
        to the Gospel: The Theology of Acts.*
        Edited by I. H. Marshall and D.
        Peterson. Grand Rapids: Eerdmans.

Greenhut, Z.
1992   "Burial Cave of the Caiaphas
        Family." *Biblical Archaeology Review*
        18/5:28–36, 76.

Greenwood, L. H. G.
1935   *Cicero*, vol. 8: *The Verrine Orations*,
        vol. 2: *Against Verres*, part 2, books
        3–5. Loeb Classical Library 293.
        Cambridge: Harvard University
        Press.

Haacker, K.
1980   "Dibelius und Cornelius: Ein
        Beispiel formgeschichtlicher
        Überlieferungskritik." *Biblische
        Zeitschift* 24:234–51.

Haenchen, E.
1954   "Schriftzitate und Textüberlieferung
        in der Apostelgeschichte." *Zeitschrift
        für Theologie und Kirche* 51:153–67.
1987   *The Acts of the Apostles: A
        Commentary.* Translated by B. Noble
        and G. Shinn. Oxford: Blackwell.

Hamm, D.
2003   "The Tamid Service in Luke-Acts:
        The Cultic Background behind
        Luke's Theology of Worship."
        Catholic Biblical Quarterly 65:215–
        31.

Hanson, R. P. C.
1985   "The Journey of Paul and the Journey of Nikias: An Experiment in Comparative Historiography." Pp. 22–26 in *Studies in Christian Antiquity*. Edited by R. P. C. Hanson. Edinburgh: T&T Clark.

Harnack, A.
1908   *Die Apostelgeschichte*. Beiträge zur Einleitung in das Neue Testament 3. Leipzig: Hinrichs.

Harrison, E. F.
1975   *Acts: The Expanding Church*. Chicago: Moody.

Hauser, H. J.
1979   *Strukturen der Abschlusserzählung der Apostelgeschichte (Apg. 28,16–31)*. Analecta biblica 86. Rome: Pontifical Biblical Institute Press.

Havelaar, H.
1997   "Hellenistic Parallels to Acts 5.1–11 and the Problem of Conflicting Interpretations." *Journal for the Study of the New Testament* 67:63–82.

Hay, D. M.
1973   *Glory at the Right Hand: Psalm 110 in Early Christianity*. Society of Biblical Literature Monograph Series 18. Nashville: Abingdon.

Head, P.
1993   "Acts and the Problem of Its Texts." Pp. 415–44 in *The Book of Acts in Its Ancient Literary Setting*. Edited by B. Winter and A. Clarke. The Book of Acts in Its First Century Setting 1. Grand Rapids: Eerdmans.

Hedrick, C. W.
1981   "Paul's Conversion/Call: A Comparative Analysis of the Three Reports in Acts." *Journal of Biblical Literature* 100:415–32.

Hemer, C. J.
1975   "Euraquilo and Melita." *Journal of Theological Studies*, n.s., 26:100–111.
1985   "First Person Narrative in Acts 27–28." *Tyndale Bulletin* 36:79–109.
1987   "The Name of Felix Again." *Journal for the Study of the New Testament* 31:45–49.
1989   *The Book of Acts in the Setting of Hellenistic History*. Edited by C. H. Gempf. Wissenschaftliche Untersuchungen zum Neuen Testament 49. Tübingen. Mohr.

Hengel, M.
1971–72   "Die Ursprünge der christlichen Mission." *New Testament Studies* 18:15–38.
1974   *Judaism and Hellenism*. Translated by J. Bowden. 2 vols. Philadelphia: Fortress.
1979   *Acts and the History of Earliest Christianity*. London: SCM.
1981   *The Charismatic Leader and His Followers*. Translated by J. Greig. Edinburgh: T&T Clark.
1983   *Between Jesus and Paul: Studies in the Earliest History of Christianity*. Translated by J. Bowden. Philadelphia: Fortress.
1985   *Studies in the Gospel of Mark*. Translated by J. Bowden. Philadelphia: Fortress.
2000   "Ἰουδαία in the Geographical List of Acts 2:9–11 and Syria as 'Greater Judea.'" *Bulletin for Biblical Research* 10:161–80.

Hengel, M., and M. Schwemer
1997   *Paul between Damascus and Antioch: The Unknown Years*. Louisville: Westminster.

Heuger, N.
1984   "'Paulus auf Malta' im Licht der maltesischen Topographie." *Biblische Zeitschrift* 28:86–88.

Hoehner, H. W.
1977   *Chronological Aspects of the Life of Christ*. Grand Rapids: Zondervan.

Holtz, T.
1968   *Untersuchungen über die alttestamentliche Zitate bei Lukas*. Texte und Untersuchungen 104. Berlin: Akademie.

Horgan, M. P.
1979   *Pesharim: Qumran Interpretations of Biblical Books*. Catholic Biblical Quarterly Monograph Series 8. Washington, DC: Catholic Biblical Quarterly Association of America.

Horsley, G. H. R.
1994   "The Politarchs." Pp. 419–31 in *The Book of Acts in Its Graeco-Roman Setting*. Edited by D. W. J. Gill and C. Gempf. The Book of Acts in Its First Century Setting 2. Grand Rapids. Eerdmans.

Horst, P. W. van der
1977   "Peter's Shadow: The Religio-Historical Background of Acts v.15." *New Testament Studies* 23:204–12.

1985   "Hellenistic Parallels to the Acts
        of the Apostles (2:1–47)." *Journal
        for the Study of the New Testament*
        25:49–60.
1989   "Hellenistic Parallels to Acts
        (Chapters 3 and 4)." *Journal for the
        Study of the New Testament* 35:37–46.
1994   "The Altar of the 'Unknown God'
        in Athens (Acts 17.23) and the
        Cults of the 'Unknown Gods' in the
        Greco-Roman World." Pp. 165–202
        in *Hellenism–Judaism–Christianity*.
        Edited by P. W. van der Horst.
        Kampen, Neth.: Kok Pharos.

Horton, F. L., Jr., and J. A. Blakely
2000   "'Behold Water!' Tell el-Hesi and the
        Baptism of the Ethiopian Eunuch."
        Revue biblique 107:56–71.

Hubbard, M. V.
2005   "Urban Uprisings in the Roman
        World: The Social Setting of the
        Mobbing of Sosthenes." *New
        Testament Studies* 51:416–28.

Hurtado, L. W.
2003   *Lord Jesus Christ: Devotion to Jesus
        in Earliest Christianity*. Grand
        Rapids: Eerdmans.

IG   *Inscriptiones graecae*. Berlin: Reimer,
        1873–.

IGRR *Inscriptiones graecae ad res romanas
        pertinentes*. Edited by R. Cagnat et al.
        3 of 4 vols. published. Rome: L'Erma,
        1964.

ILS   *Inscriptiones latinae selectae*. Edited
        by H. Dessau. 3 vols. in 5. Berlin:
        Weidmann, 1896–1916.

Inschr.   *Die Inschriften von Ephesos*. Edited
Eph.   by H. Wankel. 8 vols. in 10. Bonn:
            Habelt, 1979–84.

Jeremias, J.
1937   "Untersuchungen zum
        Quellenproblem der
        Apostelgeschichte." *Zeitschrift für die
        neutestamentliche Wissenschaft* 36.
1969a   *Jerusalem in the Time of Jesus: An
        Investigation into Economic and
        Social Conditions in the Time of
        Jesus*. London: SCM.
1969b   "Paulus als Hillelit." Pp. 88–94
        in *Neotestamentica et semitica:
        Studies in Honor of Matthew Black*.
        Edited by E. E. Ellis and M. Wilcox.
        Edinburgh: T&T Clark.

Jervell, J.
1972   *Luke and the People of God*.
        Minneapolis: Augsburg.
1996   *The Theology of the Acts of the
        Apostles*. New Testament Theology.
        Cambridge: Cambridge University
        Press.
1998   *Die Apostelgeschichte*. Kritisch-
        exegetischer Kommentar über
        das Neue Testament 3. Göttingen:
        Vandenhoeck & Ruprecht.

Jewett, P.
1979   *A Chronology of Paul's Life*.
        Philadelphia: Fortress.
1997   "Mapping the Route of Paul's
        'Second Missionary Journey' from
        Dorylaeum to Troas." *Tyndale
        Bulletin* 48:1–22.

Johnson, L. T.
1992   *The Acts of the Apostles*. Sacra pagina
        5. Collegeville, MN: Liturgical Press.

Jones, D. L.
1970   "The Title *Christos* in Luke-Acts."
        Catholic Biblical Quarterly 32:69–76.

Judge, E. A.
1971   "The Decrees of Caesar at
        Thessalonica." *Reformed Theological
        Review* 30:1–7.

Käsemann, E.
1964a   "Ministry and Community in the
        New Testament." Pp. 89–94 in *New
        Testament Essays*. Edited by E.
        Käsemann. London: SCM.
1964b   "The Disciples of John the Baptist
        in Ephesus." Pp. 136–48 in *New
        Testament Essays*. Edited by E.
        Käsemann. London: SCM.
1969   *New Testament Questions for Today*.
        Philadelphia: Fortress.

Keck, L. E., and J. L. Martyn (eds.)
1966   *Studies in Luke-Acts: Essays
        Presented in Honor of Paul Schubert*.
        Nashville: Abingdon.

Kee, H. C.
1990   "The Transformation of the
        Synagogue after 70 CE." *New
        Testament Studies* 36:1–24.

Kern, P. H.
2003   "Paul's Conversion and Luke's
        Portrayal of Character in Acts 8–10."
        Tyndale Bulletin 54:63–80.

Kilgallen, J. J.
1976   *The Stephen Speech: A Literary and
        Redactional Study of Acts 7,2–52*.
        Analecta biblica 67. Rome: Pontifical
        Biblical Institute Press.
1998   "Your Servant Jesus Whom You
        Anointed (Acts 4,27)." *Revue biblique*
        105:185–201.

2000 "The Apostles Whom He Chose because of the Holy Spirit: A Suggestion regarding Acts 1,2." *Biblica* 81:414–17.

2002 "'With Many Other Words' (Acts 2,40): Theological Assumptions in Peter's Pentecostal Speech." *Biblica* 83:71–87.

2003a "Hostility to Paul in Pisidian Antioch (Acts 13,45)—Why?" *Biblica* 84:1–15.

2003b "Acts 17,22b–31—What Kind of Speech Is This?" *Revue biblique* 110:417–24.

Kim, S.
1981 *The Origin of Paul's Gospel*. Grand Rapids: Eerdmans.

Kistemaker, S.
1990 *Acts*. New Testament Commentary. Grand Rapids: Baker Academic.

Klauck, H.-J.
1982 "Gütergemeinschaft in der klassiken Antike, Qumran und im Neuen Testament." *Revue de Qumran* 11:47–79.

2000 *The Religious Context of Early Christianity: A Guide to Greco-Roman Religions*. Translated by B. McNeil. Studies of the New Testament and Its World. Edinburgh: T&T Clark.

2003 *Magic and Paganism in Early Christianity: The World of the Acts of the Apostles*. Minneapolis: Fortress.

Knibbe, D.
1995 "Via sacra ephesiaca: New Aspects of the Cult of Artemis Ephesia." Pp. 141–54 in *Ephesos: Metropolis of Asia*. Edited by H. Koester. Valley Forge, PA: Trinity.

Kodell, J.
1974 "'The Word of God Grew'—the Ecclesial Tendency of *logos* in Acts 6:7; 12:24; 19:20." *Biblica* 55:505–19.

Kraabel, A. T.
1981 "The Disappearance of the 'God-Fearers.'" *Numen* 28:113–26.

Kraus, T. J.
1999 "'Uneducated,' 'Ignorant,' or Even 'Illiterate'? Aspects and Background for an Understanding of ΑΓΡΑΜΜΑΤΟΙ and ΙΔΙΩΤΑΙ in Acts 4.13." *New Testament Studies* 45:434–49.

Kreitzer, L. J.
1987 "A Numismatic Clue to Acts 19:23–41: The Ephesian Cistophorai of Claudius and Agrippina." *Journal for the Study of the New Testament* 30:59–70.

Kremer, J.
1973 *Pfingstbericht und Pfingstgeschehen: Eine exegetische Untersuchung zu Apg 2,1–13*. Stuttgarter Bibel-Studien 63–64. Stuttgart: Katholisches Bibelwerk.

Kümmel, W. G.
1972 *The New Testament: The History of the Investigation of Its Problems*. Translated by S. M. Gilmour and H. C. Kee. Nashville: Abingdon.

Kurz, W.
1997 "Effects of Variant Narrators in Acts 10–11." *New Testament Studies* 43:570–86.

Lachs, S. T.
1977 "The Pharisees and Sadducees on Angels: A Reexamination of Acts xxiii 8." *Gratz College Annual of Jewish Studies* 6:35–42.

Ladouceur, D. J.
1980 "Hellenistic Preconceptions of Shipwreck and Pollution as a Context for Acts 27–28." *Harvard Theological Review* 73:435–49.

Lake, K., and H. J. Cadbury
1933 *The Acts of the Apostles*, vol. 4: *English Translation and Commentary*. Edited by F. J. Foakes-Jackson and K. Lake. London: Macmillan.

Larkin, W. J., Jr.
1995 *Acts*. IVP New Testament Commentary 5. Downers Grove, IL: InterVarsity.

Leary, T. J.
1990 "The 'Aprons' of St. Paul—Acts 19:12." *Journal of Theological Studies* 41:527–29.

Le Cornu, H., and J. Shulam
2003 *A Commentary on the Jewish Roots of Acts*. 2 vols. Jerusalem: Academon.

Lentz, J. C., Jr.
1993 *Luke's Portrait of Paul*. Society for New Testament Studies Monograph Series 77. Cambridge: Cambridge University Press.

Leon, H. J.
1960 *The Jews of Ancient Rome*. Philadelphia: Jewish Publication Society. Reprint, Peabody, MA: Hendrickson, 1995.

Levine, L. I.
2005 *The Ancient Synagogue: The First Thousand Years*. New Haven: Yale University Press.

Levinskaya, A.
1995   *The Book of Acts in Its Diaspora Setting*. The Book of Acts in Its First Century Setting 5. Grand Rapids: Eerdmans.

Lincoln, A. T.
1984–85   "Theology and History in the Interpretation of Luke's Pentecost." *Expository Times* 96:204–9.

Litwak, K. D.
2005   *Echoes of Scripture in Luke-Acts: Telling the History of God's People Intertextually*. Journal for the Study of the New Testament: Supplement Series 282. New York: T&T Clark.

Llewelyn, S. R.
2001   "The Use of Sunday for Meetings of Believers in the New Testament." *Novum Testamentum* 43:205–23.

L&N   *Greek-English Lexicon of the New Testament: Based on Semantic Domains*. Edited by J. P. Louw and E. A. Nida. 2 vols. 2nd edition. New York: United Bible Societies, 1989.

Longenecker, B.
2004   "Lukan Aversion to Humps and Hollows: The Case of Acts 11:27–12:25." *New Testament Studies* 50:185–204.

Longenecker, R. N.
1981   "The Acts of the Apostles: Introduction, Text and Exposition." Vol. 9 / pp. 207–573 in *The Expositor's Bible Commentary*. Edited by F. E. Gaebelein. Grand Rapids: Zondervan.

Löning, K.
1974   "Die Korneliustradition." *Biblische Zeitschrift* 18:1–19.

Lösch, S.
1931   "Die Dankesrede des Tertullus: Apg 24.1–4." *Theologische Quartelschrift* 112:295–319.

Lovestam, E.
1962   *A Study of Acts 13:32–37*. Lund, Sweden: Gleerup.

LSJ   *A Greek-English Lexicon*. By H. G. Liddell, R. Scott, and H. S. Jones. 9th edition. Oxford: Clarendon, 1968.

Lyons, W. J.
1997   "The Words of Gamaliel (Acts 5,38–39) and the Irony of Indeterminacy." *Journal for the Study of the New Testament* 68:23–49.

Maddox, R.
1982   *The Purpose of Luke-Acts*. Forschungen zur Religion und Literatur des Alten und Neuen Testaments 127. Göttingen: Vandenhoeck & Ruprecht.

Malherbe, A. J.
1985–86   "'Not in a Corner': Early Christian Apologetic in Acts 26:26." *Second Century* 5:193–210.

MAMA   *Monumenta Asiae Minoris antiqua*. Manchester, UK: Manchester University Press, 1928–.

Manson, T. W.
1938   "Sadducee and Pharisee: The Origin and Significance of the Names." *Bulletin of the John Rylands Library* 22:144–59.

Marguerat, D.
1998   "Voyages et voyageurs dans le livre des Actes et la culture gréco-romaine." *Revue d'histoire et de philosophie religieuses* 78:33–59.

2002   *The First Christian Historian: Writing the "Acts of the Apostles."* Translated by K. McKinney, G. J. Laughery, and R. Bauckham. Society for New Testament Studies Monograph Series 121. Cambridge: Cambridge University Press.

Marshall, I. H.
1970   "The Resurrection in the Acts of the Apostles." Pp. 92–107 in *Apostolic History and the Gospel*. Edited by W. Gasque and R. Martin. Grand Rapids: Eerdmans.

1977   "The Significance of Pentecost." *Scottish Journal of Theology* 30:347–69.

1980   *The Acts of the Apostles: An Introduction and Commentary*. Tyndale New Testament Commentaries 5. Grand Rapids: Eerdmans.

2002   "The Meaning of the Verb 'Baptize.'" Pp. 8–24 in *Dimensions of Baptism: Biblical and Theological Studies*. Edited by S. E. Porter and A. R. Cross. Journal for the Study of the New Testament: Supplement Series 234. Sheffield: Sheffield Academic Press.

Marshall, I. H., and D. Petersen
1998   *Witness to the Gospel: The Theology of Acts*. Grand Rapids: Eerdmans.

Mastin, B. A.
1976   "Scaeva the Chief Priest." *Journal of Theological Studies* 27:405–12.

McDonald, W. A.
1940   "Archaeology and St. Paul's Journeys in Greek Lands." *Biblical Archaeology* 3:18–24.

McKelvey, R. J.
1969   *The New Temple: The Church in the New Testament.* Oxford Theological Monographs. Oxford: Oxford University Press.

McKnight, S.
2001   "Jesus and the Twelve." *Bulletin for Biblical Research* 11:203–31.

Mealand, D.
1977   "Community of Goods and Utopian Allusions in Acts II–IV." *Journal of Theological Studies* 28:96–99.

1989   "The Phrase 'Many Proofs' in Acts 1,3 and in Hellenistic Writers." *Zeitschrift für die neutestamentliche Wissenschaft* 80:134–35.

1990   "Acts 28.30–31 and Its Hellenistic Greek Vocabulary." *New Testament Studies* 36:583–97.

Meier, J.
1991   *A Marginal Jew: Rethinking the Historical Jesus,* vol. 1: *The Roots of the Problem and the Person.* Anchor Bible Reference Library. New York: Doubleday.

2001   *A Marginal Jew: Rethinking the Historical Jesus,* vol. 3: *Companions and Competitors.* Anchor Bible Reference Library. New York: Doubleday.

Menard, J. E.
1957   "*Pais Theou* as Messianic Title in the Book of Acts." *Catholic Biblical Quarterly* 19:83–92.

Menzies, R. P.
1991   *The Development of Early Christian Pneumatology with Special Reference to Luke-Acts.* Journal for the Study of the New Testament: Supplement Series 54. Sheffield: Sheffield Academic Press.

Metzger, B. M.
1944   "St. Paul and the Magicians." *Princeton Seminary Journal* 38:27–30.

1970   "Ancient Astrological Geography and Acts 2:9–11." Pp. 123–33 in *Apostolic History and the Gospel.* Edited by W. Gasque and R. Martin. Grand Rapids: Eerdmans.

1971   *A Textual Commentary on the Greek New Testament.* New York: United Bible Societies.

Michiels, R.
1985   "The 'Model of Church' in the First Christian Community of Jerusalem: Ideal and Reality." *Louvain Studies* 10:303–23.

Miles, G. B., and G. Trompf
1976   "Luke and Antiphon: The Theology of Acts 27–28." *Harvard Theological Review* 69:259–67.

MM   *The Vocabulary of the Greek Testament.* By J. H. Moulton and G. Milligan. London: Hodder & Stoughton, 1930. Reprint, Peabody, MA: Hendrickson, 1997.

Moessner, D. P.
1988   "The Ironic Fulfillment of Israel's Glory." Pp. 35–50 in *Luke-Acts and the Jewish People: Eight Critical Perspectives.* Edited by J. Tyson. Minneapolis: Augsburg.

1989   "Paul in Acts: Preacher of Eschatological Repentance to Israel." *New Testament Studies* 34:96–104.

1996   "The Script of the Scriptures in Acts: Suffering as God's Plan (βουλή) for the World for the Release of Sins." Pp. 218–50 in *History, Literature, and Society in the Book of Acts.* Edited by B. Witherington III. Cambridge: Cambridge University Press.

Mommsen, T.
1901   "Die Rechtsverhältnisse des Apostels Paulus." *Zeitschrift für die neutestamentliche Wissenschaft* 2:81–96.

Moore, T. S.
1997   "To the End of the Earth: The Geographical and Ethnic Universalism of Acts 1:8 in Light of Isaianic Influence on Luke." *Journal of the Evangelical Theological Society* 40:389–99.

Mosley, A. W.
1965–66 "Historical Reporting in the Ancient World." *New Testament Studies* 12:8–25.

Moule, C. F. D.
1959   *An Idiom-Book of New Testament Greek.* 2nd edition. Cambridge: Cambridge University Press.

1966   "The Christology of Acts." Pp. 159–85 in *Studies in Luke-Acts: Essays Presented in Honor of Paul Schubert.* Edited by L. E. Keck and J. L. Martyn. Nashville: Abingdon.

Moulton, J. H., and N. Turner
1963   *A Grammar of New Testament Greek*,
        vol. 3: *Syntax*. Edinburgh: T&T
        Clark.
Murphy-O'Connor, J.
1983   *St. Paul's Corinth: Texts and
        Archaeology*. Good News Studies 6.
        Wilmington, DE: Glazier.
Mussner, F.
1966   "In den letzten Tagen (Apg 2,17a)."
        Biblische Zeitschrift 5:263–65.
NA²⁷   *Novum Testamentum Graece*. Edited
        by (E. and E. Nestle), B. Aland, et
        al. 27th revised edition. Stuttgart:
        Deutsche Bibelgesellschaft, 1993.
Nauck, W.
1956   "Die Tradition und Komposition
        der Aeropagrede." *Zeitschrift für
        Theologie und Kirche* 53:11–52.
NewDocs   *New Documents Illustrating Early
        Christianity*. Edited by G. H. R.
        Horsley and S. Llewelyn. North Ryde,
        NSW: Ancient History Documentary
        Research Center, 1976–.
Neyrey, J.
2003   "'Teaching You in Public and from
        House to House' (Acts 20.20):
        Unpacking a Cultural Stereotype."
        *Journal for the Study of the New
        Testament* 26:69–102.
NIDNTT   *The New International Dictionary
        of New Testament Theology*. Edited
        by L. Coenen, E. Beyreuther, and
        H. Bietenhard. English translation
        edited by C. Brown. 4 vols. Grand
        Rapids: Zondervan, 1975–86.
Noack, B.
1962   "The Day of Pentecost in Jubilees,
        Qumran, and Acts." *Annual of the
        Swedish Theological Institute* 1:73–
        95.
Nobbs, A.
2006   "What Do Ancient Historians Make
        of the New Testament?" *Tyndale
        Bulletin* 57:285–90.
Nock, A. D.
1933   "Note XIV: Paul and the Magus." Pp.
        164–88 in *The Acts of the Apostles*,
        vol. 5: *Additional Notes to the
        Commentary*. Edited by F. J. Foakes-
        Jackson and K. Lake. London:
        Macmillan.
Nolland, J.
1977   "Luke's Readers: A Study of Luke
        4.2–28; Acts 13.46; 18.6; 28.28
        and Luke 21.5–36." DPhil diss.,
        Cambridge University.

O'Brien, P. T.
1999   "Mission, Witness, and the Coming
        of the Spirit." *Bulletin for Biblical
        Research* 9:203–14.
Ogilvie, R. M.
1958   "Phoenix." *Journal of Theological
        Studies*, n.s., 9:308–14.
OGIS   *Orientis graeci inscriptiones selectae*.
        Edited by W. Dittenberger. 2 vols.
        Leipzig: Hirzel, 1903–5.
Omerzu, H.
2002   *Der Prozeß des Paulus: Eine
        exegetische und rechtshistorische
        Untersuchung der Apostelgeschichte*.
        Beihefte zur Zeitschrift für die
        neutestamentliche Wissenschaft 115.
        Berlin: de Gruyter.
O'Neill, J. C.
1961   *The Theology of Acts in Its Historical
        Setting*. London: SPCK.
Oster, R. E.
1976   "The Ephesian Artemis as an
        Opponent of Early Christianity."
        Jahrbuch für Antike und Christentum
        19:24–44.
O'Toole, R. F.
1978   *Acts 26, the Christological Climax of
        Paul's Defense*. Analecta biblica 78.
        Rome: Pontifical Biblical Institute
        Press.
1979   "Christ's Resurrection in Acts 13,13–
        52." *Biblica* 60:361–72.
1984   *The Unity of Luke's Theology: An
        Analysis of Luke-Acts*. Good News
        Studies 9. Wilmington, DE: Glazier.
Overbeck, F.
1919   *Christentum und Kultur*. Edited by
        C. A. Bernoulli. Basel: Schwabe.
Palmer, D. W.
1993   "Acts and the Ancient Historical
        Monograph." Pp. 1–29 in *The Book
        of Acts in Its Ancient Literary Setting*.
        Edited by B. W. Winter and A. D.
        Clarke. The Book of Acts in Its First
        Century Setting 1. Grand Rapids:
        Eerdmans.
Pao, D. W.
2000   *Acts and the Isaianic New Exodus*.
        Wissenschafliche Untersuchungen
        zum Neuen Testament 2.130.
        Tübingen: Mohr.
Parker, F.
2003   "The Terms 'Angel' and 'Spirit' in
        Acts 23,8." *Biblica* 84:344–65.
Parsons, M. C., and R. I. Pervo
1993   *Rethinking the Unity of Luke and
        Acts*. Minneapolis: Fortress.

Pelikan, J.
2005   *Acts.* Brazos Theological Commentary on the Bible. Grand Rapids: Brazos.

Penner, T.
2004   *In Praise of Christian Origins: Stephen and the Hellenists in Lukan Apologetic Historiography.* Emory Studies in Early Christianity. London: T&T Clark.

Pervo, R. I.
1987   *Profit with Delight: The Literary Genre of the Acts of the Apostles.* Philadelphia: Fortress.

Pesch, R.
1966   *Die Vision des Stephanus: Apg 7,55–56 im Rahmen der Apostelgeschichte.* Stuttgarter Bibel-Studien 12. Stuttgart: Katholisches Bibelwerk.

1986a   *Die Apostelgeschichte (Apg 1–12).* Evangelisch-Katholischer Kommentar zum Neuen Testament 5.1. Zurich: Benzinger/Neukirchen-Vluyn: Neukirchener Verlag.

1986b   *Die Apostelgeschichte (Apg 13–28).* Evangelisch-Katholischer Kommentar zum Neuen Testament 5.2. Zurich: Benzinger/Neukirchen-Vluyn: Neukirchener Verlag.

Peterson, D.
1993   "The Motif of Fulfillment and the Purpose of Luke-Acts." Pp. 83–104 in *The Book of Acts in Its Ancient Literary Setting.* Edited by B. W. Winter and A. Clarke. The Book of Acts in Its First Century Setting 1. Grand Rapids: Eerdmans.

1998   "The Worship of the New Community." Pp. 373–95 in *Witness to the Gospel: The Theology of Acts.* Edited by I. H. Marshall and D. Peterson. Grand Rapids: Eerdmans.

PGM   *Papyri graecae magicae.* Edited by K. Preisendanz. 2 vols. Berlin: Teubner, 1928–31.

Phillips, T. E.
2005   "Paul as a Role Model in Acts: The 'We'-Passages in Acts 16 and Beyond." Pp. 49–63 in *Acts and Ethics.* Edited by T. E. Phillips. New Testament Monographs 9. Sheffield: Sheffield Phoenix.

Pillai, C. A. J.
1980   *Apostolic Interpretation of History—a Commentary on Acts 13:16–41.* Hicksville, NY: Exposition.

Plümacher, E.
1979   "Die Apostelgeschichte als historische Monographie." Pp. 457–66 in *Les Actes des apôtres: Traditions, redaction, théologie.* Edited by J. Kremer. Bibliotheca ephemeridum theologicarum loveniensium 48. Louvain: Leuven University Press.

Pokorny, P.
1973   "Die Romfahrt des Paulus und der antike Roman." *Zeitschrift für die neutestamentliche Wissenschaft* 64:233–44.

Polhill, J. B.
1992   *Acts.* New American Commentary 26. Nashville: Broadman.

Porter, S. E.
1999   *The Paul of Acts: Essays in Literary Criticism, Rhetoric, and Theology.* Wissenschaftliche Untersuchungen zum Neuen Testament 2.115. Tübingen: Mohr. Reprint, Peabody, MA: Hendrickson, 2001.

2005   "The Genre of Acts and the Ethics of Discourse." Pp. 1–15 in *Acts and Ethics.* Edited by T. E. Phillips. New Testament Monographs 9. Sheffield: Sheffield Phoenix.

Praeder, S. M.
1984   "Acts 27:1–28:16: Sea Voyages in Ancient Literature and the Theology of Luke-Acts." *Catholic Biblical Quarterly* 46:683–706.

1987   "The Problem of First Person Narration in Acts." *Novum Testamentum* 29:193–218.

Rackham, R. B.
1901   *The Acts of the Apostles: An Exposition.* Westminster Commentaries. London: Methuen. Reprint, Grand Rapids: Baker Academic, 1978.

Ramsey, W. M.
1895   *St. Paul the Traveller and Roman Citizen.* London: Hodder & Stoughton.

Rapske, B.
1994a   "Acts, Travel, and Shipwreck." Pp. 1–47 in *The Book of Acts in Its Graeco-Roman Setting.* Edited by D. W. J. Gill and C. Gempf. The Book of Acts in Its First Century Setting 2. Grand Rapids: Eerdmans.

1994b   *The Book of Acts and Paul in Roman Custody.* The Book of Acts in Its

First Century Setting 3. Grand
Rapids: Eerdmans.

1998   "Opposition to the Plan of God and
Persecution." Pp. 235–56 in *Witness
to the Gospel: The Theology of Acts*.
Edited by I. H. Marshall and D.
Peterson. Grand Rapids: Eerdmans.

Ravens, D.

1995   *Luke and the Restoration of Israel*.
Journal for the Study of the New
Testament: Supplement Series 119.
Sheffield: Sheffield Academic Press.

Reeder, E. D.

1987   "The Mother of the Gods and
a Hellenistic Bronze Matrix."
American Journal of Archaeology
91:423–40.

Reese, B.

1975   "The Apostle Paul's Exercise of
His Rights as a Roman Citizen as
Recorded in the Book of Acts."
Evangelical Quarterly 47:138–45.

Reich, R.

1991   "Ossuary Inscriptions from the
Caiaphas Tomb." *Jerusalem
Perspective* 4/4–5:13–22.

Reicke, B.

1948   "Die Mahlzeit mit Paulus auf
den Wellen des Mittelmeers Act
27,33–38." *Theologische Zeitschrift*
4:401–10.

Rengstorf, K. H.

1995   "The Election of Matthias." Pp.
178–92 in *Current Issues in New
Testament Interpretation*. Edited by
W. Klassen and G. F. Snyder. New
York: Harper.

Ridderbos, H. N.

1962   *The Speeches of Peter in the Acts of
the Apostles*. London: Tyndale.

Riesner, R.

1998   *Paul's Early Period: Chronology,
Mission Strategy, Theology*. Grand
Rapids: Eerdmans.

Robbins, V. K.

1978   "By Land and by Sea: The We-
Passages and Ancient Sea Voyages."
Pp. 215–42 in *Perspectives on
Luke-Acts*. Edited by C. H. Talbert.
Edinburgh: T&T Clark.

Robert, J., and L. Robert

1970   "Bulletin épigraphique." *Revue des
études grecques* 83/633:474–75.

Robertson, A. T.

1934   *A Grammar of the Greek New
Testament in the Light of Historical
Research*. Nashville: Broadman.

Robinson, A. B., and R. W. Wall

2006   *Called to Be Church: The Book of
Acts for a New Day*. Grand Rapids:
Eerdmans.

Robinson, E., and E. Smith

1856   *Biblical Researches in Palestine*, vol.
2. London: Murray.

Robinson, T. A.

1988   *The Bauer Thesis Examined: The
Geography of Heresy in the Early
Christian Church*. Lewiston, NY/
Queenston, ON: Mellen.

Roloff, J.

1988   *Apostelgeschichte*. 2nd edition.
Das Neue Testament Deutsch
5. Göttingen: Vandenhoeck &
Ruprecht.

Ropes, J. H.

1926   *The Acts of the Apostles*, vol. 3: *The
Text of Acts*. Edited by F. J. Foakes-
Jackson and K. Lake. London:
Macmillan.

Rordorf, W.

1977   "Sonntagnachtgottesdienste der
christlichen Frühzeit?" *Zeitschrift für
die neutestamentliche Wissenschaft*
68:138–41.

Rosner, B.

1993   "Acts and Biblical History." Pp. 65–
82 in *The Book of Acts in Its Ancient
Literary Setting*. Edited by B. W.
Winter and A. D. Clarke. The Book
of Acts in Its First Century Setting 1.
Grand Rapids: Eerdmans.

1998   "The Progress of the Word." Pp.
215–33 in *Witness to the Gospel: The
Theology of Acts*. Edited by I. H.
Marshall and D. Peterson. Grand
Rapids: Eerdmans.

Rothschild, C. K.

2004   *Luke-Acts and the Rhetoric of History*.
Wissenschaftliche Untersuchungen
zum Neuen Testament 2.175.
Tübingen: Mohr.

Sanders, E. P.

1992   *Judaism: Practice and Belief: 63
B.C.E.–66 C.E.* London: SCM

Sanders, J. T.

1987   *The Jews in Luke-Acts*. Philadelphia:
Fortress.

Schille, G.

1984   *Die Apostelgeschichte des Lukas*.
2nd edition. Theologischer
Handkommentar zum Neuen
Testament 5. Berlin: Evangelische
Verlagsanstalt.

Schnabel, E. J.
2002   *Urchristliche Mission*. Wuppertal: Brockhaus.
2004   *Early Christian Mission*. 2 vols. Downers Grove, IL: InterVarsity/ London: Apollos.

Schneider, G.
1977   "Der Zweck des lukanischen Doppelwerks." *Biblische Zeitschrift* 21:45–66.
1980   *Die Apostelgeschichte*, vol. 1: *Einleitung, Kommentar zu Kap. 1,1–8,40*. Herders Theologischer Kommentar zum Neuen Testament 5.1. Freiburg im Breisgau: Herder.
1982   *Die Apostelgeschichte*, vol. 2: *Kommentar zu Kap. 9,1–28,31*. Herders Theologischer Kommentar zum Neuen Testament 5.2. Freiburg im Breisgau: Herder.

Schreiber, S.
2002   "Aktualisierung göttlichen Handelns am Pfingsttag: Das frühjüdische Fest in Apg 2,1." *Zeitschrift für die neutestamentliche Wissenschaft* 93:58–77.

Schröter, J.
2005   "Lukas als Historiograph: Das lukanische Doppelwerk und die Entdeckung der christlichen Heilsgeschichte." Pp. 237–62 in *Die antike Historiographie und die Anfänge der christlichen Geschichtsschreibung*. Edited by E.M. Becker. Beihefte zur Zeitschrift für die neutestamentliche Wissenschaft 129. Berlin: de Gruyter.

Schürer, E.
1973–87   *The History of the Jewish People in the Age of Jesus Christ (175 B.C.–A.D. 135)*. Translated by T. A. Burkill et al. Revised and edited by G. Vermes and F. Millar. 3 vols. in 4. Edinburgh: T&T Clark.

Schwank, B.
1990   "Also doch Malta? Spurensuche auf Kefalonia." *Bibel und Kirche* 45:43–46.

Schweizer, E.
1966   "Concerning the Speeches in Acts." Pp. 208–16 in *Studies in Luke-Acts: Essays Presented in Honor of Paul Schubert*. Edited by L. E. Keck and J. L. Martyn. Nashville: Abingdon.

Schwemer, A. M.
1998   "Paulus in Antiochien." *Biblische Zeitschrift*, n.s., 42:161–80.

Scobie, C. H. H.
1972–73   "The Origins and Development of Samaritan Christianity." *New Testament Studies* 19:39–414.

Scott, J. J., Jr.
1997   "The Church's Progress to the Council of Jerusalem according to the Book of Acts." *Bulletin for Biblical Research* 7:205–24.

Scott, J. M.
1995   *Paul and the Nations: The Old Testament and Jewish Background of Paul's Mission to the Nations with Special Reference to the Destination of Galatians*. Wissenschaftliche Untersuchungen zum Neuen Testament 84. Tübingen: Mohr Siebeck.
2000   "Acts 2,9–11 as an Anticipation of the Mission to the Nations." Pp. 87–123 in *The Mission of the Early Church to Jews and Gentiles*. Edited by J. Ådna and H. Kvalbein. Wissenschaftliche Untersuchungen zum Neuen Testament 127. Tübingen: Mohr Siebeck.

Seccombe, D.
1998   "The New People of God." Pp. 349–72 in *Witness to the Gospel: The Theology of Acts*. Edited by I. H. Marshall and D. Peterson. Grand Rapids: Eerdmans.

Shauf, S.
2005   *Theology as History, History as Theology: Paul in Ephesus in Acts 19*. Beihefte zur Zeitschrift für die neutestamentliche Wissenschaft 133. Berlin: de Gruyter.

Sherwin-White, A. N.
1939   *The Roman Citizenship*. Oxford: Oxford University Press.
1963   *Roman Society and Roman Law in the New Testament*. Oxford: Clarendon.

SIG   *Sylloge inscriptionum graecarum*. Edited by W. Dittenberger. 3rd edition. 4 vols. Leipzig: Hirzel, 1898– 1901, 1915–24.

Simon, M.
1953   *St. Stephen and the Hellenists in the Primitive Church*. New York: Longman, Green & Unwin.

Smalley, S. S.
1961–62   "The Christology of Acts." *Expository Times* 73:358–62.
1973   "The Christology of Acts Again." Pp. 79–93 in *Christ and Spirit in the New*

Testament. Edited by B. Lindars and S. Smalley. Cambridge: Cambridge University Press.

Smith, J.
1880   *The Voyage and Shipwreck of Paul.* 4th edition. London: Longmans, Green.

Smith, M.
1971   "Zealots and Sicarii: Their Origins and Relation." *Harvard Theological Review* 64:1–19.

Soards, M. L.
1994   *The Speeches in Acts: Their Content, Context, and Concerns.* Louisville: Westminster/John Knox.

Spencer, F. S.
1992   *The Portrait of Philip in Acts: A Study of Roles and Relations.* Journal for the Study of the New Testament: Supplement Series 67. Sheffield: Sheffield Academic Press.
2004   *Journeying through Acts: A Literary-Cultural Reading.* Peabody, MA: Hendrickson.

Squires, J. T.
1993   *The Plan of God in Luke-Acts.* Society for the New Testament Monograph Series 76. Cambridge: Cambridge University Press.
1998   "The Plan of God in the Acts of the Apostles." Pp. 19–39 in *Witness to the Gospel: The Theology of Acts.* Edited by I. H. Marshall and D. Peterson. Grand Rapids: Eerdmans.

Staats, R.
1975   "Die Sonntagnachtgottesdienste der christlichen Frühzeit." *Zeitschrift für die neutestamentliche Wissenschaft* 66:242–63.

Stählin, G.
1980   *Die Apostelgeschichte.* Das Neue Testament Deutsch 5. Göttingen: Vandenhoeck & Ruprecht.

Stanton, G.
1974   *Jesus of Nazareth in New Testament Preaching.* Society for the Study of the New Testament Monograph Series 27. Cambridge: Cambridge University Press.
1994   "Jesus of Nazareth: A Magician and a False Prophet Who Deceived God's People?" Pp. 164–80 in *Jesus of Nazareth, Lord and Christ: Essays on the Historical Jesus and New Testament Christology.* Edited by J. B. Green and M. Turner. Grand Rapids: Eerdmans.

Steck, O. H.
1967   *Israel und das gewaltsame Geschick der Propheten: Untersuchungen zur Überlieferung des deuteronomistischen Geschichtsbildes im Alten Testament, Spätjudentum und Urchristentum.* Wissenschaftliche Monographien zum Alten und Neuen Testament 23. Neukirchen-Vluyn: Neukirchener Verlag.

Stendahl, K.
1963   "The Apostle Paul and the Introspective Conscience of the West." *Harvard Theological Review* 56:199–215.
1976   *Paul among Jews and Gentiles, and Other Essays.* Philadelphia: Fortress.

Stenschke, C. W.
1999   *Luke's Portrait of Gentiles prior to Their Coming to Faith.* Wissenschaftliche Untersuchungen zum Neuen Testament 2.108. Tübingen: Mohr.

Sterck-Degueldre, J.-P.
2004   *Eine Frau namens Lydia: Zu Geschichte und Komposition in Apostelgeschichte 16.11–15, 40.* Wissenschaftlitche Untersuchungen zum Neuen Testament 2.176. Tübingen: Mohr.

Sterling, G. E.
1992   *Historiography and Self-Definition: Josephos, Luke-Acts, and Apologetic Historiography.* Novum Testamentum Supplement 64. Leiden: Brill.

Stipp, H.-J.
1999   "Vier Gestalten einer Toten-erweckungserzählung (1 Kön 17,17–24; 2 Kön 4,8–37; Apg 9,36–42; Apg 20,7–12)." *Biblica* 80:43–77.

Stoops, R. F.
1989   "Riot and Assembly: The Social Context of Acts 19.23–41." *Journal of Biblical Literature* 108:73–91.

Stott, J. R. W.
1990   *The Message of Acts.* Bible Speaks Today. Downers Grove, IL: InterVarsity.

Strauss, M. L.
1995   *The Davidic Messiah in Luke-Acts: The Promise and Its Fulfillment in Luke's Christology.* Journal for the Study of the New Testament: Supplement Series 110. Sheffield: Sheffield Academic Press.

Str-B   *Kommentar zum Neuen Testament aus Talmud und Midrasch*. By H. L. Strack and P. Billerbeck. 6 vols. Munich: Beck, 1922–61.

Strelan, R.
2000   "Recognizing the Gods (Acts 14:8–10)." *New Testament Studies* 46:488–503.
2001   "The Running Prophet (Acts 8:30)." *Novum Testamentum* 43:31–38.

Sweeney, J. P.
2002   "Stephen's Speech (Acts 7:2–53): Is It as 'Anti-temple' as Is Frequently Alleged?" *Trinity Journal*, n.s., 23:185–210.

Sylva, D. D.
1987   "The Meaning and Function of Acts 7:46–50." *Journal of Biblical Literature* 106:261–75.

Taeger, J.-W.
1982   *Der Mensch und sein Heil: Studien zum Bild des Menschen und zur Sicht der Bekehrung bei Lukas*. Studien zum Neuen Testament 14. Gütersloh: Mohn.

Tajra, H. W.
1989   *The Trial of St. Paul: A Juridical Exegesis of the Second Half of the Acts of the Apostles*. Wissenschaftliche Untersuchungen zum Neuen Testament 2.35. Tübingen: Mohr.

Talbert, C. H.
1966   *Luke and the Gnostics: An Examination of the Lucan Purpose*. Nashville: Abingdon.
1997   *Reading Acts: A Literary and Theological Commentary on the Acts of the Apostles*. New York: Crossroad.

Talbert, C. H., and J. H. Hayes
1995   "A Theology of Sea Storms in Luke-Acts." Pp. 321–36 in *Society of Biblical Literature Seminar Papers, 1995*. Edited by E. H. Lovering. Atlanta: Scholars Press.

Tannehill, R.
1985   "Israel in Luke-Acts: A Tragic Story." *Journal of Biblical Literature* 104:69–85.

Taylor, J.
1999   "The Gate of the Temple Called 'the Beautiful.'" *Revue biblique* 106:549–62.

TDNT   *Theological Dictionary of the New Testament*. Edited by G. Kittel and G. Friedrich. Translated by G. W. Bromiley. 10 vols. Grand Rapids: Eerdmans, 1964–76.

Teeple, H. M.
1957   *The Mosaic Eschatological Prophet*. Society of Biblical Literature Monograph Series 10. Philadelphia: Society of Biblical Literature.

Thompson, R. P.
1998   "Believers and Religious Leaders in Jerusalem: Contrasting Portraits of Jews in Acts 1–7." Pp. 325–44 in *Literary Studies in Luke-Acts: Essays in Honor of Joseph B. Tyson*. Edited by R. P. Thompson and T. E. Phillips. Macon, GA: Mercer University Press.

Tiede, D.
1980   *Prophecy and History in Luke-Acts*. Philadelphia: Fortress.
1986   "The Exaltation of Jesus and the Restoration of Israel in Acts 1." *Harvard Theological Review* 79:278–86.

Towner, P.
1998   "Mission Practice and Theology under Construction (Acts 18–20)." Pp. 417–36 in *Witness to the Gospel: The Theology of Acts*. Edited by I. H. Marshall and D. Peterson. Grand Rapids: Eerdmans.

Trebilco, P.
1989   "Paul and Silas—'Servants of the Most High God.'" *Journal for the Study of the New Testament* 36:51–73.
1994   "Asia." Pp. 291–362 in *The Book of Acts in Its Graeco-Roman Setting*. Edited by D. W. J. Gill and C. Gempf. The Book of Acts in Its First Century Setting 2. Grand Rapids: Eerdmans.
2004   *The Early Christians in Ephesus from Paul to Ignatius*. Wissenschaftliche Untersuchungen zum Neuen Testament 166. Tübingen: Mohr.

Turner, M. M. B.
1996   *Power from on High: The Spirit in Israel's Restoration and Witness in Luke-Acts*. Journal of Pentecostal Theology Supplement Series 9. Sheffield: Sheffield Academic Press.
1998   "The 'Spirit of Prophecy' as the Power of Israel's Restoration and Witness." Pp. 327–48 in *Witness to the Gospel: The Theology of Acts*. Edited by I. H. Marshall and D. Peterson. Grand Rapids: Eerdmans.

Unnik, W. C. van
1960–61 "The 'Book of Acts' the Confirmation of the Gospel." *Novum Testamentum* 4:26–59.
1966 "Der Ausdruck ἕως ἐσχάτου τῆς γῆς [Apostelgeschichte 1:8] und sein alttestamentlicher Hintergrund." Pp. 335–401 in *Studia biblica et semitica: Theodoro Christiano Vriezen qui munere professoris theologiae per xxv annos functus est, ab amicis, collegis, discipulis dedicata.* Wageningen, Neth.: Veenman.
1979 "Luke's Second Book and the Rules of Hellenistic Historiography." Pp. 37–60 in *Les Actes des apôtres: Traditions, redaction, theologie.* Edited by J. Kremer. Bibliotheca ephemeridum theologicarum loveniensium 48. Louvain: Leuven University Press.

van der Horst, P. W. *See* Horst, P. W. van der

Van Elderen, B.
1970 "Some Archaeological Observations on Paul's First Missionary Journey." Pp. 151–61 in *Apostolic History and the Gospels: Essays Presented to F. F. Bruce.* Edited by W. W. Gasque and R. P. Martin. Grand Rapids: Eerdmans.

Vermes, G.
1973 *Jesus the Jew: A Historian's Reading of the Gospels.* Philadelphia: Fortress.

Vielhauer, P.
1966 "On the 'Paulinism of Acts.'" Pp. 33–50 in *Studies in Luke-Acts: Essays Presented in Honor of Paul Schubert.* Edited by L. E. Keck and J. L. Martyn. Nashville: Abingdon.

Viviano, B. T., and J. Taylor
1992 "Sadducees, Angels, and Resurrection." *Journal of Biblical Literature* 111:496–98.

Vogeli, A.
1953 "Lukas und Euripides." *Theologische Zeitschrift* 9:415–38.

Vos, C. S. de
1999 "Finding a Charge That Fits: The Accusation against Paul and Silas at Philippi (Acts 16.19–21)." *Journal for the Study of the New Testament* 74:51–63.

Walker, W. T.
2001 "Urban Legends: Acts 10:1–11:18 and the Strategies of Greco-Roman Foundation Narratives." *Journal of Biblical Literature* 120:77–99.

Wall, R. W.
2000 "The Function of LXX Habakkuk 1:5 in the Book of Acts." *Bulletin for Biblical Research* 10:247–58.

Wallace, D. B.
1996 *Greek Grammar beyond the Basics: An Exegetical Syntax of the New Testament.* Grand Rapids: Zondervan.
2000 *The Basics of New Testament Syntax: An Intermediate Greek Grammar.* Grand Rapids: Zondervan.

Warnecke, H.
1987 *Die tatsächliche Romfahrt des Apostels Paulus.* Stuttgart: Katholisches Bibelwerk.

Weatherly, J. A.
1994 *Jewish Responsibility for the Death of Jesus in Luke-Acts.* Journal for the Study of the New Testament: Supplement Series 106. Sheffield: Sheffield Academic Press.

Wedderburn, A. J. M.
1994 "Traditions and Redaction of Acts 2:1–13." *Journal for the Study of the New Testament* 55:27–54.

Wehnert, J.
1990 "Gestrandet: Zu einer neuen These über den Schiffbruch des Apostels Paulus auf dem Wege nach Rom (Apg. 27–28)." *Zeitschrift für Theologie und Kirche* 87:67–99.

Weiser, A.
1981 *Die Apostelgeschichte Kapitel 1–12.* Ökumenischer Taschenbuchkommentar zum Neuen Testament 5.1. Gütersloh: Mohn.
1985 *Die Apostelgeschichte Kapitel 13–28.* Ökumenischer Taschenbuchkommentar zum Neuen Testament 5.2. Gütersloh: Mohn.

Wenham, G. J.
1981 "The Theology of Unclean Food." *Evangelical Quarterly* 53:6–15.

Wenk, M.
2000 *Community-Forming Power: The Socio-Ethical Role of the Spirit in Luke-Acts.* Journal of Pentecostal Theology Supplement Series 19. Sheffield: Sheffield Academic Press.

Whiston, W. (trans.)
1987 *The Words of Josephus: Complete and Unabridged.* New updated edition. Peabody, MA: Hendrickson.

Wikenhauser, A.
1948 "Doppelträume." *Biblica* 29:100–111.
1961 *Die Apostelgeschichte*. 4th edition. Regensburger Neues Testament 5. Regensburg: Pustet.

Wilckens, U.
1974 *Die Missionsreden der Apostelgeschichte: Form- und traditionsgeschichtliche Untersuchungen*. 3rd edition. Wissenschaftliche Monographien zum Alten und Neuen Testament 5. Neukirchen-Vluyn: Neukirchener Verlag.

Wilcox, M.
1972–73 "The Judas Tradition in Acts i.15–26." *New Testament Studies* 19:438–52.
1977 "'Upon the Tree'—Deut. 21:22–23 in the New Testament." *Journal of Biblical Literature* 96:85–99.

Williams, D. J.
1990 *Acts*. New International Biblical Commentary 5. Peabody, MA: Hendrickson.

Wilson, M.
2003 "Cilicia: The First Christian Churches in Anatolia." *Tyndale Bulletin* 54:15–30.

Wilson, R. M.
1979 "Simon and Gnostic Origins." Pp. 485–91 in *Les Actes des apôtres: Traditions, redaction, théologie*. Edited by J. Kremer. Bibliotheca ephemeridum theologicarum loveniensium 48. Louvain: Leuven University Press.

Wilson, S. G.
1973 *The Gentiles and the Gentile Mission in Luke-Acts*. Society for New Testament Studies Monograph Series 23. Cambridge: Cambridge University Press.
1983 *Luke and the Law*. Society for New Testament Studies Monograph Series 50. Cambridge: Cambridge University Press.

Windisch, H.
1922 "The Case against the Tradition." Pp. 298–348 in *The Acts of the Apostles*, vol. 2: *Prolegomena II: Criticism*. Edited by F. J. Foakes-Jackson and K. Lake. London: Macmillan.

Winter, B. W.
1993 "Official Proceedings and the Forensic Speeches in Acts 24–26." Pp. 305–36 in *The Book of Acts in Its Ancient Literary Setting*. Edited by B. W. Winter and A. D. Clarke. The Book of Acts in Its First Century Setting 1. Grand Rapids: Eerdmans.
1994 "Acts and Roman Religion, B: The Imperial Cult." Pp. 93–103 in *The Book of Acts in Its Graeco-Roman Setting*. Edited by D. W. J. Gill and C. Gempf. The Book of Acts in Its First Century Setting 2. Grand Rapids: Eerdmans.
1996 "On Introducing Gods to Athens: An Alternative Reading of Acts 17.18–20." *Tyndale Bulletin* 47:71–90.
2006 "Rehabilitating Gallio." *Tyndale Bulletin* 57:291–308.

Winter, B. W., and A. D. Clarke (eds.)
1993 *The Book of Acts in Its Ancient Literary Setting*. The Book of Acts in Its First Century Setting 1. Grand Rapids: Eerdmans.

Witherington, B., III
1998 *The Acts of the Apostles: A Socio-Rhetorical Commentary*. Grand Rapids: Eerdmans/Carlisle, UK: Paternoster.

Wright, N. T.
2003 *The Resurrection of the Son of God*. Minneapolis: Fortress.

Yamauchi, E. M.
1980 *New Testament Cities in Western Asia Minor: Light from Archaeology on Cities of Paul and the Seven Churches of Revelation*. Grand Rapids: Baker Academic. Reprint, Eugene, OR: Wipf & Stock, 2003.
2006 "Acts 8:26–40: Why the Ethiopian Eunuch Was Not from Ethiopia." Pp. 351–65 in *Interpreting the New Testament Text: Introduction to the Art and Science of Exegesis*. Edited by D. L. Bock and B. M. Fanning. Wheaton: Crossway.

Zeigan, H.
2005 *Aposteltreffen in Jerusalem: Eine forschungsgeschichtliche Studie zu Galater 2,1–10 und den möglichen lukanischen Parallelen*. Arbeiten zur Bibel und ihrer Geschichte 18. Leipzig: Evangelische Verlagsanstalt.

Zeisler, J. A.
1979 "The Name of Jesus in the Acts of the Apostles." *Journal for the Study of the New Testament* 4:28–41.

Zwann, J. de
1922 "The Use of the Greek Language in Acts." Pp. 30–65 in *The Acts of*

the Apostles, vol. 2: *Prolegomena II: Criticism*. Edited by F. J. Foakes-Jackson and K. Lake. London: Macmillan.

Zwiep, A. W.

2004   *Judas and the Choice of Matthias: A Study on Context and Concern*

of Acts 1:15–26. Wissenschaftliche Untersuchungen zum Neuen Testament 2.187. Tübingen: Mohr.

Index of Subjects

Index of Authors

Index of Greek Words

Index of Scripture and Other Ancient Writings

Old Testament

Genesis
1–2   565
1:20   388n5
1:24   388n5, 566n4
2:7 LXX   97
2:7   565n3, 574
2:13   341
4:7   396
4:10   246n1
4:23   110
5:24   67
6:18   315
6:20 LXX   388n5
7:18   264
8:21   432
8:22   478
9:3–4   506
9:4   506
9:11   315
10   324
10–11   566
10:1–32   566n4
10:5   103n14
10:20   103n14

11:1–9   95
11:7   101, 366, 611
11:9   101, 366, 610, 611
11:26   284
11:27–28   282
11:28   283
11:31   283
11:32   284
11:31–12:4   282
12:1   282
12:1–3   180, 720n6
12:3 LXX   181
12:3   464, 504, 722
12:4   284
12:7   283, 289
13   283
13:15   283, 289
14:18   303
14:19   303
14:22   303
15:2   283
15:7   282, 283
15:12 LXX   388

15:13   284
15:13–14   179, 284
15:14   285
15:18   283
15:18–20   289
16:6   259
16:7   426
16:7–11   239
17   283
17:1–14   285
17:2   264
17:7   315
17:8   283, 289
17:9–10   487
17:9–14   406
17:10–12   285–86
17:10–14   494, 497
17:20   264
18:26–32   738
19:11   359
19:24   98n8, 116
19:32–38   105
21–36   286
21:4   285, 286

21:17   239
21:27–30   289
22   180, 630
22:1–2   360, 389
22:10–18   239
22:11   357, 716
22:11–12   360
22:18   179, 180
22:18 LXX   181
23   288
24:6   629
24:7   283, 289
24:25   287
24:32   287
25:24   94
26:3   315
26:4   180
26:26–32   289
26:29 LXX   514
27:12 LXX   566
27:38   141
27:42 LXX   197
28:12   114
31:11–13   239, 357

New Testament

Old Testament Apocrypha

Old Testament Pseudepigrapha

New Testament Apocrypha

Rabbinic Writings

Targums

Qumran / Dead Sea Scrolls

Papyri

Josephus

Philo

Classical Writers

Achilles Tatius

The Adventures of Leucippe and Cleitophon

1.1 732
1.3 428
2.23 428
3.2 736, 737
3.2.9 736
3.3 739
3.4–5 738
3.9–11 421n1

Aelius Aristides

Orations

70 541

Sacred Tales

2.12–13 738
2.68 739

Aeschylus

Agamemnon

1624 716n3

Eumenides

28–29 536
647–48 570

Ammianus Marcellinus

Res gestae

22.13 608n4

Apollonius of Rhodes

Argonautica

4.640–42 475n5

Apollonius of Tyana

Letters

32 612

Appian

Civil Wars

1.100 386
3.54 694n5
3.54.222 710

Apuleius

Apology

47 538

The Golden Ass

8.26–30 536

Aratus

Phaenomena

5 568

Aristobulus

frg. 4 565

Aristotle

Nicomachean Ethics

1110A 736
1168B 215
1168B.31 153

Politics

1273B–74A 562
1291A 440, 551n1
1335B 440

Arrian

Anabasis

4.9.7 743

Artapanus

On the Jews

frg. 3 290n7, 421n1
3.6–8 291n9

Artemidorus

Onirocritica

3.53 160

Athenaeus

Deipnosophistae

6.234 221

Augustus

Res gestae divi Augusti

in toto 1, 102

Cato

On Agriculture

120 105

Chariton of Aphrodisias

Chaereas and Callirhoe

1.1.16 476n6
1.5.2 540
1.11.6–7 563
1.14.1 476n6
3.1.1 540
3.2.15–17 476n6
3.4.4–18 492
3.4.18 430, 462
5.1–2 430
5.9.9–10 540
8.7.1–16 492

Cicero

De inventione rhetorica

1.14.19 659n2

De legibus

2.8.19 538

De natura deorum

3.2.5 393
3.18[45] 523

Epistulae ad Atticum

1.13.1 747
1.19.10 49
1.20.6 49
2.1.1–2 49
2.12.2 747
2.13.1 747

Epistulae ad familiares

5.12.10 49

In Pisonem

36.89 555

In Verrem

1.20[54] 450
2.4.117–19 745
2.5.62 §§161–62 544n6
2.5.66 664
2.5.66 §170 544n6
5.62 539

Pro Flacco

26.62 560
28 538
280.67–69 580

Pro Rabirio

4.12 544n6

Tusculanae disputationes

1.31.7 571

Cleanthes

Hymn to Zeus

in toto 586

Cleomedes

De motu circulari

2.1 160
2.91 160

Demosthenes

1 Philippic

4 10[43] 563

On the Crown

43 194

Orations

18 194

Demosthenes Ophthalmicus

Aëtius

7.33 388

Dio Cassius

Roman History

39.20 608n4
40.11 417n4
51.19 703n2
53.16.18 712
56.25.5–6 553
57.15.8 553
60.6.6 578, 751
60.17 665
60.24.4 544
60.28.6 694n5, 757
61.35 580
62.5 431
66.15 710

Dio Chrysostom

Man's First Conception of God (Olympic Discourse)

12.28 568

Church Fathers